1001

GREAT

FAMILY WALKS

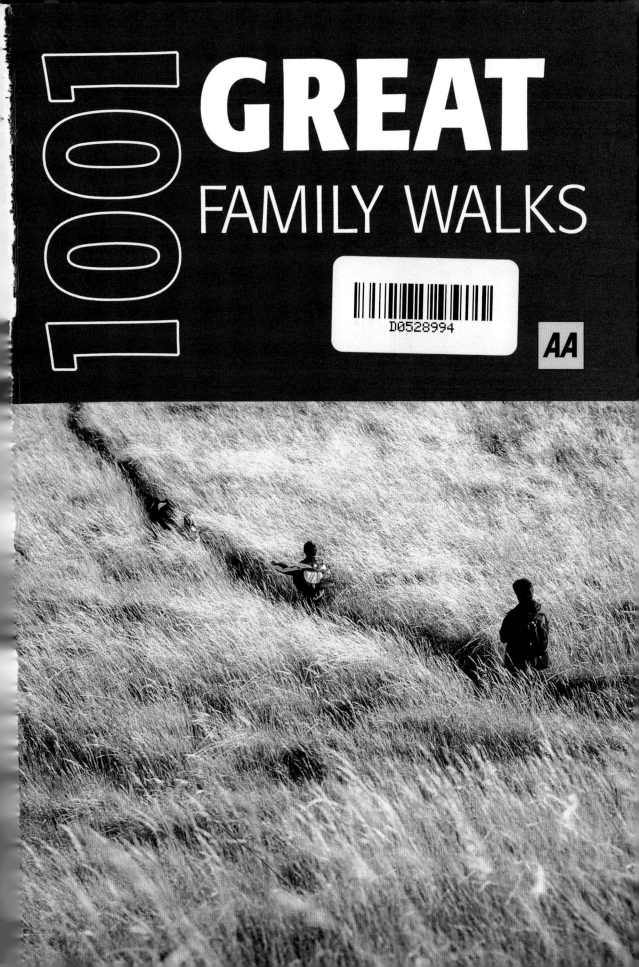

D0528994

AA

Produced by AA Publishing
© Automobile Association Developments Limited 2005
First published 2003. First published in this form 2005. Reprinted with amendments 2007.

Published by AA Publishing (a trading name of Automobile Association Developments Limited, whose registered office is Fanum House, Basing View, Basingstoke, Hampshire RG21 4EA; registered number 1878835)

ISBN-10: 0-7495-5309-X
ISBN-13: 978-0-7495-5309-8

A03199

A CIP catalogue record for this book is available from the British Library.

Many of these routes appear in other walks books from AA Publishing, including 1,001 Walks in Britain

Visit AA Publishing's website www.theAA.com/travel

Colour reproduction by Keene Group, Andover
Printed and bound in Italy by G. Canale & C. SpA

The images are held in AA Publishing's own library (AA WORLD TRAVEL LIBRARY) with contributions from the following photographers:
Front cover – cl Vic Bates; c Steve Day; cr Chris Mellor; bl Anthony J Hopkins; bc James A Tims; br Harry Williams
Page 1 Max Jourdan; page 3 left AA; page 3 right Wyn Voysey

Page i Steve Gregory; page ii Steve Day; page iii Andy Tryner; page iv top Rupert Tenison; middle top Rick Strange; middle bottom C Nicholls; bottom AA; page v top Tom Mackie; middle top Derek Forss; middle bottom Jeff Beazley; bottom Jim Henderson; page vii Rupert Tenison; page viii Vic Bates; page ix Colin Molyneux; page x Caroline Jones; page xi M. Birkitt; page xii Martin Trelawny; page xiii Cameron Lees; page xiv Ken Paterson; walking in safety page Jason Ingram

AA Publishing would like to thank Chartech for supplying aqua3 OS maps for this book. For more information or to order maps visit their website at www.aqua3.com

1001

GREAT
FAMILY WALKS

contents

southwesr

southeast

wales

central

contents

eastern

northwest

northeast

scotland

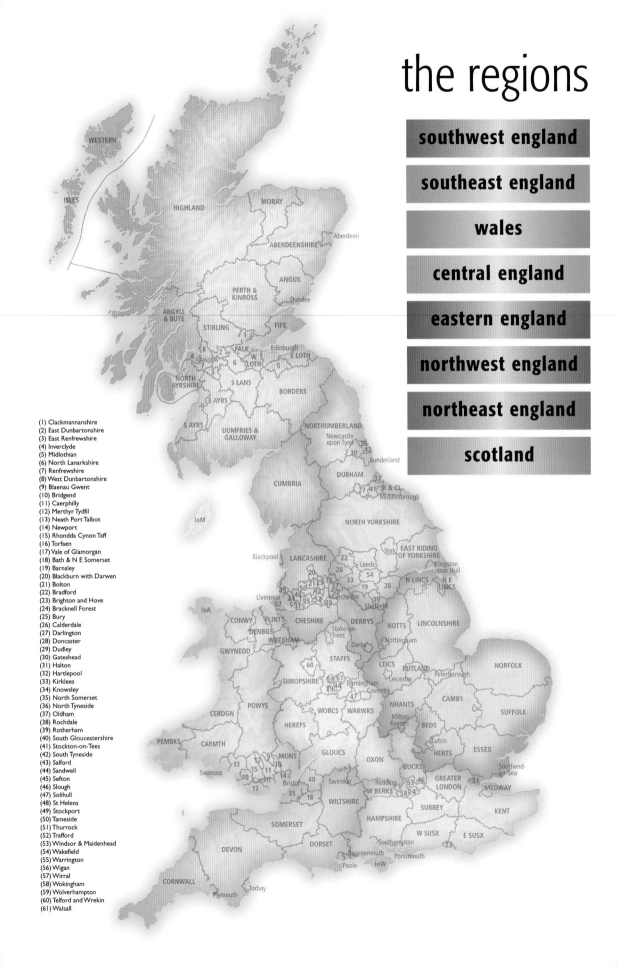

The southwest is defined by its coastline, its villages and its country towns rather than by great cities or industrial conurbations. Even the metropolitan centres reflect the culture of rural and maritime England.

southwest
england

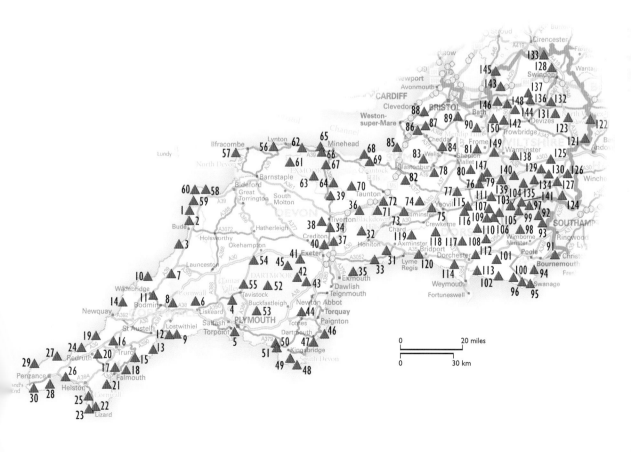

There is an air of industriousness in the southeast.
Amid the hustle and bustle there are green oases of
peace to discover, a long and complex history to
unravel, ancient ways to travel and mysteries to
ponder.

southeast
england

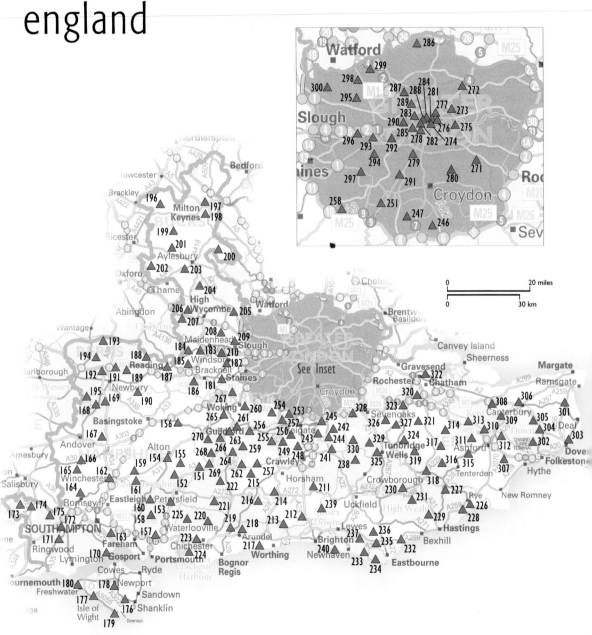

wales

Modern Wales has a buzz, a street credibility born of a new confidence, expressed through art, music and language. But it is still a land of dragons, of druidic landscapes, of mythical warriors, and of poetry.

This is Shakespeare country, land of Oxford's dreaming spires, warm Cotswold stone and fine cathedral cities. Staffordshire claws its way into the Peak District, while Shropshire throws up hills on the Welsh border.

central
england

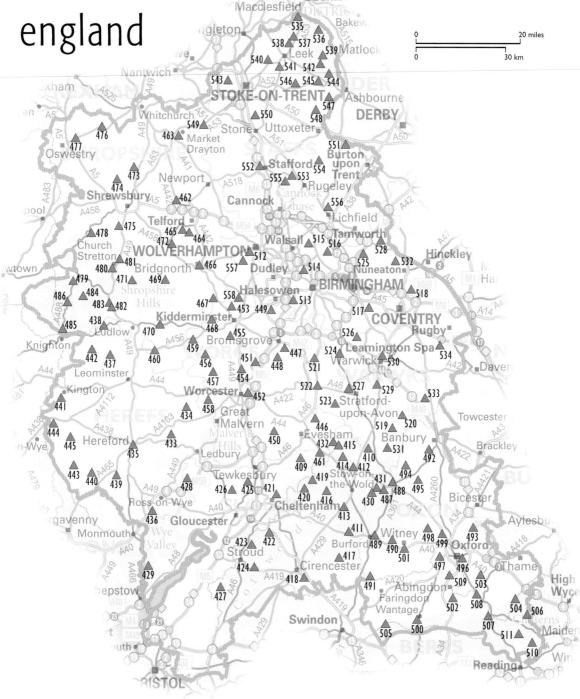

From the ancient oaks of Sherwood Forest, across the Fens to the

Norfolk Broads and the North Sea coast, and up to the

Lincolnshire Wolds there is a surprising variety of landscapes in

the eastern side of England.

eastern england

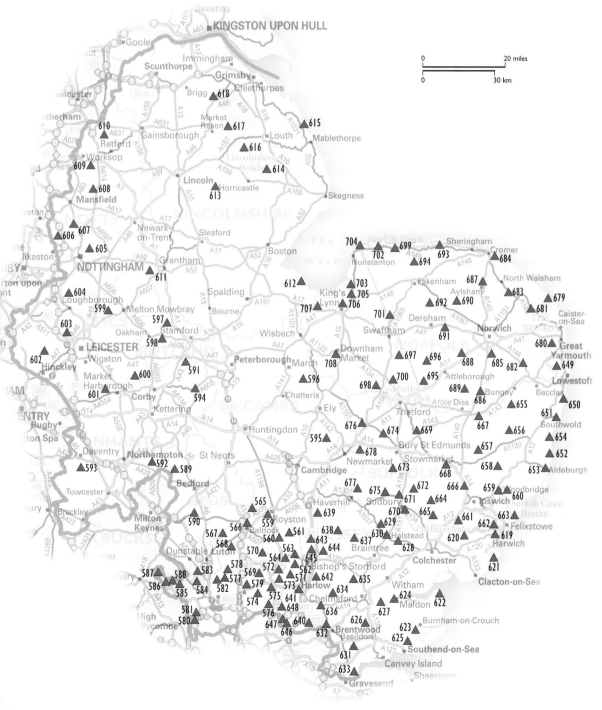

This is a region of great industrial towns and cities, high moors and the great sands of Morecambe Bay. This is walking country, which boasts two national parks: the Lake District and a healthy chunk of the Peak District.

northwest
england

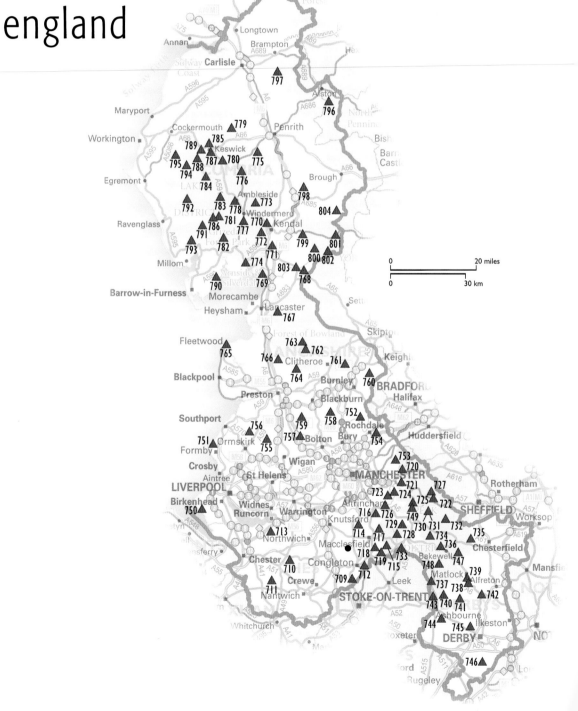

Perhaps the northeast of England and Yorkshire display the strongest personalities of all the English regions. They are certainly among the proudest and the new century has brought a renewed spirit of creativity.

northeast
england

scotland

Almost half the size of England, yet with barely one fifth of its population, Scotland is a country of huge spaces and mountains on a grand scale. It is also a nation steeped in history, and cultural diversity.

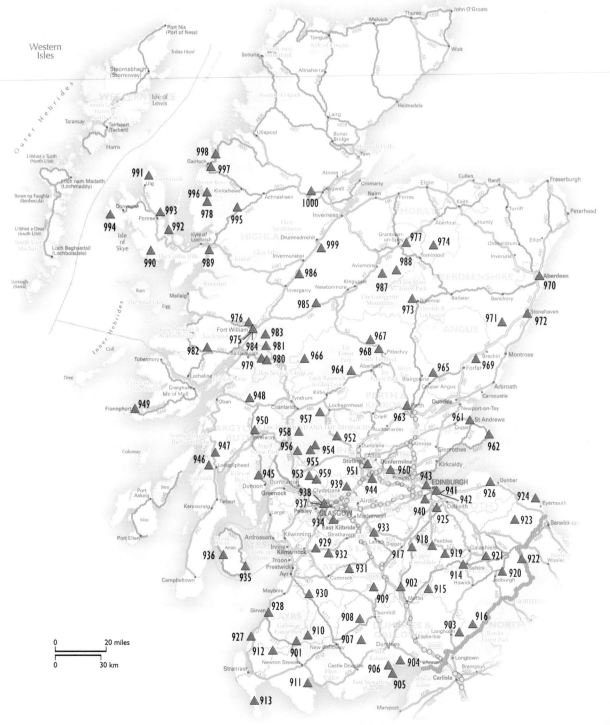

using this book

This collection of walks is easy to use. Use the Contents page to select your walk, then turn to the map and directions of your choice.

---

241 LINGFIELD *POWER AND FLOUR AT HAXTED*

Surrey · SOUTH-EAST ENGLAND

5½ miles (8.8km) 2hrs **Ascent:** 66ft (20m) ▲
Paths: Field edge paths can be overgrown or muddy, farm tracks and country lanes, 15 stiles
Suggested map: aqua3 OS Explorers 146 Dorking, Box Hill & Reigate; 147 Sevenoaks & Tonbridge
Grid reference: TQ 385435
Parking: Free council car park in Gun Pit Road, Lingfield

A lowland walk and a remarkable water mill.
❶ Walk down High Street, turn **L** into Old School Place, and take footpath through churchyard. Turn **R** into Vicarage Road, cross over into Bakers Lane, and continue beyond Station Road on to footpath across **railway**. Swing **L** as you approach **Park Farm**, then fork **L** on to gravelled farm track.
❷ Proceed over stile into open field. After few paces further on, dodge through gate on **L**; continue with hedge on R. At top corner of field, turn **R** through small gate, heading past prominent oak tree towards gates on far side of field.
❸ Cross lane, climb stile opposite, and take waymarked route beside **Eden Brook**. Cross brook on wooden bridge, then head across field to stile by metal gates. Turn **R** along road to **Haxted Mill**.
❹ Turn **R** over stile on to Vanguard Way, recross river; bear **L** towards stile on far side of next field. Turn **L** on to road then fork **L** just beyond bridge.

❺ Turn **R**, along drive towards **Starborough Farm**. At farm, take stile by metal gates, cross drive to Badger House, and then follow waymarked path across field towards corner of small wood. Cross footbridge and stile, and follow path along **L-H** edge of next 4 fields.
❻ Turn **R** in corner of 4th field, keeping hedge on L. Continue over bridge and stile into **Lingfield Hospital School** sports ground. Keep ahead to gap in far hedge, then cross lane, where footpath continues at stile.
❼ Cross 2 small fields, enter woods by stile, and pass children's adventure playground. Beyond woods, bear **R** through gates near school buildings, and follow winding path through fields to **railway crossing** near Lingfield Station. Turn **R** up Station Road then, just opposite station, turn **L** up path to **Star Inn**. Cross over Church Road, and turn **R** through charming 16th-century Old Town into churchyard. Finally, retrace your steps to car park.

---

❶ Information panels
Information panels show the total distance and total amount of ascent (that is how much ascent you will accumulate throughout the walk). An indication of the gradient you will encounter is shown by the rating 0-3. Zero indicates fairly flat ground and 3 indicates undulating terrain with several very steep slopes.

❷ Minimum time
The minimum time suggested is for approximate guidance only. It assumes reasonably fit walkers and doesn't allow for stops.

❸ Walk theme
There are ten themes, each theme is identified by a different icon. The themes are architecture/urban, famous footsteps, historic, industrial heritage, mystery/ancient, nature/woodland, parkland, rural, spectacular, and wilderness.

❹ Start points
The start of each walk is given as a six-figure grid references prefixed by two letters indicting which 100km square of the National Grid it refers to. You'll find

more information on grid reference on most Ordnance Survey maps.

❺ Abbreviations
Walk directions use these abbreviations:
L – left
L–H – left-hand
R – right
R–H – right-hand
Names which appear on signposts are given in brackets, for example ('Bantam Beach').

❻ Suggested maps
Details of appropriate maps are given for each walk, and usually refer to 1:25,000 scale Ordnance Survey Explorer maps. We used laminated aqua3 versions of these maps to walk the routes as they are longer lasting and water resistant. We strongly recommend that you always take the appropriate OS map with you. Our hand-drawn maps are there to give you the route and do not show all the details or relief that you will need to navigate around the routes provided in this collection. You can purchase OS maps at all good bookshops, or by calling Stanfords on 020 7836 2260. You can

purchase acqua3 maps at www.aqua3.com.

❼ Car parking
Many of the car parks suggested are public, but occasionally you may find you have to park on the roadside or in a lay-by. Please be considerate when you leave your car, ensuring that access roads or gates are not blocked and that other vehicles can pass safely. Remember that pub car parks are private and should not be used unless you are visiting the pub or you have the landlord's permission to park there.

Cornwall

1 MORWENSTOW *THE PARSON-POET*

7 miles (11.3km) 4hrs **Ascent:** 1,640ft (500m)
Paths: Generally good, but inland paths and tracks can be very muddy during wet weather
Suggested map: aqua3 OS Explorer 126 Clovelly & Hartland
Grid reference: SS 206154
Parking: Morwenstow: Follow signposted road from the A39 about 2½ miles (4.4km) north of Kilkhampton. Small free car park by Morwenstow Church and Rectory Farm Tearooms

A walk in the footsteps of the eccentric Victorian poet, Reverend Robert Stephen Hawker.

❶ Follow signposted track from car park to coast path; turn **L**. Reach **Hawker's Hut** in about 100yds (91m). Continue along coast path to **Duckpool**.

❷ Reach inlet of **Duckpool**, walk up road along bottom of valley to T-junction. Turn **L**. At junction, go **R** to cross bridge beside ford. Follow lane **L** for 150yds (137m), then bear **L** on broad track through woodland.

❸ Cross stile on **L**, cross wooden footbridge, climb slope, then turn **R** and up track. Turn **L** at T-junction; keep ahead at next junction. Shortly go **R** through metal gate.

❹ Follow field track to surfaced lane at **Woodford**. Turn **L** and go downhill past **Shears Farm** then **R** and uphill to junction with road. Turn **L** past bus shelter.

❺ Turn **L** along path between cottages to kissing gate. Turn **R** then immediately **L** and follow field edge to stile on **L**. Cross stile, then next field, bearing slightly **L**, to reach hedge on opposite side.

❻ Cross 2 stiles; go straight up next field (often muddy) to hedge corner. Go alongside wall to hedged track and on to junction with surfaced lane.

❼ Go through gate opposite; turn **R** through gap. Go **L** to stile, **L** across next field to far **L-H** corner, then up to **Stanbury House**. Turn **R** to surfaced lane.

❽ Go **L** along lane then over narrow stile on **R**. Go straight across next 2 fields to stile and gate into farm lane behind **Tonacombe House**.

❾ Go **R** then bear off **L** along muddy track. Cross 2 fields; descend into wooded valley. Keep **R**, cross stream, then go **R** and up to stile (steep).

❿ Cross over fields to meadow behind **Bush Inn**. Go down **L** side of buildings, then up to road. Turn **L** for **Morwenstow Church** and car park.

2 BUDE *A WILD-FLOWER FIESTA*

5 miles (8km) 2hrs 30min **Ascent:** 262ft (80m)
Paths: Excellent throughout. The National Trust is carrying out regeneration of some eroded sections; please heed notices
Suggested map: aqua3 OS Explorer 111 Bude, Boscastle & Tintagel, and 126 Clovelly & Hartland
Grid reference: SS 204071
Parking: Crooklets Beach car park. Follow signs for Crooklets. Large pay-and-display car park, can be very busy in summer

A wild-flower stroll along the coast.

❶ Go towards **Crooklets Beach**, cross bridge and head for some steps. Pass in front of beach huts, then turn **L** along stony track between walls. Go up some steps and on to coast path, signposted 'Maer Cliff'.

❷ Go through gate and along track behind white building, called **The Bungalow**. Bear off to **L**, by signpost, down path to sea at wide, stony **Northcott Mouth beach**. From here, bear **R** along track that will take you back inland, past group of houses on **L**, and continue uphill passing some more houses.

❸ Where track bends round to **R**, leave it and keep straight ahead to gate. Keep outside **L** edge of **overgrown bridleway** ahead.

❹ Reach field gate and follow track through fields. Keep **L** at junction with another track, then continue to T-junction with public road. Turn **L** and walk down road (with care) to beach at **Sandy Mouth**.

❺ Pass National Trust information kiosk and descend towards beach. Go **L** and uphill and follow coast path back to **Northcott Mouth beach**, and red lifeguard hut passed earlier.

❻ Follow roadside path just past lifeguard hut and retrace your steps to white **Bungalow** passed earlier. Go along track behind building, then keep ahead along broad track with field hedge on your **L**.

❼ At field corner by footpath sign go through gate ahead then turn **L** and follow field edge into hedged-in path. Continue between trees to lane by house at **Rosemerrin**. Continue to road.

❽ Turn **R** along road, with **Maer Lake Nature Reserve** (often flooded in winter) down to your **L**. Cross at junction with **Maer Down Road**, go **L**, then **R**, and return to car park.

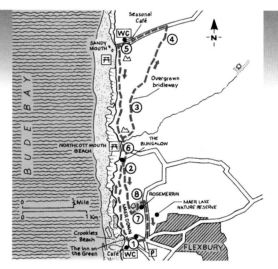

3 CRACKINGTON HAVEN *A GEOLOGICAL PHENOMENON*

3½ miles (5.7km) 1hr 45min **Ascent:** 270ft (82m)
Paths: Good coastal footpath and woodland tracks. Can be very wet and muddy
Suggested map: aqua3 OS Explorer 111; Bude, Boscastle & Tintagel
Grid reference: SX 145969
Parking: Crackington Haven car park. From the A39 at Wainhouse Corner, or from Boscastle on the B3263. Can be busy in summer. Burden Trust car park, along B3263 road to Wainhouse

A coastal and inland walk with spectacular sea cliff views of the North Cornish coast.

❶ From **Crackington Haven** car park entrance go **L** across bridge, then turn **R** at telephone kiosk. Follow broad track round to **L**, between signpost and old wooden seat, then go through kissing gate on to coast path.

❷ Keep **L** and follow path up sheltered valley on inland side of steep hill, then continue on cliff path (breathtaking view of folded strata and quartzite bands of **Cambeak's cliff**).

❸ Where stretch of low inland cliffs begins, just beyond signpost and shortly before 2nd signpost, go **L** along path to reach road by National Trust sign for **'The Strangles'**. Looking back from here you can see such fantastic features as **Northern Door**, promontory of harder rock pierced by its natural arch where softer shales have been eroded by sea. Track down to beach is worthwhile despite steep return. You can view remarkable coastal features from sea level.

❹ Go **L**, walking past farm entrance to Trevigue (16th-century farmhouse), then, short distance along, turn **R** down drive by **Trevigue** sign. Bear off to **L** across grass to go through gate by signpost.

❺ Go directly down field, keeping **L** of telegraph pole, to reach stile. Continue downhill to edge of wood. Go down tree-shaded path to junction of paths in shady dell by river.

❻ Turn sharp **L** here, following signpost towards **Haven**, and continue on obvious path down wooded river valley, descending into **East Wood** (and **Trevigue valley**, much of which is now nature reserve).

❼ Cross footbridge, then turn **L** at junction with track. Cross another footbridge and continue to gate by some houses. Follow track then surfaced lane to main road, then turn **L** to return to car park.

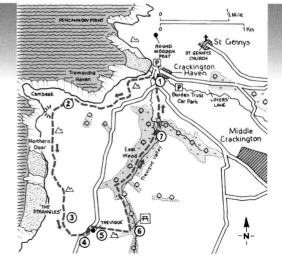

Cornwall

COTEHELE TUDORS AND VICTORIANS

4 miles (6.4km) 3hrs **Ascent:** 164ft (50m)

Paths: Excellent woodland tracks, can be muddy in places
Suggested map: aqua3 OS Explorer 108 Lower Tamar Valley & Plymouth
Grid reference: SX 436683
Parking: Calstock Quay car park. Bear R at junction at bottom of steep descent into the village. Free car park, but limited spaces. Often full by mid-morning

A stroll along the River Tamar from a Victorian viaduct to Tudor Cotehele House.

1 From car park walk to **L** of **Tamar Inn**, then turn **L** into **Commercial Road**. Shortly take 2nd turning **L** and go along **Lower Kelly Lane** and beneath **Calstock Viaduct**.

2 Keep **L** at fork just past large house with veranda. Beyond row of cottages, branch **L**, signposted 'Cotehele House', and follow broad track uphill and beneath trees.

3 Go **R** at junction, signposted 'Cotehele House'. Pass above dovecote in Cotehele Gardens, then turn **L** at T-junction. Go through gate and turn **R** for entrance to National Trust's **Cotehele House**, dating mainly from late 15th and early 16th centuries and home of Edgcumbe family.

4 Follow road from **Cotehele House**, then branch **L** and downhill to reach **Cotehele Quay**. (You can

continue from Quay for just under ½ mile (800m) to visit **Cotehele Mill**, restored to working order.)

5 Follow path that starts beside car park and just beyond Cotehele Quay Gallery. Pass little chapel and then viewpoint to **Calstock**. At junction, go **R**, signposted '**Calstock**'. Shortly branch **L** up rising track.

6 Go **R** at junction; descend to wooden footbridge over stream. At T-junction with another track, turn **L** and walk up track for about 55yds (50m).

7 Turn sharply **R** and go up rising track along side of stone wall. Pass stone pillar and old well on your **L**, then pass junction with track coming in from **L**. Join surfaced lane just before big house with veranda, passed earlier. Retrace your steps to **Cotehele Quay** where preserved sailing barge, Shamrock, and National Maritime Museum's exhibition rooms commemorate great days of Tamar trade.

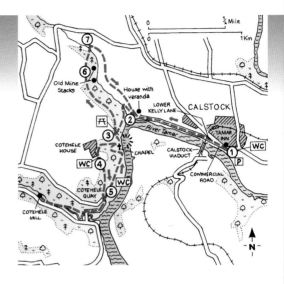

MOUNT EDGCUMBE CORNISH SHORES

8 miles (12.9km) 4hrs **Ascent:** 328ft (100m)

Paths: Good throughout. Muddy in places in wet weather, 8 stiles
Suggested map: aqua3 OS Explorer 108 Lower Tamar Valley & Plymouth
Grid reference: SX 453534
Parking: Cremyll car park. Alternatively reach Cremyll by ferry from the Plymouth side. Daily service between Admiral's Hard, Stonehouse, Plymouth and Cremyll

A walk round the Mount Edgcumbe estate.

1 Go **L** along footway opposite car park entrance. Where it ends at fountain, cross back **L**; go through by telephone box signed '**Empacombe**'. Keep **L** past Old School Rooms. Turn **R** at junction; pass obelisk and follow path by tree-hidden creek to **Empacombe**.

2 At surfaced lane, by house, keep ahead; go down to **Empacombe Quay**. Turn **L** beyond low wall (control dogs); skirt edge of harbour to stile on to wooded path. Continue round **Palmer Point** and on to public road.

3 Go through kissing gate opposite, signposted '**Maker Church, Kingsand**'. Follow track ahead; shortly bear **R**, up field (no obvious path) heading between telegraph poles, to faint path into **Pigshill Wood**. Bear **R** along track, go **L** at signposts and climb uphill following footpath signs. Cross track, then go up steps to more steps on to public road. Cross, carefully; follow path to **Maker Church**.

4 Turn sharp **R** in front of church, follow field edge, then cross stile on **L**. Follow next field edge and cross stile on **L**; follow path past house and across lane into field. Cross 2 fields to lane. Turn **R**; go **L** at junction.

5 Where road levels, bear **L** down track at public footpath signpost. Keep ahead at junction; after long level stretch, go **L** at junction to Kingsand via Devonport Hill and Kingsway. To explore **Kingsand** and **Cawsand**, bear **L** (Heavitree Road).

6 To return to **Cremyll**, at Kingsway go through gate into **Mount Edgcumbe Country Park**. Follow track to public lane at Hooe Lake Valley.

7 Rejoin coast path, signposted along lane. Keep to upper path at junction, merge with track from **L**; continue through woods.

8 After passing beneath arch, bear **R** from main track and down path to coast. Follow coast path back to **Mount Edgcumbe** and **Cremyll**.

BODMIN MOOR ROCKY BOUNDS

3 miles (4.8km) 2hrs 30min **Ascent:** 230ft (70m)

Paths: Moorland tracks and paths and disused quarry tramways
Suggested map: aqua3 OS Explorer 109 Bodmin Moor
Grid reference: SX 260711
Parking: The Hurlers car park on south west side of Minions village

A walk across the wilds of Bodmin Moor.

1 Leave car park by steps at top end beside information board (**Hurlers stone circles**). Cross grass to track. Turn **R**; follow track, passing **Hurlers** (**R**) and **Pipers** stones further on.

2 At 3-way junction, by large granite block, take **R-H** track down through shallow valley bottom; climb uphill on track towards **Cheesewring Quarry**. At junction with another track, cross over and follow grassy track uphill towards quarry. At first green hillock, go **R**, then **L** to **Daniel Gumb's Cave** (18th-century stone-worker's rock house). Return to path; follow path alongside fenced-in rim of quarry to Cheesewring rock formation.

3 Retrace steps towards valley bottom.

4 Short distance from valley bottom, level with thorn trees (**R**) and just before fenced-off mound (**L**), turn **R** along path. Keep **L** of thorn trees and leaning granite block and soon find beginnings of grassy track. Follow

track, keeping to **R** of solitary thorn tree and gorse bushes. Track becomes clearer.

5 Track begins to strand. At leaning rock, split like whale's mouth, keep **R** along path through scrub, with rocky heights of Sharp Tor ahead. Keep to path round slope, with **Wardbrook Farm L** and **Sharptor** ahead. Reach road; turn **R** to reach open gateway.

6 Go to **R** of fence by gateway and follow path alongside fence past 2 slim granite pillars. Join disused tramway and follow.

7 Pass piles of broken rock and, about 30yds (27m) beyond, turn sharp **R** at wall corner. Follow green track uphill and alongside wall. Where wall ends keep on uphill to broad track.

8 Turn **L** along track to **Cheesewring Quarry**. For main route, turn **L** and follow track to Minions village. Pass **Minions Heritage Centre** (converted mine engine house). At main road, turn **R** through village to return to car park.

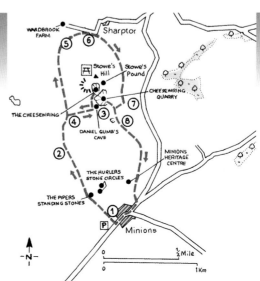

Cornwall

7 CAMELFORD *Moors and Meadows*

5 miles (8km) 3hrs Ascent: 164ft (50m)
Paths: Well-marked paths. Some field sections poorly defined, 28 stiles, some in triplicate and very high
Suggested map: aqua3 OS Explorer 109 Bodmin Moor
Grid reference: SX 106836
Parking: Church car park at north entrance to Camelford, or small car park opposite the North Cornwall Museum

Riverside, woodland and quiet fields.

❶ From between Town Hall and Darlington Inn, cross main street, carefully; turn up Fore Street. Shortly go **L** through low archway ('The Moors') and ('To River and **Advent Church**'). Follow riverside path.
❷ At surfaced lane, beside bridge, turn **R** and uphill. At top, before **Fenteroon Farm**, go **L** and through gate ('Public Footpath'). Follow 1st field edge; cross next field. Cross high stile; descend through woods towards river. Ignore stile on R; instead keep down to signpost in valley bottom. Cross meadow ahead; go **L** over bridge and through trees. Bear steeply up **L**, then **L** again, by signpost, to stile into lane. Turn **R**.
❸ Pass Trethin Manor entrance, veer **L** over stile; through meadow and past **fish pond**. Cross clapper bridge and stile; go up field to Advent churchyard.
❹ From east end of churchyard (opposite where you entered) go over wooden stile and slightly **R** across field, to several stiles. Cross meadow; follow **R-H** field edges to 3 stiles in hedge. Bear **L** across middle of field to far corner and on to surfaced lane. Turn **L**.
❺ Turn **L** before stream and T-junction by **Watergate Farm**. Cross stiles and alongside stream on stone flags. Pass enclosure, follow stream for short distance, then skirt gorse and fenced-in trees to hidden stiles into field. Go straight up field slope; continue to stile into next field. Continue to lane at **Moorgate**.
❻ Cross lane, go through several fields, then continue along stony track to another lane at **Aldermoor Farm**. Turn **L** along lane.
❼ Turn **R** opposite buildings at **Treclago Farm**; go up lane. At junction, keep ahead along track (possibly muddy). Descend meadow to gate, cross wooden footbridge over stream, then climb steeply uphill to surfaced lane (College Road). Follow to **Camelford**.

8 CARDINHAM *Through the Woods*

5 miles (8km) 3hrs 30min Ascent: 328ft (100m)
Paths: Generally clear woodland tracks and field sections, 6 stiles
Suggested map: aqua3 OS Explorer 109 Bodmin Moor
Grid reference: SX 099666
Parking: Cardinham Woods car park

A long woodland walk in quiet countryside between Bodmin town and moor.

❶ From **Cardinham Woods** car park, head for west side of main bridge over Cardinham Water; bear **R** through wooden barrier to 3-way junction. Keep to **R**; follow track through woods (Cardinham Water on R).
❷ At junction of tracks, keep **R** and cross hidden tributary stream from L; turn **L** up track. Pass picnic tables by rock face on bend.
❸ Turn **R** at junction; pass purple marker post. At next junction, keep ahead along grassy track through **Lidcutt Wood**. Cross stile and on through woods.
❹ Enter field; turn sharp **R** and uphill by signpost to gate on to concrete track. Turn **L**; follow track to surfaced road. Turn **R** along road; follow over brow of hill and down into valley.
❺ Beyond junction, pass public footpath sign, cross river, then go **R** at another public footpath sign. Cross ditch and stile. Head diagonally up field, aiming to **R** of Cardinham church tower, to stile. Go along grassy ride beside church. Turn **R** at road.
❻ At public footpath sign opposite **cemetery**, go **R** and through gate into field. Keep parallel to fence; turn **L** in front of house and follow old track, keeping L of tree. Go through wooden gate; keep alongside hedge on R. Where track bends R, turn **L** and downhill between trees; cross meadow to stile. Notices indicate keep to **R-H** edge of field to stile.
❼ Bear slightly to **L** across next field to wooden gate beside horse jump. Keep ahead from meadow to bridge over stream by water jump; follow path through trees. Go through gate to T-junction with track at **Milltown**. Turn **R**, down surfaced lane; keep **L** at junction. Pass **Milltown Farm**, then junction on L to black-and-white wooden barrier. Go up slope; turn **R** at junction with forestry track.
❽ Follow track then surfaced lane from **Target Cottage** to car park.

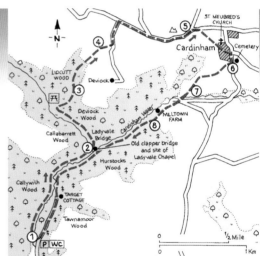

9 POLRUAN *A Glimpse of Old Cornwall*

4 miles (6.4km) 3hrs 30min Ascent: 754ft (230m)
Paths: Good throughout. Can be very muddy in woodland areas during wet weather
Suggested map: aqua3 OS Explorer 107 St Austell & Liskeard
Grid reference: SX 126511
Parking: Polruan. An alternative start to the walk can be made from the National Trust Pencarrow car park (► ❹, SX 149513) . You can also park at Fowey's Central car park, then catch the ferry to Polruan

A woodland and coastal walk from Polruan through the ancient parish of Lanteglos.

❶ Walk up from **Quay** at **Polruan**; turn **L** along **East Street**, by telephone box and seat. Go **R**, up steps signposted 'To the Hills' and 'Hall Walk'. Go **L** at next junction, then keep along path ahead. Keep **R** at junction and pass National Trust sign ('North Downs').
❷ Turn **R** at T-junction with track, then shortly bear **L** along path, signposted '**Pont** and **Bodinnick**'. Reach wooden gate on to lane. Don't go through gate but instead bear **L** and go over stile. Follow path, established by National Trust, and eventually descend steep wooden steps.
❸ At T-junction with track, turn **R** and climb uphill. It's worth diverting **L** at T-junction to visit **Pont**. Follow this route to reach lane. Go **L** for short distance then, on bend by Little Churchtown Farm, bear off **R** through gate ('Footpath to Church'). Climb steadily to reach handsome medieval **Church of St Winwaloe** (or Willow). Novelist Daphne du Maurier was married here in 1932.
❹ Turn **L** outside church and follow narrow lane. At T-junction, just beyond **Pencarrow car park**, cross road and go through gate, then turn **R** along field edge on path established by National Trust, to go through another gate. Turn **L** along field edge.
❺ At field corner, turn **R** on to coast path and descend very steeply. (To continue to Pencarrow Head go **L** over stile here and follow path on to headland. From here coast path can be re-joined and access made to **Great Lantic Beach**.) Follow coast path for about 1¼ miles (2km), keeping to cliff edge and ignoring any junctions.
❻ Where cliff path ends, go through gate to road junction. Cross road then go down School Lane. Turn **R** at 'Speakers Corner', then turn **L** down Fore Street to reach **Quay** at Polruan.

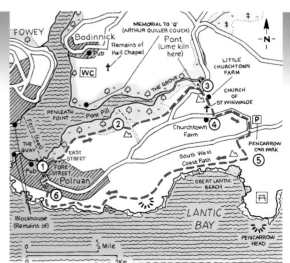

Cornwall

PORT QUIN *A ROLLERCOASTER PATH*

6 miles (9.7km) 4hrs **Ascent:** 984ft (300m) **3**

Paths: Good coastal and field paths. Several sections of coast path run very close to unguarded cliff edges. May not be suitable for children and dogs. 14 stiles

Suggested map: aqua3 OS Explorer 106 Newquay & Padstow

Grid reference: SW 999809

Parking: Port Isaac. Large car park on outskirts of village, can be busy in summer. Allowed on Port Isaac's stony beach, but this is tidal so check tides! Small car park at Port Quin

An exhilarating hike between two villages.

❶ Exit car park by lower terrace; turn **L** along track, keeping **R** where it branches ('Coast Path'). At road, keep ahead and down Fore Street to The Platt at entry to **harbour**. Just past Port Isaac Fishermen Ltd, turn **R** up Roscarrock Hill Lane ('Coast Path').

❷ At top of lane, pass footpath sign on L; shortly, keep to **R** of gateway to terrace of houses; bear **R** ('Coastal Footpath'). Follow path round **Lobber Point**.

❸ Descend to Pine Haven Cove; cross stile. (Wooden fence skirts along inside edge of path from here.) Climb uphill and round edge of enormous gulf. Cross stile at end of fenced section and cross **Varley Head**. (Path ahead runs close to cliff edge and is fenced on inside.)

❹ Beyond bench descend steep steps (hand rail) into **Downgate Cove** and **Reedy Cliff**. Follow coast path up to seaward edge of **Kellan Head** (steep). Continue along path to **Port Quin**.

❺ Turn **L** at **Port Quin**; go up road past car park entrance. At bend in road bear **L** ('Public Footpath to **Port Isaac**'). Pass cottages and keep up slope to gate with stone stile (dogs under strict control). Follow path alongside hedge; climb to stile between 2 gates. Keep alongside **R-H** edge of next fields.

❻ Cross stile beside gate; turn **L** and follow **L** field edge to stile. Go **L** over stile; descend into wooded valley bottom. Cross footbridge over stream, then go over stile. Proceed and climb (steeply) through gorse to open field slope. Continue across field (no obvious path), aiming to L of pole that comes into view.

❼ Cross stone stile; follow hedged-in path downhill to junction with lane at Point ❷. Turn **R** and retrace steps to **Port Isaac** and on to car park.

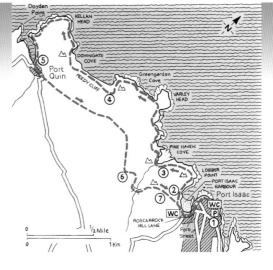

WADEBRIDGE *ALONG THE RIVER CAMEL*

6 miles (9.7km) 3hrs 30min **Ascent:** 328ft (100m) **1**

Paths: Farm and forestry tracks and well-surfaced old railway track

Suggested map: aqua3 OS Explorer 106 Newquay & Padstow

Grid reference: SW 991722

Parking: Wadebridge main car park. Small parking area at end of Guineaport Road at start of the Camel Trail

A gentle woodland walk along the famous old railway trackbed of the Camel Trail and through woodlands.

❶ From car parks in **Wadebridge**, walk along Southern Way Road past **Betjeman Centre**, housed in old railway station, containing memorabilia of famous Poet Laureate, Sir John Betjeman, and continue along Guineaport Road to start of **Camel Way/Trail**. Start from here if adjacent parking is used.

❷ Do not follow the **Camel Way/Trail**. Instead, where road forks just past row of houses, keep **R** and shortly, at junction, where road curves up to **R**, keep ahead along unsurfaced track, signposted 'Public Footpath to Treraven'. Follow track steadily uphill. Go through wooden gate and follow **R-H** field edge to go through another gate. Keep ahead along track to reach junction with wider track. Continue ahead and follow track.

❸ Go **L** in front of **Treraven Farm**, then, in about 15yds (14m), at junction, keep **R** and continue along track to reach bend on minor public road by building.

❹ Keep straight ahead along road, with care, then turn **L** at crossroads, signposted '**Burlawn**'. At next junction, go **L** and follow road through little hamlet of Burlawn. Go steeply downhill on narrow lane overshadowed by trees.

❺ At **Hustyn Mill**, beyond little footbridge, turn **L** off road and follow broad woodland track. Stay on main track to where it reaches surfaced road at **Polbrock Bridge**.

❻ Turn **L** over bridge across **River Camel** and, in short distance, go off **L** and down steps to join Camel Trail, which runs through some of Cornwall's most scenic landscape with diversity of animals and bird life. Turn **L** here and follow unwavering line of **Camel Way/Trail** to return to **Wadebridge**.

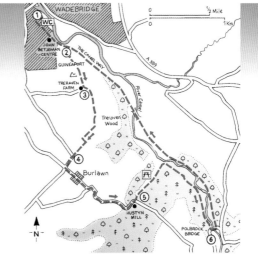

FOWEY *DAPHNE DU MAURIER'S WORLD*

7½ miles (12.1km) 4hrs **Ascent:** 820ft (250m) **3**

Paths: Field paths, rough lanes and coastal footpath, can be very muddy on inland tracks during wet weather, 12 stiles

Suggested map: aqua3 OS Explorer 107 St Austell & Liskeard

Grid reference: SX 118511

Parking: Readymoney Cove car park, reached by continuing on from entrance to Fowey's main car park

In the footsteps of Daphne du Maurier.

❶ From bottom end of car park proceed to walk down St Catherine's Parade; turn **R** towards inlet of **Readymoney Cove**. Continue to end of road, above beach and follow Love Lane uphill (Saints Way). Continue past 1st junction, ignoring options by National Trust sign ('Covington Woods').

❷ Turn **L** at next junction; climb wooden steps to **Allday's Field**. Follow **R-H** field edge. At field gap follow track ahead to lane end at **Coombe Farm**. Follow lane ahead.

❸ At road, turn **R**; continue to **Lankelly Farm**. Pass junction on R; follow Prickly Post Lane. Shortly turn **L** on to gravel drive; keep **L** and along fenced-in path.

❹ Go up rough track by derelict buildings at **Trenant**; cross stile on **L**. Keep ahead alongside field edge; follow path to stile into field below **Tregaminion Farm**. Go up field to gate, continue between buildings; turn **R**, then **L**, to T-junction with road by entrance gate to **Church of Tregaminion**.

❺ Turn **R**; shortly go **L** into field. Reach junction on edge of woods. On main route, keep **L** along field edge and follow coast path to Gribbin Head.

❻ Enter wooded National Trust property of Gribbin. Keep **L** at junction. Go through gate and cross to **Gribbin Daymark**. Go **L** and down faint track, then follow coast path to **Polridmouth**.

❼ Follow coast path ('Lankelly Cliff'). At open ground, follow seaward field edge. Go steeply into, and out of, **Coombe Hawne**. Enter Covington Wood, keep **L** at junction and pass **Rashleigh Mausoleum**.

❽ Turn **R** at junction to reach **St Catherine's Castle**. Return along path; go down steps at 1st junction on **R**. Go down wooden steps to **Readymoney Beach**. Return to car park via St Catherine's Parade.

Cornwall

Cornwall • SOUTHWEST ENGLAND

13 DODMAN POINT ANCIENT WALLS

4½ miles (7.2km) 3hrs **Ascent:** 377ft (115m) ▲2
Paths: Good coastal paths. Inland paths can be muddy, 9 stiles
Suggested map: aqua3 OS Explorer 105 Falmouth & Mevagissey
Grid reference: SX 011415
Parking: Gorran Haven car park, pay at kiosk

A circuit of the headland of Dodman Point, with its Iron-Age earthwork.
❶ Turn **L** out of car park and walk down to **Gorran Haven** harbour. Just before access to beach, turn **R** up Fox Hole Lane, then go up steps (*'Vault Beach'*). Go up more steps, then through gate. Follow coast path ahead, past sign for Lamledra (National Trust).
❷ Keep **L** at junction below rocky outcrop. Alternative path (steep) leads up **R** from here, past memorial plaque, to rejoin main coast path. On main route, go down steps and follow path along slope. At junction, keep **R**. **L**-**H** track leads down to **Vault Beach**; regain coastal path by another track leading uphill. Keep **L** at next junction.
❸ Go **L** over stile and follow path through scrubland. Keep ahead at junction (*'Dodman Point'*), then go over stile on to open ground. Continue on footpath to summit of Dodman Point.
❹ On approaching large granite cross on summit of Dodman, reach 1st junction from where path going **R** leads to Watch House. Continue towards cross on summit; just before cross and at next junction and arrow post, go **R** along coast path.
❺ Go over stile beyond gate with access notice pinned to it. Reach junction shortly. Turn **R** and follow path between high banks of **Bulwark**.
❻ Keep ahead where path comes from **R**. Follow hedged track to kissing gate and lane at Penare. Turn **R** along lane.
❼ At junction leave road and go through field gate (*'Treveague'*). Keep across 2 fields; at road end by houses, turn **R** (*'Gorran Haven'*). Go **L** at another signpost then along drive behind house, bearing **R**. Go **L** through gate and along path above small valley.
❽ Cross muddy area by stepping stones, then go through gate. Follow driveway to T-junction with public road. Turn **R** and walk down (carefully), to Gorran Haven car park.

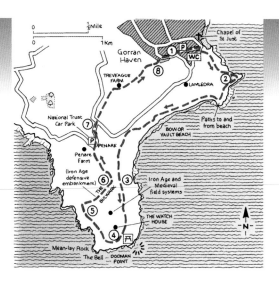

14 BEDRUTHAN GIANT STEPS AND STAIRCASES

4½ miles (7.2km) 2hrs 30min **Ascent:** 131ft (40m) ▲2
Paths: Coastal paths and field paths. Coast path very close to unguarded cliff edges in some places. Take care in windy weather and with children and dogs. 1 stile
Suggested map: aqua3 OS Explorer 106 Newquay & Padstow
Grid reference: SW 850691
Parking: National Trust car park at Carnewes. Or at the National Trust Park Head car park, grid reference: SW 851706, from where the walk can also be started at Point ❺

Exploring Bedruthan Steps and Park Head.
❶ From **car park**, go through gap in wall on **R** of National Trust house; shortly, bear **L** at junction. Follow to crossing of paths; go straight across and down grassy path to **Carnewes Point** (dramatic views). Return to crossing; follow path **L** along cliff edge. (Heed warning notices.) At junction with cobbled path, go **L**; descend to dip at Pendarves Point.
❷ At junction in dip, go down **L** to top of cliff staircase. On re-ascending staircase, go back uphill to junction with coast path; keep **L** past National Trust sign (*'Carnewes'*). Follow coast path along fence and below parking area with picnic tables above.
❸ Pass **Redcliff Castle**; where paths forks by signpost, follow either to where they rejoin. Keep **R** of stone wall with tamarisk trees, to wooden kissing gate. Continue along clifftop to set of wooden gates on **R**.
❹ Go **R** and through smaller gate; follow permissive footpath along field edges. Just before buildings at Pentire, turn **R** through gate and follow field edges to **Park Head car park**.
❺ Turn **L**; go **L** down surfaced lane. Before **Pentire** buildings go through gate on **R** (*'Porthmear Beach and Park Head'*). Bear **L** across field to stile and gateway. Bear **R** down next field to kissing gate (bottom corner). Go through gate and follow path through wetland area to coast path above Porth Mear.
❻ Go **L**; follow coast path then round Park Head. Take care near cliff edges. At memorial plaque above **High Cove**, divert to promontory of **Park Head** itself. Return to plaque and follow coast path south to Point ❹. Retrace steps to Point ❷, in dip above crest of cliff staircase. Follow cobbled walkway uphill and back to **Carnewes car park**.

15 NARE HEAD HIDDEN CORNWALL

7 miles (11.3km) 5hrs **Ascent:** 1,312ft (400m) ▲3
Paths: Good coastal footpath, field paths and quiet lanes. Field stiles are often overgrown, 30 stiles
Suggested map: aqua3 OS Explorer 105 Falmouth & Mevagissey
Grid reference: SW 906384
Parking: Carne Beach car park. Large National Trust car park behind beach

A walk through fields and along the coast through remote and endearing landscapes.
❶ Turn **L** out of car park and walk carefully up road. Past steep bend, turn **R**, go up steps and on to coast path. Follow to **Paradoe Cove**; continue past **Nare Head**.
❷ Above **Kiberick Cove**, go through gap in wall. Keep ahead through dip to stile. Follow coast path to **Portloe**. Go **L** up road from cove, past Ship Inn.
❸ Just after sharp **L**-**H** bend, where road narrows, cross high step stile to **R**. Cross field to stile; follow next field edge. Pass gate; shortly go **R** and over stile. Cross next field to stile into lane.
❹ Go **R** along road past **Camels Farm** for 200yds (183m), then **L** over stile and follow field edge to another stile. Follow next field edge; just before corner, go **R** over stile. Turn **L** through gap, then diagonally **R** across 2 fields to stile. At road junction, go along road (*'Carne and Pendower'*).
❺ Just past **Tregamenna Manor Farm**, on bend, cross stile by gate. Cut across corner of field, then **R** over stile. Cross next field to stile; continue to T-junction with lane. (Turn **R** to visit **Veryan**.)
❻ Otherwise, turn **L**; just past Churchtown Farm, go **L** over stile. Follow field edge to stile into lane. Go immediately **L** over 2 stiles; follow path, past Carne Beacon, to lane.
❼ At corner junction keep ahead down lane (*'Carne Village Only'*). Bear **R** down driveway past Beacon Cottage. Go through gate (*'Defined Footpaths Nos 44 & 45'*). Follow track to **R** between garage and house; follow grassy track, keeping ahead at junction (*'Carne Beach'*). Go through gate (dogs on leads) and follow path alongside bank and hedge.
❽ Abreast of gate on **R**, bear **L** and downhill through scrub (path not evident initially). Soon pick up path leading through gorse to join coast path back to **Carne Beach** and car park.

Cornwall

BISHOP'S WOOD *A FORESTRY ESTATE*

3½ miles (5.7km) 2hrs 30min **Ascent:** 164ft (50m)

Paths: Forest tracks and paths. Can be very muddy after rain

Suggested map: aqua3 OS Explorer 105 Falmouth & Mevagissey

Grid reference: SW 820477

Parking: Forestry car park, north of Idless, near Truro. Car park gates are closed at sunset. Working woodland, please take note of notices advising work in progress

Enjoy the local flora and fauna on this gentle stroll through richly diverse woodlands near Truro.

❶ Leave top end of forestry car park at southern end of forestry car park via wooden barrier and go along broad track. In a few paces at fork, keep to **R** fork and follow track above **Woodpark** and along inside edge of Lady's Wood. (Little stream runs below this track which can be very muddy after rain.) Beech trees dominate here and provide good cover. Further into wood you will find that oak, hazel, birch, Japanese larch and holly grow on either side of track that you are walking along.

❷ Keep on main track, parallel to river, ignoring branch tracks leading off to **L**.

❸ Just before northern end of woodland you reach fork of tracks. Keep on main track as it bends to **L** and uphill. Track levels off and at open area merges with

broad forestry ride. Continue walking ahead along this ride.

❹ At forestry notice indicating remains of **Iron-Age encampment**, go **L** along path beneath conifer trees to reach substantial bank and ditch of encampment which is densely covered with coppiced oaks, identified by multiple growths at their base. Mix of broadleaved trees that makes up most of area indicates long-established forestry. Return to main track and turn **L**.

❺ At bend beside wooden bench, where tracks lead off to L and R, go **R** and follow public footpath uphill. At path crossing, turn **L** and follow path through scrubland and young pine trees.

❻ Re-enter mature woodland of **St Clement Wood** and follow track downhill. Keep **R** at junction, then go **L** at next junction. Reach T-junction with broad track. Turn **R** and follow track to car park.

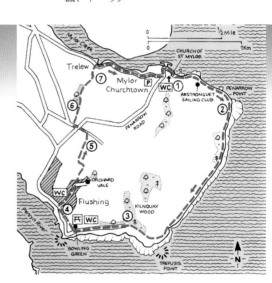

MYLOR CHURCHTOWN *A WATERSIDE WALK*

4 miles (6.4km) 3hrs **Ascent:** 164ft (50m)

Paths: Good paths throughout. Wooded section to Trelew Farm is often very wet, 7 stiles

Suggested map: aqua3 OS Explorer 105 Falmouth & Mevagissey

Grid reference: SW 820352

Parking: Mylor Churchtown car park

To Flushing on a quiet peninsula dominated by ships and sails.

❶ From car park entrance at **Mylor Churchtown**, turn **R** to start of surfaced walkway ('Flushing'). Follow walkway; by gateway of house, bear **L** along path ('Flushing'). Pass in front of **Restronguet Sailing Club**, go up steps, then **L** along coast path.

❷ Follow path round **Penarrow Point**; continue round Trefusis Point. Reach gate and granite grid stile by wooden shack at **Kilnquay Wood**. Continue to reach lane.

❸ Follow lane L; go **R** through gap beside gate and continue along road. Where road drops towards water's edge, bear **R** up slope to 'Bowling Green'. (Strictly no dog fouling.) Continue past pavilion and toilets and go down walkway; turn **L** by junction and signpost for **Flushing**.

❹ Turn **R** at street junction; go along Trefusis Road past Seven Stars Inn. At junction by Royal Standard

Inn, keep **R** past Post Office; go up Kersey Road. At top, by **Orchard Vale**, go **L** up steps ('Mylor Church'). Cross stile; keep to field edge to house and stile.

❺ Go **R** through gate, then turn **L** over cattle grid and follow drive to **Penarrow Road**. Cross carefully, go down road opposite, then **R** down steps and on down field edge. Keep ahead where field edge bends L to reach woods.

❻ Enter woodland; keep **R** at junction to follow rocky path (often mini stream after heavy rainfall). Go through gate, keep **L** at junction, then cross proper stream. Go through tiny gate; turn **R** down farm track to surfaced lane at **Trelew**.

❼ Turn **R** along lane, passing old water pump. At slipway, keep ahead along Wayfield Road. Continue between granite posts and on to public road into Mylor Churchtown. Cross road with care (blind corner) to go through churchyard of St Mylor Church (not public right of way). Turn **R** at waterfront to find car park.

ST ANTHONY'S HEAD *GUNS AND GUIDING LIGHTS*

6½ miles (10.4km) 4hrs **Ascent:** 230ft (70m)

Paths: Excellent coastal and creekside footpaths. May be muddy in places during wet weather, 12 stiles

Suggested map: aqua3 OS Explorer 105 Falmouth & Mevagissey

Grid reference: SW 848313

Parking: National Trust St Anthony Head car park. Alternative parking on the route at Porth Farm (Point ❸, SW 868329)

Visit a church, lighthouse and gun battery.

❶ Leave **St Anthony Head** car park at far end; keep ahead along lane past row of holiday cottages (L). Follow coast path, parallel with old military road alongside **Drake's Downs**, to where it passes above **Porthbeor Beach** at junction with beach access path.

❷ Follow coast path round **Porthmellin Head** and **Killigerran Head** to **Towan Beach**. At junction with beach access path, turn **L** and inland. Bear **L** before gate; go through roofed passageway, to road.

❸ Cross road and through gapway ('Porth Farm'), then down surfaced drive. Turn into entrance to National Trust car park, bear **L** along path, ('Place via Percuil River'). Cross footbridge, turn **R** and follow edge of **Froe Creek** to stile into woods. Follow path alongside **Porth Creek** and through **Drawler Plantation**, ignoring side paths ('Bohortha').

❹ Pass jetty for St Mawes ferry. Continue to kissing

gate and on to road end in front of **Place House**. Go **L** along road and uphill.

❺ Turn **R** and cross stile by red gate ('**Church of St Anthony** and **St Anthony Head**'). Follow path past gravestones to church (control dogs). Go up steps opposite church door; follow path uphill. Bear **R**; at T-junction with track, turn **R**. Follow track ahead; at bend, bear **L**. Cross stile by gate. Follow field edge uphill. Cross stile (seat to L) and keep ahead and downhill until water's edge.

❻ Turn **L**; follow coast path around **Carricknath Point**. Past **Great Molunan Beach**, cross causewayed dam above quay; at junction, keep **R** and follow coast path signs. At junction with surfaced track from L, keep ahead to **St Anthony Lighthouse**.

❼ Return to junction and climb steep track to car park. Halfway up, another track leads **R** to Battery Observation Post and bird hide above Zone Point.

19 ST AGNES *HIGH CLIFFS AND A HIGH HILL*

5 miles (8km) 3hrs Ascent: 623ft (190m)
Paths: Good coastal footpaths and inland tracks
Suggested map: aqua3 OS Explorer 104 Redruth & St Agnes
Grid reference: SW 699512
Parking: St Agnes Head. Number of parking spaces along the clifftop track. Start the walk from any of these

A bracing walk along the cliffs at St Agnes, then inland to the top of St Agnes Beacon.

❶ Join coastal footpath from wherever you park along cliff top. Follow stony track across little promontory of **Tubby's Head**, former Iron-Age settlement. Branch off R on to narrower path about 100yds (90m) before old mine buildings (these are remains of **Wheal Coates** mine). Cross stone stile and continue to **Towanroath mine engine house**.

❷ About 50yds (46m) beyond **Towanroath** branch off R at signpost and descend to **Chapel Porth Beach**.

❸ Cross stream at back corner of car park, follow path up **Chapel Combe** next to stream. Pass below mine building and where path forks among trees, go L through wooden kissing gate.

❹ Cross bridge then turn R onto track. Continue along grassy track and where track narrows, keep ahead at fork. Keep alongside field and on to track;

turn L over wooden stile by gate onto track. After around 50yds (46m), reach junction with wide track. Turn L and continue to public road.

❺ Turn R along public road, and keep ahead at junction. In 200yds (183m), next to entrance to **Sunholme Hotel**, continue up stony track on L. After 50yds (46m), at junction, go L and follow path rising to obvious summit of 629ft (192m) **St Agnes Beacon**, used traditionally for lighting of signal fires and for celebratory bonfires. Views from top of **Beacon** reach as far as tors of Bodmin Moor.

❻ From summit of **Beacon** follow lower of 2 tracks, heading northwest, down towards road. Just before you reach road turn R along narrow path, skirting base of hill, eventually emerging at road by seat.

❼ Cross over and follow track opposite, across New Downs, directly to edge of cliffs, then turn L at junction with coast path and return to car park.

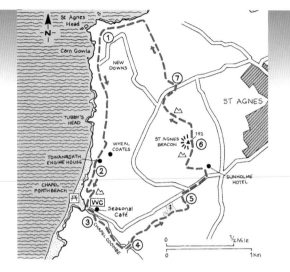

20 REDRUTH *MINES AND METHODISM*

4 miles (6.4km) 2hrs 30min Ascent: 442ft (135m)
Paths: Field paths, rough tracks and surfaced lanes. Can be muddy after rain, 6 stiles
Suggested map: aqua3 OS Explorer 104 Redruth & St Agnes
Grid reference: SW 699421
Parking: Several car parks in Redruth

A walk through Cornwall's mining heartland, visiting Gwennap Pit.

❶ From any of car parks, go to **Fore Street**. Walk up to 3-way junction (railway station to R) and take Wesley Street (middle branch) to L of Redruth Methodist Church ('To Victoria Park'). Shortly turn R (**Sea View Terrace**); Pednandrea Mine chimney stack is up to L along road. Pass Basset Street (R); where streets cross, go L up **Raymond Road** to T-junction with **Sandy Lane**.

❷ Cross road carefully; follow track opposite, ('Public Bridleway' and 'Grambler Farm'). Go through gate by farm; continue to open area. Bear L following much narrower track between hedges. At junction with another track turn L ('Gwennap Pit').

❸ Go R, following **Gwennap Pit** signposts; cross stile by gate, then go through small wooden gate. Keep ahead (free-ranging pigs may be in area; dogs under strict control). Cross stile at next gate; follow

field edge ahead. Cross final field towards house, then walk down lane past house to junction of surfaced roads at **Busveal**. Cross and follow road opposite to **Gwennap Pit**.

❹ Follow road away from **Gwennap Pit**. Turn off to R along broad track ('Public Bridleway'). Keep ahead at 2 crossings; at final crossing beside ruined building, turn R and follow stony track up hill to **Carn Marth**.

❺ Pass flooded quarry (viewpoint far side); just beyond trig point, bear R on path alongside fenced-in rim of deep quarry. At surfaced road, turn L, L again at next junction, then follow lane to T-junction with road at **Calhill Farm**. Turn R; walk along **Sandy Road** (watch for traffic) for 275yds (251m).

❻ Go L at junction ('cycle route'); follow lane R, then L into avenue of houses. At crossroads turn R (Trefusis Road). At next junction turn L (**Raymond Road**), then R (**Sea View Terrace**). Turn L down Wesley Street and on into **Fore Street**.

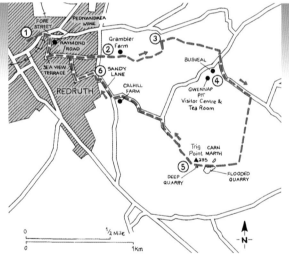

21 HELFORD *HIDDEN CREEKS*

5 miles (8km) 3hrs Ascent: 328ft (100m)
Paths: Good woodland paths and tracks and field paths. Short section of quiet lane, 10 stiles
Suggested map: aqua3 OS Explorer 103 The Lizard
Grid reference: SW 759261
Parking: Helford car park. Large car park overlooking creek. Can become busy in summer. Only authorised cars are allowed beyond the car park into the village of Helford

A circuit of peaceful tidal creeks.

❶ On leaving car park, turn L along path ('Coast Path'). Go through metal gate; follow sunken lane. Descend steps, then turn R along lane. At steep R-H bend, bear ahead along track. Follow path through trees, keeping L at any junctions.

❷ Leave wooded area via metal gate, then turn L along field edge to stile. Follow bottom edge of next 2 fields. Cross fence at field gap beside white pole and red post and triangle (navigation marks). Follow field edge. Go through kissing gate, then follow field edge (seat and viewpoint on L), to where it ends at beginning of wide track (to make short circuit of **Dennis Head**, follow track ahead to stile on L).

❸ To continue on main route, turn R at start of wide track; follow L-H field edge and then path across open field. Join track behind house, then go through kissing gate and descend to **St Anthony's Church**. Follow

road alongside **Gillan Creek**.

❹ Just beyond where road curves round bay, go up R between granite gate posts by public footpath sign. Follow broad track through trees to houses at **Roscaddon**. Keep ahead along track leading to Manaccan at T-junction opposite Manaccan church.

❺ Go through churchyard and on through gate opposite to road (village shop L). Bear R to junction (**New Inn** L), then go up R, past school. Keep uphill, then turn L along Minster Meadow, cross stile, and through 2 fields to reach road.

❻ Go diagonally L to stile opposite, cross field, then go L following signposts to woods. Follow path ahead. At junction keep ahead, cross stile and reach 2nd junction.

❼ Bear down R following broad track through trees to buildings at Helford. Keep ahead at surfaced road and follow road uphill to car park.

Cornwall

CADGWITH *THE SERPENTINE ROUTE*

4½ miles (7.2km) 3hrs **Ascent:** 230ft (70m)

Paths: Very good. Occasionally rocky in places. Rock can be slippery when wet
Suggested map: aqua3 OS Explorer 103 The Lizard
Grid reference: SW 720146
Parking: Cadgwith car park. About 350yds (320m) from Cadgwith. Busy in summer

A wandering route between coast and countryside through the serpentine landscape of the Lizard Peninsula.

❶ Go **L** along grassy ride below car park, to stile. Continue over another stile, then branch **R**. Turn **R** at lane, then on corner, go up track and continue to main road at little village of **Ruan Minor**.

❷ Go **L** and, just beyond shop, turn **L** down surfaced path. Rejoin main road by thatched cottage (there are toilets just before road). Cross diagonally **R**, then go down lane past **Church of St Ruan** (small building of mainly local serpentine stone).

❸ Just past old mill and bridge, go **R** at T-junction to reach car park at Poltesco. From far end of car park follow track, signposted 'Carleon Cove'. Go **R** at junction.

❹ Turn **L** at T-junction just above cove (once site of water wheels, steam engines, machine shops and factory where serpentine was processed), and again turn **L** where path branches in about ¼ mile (400m). Continue along cliff-edge path to archetypal Cornish village of **Cadgwith**.

❺ Follow narrow path, signposted 'Coast Path'. By house gateway, go **L** up surfaced path ('Devil's Frying Pan'). At an open area turn **L**, pass Townplace Cottage, cross meadow and reach **Devil's Frying Pan** itself, vast gulf in cliffs caused by collapse of section of coast undermined by sea.

❻ At junction, just past chalet studio, follow path inland to T-junction with rough track. Turn **L** and, at public lane, go **L** again to reach entrance to **Church of Holy Cross** standing on raised ground at Grade, after 1 mile (1.6km).

❼ Follow edge of field behind church, then cross next field to reach lane. Ancient **St Ruan's Well** is opposite diagonally **L**. Turn **R** for 200yds (183m), then branch off **R** between stone pillars to return to car park.

LIZARD POINT *LIGHTHOUSES AND LIFEBOATS*

6½ miles (10.4km) 4hrs **Ascent:** 220ft (67m)

Paths: Coastal footpaths, inland tracks and lanes. Please take note of path diversion notices at any erosion repair areas, 3 stiles
Suggested map: aqua3 OS Explorer 103 The Lizard
Grid reference: SW 703125
Parking: Large car park at centre of Lizard village. Donation box. Can be busy in summer

Around Britain's most southerly point.

❶ Walk past public toilets at bottom end of car park and go along surfaced lane ('To Caerthillian and Kynance Coves'). In 50yds (46m) bear **R** at junction and go along track ('Public Footpath Kynance Cove'). Shortly, at public footpath sign, bear **L** behind chalet; go up some steps, then follow hedge-top path.

❷ Descend steps and go through privet grove. Negotiate 2 more sets of steps then bear slightly **R** across field towards roof of house (just visible). Go over step stile to surfaced road.

❸ Follow road past house, ('Carn Goon'). Shortly bear **R** along track. Reach T-junction with wide track and cross to reach bottom end of National Trust car park for Kynance Cove. Pass in front of information kiosk; turn **R** and follow track to **Kynance Cove**.

❹ Walk back up from cove to where path goes **R** ('Coastal Path To **Lizard Point**'). Follow cobbled and stepped path uphill, then continue along coast path for about 1¼ miles (2km). Pass above Pentreath Beach and **Caerthillian Cove** and continue to rocky **Lizard Head**, then **Lizard Point** and car park and cafés.

❺ Cross car park and follow coast path past lighthouse. Descend steeply into **Housel Cove** and ascend (also steeply), ignoring link path inland to **Lizard** village. Pass old **Marconi Wireless Station**, at Pen Olver, **Old Lloyds Signal Station**, then **National Coastwatch Institution Lookout** at Bass Point.

❻ Follow track past houses, then bear **R** and follow narrow coast path past Hot Point and on to lifeboat house at Kilcobben Cove.

❼ Go down steps on far side of lifeboat station and follow coast path to Church Cove. Follow public lane inland past **Landewednack Church**; continue uphill to junction with main road on bend by granite cross and seat. Go **L** along Beacon Terrace to car park.

PORTREATH *CLIFFS AND DEEP WOODS*

4 miles (6.4km) 3hrs **Ascent:** 459ft (140m)

Paths: Good coastal path, woodland path, farm tracks
Suggested map: aqua3 OS Explorer 104 Redruth & St Agnes
Grid reference: SW 656453
Parking: Portreath Beach

Along spectacular cliffs and through woods.

❶ Turn **R** outside **Portreath Beach** car park, cross bridge and turn **R** up **Battery Hill** ('Coast Path'). Follow lane uphill to houses above beach. Go **L** in front of garage ('North Coast Foot Path').

❷ Follow path through gate; keep straight uphill to cliff top (take care). Turn **L** to wooden gate; follow path round cliff edge above **Ralph's Cupboard**. Continue by steep paths into and out of **Porth-cadjack Cove**.

❸ At car parking area above **Basset's Cove** follow broad track inland. At road, cross and turn **L** for 40yds (37m); watch for fast-moving traffic. Reach granite grid stile on **R**, cross stile. Follow narrow path into **Tehidy Woods**.

❹ Keep ahead at crossing. Soon pass R-H junction, then L-H junction ('Pedestrians Only'). Keep straight ahead to reach T-junction with broad track. Turn **L**.

❺ Reach junction and 4-way signpost beside 2 seats (café ¼ mile/400m down R-H signposted track). On main route, keep ahead ('East Lodge'). Reach junction by seat. Go **R** and through wooden kissing gate. Cross golf course (watch for golf balls). Go through metal kissing gate; follow track by **golf course**.

❻ Shortly beyond end of **golf course** section, bear **L** into woods by staggered wooden barrier, ('Pedestrians Only'). Stay on main path, ignoring side paths, then bear **R** to car park and public road. Cross diagonally **R**, then go **L** between wooden posts (red marks). Follow track ahead (often muddy).

❼ Go **R** on to wider track by field gate. Next section can be muddy in rain. Pass holiday chalets and reach T-junction above farm buildings (**Feadon Farm**).

❽ Turn **L**, then shortly **R** down track. At farmyard go sharp **L** by public footpath sign; follow path through woods to surfaced road. Past 'Glenfeadon Castle' turn **L** (**Glenfeadon Terrace**), pass beneath bridge, then at junction keep ahead (Tregea Terrace) and return to **Portreath Beach** car park.

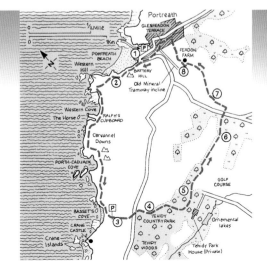

Cornwall

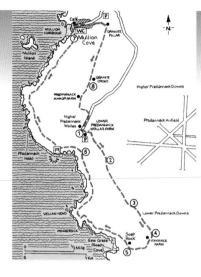

25 MULLION COVE *WILDFLOWER HAVEN*

7 miles (11.3km) 4hrs **Ascent:** 164ft (50m) ▲
Paths: Good inland tracks and paths, can be muddy during wet weather. Coastal footpath, 21 stiles
Suggested map: aqua3 OS Explorer 103 The Lizard
Grid reference: SW 669162
Parking: Predannack Wollas Farm car park (National Trust)

The Lizard Peninsula heathland supports some of Britain's most remarkable wild flowers.

❶ Leave **Predannack Wollas Farm** car park by bottom end. Follow winding track ahead for just under ½ mile (800m) to gate. (Ignore signposted track L just before gate.) Beyond gate, bear **L** to stile. Follow edge of next field to stile; continue to open ground by gate in fence on **R**.

❷ Cross stile next to gate; bear away from fence along path to English Nature's Kynance Farm Nature Reserve. Keep ahead towards distant buildings.

❸ Watch for gap in hedge on **L**, go through, then cross field to rough track. Turn **R** along track then bear **L** and follow edge of scrub.

❹ Go through gate; follow track **R**. Merge with another track; just before ford, bear **R** along track towards coast (**Kynance Farm** R).

❺ At crossing with coast path, go **R** and uphill; cross

stile on to cliff top. Follow coast path round edge of cliffs at **Pengersick** and **Vellan Head**.

❻ Go **L** at junction, just past National Trust sign ('Predannack'). (You can return to car park by following inland path from here.) Cross stream in dip; climb up **L**, then continue along coast path to **Mullion Cove** and **Harbour**.

❼ Go up road from **Mullion Harbour**; beyond public toilets and shop, turn **R** at coast path sign. Keep to **R** of entrance to holiday residential site; follow track uphill. On bend and just before granite pillar, go **R** and over stone stile. Follow path ahead through thorn tree grove, then through fields.

❽ Pass tall granite cross, then reach lane. Turn **R** along lane towards farm. Before **Predannack Manor Farm** entrance, go **L** over stile by field gate, then **R** along field edge. Cross stile, then **L** along hedged-in path; cross stile and 2 fields to lane (watch for traffic). Turn **R** to **Lower Predannack Wollas Farm** car park.

26 PRUSSIA COVE *THE SMUGGLER KING*

4 miles (6.4km) 3hrs **Ascent:** 394ft (120m) ▲
Paths: Good field paths and coastal paths, 18 stiles
Suggested map: aqua3 OS Explorer 102 Land's End
Grid reference: SW 554282
Parking: Trenalls, Prussia Cove. Small privately-owned car park. Or car park at Perranuthnoe, from where the walk can be started at Point ❺

Through the coastal domain of John Carter, the famous Cornish smuggler.

❶ From car park entrance walk back along approach road, past large house (watch for traffic). After 2nd bend, by camp site entrance, look for stile on **L**, past field gate.

❷ Cross stile; follow field edge, bearing **R**, where it bends **L**, to stile in hedge opposite. Walk down edge of next field, behind **Acton Castle** (private dwellings); turn **R** along field edge to stile into adjacent lane. Turn **R**.

❸ Turn **L** along track at junction in front of bungalow entrance at **Trevean Farm**. At L-H bend go on to stony track for short distance; at public footpath sign, ascend to **R**, up narrow steps, then **L** along field edge.

❹ At **Trebarvah**, cross farm lane, pass in front of barns (view of St Michael's Mount ahead), then follow field edge to hedged-in path. Follow path ahead through fields, then pass houses to reach main road

opposite **Victoria Inn**. Go **L** and follow road to car park above **Perranuthnoe Beach**.

❺ For beach and **Cabin Café**, keep ahead. On main route, go **L**, just beyond car park, and along lane. Bear **R** at fork, then **R** again just past house at junction.

❻ Go down track towards sea and follow it **L**. At field entrance, go down **R** (signposted), turn sharp **L** through gap and follow coast path along edge of **Trebarvah** and **Stackhouse Cliffs**.

❼ At National Trust property of Cudden Point, follow path uphill, then across inner slope of headland above **Piskies Cove**.

❽ Go through gate and pass ancient fishing huts. Follow path round edge of **Bessy's Cove** inlet of **Prussia Cove**, to track by thatched cottage. Cove can be reached down path on **R** just before this junction. Turn **R** and follow track, keeping **L** at this junction, to return to car park.

27 ST IVES *CHURCH PATHS AND COASTGUARD WAYS*

8 miles (12.9km) 3hrs **Ascent:** 394ft (120m) ▲
Paths: Coastal path, can be quite rocky. Field paths, some stiles. Very scenic coast and small inland fields
Suggested map: aqua3 OS Explorer 102 Land's End
Grid reference: SW 522408
Parking: Upper Trenwith car park St Ives or Porthmeor Beach, Smeaton's Pier and Porthmeor car park

A long coastal walk following old paths.

❶ Walk along harbour to Smeaton's Pier. Before pier entrance, turn **L** (Sea View Place). Where road bends, keep ahead into Wheal Dream. Turn **R** past **St Ives Museum**; follow walkway to **Porthgwidden Beach**.

❷ Cross car park above beach; climb to **National Coastwatch lookout**. Go down steps, behind building at back, then follow footway to **Porthmeor Beach**. Go along beach to car park.

❸ Go up steps beside public toilets; turn **R** along track past bowling and putting greens. Continue to **Carrick Du** and **Clodgy Point**.

❹ From square-cut rock on **Clodgy Point** walk uphill and through low wall. Follow path **R** and across boggy area. In ½ mile (800m) go **L** at junction.

❺ Reach T-junction with track just past National Trust sign ('Hellesveor Cliff'). Turn **R**; follow coast path. (Short version of walk goes **L** and inland.)

❻ Keep **R** at junction past old mine stack and shed

(L). Continue to **River Cove**. On other side, go **L** at junction and inland through woods.

❼ At junction, go **L** over cattle grid; follow signs past **Trevail Mill**. Go through metal gate and climb.

❽ Cross track; follow path opposite. Shortly go **L** over stile by black-and-white pole. Follow field edges over stiles.

❾ Follow **R-H** edge of field containing parish boundary stone. Cross 2 stiles; at hedge corner, bear **R** across field; continue to **Trevalgan Farm**. Cross behind farm to stile; continue to **Trowan Farm**.

❿ Go **L** over stile before house; turn **R**. Go through farmyard to lane; turn **L** then **R**, over stile. Follow field paths over more stiles.

⓫ Go over stile and through metal gate, pass field gap, then **L** and down hedged-in path. Cross stile and pass between hedges to **Burthallan lane**.

⓬ Turn **R** to reach T-junction with main road. Turn **L**; follow road downhill to **Porthmeor Beach** and start.

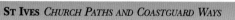

Cornwall

LAMORNA COVE *MERRY MAIDENS*

6 miles (9.7km) 3hrs 30min **Ascent:** 558ft (170m)
Paths: Good coastal footpaths, field paths and rocky tracks
Suggested map: aqua3 OS Explorer 102 Land's End
Grid reference: SW 450241
Parking: Lamorna Cove

A coastal and inland walk passing an ancient stone circle along the way.

❶ From far end of seaward car park, at end of terrace above **Lamorna Cove**, follow coast path through short rocky sections. Continue along path past tops of **Tregurnow Cliff** and **Rosemodress Cliff**.

❷ Pass above entrance ramp and steps to **Tater-du Lighthouse**. Pass large residence (R); where track bends R, keep **L** along coast path, at signpost.

❸ Descend steeply (care when muddy) from **Boscawen Point** to **St Loy's Cove**. Cross section of boulders (may be slippery when wet). Follow path inland through dense vegetation and by stream. Cross private drive then climb steeply uphill. Cross stile on to track, turn **R** over stile and follow path through trees.

❹ By wooden signpost and old tree, go **R** and cross stream on large boulders; follow hedged-in path **L**. Shortly, by wooden signpost, go **R** and up to surfaced lane. Turn **L**; follow lane uphill. At junction with bend

on another track, keep ahead and uphill. At **Boskenna Farm** buildings follow lane L; keep ahead.

❺ From lane, at entrance drive to bungalow on R, right of way goes through field gate, then cuts across field corner to stile in wire fence. Beyond, right of way (no path) leads diagonally across field to top **R-H** corner, where stile leads into lay-by with granite **cross** at edge. An alternative route is to continue along farm lane; turn **R** along public road, taking care, to lay-by.

❻ Follow road to **Tregiffian** burial chamber on R, then **Merry Maidens** stone circle. From circle continue to field corner, cross stile and follow path diagonally **R** across next field towards buildings. Cross stile on to road, then down **R-H** of 2 lanes (surfaced, 'No Through Road' sign).

❼ Where lane ends, keep ahead on to public bridleway. Follow track downhill to public road. Turn **R** and walk down road, with care, passing Lamorna Wink Inn, to car park.

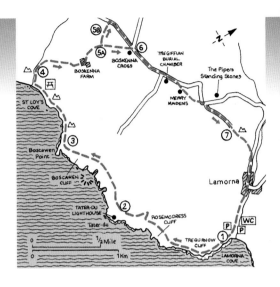

PENDEEN *THE TINNERS' TRAIL*

5 miles (8km) 4hrs **Ascent:** 328ft (100m)
Paths: Coastal footpath, field paths and moorland tracks
Suggested map: aqua3 OS Explorer 102 Land's End
Grid reference: SW 383344
Parking: Free car park in centre of Pendeen village, opposite Boscaswell Stores, on the B3306

Through tin and copper mining country.

❶ Turn **L** out of car park and follow road to entrance of **Geevor Tin Mine**. Go down drive to reception building and keep to its **L** down road between buildings, signposted 'Levant'.

❷ Just beyond buildings, turn **L** along narrow path that soon bears R and becomes unsurfaced track between walls. Turn **L** at huge boulder and head towards very tall chimney stack ahead. Continue across broken ground to National Trust's **Levant Engine House**.

❸ Follow bottom edge of Levant car park and then rough track to reach **Botallack Count House**. Keep on past **Manor Farm** and reach public road at **Botallack**. Turn **L**.

❹ Go **L** at main road (watch out for fast traffic) then turn **L** along Cresswell Terrace to stile. Follow field paths to old mining village of **Carnyorth**. Cross main road, then follow lane opposite, turning **R** at junction,

to reach solitary house.

❺ Keep **L** of house, go over stile and cross field to opposite hedge to reach hidden stile. Follow path through small fields towards radio mast. Cross final stile on to rough track.

❻ Go **L**, then immediately **R** at junction. Keep on past **radio mast**, then follow path through gorse and heather to rocky outcrop of **Carn Kenidjack** (not always visible when misty).

❼ At junction abreast of **Carn Kenidjack**, go back **L** along path past small granite parish boundary stone, eventually emerging on road. Turn **R** and in about 140yds (128m), go **L** along obvious broad track opposite house.

❽ Keep **L** at junction. By 2 large stones on L, bear off **R** along grassy track. Go **L** over big stone stile directly above **Church of St John**, built by mining community in 1850s, and descend to main road. Turn **R** to car park.

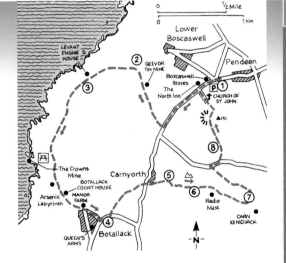

PORTHCURNO *GOLDEN BEACHES AND CLIFFS*

3½ miles (5.7km) 2hrs 30min **Ascent:** 164ft (50m)
Paths: Coastal footpath
Suggested map: aqua3 OS Explorer 107 St Austell & Liskeard
Grid reference: SW 384224
Parking: Porthcurno, St Levan and Porthgwarra

Between sandy coves and granite cliffs on the Land's End Peninsula.

❶ From car park, walk back up approach road; just beyond Porthcurno Hotel, turn **L** along track and follow to cottages. Pass to their **R** and go through kissing gate. Follow field path past granite cross.

❷ Enter **St Levan churchyard** by granite stile. Go round far side of church to entrance gate and on to surfaced lane; cross and follow path opposite ('Porthgwarra Cove'). Cross footbridge over stream; shortly, at junction, take **R** fork and follow path to merge with main coast path and keep ahead.

❸ After path begins to descend towards **Porthgwarra Cove**, branch **R** up wooden steps. Reach track and turn up **R**, at road, turn **L**.

❹ Go round sharp L-H bend; at footpath signpost, go **R** down path and cross stone footbridge. Continue uphill to reach bend on track, just up from granite houses.

❺ Turn **L**, cross stile beside gate, then down surfaced lane to **Porthgwarra Cove**. Opposite shop and café, go **R** down track ('Coast Path'); take path L in front of house. Go **R** at junction and climb steps.

❻ Continue along coast path, partly reversing previous route past Point **❸**. Keep **R** at junctions; eventually descend past **St Levan's Well** to just above **Porth Chapel Beach**. (Control dogs on beach.) Follow coast path steeply over **Pedn-mên-an-mere**; continue to **Minack Theatre** car park.

❼ For surefooted walkers, cross car park and go down track to **L** of Minack compound; descend steep cliff steps (take care). When path levels off, continue to junction. **R** fork leads to Porthcurno Beach and back to car park. Continuation leads to road opposite Beach Café, where **R** turn leads to car park. For less challenging alternative, turn **L** out of Minack car park. Follow approach road to T-junction with public road. Turn **R** and walk down road, watching out for traffic.

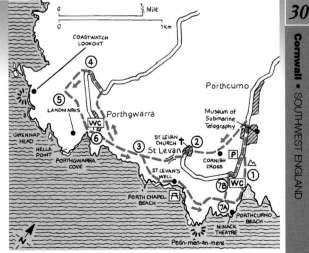

Devon

31 COLYTON A CHEQUERED HISTORY

4¼ miles (6.8km) 2hrs 30min **Ascent:** 197ft (60m)
Paths: Fields and country lanes, one narrow boggy track, 9 stiles
Suggested map: aqua3 OS Explorer 116 Lyme Regis & Bridport
Grid reference: SY 245940
Parking: Paying car park in centre of Colyton (Dolphin Street)

Along the River Coly and Umborne Brook.

1 From car park turn **R**, then 1st **L** (Lower Church Street). Turn **L** at Gerrard Arms (Rosemary Lane), **R** (Vicarage Street), then **R** towards river; cross bridge.

2 Turn **L** through kissing gate and along river bank on **East Devon Way** (EDW). Follow path through 2 kissing gates. Ignore next footpath sign R; go ahead through 2 gates, following river.

3 At junction of footpaths at end of field keep river **L**; take kissing gate in corner on to concrete walkway. Go through kissing gate and across field to 2 gates and footbridge below 3 oaks. Cross another footbridge/gate to bridge over river on **L**.

4 Turn **R**, through gate to lane; turn **R**. At Cadhayne Farm (R) turn **L** through gate opposite farmyard. Walk uphill, through gate at top and straight on. Lane veers L; turn **R** along muddy lane (**Tritchayne**).

5 Cross; walk downhill along **Watery Lane**. At **Tritchmarsh**, lane becomes grassy track; follow

footpath sign **R** on wooden walkway. Go **L** to gate and **L** round field. Ignore next stile L; take small gate/bridge/gate to **R**; cross paddock and **Umborne Brook** via gate and walkway to **Lexhayne Mill**. Path runs to kissing gate and over stile in wire fence. Cross next stile; head diagonally **R** for drive to **Lexhayne Farm**. Go **L**, then **R** (signed) through hedge gap.

6 Cross diagonally down field towards bottom corner, over double gate/bridge and footbridge over brook. Walk **L**; cross stile; cross brook via double gate/footbridge with **Colyton church** ahead.

7 Aim for stile in fence ahead **R**. Keep ahead; cross brook via double gate/bridge, then **L**. Cross stile and 2 stiles/footbridges, then diagonally across upper part of next field. Cross stile, go downhill; over stile to road.

8 Turn **L**; pass picnic area at **Road Green**, then over bridge. Take 1st **L** (Vicarage Street); go straight on, past church (L), through town centre and down Silver Street to car park.

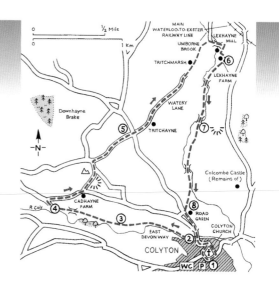

32 BROADHEMBURY AN UNSPOILT VILLAGE

5½ miles (8.8km) 2hrs 30min **Ascent:** 360ft (110m)
Paths: Country lanes, pastures and woodland paths, 7 stiles
Suggested map: aqua3 OS Explorer 115 Exeter & Sidmouth
Grid reference: SY 095068
Parking: Unsurfaced car park at Knowles Wood

Beech woods and rolling farmland around an unspoilt thatched village.

1 Return to road; turn **L** uphill. Shortly bridleway sign points **R** through another parking area, then path reaches signpost and metal gate (L), indicating you have reached **Devon & Somerset Gliding Club**. Ignore gate; continue on bridleway.

2 Pass through next metal gate on to airfield. Turn **R** along edge, keeping to R of clubhouse. Follow tarmac drive **L** over cattle grid and down lane to road.

3 Turn **R**; pass **Barleycombe Farm** (L), then follow bridleway signs **R** through gate, **L** through another and into field. Track follows bottom of field. Path curves **R** through beech trees and metal gate, then runs straight across next field towards beech tree and gate. Shortly bear **R** along grassy path (ignore gate ahead) and through 2 metal gates (coniferous plantation to R).

4 Path ends at lane; turn **R** downhill into

Broadhembury. At **St Andrew's Church** cross road and go through churchyard, then under lychgate and downhill to **Drewe Arms** on your L.

5 From pub, turn **L** down main street to bridge and ford. Turn **R** up lane, past playground and up hill.

6 Past 2 thatched cottages go **L** over stile in hedge and up field, aiming for stile in top **L** corner. Go over and ahead, keeping old farmhouse and barn to R. Cross next stile, then another. Turn **R**, round edge of field, and over small stile into small copse. Another stile leads into next field; look across to locate next stile in beech hedge opposite, which leads to green lane.

7 Turn **R**; walk uphill between conifers (L), and fields until metal gate leads on to open gateway and back on to airfield.

8 Turn **L** along edge of field. Go **R** over 2nd iron gate to rejoin bridleway which leads back to road. Turn **L** downhill to your car.

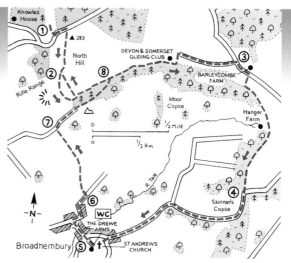

33 BRANSCOMBE THE EAST DEVON CLIFFS

6¼ miles (10.1km) 3hrs 30min **Ascent:** 492ft (150m)
Paths: Coast path (one steep ascent), country lanes, 14 stiles
Suggested map: aqua3 OS Explorer 115 Exeter & Sidmouth
Grid reference: SY 167890
Parking: Unsurfaced car park at Weston

Along the coast near Branscombe.

1 From car park take track over stile on to East Devon Heritage Coast path ('Weston Mouth'). After ½ mile (800m), at stile and gate, go straight on; veer **L** across field; join coast path at another stile.

2 Go **L**, steeply uphill (wooden steps), to top of **Weston Cliff**. Kissing gate leads on to **Coxe's Cliff**; path runs diagonally away from coast via deep combe towards another stile in top **L** corner of field. Cross next field and stile on to grassland above Littlecombe Shoot.

3 Pass coast path marker ahead and 2 stands of gorse (L). Turn diagonally **L**, away from cliff, towards gap in gorse hedge. Head for gate in top **L** corner of next field; turn **L** down track to lane at Berry Barton.

4 Turn **R** down lane to **Fountain Head** pub. Turn **R** again down valley, passing thatched cottages and **St Winifred's Church** (R). Continue downhill past post office and **Forge** to St Branoc's Well and village hall.

5 Turn **R** opposite Parkfield Terrace down lane ('Branscombe Mouth'). Shortly farm gate leads to well-signposted path through field to footbridge and gate. Go through next meadow and gate. Turn **R** over wooden bridge and gate to **Branscombe Mouth**.

6 Turn immediately **R** through kissing gate to join coast path signs uphill beneath coastguard cottages (now private). Go through open gateway and **L** into woods via stile. Ignore paths L and R until, after 2 stiles and ½ mile (800m), signpost points **L** between grassy hummocks towards cliffs.

7 Follow coastal footpath signs to rejoin cliff edge, over stile on to Littlecombe Shoot. Retrace steps over 2 stiles to Coxe's Cliff, then stile and kissing gate on to **Weston Cliff**. Turn immediately **R** through kissing gate into wildflower meadow.

8 Pass cottage and outbuildings (R) over 2 stiles and on to track leading to tarmac lane. Go **L** to Weston and your car.

Devon

BICKLEIGH *THE EXE VALLEY WAY*

4¼ miles (6.8km) 2hrs Ascent: 509ft (155m)
Paths: Country lanes, one long, steep, muddy track
Suggested map: aqua3 OS Explorer 114 Exeter & the Exe Valley
Grid reference: SX 939075
Parking: Bickleigh Mill just off A396 at Bickleigh Bridge

Leave the crowds behind at Bickleigh Bridge and explore the lovely Exe Valley.

1 From public parking area at edge of **Bickleigh Mill** go back, with care, to A396 and cross bridge. Turn **L** down A3072, following brown tourist sign (**Bickleigh Castle**). Take 1st lane **L**, running along edge of flood plain on **Exe Valley Way** (EVW). **Bickleigh Castle** is R. Go straight on past **Way Farm**.

2 Just after **Way Farm** buildings turn **R** to leave **Exe Valley Way** ('Lee Cross & Perry Farm'). Take care here as this is a very narrow lane, carrying busy traffic, especially from local working farms. This ancient lane climbs steeply uphill and after 700yds (640m) comes to farm at **Lee Cross**.

3 Immediately after house keep straight ahead along road. Pass **Perry Farm** and continue until you reach T-junction; turn **L** on to green lane. Continue down this lane until you reach another T-junction. Turn **R**; lane levels off and becomes easier.

4 Where green lane meets tarmac lane turn **L** and proceed steeply downhill (EVW). Views over River Exe and Silverton church beyond are glorious. Follow lane down until you see **Tray Mill Farm** on L.

5 Way home is straight on along lane, but it's worth doing small detour to river. Turn **R** through farmyard (no sign) and pass through metal gate on to concrete standing. Ahead is suspension bridge over river; cross it and go straight on to reach dismantled railway track. Do not turn L along track – which would take you straight back to your car – it's privately owned and has no public right of way.

6 Path goes straight on here to meet A369. Turn **L**, then **R** to walk through **Bickleigh** village back to mill (road is busy; it's better to retrace steps to **Tray Mill Farm** and take quieter route back to **Bickleigh Mill**).

7 Back on lane by **Tray Mill Farm**, turn **R** and walk along lane, past **Bickleigh Castle**, turning **R** at A3072, and **R** again over bridge to return to your car.

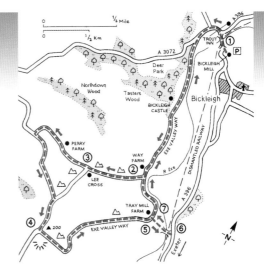

OTTERTON *BIRD LIFE AT THE RESERVE*

4¼ miles (6.8km) 2hrs Ascent: 164ft (50m)
Paths: Good level paths, coastal section and lanes, 2 stiles
Suggested map: aqua3 OS Explorer 115 Exeter & Sidmouth
Grid reference: SX 077830
Parking: By side of broad, quiet lane near entrance to South Farm

Along the River Otter towards High Peak.

1 Walk through kissing gate to **R** of gate to **South Farm**. Turn **R** following signs ('Coast Path Ladram Bay'). Sandy path runs along field edge (views R over saltmarshes of Otter Estuary Nature Reserve and River Otter).

2 At end of field shallow flight of wooden steps leads to walkway and footbridge, and up into next field (good views downriver to shingle bank at Budleigh Salterton).

3 Path continues gently downhill until it turns sharply **L** following line of coast.

4 After 1 mile (1.6km) path rises; ahead is Lyme Bay, including High Peak (564ft/157m – one of highest points on South Devon coast). Follow coast path: red sandstone cliffs extremely friable and 'chunks' continually tumble seawards, but path is safe. Pass through small gate by ruined lookout building, and downhill.

5 Turn **L** to leave coast path on 'Permissive path to Otterton'; this leads over stile; turn immediately **L** and follow path **R** around **water treatment works**, and up gravelly lane to **Stantyway Road**. Lane veers R, but turn **L** up grassy track, following signs to Otterton and **River Otter**. Track soon veers R and gives way to tarmac lane.

6 After 400yds (366m) **Colliver Lane** and **River Otter** signed to L. Turn **L** here; follow narrow, wooded green lane, which ends at stile. Go through, then almost immediately another; follow signs along edge of next field, which you leave over stile on to track.

7 Turn immediately **L** between 2 brick pillars, then **R** under large oak tree. Descend steps and cross **River Otter** on Clamour Bridge (wooden footbridge).

8 Turn **L** and follow river south; over small leat (look out for aqueduct coming across meadows on R), through gate and continue to White Bridge; go through kissing gate, turn **L** and find your car.

CULMSTOCK *OVER THE BORDER TO SOMERSET*

8 miles (12.9km) 3hrs 30min Ascent: 590ft (180m)
Paths: Rough pasture, green lanes and woodland tracks, 16 stiles
Suggested map: aqua3 OS Explorer 128 Taunton & Blackdown Hills
Grid reference: ST 103136
Parking: Fore Street, Culmstock, near entrance to All Saints Church

A long walk from Culmstock to the Wellington Monument.

1 Walk along Fore Street with church to L. As street bends R, take lane ahead around church wall. At 'Cobblestones' turn **R** towards kissing gate. Make for bottom **L** corner of field. Go down steps to river; don't cross.

2 Turn **R** through kissing gate towards stile below ash trees. Take wooden footbridge across river. Turn **L**, then **R**; cross stile in hedge. Cross next stile towards stables, on to lane. Turn **R**.

3 Past cream-coloured house (R), turn **L** through wooden gate. Walk up field with hedge to L. When hedge veers L aim for top **R** corner of field and stile. Cross stile; continue uphill across field. Through gate, follow track L of **Pitt Farm**. Where gate leads to farm drive, turn **L**; where drive meets lane, turn **R** uphill.

4 Lane becomes rough track and turns **L**; just round corner turn **R** through small gate and climb to

trig point on **Culmstock Beacon**.

5 Pass to **R** of trig point; follow ridge on flinty track. Keep out in open; aim for communications tower ahead to **R**. Cut **R** towards mast from broad grassy ride, through metal gate into beech woods and take track ahead. Path eventually leaves woods and runs downhill to join tarmac road; carry on to larger road on sharp bend. Continue straight ahead.

6 When road curves R turn **L** over stile and up field; over 2 stiles, then 3rd in top corner to monument. Turn **R** down approach track to road; turn **R** again.

7 Before road bends R take footpath signed **L** over stile. Cross field and next stile on to grassy path. Cross 2 stiles and field into beech wood by stile. Leaving woodland by another stile, carry straight on and over 2 more stiles to lane. Turn **R**.

8 Shortly turn **R** downhill, then **R** at 1st junction. Go ahead through **Whitehall**; follow lane to house at Point **3**. Turn **L** past house and retrace steps.

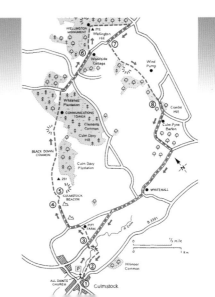

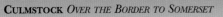

37 KILLERTON *The National Trust*

4¼ miles (6.8km) 2hrs 15min Ascent: 131ft (40m) ⚠
Paths: Good footpaths, bridleways and farm tracks, 3 stiles
Suggested map: aqua3 OS Explorer 114 Exeter & the Exe Valley
Grid reference: SX 977001
Parking: National Trust car park plus overflow car park

Around the Killerton Estate.

❶ From car park return to road and turn **R** to gate and cattle grid at entrance drive to **Killerton House**. Follow public footpath sign towards house, passing stables and courtyard on **R**.

❷ Leave main approach drive as it gets closer to **Killerton House**. Pass house on **R-H** side. Continue straight on, past walled gardens and ornamental lawns. Shortly after, cross stile on **R**; continue through small gate in hedge ahead to large sloping field.

❸ Turn **R** uphill, keeping by hedge, then metal fence on **R**. At top of field ignore public footpath sign ('Bluebell Gate'); turn **L** down across field to enter **Columbjohn Wood** through gate ('Beware of walkers').

❹ Take bridlepath **L**, and immediately branch **L** on higher path, leading gradually downhill. Leave wood by another gate; keep straight on to meet and follow farm track. After 250yds (229m) cross stile on **R** to enter field. Keeping wood on **R**, pass cottage to 16th-century **Columbjohn Chapel**.

❺ Cross another stile to grassy drive opposite chapel; look at old gatehouse archway. Retrace steps through field back to farm track.

❻ Turn **L** and follow track through woods and fields around edge of estate. **River Culm** is on **L**, but you will be more aware of main **Penzance-to-Paddington railway**. Track reaches road by **Ellerhayes Bridge**.

❼ Do not go on to road; turn **R** to follow edge of parkland and woods, keeping road on **L**. Pass through several gates ('National Trust bridlepath') to join gravel track which passes entrance to **Chapel of Holy Evangelists**, built in Norman style in 1842 for Acland family, their tenants and employees, and to replace one at Columbjohn.

❽ Continue on to road. Turn **R** through cutting, and again branch **R**, following signs to Killerton House, to reach car park.

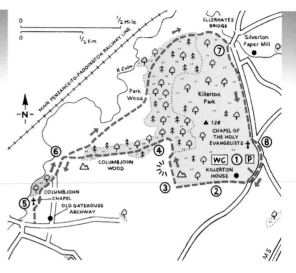

38 WITHLEIGH *Watching for Buzzards*

3¾ miles (6km) 2hrs Ascent: 150ft (45m) ⚠
Paths: Waymarked paths, tracks and quiet lanes, 3 stiles
Suggested map: aqua3 OS Explorer 114 Exeter & the Exe Valley
Grid reference: SX 905121
Parking: A narrow lane (No Through Road) leads to car park from B3137 near sign to Withleigh church

A walk through peaceful hillside woods and along river banks.

❶ From car park cross stile into field, and turn **R**. At hedge ahead turn **L** and walk towards wood. Drop down steeply **R**, heading for gate and stone water trough near by.

❷ Once through gate go ahead, keeping hedge **L**. Cross next stile and continue with tiny River Dart on **R**. Before bridge turn **L** at waymarker, through small gate into another field. Turn **R**, keeping high hedge **R**.

❸ Leave field through next gate on to broad track which rises through **Cross's Wood**. Soon after passing bench, waymarker directs you **L**, off track and back into woods up steep path (overgrown and muddy in places). Continue to climb to wide track at top of woods.

❹ Turn **R** to follow track gently downhill, through gate into open area where it zig-zags more steeply downhill between gorse, broom and bracken.

❺ Continue on to valley bottom and join riverside track, passing through gate with sign asking horse-riders to dismount. Before bridge ahead turn **L** on broad track. Shortly turn **R** over stile and double-plank bridge to enter field.

❻ Keep high hedge to **L** and walk through field to reach small gate into Huntland Wood. Follow path steeply uphill. Path levels off and leads through beautiful upper part of wood before descending gradually to leave at lane.

❼ Turn **R** and go downhill, cross River Dart at **Worthy Bridge**, turn **R** at next junction and past some houses. Where lane bends **L**, go ahead through gate on to track; follow track (river to **R**) through gate and into **Thongsleigh Wood**.

❽ Continue along track, with river **R**. At gate leave wood and enter meadows; path is faint here but continues ahead. Next gate (rather decrepit) leads on to lane. Turn **R** over **Groubear Bridge** and climb back up ancient rocky lane to car park.

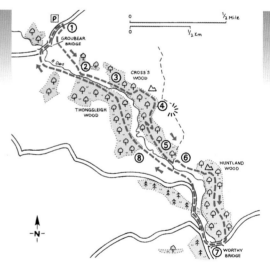

39 BAMPTON *A Little-Known Corner*

5½ miles (9km) 2hrs 30min Ascent: 425ft (130m) ⚠
Paths: Rough fields, tracks and lanes, 11 stiles
Suggested map: aqua3 OS Explorer 114 Exeter & the Exe Valley
Grid reference: SX 956223
Parking: Station Road car park by church in centre of Bampton

A walk deep into the northeast Devon countryside.

❶ Leave car park by toilets, cross road and turn **L** up lane ('Dulverton'). Shortly follow **Exe Valley Way (EVW)** signs **R** up drive, **L** through gate and up field keeping **R**. Cross stile; go **L** on track to double stile in top corner of field. Cross, turn immediately **R** over another, then **L** through trees and **R**, uphill (keeping trees **R**).

❷ Follow EVW signs over next stile, across field to another stile (top **L**) and **L** around field to open gateway. Turn **L**, then immediately **R**, keeping hedge on **L** to metal gate at hilltop.

❸ Continue downhill through fields and 3 gates to **Coldharbour Farm**. Follow footpath signs **L** before farmhouse then ahead on grassy track, through gate and downhill to lane through another gate.

❹ EVW goes **L** here but turn **R** up lane to **Blight's Farm** on **R**. Turn **L** through gate and up track to **Surridge Farm**. Turn **L** through metal gate, then another at hilltop, continuing downhill through another gate on to green lane (muddy in winter).

❺ Lane joins track; turn **L** and over dismantled railway towards **Ashtown Farm** then **R** down drive under trees. Turn **R**; follow lane uphill past Old Vicarage to **Morebath**.

❻ Turn **L** down B3190 (no pavement). At **Bonny Cross** go **R** ('Bampton'); pass **Lodfin Cross** and **old station**. When road bends **R** take track ahead, slightly uphill.

❼ At hilltop, footpath sign leads **R** over stile. Go down field, over stile then straight on, over stile and through gate at top of next field. Turn immediately **L** through another gate. Cross field diagonally towards **L-H** gate at top. Pass through next 2 fields to stile in hedge at top, then down path towards **Bampton**. Cross next stile and field to road over another stile.

❽ Turn **L**; cross to take old road into town. Turn **R**; go ahead towards church and your car.

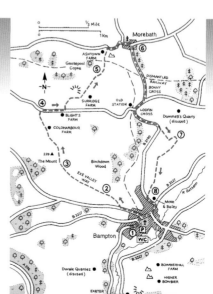

Devon

BRAMPFORD SPEKE *The Meandering Exe*

3½ miles (5.7km) 1hr 30min **Ascent:** Negligible

Paths: Grassy field paths, tracks and country lanes, 5 stiles
Suggested map: aqua3 OS Explorer 114 Exeter & the Exe Valley
Grid reference: SX 927986
Parking: On laneside near St Peter's Church, Brampford Speke

Water-meadows, ox-bow lakes and herons.

❶ Follow **Exe Valley Way** (EVW) footpath signs through churchyard to **L** of church. Leave via metal gate; follow path through kissing gate and on to lane at kissing gate under lychgate.

❷ Turn **R** and follow footpath signs downhill; cross River Exe over wooden bridge. Turn **L** across meadow, following footpath signs. Ignore footpath signpost pointing **R**; go through gateway in hedge, keeping close to river (on **L**).

❸ Follow river as it loops around flood plain. Cross old railway line via 2 kissing gates (old railway bridge piers in river on **L**).

❹ Immediately through 2nd gate drop down **L** to river; continue straight on. Cross stile, then double stile, then 2nd double stile with plank bridge.

❺ After 1 mile (1.6km) path veers **R** away from river and down green lane to kissing gate. Turn immediately **L** along another green lane. At next footpath post go

R, then straight on (ignoring EVW signs **L**) along green lane, which crosses arable farmland, ending at road on edge of Rewe.

❻ Turn **R** along lane towards Stoke Canon to pass old cross at **Burrow Farm**. Carry straight on to pass **Oakhay Barton**. Note Stoke Canon level crossing on Exeter–Tiverton line ahead.

❼ Just before level crossing follow footpath sign **R** through kissing gate and along fenced path. Pass through another kissing gate and metal gate to join **dismantled railway** line. Pass through another kissing gate and go straight on. River Exe loops in on **L**; **Brampford Speke church** is ahead above river. Kissing gate leads over small bridge and into copse. Another kissing gate leads back into meadows (marshy in winter, but small wooden footbridge, **R**, can be used) and to footbridge over Exe.

❽ Once over bridge, retrace steps up path, turning **L** at lychgate; back through churchyard to car park.

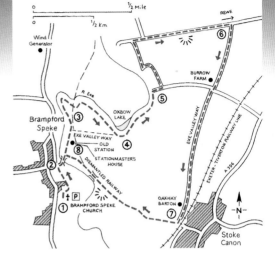

STEPS BRIDGE *A Dartmoor Outlier*

5 miles (8km) 2hrs 45min **Ascent:** 393ft (120m)

Paths: Woodland paths, open fields and country lanes, 7 stiles
Suggested map: aqua3 OS Explorer 110 Torquay & Dawlish
Grid reference: SX 804883
Parking: Free car park (and tourist information) at Steps Bridge

A climb up Heltor Rock and a church.

❶ Cross road, following signs ('youth hostel'). Turn **R** up track, then **L** at youth hostel, turn **R**, following signs ('**Heltor Farm**'). Path leads uphill through woodland. At T-junction turn **L** and over steps by gate into field.

❷ Follow footpath posts up field. Go through gate and between gateposts (**Heltor Rock** to **L**). Pass signs ('**Lower Heltor Farm**') at gate to green lane; turn **L**.

❸ Follow footpath signs **L** then **R** round farmhouse to track. Turn **L** up farm drive.

❹ At top turn **L** ('Bridford'). Soon turn **L** over stile up narrow path to **Heltor**. Retrace steps to road; turn **L**.

❺ Lane bends **L**, then **R**, to edge of Bridford. Turn **R** down lane ('Parish Hall & Church'). Follow path round churchyard, and down steps and **R** to **Bridford Inn**.

❻ Turn **L** from pub; follow lane through village. Take **L** 3rd lane (Neadon Lane) on **R**, by telephone box. Past where bridleway joins (**L**) lane dips **R**, downhill; take **L**

fork ahead passing **Westbirch Farm** (**R**). Turn **L** at track to Birch Down Farm. Cross 2 stiles by barn; cross field, keeping wire fence (**R**). Cross stile and up **R-H** edge of next field to stile in top corner; cross wall and straight on through gorse bushes, towards footpath signpost. Cross stile by trees.

❼ Continue along top of field, through 2 gates and down lane to **Lower Lowton Farm**. Turn **R** to footpath signpost; follow bridleway **R** ('**Woodlands**'). Keep to bridleway past barn (**L**); turn **R** through gate and downhill on lane. Cross track between fields via 2 gates, then through gate. Continue down banked lane to surfaced lane.

❽ Turn **L** through middle gate ('Byway to **Steps Bridge**'). At edge of **Bridford Wood** (by National Trust sign) turn **R** following footpath signposts. (Many junctions; you want to keep **L** and head downhill.) Cross track (**R**; sign) turn **R**; cross sandy track, keeping downhill. Path runs to **L**, high above river to **Steps Bridge**, to road opposite café. Turn **L** to return to car park.

LUSTLEIGH *Wooded Bovey Valley*

5 miles (8km) 3hrs **Ascent:** 754ft (230m)

Paths: Steep rocky ascents/descents, rough paths and woodland
Suggested map: aqua3 OS Outdoor Leisure 28 Dartmoor
Grid reference: SX 774815
Parking: By side of lane at Hammerslake

Exploring wooded Bovey Valley.

❶ With Lustleigh behind, walk ahead from car; turn **L** up path between houses 'Loganstones' and 'Grove', following bridleway signs ('Cleave for **Water**'). At gate go ahead ('**Hunter's Tor**'); climb to top.

❷ Turn **R** through woodland; vegetation clears then follow path straight on over highest part of ridge and across remains of **Iron Age fort** to **Hunter's Tor**.

❸ Through gate **R** of tor; follow signed path **R** to another signed path **L**. Follow track downhill through gate; immediately **R** through another and downhill towards **Peck Farm**. Go through gate and down drive.

❹ Shortly after turn **L** through gate ('**Foxworthy Bridge**'); continue along wooded track. Pass through 2 gates to **Foxworthy**; turn **R**.

❺ Go **L** ('**Horsham**'). Follow track into woodland through gate. After 5 minutes follow signs **R** ('**Horsham** for Manaton & **Water**') to River Bovey. Follow riverbank **L** to crossing (on boulders) at

Horsham Steps. If concerned about crossing river here, don't turn **L** for '**Horsham**' at Point ❺, go **R** down drive, which crosses river. Take 1st footpath **L** and follow river to rejoin main route at Point ❻.

❻ Cross, carefully; enter **nature reserve**. Follow path uphill through woodland and over stile. Keep **L** at 2 junctions; pass through gate by 2 cottages (note tree-branch porch) following signs ('**Water**') through **Letchole Plantation**.

❼ At crossroads of tracks turn **R** ('Manaton direct') to lane by cottages at **Water**. Take 2nd lane **R** to Kes Tor Inn.

❽ Retrace steps to crossroads. Go downhill to split in track. Keep **L** through gate; continue down path ('**Clam Bridge** for **Lustleigh Cleave**'). Cross river on split-log bridge; go uphill to signpost **L** ('Lustleigh via **Hammerslake**'). Go **L** and **L** again at next signpost (steep). Pass boulder; follow signs for **Hammerslake**. At gate turn **R** down path back to lane at start.

Devon • SOUTHWEST ENGLAND

43 BOVEY TRACEY *DARTMOOR'S NATIONAL PARK*

3 miles (4.8km) 1hr 30min **Ascent:** 196ft (60m)
Paths: Woodland and field paths, 4 stiles
Suggested map: aqua3 OS Explorer 110 Torquay & Dawlish
Grid reference: SX 814782
Parking: Car park on the B3344 at lower end of Fore Street, Bovey Tracey, with tourist information office

Woodlands and an old railway line.

❶ Cross road; turn **R**, following signs ('Town centre shops'). Before bridge turn **L** along concrete walkway into Mill Marsh Park, past children's playground and through arboretum, past sports field to busy **A382** at **Hole Bridge** via kissing gate. Cross road carefully.
❷ Go through kissing gate; turn **R** to enter National Trust's **Parke Estate** on dismantled railway line. Follow path over river.
❸ Turn immediately **L** down wooden steps and over stile to follow river (**L**). Cross stile at end of field; continue through wooded strip, down steps and over footbridge and stile into next field.
❹ Signs point **L** for **Parke** and **R** for 'Railway Walk'; go straight on following **Riverside Walk** through field into woodland, then on raised walkway to river. Path winds on, then runs between woods with fields (**R**), then over footbridge to meet river at weir. Follow bank, ignoring broad track **R**. Two kissing gates lead out of

National Trust land and past footbridge (**L**). Shortly footpath turns **R** to cross railway track. Turn **L** and straight on to lane via kissing gate.
❺ Turn **L** ('Manaton'); pass between old railway bridge piers. Walk across **Wilsford Bridge**, ignoring signs ('Lustleigh') **R**. Continue up lane past **Forder gatehouses**, then uphill until lane bends **R**.
❻ Turn **L** over stile; re-enter **Parke Estate**. Wooded path is narrow. Go through wood and kissing gate to large field. Keep to **R** edge, heading downhill, to leave via kissing gate and down wooded path parallel to road.
❼ Path ends at kissing gate; turn **L** to cross parkland and driveway to **Parke** car park. Walk downhill to cross lower drive, then **L** to walk below house, ending at 5-bar gate. Turn **R** ('Riverside Walk') to cross river at **Parke Bridge**; keep ahead to join old railway track.
❽ Turn **R**; follow track until it crosses River Bovey to meet **A382**. Cross road to enter Mill Marsh Park and retrace steps to car.

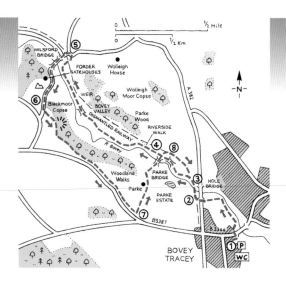

44 DARTINGTON *A MEDIEVAL MANSION*

5 miles (8km) 2hrs 30min **Ascent:** 164ft (50m)
Paths: Fields, woodland tracks and country lanes, 4 stiles
Suggested map: aqua3 OS Explorer 110 Torquay & Dawlish
Grid reference: SX 799628
Parking: Opposite entrance to Dartington Hall
Note: Larger organised groups should seek permission from the Property Administrator (01803 847000) at least 10 days in advance. All paths on Dartington Hall Estate are permissive unless otherwise marked

Around the Dartington Hall Estate.

❶ From car park turn **L** downhill. Follow pavement to River Dart.
❷ Turn **L** over stile and follow river northwards (can be very muddy after rain). Pass over stile, through strip of woodland and over another stile into meadow. At end cross stile to wooded track.
Walk along river edge of next field (**Park Copse** to **L**). At end of field cross stile into **Staverton Ford Plantation**. Where track veers **L** go through gate in wall ahead, then **R** to follow wooded path back towards river. Keep on path as it runs parallel with river, becoming broad woodland track through **North Wood**. When you see buildings through trees on **R**, leave track and walk downhill to metal gate and lane.
❹ Turn **R** to cross **Staverton Bridge**. At level crossing turn **R** to pass through **Staverton Station**

yard into park-like area between railway and river. Follow path across single-track railway and walk on to lane by Sweet William Cottage.
❺ Turn **R** and follow lane to end. Go ahead on small path to pass **Church of St Paul de Leon** (9th-century travelling preacher). Turn **L** at lane to pass public toilets, and **L** at junction to **Sea Trout Inn**. After break retrace steps to metal gate past **Staverton Bridge**.
❻ Turn immediately **R** to rejoin track. Follow until it runs downhill and bends **L**. Walk towards gate on **R**. Turn **L** on narrow concrete path. Keep on concrete path, which leaves woodland and runs between wire fences to concrete drive at **Dartington Crafts Education Centre**. Follow drive to road.
❼ Turn **L** to pass **Old Parsonage Farm**. Keep on road back to **Dartington Hall**, passing gardens and ruins of original church (**R**), until car park on **L**.

45 GRIMSPOUND *3,500 YEARS ON DARTMOOR*

6 miles (9.7km) 3hrs 15min **Ascent:** 656ft (200m)
Paths: Heathery tracks and grassy paths, 3 stiles
Suggested map: aqua3 OS Outdoor Leisure 28 Dartmoor
Grid reference: SX 682819
Parking: Small unmarked quarry on **L** of B3212

From Bronze-Age Grimspound to the Golden Dagger tin mine.

❶ Follow narrow heathery path leading directly away from car park towards **Birch Tor** (on horizon).
❷ Path leads straight on from tor downhill to meet track at right-angles. Turn **L** towards **Headland Warren Farm** in valley ahead. Follow path along granite wall (**R**) to wooden signpost.
❸ Go straight on uphill to cross road. Take small path leading off **R**, up to **Grimspound**. Walk to **R**, then through 'entrance' in perimeter wall.
❹ At centre of enclosure turn **R** and climb steeply uphill to gain **Hameldown Tor**. Path on ridge top leads to **Broad Barrow** then **Two Barrows** where you reach wall running ahead and downhill **R**.
❺ Turn **R** to follow wall down valley side. Wall gives way to line of small beech trees (superb views towards Soussons Wood and Warren House Inn). Cross stock fence via stile to join path, and over another stile on to

road. Turn **R** to reach drive to **Challacombe Farm**.
❻ Turn **L** up concrete drive. At T-junction turn **L** to pass farm and through small gate. Keep **R** through next gateway (signs to **Bennett's Cross**) and along field edge.
❼ Next gate/stile takes you into edge of **Soussons Wood**. Shortly reach remains of **Golden Dagger tin mine** (detailed information board). It's worth exploring here. Follow main track on. When it veers **L** continue ahead on smaller bridleway ('**Bennett's Cross**') and go up valley through gate back on to low-lying yet open moorland, through masses of mining remains.
❽ At junction of tracks either turn **L** over stream, crossing by ruined building and ascending to **Warren House Inn**, or go straight on, keeping **R** where path splits shortly. Follow narrow indistinct path uphill to grassy gully. Climb out at top, turn **L** then **R** up to **Bennett's Cross** car park. Walk **R** up road to car.

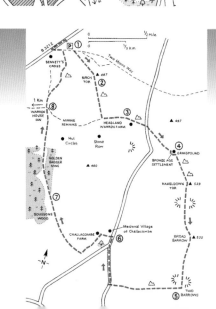

Devon

COLETON FISHACRE *WARTIME SECRETS*

4½ miles (7.2km) 3hrs Ascent: 525ft (160m)

Paths: Varying coast path, tracks and lanes, steep steps, 9 stiles
Suggested map: aqua3 OS Outdoor Leisure 20 South Devon
Grid reference: SX 910513
Parking: National Trust car park at Coleton Camp

The delights of Coleton Fishacre.

1 At car park, turn **R**; park along **R** edge. Through kissing gate in top **R** corner to take path towards gate and stile ('National Trust Coleton Barton Farm'). Go along field edge and over stile down to another stile at bottom of field, then **L** diagonally to another stile. Walk uphill to coast path (signs to **Pudcombe Cove R**).

2 Turn **R**; follow path along cliff. Cross stile, walk steeply downhill and over footbridge to gate at bottom of **Coleton Fishacre** gardens (no public right of way into gardens here).

3 Turn **L**, following coast path signs; pass steps to cove and go up steps; leave estate over stile and on to Coleton Cliffs. At next stile, path drops, then climbs above **Old Mill Bay**, followed by steep climb to **Outer Froward Cove**. Path undulates, then climbs to back of **Froward Cove**.

4 Turn **L**, following signs ('Kingswear') and ('Brownstone car park'). Cross stile; walk uphill; cross

another stile. Take next coast path sign **L**, downhill through wooded section. Path undulates towards sea.

5 Lookout at **Inner Froward Point** is next landmark, followed by 104 steps up cliff. Follow tramway uphill; keep to walkway and steps to pass disused wartime buildings. At top is junction of paths and wooden footpath sign.

6 Turn **L** for Kingswear; walk through woodland behind Newfoundland Cove, over stile and down broad woodland track (estuary **L**). Go down 84 steps to **Mill Bay Cove**; turn **R** down tarmac way. Turn **L** over stile and climb 89 steps to lane, then 63 to another lane.

7 Turn **R** ('Brownstone'). Shortly lane forks; take **R** fork downhill ('Access only to The Grange') to **Home Cottage**.

8 Follow footpath signs **R** up path to concrete lane and on to pass **Higher Brownstone Farm**. Walk up lane passing National Trust car park, then gates to **Coleton Fishacre**, and back to car park.

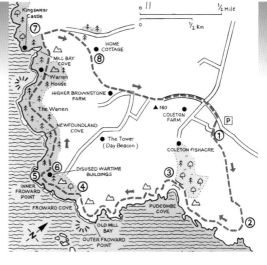

DARTMOUTH *A PORT AND A CASTLE*

3 miles (4.8km) 2hrs Ascent: 115ft (35m)

Paths: Easy coastal footpath and green lanes
Suggested map: aqua3 OS Outdoor Leisure 20 South Devon
Grid reference: SX 874491
Parking: National Trust car parks at Little Dartmouth

Along the cliffs to Dartmouth Castle.

1 Car parks at **Little Dartmouth** are signposted off B3205 (from A379 Dartmouth-to-Stoke Fleming road). Go through **R-H** car park, following signs ('Coast Path Dartmouth'). Continue through kissing gate, keeping hedge **R**. Walk through next field, then kissing gate to coast path.

2 Turn **L** (lovely views west to start and east towards Day Beacon above Kingswear). Coast path runs inland from cliff edge, but go ahead to walk above Warren Point.

3 Continue **L** to pass above **Western Combe Cove** (steps down to sea) then **Combe Point** (take care; long drop to sea from here).

4 Rejoin coast path through open gateway in wall; follow above **Shinglehill Cove**. Path turns inland, passes through gate, becomes narrow and overgrown, and twists along back of **Willow Cove**. It passes through wooded section (with field on **L**), then

climbs around back of **Compass Cove**. Keep going to pass through gate. Keep **L** to reach wooden footpath post, then turn sharp **R**, down valley to cliff edge. Follow path on, through gate near **Blackstone Point**.

5 Leave path **R** to clamber down on to rocks here (superb view over mouth of estuary). Retrace steps and continue on coast path as it turns inland side of estuary and runs through deciduous woodland.

6 Path meets surfaced lane opposite **Compass Cottage**; go **R** on to lane and immediately **R** again steeply downhill, keeping wall to **L**. At turning space go **R** down steps to **castle** and **café**.

7 Retrace your route up steps to tarmac lane at Point **6**, then **L** to pass **Compass Cottage**, and straight on up steep lane ('**Little Dartmouth**') and through kissing gate on to National Trust land.

8 Path runs along top of field and through 5-bar gate on to green lane. Go through gate and farmyard at **Little Dartmouth**; continue on lane to car park.

EAST PRAWLE *THE DEEP SOUTH*

4 miles (6.4km) 2hrs Ascent: 394ft (120m)

Paths: Green lanes, fields and coast path, rocky in places, 3 stiles
Suggested map: aqua3 OS Outdoor Leisure 20 South Devon
Grid reference: SX 781365
Parking: Around green in East Prawle (honesty box contributions)

A land of shipwrecks and smugglers,
gannets and skuas.

1 Walk down lane towards sea, leaving green (**L**) and phone box on **R**, following footpath ('Prawle Point'). Shortly lane turns **L**; go ahead along rutted green lane ('Public Bridleway Gammon Head').

2 Green lane ends at T-junction (metal gate opposite); turn **L** down narrow grassy path between old walls (views ahead). Follow path to footpath post.

3 Turn **R** and immediately downhill to coast path high above secluded **Maceley Cove**, with Gammon Head **R**. Turn **L** and walk along path above **Elender Cove** (steep access to both beaches but take care).

4 Path leads through kissing gate and on around **Signalhouse Point**. Steep ascent rewarded with fine views ahead to wreck of Demetrios on rocks, with Prawle Point beyond. Follow footpath posts through kissing gate and across grassy down, keeping to **R** of **coastguard lookout** ahead.

5 At **coastguard lookout** enjoy superb views east to Lannacombe, Mattiscombe Sand and start. Take time to explore visitor centre (excellent details about area). To continue, follow grassy path inland towards old coastguard cottages.

6 Turn **R** through gate to pass in front of cottages and along edge of level, grassy wavecut platform which lies below original Pleistocene cliffs here. Pass through kissing gate and along level meadows above low cliffs. Go through next kissing gate, past next footpath post and over ivy-covered stile. Pass around edge of next field (Maelcombe House now ahead).

7 Follow path as it turns inland and, shortly, cross stone wall. Turn immediately **L** up edge of field. At end of hedge go **L** up track.

8 Take 1st stile **R** to go up field (wonderful views back to coast). Cross stone stile at top and continue **R** up narrow rocky track to join lane, ascending **R** steeply back to village.

Devon

49 EAST PORTLEMOUTH *The Kingsbridge Estuary*

4 miles (6.4km) 2hrs Ascent: 377ft (115m)
Paths: Good coast path, field paths and tracks
Suggested map: aqua3 OS Outdoor Leisure 20 South Devon
Grid reference: SX 746385
Parking: Near phone box in East Portlemouth or in small parking bay

A stroll around sleepy East Portlemouth.
❶ Park on verge near phone box at **East Portlemouth** (or parking area – contributions to village hall fund). Walk through parking area and downhill on narrow tarmac footpath ('Salcombe'), which leads to steps.
❷ Reach lane at bottom; turn R to visit **Venus Café** or to catch ferry to **Salcombe**. To continue with walk, turn L along lane as it follows edge of estuary (official route of coast path, passing exclusive residences in almost sub-tropical surroundings).
❸ Lane leads to beach at **Mill Bay**. Follow coast path signs for Gara Rock along edge of wood (lovely views across estuary, and glimpses of little coves).
❹ At **Limebury Point** reach open cliff. From here there are great views to South Sands and Overbecks opposite and craggy Bolt Head. Coast path veers eastwards below **Portlemouth Down**.
❺ Path undulates steeply (rocky in places). Keep

going until bench and viewpoint over beach at Rickham Sands. Just beyond, as coast path continues R along cliffs (reasonable access to beach), take L fork and climb up below lookout to reach wall in front of **Gara Rock Hotel**.
❻ Turn L to hotel drive; walk straight on up lane. Shortly turn L through gate in hedge ('Mill Bay'). Walk across field (roped-off area indicates car park for beach) with views to **Salcombe** and Malborough church beyond. Go through small copse, then gate and across farm track. Go through metal gate down public footpath.
❼ This leads on to beautiful bridlepath, running downhill beneath pollarded lime trees (grassy combe to R). Path leads past car park to **Mill Bay**.
❽ Turn R along lane. To avoid steps, watch for footpath sign pointing R, up path to regain **East Portlemouth** and your car; if not, continue along lane and retrace steps up steep tarmac path.

50 KINGSTON *Peace and Solitude*

5½ miles (8.8km) 2hrs 30min Ascent: 394ft (120m)
Paths: Fields, tracks and good coast path, 7 stiles
Suggested map: aqua3 OS Outdoor Leisure 20 South Devon
Grid reference: SX 635478
Parking: By the church in Kingston village

A magical part of the county's south coast that is seldom visited.
❶ With church L, follow lane uphill to Wonwell Gate and turn R down lane ('Wonwell Beach'). When it bends L then R, turn L through gate/stile and straight on, keeping hedge L. Pass through hedge into next field; follow sign R, diagonally across field to enter **Furzedown Wood** over stile into green lane.
❷ This leads into next field; cross, then go over stile into **Wrinkle Wood** and follow path downhill to lane.
❸ Turn L; limited parking for beach here. Walk down to **Erme estuary** (attractive spot for picnic).
❹ Retrace steps and follow coast path signs up steps R ('Bigbury'). Follow wooded path, which leads on to and along back of **Wonwell Beach**. Go up steps, over stile and straight on along estuary to **Redcove Point** (superb views to Battisborough Island opposite).
❺ Path veers eastwards over stile (National Trust Scobbiscombe Farm), then sweeps across broad

grassy area above **Fernycombe Beach** to **Beacon Point** (glorious views ahead). Walk through small gate, into combe and up to gate. Pause at bench overlooking **Hoist Beach**, before path drops down into combe and climbs up through another gate.
❻ Follow steep (often slippery) descent to Westcombe Beach. Take great care here, parts are stepped (steps sandy and it's easy to skid).
❼ Turn L over stile at back of beach, following signs for **Kingston** (permissive path, unmarked on maps). Path has wire fence (L) and stream (R); walk over wooden footbridge (R) to cross stream and enter willow plantation. Path twists out through strip of woodland.
❽ Cross stile and go straight on up, gradually ascending green lane (bridleway to **Kingston**). Continue on to pass ponds at **Okenbury** R (muddy in places). Track runs into tarmac lane, and back uphill into **Kingston**. Turn R, then L to church and car.

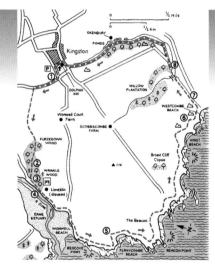

51 BIGBURY-ON-SEA *Burgh Island Paradise*

3 miles (4.8km) 1hr 45min Ascent: 246ft (75m)
Paths: Fields, tracks (muddy in winter) and coast path, 4 stiles
Suggested map: aqua3 OS Outdoor Leisure 20 South Devon
Grid reference: SX 651442
Parking: Huge car park at Bigbury-on-Sea

An Art Deco dream and Devon's oldest inn.
❶ Leave car park through entrance. Follow coast path signs R, L towards road, then L again up grassy area. Turn L before bungalow, then L (unmarked path) to road. Turn R and walk steeply uphill to **Mount Folly Farm**.
❷ Turn L along track ('Ringmore'). At top of field is junction of paths; go through gate L, then through gate ahead, keeping downhill. Cross stile; walk downhill through kissing gate. Cross farm track and up field to stile, then descend steps into narrow lane.
❸ Cross over, following signs ('Ringmore'), through L of 2 gates. Walk down into next combe, keeping hedgebank R. Cross stream at bottom on concrete walkway, and over stile. Ignore path L; go ahead, uphill, through plantation and gate on to path between fence and hedge.
❹ Pass through kissing gate; turn R through open gateway. Turn L uphill to metal gate/stile to join track

leading to **Ringmore**. Turn R at lane, then L at church to Journey's End (R).
❺ From pub turn R down narrow lane which gives way to footpath, which winds round to tarmac lane. Turn L downhill. Walk on down track ('Lower Manor Farm'); keep going down past 'National Trust Ayrmer Cove' notice. After small gate track splits; keep L (unsigned) and straight on.
❻ Turn L through kissing gate; walk towards cove on path above combe (L). Pass through gate and over 2 stiles to beach.
❼ Follow coast path ('Challaborough') L over footbridge then climb steeply uphill to cliff top (views over **Burgh Island**). Cliffs crumbly here – take care. Path is narrow, with wire fence L, leading to Challaborough (holiday camp).
❽ Turn R along beach road and follow track leading uphill along coast towards Bigbury. Go straight on to tarmac road, then R on gravel path to car park.

Devon

PRINCETOWN *DARTMOOR'S HIGHEST TOWN*

7 miles (11.3km) 3hrs **Ascent:** 328ft (100m)
Paths: Tracks, leat-side paths and rough moorland
Suggested map: aqua3 OS Outdoor Leisure 28 Dartmoor
Grid reference: SX 588735
Parking: Main car park in Princetown (honesty box)

There was great industrial activity here in the late 18th and early 19th centuries.

❶ Leave car park past toilets; turn **R** to pass **High Moorland Visitor Centre**. Cross road and follow lane between 2 pubs and their car parks behind. Shortly small gate leads to track which ascends to **South Hessary Tor** (splendid views to Plymouth Sound ahead; prison behind).

❷ Follow track as it drops gently, passing boundary stones. It crosses 2 other tracks (look L for view of Devonport Leat) before dropping to **Nun's Cross. Nun's Cross Farm** (c 1870) is L.

❸ Turn 90 degrees **R** at cross to go over bumpy area of disused tin workings to find end of tunnel where leat emerges (near remains of cottage under beech and 3 hawthorn trees). Walk along **R** bank of leat.

❹ Where leat bends north cross it on **Older Bridge** (granite slabs); walk along **L** bank (Burrator reservoir L). Follow leat. There are various crossing places;

cross back to **R** bank before descending to Meavy valley. Leat picks up speed as it rushes downhill here; path steep and rocky.

❺ **River Meavy** is crossed via aqueduct and leat turns L. Take grassy path **R** leading uphill away from river (tin workings in valley worth exploration). Path passes through tumbledown wall; turn **L** and climb up to **Black Tor**.

❻ Go straight on past **Logan Stone** (balanced so it can be rocked on its base), and on across open moorland to road, (views of Brentor, Swelltor Quarries and **disused railway line** ahead). Turn **R** at road.

❼ Shortly, opposite blocked off parking place, turn **L** and cross grass, aiming for mast on North Hessary Tor (boggy in places, but passable).

❽ At railway track turn **R**; walk back to edge of town. Path splits; keep **L** and through small gate to tarmac road. Pass Devon Fire & Rescue Service building to car park on **R**.

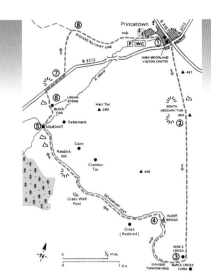

CADOVER BRIDGE *MYSTERIES OF THE DEWERSTONE*

3½ miles (5.7km) 1hr 45min **Ascent:** 180ft (55m)
Paths: Woodland paths, some rocky, and rough moorland, 4 stiles
Suggested map: aqua3 OS Outdoor Leisure 28 Dartmoor
Grid reference: SX 555646
Parking: Free car park at Cadover Bridge

Industrial archaeology and a hard climb past the eerie Dewerstone Crags.

❶ From car park, walk away from **Cadover Bridge**, (river on R). Cross stile into willow plantation.

❷ Wooden ladder down bank leads to short stretch of pasture. Stile and footbridge lead into **North Wood** oak woodland. Choice of route here; keep to path with large pipe set in ground.

❸ Leave **North Wood** over stile and follow path through open brackeny area; **River Plym** below on R. (Note group of **Dewerstone Crags** ahead on other side of valley.) Path leads into mixed silver birch and oak past ruined building, then forks. Take **R** fork slightly downhill to track and gate.

❹ Turn **R** inside wire fence, following footpath sign ('Shaugh Bridge'). Stay within woods as path twists downhill. Path leads over stile past notice ('Hazardous Area: Proceed with Caution' – can be slippery. Pass settling tank (R); path ends at road.

❺ Turn immediately **R**; take **L** fork then down steps into Shaugh Bridge car park. Turn **R**; walk through car park towards river.

❻ Cross river via railed wooden footbridge; enter **Goodameavy** (National Trust). Follow path **R**. It becomes rocky track leading above river and winds steeply uphill. Where path goes straight ahead and there is sharp bend R, keep **R** and uphill until you see top of **Dewerstone Crags** through trees R.

❼ Path becomes rocky scramble **L** and up to leave woods and on to moorland to **Dewerstone Rock**.

❽ Turn 90 degrees **R** at rock; follow grassy path along ridge passing Oxen Tor and over **Wigford Down**, keeping **Cadworthy Wood** and Plym Valley R. Keep straight on to boundary wall of wood, then **L** to follow wall around fields. Eventually wall veers R; walk downhill past **Cadover Cross** (views of china clay works beyond). Head towards bridge, cross over on road and walk back to car.

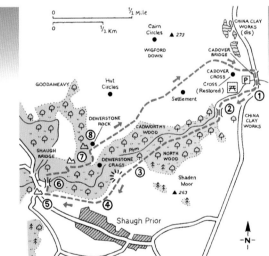

MELDON RESERVOIR *DARTMOOR'S HIGHEST TORS*

4¼ miles (6.8km) 2hrs 45min **Ascent:** 722ft (220m)
Paths: Grassy tracks and open moorland
Suggested map: aqua3 OS Outdoor Leisure 28 Dartmoor
Grid reference: SX 563917
Parking: Car park at Meldon Reservoir (voluntary contributions)

An ancient oak woodland and views of Yes Tor and High Willhays.

❶ Walk up stone steps by toilets, through gate and **L** on tarmac way towards dam, ('Bridleway to Moor'). Cross dam.

❷ Turn **R** along track. Stile leads to waterside picnic area. Don't cross stile, but leave track here to go straight on, following edge of reservoir through single valley and over footbridge. Narrow path undulates in steepish descent at end of reservoir to meet broad marshy valley of West Okement River; **Corn Ridge** 1,762ft (537m) lies ahead.

❸ Cross footbridge; take path along **L** edge of valley, keeping to bottom of slope on **L**. Path broadens uphill and becomes grassy as it rounds **Vellake Corner** above river below R.

❹ At top of hill, track levels; you can glimpse **Black Tor Copse** ahead. Follow river upstream past waterfall and weir, R of granite enclosure, and along **L** bank

through open moorland to enter **Black Tor Copse**.

❺ Retrace steps out of trees and veer **R** around copse edge, uphill aiming for **L** outcrop of **Black Tor** on ridge above. Walk through bracken to tor; no definite path here, but it's straightforward. Outcrop on R rises to 1,647ft (502m).

❻ Return to grassy area north of tor. Turn **R** to continue away from river valley behind, aiming for track visible ahead over **Longstone Hill**. To find track go slightly downhill from tor to small stream. Turn **L**, then **R** towards 3 granite blocks marking track.

❼ Intermittent track runs straight across open moor (good views of quarry ahead). Where **Red-a-Ven Brook** Valley appears below R, enjoy view of Row Tor, West Mill Tor and Yes Tor. High Willhays, Dartmoor's highest tor, lies just out of sight to R. Track veers **L** around end of hill and drops back to reservoir.

❽ Turn **R** to rejoin track back over dam and back to car park.

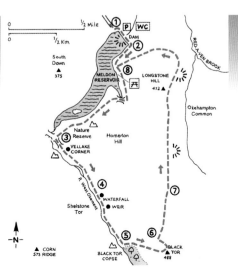

Devon

Devon • SOUTHWEST ENGLAND

---

55 BRENT TOR *The Devil Versus the Church*

4 miles (6.4km) 2hrs **Ascent:** 425ft (130m)
Paths: Tracks and green lanes, open fields and lanes
Suggested map: aqua3 OS Explorer 112 Launceston & Holsworthy
Grid reference: SX 495800
Parking: Lay-by past cattle grid outside Mary Tavy on moorland road to North Brentor village

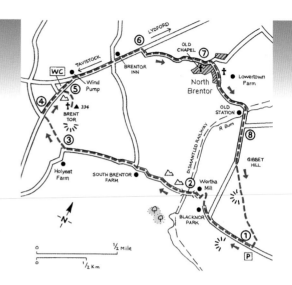

To the Church of St Michael de Rupe.

① Walk straight ahead from car towards **Brent Tor**. Where lane veers R turn **L** along unfenced lane (dead end and weak bridge signs). Go downhill and over cattle grid. Tarmac lane becomes track passing **Blacknor Park** (L), to cross old railway line.

② Stony track goes uphill, levels off and runs into green lane. At next T-junction of tracks turn **L** passing **South Brentor Farm** and lane (R); keep straight on slightly uphill – under beech trees – passing 'Hillside' on L.

③ Just past white cottage on L lane bends L. Turn **R** through wooden gate (no sign) and along bottom of field, keeping hedge L. Brent Tor above to R. Pass through double metal gates to Tavistock to Lydford road (take care).

④ Turn **R** to car park, toilets and information board for **Brent Tor** (L).

⑤ Turn **R** and take path up to **Church of St Michael**

de Rupe, then retrace steps to road and turn **R** to pass **Brentor Inn** on L. According to legend, Devil is closely associated with church while it was being built.

⑥ Reach 2 white cottages on either side of road and turn **R** down tarmac lane ('Brentor and Mary Tavy'). Lane runs downhill, with moor rising steeply up behind village ahead.

⑦ At edge of houses go straight on, keeping old chapel R, to war memorial. Turn **R** slightly downhill to pass phone box, church and village hall. Follow lane as it veers **R** to cross old railway line (old station with platform canopy below to R).

⑧ Cross cattle grid on to open moor and up lane. Where lane bends R and you see 2 big granite gateposts in beech-lined wall R, cut **L** diagonally over edge of **Gibbet Hill** on indistinct grassy track. Lane leads back to car, but this is more pleasant route. At crest of hill you will see route back to car on lane below to R.

---

56 HEDDON GATE *Exmoor's Spectacular Valley*

5 miles (8km) 2hrs 45min **Ascent:** 787ft (240m)
Paths: Wooded tracks, exposed coast path and quiet lanes, 2 stiles
Suggested map: aqua3 OS Outdoor Leisure 9 Exmoor
Grid reference: SS 655481
Parking: National Trust car park at Heddon Gate

Oakwoods, rushing rivers and high cliffs.

① Walk towards **Hunter's Inn**. To R is wooded track ('Heddon's Mouth') through gate. Walk down track, which splits; keep **L** ('Heddon's Mouth beach'). Keep to path nearest river. Coast path (unsigned) joins from R.

② Turn **L** over footbridge, then **R** and walk towards coast to 19th-century lime kiln above rocky beach. Retrace steps, keeping river to L, to pass 2 footbridges. Keep going until next coast path sign ('Combe Martin') directs you **R**, sharply uphill.

③ Steep zig-zag climb is rewarded with amazing views across valley and inland. Keep going along narrow path, running parallel to valley to coast above **Heddon's Mouth**, then turn **L** towards **Peter Rock**. Cliffs here are over 650ft (200m) high and sheer; path is narrow and exposed – take care. Continue along path, which runs inland to meet wall.

④ Turn **R** ('Combe Martin'). Follow coast path signs through gate, then **R**, along short wire-fenced section

and over stile to rejoin cliff edge. Cross stile above **Neck Wood**, then leave National Trust lands via stile and kissing gate. Coast path continues ahead.

⑤ Turn **L** and walk uphill, then **L** again where path meets grassy path. Proceed uphill, following fence, to parking area and barrier at **Holdstone Down Cross**, on edge of Trentishoe Down.

⑥ Turn **L** along narrow lane, following signs for **Trentishoe church** (signpost misleadingly points back way you have come). Walk along lane until you see church above you on L (good place for break).

⑦ Continue downhill below **Sevenash Cottage** to pass place where 'Access to coast path' sign points L. Walk down **Trentishoe Hill** (unsuitable for vehicles) which runs through wooded Trentishoe Cleave.

⑧ Turn **L** at valley bottom by 2 pretty white cottages. Walk along lane past footpath sign to **Heddon Valley** on L, cross small river, then Heddon river just before **Hunter's Inn**. Turn **R** to find car.

---

57 LEE BAY *North Devon Coast Classic*

8 miles (12.9km) 4hrs 15min **Ascent:** 426ft (130m)
Paths: Fields, tracks and coast path, 15 stiles
Suggested map: aqua3 OS Explorer 139 Bideford, Ilfracombe & Barnstaple
Grid reference: SS 452458
Parking: Car park at Mortehoe

'Fuchsia valley' and craggy Morte Point.

① Take lane opposite ('Lighthouse & Lee'). Pass **Rockham Bay Hotel** to lane end at private road to Bull Point lighthouse.

② Follow signs through gate (R) across **Easewell Farm** campsite and complex. Exit via gate (pond R); cross field to **Yarde Farm** via stile. Turn **L** along rocky track uphill to gate/stile into field. Keep wall L; cross stile in muddy bottom corner on to farm track.

③ Turn **L**, following signs through **Damage Barton Farm** veering R towards **Warcombe Farm** and **Borough Wood**. Shortly footpath sign on building ahead directs you **L**, then another sign points **R**, then **L** through gate. Walk uphill to footpath post. Go **R** towards another signpost, fork **R** through rough area, then follow coast path signs through gate. Cross field to hedge; look for next signpost atop small hill. Cross stile in next hedge; walk across field to lane via stile.

④ Cross lane and stile, leading into 'Open Access

area' and viewpoint. Follow signs to Lee across meadow. Cross stile; go downhill into **Borough Valley**. At bottom turn **L**.

⑤ Follow valley down to leave woods; turn **R** over bridge and stile. Cross field then stile; turn **R** up lane to **Grampus** pub.

⑥ Retrace steps past toilets to cove at Lee Bay. Turn **L** uphill; join coast path through gate. Follow footpath signs to stile/footbridge/stile at bottom of combe, then up steps and over stile into another combe and rocky cove. Cross footbridge; walk up to **Bull Point**.

⑦ Follow footpath signs L of **lighthouse** towards Morte Point. Go through gate down into combe (97 steps up other side). Cross Windy Lag and down to **Rockham Bay** (steps lead to beach). Cross 2 stiles and continue to Morte Point.

⑧ Follow coast path signs past **Windy Cove**. Cross stile, pass **Grunta Beach**; follow signs **L**, uphill, to join road below **Mortehoe**. Go uphill and **R** to car park.

Devon

CLOVELLY WITHOUT THE CROWDS

5 miles (8km) 2hrs 15min **Ascent:** 410ft (125m) ⚠
Paths: Grassy coast path, woodland and farm tracks, 4 stiles
Suggested map: aqua3 OS Explorer 126 Clovelly & Hartland
Grid reference: SS 285259
Parking: National Trust car park at Brownsham

Pheasants and follies – and a different way into Clovelly.

❶ Leave car park over stile opposite entrance. Walk along field and through gate into woods. Follow signs ('Footpath to coast path') to pass bench. Keep ahead ('Mouth Mill & coast path'). Cross stile to coast path.
❷ Go R over stile into field on **Brownsham Cliff**. Keep to L edge, across stile, down steps and L round next field. Cross stile; go downhill through woodland. Leave trees; turn L towards sea at **Mouth Mill**.
❸ Follow coast path across stream by stepping stones. Clamber up rocky gully L and turn R on to track, on bend. Keep going L, uphill.
❹ Shortly follow coast path signs L, then immediately R. Go L up steps to follow path uphill towards cliffs below **Gallantry Bower**.
❺ Follow signed path through woodland to pass folly ('Angel's Wings'). Where path leads straight on to church, keep L following signs and via gate through

edge of **Clovelly Court estate** (R). Pass into woods via kissing gate. Path winds down and up past shelter, then through kissing gate into field. Keep to L; continue through gate and oak trees to road at gate. Follow coast path signs on to road leading to top of **Clovelly** village below **Visitor Centre**.
❻ Walk up **Wrinkleberry Lane** (R of Hobby Drive ahead) to lane, past school and on to road. Turn R; where road bends R go through gates to **Clovelly Court**. At T-junction follow bridleway signs L ('Court Farm' & sawmills') through farm, metal gate (sometimes open) and along track. Pass through small wooded section and walk on to hedge at end of field.
❼ Turn R, then L through gate (by footpath sign). At bottom of field go through gate into plantation, downhill.
❽ Turn L at forest track, following bridleway signs. Turn R up track to Lower Brownsham Farm. Turn L for car park.

MORWENSTOW A TOUGH TREK INTO CORNWALL

5¾ miles (9.2km) 3hrs 30min **Ascent:** 328ft (100m) ⚠
Paths: Rugged coastal footpath, fields and tracks, 14 stiles
Suggested map: aqua3 OS Explorer 126 Clovelly & Hartland
Grid reference: SS 213179
Parking: Welcombe Mouth, bumpy track passable with care

A strenuous coastal walk to Morwenstow.

❶ Walk L up coast path. Cross 2 stiles, then walk down to **Marsland Mouth** and cross Marsland Water.
❷ Follow coast path markers inland; turn R and up on to **Marsland Cliff**. Path runs along cliff, down steps into combe, over bridge, then up other side (**Cornakey Cliff**). Proceed along field edge, crossing 4 stiles; drop down into combe via footbridge/stile and up other side to top of **Henna Cliff**.
❸ At next stile, turn L inland, keeping wire fence R. At bank at field end turn R; turn L through 2 gates and across field towards **Westcott Farm**.
❹ At hedge break before farm turn R, downhill. Pass through hedge gap towards footpath sign. Enter wood; cross stile/footbridge. Walk uphill past vicarage; cross stile into graveyard. Turn R towards church, then L and L again to exit via lychgate. Continue to Bush Inn (R).
❺ Return to hedge break approaching **Westcott Farm** at Point ❹. Keep ahead, uphill, following signs

('Alternative path avoiding farm'). Cross bank over steps. Turn R; go through open gateway at top R of field (follow yellow arrows). Turn L through gate; cross field. Cross stile; walk round barn (R). Arrow ahead directs you through gate and down drive to road.
❻ Turn L towards **Cornakey Farm**; follow sign ('Alternative path avoiding farmyard') through gate R. Turn L through gate; down steps. Turn R into lane.
❼ At next gate, arrows point along bank (R). Pass through gate; walk diagonally across field, downhill. Cross hedgebank via steps; go straight over field. Cross stile into wooded area; go down to cross footbridge and up, out of wood on far side (R) over grassy area before **Marsland Manor**. Pass through trees; go R following signs to stile on to lane.
❽ Turn L and shortly L again ('Marsland Mouth') on track. Go through gate and downhill. At cottage on R, keep L following marker posts to coast path. Continue ahead; cross stream and retrace steps to start.

HARTLAND QUAY AROUND THE POINT

8¾ miles (14.1km) 5hrs 30min **Ascent:** 328ft (100m) ⚠
Paths: Coast path through fields; country lanes, 35 stiles
Suggested map: aqua3 OS Explorer 126 Clovelly & Hartland
Grid reference: SS 259245
Parking: Car park in centre of Hartland village

Along the coast path overlooking Lundy.

❶ Leave car park past **Hart Inn** (R); turn R (North Street). Turn L down narrow lane ('Hartland Point'). Pass **Pattard Bridge**; follow lane R. Past lane to R, take footpath sign R up steps and over stile. Walk up field; cross bank to rejoin lane.
❷ Turn R and R again at Youltree Cross. Turn L at Moor Cross ('Exmansworthy'). Lane veers R; take next lane L. Pass Exmansworthy Farm; turn R through car park on to path; cross stile following signs ('Coast Path') to lane (ends at stile into open fields). Follow sign L; go ahead to coast path.
❸ Go L over stile, cross 6 more, then R downhill. Keep to field edge; cross stile. Go downhill; cross another stile. Cross 2 more to **Shipload Bay**.
❹ Follow coast path through gate and past signs L ('Titchberry'). Cross 6 more stiles. Turn R towards sea, pass round gate then between fence and cliff, R of radar tower, to **Barley Bay**.

❺ Follow coast path signs (Hartland Quay). Take path L, then L again along field edge (**Blagdon Cliff**) and over stile. Walk round next stile and on above **Upright Cliff**. Cross stile; descend into combe then round stile. Cross stream. Steps lead up other side to stile. Turn R; follow coast path signs R over stile into **Smoothlands valley**.
❻ Climb out of **Smoothlands** on to **Blegberry Cliff**. Descend into combe; cross stream via kissing gate and up other side and over stile. Cross next stile; descend to combe at **Blackpool Mill**. Pass cottage (R).
❼ Turn R; cross stream on bridge. Cross stile; turn R on to **Warren Cliff** through gate. Pass **ruined tower**; at gate turn R for Hartland Quay.
❽ Turn L inside hedge. At field end cross stile; go ahead. Leave field over stile; pass cottages. Go through kissing gate, stile, then another, to **St Nectan's churchyard**. Leave via lychgate; go ahead following road back to **Hartland** village.

Somerset

61 THE CHAINS *BRONZE-AGE FARMERS*

5¾ miles (9.2km) 3hrs Ascent: 700ft (210m)
Paths: Narrow moorland paths following fences and some tracks, 4 stiles
Suggested map: aqua3 OS Outdoor Leisure 9 Exmoor
Grid reference: SS 728401
Parking: Unmarked roadside pull-off on B3358 on Chains Hill

Experience quintessential Exmoor among the barrows and tumuli of its Bronze-Age farmers.

❶ At Simonsbath end of pull-off is gate with bridleway sign ('Chains Barrow'). Go up **R-H** edges of 2 fields; head **L**, to gate. Way across following rough moorland is marked by yellow-topped posts. Go uphill, parallel with hedge on **L**. Marked way bends slightly **R**, up crest of moorland spur. At top is bank with gateway.
❷ Signpost indicates path over moor to **Chains Barrow**. Return to gateway and follow fenced bank leading across moor top to **Pinkery Pond** (crossed by dam).
❸ Follow fence as it continues uphill to corner of access land. Continue across moorland for 350yds (320m) to join high bank; follow **L**, to **Wood Barrow**.
❹ Gate ahead leads into Devonshire. Beyond, Wood Barrow is one of many barrows used by Saxons as markers of Devon's boundary. In front of Woodbarrow

Gate turn **L** on signed bridleway track, with high bank on R, which leads off moor. Bear **L** around sheep-pen made of disused metal crash barriers. Gate leads on to B3358.
❺ Cross to track ('**Mole's Chamber**') which climbs ¼ mile (400m) to signpost. Bear **L** across moorland for 550yds (503m). Field corner soon comes into sight: on R is high banking with fence in front; on L is lower banking with fence on top; between is destination gate. Go straight downhill to stream, with peaty track starting beyond it. Follow up then bend **R**, to end of tarred road.
❻ Turn **L**, away from road. Faint track runs down across stream to gate with blue paint-spot. Path runs down to **R** of stream, gradually slanting up to gate. Join larger track, but immediately after gate keep ahead as it bends R. Green track runs parallel with river down on L, to signposted gate. Turn **L** on tarred track, to join B3358. Turn **L** to parking pull-off.

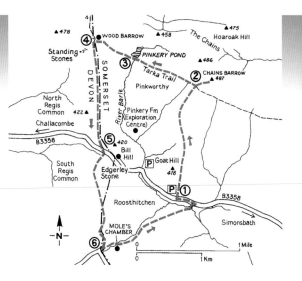

62 DOONE VALLEY *FACT AND FICTION*

8¾ miles (14.1km) 4hrs 30min Ascent: 1,250ft (380m)
Paths: Some steep ascents and descents, pathless open moor, 1 stile
Suggested map: aqua3 OS Outdoor Leisure 9 Exmoor
Grid reference: SS 820464
Parking: Car park (free) at Robbers Bridge

Visit the tiny church celebrated in R D Blackmore's classic novel, Lorna Doone.

❶ Cross Robber's Bridge; follow road to **Oareford**. Turn **L** on bridleway ('Larkbarrow'). After 1 mile (1.6km), at gate on to open moor with faint track ahead, bear **L**. Follow fence, heading over moorland crest to corner of large field.
❷ Go through gate on **L**, then narrow gate on **R** to rougher moorland. Take green path ahead. Bear slightly **R** on smaller path to go through shallow col or gap. Wider path appears from R. Bear **L** to gate in bank marking edge of Exmoor Park Access Area.
❸ Path ahead leads down, with bank on L, to signpost. Turn **R** ('Doone Valley') on clear path that climbs to gate in Access Area bank – it runs down to footbridge over Badgworthy Water.
❹ Turn **R**, downstream. After plank footbridge, gate leads into hummocks of lost **medieval village**. Go ahead to wide path; turn **R**. Continue down valley to

footbridge leading to **Cloud Farm**.
❺ Pass to L of Cloud Farm, on to track that goes through farm shed, then climbs out of valley. Where it ends, follow lower side of field to edge of wooded combe. Turn **R** heading for gate on L. Track passes above combe and turns down beyond it. Where track bends R, keep straight downhill through waymarked gates; turn **L** on valley road below beside Oare church.
❻ Turn **R** ('Porlock'); follow road, then cross **Oare Water**. Turn **R** along riverside to cross small stream (no footbridge, although marked on OS map). Further on, turn **L** to house, then **R** between gorse bushes. Grass path leads straight up sharp spur and beside fence to stile; keep ahead, over heather, to plantation.
❼ Turn **R** along track; at plantation's corner keep ahead on smaller track ('Oareford'). This bends L near field corner; keep ahead on path towards trees. Pass **R** of trees, to gate. Path leads down to footbridge into Oareford. Turn **L** to return to car park.

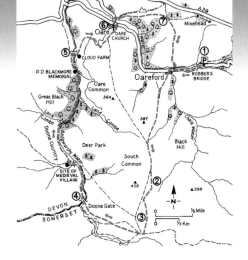

63 TARR STEPS *BRONZE-AGE TRACKWAYS*

5¼ miles (8.4km) 2hrs 30min Ascent: 700ft (210m)
Paths: Riverside paths and field tracks, some open moor, no stiles
Suggested map: aqua3 OS Outdoor Leisure 9 Exmoor
Grid reference: SS 872323
Parking: Just over ¼ mile (400m) east of Tarr Steps – can be full in summer. (Parking at Tarr Steps for disabled people only)

Visit one of the world's 'oldest' bridges.

❶ Leave bottom of car park by footpath on L-H side ('Scenic Path'). This leads down to **L** of road to Little River, crossing 2 footbridges to **Tarr Steps**, over River Barle, ahead.
❷ Cross Steps, turning upstream at far side ('Circular Walk'). Follow river bank path past wire footbridge. After ¾ mile (1.2km) cross side-stream on stepping stones, then reach footbridge over river.
❸ Cross, and continue upstream (river now L). After ¾ mile (1.2km) path crosses wooden footbridge, then divides at signpost.
❹ Turn **R**, uphill ('Winsford Hill'). Wide path goes up through woods with stream on R. Where it meets track turn briefly **R** to ford stream; continue uphill on narrower signed path. At low bank with beech trees turn **R** to gate; follow foot of tarred lane. Go up to cattle grid on to open moor. Bear **R** on faint track

heading up between gorse bushes. After 250yds (229m) reach 4-way signpost.
❺ Turn **R** ('Knaplock') and slant down to hedge corner. Follow hedge briefly, then take path that slants gradually up into moor. After 170yds (155m) sign points back down towards moor-foot banking. Beech bank crosses ahead: aim for lower end, where soft track leads forward, with occasional blue paint-spots. After ¼ mile (400m) track turns downhill, then back to **L** (becomes firmer as it reaches **Knaplock Farm**).
❻ At farm buildings turn downhill ('Tarr Steps'), on to muddy farm track. Where this turns off into field, continue ahead on stony track, **Watery Lane**. After initial descent this becomes smooth path down to River Barle. Turn **L**, downstream. When path rises above river, look for fork on **R** ('Footpath'). This rejoins river to pass through open field. Cross road and turn **L** up scenic path to return to car.

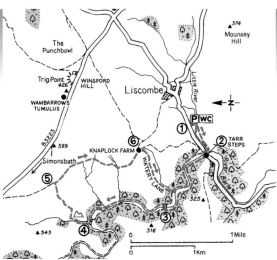

Somerset

WIMBLEBALL LAKE *Woodland Water*

6 miles (9.7km) 3hrs **Ascent:** 750ft (230m)
Paths: Rough descent, long climb, easy track between, 1 stile
Suggested map: aqua3 OS Outdoor Leisure 9 Exmoor
Grid reference: SS 969285
Parking: Frogwell Lodge car park, Haddon Hill

Natural and artificial landscapes merge on this route through wooded valley, heath and across the Wimbleball Dam.

1 Leave car park by small gate **L** of toilets. Turn **R** to cross tarred track; head downhill on small path running through gorse, grass and heather until open birch woods give rise to easier going. If you lose path keep going downhill. Above reservoir is stony track.

2 Turn **L**. Track emerges on to open grassland and starts rising to **L**. Look for stile down on **R**, into woodland. Cross; turn **L** on path that emerges near **Wimbleball Dam**. Side-trip to dam gives fine views of **Hartford Bottom** below.

3 Return along dam and turn **R** into tarmac road ('Bury 2½'). At bottom keep ahead on concrete path ('Bridleway'). With bridge ahead, bear **L** on to grass track ('Bridleway to Bury') which leads to ford; watch for footbridge on **R**. Cross then take track between houses; turn **L** into **Hartford**.

4 Turn **L** ('Bury 2') on track, passing through woods beside **River Haddeo**. Track now stony to village of **Bury**.

5 Turn **L** to packhorse bridge beside road's ford. Ignore riverside track on **L**; continue for 180yds (165m); turn **L** at bridleway sign. Pass between houses to sign for Haddon Hill, and sunken track which climbs steeply; stream at bottom flows over orange bedrock. At top track continues between hedges, before turning **L** for short climb to **Haddon Farm**.

6 Pass to **L** of farm's buildings, on to access track. After ¼ mile (400m) reach corner of wood. Shortly stile above leads into wood. Ignore pointing signpost but bear **L** to go up **L**-H side of wood to gate on to open hill. Go up alongside wood to top corner.

7 Take track bearing **L** to cross crest of hill. Turn **R**, on wide track running to top of **Haddon Hill**. Continue downhill to car park.

PORLOCK *Wildwood and Sea Views*

6 miles (9.7km) 3hrs 15min **Ascent:** 1,200ft (370m)
Paths: Initial stiff climb then smooth, well-marked paths, no stiles
Suggested map: aqua3 OS Outdoor Leisure 9 Exmoor
Grid reference: SS 885468
Parking: Pay-and-display at Porlock Central car park; free parking at Whitstone Post, Point **5**

A stiff climb through the wildwood for a sudden sea view.

1 From car park follow signs for public library; turn **L**. Before church turn **R** (Parsons Street). At parking area with toilets, bridleway sign for Hawkcombe points upstream to footbridge.

2 Path climbs through bamboo and laurel, to join bridleway from below, up through wood, passing below wall with bench. At top of low wall paths divide.

3 Turn **L**, still climbing; immediately bear **R** on to sunken path. Emerge at white house ('Halsecombe'), keep ahead to field gate marked with blue spot. Follow **L** edge of field, to **L**-H of 2 gates, leading back into woodland. Take bridleway ahead (occasional blue waymarkers). Track becomes terraced path, running near top edge of wood for 1 mile (1.6km) to reach track.

4 Turn **L** down track, then **R** into narrow path ('**Whitstone Post**', which runs through bracken and heather into head of Hawk Combe. As path enters hawthorn thicket bear **R** to road signpost at Whitstone Post.

5 Cross main A39 into parking area; turn **R** on wide path. After 110yds (100m) turn **L** down track. Where it turns **L**, turn **R** into smaller track. This contours through gorse and heather (superb views over Porlock Bay), then rejoins A39 at cattle grid.

6 Turn **L**, then **R** into track (bridleway to Porlock). Cross 2 cattle grids to Point **4** of upward route. Keep on down track for 125yds (114m); turn **L** on to terraced path which runs downhill for ¼ mile (400m), to wider path. Turn **R** down to stream.

7 Path runs downstream. On reaching houses it becomes tarred lane and descends through wood. At high wall on **R** sign points to footbridge. Over this, path ascends through woods. Bear **L** on path ('No Horses') and descend to join street at parking area. Turn **L** to cross stream; turn **R** into Mill Lane and Porlock.

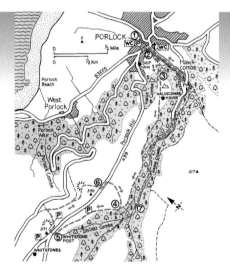

HORNER *Exmoor's Red Deer*

4½ miles (7.2km) 2hrs 30min **Ascent:** 1,000ft (300m)
Paths: Broad paths, with some stonier ones, steep in places, no stiles
Suggested map: aqua3 OS Outdoor Leisure 9 Exmoor
Grid reference: SS 898455
Parking: National Trust car park (free) at Horner

On the trail of Exmoor's red deer in the woodlands under Dunkery Beacon.

1 Leave National Trust car park in Horner village past toilets; turn **R** to track leading into **Horner Wood**, crossing bridge and passing field before rejoining **Horner Water**. Take footpath alongside stream instead of track, leading to same place. Ignore 1st footbridge; continue along track to where sign, ('Dunkery Beacon') points **L** towards 2nd footbridge.

2 Ignore footbridge. Keep on track, then fork **L** on path alongside **West Water**. This rejoins track; after ½ mile (800m) bridleway sign points back to **R**. Look down to **L** for footbridge.

3 Cross on to path that slants up to **R**. After 200yds (183m) turn **L** on to smaller path that curves up left alongside **Prickslade Combe**. Path reaches little stream at cross-path, with wood top visible above. Turn **L**, across stream, on path contouring through top of wood, which emerges into open to tree with bench

and fine view over top of woodlands to Porlock Bay.

4 Continue ahead on grassy track, with car park of **Webber's Post** visible ahead. Deep valley of **East Water** lies ahead. Turn down **L** on path back into birchwoods, to meet larger track in valley bottom.

5 Turn downstream, crossing footbridge over East Water, beside ford. Shortly bear **R** on to ascending path. At top of steep section turn **R** on sunken path climbing to Webber's Post car park.

6 Walk to **L**, round car park, to path ('Permitted Bridleway') to Horner. (Do not take pink-surfaced, easy-access path immediately to **R**.) After 80yds (73m) bear **L** on to wider footpath. Keep ahead down wide, gentle spur, with deep valley of **Horner Water** on **L**. As spur steepens, footpath meets crossing track ('Windsor Path').

7 Turn **R** for about 30 paces, then take descending path ('Horner'). Path widens and finally meets wide track with wooden steps; turn **L** into Horner.

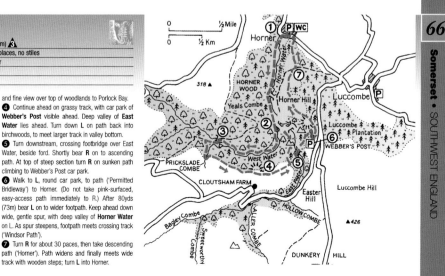

Somerset · SOUTHWEST ENGLAND

67 LYPE HILL *To Brendon's Heights*

5¾ miles (9.2km) 3hrs Ascent: 850ft (260m)
Paths: A rugged track, then little-used field bridleways, 4 stiles
Suggested map: aqua3 OS Outdoor Leisure 9 Exmoor
Grid reference: SS 923387
Parking: Village car park (free) on A396 at Wheddon Cross

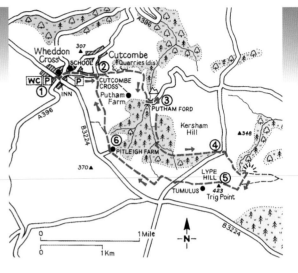

A sunken lane from Wheddon Cross leads up to Lype Hill, the high point of the Brendons.

❶ From main crossroads head towards Dunster; bear **R** at war memorial to pass car park on R-H side. After school, bear **R**, following signpost to Puriton (Popery Lane). Sunken lane runs to **Cutcombe Cross**; keep ahead ('Luxborough via **Putham Ford**') then bear **L** at sign into Putham Lane.

❷ Horses and tractors use track. At bottom it crosses ford, with footbridge alongside. Keep ahead on to lane heading uphill.

❸ At top, field gate on **R** has inconspicuous footpath signpost, leading to green track that runs below, then into wood. Look for footpath sign and stile beside stream below. Cross water and take path on **R**, into open space. Slightly wider path above slants up along bracken clearing. After stile it follows foot of wood, to join forest road, then tarred lane.

❹ Turn **L**, down wide verge; take upper of 2 gates on **R**, with stile and footpath sign. Head up side of wooded combe and across top. Sea view on **L**, stile and gate ahead. Don't cross; turn **R**, and **R** again across top of field to gate by trig point on **Lype Hill** and views of Dunkery Beacon, Wales and Dartmoor.

❺ Through gate keep ahead across field, with tumulus 70yds (64m) on **L**; after gate bear **L**, following fence on **L** to its corner. Gate ahead leads on to road. Cross to signposted gate; bear **L** to field's far corner. Turn **L** alongside beech bank to waymarked gate. Turn **R**, with fence on **R**, and head down along field edges towards **Pitleigh Farm**. Gate in deer fencing leads on to driveway **L** of farm.

❻ Cross driveway on to green track. This becomes fenced-in field edge to deer-fence gate on **L**. Turn **R** to continue as before with hedges now on **R**. After 2 fields reach hedged track. This runs down to crossroads in Popery Lane.

68 KILVE *Along the Quantock Coastline*

3 miles (4.8km) 1hr 30min Ascent: 250ft (80m)
Paths: Tracks, field paths, and grassy cliff top, 7 stiles
Suggested map: aqua3 OS Explorer 140 Quantock Hills & Bridgwater
Grid reference: ST 144442
Parking: Pay-and-display at sea end of Sea Lane

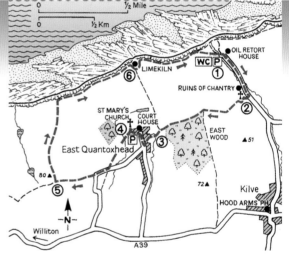

A stimulating walk including Tudor villages, breezy cliffs, industrial remnants and geology underfoot.

❶ From car park head back along lane to **ruined chantry**. Turn into churchyard through lychgate. Pass to **L** of church, to kissing gate.

❷ Signposted track crosses field to gate with stile; bear **R** to another gate with stile and pass along foot of **East Wood**. (At far end, stile allows wandering into wood, April to August only.) Ignoring stile on **L**, keep ahead to field gate with stile and track crossing stream.

❸ Track bends **L** past gardens and ponds of **East Quantoxhead** to tarred lane. Turn **R**, towards Tudor **Court House**, but before gateway bear **L** into car park. Pass through to tarred path beyond 2 kissing gates. In open field path bears **R**, to **St Mary's Church**.

❹ Return to 1st kissing gate but don't go through; instead bear **R** to field gate, and cross field beyond to

lane. Turn **R** and, where lane bends **L**, keep ahead on to green track. At top, turn **R** at 'Permissive path' notice-board.

❺ Follow field edges down to cliff top, and turn **R**. Clifftop path leads to stile before sharp dip, with ruined **limekiln** opposite, built around 1770 to process limestone from Wales. Most of rest of Somerset is limestone, but it was easier to bring it by sea across Bristol Channel.

❻ Turn round head of dip, and back **L** to cliff top. Here iron ladder descends to foreshore: you can see alternating layers of blue-grey lias (type of limestone) and grey shale. Fossils can be found here, but note that cliffs are unstable – hard hats are now standard wear for geologists. Alternatively, given suitably trained dog and right sort of spear, you can pursue traditional sport of 'glatting' – hunting conger eels in rock pools. Continue along wide clifftop path until tarred path bears **R**, crossing stream into car park.

69 HOLFORD *A Quantock Amble*

5½ miles (8.8km) 2hrs 40min Ascent: 700ft (210m)
Paths: Wide, smooth paths, with one slightly rough descent, no stiles
Suggested map: aqua3 OS Explorer 140 Quantock Hills & Bridgwater
Grid reference: ST 154410
Parking: At back of Holford (free)

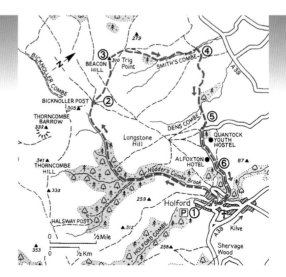

A ramble in the Quantocks in the footsteps of Wordsworth and Coleridge.

❶ Two tracks leave road beside car park. Take **R-H** track, marked with bridleway sign, which becomes earth track through woods, with **Hodder's Combe Brook** on **R**. After ¾ mile (1.2km) track fords stream and forks. Take **R-H** option, entering side-valley. Path runs up valley floor, rising through oakwoods floored with bilberry ('whortleberry'), then mixed heather and bracken, to Quantock ridge. As ground eases, keep ahead over 2 cross-tracks to **Bicknoller Post**.

❷ To **R** (north) of col ridge divides: take **L-H** branch ('Beacon Hill'); pass to **L** side of marker stake on broad track. Keep ahead on widest track. Bear **L** to trig point on **Beacon Hill**.

❸ At trig point turn half-**R** to marker-post on main track. Smaller path descends ahead, into **Smith's Combe**. Weaving path crosses stream several times.

❹ At foot of valley, with green fields below, is 4-way

'Quantock Greenway' signpost: turn **R** (green arrow), uphill. Path runs around base of hills, with belt of trees below, then green fields. At 1st spur crest is another signpost, 3-way: keep ahead for Holford. Path drops to cross stream, **Dens Combe**. After ¼ mile (400m) it drops towards gate leading on to tarmac.

❺ Don't go through gate; strike uphill to another 'Quantock Greenway' signpost. Keep uphill (green arrow) to pass above pink house on to tarred lane. Take track ahead below several houses. Sign indicates Quantock Hills Youth Hostel down to **L**, but stay on lane; it runs out past Alfoxton, with walled garden of grand house (once poet William Wordsworth's, now hotel) on **L** and stable block on **R**. At foot of hotel driveway is parking area.

❻ Follow lane for 650yds (594m) then, as it bends **R**, look out for waymarker and railings down in trees. Below is footbridge leading across into Holford. Turn **R**; at 1st junction turn **R** again, to car park.

Somerset

WIVELISCOMBE *WOOL TOWN AND THE TONE*

6 miles (9.7km) 3hrs 15min **Ascent:** 1,000ft (300m)
Paths: Tracks, a quiet lane, a few field edges, 1 stile
Suggested map: aqua3 OS Explorer 128 Taunton & Blackdown Hills
Grid reference: ST 080279
Parking: North Street, Wiveliscombe

A pretty village and a wooded riverside on the edge of the Brendons.

❶ Turn **L** out of car park into Square; head down High Street and turn **L** at traffic lights (Church Street). Turn **R**, down steps under arch, to Rotton Row. Continue to South Street; turn **L** along pavement.

❷ At end of 30mph limit turn **R**, into lane; go ahead through gate with footpath sign. Cross stile ahead, and bottom edges of 2 fields. Stile in hedge ahead has grown over, so head up to **L** to gateway before returning to foot of field to reach farm buildings. Go up **L-H** edge of field above to gate on to B3227.

❸ Turn **L**, then **R** into lane heading downhill. After ¾ mile (1.2km) it crosses **River Tone** and bends **L** at **Marshes Farm**. Keep ahead, on track marked by broken bridleway sign. Do not turn **R** here into track towards **Wadham's Farm**; keep uphill to deeply sunken lane. Turn **R**, descending towards farm, but at 1st buildings turn **L** (track runs up River Tone). With

houses visible ahead, turn **R** at T-junction; cross footbridge and turn **L** to **Challick Lane**.

❹ Continuing track upstream is currently beside River Tone: polite enquiry at farm will let you through between buildings. Track continues upstream through pleasant woodland to **Washbattle Bridge**.

❺ Turn **R**, along road, for 200yds (183m). Signed forest road leads uphill on **R**. At highest point, with pheasant fence alongside, bear **L** on to wide path that continues uphill. At wood edge cross bottom corner of field to woodland opposite then turn uphill alongside to gate.

❻ Go through gate and turn **L**, with hedge beside it on **L**. Next gate opens on to hedged track which turns **R**, and passes **reservoir** at summit of **Maundown Hill**. At top of tarred public road turn **R** on to track that becomes descending, hedged path. At signposted fork turn **L** on to contouring path. Soon lane leads down into town, with car park near by on **R**.

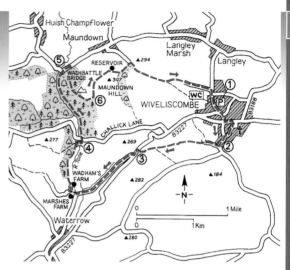

STAPLEY *CLOSE TO THE BORDER*

3 miles (4.8km) 1hr 40min **Ascent:** 500ft (150m)
Paths: Field edges, small woodland paths, 8 stiles
Suggested map: aqua3 OS Explorer 128 Taunton & Blackdown Hills
Grid reference: ST 188136
Parking: Small pull-in beside water treatment works at east end of Stapley; verge parking at walk start

Stapley's little valley looks down over the county boundary into Devon.

❶ Phone box marks start of walk. Some 20 paces below it lane runs between houses. After 100yds (91m) keep ahead on to shady path. At stile bear **R** to ford with footbridge.

❷ Head up wide track. At junction cross on to waymarked path, which heads uphill, following bank, to stile. In field beyond bear **R**, to field corner and stile back into woodland. Path runs along top edge of **Pay Plantation**, emerging near **Beerhill Farm**.

❸ Bear **L** for 100yds (91m) to waymarked gate, and 2nd just beyond. Pass to **R** of cowshed to reach small pool. Pass **R** of pool, to gate; follow top edge of wood to **Rainbow Lane**.

❹ Cross lane to signposted stile. Pass along **L** edge of long narrow field; over on **L**, **Luddery Hill Farm** is built of flinty-looking chert. Stile leads into ash wood. Path runs along top edge of wood. With isolated house

visible ahead, waymarker indicates diverted right of way bearing **R**. Path slants downhill, to meet driveway at bend. Cross on to wide path just above driveway. At end of wood turn down **R**, to rejoin driveway to road below.

❺ Cross into trackway of **Biscombe Hill Farm**. Bear **L** to field gate, and go down **R** edge of field to muddy hedge gap on **R**. Slant down following field to stile at bottom **R-H** corner, with stepping stones across stream beyond. Go up **R-H** edge of next field to stile leading on to sunken track; turn **L** and follow it up to lane.

❻ Turn **R**, up road. Where it levels and bends **L**, turn **R** into driveway of **Craigend Cottage**. Turn **L** along field tops, with hedge bank on your **L** and view of Devon over your **R** shoulder. After stile, field gate leads to tractor track. After short, muddy passage past **Stapley Farm** reach village road at phone box.

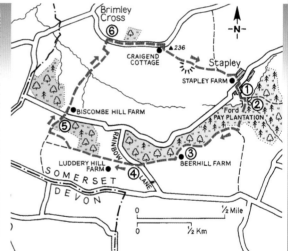

BLACKDOWN HILLS *PRIOR'S PARK WOODLANDS*

5 miles (8km) 2hrs 40min **Ascent:** 700t (210m)
Paths: Rugged in Prior's Park Wood, otherwise comfortable, 7 stiles
Suggested map: aqua3 OS Explorer 128 Taunton & Blackdown Hills
Grid reference: ST 211182
Parking: Roadside pull-off between post office and White Lion, Blagdon Hill

Prior's Park Wood is at its best with autumn's colours or spring's bluebells.

❶ Walk starts at phone box opposite White Lion, handsome 17th-century inn. Cross stile and follow **L** edge of triangular field to another stile into Curdleigh Lane. Cross into ascending **Quarry Lane**. Bend **L** between buildings of Quarry House, on to track running up into **Prior's Park Wood**.

❷ From mid-April **Prior's Park Wood** is delightful with bluebells and other wild flowers. It is also fine (but possibly muddy) in late October and November. Where main track bends **L** and descends slightly, keep uphill on smaller one. This eventually declines into muddy trod, slanting up and leftwards to small gate at top of wood.

❸ Pass along wood's top edge to gate. Red-and-white poles mark line across next field to another gate. After 50yds (46m) turn **R**, between buildings of **Prior's Park Farm**, to its access track and road. Turn **L** and

follow road with care (it's fairly fast section), towards **Holman Clavel Inn**.

❹ Just before inn turn **L** into forest track. Where track ends small path runs ahead, zig-zagging down before crossing stream. At wood's edge turn **R** up wider path to B3170.

❺ At once turn **L** on lane ('Feltham'). After ½ mile (800m), wide gateway on **L** leads to earth track. This runs along top of Adcombe Wood then down inside it, giving very pleasant descent.

❻ Once below wood follow track downhill for 180yds (165m). Look for gate with signpost on **L-H** side. Go through it and follow hedge on **R** to stile and footbridge, then bend **L**, below foot of wood, to another stile. Ignore stile into wood on **L**, but continue along wood's foot to next field corner. Here further stile enters wood but turn **R**, beside hedge, to concrete track. Turn **L** – track becomes Curdleigh Lane, leading back into **Blagdon Hill**.

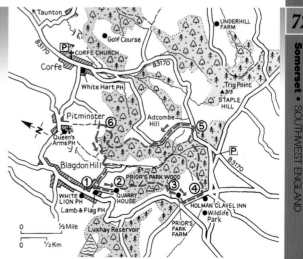

Somerset

73 ILMINSTER A WALK IN THE WOODS

5¾ miles (9.2km) 2hrs 40min **Ascent:** 500ft (150m)
Paths: Tracks, wide paths, and riverside field edges, 12 stiles
Suggested map: aqua3 OS Explorer 128 Taunton & Blackdown Hills
Grid reference: ST 362144
Parking: Pay-and-display in Ditton Street, signposted from nearby Market Cross

A pleasing riverside and woodland ramble.
❶ From car park aim for town centre and head uphill on North Street. With ancient **Bell Inn** on L, continue on path (Old Road), rising past beacon fire-basket and mobile phone mast before descending to **B3168**.
❷ Cross with care into hedged byway. Where it forks, keep **R**, to **Eames Mill**. Turn **R**, along waymarked access track. After 220yds (201m) concrete track turns back **L**. Just before bridge turn **L** over stile; follow **River Isle** upstream. Rights of way don't allow more straightforward route.
❸ Cross weir then head upstream with river to **L**. After 1 mile (1.6km) reach car park of Powrmatic works, and **B3168** beyond.
❹ Cross on to track ('**Industrial Estate**'). Pass along river bank to **L** of buildings, then between piles of ironwork to footbridge. With river on **R**, head upstream on fenced way to re-cross on another

footbridge. Continue over stiles along **R-H** bank. With tower of **Donyatt church** ahead, cross diagonally **R** to gate on to road.
❺ Turn **L** through village, and bear **L** past church. Head straight up **Herne Hill** as lane becomes track, then field-edge path, then earth path through Herne Hill Wood, whose summit is under tall beeches. Wide avenue ahead leads to field corner. Continue inside wood, passing bench and trig point on R, and going down to wood's foot. Turn back **L** for 90yds (82m) to gate on **R**.
❻ Wide path runs towards Ilminster, with sports fields below. Turn **L**, between sports fields and town, for 200yds (183m) to yellow litter bin. Gap on **R** leads to path alongside remnant of Chard–Taunton **Canal**. Turn **R** behind tennis courts; after 250yds (229m) turn **L** into Abbots Close and on to tarred path. This leads to West Street, arriving at **Crown Inn**. Turn **R** and bear **R** into Silver Street, to reach town centre.

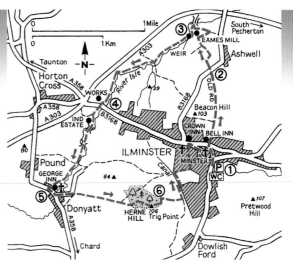

74 EAST LAMBROOK IN PRAISE OF APPLES

4¾ miles (7.7km) 2hrs 30min **Ascent:** 350ft (110m)
Paths: Little-used field paths (some possibly overgrown by late summer), 24 stiles
Suggested map: aqua3 OS Explorer 129 Yeovil & Sherborne
Grid reference: ST 431190
Parking: Street parking in East Lambrook village

A gentle, secluded ramble around the fields and fragrant apple orchards of Somerset.
❶ Head into village, eventually turning **L** on to track. After 1 field, track leads **L** to lane (**Hawthorn Hill**). Turn **R** to **The Cottage**, where gate with stile leads into orchard on your **L**. Follow **L** edge and next field. Cross following field, keeping 70yds (64m) from L edge, to gate. Bear **R** to stile-with-footbridge and orchard. At far end gate leads on to **Stockditch Road**.
❷ Turn **L** for 40yds (37m), into overgrown track. Edge of another orchard leads to 2 stiles and footbridge. Follow **L** edges of 2 fields to road; turn **R** to **Rusty Axe pub**.
❸ Keep ahead, on to track, past houses. On crossing crest turn **L** on green track. At next field follow hedge on **L** (ignoring waymarker for different path). Two stiles lead into long field with stumps of former orchard. Keep to **L** of house to join quiet country lane.

❹ Cross into tarred driveway of **Lower Burrow Farm**; follow waymarkers between farm buildings. Bear **L**, slanting uphill, to gateway. Cross next field to double stile. In next field bear **R** to gate and stile. **Burrow Hill Farm** is 1 field ahead. Turn **L**, up side of field and across top to gate. Go up field to poplars and summit of **Burrow Hill**.
❺ Drop to lane at **Pass Vale Farm** and then turn **L** for ¼ mile (400m) to waymarked field gate on **R**. Follow **L** edges of 2 fields to footbridge with brambly stile. Turn **L** beside stream to another brambly stile and turn **R** to lane.
❻ Turn **L** to gate on **R** ('**East Lambrook**'). Follow **L** edges of 3 fields, then bear **L** over stile and footbridge to 2nd bridge beyond. In next large field, follow waymarkers down **R-H** side and across far end to orchard. Do not cross obvious stile out of orchard but turn **R**, to its far end, where lane leads back into East Lambrook.

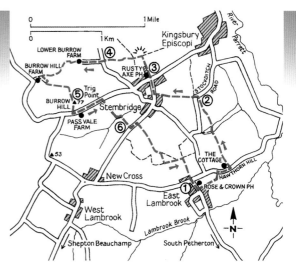

75 HAM HILL GOLDEN STONE

4 miles (6.4km) 2hrs **Ascent:** 700ft (210m)
Paths: Well-trodden and sometimes muddy, 5 stiles
Suggested map: aqua3 OS Explorer 129 Yeovil & Sherborne
Grid reference: ST 478167
Parking: Main car park on western escarpment of Ham Hill

Ascending the hill whose warm-coloured limestone forms the towns and villages of Somerset.
❶ Turn **L** out of car park; follow road to junction. Bear **L** then take path on **R** ('Norton Sub Hamdon'), which leads through woods around side of Ham Hill. When open field appears ahead, turn **R**, downhill. Ignore 1st gate on L and continue to 2nd.
❷ Descend grassland into small valley with hummocks of **medieval village** of Witcombe. Head up valley floor, passing to **L** of willow clump. Grassy path climbs **R-H** side of valley to field corner. Turn **L** on track leading to lane near **Batemoor Barn**.
❸ Hollow Lane descends directly opposite the barn. Stile to **R** passes along field edges, then wood. Shortly, turn **R** to stile. Clear path runs just below top of wood, then down to edge of **Montacute village**. Turn **L** near entrance to **Montacute House**, to reach **King's Head Inn**.

❹ Turn **L**, past church; after duck pond turn **R** on to permissive path. Kissing gate leads you to bottom of **St Michael's Hill**. Turn **L** to stile into woods.
❺ Path ahead is arduous. For gentler way up hill, turn **L** around base to descending track. Otherwise head slightly **L** up steep path, to join same track just below summit tower. The **Tower's** open and spiral staircase are worth climb. Descend spiralling track to gate at hill's foot.
❻ Turn half-**R** and go straight down field to gate leading on to track corner. Turn **L** and follow track round field corner. After 90yds (82m) take **R** fork. Earth track runs close to foot of woods, passing ruins of pump house, and diminishing to path; it then climbs steps to join higher one. Turn **R** to continue close to foot of woods until path emerges at gate. Steps lead up to **Prince of Wales pub**. Turn **L** along its lane, passing through hummocks of former quarries, to car park and start.

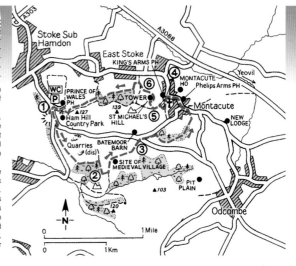

Somerset

CUCKLINGTON *DEEPEST SOMERSET*

5½ miles (8.8km) 2hrs 45min **Ascent:** 600ft (180m) ⚠
Paths: Little-used field paths, which may be overgrown, 11 stiles
Suggested map: aqua3 OS Explorer 129 Yeovil & Sherborne
Grid reference: ST 747298
Parking: Lay-by on former main road immediately south of A303

Up hill and down, taking in a church with over a thousand years of history.

❶ With back to A303, turn **R** on lane to where track runs ahead into wood. At far side, fenced footpath runs alongside main road. Turn **L** up path, then **R** into fenced-off path that bends **L** to **Parkhouse Farm**. After passage to **L** of buildings, turn **L** again to lane.

❷ Turn back **R**, following field edge back by farm track. Go through gate; turn **L** through gate. Heading towards Stoke Trister church, follow **L** edge of field; go straight up 2nd field, turning **R** along lane to church.

❸ Continue to stile. Go uphill past muddy track, but turn **R** alongside hedge immediately above. Follow around **Coneygore Hill**, over stile, then to 2nd; go straight down to **Stileway Farm**.

❹ Turn **L** by top of farm buildings. Continue into field track but immediately take gate above; pass along base of 2 fields, to gate by cattle trough. Head uphill, with hedge to **L**, to steeper bank around Coneygore Hill. Turn **R** and follow banking to stile. Keep on to gap between bramble clumps; slant down **R** to gate in corner leading on to green track and then to lane near **Manor Farm**.

❺ Turn downhill past thatched cottage and red phone box; bear **R** for **Cucklington**. There are field paths on **L**, but use lane to cross valley and climb to Cucklington. Gravel track on **L** leads to Cucklington church.

❻ Pass **L** of church; cross 2 fields, passing above **Cucklington Wood**. In 3rd field slant to **R** to join track to **Clapton Farm**.

❼ After Tudor manor house track bends **R**, uphill. Turn **L** between farm buildings to gate, then turn **L** down wooded bank. Turn **R**, along base of bank, to gap in hedge. Bear **L** past power pole to field's bottom corner. Cross 2 streams; bear **L** to cross 3rd and stile beyond. Go straight up to stile by cattle trough and lane you parked on.

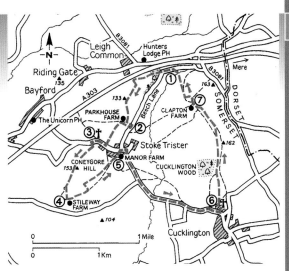

SOUTH CADBURY *CADBURY CASTLE AS CAMELOT?*

6¾ miles (10.9km) 3hrs 30min **Ascent:** 1,000ft (300m) ⚠⚠
Paths: Well-used paths, 6 stiles
Suggested map: aqua3 OS Explorer 129 Yeovil & Sherborne
Grid reference: ST 632253
Parking: Cadbury Castle car park (free), south of South Cadbury

Cadbury Castle hill fort gives wide views of Somerset and a glimpse of pre-history.

❶ Turn **R** out of car park to 1st house in South Cadbury. Track leads up to **Cadbury Castle**. Ramparts and top of fort are access land; stroll around at will.

❷ Return past car park. After ¼ mile (400m) pass side road on **L**, to stile signposted '**Sigwells**'. Walk down to reach stile and footbridge. Cross then follow **L** edge of field, then uncultivated strip. Track starts ahead, but take stile on **R** to follow field edge next to it, to gate with 2 waymarkers. Faint track leads along top of following field. At end turn down into hedged-earth track which leads out past **Whitcombe Farm** to rejoin road.

❸ Turn **L** to junction below Corton Denham **Beacon**. Turn **L** to slant uphill for ¼ mile (400m). Track on **R** leads to open hilltop and summit **trig point**.

❹ Head along steep hill rim to stile with dog slot. Continue along top of slope (Corton Denham below). Pass modern 'tumulus' (small, covered reservoir). Above 5 large beeches slant down to waymarked gate. Green path slants down again, until gate leads to tarred lane; follow to road below.

❺ Turn **L** on road, between high banks for 110yds (100m) to stile ('**Middle Ridge Lane**'). Keep to **L** of trees to field gate, with stile beyond leading into lane. Go across into stony track that climbs to ridgeline.

❻ Turn **R**; walk along **Corton Ridge** with hedge on **R** and view on **L**. After 650yds (594m) Ridge Lane starts on **R**, but go through small gate on **L** to continue along the ridge. After small gate, green path bends around flank of **Parrock Hill**. With **Cadbury Castle** now on **L**, ignore 1st green track down to **L**. Shortly main track turns down **L** into hedge end and waymarked gate. Hedged path leads down to road.

❼ Cross road ('**South Cadbury**'). Shortly turn **R**, again for **South Cadbury**; follow road round base of **Cadbury Castle** to car park.

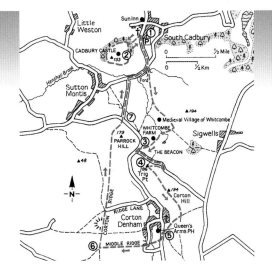

POLDEN HILLS *EDGE OF THE LEVELS*

4½ miles (7.2km) 2hrs 15min **Ascent:** 450ft (140m) ⚠
Paths: Initially steep then easy tracks and paths, 3 stiles
Suggested map: aqua3 OS Explorer 141 Cheddar Gorge
Grid reference: ST 480345
Parking: Car park (free) at Street Youth Hostel, just off B3151; another car park on south side of road

From Polden's edge down on to the Somerset Levels and up again.

❶ From parking area on youth hostel side, cross and turn **R** on woodland path. Shortly smaller path descends on **L** by steps. At foot of wood turn **R**; at field corner go down short way to track which runs along base of wood to lane.

❷ Go down to **Lower Ivythorn Farm** entrance; turn **L** into track. After ½ mile (800m) this reaches corner of unsurfaced track. Turn **R**. After ¼ mile (400m) track turns **L** into field. Follow edge, with ditch and fence **L**, to gate. In next field continue alongside ditch to corner. Former footbridge is derelict. Take gate on **L**, then turn **R** on field track, passing **L** of Hurst Farm, to tarred lane.

❸ Turn **R** to bridleway sign on **L**. Follow green track to Ham Lane. This leads to crossroads of B3151 in **Compton Dundon** (Castlebrook Inn to **R**).

❹ Cross busy B3151 and pass between ancient market cross (**R**) and Victorian obelisk (**L**) into Compton Street. At 1st junction keep to **L**, towards **Hood Monument** above. As street climbs, turn **R** and **L** up lane beyond. Where it reaches woodland turn off through waymarked gate ('Reynolds Way'). Path slants up into wood. Shortly before it arrives at road, turn **L** along top of steep ground, to **Hood Monument**.

❺ Continue down through wood to minor road, with main road 50yds (46m) away on **L**. Ignore path descending opposite but turn **R** for few steps to footpath sign and kissing gate. Grass path heads up crest of **Collard Hill**, (wide views to **L**).

❻ From summit go straight on down to stile and signposted crossroads of B3151. Cross both roads. Ridge road signposted for youth hostel; path is just to **R**, crossing glade into woodland. Keep to **R** of hummocky ground to wood's edge; follow this path to car park.

79 ALFRED'S TOWER *THREE COUNTY CORNER*

8½ miles (13.7km) 4hrs **Ascent:** 950ft (290m)

Paths: Some tracks and some small paths and field edges, 7 stiles

Suggested map: aqua3 OS Explorer 142 Shepton Mallet

Grid reference: ST 755314

Parking: Penselwood church; some verge parking at Bleak Farm

An expedition through Somerset, Dorset and Wiltshire, to Stourhead and Alfred's Tower.
❶ Go through churchyard to road beyond. Turn **L** through **Bleak Farm** village, then **L** into sunken track, ending at top of tarred lane. Turn **L** through white gate ('Pen Mill Hill'). Head down to kissing gate in dip; follow track past pond to road.
❷ Cross into path ('Coombe Street'). Pass below **Orchard Cottages**, then turn **L** over 2 stiles. Cross stream in dip to stile below thatched cottage. Woodland path bends **R** to footbridge over **River Stour**.
❸ From here to Point ❹ is marked ('Stour Valley Way'). Go on to tarred lane; turn **L**. Keep ahead into hedged way to stile. Go up and round **L** to another stile. Lane beyond leads to T-junction; go across and turn **L** on to bridleway. Go through gate to follow **L** edge of field into hedged track, emerge opposite **Bonham House**.
❹ Turn **L**; at 2nd signpost bear **R** to road below. Follow to **R**, to rustic rock arch. Take track on **L**

('Alfred's Tower').
❺ Track bends **R** and heads into wooded valley with **Alfred's Tower** visible ahead, reaching open ground at hilltop, with road ahead. Turn **L**, in grassy avenue, to **Alfred's Tower**.
❻ Join road ahead for 220yds (201m), down to sunken path on **L** ('Penselwood'). Follow, ignoring paths on both sides, on to track down to major junction. Bear **R** to lane, then **R** again, on road ('Penselwood'), which leads over hilltop with hill fort. Descend until open ground appears on **L**.
❼ Cross stile; head downhill with **Castle Wood L**, and young trees **R**. Move into wood to join track along its edge. At corner of wood, waymarked gate on **R** leads into fields.
❽ Follow **L** edge of 1st field to 2 gates on **L**; keep ahead to gate and 2nd gate beyond. Track leads out to road. Turn **R** to sharp R-H bend, where gate starts field path to Penselwood church.

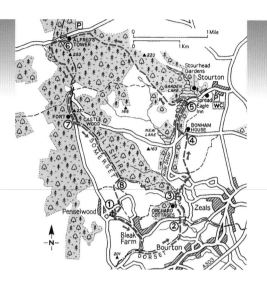

80 BRUTON *GOLDEN WOOL*

4½ miles (7.2km) 2hrs 15min **Ascent:** 500ft (150m)

Paths: Enclosed tracks, open fields, an especially muddy farmyard

Suggested map: aqua3 OS Explorer 142 Shepton Mallet

Grid reference: ST 684348

Parking: Free parking off Silver Street, 50yds (46m) west of church; larger car park in Upper Backway

A walk around and above beautiful Bruton, a typical Somerset wool town.
❶ With church **L** and bridge **R**, head down Silver Street to car park in Coombe Street. Old packhorse bridge over River Brue leads into Lower Backway. Turn **L** for 350yds (320m), ignoring arch leading towards footbridge; take path between railed fences to 2nd footbridge. Turn **R** along river to **West End**.
❷ Turn **R** over river and **R** again into end of High Street; immediately turn uphill on to walled path ('Mill Dam'). At lane above turn **R** along track ('Huish Lane'). Just after footbridge fork **L**; hedged track is steep and muddy, bending **R** then **L** to lane (**Wyke Road**).
❸ Turn **R**, then **R** again; after 220yds (201m) turn **R** past farm buildings on to uphill track (**Creech Hill Lane**), which becomes hedged tunnel, then emerges at **Creech Hill Farm**. Pass along front of farm and out to **B3081**. Turn **L** over hill crest to triangular junction.
❹ Turn **R** for 40yds (37m) to public bridleway sign

and gate on **R**. Go down combe below; at foot keep **L** of **Green's Combe Farm** and above intermittent wall; turn down through gate between farm buildings.
❺ Continue down farm's access track for ¼ mile (400m) until it bends **R**. Keep ahead through field gate with blue waymarker, on to green track. After 200yds (183m), beside 3 stumps, turn downhill, to **L** of hazels, to gate. Pass through small wood to gate and waymarked track. When this emerges into open field follow fence above to join **B3081**. Turn **L**, uphill, to **Coombe Farm** entrance.
❻ Ignoring stile on **L**, go through ivy-covered wall gap, then down driveway; turn **L** on to wide path under sycamores. Path rises, with gate on **L**. At open grassland, keep to **L** edge to descending path that becomes St Catherine's Lane. Weavers' cottages are on **R** as street descends into **Bruton**. Turn **L** along High Street. At end turn **R** down Patwell Street to Church Bridge.

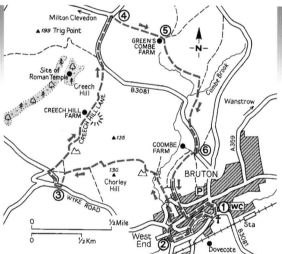

81 NUNNEY *VILLAGE, CASTLE AND COMBE*

3 miles (4.8km) 1hr 15min **Ascent:** 100ft (30m)

Paths: Broad, riverside path, pasture, then leafy track, 8 stiles

Suggested map: aqua3 OS Explorer 142 Shepton Mallet

Grid reference: ST 736456

Parking: Short-stay parking at Nunney Market Square; small lay-by at end of a public footpath 150yds (137m) up Castle Hill

Through woodland and pasture, visiting a stone-built village with a moated castle.
❶ From Nunney's Market Square cross brook and immediately turn **R** to **Nunney Castle** (entry free). Inspect castle, then return and pass **R**, across footbridge, to church. Further on, where street starts uphill, turn **L** into Donkey Lane.
❷ Follow lane past high wall on **L**, to gate with signpost ahead, leaving track after 150yds (137m) for small gate ahead into woods. Wide path leads downstream with **Nunney Brook** on **L**. After about ¾ mile (1.2km) track runs across valley.
❸ Turn **L** to cross brook; immediately turn **R** over broken stile. Continue along stream on path. After 350yds (320m) path climbs away from stream to join track above. Turn **R** on this, to cross stream on high-arched bridge. Track bends **R**, through gate: before next gate look for grey gate (**L**) with waymarking arrow.

❹ Go up R-H side of narrow field to field gate (no stile). Continue uphill on **L-H** edge for 50yds (46m), to stile in hedge. This, and following stiles, have waymarkers giving direction across next field. Turn half-**R** as arrow indicates, slanting up to hedge and follow it along top of field to stile at corner. At crest of broad ridge there are views ahead to hills in west.
❺ Turn **L** around field to stile in next corner. Cross, turn half-**R** and go straight across field to double stile at furthest corner. Cross and follow **L-H** edge of long field ahead. At corner cross stile between 2 gateways and turn **R**. After 400yds (366m), before end of field, watch out for stile on **R**.
❻ This leads into narrow track between overarching hedges. It bends to **L** then **R**, then descends to become street leading into **Nunney**. Street runs down to join Donkey Lane on outward route, with church 300yds (274m) ahead.

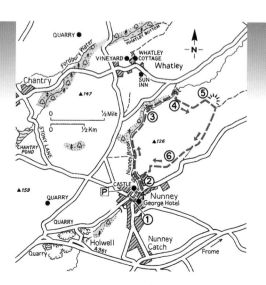

Somerset

BURROW MUMP *On the Levels*

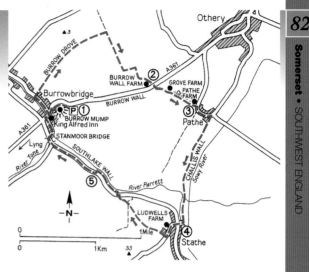

5¼ miles (8.4km) 2hrs 15min **Ascent:** 150ft (50m)
Paths: Tracks, paths, unfrequented field edges, 6 stiles
Suggested map: aqua3 OS Explorer 140 Quantock Hills & Bridgwater
Grid reference: ST 360395
Parking: National Trust car park (free) at Burrow Mump

A gentle wander around the Somerset Levels near Burrowbridge leading up to a 'mump'.

1 Gate leads on to base of **Mump**. Keep to **R** to small gate and steps down to Burrow Bridge. Before bridge turn **R** into Riverside. After 350yds (320m) turn **R** into **Burrow Drove**, which becomes tractor track. On either side and between fields are deep ditches, coated in bright green pondweed. At T-junction is 19th-century brick culvert on **L**. Turn **R** on new track, passing behind **Burrow Wall Farm** to meet busy A361.

2 'Public footpath' sign points to track opposite. After 30yds (27m) turn **L** over stile. With bushy **Burrow Wall** R, cross field to **Grove Farm** (usually muddy). Go through 2 gates; continue along fields beside woodland on **L**. At end of 2nd field rusty gate leads up between brambles to green track: turn **R** to lane near **Pathe Farm**.

3 Turn **R** along lane, ignoring track on R, to side-lane on R. Here cross bridge to hedge-gap on **R** and very narrow footbridge. Continue through several fields, with wide rhyne (ditch) on R. Near by, on **L**, is low banking of **Challis Wall**, concealing **Sowy River**. Ditch on R gradually gets smaller. When it finally ends bear **R** to **River Parrett** and follow to latticework road bridge. Cross into edge of **Stathe**.

4 Keep ahead through village, past phone box and **Ludwells Farm**, to stile on R ('Macmillan Way'). Follow R edge of field to gate; cross to hedge opposite and follow round to **L**, to stile. Continue with hedge on R to gate, where hedged track leads to road. Turn **L**, scrambling up banking, to walk on **Southlake Wall** between road and river.

5 As road turns away from river, rejoin it. Once across Stanmoor Bridge waymarker points to R for riverbank path to **Burrowbridge**. Turn **R** and, this time, climb to top of **Burrow Mump** for overview of entire walk and much of Somerset.

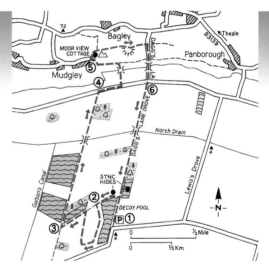

WESTHAY *A Peatland Reserve*

4¾ miles (7.7km) 2hrs 15min **Ascent:** 250ft (80m)
Paths: Mostly smooth, level paths and tracks, 2 stiles
Suggested map: aqua3 OS Explorer 141 Cheddar Gorge
Grid reference: ST 456437
Parking: Free car park at Decoy Pool, signposted from public road
Note: To bypass rough part, follow lane between Points **4** and **6**

A nature ramble through peat marshland.

1 Head into reserve on broad track, with **Decoy Pool** behind reeds on **L**. At end of lake kissing gate leads to Somerset Trust for Nature Conservation (**STNC**) **hides**, with broad path continuing between high reedbeds. Ignore gate on **L** ('No Visitor Access'); go through kissing gate further on.

2 Fenced track runs through peat ground, where birches are being felled to re-create blanket bog. Track turns R; now take kissing gate on **L** for path through trees. At end, new track leads back through peat. At end turn **L** to gate on to next of 'droves' (raised trackways through peatland).

3 Turn **R**, passing hides and crossing bridge over wide North Drain; land on each side now comprises water-meadows. Track leads to lane.

4 To omit field paths above (which are rough, but give splendid view over reserve), turn **R**, going along road for 650yds (594m) to junction, Point **6**. Otherwise turn **R** as far as R-H bend; continue for 175yds (160m) to gates on both sides of road. Go through **L-H** one (with red-painted marker); cross to gate and bridge over ditch. Follow **L** edge of next field to corner. Turn **L** through gate and follow field edges to orchard. Turn **R**, up to end of tarred lane.

5 Turn **L** along road to uphill path to L of **Moor View Cottage** (overgrown and steep) to stile on **R**. Cross tops of 5 fields. In 6th field drop slightly to pass below farm buildings (helpful signpost here). Gate leads into orchard, with signposted gate on to **Dagg's Lane** just above. Turn down lane to road below.

6 Directly opposite Dagg's Lane is track (**Dagg's Lane Drove**), which runs between meadows then re-enters reserve, passing between pools. Look out for path on **L** signposted to hide. Return from hide and rejoin drove track, which leads back to car park.

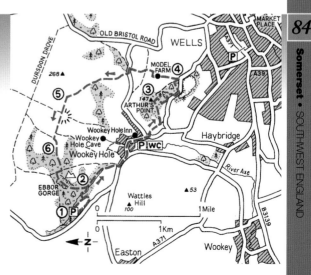

EBBOR GORGE *Coleridge's Inspiration*

4¾ miles (7.7km) 2hrs 30min **Ascent:** 700ft (210m)
Paths: Small paths and field edges, with a rugged descent, 9 stiles
Suggested map: aqua3 OS Explorer 141 Cheddar Gorge
Grid reference: ST 521484
Parking: Lane above Wookey Hole (optional, small fee)

The small but sublime limestone gorge that inspired the poet, Samuel Taylor Coleridge.

1 From notice-board at top end of car park descend stepped path. After clearing, turn **L** ('The Gorge'). Wide path crosses stream to another junction.

2 Turn **R**, away from gorge; follow valley down to road. Turn **L**, passing through village of Wookey Hole. At end of village, road bends R; take kissing gate on **L** ('West Mendip Way' waymarker post). After 2 more kissing gates turn **L** up spur to stile and top of **Arthur's Point**.

3 Bear **R** into woods again. Beware: hidden in brambles ahead is top of quarry crag; turn **R**, down to stile. Go down field edge to kissing gate; bear **L** between boulders back into wood. After sharp rise bear **R**, to join Lime Kiln Lane below, which bends **L** with path on **L** diverting through bottom of wood. This emerges at end of short field track; follow down to footpath signpost.

4 Turn sharp **L**, on track that passes through **Model Farm**. Follow track through farm, turning **R** by houses to continue to a track to Tynings Lane. Turn **L** to signposted stile on your **R**. Go up with fence R, then bear **L** to gate with stile. Go straight up next, large field, aiming for gateway with tractor ruts. Track leads up through wood and field to gate. Slant upwards in same direction to another gate next to stile 100yds (91m) below field's top L corner.

5 Small path runs along tops of 3 fields with long view across Levels to L. With stile on R and gate and trough in front, turn downhill with fence on R; follow it to stile leading into **Ebbor Gorge** Nature Reserve.

6 2nd gate leads into wood. At junction with red arrow and sign ('Car Park') pointing forward, turn **R** into valley and go down – it narrows to rocky gully. At foot of gorge turn **R** ('Car Park'). You are now back at Point **2** of outward walk. Cross stream, turn **L** at T-junction to wood edge and back **R** to car park.

85 HUNTSPILL COAST, FLATLANDS AND MUD

4½ miles (7.2km) 1hr 45min **Ascent:** Negligible
Paths: Town paths, wide, surfaced track and fields, 17 stiles
Suggested map: aqua3 OS Explorer 153 Weston-super-Mare
Grid reference: ST 305455
Parking: Street parking at Huntspill church

A coastal walk that will heighten your understanding of flatlands and mud.
❶ Head away from church with houses on R and trees on L (sea somewhere behind). Church Road bends R then back L: at next bend keep ahead in Longlands Lane, which becomes ditched track under poplars. Join concrete track that bends R to **Maundril's Farm**.
❷ Turn **L** on waymarked footpath between huge sheds. Cross track to stile; turn half-**R** to cross field to footbridge. Fenced path leads to street and continues beyond it, passing end of 2nd street, to reach 3rd.
❸ Tarred path continues opposite, emerging into field. Fenced-off way runs round edge of field to stile. Continue along **R-H** edge of field to corner.
❹ Walled way leads out to R: take it if you wish to cross bridge to visit Highbridge. Opposite **Highbridge Inn** is handsome Victorian warehouse in brick and stone. (Find toilets by bearing L at roundabout to car

park.) Main walk continues from Point ❹ along field edge near **River Brue**, with its banks of brown mud, to reach sea lock.
❺ Bear **L** to stile; follow path on flood bank alongside tidal river. As banking reaches sea, stile and gate on **R** lead on to concrete top of more sea defences.
❻ Follow concrete track along shoreline for 1 mile (1.6km). Where concrete disappears under grass bear **L** to gate; cross earth barrier to tarred lane. After 150yds (137m) this leaves shore to pass litter bin.
❼ Cross stile here; head towards Huntspill church on faint field path with hedge and ditch to L. Cross footbridge on **L** – here field boundaries are made of water. Turn **R** alongside hedge to join track. After 300yds (274m) watch out for footbridge on **R**. Turn **L** towards church; bear **R** towards house with white gables, to narrow footbridge. Head straight towards church over several stiles, to enter churchyard through kissing gate.

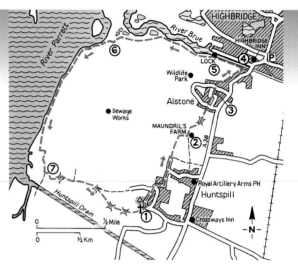

86 CROOK PEAK THE WESTERN MENDIPS

6 miles (9.7km) 3hrs **Ascent:** 900ft (270m)
Paths: Field edges, then wide clear paths, 6 stiles
Suggested map: aqua3 OS Explorer 153 Weston-super-Mare
Grid reference: ST 392550
Parking: On road between Cross and Bleadon, west of Compton Bishop; also street parking in Cross and on A38

A high-level ridge wander in the western Mendips to Somerset's shapeliest summit.
❶ Cross road to wide gate on **R** (not small gate ahead). Wide path contours round through brambly scrub, crosses ridgeline and drops through wood to its foot. Go down through gate into **Compton Bishop** and turn **L** to church.
❷ Lane turns down, before church, to crossroads. Take track opposite and follow it round bend to its end. Contour base of high slope of **Wavering Down**. Cross stile, pass through wrought-iron gate into narrow paddock, and cross another stile into large field; keep along bottom edge. At its corner keep ahead over stile, then through 2 gates, then go 40yds (37m) uphill around fence corner to another stile on same level. Follow bottom edge of field to track and turn **R**, down to road. Turn **L** through **Cross** village.
❸ At 'Give Way 150yds' sign (warning of **A38**

ahead) turn **L** up enclosed path, which turns **R** above fence, then slants up to rejoin same fence higher up. It enters woodland, running above bank of hornbeams: watch out for waymarker where path bears **R** to pass through this bank. After gate ignore stile above to stay on main track, which emerges at top of car park on **Winscombe Hill**.
❹ Turn **L**, away from car park, on broad track uphill. This rises through **King's Wood**, then dips slightly to pass pantiled **Hill Farm**, before rising to trig point on **Wavering Down**. Continue with wall on **R**, walking next to wall for views over it, to cross **Barton Hill**. In dip below **Crook Peak** waymarkers point to L and R, but keep ahead to climb slightly crag-topped summit.
❺ Turn **L** and (with small rocky drop to L) head down on to long gentle ridge – outcrops of limestone poke out through shallow grass of path. At railed barrier turn **R** on path back to car park.

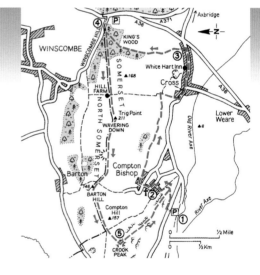

87 DOLEBURY WARREN AN IRON-AGE HILL FORT

5¼ miles (8.4km) 2hrs 30min **Ascent:** 600ft (180m)
Paths: Wide and mostly mud-free, 4 stiles
Suggested map: aqua3 OS Explorer 141 Cheddar Gorge
Grid reference: ST 444575
Parking: Pull-off near church; street parking around main Shipham crossroads

A walk through woodland and heathland on the northern rim of the Mendips.
❶ From main crossroads in centre of Shipham head uphill on Hollow Road ('Rowberrow'). At top bear **R** (Barn Pool), then turn **R** again (Lipiatt Lane). Continue walking up hill, then at its end keep ahead on path with waymarker for Cheddar, to descend sunken path to stream.
❷ Just before stream turn **L** on path ('Rowberrow'). Stay to L of stream (ignoring R fork) – path becomes tarred track. After 3 houses and limekiln bear **R** into forest at notice-board ('Rowberrow Warren').
❸ Track bends to **R**, climbing. At corner of open field turn **L** into smaller track that descends with this field above on its R. At junction keep ahead, uphill, then turn **L** on forest track with bridleway sign.
❹ After 350yds (320m) track ends; bear **L** down path with forest on R. Where it joins stony track and

path below, bear **R** on stony track, with wall to L. At T-junction turn **L** to gate on L with National Trust sign.
❺ Follow grassy ridgeline ahead, passing along **L** side of fenced enclosure of scrubland. At its end, bear **R** ('Limestone Link' waymarker) to pass to R of tall pine clump. Emerge on to more open grassland (wide views). Highest point of ridge is rim of **Dolebury hill fort**.
❻ Green track runs down through fort and into woods below. It bends **L**, then back **R**, emerging at gate on to tarred lanes. Take lane on **R**, down to **A38**. Cross to signposted bridleway, which rises to lane. Turn **L** – ground on L consists of broken screes from disused **Churchill Quarry** below. Ignore turnings L and R and follow enclosed track down to Star.
❼ Cross **A38** on to grass track to stile; go up grassy spur above. Keep to L of some trees to stile; pass to **R** of football pitch, to short path out to edge of **Shipham**. Turn **R**, to village centre.

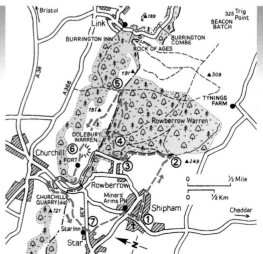

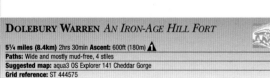

Somerset

GOBLIN COMBE *CRAG TOPS AND HOLLOWS*

5¼ miles (8.4km) Ascent: 400ft (210m)
Paths: Tracks and paths, one steep-stepped ascent, 3 stiles
Suggested map: aqua3 OS Explorer 154 Bristol West & Portishead
Grid reference: ST 459653
Parking: Goblin Combe car park (free) on Cleeve Hill Road (turn off A370 at Lord Nelson pub)

A walk full of crag tops and hollows.

❶ From parking area turn **R** into Plunder Street; bear **L** past **Goblin Combe** Environmental Centre to pass through gateway marked 'Footpath to Wrington only'. Earth track leads up combe bottom, with grey crags above (L).

❷ After ¾ mile (1.2km) track passes through gap in wall. By permissive paths map, turn **L** up path. Steps lead to top of slope, where small path turns **R** beside broken wall. On R, yew trees conceal drop beyond. After 100yds (91m) path bears **R** to open crag top. Turn **L** for 270yds (247m) into clearing. After another 100yds (91m) is barrier with stile. Track leads down to notice-board near **Warren Farm** outbuildings.

❸ Turn **R** on green track; it goes uphill, then descends and bears **L** to floor of wooded combe. Turn **R** for 110yds (100m) to junction of combes and tracks.

❹ Turn sharp **L**, past tree-trunk obstructions, on green track in bottom of new combe. With wood edge visible ahead, bear **L** to barrier and turn **R** on track beyond, running along wood edge. After corner of **Spying Copse** track runs into open pasture. It turns **R** then **L**; after another 100yds (91m) watch for kissing gate on **R**-H side: grassy way leads across field to lane (Wrington Hill).

❺ Turn **R** for ¾ mile (1.2km); as road leaves beeches of **Corporation Woods**, turn back **L** on track following signpost ('Congresbury Woodlands'). After bungalow on R-H side track descends to **Woolmers House**.

❻ After passing kennels, turn **R** on waymarked track; go through 2 gates into **King's Wood**. Broad path ahead leads to waymarked footbridge. After another 50yds (46m) bear **L** with waymarkers. Path runs down to stile at foot of wood. Bear slightly **L** towards gap in trees and gate, but turn **R** along foot of field. Stile on **L** leads to tarred lane and car park.

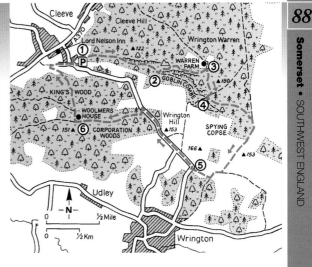

WOOLLARD *HUNSTRETE AND COMPTON DANDO*

6¼ miles (10.1km) Ascent: 700ft (210m)
Paths: Tracks, field paths, woodland paths, and byways, 15 stiles
Suggested map: aqua3 OS Explorer 155 Bristol & Bath
Grid reference: ST 632644
Parking: Street parking near bridge in Woollard; also opposite pub in Compton Dando (Point ❻)

Serenity in a rich landscape nestling between the cities of Bristol and Bath.

❶ At southern end of **Woollard** bear **R** at 'Circular Walk' sign. Byway initially underwater; path parallels it on R. After byway becomes Birchwood Lane, turn **L** into **Lord's Wood**, on path (Three Peaks Way). Go downhill, crossing track, to pool. Pass to **L** of this, to waymarker and track junction. Track opposite leads up to edge of wood.

❷ Turn **R**; drop to hidden footbridge under trees. Head uphill, passing R-H edge of plantation, to **Pete's Gate** beside corner of **Hunstrete Plantation**. Turn **L** to field gate. Right of way bears R, but, with no sign of path, keep ahead to lane and turn **R** into Hunstrete.

❸ Turn **L** beside Cottage No 5. Ignoring waymarking arrow, go down **R**-H side of field to stile into **Common Wood**. Track ahead passes through paintball sports area. Where it crosses stream and bends **L**, take waymarked path rising to top of wood. Pass through small col with lone ash tree, down to hedge corner. Go straight downhill to signpost; turn **R** to join lane at **Marksbury Vale**.

❹ Turn **L** towards **Court Farm**; before buildings, turn **R** over stile, and take **R**-H track for 100yds (91m) to stile. Pass to **R**-H side of farm buildings to enclosed track following **Bathford Brook**. Head downstream to track at **Tuckingmill**.

❺ Follow track past manor house to ford. Cross footbridge and turn **R**, alongside stream, which is again line of underwater byway – rejoin as it emerges; it leads to road, with **Compton Dando** away to L.

❻ Turn **R** into Church Lane; go through lychgate. Stile leads down. Turn **L** behind mill house and pass to L of mill pond, to footbridge over **River Chew**.

❼ Bear **L** into woodland ('Park Copse'). At top follow **R**-H edge of field round to stile. In lane beyond turn **L**; it becomes hedged track and runs alongside tiny gorge as it descends to **Woollard**.

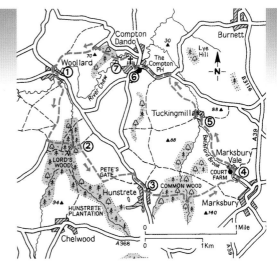

WELLOW *COTSWOLDS MEET MENDIPS*

6½ miles (10.4km) Ascent: 984ft (300m)
Paths: Byways, stream sides and some field paths, 12 stiles
Suggested map: aqua3 OS Explorer 142 Shepton Mallet
Grid reference: ST 739583
Parking: Street parking in village centre, or large car park below Peasedown road

A green valley walk, tracing a legacy of abandoned industry and failed technology.

❶ Head past church and under **viaduct**. Immediately after Wellow Trekking, track starts just above road. Where it becomes unclear, cross to hedge opposite; continue above it. New track runs through wood, then down to valley floor. Where bridleway sign points R, turn **L** to pass under railway bridge.

❷ Just before **Lower Twinhoe Farm** turn **L** on to signposted track at hilltop, track leads into thistly ground. Bear **R**, before **Middle Twinhoe**, to small gate. Turn **R** along farm's driveway to lane. Turn **L**, then **R** around farm buildings and **L** towards Upper Twinhoe. Just before farm, signed track descends to **R**.

❸ After 130yds (118m) turn **L** through double gate and along field top. Path slants down through woodland towards **Combe Hay**. From woodland edge follow lower edge of field to stone bridge into Combe Hay village. Follow main road **L**, to pass **Manor House**.

❹ After last house of **Combe Hay**, find gap in wall on **L**. Bear **R**, down to **Cam Brook** and footbridge. Cross and continue with stream down to R through field and wood. Follow stream along another field to stile, then along foot of short field to gateway.

❺ Don't go through gateway, but turn up field edge to stile on **R**. Slant up **L** across next field to nettled way between thorns. At top bear **R** on rutted track to lane. Turn uphill to **White Ox Mead**; follow lane to stile. Slant up to another stile; turn up tarred track to where it divides near shed without walls.

❻ Keep ahead on rutted track along hill crest. Ignore waymarked stile to pass under electric cables. Here small metal gate on **R** leads to hoof-printed path down beside fence. At foot of field turn **L**, then **L** again (uphill), round corner to gate. Turn **L** across field top and down edge to street leading into **Wellow**.

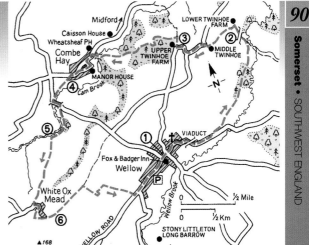

Dorset

91 HENGISTBURY HEAD *HEIGHTS AND HUTS*

3¼ miles (5.3km) 2hrs Ascent: 109ft (33m) ▲
Paths: Grass, tarmac road, soft sand, woodland track, some steps
Suggested map: aqua3 OS Explorer OL 22 New Forest
Grid reference: SZ 163912
Parking: Car park (fee) at end of road, signed 'Hengistbury Head' from B3059

An easy coastal loop with much to see.
❶ From corner of car park take grassy path towards sea, with fenced-off lines of **Double Dikes** to L. At sea-edge you can see to towers of **Bournemouth**, chalky Foreland and Durlston Head to west; Christchurch Bay and Isle of Wight are to east.
❷ Turn L and follow road along cliffs. Priory Church in Christchurch dominates view inland across harbour, with St Catherine's Hill behind. Follow road up hill. Pause to admire boggy pond to R, home to rare natterjack toad. Road narrows; climb up some steps, passing numbered post marking **Stour Valley Way**. As you climb, views back along coast are fabulous; also views across shallows of **Christchurch Harbour**, with windsurfers and sailing dinghies.
❸ On top of **Warren Hill** viewing platform indicates you're 75 miles (120km) from Cherbourg and 105 miles (168km) from Jersey. Keep R along path, passing deserted coastguard station and following top

of cliffs. Descend into deep hollow, where sea appears to break through. Keep straight on, following curve of head, with views across to Needles. At end, path turns down through trees; descend steps. Walk along sand on sea side of beach huts to point. Stone groynes form little bays.
❹ At end of spit you're not far from opposite shore (ferry runs across to pub from end of pier, passed further on). Turn round end of point, passing old Black House; walk up inner side of spit, overlooking harbour.
❺ If you've had enough beach and breeze, catch land train back to car park from here (times vary seasonally). Otherwise, join metalled road which curves round to R past freshwater marsh and lagoon.
❻ At post marked '19' turn R on to sandy path and follow through woods, crossing small ditch, to emerge back on road. Turn R, passing reedbeds on R and bird sanctuary on L. Continue past thatched barn and follow road to **café**, **ranger station** and car park.

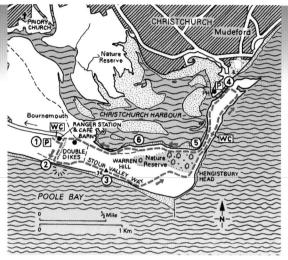

92 PENTRIDGE *DOWN, DITCH AND DYKE*

3½ miles (5.7km) 2hrs Ascent: 475ft (145m) ▲
Paths: Steep, muddy farmland, grassy sward, farm roads, 4 stiles
Suggested map: aqua3 OS Explorer 118 Shaftesbury & Cranborne Chase
Grid reference: SU 034178
Parking: Lay-by in Pentridge or start from car park at Martin Down

A stiff climb leads to a dramatic defensive earthwork.
❶ From lay-by walk past turning up to church; climb stile on L by footpath sign. Head up field to stile; cross and enter narrow footpath, which leads between hedges, straight up **Pentridge Hill**. Cross another stile into field and keep straight ahead. Admire view, with green curve of **Pentridge Down** to L. Keep straight on to top of hill (**Penbury Knoll**), passing to L of clump of trees.
❷ At top turn L on to **Jubilee Trail** footpath, which runs along ridge of down beside ancient hedge line. (Fabulous views on either side – **Pentridge** largely hidden in trees.) After ½ mile (800m) path starts to descend.
❸ Turn R, through gate into copse, following **Jubilee Trail** marker, and descend along field edge. Soon bear L across field to fingerpost in hedge, to turn R down muddy track (good views of **Bokerley Dyke** to

L). Descend through woodland to gate at bottom. Go through and turn R, on to bridleway. Pass metal gate and immediately hook back L on chalky track. As you descend, **tumuli** appear to R.
❹ Cross **Grim's Ditch** and **Bokerley Dyke** on to nature reserve of **Martin Down**, and immediately turn L on to grassy path, which runs along east side of ditch. Follow downhill for ½ mile (800m).
❺ At crossroads of tracks turn L on to **Jubilee Trail**, by fingerpost announcing it's 90 miles (144km) to Forde Abbey. Nettly path runs up side of mixed woodland. At end of woods go ahead, through gate. Follow field boundary up to top and cross stile.
❻ Turn R and go through farm gate into green lane. **Pentridge Down** emerges to L, with village hidden by trees. Pass through another gate on to farm track between high hedges. Continue down to bottom and follow it round to L. Walk back into village along main street to return to car.

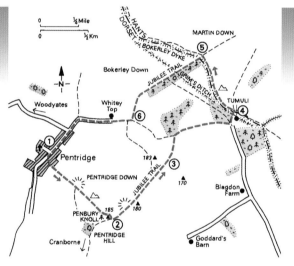

93 HORTON *THE REBEL KING*

7½ miles (12.1km) 4hrs Ascent: 426ft (130m) ▲
Paths: Field paths, tracks, some road, 15 stiles
Suggested map: aqua3 OS Explorer OL 22 New Forest; Explorer 118 Shaftesbury & Cranborne Chase
Grid reference: SU 034072 (on Explorer 118)
Parking: Lay-by with phone box, just west of Horton

A luscious landscape, where once a rebel was roused.
❶ Go towards village; turn L over stile by pump. Head towards **Horton Tower**, crossing 2 more stiles. Go up hill, diagonally L. Cross fence at top corner; turn R to view tower.
❷ Retrace steps; stay on track through gate into **Ferndown Forest**. After ¼ mile (400m) join firmer track. Shortly, turn R between trees. Cross stream and track to gate.
❸ Pass this, go through bank and turn L along forest ride. Turn R before edge of wood; follow path for ¾ mile (1.2km). Bear L at bottom, down track. Turn L at road; pass **Paradise Farmhouse**.
❹ Turn L between houses; follow track to **Holt Lodge Farm**. With buildings L, bear half-R across yard to lane.
❺ At end bear L into field, (hedge to R). Cross stile; go through gate to **Early's Farm**. Turn immediately L to gate, and R, in front of house, into lane. At junction

after **Chapel Farm**, turn L, signed 'Long House'. Turn R at gate; cross stile. Bear L around field, cross stile by bungalow and another to road.
❻ Turn L, then R into lane by **Pee Wee Lodge**. Keep straight on at junction; fork R into **Grixey Farm**. Follow waymarker up hill, crossing 2 stiles. With copse L, go up field. Cross stile and turn L on to road.
❼ After ½ mile (800m) bear L ('Monmouth's Ash Farm'); take path to R of bungalow. Keep straight on bridleway over heath and down into woodland. After 1 mile (1.6km) track emerges from woods.
❽ Past **Woodlands Manor Farm** turn L along road with fence. Bear R beside lake; stay on road. After it becomes track, look for 2 stiles in hedge on R, just after farm. Cross and go diagonally across field to another stile. Cross top of next field and stile, turning R to road.
❾ Turn L through **Haythorne**; before road descends, go R, through trees, to gate and down field, to vineyard. Turn L and L again to return to car.

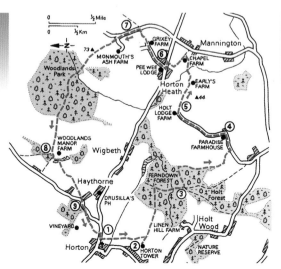

Dorset

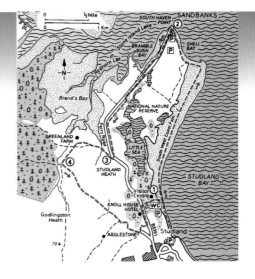

STUDLAND *SAND AND HEATH*

7 miles (11.3km) 4hrs **Ascent:** 132ft (40m)
Paths: Sandy beach, muddy heathland tracks, verges, no stiles
Suggested map: aqua3 OS Explorer OL 15 Purbeck & South Dorset
Grid reference: SZ 033835
Parking: Knoll car park, by visitor centre, just off B3351

Easy walking through a nature reserve over beach and heath.

1 From car park go past visitor centre to sea. Turn **L** and walk up beach for about 2 miles (3.2km). Dunes hide edge of heath to L, but there are views to Tennyson Down on Isle of Wight, and cliffs of Bournemouth come away ahead. Continue round tip of sand bar into **Shell Bay**. Poole opens out ahead – more precisely, spit of Sandbanks with good views of nature reserve island of Brownsea, with Branksea Castle at eastern end.

2 Turn inland at **South Haven Point**, joining road by phone box. Pass boatyard and toll booth; bear **R** at gate on to bridleway, leading down to houseboats. Turn **L** along tranquil inner shore of Poole Harbour and past **Bramble Bush Bay**. Choose any of various tracks leading back up to road. Cross over and follow verge until end of woods on L; pick up broad muddy track on heath. After ½ mile (800m) this bends **L**, with views across to Little Sea. Where track bends sharply **R** to meet road, stay straight ahead on footpath for few more paces.

3 Cross road by bus stop and head down track, indicated by fingerpost. Go past marshy end of **Studland Heath** and up to junction by **Greenland Farm**. Bear **L** and, just round next corner, turn **L** through gate on to heath. Go straight along old hedge-line, pass barn on L, and reach fingerpost.

4 Turn **L** across heath (not shown on fingerpost), aiming for distant lump of **Agglestone**. Go through gate by another fingerpost; continue along muddy track over top, passing **Agglestone** away to R. Go down into woods, turn **R** over footbridge and pass through gate into lane. Pass several houses then, where blue markers indicate public bridleway, turn **L** into field. Head diagonally **R** into green lane and go through gate at bottom. Turn **L** along verge, pass **Knoll House Hotel** and turn **R** at signpost to return to car park.

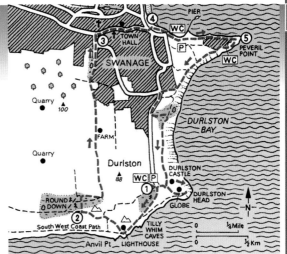

SWANAGE *THE EXTRAORDINARY COLLECTOR*

4¼ miles (6.8km) 3hrs **Ascent:** 509ft (155m)
Paths: Grassy paths, rocky tracks, pavements, 4 stiles
Suggested map: aqua3 OS Explorer OL 15 Purbeck & South Dorset
Grid reference: SZ 031773
Parking: Durlston Country Park (charge)

A coastal town that not only exported stone but imported it too.

1 Take footpath below visitor centre car park, signed (**lighthouse**). Steps lead down through trees. With sea ahead, follow path to **R**, joining coastal path. Keep **R**, towards **lighthouse**, on own path. Climb up other side, looking back and down towards **Tilly Whim Caves**. Pass **lighthouse**, turn **R**, then go through kissing gate; follow path with butterfly markers up steep side of **Round Down**.

2 At top bear **R**, heading inland and parallel with wall. Go down slope, through gate and across footbridge; turn up **R**. At wooden gate turn **L** over stile, following butterfly marker. After another stile you can see Purbeck Hills ahead. Cross stile and go down track. Beyond stile by farm, track narrows and starts climbing. Continue ahead on to road and follow into town (prominent church before you).

3 Turn **R** on to main road. Continue along street; look out for metal plaque above front door of No 22A, home of Taffy Evans, who died with Captain Scott on return from South Pole; elaborate Wesley memorial; and **Town Hall** with Wren frontage, donated by George Burt who collected stonework from old buildings.

4 At square bear **L** beside Heritage Centre, towards harbour. Turn **R** and pass entrance to **pier**. Keep **L** at yellow marker; bear **R**, up hill, past modern apartment block and stone tower, to **Peveril Point**, with coastguard station.

5 Turn **R**; walk up grassy slope along top of cliffs. Take path in top corner and follow Victoria's head markers to road. Turn **L** through area of Victorian villas. Erosion of coastal path means well-signed detour here, along street, down to **L** and **L** into woodland ('**lighthouse**'). Follow path for about ½ mile (800m) along cliff top to **Durlston Head**. Pass **Durlston Castle** on L and turn down to examine stone globe of world. Climb back up hill to return to car park.

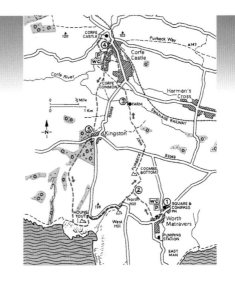

CORFE CASTLE *CIVIL STRIFE*

9 miles (14.5km) 3hrs **Ascent:** 1,083ft (330m)
Paths: Village lanes, rocky lanes (slippery after rain), moorland tracks, grassy paths, steep cliff path with steps, 34 stiles
Suggested map: aqua3 OS Explorer OL 15 Purbeck & South Dorset
Grid reference: SY 974776
Parking: Car park just north of Worth Matravers (honesty box)

A quarry village and a condemned castle.

1 Turn **R** down street; go **R**, up path by fingerpost. Cross stile; turn **L** through gap in wall. Turn **R** at end, cross wall and continue down next field. At bottom bear **L** over stile, down narrow cutting.

2 Cross 2 stiles; turn **R** on to **Purbeck Way**. Follow track up valley, bending **L** at **Coombe Bottom** and **R** through gate and up hill. Go through gate at top; bear **R** on to track. At farm turn **L** then **R** to road. Cross; turn **L** down track ('**Purbeck Way**'). Continue to bottom. By trees turn **L**, cross footbridge and turn **R**. Pass farm; go round to heath.

3 After footbridge, cross **Corfe Common** towards castle. Bear **L** at marker, **R** to gate. Cross B3069, go through gate and ahead, later bear **R** behind house. Go through gate; follow path towards village centre. After it narrows turn **R**, through gate; cross fields into playground. Turn **L** then **R** into West Street to square.

4 Turn **L** by **castle** on path below walls. Go **L** up road; **L** again by gate and over stile. Cross fields to car park; **L** then **R** on to West Street. At end, cross cattle grid. Bear **L** on path across heath. Cross duckboards and uphill, bearing **R** between stone block and tumulus. Go down other side and through gate. Cross 2 bridges, go up through gap between trees; cross field and into lane. Cross another field, cross road and up hill. Walk up field, towards **Kingston Church** tower.

5 At top, go through gate; turn **R**. After junction of lanes, turn **L**, through trees; **L** to road. Turn **R**; take track on **L** ('**Houns Tout**'). Follow to sea and along cliff. Descend steps; cross stile at bottom. Head inland to road. Turn **R** and follow round; bear **L** on to track ('**Coastal Path**'). Beside house bear **L**. Go through gate; continue ahead up road. Where this goes R, keep on up to Beacon Bottom. Shortly, turn **R** over stile; retrace steps to car park.

Dorset

97 CRANBORNE CHASE THE ROYAL FOREST

4 miles (6.4km) 2hrs Ascent: 165ft (50m)
Paths: Woodland paths and tracks, quiet roads, farm paths, 3 stiles
Suggested map: aqua3 OS Explorer 118 Shaftesbury & Cranborne Chase
Grid reference: SU 003194
Parking: Garston Wood car park (free), on Bowerchalke road 2 miles (3.2km) north of Sixpenny Handley

Extensive plantations on the rolling landscape of a Norman royal hunting forest provide superb walking.

❶ Go through gate in corner and take track leading up through woods. Go ahead through kissing gate emerging at corner of field. Keep **R**, up edge of field; continue straight on.

❷ At junction of tracks turn **L**; walk alongside hedge, on waymarked bridleway, through rolling farmland. Muddy farm track leads downhill. Where it sweeps **L** into farm, go ahead on grassy track. Pass cow byres (**L**), with **Upwood** farmhouse in trees ahead; turn **R** along lane. Continue through gate, along avenue of sycamores between high banks and hedges.

❸ Pass house on **R**; bear **L** on steep path straight down hill to road, in **Deanland**. Turn **R**, pass phone box and reach gate on **L** (yellow marker). Go through, bear diagonally **R** across small field to cross stile, then

bear **L** up edge of field (woods **L**).

❹ Look for stile on **L**, but turn directly **R** here; cross field, parallel with road. Over brow of hill ahead, settlement of **New Town** can be seen. Head for stile in bottom corner of field. Turn **L** up lane, which becomes woodland track. Follow for ½ mile (800m). By entrance to conifer wood (**Great Forlorn**), look for yellow marker and turn **R** up hill. After steep climb it levels, with fields on **L**. Keep straight on with good views to **West Chase** house, at head of its own valley. Descend steadily; cross stile to road by lodge house.

❺ Cross straight over on to broad track and immediately turn up to **R** on narrow path beside fence. Follow steep path uphill through woods – it levels out towards top, with fields on **L**. At junction of tracks keep **L** then bear **R**, continuing along edge of wood, and eventually descending to reach road. Turn **R** to return to car park at **Garston Wood**.

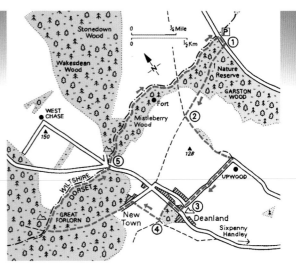

98 BADBURY RINGS ROADS AND RESIDENTS

7½ miles (12.1km) 4hrs Ascent: 459ft (140m)
Paths: Farm tracks, roads, grassy lanes and fields, 15 stiles
Suggested map: aqua3 OS Explorer 118 Shaftesbury & Cranborne Chase
Grid reference: ST 959031
Parking: Car park (donation) at Badbury Rings, signposted off B3082 from Wimborne to Blandford

An easy, longish walk on the edge of the Kingston Lacey Estate.

❶ Walk up hill to **Badbury Rings**, then head down track by which you drove in. Cross **B3082** and go down road towards **Shapwick** – its straightness gives away its Roman origins. Pass **Crab Farm**, with Charborough Tower on distant horizon.

❷ At junction with Park Lane turn **R**, then **R** again by Elm Tree Cottage to go up Swan Lane (grassy track). Turn **L** over stile before gate. Go over field, cross stile, and along edge of next field. Cross stile into yard of **Bishops Court Dairy**; turn **R** past 1st barn. At gates bear **L** over stile, then **R** across field, heading for stile half-way along hedge. Cross and bear **R** to top corner of field.

❸ Cross stile and turn **L** down broad bridleway. After about ½ mile (800m) pass line of trees. Turn **R**, up track between high hedges (following blue public bridleway marker). Continue downhill. Follow track to

L, by side of stream.

❹ Go through gate and reach church on your **L**. Continue towards **Tarrant Abbey Farm** barns. Go **L** through gate and continue diagonally across field to track between fences. Follow uphill, passing above farmhouse. At top of track cross stile and go over next field. Cross road and walk down edge of field. Cross another road into green lane. Bear **L** across stile, then diagonally across field. Go through gate on to road and turn **R**.

❺ Walk on to old **Crawford Bridge**, just to admire it. Retrace steps and turn **R** at footpath sign. Cross stile and walk straight across meadows for 1 mile (1.6km). Reach fence on **L**; walk around it to gate. Go through and follow track to **R**. Cross stile behind farm and walk along road into village.

❻ Pass **Anchor pub** and turn **L**, passing Piccadilly Lane (R-H side). Go straight up road, now retracing route back to car park at **Badbury Rings**.

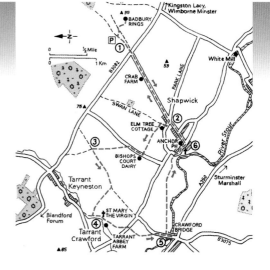

99 TARRANT GUNVILLE CHALK DOWNS AND TOMBS

5 miles (8km) 2hrs Ascent: 360ft (110m)
Paths: Quiet country lanes, farm and woodland tracks, no stiles
Suggested map: aqua3 OS Explorer 118 Shaftesbury & Cranborne Chase
Grid reference: ST 925128
Parking: Up broad lane beside village hall in Tarrant Gunville

A stroll across open farmland in search of an ancient tomb.

❶ Turn **L** on main street, passing phone box on **R**. Turn **R** by old forge ('Everley Hill'); go up road. Where it swings **R**, keep ahead up lane. Pass gates of **Manor** House, on **L**. At junction keep ahead on farm track.

❷ Pass old farmhouse on **R**, with small labourer's cottage in yard. At fingerpost bear **R** on track, passing old hedge on **R**. Route climbs uphill, passing end of **Pimperne Wood** on **L**.

❸ At junction of tracks at top turn **2nd-L** on to muddy bridleway along edge of wood. At end stay on grassy track. Where farm road bends **R** follow blue markers ahead up edge of fields. At crest of hill, bristling radio mast of Blandford army camp is in view ahead. Beyond rolling **Pimperne Down** to **R** Hambledon Hill falls away sharply to north. Continue to where track meets metalled farm road.

❹ Turn **L** on to grassy track, passing shell of barn and water tower. Go through gate to **Pimperne Long Barrow**. Walk around southern end and up other side, heading diagonally **R** across field. Cross broken fence aiming for grassy track (signified by blue marker of public bridleway). Follow through field, with woods to L-H side.

❺ Just over brow of hill, where track veers **R**, bear **L** down edge of field, passing into woods at bottom and continuing up opposite slope. At top of hill, by metal gate, go ahead down green path, which becomes lane – pass dwellings on **R** and skirt edge of **Gunville Park**. At junction of lanes turn **R** and retrace steps towards the village of **Tarrant Gunville**.

❻ Bear **R** before bottom of hill through 2 gates into churchyard. Leave church and go down path and some steps, turning **L** at bottom. Turn **R** at end, to retrace steps back into village.

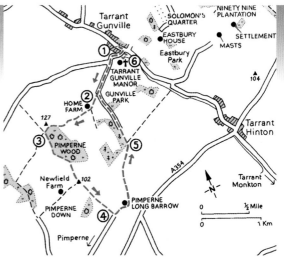

Dorset

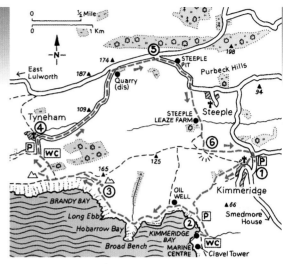

KIMMERIDGE *Coal, Oil and a War-Time Village*

7½ miles (12.1km) 3hrs 30min Ascent: 1,165ft (355m)
Paths: Grassy tracks and bridlepaths, some road walking, 12 stiles
Range walks open most weekends throughout year and during main holiday periods; call 01929 462 721 ext 4819 for further information. Keep strictly to paths, between yellow-marked posts
Suggested map: aqua3 OS Explorer OL 15 Purbeck & South Dorset
Grid reference: SY 918800
Parking: Car park (free) in old quarry north of Kimmeridge village

A coastal walk by army ranges.
❶ Turn **R** up road, then **L** over stile ('**Kimmeridge**') – enjoy sweeping views as you descend. Go through gate by church, then another at bottom. Turn **R** past houses; go through gateway and bear **L**. Go through gate below coppice, then bear **L** along hedge, following it round to pair of stiles. Bear **R** across these and follow path along hedge towards sea. Turn **L** on to road, go past houses and turn **R**, across car park.
❷ Bear **L** to **marine centre** (closed in winter), otherwise turn **R** on coastal path to continue. Descend steps, cross bridge and bear **R** ('**Range Walks**'). Pass cottages on R, and **oil well**. Go through gate on to range walk and continue around coast on track between yellow posts, crossing several cattle grids. Cliffs of **Brandy Bay** stagger away to west.
❸ After a mile (1.6km) cross stile and follow path as

it zig-zags uphill. Continue around top of Brandy Bay on cliff path. Beside stile and marker stone turn down to R ('**Tyneham**'). Soon cross stile to **L** and follow track down into farming village of **Tyneham**.
❹ After exploring, take exit road up hill. At top, by gate, turn **R** over stile and go along path parallel with road.
❺ Emerge at gate and turn **R** down road; go past **Steeple Pit**. Where road turns sharp **L**, go straight ahead down gravel drive through **Steeple Leaze Farm** and take gravel track ahead, leading straight up hill. Go through gate and keep **L** up muddy path that winds through gorse and scrub. Cross stile at top and continue straight ahead, with superb views over Kimmeridge.
❻ Turn **L** across stile and go straight along edge of field, following ridge of hill, for ½ mile (800m), with views to Smedmore House and ruins of Corfe Castle. Go through gate and turn **R** to return to car park.

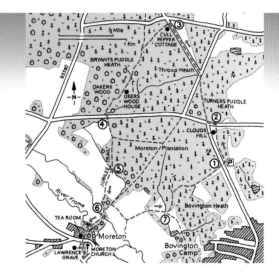

CLOUDS HILL *Following T E Lawrence*

6 miles (9.7km) 3hrs Ascent: 279ft (85m)
Paths: Heathland tracks, forest, field and woodland paths, 9 stiles
Suggested map: aqua3 OS Explorer OL 15 Purbeck & South Dorset
Grid reference: SY 825904
Parking: Car park on road between Bovington Camp and Clouds Hill

The retreat of a famous British soldier.
❶ Facing back of car park, turn **L** (yellow marker) along fence through pines. Shortly, stone on **L** marks where Lawrence was fatally injured. Stepping stones lead across marshy sections. Path becomes sandy heading uphill by fence. **Clouds Hill** is **L**. Keep **R**, round fence; bear **L** to road.
❷ Turn **L**; at junction cross over and turn **R** through gate. Walk across **Turners Puddle Heath** Nature Reserve. Go through gate at other side; walk up road ahead ('**Briantspuddle**').
❸ After ½ mile (800m), before junction, turn **L** down path between **Cull Pepper Cottage** and garage. Go through gap on to path; bear **L** on track across **Bryants Puddle Heath**. Keep straight on at crossing of tracks, following Hardy Way signs. Go straight on through gate into **Oakers Wood**. Pass **Okers Wood House**; stay on drive, which bends to meet road.
❹ Cross road; go on through more woods, with field

opening on **R**. At end of field continue ahead on woodland path. Shortly, by water tank, look for **Jubilee Trail** waymarker; turn **R**, walking down through pine trees. Follow trail through rhododendrons, later bearing **R** over streambed.
❺ Cross stiles and footbridge at end of woods. Bear **R** across field. Cross another footbridge; bear diagonally **R** to stile in fence. Head straight on; cross stile by trough; keep **L** round edge of next field.
❻ Cross stile in corner; turn **R** into lane. Cross 2 bridges; keep **R** to cross bridge over ford. Pass former post office to 3-way gate junction. Walk ahead to graveyard (**Lawrence's grave**). Return past junction; turn **R** for **Moreton** church. Retrace route to Point ❻; keep ahead. At junction of tracks turn **R**; at end, bear **L**. Track leads past cottages into woodland and heath.
❼ Turn **L** up sandy track. Where it divides turn **R**, up hill. At top cross stile; turn **L** along fence. Cross stile at end; cross road bearing **L** back to car park.

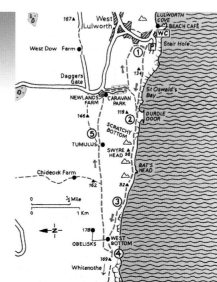

LULWORTH *To Durdle Door*

6¾ miles (10.9km) 3hrs 30min Ascent: 1,247ft (380m)
Paths: Stone path, grassy tracks, tarmac, muddy field path, 8 stiles
Suggested map: aqua3 OS Explorer OL 15 Purbeck & South Dorset
Grid reference: SY 821800
Parking: Pay-and-display car park (busy), signed at Lulworth Cove

An exhilarating walk on a spectacular piece of coastline.
❶ Find stile at back of car park. Cross and take paved footpath up steps to top of 1st hill. Continue along brow, and down other side. Pass below **caravan park**; cross stile.
❷ Reach cove of **Durdle Door**, almost enclosed from sea by line of rocks. Flight of steps leads down to sea here, but carry on walking straight ahead on coast path and natural stone arch of Door is revealed in 2nd cove below. **Swyre Head** looms close; path you take ascends straight up side. Walk down to bottom then climb back up to **Swyre Head**. Path leads steeply down again on other side, to short stretch overlooking **Bat's Head**. Climb next steep hill. Continue along path behind cliffs, where land tilts away from sea.
❸ Path climbs more gently up next hill. Pass navigation **obelisk** on R; follow path as it curves round contour above **West Bottom**.

❹ At marker stone that indicates Whitenothe ahead turn **R**, over stile, and follow fence inland. Path curves round so it's parallel with coast on level greensward. Pass 3 stone embrasures with shell sculptures inside, and 2nd **obelisk**. Go through gate. Keep straight ahead along top of field and across junction of paths ('Daggers Gate'). Go through gateway and straight on. Path starts to descend gently. In next field, path becomes more tracklike. Bear **R** passing close by **tumulus** and reach stile.
❺ Cross and walk along top of field, above **Scratchy Bottom**. Cross stile into green lane leading to **Newlands Farm**. Follow road to farm and turn **R** into **caravan park**. Go straight ahead on road through here. At far side cross stile and turn **L** ('West Lulworth'). Stay along field edge, cross stile and walk above farm lane, around end of hill. Keep straight on at fingerpost and reach stiles above car park. Turn **L** and retrace route to car park.

Dorset

103 ASHMORE *ROAMING THE WOODS*

5¾ miles (9.2km) 3hrs **Ascent:** 427ft (130m)
Paths: Forestry and farm tracks, woodland and field paths, 1 stile
Suggested map: aqua3 OS Explorer 118 Shaftesbury & Cranborne Chase
Grid reference: ST 897167
Parking: At Washers Pit entrance to Ashmore Wood

A gentle amble through plantations of mixed woodland to a village highpoint.

❶ With back to road, walk past gate; follow forestry road as it curves past **Washers Pit Coppice** on L and **Balfour's Wood** on R. After ½ mile (800m) ignore crossing bridleway and stay ahead on track. You're now in **Stubhampton Bottom**, following winding valley through trees.

❷ Where main track swings up to L, keep ahead, following blue public bridleway marker, on rutted track along valley floor. Path from **Stony Bottom** feeds in from L – keep straight on. Where area of exposed hillside appears on L, follow blue markers on to narrower track to **R**, which runs down through woodland parallel and below forestry road. At **Hanging Coppice**, fingerpost shows where **Wessex Ridgeway** path feeds in from R – again, keep ahead. Path soon rises to emerge at corner of field.

❸ Turn **L** at fence (following blue marker); walk uphill.

Follow path along edge of forest, with good views to south east of rolling hills and secretive valleys.

❹ After ¾ mile (1.2km) turn **L** at marked junction of tracks and walk through woods. Cross track and keep straight on, following marker, to meet track. Go straight on, following signs for **Wessex Ridgeway**, and passing under beech tree. Go through old gate. Continue up track for about 1 mile (1.6km), through farmland and across exposed open hilltop, with houses of **Ashmore** appearing. At end of track turn **R**; walk into village to duck pond.

❺ Retrace route but stay on road out of village, passing **Manor Farm** (R) and heading downhill. Just before road narrows, bear **L** through gate (blue marker). Walk along top of field, pass gate on L and bear down to **R** to lower of 2 gates at far side. Cross stile and walk ahead on broad green track. Go through gate into woods; immediately turn **R**, following steep bridleway down side of hill to car park.

104 COMPTON ABBAS *WILDFLOWERS AND BUTTERFLIES*

4½ miles (7.2km) 2hrs **Ascent:** 820ft (250m)
Paths: Downland tracks, muddy bridleway, village lanes, 3 stiles
Suggested map: aqua3 OS Explorer 118 Shaftesbury & Cranborne Chase
Grid reference: ST 886187
Parking: Car park on road south of Shaftesbury, near Compton Abbas Airfield

Over the preserved downs around Compton Abbas, in search of butterflies and wild flowers.

❶ Take rough track from bottom **R** corner of car park, walking downhill towards **Compton Abbas**. Pass old chalk **quarry** and continue downhill. Turn **R** up steps; cross stile to **Compton Down**. Bear **L** and uphill towards fence. Follow track that contours round, just below top of hill, heading towards saddle between down and **Melbury Hill**.

❷ Pass steep, natural amphitheatre to L, go across saddle and turn **L** at fence. Follow to top of **Melbury Hill**. Pass scar of ancient **cross dyke** on L as you climb; look down other side to Melbury Abbas church.

❸ **Trig point** marks top of hill, with fantastic views all around, including Shaftesbury to north and ridges of Hambledon Hill to south east. Retrace route downhill, with views over Melbury Down and to Compton Abbas Airfield. Turn **R** on to farm track. After

short distance bear **L**, down steep path, to gate. Go through and bear immediately **L** through 2nd gate. Go straight along muddy field edge towards **Compton Abbas**. Pass through gate on to road.

❹ Turn **L** and follow road **R** round sharp bend. Pass tower of original church, in small graveyard. Continue along lane, passing houses, with spire of modern church ahead in trees. Descend between hedges; turn **L** at junction. Follow winding road through bottom of village, passing thatched cottages.

❺ Pass **Clock House**; turn **L** up bridleway ('Gore Clump'). Gravel track gives way to tree-lined lane between fields. Go through gate and continue straight on. Cross stile by gate and continue ahead along edge of field. In corner, turn **L** along fence and walk up track above trees to gate. Pass through this on to **Fontmell Down**. Continue ahead on rising track. After ½ mile (800m) ignore stile to R and keep ahead along fence to top of hill and stile into car park.

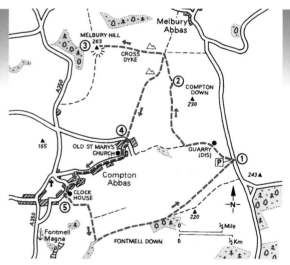

105 HAMBLEDON HILL *A FAMOUS LANDMARK*

4½ miles (7.2km) 3hrs **Ascent:** 541ft (165m)
Paths: Village, green and muddy lanes, bridleways, hillside, 6 stiles
Suggested map: aqua3 OS Explorer 118 Shaftesbury & Cranborne Chase
Grid reference: ST 860124
Parking: Lay-by opposite Church of St Mary's

Take the gentle route up a famous sculpted landmark.

❶ With church to L, walk up street. Pass farmhouse on corner of Main Street and Frog Lane. Cross road into lane opposite (Courteney Close). Pass converted chapel, fork **L** and go through gate. Keep **R** along hedge. Where gardens end keep straight ahead through gate and across field.

❷ Turn **R** at fence, cross stile and turn **L**. Go through gate and bear **L** up grassy lane between hedges. Pass **Park Farm** and keep ahead. At junction bear **R** into **Bessells Lane**.

❸ At end of **Bessells Lane**, by **Lynes Cottage**, bear **R** and immediately **L** up muddy bridleway, keeping with line of trees to L. At top go through gate; bear **L** down narrow lane at road turn **L** and head into **Child Okeford**. Just past post box turn **L** and cross stile. Bear **R** along edge of park, towards church tower. At fence turn **L**.

❹ Cross drive and keep straight on (glimpses of chimneys of Victorian manor house to L). At corner cross stile and keep ahead down path. Cross stone stile by road and immediately turn **L** up lane, which becomes track, climbing steeply through trees.

❺ Pass millennium **totem pole** and follow lane **R** and uphill. Go through gate and keep straight on up. Path levels out below earthworks that ring top of hill. Go through gate, emerge from track and go straight on up hill, through gate and across bridleway.

❻ At trig point turn **L** to explore ancient settlement. Return to trig point, turn **L** over top of hill and go down slope, following bridleway.

❼ Meet track by wall at bottom. Turn **L** and go through gate, with village ahead. Follow track down to cricket pavilion. Go through gate and turn **R**, on to road. Follow down past thatched barn and turn **R** to return to car. Alternatively, turn **L** at pavilion, and soon turn **R** by Hill View Cottage, to **pub**.

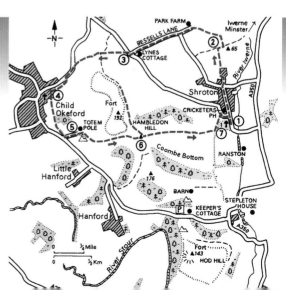

Dorset

HAMMOON TWO ANCIENT VILLAGES

4¼ miles (6.8km) 2hrs **Ascent:** 98ft (30m)
Paths: Field boundaries, grassy tracks, firm road, grassy bridleways, 15 stiles
Suggested map: aqua3 OS Explorer 129 Yeovil & Sherborne
Grid reference: ST 822120
Parking: Lay-by on Hayward Lane by old brick railway bridge

A loop around the River Stour.

❶ Go through gate and follow blue markers up farm road, passing **Bere Marsh Farm**. Pass house on L; go straight on through gate.

❷ Where road swings L stay ahead. Bear **R** of **burial ground**, down broad ride. Follow bridleway (blue markers) across fields for 1 mile (1.6km) to **Hammoon**, passing **Diggers Copse** (R). Initially, bridleway is parallel with route of **former railway** on L. After 6th gate pass **Downs Farmhouse**. Track becomes road. Bend **L** then **R** to emerge opposite stump of ancient cross. Cross over to look at Hammoon's church; walk up lane to admire **Manor Farm** (private).

❸ Return to main road and turn **L**. After crossing weir climb stile on **R**. Head across field bearing **R**, away from tree line, to river. Cross footbridge; look **L** to see red brick **Fontmell Parva House**. Go diagonally up field to gateway (yellow marker); bear **R** along edge

of field, above river. Go through another gateway and straight on, to line of trees. Walk up **R** side of trees, past **chicken farm** (L).

❹ Turn **L** at corner of field across stile; go down lane. At road turn **R** into **Child Okeford** (Saxon Inn is further down, on L). Turn **R** through gateway and immediately go **L** across stile. Walk down beside fence, behind houses, to cross pair of stiles into field. Continue along top, cross another stile and go along path behind hedges.

❺ Emerge at lane; turn **R**. Turn **L** at stile into field. Cross it and 2nd stile; follow edge of field to **R**. Cross pair of stiles, go over muddy track, cross 2 more stiles and bear **L** beside stream. Walk along edge of field, cross stile and keep straight on. Cross another pair of stiles then bear diagonally **L** across field to raised footbridge. Cross and keep straight on across concrete bridge; bear **R** towards bridge in hedge. Cross and bear **L** to corner of field, to return to start.

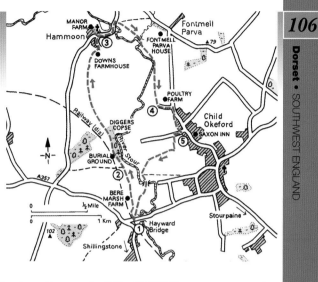

FIDDLEFORD ANCIENT MILLS AND A MANOR HOUSE

5¼ miles (8.4km) 3hrs **Ascent:** 429ft (150m)
Paths: Grassy paths, muddy woodland tracks, a rutted lane, roadside walking, pavements, 9 stiles
Suggested map: aqua3 OS Explorer 129 Yeovil & Sherborne
Grid reference: ST 781135
Parking: Signposted Sturminster Newton Mill, off A357 just west of Old Town Bridge to south of town

Two ancient mills and an extraordinary manor house, along the banks of the River Stour.

❶ Go past mill and over bridges, to **R** of pond, and through gate into field. Keep **L** up edge, parallel with **Stour**. Go through gate and up avenue of trees. Bear **L** along path, then go past playground into Ricketts Lane. Cross high street; turn **R**.

❷ Turn **L** by Old Malt House, to **church**. At end of churchyard bear **R**, through gate, down steps and into lane, bending **L**. Take path (**R**) to **Fiddleford Mill**. Go through gate and over field, above river. Cross stile; bear **L** along hedge. Continue ahead. At far **R-H** corner cross 2 footbridges and mill-race; bear **R**, past mill. Go down drive, turn **R** and **R** again through car park to **Fiddleford Manor**. Return to lane; turn **R**.

❸ At main road turn **R**; cross to bridleway, walking uphill into **Piddles Wood**. At top turn **R** on to track; follow round hill. Descend, passing 2 fingerposts. Go

through gate into car park; bear **L** to road.

❹ Turn **R** and immediately **L** through farmyard ('Broad Oak'). Go ahead through 2 fields into lane. At end turn **L** down road.

❺ At bottom turn **R** down muddy, overgrown lane – **Gipsy's Drove**. Follow for ¾ mile (1.2km). Turn **R** through gate before farm. At bottom go through gate and straight over field. Cross stile, then go straight on down field edge. Cross stile on to path. Bear **R** along tree line; cross 2 stiles to lane.

❻ Turn **L**; in **Newton**, turn **L** then **R** into Hillcrest Close. Where this bends R, go straight down lane. Climb fence (by yellow marker); continue down field, with hedge to R. Leave via gate at bottom, cross **A357** and turn **R**. After town sign turn **L** up track ('Newton Farm'). At fingerpost cross stile on **R**; walk across field. Cross stile, go through woods behind barn, and down steps by fence to another stile. Bear **R** on road then **L** through gate. Cross picnic area to car park.

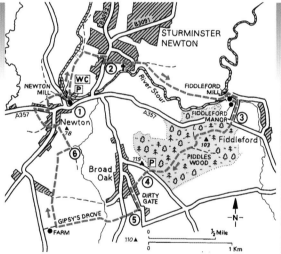

MILTON ABBAS RIDGEWAY PANORAMAS

6½ miles (10.4km) 3hrs **Ascent:** 755ft (230m)
Paths: Village high street, easy forest roads, muddy bridleways, minor road, farm tracks, 2 stiles
Suggested map: aqua3 OS Explorer 117 Cerne Abbas & Bere Regis
Grid reference: ST 806018
Parking: On main street of Milton Abbas

Walk from a planned village into the surrounding hills and woods.

❶ From church take road up hill. Where pavement ends turn **L** through woodland. At top turn **R**, into estate road, and **R** again, to road into village by **Hill Lodge**.

❷ Cross over and go down private road. Follow down to Forestry Commission signboard and bend **L** then **R**. Before gateway turn **L** up steep path ('Jubilee Way'). Pass **Park Farm** on L and descend to track. Turn **L** and soon up to **R**. Bear **R** at top, on to track. Where this forks, keep **R** to descend through **Charity Wood**. At crossroads keep ahead. At fingerpost bear **R**, up bridleway.

❸ Emerge at field to follow path down, with **Higher Clenston Cottages** ahead. At bottom turn **R** through **Winterborne Clenston**. Turn **L** to church. Retrace steps to 1st barn; turn **L** up steep road. This becomes track, passing below **Clenston Lodge**.

❹ Continue on to gate into **Oatclose Wood**. Path bends to **R**. Keep **R** at 1st fork, **L** at 2nd. Where path divides keep **L**, following blue markers. Where track curves **R**, keep **L**. Cross forest road, after which path narrows and bends **R**, to field by gate. Turn **R** down edge and, at bottom, turn **L** along track.

❺ At junction turn **R**. After ½ mile (800m) track climbs. As it curves **R** look for path on L; follow this to field corner. Turn **L** up steep track. Continue up edge of field; swing **R** at top. Descend to road.

❻ Cross over and walk straight up lane, passing Luccombe **business units**. Pass cottage and turn **R** through gateway, up track. Where it almost meets road, bear diagonally **L** to cross stile in fence. Bear **L** over 2nd stile and enter woods. There's no clear path – keep downhill and bear **L** to village street above school. Turn **L** to return to your car.

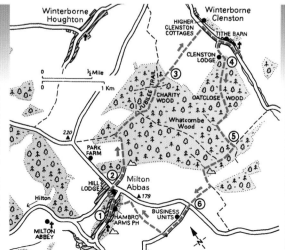

Dorset

109 IBBERTON *LIVING ON THE EDGE*

4¼ miles (6.8km) 2hrs **Ascent:** 591ft (180m)
Paths: Quiet roads, muddy bridleways, field paths, 2 stiles
Suggested map: aqua3 OS Explorer 117 Cerne Abbas & Bere Regis
Grid reference: ST 791071
Parking: Car park at Ibberton Hill picnic site

From the tops of Bulbarrow Hill to the valley floor and back, via an atmospheric church.

❶ Turn **L** along road, following route of **Wessex Ridgeway**, with Ibberton below R. Road climbs gradually, with **masts** on **Bulbarrow Hill** ahead.
❷ After 1 mile (1.6km) pass car park on L. At junction bear **R** and immediately **R** again ('Stoke Wake'). Pass another car park on R (woods of **Woolland Hill** on R). Pass **radio masts** to L and reach small gate into field on R, near end of wood. Before taking it, go extra few steps to road junction ahead for view of escarpment to west.
❸ Go through gate and follow uneven bridleway down. Glimpse spring-fed lake through trees on R. At bottom path swings **L** to gate. Go through, on to road. Turn **R**, continuing downhill. Follow road into **Woolland**, passing **Manor House** (L) and Old Schoolhouse (R).
❹ Just beyond entrance to **Woolland House** turn **R** into lane and immediately **L** through kissing gate. Path immediately forks. Take **L-H** track, down through marshy patches and young sycamores. Posts with yellow footpath waymarkers lead straight on across meadow, with **Chitcombe Down** up to R. Cross footbridge over stream. Go straight on to cross road. Keeping straight on, go through kissing gate in hedge. Bear **L** down field, cross stile and continue down. Cross footbridge and stile to bear **L** across next field. Go through gate to road junction. Walk straight up road ahead and follow it R, into Ibberton. Bear **R** to **Crown Inn**.
❺ Continue up road through village. Path becomes steep. Steps lead up to **church**. Continue up steep path. Cross road and go straight ahead through gate. Keep straight on along fence, climbing steadily. Cross under power lines; bear **L** up next field, to small gate in hedge. Turn **L** up field edge, then go through gate at top on to road, finally turning **L** to return to car park.

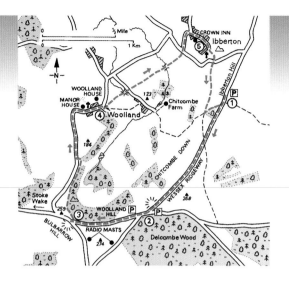

110 HIGHER MELCOMBE *A LOST VILLAGE*

5 miles (8km) 2hrs 30min **Ascent:** 443ft (135m)
Paths: Farmland, woodland track, ancient bridleway, road, 13 stiles
Suggested map: aqua3 OS Explorer 117 Cerne Abbas & Bere Regis
Grid reference: ST 765031
Parking: Small parking area on north side of village hall

A hilly rural circuit, where, centuries ago, labour economics determined settlement.

❶ Turn up road and go immediately **L** down waymarked path. Cross stile, bear **R** down edge of field and cross stile at bottom. Continue straight up next field, cross stile and road to go through gate. Keep straight on to pair of stiles in hedge.
❷ Go through stiles then bear **R**, across field. Descend and go **R**, through gate in corner. Follow track beside hedge; go through gate and bend **L**.
❸ Go into **farm**; turn immediately **L** through furthest of 3 gates ('Wessex Ridgeway'). Walk along edge of field, above wood. Go through gate and keep ahead along top of ridge (superb views of Blackmoor Vale). Track descends abruptly. Turn **R**, through gate, to crossroads of tracks at **Dorsetshire Gap**.
❹ Turn **L** down bridleway through deep cleft ('Higher Melcombe'). Keep straight on through 3 fields. Ridges and hummocks in field to R are only sign of medieval village. Pass **Higher Melcombe farm**, then go through gate and turn **L**, on to minor road. Bear **R**; walk down avenue of trees (hill track leads to **Giant's Grave** on R). Descend past houses to junction.
❺ Turn **L**; walk on road into **Melcombe Bingham**. Pass houses then turn **R**. Go through gate to take path straight ahead across field. Pass end of strip of woodland and maintain direction up fence towards hut. Cross fence at top. Continue ahead, down field towards **Bingham's Melcombe**. Cross stile and turn **R**. Follow drive round and down to church.
❻ Retrace route to stile; keep straight on past, up field. Before end turn **L** through gate; bear **R** along path. Where this divides bear **L**. Go through gate and descend on track. Go straight ahead to cross footbridge. Keep straight on, bear **R** over stile in fence and continue down field. At bulging trees turn **L** over stile. Keep ahead then cross stile on to road. Turn **R** to return to car.

111 MARNHULL *DAIRIES AND PASTURES*

4 miles (6.4km) 2hrs 30min **Ascent:** 115ft (35m)
Paths: Village roads, pasture (wellies advised in winter), 14 stiles
Suggested map: aqua3 OS Explorer 129 Yeovil & Sherborne
Grid reference: ST 774193
Parking: Small car park (free) in Marnhull village, opposite butcher

On the level through pastures that owe their presence to mechanised farming.

❶ Turn **L** out of car park and walk along Burton Street. Pass **Blackmoor Vale pub**; keep straight on, down **Ham Lane**. Follow footpath sign straight ahead down field, with trees on L.
❷ At bottom of field track curves L and disappears – turn **R** here to walk down field edge. Cross stile and bear **L** to cross footbridge over **River Stour**. Continue straight ahead. Cross stile in hedge, then cross another stile; bear **L** across field towards **Hamwood Farm**.
❸ Keep to **R** of biggest barn, to pass through farmyard with farmhouse to L-H side. Cross lane, go through gate and head diagonally **R** towards stile, passing close to telegraph pole. Cross bridge and head **R**, across field, towards **Crib House Farm**. Cross over pair of stiles then go **L**, around field edge. Climb stile in corner and turn **L** down road. Just before farmyard turn **R**, through 1st gate. Bear **R** across field. Cross another bridge and make for **Gomershay Farm**. Turn **R** past 1st byre, then turn **L** and **R** through farmyard. At other side of barns turn **L** and pass farmhouse itself. Continue up lane, passing small barn. By old truck bear **R** over brow of field, then cross bridge over river.
❹ At other side of footbridge keep to **R**, past curve of stream; head straight up through gate. Walk up next field and cross stile on to lane. Follow to junction by **Chantry Farm**. Cross road and go into field. Head diagonally **L**, cross stile in bottom corner; walk along edge of next field.
❺ Cross stile into road and turn **R** back into Marnhull village. Go past school to parish church. Turn **L** down **Church Hill**. Follow road as it winds through village, eventually becoming Burton Street by Methodist church. Walk past post office and return to car park.

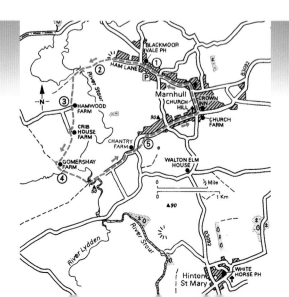

Dorset

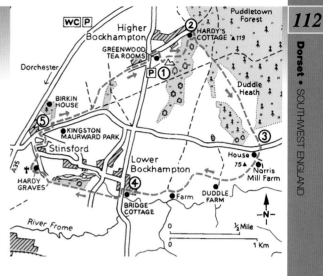

HIGHER BOCKHAMPTON *BY HARDY'S COTTAGE*

5 miles (8km) 2hrs **Ascent:** 328ft (100m)
Paths: Woodland and heathland tracks, muddy field paths and bridleways, firm paths, road, 15 stiles
Suggested map: aqua3 OS Explorer 117 Cerne Abbas & Bere Regis
Grid reference: SY 725921
Parking: Thorncombe Wood (donations) below Hardy's Cottage

Across wooded heath and farmland to where Thomas Hardy, quite literally, left his heart.

❶ Take steep woodland path to **R** of display boards ('Hardy's Cottage'). Turn **L** at fingerpost; follow route to crossroads of tracks, marked by monument. Turn **L** for **Hardy's Cottage**.

❷ Retrace route up behind cottage; bear **L** ('Rushy Pond'). At crossroads take path ('Norris Mill'). Where path forks bear **R**. Cross track then head down between rhododendrons. Emerge on to heathland; stay on path. Follow markers to **R**. Descend, cross stile and bear **R**. Cross pair of stiles; turn **L** up field, towards house.

❸ Cross road on to farm track. Bear **R** before barns, cross stile and continue up track. After gate bear **R** over field. Cross pair of stiles in hedge, then fields and drive, passing **Duddle Farm** (L). Cross bridge and stile down into field. Go straight on; bear **L**, following track round hill. Cross stile by converted barn; walk up

drive. At fingerpost keep straight on through gate ('**Lower Bockhampton**'). Bear **L** through another gate then walk down field to gate at far corner. Go through and straight on (river L). Go through farmyard to road.

❹ Turn **L** by **Bridge Cottage**. Cross stream; immediately turn **R**, on to causeway. After ½ mile (800m) turn **R** ('Stinsford'). Walk up and turn **L** into churchyard, just below church. Pass **church** (L), and **Hardy graves** (R). Hardy's heart was buried here. Leave by top gate and walk up road. Pass piggery; turn **R** along road. Turn **L** at end to main road by house.

❺ Turn **R**, up road. After entrance to **Birkin House**, bear **L** through gate and **R** on to path through woodland, parallel with road. Descend, cross stile and bear **L** to fingerpost. Go through gate and bear diagonally **R** up field ('Higher Bockhampton'). At top corner keep on through gate and turn **R** towards barn. Pass this and bear **R** on to track to road. Turn **L**, **R** by post box, and **R** again to car park.

OSMINGTON *THE WHITE HORSE*

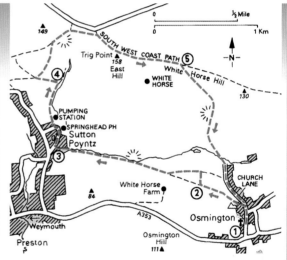

4 miles (6.4km) 2hrs **Ascent:** 568ft (173m)
Paths: Farm and village lanes, woodland paths, field paths, 9 stiles
Suggested map: aqua3 OS Explorer OL 15 Purbeck & South Dorset
Grid reference: SY 724829
Parking: Church Lane in Osmington, just off A353

Osmington's white horse is the only one depicting a rider – King George III.

❶ From **Osmington church** walk down street of pretty thatched cottages. At junction keep on down **Church Lane**. Opposite Forge Barn, at end of wall, turn **L** up steep flight of steps ('Sutton Poyntz'). Path rises through woodland. After 2nd set of steps bear **R** on path which undulates through trees. Cross stile and continue straight on to end of field.

❷ Cross stile and turn immediately **R** to cross 2nd stile and walk down field. Turn **L** through gate; head across field. Cross farm track and bear ahead and **R**. Cross pair of stiles and continue along bottom of field (**White Horse** to R). Continue though gap. At end of next field bear **L**, through gateway, then straight on (yellow marker), towards **Sutton Poyntz**. Veer **R**, cross stream and bear **L** through gate. Follow path to stile and continue to road.

❸ Turn **R**, pass Mill House and mill on L. Pass village

pond and **Springhead pub** on R. Bear **L** and **R** up lane by Springfield Cottage. Go through gate and follow track ahead. Go through another gate, with **pumping station** on R, below bottom of steep combe where spring emerges.

❹ Cross stile by gate; turn **L** up grassy lane. About half-way up hill turn **R**, up track (upper of 2) that leads to top above combe (great views along valley and down to Weymouth Bay and Portland). Keep **R** on green track, go through gate and keep **L** along field edge. Follow path to **R** and walk up field (lane soon joins from L). Stay on this track past trig point. Go through gate and keep straight on (good view to strip lynchets on hillside ahead).

❺ Go through gate and bear down to **R** ('Osmington'). Track leads down hill, through gate – look back to see **White Horse** again. Follow lane back up through village to car.

ABBOTSBURY *DORSET'S OTHER HARDY*

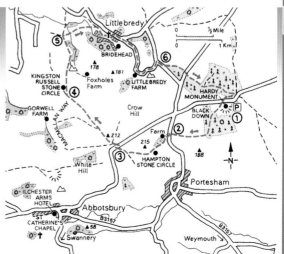

7 miles (11.3km) 3hrs 30min **Ascent:** 784ft (228m)
Paths: Field tracks, quiet roads, woodland tracks, 10 stiles
Suggested map: aqua3 OS Explorer OL15 Purbeck & South Dorset
Grid reference: SY 312876
Parking: By Hardy Monument, signed off road between Portesham and Winterbourne Abbas

A long walk over rolling farmland.

❶ Turn **L** down path by entrance ('Inland Route'). Follow track through woods. At bottom turn **R**; bear **L**, before gate, over stile. Walk up edge of 2 fields. At corner cross stile and immediately another. Walk alongside fence to hedge.

❷ Turn **L** on to road and **R** towards farm. After farm bear **L** through gate and up track, then through another gate and bear **R**. Pass **Hampton Stone Circle**; keep straight on. Cross stile; bear along fence and down steps ('West Bexington'). Follow path along hillside and up through gate to road.

❸ Turn **R**; take 1st road **L**. Soon bear **R** along track. Go through gate (blue marker); walk ahead down hedge. Head up through 3 fields.

❹ Go through gate to junction of tracks. Bear **R** across field, passing lichen-covered **Kingston Russell Stone Circle**. Go through gate and bear slightly **L** over hill, passing earthworks on L. At bottom

go straight down to gate. Go through and bear **L**, then go through gate to **R** and down hill.

❺ When you reach middle of field turn **R**. Cross footbridge; go through gate. Cross stream and walk straight ahead up field. Bear **L** along hedge. Cross double stile and head diagonally **L**. Cross another footbridge over stream. Turn **R**, bear **L** up through trees, then go **R**, to stile. Cross and go over hill towards **Littlebredy**. Cross stile by fingerpost and go straight on. Pass church, go **L** through gate and turn **R** on to road. Bear **R** at junction, passing **Bridehead** house. Continue past **Littlebredy Farm** and up hill. At junction turn **R**.

❻ Soon bear **L** on bridleway; follow track by woods. Cross road; go ahead. Descend through steep combe; after track divides, turn up to **R**. After ½ mile (800m), before road, turn **R** and **R** again on to footpath. Cross bridge and follow woodland path up to **L**. Stay on this to reach road opposite **Hardy Monument**.

Dorset

115 PURSE CAUNDLE *In the Doghouse*

5 miles (8km) 2hrs **Ascent:** 427ft (130m)
Paths: Muddy field paths, farm tracks, country roads, wet bridleway (wellies recommended), 13 stiles
Suggested map: aqua3 OS Explorer 129 Yeovil & Sherborne
Grid reference: ST 695175
Parking: Limited space by war memorial, Purse Caundle

Over hill and down valley from a village dominated by a fine manor house.

❶ Park your car by **church**. Walk up street to admire **manor house**. Return, pass phone box and turn **L** through gate. Go up edge of field, cross stile and turn **R** to continue on this line, up through gateway and across another field. After 2nd gateway bear **R** up field. Cross stile in corner and turn **R**. Cross stile and pass lake to **L**. Cross stile at far side; bear **R** along field edge.

❷ Cross stile at corner and go on down edge of field. Path curves down and up to gate. Go through gate and swing **L**, up bridleway. This narrows and is shared with stream. Go through gate and keep straight on up hill. Go through gate in top corner; follow muddy track. Becomes hedged lane; follow for ½ mile (800m) to pass **Manor Farm**. Continue through gate.

❸ Turn **L** at fingerpost over stile. Bear **L** down field to cross 3 stiles and footbridge in middle of hedge.

Head diagonally **L** down next field. Cross pair of stiles and footbridge in corner; immediately turn **R** over stile and footbridge. Walk ahead up field edge.

❹ At top turn **R**, then bear **R** along bottom of young plantation. Go through gateway and turn **L** up edge of field. Follow path round behind **Frith Farm Cottages**, down to gate. Turn **L** on road; follow for ½ mile (800m), beside stone wall of **Stalbridge Park**.

❺ At crossroads turn **L**, towards **Frith Farm**. Soon bear **R**, following markers. Path bends **L**, through gate to covered reservoir. Pass and turn **R**, through gate. Descend steps and bear **L** down edge of field (views to manor). Continue on through gap.

❻ When you reach bottom bear **L** into woodland (but stay on path). Walk down ridge, then cross ditch on **L** and continue down edge of field. Go through gateway and retrace your outward route to **church** and your car.

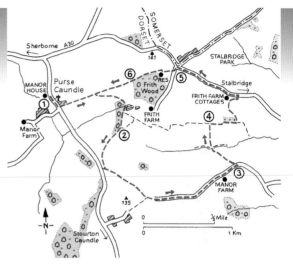

116 SHERBORNE *Raleigh's Country Retreat*

6½ miles (10.4km) 3hrs **Ascent:** 443ft (135m)
Paths: Country lanes, green lane, field paths, estate tracks, 9 stiles
Suggested map: aqua3 OS Explorer 129 Yeovil & Sherborne
Grid reference: ST 670157
Parking: On road by church, Haydon village, 2 miles (3.2km) southeast of Sherborne

Around Sherborne, former home of a pirate, politician and poet, Sir Walter Raleigh.

❶ With **church** on **L**, walk along road and out of **Haydon**. At junction continue ahead ('Bishop's Caundle'). At minor junction cross stile, ahead. Turn **R**, up field edge, towards **Alweston**. Cross stile; bear diagonally **L** over field. Cross stile in corner, go down path; proceed on road, which curves to meet **A3030**.

❷ Turn **R**; turn **L** over stile in hedge. Cross field to gap. Bear diagonally **R** over next field. Halfway along far side go through hedge via stile at corner (yellow marker). Keep ahead along hedge, crossing stiles and footbridges. Continue by wall towards **Folke church**. Cross 2 stiles, go through gate and turn **R** up lane into village, passing church entrance and raised pavement on **R**. Keep **L** at junction; follow lane round to **L**.

❸ Follow road as it bends sharply **L**; turn **R** up signed bridleway. Follow for 1 mile (1.6km), ascending. It becomes broader and muddier, reaching

main road via gate.

❹ Turn **L** then **R** through gate directly beside **lodge**, up lane. Continue down through woods, with park wall to **R**. Where drive sweeps **R** by cottage, keep straight on, up track, passing sports fields on **L**. Go through 2 gates, cross road and through another gate by lodge on to tarmac track. Follow down steep gorge to main road. Take path immediately **R**, through gate; walk up hill above castle gateway.

❺ Pass through gate into **Sherborne Park**. Follow grassy track ahead, downhill. Go through kissing gate and ahead on estate track (superb views of **castle**). Go up track to thatched lodge, then go through wooden gate and up hill.

❻ At top keep **R**, through gate into woods. Follow track round. Proceed on to tarmac path; pass huge barn on **L**. Follow track **R**; keep ahead at junction. Descend to lodge; go through gate and straight on to return to car.

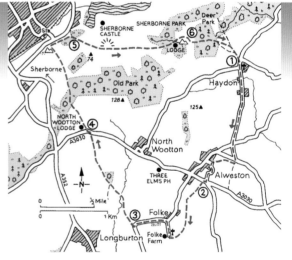

117 CERNE ABBAS *Giant Steps*

5½ miles (8.8km) 2hrs 30min **Ascent:** 591ft (180m)
Paths: Country paths and tracks, minor road, main road, 2 stiles
Suggested map: aqua3 OS Explorer 117 Cerne Abbas & Bere Regis
Grid reference: ST 659043
Parking: Car park (free) opposite church in Minterne Magna

A valley walk from Minterne Magna to see a famous chalk hill carving.

❶ Turn **R** and walk up road through village. Where it curls **L**, turn **R** through gate on to bridleway and go up hill. At top go through gate and bear **L**. Follow blue marker diagonally up to **R**. Go through gate, walk on past trees, then bend up, round field towards trees.

❷ Go through gap and take track down diagonally **L** through woods. At bottom turn **L** along road. After bend take footpath **R**, across field. After trees veer **L**, towards white gate. Cross road, pass **R** of gate, and continue down field. Pass another white gate then continue ahead on road. At end bear **R** on to **A352**.

❸ Cross to car park for best view of **Giant hill carving**. Take road down to village; turn **L** signposted 'Pottery'. Turn **R** by **church** ('Village Centre'). Continue over slab bridge and pass old mill. Bear **L**, to high street. Turn **L**, and **L** again in front of **Royal Oak**, to church. Walk up Old Pitch Market to Abbey. Turn **R** into

churchyard and bear **L**. Go through gate signposted 'Giant's Hill'; bear **L**.

❹ Cross stile, then turn **R** up steps. Follow path to **L**, round contour of hill, below fence. As path divides, keep **R**, up hill, towards top. Bear **L** along ridge, cross stile by fingerpost and head diagonally **R**, towards barn.

❺ At barn turn **L** and go down through gate. Turn **R** and follow bridleway along hillside with great views towards Minterne Parva. Keep ahead at junction of tracks; dip down through gateway above woods. Keep straight on; go through gate near road. Turn **L** along grassy track. At gateway turn **L** on to gravel lane.

❻ Directly above **Minterne House**, turn **L** through gate and bear **L**. Go through gate and turn **L**, downhill. Continue down through several gates and bear **R** at fingerpost down broad track. Cross stream, then walk up past **church** to return to car park.

Dorset

WINYARD'S GAP THE MONARCH'S WAY

3¼ miles (5.3km) 1hr 30min Ascent: 410ft (125m) **2**
Paths: Field paths, some roads, 1 stile
Suggested map: aqua3 OS Explorer 117 Cerne Abbas & Bere Regis
Grid reference: ST 491060
Parking: Lay-by north of Chedington, opposite Court Farm

A short walk in Dorset's northern uplands following the route of an historic royal escape.

❶ Go through gate at back of lay-by; bear **R** on path up through woods. At top of ridge turn **L** for **memorial**. Turn **L** down steps, go back through gate and turn **R** along road. Pass **Winyard's Gap Inn** on **R**; at junction, cross over and walk up road ahead. Keep **R**, following lane over top of ridge between high banks (**Crook Hill** ahead). After about ½ mile (800m) bear **L** through gate ('**Monarch's Way**').

❷ Bear **L** along top of field, with **Chedington Woods** falling away on **L**, and **Crook Hill** ahead and **R**. Go through gate at foot of hill; bear **R** through woods, round base. Cross stile and bear **L** down field. At farm road near trees, turn **R**. Follow up to lane and turn **R**.

❸ Shortly, on corner, go **L** through gate and hook back down fence on bridleway. Go through 2 gates at

bottom and continue down field, parallel with top hedge. **Twelve Acre Coppice** (R) is a lovely stretch of mixed woodland. At bottom cross stream via bridge, then go through gate and ahead up track. Go through gate to **L** of barn (blue marker) and turn **R** on farm road, through farmyard. At lane go straight ahead, passing **Home Farm** on **L**, into **Weston**.

❹ Just before **Weston Manor Farm** detour **R** through gate (blue marker). Turn **L** through gate; turn **R** to resume track straight up hill, with radio mast topping ridge ahead. After short tunnel of trees bear **R** through gate along track, part of **Monarch's Way** commemorating Charles II's flight from Cromwell's army. Go through gate and stay on track. Go through another gate with ponds to **R**. Pass through 2nd gate to **L** of barn, walk past **Hunter's Lodge Farm** and up drive to road. Turn **R** on main road; follow back down to inn, with care. Turn **L** to return to lay-by and your car.

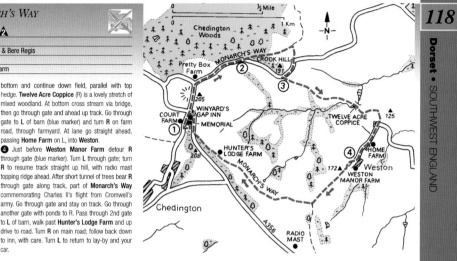

THORNCOMBE FORDE ABBEY

5 miles (8km) 2hrs 30min Ascent: 443ft (135m) **1**
Paths: Field paths, country lanes, 18 stiles
Suggested map: aqua3 OS Explorer 116 Lyme Regis & Bridport
Grid reference: ST 373029
Parking: At crossroads south west of Thorncombe

The going is fairly easy through this area renowned for its soft fruit.

❶ Turn **L** (northeast) and walk down into **Thorncombe**. Turn **L** up Chard Street and take footpath on **R** through churchyard. Bear **R** down lane, then **L** on gravel track beside wall, opposite Goose Cottage. Cross stile into field, pass **barn** on **L**, then go straight on down hedge.

❷ Cross stile in corner; go straight across field. Cross stile, then 2nd stile on **R**. Ford stream and bear **L**, up field. Cross stile on **L**; continue ahead. Cross another stile on **R**; bear **R** round edge of field. Track veers **R** through hedge. Cross 2 more stiles; continue straight on. By trough turn **L** over pair of stiles; go straight ahead up field edge. Go through gate and bear **R**, towards house.

❸ Emerge through gate on to road; turn **L**. At junction turn **R** on to path; head for woods. Turn **L**

before edge of woods; at corner go **R**, through gate. Head diagonally **L** to bottom corner, opposite **Forde Abbey** gates. Cross stile; turn **R** on road to cross River Axe.

❹ Turn immediately **L** on to footpath; follow past back of **Abbey**. At far corner cross footbridge over river; bear **R** towards lone cedar, then **L** up slope to stile ('**Liberty Trail**'). Cross, then walk along top of woods. Cross stile; bear **L** across fields towards another cedar.

❺ Meet road by **fruit-pickers' camp**. Go across, through gate and up field. Towards top R-H corner bear **R** through gate; keep on this line. Cross pair of stiles in corner, pass **Forde Abbey Farm** on **L** and keep straight on by hedge. Cross stile and walk down track.

❻ At junction of tracks keep straight on. Where track forks bear **L**, go through gate and **L** across field. Cross stile in hedge; turn **R** up field. Follow for ½ mile (800m) to return to car.

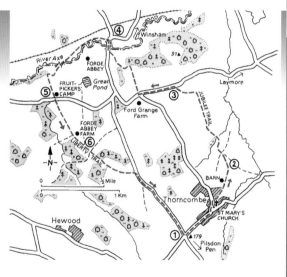

SEATOWN GOLDEN CAP IN TRUST

4 miles (6.4km) 2hrs 30min Ascent: 1,007ft (307m) **3**
Paths: Field tracks, country lanes, steep zig-zag gravel path, 7 stiles
Suggested map: aqua3 OS Explorer 116 Lyme Regis & Bridport
Grid reference: SY 420917
Parking: Car park (charge) above gravel beach in Seatown; beware, can flood in stormy weather

Climb a fine top, owned by one of the country's most popular charities.

❶ Walk back up through **Seatown**. Cross stile on **L**, on to footpath ('Coast Path Diversion'). Cross stile at end, bear **L** to cross stile and footbridge into woodland. Cross pair of stiles at other side; bear **R** up hill ('**Golden Cap**').

❷ Where track forks keep **L**. Go through trees and over stile. Bear **L**, straight across open hillside, with National Trust's **Golden Cap** ahead of you. Pass through line of trees and walk up fence. Go up some steps, cross stile and continue ahead. At fingerpost go **L** through gate; follow path of shallow steps up through bracken, heather, bilberry and bramble to top of **Golden Cap**.

❸ Pass trig point and turn **R** along top. Pass stone memorial to Earl of Antrim. At marker stone turn **R** and follow zig-zag path downhill (great views along bay to Charmouth and Lyme Regis). Go through gate and bear **R** over field towards ruined **St Gabriel's Church**.

In bottom corner turn down through gate, passing ruins on **R**; go through 2nd gate. Go down track, passing cottages on **L**, and bear **R** up road ('Morcombelake'). Follow up between high banks and hedges. Continue through gateway.

❹ At road junction, turn **R** down **Muddyford Lane** ('**Langdon Hill**'). Pass gate of **Shedbush Farm** and continue straight up hill. Turn **R** up concreted lane towards **Filcombe Farm**. Follow blue markers through farmyard, bearing **L** through 2 gates. Walk up track, go through 2 more gates and bear **L** over top of green saddle between **Langdon Hill** and **Golden Cap**.

❺ Go **L** through gate in corner and down gravel lane (**Pettycrate Lane**) beside woods ('**Seatown**'). Ignore footpath to **R**. At junction of tracks keep **R**, downhill, with patchwork of fields on hillside ahead. Pass **Seahill House** on **L** and turn **R**, on to road. Continue down road into **Seatown** village to return to car.

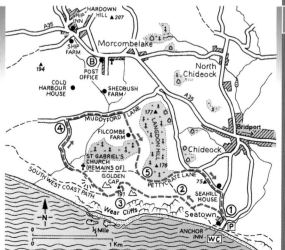

Wiltshire

121 THE CHUTES *Border Paths Around and About*

8 miles (12.9km) 4hrs 15min **Ascent:** 1,099ft (335m)
Paths: Bridle paths, downland tracks, field paths, roads, 8 stiles
Suggested map: aqua3 OS Explorer 131 Romsey, Andover & Test Valley
Grid reference: SU 308530
Parking: Lower Chute Club

Explore the Wiltshire/Hampshire border.

❶ Turn **L** out of car park, then **R** at T-junction. Fork **L** at war memorial, then turn **L** by 'Chute Cadley' village sign. Keep **L**; take bridle path, track, through edge of woodland. Continue between hedgerows; descend into **Chute Standen**.

❷ Turn **R** at T-junction. Where lane swings **L** to **Standen House**, keep on grassy track (**Breach Lane**). At T-junction, turn **R** then **L** along woodland edge. Continue for ½ mile (800m) to **Chute Causeway**.

❸ Cross causeway and descend track to lane in **Hippenscombe Bottom**. Turn **L**, then **R** through gate; swing **R**, then **L** between farm buildings. Fork **R** along track, then **L** and ascend to crossing of ways.

❹ Turn **R** on track. At **Fosbury Farm**, bear **R**; walk beside woodland. Follow track into woods; go through earthworks into **Fosbury Ring** (top of **Knolls Down**).

❺ Fork **L**, exit ring and walk down **L-H** field edge. Go through gap in corner and maintain direction around

edge of field. Descend to **cottage** in corner. Turn **R** along lane; cross stile on **L**. Keep to **R-H** field edge to stile and lane; turn **R** into **Vernham Dean**.

❻ Take waymarked track beside house ('**Underwood**'). Follow **L-H** field edge; before gap in corner, turn **R** down hedged track. Follow track into woodland, then follow waymarker uphill across field and through plantation to stile. Turn **L** along top of escarpment to gate in corner and road.

❼ Turn **R**; where road swings sharp **L** by junction, keep ahead over stile. Initially head towards barn, but fork **L** across depression and continue to another stile. Cross next field to stile; walk down track between fields. Bear slightly **L**, then along **R-H** field edge to cross stile by cattle grid.

❽ Keep to **R-H** field edge; cross stile on **R** just before corner. Continue by woodland, eventually joining drive (becomes metalled lane). Turn **R** at T-junction; retrace steps to car park.

122 GREAT BEDWYN *A Working Windmill*

5½ miles (8.8km) 2hrs **Ascent:** 147ft (45m)
Paths: Field paths, woodland tracks, tow path, roads, 1 stile
Suggested map: aqua3 OS Explorer 157 Marlborough & Savernake Forest
Grid reference: SU 279645
Parking: Great Bedwyn Station

A peaceful canal walk, visiting Wiltshire's only working windmill.

❶ Walk back to main road in **Great Bedwyn** and turn **R**, then **L** down Church Street. Pass **Lloyd's Stone Museum** and church; take footpath **L** between 2 graveyards. Climb stile, cross field to kissing gate; carefully cross railway line to further kissing gate. Cross footbridge, then bridge over **Kennet and Avon Canal** and descend to tow path.

❷ Turn **R**, pass beneath bridge and continue along tow path for 1½ miles (2.4km), passing 3 locks, to Lock 60. Cross canal here, turn **L**, then follow wooded path **R** and through tunnel beneath railway. Ascend steps to **Crofton Pumping Station**.

❸ Retrace steps to tow path and Lock 60. Take footpath **R**, waymarked to **Wilton Windmill**; walk by **Wilton Water** along edge of fields. Eventually, turn **R** down short track to lane by village pond in **Wilton**.

❹ Turn **L**, then just past **Swan Inn**, follow lane **L**

('**Great Bedwyn**'). Climb out of village and fork **R** to pass **Wilton Windmill**. Continue along lane and turn **L** on to track, opposite lane to Marten. Just before wooded track snakes downhill, turn **R** along bridle path (unsigned) beside woodland.

❺ At staggered crossing of paths, turn **R**; in 50yds (46m), turn **L** ('**Great Bedwyn**'). Proceed down well-surfaced track; go through gate into **Bedwyn Brail**. Continue through woods, following signs ('**Great Bedwyn**'). Go straight across clearing before forking **L** to re-enter woods in **L-H** corner of clearing.

❻ On emerging in field corner, keep **L** along field boundary, go through gap in hedge and descend along **L-H** side of next field (**Great Bedwyn** visible ahead). Near bottom of field, bear half **R**, downhill to canal.

❼ Pass through gate by bridge and Lock 64 and turn **R** along tow path. Go through car park to road, then turn **L** over canal and rail bridges before turning **R** back to Great Bedwyn Station.

123 SAVERNAKE *A Royal Forest*

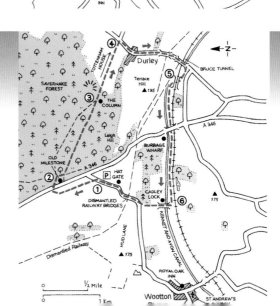

5½ miles (8.8km) 2hrs 30min **Ascent:** 213ft (65m)
Paths: Woodland tracks, tow path, bridle paths, country lanes
Suggested map: aqua3 OS Explorer 157 Marlborough & Savernake Forest
Grid reference: SU 215646
Parking: Hat Gate 8 picnic area off A346 south of Marlborough

Through an ancient forest landscape high above Marlborough.

❶ From car park, turn **R**, then almost immediately **L** past wooden barrier. Follow wooded path for 500yds (457m), then bear **R** to reach **A346**. Cross over near old milestone and take track beyond wooden barrier, signed to **Tottenham House**.

❷ In 150yds (137m), at major crossing of routes, turn **R** and after similar distance at more minor crossing of paths, turn **L**. Follow this straight track (can be very muddy in places) for ¾ mile (1.2km) to **The Column**, an elegant classical column, built by Thomas Bruce in memory of his uncle, Charles Bruce, former Earl of Ailesbury.

❸ Maintain direction towards **Tottenham House**, which is visible in distance. **Savernake Forest** consists of 2,300 acres (931.5ha) of mixed woodland (grand oaks, chestnuts and beeches), managed by Forestry Commission. (Local tradition has it that Henry

VIII married Jane Seymour at Savernake, where great barn was hung with tapestries and transformed into banqueting hall for wedding feast.) On leaving woodland, continue along wide fenced track, eventually reaching gate and road opposite drive to **Tottenham House**.

❹ Turn **R**, walk through hamlet of **Durley** and keep to lane across old railway bridge, then main railway bridge, and shortly take footpath on **R**, waymarked 'Wootton Rivers'. You are now walking above **Kennet and Avon Canal** as it passes through **Bruce Tunnel**.

❺ Walk down some steps, pass through narrow and low tunnel under railway line and join canal tow path just below entrance to **Bruce Tunnel**. Turn **L** along tow path for about 1½ miles (2.4km), passing beneath **A346** at **Burbage Wharf** to reach **Cadley Lock**.

❻ Turn **R** over bridge No 105 and follow metalled track to T-junction. Turn **R** and keep to road, passing 2 dismantled railway bridges, back to car park.

DOWNTON *ADMIRAL LORD NELSON*

5 miles (8km) 3hrs **Ascent:** 229ft (70m)
Paths: Riverside paths, downland tracks, metalled lanes, 6 stiles
Suggested map: aqua3 OS Explorers 130 Salisbury & Stonehenge; 131 Romsey, Andover & Test Valley
Grid reference: SU 180214 (on Explorer 130)
Parking: Plenty of roadside parking in High Street

Discover an 18th-century estate associated with Lord Nelson.

❶ Head west along High Street, cross river bridge and take footpath **R** ('Charlton All Saints'). Walk alongside river, go through kissing gate and keep to footpath as it swings away from river along causeway through water-meadows. Path widens to track; as this bears **L** towards bridge, fork **R** along path to stile and footbridge.

❷ Turn **R** along concrete track; as it bears **L** towards farm buildings, fork **R** across stile and keep to **R-H** field edge to small bridge and stile. Head across field to stile; cross next field to stile by house. Cross drive and stile opposite. Walk beside hedge on **R**, following it **L**; continue ahead to public footbridge.

❸ Cross stile and further footbridge to join footpath through marshland. Pass through gate; cross series of footbridges across weirs and streams to mill. Turn **L** in front of mill and follow driveway. Shortly, take waymarked footpath **L** (bear **R** to chapel), uphill through woodland, eventually reaching fork of paths.

❹ Take main path **R** to stile on woodland edge. Bear half **R** across field to gate (**Trafalgar House**, given to Nelson's heirs in recognition of his services is to R), and follow woodland path for ¼ mile (400m) to metalled lane. Turn **L** uphill and shortly **L** at junction opposite lodge.

❺ Cross bridge over disused railway line and take arrowed bridle path **R**. Do not follow course of old railway, instead keep to **R-H** edge of 2 fields to road.

❻ Turn **R** under bridge; then **L** to follow old embankment. When this ends, maintain direction over hill and descend to cross path.

❼ Descend into valley; as you start climbing, take path to **L** of embankment. Eventually, go through gap in hedge at rear of houses and bear **R** along fenced path. Cross road and continue down path to gate. Walk down drive and turn **L** back to High Street.

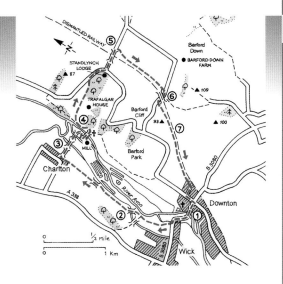

AMESBURY *GLIMPSES OF STONEHENGE*

6½ miles (10.4km) 3hrs **Ascent:** 518ft (158m)
Paths: Tracks, field and bridle paths, roads, 3 stiles
Suggested map: aqua3 OS Explorer 130 Salisbury & Stonehenge
Grid reference: SU 149411
Parking: Free parking at Amesbury Recreation Ground car park

A downland and riverside ramble.

❶ Take footpath to **R** of play area, cross footbridge. Bear **R** to cross main footbridge over **River Avon**. At crossing of tracks, take track ('Durnford'); pass **R** of cottages. Head uphill to junction; continue straight on, downhill to gate. Turn **R** along field edge and bear **L** in corner to join path through valley bottom by stream.

❷ Shortly, cross footbridge on **R**; follow path through marshy ground to cross bridge over Avon. Bear **R** over bridge; keep **L** through paddock beside thatched cob wall of **Normanton Down House** to stile. Bear **R** along drive to road. Turn **L** then, in ¼ mile (400m), turn **R** up farm road towards **Springbottom Farm**.

❸ Either walk up tarmac road or join path through spinney on **R**, latter giving views to Stonehenge. Pass barns and descend to footpath. Beyond barns, bear **L** with red byway arrow on to track beside paddocks.

❹ Keep to track through downland valley (Lake Bottom) for ¾ mile (1.2km). Where it becomes metalled at Lake, take arrowed path **R**, up **L-H** edge of field into woodland; bear **L** uphill to stile. Keep **R** along field edge to further stile.

❺ Cross lane and take bridle path **R** in front of thatched house. Head downhill, cross drive and bear **L**; cross 2 footbridges over Avon. Pass beside **Durnford Mill**; follow drive out to lane.

❻ Turn **L** and walk through **Great Durnford**, passing church and drive to **Great Durnford Manor**, following lane **R**, uphill through woodland. Descend and take waymarked bridle path **L** beside house.

❼ Ascend through edge of **Ham Wood**. On leaving wood, bear **R** along path to gate. Keep **R** along edge of 2 fields to gate.

❽ Continue through pastureland; bear **R** across field towards waymarker post at field boundary. Ignore public footpath to **R** ('Stockport'); walk down field edge to gate to rejoin outward route. Retrace steps into Amesbury.

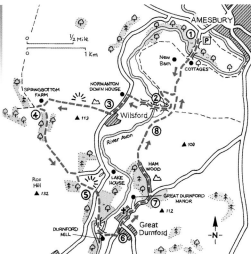

PITTON *CLARENDON'S LOST PALACE*

7½ miles (12.1km) 3hrs **Ascent:** 410ft (125m)
Paths: Field paths, woodland tracks, country lanes, 9 stiles
Suggested map: aqua3 OS Explorer 130 Salisbury & Stonehenge
Grid reference: SU 212312
Parking: Pitton village hall

Exploring ancient woodland for the remains of Clarendon Palace.

❶ From car park, cross lane and walk up cul-de-sac to **R** of **pub**. In 100yds (91m), take footpath **R**, heading uphill between houses to stile. Proceed across narrow track to stile, then go ahead along **R-H** field edge to stile and gate.

❷ Cross track and continue along another track to **R** of woodland. It narrows to path and soon reaches stile and enters **Church Copse**. Where fenced path joins track bear **R** then, at junction on woodland fringe, keep straight on downhill into **Farley** village.

❸ At road, turn **R** and pass **All Saints Church** and almshouses. Leave village and, just before 30mph sign, cross stile on **L** and follow hedge **R** to stile to rear of bungalow. Walk down drive, cross lane to gate and follow path through narrow field to stile and gate.

❹ Cross footbridge and stile ahead, then proceed across next field (on **L** of power cables), to stile and gate. Take track immediately **R** and follow this byway to crossing of tracks. Turn **L** alongside fenced enclosure and, on emerging from wood, head straight across 2 fields and enter further woodland.

❺ Walk through woodland alongside clearing to your **R**, and cross lane back into wood. Leave wood and follow track **R**, then **L** around field edge and soon re-enter wood. Keep ahead where **Clarendon Way** merges from **R** and continue to ruins of **Clarendon Palace**, which began life as Saxon hunting lodge.

❻ From **palace** remains, retrace your steps through wood, keeping **L** along **Clarendon Way**. Follow path for nearly 1 mile (1.6km) through wood. On emerging, keep straight on down track and cross lane by barn.

❼ Pass beside cottages and woodland to your **R**, then walk down fenced path, soon to follow diverted footpath signs to sewage pumping station. At lane turn **L**, then **R**, back to village hall.

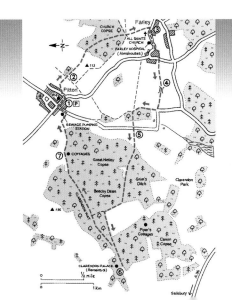

Wiltshire • SOUTHWEST ENGLAND

127 SALISBURY *A HISTORIC TRAIL*

3 miles (4.8km) 2hrs (longer if visiting attractions) **Ascent:** Negligible ⚠
Paths: Pavements and metalled footpaths
Suggested map: aqua3 OS Explorer 130 Salisbury & Stonehenge; AA Salisbury streetplan
Grid reference: SU 141303
Parking: Central car park (signed off A36 Ring Road)

Around a cathedral city.

❶ Join Riverside Walk and follow path through **Maltings Shopping Centre**. Keep by Avon tributary stream to St Thomas Square, close to Michael Snell Tea Rooms and St Thomas' Church. Bear **R** to junction of **Bridge Street**, Silver Street and **High Street**.

❷ Turn **L** along Silver Street and cross pedestrian crossing by Haunch of Venison pub to Poultry Cross. Keep ahead along Butcher Row and Fish Row to pass **Guildhall** and **tourist information centre**. Turn **R** along **Queen Street** then **R** along **New Canal**.

❸ Return to crossroads; continue along **Milford Street** to pass Red Lion. Turn **R** along **Brown Street**, then **L** along Trinity Street to pass Trinity Hospital. Pass Love Lane into Barnard Street and follow road **R** to St Ann Street, opposite **Joiners' Hall**.

❹ Walk down **St Ann Street**; keep ahead on merging with Brown Street to T-junction with St John Street. Cross over and go through **St Ann's Gate** into

Cathedral Close. Pass **Malmesbury House** and Bishops Walk and take path diagonally **L** across green to cathedral's main entrance.

❺ Pass entrance, walk beside barrier ahead and turn **R**. Shortly, turn **R** along **West Walk**, passing **Salisbury and South Wiltshire Museum**. Discover Salisbury and **Regimental Museum**. Keep ahead into Chorister Green to pass **Mompesson House**.

❻ Bear **L** through gates into **High Street** and turn **L** at crossroads along **Crane Street**. Cross **River Avon** and turn **L** along metalled path beside river through **Queen Elizabeth Gardens**. Keep **L** by play area; soon cross footbridge to follow Town Path across water-meadows to **Old Mill** (hotel) in **Harnham**.

❼ Return along Town Path, cross footbridge and keep ahead to **Crane Bridge Road**. Turn **R**, recross **Avon** and turn immediately **L** along riverside path to **Bridge Street**. Cross and follow path ahead towards Bishops Mill. Walk back through **Maltings** to car park.

128 LYDIARD PARK *SWINDON'S SURPRISE*

3¼ miles (5.3km) 2hrs **Ascent:** 65ft (20m) ▲
Paths: Field paths (can be muddy), tracks and metalled lanes, 11 stiles
Suggested map: aqua3 OS Explorer 169 Cirencester & Swindon
Grid reference: SU 101844
Parking: Free parking at Lydiard Country Park

A rural ramble from a Palladian mansion and country park on Swindon's urban fringe.

❶ Turn **L** out of car park, pass **Forest Café** and wooden barrier and continue along track to **Lydiard House**, home of Bolingbroke family who lived here from Elizabethan times (present house built in 1743), and **church**. At **church**, bear **L** through car park, ignoring stile on R, and go through gate. Walk beside walled garden and follow path **L** into woodland.

❷ Just before small clearing, turn **R** (marked by red striped post) to reach kissing gate and cattle grid on woodland edge. Proceed ahead across field on defined path to stile and plank bridge in **R-H** corner.

❸ Continue through edge of small plantation, passing beneath electricity cables, with turn **L** across stile in corner of plantation. Follow waymarker across field to stile and turn **R**, following path within edge of woodland. Bear **L**, then **R**, climb wooden steps and,

emerging in corner of field, turn **L** with red striped post marker and cross stile.

❹ Go across gap (often muddy) between 2 fields to waymarker, then follow **R-H** field edge to stile and gate. Follow farm track ahead; just beyond 1st of 2 metal barriers, turn **R** down track to road.

❺ Turn **R** then, in about 200yds (183m), take arrowed footpath to **L** through gate. Bear half **L** to double stiles and maintain your direction to further stile. Turn sharp **R** along field edge to reach gate by barn, then bear half **L** across field, passing beneath electricity power cables to stile in corner.

❻ Cut diagonally across road to stile and gate. Bear **R** around field edge, alongside small copse to stile. Almost immediately turn **L** through gate and walk down long narrow field. Swing **R** with field boundary and eventually turn **R** across stile by cattle grid encountered on outward route. Retrace steps back to country park and car park.

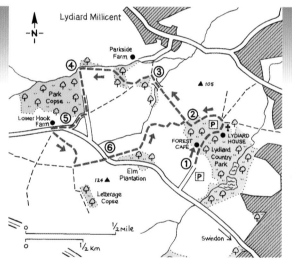

129 GREAT WISHFORD *GROVELY WOOD*

5 miles (8km) 2hrs 30min **Ascent:** 370ft (113m) ▲
Paths: Woodland paths and downland tracks
Suggested map: aqua3 OS Explorer 130 Salisbury & Stonehenge
Grid reference: SU 080353
Parking: Roadside parking in South Street, Great Wishford

Learn all about Wiltshire's oldest surviving custom on this peaceful walk through ancient woodland.

❶ Return along South Street to **Church** of St Giles and turn **L** at T-junction. Walk past **Royal Oak**. Go under railway bridge and immediately turn **R** along waymarked bridle path beside cemetery. Ascend track to gate.

❷ Walk along **L-H** field edge to gate, then bear **R** around top of field making for gate that leads into woodland. Turn immediately **L** along woodland track, then turn **L** at next T-junction and walk down well-defined track (permissive bridle path) to another T-junction. Turn **R** up metalled lane.

❸ At major junction, turn sharp **L** on to gravel track. Follow it **L**, pass beside metal barrier and join metalled track running down broad beech avenue (**First Broad Drive**) along course of old Roman road, or Lead Road, which traversed Wessex from lead mines of Mendips

in Somerset to join other ancient routes at Old Sarum, such as Harrow Way to Kent. You are now walking through **Grovely Wood**, a fine stretch of woodland that was once used as royal hunting forest and which, together with New Forest and Cranborne Chase, formed very significant preserve.

❹ After 1 mile (1.6km), at crossing of public bridle paths, turn **L** and keep to main track downhill through woodland, ignoring all cross paths and forks. Eventually emerge from **Grovely Wood** and follow track downhill towards **Great Wishford**, most southerly of delightful series of villages that nestle in valley of River Wylye. Village is famous for its Oak Apple Day celebrations (29 May), when county's only ancient custom still taking place is enacted by villagers. Pass beneath railway line to lane. Turn **L**, then fork **R** along South Street.

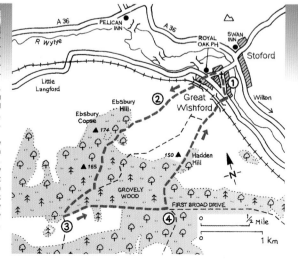

Wiltshire

OLD SARUM MEDIEVAL CITY

6 miles (9.7km) 2hrs **Ascent:** 557ft (170m)
Paths: Footpaths, tracks, bridle paths, stretches of road, 12 stiles
Suggested map: aqua3 OS Explorer 130 Salisbury & Stonehenge
Grid reference: SU 139326
Parking: English Heritage car park (closes 6pm; 4pm winter)

Explore the Avon Valley and Old Sarum.
❶ From car park walk down access road through outer bank of fortified site. Ignore gates on L, which provide access to upper and lower ramparts. Go through 2 gates leading to waymarked and fenced bridle path; follow to road.
❷ Go through gate opposite; follow track. Pass cottage (**Shepherds Corner**); ascend track. Shortly descend to **Keeper's Cottage** and crossing of paths.
❸ Keep straight on, heading uphill and between fields into wooded area. At crossing of bridle paths, turn **L** and descend path. At boundary marker, bear **R** and continue to road.
❹ Turn **L**, then shortly turn **R** down metalled lane (cul-de-sac). Cross Avon and 2 further footbridges, then follow metalled path and drive to road. For **Wheatsheaf** turn **L**. Turn **R**; shortly, turn **L** up lane.
❺ Just before **cottages and barns**, turn **L** over stile and walk down L-H field edge, crossing 2 more stiles

and fields. Maintain direction across next field, cross track; go through hedge ahead, then to stile and road.
❻ Cross road diagonally and take path down wooded track. Pass L of '**The Bays**' to stile; turn **R** between stream and fence. Cross double stiles in corner; turn sharp **L** over stile and **R** beside stream to white gate and metalled drive. Turn **L** and skirt **Home Farm** and Little Durnford Manor to gate and road.
❼ Turn **R**; follow road for ¾ mile (1.2km) to staggered crossroads. Keep ahead towards Stratford sub Castle, eventually crossing stile on **L**. Follow R-H field edge around churchyard, cross stile, path and another stile; bear half-**R** to gate in field corner. Head down next field, pass barn; cross stile to fenced track.
❽ Turn **L** uphill towards tree-covered ramparts. Keep **L** at junction of paths by gate, then shortly fork **R** and climb on to outer rampart. Turn **R** and follow path to gate and Old Sarum's access road. Turn **L** back to car park.

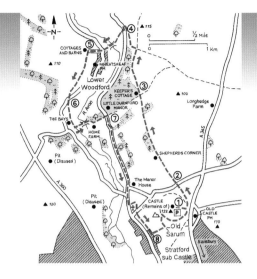

ALTON BARNES PEWSEY VALE AND DOWN

7 miles (11.3km) 3hrs **Ascent:** 492ft (150m)
Paths: Tracks, field paths, tow path, metalled lanes, 4 stiles
Suggested map: aqua3 OS Explorer 157 Marlborough & Savernake Forest
Grid reference: SU 115637
Parking: Tan Hill car park

A ramble on chalk downland.
❶ From car park, cross road to gate and follow track along L-H field edge to stile and gate. Ascend to further stile and gate, continue uphill and descend through earthworks to T-junction with **Wansdyke**.
❷ Turn **L** and continue with earthworks on **L**. Begin to descend, cross wooden barrier, then go through gate and bear **L** off **Wansdyke** on to metalled track. Just after track becomes concrete, fork **R** through gate and follow grassy track downhill to stile and gate.
❸ Rejoin main track by barn. Pass more barns and continue down to road. Turn **L** and take footpath **R** just before turning for **Stanton St Bernard**. Footpath becomes metalled lane. At T-junction, turn **R** and pass church, then swing **R** to **Pewsey Vale Riding School**. Turn **L** and follow track to **Kennet and Avon Canal**.
❹ Cross canal and bear **L** through gate to tow path. Keep to tow path for 1 mile (1.6km), passing **Barge Inn**, and bear **R** up to road at **Honeystreet**. Turn **L**

over bridge into **Alton Barnes**. In 100yds (91m), turn **R** ('**St Mary's Church**').
❺ Just before church, turn **L** through turnstile and walk down cobbled path. Follow path **R**, cross 2 footbridges via turnstiles then, where path turns **R** to All Saints Church in Alton Priors, turn **L** across field to kissing gate and road.
❻ Turn **L**; just beyond village sign, take footpath **R** up R-H field edge. At kink in field boundary, follow field perimeter, heading towards white sign beyond boundary. At road, ascend and fork **L** up track to gate leading to **Pewsey Down**.
❼ Follow waymarker uphill. Path swings **L** around hillside, then **R** up valley. Take path **L** to **White Horse**, Point ⒶA.
❽ Continue over hill; bear **R** down combe towards road. Before bearing **L** over wooden barrier and follow R-H field edge to stile. Turn **R** through gate and cross road to car park.

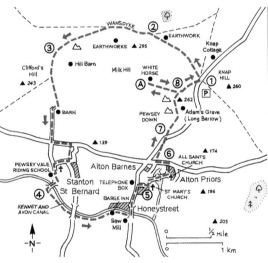

AVEBURY PAGAN PASTURES

5 miles (8km) 2hrs 30min **Ascent:** 262ft (80m)
Paths: Tracks, field paths, some road walking, 3 stiles
Suggested map: aqua3 OS Explorer 157 Marlborough & Savernake Forest
Grid reference: SU 099696
Parking: Large National Trust car park in Avebury

Explore the famous stone circle and some fine prehistoric monuments.
❶ From car park, walk back to main road and turn **R**. In 50yds (46m), cross and go through gate ('**West Kennett Long Barrow**'). Pass through another gate; follow path alongside **River Kennet**. Go through 2 more gates and cross 2 stiles, your route passing **Silbury Hill**, Europe's largest artificial prehistoric mound.
❷ Beyond gate, walk down R-H field edge to gate and **A4**. Cross straight over (carefully) and turn **L**, then almost immediately **R** through gate. Walk down gravel track and cross bridge over stream, track soon narrowing to footpath. Go through kissing gate and turn sharp **L**.
❸ To visit **West Kennett Long Barrow**, 2nd largest barrow in Britain at 300ft (91m) in length, shortly turn **R**. Otherwise go straight on around L-H field edge to gate and continue along track. At staggered junction,

keep ahead across stile and walk along R-H field boundary. Keep **R** in corner by redundant stile and cross stile on your **R** in next corner and proceed up narrow footpath.
❹ At T-junction, turn **L** and descend to road. Turn **L**, then just beyond bridge, take bridle path sharp **R**. Follow R-H field edge to gap in corner and keep **L** through next field. At top you'll see **tumuli** (R) and **The Sanctuary**, site of major wooden buildings, possibly used for religious and burial rites (L). Continue to **A4**.
❺ Cross A4 (care) and head up **Ridgeway**. After 500yds (457m), turn **L** off Ridgeway on to byway. Bear half **R** by clump of trees on **tumuli** and keep to established track, eventually reaching T-junction by series of farm buildings (**Manor Farm**).
❻ Turn **L** ('**Avebury**'), and follow metalled track through earthwork and straight over staggered crossroads by **Red Lion Inn**. Turn **L** opposite National Trust signpost and walk back to car park.

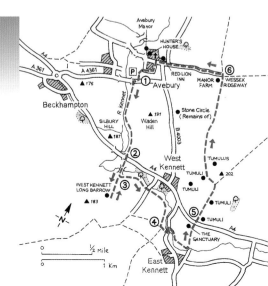

133 CRICKLADE *THE INFANT THAMES*

5½ miles (8.8km) 2hrs 30min **Ascent:** Negligible
Paths: Field paths and bridle paths, disused railway, town streets, 15 stiles
Suggested map: aqua3 OS Explorer 169 Cirencester & Swindon
Grid reference: SU 100934
Parking: Cricklade Town Hall car park (free)

An easy ramble across water-meadows.

1 Turn **R** out of car park, keep ahead at roundabout and walk along High Street. Pass **St Mary's Church** then turn **L** along North Wall before river bridge. Shortly, bear **R** to stile and join Thames Path. Cross stile and continue along field edge to houses.

2 Go through kissing gate on **R** and bear **L** across field to gate. Follow fenced footpath, cross bridge and pass through gate immediately on R-H side. Cross river bridge; turn **L** through gate. Walk beside infant Thames, crossing 2 stiles to enter **North Meadow**.

3 Cross stile by bridge. Go through gate immediately **R** and keep ahead, ignoring Thames Path **L**. Follow path beside **disused canal**. Cross footbridge and 2 stiles; at fence, bear **R** to cross footbridge close to house ('The Basin'). Cross stile and bear **R** along drive.

4 Cross bridge and turn **L** through gateway. Shortly, bear **R** to join path along **L** side of old canal. Keep to

path for ½ mile (800m) to road. Turn **L** into Cerney Wick to T-junction.

5 Cross stile opposite; keep ahead through paddock to stile and lane. Cross lane and climb stile opposite, continuing ahead to further stile. Shortly, cross stile on **R** and follow path beside lake. Bear **R**, **L** then bear off **L** (yellow arrow) into trees where path becomes track.

6 Cross footbridge and proceed ahead along field edge to stile. Turn **L** along old railway ('Cricklade'). Cross **Thames** in 1 mile (1.6km) and keep to path along former trackbed to bridge.

7 Follow gravel path to Leisure Centre. Bear **L** on to road, following it **R**; turn **L** opposite entrance to **Leisure Centre** car park. Turn **R**, then next **L** and follow road to church.

8 Walk beside barrier and turn **L** in front of The Gatehouse into churchyard. Bear **L** to main gates and follow lane to T-junction. Turn **R** to return to car park.

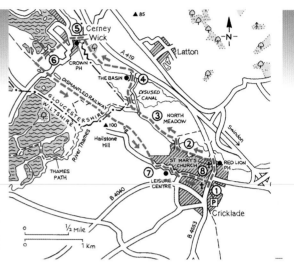

134 DINTON *UNSPOILT NADDER VALLEY*

5¼ miles (8.4km) 3hrs **Ascent:** 360ft (110m)
Paths: Tracks, field and woodland paths, parkland, 15 stiles
Suggested map: aqua3 OS Explorer 130 Salisbury & Stonehenge
Grid reference: SU 009315
Parking: Dinton Park National Trust car park

Architecture, history and varied scenery.

1 Leave car park, cross and follow lane to **B3089**. Turn **L**, pass **Little Clarendon**, and continue for ¼ mile (400m). Take path **R** by bus shelter.

2 Follow track to kissing gate and cross railway line to further gate. Keep to track; bear **L** alongside stream to **Dinton Mill**. Pass **L**, cross footbridge over **River Nadder** and follow drive to lane.

3 Turn **R** and follow metalled lane into **Compton Chamberlayne**. Take footpath **R**, opposite entrance to **Compton House**. Ascend, pass round gate and continue along track to **Home Farm** and junction of tracks.

4 Turn **R**, follow track **L** around buildings and remain on track (views of regimental badges etched into chalk). Walk beside woodland; near field corner, follow path into trees and continue close to woodland fringe. Pass reservoir to reach track.

5 Turn **R**; walk downhill to lane. Turn **L** then, at

sharp **L** bend, take path **R** and enter field (stile **L**). Bear half-**R** to stile. Cross track, pass through kissing gate and walk across rough grassland, then bear **L** to gate.

6 Turn **R** along field edge, go through kissing gate and bear **L** down R-H side of field. At waymarker, follow path **L**, downhill to stile. Descend through scrub, cross footbridge, then stile, and walk ahead to further stile. Bear **L** along riverbank, cross stile and continue to bridge over mill stream.

7 Pass before **Mill Farm** on path. Cross footbridge and stile; bear diagonally **R** towards railway. Cross line via stiles; bear slightly **R** to stile and woodland. Walk through to stile and keep ahead, to rear of barn, to stile. Continue ahead to stile; cut across pasture, keeping to **R** of 2nd telegraph pole to stile and road.

8 Cross stile opposite into **Dinton Park**; turn **R** alongside hedge. Bear **L** along path, pass pond and head towards **church**. Go through 1st gate on **R** and return to car park.

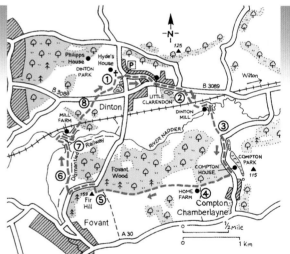

135 WARDOUR *OLD AND NEW CASTLES*

3½ miles (5.7km) 1hr 30min **Ascent:** 278ft (85m)
Paths: Field and woodland paths, parkland tracks, 13 stiles
Suggested map: aqua3 OS Explorer 118 Shaftesbury & Cranborne Chase
Grid reference: ST 938264
Parking: Free parking at Old Wardour Castle

Rolling parkland around medieval ruins.

1 From parking area turn **L** along drive and pass between **castle** and **Cresswell's Pond**. Pass Gothic Pavilion then at Wardour House (private) bear **R** with trackway. Gently climb wide track, skirting woodland then at fork keep **L**. At end of woodland, cross stile by field entrance and walk ahead along R-H side of field, heading downhill to stile.

2 Follow path beside **Pale Park Pond** to further stile, then ascend across field to stile and woodland. Shortly, bear **L**, then **R** to join main forest track. Keep **R** at fork and soon leave **Wardour Forest**, passing beside gate on to gravel drive.

3 At end of drive cross stile on **R**. Head downhill across field to metal gate and follow waymarked path through **Park Copse**, soon to bear **L** down grassy clearing to stile beside field entrance. Follow R-H edge towards **Park Gate Farm**.

4 Cross stile on to farm drive and turn **R** (yellow

arrow) to cross concrete farmyard to gate. Follow path beside hedge to further gate, with River Nadder on **L**, then proceed ahead along R-H field edge to stile. Bear diagonally **L** across field, aiming for L-H side of cottage. Go through gate and maintain direction to reach stile.

5 Cross farm drive and stile opposite and head straight uphill, keeping **L** of tree, towards stile and woodland. Follow path **R** through trees and soon bear **L** to pass building on **L**. New Wardour Castle is visible on **R**. Keep close to bushes across grounds towards main drive; turn **R** along gravel path and follow sign ('Chapel').

6 Join track and walk past **New Wardour Castle**. Where track forks, keep to **R** of stile beside gate. Follow grassy track ahead across parkland towards **Old Wardour Castle**. Climb stile beside gate and proceed ahead, following track uphill to T-junction of tracks. Turn **L**; follow outward route back to car park.

CALNE *EXPLORING BOWOOD PARK*

7 miles (11.3km) 3hrs 30min **Ascent:** 360ft (110m)
Paths: Field, woodland and parkland paths, metalled drives, pavement beside A4, former railway line, 3 stiles
Suggested map: aqua3 OS Explorer 156 Chippenham & Bradford-on-Avon
Grid reference: ST 998710
Parking: Choice of car parks in Calne

A visit to one of Wiltshire's grandest houses.
❶ Locate **new library** on **The Strand** (**A4**); walk south along New Road to roundabout. Turn **R** along Station Road; take footpath **L** opposite **fire station**. Turn **R** at **Wenhill Lane**; follow it out of built-up area.
❷ Near **cottage**, follow waymarker **L** and walk along field edge. Just beyond cottage, climb bank and keep **L** along field edge to bridge and stile. Keep to **L-H** field edge and bear **L** to stile. Follow path **R**, through rough grass around **Pinhills Farm** to stile opposite **bungalow** and turn **L** along drive.
❸ At junction, turn **R** along drive; continue for 1 mile (1.6km). Near bridge, take footpath **R**, through kissing gate and walk through parkland beside land. Cross bridge, go through gate; turn **R** by **Bowood Lake**.
❹ Follow path **L** to gate and cross causeway between lakes to gate. Keep straight on up track; follow **L**, then **R** to cross driveway to **Bowood House**.

❺ Beyond gate, keep ahead along field edge, then follow path **L** across **Bowood Park**. Keep **L** of trees and field boundary to gate. Turn **R** along drive beside **Bowood Golf Course**. Where drive turns sharp **R** to cottage, keep straight into woodland.
❻ Follow path **L**, downhill through clearing (often boggy) along line of telegraph poles. Bear **R** with path back into woodland and follow uphill beside golf course. Turn **R** through break in trees; go through main gates to **Bowood House** into **Derry Hill**.
❼ Turn immediately **R** along Old Lane. At **A4**, turn **R** along pavement. Shortly, cross to opposite pavement and continue downhill. Pass beneath footbridge and take drive immediately **R**.
❽ Join former **railway** line at Black Dog Halt. Turn **L** and follow back towards **Calne**. Cross disused Canal and turn **R** along tow path. Where path forks keep **R** to Station Road. Retrace steps to town centre.

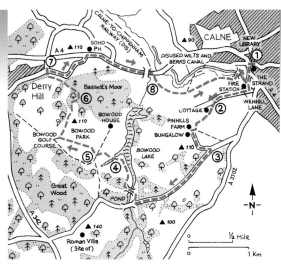

BREMHILL *MAUD HEATH'S CAUSEWAY*

4 miles (6.4km) 1hr 30min **Ascent:** 295ft (90m)
Paths: Field paths, bridle paths, metalled roads, 13 stiles
Suggested map: aqua3 OS Explorer 156 Chippenham & Bradford-on-Avon
Grid reference: ST 980730
Parking: Bremhill church

Follow field paths to a hilltop monument and the start of Maud Heath's Causeway.
❶ With your back to **St Martin's Church**, turn **R** and walk downhill through village. Start climbing and take arrowed path **L** across stile. Proceed straight on below bank along field edge to stile in corner. Bear diagonally **R**, uphill across field to gate and lane.
❷ Cross stile opposite and paddock to further stile. Bear half-**L** to stile in field corner and walk along **L-H** edge to gate; maintain direction to stile. In next field look out for and pass through gate on your **L** and head across field to gate and lane.
❸ Turn **L**, then immediately bear **R** along track to gate. Join waymarked bridle path along **R-H** field edge to gate. Maintain direction through several fields and gates to reach **monument to Maud Heath** on top of **Wick Hill**. It commemorates local widow who, in 1474, made bequest of land and property to provide income to build and maintain causeway from Wick Hill

through Avon marshes to Chippenham.
❹ Continue to cross lane via stiles, passing stone tablet and inscription indicating beginning of Maud Heath's Causeway. Follow bridle path along crest of hill through 7 fields via gates and bear **L** before woodland to gate and lane at top of **Bencroft Hill**.
❺ Turn **L**, pass **Bencroft Farm** and bungalow, then take waymarked path **R**, through woodland to gate. Continue ahead through plantation, bearing **L** on nearing gate to cross stile. Proceed across field on defined path, cross double fence stiles and remain on path to stile to **L** of bungalow.
❻ Turn **L** along lane, heading uphill to junction beside **Dumb Post Inn**. Turn **R**, then **L** along drive to **thatched cottage**. Go through squeeze-stile and keep to **L-H** edge of field through gate and squeeze-stile to reach stile in field corner. Walk in front of **Manor Farm** to reach gate leading into Bremhill churchyard. Bear **R** along path back to car.

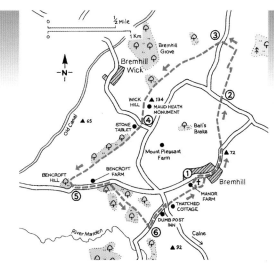

HEYTESBURY *THE CHALK STREAM*

4 miles (6.4km) 2hrs **Ascent:** 49ft (15m)
Paths: Field paths and bridleways, 10 stiles
Suggested map: aqua3 OS Explorer 143 Warminster & Trowbridge
Grid reference: ST 926425
Parking: Plenty of room along wide village street

A gentle stroll along the River Wylye.
❶ Head east along street, pass **Angel Inn** and turn **R** down Mantles Lane. Where it curves **R** to become Mill Lane, take footpath **L** along drive beside River Wylye. Bear **R** on to footpath in front of **Mantles Cottage**, go through walk-through stile and walk along **R-H** edge of pasture; soon bear slightly **L** on nearing **Mill Farm** to gate.
❷ Beyond further gate, turn **R** across bridge; follow yellow arrow **L** and cross footbridge. Follow Wessex Ridgeway marker ahead at junction then, just before footbridge, turn **L** through gap and bear **R** along field edge. At white wooden arrow, bear half-**L** across field towards thatched cottages to river bank; bear **R** to stile and junction of paths.
❸ Turn **L** across footbridge, pass **Knook Manor** and **St Margaret's Church**, then turn **R** by post-box and pass **East Farm** on track (messy after rain). Go through **L-H** of 2 gates and proceed along **R-H** field

edge to another gate. Continue into **Upton Lovell**.
❹ At crossroads, take signed footpath **R**; just before drive to Hatch House, follow path **L** to footbridge over river. Go through gate and ahead along field edge to metal gate. Cross stile on **L**, walk along hedged path and cross railway (care) via gates and steps. Continue to lane in **Corton**.
❺ Turn **L** through village, passing **Dove Inn**. At T-junction, take arrowed path across stile on **R**. Head across field on defined path to stile; keep ahead along fenced path to further stile and proceed along **R-H** edge of field. Shortly, climb stile and turn **L** along field edge to stile and pass beneath railway.
❻ Cross footbridge, then stile and walk beside **R-H** fence to gate. From here, follow track ahead. Cross another stile and keep to track until lane. Turn **R**; go through complex of buildings at Mill Farm and across river to rejoin outward route beside River Wylye back into **Heytesbury**.

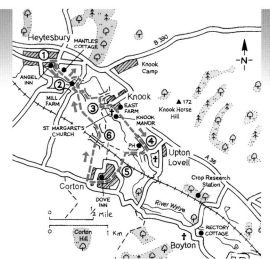

139 EAST KNOYLE *WREN'S BIRTHPLACE*

5 miles (8km) 2hrs 30min Ascent: 590ft (180m)
Paths: Field paths, woodland bridle paths, metalled lanes
Suggested map: aqua3 OS Explorer 143 Warminster & Trowbridge
Grid reference: ST 879305
Parking: East Knoyle village hall, adjacent to church

Savour the views on this undulating ramble.

❶ Turn **L** out of car park; **L** up Wise Lane. Bear **L**; take drive **R**. Continue on track where drive veers **L**.

❷ Keep ahead uphill; bear **L** along metalled drive. At **Clouds House** stable buildings, take unmarked path **R**, downhill, passing garage to lane in **Milton**. Cross and bear **L** along lower lane.

❸ Pass thatched cottage on **R**; climb bank to stile. Turn **R** behind cottage to gate; climb through woodland edge. At top, bear half-**L** on path then descend to bridle path. Turn **L**, then **R** at next junction; follow path downhill to lane.

❹ Turn **L**, then **R** at T-junction. Take bridle path **L** beyond **Chapel Farm**, forking **R** along track to gate. Continue along field edge, following **L** to gate in field corner. Descend off **Cleeve Hill**, through 2 gates and **Manor Farm** to lane in **West Knoyle**.

❺ Keep ahead. Continue through village, passing **village hall**; beyond 'The Willows', turn **L** to gate

beside **Puckwell Coppice**. Follow track ahead to information board. Take footpath to **R**, through gate.

❻ Proceed ahead, cross footbridge and keep **R** at fork of paths. Bear **L** with footpath that exits wood to **R**; descend through trees to footbridge. Bear **L** and follow grassy swathe to gap in field corner. Continue then turn **R** along 1st swathe to gate.

❼ Bear slightly **R** to kissing gate, cross footbridge and keep on to fence stile. Turn **R** along track, then **L** through gate; bear diagonally **R**, then descend to fence stile and copse. Cross footbridge and wire fence; keep ahead, uphill through trees to field. Continue beside woodland to gate in top L-H corner.

❽ Follow bridleway uphill through woodland. At junction, turn **L**; at top, bear **R** into cul-de-sac to lane. Turn **L** for **Fox and Hounds**. Turn **R** to **Windmill Hill**, ahead at crossroads and descend into **East Knoyle**. Take footpath by **Wren's Cottage**, cross lane and steps into churchyard. At road, turn **R**; return to start.

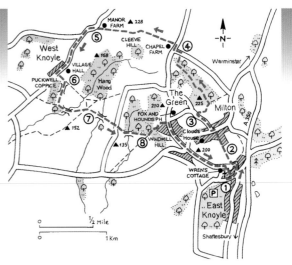

140 FONTHILL *FANTASTIC FOLLY*

4¼ miles (6.8km) 2hrs Ascent: 278ft (85m)
Paths: Tracks, field and woodland paths, parkland, some road walking
Suggested map: aqua3 OS Explorer 143 Warminster & Trowbridge
Grid reference: ST 933316
Parking: Lay-by close to southern end of Fonthill Lake

Explore Fonthill Park, ridge-top woodlands and pastures around Fonthill Bishop.

❶ With your back to lay-by, turn **R** along road (this can be busy) that traverses **Fonthill Park** beside its beautiful tree-fringed lake for just over ½ mile (800m). Pass beneath magnificent **stone arch** and shortly bear **R** to B3089. Keep to **R** along pavement into pretty little village of **Fonthill Bishop**.

❷ Turn **R** just beyond bus shelter on to track. On passing 'Private Road' sign for Fonthill Estate, turn **L** through small **business park** on unsigned footpath. (William Beckford acquired estate in mid-18th century. His son built Gothic fantasy palace, one of most remarkable buildings in country, in woodland west of lake. It eventually collapsed during a storm.) Keep **L** and soon join track that bears **R** uphill towards woodland. Follow grassy track beside **Fonthill Clump** and keep to main track above valley. In ½ mile (800m) bear **R** downhill into **Little Ridge Wood**.

❸ Track gives way to path. At T-junction, bear **L** and keep **L** at next 2 junctions, following wide path to gate and lane. Turn **R** through hamlet of **Ridge**. Pass **telephone box**, walk uphill and bear off **R** with yellow arrow along drive to **Fonthill House**, which lies above sweeping pastureland.

❹ In ¼ mile (400m), fork **L** with footpath sign to follow track by paddocks to pass beside gate. In 20yds (18m) fork **R** with yellow arrow and walk beside woodland. On entering field, turn **L** along field edge (path becomes defined grassy track around field edge). Gradually descend towards woodland.

❺ Enter wood and bear **L** along gravel track beside **Fonthill Lake**, which was used as location for filming Joanne Harris's novel *Chocolat*. Cross weir to gate. Disregard track which goes ahead uphill and bear off **R** along lakeside edge. Follow well-established path through 2 gates, eventually returning to parking area.

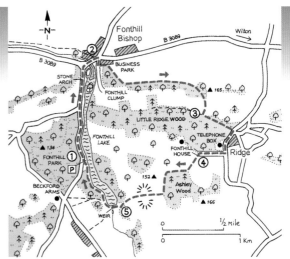

141 TOLLARD ROYAL *AROUND RUSHMORE PARK*

4½ miles (7.2km) 2hrs Ascent: 616ft (188m)
Paths: Field and woodland paths, bridle paths and tracks
Suggested map: aqua3 OS Explorer 118 Shaftesbury & Cranborne Chase
Grid reference: ST 944178
Parking: By pond in Tollard Royal

A walk in the heart of Cranborne Chase.

❶ Facing pond turn **L** along track and take waymarked path **R** across footbridge to stile. Follow narrow path half-**L** uphill through scrub and along field edge; soon bear **R** to gate in top corner. Continue, pass to **R** of copse; bear **L** through gates into adjacent field. Keep to R-H edge, downhill to gate and stile.

❷ Bear diagonally **L** and descend to gate and junction of paths in valley bottom. Take track **R**, through gate and continue to fork of tracks. Ascend track ahead and follow it beside woodland for ½ mile (800m). Bear **R** through trees to metalled lane.

❸ Turn **R**, then **L** before gates to **Rushmore Park**. Keep to established track, heading downhill to crossing of paths by **golf course**.

❹ Turn **R**, pass in front of cottage and keep to path through rough grass alongside fairway. Bear **R** on to track and follow it **L** to reach redundant gateposts. Pass beside gate posts and follow track **R**. Where this

peters out, keep ahead beside woodland, bearing **R** to pass green on **L**.

❺ Bear **R** through gate into woodland and follow yellow waymarker **R** through trees. Ill-defined at first, path soon bears **L** to become clear route (yellow arrows) through **Brookes Coppice**, to reach T-junction with track.

❻ Turn **L**, cross drive and stile opposite and bear half-**R** across parkland to stile beyond avenue of trees. Bear slightly **L** downhill to gate in field corner. Shortly take 2nd arrowed path sharp **R**.

❼ Follow track through **Tinkley Bottom** to gate and pass below **Rushmore Farm**. On passing through 2nd of 2 gateways, turn immediately **L** and walk uphill to pair of gates. Go through L-H gate; keep **R** through 2 paddocks to reach gate.

❽ Take path ahead and bear diagonally **R** downhill to gate and B3081. Keep ahead into **Tollard Royal** back to pond and your car.

Wiltshire

HOLT *A WALK WITH GOOD MANORS*

3 miles (4.8km) 1hr 30min **Ascent:** 147ft (45m)
Paths: Field paths, metalled track, country lanes, 8 stiles
Suggested map: aqua3 OS Explorer 156 Chippenham & Bradford-on-Avon
Grid reference: ST 861619
Parking: Holt Village Hall car park

A stroll from a Wiltshire industrial village to a 15th-century moated manor house.

❶ Turn **L** out of car park, then **R** along B3107 through village. Just before **Old Ham Tree pub** and village green, turn **R** along Crown Corner. At end of lane take waymarked path **L** along drive. Follow fenced path beside 'Highfields' to stile.

❷ Keep to **R** along edge of field, then keep ahead in next field towards clump of fir trees. Continue following worn path to **R**, into further field. Keep **L** along field edge to stile in top corner. Maintain direction to ladder stile and cross metalled drive and stile opposite. Bear diagonally **L** through field to hidden stile in hedge, level with clump of trees to **R**.

❸ Turn **R** along lane. At junction, turn **R** towards **Great Chalfield** and go through kissing gate almost immediately on **L**. Take arrowed path **R**, diagonally across large field towards **Great Chalfield Manor** visible ahead.

❹ Cross stile and bear half-**R** downhill to stile. Cross stream via stepping stones, then stile and bear diagonally **L** across field to gate. Cross bridge and keep ahead beside hedge to metalled track by barn.

❺ Turn **R**, then **R** again when you reach lane, passing in front of **Great Chalfield Manor**. At sharp **R-H** bend, go through gate ahead and bear **R**, then half-**L** across field to cross footbridge over stream. Continue straight on up field beside woodland to gate in field corner.

❻ Follow **L-H** field edge to gate, then follow path straight ahead towards chimney on skyline. Go through gate, bear immediately **R** to gate in hedge and turn **R** along path around field edge.

❼ Ignore stile on **R**; continue to field corner and raised path beside water. Go through gate and turn **L** along field edge to further gate on **L**. Join drive past Garlands Farm and pass between small **factory buildings** to road and turn **R** back to car park.

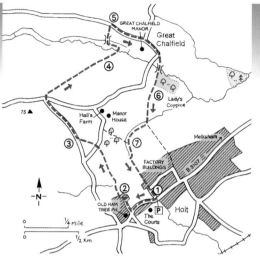

CASTLE COMBE *A PICTURE-BOOK VILLAGE*

5¾ miles (9.2km) 2hrs 30min **Ascent:** 515ft (157m)
Paths: Field and woodland paths and tracks, metalled lanes, 10 stiles
Suggested map: aqua3 OS Explorer 156 Chippenham & Bradford-on-Avon
Grid reference: ST 845776
Parking: Free car park just off B4039 at Upper Castle Combe

Through the hilly and wooded By Brook Valley from a famous Wiltshire village.

❶ Leave car park via steps and turn **R**. At T-junction, turn **R**; follow lane into Castle Combe. Keep **L** at **Market Cross**, cross By Brook and continue along road to take path ('Long Dean'), across 2nd bridge on **L**.

❷ Cross stile and follow path uphill then beside R-**H** fence above valley (**Macmillan Way**). Beyond open area, ascend through woodland to stile and gate. Cross further stile; descend into **Long Dean**.

❸ Pass mill and follow track **R** to cross river bridge. At **mill house**, keep **R** and follow sunken bridleway uphill to gate. Shortly enter pasture and follow path around top edge, bearing **L** to stile and lane.

❹ Turn **L** and descend to **A420** at **Ford**. Turn **R** along pavement and **R** again into **Park Lane**. (To visit **White Hart** in **Ford**, take road ahead on **L**, 'Colerne'.) Climb gravel track and take footpath **L** through squeeze stile.

❺ Keep **R** through pasture and continue through trees to water-meadow in valley bottom. Turn **L**, cross stream and ascend grassy slope ahead, bearing **L** beyond trees towards waymarker post. Follow footpath along top of field to stile and gate, then walk through woodland to gate and road.

❻ Turn **L**, then immediately **L** again ('North Wraxall'). Keep to road for ¼ mile (400m) and take arrowed bridleway **R**. Follow track then, just before gate, keep **R** downhill on sunken path to footbridge over **Broadmead Brook**.

❼ Shortly, climb stile on **R** and follow footpath close to river. Cross stile and soon pass beside **Nettleton Mill House**, bearing **R** to hidden gate. Walk beside stream and cross stile to **golf course**.

❽ Turn **R** along track, cross bridge. Turn **R**. At gate, follow path **L** below golf course. Follow wall to stile on **R**. Descend steps to drive and keep ahead to **Castle Combe**. Turn **L** at **Market Cross** and retrace steps.

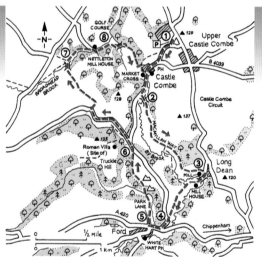

LACOCK *BIRTHPLACE OF PHOTOGRAPHY*

2 miles (3.2km) 1hr **Ascent:** 16ft (5m)
Paths: Field paths and tracks; some road walking, 6 stiles
Suggested map: aqua3 OS Explorer 156 Chippenham & Bradford-on-Avon
Grid reference: ST 918681
Parking: Free car park on edge of Lacock

A stroll around England's finest medieval village with a riverside walk and a visit to Lacock Abbey.

❶ From car park entrance, cross road and follow gravel path into village, passing entrance to **Lacock Abbey** and **Fox Talbot Museum**, housed in beautifully restored 16th-century barn, commemorating William Henry Fox Talbot, pioneer of photography. Abbey began as Augustinian nunnery and was eventually sold to Talbot family. Turn **R** into **East Street** opposite **Red Lion** and walk down to Church Street. Turn **L**, pass timber-framed Sign of the Angel Inn with its medieval layout and magnificent 16th-century doorway and turn **L** into **West Street** opposite George Inn, which dates back to 1361. Shortly, follow road **L** into High Street.

❷ Pass National Trust shop and turn **L** to walk back down along East Street. Turn **R** on Church Street and bear **L** in front of **St Cyriac's Church** with its fine

wagon roof and grandiose Renaissance tomb of Sir William Sharrington, to reach ancient packhorse bridge beside ford across Bide Brook. Follow path beside stream then continue up lane beside cottages to end of road.

❸ Go through kissing gate on your **R** and follow tarmac path across field to gate and pass stone cottages at **Reybridge**. Turn **L** along lane, then **R** again to cross bridge over **River Avon**.

❹ Immediately cross stile on your **R** and bear diagonally **L** to far corner where you rejoin river bank to reach stile. Walk beside river for 300yds (274m) to further stile and cross field following line of telegraph poles to stile. Keep straight on to stile beside gate then head towards stone bridge over Avon.

❺ Climb stile and turn **R** across bridge. Join raised pavement and follow this back into village and car park.

145 SHERSTON COTSWOLDS FRINGE

6½ miles (10.4km) 3hrs **Ascent:** 131ft (40m) ▲
Paths: Field and parkland paths, tracks, metalled lanes, 11 stiles
Suggested map: aqua3 OS Explorer 168 Stroud, Tetbury & Malmesbury
Grid reference: ST 853858
Parking: Sherston High Street; plenty of roadside parking

A pastoral ramble.

❶ On High Street, walk towards village stores, pass **Rattlebone Inn**; turn **R** into Noble Street. Pass Grove Road; take footpath **L** up steps. Cross cul-de-sac; follow footpath to gate then to rear of houses to gate.

❷ Bear diagonally **R** across field to gate and lane. Turn **R**, cross over river and turn **L** ('Foxley'). At end of woodland on L, take footpath **L** through gate. Follow track across **Pinkney Park** to gate.

❸ Keep ahead, bearing **L** beside wall to gate. Follow track ahead towards farm buildings; where drive curves L, turn **R** into farmyard. Keep **R** to join path to stile. Turn **L** around field edge to stile; keep to **L-H** field edge to stile in corner.

❹ Bear half-**R** across field; follow path along field edge above **Avon** to stile. Cross further stile; walk beside fence (**Easton Grey House** L), and head downhill to gate and lane.

❺ Turn **L** into **Easton Grey**. Cross river bridge, turn

R uphill to footpath ahead on reaching entrance gates on R. Cross gravelled area, go through gate and ahead to stile. Continue across next field; descend to follow track into next field.

❻ Turn **R** along field edge; bear off **R** downhill through scrub to footbridge. Keep ahead beside ruin to gate. Cross stile and continue to further stile and gate. Follow track downhill to stile; turn **R** along track (**Fosse Way**). Continue for ½ mile (800m) to road.

❼ Cross over; follow byway to another road. Bear **L** and keep ahead where lane veers L. Follow rutted track for ½ mile (800m), then cross arrowed stile on **R**. Head across field to gate and bear diagonally **R** across large paddock to stile.

❽ Join track, cross racehorse gallop and go through **L-H** gate ahead. Walk through scrub to another gate; keep to track ahead to road. Turn **L** and continue to crossroads. Proceed straight on to next junction; keep ahead, following lane back into **Sherston**.

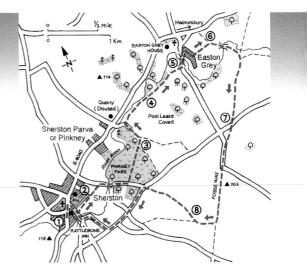

146 BOX BRUNEL'S GREAT TUNNEL

3¼ miles (5.3km) 1hr 45min **Ascent:** 508ft (155m) ▲
Paths: Field and woodland paths, bridle paths, metalled lanes, 15 stiles
Suggested map: aqua3 OS Explorer 156 Chippenham & Bradford-on-Avon
Grid reference: ST 823686
Parking: Village car park near Selwyn Hall

A hilly walk around Box Hill.

❶ Facing recreation ground, walk to **L-H** side of **football pitch**; join track in corner close to railway line. At lane, turn **L**, pass beneath railway, cross bridge and take arrowed footpath, to **R**, before 2nd bridge.

❷ Walk by river, cross footbridge and turn **L**. Cross footbridge and continue to stile. Walk through water-meadows close to river, go through squeeze stile and maintain direction. Shortly, bear **L** to squeeze stile in field corner. Follow **R-H** field edge to stile and keep ahead; pass **Quarryman's Arms**.

❸ Turn **R**, then **R** again at junction. Cross river, pass **Drewett's Mill** and ascend lane. Past **Mills Platt Farm**, take arrowed footpath ahead across stile. Continue uphill to stile; cross **A4**. Ascend steps to lane and proceed straight on up Barnetts Hill. Keep **R** at fork, then **R** again; pass **Quarryman's Arms**.

❹ Keep **L** at fork; continue beside **Box Hill Common** to junction. Take path ahead into woodland. Almost immediately, fork **L** and follow path close to

woodland edge. As it curves R into beech wood, bear **L** and follow path through gap in wall, then **R** at junction of paths.

❺ Follow bridlepath to fork. Keep **L**, then turn **R** at T-junction and take path **L** to stile. Cross further stile and descend into **Thorn Wood**, following stepped path to stile at bottom.

❻ Continue through scrub to stile; turn **R** beside fence to wall stile. Bear **R** to further stile, then **L** uphill to stile and **A361**. Cross and follow drive ahead. Where it curves L by stables, keep ahead along arrowed path to house. Bear **R** up garden steps to drive and continue uphill to T-junction.

❼ Turn **L**; on entering **Henley**, take path **R**, across stile. Follow field edge to stile; descend to allotment and stile. Continue to stile and gate.

❽ Follow drive ahead, bear **L** at garage; take path **R**, into Box. Cross main road and continue to **A4**. Turn **R**, then **L** down access road back to Selwyn Hall.

147 STOURHEAD A GARDENER'S PARADISE

3 miles (4.8km) 1hr 30min **Ascent:** 262ft (80m) ▲
Paths: Parkland and woodland paths and tracks, 2 stiles
Suggested map: aqua3 OS Explorers 142 Shepton Mallet; 143 Warminster & Trowbridge
Grid reference: ST 779340 (on Explorer 142)
Parking: Free National Trust car park at Stourton

A gentle walk through the Stourhead Estate.

❶ Leave car park via exit and turn **L** down lane into Stourton village passing **Spread Eagle Inn**, **St Peter's Church** and entrance to **Stourhead Gardens**. (Note: National Trust members or those paying to visit Gardens and Stourhead House should access village via visitor centre.) Continue along lane, pass beneath **Rock Arch** and turn immediately **R** along track.

❷ Pass beside lake, cross cattle grid and follow track to **Beech Cottage**. Keep **L** along track, to stile beside gate and ignore Stour Valley Way signposted to R. At fork, bear **R** through gate ('Alfred's Tower').

❸ Proceed ahead on grassy track along top of field to further gate and stile, noting **ruins of Tucking Mill** and Cottages on your L. Walk through woodland and take 1st track **R** (by silver National Trust sign) into coniferous woodland. Ascend steeply to reach Broad Ride, wide grassy swathe through woodland.

❹ Turn **L** to gate and Iron-Age **hill fort** at Park Hill.

Do not cross stile, but bear **R** along narrow path beside fence to reach track. Turn **R** and shortly turn sharp **L** downhill through woodland to stile and **Six Wells Bottom**.

❺ Turn **R** and bear diagonally **L** across valley bottom, keeping **L** of lake, heading uphill to gate on edge of woodland. Continue up track to gate and turn immediately **L** up bank to pass **Obelisk**, with **Stourhead House** clearly visible now to your R.

❻ On reaching track, turn **R** towards **Stourhead House**. At junction of tracks, turn **R** through gate and pass in front of house.

❼ Pass underneath gatehouse and turn **L** up lane back to car park. National Trust members and visitors who have paid to enter Stourhead gardens and house can bear **R** just before gatehouse and walk through walled garden and across bridge to return to car park via visitor centre.

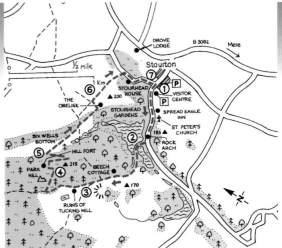

Wiltshire

CORSHAM *A WEALTHY WEAVING TOWN*

4 miles (6.4km) 2hrs **Ascent:** 114ft (35m)
Paths: Field paths and country lanes, 10 stiles
Suggested map: aqua3 OS Explorer 156 Chippenham & Bradford on Avon
Grid reference: ST 871704
Parking: Long stay car park in Newlands Lane

Explore this unexpected architectural town and adjacent Corsham Park.

① Turn **L** out of car park, then **L** again along Post Office Lane to High Street. Turn **L**, pass **tourist information centre** and turn **R** into Church Street. Pass impressive entrance to **Corsham Court** and enter St Bartholomew's churchyard.

② Follow path **L** to gate; walk ahead to join main path across **Corsham Park**. Turn **L**; walk along south side of park, passing **Corsham Lake**, to stile and gate. Keep ahead on fenced path beside track to kissing gate and proceed across field to stile and lane.

③ Turn **L**, pass **Park Farm**, splendid stone farmhouse on **L**, and shortly take waymarked footpath **R** along drive to pass **Rose and Unicorn House**. Cross stile and follow **R-H** field edge to stile, then bear half-**L** to stone stile in field corner. Ignore path arrowed **R** and head straight across field to further stile and lane.

④ Take footpath opposite, bearing half-**L** to stone stile to **L** of **cottage**. Maintain direction and pass through field entrance to follow path along **L-H** side of field to stile in corner. Turn **L** along road for ½ mile (800m) to **A4**.

⑤ Go through gate in wall on **L** and follow worn path **R**, across centre of parkland pasture to metal kissing gate. Proceed ahead to reach kissing gate on edge of woodland. Follow wide path to further gate and bear half-**R** to stile.

⑥ Keep ahead on worn path across field and along field edge to gate. Continue to further gate with fine views **R** to **Corsham Court**. Follow path **R** along field edge, then where it curves **R**, bear **L** to join path beside churchyard wall to stile.

⑦ Turn **L** down avenue of trees to gate and town centre (**almshouses** on **L**). Turn **R** along Pickwick Road, then **R** again along pedestrianised High Street. Turn **L** back along Post Office Lane to car park.

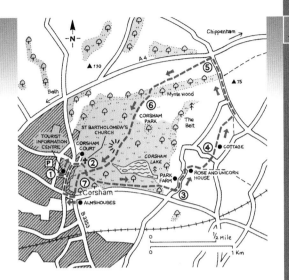

LONGLEAT *WOODLAND AND WILDLIFE*

5¼ miles (8.4km) 2hrs 30min (longer if visiting attractions) **Ascent:** 508ft (155m)
Paths: Field, woodland and parkland paths, 4 stiles
Suggested map: aqua3 OS Explorer 143 Warminster & Trowbridge
Grid reference: ST 827422
Parking: Heaven's Gate car park, Longleat Estate

Glorious woodland and parkland walking.

① Cross road and follow path into trees. Disregard straight track **L**, bear **R**, then **L** along wide worn path through mixed woodland to double gates and reach viewpoint at **Heaven's Gate**.

② Facing **Longleat**, go through gate in **L-H** corner. Shortly, at crossing of paths, turn **R**, then keep **R** at fork and head downhill through woodland to metalled drive by thatched **cottage**. Turn **R**, keeping ahead where drive bears **L**; shortly follow path **L**, heading downhill close to woodland edge to pass between garage and cottage to lane.

③ Turn **L** on **White Street** to crossroads; turn **R** downhill. Ascend past **church** to T-junction; turn **R**. Turn **L** opposite **school**; follow bridleway up track and between sheds to gate. Bear **L** with track, pass through 2 gates; bear slightly **R** to stile on woodland edge.

④ Follow path through copse then bear off **R** diagonally downhill to stile and gate. Turn **L** along field edge to reach track. Turn **R**, go through gate beside thatched cottage and follow metalled lane (**Pottle Street**). In 200yds (183m), cross stile on **R** and field to stile and rejoin lane.

⑤ Turn **R** and follow quiet lane to crossroads. Proceed straight across and follow road through **Horningsham** village, passing thatched chapel, to crossroads opposite **Bath Arms**.

⑥ Go straight across crossroads, walk down estate drive and pass through gatehouse arch into **Longleat Park**. With house ahead, walk beside metalled drive with lakes and weirs to **R**. At T-junction in front of house, keep ahead **L** past house and follow path **L** to reach other tourist attractions.

⑦ For main route, turn **R** and walk beside drive, heading uphill through **Deer Park**. Begin to climb steeply, then take metalled drive **R** beyond white barrier. Ascend **Prospect Hill** and reach **Heaven's Gate** viewpoint. Retrace steps back to car park.

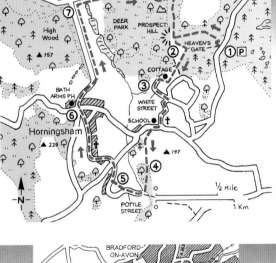

BRADFORD-ON-AVON *A MINIATURE BATH*

3½ miles (5.7km) 1hr 45min **Ascent:** 164ft (50m)
Paths: Tow path, field and woodland paths, metalled lanes
Suggested map: aqua3 OS Explorers 142 Shepton Mallet;156 Chippenham & Bradford on Avon
Grid reference: ST 824606 (on Explorer 156)
Parking: Bradford-on-Avon Station car park (charge)

Combine a visit to this enchanting riverside town with a canal-side stroll.

① Walk to end of car park, away from station, and follow path **L** beneath railway and beside River Avon. Enter **Barton Farm Country Park** and keep to path across grassy area to information board. Here you can visit craft shops in former medieval farm buildings and marvel at great beams and rafters of Bradford-on-Avon's magnificent tithe barn, 2nd largest in Britain. With packhorse bridge **R**, keep ahead to **R** of **tithe barn** to **Kennet and Avon Canal**.

② Turn **R** along tow path. Cross bridge over canal in ½ mile (800m) and follow path **R** to footbridge and stile. Proceed along **R-H** field edge to further stile, then bear diagonally **L** uphill away from canal to kissing gate.

③ Follow path through edge of woodland. Keep to path as it bears **L** uphill through trees to reach metalled lane. Turn **R** and walk steeply downhill to **Avoncliff** and canal.

④ Don't cross aqueduct, instead pass Mad Hatter Tea Rooms, descend steps on your **R** and pass beneath canal. Keep **R** by **Cross Guns** and join tow path towards Bradford-on-Avon. Continue for ¾ mile (1.2km) to bridge passed on your outward route.

⑤ Bear off **L** downhill along metalled track and follow it beside River Avon back into **Barton Farm Country Park**. Cross packhorse bridge and railway to Barton Orchard.

⑥ Follow alleyway to Church Street and continue ahead to pass **Holy Trinity Church** and **Saxon Church of St Laurence**, jewel in Bradford-on-Avon's crown and not to be missed. Founded by St Aldhelm, Abbot of Malmesbury in AD 700, this building dates back to 10th century. Cross footbridge and walk through St Margaret's car park to road. Turn **R**, then **R** again back into station car park.

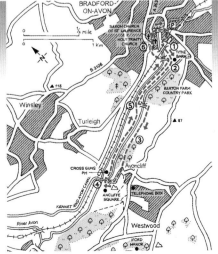

151 BRAMSHOTT *FOLLOWING FLORA'S FOOTSTEPS*

4 miles (6.4km) 2hrs **Ascent:** 295ft (90m) ▲

Paths: Woodland paths and heathland tracks, 3 stiles

Suggested map: aqua3 OS Explorer 133 Haslemere & Petersfield

Grid reference: SU 855336

Parking: Unsurfaced car park on edge of Bramshott Common

This heath and woodland beauty spot was much loved by writer Flora Thompson.

❶ From car park, take path beyond low wooden barrier. Gradually descend. At bottom, main bridleway (blue arrow) directs you L along sunken track. Ignore this if wet and muddy and climb path ahead beneath trees. At fork, keep L down to river and footbridge.

❷ Cross bridge. Turn R along footpath parallel with river. Pass **wishing well** and house. Proceed through valley bottom to L of 3 **ponds**, to reach lane by ford.

❸ Just before lane, turn L, pass memorial stone and steeply ascend through woodland. As it levels out, cross path, then track. Shortly merge with gravel track. Keep L, pass bridleway on L, then, where track begins to curve L downhill, keep ahead through trees.

❹ Cross path. In a few paces, at broad sandy track bordering open heathland, turn R. On reaching fork, bear L over common. Path soon widens and descends to T-junction (fingerpost visible on R at next junction).

❺ Turn L. Follow open heathland trail, edged by bracken and gorse, and eventually merge with wider sandy trail. Keep L then, on reaching bench and junction of ways on the common fringe, proceed ahead through mixed woodland.

❻ At crossing of paths by line of telegraph poles, turn L with bridleway signs. Keep ahead at junction of paths, following bridleway (blue arrow) close to woodland fringe. Stay with telegraph poles, ignoring bridleway R as both merge later. Beyond this point ignore bridleway R; continue to crossing of bridleways.

❼ Turn R; keep straight on at next crossing of routes, following footpath marker alongside a garden to stile on woodland edge. Walk along the L-H edge of pasture to stile in field corner.

❽ Steeply descend into woodland and cross gravel track to reach stile. At track beyond, turn R downhill to river and footbridge encountered on outward route. Retrace your steps back to car park.

152 THE HANGERS *LOOKING FOR EDWARD THOMAS*

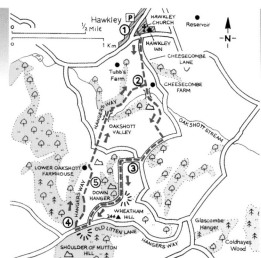

3 miles (4.8km) 2hrs **Ascent:** 682ft (208m) ▲

Paths: Field and woodland paths, rutted, wet and muddy tracks (in winter) and short stretches of road, 29 stiles

Suggested map: aqua3 OS Explorer 133 Haslemere & Petersfield

Grid reference: SU 746291

Parking: By village green and church in Hawkley

Explore the beech-clad hills and vales that so inspired Hampshire's great poet.

❶ With your back to **Hawkley** church, walk L beside green to road junction. With **Hawkley Inn** to your L, cross straight over down Cheesecombe Farm Lane ('Hangers Way'). Shortly, bear off R along concrete path. Descend to stile and keep straight on at fork of paths, with **Cheesecombe Farm** to L.

❷ Cross **Oakshott Stream** and keep L along field edge beside woodland. Steeply ascend to stile, keep R to further stile, then turn L beside fence and drop down to track. Turn R, to reach lane, then R again for 55yds (50m) to take waymarked right of way beside Wheatham Hill House.

❸ Climb long and steep, chalky track up through **Down Hanger** (be warned this gets very wet and muddy), with views unfolding east along the South Downs. At top of **Wheatham Hill**, turn R at T-junction

of tracks along **Old Litten Lane**. In 300yds (274m), take **Hangers Way** right over stile. For Edward Thomas memorial stone and South Downs views, continue along track for 200yds (183m) and turn L with waymarker. Pass beside wooden barrier and drop down to clearing on **Shoulder of Mutton Hill**.

❹ On return route, follow short section of **Hangers Way**, this is a 21-mile (33.6km) long-distance trail that traverses East Hampshire, from Queen Elizabeth Country Park to Alton. Follow trail as it descends through edge of beech wood and steeply down across lush meadowland, eventually joining drive to **Lower Oakshott Farmhouse** and road.

❺ Turn R, then L over stile and follow defined **Hangers Way** path through Oakshott Valley, crossing stiles, plank bridges and delightful meadows to reach junction of paths before **Cheesecombe Farm**. Turn L to stile and retrace your steps back to **Hawkley**.

153 BUTSER *AN ANCIENT FARM*

6¾ miles (10.9km) 3hrs **Ascent:** 756ft (252m) ▲

Paths: Woodland paths, bridleways and forest tracks, 4 stiles

Suggested map: aqua3 OS Explorer 120 Chichester

Grid reference: SU 718185

Parking: Large pay-and-display car park at country park

Discover a unique archaeological farmstead.

❶ From car park, follow Woodland Trail (green-topped posts) to R. On reaching road, turn R then L on to gravel path. Walk up slope and turn R along **South Downs Way**. Descend to metalled track. Turn L and immediately fork R down track.

❷ Gently climb between fields, bridleway soon curving L around woodland; gradually bear R between fields, noting 18th-century windmill on skyline to R.

❸ At road, turn R to visit **Butser Ancient Farm**, or turn L and follow road (some blind bends) for ½ mile (800m) into **Chalton**. Turn L at junction, ('Ditcham').

❹ At fork, bear L along byway. Continue between fields; soon descend through trees to join road. Turn L. Walk parallel to railway for ¼ mile (400m), to stile on R. Bear half-L across field and enter woodland.

❺ At junction of paths continue ahead and then steadily climb wide forest track. On descent, fork L then almost immediately fork R down narrow

signposted footpath. Climb stile and continue down to road (**South Downs Way**).

❻ Turn R then, in 100yds (91m), take footpath L and head steeply down through trees to stile. Bear half-R across field to stile by gate then follow path round to L, passing pond, into **Buriton**.

❼ Turn L along High Street then, just past post office, take footpath L. Go round village hall and continue to reach gate. Very carefully cross railway line. Go through gate; follow path to junction with bridleway. Turn R and steeply ascend to road. Cross straight over into **Hall's Hill car park**.

❽ Go through gate and up track (**South Downs Way**) into Queen Elizabeth Country Park. Gradually ascend then, just after track merges from R, fork R and go through gate. Go through **Benhams Bushes car park**, follow short stretch of road then bear L with **South Downs Way**. Rejoin road at Bottom Fields. Turn R, (**Hangers Way**) and retrace outward route.

Hampshire

CHAWTON JANE AUSTEN'S INSPIRATION

5 miles (8km) 2hrs 30min **Ascent:** 134ft (41m) ▲
Paths: Field paths, old railway track, some road walking, 16 stiles
Suggested map: aqua3 OS Explorer 133 Haslemere & Petersfield
Grid reference: SU 708375
Parking: Free village car park opposite Jane Austen's House

A gentle ramble around the pastoral countryside that surrounds Chawton.

❶ Turn **L** out of car park, opposite **Jane Austen's House**. Walk along dead-end lane, pass **school**, then **R** into **Ferney Close**. Keeping to **L**, bear **L** along path beside Ferney Bungalow to stile. Continue along **L-H** field edge to stile and cross (with care) **A32**.

❷ Climb steps and stile; walk along **L-H** field edge, leading to stile on **L**. Through copse, following path **R**, then **L** between fields to reach track (**former railway track bed**). Keep ahead at crossing of paths (track now earth and shaded by trees).

❸ On reaching bridge, bear **L** with main path towards silos, path soon passing behind them to reach stile. Cross **A32**; join track leading to **Manor Farm**. At crossing of tracks, by **play area**, turn **R**. Take narrow path **L** at bottom of play area to reach track.

❹ Turn **R** into lane in **Upper Farringdon**, opposite **Massey's Folly**. Turn **L** into churchyard and leave by main gate, turning **L** along lane. Keep ahead along **Gaston Lane** for ½ mile (800m) to track on **L**.

❺ Turn **L** then, shortly, take grassy track **R** to gate; climb stile ahead into open pasture. Keep **R** of brook; cross stile; then bridge over **brook** on **L**. Keep going, with brook to **R**, to stile at end of field.

❻ Turn immediately **L**. Go through gate to join permissive path between fences. Follow it **R**, towards **Whitehouse Farm**. At junction of paths by track, turn **L** through gate and keep to **R-H** field edge to gate.

❼ Bear **R** across field to stiles set in hedge; maintain direction across 3 more fields and stiles towards **Eastfield Farm**. Skirt round farm via yellow-topped squeeze stiles through several fields to reach stile beside woodland, beyond corrugated iron shed.

❽ Go through copse to stile. Bear half-**L** across field to further stile. Continue ahead to stile in wall. Walk along narrow footpath back to main village street. Turn **L** back to car park.

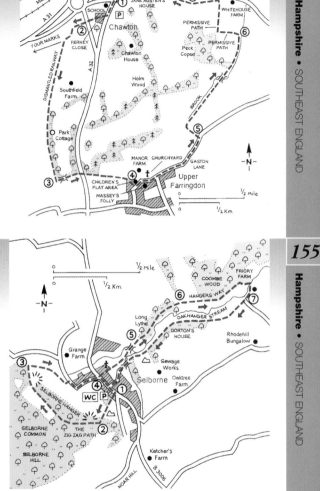

SELBORNE IN THE FOOTSTEPS OF GILBERT WHITE

3½ miles (5.7km) 1hr 30min **Ascent:** 361ft (110m) ▲
Paths: Woodland, field paths, stretch of metalled road, 7 stiles
Suggested map: aqua3 OS Explorer 133 Haslemere & Petersfield
Grid reference: SU 741334
Parking: Free National Trust car park behind Selborne Arms

Enjoy the beech hangers that inspired the eminent naturalist.

❶ Take arrowed footpath ('Zig-Zag Path & Hangers') by car park entrance and gently ascend to gate at base of **Selborne Hill** & **Common**. Bear **L** to follow impressive **Zig-Zag** path uphill, pausing at regular intervals to catch your breath and to admire unfolding views across village.

❷ At top, take stepped path **R**. After few paces, keep **R** at fork to follow lower path through beech hangers. Shortly, look out for metal bench, by path ascending from **R** – savour views. Continue along path, descending to junction of paths, by National Trust sign.

❸ Turn **R** downhill along track then, where this curves **L**, bear **R** across stile into pasture. Keep to **L-H** edge, cross 3 more stiles and follow path to lane. Turn **R** and follow it back into village, opposite church. Turn **L** along B3006 road for The Wakes and car park, if you wish to cut walk short.

❹ Cross B road and follow Hangers Way sign through churchyard to gate. Follow defined path to footbridge over **Oakhanger Stream**.

❺ Keep to **Hangers Way** through gate and along edge of meadowland to gate, then pass through stretch of woodland to kissing gate and fork of paths.

❻ Proceed straight ahead (yellow arrow), leaving **Hangers Way**. Eventually pass alongside fence to stile on edge of **Coombe Wood**. Keep close to woodland fringe to stile, then bear **L** along field edge to stile and turn **R** along bridleway towards **Priory Farm**. Keep to track through farmyard to metalled drive.

❼ After few paces, where it curves **L**, bear **R** along track beside bungalow. Cross stile and follow grassy track uphill along field edge, through gate, eventually reaching gate and woodland. Follow track (can be muddy) through beech woodland. Leave wood, passing house called **Dorton's**, and climb lane steeply back to **Selborne**, turning **L** for car park.

ODIHAM A CASTLE AND A CANAL

4 miles (6.4km) 2hrs **Ascent:** 147ft (45m) ▲
Paths: Canal tow path, field edge and woodland, 20 stiles
Suggested map: aqua3 OS Explorer 144 Basingstoke, Alton & Whitchurch
Grid reference: SU 740510
Parking: Odiham High Street or signed pay-and-display car parks

A lovely walk combining the elegant country town of Odiham with a castle and the Basingstoke Canal.

❶ Head east along High Street and then take **L** fork, London Road, leading to **Basingstoke Canal**. Pass **Water Witch pub** and cross bridge, then drop down **L** to walk along tow path. Follow waterway parallel with A287 for just over 1 mile (1.6km) to North Warnborough.

❷ Pass **Jolly Miller pub** and go under road bridge. Keep to tow path, passing swing bridge, then in 300yds (274m) pass ruins of **Odiham Castle** (or King John's Castle) on your **R**. Pass over **River Whitewater** and continue for ½ mile (800m) to Greywell Tunnel, famous for its roosting bat population and best visited at dusk. Take path **L** over its portal and drop down to road.

❸ Turn **R** into **Greywell**, then **L** at junction to pass **Fox and Goose pub**. Walk through village and turn **L** through lychgate to **St Mary's Church**. Walk down path to church and turn **L** through gate opposite. Keep to **R-H** field edge then, in 200yds (183m), turn **L** to stile and bridge over **River Whitewater** and enter Greywell Moors Nature Reserve.

❹ Walk through wood, passing memorial to the eminent biologist EC Wallace, and keep ahead across 2 stiles in field. Proceed in easterly direction across field to stile and road. Turn **L** for 50yds (46m), then **R** with footpath sign. Walk along **L-H** field edge to stile, then bear diagonally across paddock to stile and maintain direction across next field to further stile.

❺ Cross road to stile opposite and walk across field, heading to **R** of 3 chimneys, to stile. Join path alongside **school** and then turn **R** to **West Street**. Turn **L**, passing **school**, then as road veers **L**, bear **R** up West Street to roundabout. Go straight over and back along Odiham High Street.

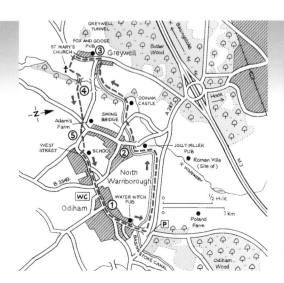

Hampshire

Hampshire • SOUTHEAST ENGLAND

157 SOUTHWICK *PORTS DOWN'S FORTRESS FOLLIES*

6 miles (9.7km) 3hrs Ascent: 390ft (119m)

Paths: Field, woodland paths and stretches of road, 17 stiles
Suggested map: aqua3 OS Explorer 119 Meon Valley
Grid reference: SU 627085
Parking: Free car park by Southwick Village Hall, close to HMS *Dryad*

A ramble from Southwick to Fort Nelson.

❶ From car park, turn **R** to junction and **L** to roundabout. Go straight over, taking narrow lane for **Portchester**. Climb steeply, bearing **R** by quarry then, where road veers sharp **L**, take lane **R**.

❷ Descend for 150yds (137m). Go **L** through gap in hedge. Take footpath diagonally across field, (head just to **R** of **Nelson's Monument**). Keep ahead across next field to stile and lane. Turn **L**, pass **Nelson's Monument**, then **R** at crossroads ('**Fort Nelson**').

❸ Visit fort. Retrace route back to Monument and continue down lane for 50yds (46m). Take footpath **L** over stile. Head towards **R** corner of fort, cross stile and skirt edge of fort to further stile. Bear half-**R** across field, between house and pylon, to road.

❹ Turn **R** downhill, then **R** again at next junction. After 200yds (183m) bear **L** through **St Nicholas's churchyard**. Rejoin road; continue past barns and pond. Shortly, beside lay-by, bear **L** over stile. Follow footpath along **L-H** field edge. Continue on between fields, then by **Grub Coppice** to cross bridge.

❺ Climb stile, keep to **R-H** field edge to stile on **R**. Cross next stile. Keep to **L-H** field edge to further stile. Turn **L** over stile by stream and bear **R**, around field edge to stile and road. Cross stile opposite. Walk along **R-H** field edge close to stream. Follow field boundary **L**; shortly bear **R** across bridge and stile to join track.

❻ Go between farm buildings, through gate and bear **L** to **B2177**. Cross and take footpath **R** on track. It becomes grassy and bears **R** into woodland. Take 2nd footpath **R**, emerge from trees and head across narrow field. Cross bridge, bear **R**, then half-**L** making for large oak. Swing **L** and descend steps to lane.

❼ Cross and bear half-**R** across field towards church tower. Cross bridge and continue through plantation. Beyond another bridge, walk up drive to road. Turn **L** then, **R** into Southwick. Keep **L** at junction and **L** again to car park.

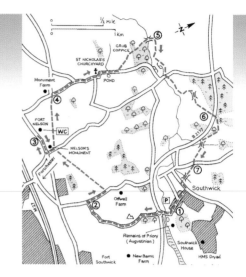

158 HAMBLEDON *THE CRADLE OF CRICKET*

6 miles (9.7km) 2hrs 45min Ascent: 420ft (140m)

Paths: Field paths, farm tracks and stretches of road, 18 stiles
Suggested map: aqua3 OS Explorer 119 Meon Valley
Grid reference: SU 646150
Parking: Street parking near Hambledon village centre

To Hambledon Cricket Club.

❶ From village hall turn **L**. Turn **L** opposite **Old Post Office** to church. Follow footpath to **R**, through churchyard to Church Lane. Take road opposite (**R** of school). Where it turns **L**, stay on waymarked footpath.

❷ Cross drive and keep ahead between fences (**Hambledon Vineyard** to **L**). At track, bear **L**. In 50yds (46m) proceed on footpath. In 50yds (46m), cross stile on **R**. Head towards **R-H** edge of trees opposite.

❸ Climb stile. Bear **R** through trees into field. Turn **L** along field edge. In 20yds (18m), bear diagonally **R** to corner of fenced copse. Continue across field towards 2 aerials. Cross road via stiles to enter **Ridge Meadow** (**Hambledon Cricket Club**).

❹ Keep to **R-H** edge of ground; exit in corner on path (sometimes overgrown). Shortly, pass by wood. Where path bears **L**, go **R** through hedge, by waymarker. Cross field in northeasterly direction to stile. Join track leading to **Hermitage Farm**. Follow to road.

❺ Turn **R** for ½ mile (800m) to where footpath crosses road. Turn **L** through gate; bear **L** around field edge to stile. Turn sharp **R** along edge of next field; maintain direction across 2 stiles to lane. Turn **R** to **Bat and Ball**, **cricket ground** and crossroads.

❻ Turn **R**. In 250yds (229m), opposite road to **Chidden**, cross stile **L**. Head uphill across field to stile. Turn **R** on track, ('**Monarch's Way**'). Follow it **L** over **Broadhalfpenny Down** to **Scotland Cottage**. Where drive bears **R**, stay on path. Descend to track. Turn **R**.

❼ Bear **L** at fork. In 250yds (229m), at T-junction, turn **R** to **Glidden Farm**. Beyond gate, turn **L** around slurry pit; walk down track. Cross stile; pass barn; keeping to track across fields and stiles. Pass beneath power cables; cross track; turn **L** to stile. Cross paddock and bear to **L** of fir trees.

❽ Climb stile to rear of outbuildings (**Stud Farm**) on to access road. Bear **R** to road. Turn **R**. Keep **L** downhill to **Hambledon**. Turn **L** through village to hall.

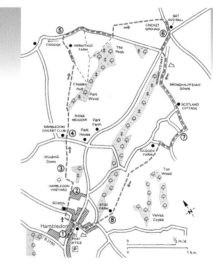

159 ALRESFORD *A WATERCRESS WALK*

4 miles (6.4km) 1hr 45min Ascent: 240ft (73m)

Paths: Riverside paths, tracks, field, woodland paths and roads
Suggested map: aqua3 OS Explorer 132 Winchester
Grid reference: SU 588325
Parking: Pay-and-display car park off Station Road, New Alresford

Exploring New Alresford – the 'new' market town at the heart of Hampshire's watercress industry.

❶ From car park walk down **Station Road** to T-junction with **West Street**. Turn **R** then **L** down **Broad Street**. This is a sumptuous street, which is lined with limes and elegant colour-washed houses. Mary Russell Mitford, authoress of *Our Village*, was born at number 27 in 1787. Keep **L** at bottom of road and proceed along **Mill Lane**. Halfway down follow Wayfarer's Walk banner **L** and soon join river bank and pass **Fulling Mill Cottage** straddling the **River Arle**. It is 300 years old and it was where the homespun wool was scoured and washed, pounded with mallets, stretched, brushed and sheared.

❷ Continue to bottom of Dean Lane and then keep along riverside path. Cross footbridge over **River Arle**, and drop down to pass some cottages. Shortly, cross lane on to wide track and soon follow it as it leads gently downhill to reach junction of tracks. Bear **R** uphill to lane.

❸ Turn **L**, descend to **Fobdown Farm** and take track on **R** beside the farm buildings. On reaching T-junction of tracks, turn **R** and follow established track for just over ½ mile (800m), gently descending into **Old Alresford**.

❹ Pass **watercress beds** on your **R** and follow (now metalled) lane **L**, past houses. Alresford has ideal conditions for growing watercress and is 'Watercress Capital' of England and you'll see several watercress beds. Turn **R** beside the green to **B3046**. Cross straight over and follow pavement right to reach lane opposite 18th-century **St Mary's Church**.

❺ After you have visited the church, cross road and turn **L** along pavement to grass triangle by junction. Bear **L** along lane and take footpath ahead over stream and beside watercress beds back to **Mill Lane** and **Broad Street**.

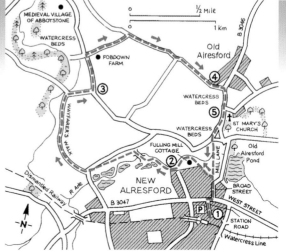

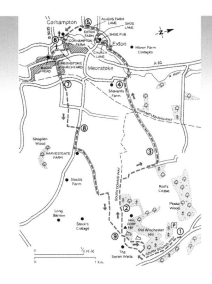

WINCHESTER *MEON VALLEY MEANDER*

5½ miles (8.8km) 2hrs 15min **Ascent:** 472ft (144m)
Paths: Field paths, footpaths, tracks and sections of road, 9 stiles
Suggested map: aqua3 OS Explorer 119 Meon Valley
Grid reference: SU 645214
Parking: English Nature car park off Old Winchester Hill Lane

An exhilarating walk and a favourite haunt of historians and naturalists

1 From car park go through gate on to downland. Turn **L** between information boards. Follow path around reserve perimeter. Merge with **South Downs Way** (**SDW**). Bear **R** towards **hill fort**. Go through gate, follow **SDW** markers **L**, then **R** over centre of **hill fort**.

2 Descend and keep **L** at fork by rampart, heading downhill to stile. Pass beneath yew trees and beside gate. Continue downhill; walk along edge of field then bear **L** on to track. At junction turn **L** along track.

3 When it enters field, proceed. Go under **disused railway** (in winter use steps). Continue to T-junction.

4 Bear **R** and cross footbridge over **River Meon** to **A32**. Cross over into **Church Lane** and continue into **Exton**. Turn **L** along Shoe Lane; **R** at junction beyond **Shoe pub**; shortly turn **L** (**Allens Farm Lane**).

5 At sharp R-H bend, keep ahead along path beside **Exton Farm**. Go through gate; bear **L** along R-H edge

of paddocks to stile. Pass beside **Corhampton Farm** and **Church**, bearing **L** to **A32**.

6 Cross over. Walk **L** along pavement; turn **R** by shop. Take metalled path beside last house on **R** and enter churchyard. Turn **L** along lane to T-junction beside **Bucks Head**. Turn **L**, then **L** again at junction. Follow lane **R** (Pound Lane); soon cross old railway.

7 At crossroads climb stile on **L**. Proceed ahead across field; pass behind gardens, eventually reaching stile and lane. Climb stile opposite and keep to R-H field edge to stile. Maintain direction to stile, then bear diagonally **L** towards house and road.

8 Turn **R**. Take track **L** beside **Harvestgate Farm**. At top, bear **L** uphill along field edge then sharp **R** following path by hedge into next field. Over stile on **L** into Nature Reserve. Ascend steeply to ramparts.

9 Cross stile and go **R** to join outward route by fort entrance. Go through gate opposite information board, follow path. Bear **R** to gate; retrace steps to car park.

TICHBORNE *A CIVIL WAR BATTLEFIELD*

6½ miles (10.4km) 3hrs **Ascent:** 426ft (130m)
Paths: Field paths, downland tracks and some road walking
Suggested map: aqua3 OS Explorer 132 Winchester
Grid reference: SU 583286
Parking: Cheriton. Roadside parking on village lane east of B3046

A gentle walk across a Civil War battlefield and through the Itchen Valley.

1 From village lane, cross small bridge near Freeman's Yard; bear **R** in front of school. Just beyond house ('Martyrwell'), turn **L** along narrow fenced path, leave village via stile. Turn **R** around field edge to stile and crossing of paths.

2 Proceed along grassy track to crossing of routes. Fields to **R** were site of **Battle of Cheriton** (1644). Turn **L** downhill and keep to track to lane by barn.

3 Cross lane and walk along farm track. Path merges from **L**, beyond which you climb to junction of paths. With views across Itchen Valley, turn **L** downhill, following track to **B3046**.

4 Turn **R** then, in few paces, cross road and take path **L**, across field parallel with river. Cross stile and proceed to stile on edge of copse. Walk through trees, cross stile and keep to L-H edge of pasture (**Tichborne House** is to **L**) to stile by drive entrance.

5 Turn **R**; keep ahead. Where metalled road curves **L**, stay on track. Just before woodland, bear **R** on grassy track into field. Walk along L-H edge, then R-H edge of adjacent field. Cross 2 stiles to join bridleway.

6 Turn **L**, pass **Vernal Farm**. Cross **River Itchen** to lane. Take path opposite, uphill along field edge. In top L-H corner, follow track **L** into field. Turn **L** along field edge, downhill towards **Tichborne church**. Ignore tracks **R** and **L**, continue to lane (**Tichborne Arms L**).

7 Just before lane, take path **L** uphill to church. On leaving church, follow access lane downhill to T-junction. Turn **R** and follow lane for 1 mile (1.6km), close to **Tichborne Park** and river, to **Cheriton Mill**.

8 Follow **Wayfarer's Walk R**, beside **mill** to gate. Walk in front of cottage to stile and continue ahead parallel with river. Cross double stiles and proceed to stile by gate. Continue to further stile; turn **L** along lane to **B3046** in **Cheriton**. Cross over to reach village lane and car park.

WINCHESTER *ALFRED'S ANCIENT CAPITAL*

3½ miles (5.7km) 1hr 30min **Ascent:** 499ft (152m)
Paths: Established riverside paths through water-meadows, 3 stiles
Suggested map: aqua3 OS Explorer 132 Winchester
Grid reference: SU 486294
Parking: Pay-and-display car parks in city centre

Winchester's historic streets, Cathedral Close and the beautiful Itchen Valley.

1 From King Alfred's statue on **Broadway**, walk towards city centre, passing **Guildhall** (tourist information centre) on **L**. Join High Street, then in 100yds (91m), turn **L** along Market Street. Continue ahead into Cathedral Close to pass cathedral main door.

2 Turn **L** down cloister, then **R** through Close ('**Wolvesey Castle**'), to Cheyney Court and exit via Prior's Gate. Turn **L** though Kingsgate, with tiny **Church of St Swithun** above, then bear **L** down **College Street** and shortly pass entrance to **Winchester College**. Beyond road barrier, bear **R** along College Walk then turn **R** at end of wall, along track.

3 Go **L** through gate by private entrance to **College**. Follow path beside **River Itchen** for ½ mile (800m) to gate and road. Cross over and follow gravel path, alongside tributary, to gate and cross open meadow towards **Hospital of St Cross**.

4 Keep **L** alongside wall and through avenue of trees to stile. Proceed ahead along gravel path to 2 further stiles and join farm track leading to road. Turn **L** and walk length of now gated road (traffic-free), crossing **River Itchen** to reach junction of paths by **M3**.

5 Turn **L** along path. Pass gate on **R** (access to **St Catherine's Hill**). Keep **L** at fork and drop down to follow narrow path by **Itchen Navigation**. Go through car park to road.

6 Turn **L** across bridge and take footpath immediately **R**. Keep to path beside water, disregarding path **L** (College nature reserve). Soon cross bridge by rowing sheds to join metalled track.

7 Turn **L**, then **L** again at road. Follow road **L** along College Walk then bear **R** at end ('Riverside Walk'). Pass Old Bishops Palace (**Wolvesey Castle**) and follow metalled path beside Itchen and up steps to Bridge Street, opposite **City Mill** (National Trust). Turn **L** back to King Alfred's statue.

Hampshire

163 BURSLEDON *THE HAMBLE ESTUARY*

6 miles (9.7km) 3hrs **Ascent:** 164ft (50m)
Paths: Riverside, field and woodland paths, some stretches of road
Suggested map: aqua3 OS Outdoor Leisure 22 New Forest
Grid reference: SU 485067
Parking: Pay-and-display car park by Quay in Hamble

Exploring both sides of the Hamble estuary.
1 From quayside car park, walk to pontoon and take passenger ferry across estuary to **Warsash** (weather permitting Monday–Friday 7am–5pm; Saturday, Sunday 9am–6pm). Turn **L** along raised gravel path beside estuary and mudflats. Cross footbridge and continue to gravelled parking area. During exceptionally high tides path may flood, so walk through car park and rejoin it by marina.
2 At boatyard, keep **R** of boat shed. Bear **L** beyond, between shed and TS Marina. Bear **R** in front of sales office to rejoin path. Reach lane, turn **L**, pass **Victory Cottages** (R). Continue by Moody's Boatyard to A27.
3 Turn **L** and cross **Bursledon Bridge**. (Turn **R** before bridge to visit **Bursledon Brickworks**.) Pass beneath railway and turn **L** ('the Station'). Turn **L** into Station Road, then **L** again into station car park ('**Jolly Sailor**'). Climb steep path to road. Turn **L** at junction, then **L** again to reach pub.

4 Return along lane and fork **L** along High Street into Old Bursledon. Pause at excellent **viewpoint** at **Hacketts Marsh**, then bear **L** at **telephone box** along High Street. Pass Vine Inn and **Salters Lane**, then at R bend, bear **L** by Thatched Cottage along footpath.
5 Join metalled lane by drive to Coach House then, as lane curves L, continue beside house (Woodlands), following path downhill to stream. Proceed uphill through woodland (**Mallards Moor**). At junction of paths on woodland fringe bear **L** with bridleway. At concrete road bear **R**, then **L** to join fenced path.
6 Cross **railway bridge** and soon pass barrier to road. Keep **L** round sharp L-H bend. Look out for waymarked footpath on **R** and follow path behind houses for ½ mile (800m).
7 Join metalled path, passing modern housing to road. Follow to Hamble Lane. Turn **L** on to High Street. At roundabout, bear **R** on Lower High Street to Quay and car park.

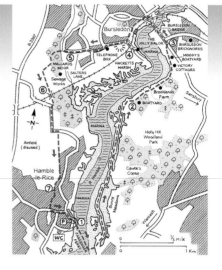

164 ROMSEY *A GRAND ABBEY*

5½ miles (8.8km) 2hrs 30min **Ascent:** 120ft (40m)
Paths: Tow path, field and woodland paths, some roads, 14 stiles
Suggested map: aqua3 OS Explorer 131 Romsey, Andover & Test Valley
Grid reference: SU 352212
Parking: Romsey town centre, several pay-and-display car parks

Explore a market town and the Test Valley.
1 From Market Square head east along the Hundred and continue into Winchester Road. At roundabout, turn **L** up steps to join footpath to **Timsbury**. Walk alongside old canal as it passes under railway and then road bridge, and leave town into open meadowland.
2 At crossing of paths (with bridge R), turn **L** and walk along **L-H** field edge. Bear **R** across bridges in corner and follow path beside stream to **River Test**. Turn **L** along river bank, cross wooden bridge and walk alongside opposite bank to stile and track by bridge and house. Turn **R** to A3057 and turn **R**.
3 Follow pavement and cross **Test**, then take footpath immediately **R** alongside river. Pass bridge, then follow official diversion **L** around house to track. Turn **L** to main road and **Duke's Head** on L.
4 Cross road to join B3084, ('**Roke Manor**'). Carefully walk along this road, which is often busy (some verges) for ½ mile (800m), then just beyond

railway bridge, fork **L** for **Roke Manor**. Pass entrance to **Manor** and take drive on L.
5 Pass Roke Manor Farm, then on nearing **Manor** bear half-**R** along road for 100yds (91m). Take footpath **R** (can be overgrown) and shortly bear **R** through hedge, then **L** around field. Skirt copse on L to locate **Test Way** sign and turn **L** through gate.
6 Walk into **Squabb Wood** on bracken-lined path, cross 2 plank bridges and reach junction of paths. Keep **L** with **Test Way** and proceed through wood, via plank bridges and stiles, looking out for **Test Way** markers.
7 Leave wood and bear half-**R** across field to stiles and footbridge, then bear slightly **R** to further stiles and footbridge. Keep to **L-H** edge of field, pass through 2 kissing-gates and walk along track to gate. Turn **L** between houses to **River Test** by **Saddler's Mill**.
8 Bear **L** by mill to leave **Test Way**. Cross river; follow tarmac path. Shortly pass **War Memorial Park**. Keep on road close to Abbey back to Market Square.

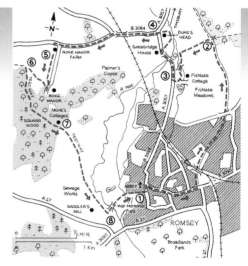

165 HORSEBRIDGE *A PALACE BY THE TEST*

3 miles (4.8km) 1hr 15min **Ascent:** 138ft (42m)
Paths: Former railway track, field paths, tracks and road, 3 stiles
Suggested map: aqua3 OS Explorer 131 Romsey, Andover & Test Valley
Grid reference: SU 345305
Parking: Test Way car park at Horsebridge, opposite John of Gaunt

Enjoy the fine downlands around King's Somborne, once the haunt of Norman kings.
1 This walk starts at Horsebridge, situated beside the **River Test** at the exact point where the original Roman road from Winchester to Old Sarum crossed the river. It is believed that the Normans revived the old road to provide easy access to the hunting grounds near by. Leave car park at **Horsebridge** and turn **L**, opposite **John of Gaunt pub**. Go across **River Test** and turn **R** along **Test Way**, dropping down on to old railway line. In ¾ mile (1.2km), pass beside gate and turn **R** along **Clarendon Way**.
2 Climb out of valley, track becoming metalled at top. Where track leads off R, keep straight ahead, then just before junction of lanes, turn **R** with waymarker down **L-H** edge of field towards **King's Somborne** (it takes its name from 'som' (swine) who drank at or crossed 'bourne' (stream).
3 Turn **R** along lane, then **R again** at A3057 into

King's Somborne village. Turn **L** along Church Road opposite **Crown Inn**. Just beyond churchyard wall, take narrow footpath **R** alongside churchyard.
4 Go through gate and enter rough grassland. This is where John of Gaunt's palace is supposed to have existed. Cross to further gate and enter playing field. Bear diagonally **L** across field to top **L-H** corner and join grassy path leading to close of houses. Turn **R** then, in a few paces, bear **L** along narrow-fenced path between properties to main road.
5 Cross straight over and go through gate into pasture. Take footpath No 7 **half-R** across field to its boundary. Keep to path that leads you through gardens, via small gates, to field.
6 Continue straight ahead towards house and shortly cross drive in front of it. Maintain direction through further pasture to reach stile and lane in Horsebridge. Turn **R**, then **R** again at junction and turn **L** back into Test Way car park.

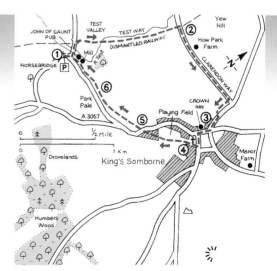

Hampshire

STOCKBRIDGE *A Testing Trail*

7 miles (11.3km) 3hrs 30min Ascent: 492ft (150m) ⚠

Paths: Wide byways, field paths and railway track, 4 stiles

Suggested map: aqua3 OS Explorer 131 Romsey, Andover & Test Valley

Grid reference: SU 355351

Parking: Along Stockbridge High Street

An invigorating downland walk to Danebury Ring from the River Test's fishing capital.

❶ Walk west along main street (**A30**), crossing numerous braided streams of **River Test**. Pass Carbery Guest House and soon bear off to **L**, going uphill beside **Roman Road**. Keep ahead at end of the road, walking along narrow defined path that climbs **Meon Hill**.

❷ Just before reaching **Houghton Down Farm** on **L**, look out for stile in hedge on **R**. Cross this and walk along **R-H** edge of small plantation to stile. Cross **A30** (which can be busy so take care) and stile opposite then walk along **R-H** edge of large field, enjoying open downland views.

❸ Ignore stile on **R** and keep to main path, eventually bearing **L** with field edge to grassy track leading to gate and stile. Turn immediately **R** along wide, hedged track and follow this for ¾ mile (1.2km) to road junction. To visit **Danebury Hill Fort**, turn **L**

along road for 200yds (183m), then **L** again along drive to car park and access to **Danebury Hill**.

❹ Retrace your steps back to road junction you passed before **Danebury Hill** and take byway to **L** beneath height barrier. Remain on this track as it descends back into Test Valley. Eventually it becomes metalled as it enters village of **Longstock**.

❺ At T-junction by church turn **L**, then **R** beside **Peat Spade pub**, along 'The Bunny'. Cross numerous streams that make up **River Test**, notably one with thatched fishing hut and replica metal eel traps.

❻ Just before crossing bridge over **disused Test Valley railway**, and reaching **A3057**, take narrow footpath on **R**. Walk along old **railway trackbed** (here forming part of **Test Way**) for about 1 mile (1.6km) to **A3057**. Taking great care, turn **R**, walking along roadside for 100yds (91m) to roundabout, then follow grassy verge to next roundabout by **White Hart Inn**. Turn **R** here to walk back into **Stockbridge**.

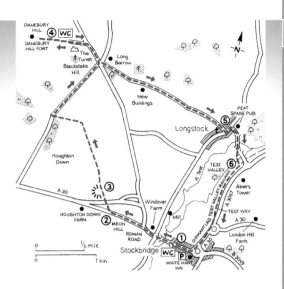

LONGPARISH *Murder in Harewood Forest*

7½ miles (12.1km) 3hrs 30min Ascent: 295ft (90m) ⚠

Paths: Field, woodland paths and tracks, sections of Test Way

Suggested map: aqua3 OS Explorer 144 Basingstoke, Alton & Whitchurch

Grid reference: SU 426439 **Parking:** Car park at St Nicholas Church or by village hall

In search of Deadman's Plack, which marks the spot where King Edgar murdered his friend, Athelwold, in AD 963.

❶ Walk through churchyard; exit via gate; follow **Test Way** across water-meadow. Go through 2 gates. Turn **L** along lane into **Forton**. Take sharp **R-H** bend by barn to T-junction. Pass through gate opposite to field path; bear **R** along track.

❷ Cross **old railway**; follow track between fields. At copse, leave track. Bear **L** with waymarker along field edge. Shortly, cross track to follow path along **L-H** edge of base of shallow valley. At copse, keep **L** and continue to reach gate and lane.

❸ To see **Deadman's Plack**, turn **L** before gate. Follow path uphill into woodland. Ignore 2 tracks on **R**. Take 3rd path. Where it forks, keep **R**; follow path for 300yds (274m), take path on **R** leading to monument.

❹ Retrace your steps back to lane. Turn **L**; after 50yds (46m), cross stile in hedge on **R**; follow path between fields, by woodland. Bear **L** by birch trees to

join main track through **Harewood Forest**. Keep ahead at crossing of paths by conifer tree. Eventually join gravel drive leading to **B3400**.

❺ Turn **R** then **L** up drive to **Andover Down Farm**. Keep to **R** of farm and industrial site. Bear **L** at gates to house; follow track **R**. Head downhill towards **Faulkner's Down Farm**.

❻ At farm, bear **R** along metalled drive, ('**Test Way** – '**TW**'). Proceed downhill. Turn **R** ('Private Road, No Thoroughfare') on to track between fields. Go through gap in hedge ('**TW**'). Follow **L-H** field edge to stile near **cottages**. Bear **L** through gate; follow drive to **B3400**.

❼ Cross road and stile opposite. Follow grassy track ('**TW**') beside arable land. Gently climb, then descend, to join stony track. Shortly, bear **L** ('**TW**') along narrow path to metalled track.

❽ Turn **L**, cross **railway**. Keep **L** at fork on to gravel track. Follow it **L**. Shortly reach junction of tracks. Turn **R** ('**TW**') to reach **Longparish**. At village lane, turn **R**, passing **Plough Pub**, back to church or village hall.

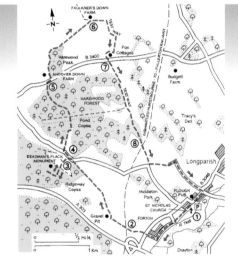

ASHMANSWORTH *The Hampshire Highlands*

5½ miles (8.8km) 2hrs 30min Ascent: 609ft (203m) ⚠

Paths: Ridge tracks, field paths and country road

Suggested map: aqua3 OS Explorers 131 Romsey, Andover & Test Valley; 144 Basingstoke, Alton & Whitchurch

Grid reference: SU 416575

Parking: Along village street by the Plough

Hidden combes and heady heights on the North Hampshire Downs.

❶ Walk north along village street, keeping ahead at fork ('Newbury'). In ¼ mile (400m), just before you reach a house, turn **L** along byway ('Wayfarer's Walk'– '**WW**'). With superb views unfolding across Berkshire, keep to ancient track along ridge and beside **Bunkhanger Copse** to lane.

❷ Turn **R**. In ¼ mile (400m), bear **L** with **WW** marker, just before lane begins to descend. Follow stony track along ridge, bearing **L** then **R** to cross open downland to crossing of paths.

❸ Cross stile on **L** and head straight across pasture, called **Pilot Hill**, to stile. Bear **L** along field edge, then **R** on to stony track alongside woodland. Steeply descend into combe, keep ahead at crossing of tracks and gradually climb, track eventually merging with metalled lane.

❹ Turn **R** into **Faccombe** and turn **L** along village street. Pass estate office and lane on **R** ('**Jack Russell Inn**') then turn **L** ('**Ashmansworth**') by the side of **Faccombe Manor**. In 200yds (183m), take arrowed path **L** beside double gates.

❺ Keep to **L-H** field-edge, following track **R**, and steeply descend through woodland. At junction of tracks, bear **R** to pass 2 brick-and-flint farm buildings (**Curzon Street Farm**).

❻ Proceed straight on at crossing of tracks. Keep to main track as it steeply ascends valley side into woodland. Emerge from trees and keep to track beside Privet Copse. Continue ahead at junction of tracks, across field and track to join narrow path (marked with yellow arrow on post) through copse.

❼ Drop down on to track, bear **L**, then immediately **R** and steeply climb to gap beside gate. Turn **L** along lane, following it uphill into **Ashmansworth**.

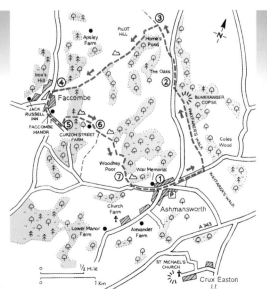

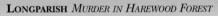

166

Hampshire • SOUTH-EAST ENGLAND

167

Hampshire • SOUTH-EAST ENGLAND

168

Hampshire • SOUTH-EAST ENGLAND

169 HIGHCLERE CASTLE *ABOVE THE CASTLE*

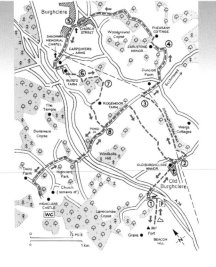

6½ miles (10.4km) 3hrs **Ascent:** 767ft (234m) ▲
Paths: Tracks, field and woodland paths, some roads, 6 stiles
Suggested map: aqua3 OS Explorers 144 Basingstoke, Alton & Whitchurch; 158 Newbury & Hungerford
Grid reference: SU 463575 (on Explorer 144)
Parking: Beacon Hill car park off A34

A hilltop grave and a decorated chapel.

❶ Climb **Beacon Hill** at start or finish. Leave car park via access road. Cross **A34 bridge** to T-junction. Take footpath opposite, downhill to gate. Walk along field edge to **Old Burghclere**. Pass beside church wall and **Old Burghclere Manor** to lane. Proceed ahead, cross railway bridge and take path **L**.

❷ Keep to **L-H** field edge. Enter woodland. Shortly, bear **L** on to track bed. Turn **R**. Follow track to bridge.

❸ Bear **L** up chalky path to track. Turn **R** over bridge. Descend to lane, turn **L** then **R**, ('Ecchinswell'). In 50yds (46m), take waymarked bridleway **L**. Keep to path until gravel drive. Turn **L**.

❹ Follow track to **Earlstone Manor**. Proceed through or close to woodland for 1 mile (1.6km) to road. Turn **R**, then **L** along **Church Street** in Burghclere, ('Sandham Memorial Chapel').

❺ Turn **L** by church; keep to road, passing **Memorial Chapel** and **Carpenters Arms**, before turning **L** along metalled dead-end lane. Pass cottage; take footpath **R** between gardens to stile. Skirt round **Budd's Farm** across 3 fields via 3 stiles; join path through trees to stile.

❻ Turn **R** along field edge, following it **L** in corner. Descend to fingerpost. Follow **L-H** path into woodland. If route is boggy, keep to field edge, looking out for gap and path **R** into woodland. Cross to stile keep ahead across field. Bear **R** through gap into field.

❼ Ignore path **L**. Continue, with woodland on **R**, to waymarker. Turn **R** towards **Ridgemoor Farm**. Pass pond to gate and track. Turn **R**, then where it bears **R**, turn **L** on sunken path to track. To visit **Highclere Castle**, turn **R** to road; cross **A34**; enter parkland; follow drive to house. Retrace steps and keep ahead.

❽ Turn **L** to crossroads, then **R**. Head uphill; keep to undulating track for ½ mile (800m) to Old Burghclere. Turn **L** along lane; then **R** along drive to Old Burghclere Manor. Retrace outward steps to car park.

170 EXBURY *HAMPSHIRE'S GREAT GARDEN*

6 miles (9.7km) 3hrs **Ascent:** 114ft (35m) ▲
Paths: Fields, woodland and foreshore paths, some roads, 8 stiles
Suggested map: aqua3 OS Outdoor Leisure 22 New Forest
Grid reference: SZ 455985
Parking: Pay-and-display car parks at Lepe Country Park

Walk along the Solent to a woodland garden.

❶ Walk west from car park on road. Keep **L** along path, pass **The Watch House**. At lighthouse, bear **R** to reach lane. Turn **L**. As road curves **L**, cross stile on **R**. Walk along field edge, then bear **L** over bridge.

❷ Keep by fence to stile, go straight across field. Briefly pass by woodland. Follow path to stile near telegraph pole. Cross next stile, path leading to stile on woodland edge ahead. Continue through trees, bearing **R** beyond footbridge, then **R** with waymarker post to join bridleway arrowed to **L**.

❸ Enter field, walk up **L-H** edge, skirting **East Hill Farm** to track. Where track curves sharp **L**, turn **R** through gate. Follow path ahead. Enter field; turn **R**. Follow field edge to T-junction. Turn **L** to stile and lane.

❹ Turn **R** through gate by cattle grid; take footpath **L** through gate (by cattle grid) to join track to **Gatewood Farm**. Bear **R** at fork; walk around farm; remain on track for ¾ mile (1.2km) to gate and lane.

Go straight across for **Exbury Gardens** (tea room).

❺ On leaving gardens, turn **R** along road then, where road bends **L**, keep ahead ('Inchmery Lane'). Continue to waymarked path and stile on **L**.

❻ Proceed across grassland into woodland, following path **R**, through trees. At crossing of paths, turn **L** through woodland fringe. On leaving trees, turn **R** along field edge by woodland to stile. Maintain course, bearing **R** with waymaker, and soon follow path through scrub into woodland. Cross footbridge and bear **L**, eventually reaching lane.

❼ Turn **L** and follow it to shore. Proceed along foreshore (follow fingerpost) close to high tide line and continue below Inchmery House. Pass **Lepe House** and rejoin outward route. Final stretch along foreshore may be impassable at high tide, so keep to lane around **Inchmery House**, then, just before road junction, turn **R** beside barrier down to foreshore to pick up path past **Lepe House**.

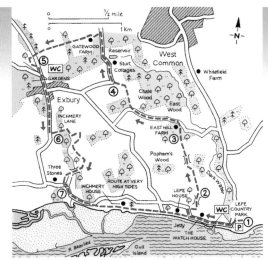

171 LYNDHURST *NEW FOREST TRAILS*

6 miles (9.7km) 3hrs **Ascent:** 210ft (64m) ▲
Paths: Grass and gravel forest tracks, heathland paths, some roads
Suggested map: aqua3 OS Outdoor Leisure 22 New Forest
Grid reference: SU 266057 **Parking:** Brock Hill Forestry Commission car park, just off A35

Ancient oaks and towering conifers.

❶ Take path (south end of car park beyond information post). In 100yds (91m) turn **R** (by post) on to track. Cross, then, where it curves **L**, keep ahead to gate/A35. Cross, go through gate; proceed to junction. Turn **R**. Follow path to road. Cross into Knightwood Oak car park; follow sign to **Knightwood Oak**.

❷ Return to car park, bear **R** and **R** again by fallen tree on to path into mixed forest. Cross stream and soon reach track. Bear **L** and keep ahead, passing Reptile Trail signs, to fork. Keep **L** and soon reach gate and road. Turn **R** to view **Portuguese Fireplace**.

❸ Return via Holidays Hill Inclosure to fork. Bear **L**. Follow track to **New Forest Reptile Centre**. Walk along access drive. At barrier (**L**), descend on to path; follow it across bridge.

❹ Keep to main path for ¾ mile (1.2km), skirting walls to **Allum Green** and several clearings; ascend through trees to crossing of paths; turn **R**. Shortly, bear half-**R** across clearing and footbridge, proceed through woodland edge to telegraph pole. Bear **R** for 20yds (18m) then **L** through gate to A35.

❺ Turn **L**, then **R** across road to gate. Proceed to garden boundary; turn **R**, narrow path leading to lane in **Bank**. Turn **R**, pass **Oak Inn**; walk through hamlet. Just before sharp **L-H** bend (by cattle grid), bear **R** beside barrier; walk ahead on path.

❻ Go through trees and scrub to fork on edge of clearing. Keep **R** to follow path. Negotiate boggy area; at fork, keep **L**; follow path to lane at **Gritnam**.

❼ Proceed, passing **Jessamine Cottage** then, where lane bends **R**, keep ahead across grassland into trees. Bear slightly **R**; walk by thick birch copse. Remain on path (ill-defined in places); eventually join grassy path. Turn **L**; continue to bridge.

❽ Ignore path immediately **L**, keep ahead, following path through **Brinken Wood**. Enter clearing; proceed to cross bridge over **Warwickslade Cutting**. At gravel track, turn **R** then take 1st path **L**. Soon merge with start of Tall Trees Trail, opposite **Brock Hill** car park.

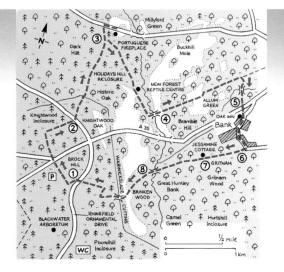

Hampshire

MINSTEAD *CHURCH TREASURES*

5¼ miles (8.4km) 2hrs 30min **Ascent:** 361ft (110m) ▲
Paths: Field paths, bridleways, forest tracks, roads, 5 stiles
Suggested map: aqua3 OS Outdoor Leisure 22 New Forest
Grid reference: SU 280109 **Parking:** Minstead church or by village green

A New Forest walk starting at Minstead church – the burial place of Sir Arthur Conan Doyle.

❶ Go through gate on **R** of churchyard; walk to gate. Keep ahead; enter wood. Exit via gate. Bear **R** then **L** to road. Cross ford. Stay on lane. Go **L** by phone box.
❷ At crossroads, go straight over, following sign ('Acres Down Farm'). Cross ford; at crossroads, just past farm, turn **R**. Almost immediately take **L** fork, ('Acres Down Car Park'). Pass car park; follow signposts (heading for Bolderwood).
❸ Swing **R** through gate. Ignore junction R, over stream; just beyond track merging from L, turn **R** along grass track. Walk through coniferous trees, then cross gravel track and bear slightly **R**. Path swings **R**, then **L**, eventually reaching fork at top of short rise.
❹ Bear **L**, then at indistinct fork, take more distinct path **R**. Maintain direction across track; in 50yds (46m), fork **R**, vaguely parallel to track. Continue with less woodland to **L**; eventually exit woods via gate.

❺ Turn **R**, join track from L. Almost immediately fork **L**. With woodland to R, keep on well-defined track, ignoring routes L and R, for ½ mile (800m). Fork **R** through gorse and merge with track from R. Swing **R**, ignore track L to road, but keep ahead to reach road.
❻ Cross; walk **L** down verge. Pass **Grovewood House**; turn **L** down bridleway ('**King's Garn**'). Pass house; take **L** fork and join track merging from R. Continue downhill; just before reaching road, turn **L** over stile; continue between boundaries.
❼ Drop down to bridge and stile. Enter woodland and turn **R** through gate. Cross stream; go up steps; fork **R** through gate. Cross plank bridge, go through gate and continue gentle ascent. Join path from R and proceed into car park. Fork **R**, pass **Furzey Gardens**; walk down to road.
❽ Turn **R**, then **R** again. Take footpath **L**. Walk along **L-H** field edge to bridge and stile. Maintain direction through next field to road. Turn **R** into Minstead, then **R** after pub back to church.

ROCKBOURNE *ROMAN REMAINS*

4½ miles (7.2km) 1hr 45min **Ascent:** 295ft (90m) ▲
Paths: Field paths, woodland bridleways and tracks, 9 stiles
Suggested map: aqua3 OS Outdoor Leisure 22 New Forest or OS Explorer 130 Salisbury & Stonehenge
Grid reference: SU 113184
Parking: Rockbourne village hall car park

Roman discoveries link Rockbourne and Whitsbury, by the Wiltshire border.

❶ Turn **L** out of car park. Take lane **R** towards **Manor Farm**. Turn **R**, signed to church. Cross drive to path to **St Andrew's Church**. Keep by **R-H** edge of churchyard to junction of paths. Proceed behind houses, ignoring 2 paths R. Cross stile. Go **R** through gate.
❷ Follow field edge to junction of paths. Keep on **L** to gate. Maintain direction over 2 stiles and by field edge to stile in corner. Climb stile immediately **R**. Bear **L** by edge of meadow to stile. Pass in front of thatched cottage to stile and track, opposite **Marsh Farm**.
❸ Bear **L**, then **R** through gate. Keep to **L** through pasture to gate. Bear half **R** to gate in corner; proceed along field edge, eventually reaching stile and lane. To visit **Roman Villa**, turn **R** to T-junction, and turn **R** into entrance. Retrace steps.
❹ Take track opposite. Enter copse; at junction of tracks, take arrowed path **L** up bank into field. Keep to

L-H edge; head across field to track. Turn **R**, then **L** downhill through woodland edge. Pass house to lane.
❺ Turn **R**, then **L** along bridleway; ascend through **Radnall Wood**. At fork of paths, bear **L** (blue arrow). Pass behind **Whitsbury House** to lane. Turn **L**, then **R** along track between properties to lane. Turn **R** then **R** (by fingerpost) on bridleway through **Whitsbury Wood**.
❻ At junction with track, bear **L**; walk beside paddocks to bungalow. Turn **L** along track between paddocks towards **Whitsbury church**. Turn **L** at T-junction and shortly enter churchyard. Go through gate opposite church door to lane.
❼ Turn **L** for **Cartwheel Inn**, otherwise turn **R**, then **L** along farm drive and keep ahead, bearing **L**, then **R** between paddocks, uphill to gate. Turn **L** along field edge then head across field to track.
❽ Turn **R** and follow track **L** to junction of tracks. Cross stile opposite and walk back to Rockbourne church. Retrace steps back to village hall.

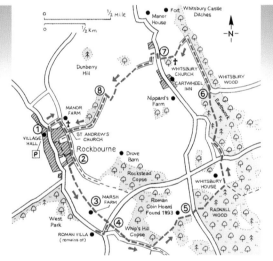

BREAMORE *AN HISTORIC HOUSE*

9 miles (14.5km) 4hrs **Ascent:** 315ft (105m) ▲
Paths: Field paths, water-meadows, woodland trails, 9 stiles
Suggested map: aqua3 OS Outdoor Leisure 22 New Forest; OS Explorer 130 Salisbury & Stonehenge
Grid reference: SU 151187 (on Outdoor Leisure 22)
Parking: Car park near Breamore House and Countryside Museum

Explore a classic estate village.

❶ Walk past **Countryside Museum**; turn **R** by parkland wall. Cross drive; walk to church. Bear **R** then **L** through **churchyard** to gate. Cross pasture, then stile. Bear half-**L** to stile. Bear half-**L** to **L-H** edge to gate; turn **R** through copse to stile.
❷ Head across 2 fields, via stiles; cross busy **A338**. Cross another footbridge and path beyond lay-by. Cross field to swing gates and footbridge. Proceed through **South Charford Farm**.
❸ Turn **R** along track, follow it **L** (arrow on gate post), then **R** and **L** across valley. Bear **L** across old sluice; cross meadow beside stream (can be boggy) to stile. Cross footbridge; keep alongside stream to stile. Follow path to R of drainage channel then, on nearing **River Avon**, turn **L** across bridge to gate.
❹ Cross Avon and lane. Ascend path to **St Mary's Church**. Continue uphill, soon to walk parallel with **Hale House's** drive. Turn **R** at lane and **L** by Garden Cottage.

❺ At end of lane, fork **R** down drive; in front of Hemmick Court. Head downhill; then climb through woodland. At crossing of bridleways, turn **R**; proceed through **Stricklands Plantation**. Pass beneath pylon; soon descend to junction of tracks.
❻ Turn **L**. Follow drive to T-junction of tracks. Turn **R**; descend to drive. Turn **L**. Cross stile to R of gate; cross pasture to stile. Keep to **R-H** field to gate; bear **L** through woodland to bridge. Ascend between houses to track. Turn **R**, then **L** at junction to lane.
❼ Turn **R** downhill following lane ('Breamore'). Cross Avon Valley to **A338**. Turn **R**; pass **Bat and Ball** and immediately cross road to follow lane **L**. Pass behind **school** to join track by common land.
❽ Bear **R** on to common, following **R-H** path towards **pavilion**. Follow path **R**. Just before cottages and track, turn **L** to footbridge and drive. Bear **R** to lane, opposite Orchard Cottage. Turn **L**; take footpath **R** over field to lane. Turn **L**, then **L** again at T-junction to car park.

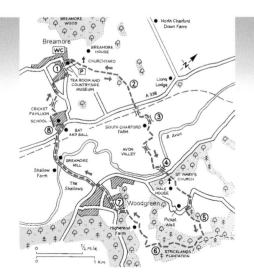

Hampshire

175 FRITHAM *A FOREST WALK*

6 miles (9.7km) 3hrs Ascent: 404ft (123m)	
Paths: Gravel forest tracks, heathland and woodland paths	
Suggested map: aqua3 OS Outdoor Leisure 22 New Forest	
Grid reference: SU 230141 **Parking:** Forestry Commission car park beyond Royal Oak	

A hidden hamlet in the New Forest.

1 From car park turn **L** and head downhill on road. The road eventually becomes gravelled and passes **Eyeworth Pond** to R. Continue past Eyeworth Cottage and **Eyeworth Lodge**, then take footpath on **R** beyond **Oak Tree Cottage** at end of track.

2 Bear **L** then, at fork, keep **L** through trees close to field boundary. As boundary swings further L, bear **R** along track between coniferous and deciduous woods. At T-junction by large single fir, turn **L** along grassy track. Cross ford; proceed to junction.

3 Turn **R** on to gravel track then, where it bears sharply R, keep ahead with grassy track. Ascend into more open countryside; continue to climb along meandering path, ignoring paths L and R, across edge of Fritham Plain. Path bears **R** towards trees to track. Turn **L**, then **R** and enter **Sloden Inclosure**.

4 Walk through inclosure; descend across heathland towards cottage. Cross bridge; bear **R** then, just before **Holly Hatch Cottage**, turn **L** through gate.

At fork, bear **R** along grassy track and gently climb through **Holly Hatch Inclosure** to track.

5 Turn **L**, then in about 400yds (366m), turn **R** at major junction; shortly reach gate on woodland edge and turn **L**, on to wide track beside wood then keep **L** at fork. Track soon becomes concrete and passes to R of **Cadmans Pool**. Cross over metalled road and take **L** turn along grassy track to enter more woodland.

6 In 50yds (46m), turn **R** and keep ahead. As footpath becomes indistinct, maintain direction. Soon bear **L** on to gravel track. Continue to gate. Walk across area of concrete, taking path in bottom **R-H** corner that leads into **South Bentley Inclosure**.

7 Descend to gate (75); turn **R**. Cross stream; proceed along indistinct path, soon bear half-**L** through copse to reach larger stream. Walk along **R-H** bank; cross bridge.

8 Continue ahead, path passing house and gate to become gravelled drive. Proceed to junction by Royal Oak; turn **L** to car park.

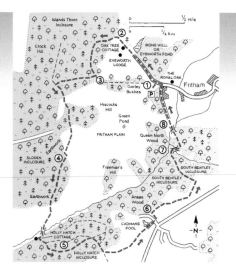

176 GODSHILL *TO APPULDURCOMBE*

4½ miles (7.2km) 2hrs Ascent: 639ft (195m)	
Paths: Downland, woodland paths, tracks, metalled drive, 6 stiles	
Suggested map: aqua3 OS Explorer 29 Isle of Wight	
Grid reference: SZ 530817	
Parking: Free car park in Godshill, opposite Griffin Inn	

To the ruins of a Palladian mansion.

1 From car park in Godshill, cross road and walk down Hollis Lane beside **Griffin Inn**. Just before Godshill Cherry Orchard, take footpath **L**, signed to **Beech Copse**. Keep to **R** of pub garden to stile. Continue to further stile; keep to path gently uphill through valley to stile on edge of **Beech Copse**.

2 Just beyond, at fork, bear **R** uphill through trees to junction of paths by gate. Turn **R** through gate; walk towards **Sainham Farm**. Keep **L** of farm to gate; turn **L** uphill, **Worsley Trail** ('Stenbury Down'). Climb fenced track, passing via 2 large metal gates; enter copse.

3 At junction of paths below **Gat Cliff**, take bridleway GL49 **R** through gate by fingerpost ('Stenbury Down'). Shortly, disregard footpath R and keep to bridleway as it veers **L** and climbs to gate. Skirt around base of **Gat Cliff** and then **Appuldurcombe Down**, path follows field edges before climbing steeply by stone wall to gate and open

grassland on top of **Stenbury Down**.

4 Keep **L** beside hedge to gate; shortly turn **R** along track towards radio station. Pass to **L** of building, then just before reaching stile and footpath on R, turn **L** (unsigned) along field edge. Head downhill; at field boundary, bear **L** to descend steps to track.

5 Turn **L** and descend to T-junction. Turn **L**. Where lane curves R, keep ahead, past **Span Lodge** and barn to stile. Continue between fields to stile. Keep to **L-H** field edge in front of **Appuldurcombe House**, ignoring waymarked path R, to reach stile by house entrance.

6 Take footpath to **L** of car park, ('Godshill'). Walk along drive to **Appuldurcombe Farm** then, where it curves L, keep ahead via 2 gateways. Soon go through **Freemantle Gate** on edge of Godshill Park.

7 Proceed downhill towards **Godshill Park Farm**. Ignore paths R and L, pass in front of **Godshill Park House** and join drive to **A3020**. Cross and turn **L** along pavement back to car park.

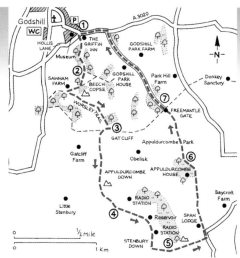

177 BRIGHSTONE *WILD AND BEAUTIFUL SHORE*

8¼ miles (13.3km) 4hrs Ascent: 941ft (287m)	
Paths: Field and clifftop paths, woodland tracks, 10 stiles	
Suggested map: aqua3 OS Outdoor Leisure 29 Isle of Wight	
Grid reference: SZ 385835	
Parking: National Trust car park at Brookgreen	

From downland to the seashore.

1 From car park, turn **L** along A3055 to stile on **R** ('Hamstead Trail') and walk across field to track. Keep ahead by cottages and continue. At crossing of tracks, head uphill on metalled track. Bear **L** then **R** around **Dunsbury Farm** to T-junction.

2 Turn **R**, then **L** through gate and ascend steeply between trees to gate. Merge with track at junction and bear **R**. Go through gate and continue to climb, shortly bearing **R** (marked by blue byway sign) to follow track downhill beside line of telegraph poles. Keep **R** at chalk track; go through gate and cross B3399 to gate and bridleway, ('Shorwell').

3 Climb steadily across downland to gate. Continue along main track, **Tennyson Trail**, to top of **Mottistone Down**. Descend to car park and turn **R** along lane. In few paces turn **L** along stony track.

4 Follow **Worsley Trail** uphill beside **Brighstone Forest**. At 2nd junction of paths (by fingerpost), take

bridleway **R** through gate and descend Limerstone Down on gorse-edged path. On reaching waymarker post, take bridleway **R** for **Brighstone**.

5 Head downhill through bracken to join sandy path between trees to **Brighstone**. Cross lane, walk along **North Street**, passing museum, to B3399. Turn **L**, then **R** beside **Three Bishops pub** into **Warnes Lane**.

6 Keep **L** of car park along metalled path to road. Turn **R**, then **L** with waymarker and cross footbridge. Keep to **L-H** edge of playing field and to rear of gardens to lane. Cross straight over and follow fenced path to **Chilton Lane**.

7 Turn **L**, pass **Chilton Farm** and keep ahead at sharp **R-H** bend along track to A3055. Pass through car park opposite and follow path to coast. Turn **R** along coast path and soon cross stile on to National Trust land ('**Sud Moor**'). Keep to coast path, crossing 6 stiles to reach **Brookgreen**. Bear **R** along beside Chine and cottages and turn **L** to stile and car park.

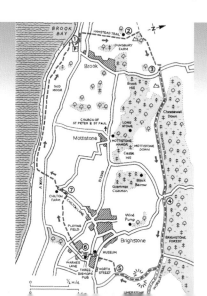

Hampshire

CARISBROOKE'S CASTLE *A Royal Prisoner*

6½ miles (10.4km) 2hrs 30min **Ascent:** 764ft (233)m
Paths: Field and downland paths and tracks, some roads, 4 stiles
Suggested map: aqua3 OS Outdoor Leisure 29 Isle of Wight
Grid reference: SZ 489876 **Parking:** Car park close to Carisbrooke Priory

King Charles I was imprisoned in the castle until his trial and execution in London, 1648.
❶ From car park (facing **Carisbrooke Priory**) turn **L** and walk along road. Take 1st **L-H** footpath. Shortly veer **L**, ascending through trees. On reaching **castle**, bear **L**; follow path alongside castle walls. Turn **L** towards car park; follow footpath ('**Millers Lane**').
❷ Turn **R** at road, pass **Millers Lane**; walk to stile and path on **L** ('**Bowcombe**'). Cross field to next stile; proceed across pastures, crossing several more stiles. Level with **Plaish Farm**, making for stile and junction.
❸ Bear **R**; follow enclosed path, shortly bending **L**. At **Bowcombe Farm**, turn **L**. Follow signs ('**Gatcombe**'). Pass footpath on **L**; stay on track as it curves **R**, avoiding track ahead. Veer away from track at corner of **Frogland Copse**; follow field edge to gate.
❹ Pass through trees to gate; continue up slope, skirting field boundary. Keep ahead in next field towards gate and bridleway sign. Walk along edge of **Dukem Copse**; look for turning on **L** to **Gatcombe**.

❺ Go through gate; continue along field edge. On reaching path to **Garston's**, descend to **R**; then swing **L** to gate. Follow bridleway for **Gatcombe**; turn **R** to **Newbarn Farm**. Bear **R** at entrance and, at lane, keep **R** along bridleway. At edge of **Tolt Copse** ignore path **R** and bear **L**, soon to leave **Shepherd's Trail**, proceed along bridleway towards **Sheat Manor**.
❻ Before manor, at junction of paths, turn **L**, following path past cottages. Bear **L** and keep to curving path as it ascends to woodland. Proceed through wood and down to lane by **St Olave's Church**.
❼ Turn **L** along Gatcombe Road, pass **Rectory Lane**, then turn **R** at crossing of ways, rejoining **Shepherd's Trail** for **Carisbrooke**. Pass between properties and ascend through trees. Pass over track; go through gate; follow path round **L-H** field edge.
❽ Go through gate; keep by field edge. Path later enclosed by fence and hedge to reach sign ('**Carisbrooke** and **Whitcombe Road**'). Keep to path; eventually reach junction. Continue to reach car park.

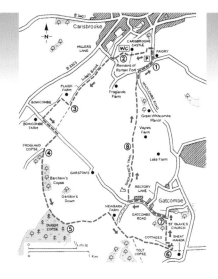

BLACKGANG CHINE *The Peeping Pepper Pot*

5½ miles (8.8km) 2hrs **Ascent:** 745ft (227m)
Paths: Field paths, downland tracks, coast path, 12 stiles
Suggested map: aqua3 OS Outdoor Leisure 29 Isle of Wight
Grid reference: SZ 490767
Parking: Free parking in viewpoint car park above Blackgang Chine

Around the Isle of Wight's most southerly point.
❶ From car park, cross road; climb steps to stile. Bear **L** around field edge, ('**St Catherine's Oratory**'). Cross stile; steadily climb grassy downland to stile. Ascend to **old lighthouse** (Pepper Pot), ignore stile by trig point just beyond; and, keeping fence on **R**, continue downhill to reach gate.
❷ Go through gate and proceed on broad grassy swathe to **Hoy's Monument**. Return for 55yds (50m) and take bridleway **L**. Descend steeply through trees and bear **L** with main path downhill to gate. Follow bridleway **L** then bear **R** along driveway.
❸ Proceed at crossing of tracks (**Downcourt Farm** drive is to **R**), heading downhill to gate by house. Walk along **R-H** field edge to gate. Head downhill on hedged path. At T-junction, turn **R**. Go through gate, path soon emerging into field.
❹ Keep to **L-H** field edge, beside overgrown gully. Go through 1st gate on **L**. In few paces, turn **R**. Take

path **L** just before gate. Go through trees; cross bridge and keep **R**. Gradually ascend stony path (very wet in winter), which bears **L** then steepens to reach stile.
❺ Walk ahead, following defined path uphill beside hedge to 2 stiles in field corner. Cross **R-H** stile and immediately turn **R**, down on to path that heads diagonally uphill across face of **Head Down** to stile. Turn **L** along to stile and track
❻ Turn **L**, then almost immediately **R** along hedged bridleway. Head downhill, path becoming metalled as it enters **Niton**. Just before lane, bear **R** into **churchyard**. Keep **L**, exit **churchyard** by small gate and turn **R** alongside A3055.
❼ Take footpath beside last house on **L**; ascend steeply through trees to stile. Keep ahead over grassland to stile. Follow **L-H** field edge to next stile.
❽ Turn **R** along coastal path, cross 2 stiles. Soon emerge on to open cliff top. Stay on narrow path close to cliff edge for nearly 1 mile (1.6km) to car park.

FRESHWATER BAY *Tennyson's Island Retreat*

6 miles (9.7km) 3hrs **Ascent:** 623ft (190m)
Paths: Downland, field and woodland paths, some road walking and stretch of disused railway, 4 stiles
Suggested map: aqua3 OS Outdoor Leisure 29 Isle of Wight
Grid reference: SZ 346857
Parking: Pay-and-display car park at Freshwater Bay

In the footsteps of a Romantic poet.
❶ From car park, turn **R** along road, then **L** before bus shelter along metalled track, ('Coastal Footpath'). As it bears **L**, keep ahead through kissing gates and soon begin steep ascent on concrete path on to **Tennyson Down**. Keep to well-walked path to **memorial cross** at its summit.
❷ Continue on wide grassy swathe, which narrows between gorse bushes, to reach replica of **Old Nodes Beacon**. Here, turn very sharp **R** down chalk track. At junction (car park **R**) keep ahead on narrow path.
❸ Path widens, then descends to gate into woodland. Proceed close to woodland fringe to further gate and enter more open countryside. Pass disused excavations on **R** then shortly, turn sharp **L** down unmarked path. Cross stile, then keep **L** along field boundary and bear sharp **L** to stile. Cross next field to stile and turn **R** along field edge to stile.
❹ Cross farm track, go through gate and walk along

track (F47) beside **Farringford Manor Hotel**. Pass beneath wooden footbridge and continue downhill to gate and road. (Turn **L** to visit hotel.) Turn **R**, pass **thatched church** and turn **L** down **Blackbridge Road**. Just before Black Bridge, turn **L** into **Afton Marshes** Nature Reserve.
❺ Join nature trail, following **L-H** path beside stream to A3055 (can be very wet in winter). Turn **L**. Almost immediately cross to join footpath F61 along old railway. In ½ mile (800m) reach the **Causeway**.
❻ Turn **R** and follow the lane to B3399. Turn **L** and shortly cross into unmetalled **Manor Road**. In few paces, bear off **L** ('Freshwater Way'), and ascend across grassland towards **Afton Down**.
❼ Keep ahead at junction of paths beside golf course, soon to follow gravel track **R** to clubhouse. Go through gate, pass in front of building and walk down access track, keeping **L** to A3055. Turn **R** downhill into **Freshwater Bay**.

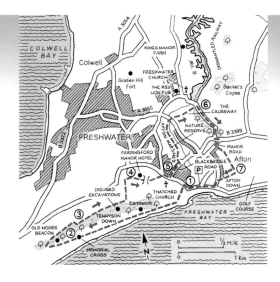

Berkshire

Berkshire • SOUTHEAST ENGLAND

181 SUNNINGDALE *A CONSTITUTIONAL CRISIS*

4 miles (6.4km) 1hr 45min **Ascent:** Negligible ⚠️
Paths: Enclosed woodland paths, estate drive, paths and tracks, path across golf course and polo ground, no stiles
Suggested map: aqua3 OS Explorer 160 Windsor, Weybridge & Bracknell
Grid reference: SU 953676
Parking: On-street parking in Sunningdale village

Skirt the grounds of Edward VIII's favourite home, Fort Belvedere.

❶ From **Nags Head** turn **L**. Walk down High Street, keeping Anglican **church** on R and Baptist **church** on L. Pass Church Road and proceed along Bedford Lane. Cross brook. Turn **R** by bungalows to follow path cutting between hedgerows and fields. Look for large, shuttered house (R) just before **A30**. Bear **L**. Walk to sign on R for Shrubs Hill Lane and Onslow Road.

❷ Follow path to junction by panel fence. Turn **R** by bridleway/footpath sign. Curve **L**, make for roundabout and swing **L**, looking for footpath by house (Highgate). Follow it through woodland and when you join wider path on bend, keep **L**. Skirt **golf course**, cutting between trees and bracken. Emerge from woodland and follow path across fairways, keeping **L** at junction by bunker. Veer **L** at 1st fork, into trees, and follow path to junction with tarmac drive.

❸ Turn **L** and pass through **Wentworth Estate**, cutting between exclusive houses with secluded landscaped grounds and imposing entrances. On reaching **A30**, turn **L** and follow road west. Walk down to **Berkshire/Surrey border** and bear sharp **R** to join right of way. Follow shaded woodland path between beech trees and exposed roots. Beyond wood you reach buildings of **Coworth Park**.

❹ Draw level with bridge, turn **L** and then follow well-defined footpath across broad expanse of parkland, part of which is used as a **polo ground**, crossing track on far side. Enter woodland, turn **L** at road and pass several houses. When you reach speed restriction sign, bear **R** to join byway by Sunningdale **Bowling Club**. Proceed ahead on tarmac drive and continue ahead. Turn **L** at road, swinging **L** just after fork. Pass Coworth Road and return to centre of **Sunningdale**.

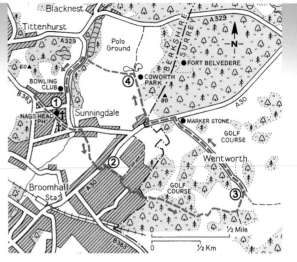

182 WINDSOR GREAT PARK *A ROYAL RAMBLE*

5½ miles (8.8km) 2hrs 30min **Ascent:** 160ft (49m) 🔼
Paths: Park drives and rides, woodland paths and tracks
Suggested map: aqua3 OS Explorer 160 Windsor, Weybridge & Bracknell
Grid reference: SU 947727
Parking: Car park by Cranbourne Gate

Royal footsteps on the Long Walk.

❶ From car park, cross **A332** to **Cranbourne Gate** and enter park. Follow drive beside trees planted to commemorate Queen Victoria's Golden Jubilee (1887) and Edward VII's coronation (1902). Turn **R** at 1st crossroads ('**Cumberland Lodge**'); follow drive to next junction by 2 ponds.

❷ Keep **L** here ('**The Village**'). Pass **Post Office** and General Store, walk between spacious green and playing field and then turn **R** to join **Queen Anne's Ride**. Look back for another view of Windsor Castle. Pass alongside **Poets Lawn** and follow ride to tarmac drive. Turn **L**; keep **L** at fork, then **L** again after a few paces at crossroads.

❸ **Poets Lawn** is now on L. Continue ahead at next intersection; then turn **R** to follow broad, hedge-lined footpath. Ahead lies **Royal Lodge** and to L of it is famous **Copper Horse** statue. Take next grassy ride on **L** and head for deer gate. Keep ahead towards

statue and when you draw level with it, bear **L**. Figure of George III points the way. Follow woodland path and merge with clear track running down to drive. Pass through automatic gate and keep **R** at immediate fork.

❹ Walk to **Queen Anne's Ride**, which crosses drive just before house. On L is millstone. Bear **R** and follow ride to **Russel's Pond**. Here, veer away from ride and keep beside pond and fence. Walk ahead between fields, making for woodland. Drop down to road at **Ranger's Gate**. Cross at lights and take tarmac drive.

❺ Veer half-**L** about 100yds (91m) before some white gates and follow path across grass and alongside trees. Follow it up slope and through wood. Keep to sandy track and at point where it bends L, go straight on along path between trees. As it reaches gate, turn **L** and keep alongside fence. (Path can be overgrown in places.) Follow fence to drive and on R is outline of **Cranbourne Tower**. Bear **L** and return to car park.

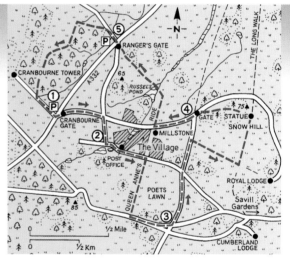

183 MAIDENHEAD THICKET *DANGER AT DUSK*

3½ miles (5.7km) 1hr 30min **Ascent:** 82ft (25m) ⚠️
Paths: Field and woodland paths, some road walking, 2 stiles
Suggested map: aqua3 OS Explorers 160 Windsor, Weybridge & Bracknell; 172 Chiltern Hills East
Grid reference: SU 838800 (on Explorer 172)
Parking: By green in village of Littlewick Green

A pretty walk through extensive woodland, once the haunt of highwaymen.

❶ Head for southeast corner of green in centre of **Littlewick Green**, turn **R** into School Lane and follow it to woodland edge. Emerging from trees, bear **L** to join tarmac track across fields. Cross road leading to business park and continue over farmland to next road. Turn **L**, pass houses lining route and walk almost to **A4**, keeping **R** at junction just before it.

❷ Cross over and enter **Maidenhead Thicket**. Claude Duval (1643–70), one of the best-known highwaymen, preyed upon travellers in this area. Dick Turpin (1705–39) also travelled this way, waiting in the shadows to ambush passing coaches. From here he would gallop to his aunt's cottage at nearby Sonning where he stabled his horse, Black Bess, before going into hiding until the dust settled. Follow path between trees and clearings. At bridleway, veer **R** and follow main route along to junction. Turn **L** and

follow hard path to reach lodge to **Stubbings House**.

❸ Cross 2 stiles to R of it and then follow path out across fields. Footpath graduates to track before arriving at buildings of **Stubbings Farm**. On reaching road at **Burchett's Green**, turn **L** and pass some houses, one of which has white weatherboarded tower. Follow lane and veer half-**R** just beyond entrance to **Old Oak Farm**.

❹ Follow path between hedgerows and trees and further on it runs alongside houses and bungalows. Along this stretch path broadens to track. Sound of traffic on **A4** gradually becomes audible. At junction go straight over into Jubilee Road and follow it towards cricket ground at **Littlewick Green**. On reaching edge of green, bear **R** to join waymarked footpath running alongside ground and past front of Littlewick Green cricket club. At road turn **L**, passing **Cricketers Inn**. Alternatively, follow road round eastern edge of green to start and your car.

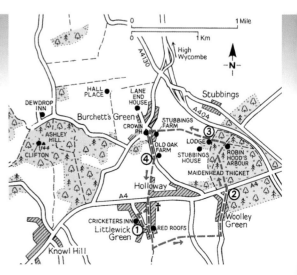

Berkshire

WARGRAVE TO BOWSEY HILL

6 miles (9.7km) 2hrs 15min **Ascent:** 248ft (76m)
Paths: Stretches of road, field and woodland paths,13 stiles
Suggested map: aqua3 OS Explorer 171 Chiltern Hills West
Grid reference: SU 786785
Parking: Public car park in School Lane, just off A321

Head for peaceful Bowsey Hill.

1 Turn **L**. Walk along School Lane, (**B477**). On 1st bend, bear **L** into Dark Lane, head up hill; turn **R** at T-junction. Follow road; turn **L** ('**Crazies Hill**'). Bear **R** by **East Lodge**, follow lane to bend; bear **L** over stile to join waymarked path. Keep alongside fence, and across fields towards trees. Cross stile; turn **R** at road, veering **L** opposite house, '**Crouch End**'.

2 Keep close to **L** boundary of field; look for stile in bottom corner. Descend steeply to 2 stiles and bridleway beyond. Cross stile almost opposite; climb hillside. Look for stile further up slope and keep ahead on higher ground, following path alongside fence. Descend to kissing gate at road; turn immediately **R**. Head uphill passing **Worley's Farm**.

3 Take next waymarked path on **R**, just before row of trees, and aim little to **L** as you cross field, lining up with white house in distance. Head towards stile in hedge and maintain direction, keeping to **L** of house.

Look for stile; follow enclosed path to road. Turn **R**, then **L** beside village hall; after few paces, bear **L** by Old Clubhouse. Follow path by paddock to stile by road. Bear **R**, past entrance to **Thistle House** and bridleway into trees on **R**.

4 Continue for several paces to stile on **L**. Join woodland path (watch for white arrows on tree trunks) eventually reaching waymarked junction. Turn **R** here, avoid path on **R** and keep going to next waymarked junction, on edge of wood. Bear **L**; walk down to flight of steps and footbridge. Make for woodland perimeter; turn **R** along field edge.

5 Cross bridleway via 2 stiles. Proceed along woodland edge. Look for hedge gap on **R**; cross into adjoining field; maintain direction. Make for kissing gate and footbridge in field corner. Proceed to kissing gate. Follow path across field, heading towards trees. Make for kissing gate leading out to road. Turn **R**. Follow it to **A321**, turn **L**. Walk to School Lane.

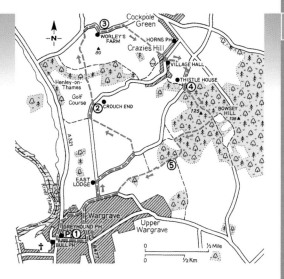

DINTON PASTURES WATER AND WILDLIFE

3 miles (4.8km) 1hr 30min **Ascent:** Negligible
Paths: Lakeside and riverside paths, some road walking, no stiles
Suggested map: aqua3 OS Explorer 159 Reading, Wokingham & Pangbourne
Grid reference: SU 784718
Parking: Large car park at Dinton Pastures

Enjoy this popular country park, visiting six lakes along the way.

1 With Tea Cosy café and Countryside Service office on **R** and **High Chimneys** behind you, cross car park to large map of site. Follow wide path and keep **R** at fork ('wildlife trails'). Pass enclosed play area on **L**; keep Emm Brook on **R**.

2 Swing **L** on reaching water; follow path alongside lake. When it veers **R**, turn **L** across bridge to sign ('**Tufty's Corner**'). Bear **R** here and keep **L** at fork after few paces. Follow path beside **White Swan Lake** to waymark post by patch of grass and flight of steps. Avoid steps but take **L-H** path and follow it to lake known as **Tufty's Corner**. On reaching junction by bridge, turn **R** and keep **River Loddon** on **L**.

3 Walk to next bridge. Don't cross it, instead continue on riverside path. **White Swan Lake** lies over to **R**, glimpsed between trees. Further on, path curves to **R**, in line with river, before reaching sign

('private fishing – members only'). Join track on **R** here and bear **L**. Pass alongside Herons Water to sign ('**Sandford Lake, Black Swan Lake** and **Lavell's Lake** – Conservation Area'). Turn **L**; keep **Sandford Lake** on **R**. When path curves **R**, go out to road.

4 To visit **Berkshire Museum of Aviation**, bear **L** and pass **Sandford Mill**. Take road ('No Through Road') on **L**, pass cottages and continue ahead when road dwindles to path. **Museum** is on **L**. Retrace route to Sandford Mill; keep ahead to footpath and kissing gate on **L**. Keep **L** at 1st fork, then **R** at 2nd and head for **Teal hide**. Return to road, cross over and return to lakeside path.

5 Continue with **Sandford Lake** on **R**. On reaching '**Sandford Lake**' sign veer **L** over bridge and turn **L**. **Sailing Club** on **L**. Continue on path and look out across lake to **Goat Island**, noted for its population of goats. On reaching picnic area, turn **L** and retrace your steps back to main car park.

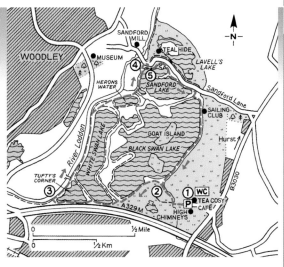

WOKINGHAM TO THE COUNTRY

6½ miles (10.4km) 2hrs 45min **Ascent:** Negligible
Paths: Streets, forest and field paths, tracks, 1 stile
Suggested map: aqua3 OS Explorer 159 Reading, Wokingham & Pangbourne
Grid reference: SU 813686
Parking: Public car parks in Rose Street and Denmark Street

A typical market town and open countryside.

1 With **Town Hall** on **R**, walk down Denmark Street. Pass Wokingham Memorial Clinic; keep **R** at **Dukes Head**. Walk to roundabout, cross Kendrick Close and follow Finchampstead Road. Pass under railway. Take footpath on **L** at next roundabout. Head for gate, veer **R** by some loose boxes and follow fenced track. Make for line of houses and continue to Lucas Hospital.

2 Look for stile here and head diagonally **R** across paddock to wrought iron gate and tarmac drive leading to **Ludgrove School**. Turn **R**, pass white gateposts and bear **L** just beyond them at galvanised gates. Begin lengthy stretch of track walking, keeping **railway line** on **R**. Eventually pass old wartime Nissen hut and cottage on **R**. Continue for about 80yds (73m) then turn **R** by some wooden posts.

3 Follow track between plantations, avoid path ahead at **L-H** bend and keep **R** at next fork. Make for road and turn **L**. Pass Kingsbridge Cottages and Grove

Close before reaching site of former pub, '**Who'd a Thot It**'. Continue along road to St Sebastian's Church, and turn **L** into Heathlands Road. Pass entrance to **Heathlands Court** and swing **L** just beyond it to join byway for sign for Bramshill Forest.

4 Swing **R** at next waymarked junction and when path bends **R**, go through deer gate and continue on across market gardens. Continue between fences and fields and follow path to **L** of entrance to **Ludgrove School**. Cut between laurel bushes and holly trees, cross over drive leading to school and continue towards Wokingham. Keep ahead to railway footbridge and veer **R** on far side, following Gypsy Lane.

5 Pass **Southfields School**, cross Erica Drive and continue to next main junction. Cross Murdoch Road and follow Easthampstead Road towards town centre. Bear **R** at T-junction and walk along to **Ship Inn**. Keep **L** here, following Wiltshire Road, and turn **L** into Rose Street. Follow it back to Market Place.

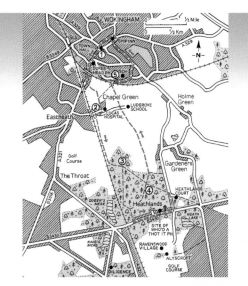

Berkshire

187 READING ON THE WILDE SIDE

3 miles (4.8km) 1hr 15min Ascent: Negligible
Paths: Pavements, river and canal tow path, no stiles
Suggested map: aqua3 OS Explorer 159 Reading, Wokingham & Pangbourne. A good street map of Reading
Grid reference: SU 716735
Parking: Reading Station, Chatham Street, Garrard Street, Hexagon

A canal-side trail past Reading Gaol, where Oscar Wilde served time.

❶ Start by statue of Queen Victoria and, with your back to Town Hall, turn **R**, pass **tourist information centre** and museum. Cross Valpy Street; turn **R** into Forbury Road. Walk to roundabout, with Rising Sun pub on corner, and turn **L** towards **railway bridge**. Pass beneath line and cross road at pedestrian lights. Avoid King's Meadow Road and make for **Reading Bridge**.

❷ Take steps on **R** just before bridge and join **Thames Path**, heading downstream with river on **L**. Pass **Caversham Lock** as sound of traffic begins to fade and surroundings becomes leafier. Skirt **King's Meadow**, with smart apartment buildings and lines of houses on opposite bank. Pass boat yard and continue under tree branches. Eventually reach Kennet Mouth and here distinctive Sustrans waymark directs you over bridge (in direction of Bristol!).

❸ Cross **Horseshoe Bridge** and turn **L** on far side, heading for central Reading. Pass beneath Brunel's **railway bridge**, continue to **Fisherman's Cottage** and Blakes Lock, and leave canal tow path at next bridge. Turn **R** along **King's Road**, passing listed façade of **Huntley and Palmer's** biscuit factory, then turn immediately **R** and cross bridge built by Reading Gas Company (1880). Join tow path and keep vast hulk of the Prudential building over on **L** bank.

❹ Pass under **King's Road**, keep to **R** and follow Chestnut Walk. **Reading Gaol** is **R**. Walk to ruins of **Reading Abbey** and turn **R**. Keep beside gaol and enter **Forbury Gardens** through flint arch. Keep to **L** edge, with statue of lion on **R**. Look for abbey gateway on **L**, with Reading Crown Court adjacent, and exit at Victoria Gate. Walk ahead to outer gate of **Reading Abbey**, pass Church of St Laurence-in-Reading on **R** and return to **tourist information centre** and statue.

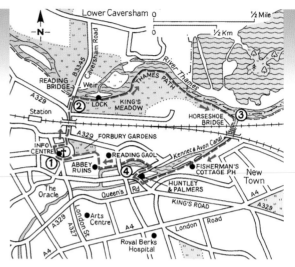

188 PANGBOURNE FASHIONABLE RIVERSIDE RESORT

3 miles (4.8km) 1hr 30min Ascent: Negligible
Paths: Field and riverside paths, stretches of road, section of Thames Path, 4 stiles
Suggested map: aqua3 OS Explorer 159 Reading, Wokingham & Pangbourne
Grid reference: SU 633765
Parking: Car park off A329 in Pangbourne, near railway bridge

The Pang and a National Trust meadow

❶ From car park turn **R** to mini-roundabout; walk along to church and adjoining cottage. Retrace your steps to main road, keep **Cross Keys pub** on **R** and turn **R** at mini-roundabout. Cross **Pang**; bear **R** at next major junction into The Moors. At end of drive continue ahead on waymarked footpath. Pass alongside various houses and patches of scrub; then go through tunnel of trees. Further on is gate with map and information board. Beyond gate **River Pang** can be seen.

❷ Follow riverside path. Make for footbridge. Don't cross it, instead, turn sharp **L** and walk across open meadow to stile in far boundary. Once over, keep alongside hedge on **L** and, as you approach a World War II pill box, turn **R** at path intersection and cross footbridge. Head for another footbridge on far side of field and then look for 3rd bridge with white railings, by field boundary. Cross bridge and stile beyond it; then head across field to far boundary.

❸ Exit to road and bear **L**. Follow lane between hedges and oak trees and proceed to **A329**. Go diagonally **R** to footpath by sign ('Purley Rise') and follow path north towards distant trees. Turn **R** at next bridge; follow concrete track as it bends **L** to run beneath railway line. Once through it, bear **R** to stile; then follow track along **L** edge of field, beside rivulet. Ahead on horizon are hanging woods on north bank of Thames. Pass double gates and bridge on **L**; continue on footpath as it crosses gentle lowland landscape. Cross stile; walk across next field to reach river bank.

❹ On reaching **River Thames**, turn **L** and head towards **Pangbourne**. Follow **Thames Path** to **Pangbourne Meadow** and up ahead now is **Whitchurch Bridge**. As you approach it, begin to veer away from river bank towards car park. Keep **L** when you get to road, pass beneath **railway line** and turn **R** at next junction. Bear **R** again at mini-roundabout and return to car park.

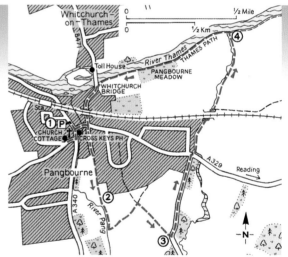

189 FRILSHAM THE POT KILN

3½ miles (5.7km) 1hr 30min Ascent: 99ft (30m)
Paths: Tracks, paths and stretches of country road, no stiles
Suggested map: aqua3 OS Explorer 158 Newbury & Hungerford
Grid reference: SU 551731
Parking: Space at side of Pot Kiln (but ask permission)

A delightful woodland walk to a traditional local pub.

❶ The Pot Kiln, from the outside, could almost pass for a farm or a private house but is famous for being a traditional pub – certainly worth walking up a thirst for! Go to end of car park at side of Pot Kiln and follow track. Keep microbrewery on **R**, pass several houses, including Laurel Bank Cottages. Avoid public footpath on **L** and continue to 2 cottages at **R** angles to byway. Bear **L** just beyond them and follow footpath between holly trees. Disregard turning on **L** and keep **R** at next fork. Head for road and turn **L**. Walk through Frilsham village, pass Beechfield, a residential development, and turn **L** at sign for Hermitage and Bucklebury.

❷ When lane bends **R**, go straight ahead, following path deep into woods. Pass through gate and continue on bridleway to next waymark. Branch off to **L** at this point, following path down wooded slope to road. Cross over to gateway and continue on this track for about ¾ mile (1.2km). Piles of logs can often be seen lining route, waiting to be transported to sawmills. Pass waymarked track on **R** and then one on **L** – don't be tempted to turn off but continue on main track, following it through ornamental woodland to next waymarked junction.

❸ Bear **L** here and cut through bluebell woods to gate. Cross over field to gate in next boundary, with traffic on **M4** visible in distance. Veer half-**L** in field and away to **R** in distance, you can just make out façade of Yattendon Court, up among trees. Cross over field and make for bridleway on **R**, running into trees.

❹ Beyond wood, follow path between fences and swing **L** at next waymarked junction. Walk along to next junction, where there are footpath and bridleway signs, and veer **R**. Follow track round side of **Magpie Farm** and on reaching road, turn **L**. Return to car park by **Pot Kiln**.

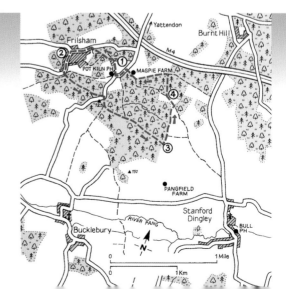

Berkshire

BRIMPTON *THROUGH WASING PARK*

6 miles (9.7km) 2hrs 45min **Ascent:** 150ft (46m)
Paths: Field and woodland paths and tracks, parkland drives, meadow, road and riverside, 11 stiles
Suggested map: aqua3 OS Explorer 159 Reading, Wokingham & Pangbourne
Grid reference: SU 567628
Parking: Limited spaces in lay-by opposite Pineapple pub

A walk through lovely parkland overlooking the Kennet Valley.

❶ Follow path across 2 stiles to road. Cross to join byway, follow it **R** and across **common**. When it swings sharp **L**, keep ahead. Take path to **R** of Woodside; bear **L** at T-junction; follow path. Where it joins track, veer **L** at waymark, following field-edge path. Look for opening in trees ahead; cross bridge; turn **R** at track, following signs ('**Wasing Church**').

❷ Take track, turn **L** at bend; cut through wood. Turn **R** and proceed to road. Bear **L** to junction, then **R** over **Enborne** to fork. Keep **L** and turn **R** at 'Wasing Estate' sign. Veer **L** along grassy track to junction; bear **L**.

❸ Follow path to road; turn **R**, then **L** to join path. Keep to **L** edge of field, through kissing gate in top corner; veer **R**. Turn **R** to reach housing estate. Bear **R** at road; walk along to church, following path beside it. On reaching field corner, keep ahead, swinging **L** by power lines. Head south to Hyde End Lane.

❹ Turn **L**, keeping **R** at fork. Look for stile to **L** of footbridge; go across meadow. Follow river bank to reach footbridge and stile. Cross over and take path to stile and bridge. Cross over road and follow track, taking path to **L** of it along woodland edge and making for bridge in far **R** corner. Follow line of trees to stile; cross next pasture towards buildings. Approaching gate and cottage veer **L** to stile. Cross to another stile by road.

❺ Turn **R** over bridge; bear **L** to gate leading into Ashford Hill Meadows, veering **L** across pastures. After 75yds (68m) it becomes enclosed by trees, look for fork, and branch **L** to footbridge. Begin crossing field, after about 120yds (109m), make for gate on **L**. Swing **R** and keep **L** at fork after about 50yds (45m). Look for stile at fence corner and continue through trees. Head for stile, turn **L**. Cross over field to next stile. Proceed; when lane bends **R**, bear **L** and continue to road. Continue to return to lay-by.

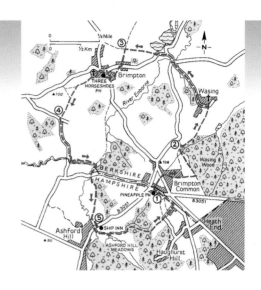

HERMITAGE *A WRITER'S WARTIME REFUGE*

6 miles (9.7km) 2hrs 45min **Ascent:** 320ft (98m)
Paths: Field and woodland paths and tracks, some road, 4 stiles
Suggested map: aqua3 OS Explorer 158 Newbury & Hungerford
Grid reference: SU 505730
Parking: Limited parking in Hermitage

Explore dense woodland and pass the former home of DH Lawrence on this spectacular walk near Newbury.

❶ From **village hall** in **Hermitage** turn **R**, then **R** again into Doctors Lane. Cross stile by private road sign and head across field to next stile. Pass beneath power lines and make for stile in boundary of woodland ahead. Follow footpath through trees as far as cottage. Turn **L** when you reach track and veer **R** after about 60yds (55m) at public footpath sign. Drop down through woodland to lane and keep to **R**. Walk along lane to hamlet of **Oare** and turn **R** by small pond.

❷ Head towards buildings of **Little Hungerford**, cross stile and turn **R** at road. Bear **L** into Chapel Lane and follow road round R-H bend. Pass Pond Lane and DH Lawrence's former home on corner as you head for next road junction. **Chapel Farm Cottage** is clearly identified – its front entrance is in Pond Lane and its rear garden backs on to Chapel Lane. Turn **L** and walk along to a public footpath sign on **R**. Follow track deep into **Box Wood** and eventually reach junction.

❸ Bear **R** here and follow track through trees to next road. Cross over by bungalow and continue on next section of track. Turn **R** at next road and walk along to turning for **Boar's Hole Farm** on **L**. Follow track to farm and continue south to L-H bend. Go through gate on **R** and make for gate and house in field corner. Keep to **R** of house and turn **R** at track bend, passing through metal gate.

❹ Follow woodland track and keep **R** at fork. Go across stream and pass **L** turning. Take next **L** path by stream and pass over staggered junction. Turn **R** by pond, then 1st **L**, cutting through trees. Swing **R** at next junction and follow track as it runs up by seat. Keep **L** at junction and make for road by cottage. Opposite are earthworks of **Grimsbury Castle**. Turn **R** and walk along to road junction. Bear **L** and return to Hermitage.

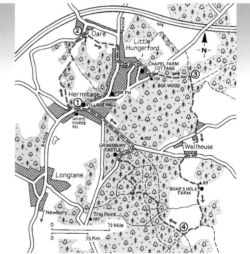

DONNINGTON CASTLE *CIVIL WAR STRONGHOLD*

3 miles (4.8km) 1hr 45min **Ascent:** 165ft (50m)
Paths: Paths and tracks through woods
Suggested map: aqua3 OS Explorer 158 Newbury & Hungerford
Grid reference: SU 463709
Parking: Car park at Snelsmore Common Country Park

A country park and a castle.

❶ Keep toilets on **R** and walk ahead to barrier and country park sign. Veer **R** at fork and picnic tables and benches. Follow track to kissing gate. Beyond, track curves to **L** and then runs straight to **L** curve. Pass path on **R** here and continue for few paces to bridleway.

❷ Turn sharp **R** and keep **L** at next fork, avoiding path on extreme **L**. Keep to **R** of wooden seat and descend bank between bracken. Cut through trees at bottom to gate and follow path ahead as it upgrades to track. Pass **Honey Bottom Cottage** and go straight ahead when track bends **R**. Follow path along woodland edge until reaching wooden kissing gate on **R**.

❸ Head down field slope towards **Bagnor**, following waymarks. Make for gate and follow grassy path to road. Turn **L**, pass **Blackbird Inn** and follow track at end of car park. Go through kissing gate and take tarmac path over **A34** to golf course. Keep **L** at fork on far side of footbridge, heading towards woodland and

intersection. Cross drive and follow waymarked path on **R**, threading through trees. Keep greens and fairways on **R**. Emerge from woodland at gate and climb slope to **Donnington Castle**.

❹ Look for gate behind it, leading to track. Turn **L**. Pass between barns of **Castle Farm**. Bear **L** down tarmac bridleway. Re-cross bypass and sweep **R**, following drive as it dwindles to track. Keep **R** at fork and cut between fences. On **L** are extensive fairways. Follow track towards house and keep to **L** of it.

❺ Pass through gate on to **Snelsmore Common** and keep ahead at waymarked junction. Pass beneath power lines and continue between bracken and gorse bushes. Keep **R** at next fork and follow waymark pointing towards car park. A useful landmark is fire control tower. Merge with another path at next waymark and, within sight of road and just before stile, look for gate on your **L**. Go through it and return to car park.

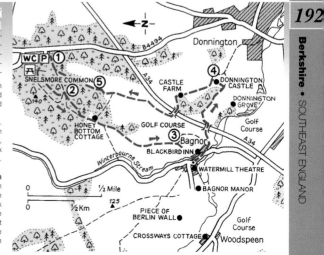

Berkshire

193 FARNBOROUGH *THE OLD RECTORY*

7½ miles (12.1km) 3hrs **Ascent:** 150ft (46m)

Paths: Bridleways, field paths, tracks and quiet lanes, no stiles
Suggested map: aqua3 OS Explorer 170 Abingdon & Wantage
Grid reference: SU 471825
Parking: Room to park in West Ilsley's main street

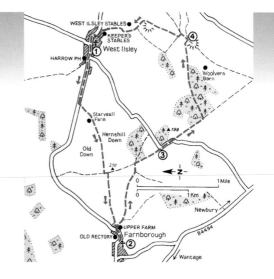

To the former home of a poet, John Betjeman.
❶ Follow road out of **West Ilsley**, heading west. Take 1st bridleway on **L** and make for gate. Continue ahead with field boundary on R. Bear **L** at next junction, and then almost immediately **R** to follow path across large field. Look for boundary corner ahead and keep ahead in next field, with fence on R. Follow path across field to road by **Upper Farm**, veer **L** and walk along to **Farnborough church** and **Old Rectory**.
❷ Walk along road to farm, rejoin track beside outbuildings and look for waymark and galvanised gates after about 60yds (55m). Field footpath and 2 tracks can be seen here. Keep **R**, alongside farm. Cut between trees, bushes and margins of vegetation and cross track further on. Continue ahead to junction with byway and bridleway. Keep going through woodland, following Ilsley Downs Riding Route. Make for next junction, where you can see field beyond the trees, bear **R** and follow clear path through woods.

❸ Keep **R** at road and when it bends R, keep ahead along bridleway running across fields towards trees. At length, bridleway becomes byway. Keep ahead on reaching bend and walk along to on **L**. Take it into woodland and down slope. As you approach gap in hedge, with field ahead, veer **R** to follow path running through trees. Eventually it climbs gently to junction. Walk turns **L**, but it is worth stepping to R for several paces to admire timeless view of **Woolvers Barn** and Woolvers Down.
❹ Follow byway, avoiding public footpath on R, and take next bridleway on **L**. Keep **R** at next junction and cut between hedges. When track bends **L**, there is memorable view of **West Ilsley** sitting snug in its downland setting. Keep **R** at next junction, following track alongside **West Ilsley Stables**. Walk down to and turn **L**. As it bends R by bridleway sign, go straight on by **Keeper's Stables**. Swing **L** as you reach centre of **West Ilsley** and pass **All Saints Church**.

194 CHADDLEWORTH *A NAG'S TALE*

6 miles (9.7km) 2hrs 30min **Ascent:** 269ft (90m)

Paths: Field paths and tracks, stretches of road, 8 stiles
Suggested map: aqua3 OS Explorer 158 Newbury & Hungerford
Grid reference: SU 416773
Parking: Permission given by landlord to park at Ibex pub

An exhilarating walk into racing country.
❶ From **Ibex** take path opposite pub, emerging at next road by Box Hedge Cottage. Keep **R** and follow lane between cottages to steps and footpath on **R**. Grassy path cuts between fields, towards houses. Keep to **R** of village hall and cross next road to gate.
❷ Skirt field, avoid footpath on L and proceed beside oak trees. On reaching stile, cross over and keep paddock on **L**. Turn **L** at next path junction; keep along field edge. Eventually path broadens to track. Keep ahead at road; just before it bends R, look for waymarked track on **L**, descending to **Manor Farm**.
❸ Cross road; follow path up slope to stile. Continue ahead, keeping fence on L, and make for brow of hill. Descend field slope; make for bushes in field corner, concealing 2 stiles. Head straight down next field, cross stile and continue ahead in line with row of telegraph poles towards road. Cross stile and head towards **Whatcombe** and South Fawley. Turn **L** at

entrance to **Whatcombe** and, on reaching stud, keep **L** and take waymarked bridleway.
❹ Ascend, keeping to **R** of trees ahead. Make for gateway into plantation and cross next field by cutting off corner. If muddy, follow **L** boundary. Look for waymark in trees, descend bank to path. Turn **L**. On reaching track, proceed keeping to **L** of farm outbuildings. Pass to **R** of **Henley Farm**; follow byway down to cottages. Cross road to single-track lane; bear **L** at next junction.
❺ Take 1st lane on **R** and climb steeply to **L-H** bend. Walk to next junction, turn **R** and pass sign ('**Chaddleworth**'). Church is on **L**. Turn **R** towards Great Shefford; then take 1st **L** path. Look for transformer, enter field, via squeeze stile and cross, keeping to **R** of house and alongside line of trees.
❻ Cross stile in corner. Turn **L** at footpath sign. Follow field edge to next waymark and drop down to housing estate. Turn **R** at road. Retrace steps to start.

195 COMBE GIBBET *A GRISLY TALE*

7 miles (11.3km) 3hrs **Ascent:** 560ft (171m)

Paths: Woodland paths, field and downland tracks, some road and stretch of Wayfarer's Walk, 5 stiles
Suggested map: aqua3 OS Explorer 158 Newbury & Hungerford
Grid reference: SU 379615
Parking: Small car park to east of Walbury Hill

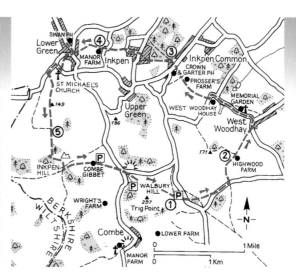

Climb to the scene of a 17th-century double murder – and punishment.
❶ Cross road to gate; go down field towards corner of wood on R. Edge round it and head for trees. Follow path as it veers to **L** of woodland, making for gate in fence. Walk down lane to 2nd bridleway on **L**. Follow it between fields, sweeping **R** to **Highwood Farm**.
❷ Join concrete track; follow it to road. Turn **L**, keep **L** at next junction and pass St Laurence's Church. Pass **West Woodhay House** and Kintbury turning; follow road round **L** bend. Turn **R** 80yds (73m) beyond it; continue to **Prosser's Farm**. Keep ahead at road, cross and follow track to cottage. Keep **R** at 1st fork, then **L** at 2nd fork.
❸ Follow woodland trail to junction of paths by stone; swing **L** to keep to path, skirting woodland. Emerge from trees, pass houses; turn **R** at 1st kissing gate. Follow path across field to kissing gate. Cross road; follow lane beside gate and round to **R**. Make for

gate on L, pass tennis court and walk along edge of lawn to kissing gate. Cross field to another; keep **L** at road towards **Manor Farm**; cross stile ahead at bend.
❹ Shortly, veer **L** to gate. Follow path between hedge and fence, through 2 kissing gates; follow section of boardwalk. Look for tree house on R, pass beech hedge; follow drive to road. Bear **L** to stile and follow fence; cross into next field, towards **St Michael's Church**, and stile. Turn **R**, to junction. Bear **L** pass ('Inkpen village') sign; swing **L** to follow waymarked track. Continue to next waymark and keep line of trees on R before crossing fields. Make for next waymark and keep ahead between trees.
❺ Climb to reach stile. Aim diagonally **L**, ascending towards cleft in ridge of **Inkpen Hill**. At summit keep fence **R** and make for gate ahead. Head **L** to join byway. Follow track to **Combe Gibbet**; cross 2 stiles at either end of it. Keep on track to road, cross and follow Wayfarer's Walk. Keep on track, back to start.

Buckinghamshire

STOWE *MAJESTIC PARADISE*

4½ miles (7.2km) 2hrs **Ascent:** Negligible
Paths: Field paths, estate drives, stretches of road, 5 stiles
Suggested map: aqua3 OS Explorer 192 Buckingham & Milton Keynes
Grid reference: SP 684357
Parking: On-street parking in Chackmore

Savour the delights of Stowe, with its famous 18th-century landscape garden.

❶ Walk through **Chackmore**, pass **Queens Head** and continue through village. At speed derestriction signs, keep ahead for few paces and look for path on L. Aim diagonally **R** in field, passing under power lines. Make for stile beneath branches of oak in corner where waymarks indicate that path forks.

❷ Cross field towards 2 stiles, making for one on L, beyond which is plank bridge. Keep to **R** boundary of elongated field and when it widens, go diagonally **R** to far corner. **Stowe Castle** is visible to R and outline of **Corinthian Arch** to L. Join track, pass under telegraph wires and look for gap and waymark as track curves **R** by hedge corner. Veer over to **R** in field and look for path ('Farey Oak'). Avoid this route and make for footbridge and stile few paces away.

❸ Cross into field and head up slope, keeping to **L** of 2 distant houses. Head for single-storey dwelling in top corner and as you climb slope, outline of **Gothic Temple** looms into view. Go through gate at **Lamport** and continue ahead on bridleway. The **Bourbon Tower** is clearly visible. Pass through gate and keep ahead towards monument commemorating Duke of Buckingham. Merge with another path and keep sports ground on R.

❹ Make for gate leading out to avenue of trees running down towards **Grecian Valley**. Cross over and follow grass track up to clump of trees. Bear **L** here and follow avenue (part of **Roman road**). Pass magnificent façade of **Stowe School** and keep along main drive. On reaching **Boycott Pavilions**, branch off half-**L** at stile and sign for **Corinthian Arch**. Down below lies **Oxford Water**, crossed by stone bridge.

❺ Follow drive through parkland. Drive eventually reaches **Corinthian Arch**. Line up with arch and enjoy views of **Stowe School**. Walk down avenue to road junction, swing **L** and return to **Chackmore**.

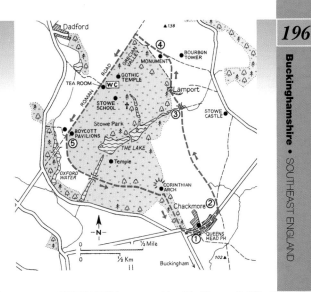

MILTON KEYNES *CITY OF THE FUTURE*

3 miles (4.8km) 2hrs **Ascent:** Negligible
Paths: Paved walkways, boulevards and park paths
Suggested map: aqua3 OS Explorer 192 Milton Keynes & Buckingham, or street map from tourist information centre
Grid reference: SP 842380 **Parking:** Car park at Milton Keynes Station

A unique city walk.

❶ With your back to **station**, aim slightly **L**, line up with row of flag-poles and make for 2 underpasses. Head along **Midsummer Boulevard**, passing sculpture on L. Make for next subway and cross **Witan Gate** and Upper 5th Street. Swing **L** just before next subway. Keep **church** L and continue to **Silbury Boulevard**, passing under subway.

❷ Turn **R**, pass Milton Keynes **Library and Exhibition Gallery**. Pass North 9th Street and statue of Lloyds black horse. Swing **R** and pass under road to approach **shopping centre** at Deer Walk. Don't enter complex here, instead turn **L** and walk along to next entrance at Eagle Walk. Go straight through, pass map of centre and emerge at Midsummer Boulevard.

❸ Turn **L** to Field Walk and turn **R** here to cross boulevard. Bear **L** to reach tourist information centre, **Milton Keynes Theatre** and city gallery. Continue ahead under subway and cross footbridge into **Campbell Park**. Skirt round pond and make for beacon that represents highest point in park. As you approach it, turn sharp **R** and follow path as it through park. Roughly 30yds (27m) before circular seat bear sharp **R** to join grassy path alongside fence. Make for kissing gate and turn **R**. Walk along to next path junction, with kissing gate on R. Turn **L** here, back towards town centre. Keep to **L** to join wide concrete ride and follow waymarked city centre route.

❹ Cross bridge to Bankfield roundabout. Proceed on **Avebury Boulevard**. Cross **Secklow Gate** and Lower 10th Street. Turn **R** into Lower 9th Street. Pass **The Point** and bear **L** into Midsummer Place **shopping centre**. Cross concourse and pass police station. The Church of Christ the Cornerstone can be seen from here. Keep **L** and return to **Avebury Boulevard**, turning **R** to underpass. Walk to **Grafton Gate**, veer **R** just before it and head for **Midsummer Boulevard**. Go through underpasses and return to railway **station**.

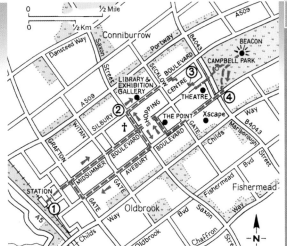

BLETCHLEY PARK *IN SEARCH OF SECRETS*

5 miles (8km) 1hr 45min **Ascent:** Negligible
Paths: Roads, park and field paths, canal tow path and riverside walk, 2 stiles
Suggested map: aqua3 OS Explorer 192 Buckingham & Milton Keynes
Grid reference: SP 868337
Parking: Bletchley Station and approach road

Puzzle over the enigma of Station X on this urban walk around Bletchley.

❶ From **station** car park cross road; take path to **Bletchley Park**. On leaving former Station X walk along Wilton Avenue; turn **L** into Church Green Road. Bear **L** at junction with Buckingham Road and head towards Central Bletchley. Turn **R** into Water Eaton Road; pass under **railway line**. Bear **R** at footpath sign, just before next railway bridge.

❷ Pass pond, **Pulmans Swannery**, on R; follow fenced path to stile. Continue to fork, keep **R**. Follow track anti-clockwise around edge of lake. Avoid ford and footbridge and continue on lakeside path. At southwest corner of lake, look for steps and footbridge on R. Turn **L** immediately beyond them; follow path parallel to power lines. Bear **L** at grassy track and follow it towards **railway line**. Turn **R** immediately before stile keeping to R of house. Swing **L** at fence to reach stile then walk ahead, keeping **railway line** L.

❸ Pass through tunnel of trees and beside farmland. At drive to **Slad Farm**, exit to road. Bear **L**. Cross railway bridge and turn immediately **R** at gate. Follow path for short distance to field corner and swing **L** to join bridleway. Keep houses on L, beyond trees and hedgerow. At road, between 2 roundabouts, cross over to canal bridge and swing **L** to follow **Broad Walk**. At sign for **Riverside Walk**, turn **R** then swing **L** after about 75yds (69m).

❹ Draw river away to R. Draw level with farm over to R, cross footbridge over pond and turn **L**. Head for The **Watermill** and **Mill Farm**, avoiding car park for **Waterhall Park**. Cross bridge over **Grand Union Canal** and keep **R**. Ahead now are cottages. Turn **L** in front of them and keep **R** at main road junction, heading towards **Plough Inn**. Cross road at roundabout, following sign for **station**. Continue through residential area. Pass under 2 bridges, go straight over at junction and to **station** car park.

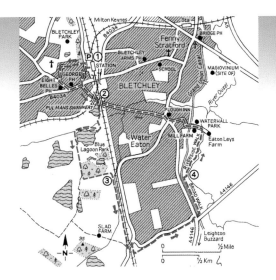

Buckinghamshire

199 THE CLAYDONS *LADY WITH THE LAMP*

5½ miles (8.8km) 2hrs **Ascent:** 160ft (49m) ▲
Paths: Field paths and tracks, several stretches of road
Suggested map: aqua3 OS Explorer 192 Buckingham & Milton Keynes
Grid reference: SP 739255
Parking: On-street parking in road leading to St Mary the Virgin Church, East Claydon

Visit a National Trust house and the bedroom occupied by Florence Nightingale.
❶ Walk along Church Way into village centre. Keep R at next junction, following **Sandhill Road**. Pass houses and swing L through gate, before brick and timber cottage. Keep ahead towards next gate; look for gate and waymark few paces to L of it. Keep ahead in field, with boundary on R. Make for gate in corner on L, following track along field perimeter, towards **Home Farm**. Look for plank bridge and stile to L of track; cross cemetery to stile by road.
❷ Bear L. Follow road for 600yds (549m). Pass entrance to **Home Farm** (R) and footpath (L). Turn L. Follow drive to **Claydon House**. At cattle grid just in front of it, bear R through 2 gates then L. Keeping **Claydon House** and church L, continue beside ha-ha, with lake to R. Cut through parkland to gate, merge with drive to **Claydon House** and follow to road.

❸ Turn R and pass lay-by. Keep ahead to stile in L boundary. Head diagonally L towards hedge corner, making for stile close to it. Maintain direction and make for extreme L corner of **Home Wood**. Cross 2nd stile and look for 3rd stile by woodland edge. Keep telegraph wires (L) and look for waymark in corner. Cross stile, keeping to L of hedge. Make for gate and stile ahead. Cross tarmac drive to **Muxwell Farm**.
❹ Beyond gate, head diagonally L and look for waymark in line of trees across pasture. Veer R in next field, making for stile and post in boundary. Walk diagonally R across field to far corner, pass through gap and keep to R edge of pasture. Bear R at gateway to track and turn L. Walk along to road and turn R.
❺ Walk through **Botolph Claydon**. Bear L at junction, following signs, ('**East Claydon** and **Winslow**'). Pass Botolph Farmhouse, **library** and hall. Follow pavement to sign ('footpath only, no horses'). Take path back to **East Claydon**.

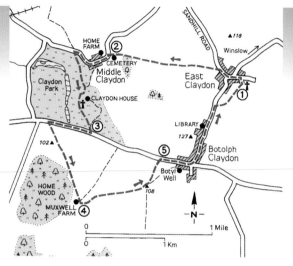

200 MENTMORE *CRIME OF THE CENTURY*

6½ miles (10.4km) 2hrs 45min **Ascent:** 180ft (55m) ▲
Paths: Field paths and tracks, roads and canal tow path, 2 stiles
Suggested map: aqua3 OS Explorers 181 Chiltern Hills North; 192 Milton Keynes & Buckingham
Grid reference: Grid reference: SP 907196 (on Explorer 181)
Parking: Limited parking in vicinity of Stag pub at Mentmore

Enjoy an amble in the Vale of Aylesbury, passing the site of the Great Train Robbery.
❶ Walk back to junction by **Stag**, turn R and pass one of **Mentmore Towers**' entrances. Follow road round to L, then R by Church of St Mary the Virgin. Continue along road; bear R at stile, just beyond **Vicarage Cottage**. Go down field, keeping fence to R; look for stile in bottom boundary.
❷ Veer R briefly to plank bridge; swing L to skirt field, keeping ditch on R. On reaching next plank bridge and waymark, look for pond. Follow path alongside it into next field and pass under telegraph wires to next plank bridge in boundary. Keep ahead and pass under electricity cables. Houses of **Ledburn** can be seen ahead. Make for footbridge; in next field aim slightly L, towards house. Keep to L of it, turning R at road.
❸ Walk through **Ledburn**, making for L bend. On L is **Cornfield Cottage**. Cross road to kissing gate and follow track running across farmland. As it curves L,

keep ahead, following path across field. On reaching track, turn R and follow it to **Sears Crossing**. Cross **railway bridge**, follow track over railway. Turn L.
❹ Bear R at sign for Grove Church and Farm and down to **Grand Union Canal** at **Church Lock**. Pass Church Lock Cottage before turning R to join tow path. Follow **Grand Union** for about 1 mile (1.6km) and, about 140yds (128m) before bridge, with **weir** on the L, leave tow path at plank bridge and bear R for few paces to field corner.
❺ Swing L and keep boundary on R. Make for 2 gates leading out to road, then L at turning for Wing and **Ledburn**. Follow road to **Bridego Bridge**, pass beneath **railway**; keep ahead to **Rowden Farm**.
❻ Bear L at next junction for Mentmore. Pass Mentmore Courts and **Stud House** before turning **L** at end of stretch of pavement. Opposite junction are 2 wooden gates leading into field. Follow road round to R and return to playground and parking area.

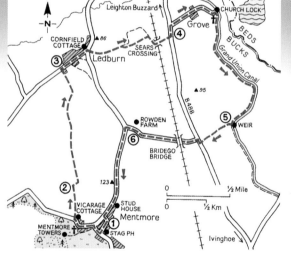

201 QUAINTON *MAKING TRACKS*

5 miles (8km) 2hrs **Ascent:** Negligible
Paths: Mainly field paths, some stretches of road, parts of North Buckinghamshire Way and Midshires Way, 22 stiles
Suggested map: aqua3 OS Explorer 181 Chiltern Hills North
Grid reference: SP 736189
Parking: Brill Tramway Path car park, parking on extreme L. Permission given by Buckinghamshire Railway Centre

Recall the great days of steam.
❶ Leave car park, turn L and cross road bridge over **railway**. Entrance to site is on R. Exit **railway centre**, bear R and follow Station Road towards **Quainton**. Pass houses and, when road curves to L by bus stop, turn R at footpath sign and stile to follow track between fields. **Quainton** and windmill are L. Go through gateway. Turn R to join **North Buckinghamshire Way**.
❷ Follow field edge to gate. Continue to stile in far boundary. Cross 3 more stiles before reaching **railway line; Quainton Road Station** lies to R. Cross 2 stiles and follow track to R-H bend. Outline of Waddesdon Manor can be seen to R of church. As track bends R, cross stile into field. Turn immediately R.
❸ Skirt **Glebe Farm** and cross track via 2 stiles, continuing on **North Buckinghamshire Way**. Aim diagonally R to 2 stiles and continue alongside

hedgerow in next field. Cross 2 stiles and join enclosed path running into **Waddesdon**. On reaching A41, turn R, crossing Quainton Road and Frederick Street. Pass **Lion Pub**, church and post office before reaching parish church of St Michael and All Angels on R.
❹ Follow road out of village, passing **Bell** pub. Keep to A41 and look for old stone milepost. In 50yds (46m), beyond speed derestriction sign, turn R at stile and waymark. Cut through trees to 2nd stile and continue ahead in field. Cross concrete farm track, pass under power lines and aim for stile in boundary hedge. **Littleton Manor Farm** can be seen near by.
❺ Aim slightly L in next field to reach stile. Go diagonally L across next pasture to far corner. Look for narrow gap in hedgerow, cross 2 stiles and walk ahead, passing beside corrugated animal shelters. Make for 2 stiles, turn R and follow road back to start.

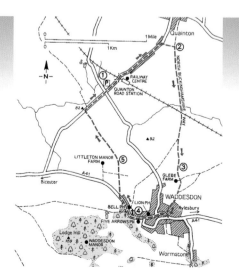

Buckinghamshire

BRILL *A FARMHOUSE DEN OF THIEVES*

4½ miles (7.2km) 1hr 30min **Ascent:** 350ft (107m)
Paths: Field paths and tracks, several stretches of road, 8 stiles
Suggested map: aqua3 OS Explorer 180 Oxford, Witney & Woodstock
Grid reference: SP 653141
Parking: Room to park by windmill

Pass the hideout of the Great Train Robbers.
❶ From car park go down lane, South Hills, beside **Pheasant Inn**, keeping **windmill** visible on R. At lock-up garage and signpost ('Leyhill'), swing **L** to join track. Follow it round to **R** to pair of garages and cross low stile to **R**. On R is cottage. Keep to enclosed footpath and head for 2 more stiles before crossing rolling grassland. Head towards large house and stile to **L** of it. Cross over to road and turn **R**.
❷ Pass footpath, then look for bridleway and footpath sign further down on R; cross into field at stile. Head diagonally **R** down field to plank bridge and stile. Aim broadly **L** at adjoining field, making for stile just to **R** of bottom corner. Turn **L** and follow footpath through undergrowth to cottage. Keep **L** and bear **R** after few paces into **Oakley**. Walk along **Little London** Green to road; turn **R**.
❸ Take 1st path on L, opposite **Little London Farm**. Head diagonally **L** in field, pass under power lines and

make for gateway. Cross next field to waymark and gate; then continue ahead across next pasture to stile and track. Bear **L** and walk up track towards **Leatherslade Farm**. As you approach farm gate, take bridlepath to **L** of it, and skirt house and outbuildings. This is a modern house, built to replace the original farmhouse used by the gang after the robbery.
❹ Once clear of farmhouse buildings, keep climbing gently, passing public footpath on R. Cut between trees and banks of vegetation and make for next galvanised gate. Continue ahead, with field boundary on R. Pass several more footpaths on R and keep going until you reach gate in top boundary. Follow track ahead to road by entrance to house, 'Fairview'.
❺ Keep **L** and keep ahead to **Brill**. Pass Wesleyan chapel, to R, across green is church. The **Red Lion** can also be seen. Pass turning on L to **Oakley** and look for barometer in wall. Bear **L** into Windmill Street and return to car park.

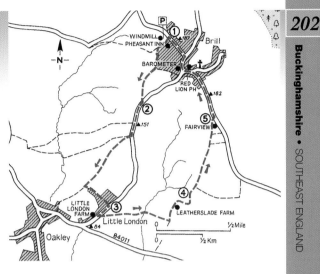

HARTWELL *A GREEN ABODE*

5 miles (8km) 2hrs **Ascent:** 180ft (55m)
Paths: Field and riverside paths, tracks and lanes, 6 stiles
Suggested map: aqua3 OS Explorer 181 Chiltern Hills North
Grid reference: SP 783123
Parking: Space in Eythrope Road, Hartwell

By the River Thame and through the grounds of Hartwell House.
❶ From A418 turn into Bishopstone Road and keep to L of church. Walk along to footpath beside Manor Farm Close and cross pasture to kissing gate leading out to recreation ground. Pass ornate gate pillars on L, recalling village men who died in world wars. Exit to road by railings. Cross over to footpath sign and gate for Woodspeen and follow drive to timber garage and shed. Bear **R** to gate and follow path to road. Turn **R**, walk up to **A418**. **Rose and Crown** is on R.
❷ Swing **L** at corner. Follow path beside stone wall. Head for road, bear **R** and walk to **Hartwell House** entrance. Veer **L** at gate pillars. Follow waymarked path through hotel grounds. Go through kissing gate, keep church R and graveyard L. Turn **R** at road and pass pavilion. Avoid **North Bucks Way** to L, pass **Lower Hartwell Farm**. Turn **L** at footpath. Cross 2 fields via 3 stiles. Turn **R** just beyond plank bridge.

❸ Skirt field, making for stile ahead. Keep hedge on L and continue on **North Bucks Way**, heading towards **Waddon Hill Farm**. Cross stile, walk ahead alongside timber barns; turn **L** at waymark. Follow track across fields. When it eventually sweeps L, leave it and go proceed along a path to stile. Cross meadow and head for **River Thame**. Swing **L** at river bank to gate and join **Thame Valley Walk**.
❹ After about 60yds (55m) path reaches 2nd gate, where river begins wide loop away to R. Follow stream to next gate and rejoin river bank. Follow **Thame**, avoiding bridleway branching away from river, and continue on waymarked trail. Make for footbridge and weir, on opposite bank is ornate **lodge**. Join concrete track and follow it towards trees.
❺ Once in trees, river is on L and **Eythrope Park** is on R. Bear **R** at next junction. To continue, keep **L** and follow tarmac drive. Begin moderate lengthy ascent before reaching **Stone**.

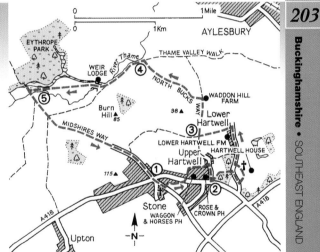

CHEQUERS *COUNTRY SEAT OF OUR CHOSEN LEADERS*

5 miles (8km) 2hrs **Ascent:** 378ft (115m)
Paths: Field and woodland paths and tracks, stretch of Ridgeway, 9 stiles
Suggested map: aqua3 OS Explorer 181 Chiltern Hills North
Grid reference: SP 842069
Parking: Limited spaces at Butler's Cross

Savour glimpses of an Elizabethan mansion – rural retreat of the Prime Minister.
❶ From **Butler's Cross** follow Chalkshire Road, keeping **Russell Arms** on R. Walk to row of cottages and take path opposite sign ('Aylesbury Ring'). Cross 4 stiles and pass path on R. Continue to drive on bend and keep ahead, passing **Springs Cottage**. Ahead now are 2 stiles. Veer **L** to further stile, and then swing **L** and head up field slope to **Ellesborough** church. Cross stile into churchyard and keep to R of church. Cross road to bus stop and veer **R** for several paces to kissing gate.
❷ Follow path diagonally up slope to stile, sweeping round to R of **Beacon Hill**. Make for stile and continue through woodland, up flight of steps to edge of trees. Cross field at top, heading for next wood and take track between trees. Cross track leading to **Chequers**, make for stile and initially follow field boundary. After several paces, leave wood on L and stride out across field to kissing gate. Bear **L** across field to kissing

gate. Keep woodland on R and **Chequers** in view across field. Follow path to Ridgeway waymark then cross field and drive to house. Continue to kissing gate.
❸ Cross road and follow **Ridgeway** through woodland. On reaching 4-way junction, turn **L** and follow path alongside hill. After ½ mile (800m), several paths converge. Turn **L** at road, then **R** where it joins another road. Keep to **R** edge and pass lodge house. Follow path north as road diverges to northwest. Continue through woodland to gate. Bear **L**, leaving National Trust land at 2nd gate. Follow path and drive to road by **Coombe Hill Farm**.
❹ Turn **R**, cross over to barrier and join long path half-**R** up large field. Bear **R** at track, following it to road opposite **Ellesborough** church. Enter churchyard, keep to R of church and make for iron gate. Pass cottages on L. Go downhill to pavement and return to **Butler's Cross**.

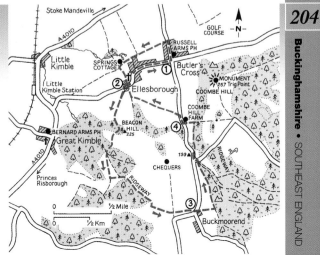

Buckinghamshire • SOUTHEAST ENGLAND

205 JORDANS *WATER OF PEACE*

6¾ miles (10.9km) 2hrs 45min **Ascent:** 98ft (30m)
Paths: Paths across farmland and some road walking, 12 stiles
Suggested map: aqua3 OS Explorer 172 Chiltern Hills East
Grid reference: SU 991937
Parking: Car park off main street, almost opposite church

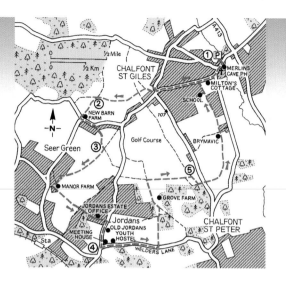

Visit a Quaker settlement and museum recalling the life of poet William Penn.
❶ From car park turn **R** and walk through village. After ¾ mile (1.2km), bear **R** into Back Lane, shortly swinging **L**. Keep **L** at fork, avoid stile in boundary; continue to wide gap in hedge, just before field corner. Cross into adjoining field and proceed in same direction, following path for about 60yds (55m) to stile. Keep ahead in next field, with hedge on **L**, heading for stile. Follow path across fields and between trees until reaching stile and waymark.
❷ Turn **L**; skirt field to gate and stile. Path runs through trees to next stile and drive beyond. Follow it by **New Barn Farm** to road. Turn **L** and **L** again at junction. Bear **R** just beyond **L** bend. Follow waymarked track to Willow Court Stables. Go through kissing gate. Follow path by paddocks.
❸ At path crossroads, turn **R**. Go through kissing gate, under power cables. Make for stile and gate; cross

recreation ground. Keep ahead, cross drive to **Manor Farm**. Follow tree-lined path. Head for path junction; proceed between houses. Cross Copse Lane. Follow Seer Green Lane into village. Continue to junction. Turn **R** towards **Seer Green**. Pass **Old Jordans Guest House**; follow road to **Meeting House**.
❹ Turn **L** into **Welders Lane**; pass **youth hostel**. Continue along lane to track on **L**, ('Grove Farm'). Keep ahead to stile on **L**, just before private property sign. Head diagonally across paddock, passing under power cables. Cross 4 stiles. Turn **R** and follow fenced path to gate. Keep along woodland edge, pass path on **R** and continue to junction by corner of wire fence.
❺ Swing **R**; go through trees to stile by road. Cross; follow enclosed path. Eventually reach track by bungalow, '**Brymavic**'. Cross and continue on path as it skirts bowling green, playing fields and recreation ground. Look for path in corner and keep to **R** of a **school**. Go down to road, turn **R** to return to car park.

206 WEST WYCOMBE *DISRAELI'S DES RES*

7 miles (11.3km) 2hrs 45min **Ascent:** 280ft (85m)
Paths: Field, woodland and parkland paths, some roads, 5 stiles
Suggested map: aqua3 OS Explorer 172 Chiltern Hills East
Grid reference: SU 826952
Parking: Car park by church and mausoleum at West Wycombe

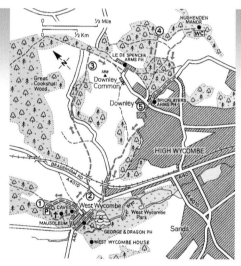

Visit Hughenden Manor, home of famous British statesman Benjamin Disraeli.
❶ From car park pass to immediate **R** of **church**. Continue to **mausoleum** and line up with **A40** below. Take grassy path down hillside, avoiding path on **R** and walk to fork. Keep **R** to steps; descend to road. Bear **L** and pass Church Lane on **R**. Take next path on **R**; keeping to field **R-H** boundary. Look for stile and maintain same direction to stile by road.
❷ Cross over, making for gate; pass under **railway**. At field keep ahead keeping **R** of fence. Follow path to stile; cross track and continue up slope. Make for 2 stiles by gate and barns. Join lane, swing **R** at waymark and follow ride through woodland. Eventually reach a stile with path crossing field beyond.
❸ On reaching track, turn **R** and cut through wood. Veer **L** at fork and head for road. Bear **L** into **Downley**. Turn **L** for **pub** or **R** to continue. Pass houses; when track bends **L**, keep ahead briefly, veering **L** at

waymark. Cross common, following path through clearings and into trees. At National Trust sign, turn sharp **L** and follow path through woods. Avoid path on **L** following white arrows. Pass gate and continue ahead, up moderately steep slope to junction.
❹ Keep **R**; follow path to track. Swing **L** to visit **Hughenden Manor** or **R** to continue. Follow path through parkland, making for trees. Bear immediately **L**, up slope. Look for house; turn **R** at road. Pass **Bricklayers Arms** and straight ahead at junction.
❺ Keep ahead through housing estate. Go forward for several paces at road, bearing **R** at 1st footpath sign. Follow path as it bends **L** and leads to junction. Swing **L** for several steps; veer **R** by houses, heading through trees to galvanised gate. Take sunken path to **R** of gate, follow it to fork and continue ahead. Head for lane and follow it towards **West Wycombe**. Cross **Bradenham Road**; proceed into village. Turn **R** into West Wycombe Hill Road. Head uphill to car park.

207 TURVILLE *THE ROLLING CHILTERNS*

3 miles (4.8km) 1hr 30min **Ascent:** 150ft (45m)
Paths: Field and woodland paths, some road walking, 9 stiles
Suggested map: aqua3 OS Explorer 171 Chiltern Hills West
Grid reference: SU 767911
Parking: Small parking area in centre of Turville

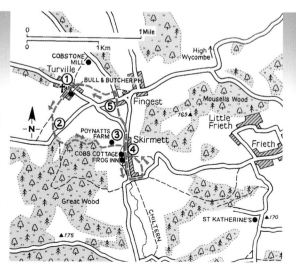

Enjoy views, made famous by film.
❶ The walk starts from **Turville**, one of Britain's most frequently used film and television locations, including *Chitty Chitty Bang Bang, The New Avengers* and *The Vicar of Dibley*. Take lane just to **L** of church entrance, with Sleepy Cottage on corner. Pass Square Close Cottages and school before continuing on Chiltern Way through trees. Climb to gate. Keep ahead along field edge to waymark in boundary. Branch half-**L** at this point, heading diagonally down field to stile.
❷ Cross road to further stile. Follow track through trees, passing gas installation on **R**. Pass bench on **L** before exiting trees. Avoid path branching off to **R** and continue up field slope to next belt of trees. **Turville** is clearly seen over to **L**. Enter woodland; at junction keep **L**. Follow clear wide path as it contours round slopes. Descend hillside, keeping to woodland edge. Follow fence and bear **L** at next corner, heading to stile by **Poynatts Farm**.

❸ Walk along drive to road; bear **R** and enter **Skirmett**. On **R** is **Cobs Cottage** and next door is Ramblers. Pass **The Frog Inn** and follow road south to next junction. Houses, telephone box and post box line route. Turn **L**, pass stile on **R** and walk along to next **L** footpath. Follow field edge to bungalow and stile, cross over to drive and make for road.
❹ Bear **R**, heading out of village, to junction with Watery Lane. Signs ('Except for access') can be seen now. Look for stile and footpath immediately to **R** of it. Cross field to stile in corner and make for boundary hedge ahead in next field. Cross stile and head diagonally **R** to hedge by houses. Once over stile, take road opposite ('Ibstone and Stokenchurch').
❺ Walk up road for about 120yds (110m) and swing **L** at 1st waymarked junction. Follow Chiltern Way between trees, offering glimpses of Chilterns. Cross stile and head diagonally down field towards **Turville**. Make for track; follow it to village green.

Buckinghamshire

BURNHAM BEECHES *SPACE IN A BUSTLING WORLD*

4½ miles (7.2km) 1hr 45min **Ascent:** 150ft (46m) ⚠️
Paths: Woodland paths and drives, field paths, tracks and stretches of road, 9 stiles
Suggested map: aqua3 OS Explorer 172 Chiltern Hills East
Grid reference: SU 957850
Parking: Car park at Burnham Beeches

Enjoy the spacious clearings and sunny glades of a National Nature Reserve.

❶ Follow drive away from **Farnham Common**, keeping car parking area on your L. Pass refreshment kiosk and veer **R** at fork just beyond. Soon reach gate where you enter National Nature Reserve's car-free zone. Follow **Halse Drive** as it curves **L** and down between trees. When you reach bottom of hill swing **L** into **Victoria Drive**.

❷ Follow broad stony drive between beeches, avoiding turnings either side of route; eventually reach major junction with wide path on L and R. On R is large beech tree with 'Andy 6.9.97' carved on trunk. If you miss path, you shortly reach road. Bear **R** and go up slope, keep **L** at fork and cross several clearings to reach road at junction with Green Lane and **Park Lane**.

❸ Cross road to stile and waymark and go straight ahead, keeping boundary on L. Make for stile and descend into field dip, quickly climbing again to pass alongside grounds of **Dorney Wood**. Walk ahead to field corner, cross stile and turn **R** at road. Head for waymarked footpath on **L** and cross field to gap in trees and hedgerow. Turn **R** and skirt fields, making for belt of trees and banks of undergrowth. Path cuts between 2 oak trees in next field before reaching gap in hedgerow.

❹ Cross stile out to road; turn **L**. Pass Common Lane and Horseshoe Hill; turn **R** at next bridleway. Follow track through wood to next road at **Littleworth Common**. Cross stile to **R** of Blackwood Arms and follow Beeches Way. Beyond next stile continue ahead alongside wood, crossing 2 stiles before following fenced path. Go through gate and take path between trees of **Dorney Wood**.

❺ On reaching stile, cross over to road and continue on Beeches Way. Make for next major intersection and keep **R** along Halse Drive. Pass **Victoria Drive** and retrace your steps back to car park.

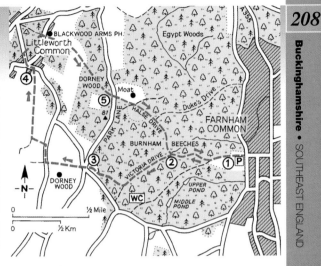

STOKE POGES *A GARDEN GRAVEYARD*

4 miles (6.4km) 1hr 45min **Ascent:** Negligible ⚠️
Paths: Semi-residential paths and drives, field tracks and paths, some road walking and stretches over golf courses, 9 stiles
Suggested map: aqua3 OS Explorer 172 Chiltern Hills East
Grid reference: SU 977825
Parking: Opposite Memorial Gardens

An ornamental landscape.

❶ From car park, turn **R** along road. When pavement ends, cross over. At waymark and kissing gate by oak tree, go through gate and follow path as, initially, it runs parallel with road. Pass entrances to various houses and through 2 gates before joining residential drive – Duffield Park. At road junction bear **R**; then take 1st footpath on **L**, by sign ('Snitterfield House').

❷ Follow drive and, avoiding stile L and turning R, proceed for few paces to **R-H** stile just before sign for house. Cross paddock to stile, make for boundary. Cross stile and footbridge. Keep by **R-H** edge of field. Look for stile by oak tree in corner. Cross next field to gap in hedge by road. Turn **L**, pass **hospital** entrance. Just beyond it, on R, is private drive sign and electricity transformer; bear **R** to stile and gate. Follow track.

❸ Cross next stile after about 50yds (46m) and proceed to **Bell Farm**. Pass outbuildings and keep ahead on grassy track to stile and gate. Turn **L** and follow bridleway ('Galleons Lane') to plank bridge and stile on L. Route now crosses **golf course**. Cut across fairways to wide path and follow it to club car park. Take drive, veering **R** to stile by row of houses and follow track to road. Bear **R** and walk along to **Plough**.

❹ Swing **L** into Plough Lane; when it bends R, keep ahead along public bridleway. Cross next road to kissing gate and continue on waymarked path. Keep ahead, crossing old driveway to **Sefton Park** and golf course before reaching kissing gate. At road, turn **L** and walk to Rogers Lane on **R**. Make for kissing gate on corner and follow outline of path ahead to 2nd gate.

❺ Branch half-**R** and follow path towards **Clock House**. Go through 4 gates before reaching road. Cross to kissing gate. Follow straight path across **Gray's Field**. Keep to **R** of **monument** and look for gate into churchyard. Walk through it to car park.

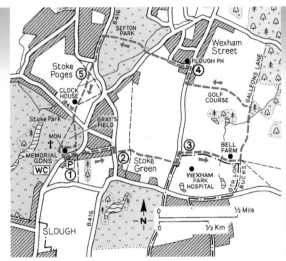

DORNEY *MEDIEVAL VILLAGE MANOR HOUSE*

5 miles (8km) 1hrs 45min **Ascent:** Negligible ⚠️
Paths: Roads, firm paths and Thames tow path
Suggested map: aqua3 OS Explorer 160 Windsor, Weybridge & Bracknell
Grid reference: SU 938776
Parking: Large car park at Dorney Common

Take a stroll by the Thames and visit Dorney Court – unchanged for 600 years.

❶ From car park follow road across **Dorney Common**, towards **Dorney** village. Pass Wakehams, a timber-framed house with a well, and away to R is a fine view of Windsor Castle. Keep **L** at T-junction, cross cattle grid and join pavement. Walk through **Dorney**, keeping **Palmer Arms** on your R. Bear **L** into Court Lane and pass entrance to **Dorney Court**. Follow path parallel to road; shortly reach **Church of St James the Less**.

❷ Continue on path and when road bends R, keep ahead at sign for Dorney Lake, Park and Nature Reserve. Keep to **R-H** side of drive and follow parallel path as it sweeps away to **R** by plaque and grove of trees. Further on path passes over conveyor belt carrying sand and gravel from nearby quarry works. Make for some trees and reach Thames Path by Sustrans waymark.

❸ Turn **L**. Follow national trail, keeping **Bray Marina** on opposite bank. Further downstream the imposing cream façade of **Bray film studios** edges into your view. Continue on leafy Thames Path and soon you will catch sight of **Oakley Court** across water on Berkshire bank.

❹ Beyond hotel can be seen cabin cruisers and gin palaces of **Windsor Marina** and next to it lines of caravans and mobile homes. Through trees on Buckinghamshire bank is outline of Eton College's new boathouse and rowing lake. To gain closer view, briefly follow path beside river boathouse and slipway, walk towards lake and retrace your steps to Thames Path. On opposite bank is Windsor Race Course Yacht Basin and ahead is **Chapel of St Mary Magdalen**. Follow path alongside **chapel** to kissing gate and about 50yds (46m) beyond it reach lane. With Old Place opposite and avenue of chestnut trees on R, turn **L** and return to car park.

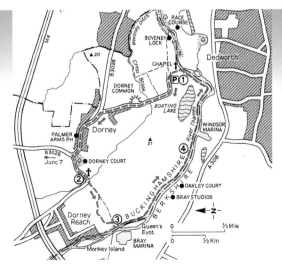

211 CUCKFIELD *Across Haywards Heath*

5 miles (8km) 2hrs 30min **Ascent:** 230ft (70m)
Paths: Field, woodland and parkland paths, minor roads, 7 stiles
Suggested map: aqua3 OS Explorers 134 Crawley & Horsham; 135 Ashdown Forest
Grid reference: TQ 304246 (on Explorer 135)
Parking: Free car park in Broad Street, Cuckfield. 4 hour limit 8am–6pm, Monday to Saturday

Head across country to Cuckfield Park.

1 Turn **L** out of car park into Broad Street. Bear **L** at mini-roundabout. Proceed to Church Street. Make for lychgate by **parish church**; enter churchyard. Head for kissing gate on far side, turn **L**; follow track.

2 Pass **Newbury Pond** and cross stile to **R** of gate. Keep to field boundary before crossing stile to join enclosed path running between holly trees. Cross another stile and keep ahead until turning on **R**. Follow path to busy **A272**, cross over to stile. Follow path through trees. Walk along to **Copyhold Lane**; bear **R**.

3 Pass **Lodge Farm** and, when lane swings to **L**, keep ahead at public bridleway sign, ignoring path on **R** by Copyhold Cottage. Walk ahead into trees and follow woodland path down to lane. Keep ahead, then cross stream and bear **R** on to footpath, crossing footbridge. Once in field, keep to **R** edge and make for corner.

4 Avoid stile and bear **L**, following field boundary. Cross into next field via gap in hedge and make for stile in corner. Continue to skirt farmland; shortly reach footpath sign on bend of track. Keep ahead, passing house on **R**, and soon reach **A272** at Ansty.

5 Cross over and follow Bolney Road, turning **R** by St John's Church into Deaks Lane. Pass Ansty Farm and head out of village in northerly direction. Keep to lane for over 1 mile (1.6km) and turn **R** opposite house, 'The Wyllies'. Pass through gate and follow High Weald Landscape Trail to footbridge.

6 Climb steeply through woodland to reach fence. Turn **R** and walk along fence corner by gate. Continue ahead, merging with grassy track to reach gate and stile – edge of **Cuckfield Park**. Cut between trees and carpets of bracken, dropping down to footbridge. Ascend steep bank to reach wrought iron kissing gate and keep fence on **R**. Continue to kissing gate and head towards **Cuckfield's** prominent **church** spire. On reaching South Street, turn **L** and return to village centre.

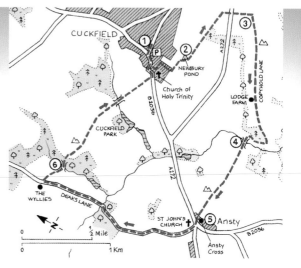

212 DEVIL'S DYKE *A Grand View*

3 miles (4.8km) 1hr 30min **Ascent:** 656ft (200m)
Paths: Field and woodland paths, 6 stiles
Suggested map: aqua3 OS Explorer 122 South Downs Way – Steyning to Newhaven
Grid reference: TQ 268112
Parking: Summer Down free car park

A fine walk with glimpses over the most famous of all the dry chalk valleys, the South Downs.

1 From **Summer Down** car park go through kissing gate and veer **R**. Join **South Downs Way** and follow it alongside lines of trees. Soon path curves **L** and then drops down to road. Leave **South Downs Way** here, as it crosses over to join private road to **Saddlescombe**, and follow verge for about 75yds (68m). Bear **L** at footpath sign and drop down bank to stile.

2 Follow line of tarmac lane as it curves **R** to reach waymark. Leave lane and walk ahead alongside power lines, keeping line of trees and bushes on **R**. Look for narrow path disappearing into vegetation and make for stile. Descend steps into woods and turn **R** at junction with bridleway. Take path running off half-**L** and follow it between fields and wooded dell. Pass over stile and continue to stile in **L** boundary. Cross footbridge to further stile; now turn **R** towards **Poynings**.

3 Head for gate and footpath sign and turn **L** at road. Follow parallel path along to **Royal Oak**; then continue to **Dyke Lane** on **L**. There is **memorial stone** here, dedicated to George Stephen Cave Cuttress, a Poynings resident for over 50 years, and erected by his widow. Follow tarmac bridleway and soon it narrows to path. On reaching fork, by National Trust sign for **Devil's Dyke**, veer **R** and begin climbing steps.

4 Follow path up to gate and continue up stairs. From higher ground there are breathtaking views to north and west. Make for kissing gate and head up slope towards inn. Keep **Devil's Dyke pub** on **L** and take road round to **L**, passing bridleway on **L**. Follow path parallel to road and look to **L** for definitive view of **Devil's Dyke**.

5 Head for **South Downs Way** and turn **L** by National Trust sign for **Summer Down** to stile and gate. Follow trail, keeping **Devil's Dyke** down to **L**, and eventually reaching stile leading into **Summer Down car park**.

213 BEEDING'S *Royal Escape Route*

2¾ miles (4.4km) 1hr 30min **Ascent:** Negligible
Paths: Riverside, field and village paths, some road, 10 stiles
Suggested map: aqua3 OS Explorer 122 South Downs Way – Steyning to Newhaven
Grid reference: TQ 185105
Parking: Free car park at Bramber Castle

Take a leisurely stroll through the peaceful Adur Valley to an historic bridge.

1 Follow drive to roundabout. Turn **R** into **Castle Lane** and follow it through woodland. On reaching junction with Roman Road, turn **R** to join footpath.

2 Head up through trees, passing galvanised gates on **L** and **R**. Rooftops of houses and bungalows peep into view along here. Continue ahead at next signpost and **River Adur** can be glimpsed between trees on **R**. Pass footpath on **L** and make for stile ahead. Follow grassy path to next stile and footpath sign. Cross over and turn **R** towards footbridge spanning the **Adur**.

3 Cross stile and bridge. Bear **R**, following river bank towards **Upper Beeding**. Branch off **L** to footbridge and stile to visit Priory **Church of St Peter**. Returning to main walk, continue towards **Upper Beeding**. Cross stile by gate and continue to kissing gate. Follow path to Bridge Inn at Beeding and cross **Beeding Bridge**. It's worth stopping here to consider

its importance as a river crossing. In October 1651 Charles II, defeated and on the run, crossed the bridge en route to France. As the King and escort arrived in Bramber, they were horrified to find troopers near the river bank. Cautiously, they managed to cross the bridge undetected but it was a narrow escape.

4 Swing **L** and join R-H bank, heading downstream. Cross stile and follow riverside path. Continue to R-H stile and enter field. Keep hedge on **R** and at fence corner go straight on, out across field.

5 As you approach **A283**, turn **R** in front of stile and head towards trees, with ruins of **Bramber Castle** peeping through. Make for stile and bear **R**. Follow track as it bends **L** and crosses 2 stiles before joining tarmac drive running through trees to road. Turn **L**, pass **St Mary's House** and walk along High Street, passing Castle Inn Hotel. When you reach **Old Tollgate Restaurant and hotel**, cross road and follow steps up to car park.

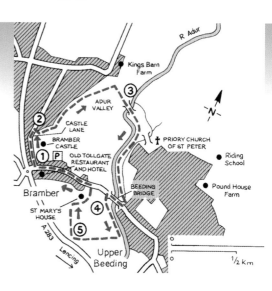

SHIPLEY *HILAIRE BELLOC'S SUSSEX*

7 miles (11.3km) 3hrs Ascent: 98ft (30m)
Paths: Field and woodland paths, country roads, 9 stiles
Suggested map: aqua3 OS Explorers 121 Arundel & Pulborough, 134 Crawley & Horsham
Grid reference: TQ 144218 (on Explorer 134) **Parking:** Small free car park at Shipley

Around the home of a writer with a love for the Sussex countryside.

1 From car park turn **R**; follow road round **L** bend. After 100yds (91m) bear **R** through kissing gate, follow **R-H** boundary of field. Look for gate into **Church Wood**. Follow path through trees to stile; keep ahead, skirting field. Exit to road.

2 Cross then follow woodland path to field. Proceed to footpath fingerpost. Bear **R**; follow drive towards **Knepp Castle**. At **L** turning, swing **R**; head across pasture. Make for white gate and turn **R**, passing **New Lodge**. Follow drive alongside Kneppmill Pond.

3 Cross **A24**; look for footpath sign and gate. Proceed to stile in **R** corner of field. Join woodland path; bear **R** at waymark. Make for stile at corner of wood and skirt field, keeping to **R** edge. At hedge corner, proceed across field to reach footpath sign; bear **R**. Follow hedge to gate leading into churchyard. Pass church door; turn **R** at footpath sign.

4 Make for kissing gate in **churchyard**; follow path

south. Cross **River Adur**, bend **L** to track; continue in southerly direction. Track becomes tarmac drive as it passes through **Butcher's Row**. Follow it southwest, keeping **R** at junction with 2 tracks and footpath. Bear **L** at next junction; follow **Rookcross Lane**. Pass **Rookcross Farm** before veering **R** at private drive sign.

5 Follow **L** edge of field to stile in 1st corner. Cross it; turn **R**, keeping to field edge until reaching stile. Cross; keep to **L** boundary of next field. Make for stile in corner; recross **A24**. Head for stile and footpath sign; cross pasture to gateway in **L** corner. Pass into adjacent field to bungalow; then bear immediately **R**. Cross 2 stiles to reach Crown car park.

6 Turn **R** on leaving, through **Dial Post** and **L** into Swallows Lane. Once leaving village, branch **L** and follow road to **New Barn Farm**. Beyond outbuildings, continue to road.

7 Turn **L** into **Pound Lane** and pass footpath to church. Continue to **R-H** bridleway. Follow path to **windmill**, continue to road. Turn **R** for car park.

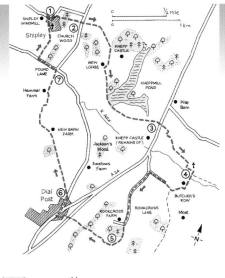

LOXWOOD *THE LOST ROUTE*

4½ miles (7.2km) 2hrs Ascent: 82ft (25m)
Paths: Field paths, tracks and tow path, 6 stiles
Suggested map: aqua3 OS Explorer 134 Crawley & Horsham
Grid reference: TQ 041311
Parking: Free car park by Wey and Arun Junction Canal, next to Onslow Arms, Loxwood

Cross pasturelands to discover how a forgotten canal, which once led from London to the sea, is being brought back to life.

1 From car park by **Onslow Arms** turn **R** at B2133, cross canal and then walk along road to **R-H** footpath. Follow tarmac path between hedges and continue ahead by **Loxwood Surgery**. Cut through residential housing development and bear **R** at T-junction.

2 Pass **Burley Close** and turn **L** into **Spy Lane**. Follow road between houses and bungalows and look for **Emmanuel Fellowship Chapel** on **R**. Bear **R** immediately beyond chapel, over stile and skirt Emmanuel Fellowship playing field.

3 Follow path to next stile and pass through tongue of woodland. Make for **R-H** boundary of field, aiming for stile in corner. Turn **L** immediately to finger post and stile. Cross pasture to next stile and waymark and continue over farmland, passing **Songhurst New Farm**. Head for field corner and look for stile just to **R**

of galvanised gate. Join single-track lane and follow it north, passing small brick-built house on **R**. Down to **L** is **Mallards Farm**.

4 Turn **L** on reaching **Sussex Border Path** and pass **Songhurst House**. Head for road and then bear **L** opposite **Sir Roger Tichborne pub**. Walk along until you reach **Oakhurst Lane** and then follow **Sussex Border Path** up gentle slope to **Oakhurst Farm**. Pass between timber barns and then keep ahead through gate when track curves **R**. Follow field path ahead, aiming for woodland. Keep to bridleway and head for route of **Wey and Arun Junction Canal**.

5 Turn **L** here and follow **Wey South Path** alongside canal. Continue on this old tow path, passing through several gates. Disregard any turnings and continue ahead, keeping to route of canal. Pass footbridge and continue, eventually you will reach B2133. Cross over, keeping to **L** of Onslow Arms and return to car park.

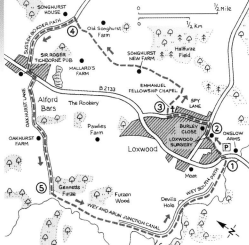

AMBERLEY *A DOWNLAND RAMBLE*

5½ miles (8.8km) 2hrs Ascent: 262ft (80m)
Paths: Riverside paths, downland tracks and some roads, 2 stiles
Suggested map: aqua3 OS Explorer 121 Arundel & Pulborough
Grid reference: TQ 026117
Parking: Amberley Museum car park by Amberley Station. Visit the museum, then leave your car here while on walk. Parking by kind permission of Amberley Museum management

Visit Amberley Museum on the Downs.

1 Turn **L** out of car park; pass under the **railway bridge**. Start crossing road bridge spanning **Arun** then bear **L** at footpath sign to stile by galvanised gate. Once over, cross water-meadows to next stile and, few paces beyond, bear **L** at footpath sign.

2 Follow path between trees, turn **R** on reaching lane, pass **Sloe Cottage**. Turn **L** just beyond caravan site to join bridleway. Follow path as it runs above camping ground and make for gate and bridleway sign. Cross track here and join rough lane.

3 Stay on lane as it climbs gradually. Pass ruined farm outbuildings and keep ahead, lane dwindling to track along stretch. Veer **L** at fork and follow waymarked public right of way. Head for signposted crossroads and take **L-H** public bridleway.

4 Walk down chalk track, pass through gate; continue steep descent. Look for 2 gates below, set

some distance apart. Cross to **R-H** gate and bridleway sign. Follow bridleway as it bends **L**, climbing steeply towards **Downs Farm**. Keep fence on **L** and follow bridleway as it merges with wide track.

5 Keep **L** at next junction and follow **South Downs Way** towards entrance to **Downs Farm**. Veer to **R** of gateway and join narrow footpath, which begins steep descent. Keep on slope until reaching tarmac lane; bear **R**. On **R-H** side is house, 'Highdown'.

6 Veer **L** at fork and follow **High Titten** between trees and hedgerows. **Amberley Museum** can be spotted at intervals along stretch. On reaching road junction, turn **R** and follow tarmac path parallel to road. Bear **L** at **South Downs Way** sign and follow concrete track over **railway line** to galvanised gate.

7 Turn **L**. Follow bridleway to **River Arun**. Swing **L**, veering slightly away from river bank, to join drive. Turn **L** at road. Bear **R** to return to **Amberley Museum**.

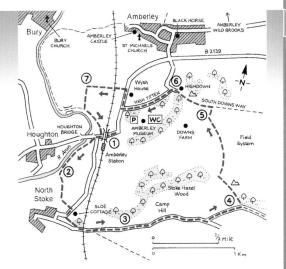

217   CLIMPING *COUNTRYSIDE MEETS COAST*

4 miles (6.4km) 2hrs Ascent: Negligible ⚠
Paths: Field paths, roads and stretches of beach, 1 stile
Suggested map: aqua3 OS Explorer 121 Arundel & Pulborough
Grid reference: TQ 005007
Parking: Car park at Climping Beach

An invigorating walk on the last surviving stretch of undeveloped coast between Bognor Regis and Brighton.
❶ From beach car park take road heading away from sea, passing entrance to **Bailiffscourt Hotel** on L-H side. Continue walking along road until you reach **The Black Horse pub** and then take next footpath on R, by thatched cottages.
❷ When track swings L, continue walking ahead across field to junction with byway. Go straight over and follow path through fields, heading for derelict outbuildings.
❸ Join track on bend and turn **R**. As it swings R, take signposted path; begin by following boundary hedge. Stride across field, cross concrete footbridge and bear L at footpath sign to follow deep ditch known as **Ryebank Rife**. When path veers away from ditch, cross field to line of trees. There is stile here, followed by footbridge.

❹ Turn **R** and walk along road to turning on **R** for **Littlehampton Golf Club**. Route follows this road but before taking it, continue ahead briefly, to look at footbridge crossing Arun. Buildings of Littlehampton can be seen on far side and you may like to extend walk by visiting town.
❺ Continuing main walk, follow road towards **West Beach** and **golf club**, veering **R** at car park sign. Follow enclosed path to kissing gate and briefly cross golf course to enter wood. Greens and fairways are visible as you pick your way between trees. Keep to path; eventually reach house, 'The Mill'. Avoid path on R here and keep **L**.
❻ Continue on footpath and soon it reaches **West Beach**. Look for interpretation board, which explains how this stretch of coastline has been shaped and influenced by climatic conditions and the sea. Follow footpath sign towards **Climping**, skirting beach and avoiding byway on R as you approach beach car park.

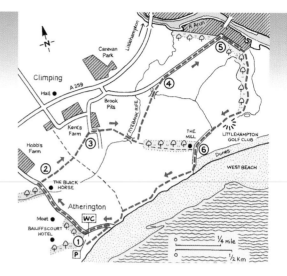

218   ARUNDEL *SUSSEX STRONGHOLD*

3¼ miles (5.3km) 2hrs Ascent: 197ft (60m) ⚠
Paths: Riverside and parkland paths, some road walking, 2 stiles
Suggested map: aqua3 OS Explorer 121 Arundel & Pulborough
Grid reference: TQ 020071
Parking: Mill Road fee-paying car park, Arundel **Note:** Arundel Park is closed annually on 24th March

Along the River Arun to Arundel Park.
❶ From car park in **Mill Road** turn **R** and walk along tree-lined pavement. Pass **bowling green** – glance to L reveals dramatic view of historic **Arundel Castle** with its imposing battlements. There has been a castle here since the 11th century, though most of the present fortification is Victorian. Arundel Castle is the principal ancestral home of the Dukes of Norfolk. The castle was attacked by parliamentary forces during the Civil War but was extensively rebuilt and restored in the 18th and 19th centuries.
❷ Follow road to stone bridge, cross over via footbridge and turn **R** to join riverside path. Emerging from cover, path cuts across lush, low-lying ground to reach western bank of **Arun**. Turn **L** and walk beside reed-fringed **Arun** to **Black Rabbit pub**, which stands out against curtain of trees.
❸ From **Black Rabbit**, follow minor road in roughly westerly direction back towards **Arundel**, passing

entrance to **Wildfowl and Wetlands Trust**. Make for gate leading into Arundel Park and follow path alongside **Swanbourne Lake**. Eventually lake fades from view as walk reaches deeper into park. Ignore turning branching off to L, just before gate and stile, and follow path as it curves gently to **R**.
❹ Turn sharply to **L** at next waymarked junction and begin fairly steep ascent, with footpath through park seen curving away down to L, back towards lake. This stretch of walk offers fine views over Arundel Park. Head for a stile and gate then immediately **R** up bank. Cross grass, following waymarks and keeping to L of **Hiorne Tower**. On reaching driveway, turn **L** and walk down to Park Lodge. Keep to **R** by private drive and make for road.
❺ Turn **L**, pass **Arundel Cathedral** and bear **L** at road junction by entrance to **Arundel Castle**. Go down hill, back into centre of **Arundel**. You'll find **Mill Road** at bottom of High Street.

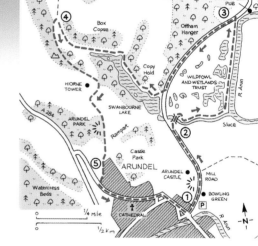

219   SLINDON *TREASURES IN TRUST*

4 miles (6.4km) 2hrs Ascent: 82ft (25m) ⚠
Paths: Woodland, downland paths and tracks, 4 stiles
Suggested map: aqua3 OS Explorer 121 Arundel & Pulborough
Grid reference: SU 960076
Parking: Free National Trust car park in Park Lane, Slindon

Tour and explore a sprawling National Trust estate on this glorious woodland walk.
❶ From car park walk down towards road and turn **R** at sign ('No riding') passing through gate to join wide, straight path cutting between trees and bracken. Path runs alongside sunny glades and clearings and between lines of beech and silver birch trees before reaching crossroads.
❷ Turn **R** to 2nd crossroads and continue ahead here, keeping grassy mound and ditch, all remains of **Park Pale**, on R. Follow broad path as it begins wide curve to R; boundary ditch is still visible here, running keep ahead, soon skirting fields. As you approach entrance to **Slindon campsite**, swing **L** and follow track down to road.
❸ Turn **L** and follow road through woodland. Pass **Slindon Bottom Road** and turn **R** after few paces to join bridleway. Follow path as it cuts between fields and look for path on **R**.

❹ Cross stile, go down field and up other side to next stile to join track. Turn **R**. Follow this track as it bends L. Walk along to **Row's Barn**, cross stile and continue on track. **Nore Folly** can be seen over to L.
❺ Continue ahead on track, following it to double gates and stile. Pass to R of **Courthill Farm**, turn **R** and follow lane or parallel woodland path to next road. Bear **L** and pass **Slindon College** and **St Richard's Catholic Church** on R before reaching **Church Hill**.
❻ To visit **Newburgh Arms**, continue ahead along Top Road. Otherwise, follow **Church Hill**, pass church and make for **pond**. Look for mallard ducks here. Follow obvious waterside path to enter woodland. At fork, by National Trust sign for **Slindon Estate**, keep **L** and walk through trees to car park. To celebrate its centenary in 1995, the National Trust chose the **Slindon Estate** to launch its 100 Paths Project, which offers many miles of footpaths and bridleways – just perfect for country walking.

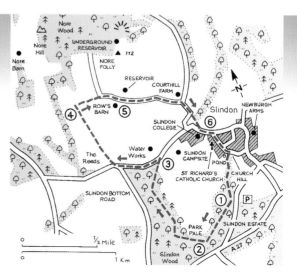

GOODWOOD *GLORIOUS GOOD GOING*

3½ miles (5.7km) 1hr 30min **Ascent:** 328ft (100m) ▲

Paths: Woodland tracks and field paths, section of Monarch's Way and one lengthy stretch of quiet road, 4 stiles

Suggested map: aqua3 OS Explorers 120 Chichester, South Harting & Selsey; 121 Arundel & Pulborough

Grid reference: SU 897113

Parking: Counter's Gate free car park and picnic area at Goodwood Country Park or large free car park opposite racecourse

A lovely woodland walk beside one of Britain's best-known racecourses.

❶ Make for western end of **Counter's Gate** car park and look for footpath sign by opening leading out to road. Cross over to junction of 2 clear tracks, with path on R. Follow **R-H track** ('public footpath'), which is part of **Monarch's Way**, to gate and stile. Continue to next gate and stile then cross clearing in woods.

❷ Cut through remote, thickly wooded country, following gently curving path over grassland and down between trees to reach gateway. Village of **East Dean** can be seen nestling down below. Head diagonally **R** down steep field slope to stile in corner.

❸ Cross into adjacent field and follow boundary to 2nd stile leading out to road. Bear **L** and walk down into **East Dean**, passing **Manor Farm**. Keep R at junction in village centre and, if it's opening time,

follow road towards Petworth in order to visit **Hurdlemakers Inn**.

❹ Leave **East Dean** by keeping pond on R-H side and follow road towards neighbouring **Charlton**. On reaching village, pass **Fox Goes Free** pub and **Woodstock House Hotel** and take next **L** turning. Follow lane to stile on **R** and turning on **L**. To visit **Open Air Museum** at Singleton, cross over into fields and follow straight path. Return to this stile by same route and take road opposite.

❺ Walk along to junction and turn **R** by war memorial, dedicated to fallen comrades of Sussex Yeomanry in both World Wars. Follow **Chalk Road**, which dwindles to track on outskirts of **Charlton**. Once clear of village, track climbs steadily between trees. Follow track eventually to reach road and cross over to **Counter's Gate** car park.

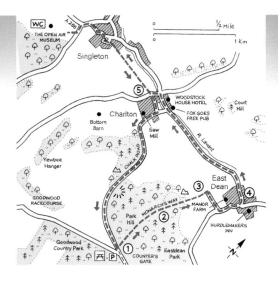

MIDHURST *TOWN AND COUNTRY*

3 miles (4.8km) 2hrs **Ascent:** 123ft (37m) ▲

Paths: Pavements, field, riverside tracks and country road, 4 stiles

Suggested map: aqua3 OS Explorer 120 Chichester, South Harting & Selsey

Grid reference: SU 886217

Parking: Car park by tourist information centre in North Street

Follow the River Rother to the ruins of Cowdray House.

❶ From car park by tourist information centre turn **L** and walk along **North Street**, passing post office. Bear **L** into **Knockhundred Row** ('South Pond'). Walk along **Church Hill** and into South Street, passing historic **Spread Eagle Hotel**.

❷ Turn **L** by **South Pond** into **The Wharf**, following bridleway beside industrial buildings and flats. Bear **R** at next waymarked junction, cross bridge and pass **cottage** on **L**. Keep wooden fencing on R and avoid path to L. Make for stile. Keep ahead along field boundary, keeping trees and vegetation on R. Cross 2 stiles in field corner; follow path to R of **polo stables**.

❸ Keep **L** and follow wooded stretch of road. Pass cottages and on reaching bend turn **L** at bridle path ('Heyshott and Graffham'). Follow track as it curves to **R**.

❹ Veer **L**, just before entrance to house, and follow waymarked path as it climbs quite steeply through

trees, passing between woodland and bracken. Drop down slope to waymarked path junction and turn **L** to join sandy track. Keep **L** at fork; follow track as it curves **L**, then **R**.

❺ On reaching road, turn **L** and, when it bends L by some gates, keep ahead along bridleway towards **Kennel Dairy**. Keep to **L** of outbuildings and stable blocks and walk ahead to galvanised gate. Continue on track. When it reaches field gateway, go through gate to **R** of it, following path as it runs just inside woodland.

❻ Continue along to junction, forming part of outward leg of walk, turn **R** and retrace your steps to bridge. Avoid path on L, running along to **South Pond**, and veer over to **R** to rejoin riverbank. Keep going until you reach footpath on **L**, leading up to ruins of St Ann's Hill. Follow path beside **Rother**, heading for kissing gate. Turn **L** and make for bridge, cross to access **Cowdray House**. After visiting house, continue along causeway path to car park.

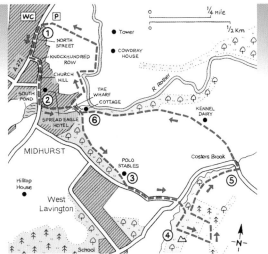

BLACK DOWN *ALFRED, LORD TENNYSON*

4½ miles (7.2km) 2hrs **Ascent:** 315ft (95m) ▲

Paths: Woodland paths and tracks, some minor roads

Suggested map: aqua3 OS Explorer 133 Haslemere & Petersfield

Grid reference: SU 922306

Parking: Free car park off Tennyson's Lane, near Aldworth House to the southeast of Haslemere

Follow in the footsteps of the distinguished Victorian poet Alfred, Lord Tennyson on this gloriously wooded, high-level walk in the northwest corner of Sussex.

❶ Turn **L** out of car park and then **L** again to join **Sussex Border Path**. Keep **L** at junction and swing **R** at fork.

❷ Follow long distance border trail to triangular green and veer **R** here. Keep **L** at fork, still on **Sussex Border Path**, and pass over crossroads. Veer **L** just beyond it at fork and drop down to rhododendron bushes. Turn sharp **L** here and follow path through tunnel of trees.

❸ Bear **L** at drive and when, after few paces, it curves **R**, keep ahead through trees to join road.

❹ Turn **L** towards entrance to **Sheetland**. Avoid turning and follow lane for about 1 mile (1.6km), passing entrance to **Cotchet Farm** on L. Continue along **Fernden Lane**.

❺ Make for signposted bridleway on **L** and after few paces you reach National Trust sign ('**Black Down**'). Keep **L** here and follow sunken path as it climbs between trees, steeply in places. On higher ground, follow path as it winds pleasantly between bracken and silver birch. Walk along to seat, which takes advantage of magnificent view, partly obscured by trees. Keep seat and view on R and walk along to seat at what is known as **Temple of the Winds**.

❻ Do not retrace your steps but take path running up behind seat to junction. Don't turn L; instead head north on bridleway. Avoid path running off sharp R and flight of steps and veer **L** or **R** at waymarked fork. Both paths soon merge again.

❼ Continue ahead and veer **R** at next fork. Keep ahead at next junction, now following part of **Sussex Border Path** again. Veer to **R** at fork, still following long distance trail, and head for road by car park entrance.

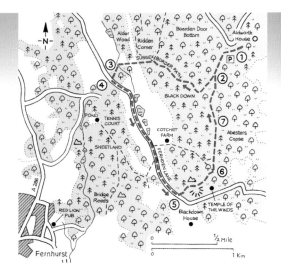

223 CHICHESTER *ESPYING THE SPIRE*

4½ miles (7.2km) 2hrs **Ascent:** Negligible
Paths: Urban walkways, tow path and field paths, 4 stiles
Suggested map: aqua3 OS Explorer 120 Chichester, South Harting & Selsey
Grid reference: SZ 857044
Parking: Fee-paying car park in Avenue de Chartres

Enjoy the ancient treasures of a cathedral city.
❶ Leave car park. Cross footbridge over **Avenue de Chartres**. Head towards city centre. Turn **R** at city map and **L** into **South Street**. Bear **L** into **Canon Lane**, just beyond **tourist information centre**. Turn **R** into St Richard's Walk then approach **cathedral**.
❷ Swing **L** at cloisters and **L** again (keep stone wall L). Make for West Door. Pass Bell Tower to reach **West Street**; bear **R**. Opposite is pub. Proceed on **West Street**. At Market Cross, turn **L** into **North Street**. Bear **R** just beyond Council House into **Lion Street**.
❸ Walk to St Martin's Square (opposite is St Mary's Hospital). Turn **R**; proceed to East Street (Corn Exchange on L.) Go over into North Pallant. Walk to Pallant House. Keep ahead into South Pallant. Follow road round to **R**, passing **Christ Church** on L. Turn **L** at next junction, head for traffic lights; continue south into Southgate.
❹ Cross **railway**; then swing **L** to reach canal basin. Follow tow path to **Poyntz Bridge**; continue to next

bridge, carrying **A27**. Continue to next footbridge and follow path to road. Confusingly bridge is labelled Poyntz Bridge on OS maps.
❺ Bear **L** briefly to stile by car park entrance. Cross into field. Keep field boundary on immediate **R** and make for footbridge and stile. Continue ahead, with trees and bushes on L. Make for stile in field corner; cross next field, maintaining direction. Aim for stile in wooded corner and just beyond it is busy **A27**.
❻ Cross with extreme care to footpath opposite. Turn **R** at junction; follow tarmac path to recreation ground. Cross to far side of green, keeping **cathedral** spire straight ahead. Look for Cherry Orchard Road, with post-box and telephone box on corner.
❼ Bear **L** at crossroads into **Kingsham Avenue**; follow it into Kingsham Road. Turn **R** at T-junction, pass bus station and, on reaching one-way system, cross at lights. Bear **R** into Southgate, then **L** into **Avenue de Chartres**. Car park is on **L**.

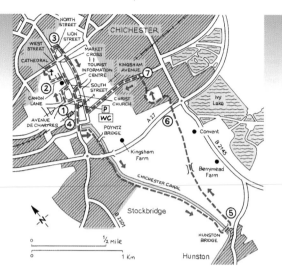

224 WEST ITCHENOR *HARBOUR SAILS AND TRAILS*

3½ miles (5.7km) 1hr 30min **Ascent:** Negligible
Paths: Shoreline, field tracks and paths, 1 stile
Suggested map: aqua3 OS Explorer 120 Chichester, South Harting & Selsey
Grid reference: SU 797013
Parking: Large pay-and-display car park in West Itchenor

Chichester Harbour's plentiful wildlife and colourful yachting activity form the backdrop to this waterside walk.
❶ From car park walk along to road. Bear **L**, heading towards harbour front. Pass **Ship Inn** and head to water's edge. Look for **harbour office** and **toilets** and follow footpath to **L** of **Jetty House**.
❷ Cut between hedging and fencing to reach boatyard then continue ahead on clear country path. Keep **L** at next junction; shortly path breaks cover to run hard by harbour and its expanses of mud flats. Cross **Chalkdock Marsh** and continue on waterside path.
❸ Keep going until you reach footpath sign. Turn **L**, by sturdy old oak tree, and follow path away from harbour edge, keeping to **R-H** boundary of field. Cross stile to join track on bend and continue ahead, still maintaining same direction. Pass **Itchenor Park House** on R and approach some farm outbuildings.
❹ Turn **R** by brick-and-flint farm outbuilding and

follow path, soon merging with concrete track. Walk ahead to next junction and turn **L** by white gate. Join to road. Bear **R** here, pass speed restriction sign and soon you reach little **Church of St Nicholas**.
❺ Follow road along to **Oldhouse Farm** then turn **L** at footpath sign to cross footbridge. Keep to **R** of several barns and follow path straight ahead across field. Pass line of trees and keep alongside ditch on **R** into next field. Path follows hedge line, making for field corner. Ahead are buildings of **Westlands Farm**.
❻ Turn sharp **L** by footpath sign and follow path across field. Skirt woodland, part of **private nature reserve**, and veer **L** at entrance to Spinney. Follow residential drive to **Harbour House**.
❼ Turn **R** just beyond it and follow path along harbour edge. Keep going along here until you reach **Itchenor Sailing Club**. Bear **L** and walk up drive to road. Opposite you should be **Ship Inn**. Turn **L** to return to car park.

225 KINGLEY VALE *VIEWS AND YEWS*

5 miles (8km) 2hrs **Ascent:** 440ft (134m)
Paths: Mostly woodland paths and downland tracks
Suggested map: aqua3 OS Explorer 120 Chichester, South Harting & Selsey
Grid reference: SU 814215
Parking: Free car park at Stoughton Down

Discover a magical ancient forest teeming with wildlife high up on the South Downs.
❶ From car park make for bridleway near exit and follow it away from road, skirting dense beech woodland. There are striking views on L over pastoral, well-wooded countryside. Keep **R** at fork and follow stony path as it curves to R. Veer **R** at next waymarked fork and begin gradual ascent beneath boughs of beech trees.
❷ Eventually break cover from trees at major junction of waymarked tracks. Go straight on, looking to R for spectacular views. Continue to next bridleway sign at fork and join path running parallel to track. Cut between trees and keep going until gap on **R**. Keep to waymarked track as it runs down slope. Rejoin enclosed track, turning **L** to follow it up slope towards **Bow Hill**.
❸ On reaching **Devil's Humps**, veer off path to enjoy magnificent vistas across downland countryside.

Immediately below are trees of Kingley Vale. This was a wartime artillery range but Kingley Vale became a nature reserve in 1952 and today it is managed by English Nature. Head along footpath in westerly direction, with **nature reserve** on L. Continue between carpets of bracken and lines of beech trees.
❹ Turn **R** at next main junction and follow bridle track along field edge. On L are glimpses of Chichester Harbour, with its complex network of watery channels and sprawling mudflats. Pass several ancient burial **tumuli** then descend through area of beech woodland. Keep going until you reach road. Turn **R** and walk through pleasant village of **Stoughton**.
❺ Pass entrance to **St Mary's Church** on L, followed by **Hare and Hounds** pub. Continue through village and on R is **Monarch's Way**. Follow road out of **Stoughton**, all way to **L-H** bend where you'll see entrance to car park on Stoughton Down on **R**.

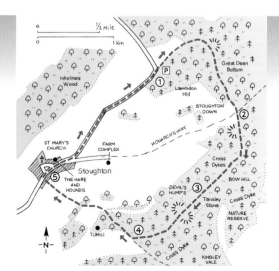

RYE *WIDE SKIES AND LONELY SEAS*

4½ miles (7.2km) 2hrs **Ascent:** Negligible

Paths: Level paths and good, clear tracks, no stiles
Suggested map: aqua3 OS Explorer 125 Romney Marsh, Rye & Winchelsea
Grid reference: TQ 942190
Parking: Spacious free car park at Rye Harbour

Wide skies, lonely seas and lagoons form the backdrop to this remote coastal walk, which is excellent for birdwatching.

1 Keep **Martello Tower** and entrance to holiday village on your **R** and enter **Rye Harbour Local Nature Reserve**. In late May and June the shingle is transformed by a colourful array of flowers. Salt marsh, vegetation along the river's edge and grazing marsh add to the variety and the old gravel pits now represent an important site for nesting terns, gulls, ducks and waders. The **Rother** can be seen on **L**, running parallel to path. Head for **Lime Kiln Cottage information centre** and continue on firm path, with Rother still visible on **L**. **Camber Sands** (popular holiday destination) nudges into view beyond river mouth.

2 Follow path to beach, then retrace your steps to point where permissive path runs off to **L**, cutting between wildlife sanctuary areas where access is not allowed. Pass entrance to Guy Crittall hide on **R**. From here enjoy superb views over **Turnery Pool**. Continue west on clear path and gradually it edges nearer shore.

3 Ahead now is outline of old abandoned lifeboat house and, away to **R** in distance, unmistakable profile of **Camber Castle**. Keep going on clear path until you reach waymarked footpath on **R**, running towards line of houses on eastern edge of **Winchelsea**.

4 Take this footpath and head inland, passing small pond on **R**. Glancing back, old lifeboat house can be seen. Turn **R** at next junction, pass **Watch House** and continue on track as it runs alongside several lakes. Pass to **L** of some dilapidated farm outbuildings and keep going along track. Lakes are still seen on L-H side, dotted with trees, and silent fishermen can often be seen along here. Begin approach to **Rye Harbour** and on **L** is church spire.

5 On reaching road in centre of village, turn **L** to visit parish church before heading back along main street. Pass **Inkerman Arms** and return to car park.

GREAT DIXTER *GLORIOUS GARDENS*

3½ miles (5.7km) 1hr 30min **Ascent:** 98ft (30m)

Paths: Field paths and quiet roads, 11 stiles
Suggested map: aqua3 OS Explorer 125 Romney Marsh, Rye & Winchelsea
Grid reference: TQ 828245
Parking: Free car park on corner of Fullers Lane and A28, Northiam **Note:** Great Dixter. Seasonal opening

A pleasant walk on the Sussex/Kent border, and a visit to an historic house and garden.

1 Turn **R** out of car park and walk along Fullers Lane towards **St Mary's Church**. Take path on **L** ('Goddens Gill'); keep to **R** edge of field. Cross stile in corner and look for oasthouse on **R**. Make for path on far side of field and listen for between fences towards thatched cottage. Cross stile to road.

2 Turn **L** and head for **A28**. Bear **L** and walk to **Crown and Thistle**. Then, cross road and take signed turning ('Great Dixter'). Pass telephone box and straight on at crossroads, following Great Dixter Road.

3 Pass **Unitarian Chapel** and avoid path on **R**. Keep **L** at junction with Higham Lane and continue to follow signs for **Great Dixter**. Disregard turning on **R** and keep ahead, following path between trees and hedges, parallel to main drive to house.

4 Pass toilets and head towards cattle grid. Cross stile just to **L** of it and follow path ('Ewhurst'). Follow waymarks and keep hedge on **L**. Cross stile in field corner; then head diagonally down field slope to next stile. Follow clear path down field slope.

5 Make for footbridge; then turn **L** to join **Sussex Border Path**. Path skirts field before disappearing into woodland. Emerging from trees, cut straight across next field to 2 stiles and footbridge. Keeping woodland on **L**, look for gap in trees. Cross stream to a stile and bear **R**. Follow **R** edge of field and keep on **Sussex Border Path** until reaching road.

6 Cross over lane to drive. Bear immediately **L** and then follow path to stile. Pass alongside woodland then veer slightly away from trees to stile in approaching boundary. Cross it and go straight ahead up field slope. Take 1st footpath on **R** and follow it to gap in field corner. Cross footbridge under trees and continue along **R-H** edge of next field to join drive. Bear **L** and follow it to road. Turn **L**, then **R** to return to car park.

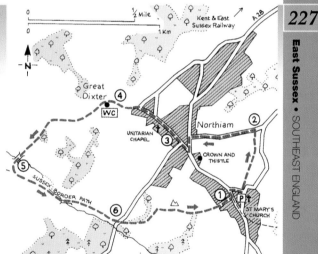

WINCHELSEA *ABANDONED BY THE SEA*

4½ miles (7.2km) 2hrs **Ascent:** 197ft (60m)

Paths: Field paths and pavements, 19 stiles
Suggested map: aqua3 OS Explorer 124 Hastings & Bexhill or 125 Romney Marsh, Rye & Winchelsea
Grid reference: TQ 905173
Parking: Roadside parking near St Thomas's Church at Winchelsea

Explore a Cinque Port before following an historic line of defence.

1 With **New Inn** on **L** and ruined **St Thomas's Church** on **R**, follow road round **R-H** bend. Head down to Strand Gate; then take road to junction with A259. Turn **R** and follow pavement.

2 When road bends **L**, turn **R** at sign ('Winchelsea Beach'). Cross **Royal Military Canal** and bear immediately **R**. Follow tow path across empty landscape. Cross stile and avoid concrete footbridge. Eventually, canal begins to curve **L**. Here you will find a stile and galvanised gate.

3 Bear **R** few paces beyond it at footbridge. Cross 2nd footbridge over ditch and make for stile. Pass birdwatching hide and continue along path, making for next footbridge.

4 Turn **R** here, veer **R** then follow path as it curves **L** through reedbeds. Begin moderate climb and head towards house. Keep to **L** of it and follow path through trees. Join drive, pass **Ashes Farm** and look for stile on **L**. Go diagonally across field to stile, then bear **R** briefly to 2 more stiles. Skirt field to next stile and exit to road. Keep **R** here ('Winchelsea') and soon pass below hilltop windmill, avoiding **1066 Country Walk**, which meets road at this point.

5 Go straight ahead over stile when lane bends **L** and cross field. Look for stile and keep alongside some trees to next stile. Continue ahead, pass old pill box and head down gentle field slope to road.

6 Turn **R** for few paces to stile on **L**. Bear **R**, still on **1066 Country Walk**, and cross next stile. Keep to **R** of **Wickham Manor** and look for stile in far boundary. Cross drive to stile and keep ahead across fields. Make for stile and gate in bottom **L** corner and follow **1066 Country Walk** waymarks. Path veers over to **R** to 2 stiles. Bear **L** and begin moderate ascent to stone stile. Turn **R** at road. Follow it round to **L** and return to centre of **Winchelsea**.

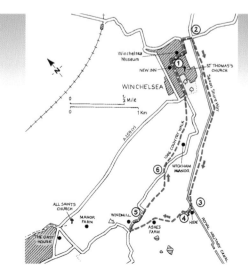

229 BATTLE *Famous Battlefield*

6 miles (9.7km) 3hrs **Ascent:** 230ft (70m)
Paths: Field and woodland paths, some road walking, 23 stiles
Suggested map: aqua3 OS Explorer 124 Hastings & Bexhill
Grid reference: TQ 747161
Parking: Pay-and-display car park in Mount Street, Battle

Discover the field where two men fought for the English crown.

❶ Look for path and bungalow, 'Little Twitten'. Turn **R** after few paces and follow Malfosse Walk. As it branches to L, continue for few paces then veer **R**.

❷ Cross stile; then follow waymarked path across several pastures to gate. Pass through **railway** tunnel and veer **L**, following woodland path. Cross track, make for stile; continue ahead across field to stile by road.

❸ Turn **L**. As you approach car park at **Battle Great Wood**, look for gap in hedge by entrance. Cross field towards woodland. Head for footbridge and stile. Go half **R** across field to 2 stiles. Follow path as it crosses 8 stiles. Keep alongside trees to 2 footbridges. Cross **R-H** bridge. Turn **L** after several paces then immediately **R**. Continue on path as it runs beside stream. Cross next stile, then field to stile by **A21**.

❹ Cross to stile and follow path across fields. On reaching gate and footbridge, follow path into **Sedlescombe**, passing recreation ground. Turn **L** at road and walk into village.

❺ Return to footbridge and keep ahead. After about 120yds (109m) look for several stiles over to **L**. Turn **R** to footbridge and stile then cross some rough ground. Make for 2 stiles in field corner and go straight across next pasture to stile by road. Cross over and join track opposite. Keep **L** when track forks. Go through gate at **Beanford Farm**; bear **R**.

❻ Pass through 2nd gate. Follow sunken path curving **L** through belt of trees. On reaching broad grassy ride, continue for few paces then veer **R** at fork. Turn **L** at next ride; follow it to major junction of tracks. Bear **R** for several steps then swing **L** up hill.

❼ Turn **R** at crossroads of tracks. Follow **1066 Country Walk** through trees. Ride gradually narrows before reaching Marley Lane. Go straight on towards **Battle**, cross **railway** and turn **R** at main road. Walk along to **Battle Abbey** and continue to Mount Street.

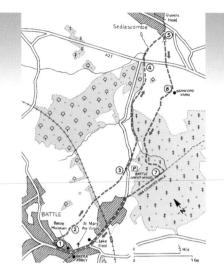

230 BURWASH *Kipling's Place*

4¾ miles (7.7km) 2hrs **Ascent:** 345ft (105m)
Paths: Field and woodland paths, stretches of minor road, 16 stiles
Suggested map: aqua3 OS Explorers 124 Hastings & Bexhill; 136 The Weald
Grid reference: TQ 674246 (on Explorer 124)
Parking: Free car park off A265 in Burwash village

Visit the home of Rudyard Kipling on this walk in the Dudwell Valley.

❶ Make for footpath behind **toilet block**, heading for stile. Follow path down slope; look for gap in trees on **R**. Cross stile at junction and continue ahead. Make for next stile and keep boundary hedge on R. Look for stile on **R** and head diagonally down field, keeping fenced spinney on R. Make for stile in field corner, follow field edge to next stile, and exit to road.

❷ Turn **R**; follow lane along to **Bateman's** (National Trust). Keep **L** in front of house and make for **Park Farm**. Veer **L** through gate then head up field slope, keeping trees on immediate R. Look for gate and bridleway post on **R**, passing through wood to track.

❸ Bear **L**, then immediately **R**. Follow bridleway, keeping **L** at fork. Pass cottage and walk along to road. Turn **R**, eventually pass **Willingford Farm**; then climb quite steeply to small white house on R.

❹ Go through kissing gate and head straight along top of field. Make for kissing gate in corner. Head diagonally **L** in next field, towards buildings of **Burnt House Farm**. Right of way leads to farm buildings and then sharply **R**, but you may find route has been diverted across paddock. Whichever, make for galvanised gate by trees and go straight ahead in next pasture, keeping wrought iron fence and farm to L.

❺ Make for gate ahead and cross field, keeping to **L** boundary. Path cuts across next field to stile. Pass through woodland to field; head down to gap in hedge. Follow surfaced lane, which quickly becomes grassy track, passing some dilapidated farm outbuildings.

❻ Cross stile by waymark and keep **R** here. Look for another stile shortly, turn **L** and skirt round field edge. Veer over to stile towards far end, cross footbridge; turn **L**. Follow path along to pond, pass gate and continue for few paces to track. Turn **L** and head back to **Bateman's**. Turn **R** by house. Retrace your steps back to the car park in **Burwash**.

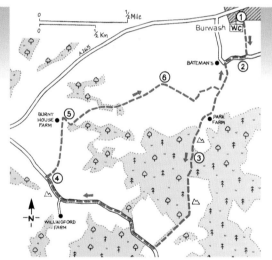

231 BRIGHTLING *A Folly Trail*

5 miles (8km) 2hrs 30min **Ascent:** 197ft (60m)
Paths: Parkland paths, woodland bridleways and lanes, 3 stiles
Suggested map: aqua3 OS Explorer 124 Hastings & Bexhill
Grid reference: TQ 683210
Parking: Darwell Wood, south of Brightling, and begin at Point ❹

Step into the colourful world of 'Mad Jack' Fuller – folly-builder extraordinaire.

❶ Go through churchyard, opposite Wealden House, to road. Turn **R**, pass **Brightling Park**; make for **L** turning, ('Robertsbridge'). Go through kissing gate by junction and sign. Follow path over fields to footpath junction and sign.

❷ Turn **R**. Follow field edge to **Tower**. Cut through trees; descend slope to stile and road. Bear **R** briefly; turn **L** by barns and outbuildings. Cut between ponds and lakes, looking for **cricket ground** by track. **The Temple** can be seen on **R** at intervals. Pass turning to farm outbuildings and continue on main bridleway, veering **R** when it forks. Cut through area of pheasant-rearing woodland. Make for footbridge.

❸ Turn **L** and join footpath, keeping alongside trees. Veer away from wood when you see house on R. Look for stile in boundary; make for cottage. Cross next stile and exit to road. Turn **R** and proceed to row of cottages. Make for parking area just beyond and look for 2 tracks running into **Darwell Wood**.

❹ Take **L-H** bridle track, when it eventually forks, keep **R**. Begin to swing **L** as track curves around to R, still on bridleway. Keep **R** at next waymark and continue along forest path. When it swings sharply to R, at hairpin bend, look for bridleway sign on **L**. Follow path through wood. On emerging, cross over pipe linking Mountfield and Brightling gypsum mines.

❺ Follow track to **L**, then veer **R** at fork. Cross **Darwell Stream**. Bear **L**, following woodland path to road. Turn **R** to view **Darwell Reservoir** and **L** to proceed. Follow **Kent Lane**, recross conveyor belt; head to **Hollingrove**. On **R** is house (former chapel).

❻ Keep **L** at junction and walk along lane for short distance, passing Glebe Cottage. Take stony track on **R** and veer **L** shortly in front of part tile-hung house. Walk to turning for **Tower**. Retrace route across fields; follow road to **Brightling church**.

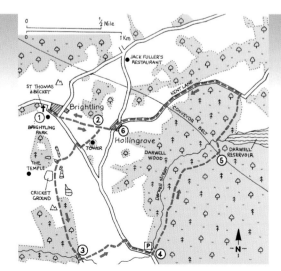

PEVENSEY *ROMANS AND NORMANS*

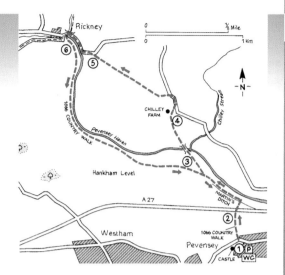

4½ miles (7.2km) 1hr 45min **Ascent:** Negligible ⚠
Paths: Field paths, brief stretch of road and riverside, 4 stiles
Suggested map: aqua3 OS Explorer 124 Hastings & Bexhill
Grid reference: TQ 645048
Parking: Pay-and-display car park by Pevensey Castle

Visit a Norman castle within a Roman fort and the eerie Pevensey Levels.

❶ On leaving car park, go straight ahead on bend, keeping Priory Court Hotel on R. Castle walls rise up L. Bear off to R just beyond hotel to follow **1066 Country Walk**.

❷ Cross **A27** and keep on trail, following sign 'Rickney'. Go through 2 gates; follow path as it bends L. Continue between fencing and hedging. Keep **Martin's Ditch** on L. Go through galvanised gate. Make for signpost and veer off diagonally R, leaving **1066 Country Walk** at this point.

❸ On reaching river bank footpath sign, at confluence of **Pevensey Haven** and **Chilley Stream**, continue for short distance to footbridge. Cross and aim half-L, making for house. Head for gap in line of bushes then go across rough, thistle-strewn ground to 2 stiles in corner by trees. Bear R to galvanised gate, then turn **L** and cross field, keeping house on L. On

reaching gate, turn **R** and walk along track to road.

❹ Swing **L** at lane and follow it until it curves R. Go through gate on **L**, reaching 2nd gate beyond. Follow path to gates; pass via **R-H** one. Keep ahead to gate in field corner and continue, keeping boundary on L. Make for footbridge on **L**. Cross and bear **R**. Follow edge of pasture to 2 stiles; exit to road.

❺ Keep **L** and walk along to village of **Rickney**. Avoid **1066 Country Walk** as it runs off north; cross road-bridge. Bear **L** at sign for Hankham; immediately cross bridge. Swing **L** after few paces; follow **1066 Country Walk**.

❻ Go through galvanised gate and follow path as it heads for **Pevensey Haven**. Make for another gate and continue beside or near water. On reaching gate, keep ahead and look for fingerpost, indicating path on R. Avoid path and continue ahead, still on **1066 Country Walk**. Retrace your steps to **A27**. Cross over and return to **Pevensey**.

CUCKMERE HAVEN *SNAKE RIVER AND SEVEN SISTERS*

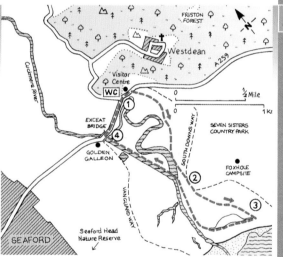

3 miles (4.8km) 1hr 30min **Ascent:** Negligible ⚠
Paths: Grassy trails and well-used paths. Mostly beside the Cuckmere or canalised branch of river
Suggested map: aqua3 OS Explorer 123 South Downs Way – Newhaven to Eastbourne
Grid reference: TV 518995
Parking: Fee-paying car park at Seven Sisters Country Park

Follow a breezy trail beside the Cuckmere River as it winds in erratic fashion towards the sea.

❶ Make for gate near entrance to **Seven Sisters Country Park**. This is the focal point of the lower valley and is an amenity area of 692 acres (280ha) developed by East Sussex County Council. There are artificial lakes and park trails, and an old Sussex barn near by which has been converted to provide a visitor centre. Next follow wide, grassy path towards beach. Path gradually curves to **R**, running alongside concrete track. Cuckmere River meanders beside you, heading for open sea. Continue walking ahead between track and river and make for **South Downs Way** sign.

❷ Avoid long distance trail as it runs in from L, pass it and **Foxhole campsite** and keep ahead, through gate towards beach. Veer **L** at beach and **South Downs Way** sign. On reaching next gate, don't go

through it. Instead, keep **R** and follow beach sign. Pass couple of wartime pill boxes on L, an evocative reminder of less peaceful times, and go through gate. Join stony path and walk ahead to beach, with white wall of Seven Sisters rearing up beside you.

❸ Turn **R** and then cross shore, approaching Cuckmere Haven Emergency Point sign. Branch off to **R**, to join another track here. Follow this track for about 50yds (46m) until you come to junction and keep **L**, following Habitat Trail and Park Trail. Keep beside Cuckmere where the landscape is characterised by meandering channels and waterways, all feeding into river. Pass turning to **Foxhole campsite** and follow footpath as it veers **L**, in line with Cuckmere. Make for kissing gate and then continue on straight path alongside of river.

❹ Keep ahead to road at **Exceat Bridge** and on L is **Golden Galleon** pub. Turn **R** and follow **A259** to return to car park at **country park**.

BIRLING GAP *TO BEACHY HEAD*

7½ miles (12.1km) 3hrs **Ascent:** 536ft (163m) ▲
Paths: Downland paths and tracks, clifftop greensward, no stiles
Suggested map: aqua3 OS Explorer 123 South Downs Way – Newhaven to Eastbourne
Grid reference: TQ 554959
Parking: Free car park at Birling Gap

A magnificent clifftop walk exploring a scenic stretch of the Sussex coast.

❶ Walk away from car park, keeping road on L. Ignore South Downs Way sign by road and continue on grassy path. Keep to **R** of next car park and follow path between trees.

❷ Keep parallel to road; when you see junction with concrete track, take next **L** path to meet it. Follow signposted bridleway ('Cornish Farm and Birling Manor'). Glance back for view of old Belle Tout lighthouse. Pass fingerpost and continue ahead. Follow concrete track as it bends **R**, avoiding bridleway going straight on. Look for gate on R and head east, keeping fence on R.

❸ Make for another gate and proceed. Pass alongside lines of bushes before reaching next gate. Traffic on A259 zips by on skyline. Pass access track to Bullockdown Farm. Along here you can see flint walls enclosing fields and pastures.

❹ Pass through gate to road. Turn **R**, following wide grassy verge. On reaching 2 adjoining gates on **R**, cross road and take grassy path to waymarked junction. Follow path towards Eastbourne ('seafront') and soon you meet South Downs Way.

❺ Bear sharp **R** here; follow long distance trail as it climbs between bushes and vegetation. Keep **R** when another path comes in from L and make for viewpoint, with views of Beachy Head lighthouse. Keep grass, up slope to trig point. In front of you are Beachy Head Inn and South Downs Countryside Centre.

❻ Return to South Downs Way and follow west. Path can be seen ahead, running over cliff top. Keep Belle Tout lighthouse in your sights and follow path up towards it. Keep to **R** of old lighthouse and soon car park at Birling Gap edges into view, as do famous Seven Sisters cliffs. Bear **R** at South Downs Way post. Follow path down and round to **L**. Swing **L** just before road and return to car park at Birling Gap.

232

East Sussex • SOUTHEAST ENGLAND

233

East Sussex • SOUTHEAST ENGLAND

234

East Sussex • SOUTHEAST ENGLAND

235 WILMINGTON *MYSTERY OF THE LONG MAN*

6¼ miles (10.1km) 2hrs 30min **Ascent:** 465ft (152m)
Paths: Downland paths and tracks, stretch of country road, 1 stile
Suggested map: aqua3 OS Explorer 123 South Downs Way – Newhaven to Eastbourne
Grid reference: TQ 543041
Parking: Long-stay car park at Wilmington

Visit the legendary chalk figure, which still puzzles archaeologists and historians.

❶ Make for car park exit; follow path parallel to road, heading towards **Long Man**. Bear **L** at next gate and take **Wealdway** to chalk figure. Climb quite steeply, curving to **R**. Go through gate, avoid **Wealdway** arrow and keep ahead towards escarpment, veering **R** just below **Long Man**.

❷ Go through next gate, cross track. Bear **L** at fence. After few paces, reach gate and sign for **South Downs Way**. Pass small reservoir; follow track to road.

❸ Turn **L** then walk to signpost ('**Lullington church**'), following path beside cottages. After visiting **church**, retrace steps to road. Turn **R**. Head down lane, looking for **Alfriston church** on R. Pass turning to village on R and continue ahead towards Seaford. Look out for post box and swing **L** ('Jevington').

❹ Follow bridleway as it climbs steadily between tracts of remote downland. Keep **L** at next main

junction and there is moderate climb. Avoid bridle track branching off to L and proceed towards Jevington. **Lullington Heath National Nature Reserve** is on R now. Pass bridleway to Charleston Bottom on R and keep on track as it climbs quite steeply. Pass 2nd sign and map for nature reserve and make for junction with **South Downs Way**.

❺ Turn **L** and then follow enclosed path to gate. Go straight ahead alongside woodland and pass through 2nd gate. Path begins gradual curve to **L** and eventually passes along rim of dry valley, **Tenantry Ground**. Keep fence on your **L** and look for gate ahead. Swing **R** as you approach gate to reach stile then follow path alongside fence, crossing top of **Long Man**.

❻ To your **R**, you can just make out chalk figure down below. Continue keeping fence on **R** and descend to gate. Turn **R** here and retrace your steps to car park at **Wilmington**.

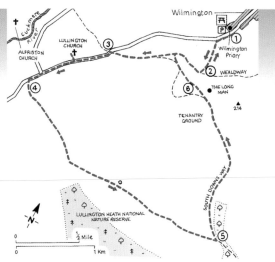

236 ARLINGTON *A LAKESIDE TRAIL*

3 miles (4.8km) 1hr 30min **Ascent:** 82ft (25m)
Paths: Field paths and trail, some brief road walking, 13 stiles
Suggested map: aqua3 OS Explorer 123 South Down Ways – Newhaven to Eastbourne
Grid reference: TQ 528074
Parking: Arlington Reservoir

Combine a delightful walk with a little birdwatching by the Cuckmere River.

❶ From car park walk towards information boards then turn **R** to join waymarked bridleway. Cut through trees to tarmac lane; look for bridleway sign. Follow lane and soon reservoir edges into view again. On reaching gate signed ('No entry – farm access only') bear **R** and follow bridleway and footpath signs.

❷ Skirt buildings of **Polhill's Farm** and return to tarmac lane. Turn **R** and walk along to kissing gate and 'circular walk' sign. Ignore gate and keep on lane. Continue for about 100yds (91m) and then branch **L** over stile into field. Swing half-**R** and look for 2nd stile to **R** of pond. Cross 3rd stile and go across pasture to 4th stile.

❸ Turn **L** here and follow road as it bends **R**. Cross **Cuckmere River** then bear **L** to join **Wealdway**, following sign ('Arlington'). Walk along drive and when it curves to R, by houses, veer **L** over stile.

Arlington **church** spire can be seen now. Continue ahead, when you reach R-H fence corner, following waymark. Cross several stiles and footbridge. Keep to R of **church**, cross another stile and pass Old School on your R.

❹ Walk along lane to **Yew Tree Inn**, then retrace your steps to **church** and cross field to footbridge. Turn **R** immediately beyond it to stile in field corner. Cross pasture to obvious footbridge and continue to 2nd footbridge where there are 2 stiles. Head across field towards line of trees, following vague outline of path. **Reservoir's** embankment is clearly defined on L, as you begin gentle climb.

❺ Cross stile by galvanised gate and go through kissing gate on immediate **R**. Follow path alongside lake and pass bird hide on L. Turn **L** further on and keep to bridleway as it reveals glimpses of lake through trees. Veer **L** at fork and follow path alongside **reservoir** and back to the start.

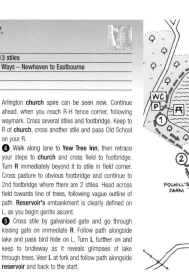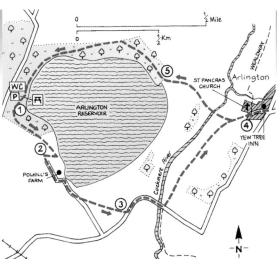

237 FIRLE *FINE DOWNLAND VIEWS*

4¼ miles (6.8km) 2hrs **Ascent:** 476ft (145m)
Paths: Tracks, paths and roads
Suggested map: aqua3 OS Explorer 123 South Down Ways – Newhaven to Eastbourne
Grid reference: TQ 468075
Parking: Free car park in Firle

Climb high above Firle Place, a Palladian mansion, and look towards distant horizons on this superb downland walk.

❶ Turn **L** out of car park, pass **Ram Inn** and follow road round to **R**, through village of **Firle**. Walk along to village stores and footpath to Charleston, once the home of Duncan Grant and Clive and Vanessa Bell, members of the Bloomsbury set. Pass turning to Firle's **Church of St Peter** and continue heading southwards, out of village.

❷ Turn **R** at junction of concrete tracks and make for road. Bear **L** then head for downland escarpment and begin long climb, which is steep in places. On reaching car park at top, swing **L** to gate and join **South Downs Way**.

❸ Head eastwards on long distance trail and, as you approach kissing gate and adjoining gate, turn sharp **L**.

❹ Follow path in northwesterly direction, down steep slopes of escarpment. On reaching wooden

post, where path forks, take lower grassy path and follow it as it descends in wide sweep. Drop down to gate and walk ahead, keeping fence on L. Skirt around **Firle Plantation** and follow track eventually leading to junction.

❺ Bear **L** and walk along track, keeping dramatic escarpment on your **L**. As you approach village of **Firle**, track curves to **R** towards buildings of **Place Farm**. Cross over junction of concrete tracks and retrace your steps back to car park at other end of village. At the centre of the village is **Firle Place**. The house dates from the 18th century and is surrounded by glorious parkland and a backdrop of hanging woods. The estate is an example of a 'closed village' and a reminder of the autocracy of powerful landowning families. This system made it virtually impossible for outsiders to move into the village system and consequently severely regulated the development of **Firle**.

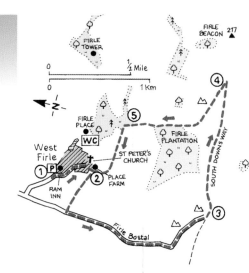

East Sussex

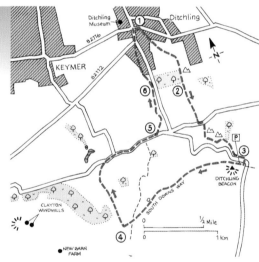

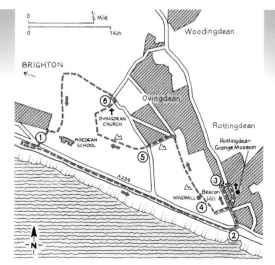

ASHDOWN FOREST *VISITING WINNIE-THE-POOH*

7 miles (11.3km) 3hrs **Ascent:** 170ft (55m)
Paths: Paths and tracks across farmland and woodland, 20 stiles
Suggested map: aqua3 OS Explorer 135 Ashdown Forest
Grid reference: TQ 472332
Parking: Pooh free car park, off B2026 south of Hartfield

Exploring the haunts of AA Milne's Pooh.

❶ Follow path ('Pooh Bridge'), take 3rd turning on R; descend to stile. Cross tree-ringed field to stile near corner, follow woodland path to another stile; head diagonally R across field to 4th stile by gate. Cross drive to 5th stile and gate, then aim R to another gate. Go forward to stile and road.

❷ Turn L, then R opposite The Paddocks; follow path through **Five Hundred Acre Wood** to reach **Wealdway**. Proceed, passing Kovacs Lodge. Climb quite steeply; make wide sweep to L. Follow track round to R to fork, veer L and approach private drive sign.

❸ Take R-H path and skirt farm. Rejoin drive and keep R, following **Wealdway** as it cuts across farmland. Pass turning to Buckhurst then bear L over stile to follow **High Weald Landscape Trail**. Cross field to gate and stile; cut through wood to brick bridge.

❹ Turn R; follow fence, passing paddocks. Veer R via gateway in field corner; make for next field. Head

diagonally L across farmland to stile. Keep to R-H edge of field to stile, then cross footbridge and continue by field edge. Turn L at stile and enter Hartfield.

❺ Bear R at B2026, then L. Cross stile in field corner and continue over next stile to Forest Way. Turn L; follow old trackbed until gate on L. Cross pasture to gate; follow woodland bridleway. Emerging from trees, continue to Culvers Farm.

❻ Make for road then turn L. Walk to 1st R-H footpath ('Pooh Bridge'). Cross stile; follow track ahead to 3 stiles before crossing field. Follow waymarks and make for stile in corner. Cross drive to another stile; head diagonally down field to stile in corner. Continue on path, heading for next stile. Follow route south.

❼ When it sweeps L towards Cotchford Farm, proceed along public bridleway to **Pooh Bridge**; follow track as it climbs alongside woodland and paddocks. Turn L at road and when it bends around to R, go ahead into trees. Follow footpath through wood, back to start.

DITCHLING *DELIGHTFUL DOWNS*

5½ miles (8.8km) 2hrs 30min **Ascent:** 600ft (183m)
Paths: Field paths, bridleways and a stretch of road, 11 stiles
Suggested map: aqua3 OS Explorer 122 South Downs Way – Steyning to Newhaven
Grid reference: TQ 326152
Parking: Free car park at rear of village hall in Ditchling

Exploring the South Downs.

❶ Turn R out of car park; follow B2116. Pass Charlton Gardens; bear R, joining path ('Downs'). Cross 3 pastures via 5 stiles; follow broad path through woodland. Keep R at fork by bridleway waymark post; pass house. Keep ahead alongside beech hedge where concrete track runs off R.

❷ Pass Claycroft House. Follow path between trees and houses. At road, turn L and proceed to bridleway on R, pointing towards **South Downs Way**. Follow path, swing L at junction; climb steep escarpment. Keep view of Weald on L and, further up, path runs by road. Look for **South Downs Way** sign ahead. Turn R.

❸ Pass by car park and over **Ditchling Beacon**. Go through gate. Look for trig point L. Head west along **South Downs Way**, pass dew pond. Make for junction of paths. **Keymer** is signed to R and Brighton to L.

❹ Follow path north towards **Keymer**, soon descending quite steeply. Keep R at fork, making for

gate out to lane. Bear L to junction, then turn R past turning for **Keymer** on L. Walk towards **Ditchling**; join Sussex Border Path at next stile on L.

❺ Cross field to stile; enter woodland. Follow path through trees, then go straight over drive and alongside barns and loose boxes. Cross grass to line of trees, curve R and briefly follow track to several stiles and footbridge. Path makes its way across elongated field towards trees.

❻ Cross stile, avoiding another stile leading out to road; continue across pasture, keeping to L of houses. Make for far L corner of field; look for opening in hedgerow. Follow path round to R, alongside row of houses. Cross stile on R and follow path to road. Bear L by grassy roundabout. Take path to R of sign for Neville Bungalows. Cut between trees, hedges and fences, following narrow path to road. Bear R towards Haywards Heath and Lindfield and walk back to centre of **Ditchling**, turning R into Lewes Road for car park.

ROTTINGDEAN *FROM THE SEA TO THE DEANS*

5 miles (8km) 2hrs **Ascent:** 305ft (92m)
Paths: Busy village streets, downland paths and tracks, 6 stiles
Suggested map: aqua3 OS Explorer 122 South Downs Way – Steyning to Newhaven
Grid reference: TQ 347032
Parking: Free car park at Roedean Bottom, at junction of A259 and B2118

Visit a picturesque village, which is famous for its artistic and literary associations.

❶ From car park cross A259; turn R towards Brighton, following path parallel to road. Look for path on L; follow it down to Undercliff. Head east towards **Rottingdean**, passing café. Continue on path until reaching steps and sign ('Rottingdean') on L.

❷ Make for village; pass White Horse pub on L. Cross A259 into **Rottingdean** High Street. Pass Black Horse, Nevill Road and Steyning Road; continue along street. As you approach The Green, look for The Dene on R.

❸ Follow road round to R and make for junction. Keep R and head back into **Rottingdean** village. Pass war memorial and village pond; look for church on L. Pass Plough Inn; walk back down to High Street. Turn L, then R into Nevill Road. Climb quite steeply; bear R into Sheep Walk.

❹ Keep **windmill** on L and follow bridleway over Downs. **Woodingdean** can be glimpsed in distance

and buildings of **Ovingdean** in foreground. Outline of **Roedean School** is visible against horizon. Continue to Longhill Road, turn L; proceed to junction.

❺ Cross over to stile; then head up slope to 2nd stile in R-H boundary. Bear L and keep going up hillside. Pass private path to **Roedean School** and continue beside wire fence to stile in field corner. Turn R and skirt pasture to next stile. Descend steeply towards **Ovingdean** church, cutting off field corner to reach stile. Cross into field and keep churchyard wall hard by you on R.

❻ Cross stile to lychgate; walk down to junction. Turn L then when road bends R, keep ahead along wide concrete track, following bridleway. Keep L at fork, then immediately L again at next fork, just beyond it. When track swings quite sharply to L, keep ahead along path. Pass path and stile, and car park by A259 looms into view. When you reach road, by entrance to **Roedean School**, cross grass to car park.

241 LINGFIELD *POWER AND FLOUR AT HAXTED*

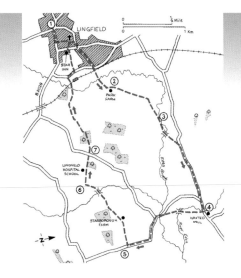

5½ miles (8.8km) 2hrs **Ascent:** 66ft (20m) 🄐
Paths: Field edge paths can be overgrown or muddy, farm tracks and country lanes, 15 stiles
Suggested map: aqua3 OS Explorers 146 Dorking, Box Hill & Reigate; 147 Sevenoaks & Tonbridge
Grid reference: TQ 385435
Parking: Free council car park in Gun Pit Road, Lingfield

A lowland walk and a remarkable water mill. ❶ Walk down High Street, turn **L** into Old School Place, and take footpath through churchyard. Turn **R** into Vicarage Road, cross over into Bakers Lane, and continue beyond Station Road on to footpath across **railway**. Swing **L** as you approach **Park Farm**, then fork **L** on to gravelled farm track.

❷ Proceed over stile into open field. After few paces further on, dodge through gate on **L**; continue with hedge on **R**. At top corner of field, turn **R** through small gate, heading past prominent oak tree towards gates on far side of field.

❸ Cross lane, climb stile opposite, and take waymarked route beside **Eden Brook**. Cross brook on wooden bridge, then head across field to stile by metal gates. Turn **R** along road to **Haxted Mill**.

❹ Turn **R** over stile on to Vanguard Way, recross river; bear **L** towards stile on far side of next field. Turn **L** on to road then fork **L** just beyond bridge.

❺ Turn **R**, along drive towards **Starborough Farm**. At farm, take stile by metal gates, cross drive to Badger House, and then follow waymarked path across field towards corner of small wood. Cross footbridge and stile, and follow path along **L-H** edge of next 4 fields.

❻ Turn **R** in corner of 4th field, keeping hedge on **L**. Continue over bridge and stile into **Lingfield Hospital School** sports ground. Keep ahead to gap in far hedge, then cross lane, where footpath continues at stile.

❼ Cross 2 small fields, enter woods by stile, and pass children's adventure playground. Beyond woods, bear **R** through gates near school buildings, and follow winding path through fields to **railway crossing** near Lingfield Station. Turn **R** up Station Road then, just opposite station, turn **L** up path to **Star Inn**. Cross over Church Road, and turn **R** through charming 16th-century Old Town into churchyard. Finally, retrace your steps to car park.

242 OXTED *NORTH DOWNS ESCARPMENT*

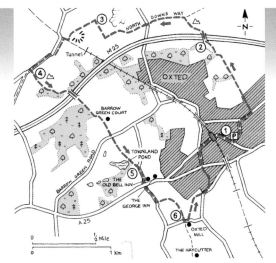

5½ miles (8.8km) 3hrs **Ascent:** 607ft (185m) 🄐
Paths: Field edge paths, farm tracks, town roads, 12 stiles
Suggested map: aqua3 OS Explorer 146 Dorking, Box Hill & Reigate
Grid reference: TQ 395529
Parking: Ellice Road car park, off Station Road East, Oxted

On the dramatic chalk downlands. ❶ Walk down Station Road East from Ellice Road car park. Turn **L** at Gresham Road then turn **R** at top into Bluehouse Lane and **L** again into Park Road. At bend, continue up signposted public footpath towards Woldingham. Cross stile beyond school playing fields, and head across field towards footbridge over **M25**.

❷ Cross **motorway**, bear **L**. Follow path to stile. Nip over and swing **L** on to **North Downs Way** National Trail. Follow waymarked trail across Chalkpit Lane and past quarry fencing, until it swings to **R** for North Downs ridge. Climb as far as waymark post beyond wicket gate and bear **L** into National Trust's Oxted Downs estate.

❸ Follow path through trees, cross stile. Turn hard **R** up rustic flight of steps. Don't miss view from seat halfway up, directly above **railway tunnel**. Swing **L** at top of steps. Follow National Trail to road at Ganger's Hill.

❹ Turn **L**, and drop back down public footpath towards **Oxted**. Join bridleway half-way down, and carry on across bridge over the **M25** on to lane past **Barrow Green Court**. Cross over **Barrow Green Road**, squeeze through wicket gate then follow footpath along edge of field past **Townland Pond** and on to Sandy Lane.

❺ Turn **R**, pass underneath A25. Cross Oxted High Street at **Old Bell Inn**. Follow Beadles Lane for 200yds (183m) then turn **L** into Springfield and fork off on to footpath on **R**. Drop gently down to Spring Lane, and picturesque **Oxted Mill** (privately owned).

❻ A 500yd (457m) diversion leads to **The Haycutter** pub. Cross straight over Spring Lane, zig-zag **R** and **L**, then take waymarked path through meadows to pub. Main route turns **L** past mill, and **L** again over stile at weir. Follow path through to Woodhurst Lane, and turn **L**. Fork **L** up narrow footpath at Woodhurst Park; cross **A25** into East Hill Road. At foot of the hill, turn **R** up Station Road West; then dive through station subway at top. Finally, turn **R** into Station Road East to return to start.

243 OUTWOOD *THE MILLER'S TRAIL*

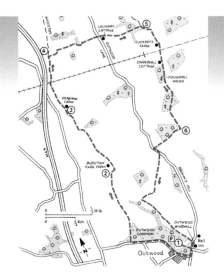

6¾ miles (10.9km) 3hrs 30min **Ascent:** 328ft (100m) 🄐
Paths: Easy field edge paths and farm tracks, 20 stiles
Suggested map: aqua3 OS Explorer 146 Dorking, Box Hill & Reigate
Grid reference: TQ 326456
Parking: National Trust car park opposite mill, Outwood

Visit England's oldest working windmill. ❶ Head out of car park towards mill. Keep turning **R**, via Millers Lane into Brickfield Road. Turn **R** down woodland bridleway 180yds (165m) beyond church; follow it out into fields towards **Burstow Park Farm**.

❷ Zig-zag **R**, then **L**, around farmhouse to metal gate. Jump stile on **L**, and walk diagonally across field. Cross another stile, turn **L** through gap in hedge, then turn **R** towards stile and footbridge at top of next field. Nip across, and bear **L** for 80yds (73m) to another stile and bridge. Bear **L** again over stile; then turn **R** towards **Henhaw Farm**, where stile leads up between farm buildings.

❸ Cross farm drive, and continue through 2 fields before crossing **railway** embankment via steep wooden steps and level crossing. Now follow fences on **L** through 3 fields, as far as metal field gate and stile.

❹ Turn **R** here, but without crossing stile. Follow footpath through several fields, separated by stiles, always keeping field edge on **L**. Cross **Outwood Lane**, walk up gravelled drive to **Laundry Cottage**; take narrow public bridleway just to **R** of metal gate.

❺ Pass blue and yellow waymarker post, and continue along easy-to-follow gravelled bridleway to **Cuckseys Farm** and **Cinderhill Cottage**. Now follow waymarked route down beside **Poundhill Wood**, and carry on for another ¾ mile (1.2km) before emerging at corner of open field that rises gently to cut off view.

❻ Turn **R** here, along woodland edge and on to track leading out to **Brown's Hill**. Turn **L**, then **R** over stile opposite Outwood Swan Sanctuary. Head diagonally across 3 fields. Bear gently **R** through gap in hedge, and continue through 1 field and into next. After 40yds (37m) turn **L** over waymarked stile and follow field boundary on **L**, past National Trust waymarker post and into woods on **Outwood Common**. Join surfaced drive at Path End cottage, and follow it back to **Outwood windmill** and start.

Surrey

CROWHURST *THE SIX WIVES*

5 miles (8km) 2hrs **Ascent:** 131ft (40m)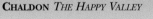
Paths: Farm tracks and well-maintained field paths, some road walking, 10 stiles
Suggested map: aqua3 OS Explorer 146 Dorking, Box Hill & Reigate
Grid reference: TQ 365453
Parking: Adjoining cricket field or in Tandridge Lane, Crowhurst

On the trail of Henry VIII.

❶ Turn **R** out of car park, and follow **Ray Lane** as far as Tandridge Lane. Turn **L**, pass **Red Barn pub** then turn **R** up tree-lined drive towards **Ardenrun**.

❷ Walk up long straight drive until it swings to **L**. Follow it for further 80yds (73m) then, just before private drive to **Ardenrun Farm**, swing hard **R** at yellow waymark on to 'Age to Age' walk. Continue for another 300yds (274m).

❸ Nip over stile on **L** and walk through 2 gently rising fields. Turn **R** at yellow ('Age to Age') waymark — with good views behind you — and follow well-maintained path straight across drive to **Crowhurst Place**. Continue beside hedge on **R**, cross small footbridge, then head diagonally across next field to junction of 2 farm tracks. To visit Crowhurst church, turn **R** for 700yds (640m), then **L** on to Crowhurst Road.

❹ Turn half-**L** here, and follow track towards **Stocks and Kingswood Farms**. Leave 'Age to Age' route and

carry straight along yellow waymarked track that winds through **Kingswood farmyard**, through small wooden gate, and along gravelled drive to picture-postcard Stocks Farm house.

❺ Gravelled drive joins surfaced lane at farm gate. Turn **L** here and, after 20yds (18m), turn **L** again, over 2 stiles in quick succession. Head diagonally across next field, and turn **L** over stile. Cross bridge and 2nd stile, then keep **L** until you cross another stile and small footbridge. Now turn **R**, walk through 2 fields, and rejoin **Tandridge Lane**.

❻ Turn **L**. After 55yds (50m), branch **R** at **Comforts Place Farmhouse entrance**. As drive swings round to **L**, cross stile and continue on lane to rural crossroads at **Oak Tree Farm**. Turn **L**. Follow unmade track past Highfield House and out to muddy lane. Beyond **Sunhill Farm** road surface improves. Lane leads to **A22**.

❼ Turn **L**. Follow main road for last 800yds (732m) into **Blindley Heath** and back to car park.

GODSTONE *DISCOVERING GILBERT SCOTT*

3¾ miles (6km) 1hr 45min **Ascent:** 278ft (85m)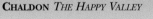
Paths: Footpaths and bridleways can be muddy in places, 4 stiles
Suggested map: aqua3 OS Explorer 146 Dorking, Box Hill & Reigate
Grid reference: TQ 350515
Parking: Adjacent to village pond. Parking limited to 3 hours, should be plenty for this walk

On the trail of one of the leading architects of the Victorian era.

❶ Directly opposite pond in **Godstone**, take public footpath beside **White Hart** pub, signposted towards **church**. Cross Church Lane and follow path through churchyard. Keep **church** on **L**, and continue along winding path as it passes **Glebe Water** to yellow waymarker post at edge of open field. Turn **R** and drop down beside field to stile, then turn **L** here on to bridleway that leads under busy **A22**.

❷ Just beyond bridge, turn **R** at **Hop Garden Cottage** and follow waymarked bridleway out on to **Jackass Lane**. Turn **R** here, opposite **Little Court Farm**, now converted into private houses. At top of hill, turn **L** for 100yds (91m) to visit **St Peter's Church**. Otherwise turn **R**, and follow Tandridge Lane to public footpath just 30yds (27m) short of **Barley Mow**.

❸ Turn **R** on to waymarked **Greensand Way**, and follow broad, sandy track between open fields to

wicket gate beside **A22**. Cross main road on level, and take footpath directly opposite. Beyond small wood, 3-way wooden signpost guides you on to bridleway straight ahead. Jump tiny ford (or use footbridge) and walk up lane past **Leigh Place pond** as far as **B2236**.

❹ Leave **Greensand Way** here, and turn **R**. Follow pavement until just beyond Church Lane, then fork **L** at bus stop, up **Enterdent Road**. After 100yds (91m) turn **R** on to public footpath into woods. The waymarked path climbs, steeply in places, to stile near adventure playground on edge of **Godstone Farm**. Follow waymarked route through farm grounds, to stile just north of car park.

❺ Turn **R** on to **Tilburstow Hill** for 100yds (91m). Just beyond **Godstone Farm** delivery entrance, turn off **L** at wooden footpath signpost. Path runs briefly through farmland on edge of **Godstone** village, then leads out into **Ivy Mill Lane**. Turn **R** for short climb back to village green, then **R** again, back to car park.

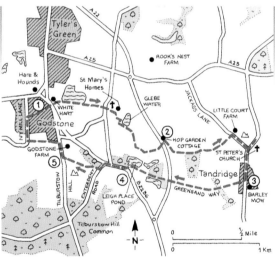

CHALDON *THE HAPPY VALLEY*

3 miles (4.8km) 1hr 30min **Ascent:** 246ft (75m)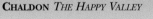
Paths: Well maintained and signposted paths, 7 stiles
Suggested map: aqua3 OS Explorer 146 Dorking, Box Hill & Reigate
Grid reference: TQ 301571
Parking: Car park on Farthing Downs, open dawn till dusk

The aptly named Happy Valley leads you through heavenly countryside — to a vision of hell in Chaldon church!

❶ Cross Downs Road from car park, turn **R** at information pagoda, and follow waymarked **London Loop** down through **Devilsden Wood**. Beyond woods, **Happy Valley** opens up in front of you. Follow woodland edge on your **R** until path bears slightly **L** and begins to lose height. Now dodge briefly into woods, and follow signposted path towards **Chaldon church**. Soon you'll be back the open and then follow woodland edge as far as wooden footpath sign. Turn **R** here, and walk through thin finger of **Figgs Wood** before crossing large open field.

❷ At far side of field, turn **L** on to **Ditches Lane** then, after 40yds (37m), fork **R** at triangle to visit **Chaldon church**. (A travelling monk visited the church in the 12th century and created its greatest treasure — a mural of the Last Judgement. The mural was

whitewashed over sometime in the 17th century and was only recently rediscovered.) Return via triangle to **Ditches Lane**, and continue for few more paces in direction you were going earlier. Now, turn **L** on to public footpath to **Piles Wood**. Cross open field, and keep straight on when you come to corner of **Piles Wood**. At far side of woods you'll come to gravelled bridleway, where you turn **L**.

❸ Follow waymarked route of Downlands Circular Walk as it drops down through **Piles Wood** to footpath cross roads. Turn **L**, towards **Farthing Downs**, and continue for 700yds (640m) along bottom of **Happy Valley**. Should you feel thirsty, take signposted route that crosses valley at this point to **The Fox**. Turn **R**, and follow **London Loop** waymarks to **Coulsdon Common**. Round trip to pub will add 1 mile (1.6km) to your walk. Otherwise, continue for further 70yds (64m), then fork **L** and climb gently up side of valley to rejoin your outward route at corner of **Devilsden Wood**.

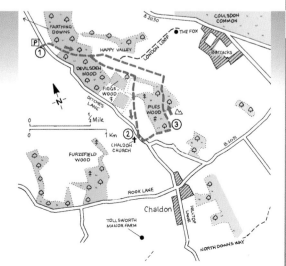

244

Surrey • SOUTHEAST ENGLAND

245

Surrey • SOUTHEAST ENGLAND

246

Surrey • SOUTHEAST ENGLAND

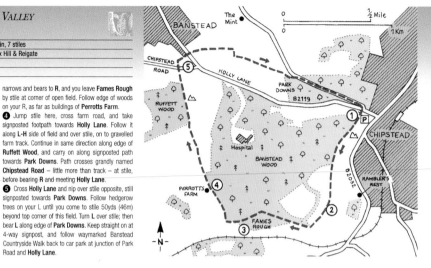

247 BANSTEAD *ACROSS CHIPSTEAD VALLEY*

3½ miles (5.7km) 2hrs **Ascent:** 295ft (90m)
Paths: Woodland and field edge paths, muddy after rain, 7 stiles
Suggested map: aqua3 OS Explorer 146 Dorking, Box Hill & Reigate
Grid reference: TQ 273583
Parking: Holly Lane, Banstead

A popular woodland route.

1 Leave car park by wicket gate at top **L-H** (southeast) corner and follow waymarked gravel path. After 80yds (73m), join public footpath towards **Perrotts Farm**. Path climbs steadily through tunnel of trees along woodland edge. (Look out for old beeches on R; these may once have formed part of old boundary hedge.)

2 At 3-way wooden signpost ½ mile (800m) from car park, you have option of diversion to **Ramblers Rest**. Continue straight along permissive path, signposted towards **Fames Rough**. 200yds (183m) further on, bear **R** at another 3-way signpost, towards **Banstead Wood**. Carry on through **Fames Rough**, turn **L** on to Banstead Countryside Walk at next 3-way signpost, and follow it to waymark, 220yds (201m) further on.

3 Here Banstead Countryside Walk dives off into undergrowth on **L**. Keep straight ahead, nipping over fallen tree trunk few paces further on. Soon path

narrows and bears to **R**, and you leave **Fames Rough** by stile at corner of open field. Follow edge of woods on your **R**, as far as buildings of **Perrotts Farm**.

4 Jump stile here, cross farm road, and take signposted footpath towards **Holly Lane**. Follow it along **L-H** side of field and over stile, on to gravelled farm track. Continue in same direction along edge of **Ruffett Wood**, and carry on along signposted path towards **Park Downs**. Path crosses grandly named **Chipstead Road** – little more than track – at stile, before bearing **R** and meeting **Holly Lane**.

5 Cross **Holly Lane** and nip over stile opposite, still signposted towards **Park Downs**. Follow hedgerow trees on your **L** until you come to stile 50yds (46m) beyond top corner of this field. **L** over stile; then bear **L** along edge of **Park Downs**. Keep straight on at 4-way signpost, and follow waymarked Banstead Countryside Walk back to car park at junction of Park Road and **Holly Lane**.

248 CHARLWOOD *JUMBO AHOY!*

4¼ miles (6.8km) 1hr 45min **Ascent:** 197ft (60m)
Paths: Byways and woodland paths, short sections on village roads and farmland, 7 stiles
Suggested map: aqua3 OS Explorer 146 Dorking, Box Hill & Reigate
Grid reference: TQ 243410
Parking: On The Street, close to Rising Sun and post office

An easy-to-follow route with something to interest everyone – especially plane spotters!

1 With recreation ground on your **R**, walk past **Pine Café** and turn **L** up Chapel Road. Continue on to byway and pass extraordinary **Providence Chapel**. Behind low picket fence, few tombstones lean drunkenly in front of small, weatherboarded chapel with a wooden verandah. The building, which dates from 1816, is straight out of an advert for Jack Daniels, and seems to have dropped in from Kentucky. Turn **L** at byway crossroads towards **Stan Hill**, and continue straight across **Norwoodhill Road**. At brow of hill, take signposted footpath on **L**, just at entrance to **Barfield Farm**.

2 Path leads to corner of **Beggarshouse Lane**, where you turn **L**, and follow lane on to tree-lined byway. At woods beyond **Greenings Farm**, turn **L** over plank bridge and waymarked stile. Follow **L-H** edge of open field, then proceed to cross farm lane at pair of

waymarked stiles. Continue over another pair of stiles until fence bears **L** at stile. Steer gently **R** here, towards stile in far corner of field then head across next field to stile into **Cidermill Road**.

3 Turn **L**, and follow wide grass verge for 75yds (69m) before turning **L** again on to signposted bridleway. Soon path dodges into **Glover's Wood** and, 200yds (183m) further on, you'll come to pair of waymarker posts. Turn hard **L** at 1st one, follow waymarked footpath across **Welland Gill**, and carry on to far side of woods.

4 Leave woods at wicket gate, and continue straight down Glovers Road. Cross Rectory Lane/Russ Hill Road, and keep ahead on footpath opposite. Path passes **St Nicholas Church** – but you must not. Inside this welcoming church are some of the finest medieval wall paintings in the country. Beyond churchyard, turn **R** past **Half Moon**, then **R** again for last 100yds (91m) back to recreation ground.

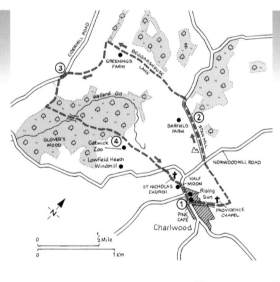

249 HOLMWOOD *HIGHWAYMEN AND HEROES*

3¼ miles (5.3km) 1hr 15min **Ascent:** 164ft (50m)
Paths: Forest and farm tracks, muddy in places, some minor roads
Suggested map: aqua3 OS Explorer 146 Dorking, Box Hill & Reigate
Grid reference: TQ 183454
Parking: National Trust car park at Fourwents Pond

Once the haunt of highwaymen, American millionaire Alfred Vanderbilt also enjoyed a spot of coach driving around Holmwood.

1 Head out of car park towards **Fourwents Pond**, and bear **R** along waterside track, keeping pond on **L**. At far corner of pond, cross small plank bridge, walk through smaller car park, and turn **R** into **Mill Road**. After 400yds (366m), turn **R** up lane ('Gable End, Applegarth and Went Cottage'). 30yds (27m) further on, fork **L** on to waymarked public footpath. Continue under set of power lines then follow blue waymarks across parting of 2 rough gravel tracks before recrossing one of them at another blue waymark. Follow path to next waymarker post and swing **L** at yellow arrow that points your way to Clematis Cottage. Turn **L** here, and join gravelled track as far as Uplands Cottage.

2 Turn **L** for 20yds (18m), then **R** on to grassy footpath. At end of footpath turn **R**, dodge through wooden post and rail barrier; turn **L** at blue-and-yellow

waymarker post, 25yds (23m) further on. Fork **R** at next junction of paths to clearing in woods and drop down grassy slope straight ahead, now following blue waymarked route on to gravelled surface at foot of hill. After 300yds (274m), keep sharp eye out for blue-and-yellow waymarker to **L** of path, and turn **R** here, on to another gravelled path.

3 This yellow waymarked route leads across the **Common** beside National Trust estate boundary, and brings you out opposite **Plough** pub at **Blackbrook**. Turn **R** on to **Blackbrook Road**, then **L** into **Red Lane** (signposted towards Leigh and Brockham) and follow it for about ½ mile (800m).

4 Turn **R** into **Brimstone Lane** at public bridleway signpost. Continue through 5-bar gate and down **R-H** side of open field, leaving through 2nd gate at far end. Follow track as far as **Lodge Farm**, then turn **R** on to **Lodge Lane**, which leads back to **Fourwents Pond**. Turn **R** here, for last 100yds (91m) back to start.

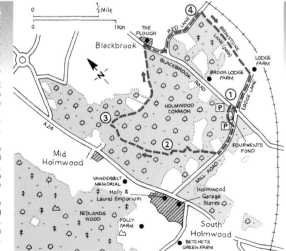

Surrey

LEIGH A PASTORAL SCENE

4 miles (6.4km) 1hr 45min **Ascent:** 73ft (22m)
Paths: Field edge and cross-field paths, 22 stiles
Suggested map: aqua3 OS Explorer 146 Dorking, Box Hill & Reigate
Grid reference: TQ 223468
Parking: Lay-by between the Plough and church in Leigh

A peaceful walk through lovely scenery.

1 With your back to **Plough**, turn **L** on to village green and take signposted footpath through churchyard and across open field to wooden footbridge. Cross brook, and waymarked stile 40yds (37m) further on; follow hedge on **R** to far corner of field. Jump stile, and turn **L** on to waymarked bridleway. After 100yds (91m), bear **R** through waymarked wicket gate towards another stile. Nip across and continue straight ahead towards far corner of field. Turn **R** over waymarked stile, and up short hill beside woods. At brow, you'll come to stile; don't jump it, but turn **R**, towards **triangulation pillar** (or trig point) across field – enjoy the views.

2 Turn hard **L** at triangulation pillar and double back to far corner of field. You could have kept straight on beside hedge that you followed earlier, but that would have been trespassing! Cross stile in corner of field, then follow succession of waymarked stiles that lead to

Dene Farm, and then across farm drive. Bear half **R** here; cross field to plank bridge and stile. Continue through next field, and out on to **Deanoak Lane**.

3 Turn **L**; then, just beyond double bend, turn **L** again, up lane towards **Stumblehole Farm**. Follow lane straight past **Tamworth Farm** and through small patch of woodland, then bear **L** at 3-way signpost on to concrete road. Continue past **Bury's Court School**. 55yds (50m) beyond **Keeper's Cottage**, look out for metal gate on **R**. Climb over here, and bear away beside infant **River Mole**. Follow waymarked route over wooden footbridge, and out on to **Flanchford Road**.

4 Turn **L**, as far as **Little Flanchford Cottages**. After few paces, take footpath on **L**, and cross stile after 150yds (137m). Now bear **R** across 2 footbridges, and continue along **R-H** edge of next 3 fields. Walk diagonally to your **L** across 4th field, to small wicket gate. Turn **L** here, for last 100yds (91m) along road and back to start.

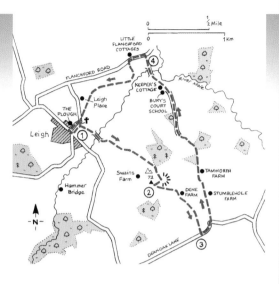

EPSOM HORSING AND COURSING

5 miles (8km) 2hrs **Ascent:** 394ft (120m)
Paths: Mainly broad, easy-to-follow bridleways
Suggested map: aqua3 OS Explorer 146 Dorking, Box Hill & Reigate
Grid reference: TQ 223584
Parking: Car park by mini-roundabout on Tattenham Corner Rd (charges apply on race days)

A walk across Epsom Downs racecourse that everyone will enjoy.

1 From the mini-roundabout near **Downs Lunch Box**, take signposted bridleway to Walton Road. Cross racecourse and continue along broad, waymarked lane, keeping an eye out for occasional cars. The Bridleway remains open on race days, though naturally there are some restrictions during races.

2 At length lane swings hard **R**. Follow waymarked bridleway as it forks off down narrow path to **L**. Bear **R** at gallops, continuing beside rustic wooden fence before rejoining broader lane down past the **Warren** – there is a lovely view across valley from here.

3 At bottom of hill, near ('Racehorses Only') sign, lies 6-way junction. Think of it as mini-roundabout and take **3rd** exit, straight ahead. Narrow track leads through scrubby trees, but it soon leads you out between wooden posts on to broader bridleway. Turn

L and then, in a few paces, fork **L**. Keep straight on at bridleway signpost, towards **Walton on the Hill**, and follow waymarked track as it swings **R** at **Nohome Farm** and begins long climb out of valley.

4 Bridleway ends at Cotton Mills, at junction of **Hurst Road** and **Ebbisham Lane**. Keep on down **Ebbisham Lane**, and turn **L** at bottom into Walton Street. Pass **Fox and Hounds** and **Mere Pond** then turn **L** at **The Bell** pub sign, up side of pond. After 30yds (27m), fork **R** at Withybed Corner and follow lane to **The Bell**.

5 Keep straight on, along path signposted to Motts Hill Lane. Continue past **Coal Post** and White Cottage; then, as lane bears R, turn **L** on to bridleway. From here you simply follow waymarked route all the way back to Epsom Lane North. Journey's end is now in sight. Go across road and continue along pavement towards car park. It finishes 100yds (91m) before you reach car park, so take care.

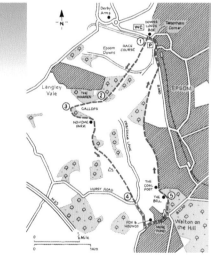

BOX HILL INVENTIONS GALORE

4 miles (6.4km) 2hrs 15min **Ascent:** 803ft (245m)
Paths: Woodland tracks, with two sections on minor roads
Suggested map: aqua3 OS Explorer 146 Dorking, Box Hill & Reigate
Grid reference: TQ 178513
Parking: National Trust car park, Fort Cottages, Box Hill Country Park

As well as its famous box trees, it was also the home of John Logie Baird, inventor of television.

1 Turn **L** out of car park. **Swiss Cottage** on **R** (now a private house) was home to John Logie Baird during the 1920s and 30s. Cross over, and follow roadside path for ½ mile (800m). Shortly after you set out, you'll see path leading down to **viewpoint**, built in memory of Leopold Salomons of Norbury Park. The commanding views of Dorking and the Mole Valley are well worth the short diversion.

2 Just before **Boxhills Tavern**, recross road and turn off to **L** on to signposted public bridleway. Ignore all turnings you pass, and follow signposted route as it drops down through **Juniper Bottom** to **Headley Road**.

3 Next few hundred paces are very steep indeed. Alternatively, turn **L** on to **Headley Road**, and rejoin route by turning **L** on to **Old London Road**. This will cut out **Mickleham** village, and shorten walk by ¾ mile

(1.2km). Otherwise, cross straight over on to public footpath and steel yourself for seemingly interminable climb up long flight of rustic steps. Just beyond top of steps path bears **R** and gradient eases slightly. Soon you come to bench seat – splendid views and a good excuse for a rest. Now follow National Trust's 'long walk' waymarks as you bear **L** and drop down past footpath crossroads with **Thames Down Link**. Clamber over stile at foot of hill, and continue past church into village of **Mickleham**. Turn **L** and follow **Old London Road**. Follow pavement on **R-H** side, which at times transforms into pleasant rural path running just few paces away from road. By time you reach junction with **Zig Zag Road**, it has returned to pavement again.

4 Cross over to junction with **Zig Zag Road**, and join signposted bridleway that climbs steadily all way back up hill to National Trust centre. Near top, you'll see old Victorian **fort** on **R**. Turn **R** at top of the hill for last 60yds (55m) back to car park.

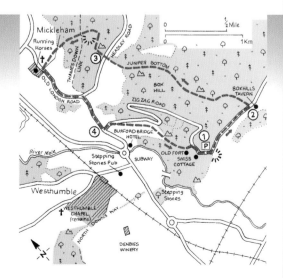

253 HEADLEY *THE HEATH HIGHLANDERS*

4½ miles (7.2km) 2hrs 15min **Ascent:** 425ft (160m)
Paths: Mainly woodland tracks
Suggested map: aqua3 OS Explorer 146 Dorking, Box Hill & Reigate
Grid reference: TQ 205538
Parking: National Trust car park, Headley Heath

A circular tour through an 8,000-year-old landscape.

❶ Face road, walk to far R-H corner of car park, and take bridleway on your R. Pass bench and follow track past **pond** to crossroads.

❷ Turn R here, and follow waymarked route down to parting of ways at foot of hill. Fork R along National Trust's waymarked route, and follow it over low rise and down to crossroads in valley bottom. Turn L along waymarked bridleway that climbs gently round to L. After 100yds (91m) turn R, following waymarked route that leaves track and climbs steeply up through woods to National Trust sign, half hidden in trees. If you reach road at **High Ashurst**, you've gone too far; turn back, and fork L after 50yds (46m).

❸ Double back to R, and wind your way down out of woods. Cross **Lodgebottom Road** at **Cockshot Cottage**, and climb steeply up narrow path to T-junction with good, level track.

❹ Turn R, and follow track as far as **Mill Way**. Just short of road, bear R on to horse margin and follow it until it leads you across road and then on to signposted byway.

❺ If you don't want to visit **Headley** village, turn R at end of byway, and rejoin route at Point ❻. Otherwise fork L here, into **Slough Lane**, and walk up to junction with **Church Lane**. Turn R on to permissive bridleway that runs beside road. Just past **Cock Horse**, fork R at bus stop on to signposted footpath. Follow it through to road junction, turn hard R into **Leech Lane**, and drop down to junction with **Tumber Street**.

❻ Turn L and cross **Mill Way** into Crabtree Lane. Follow waymarked horse track past **Broom House**, and up hill to pit on your L-H side. Bear L here, along blue waymarked track. Pass group of houses on your L and continue for 275yds (251m), until you see car park between trees on your L-H side. Turn L for short stroll back to your car.

254 POLESDEN LACEY *ROYAL ROMANCES*

4¼ miles (6.8km) 2hrs 15min **Ascent:** 607ft (185m)
Paths: Woodland and farm tracks
Suggested map: aqua3 OS Explorer 146 Dorking, Box Hill & Reigate
Grid reference: TQ 141503
Parking: National Trust car park on Ranmore Common Road

A woodland walk around a country house that was once a favourite with high society.

❶ Cross road from car park, turn L and walk for 200yds (183m) along broad roadside verge. Turn R just beyond tile-hung Fox Cottages, where 2 public footpaths meet here. Take the L-H path through woods and, ignoring all turnings, follow it through little combe. At length it draws alongside post-and-rail fence, and veers sharp L. Turn R here, through gap in fence, and continue through woodland glade. Just beyond wooden gate, turn L on to signposted Yewtree Farm Walk. Continue to gravelled forest track 100yds (91m) further on, and turn R. Just beyond you'll come to bench seat on your R. There's a great view of **Polesden Lacey**, and it's a pleasant spot for a picnic.

❷ Follow gravelled track as it winds past **Yewtree Farm**; then, 150yds (137m) beyond farm, fork L. Follow signposted bridleway across low causeway

until it climbs to meet estate road. Keep straight on, under little thatched timber footbridge. As you pass entrance to Home Farm House, look half L across open field. On far horizon, you'll see a long, low white building. Bear gently R past entrance drive to **Polesden Lacey**, and continue on to Polesden Road. Walk R to end of broad, grass verge on R-H side of road; then, 60yds (55m) further on, turn R down waymarked bridleway towards **youth hostel**.

❸ The track is relatively easy to follow now. It zig-zags R and L into **Freehold Wood** and then dives under stone-arched bridge. Continue down sunken way and then bear R at blue waymarker post at bottom of hill and climb up gently through woods to **Tanner's Hatch**.

❹ Bear L at **youth hostel** and follow yellow waymarked gravel track as it climbs up gently but steadily all the way back to **Ranmore Common Road**. Turn L for last 200yds (183m) back to car park.

255 FRIDAY STREET *AN ANCIENT LANDSCAPE*

5¼ miles (8.4km) 2hrs 30min **Ascent:** 640ft (195m)
Paths: Easily walked woodland tracks, but poor waymarking
Suggested map: aqua3 OS Explorer 146 Dorking, Box Hill & Reigate
Grid reference: TQ 130432
Parking: Woodland parking at Starveall Corner

Through wooded sandstone heaths to the highest point in southeast England.

❶ Leave car park at gate near top L-H corner. After 45yds (41m), turn L on to woodland path and follow it to crossroads. Turn L and drop down to road junction. Take road towards **Abinger Common** and Wotton then, 90yds (82m) further on, turn on to narrow, unsignposted path on your R. Cross tarmac drive, and continue as it widens into woodland ride.

❷ Leave woods and continue briefly along **Abinger Common Road**. When you reach house called St John's, fork R on to bridleway and follow it through to **Friday Street**. Pass pub and **millpond**, and drop down past letter box at Pond Cottage. Follow rough track towards Wotton, bear L past Yew Tree Cottage, and continue until you reach gate.

❸ Turn R over stile, and climb sandy track into woods. Soon it levels off, bears L past young plantation then veers R at far end. Go over 2 stiles

across Sheephouse Lane, and soon you're dropping to another stile. Nip over, and follow fence across Tilling Bourne until you reach 2 steps up to stile.

❹ Cross stile, and turn R on to Greensand Way. It brushes road at Triple Bar Riding Centre then turns L on to public bridleway. Keep R at National Trust's Henman Base Camp, and R again at **Warren Farm**, where forest road ends. Here waymarked **Greensand Way** forks R again, along narrow woodland track. Keep ahead when you reach bench and 3-way signpost at **Whiteberry Gate**, climbing steadily at first, then more steeply, until you come to barrier and 5-way junction.

❺ Track ahead dives steeply down; turn R, still following waymarked **Greensand Way** as it pushes up towards **Leith Hill Tower**. Pass **tower**, taking L-H fork towards Starveall Corner. Follow broad track back to barrier at Leith Hill Road then swing R on to signposted bridleway. After 140yds (128m), turn L for last little stretch back to car park.

Surrey

Newlands Corner *A Mysterious Affair*

3 miles (4.8km) 1hr 30min Ascent: 442ft (135m)
Paths: Easy-to-follow tracks and paths
Suggested map: aqua3 OS Explorer 145 Guildford & Farnham
Grid reference: TQ 043492
Parking: Newlands Corner

On the trail of the unsolved mystery of Agatha Christie's missing days.

① Walk back from car park towards main road and, 50yds (46m) from entrance, turn **R** on to waymarked byway. To begin with there are fine views across Weald, but soon track drops into trees and comes to junction at old World War II pill box. Swing **R** here, and follow byway as it bears **L** past old chalk pit where Agatha Christie's car was abandoned in December 1926. Look out for turning on your **R**, then carry straight on for further 200yds (183m).

② Turn **L** on to unmarked bridleway, passing **Water Lane Cottages** on your **R**. Continue to fork at **Timbercroft**, and bear **R** on to footpath towards **Silent Pool**. There are dogs and cats living here, so it's best to have your dog on lead. Fork **R** again after 100yds (91m), on to narrow, signposted public footpath. Take care as you cross quarry access road then continue as far as **A248**.

③ Cross over road and then turn **L** on to footpath which runs just inside hedge, and walk up to **A25**. Turn **L** at top and re-cross **A248** then follow **A25** footpath for 100yds (91m). Now cross busy main road and join footpath, up past **Sherbourne Farm**. Just beyond farm entrance, your waymarked path is crossed by broad, gravelled track leading up from car park. Fork **R** here if you wish to visit Sherbourne Pond and **Silent Pool**. Afterwards, return to narrow, waymarked path to continue your walk. The path climbs gently at first and then plunges into **Boxwood** and begins its serious assault on Downs. It eases off towards top, and meets **North Downs Way** National Trail at acorn waymark.

④ Turn **L** on to **North Downs Way** and then keep **R** 300yds (274m) further on, as another track forks off downhill. Now you can settle comfortably into your stride for 1 mile (1.6km) of good level walking back to busy **A25**, which is bang opposite car park.

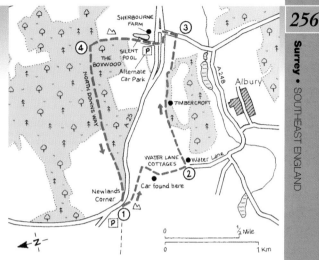

Baynards *The Railway Children*

4¼ miles (6.8km) 2hrs Ascent: 98ft (30m)
Paths: Field and forest paths, section of old railway line
Suggested map: aqua3 OS Explorer 134 Crawley & Horsham
Grid reference: TQ 078349
Parking: Lay-by on Cox Green Road, Baynards, adjacent to railway bridge at start of walk

Explore the film locations of Edith Nesbit's classic children's story.

① From lay-by, follow Downs Link signposts down on to old railway line and head north under **Cox Green Road** bridge. Soon reach wooden gate as old line approaches **Baynards Station**. Follow Downs Link as it zig-zags **L** and **R**, past station buildings, and back on to old line. There is small picnic area here, information panel, and **Thurlow Arms** is on **L**. Continue for 350yds (320m), until footpath crosses line at waymarker post.

② Turn **R** here, nip over stile and cross open field straight ahead. Keep just to **L** of corner of woodland jutting out into field, jump waymarked stile in front, and bear gently **L** along grassy track through **Massers Wood**. Leave woods at waymarked stile, and follow field boundary on your **R**.

③ At top corner of field, turn **R** over stile on to bridleway. Continue along surfaced lane at foot of hill, towards massive buildings of **Home Farm**. Follow lane as it swings to **L** past farm, and continue for 80yds (73m) beyond entrance to **Brooklands Farm** on your **L**.

④ Turn **L** here, on to gravelled track that passes back of farm and continues as grassy lane. At end of lane, carry on through 2 fields, following edge of woods on your **R** as far as buildings of **Vachery Farm**. Bear **R** here, and follow signposted bridleway until it meets farm drive at fork.

⑤ Now bear **L**, signposted towards **Vachery Farm**; then, 20yds (18m) further on, fork **R** on to signposted bridleway. Bear **R** through small wood, cross wooden footbridge over **Cobbler's Brook**, and go though small gate. Now turn **R** and follow field edge as it bears around to **L** and comes to waymarked gate.

⑥ Go through gate and continue straight ahead along waymarked bridleway. Follow it for 150yds (137m) then, as bridleway bears to **L**, dodge up to **R** and turn **L** on to **Downs Link**. Follow old railway back to **Thurlow Arms**. Retrace your steps to start.

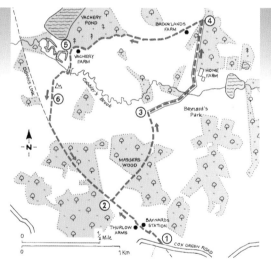

Chatley *Mast-Have Technology*

5 miles (8km) 2hrs Ascent: 230ft (70m)
Paths: Field-edge paths and heathland tracks
Suggested map: aqua3 OS Explorers 145 Guildford & Farnham; 146 Dorking, Box Hill & Reigate
Grid reference: TQ 107594
Parking: Downside Bridge, south of Cobham

A heathland walk to semaphore tower, which was built in 1822 as part of a line of hilltop stations used by the Royal Navy to signal messages between London and Portsmouth.

① Take signposted footpath just across road from car park, and cross fields to small footbridge and stile. Nip over, and continue to stile on far side of next field. Cross this one too. Follow river bank to footbridge close to some electricity lines. Beyond bridge, take signposted path across fields towards **Pointers Road**.

② Turn **R** into **Pointers Road**, and then continue ahead for 130yds (119m) beyond impressive wrought iron gates of **The Lodge**. Now turn **L**, cross over **M25** and follow tarmac lane as it winds up hill to **Chatley** semaphore tower.

③ Pass tower and follow waymarked route towards blue car park until it dives between 2 bench seats into dense fir trees. Turn **L** here on to broad sandy horse ride bordering trees. Follow ride as it crosses route to red car park, climbs to top of gentle hill, and veers around to **L**. Continue for further 350yds (320m) as far as 3-way wooden signpost.

④ Turn **R** and follow bridleway to Ockham Lane. Turn **L** and continue along Ockham Lane until road bears **L** at **Highfield Farm**. Fork **R** on to footpath to Horsley Road, and follow it over stile as far as 3-way signpost two-thirds of way along edge of long, narrow field. Turn **L** here, across field, towards Chilbrook Farm Road; walk through gap in far hedge, and follow edge of next field as far as motorway bridge. Turn **L** over **M25**.

⑤ Just beyond motorway, zig-zag **L–R** over stile and follow signposted route towards Chilbrook Farm Lane. At far corner of field, nip over stile and bear **R** on to waymarked farm road. Turn **L** into Chilbrook Farm Lane then fork **R** at pretty **Chilbrook Farm**. Go through wicket gate, and take signposted path towards **Downside Road** to reach start of walk.

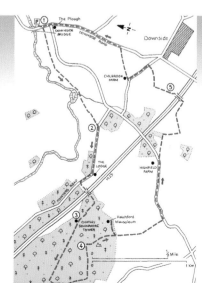

Surrey

259 FARLEY ROMANS AND CELTS

5 miles (8km) 2hrs 30min Ascent: 574ft (175m)
Paths: Forest tracks and rutted lanes, running in water after rain
Suggested map: aqua3 OS Explorer 145 Guildford & Farnham
Grid reference: TQ 051448
Parking: Forest car park (number 8) on Farley Heath

A walk through 2,000 years of history.

❶ Stand in car park, facing road, and walk to entrance on R-H side. Cross road; follow signposted public bridleway across **Farley Heath**. Keep to **R** at 1st fork; continue straight across at sandy bridleway crossroads. Keep ahead at 5-way junction. Take fork to **R** few paces further on. Then, as main track swings round hard to **L**, continue ahead on waymarked woodland footpath. Path winds down to waymark post. Turn **R** here. Follow public bridleway for further 70yds (64m) to junction with **Madgehole Lane**.

❷ Turn **R** and follow deeply rutted, sunken lane until it meets narrow tarmac road at tile-hung cottage.

❸ Turn **L**, signposted towards Winterfold, and climb through valley past rambling, half-timbered **Madgehole Farm** to **Madgehole**. Here leave tarmac and swing hard **R**, climbing steadily past young Christmas tree plantation on **L**. Follow waymarked bridleway as it winds **R**, then **L**, through **Great Copse**

and join **Greensand Way** as it swings in from your **R**.

❹ Turn **L** on to **Row Lane**. After 150yds (137m), fork **R** towards Ewhurst and Shere. Follow road over brow of hill, until you reach car park 5 on **R**. Turn **L** on to unsignposted footpath into woods; keep **R** at fork 90yds (82m) further on. Almost at once, bear **L** off main track, up narrow footpath by side of wire fence. This leads down beside garden of **Winterfold Cottage**, to another waymarker post. Fork **L**. Follow bridleway along rough cottage drive until **Row Lane**.

❺ Cross over; continue on bridleway. After 200yds (183m) it bears hard **R** on to **Ride Lane**, which leads eventually to **Farley Green**. Keep **R** at junction with **Madgehole Lane**, and proceed until gradually banks roll back as you approach **Farley Green Hall Farm**.

❻ Pass lovely old half-timbered farmhouse on **R**, and keep bearing **L** until you come to top of green. Bear **L** again, and follow **Farley Heath Road** for final stretch back to car park.

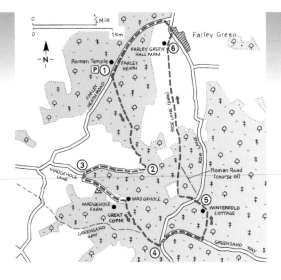

260 PYRFORD A RIVERSIDE TRAIL

3½ miles (5.7km) 1hr 30min Ascent: Negligible
Paths: Riverside tow path, some field paths and roadside
Suggested map: aqua3 OS Explorer 145 Guildford & Farnham
Grid reference: TQ 039573
Parking: Unsurfaced car park at start

A charming circuit that follows the peaceful River Wey for much of the route.

❶ Walk through car park, cross bridge at traffic lights and follow roadside pavement towards **Pyrford village**. Pavement begins on **R-H** side and crosses water-meadows on several small bridges. Enjoy views of **Newark Priory** and, in wet weather, flooded fields attract swans and other waterfowl. Now pavement switches to **L-H** side, and cross **Bourne stream**; then, as road swings hard **R** at Church Hill, keep straight on up steep woodland path to **St Nicholas Church**.

❷ Bear **R** past **church**, cross road, and take stone-flagged path through churchyard. Nip over 2 stiles at far side and follow signposted path past **Lady Place**. Bear **L** under 1st set of power lines, following field edge on **R**. Carry straight on past footpath turnings, **R** and **L**, as you approach 2nd set of power lines. Cross 2 stiles, and continue for 60yds (55m) to public footpath signpost directly under wires. Turn **R** and

head towards corner of garden that juts out into field. Bear slightly **L** here, keeping fence on **L-H** side. Continue over stile at Pyrford Green House and down gravelled drive to **Warren Lane**.

❸ Zig-zag **R** and then **L** across road, then take signposted public footpath up side of open field. Carry on over small footbridge straight ahead and follow waymarked route across Pyrford Golf Course. Watch out for flying golf balls. You'll come out on to Lock Lane, just by **Pyrford Lock**. Turn **R** here and walk across bridge by **Anchor** pub.

❹ Turn **R** again, to join easy-to-follow **River Wey** tow path. Just past **Walsham Lock**, tow path zig-zags **L** and **R** across weir. Continue walking with river on your **R**. Cross little footbridge at **Newark Lock**. From here continue along tow path; you're now on north side of river. Beyond lock, you'll come to **Newark Lane**, take **L** turn here, and cross over **Newark Bridge** to return to car park where walk began.

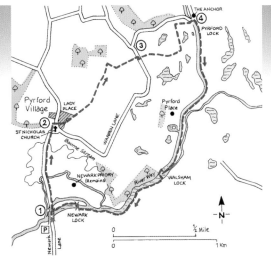

261 GUILDFORD THROUGH THE LOOKING GLASS

4¼ miles (6.8km) 2hrs Ascent: 344ft (105m)
Paths: Paved streets, downland tracks and riverside tow path
Suggested map: aqua3 OS Explorer 145 Guildford & Farnham
Grid reference: SU 991494
Parking: Farnham Road car park, next to Guildford railway station

In the footsteps of Alice and Lewis Carroll.

❶ Leave car park via footbridge at Level 5, cross Farnham Road and turn **R**. Just beyond **railway** bridge drop into subway on **L**, and follow signposts ('Town Centre via Riverside Walk'). Follow riverside walk to White House pub. Turn **L** over bridge, continue into High Street, and turn 1st **R** into Quarry Street. Pass Guildford Museum and turn immediately **L** through Castle Arch. Your route forks **R** here, into Castle Hill, but quick diversion up pedestrian path straight ahead brings you to Looking Glass statue in small garden through iron gateway on **R**. Retrace your steps and follow Castle Hill past The Chestnuts. Turn **L** at top, walk down South Hill, and turn **L** into Pewley Hill. Climb steadily past Semaphore House on corner of Semaphore Road. At end of road, continue along bridleway and follow it to striking viewpoint pillar on summit of **Pewley Down**.

❷ Fork **R** at viewpoint and then follow path off ridge, keeping hedge on **L**. Soon you'll enter tunnel of trees,

and emerge between hedges. Keep straight on at crossroads by **Pewley Down** information board, and continue for 300yds (274m) until path bears **R** and meets **North Downs Way** National Trail at acorn waymark post.

❸ Turn **R** here and follow waymarked **North Downs Way** past **South Warren Farm** to residential street called **Pilgrims Way**. Turn **L** and follow road past junction with Clifford Manor Road.

❹ Continue along **Pilgrims Way** to **A281**. Cross over and walk across **Shalford Park**, signposted towards Godalming and **Shalford**. Beyond trees you'll reach River Wey; cross footbridge, and follow tow path towards **Guildford**, with river on **R**. Cross lattice girder footbridge at Millmead Lock, and continue past Alice statue on little green near White House pub. Now, follow river bank until you reach prominent 1913 Electricity Works on opposite bank. Turn **L**, climb steps, and retrace outward route through subway to car park.

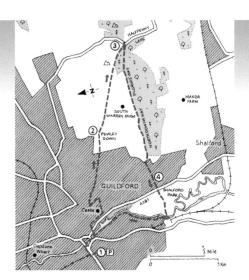

Surrey

ALFOLD *THE LOST CANAL*

4¾ miles (7.7km) 2hrs **Ascent:** 164ft (50m) ▲
Paths: Old canal tow path, field and forest paths, muddy after rain
Suggested map: aqua3 OS Explorer 134 Crawley & Horsham
Grid reference: TQ 026350
Parking: Forestry Commission car park between Alfold and Dunsfold

Take a walk through the wildwoods along a derelict canal tow path.

❶ From car park, walk back towards road for 35yds (32m) until you see track on L, marked by concrete post with small Wey South Path waymark near top. Turn L; then keep R at fork 300yds (274m) further on. Cross tarmac drive at public bridleway signpost and follow waymarked path around edge of **Firtree Copse**.

❷ Wey South Path meets canal at gate. Turn L, and follow tow path for 1 mile (1.6km). Notice gentle slope as you pass Arun 13/Wey 10 **milestone**; it's the only clue that this was once the site of a 6-lock flight.

❸ Gravelled track crosses canal at Sydney Court. Leave tow path here and turn L, following waymarked route across bridleway crossroads to **High Bridge**.

❹ Zig-zag R and L across **Rosemary Lane**; rejoin old tow path. After ½ mile (800m) look out for Arun 11½/Wey 11½ **milestone**, and continue for 150yds (137m) until **Sussex Border Path** crosses the canal.

❺ Turn L, and follow **Sussex Border Path** for 350yds (320m) until track bends sharply R. Turn L through metal field gate, and follow hedge on R. A 2nd gate leads past cottage; now, follow public bridleway signpost that points your way through 2 fields, and through another gate on to path leading out to **Rosemary Lane**. You can turn R here, for ½ mile (800m) diversion to **Crown** at Alfold.

❻ Otherwise, cross over lane and follow waymarked bridleway for ½ mile (800m). Now turn L at public footpath signpost then, just past prominent sign ('Riding by permit only'), turn R to walk along waymarked footpath through woods. Fork R a short way further on and then continue over 2 stiles and follow path just inside woodland edge until it bears L and then meets Wey South Path at waymark post. Turn L, and follow path to **Sidney Wood** car park road, before turning L again for short distance to return to your car.

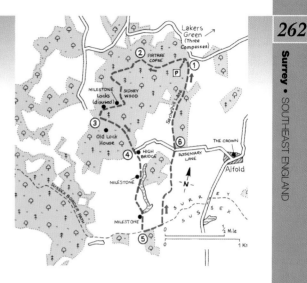

COMPTON *SURREY'S MICHELANGELO*

3¾ miles (6km) 1hr 30min **Ascent:** 262ft (80m) ▲
Paths: Sandy tracks and field paths, can be muddy
Suggested map: aqua3 OS Explorer 145 Guildford & Farnham
Grid reference: SU 963470
Parking: Lay-by in Polsted Lane, close to junction with Withies Lane

Discover the Watts Gallery, hidden in the countryside bordering Loseley Park.

❶ Take signposted public footpath from lay-by, few paces from junction of Withies Lane and **Polsted Lane**. Head through **Bummoor Copse**, and leave woods at stile. Now follow woodland edge, zig-zagging R and L over another stile until you clear woods altogether and come to waymarked stile at end of concrete road. Nip across stile and turn L. Then, just as you reach large buildings at **Coneycroft Farm**, dodge up to your R and over waymarked stile. Follow narrow path over another stile, and out on to **Down Lane**.

❷ Turn R for few paces along road. Just before **Watts Gallery**, turn R again on to signposted **North Downs Way** National Trail. This is fast, easy walking, on good sandy track. Track narrows as you pass farm buildings and begin climb towards **West Warren**. Stay with **North Downs Way** across bridleway and into woods. As you approach **East Warren**, National Trail

zig-zags L and R, and joins farm road. Follow it for another 700yds (640m) until outskirts of Guildford heave into view and trail swings L at waymark post.

❸ Turn R here; then, after 50yds (46m) fork R on to Littleton Lane. Follow it to public telephone near Littleton Youth House, and turn R on to signposted public footpath. Path leads through succession of open fields, separated by stiles. There is lake in 4th field and, beyond next stile, you'll get great views of **Loseley House** on L.

❹ Cross track to **Loseley House** at stile and 4-way signpost, and follow field edge round to L. Then, after 50yds (46m), look out for stile and yellow waymark on L. Nip across here, and continue in same direction, but now with fence on R. There's 3-way signpost at next stile; nip across. Turn R, and follow track down tree-lined avenue all way through to Little Polsted at top of **Polsted Lane**.

❺ Turn L, and follow lane back to junction and start.

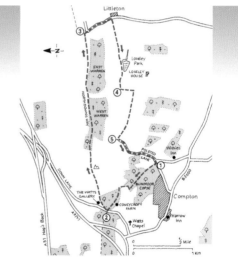

HYDON HEATH *NATIONAL TRUST'S BEGINNINGS*

3¾ miles (6km) 1hr 30min **Ascent:** 344ft (105m) ▲
Paths: Woodland paths, farm tracks and some minor roads
Suggested map: aqua3 OS Explorers 133 Haslemere & Petersfield; 145 Guildford & Farnham
Grid reference: SU 979402
Parking: National Trust car park on Salt Lane, near Hydestile

A circular walk through the varied countryside south of Godalming.

❶ Turn L along straight forest track just behind National Trust notice board in car park. At crest of hill, turn R at 8 rustic wooden posts and continue climbing for 180yds (165m) to Octavia Hill's memorial bench. Continue straight ahead, leaving bench on your L. Fork R between 3 large green inspection covers that give access to underground reservoirs on summit of hill, and drop down narrow path to chain link fence on edge of National Trust estate.

❷ Turn L here. After 60yds (55m) you'll see **Robertson obelisk** on R. The obelisk records how WA Robertson left money to the National Trust to buy this area in memory of his two brothers, who were killed in World War I. Just beyond memorial, maze of little paths will try to lead you astray. Keep as R as you can, and descend rutted path to forest crossroads close to small water **pumping station**. Turn L; then, after 200yds

(183m), fork R and continue to parting of ways 180m (165m) further on. Turn R here, and climb old sunken way as far as public bridleway marker post at top.

❸ Turn R here on to aptly named **Greensand Way**, and continue to **Maple Bungalow**.

❹ Pass **Maple Bungalow**, and follow **Greensand Way** through valley to **St Peter's Church**, **Hambledon**. 55yds (50m) beyond **church**, fork R at Court Farm Cottage and follow public footpath as it swings, first R, then L and drops down onto sunken lane to **Hambledon Road** opposite **Merry Harriers**.

❺ Turn R to walk along **Hambledon Road**. Pass Feathercombe Lane and then, after 200yds (183m), turn R on to bridleway between open fields back towards **Hydon Heath**. Track enters woods, and you climb steeply beside deer fencing on R. Keep straight on at end of fencing and, after 100yds (91m), take middle track at 3-way junction for last 350yds (320m) to car park.

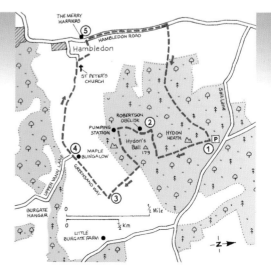

Surrey

265 PIRBRIGHT *LIVINGSTONE, I PRESUME*

4¾ miles (7.7km) 2hrs Ascent: 114ft (35m)

Paths: Country roads, woodland tracks and paths, boggy in places, patchy waymarking
Suggested map: aqua3 OS Explorer 145 Guildford & Farnham
Grid reference: SU 946560
Parking: On village green in Pirbright

A flexible figure-of-eight walk, starting from Pirbright's vast village green, in search of explorer, Henry Morton Stanley.

❶ Turn R out of car park, and bear R across green. Cross over main road, follow lane towards **church** and turn into churchyard at little gate on R. Just inside, you will see Stanley's massive, roughly hewn memorial, bearing his African name 'Bula Matari' and the single word 'AFRICA'. Leave churchyard by lychgate, and turn R along lane. Pass Old School House and **West Heath**, and then continue ahead on this lane for 200yds (183m).

❷ Turn L down signposted bridleway towards **West Hall Farm**. Follow track as it winds through farmyard and joins gated green lane. Continue past **Vines Farm** to edge of small birchwood and turn L along muddy woodland track. Bear R just beyond power lines and continue to junction of tracks near letterbox in wall at **Pirbright Lodge**.

❸ Double back hard R and follow broad track past **Long Houses**. Keep L at fork, and pass **Rails Farm** and Kiln Cottage, where track narrows briefly before bearing L on to Pirbright ranges perimeter track. As you approach military barrier at **Henley Gate**, bear L on to broad woodland track and follow it to T-junction. Turn R then, 40yds (37m) further on, turn L on to waymarked bridleway and continue until you cross small stream.

❹ Turn L on to signposted bridleway, pass **Stream House**, then follow green lane just to R of Bourne House. Continue for 300yds (274m), until waymark post points way into woods on L. Continue over stile and up side of small field, then cross plank bridge into boggy area of rough woodland. Keep straight on until you reach 2nd waymark post, then bear R on to forest road and follow it back to **Pirbright Lodge**.

❺ Turn R. Follow lane out to **A324**. Cross and turn L on to roadside pavement that leads you back to green.

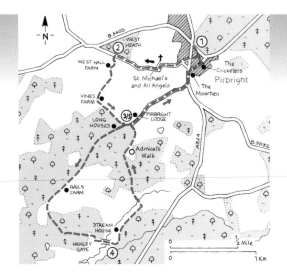

266 PUTTENHAM *ACROSS THE NORTH DOWNS*

4 miles (6.4km) 1hr 45min Ascent: 295ft (90m)

Paths: Woodland tracks and field-edge paths
Suggested map: aqua3 OS Explorer 145 Guildford & Farnham
Grid reference: SU 920461
Parking: Puttenham Common top car park

A walk in the shadow of the Hog's Back.

❶ Head into view from car park, dropping down into trees with wooden handrail on R. Fork L through woods, and bear R when path forks again 100yds (91m) further on. After 150yds (137m) you'll cross another track at tiny clearing.

❷ Turn R here and pass green-and-mauve banded waymark post. Keep straight on until you reach 2 similar posts 300yds (274m) further on. Fork R here, on to narrow path that climbs gently through bracken. Continue for 25yds (23m) beyond line of electricity wires then turn R, on to broad sandy track. After 150yds (137m), turn sharp L on to similar track. Pass large white house on R, then, ignoring all turnings, follow waymarked public bridleway to junction with **North Downs Way** National Trail.

❸ Turn sharp R here and follow **North Downs Way** over **Little Common** and straight ahead through **Puttenham** village.

❹ Turn R opposite **Good Intent**, into Suffield Lane. As lane swings to R, nip over stile by public footpath signpost on L, and follow L-H edge of open field to trees on far side. Now take waymarked route over 2nd stile to L of the woods. 2 more stiles now lead you away from woods, keeping post and wire fence on R-H side. Cross stile beside prominent oak tree and keep straight ahead, through metal field gate. Bear R down short, sharp slope towards woods, and jump stile leading out on to **Hook Lane**.

❺ Turn R, and follow road to L-H bend. Turn R again, over stile by footpath sign. Cross 3 more stiles to bring you to 'right of way' waymarker. Bear R here, and follow fence on R. Continue to small wood, step over wooden barrier into old sunken lane, and keep straight on for 150yds (137m) to small waymark post. Turn L for few paces then R at 2nd waymark. Ascend steeply, for short way back to Suffield Lane and entrance to car park.

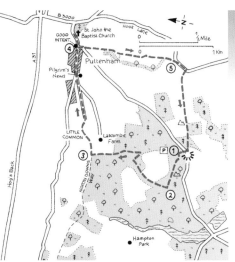

267 CHOBHAM COMMON *BIRDS AND BUTTERFLIES*

3 miles (4.8km) 1hr Ascent: 147ft (45m)

Paths: Broad bridleway tracks, can be boggy in places
Suggested map: aqua3 OS Explorer 160 Windsor, Weybridge & Bracknell
Grid reference: SU 973648
Parking: Staple Hill car park, between Chobham and Longcross

An easy-to-follow circuit of Chobham's surprisingly wild and open heathland.

❶ Cross road from car park, and turn R on to sandy track running parallel with road on R.

❷ In little more than 200yds (183m) you'll rejoin road at locked barrier. Turn hard L here, on to waymarked horse rut that will carry you straight across middle of common. Look out for the fly agaric (*Amanita uscaria*) among the many fungi that you'll see on the common. The dome-shaped cap is the colour of tomato soup, flecked with little creamy-white scales. It is so familiar from children's books that you almost expect to see a fairy on top. There are several crossroads and turnings, but simply keep walking straight ahead until you reach **Gracious Pond Road**.

❸ Turn L on to road, pass thatched buildings of **Gracious Pond Farm**, and continue to sharp R-H bend. Keep straight on here, up signposted footpath. Few paces further on track bends to R; keep straight

on again, plunging into woods at wooden barrier gate and keeping L at fork 50yds (46m) further on.

❹ Follow path as it climbs gently through conifer plantation until, just beyond power lines, another path merges from R and you arrive at waymarker post. Follow bridleway around to L, cross small brook and fork R at next waymarker post. Now simply follow bridleway, ignoring all side turnings, until you come to waymarker post at distorted crossroads junction. Bear R here until, few paces beyond wooden sleeper causeway on R, you reach another waymarker post.

❺ Swing hard L here. Follow track as it bears around to L before heading straight across in an obvious line across open heath. After about 300yds (274m) take 1st waymarked footpath on R, and follow narrow path up through gorse and over wooden sleeper causeway. At top of the hill, you'll recognise wooden barrier just few paces from road. Cross over road, back to car park where walk began.

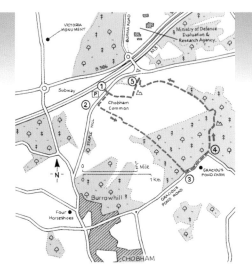

WITLEY *Woodland and Follies*

6 miles (9.7km) 2hrs 45min **Ascent:** 558ft (170m)
Paths: Woodland tracks and paths across farmland, some short sections on minor roads
Suggested map: aqua3 OS Explorer 133 Haslemere & Petersfield
Grid reference: SU 907397
Parking: Lay-by on Dyehouse Road, 60yds (55m) west of junction with Old Portsmouth Road near Thursley

A lovely rural walk along the Greensand Way.
1 Follow pavement towards Thursley, pass village hall. Turn **L** into The Street. When road bends R, turn **L** on to waymarked **Greensand Way** – signposted bridleway leads through metal gate and across field to **A3**. Cross carefully. Follow waymarked route towards Cosford Farm. As lane drops past Cosford Farm, continue along green lane to foot of hill and fork **L**. Waymarked **Greensand Way** climbs steeply through woods, crosses 2 stiles and leads to **French Lane**.
2 Cross and continue through avenue of trees, over stile and around field edge. Half-way along side of field, dodge **L** through wicket gate. Cross drive to **Heath Hall**. Follow waymarked route to edge of **Furzefield Wood**. Turn **L** through woods, then **L** on to **Screw Corner Road**.
3 Continue across A286. Follow **Greensand Way** until it turns off R, near top of hill. Keep straight on

along blue waymarked bridleway to **Parsonage Farm** Cottages. Turn **L** here. Follow footpath as it zig-zags around **Parsonage Farm**. Cross farm lane. Head for stile on far side of field. Nip over and follow path through gently curving valley until 2 stiles lead past 2 white cottages. Bear **R** up cottage drive to **Roke Lane**.
4 Turn **L**, recross A286 at **Milford Lodge**, and continue along Lea Coach Road to **Thursley Lodge**. You'll see **Witley Park** down private drive, but route lies along bridleway straight ahead. Lane drops down to junction; swing **L** past Eastlake and Lake Lodge, then bear **R** on to woodland path.
5 Turn **L** briefly on to **French Lane**, then fork **R** on to signposted bridleway which winds through **Millhanger's** landscaped grounds and up to **A3**. Cross road. Continue on to bridleway opposite. Follow it to Old Portsmouth Road. Turn **R** then **L** into Dyehouse Road and back to lay-by at start.

HINDHEAD *Travellers Beware*

3½ miles (5.7km) 1hr 30min **Ascent:** 394ft (120m)
Paths: Mostly broad, unmade forest tracks
Suggested map: aqua3 OS Explorer 133 Haslemere & Petersfield
Grid reference: SU 890357
Parking: Hillcrest car park, on A3 just east of Hindhead

A circuit at one of Surrey's best-known beauty spots and the site of a bloody murder of an unknown sailor in 1786.
1 Cross busy A3 at **car park** entrance and turn **L** on to waymarked track directly opposite. This is old **Portsmouth Road**, which climbs imperceptibly away from its modern counterpart. Just before it starts to bend to L, look out for sailor's memorial on L-H side. Now follow old road around **L-H** bend, and drop gently back down to A3.
2 Take great care crossing here, then continue up waymarked public byway opposite ('**Greensand Way**'). Continue along this rutted, stony path for ½ mile (800m) until it drops to cross-track at waymark post on edge of belt of trees.
3 Turn **L** off **Greensand Way** here, and bear gently **R** just beyond 2nd waymark post 60yds (55m) further on. Unsurfaced track is easy to follow as it winds down towards **youth hostel**. Continue straight ahead as

another track leads in from R opposite bench seat. Keep straight on through gate next to cattle grid, signposted towards **youth hostel**. The track winds through mixed woodland, crosses tiny stream at Gnome Cottage, then climbs steeply to seat by a wooden gate. Turn **R** here through gate ('Pedestrian Path Youth Hostel and Hillcrest'). Just beyond **youth hostel** entrance bear **R** along woodland path that drops down to small wooden footbridge. Cross brook here, and make short, sharp climb up boggy sunken lane opposite.
4 Turn **L** at top on to wooded track. Just after L-H bend keep to lower **L-H** fork, waymarked ('Nature Trail'). This begins ½ mile (800m) of steady, but unremitting ascent to summit, where you'll join another lane near pair of wooden gates. Turn **R** through smaller gate and then bear gently **L**, then **R** for last 125yds (114m) back to the start at **Hillcrest** car park.

WAVERLEY ABBEY *On the Pilgrim's Path*

3 miles (4.8km) 1hr **Ascent:** 164ft (50m)
Paths: Sandy and easy to follow, two sections on minor roads
Suggested map: aqua3 OS Explorer 145 Guildford & Farnham
Grid reference: SU 870455
Parking: Waverley Lane between Farnham and Elstead

By Waverley Abbey ruins in the Wey Valley.
1 The ruins of Waverley Abbey are just at the start of the walk, a stone's throw across the fields from the car park. There was a monastic community at the abbey for over 400 years until it was suppressed by Henry VIII in 1536. Later, the buildings were quarried for stone, and many wagonloads found their way into the construction of nearby Loseley House. Turn **R** out of car park, taking care to watch out for traffic, and follow **Waverley Lane** (B3001) as it zig-zags **L** and **R** over **Waverleymill Bridge**. Continue for 200yds (183m) until road bears to L. Turn **R** here, on to public byway, and follow it through metal gate and public byway signpost.
2 Keep straight ahead and follow path past Friars Way Cottage until you come to **Sheephatch Lane**. Turn **L** briefly then **R** at junction with **Tilford Street** – there's no pavement for first 400yds (366m) so go carefully. Now follow road past school, over **River Wey**

bridge and on to **Tilford** village green, where you'll find **Tilford Oak** and welcome refreshment at **Barley Mow**.
3 To continue walk, retrace your steps across river bridge. Almost at once, turn **L** at public bridleway sign just before Post Office. Path climbs gently for 500yds (457m) and brings you to tarmac lane. Turn **L**, pass **Tilhill House**, and continue up narrow sandy track straight ahead. At top of short slope, fork **R** at public bridleway waymark for 400yds (366m) climb to **Sheephatch Farm**. Cross **Sheephatch Lane**, where public byway sign points your way up gravelled track directly opposite. Track leads you through Sheephatch Copse, and soon you'll be dropping down through ancient sunken way to rejoin your outward track at metal gate and public byway signpost.
4 Turn **L** here for easy walk back to **Waverley Lane** (B3001). Watch out for traffic as you turn **L**, then retrace your outward route over **Waverleymill Bridge** and back to car park.

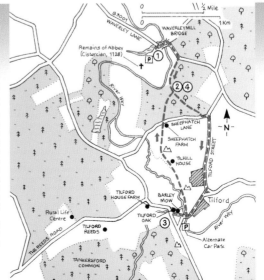

London

271 CHISLEHURST *DAYLIGHT SAVING*

3½ miles (5.7km) 2hrs **Ascent:** 98ft (30m)
Paths: Footpaths, field edges and bridlepaths
Suggested map: aqua3 OS Explorer 162 Greenwich & Gravesend
Grid reference: TQ 439708; Chislehurst rail 1 mile (1.6km)
Parking: Pay-and-display in High Street (or Queen's Head for patrons)

Explore Chislehurst, home to the inventor of British Summer Time, William Willett.

1 Walk down Chislehurst High Street, past **Prick End Pond**, cross road and turn **R** into Prince Imperial Road. Follow this as it passes row of large houses and, 50yds (46m) further on, **Methodist church**. Where houses end, take bridlepath to **R**, running through trees parallel to road. Cross Wilderness Road and look **L** to see **memorial** to Eugene, French Prince Imperial.

2 Just past golf **clubhouse** is William Willett's **Cedars** (built in 1893), identified by blue plaque. Cross road and walk up **Watts Lane** to **L** of **cricket** ground. About 150yds (137m) further on, after field, is crossroads. After few paces take narrow, tarmac path towards **St Nicholas Church**. Just before trees, turn sharp **R** and follow path to **R** of church. Exit by lychgate.

3 Walk down Hawkwood Lane to **L** of **Tiger's Head pub**. After St Mary's Church and Coopers School road bends to **L** and joins Botany Bay Lane. Continue

ahead but, when you see National Trust sign, take footpath on **L** into **Hawkwood Estate**, keeping to **R** of central fence. Path descends through woodland and along boardwalk that skirts edge of pond. It then climbs steadily alongside field (which may contain sheep). At top is view of **Petts Wood**.

4 At T-junction turn **L**. Follow bridlepath through wood. At **St Paul's Cray Road**, cross over; turn **L** and take path running parallel to road. After 500yds (457m) path emerges from woodland by **Graham Chiesman House**. Note village sign depicting Elizabeth I knighting Thomas Walsingham. Continue to **war memorial** by crossroads. Cross Bromley Lane.

5 After few paces, take footpath on **L**, just before Kemnal Road. Continue along wide track through common (you can follow pavement if this section is muddy). After you pass pond on **R**, cross road and follow footpath diagonally opposite through trees. Continue along Chislehurst High Street, back to start.

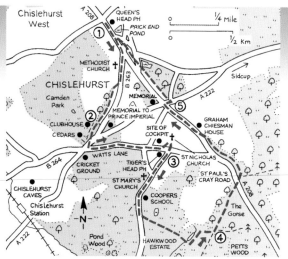

272 WANSTEAD PARK *ROYAL CONNECTIONS*

4¾ miles (7.7km) 2hrs 30min **Ascent:** Negligible
Paths: Mainly lakeside tracks that can get muddy
Suggested map: aqua3 OS Explorer 174 Epping Forest & Lee Valley
Grid reference: Grid reference TQ 406882; Wanstead tube
Parking: By Temple

Where Robert Dudley, Earl of Leicester, entertained Elizabeth I.

1 Turn **L** out of **Wanstead tube** into The Green, which becomes St Mary's Avenue. At end cross road into **Overton Drive**, which runs to **L** of **St Mary's Church**. After Bowls and Golf Club turn **R** into The Warren Drive.

2 At T-junction turn **L** and, almost immediately, enter **Wanstead Park** through gate opposite. Continue ahead downhill (**Florrie's Hill**) to reach ornamental water. Follow path to **L** of water and continue ahead as it runs to **R** of **River Roding**.

3 After ¼ mile (400m) path swings sharply to **L** round area known as **Fortifications**, once an ammunition store and now a bird sanctuary. Soon after this path traces outline of finger-shaped course of water. To **L** are steep banks of **River Roding**.

4 At meeting of paths turn **R** to continue alongside water. When path bends to **L**, you will see **Grotto** ahead.

5 At T-junction turn **R**. At end of water turn **R** again, to cross footbridge. Take **L-H** fork towards field. At crossing of paths keep ahead until you reach **boathouse**. Turn **L** here and go out through gate.

6 Immediately turn **R** to pick up path leading to **Heronry Pond**, which narrows and passes over mound. At crossing of paths turn **R** and keep ahead across grass. At next junction turn sharp **R**, towards trees.

7 Path weaves around pond to reach metal gate. Go through and take **L-H** fork to join wide, grassy track lined with sweet chestnut trees. At front of **Temple** take well-defined path on **R**. Few paces further on turn **L** and continue on this path alongside **Temple**. Keep ahead, ignoring next path on **R**.

8 At metal enclosure that surrounds **Grotto** turn sharp **L**, as if you going back on yourself; but, just beyond, take footpath that veers **R** and hugs water's edge before joining another, wider path. Turn next **L** up **Florrie's Hill** to retrace route back to **Wanstead tube**.

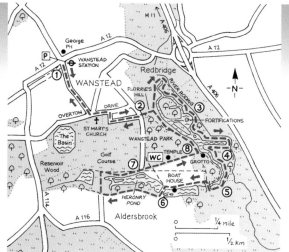

273 THREE MILLS AND THE CANALS

4¼ miles (6.8km) 2hrs 30min **Ascent:** Negligible
Paths: Gravel, tarmac and tow paths
Suggested map: aqua3 OS Explorers 162 Greenwich & Gravesend; 173 London North
Grid reference: TQ 383828 near Bromley-by-Bow tube (on Explorer 173)
Parking: Tesco car park, Three Mill Lane; Bromley-by-Bow tube ¼ mile (400m)

Discover the history of the East End waterways on this tow path walk.

1 From **Tesco** car park in Three Mills Lane take footpath to **L** of iron bridge ('Lea Navigation Tow Path') and ('Bow Flyover'). Continue ahead with river to **R**.

2 Where path ends walk up ramp on **L**, leading to A12. Turn **R**, cross A11 ahead. Turn **R** at railings. Walk down slope and across bridge to rejoin tow path, with river now to **L**. Path swings **R**, away from traffic. Ignore Greenway sign on **R** and pass under 2 pipes. Cross bridge; continue along River Lea, past **Old Ford Lock**.

3 Just before next bridge, the **Hertford Union Canal** emerges and joins at right angle on **L**. Cross over bridge. Turn **L** down to join canal path. Pass **Bottom Lock**, **Middle Lock** and, further on, **Top Lock**. Once past cottages of **Top Lock**, **Victoria Park** is visible on **R**. Continue along path until you pass under Three Colts Bridge, metal gate, 2 further bridges and 2nd metal gate.

4 Cross footbridge at T-junction of waterways to pick up southern section of **Regent's Canal**. Continue by canal towards Canary Wharf. Go under railway bridge, **Mile End Lock**, 2 more bridges and **Jonson Lock**. Pass red-brick chimney then under **railway** bridge. Continue past **Salmon Lock**. After walking under Commercial Road Bridge, turn **L**; follow steps to road.

5 Turn **R** on Commercial Road; pass **Limehouse Library** and small park on **R**. Ignore 1st gate on **R** and instead pass over bridge; take steps on **R-H** side leading down to canal. Turn **R** and follow canal tow path, the **Limehouse Cut**, keeping water **L**. Shortly pass under **A13**. Follow tarmac path under 3 more bridges until you reach A102. Walk along pavement for 50yds (46m); cross road using underpass ahead.

6 Turn **R**, walking with traffic; take 1st road on **L** to pick up canal path at **Bow Locks**. Walk over footbridge and under 2 bridges. Continue ahead towards **Mill House**. Turn **L** over bridge back to start.

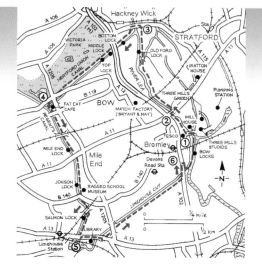

London

BOROUGH *Market Bargains*

5½ miles (8.8km) 3hrs **Ascent:** Negligible

Paths: Mainly paved

Suggested map: aqua3 OS Explorer 173 London North

Grid reference: TQ 323797 Borough tube; TQ 352979 Rotherhithe tube

A walk south of the river to two of London's famous markets.

❶ From **Borough tube** turn **L** to cross Marshalsea Road and continue along Borough High Street, ignoring L-H slip road. A few paces past **London Bridge tube** is Borough Market. Just after Bedale Road cross road into St Thomas Street.

❷ Take 1st **L** into Great Maze Pond, which runs between buildings of **Guy's Hospital**. At end turn **L** into Snowsfields. At **Rose pub** turn **R** into Weston Street and continue past original site of Bermondsey Leather Market, to **Long Lane**.

❸ Turn **L**; follow **Long Lane** until some traffic lights. On **R** is **Bermondsey Antiques Market**. Carry on ahead. Turn **R** into **The Grange**. At end turn **L** into **Grange Road**, then 1st **L** into **Spa Road**.

❹ Just before railway arch turn **R** into Rouel Road; then 1st **L** and under railway arch. At end turn **R** into St James's Road, cross road and take path on **L** via wooden posts.

❺ Turn **R**, then take 2nd road on **L**. At end, turn **R**. After 60yds (55m) turn **L** into **Southwark Park**, entering through **R-H** set of gates. Turn **R** following path as it gently swings to **L** then exit before **sports complex**. Turn **L** along Hawkestone Road to **Surrey Quays tube**.

❻ After crossing at lights take road behind station leading into Redriff Road, which then veers **L** beside **shopping complex**.

❼ Just before red **Onega Gate** turn **R** ('Russia Dock Woodland'). At bottom of steps turn **L**, past houses beside **Greenland Dock**. Turn **L** after **statue** of James Walker and, ignoring 1st path, turn **L** under bridge and continue on **L-H** path (take main path to **R** if muddy).

❽ Continue ahead ('Stave Hill') and turn next **L**. Walk in anti-clockwise direction and follow path opposite steps to **Stave Hill** that leads to Dock Hill Avenue. This crosses 2 roads before reaching Surrey Water. With this **L**, head for main road and once there, turn **L** and **Rotherhithe tube** is on your **R**.

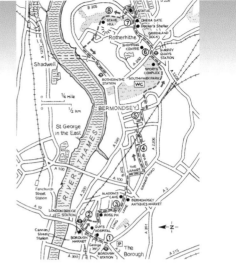

GREENWICH *Spending Measured Time*

3½ miles (5.7km) 1hr 45min **Ascent:** 154ft (47m)

Paths: Tarmac paths

Suggested map: aqua3 OS Explorer 161 London South

Grid reference: TQ 382783 Island Gardens DLR

Discover more about the background to Greenwich Mean Time on a walk through Greenwich Park.

❶ From **Island Gardens DLR** cross over **Thames** by foot tunnel. With **Cutty Sark** on your **L**, cross road ahead into Greenwich Church Street. After walking another 70yds (64m) turn **L** into market. At far end turn **R** and follow King William Walk to reach **Greenwich Park**.

❷ Enter park at **St Mary's Gate** and follow wide path, known as The Avenue, as it swings to **L**. Continue ahead, turning **L** at toilets to reach **Royal Observatory** and superb view over London and Greenwich Royal Naval College.

❸ Retrace your steps, past **Royal Observatory's** Planetarium building and café to follow broad pathway, Blackheath Avenue. Just before **Blackheath Gate**, turn **L** through some metal gates along path that skirts edge of a large pond. (Tiny path just beyond on **R** leads into area for viewing deer.)

❹ Turn **R** at next fork and exit gates to enclosure. Turn **L** and take **R-H** fork. Continue along straight path beside wall.

❺ At next junction take 2nd path on your **L** and keep ahead, straight over another set of paths, to reach another junction at which **oak tree** is protected by some railings. The oak tree dates from the 12th century and is 700 years old. It is believed that Anne Boleyn danced around it with Henry VIII, and their daughter, Elizabeth, would often play in the huge hollow trunk.

❻ Turn **R**, downhill, and **R** again at next junction on path that dips and rises. Continue ahead at next set of paths and leave park at Park Row Gate. Keep ahead along Park Row, past **National Maritime Museum** and across Romney Road.

❼ At **Trafalgar Tavern** turn **L** along Thames Path to reach **Greenwich Pier**. Retrace your steps along Greenwich Foot Tunnel, built in 1902 to link Greenwich with the Isle of Dogs, to **Island Gardens DLR**.

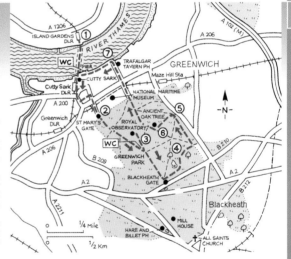

DOCKLANDS *Old and New*

3½ miles (5.7km) 1hr 45min **Ascent:** Negligible

Paths: Paved streets and riverside paths

Suggested map: aqua3 OS Explorer 173 London North

Grid reference: TQ 335807; Tower Hill tube; TQ 364803; Canary Wharf DLR or Jubilee line

Wandering through the Docklands, home to the world's oldest police force – Metropolitan Police Marine Support.

❶ Take underpass from **Tower Hill tube** that leads to **Tower of London**. In front of moat are remains of east gate of medieval wall that once surrounded City. Turn **R** and follow path, taking exit to **R** of ticket office. Turn **L** through main gates to **Tower of London** and follow cobbled path for 440yds (402m).

❷ Cross road and enter **St Katherine's Dock**. Turn **L** ('Ivory House'). Bear **R** to cross footbridge and pass some yachts and shops to cross Telford Footbridge. Take path between *Grand Turk* (18th-century warship replica) and **Dickens Inn pub**, then bear **L** through private estate and **R** into Mews Street.

❸ Turn **R** into Thomas More Street and, as road swings to **R**, it meets **Wapping High Street**. Turn **L** here passing wharfs, luxury developments and Victorian warehouses. Blue-and-white 1970s-style building on **R** is Metropolitan Police boat yard.

Continue to pass Il Bordello restaurant and **police station**.

❹ Continue ahead past **Wapping tube** and Wapping Lane. After road bends to **L** at New Crane Wharf, turn **R** into Wapping Wall ('Thames Path'). Just past **Prospect of Whitby pub**, cross bridge over Shadwell Basin.

❺ Turn **R** on to riverside path and bear to **R** of **Edward VII Memorial Park** for superb view of Canary Wharf. After blue apartment block, path bends away from river and joins Narrow Street. Path later passes **Barley Mow pub** as you cross Limehouse Basin.

❻ Turn **R** into Three Colts Street and walk to end, where you meet river again at Canary Riverside path. Continue ahead to **Canary Wharf Pier**.

❼ Walk up steps on **L** of pier, cross road to **Westferry Circus** and continue in direction of Canary Wharf, immediately ahead. Bear **R** to follow signs to **Canary Wharf DLR**, cutting through Cabot Square into Cabot Place, before arriving at station entrance.

274

London • SOUTHEAST ENGLAND

275

London • SOUTHEAST ENGLAND

276

London • SOUTHEAST ENGLAND

London

277 WHITECHAPEL *GUTS AND GARTERS*

2¾ miles (4.4km) 1hr 30min **Ascent:** Negligible
Paths: Paved streets
Suggested map: AA Street by Street London
Grid reference: Aldgate tube

Tracing the bloody path of Jack the Ripper.

❶ With **Aldgate** tube station behind you, walk towards **St Botolph's Church** on R. Cross road at pedestrian lights and continue ahead, past school on corner. Turn R along Mitre Street. Just beyond is Mitre Square (**Catherine Eddowes, 4th victim**).

❷ Continue ahead, turning L into Creechurch Lane and past some posts marking boundaries of City of London. Go across 2 main roads to reach Stoney Lane. Bear R into Gravel Lane and, at end, past parade of shops, turn L along **Middlesex Street**. Take 1st R into Wentworth Street (Petticoat Lane).

❸ Turn L into **Bell Lane** and R into Brune Street. At end turn L and L again into White's Row (**Mary Jane Kelly, 5th victim**). Cross Bell Lane and follow Artillery Lane as it narrows to form alleyway.

❹ Turn R into Sandy's Row, past synagogue, then R and L to Brushfield Street. Pass **Spitalfields Market** to reach **Christ Church Spitalfields**. Cross Commercial Street at pedestrian lights. Turn L.

❺ As road bends turn R into **Hanbury Street**, find Truman's Brewery (site of **Annie Chapman, 2nd victim**). Cross Brick Lane; continue along road for another 500yds (457m), past **Brady Recreation Centre** and along alleyway.

❻ Turn R into main road and cross over at pedestrian lights. On L **Durward Street** (**Mary Ann Nichols, 1st victim**). Continue ahead then cross busy stream of traffic on **Whitechapel Road** into **New Road**.

❼ When you get to Fieldgate Street turn R towards former synagogue; then take 3rd L into **Settles Street**. When you reach end bear R and cross over at pedestrian lights, to turn L into **Henriques Street**. (School is site of **3rd victim, Elizabeth Stride**.)

❽ Continue ahead, following road at it swings to R. At end, turn L, then immediately R into Hooper Street and R again into **Leman Street**. Cross road into **Alie Street**. At end bear R, then L along Little Somerset Street, which comes out opposite where you began at **Aldgate tube station**.

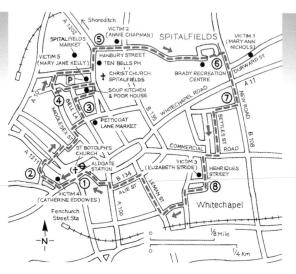

278 WESTMINSTER *CORRIDORS OF POWER*

4 miles (6.4km) 2hrs 30min **Ascent:** Negligible
Paths: Paved streets
Suggested map: AA Street by Street London
Grid reference: Westminster tube; Farringdon tube

A look at some of the city's landmarks, from Whitehall through to Smithfield.

❶ Leave **Westminster** tube following signs to Houses of Parliament. Cross Abingdon Street to **Westminster Abbey** and **St Margaret's Church**. Turn back along Abingdon Street and keep ahead as road becomes Parliament Street, then **Whitehall**. Follow it past Cenotaph to **Trafalgar Square**.

❷ Turn R and cross Northumberland Avenue. Turn R into **Strand**. Turn R at Savoy Street, to see **Queen's Chapel of the Savoy**; otherwise proceed along **Strand**, past **Somerset House**.

❸ Turn R into Surrey Street, past **Roman Baths**. Turn L into Temple Place and L again on Arundel Street. After 2 churches road becomes **Fleet Street**.

❹ After Lloyds and Child & Co turn R into Whitefriars Street. At end turn L and L again into Dorset Rise. Take next R into Dorset Buildings, past **Bridewell Theatre** and along Bride Lane to **St Bride's Church**. Cross New Bridge Street.

❺ You are now in Ludgate Hill. Turn L into Old Bailey and continue to Central Criminal Court, '**The Old Bailey**' (on the site of the notorious former Newgate Prison). Cross Newgate Street and follow Giltspur Street to reach **St Bartholomew's Hospital**.

❻ Walk under archway to hospital, with only remaining sculpture of Henry VIII, to visit St Bartholomew-the-Less, parish church where Stuart architect Inigo Jones was baptised. As you continue past central square opposite Smithfield Market, notice marks on stone wall left by Zeppelin raid during World War I. At **St Bartholomew-the-Great** turn L into Hayne Street and again into Charterhouse Street.

❼ At **St John Street** turn R and then bear L into St John's Lane. Just beyond you reach St John's Gate. Keep going to reach **Grand Priory Church**, bear L to Jerusalem Passage, then turn L at end, on to Aylesbury Street. Cross Clerkenwell Street and walk along Britton Street, turning R into Benjamin Street to reach **Farringdon tube**.

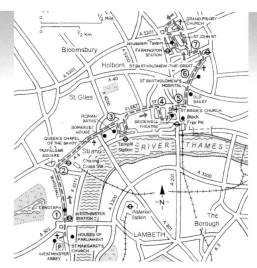

279 BALHAM *ON THE BRIGHT SIDE*

3 miles (4.8km) 1hr 30min **Ascent:** 33ft (10m)
Paths: Paved streets, tarmac and gravel paths across commons
Suggested map: aqua3 OS Explorer 161 London South
Grid reference: TQ 285731 Balham Station (tube and rail)

A circular route highlighting the greener spots of Balham and its most famous art deco property, Du Cane Court.

❶ Turn R at **Balham** station and then walk along Balham Station Road. Cross at lights, past **Bedford Arms pub**, into Fernlea Road. At mini-roundabout turn R before strip of common and pass underneath **railway** bridge. Turn L and then follow to wall of railway embankment, passing children's playground and playing fields on your R.

❷ At another bridge take R-H tarmac path running parallel to row of houses. As path bends to L, it runs alongside another **railway track** lined with trees before meeting road, Bedford Hill. Turn R and then cross over road to join path across **Tooting Bec Common**.

❸ Turn sharp L and then continue along path that hugs **railway track** and passes **Tooting Bec Lido**. Pass **Lido car park** and follow path that circles it clockwise. After crossing **car park** approach road,

take R-H path leading on to common and, at clump of trees, turn L along narrow path around lake.

❹ Beyond **children's playground** take next L to café and follow this path until you reach Hillbury Road. Turn R at crossroads and continue ahead into Manville Road. At next crossroads turn L into Ritherdon Road and continue to end.

❺ Turn R at traffic lights into **Balham High Road**, passing **Du Cane Court**. This gorgeous art deco building was named after a family of Huguenots, on whose land the site was built, and designed by architect G Kay Green in the 1930s. It contains 676 flats, over 1,000 residents, and during World War II it became home to many Foreign Office staff, no doubt impressed by the short commute. If you want to see the interior of Du Cane Court you'll have to watch one of the television adaptations of Agatha Christie's Poirot, in which the building and flats have been featured. Then pass **St Mary's Church** before reaching **station** and start of walk.

SOUTH NORWOOD *GRACE AND FAVOUR*

2¼ miles (3.6km) 1hr 30min **Ascent:** 49ft (15m) ⚠

Paths: Tarmac with some rough tracks that can get muddy

Suggested map: aqua3 OS Explorer 161 London South

Grid reference: TQ 354689

Parking: WG Grace pub by Birkbeck Tramlink or adjacent roads

Pass the tombstone of a revered cricketer, WG Grace, and South Norwood Country Park.

1 From **WG Grace pub** in Witham Road turn **R**. Continue past Tramlink bridge and entrance to **Birkbeck Station** then turn **R** into **Beckenham Cemetery**.

2 After cemetery's office turn **R** and walk along path that later swings to L. Take **L** fork and then **R-H** branch to reach **grave of WG Grace**. Look out for his large white marble tombstone 50yds (46m) on L. Carry straight on towards chapel ahead, turn **R** to join main path and then continue on through **Beckenham cemetery**.

3 At end of tarmac drive go through cemetery gates and cross **Tramlink line**. Turn **L** along footpath that crosses **Tramlink line** again before entering **South Norwood Country Park**. Turn **R** after footbridge then, at T-junction, keep ahead and stay on wide track past **visitors' centre**.

4 Just before another **Tramlink** level crossing, turn **L** to join public footpath. Follow this as it runs parallel to tram line.

5 Turn **L** at fork leading to top of **earth mound**. (At top you can see Crystal Palace, Shooter's Hill and Croydon.) To continue, turn **R**, downhill to rejoin path and walk down some steps.

6 Turn **L** before next set of steps and carry on ahead, ignoring small side paths, until you reach L-H fork. Keep ahead, over crossing of paths, and follow long, straight path with drainage ditches on each side.

7 At end, before **Tramlink line**, go over footbridge, then turn **L** and continue along path beside stream. Just after path swings to L is 5-path junction. Turn **R** and cross bridge. Ignoring 1st path on L, continue as path bends and take **L** path to jetty overlooking **lake**.

8 Continue along path and turn **R** along another path to leave park. Turn **L** along **Elmers End Road**, past **Birkbeck Tramlink**, to reach **pub** and start.

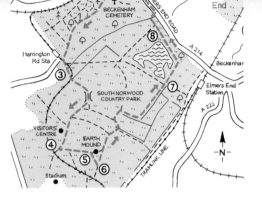

CITY OF LONDON *THE FLAMING CITY*

2¼ miles (3.6km) 2hrs **Ascent:** Negligible ⚠

Paths: Paved streets

Suggested map: AA Street by Street London

Grid reference: Monument tube; Farringdon tube

Trace the route of the Great Fire of 1666.

1 Take Fish Street Hill exit from **tube station** and bear **R** towards Monument. Then follow cobbled street for 20yds (18m) to see plaque that marks the spot on **Pudding Lane** where the fire began in 1866. Bear **R** then cross Lower Thames Street at pedestrian crossing to reach **St Magnus the Martyr Church**.

2 Few paces further to **R** of church, climb set of steps and, ignoring 1st exit, continue to arrive on west side of London Bridge. Continue ahead, away from river, along King William Street and shortly turn **L** along Arthur Street and then sharp **R** into Martin Lane, past **Olde Wine Shades**. At end turn **L** into Cannon Street. (To see houses that survived the fire, turn next **L** into Laurence Poultney Hill.)

3 Cross road and turn **R** into Abchurch Lane. At end bear **L** along King William Street towards **Bank tube station**. Keep to **L**, past front of **Mansion House**. Turn **L** into Queen Victoria Street.

4 Continue ahead, then turn **R** into Bow Lane, past

St Mary Aldermary and row of shops, to **St Mary-le-Bow** at end. Turn **L** into **Cheapside**.

5 Cross this road, turn **R** into Wood Street and take narrow alley on **R**, Milk Street. Follow it round to enter courtyard with eerie entrance to old debtors' prison. Carry on through alley, to **L** of Hole in the Wall pub, to rejoin Wood Street.

6 Cross road into Goldsmith Street and, at **Saddlers Hall** opposite, turn **L** and rejoin **Cheapside**. Turn **R** and cross pedestrian crossing to **St Paul's Cathedral**. Walk through churchyard, bear **L** to reach Ludgate Hill and turn **L**.

7 Turn **R** and **R** again into Ave Maria Lane, which becomes **Warwick Lane**. At end turn **L** along Newgate Street. At traffic lights turn **R** along **Giltspur Street**, then **L** into Cock Lane.

8 Where another road meets it, turn **R** along Snow Hill Lane, past angular building, and continue along **Farringdon Road**. At traffic lights turn **R**, to reach **Farringdon tube**, where walk ends.

SOUTH BANK *BRIDGING THE GAP*

2¾ miles (4.4km) 1hr 15min **Ascent:** Negligible ⚠

Paths: Paved streets

Suggested map: aqua3 OS Explorer 173 London North

Grid reference: TQ302796 Westminster tube

A walk along the South Bank, tracing the history of its bridges and highlighting the buildings in between.

1 Leave **Westminster tube station** by Exit 1 to follow signs to Westminster Pier. Walk up steps to your **R** and cross **Westminster Bridge**. Turn **L** along riverfront. Ahead are the 32 transparent pods of 2,100-ton **London Eye**. Just past Jubilee Gardens, on **R**, is next bridge, **Hungerford**.

2 Continue ahead past **Royal Festival Hall** and look to opposite bank of Thames for glimpse of **Cleopatra's Needle**. After National Film Theatre and its outdoor café is **Waterloo Bridge**.

3 Path bends to **R**, past **Royal National Theatre** and Hayward Gallery, before reaching craft shops and restaurants of **Gabriel's Wharf**. Turn **R** at Riviera restaurant and walk through central path lined on either side with wooden sculptures. Turn **L** at end into Stamford Street and 100yds (91m) further turn **L** again into Barge House Street.

4 Ahead, brown brickwork of **Oxo Wharf** somewhat shrouds entrance to **Oxo Tower**. Enter glass doors to your **L** and catch escalator to 8th floor for better view of skyline, or continue along ground floor to riverside exit.

5 Cross **Blackfriars Bridge** and turn **L** to follow Thames Path along wide pavement adjacent to river. The 1st boat you will pass on your L is **HMS** *President*. Next set of buildings to your **R**, after **Temple tube station**, belong to University of London. Immediately after these you'll see majestic **Somerset House**.

6 A further 200yds (183m) ahead path passes **Cleopatra's Needle** before reaching **Embankment tube**. Northumberland Avenue is next road on your **R**. About 200yds (183m) further on is Horse Guards Avenue, which are the sandwiched between formidable buildings of Old War Office and Ministry of Defence. You are now almost parallel with **London Eye**, on opposite bank of the **River Thames**. When you reach **Westminster Bridge** turn **R** into Bridge Street, to **Westminster tube** and start.

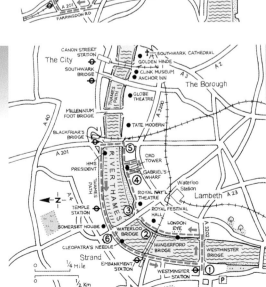

London

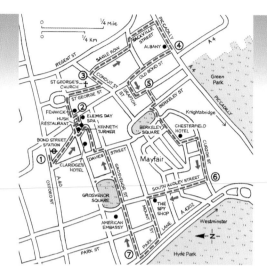

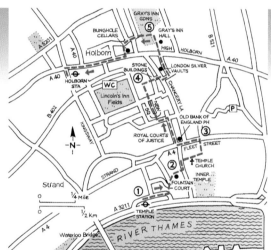

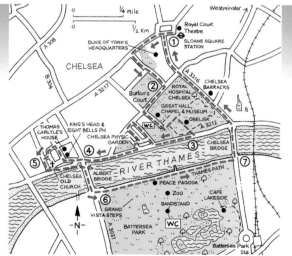

London • SOUTH-EAST ENGLAND

283 MAYFAIR *LACED WITH LUXURY*

2¾ miles (4.4km) 1hr 30min Ascent: Negligible
Paths: Paved streets
Suggested map: AA Street by Street London
Grid reference: Bond Street tube

A leisurely walk through wealthy Mayfair and plenty of opportunities to indulge yourself.

1 Turn **L** outside **Bond Street tube station** and then turn sharp **L** into pedestrianised South Molton Street. At end of road turn **L** into Brook Street. Cross over road and walk along cobbled **R-H** alley, Lancashire Court, which opens out into courtyard. Just past **Hush** restaurant you'll find **Elemis Day Spa**.

2 Turn **L** here and cross road to reach department store, **Fenwick**. Turn **R** and walk along Brook Street to reach Hanover Square. At statue of young William Pitt turn **R** into **St George Street**, walk past **St George's Church** and **L** at end on to **Conduit Street**.

3 Take next **R** into **Savile Row**, road of fine suits. At end bear **L** and then **R** into **Sackville Street**. Turn **R** along **Piccadilly** and look out for entrance to **Albany's** courtyard.

4 Just past auspicious-looking Burlington Arcade turn **R** into **Old Bond Street** and past several

exclusive shops including those of Cartier, Mont Blanc and Tiffany. Turn **L** after Asprey & Garrard into **Grafton Street**, which takes 90-degree **L** bend, becoming Dover Street.

5 Turn **R** along Hay Hill and then **R** again towards **Berkeley Square**, crossing 2 zebra crossings with square on your **R**, to reach Charles Street. Beyond **Chesterfield Hotel** turn **L** along Queen Street and then **R** into **Curzon Street**.

6 Turn **R** into **South Audley Street** and its **Spy Shop**, then, at Purdey's (royal gunmakers), turn **L** into **Mount Street**. At end turn **R** along **Park Lane**, past Grosvenor House Hotel.

7 Turn **R** into Upper Grosvenor Street, past **American Embassy** on Grosvenor Square and then turn **L** into **Davies Street**. Next, take 1st **R** into Brooks Mews and turn **L** along narrow Avery Row. This brings you on to Brook Street. From here, retrace your steps along South Molton Street, back to **Bond Street tube station**.

284 HOLBORN *THE INNS OF COURT*

1½ miles (2.4km) 1hr 30min Ascent: 49ft (15m)
Paths: Paved streets and some cobbled alleys
Suggested map: AA Street by Street London
Grid reference: Temple tube; Holborn tube
Note: Gates into the courts may be locked at the weekends

Soak up the atmosphere of these hidden alleys and squares that featured in many of Dickens' novels.

1 Turn **L** at exit to **Temple tube** and up set of steps. Turn **R** into Temple Place. At the end go **L** into Milford Lane then, shortly afterwards, go up another series of steps into **Inner Temple**. Turn **R** by Edgar Wallace pub into Devreux Court, walk under archway and go down steps to **Fountain Court**. Charles Dickens worked as a solicitor's clerk in Temple, and many of the scenes from his novel *Martin Chuzzlewit* (1843) were played out here. The place is particularly atmospheric at dusk when the Victorian lamps are lit.

2 Bear **L** under archway into **Middle Temple**, past small fountain and garden and up some steps, then bear **R** through some cloisters to reach **Temple Church**. Go through archway to **R** of church, then **L** through another archway and along cobbled alley to **Fleet Street**.

3 Turn **L** then walk along **Fleet Street** and cross over at pedestrian lights. After Old Bank of England pub turn **R** into Bell Yard and continue straight ahead on path that runs alongside **Royal Courts of Justice**. Turn **L** then bear **R** into **New Square** and follow avenue of trees.

4 Take path on far **R** along **Stone Buildings** and, keep ahead. Go through gates that lead on to **Chancery Lane**. Cross over this road and turn **R** into street called Southampton Buildings. After just 20yds (18m) this veers sharply **L**, past **London Silver Vaults**. Cross **High Holborn** and pass through gateway to Gray's Inn on your **R**. Just after **Gray's Inn Hall**, turn **L** into Field Court.

5 Continue walking to end then turn **R** and go up some steps into Jockeys Fields. Bear **L** and walk along Bedford Row and take 2nd road on your **L**, Hand Court. Just past the **Bunghole Cellars** at the end, turn **R** to walk along **High Holborn** to reach **Holborn tube**.

285 CHELSEA *WALKING WITH THE WAR HEROES*

3¾ miles (6km) 2hrs Ascent: Negligible
Paths: Paved streets and tarmac paths
Suggested map: aqua3 Explorer 161 London South
Grid reference: Sloane Square tube
Parking: Difficult – best to catch tube

A walk around Chelsea, home to the most famous pensioners in Britain.

1 From **Sloane Square tube** walk ahead, crossing Lower Sloane Street. Go past Peter Jones department store and, just afterwards, on your **L**, **Duke of York's Headquarters**. Turn **L** into Cheltenham Terrace then bear **L** into Franklin's Row.

2 Take 1st **R** along Royal Hospital Road. Just beyond lawns on **R** turn **L** into **hospital grounds** at Chelsea Gate. A few paces further on **L**, gravel path leads to the **Great Hall, chapel and museum**. Continue to the end of road and turn **L** on to some playing fields. Now head towards **obelisk**, bear **R** and leave through gates to Chelsea Embankment.

3 Turn **R** along Embankment and **R** into Tite Street, where Oscar Wilde once lived. At top turn **L** into Paradise Walk. Turn **R** and then sharp **L** towards Embankment and walk past **Chelsea Physic Garden**.

4 At traffic lights cross Oakley Street and bear **R**

along narrow Cheyne Walk. Turn **R** by quirkily-named **King's Head and Eight Bells pub** on Cheyne Row. At the end turn **L** into Upper Cheyne Row. Turn **L** again into Lawrence Street – where there is a plaque to mark Chelsea Porcelain Works – then turn **R** into Justice Walk. (Don't be fooled into thinking the sign of a red-robed judge is a pub, it merely identifies where the old courthouse used to be!)

5 Turn **L** into Old Church Street and at bottom is **Chelsea Old Church**, with statue outside of Thomas More, who worshipped here. Walk through Chelsea Embankment Gardens and cross **Albert Bridge**.

6 At sign ('Riverside Walk'), turn **L** through gate into **Battersea Park**. Follow **Thames Path**, past **Peace Pagoda** in park, along to **Chelsea Bridge**.

7 Turn **L** to cross bridge and continue ahead, passing **Chelsea Barracks** on **R** before joining Lower Sloane Street. Turn **R** to retrace your steps back to **Sloane Square tube**.

London

TRENT COUNTRY PARK *A COLOURFUL PAST*

3 miles (4.8km) 1hr 45min **Ascent:** 230ft (70m)

Paths: Mainly woodland tracks
Suggested map: aqua3 OS Explorer 173 London North
Grid reference: TQ 283971; Cockfosters tube ¼ mile (400m)
Parking: Trent Park car park off Cockfosters Road

Take a gentle stroll around Trent Mansion, now owned by the Middlesex University.

1 Take London Loop path to **L** of information board by café in **Trent Country Park** car park. 400yds (366m) after picnic tables, path swings to **R** and runs alongside a field. Continue for another 300yds (274m) and cross footbridge over ditch.

2 At the end of field bear **L** beside hedgerow. To follow nature trail, enter wooden gate opposite. Otherwise, continue along path, which then dips and rejoins wider path 50yds (46m) ahead. A few paces further on, path bends to **R** above lake. Ignore next path on your **R** and continue into wood towards **Camlet Hill.**

3 After 100yds (91m) ignore **L** fork and soon track widens and swings gently to **R** before passing **Hadley Road** car park (under trees).

4 Turn **R** at junction and, a few paces further on, cross track by water tap (beware of cars heading for car park). Follow path through **Ride Wood**, as it runs parallel with bridlepath and **Hadley Road** before swinging to **R.**

5 Go through kissing gate, cross over brook and go through another kissing gate. After walking 200yds (183m) spot house on your **L** and road, follow this for 100yds (91m).

6 Turn **R** into **Middlesex University** car park and follow this to end. Turn **L** into box-hedged gardens (known as Wisteria Walk) and continue towards stables and clock tower on your **L.** With mansion behind you, take path to **R,** which joins wider road leading to gate. Bear **R** along this towards column in centre of mini-roundabout.

7 Another 50yds (46m) further on, is **Pets Corner** and visitor centre with a fine selection of wooden rocking horses. Continue along this long, straight path, passing pond on **L.** Turn **R** along narrow path, just before stone monument, back to car park.

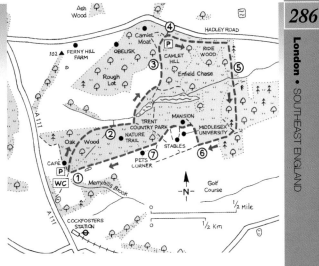

HAMPSTEAD *SPRING HAS SPRUNG*

4¼ miles (6.8km) 2hrs **Ascent:** 344ft (105m)

Paths: Mainly well-trodden heathland tracks
Suggested map: aqua3 OS Explorer 173 London North
Grid reference: TQ 264858 Hampstead tube
Parking: Car park off East Heath Road

Explore the heath — one of London's best-loved open spaces.

1 Turn **L** outside **Hampstead** tube into Back Lane and into Flask Walk. Continue downhill past **Burgh House.** Follow Well Walk, passing **Wellside** on **R.** At East Heath Road, cross and continue on heath path.

2 Follow tree-lined path for 200yds (183m), as far as junction and water tap. Continue for 100yds (91m); turn **L** at bench. Track narrows and zig-zags slightly before coming to gate indicating entrance to 112 acres (45ha) maintained by English Heritage.

3 Bear **L.** Path descends gently and opens on to heathland. Follow path to **R,** on to wider track. Pass benches and proceed into woodland. If you have a dog, it should be on lead now. Pass through wooden gate along ivy-lined path, passing 2 cottages, then bear **R** towards **Kenwood House** car park. (To detour to **Spaniards Inn** take exit on to **Spaniards Road** and inn is 300yds (274m) on **L.**)

4 To continue, bear **R** through car park following signs to **Kenwood House.** Turn **R,** through main gates. Take path on **R** of house, through ivy arch and on to wide terrace. Beyond **tea room** take **L** fork to pergola. Next, take path to **R,** passing metal gate.

5 Turn **L,** downhill, passing to **L** of lake. Keep ahead through some woodland and go through another metal gate. Continue along track ahead. Take next **L** fork and head uphill. At fork take **L-H** path, which then descends. Follow tarmac path past pond.

6 Pass 3 more **ponds;** turn sharp **R** after 3rd, along path that climbs uphill. At junction follow **R-H** path to top of **Parliament Hill.** Continue on path, through trees and between 2 **ponds.** Head uphill for 50yds (46m).

7 Turn **L.** After 250yds (229m) bear **R** on to wider track. Follow it to East Heath Road. Cross over into Devonshire Hill; turn 1st **L** into Keats Grove to visit **Keats House.** Otherwise stay on Devonshire Hill. Turn **R** at end into Rosslyn Hill and back to start.

THE ROYAL PARKS *MY KINGDOM FOR A PARK*

4¼ miles (6.8km) 2hrs 30min **Ascent:** 66ft (20m)

Paths: Mainly tarmac paths through the parks
Suggested map: aqua3 OS Explorer 173 London North
Grid reference: TQ 303803 Charing Cross tube; TQ 255794 High Street Kensington tube

A healthy, linear walk from St James's Park to Kensington Gardens.

1 From **Charing Cross Station** turn **L** into Strand and **L** again into Northumberland Street. Bear **L** along Northumberland Avenue and, very shortly, cross into Great Scotland Yard.

2 At end, turn **L** into Whitehall, cross to other side and head for arch of Horse Guards Parade.

3 Enter **St James's Park** to **L** of Guards Monument and follow path that bears **L** around lake, taking 1st **R-H** fork. Continue along this path, past weeping willow trees, to **blue bridge.** (Just across the **Blue Bridge** is **Nash Shrubberies,** which have been restored to his orginal, 'floriferous' specifications.

4 Cross bridge, stopping half-way across to enjoy views: westwards is **Buckingham Palace** and eastwards is Horse Guards Parade, where skyline looks almost fairytale-like. Turn **L,** past **Nash Shrubberies,** and leave park on **R.** Cross **The Mall** and enter **Green Park** from **Constitution Hill.**

5 Take 2nd path on **L** and continue over another set of paths. At next junction take 2nd path on **L.** Where next paths cross, take **L-H** path that inclines slightly to **Hyde Park Corner.**

6 Use underpass to first reach central island and **Wellington Arch,** and then **Hyde Park** itself. Cross road, Rotten Row, and follow **L-H** path through rose garden with cherub fountain. After 440yds (402m) follow path to **R** of **Dell Restaurant** and continue beside **Serpentine.**

7 Walk under **Serpentine Bridge** and up some steps on **R.** Cross bridge and enter **Kensington Gardens.** Take middle path and continue ahead, ignoring other paths to bandstand, but turning **R** at next opportunity.

8 At junction bear **L** along path that runs to **L** of gates to **Kensington Palace** state apartments. At end turn **L** to reach Kensington High Street. Pass **Royal Garden Hotel,** Kensington Church Street and cross Kensington High Street to **tube station** on **L.**

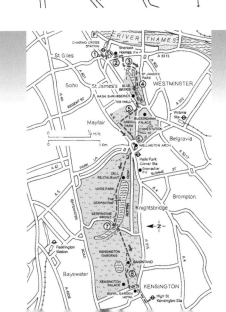

London

289 REGENT'S PARK *ROSES AND ROMANCE*

3¾ miles (5.3km) 1hr 30min Ascent: 131ft (40m) ▲

Paths: Paved streets and tarmac paths

Suggested map: AA Street by Street London

Grid reference: Baker Street tube; Warwick Avenue tube

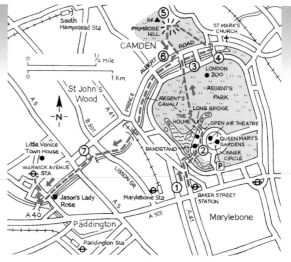

Rose gardens, an open-air theatre, panoramic views from Primrose Hill, birdsong along the Regent's Canal, and Little Venice.

❶ Take north exit from **Baker Street** tube; turn R, along Baker Street. Cross road via 2 sets of pedestrian lights. Enter **Regent's Park**. Turn R. Cross bridge over lake, then bear L, past **bandstand**.

❷ Turn L on reaching **Inner Circle** road. Beyond **The Holme** turn L, through metal gates, and over **Long Bridge**. When paths fork ahead, take R-H one and keep ahead at next crossing of paths.

❸ Go through gate, cross Outer Circle road and follow path opposite to cross Primrose Hill Bridge. Turn L along path leading down to **Regent's Canal**, then turn sharp L. Continue along this path for ¼ mile (400m), passing underneath bridge, **London Zoo** aviary and 2 bridges with ornate ironwork.

❹ At 2nd bridge turn L up path leading to **St Mark's Church**. At gate turn L along **Prince Albert Road** and past entrance to **London Zoo**. Continue for 100yds

(91m) then, at pedestrian lights, cross road to enter Primrose Hill. Take R-H path and follow it uphill to viewpoint.

❺ Follow path that bears L, leading downhill, to join path that leads to **Prince Albert Road**. Cross at zebra crossing. Turn R. At footpath ('Canalside Walk') turn L.

❻ Don't cross bridge but turn R along hedge-lined path that bends sharply to L on to tow path. Turn R. Follow tow path for ½ mile (800m). Canal banks are clad with ivy and weeping willows, and palatial homes line this stretch. Proceed under railway bridges and shortly you'll pass houseboats moored at **Lisson Green** before tow path tunnel.

❼ As canal disappears under another tunnel, walk up steps on R and continue ahead along Aberdeen Place. At end of road, cross and follow Blomfield Road into Little Venice. Cross Warwick Avenue and follow road as it bends to R, past footbridge. Turn R into Warwick Place and then L again to find **Warwick Avenue** tube 100yds (91m) ahead.

290 HOLLAND PARK *BIG SCREEN DIVERSIONS*

3¼ miles (5.3km) 1hr 30min Ascent: 66ft (20m) ▲

Paths: Paved streets and tarmac paths

Suggested map: AA Street by Street London

Grid reference: Notting Hill Gate tube

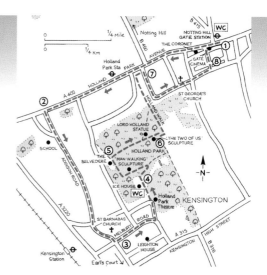

Holland Park has something for everyone: cinemas, cafés, wildlife and memorable architecture.

❶ From **Notting Hill Gate** tube head towards **Holland Park Avenue**, passing **Gate Cinema** and just beyong, **The Coronet**.

❷ About 650yds (594m) after **Holland Park** tube turn L into **Holland Park Gardens**. Just after red-brick school on R road joins **Addison Road**.

❸ Turn L past **St Barnabas Church** into **Melbury Road**. Cross Abbotsbury Road and continue to next road. Look out for huge palm trees in manicured garden on corner. Turn L here to reach gates of **Holland Park**. Take path ahead and walk through arch. On L is **ice house**.

❹ Bear R through hedged garden and, after passing under another arch, turn L to follow footpath as it descends stone steps. The strange man with rolled-up sleeves walking towards you is, in fact, a bronze **sculpture**. Follow path as it swings to R.

❺ At end of fenced path turn R along long, straight path that heads slightly uphill, flanked by lime trees. Ahead is a **statue of Lord Holland** sitting high above pond, the local watering hole for squirrels. If you're a keen birdwatcher, take a look in woods behind pond. Otherwise continue towards another **sculpture**.

❻ Make what you will of this huge bronze entitled **The Two of Us** by contemporary sculptor Stephen Gregory, then turn R. Soon go L and pass metal gate. Turn L along **Holland Walk**, this tarmac path is also used by cyclists so take care. (If you turn R here you'll end up on **Kensington High Street**.) Follow **Holland Walk** to end.

❼ Turn R and take next R, Aubrey Road. Follow it as it bends to L and later passes **St George's Church**. At crossroads continue ahead, turning into 1st road on L, Hillgate Street.

❽ After crossing Hillgate Place and its attractive rows of pastel-coloured terraced houses, turn R into **Notting Hill Gate** and back to start.

291 MORDEN HALL PARK *AN AROMATIC OASIS*

1¾ miles (2.8km) 1hr Ascent: Negligible ▲

Paths: Mainly tarmac paths

Suggested map: aqua3 OS Explorer 161 London South

Grid reference: TQ 257686 Morden tube

Parking: At garden centre off Morden Hall Road (Morden tube 550yds/500m)

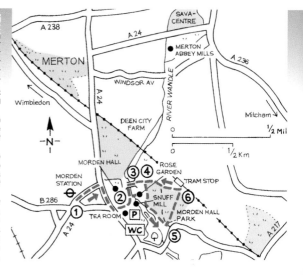

A short but lingering walk through the fragrant gardens of Morden Hall Park in suburban south London.

❶ Turn L at exit to **Morden** tube. At junction use pedestrian crossing to cross Morden Road. Bear R along Morden Hall Road. Ignore 1st entrance on L leading to **Morden Hall** (now occupied by a chain pub/restaurant outlet) and take 2nd entrance. Follow path ahead, past stable block on your R, leading to tea room and garden centre.

❷ Cross bridge, passing **Snuff Mill** Environmental Centre (primarily an educational facility for school groups), to enter lower section of rose garden. On either side of the rose garden's path you will see *Robinia pseudacacia* (false acacia). This tree is named after Jean Robin, a French botanist, but it didn't become popular until William Cobbett sold over a million trees after returning from America in the early 1800s. False acacia produces a pea-shaped, fragrant

white blossom similar to the laburnum. You can walk across grass but you need to return across bridge and turn R.

❸ Shortly afterwards, turn R over white bridge with decorative iron railings and walk along avenue of lime and chestnut trees to cross bridge over tributary of **River Wandle**.

❹ Turn R and go through metal gate leading to upper section of **rose garden**. Follow path ahead to reach another metal gate. Continue past pond, with its wilderness islands, as it curves to L to meet avenue of lime and chestnut trees.

❺ Follow path as it swings to L, becoming narrow path beside some fencing. A few paces further on, when path joins another, take L-H fork across meadow.

❻ Just before road and **tram stop**, turn diagonally L across meadow towards avenue of trees. At main path turn R and retrace your steps towards Point ❹ towards white bridge, and then back to **Morden** tube station.

London

Barnes With the Wetland Birds

3¾ miles (6km) 1hr 30min Ascent: Negligible ⚠

Paths: Riverside tow path, muddy after rain

Suggested map: aqua3 OS Explorer 161 London South

Grid reference: TQ 227767; Barnes Bridge rail ¾ mile (1.2km) or bus 283 (known as 'the Duck Bus') from Hammersmith tube

Parking: At LWC (pay if not visiting)

Explore the award-winning London Wetland Centre and join the course of the Oxford and Cambridge Boat Race.

1 Turn **L** out of **London Wetland Centre** and follow path, initially to **L** of **Barnes Sports Centre** and then beside some sports fields. At T-junction turn **L** along well-signposted **Thames Path**, alongside river in direction of **Hammersmith Bridge**.

2 About 100yds (91m) along path on **L** is stone post, denoting 1-mile (1.6km) marker of Oxford and Cambridge University Boat Race. Steve Fairbairn, who was born in 1862, founded Head of the River Race and this was the start of the world-famous, annual boat race that traditionally takes place in March.

3 The landscaped area of smart flats on **L** is called **Waterside** and, just beyond, red-brick building bears name **Harrods Village**. Once past this, as if replicating trademark Harrods colours of green and

gold, is **Hammersmith Bridge**. Continue to follow path past **St Paul's School**. On opposite side of river, Chiswick Church's green roof is visible.

4 Turn **L** through wooden gate into **Leg of Mutton Nature Reserve**. Continue along path to **R** of this stretch of water, which was once a **reservoir**. When path swerves to **L**, leave by wooden gate to **R**. Turn **L** and then follow riverside path towards **Barnes Bridge**.

5 Just past **Bull's Head pub** turn **L** into Barnes High Road. At next junction, by little pond, bear **L** into Church Road. Past **Sun Inn** is a row of village shops and 100yds (91m) further on, lychgate to **St Mary's Church**. At traffic lights continue ahead to return to **London Wetland Centre** (LWC). You can extend the walk by visiting the **London Wetland Centre**. There's an admission charge but once in there's lots to see and more than 2 miles (3.2km) of paths.

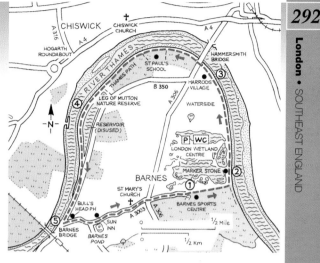

Kew Along the Thames

7½ miles (12.1km) 3hrs Ascent: Negligible ⚠

Paths: Mainly tow paths and tarmac

Suggested map: aqua3 OS Explorer 161 London South

Grid reference: TQ 19276 Kew Gardens tube

A peaceful stretch of the Thames Path.

1 From **tube**, follow road ahead past row of shops and turn **R** along Sandycombe Road, which becomes Kew Gardens Road as it bends to **L**. At main road opposite **Royal Botanic Gardens**, turn **R** and continue ahead to traffic lights. Cross **Kew Green** and head towards **church** on green.

2 Take path to **L** of **St Anne's Church** and with your back to church columns follow main path to **R**. Once across green, continue along Ferry Lane, which leads to Thames Path.

3 Turn **L** here and follow river along path that borders Kew Gardens and offers you tempting views of the gardens from the other side of a formidable walled ditch.

4 Just after field, cross ditch with metal gates to **L**, signifying boundary of **Old Deer Park**, now home of Royal Mid-Surrey Golf Course. Continue walking ahead for further mile (1.6km) on obvious track and cross **Richmond Lock** to reach other side of Thames.

5 Follow riverside path past boatyard; follow Capital Ring path as it veers away from river, passing **Brunel University** campus. At road turn **R**. Just past **Nazareth House** convent turn **R** at mini-roundabout, ('Thames Path').

6 Turn **L** alongside river towards **Town Wharf pub** and here, bear **L** and turn 1st **R** into Church Street. Go over bridge, past riverside **London Apprentice pub**. After church road swings to **L** along Park Road. Enter **Syon Park** and follow wide, tarmac road.

7 Exit park via walled path and turn **R** at road. Cross bridge and, if this path isn't flooded, turn **R** for detour along **Grand Union Canal**. Otherwise continue along road ahead bearing **R** to go through **Watermans Park** and then rejoining Thames Path.

8 Pass houseboats; turn **R** to cross **Kew Bridge**. Cross at pedestrian crossing; keep ahead. Turn **L** into Mortlake Road. Turn **R** into Cumberland Road and **L** at end to return along Kew Gardens Road to **Kew Gardens tube station**.

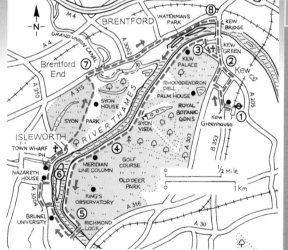

Richmond Park A Walking Safari

6¾ miles (10.9km) 2hrs 30min Ascent: 164ft (50m) ▲

Paths: Mainly tarmac paths

Suggested map: aqua3 OS Explorer 161 London South

Grid reference: TQ189728; Richmond Station (tube and rail) 1½ miles (2.4km)

Parking: Car park at Pembroke Lodge in Richmond Park

Enjoy a wonderful mix of panoramic views, wildlife haven and landscaped plantations, which are worthwhile seeing in all seasons.

1 From car park at **Pembroke Lodge** turn **R** to follow **Tamsin Trail** in general direction of **Ham Gate**. Path veers to **R** and later runs close to road.

2 At crossroads, leading to **Ham Gate**, turn **L** past **Hamcross Plantation**. At next crossroads turn **R** to visit **Isabella Plantation** (rare trees and some magnificent azaleas), otherwise continue and turn **L** at next main junction, before another plantation, and circle wood clockwise along wide track. Turn **R**, at next junction, and follow path to end of pond.

3 Turn **R** along path between 2 **ponds** and continue ahead, ignoring paths branching off that would lead you to a car park. After this, turn **R** and follow road that swings to **L** towards **Robin Hood Gate**. Deer are often spotted here but their coats give them good camouflage, especially against the bracken.

4 Turn **L** at **Robin Hood Gate**. Follow gravel path of **Tamsin Trail** past **Richmond Park Golf Course** and on to **Roehampton Gate**.

5 Continue over footbridge and, after further 500yds (457m), path winds to **R** of **Adam's Pond**, which is one of the watering holes used by deer. Follow path across upper end of park, past Sheen Gate, to **Richmond Gate**.

6 Turn **L** at **Richmond Gate**. If you have time go and look for the **Henry VIII mound**, which is sited at the highest point of the park in the formal garden of Pembroke Lodge. This prehistoric burial ground is not easy to find (take higher path past cottage) but well worth the effort, for here is a view of the dome of St Paul's Cathedral 10 miles (16.1km) away. Henry VIII was said to have stood here while his second wife, Anne Boleyn, was being beheaded at the Tower of London. Retrace your steps and continue along path to reach **Pembroke Lodge** and start.

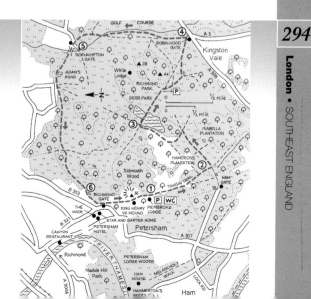

295 · HORSENDEN HILL *UP AND OVER THE HILL*

2¾ miles (4.4km) 1hr 30min **Ascent:** 180ft (55m) ▲
Paths: Mainly woodland tracks
Suggested map: aqua3 OS Explorer 173 London North
Grid reference: TQ 174697; add 650yds (594m) if joining the walk from Perivale tube at Point ⑤
Parking: Car park at Horsenden Hill

Some of London's best grassland and its wildlife are to be found on this walk.
① From car park walk back towards road. At metal barrier turn **R** down some steps and continue along tarmac path that runs parallel to **Horsenden Lane**. Continue in front of **Ballot Box pub** to reach tarmac path just past it.
② Turn **R** along tree-lined path; keep ahead as it passes **Ridding Wood** on L. After ¼ mile (400m) turn **R**, just before metal gate and houses, to enter **Horsenden Wood**.
③ Within few paces take **L-H** path at fork; keep ahead as it ascends then crosses tarmac path. Bear **R** at row of trees ahead that marks boundary of **golf course**. When ground levels towards top of hill, go to **viewpoint** ahead on L.
④ Head for **triangulation pillar** behind **viewpoint** in middle of grassy plateau. Take footpath on far **R** that leads to flight of steep, wooden steps going into thickly

wooded area. Continue down steps. At crossing of paths keep ahead, passing to **L** of oak tree, to reach road.
⑤ From car park walk back towards road. At metal **Canal** (Paddington Branch). Just after this, turn **L** again, down some steps, to tow path. Continue under bridge along **canal**, which later widens and passes **Perivale Wood** (and neighbouring Royal Mail depot).
⑥ Keep walking straight ahead for another ¼ mile (400m). Turn **L** after wooden footbridge to go through kissing gate. Carry on over bridge (**Horsenden Hill** is now visible again ahead) and follow winding footpath to go through another kissing gate. Turn **L** along footpath to R of some playing fields and continue ahead.
⑦ At end of fields bear **R** to go through gap in trees, then turn **L** over footbridge and keep to **R** edge of next meadow. Keep going towards another meadow and head for building beyond its **L** diagonal corner, **Ballot Box pub**. Cross road and turn **R** to retrace your steps along tarmac path to return to start.

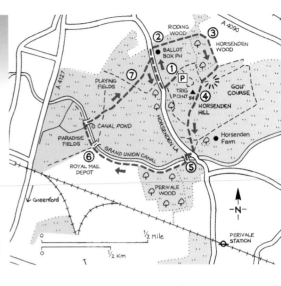

296 · OSTERLEY *MARVEL AT BRUNEL*

5 miles (8km) 2hrs 30min **Ascent:** 66ft (20m) ▲
Paths: Mixture of tow paths, tarmac paths and rough tracks
Suggested map: aqua3 OS Explorer 161 London South
Grid reference: TQ 148779; Osterley tube ¾ mile (1.2km)
Parking: Car park in Osterley Park (free to National Trust members)

In the footsteps of Isambard Kingdom Brunel.
① From car park in **Osterley Park** walk back along track heading towards entrance gates, passing **farm shop**.
② Just past **shop**, and opposite bungalow, turn **L** through gate and later another, to follow track between fields. When path ends bear **L** towards brick wall, cross track and continue to pub, **Hare and Hounds**.
③ Turn **L** along road to pass under M4. After a further 440yds (402m), just past building on your L, turn **R** to go through kissing gate and follow enclosed path alongside playing field. At end of path go through metal gate to your **R**, then cross **railway line** and follow road ahead.
④ Past bridge, go down steps on **R** to **Grand Union Canal**, then turn **R** under bridge, along tow path. During next mile (1.6km) you will pass **Hanwell Flight of 6 locks** and then Brunel's remarkable **Three Bridges** construction.

⑤ Cross **white bridge** ahead of you and continue walking along Melbury Avenue. When you reach T-junction turn **L** and then **R** at mini-roundabout.
⑥ Turn **L** along enclosed public footpath, signposted to St Mary's Avenue, beside **Plough pub**. Cross road and continue along footpath opposite, which crosses field. At far side of field climb the steps and follow road over **M4 motorway**.
⑦ Ignoring 1st metal gate along road, turn **R** through 2nd gate to re-enter **Osterley Park**. Keep going along this straight road, through farmland and avenue of small-leaved lime trees, to reach metal gate. Go past some stable buildings and main house, then take path around pond to reach car park where walk began. If you have time visit **Osterley Park House**, a neo-classical villa set in 140 acres (57ha) of park and ornamental lakes and home to some of the country's best collections of work by Scottish architect Robert Adam.

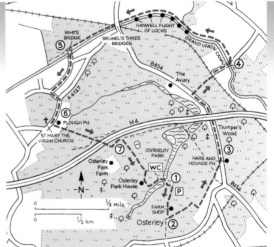

297 · HAMPTON COURT *ANYONE FOR REAL TENNIS?*

4¾ miles (7.7km) 1hr 45min **Ascent:** Negligible ▲
Paths: Gravel, tarmac and riverside tracks
Suggested map: aqua3 OS Explorer 161 London South
Grid reference: TQ 174697 Hampton Court rail
Parking: Car park in Hampton Court Road

Discover more about the game of kings on a walk through the regal landscape of Hampton Court Park.
① Cross **Hampton Court Bridge**, turn **R** through main gates to **Hampton Court Palace** and walk along wide drive. Just before palace turn **L** through gatehouse and then under arch.
② Turn **R** just before tea room, through gateway along path through gardens. At end, on R, is **real tennis court** building. Pass through another gateway and turn sharp **R** to walk alongside **real tennis court** and past entrance to it. Henry VIII played real tennis here as did Charles I. Today Prince Edward and his wife Sophie are members of the 700-strong members-only club.
③ Take central gravel path in front of palace, past fountain to railings overlooking **Long Water**, an artificial lake nearly ¾ mile (1.2km) in length. Head towards footbridge on R and go through wrought-iron gates.

④ After 220yds (201m) footpath bears **L** and joins tarmac track. Follow this, turning **L** by some farm buildings, after which path runs parallel to **Long Water**. Where lake ends continue ahead at crossing of tracks and bear **R** to skirt **L** side of **Rick Pond**. Turn **L** through metal gate, along enclosed footpath and through gate to reach **River Thames**.
⑤ Turn **L** along this riverside path and follow it for ¾ mile (1.2km) to **Kingston Bridge**. Here, join road leading to roundabout.
⑥ At end of row of houses turn **L** through gateway. Immediately after cattle grid bear **R** along grassy path running along **L** side of boomerang-shaped **Hampton Wick Pond**. Follow straight path for about ¾ mile (1.2km) back to **Hampton Court Palace**.
⑦ Bear **R** to cross footbridge and follow footpath back to real tennis court, from where you can retrace your steps to start of walk over **Hampton Court Bridge** and back into Hampton Court Road.

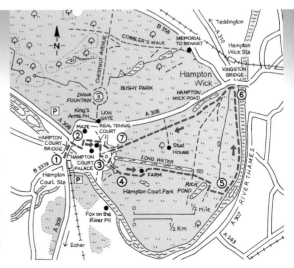

London

HARROW ON THE HILL *LITERARY HIGHS*

3½ miles (5.7km) 2hrs **Ascent:** 213ft (65m)

Paths: Footpath, fields and pavements
Suggested map: aqua3 OS Explorer 173 London North
Grid reference: TQ 153880; Harrow-on-the-Hill tube
Parking: Pay-and-display in nearby streets.

Around Harrow on the Hill, where Lord Byron and Anthony Trollope went to school.

① Follow signs for Lowlands Road exit of **Harrow-on-the-Hill Station** and go across road at pedestrian crossing. Turn **L** and then **R**, up Lansdowne Road. At top, follow public footpath ahead ('The Hill').

② Before trees, turn **R** along enclosed footpath. At road turn **L**, uphill again, along tarmac path beside churchyard. (Here, you can follow crescent-shaped path to **R** and climb steep path at end, or continue ahead to reach **St Mary's Church**.)

③ Leave by lychgate; turn **R** along Church Hill. At bottom turn sharp **L**; cross towards school library and church. Follow road as it swings to **R** after church.

④ Turn **R** on Football Lane and pick up footpath ('Watford Road'). At end of school buildings continue along path leading downhill, to reach playing fields. Look back here at Harrow School and church spires. Follow footpath sign pointing diagonally to **L** across

field (not path that follows tarmac path to **L**) to reach stile leading to busy **Watford Road**. Cross with care.

⑤ Pick up **The Ducker Footpath** opposite and carry on ahead as it passes close to **Northwick Park Hospital**, before veering to **R**, across grass.

⑥ When you get to end of hospital buildings, turn **L** along tarmac path beside brook, with playing fields to **R**. At end of this long path is **Northwick Park tube**.

⑦ Turn **L** just before tube station, along footpath which passes 2 chimneys. Follow this as it veers to **R** and passes between buildings of **Northwick Park Hospital** and **University of Westminster** campus. At end of footpath turn **L**. Cross at traffic lights. Turn **R** to follow dual carriageway for 100yds (91m) and go through gate along enclosed footpath running by side of **pitch-and-putt** golf course.

⑧ At end of this straight, long footpath turn **R** along Peterborough Road, then **L** to reach Lowlands Road. **Harrow-on-the-Hill Station** is on your R.

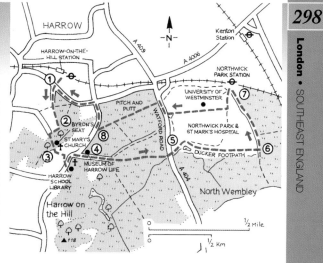

HARROW WEALD *NO SURRENDER*

4 miles (6.4km) 2hrs **Ascent:** 197ft (60m)

Paths: Clearly marked footpaths
Suggested map: aqua3 OS Explorer 173 London North
Grid reference: TQ 158936; Stanmore tube 1½ miles (2.4km)
Parking: Car park off Warren Lane

Circling the boundaries of Bentley Priory, a key wartime defence installation.

① From car park turn **R**, along **Warren Lane**. At junction cross road and continue ahead along Priory Drive. Follow road as it bends sharply to **R**. After 50yds (43m), go through kissing gate on **L** ('Bentley Way'). Continue along track, with **Bentley Priory** to **R**; go through another kissing gate.

② Where another path joins at right angles, keep ahead. Fenced area on **L** is **deer park**. At end of fencing ignore path to **L** but continue ahead as track veers **L**, crosses brook, and then reaches another kissing gate before emerging on to common.

③ Continue ahead and, at crossing of paths, turn sharp **R** across common, along waymarked path. This passes through wood and then crosses footbridge, to reach row of houses. Bear **R** and follow this meandering, tree-lined track. When it joins driveway leading to farm continue towards road ahead.

④ Turn **R**. Ignore 1st footpath sign on L and take one, just beyond, along enclosed path, just before **Honeysuckle House**. Follow path. When it reaches **A409** turn **R** and take 1st **L** into Brookshill Drive.

⑤ At end of Brookshill Drive turn **R** past buildings to **Copse Farm** ('Old Redding'). Follow track then, at T-junction, turn **R**. A few paces further on, go through wooden gate on **L-H** side and continue walking ahead along footpath through wood. It swerves to **R** of gate and later runs along side of **Harrow Weald Common**.

⑥ When footpath reaches end of common turn **R** ('Len's Avenue'). When you get to road turn **L**. After 325yds (297m) cross over and pass through large wooden gate. Go through kissing gate and then along footpath that bisects common, with grounds to military base at **Bentley Priory** on L-H side, and Heriot's Wood down hill to R. Follow this footpath as it gently descends, before joining outward path at Point **②**. Retrace your steps to car park in **Warren Lane**.

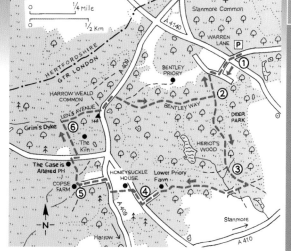

RUISLIP *THE WOODS AND LIDO*

3½ miles (5.7km) 1hr 45min **Ascent:** 115ft (35m)

Paths: Mainly non-waymarked paths through woods
Suggested map: aqua3 OS Explorer 172 Chiltern Hills East
Grid reference: TQ 080896
Parking: Young Wood car park off Ducks Hill Road

Ancient woodland, a popular lido and miniature railway.

① Enter **Young Wood** to R of car park. At crossing of paths turn **L** and, just before road, cross stile. Cross road with care and follow public footpath ('Hillingdon Trail').

② At wooden post turn **L** to go uphill. At T-junction turn **R** and immediately **L**, steadily downhill and over crossing of paths. Pass through barrier to wood at another T-junction.

③ Turn **R** along straight track that borders gardens. At end, where road meets it on L, turn **R** along path that re-enters the woods. After 200yds (183m) turn **L** along path that winds through trees and ends up at kissing gate. Take path to **L** of gate, bear **L** after another gate, and cross brook to reach edge of **golf course**.

④ Turn **R** along narrow path bordering **golf course**. Path swings to **L** and follows edge of wood. Cross footbridge over brook and bear **R** along path that skirts nature reserve.

⑤ Path eventually veers **R** into **Park Wood**. Follow this uphill and keep ahead on reasonably straight path through woods. You will see track of miniature railway line to R of fence.

⑥ Continue along footpath as it skirts fence, miniature railway and **lido**.

⑦ Turn **R** past wooden post to **miniature railway's ticket office**. Turn **L** here, along wide path that hugs southern end of **Ruislip Lido**. Continue past children's play area and follow path round to **R**, past **Water's Edge pub** and adjacent **Woodland Centre**. From car park go through gate and pick up **Hillingdon Trail** footpath again across meadowland.

⑧ At next footpath signpost turn **L** across grass and enter **Copse Wood** by wooden gate. Follow footpath as it swings round to **L** at end of some fencing. Next waymarker sign you come to is back at Point **②**. From here maintain your direction, walking ahead to retrace your footsteps back to car park.

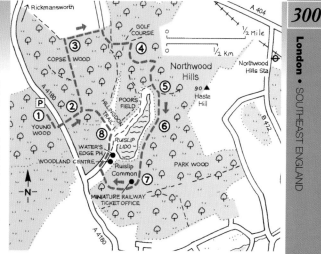

Kent

Kent • SOUTHEAST ENGLAND

301 SANDWICH *A Picturesque Trail*

3 miles (4.8km) 1hr 30min **Ascent:** 98ft (30m)
Paths: Easy town streets and field tracks, 9 stiles
Suggested map: aqua3 OS Explorer 150 Canterbury & the Isle of Thanet
Grid reference: TR 351582
Parking: Behind Guildhall in Sandwich

Enjoy the quiet English charm of Sandwich on this gentle town trail.

❶ From **St Peter's Church** in town centre, walk down St Peter's Street to The Chain. Turn **R** into Galliard Street; walk to New Street. Continue to **Guildhall**. Go **L**, through car park and up to Rope Walk, where rope makers used this long, straight area to lay out their ropes.

❷ Turn **R** and, when you reach road, cross over and turn **R** down The Butts. At main road turn **L**, cross over and turn **R** up **Richborough Road**.

❸ Walk ahead, past scrapyard, and go through gate to join footpath on **R**. Follow track round, under main road and up to **railway line**. Cross stile and cross line with care, then go over 2 more stiles and on to road.

❹ Cross over, go over another stile, then walk across field to trees, heading for 3rd telegraph pole. Path now plunges into wood and up wide track. Where it splits, fork **R** and go through trees to stile.

Now follow fence line and 2 more stiles over 2 fields to join road.

❺ Cross over and walk up track ahead. **Richborough Fort** is ahead. Path runs around fort with expansive views. At bottom of track turn **R** along end of garden. Nip over stile and back over railway, leaving it by another stile. Path now leads to **R**, over neglected-looking lock and back beside river. You will eventually rejoin road, and retrace your steps to end of **Richborough Road** where you turn **L**.

❻ Go **L** through kissing gate, pass **nature reserve** and go round edge of recreation ground. Turn **R** through gate, and on to Strand Street. Turn **L**. Then **L** again in front of **Bell Hotel** and **R** past Barbican. Walk along river bank, following line of old town wall. At bend in river, turn **R** to road. Cross over, continue along footpath, pass bowling green, then turn **R** down steps into Mill Wall Place. Cross over and go back along King Street to start.

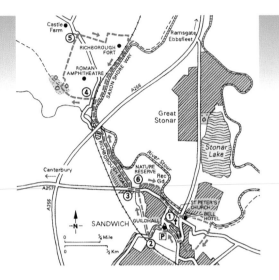

302 ELHAM *A Secret Stream*

3½ miles (5.7km) 1hr 45min **Ascent:** 115ft (35m)
Paths: Well-marked field tracks and footpaths, 9 stiles
Suggested map: aqua3 OS Explorer 138 Dover, Folkestone & Hythe
Grid reference: TR 177438
Parking: By Elham church

Walk through open countryside to an elusive stream and a hidden church.

❶ From church, walk down Duck Street, then head uphill to footpath on **R**. Cross stile and continue uphill. Nip over another stile at top of the field. Keep ahead and cross 2 more stiles to road.

❷ Cross here and follow footpath ahead, through gate, then along field edge – if it's just been ploughed you'll see plenty of flints exposed. Path goes downhill, and into next field past pylon.

❸ Go past small wood, through gate and follow guide posts over next field. Cross another stile into army training area, then walk around wood. Go straight over to yellow marker by stile, on to road and up to crossroads (you can make a detour through trees to **Acrise church**).

❹ Otherwise turn **L** and continue until you pass old **oast house**. Turn **L** just after this, then take **R-H** path to **Old Rectory** ('Private Road'). Go over stile immediately in front of house, then cross meadow. After gate, route leads diagonally over field. After 2nd gate, turn **L** and walk along field-edge. After 3rd gate path goes steeply downhill. Path now descends steeply to valley bottom, then rises again, just as steeply, to join concrete track up to farm. Where track bears **L**, go **R** through gate and up to farm buildings. Go through gate and turn **L** when you reach road.

❺ At house turn **L** and go along road under line of pylons. Just after copse lane bears **L**. Go ahead down footpath then downhill along edge of field. Walk across another field following clearly marked path. At bottom **L-H** corner go over stile with field drop.

❻ Head along edge of field, keeping fence on **R**. Follow fence and at corner follow it downhill and over another stile. After another field go **L** along field edge. You'll come to gate, which takes you over stone bridge. Walk diagonally across field in direction of church. Another gate leads to lane and church.

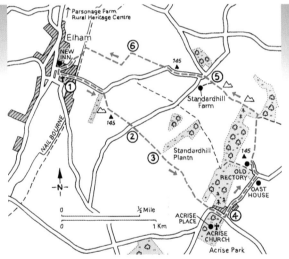

303 DOVER *Bluebirds and Butterflies*

5½ miles (8.8km) 2hrs 30min **Ascent:** 131ft (40m)
Paths: Chalky cliff paths, some sections of road. Caution: There is a danger of cliff falls – keep to the main route and dogs on leads
Suggested map: aqua3 OS Explorer 138 Dover, Folkestone & Hythe
Grid reference: TR 321412
Parking: Russell Street and St James Lane, also on cliffs by National Trust tea room

An exhilarating trail over the cliffs, which wildlife aficionados will appreciate.

❶ From **tourist information centre** on seafront, walk to **R** and at roundabout go up Bench Street. At crossing turn **L** into market square. Dover Museum is just to **L**. Turn up road on **R**. Keep going to **St Mary's Church** and then turn **R** along path that runs beside church. Keep ahead through car park, cross some water and come out on to Maison Dieu Road.

❷ Turn **R** here, and then **L**, steeply, up **Castle Hill Road**. Eventually pass entrance to **Dover Castle**. Further on, just past **Connaught Barracks**, turn **R** along Upper Road ('**Blériot Memorial**').

❸ Cross bridge over main road and then take footpath on **R**. Go down some steps, fork **L** and, in a few paces, fork **R**. Continue on this track and eventually emerge from scrub to see the sea.

❹ Turn **L** here, walk up some steps, with docks on

R. At National Trust car park follow **Saxon Shore Way** down to **R** and over cliffs. Continue past coastguard station to gate.

❺ Path now continues along cliffs and up to **South Foreland Lighthouse**. Some of the tracks branch off and lead very close to cliffs – but there is a danger of cliff falls so keep to main route. You may see some Exmoor ponies on this part of the walk. They've been introduced to the cliffs to graze the rare chalk downland and help preserve the habitat.

❻ At **South Foreland Lighthouse** turn around and retrace your steps along cliff – no hardship when you have these breathtaking views. You can take upper path here and walk past National Trust **tea room** if you fancy stopping for tea. Otherwise continue down steps and walk under main road. Go along Athol Terrace, past First and Last pub, and up on to main road and back to start.

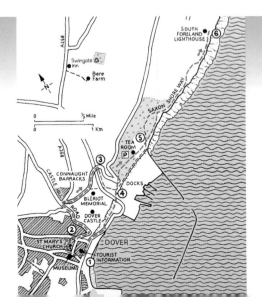

Kent

BARHAM *AN HISTORIC SPOT*

4 miles (6.4km) 2hrs **Ascent:** 98ft (30m)

Paths: Village streets, tarmac tracks and field margins, 3 stiles
Suggested map: aqua3 OS Explorer 138 Dover, Folkestone & Hythe
Grid reference: GR 208501
Parking: By Barham green

A walk around Barham and a pageant of history.

❶ From **Duke of Cumberland** pub by village green walk to main road, then turn **L** and walk along Valley Road – you'll get great views of 13th-century **church**, with its green-copper spire, on L-H side. Continue up Derringstone Hill, then turn **L** up Mill Lane.

❷ Take footpath on **R**, go through area of scrub, cross over road, nip over stile then go diagonally across field heading towards R-H edge of wood. Continue to eventually reach road.

❸ Follow road through woods. Pass 2 houses then go steeply downhill. At bottom go **L** ('Denton'). Track now opens out on **R**. Just before main road there are 2 footpaths leading off to L; take path that forks **R**.

❹ Path eventually leads into woods. Pass house, turn **L** and walk down path, with tennis courts on **R**. Turn **R** past courts and walk through grounds of 17th-century **Broome Park**, now a **hotel** and **golf club**.

Inigo Jones built the house for Sir Basil Dixwell – the man who signed the, unfulfilled, death warrant of Bonnie Prince Charlie. In the early 20th century it became the home of Lord Kitchener of Khartoum, the General who gained notoriety in World War I. He featured on the famous poster 'Your Country Needs You'. Follow path through car park then walk in front of house.

❺ Walk up track to 1st tee, cross green (look out for golf balls) and walk to marker post at trees. Turn **R** here, cross next green and go over stile into next field. Continue walking in direction of Barham church. Cross another field and come on to road, through kissing gate.

❻ Cross over to other side and walk along road almost directly ahead of you. At crossroads turn **R** and head up road, crossing stile on your **L** to follow footpath, which brings you to cemetery. Continue to road at church, turn **L**, follow road and walk back into **Barham** village centre.

BISHOPSBOURNE *JOSEPH CONRAD*

4 miles (6.4km) 2hrs **Ascent:** 328ft (100m)

Paths: Narrow lanes and field paths
Suggested map: aqua3 OS Explorer 150 Canterbury & the Isle of Thanet
Grid reference: TR 188526
Parking: On street in Bishopsbourne, especially near Mermaid Inn

Discover the country home of novelist Joseph Conrad at Bishopsbourne and the Duck Inn at Pett Bottom, where Ian Fleming penned one of his 007 novels.

❶ From **church**, walk through graveyard following Elham Valley Way. At waymarker, bear **R** across pasture for about 200yds (183m) and then cross bridge over Nail Bourne. Nip over another stile and continue through parkland of **Bourne House**, passing lake on **L**. After 650yds (594m) cross over stile and turn **L** into **Bourne Park Road**. Stroll past gates of **Bourne House** and continue until you reach 2 cottages on R.

❷ Turn **L** down lane and cross stream again. Follow lane until it peters out near farm and hop gardens, then continue ahead between hedges. Gently climb across bridge and up to top of hill. Cross stile at R-H corner of field then descend into valley walking diagonally over the fields towards the distant high

hedge (use pylon on horizon as marker). Now nip over stile, turn **R** round orchard margin and after about 300yds (274m) cut over another stile on **R**. Turn **L** and walk along road to Middle Pett Farm.

❸ Continue walking ahead, pass **Little Pett Farm** and then turn **L** to head along footpath. Cross stile at top L-H corner of field and follow signs around L-H margin of next field, turning **R** at cattle trough. Continue to cross over stile on **L**, then walk **L** around next field and continue uphill towards the corner of woodland. Follow L-H side of wood and, after about 400yds (366m), turn sharp **L**, away from wood and cross over field to marker post beside holly hedge.

❹ Fork **R** across field then turn **R** into woodland and follow track. Emerge into open fields and soon turn sharp **L**. Fork **R** at 1st telegraph pole and walk across large field heading towards chimneys of **Crows Camp** ahead. Pass to **L** of garden hedge then turn **L** at road and walk back into **Bishopsbourne**.

CANTERBURY *CHAUCER'S PILGRIMS*

3½ miles (5.7km) 1hr 45min **Ascent:** 115ft (35m)

Paths: City streets and firm footpaths
Suggested map: aqua3 OS Explorer 150 Canterbury & the Isle of Thanet
Grid reference: TR 145574
Parking: Castle Street or one of several car parks in Canterbury

Canterbury's streets have attracted pilgrims for centuries.

❶ Go **R** from Castle Street car park then **R** again past **castle**. At end turn **L** on Centenary Walk. Where this finishes go **R** and walk beside road. Cross bridge, turn **L**, go under another bridge and along river to other side of road.

❷ Cross some grassland, go over bridge and through children's play area. Walk across car park and turn **L** up road to join **Stour Valley Walk**.

❸ Go under bridge and continue to level crossing. Cross **railway**, then stroll up past **Whitehall Farm**. Walk under arch, through gate and over stream. Path bends round and main road is on your **L**. At junction turn **R** along **North Downs Way**.

❹ Go over bridge and up lane. To your **L** is **Golden Hill** – the point from which pilgrims traditionally had their first view of the city. When you come to track, turn **L** and follow it round. Go **R** along **Mill Lane** to main

road. Take underpass to cross Rheims Way, walk down **London Road**, then turn **R** into **St Dunstans Street**.

❺ Walk down into Canterbury to **Westgate**, turn **L** along **Pound Lane** and into **St Radigund Street**, with **Simple Simon's pub** on R-H side.

❻ Continue into **Northgate**, go **L** then **R** down **Broad Street**. You're now walking around outside of the city walls. Turn **R** along Burgate, past tiny 16th-century building called Pilgrim's Shop. Soon come to pedestrianised area that brings you out at Butter Market and war memorial. On your R-H side is **cathedral** entrance.

❼ Turn **L** and walk down road, pass tourist information centre and then turn **R** to Stour Street. On **R** is city **museum**, set in ancient Poor Priests' Hospital and almost opposite, down Jewry Lane, is **Canterbury Wholefoods** where you can finish your walk with tea and cakes. To return to **Castle Street**, turn **L** on Rosemary Lane and then **R**.

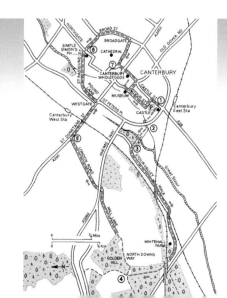

307 ALDINGTON *THE ARCHBISHOP'S PALACE*

3 miles (4.8km) 2hrs 30min **Ascent:** 66ft (20m) ▲

Paths: Waymarked tracks and badly signposted field paths, 8 stiles

Suggested map: aqua3 OS Explorer 137 Ashford

Grid reference: TQ 064355

Parking: On street in Aldington

There are memories of a palace and a notorious gang of smugglers on this walk.

❶ The **Walnut Tree Inn** at **Aldington Corner** at the start was once HQ to Aldington Gang of smugglers, probably formed by soldiers returning from the Napoleonic Wars. From pub, walk up Forge Road. At path on **L** cross stile to join **Saxon Shore Way**. Walk across field, hop over another stile, turn **L** and follow waymarker downhill. Cross stile into woods.

❷ Walk through woods, over stile and, still on **Saxon Shore Way**, follow fence line, then bear **L** and come up through pasture. Go through rusty gate on to road.

❸ Turn **R** and keep ahead. Go **L** up road, past Aldington **church**. Take track that leads to **R** past cottages. This was once the site of an **archbishop's palace**, which Henry VIII claimed for himself during the Reformation. Continue to gate, along vehicle track. Follow treeline down to stile. Follow fence line on **R**, cross stile and continue down to **Middle Park Farm**.

❹ Walk through farm where you might see some peacocks. Cross metal gate into field and continue ahead with hedgerow on **L**, walking under pylons. Continue walking along fence then take track round front of **Lower Park Farm**, over overgrown stile. Come on to shingle track and bear slightly **L** with hedgerows on **R**. Go over cattle grid and come on to road.

❺ Turn **L** down road, then turn **R** on to drive, and immediately **L** through small gate into paddock. Follow hedge by garden, and at end bear **L**. Go through clump of trees and small gate near **L-H** corner of field. Cross bridge over stream, and cross over field under pylons.

❻ Cross stream, then go diagonally across field to lone tree in corner. Climb stile then cut diagonally across field to top **L-H** corner. After going through another gap in hedge climb stile. Now go diagonally **R** across field and head down to main road. Go **L** then walk down main road and back into village.

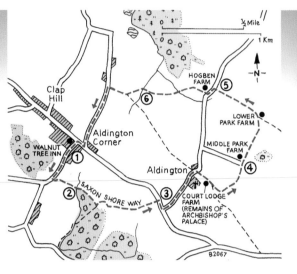

308 PERRY WOOD *A CRAFTY WALK*

4 miles (6.4km) 2hrs **Ascent:** 345ft (105m) ▲

Paths: Woodland paths and field margins, 7 stiles

Suggested map: aqua3 OS Explorer 149 Sittingbourne & Faversham

Grid reference: TQ 045556

Parking: Woodland car park in Perry Wood

A circular route through working woodland.

❶ From car park, cross road and plunge into wood, walking south along bridleway. You'll soon see evidence of recent coppicing. After few hundred paces, skirt to **L** and cross over boggy ground over boardwalk. Cross track at Keeper's Cottage gateway and bear **L** then **R**. Climb through woods, bear **L** at top and out into open heathland (it looks like woodland on OS map). Walk along ridge and climb to **observation platform** for great views.

❷ Walk past picnic area then enter orchard by stile. Continue towards bungalow at top of orchard. Skirt **L** around garden. Drop down on to tarmac lane by stile.

❸ Turn **R** to reach **Shottenden**, keep ahead at junction, pass white cottage. Continue to crossroads.

❹ Turn **L** into **Denne Manor Lane**, walk past disused oast house and continue between fields. Fork **R** under line of pylons and continue across arable fields towards telegraph pole. Maintain direction to walk through small gate and continue past fields. Your path eventually joins rough farm track, and then bears **L** to tarmac lane at **Wytherling Court**.

❺ Turn **R** and **R** again at the next 2 T-junctions. Soon come to house and turn **L** to walk along wiggly lane. Turn **R** at main road and then join footpath on **L**.

❻ Keep ahead across open fields, aiming for lone oak tree on skyline, and walk down through 1st field, crossing barbed wire fence by broken stile. Continue over next field and sheep pasture, climbing 3 more stiles to join lane.

❼ Turn **R** on to tarmac lane, where path soon dives **L** across fields, towards Georgian house. At lane, cross then go over another field and back into wood by stile.

❽ Follow path to **L**; continue to cross lane and go through paddock. Leave this at bottom corner, then scramble through overgrown area into wood, Go through garden and on to lane. Turn **R**, return through wood. Go **L** at crossroads and back to car park.

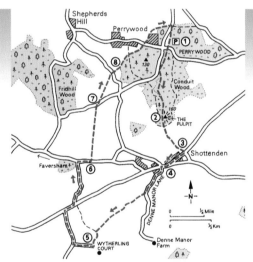

309 CHILHAM *AUSTEN'S MR DARCY'S*

5 miles (8km) 2hrs 30min **Ascent:** 131ft (40m) ▲

Paths: Parkland, field paths and woodland tracks, 8 stiles

Suggested map: aqua3 OS Explorer 149 Sittingbourne & Faversham

Grid reference: TQ 068536

Parking: Chilham car park

A countryside ramble where Jane Austen found inspiration for 'Pride and Prejudice'.

❶ From village square, walk down School Lane and cross road past **Chilham Castle** and up to **April Cottage**. Here take footpath on the **L** – waymarker on telegraph pole.

❷ Pass between gardens, then fork **R** across field to hedge in far corner. Nip over stile and into water-meadows beside **Great Stour**. Follow hedge and continue until you reach bridge. Path bears **R** here, then takes you over narrow footbridge on to busy **A28**. Turn **L** here, walk up to **East Stour Farm**, then turn **R** and walk through farmyard, cross stile and go under **railway** bridge.

❸ Follow path ahead that bears to **L** and rises up valley. Continue ahead and follow **Stour Valley Walk** as it bears **R**.

❹ At crossing of paths, continue along **Stour Valley Walk**, go through wood, and then cross stile. Continue up field and into more woodland, where soon turn **R** to follow **Stour Valley Walk**. Descend to road crossing 2 more stiles – look back for views of **Chilham Castle**.

❺ Walk to **Woodsdale Farm** and hop over stile opposite. Walk diagonally uphill to top corner (ivy-covered trees on skyline), cross another stile and then walk short distance before forking **R** along **Stour Valley Walk**. Follow this as it takes you diagonally down fields towards pair of trees in middle. Continue in same direction and cross stile on to Eggarton Lane.

❻ Turn **R**, walk down lane, and then turn **R** again under railway and up to **A28**. Cross over and walk along lane ahead. After crossing **Great Stour**, go through gates of **College of Education** and **R** into parkland of Godmersham Park.

❼ Follow public footpath through paddocks and past house. At top corner, take footpath to **R** and walk ahead, through gate and on to road. Follow road back into **Chilham**.

Kent

CHARING *PILGRIMS' WAY*

3 miles (4.8km) 1hr 30min **Ascent:** 98ft (30m)
Paths: Firm field paths and ancient trackways, 3 stiles
Suggested map: aqua3 OS Explorer 137 Ashford
Grid reference: TQ 954494
Parking: Off High Street and off Station Road, Charing

A gentle circuit taking you from Charing, once a convenient stopping place for medieval pilgrims, along the ancient ridge-top track, known as Pilgrims' Way.

❶ From **church** in centre of **Charing** village, walk to High Street, cross over road and go up School Road. At roundabout turn **R** on to **A252** and then cross road to follow public footpath that leads off to **L**. Cross stile and then walk diagonally across field and through 2 metal gates. There are 2 tracks to choose from here – strike out along **L-H** track and make your way up to some trees.

❷ When you reach hedge, climb over fence, then turn **R** and walk along **Pilgrims' Way**. It's very easy going now – this route is popular with dog walkers and horse riders. Continue on track until you reach house called **Twyford**. Where track ahead forks, go to **R** and come on to **A252**. Cross over and turn **L**. Next walk about 50yds (46m) further on then turn down

Pilgrims' Way on R-H side. Pass tarmac track on your R and continue to reach large tree.

❸ **Pilgrims' Way** now continues ahead, eventually bringing you to **Eastwell**, the burial place of Richard Plantagenet, illegitimate son of Richard III. Unless you want to walk to **Eastwell** your route now takes you to **R**, down on to bridleway. This is an immensely atmospheric lane, with a thick canopy of trees and so old that it has sunk in the middle. Take care if it's wet, as this track is chalky and can get very slippery. At tarmac road turn **R**.

❹ Just past **Pett Farm** go over stile by green gate on **L-H** side. You will soon see **Charing church** peeping through trees. Walk towards church, crossing over another stile. At bottom of field turn **R** through gap in thick hedge that brings you out to a small hut. Walk around field, along flagstone path and past children's play area. Turn **R** up fenced path and go into churchyard and back to start.

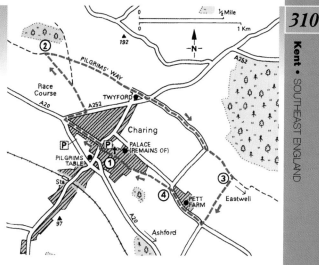

PLUCKLEY *ORCHARDS AND PERFICK VILLAGES*

3 miles (4.8km) 2hrs 30min **Ascent:** 98ft (30m)
Paths: Orchard tracks and footpaths, some field margins, 17 stiles
Suggested map: aqua3 OS Explorer 137 Ashford
Grid reference: TQ 927454
Parking: On street in Pluckley

A ramble through countryside made famous by fictional Kentish family the Larkins, created by HE Bates.

❶ From **church**, turn **R** and head up to main road. Walk uphill, turn **R** by **Black Horse** car park sign; make for gate. Cut across playing fields and through gap in hedge into orchard. Keep ahead, keeping windbreak on R-H side, then maintain direction to cross metalled track by **Sheerland Farm**.

❷ Continue through orchards to road. Bear slightly **L**, then join footpath by brick wall. Follow this, climb stile and follow fence line on **L**, to cross 2 more stiles at bottom.

❸ Route continues ahead, through gap in wall, up to another orchard and over stile. Turn **L** now and follow track with windbreak on **L**. Bear **R**, go over another stile and walk towards brick wall. Turn **R** and walk through orchard to **church**. Turn **L** and go down some steps to join road opposite **Swan pub**.

❹ Turn **R**, then nip over stile on **L** and head diagonally across field – go to **L** of lone tree. Cross stile, turn **R** and walk along field edge to cross bridge and stile. Bear **L**, then **R** at end of garden to road – you'll see duck ponds on either side. Follow tarmac lane, pass house and, at waymarker, turn **L** and walk past village green of **Little Chart Forstal**.

❺ Nip over stile on **R**, then walk down R-H side of field, climbing 2 more stiles to reach road by **riding centre**. Turn **R**, take 1st road on **L** past farm and follow it to **Rooting Manor**.

❻ Where road bends **L**, cross stile by gates, turn **L** and walk along top of field. Turn **R** as you pass through windbreak and walk up track. Follow track that leads to **L** and go through orchard, eventually bearing **R** and up to **Surrenden**. Follow track on **R**, cross stile on **L** and walk up R-H side of field to join track. Cross stile. Continue to road and cross. Walk through orchard then over playing fields. Turn **L** and return to **church**.

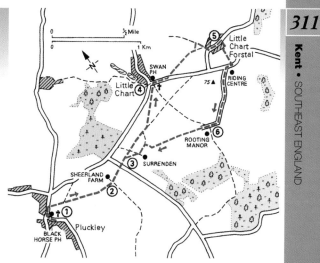

WYE *NATURAL DRAMA*

4¼ miles (7.2km) 3hrs **Ascent:** 345ft (105m)
Paths: Footpaths, wide grassy tracks and field margins, 6 stiles
Suggested map: aqua3 OS Explorer 137 Ashford
Grid reference: TQ 054469
Parking: Near Wye church

Climb the Devil's Kneading Trough for impressive views across chalk downland.

❶ From **church**, walk down Church Street, turn **L** at bottom, then **R** along Cherry Garden Lane. Keep ahead, crossing over road and continuing along track, past beech hedge.

❷ Road soon opens out and keep ahead, past **Withersdane Hall** and along footpath, with flat fields to either side. At road, cross over and continue ahead, crossing 2 stiles to track ahead – this can get very muddy. At crossing of tracks maintain direction, and follow marker post diagonally across field. Now nip over stile on to road.

❸ Walk to **R** and you'll soon see footpath on **L-H** side and sign saying 'Welcome to Wye Downs'. Walk up steps, over stile and continue winding your way up to top of hill. You get wonderful panoramic views from here. Keep walking ahead to join road, passing dramatic gorge known as **Devil's Kneading Trough** on R.

❹ Cross over, turn **L** along road, then join **North Downs Way** on R-H side. Go through gate and follow high ground, skirting valley on **L**. The soil here is fine and red, a complete contrast to the usual chalky, flinty soil of Kent. Keep ahead, but don't hurry – the views to **L** deserve some attention. After some fine walking you'll reach bench and observation point above **Wye Memorial Crown**.

❺ Take stile on **R** ('**North Downs Way**') and walk past wood on **L**. Climb another stile, then continue walking down, following some steps to join metalled road. Bear **L** and walk until track starts dropping steeply away on **R**. Turn **L** to follow bridleway.

❻ Route is easy now. Make your way down rather awkward steps, go through gate and continue ahead to reach road. Cross over and take trackway opposite, through nursery and greenhouses. At road, turn **L** then go straight ahead at crossroads. Pass **New Flying Horse Inn** then walk up Church Street to start.

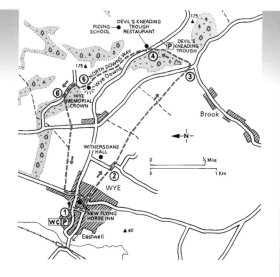

313 LENHAM... *FAST TO PARIS*

3½ miles (5.7km) 2hrs 15min **Ascent:** 49ft (15m)

Paths: Field tracks and roads, can be muddy in places, 19 stiles

Suggested map: aqua3 OS Explorer 137 Ashford

Grid reference: TQ 522899

Parking: Centre of Lenham

You don't have to be a train spotter to enjoy this rural walk

❶ From **Lenham's church** walk across churchyard and through kissing gate. Follow track diagonally across field, then cross stile. Continue in this direction, crossing fields and 2 more stiles, then walk under broad arch of **railway bridge**.

❷ Turn slightly **L**, then walk to bottom corner of next field. Cross stile and tiny wooden bridge. Bear **L** to sewage works, up ramp, then over stile. Turn sharp **R** and head to bottom of field. Don't follow Stour Valley Walk signs but walk round edge of field, over stile, then cross 3 more stiles, walk up to top of field, then down towards farmhouse, where you cross stile on to track. (It would be quicker to walk straight over to farmhouse, but you'd be straying from right of way.)

❸ Walk to **R**, then turn **R** again. Just past fruit producer's sign, hop over stile on **L**. Head uphill to gate, through scrub and turn **L** at tarmac lane. Just

past **Mount Pleasant**, converted dovecot, go to **R** down fenced track.

❹ At road, walk to **L** to tiny former **chapel**, then take lane on **R**. This sweeps past farm and down to site of new **Channel Tunnel Rail Link**. Bear to **R**, keep within fenced area and go through gate and over stile. Turn **R** then return to road.

❺ Turn **L** and continue along road for ¾ mile (1.2km), past cottages, then turn up footpath on **R**, which leads back to **sewage farm**.

❻ At **sewage farm** turn **R**, pop over 2 stiles and little bridge. Your route now goes **L**, over another stile and back to railway arch. When you reach railway turn **L** and walk parallel to **railway line**.

❼ Cross 2 little bridges and broken down stile then cross **railway line**. Walk down to bottom of field, through gap in fence and continue ahead along L-H edge of field. You cross another bridge then walk diagonally across field and back to **church**.

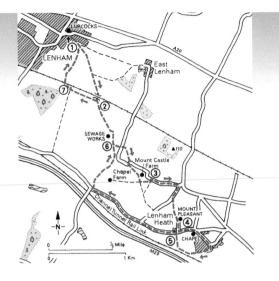

314 SUTTON VALENCE *BOWLED OVER*

3½ miles (5.7km) 2hrs **Ascent:** 148ft (45m)

Paths: Field edges and quiet lanes, 12 stiles

Suggested map: aqua3 OS Explorer 137 Ashford

Grid reference: TQ 812492

Parking: Village streets – it can get pretty crowded

A popular walk ending at John Willes' grave, the man who changed modern cricket.

❶ From **converted church** in centre of village, turn **R** down lane, then **L** at bottom to pass **ruined castle**. Continue to end of lane, and then bear **R**. Where road bears downhill, walk straight ahead along lane.

❷ Come on to surfaced area by **College Farm**. Keep walking ahead until you reach road and then turn **R**. Go downhill passing pond on R-H side. At bend, nip over stile to follow footpath on **L**.

❸ Stroll along top of field to another stile, passing pond on R-H side. Go through gap in hedge, over metal gate and on to road. Turn **L** and, after few paces, take footpath on **R**.

❹ Cross stile into field and follow fence line past tumbledown wall and up to woods ahead. Continue to some iron railings, which you follow into woods. Pass pond on your **L**, cross small bridge and continue ahead until you pop over stile into field. Bear slightly **L**,

go through gate, then head towards treeline and turn **R** to cross stile on to road.

❺ Cross road, climb another stile then continue ahead over 2 more stiles to next road. Turn **L** to follow lane uphill for 600yds (549m). Just past house turn **L** by wooden gate on to public bridleway.

❻ Your route sweeps down now, over stile and follows field edge to take you on to **Charlton Lane**. Hop over stile, cross road and walk up road ahead ('**Sutton Valence**'). Follow road past **East Sutton church** and, at another road, climb another stile into field.

❼ Take obvious path towards some trees and at waymarker go straight on along clear track. Continue to treeline in front of you, then cross stile in corner of field to join road. Walk straight on now and back to **Sutton Valence** village. To reach **St Mary's Church** walk through village, cross busy **A274** and take footpath immediately ahead. Return to village centre to finish your walk.

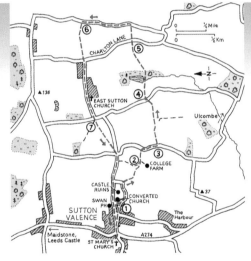

315 BETHERSDEN *OASTING AROUND*

4½ miles (7.2km) 2hrs 30min **Ascent:** 82ft (25m)

Paths: Tarmac lanes, badly signposted field tracks and one muddy farmyard, 17 stiles

Suggested map: aqua3 OS Explorer 137 Ashford

Grid reference: TQ 929403

Parking: On-street parking in Bethersden

Along quiet lanes and past oasthouses.

❶ From **churchyard**, follow footpath, then take R-H path over stile and down track. After another stile, keep ahead to trees. Nip over stile and cross road.

❷ Climb fence by metal gate and walk through salvage yard. At fork, keep to **R** and take narrow track through trees. Cross stile, walk ahead along field edge, then go **L** at marker post. At bottom of field bear **R**, then immediately **L**, and walk ahead between 2 ponds. Go through gate and cross farmyard.

❸ Follow tarmac drive to road. (Private planes land here and you'll pass a sign saying 'danger – stop, look aircraft'.) Turn **L** and continue for ¾ mile (1.2km) to main road and turn **R**. Turn **L** at **electricity sub-station**. Reach field and walk diagonally **L** towards 1st lone tree, then continue to hedge.

❹ Cross bridge, go through scrub and over stile. Turn **L** at high wire fence then go through high metal gate – you might have to push very hard to get it open.

Another gate brings you into slimy poultry yard. Walk around edge of pond; then through another gate. Cross 2 more stiles; then turn **L** in pasture where you go **R**, up track.

❺ Walk to junction, turn **R** and follow road as it bears **R** then, on corner, clamber over broken down stile and follow public footpath to **L**. Walk diagonally across 2 fields to **Wissenden Corner**.

❻ Turn **L**, walk to **Little Odiam**. Take footpath to **R**. After 2 more stiles and small bridge you reach marker post. Bear **R** and walk diagonally towards woods.

❼ At marker, cross tiny bridge and 2 stiles, then walk straight across field. Reach another bridge and stile where track goes at diagonal angle. Cross bridge in wood; then take distinct track on **L**. At another bridge and stile emerge from wood and cross pasture, then head towards bottom L-H corner of field. Cross another field to line of trees; continue to tarmac path. Proceed over 2 more stiles to return to **churchyard**.

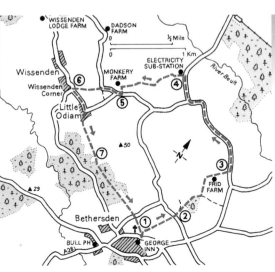

Kent

BENENDEN AN EXCLUSIVE SCHOOL

4 miles (6.4km) 2hrs Ascent: 180ft (55m) ⚠
Paths: Grassy tracks, woodland paths and field margins, 19 stiles
Suggested map: aqua3 OS Explorer 125 Romney Marsh, Rye & Winchelsea
Grid reference: TR 808327
Parking: By village green in Benenden

Enjoy the open fields and parkland on this walk past a famous girls' boarding school.
❶ From **church** turn **R**, follow footpath and go over stile. Continue over 3 more stiles, crossing fields and road to join grassy track. Go through gate at bottom, then wooden gate on **R**.
❷ You're now following the course of an old **Roman road**. Walk up **L** of field and nip over stile at top then continue through another field, keeping ahead at way signs. Pass pond and then cross over stile in hedgerow. Walk towards houses and climb stile in top **L-H** corner of field. Turn **R** and then continue until you reach main road.
❸ Turn **R**, cross by sign for **Benenden School** and follow tarmac road. Turn **L**, head along bottom of playing fields, go over stile then follow fence line on **L**. Don't cross stile ahead, instead turn **R** and walk towards **school**. Keeping the **school** on **L**, walk ahead to cross stile by house.

❹ Cross driveway and maintain direction with newer parts of **school** on **L**, then nip over stile into field and go **L** towards wood. Bear **R** to cross stile, then follow track, going past 1 stile before crossing another by wooden gate. Follow fence line, climb stile and continue to driveway. Turn **R** and walk to main road.
❺ Cross over, continue to **Goddard's Green**. Take 2nd public footpath on **R**. At house, nip over stile and keep going **L**. Route now leads across fields, over overgrown stile and through copse, which you leave by via stile. Turn **R**; follow marker to **Mount Hall Farm**.
❻ Turn **R**, follow road on to track, then continue through woods to tarmac road.
❼ Turn **L** along road and, at top of rise, nip over stile. Take track on **R** then go through gate and across field to climb another stile. Walk down track, over another stile and into woods. Cross wooden bridge, then walk to group of trees. Turn **R** and continue to climb stile by road. Turn **R** and walk back into **Benenden**.

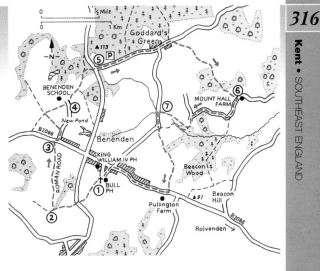

SISSINGHURST GARDENER'S DELIGHT

3 miles (4.8km) 2hrs Ascent: 33ft (10m) ⚠
Paths: Well-marked field paths and woodland tracks
Suggested map: aqua3 OS Explorer 137 Ashford
Grid reference: TQ 814409
Parking: On street in Frittenden

A lovely, easy walk to the famous garden created by Vita Sackville-West and Harold Nicholson.
❶ With your back to **Frittenden church** turn **R**, then **L** down pathway by hall. Cross stile and walk straight ahead over field, through gate and across another field. Go through kissing gate then straight ahead again – it's clearly marked. At gap in hedge cross little wooden bridge and head to telegraph pole. Branch **L**.
❷ Nip over stile, go across next field, over another stile and on to tarmac lane to turn **R** past **Beale Farm Oast**. At next house, turn **L** and walk up track until you pass old barn. Turn **R** just after barn, continue ahead over 2 more stiles and eventually cross footbridge to **R** of clump of trees. Walk few paces **L**, continue in same direction up edge of field then turn **L** again to cross another bridge. Scramble through some scrub and follow path ahead to another stile and on to road.

❸ Turn **R**, then **R** again at road junction. You pass **Bettenham Manor**, turn **L** up bridleway, over bridge, then pass **Sissinghurst Castle**, keeping building on **L**. Walk up to oast houses, then bear **L** around them, past **ticket office** and up driveway. Turn **L**, then **R** and walk by side of car parks to stile. Cross into field, then bear **R** in few paces to cross stile by some cottages.
❹ Turn **R**, walk back past cottages then bear **L** along path through trees. Continue ahead along tree-lined track. Cross stream and keep following bridleway. When you come to road, cross over and walk up **Sand Lane**.
❺ Eventually reach stile on **L-H** side, cross and then head diagonally across field to another stile in fence ahead of you. Continue diagonally, passing dip in field. Keep church spire ahead and proceed to cross another stile. Path is clear ahead, then veers to telegraph pole where you go **L**, heading for church spire. Cross bridge and walk back into village.

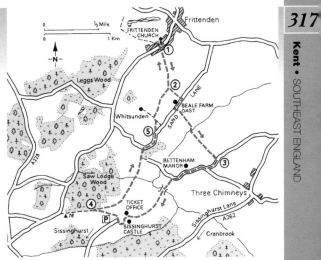

HAWKHURST SMUGGLERS' TRAIL

5 miles (8km) 2hrs 30min Ascent: 246ft (75m) ⚠
Paths: Woodland tracks and field margins, 25 stiles
Suggested map: aqua3 OS Explorer 136 The Weald, Royal Tunbridge Wells
Grid reference: TQ 763305
Parking: Car park in Hawkhurst

A circular walk from Hawkhurst, once the haunt of smugglers.
❶ Leave car park by **bus station**, turn **L** up main road, cross over then follow public footpath that runs down to **R**. Climb stile by metal gate and bear **R**, following hedge across field and past pond. Follow track through woodland, over 3 stiles and into rough pasture. Hop over stile to join track.
❷ Turn **R**, follow road; then cross to go **L** along Talbot Avenue. Pass village green, take footpath on **R** (**Sussex Border Path**) and follow it into woods to **Rowland Farm**. Walk past farm and bear **R** to top of field, crossing stile on **L**. Follow waymarker up field.
❸ Where track splits, leave **Sussex Border Path** to go **R** and through orchard. Hop over stile at top and follow track as it bears **L**, then go **R** over 2 more stiles. Cross lane and go across another field, over stile and on to **A268**.
❹ Cross road. Climb stile. Walk through **hospital** car

park then cross 2 more stiles to follow track through woods. After another stile, head sharp **L** and go back into woods. Follow track, which soon swings to **R** over stream, cross 2 more stiles, stroll across field to another stile and re-enter woods. Another stile takes you into field where there is an obvious track leading over bridge. Route now goes **L** along edge of trees.
❺ Nip over stile, then follow clear farm track on **R** to reach buildings of **Siseley Farm**.
❻ Walk past farm; then climb stile to take footpath on **L** by **Soper's Lane Farm**. Walk ahead; then turn **R** at 2nd gate, now cross 2 stiles heading for bottom corner of field. Follow track to **L**. Cross stream and head towards gap in fence. Bear **R** to **Trewint Farm**, cross road and turn **L**, then **R**, to reach **Wellington Arms**.
❼ Cross busy **A229** and walk ahead until you reach byway on **R**. Follow this past **Ockley Farm** and up into outskirts of **Hawkhurst**. Turn **R**, walk to crossroad then turn **L** to return to car park.

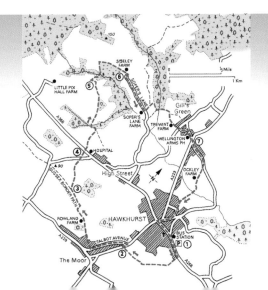

319 GOUDHURST *A Herbal High*

3 miles (4.8km) 1hr 45min **Ascent:** 164ft (50m)
Paths: Well-marked field paths, short sections of road, 12 stiles
Suggested map: aqua3 OS Explorer 136 The Weald, Royal Tunbridge Wells
Grid reference: TQ 723377
Parking: Car park in Goudhurst behind duck pond

A short but rewarding walk around one of Kent's highest villages and once the home of the Culpeper family, famous for their healing herbal remedies.

❶ From car park turn **L**, cross over road and walk along opposite to duck pond. Just past bus shelter turn **L** and then follow public footpath, crossing stile and walking downhill. There are outstanding views from here – the whole countryside seems to be sprinkled with oasthouses. Keep going down, past 2 large trees and walk to the bottom **R** of field where you cross over stile and on to narrow, tree-lined path. Follow this to stile. Go over little bridge and on to tarmac minor road.

❷ Cross over to another stile and continue ahead over pasture to tennis court. Skirt round **L** of this and, after another stile, come on to road. Turn **R**. Turn **L** through gate ('Private Road') into **Trottenden Farm**. Follow track that winds to **R**, go past pond, over stile

and walk ahead along fenced track and across pasture. Hop over stile by gate and continue ahead to another stile. At fencepost walk to **R**, round edge of meadow then cross wooden bridge, nip over another stile and into woodland. Walk uphill to another stile and continue ahead to road.

❸ Turn **R** and at corner turn **L** up public bridleway. Turn **R** at cottage and come down into field. At post by hedge turn **R** and go downhill. At bottom cross some water; then veer **L**, walking uphill towards farmhouse.

❹ Just before farm outbuildings turn **R** along track that runs by hedge. Eventually pass parkland of **Ladham House** on **L** then come to some concrete bollards. Continue walking to join road.

❺ At road turn **R**, and walk up to **B2084**. Cross over and walk along road immediately ahead. At junction keep to **R** and continue to reach main road. Turn **R** here. You can now see **St Mary's Church**. Follow road and walk back into village.

320 AYLESFORD *Ancient Sites*

5 miles (8km) 2hrs 30min **Ascent:** 230ft (70m)
Paths: Field paths and ancient trackways, some road, 12 stiles
Suggested map: aqua3 OS Explorer 148 Maidstone & the Medway Towns
Grid reference: TQ 729590
Parking: Aylesford Friary

This walk takes you to some of the most ancient sites in England.

❶ From car park turn **R** towards village, cross road and join raised pathway. Ascend steps and go round by graveyard, then follow track to tarmac road. Go **L** here, then **L** again to follow **Centenary Walk**.

❷ At marker post take **L-H** track and walk **L** around field until you come to scrub. Walk through this, turn **R** and walk ahead to patch of woodland. Keep this on **R** and continue ahead, ignoring any tracks on **R**. Eventually path bends **L** into **Eccles**.

❸ Turn **L** along residential street then take public footpath opposite No 48. Cross stile and take **L-H** track around edge of the field. Cross 2nd stile and bear **R**, then cross 3rd stile just to **L** of electricity pylon. Keep ahead across fields, going over 5 more stiles until you reach Bull Lane.

❹ Turn **R** on to Pilgrims' Way (main road) then **L** until you reach cottages. Cross over and walk up **Centenary**

Walk footpath. Follow this as it winds up to Blue Bell Hill, where there's final steep ascent. After crossing stile at top, route goes **R** along North Downs Way. (However, do take detour **L** to enjoy views from Blue Bell Hill.)

❺ Keep following **North Downs Way** until you join road. Don't cross bridge, but continue along road. Follow sign on **R** to **Kit's Coty House** (neolithic burial chamber, which dates back 5,000 years). Walk down to busy road junction, turn **L** and join Pilgrims' Way – it's on corner, by M20 sign. (Little Kit's Coty House, another neolithic burial chamber is on the main road further down to the **R**.)

❻ Follow lane, then take 1st track you see on **R** to reach road; follow ahead. Just past farmhouse take stile on **R** and walk diagonally across field. Cross another stile and bear **R** towards patch of woodland. Continue over another stile and find gate in bottom **R-H** corner. Go through and turn **R** along road. Turn **L** at junction, then **R** to return to start.

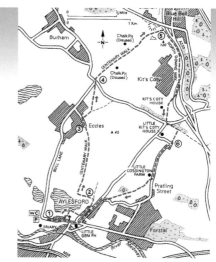

321 WEST FARLEIGH *Along the Medway*

4½ miles (7.2km) 2hrs **Ascent:** 262ft (80m)
Paths: Field paths and river walkway, some road, 12 stiles
Suggested map: aqua3 OS Explorer 148 Maidstone & the Medway Towns
Grid reference: TQ 721526
Parking: Good Intent pub car park – ask landlord's permission

A relaxing walk beside the lush banks of the Medway from West Farleigh.

❶ From **Good Intent pub** at Farleigh Green go **L**, then **L** again down footpath. Right of way has been diverted so, just before garage, veer **L** then follow path ahead. Nip over stile on **L** and across field (ignore another stile), keeping fence on your **R-H** side until you reach main road. Turn **R** and walk to road junction, then cross to **Tickled Trout pub**. Resist temptation for early refreshment and go through kissing gate on **L**, immediately before pub.

❷ Walk down field, cross over stile and then bear **R**. Follow path down to bottom of field and cross stile that lies to **R** of wartime pill box. Turn **L** and pass Tutsham Mill Cottages, then follow signs ahead for **Medway Valley Walk**. Bear to **R** in front of **Tutsham Hall** then walk through farmyard. Go over cattle grid, cross stile into field and follow **Medway Valley Walk R**, down to river bank.

❸ Nip over stile and into woods, then walk through trees until you reach small bridge that crosses muddy ground. Keep walking by river then bear to **L** to cross small stiled bridge into next field. Make for **R-H** corner of field, cross stile and squeeze through kissing gate. Continue ahead until you reach road, where you turn **R** and cross **Bow Bridge**.

❹ Immediately after crossing bridge turn **R**, walk down to river and join tow path. Now just keep following path, going through several gates until you reach **Teston Lock**, a pleasant, lively affair with rushing weir. Go under stone bridge, over stile and on to road.

❺ Turn **R** and cross bridge, then walk up some steps on **L** and follow wooded track until you cross stile and come into field. Walk ahead to cross another stile, which brings you out by **Farleigh church**. Turn **R** and walk down to main road. Walk **L** along this road then turn **R** up **Charlton Lane** and back to pub at **Farleigh Green**.

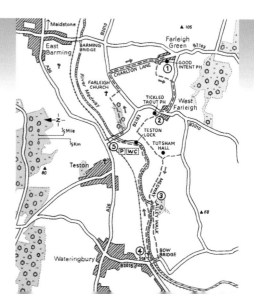

Kent

ROCHESTER *A DICKENS OF A WALK*

6 miles (9.7km) 3hrs **Ascent:** 98ft (30m) ⚠
Paths: City streets and footpaths/cycleways
Suggested map: aqua3 OS Explorer 163 Gravesend & Rochester
Grid reference: TQ 746682
Parking: Blue Boar car park and cathedral car park (fee)

Around Rochester's characterful streets.

❶ From Park-and-Ride point go **R** into pedestrianised part of High Street. Turn **L** up Crow Lane, then **R** by **Restoration House**, following signs ('Centenary Walk'). After crossing small park turn **R** and walk down hill to **cathedral**.

❷ Cross road and turn **L** round **castle**. Pass **Satis House**, then turn **R** and walk by **River Medway** until you reach Rochester Bridge. Cross bridge and, at traffic lights, go **R** along Canal Road, which runs under railway bridge.

❸ Walk along river, pass **Riverside Tavern** and follow footpath sign. This brings you out to new estate where you bear **R** along footpath/cycle track, which is part of **Saxon Shore Way**. Keep walking in same direction along track, which is intersected by roads at several points. At one point, pass rusting hull of a ship that could have come from the pages of a Dickens novel.

❹ At bend in road **Saxon Shore Way** bears **R**,

crosses industrial land, and then finally takes you close to river bank again. At river continue walking ahead as far as entrance to **Upnor Castle**.

❺ Turn **L** along Upnor's tiny, and extremely quaint, High Street, and then go to **R**. Where road joins from L, keep walking ahead to join footpath that runs to **R** of main road. Follow this to **Lower Upnor**, where you turn **R** to reach quay and great views of the **Medway**. For even better views, take a short detour up the hill to your **L**. Prehistoric wild animals once roamed these slopes, as archaeological evidence shows. One of the most interesting discoveries in the area was made in 1911, when a group of Royal Engineers working near Upnor dug up the remains of a mammoth dating back to the last ice age.

❻ Retrace rotue back into **Rochester**. After crossing Rochester Bridge walk along High Street, passing sights such as **Six Poor Travellers' Inn** and **Dickens Centre**. Continue back to Park-and-Ride point.

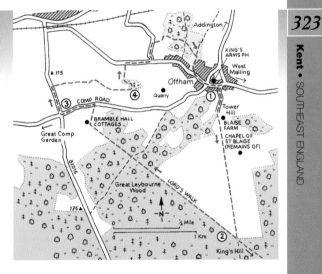

OFFHAM *JOUST A STROLL*

4½ miles (7.2km) 2hrs **Ascent:** 98ft (30m) ⚠
Paths: Easy woodland and farm paths, though not always well signed, some sections of busy road, 3 stiles
Suggested map: aqua3 OS Explorer 148 Maidstone & the Medway Towns
Grid reference: TQ 659574
Parking: On-street parking in village

An easy walk from Offham village green, where medieval knights would practise their tournament skills.

❶ With village green and its distinctive quintain on your R-H side, walk along main road and then turn **R** up Tower Hill. Go up hill to **Blaise Farm** and continue straight ahead, over 2 stiles. Your route now takes you straight along track, past site of former **chapel** dedicated to St Blaise – the patron saint of sore throats. He was once said to have miraculously healed a boy who was choking to death on a fishbone. Sadly you can't see any ruins from the footpath – it's hard to imagine that it was ever here. It's an easy stroll now to edge of wood, where you go sharp **R** along **Lord's Walk**, which runs along edge of wood.

❷ Join wide track and keep ahead gradually walking deeper into woods. Keep ahead until trees thin and you reach **Bramble Hall Cottages**. Come down to

busy road, then turn **L** and walk up to crossroads. The road ahead leads to **Great Comp Garden**, a charming garden surrounding a 17th-century manor.

❸ Turn **R** and walk up road, take great care as traffic's very busy. Keep your eyes peeled for small right of way sign at gap in hedge on **R-H** side, opposite golf course. Walk along track, through market garden. When you see hedge ahead, walk along L-H edge. Continue to typical farm oast house then walk across to small wood.

❹ Stile leads you into wood and path goes **L**, then skirts round boundary of **quarry**. Path brings you out to main road, where you turn **R** (take care, it's a very busy road). After short distance, cross over and go up lane on **L**. Continue to footpath on **R**. Follow this, crossing over 1 track, and keep walking ahead to reach 2nd junction. Turn **R** and keep ahead. Turn **L** and return to village green.

BRENCHLEY *THE IRON MEN*

4½ miles (7.2km) 2hrs 30min **Ascent:** 312ft (95m) ⚠
Paths: Orchard tracks, field margins and footpaths, 14 stiles
Suggested map: aqua3 OS Explorer 136 The Weald, Royal Tunbridge Wells
Grid reference: TQ 679418
Parking: Car park in Brenchley

This walk from Brenchley takes you back to Kent's industrial past.

❶ From car park turn **L** to war memorial. Turn **R**, then **L** at top of road and go up some steps into orchard. Walk ahead, crossing 2 stiles, then turn **L** to pass some cottages. Continue through orchard, nip over stile and on to **golf course**.

❷ Pass between greens on track, skirting corner of wood. Take track on **R**, climb stile and join track.

❸ Walk a few paces to **R** and then climb stile on **L**. Cross field and follow track to **Biggenden Farm**, where you cross stile, turn **L** and eventually reach road. Walk to **R** then take path on **L**. Cross stile and field beyond, then bear **R**. Continue towards tree line and ascend steps to **Knowle Road**.

❹ Turn **L** then, where road bends, take path on **R**. Head across field towards hedge line, maintaining direction to cross bridge and stile. Bear **L** then **R** over another bridge and stile, to join road.

❺ Turn **R** past some hop fields, then take path on **L**. Soon turn **R** through orchard to road. Turn **L** past pond, then **R** on path at vineyard.

❻ Continue to white-timbered house, nip over stile and walk between gardens to another stile. Turn **R** to join main road, then **L** and up to parking area at **Furnace Pond**.

❼ Turn **R** at **Lake Cottage** then **R** again across bridge and walk around pond. Join path on your **R** and walk up side of orchard, to turn **R** at waymarker. Continue across to lane. Turn **L** and then walk to **Hononton Farm**. Turn **R** along track, walk through orchard and then go **L** at gap in windbreak. Turn **R** at waymarker on to road.

❽ Cross over and then take track to your **L**. Follow this past house, over stile and then **R**. Cross over 2 more stiles and bridge. Eventually turn **R** to join road at **Halfway House pub**. Halfway up hill take track on your **R**. Cross field and return to **Brenchley**.

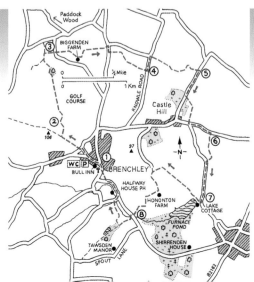

Kent

325 TUNBRIDGE WELLS *TASTING THE WATERS*

3 miles (4.8km) 1hr 30min **Ascent:** 197ft (60m)

Paths: Paved streets and tarmac paths
Suggested map: aqua3 OS Explorer 147 Sevenoaks & Tonbridge
Grid reference: TQ 582388
Parking: Car park behind The Pantiles

A simple trail through this elegant spa town, discovering the origins of its famous Pantiles and Royal patronage.

❶ From car park behind **The Pantiles**, turn **R** and walk up to main road. Cross over then walk up **Major York's Road**. Just after car park take footpath to **L** and walk across common, keeping ahead until you reach **Hungershall Park**. Turn **L**. Keep following road until you reach footpath that leads up to **R**.

❷ Follow path through trees, which eventually leads on to private road. Keep ahead and when you reach top take track ahead through trees. After horse barrier, bear **R**, pass churchyard, then turn **R** and walk around church and to busy main road.

❸ Turn **R** and then cross to walk to turning on **L** ('Toad Rock'). Path now winds uphill to rock. Now return to main road. Turn **L** and continue until you pass Fir Tree Road. On common, hidden by the trees, are Wellington Rocks.

❹ Continue along Mount Ephraim to cottages on R, which are built into rock. Turn **R** to walk across grass to picturesque **old house** that was once home to author William Makepeace Thackeray.

❺ Go along path that runs by **L** of house and walk along Mount Ephraim Road. This brings you out in front of pedestrianised shopping area. Turn **R** and walk down, past **museum and library** and war memorial. Turn **L** to walk up Crescent Road and continue until you reach **Calverley Park**, a 19th-century housing development designed by Decimus Burton. As you enter park you'll see an oak tree planted in honour of Air Chief Marshall Lord Dowding, who once lived here.

❻ Walk across Calverley Grounds to go down The Mews, then go **R** into Grove Hill Road. This brings you to roundabout; turn **L** and walk along High Street. At end go down Chapel Place, pass **Church of King Charles the Martyr**. Cross road then walk along famous **Pantiles** and back to car park.

326 SHIPBOURNE *HISTORY AND MYSTERY*

3½ miles (5.7km) 1hr 30min **Ascent:** 98ft (30m)

Paths: Easily walked fields and estate paths, short sections on roads, can be muddy in places, 8 stiles
Suggested map: aqua3 OS Explorer 147 Sevenoaks & Tonbridge
Grid reference: TQ 592524
Parking: Chaser Inn car park – ask landlord's permission

An easy walk to a moated manor house.

❶ From **Chaser Inn** walk to your **L**, go through church lychgate, following signs for the **Greensand Way**. Walk to R-H side of church and go through little gate, then over stile on your **R**. Cross field to reach another stile and follow **Greensand Way** signs, walking across field to another stile. Go a few paces to **R**, then keep straight ahead, walking up through another field.

❷ Half-way across field there is footpath sign by oak tree. Follow this, then cross another stile and go into woods along fenced path. Another stile leads you out of woods, where you turn **R** and walk around edge of field. Hop over stile then turn **R** into lane and up to entrance to **Ightham Mote**.

❸ Go through entrance and walk straight ahead, keeping manor house to L. Keep walking straight ahead, go over stile and follow footpath ('A227'). Go across field to stile and turn **R** on to A227.

❹ Walk along road and cross over at entrance to **Fairlawne Estate**. This was once the home of Sir Harry Vane, who, although a Parliamentary sympathiser, was so unpopular with Oliver Cromwell that he had him imprisoned. Sir Harry was even more unpopular with Charles II, who had him beheaded on Tower Hill. Needless to say, Sir Harry is said to haunt the grounds of Fairlawne. Go into estate and then take R-H fork that leads to pond. Go through white gate (marked 'private no entry') and walk across estate, down pleasant tree-lined walk and out on to School Lane.

❺ Turn **R** and walk along road until you see sign on R-H side for **Fairlawne Home Farm**, where you join **Greensand Way**. Walk along track until you come out on to common. Bear **R** and you will see tennis courts ahead. Keep tennis courts on your R and walk across **common**, soon to come down to **Shipbourne church** and Chaser Inn.

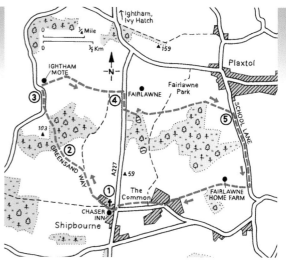

327 HADLOW *AN EXTRAORDINARY FOLLY*

4 miles (6.4km) 2hrs **Ascent:** 262ft (80m)

Paths: Field edges, woodland tracks, some stiles, 15 stiles
Suggested map: aqua3 OS Explorer 148 Maidstone & the Medway Towns
Grid reference: TQ 644526
Parking: On-street parking in Hadlow

This walk starts from a village dominated by a folly built in the 19th century by local eccentric, Walter Barton May.

❶ From centre of village walk north past **Fiddling Monkey pub**. Follow public footpath sign on **R**, walk across field and take **L-H** field edge. Cross stile and walk ahead across orchard. Cross another stile and **Goblands Farm** is ahead.

❷ Turn **L**, then take footpath on **R**, over little bridge and into field. Turn **L** and walk round field, then cross stile on **L**, followed by tiny bridge. Go straight ahead and cross another field walking in direction of oast house. Cross stile and another small bridge and walk across next field to stile. Continue in this direction over 2 more stiles then go through garden and on to lane.

❸ Turn **L**, cross main road and go through gate of **Goose Green Farm**. Follow driveway, then turn **R** through gap in fence and follow footpath across field. On reaching woodland take path that runs to **L**, through wood. Walk up to farm and into little village of **West Peckham**.

❹ Walk across village green to top L-H corner. Go through kissing gate and follow signs for **Greensand Way**. Follow track and go round to **R** of cottage and over stile. Walk around edge of field to another stile. At road, go **L** for few paces along track. Follow edge of field then cross another stile.

❺ Where **Wealdway** goes R, turn **L** and walk down to gates of **Oxen Hoath**. Walk past house, cross cattle grid and walk ahead keeping pond on L. Cross stile, walk across fields to another stile, and then hop over 3rd stile and on to road.

❻ Cross road, walk along tarmac then turn **L**, signposted for **common**. Just before you reach some cottages take lane on **R**. Follow this, cross stile then turn **L** and walk round edge of field. Cross 2 more stiles and go through kissing gate on to road. Turn **R** and walk back into village.

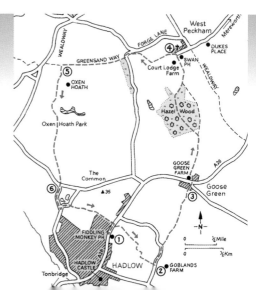

Kent

WESTERHAM CHURCHILL'S HIDEAWAY

5 miles (8km) 2hrs **Ascent:** 131ft (40m)
Paths: Mainly well-signposted woodland paths and bridleways, can be very muddy, short sections on roads, 7 stiles
Suggested map: aqua3 OS Explorer 147 Sevenoaks & Tonbridge
Grid reference: TQ 540447
Parking: Car park or on-street parking in Westerham village centre

Over thickly wooded commons to Chartwell, Winston Churchill's home.

❶ From **church** in **Westerham**, walk to village green. Cross over and head up Water Lane opposite statue of Churchill. Go over little stone stile, through gate and straight ahead across meadow. Continue into 2nd meadow and, about half-way across, turn **L** and go through kissing gate that is well hidden in hedge.
❷ Walk down narrow lane to road, turn **R**; continue to patch of common on L-H side. Turn up lane that runs to **L** of house and through trees. Soon come to hard track. Turn **R** here and follow it to French Street.
❸ Walk past April Cottage and Appletree Cottage then follow bridleway that veers to **R**. Where it branches take L-H track, then follow Greensand Way as it winds through woods, crossing minor road. Eventually cross stile on to another road, entrance to **Chartwell** is on your immediate **L**.

❹ Cross road, go up some steps and follow Greensand Way again. Eventually it bears to **R** and comes to main road, **Mariners Hill**. Cross over and follow Greensand Way – take care not to slip, as it can be muddy. At the bottom follow path round to **L** and up to **house**. Now follow tarmac track downhill and keep going to another, busier road. Turn **R** and walk along road, then turn **R** again at small sign for **Kent Hatch**. Walk along bridleway, past isolated house dated 1787, and take track that forks to **L**. Go over stile, passing sign ('Toll Riding Route') and follow Greensand Way again.
❺ Eventually landscape opens out. Cross stile then keep going straight ahead over 2 more stiles. There are lovely views of **Westerham** ahead. Hop over another stile and follow path down, past pool and over final stile, where you turn **L** and come into village. Turn **R** and walk up main street to starting point.

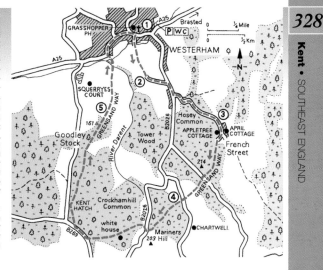

PENSHURST THROUGH PARKLAND

3½ miles (5.7km) 1hr 45min **Ascent:** 148ft (45m)
Paths: Broad tracks, short section on busy road, one badly signposted section by river, 2 stiles
Suggested map: aqua3 OS Explorer 147 Sevenoaks & Tonbridge
Grid reference: TQ 527438
Parking: On-street parking in village, also car park for Penshurst Place

A fairly easy circular walk around the magnificent estate surrounding medieval Penshurst Place.

❶ Walk up main street of village, then turn up road opposite **Quaintways** tea room. Turn **R** at public footpath sign and cross stile. There are great views of **Penshurst Place** almost immediately. The house dates back to 1341 and the Great Hall is a fabulous example of medieval architecture. It has a timber roof, a musicians' gallery and an open hearth at its centre. There have been some notable visitors to the house over the years: Elizabeth I danced here with Robert Edward Dudley; the Black Prince ate a Christmas dinner here, and the children of Charles I came here after their father was executed. Now walk to squeeze gate, cross road, then go through another squeeze gate. Bear to **R** in direction of lake. Go through 3rd squeeze gate and, keeping lake to **R**, walk around it then head towards trees.

❷ Path now veers to **L** and goes uphill. Go through 2 more squeeze gates then follow signs for **Eden Valley Walk**, which leads to **R**. This is a 15-mile (24km) linear walk that traces the route of the Eden from Edenbridge to Tonbridge.
❸ Cross stile and keep walking ahead along wide, grassy track lined with trees. At end of track cut down to **R** and continue along busy road to reach sign for **Eden Valley Walk** on R-H side, just before bridge.
❹ Go through squeeze gate and walk through pastureland, along side of **River Medway** which is on **L**. Walk by river for about ¼ mile (400m), then turn **R**, away from water, and head across pasture to little bridge. Follow footpath uphill to stile that leads on to concrete track. Turn **R** and then **L** at junction.
❺ Continue walking ahead, go through gate, then down to stile. Bear **L** and walk down track. Walk under archway, then turn **R** and walk back to village.

HEVER ROYAL PASSION

3½ miles (5.7km) 2hrs **Ascent:** 279ft (85m)
Paths: Paths, grassy tracks and field edges, some roads, 6 stiles
Suggested map: aqua3 OS Explorer 147 Sevenoaks & Tonbridge
Grid reference: TQ 476448
Parking: Car park by Hever Castle

Memories of Henry VIII and Anne Boleyn on this circular walk.

❶ Walk under lychgate and go through churchyard following **Eden Valley Walk**. Path goes downhill, across bridge and soon becomes narrow lane parallel to road, offering occasional glimpses of lake at **Hever Castle**. The lake looks natural but was actually created by William Waldorf Astor when he bought the castle in 1903. Path now bends round, goes through woodland, across another bridge and finally pops out.
❷ When you come to house, climb gate following **Eden Valley Walk** (follow it all the way to Point ❹). Pass another house then take track on R-H side, which winds round edge of meadow to woodland. When you come to tarmac road, cross it and pop over stile.
❸ Continue along enclosed track, which can get very muddy, crossing 2 more stiles and gradually heading uphill. Another stile leads you past deer fencing and through gate on to tarmac road at **Hill Hoath**.

❹ Now turn back to **R** and go through large gate, so that you seem to be doubling back on yourself. This leads to broad, grassy track. Walk ahead (don't be tempted into crossing stile on **L**) and walk between trees, passing lake on your L-H side. Soon enter much thicker woodland and track becomes narrower, but is still clear to follow.
❺ At branching of footpaths, bear **R**. Be warned, this can be very muddy. Continue down track, passing another 2 areas of woodland until you reach road.
❻ Turn **R** here and walk to **Wilderness Farm**, then take road that leads to **L** opposite farm. At another road turn **R** and walk up, past road that leads to **R**. Continue ahead to take footpath on **R** that runs alongside **Greyhound pub**.
❼ When you come to fork by 2 stiles turn **L**, then walk around edge of field and past pond. Continue ahead to lane, where you turn **L** then take footpath on **R**. Follow this back into **Hever**.

Vale of Glamorgan

331 · Dunraven *Along the Heritage Coast*

6 miles (9.7km) 2hrs 30min **Ascent:** 460ft (140m)

Paths: Easy-to-follow paths across farmland and coastline, 5 stiles
Suggested map: aqua3 OS Explorer 151 Cardiff & Bridgend
Grid reference: SS 885731
Parking: Large car park at Heritage Centre above Dunraven Beach
Note: Dogs are not allowed on Dunraven Beach in summer

A pleasant foray through rolling sand dunes.
❶ Head up lane at back of car park and pass **Heritage Centre** on R. Keep ahead on narrow path that ducks into woodland; continue to stile. Cross it and walk along field edge to gate on **L**. Go through then cross stile on **R** to continue with hedge to your R.
❷ Cross into field and keep to **L-H** side, following hedgerow, now **L**. At next stile, keep ahead, go past gate on L, to reach stile on **L**. Cross it and head diagonally **R** to stile between house and farmyard.
❸ Turn **L** on to road and walk into village. Keep **L** into Southerndown Road then fork **R** into Heol-y-slough. Follow road for ¾ mile (1.2km) then, as road bends to **L**, keep straight across common. Continue ahead where bridleway crosses track. As you join another track, maintain direction along valley floor.
❹ Path winds down through sand dunes, passing tributary valley on L, and eventually emerges on

B4524. Cross road and continue until you locate one of many paths that lead **L** towards **Portobello House**. At drive, keep **R** then fork **L** by house to continue through bracken, parallel to estuary of **Ogmore River**.
❺ Stay above small cliffs near mouth of estuary and eventually arrive at parking area above beach. From here, follow obvious route along coast around to **L**.
❻ You reach dry-stone wall, which funnels you through marked gate ('Coast Path – Emergency Vehicles Only'). Continue along coast path until, about 1¼ miles (2km) from gate, you meet with steep valley. Turn **L** into valley then immediately **R**, on to footpath that climbs steeply up grassy hillside.
❼ Stay with footpath as it follows line of dry-stone wall around to **West Farm**. Keep to **R-H** side of agricultural buildings and continue to reach upper car park. Gap in wall, at back of this, leads you to grassy track that follows road down into **Dunraven**.

332 · Castell Coch *Fairy-tale Castle*

5½ miles (8.8km) 2hrs 30min **Ascent:** 920ft (280m)

Paths: Forest tracks, disused railway line and clear paths, short section of tarmac, 2 stiles
Suggested map: aqua3 OS Explorer 151 Cardiff & Bridgend
Grid reference: ST 131826
Parking: Castell Coch

From a fairy-tale castle to a wild hillside.
❶ From car park, walk up to castle entrance and keep **R** to find information plaque and waymarker indicating woodland walk. Take this path and drop slightly before climbing steeply up to junction of tracks.
❷ Turn sharp **L** ('The Taff Trail') by picture of viaduct. Follow broad forest track around hillside then down, where it meets disused railway line. Continue along this for over 1 mile (1.6km) until you pass picnic area and come to barrier.
❸ Go through barrier then, as you come to disused bridge, turn **R** over stile ('Ridgeway Walk'). Take this up to junction by gate on L; turn **R**. Turn sharp **L** to zig-zag back across hillside, where you turn **R** again. Follow this around to **L** again, aiming at **mast** then, as you reach field edge, bear **R** again. This leads up to narrow ridge; turn **L**.
❹ Climb steeply up ridge and continue, with high

ground to L, to waymarker that directs you up narrow track to ridge top. Bear **R** and leave track until it starts to drop. Keep **R** to drop to another track; bear **L**.
❺ Follow it down through bracken to open area with stile. Cross and take track down to gate that leads on to tarmac drive. Turn **L**. Continue past houses on R-H side to junction. Turn **R** and climb up to another junction; bear **R**.
❻ Continue past **golf club**, then fork **R** on to narrow lane that drops and bears around to L. Turn **R** here to walk past Forestry Commission sign then **L**, on to narrow footpath marked by yellow-ringed post.
❼ Follow this path, ignoring tracks on both R and L, until posts become blue and you reach T-junction by sign forbidding horse riding. Turn **L** here, where posts are once again yellow, and continue downhill, past turning on L to **Countryside Visitor Centre**.
❽ Track swings around to **R** and descends to meet drive. Turn **R** to climb up drive and back to **castle**.

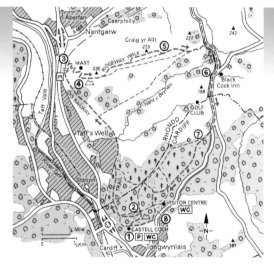

333 · Rhossili *The Highs and Lows*

4 miles (6.4km) 1hr 45min **Ascent:** 590ft (180m)

Paths: Easy-to-follow footpaths across grassy downs, 2 stiles
Suggested map: aqua3 OS Explorer 164 Gower
Grid reference: SS 416880
Parking: Large car park at end of road in Rhossili

This walk takes in the stunning views over one of Wales's finest and wildest beaches.
❶ From car park, head out on to road and continue uphill as if you were walking back out of village. You'll pass **St Mary's Church** on your L then, immediately after this, bear **L** down on broad track to gate. Go through gate and keep **L** to follow grassy track that snakes along steep hillside.
❷ Follow this through bracken, passing **Old Rectory** on your L, and eventually you'll reach sunken section with wall on your L, and **caravan park** behind. Don't be tempted to break off R just yet; instead, keep going until you come to gate. You might spot the crumbled timber skeleton of The *Helvetica* protruding from the sands below at low tide. More than one ship has fallen foul of the cruel storms that pound Rhossili. The *Helvetica* was washed up here in November 1887, but miraculously her five-man crew all survived.
❸ Turn sharp **R** here and follow grassy track steeply

up on to ridge. Of all the Gower beaches, none are blessed with quite the untamed splendour of **Rhossili Bay**. This sweeping expanse of sand runs for 4 miles (6.4km) from the Worms Head to the stranded outcrop of Burry Holms, upon which sits a ruined chapel. At top of steep section it's easy to be drawn off to R towards some obvious outcrops, but keep to top track that literally follows crest.
❹ Pass some ancient cairns and drop slightly to pass pair of megalithic cromlechs, or burial chambers. These are known as **Sweyne's Howes** and are over 4,000 years old. Continue on broad track up to high point of **The Beacon**.
❺ Keep straight ahead on clear track that starts to drop easily then steepens to meet dry-stone wall. Continue walking down side of wall and eventually come to gate you passed through on way out.
❻ Follow lane out to road, turn **R** and pass **St Mary's Church** on your R to return to car park.

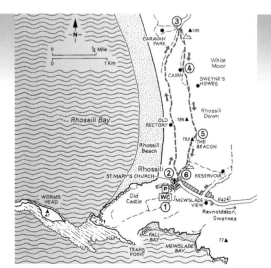

OXWICH *WOODLAND AND COAST*

4½ miles (7.2km) 2hrs **Ascent:** 480ft (146m)

Paths: Clear paths through woodland, along coast and across farmland, quiet lane, 6 stiles

Suggested map: aqua3 OS Explorer 164 Gower

Grid reference: SS 500864

Parking: Oxwich Bay

An exhilarating ramble through woodland and along delightful coastline.

1 Oxwich village was once a busy port that paid its way by shipping limestone from the local quarries, but it's now one of the prettiest and most unspoilt Gower villages, due in no small part to its distance from main roads. For maximum enjoyment it is best visited away from the main holiday season. Walk back out of the car park and turn **L** to crossroads. Turn **L** here (waymarked 'Eglwys') and pass Woodside Guesthouse and **Oxwich Bay Hotel**, on your R. This lane leads into woods and up to 6th-century **St Illtud's Church**, where gate marks end of road and start of path leading out on to **Oxwich Point**.

2 Go through gate and bear **R**, going up some wooden steps to climb steeply up through wood. As footpath levels, bear **L** to drop back down through wood and around headland until it comes out into open above **Oxwich Point**.

3 Path drops through gorse and bracken to become grassy coast path that runs easily above rocky beach. Keep sea on your L and ignore any tracks that run off to R. After approximately 1 mile (1.6km) you'll pass distinct valley that drops in from your R. Continue past this and cross succession of stiles, until you reach sandy beach of **The Sands**.

4 Turn **R**, behind beach, and follow narrow footpath to stile. This leads on to broad farm track, where you turn **L**. Continue up and around to **R** until you come to galvanised kissing gate. Go through this and keep **R** to head up lane past some houses to crossroads.

5 Turn **R** here and follow road along to fork where you keep **R**. Drop down to entrance of **Oxwich Castle** on R. This is a 16th-century mansion built by Sir Rhys Mansel on the site of a 14th-century castle, hence the name. After looking at or exploring the castle, turn **R**, back on to lane, and head down into **Oxwich** village. Keep straight ahead to car park.

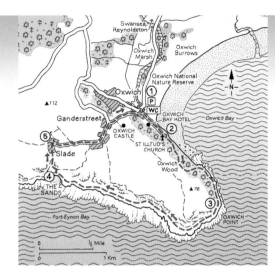

GOWER PENINSULA *THE ROCKY ROAD*

6½ miles (10.4km) 3hrs **Ascent:** 850ft (260m)

Paths: Coast path for the whole distance, 8 stiles

Suggested map: aqua3 OS Explorer 164 Gower

Grid reference: SS 467851

Parking: Large car park in Port-Eynon (buses provide logistical links on this linear route)

A linear trek along the most scenic stretch of the Gower Coast.

1 From car park head towards sea, following broad sandy track that leads past **Youth Hostel** and then on to ruins of **Salt House**, where an information board gives plenty of history on the area. Continue behind beach then fork **R** to climb steeply past quarry to **obelisk** at top.

2 Follow cliff tops along and drop to stile. Cross this to walk behind rocky beach. Keep **R** at fork to climb slightly, then drop **L** down some steps to 2nd stile. Cross this and follow path as it squeezes between impressive limestone cliffs and steep scree. You'll hurdle rocky terrace and drop beneath more crags before heading down to reach broken wall.

3 Cross wall and turn **R** to climb up steeply to good path. Turn **L** on to this and follow wall to **Foxhole Slade**. Cross iron stile in dip and climb steeply back up. (This area is owned by the National Trust.) After

200 yards (183m), next to gate on R, fork **L**. Don't be drawn out on to coast, instead continue in same direction until you join wall again and drop to stile.

4 Cross this and bear **L** back out on to cliff top. Cross stile and continue to fence, which you then follow to head of huge hollow. Cross behind this and continue along line of wall to **Mew Slade**. As wall bears R, keep straight ahead on steep path that drops awkwardly into valley.

5 Turn **L** at bottom, and drop to stile on **R**. Cross this to small cove and then follow narrow path that contours around hillside to rejoin main coast path above. Bear **L** on to this and continue to another dip. Keep high to round head of valley and then drop down, with wall on your **R**.

6 Leave wall to head back up grassy down to cliff tops where you veer around to **R** to follow them along. To continue to **Rhossili**, walk past car park to bus stop on **L** by **St Mary's Church**.

SUGAR LOAF *SWEET WALKING*

4½ miles (7.2km) 2hrs 30min **Ascent:** 1,150ft (350m)

Paths: Grassy tracks, no stiles

Suggested map: aqua3 OS Explorer OL13 Brecon Beacons National Park Eastern area

Grid reference: SO 268167

Parking: Top of small lane running north from A40, to west of Abergavenny

Escape the crowds and see another side of one of the most distinctive and popular of the Abergavenny peaks.

1 Standing in car park and looking up slope you'll see 3 obvious tracks leading away. The lowest, down to L, is tarmac drive; above this, but still heading out L, is broad grassy track. Take this and follow it for 500yds (457m) to corner of dry-stone wall.

2 This marks crossroads where you keep straight ahead, to follow wall on your L. Continue along this line for another ½ mile (800m), ignoring any R forks, and keeping wall down to your L. Eventually, you'll start to drop down into valley, where you leave wall and head diagonally towards wood. At end of the wood, keep L to descend grassy path to stream.

3 Climb out of valley, keeping to steepest, **R-H** path. This leads around shoulder and meets another dry-stone wall. Follow this, still climbing a little, until it levels by corner and gate in wall. Turn **R** here, cross

some lumpy ground and follow grassy path up.

4 As track levels, you'll be joined by another track from L. Continue ahead and climb on to rocks at western end of summit ridge. Follow ridge to white-painted trig point on **Sugar Loaf**. The Sugar Loaf and some of the land around it belongs to the National Trust, who own about 4% of the National Parks.

5 Looking back towards car park, you'll see that hillside is criss-crossed with tracks. Most will lead you back eventually, but easiest route follows path that traverses **R**, from directly below trig point. This veers **L** and drops steeply down blunt spur.

6 Follow this past insignificant R fork and then as path levels, carry straight ahead at crossroads. Keep **L** at another fork, then bear **R** at next one to follow almost sunken track along broken wall, which leads to junction by a wall. This is track that you followed on your outward leg. Bear **L** and retrace your steps back to car park.

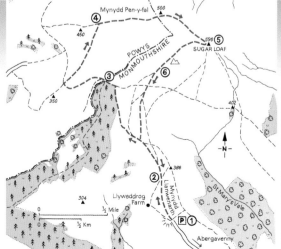

337 BLORENGE *BIRD'S-EYE VIEW OF ABERGAVENNY*

3 miles (4.8km) 1hr 30min **Ascent:** 530ft (161m) ▲
Paths: Clear tracks over open mountainside, quiet lane, no stiles
Suggested map: aqua3 OS Explorer OL13 Brecon Beacons National Park Eastern area
Grid reference: SO 270109
Parking: Small car park at Carn-y-gorfydd

A short sortie and some marvellous views.

❶ There's no easier peak to climb in the Brecon Beacons National Park but there are also few that occupy such a commanding position. The English sounding name – Blorenge – probably derives from 'blue ridge' and the mountain actually dominates a small finger of the National Park that points southwards from Abergavenny to Pontypool. It also marks a watershed between the protected mountain scenery that makes up the bulk of the National Park and the ravaged landscape that forms the southern boundary. Along the way look out and listen for red grouse as this is one of the best places in South Wales to see them as they were once managed on these moors. You'll usually be alerted to their presence by a stabbing, alarmed clucking followed by a frantic escape flight. From **Carn-y-gorfydd** Roadside Rest, walk downhill for 500yds (457m) and bear **L**, through green barrier, on to grassy track.

❷ This leads easily uphill, through a tangle of bracken, eventually allowing great views over the Usk Valley towards the outlying peak of Ysgyryd Fawr.

❸ As path levels you'll pass small **hut**. Continue along escarpment edge, on one of series of terraces that contour above steep escarpment, and enjoy the views over Abergavenny and the Black Mountains. The rough ground was formed by the quarrying of stone.

❹ Return to **hut** and bear **R**, on to clear, grassy track that climbs slightly and becomes stony. Away to **R**, you should be able to make out pronounced hump of Bronze-Age burial cairn. The path now leads easily to **trig point** and huge **cairn** that marks summit.

❺ Maintain same direction, drop down past limestone outcrop and towards **masts** on skyline. You should also be able to see the extensive spoil heaps on the flanks of Gilwern Hill, directly ahead.

❻ At masts, you'll meet road; turn **L** and continue easily downhill, for 600yds (549m), back to start.

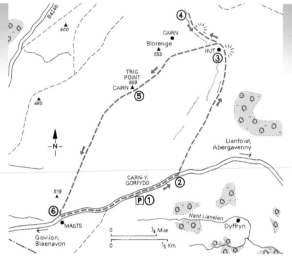

338 YSGYRYD FAWR *SUPERB VIEWS*

3½ miles (5.7km) 2hrs **Ascent:** 1,150ft (351m) ▲
Paths: Tracks through woodland and bracken, steep climb and easy traverse of airy ridge, no stiles
Suggested map: aqua3 OS Explorer OL13 Brecon Beacons National Park Eastern area
Grid reference: SO 328164
Parking: Small car park at start
Note: This walk should not be attempted in poor visibility or weather conditions

A short, steep climb and a skyline walk.

❶ This is a short walk but it is not to be underestimated; after an easy ramble, the route to the top makes a direct assault on a steep spur that offers little quarter in the fight against gravity – but the superb views are worth it. Walk through barrier at western end of car park and follow hedged track around to **R**. Climb up to gate and stile beneath large oak tree. Cross these and follow yellow waymarker that directs you off to **R**.

❷ Ascend few wooden steps and keep straight ahead at staggered crossroads, again following yellow marker posts. You'll cross over grassy forest track and then climb series of steps to cross another forest track. Continue to gate.

❸ Turn **L** here and follow moss-covered wall around. The wall drops to **L**, but continue along path and shortly you'll come alongside a tumbledown wall

on your **R**. Carry on uphill slightly to cross wall, which drops to **L**, and out on to open ground.

❹ This now undulates as it contours around hillside, eventually leading into narrow rock-strewn valley. Stay on main path to pass small **pond** on **L** and gradually veer around to **R**. You'll cross small stream and come to open area with fence on your **L**.

❺ Fork off **R** here, on faint path that leads diagonally up towards prominent shoulder. Duck under tree at head of shallow hollow, then turn **R** to climb directly upwards. The path becomes clearer as it climbs and you'll cross a couple of contouring vehicle tracks before finally making it to top.

❻ Keep straight ahead now to follow ridge along its length. Drop down narrow southern spur and bear around to **R** to join stone path. Follow this down to wall and bear **R** to return to gate at Point ❸. Retrace your steps back down through wood to car park.

339 STRUMBLE HEAD *AN INVIGORATING TRUNDLE*

8 miles (12.9km) 3hrs 30min **Ascent:** 920ft (280m) ▲
Paths: Coast path, grassy, sometimes muddy tracks, rocky paths, 21 stiles
Suggested map: aqua3 OS Explorer OL35 North Pembrokeshire
Grid reference: SM 894411
Parking: Car park by Strumble Head Lighthouse

A walk in the coast's wildest countryside.

❶ Walk back up road and cross stile on **L** on to coast path. Pass above bays of **Pwll Bach** and **Pwlluog**; drop steeply to footbridge behind pebble beach of **Porthsychan**.

❷ Follow coast path waymarkers around **Cnwc Degan** and down to bridge, where 2 footpaths lead away from coast. Continue along coast, past cottage on **R** then climbing and dropping a couple of times, before you reach **obelisk** on **Carregwastad Point**.

❸ Follow track inland and cross stile on to track; turn **R**, away from coast path. Continue with path up through gorse wall; turn **R** on to good track. Take this through succession of gates and around **L-H** bend.

❹ Ignore track to **R** and continue up cattle track to farmyard where you swing **R** then **L**, after buildings, to road. Turn **R** and follow road past large house to waymarked bridleway on **L**. Pass **Trenewydd** and go through gate on to green lane. Follow this up to

another gate and on to open ground.

❺ Turn **R** here; follow wall to gate to walled track; follow it to road. Turn **L**; climb up to car park beneath **Garn Fawr**. Turn **R**, on to hedged track, and follow this up, through gap in wall, and over rocks to trig point.

❻ Climb down and cross saddle between this tor and another, slightly lower, to south. From here head west towards even lower outcrop and pass it on **L**. This becomes clear path that leads down to stile. Cross this. Turn **L**, then **R** on to drive to road.

❼ Walk straight across and then on to coast path. Bear **R**; cross stile to drop down towards **Ynys y Ddinas**, small island ahead. Navigation is easy as you continue on coast path north, over **Porth Maenmelyn** and up to cairn.

❽ Continue along coast, towards lighthouse, until you drop to footbridge above **Carreg Onnen Bay**. Cross stile into field, then another back on to coast path and return to car park.

St David's Head *A Rocky Ramble*

3½ miles (5.7km) 2hrs Ascent: 425ft (130m)
Paths: Coast path, clear paths across heathland, 2 stiles
Suggested map: aqua3 OS Explorer OL35 North Pembrokeshire
Grid reference: SM 734271
Parking: Whitesands Beach

An easy stroll around dramatic cliffs.

❶ St David's Head is steeped in legend and peppered with the evidence of ancient civilizations. It would be difficult to imagine a more atmospheric place and for its full effect visit at sunset and watch the sky turn red over the scattered islets of the Bishops and the Clerks, located on the west of the headland. From **Whitesands Beach** head back up road, pass **campsite**, and track on L, and then take 2nd track on L. Bear **R** where it splits and continue around L-H bend to walk up to buildings. Keep **L** to walk between houses and then carry on to gate.

❷ Turn **R** on to open heathland and follow footpath along wall beneath **Carn Llidi**. Pass track that drops to **youth hostel** on R and continue around to where the path splits. Take higher track and keep going in same direction until, at corner of wall, clear track runs diagonally **L** towards coast.

❸ Follow this to coast path and turn **L** to hug cliff

tops. At **Porth Llong**, path bears **R** to climb to cairn. You'll find that the headland is a labyrinth of paths and tracks, but for maximum enjoyment try to stick as close to the cliff tops as possible as you round a number of narrow zawns. The official coast path doesn't go as far as the tip of the peninsula, but plenty of other tracks do, so follow one as far as you wish.

❹ From tip, turn **L** and make your way through rocky outcrops on southern side of headland. As you approach **Porthmelgan** you'll pick up obvious path that traverses steep hillside down into valley, which shelters small stream.

❺ Cross stream and climb up steps on other side. Continue to kissing gate where National Trust land ends and maintain your direction. Pass above **Porth Lleuog** and distinctive rocky promontory of **Trwynhwrddyn**, which is worth a visit.

❻ Path then drops steeply down to road at entrance to **Whitesands Beach**.

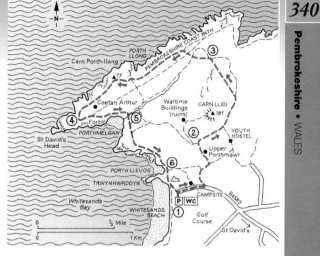

Ramsey Sound *Pounding the Hermit Monk*

3½ miles (5.7km) 2hrs Ascent: 197ft (60m)
Paths: Coast path and easy farmland tracks, 5 stiles
Suggested map: aqua3 OS Explorer OL35 North Pembrokeshire
Grid reference: SM 724252
Parking: Car park above lifeboat station at St Justinian's

Along the shores of Ramsey Sound with great views and plenty of opportunities for spotting wildlife.

❶ This is an easy but very rewarding walk with gorgeous coastal scenery and it is worth keeping a pair of binoculars handy as there are plenty of chances to spot seals, porpoises, dolphins, choughs and even Peregrine falcons along the way. Walk down to **lifeboat station** and then turn **L** on to coast path, above steps. Follow this, passing above a number of lofty, grassy promontories that make great picnic spots. After ½ mile (800m), look out for traces of Iron-Age **earthworks** on your L.

❷ Pass gate and track on your L – this is your return route – and swing around to west above **Ogof Felen**. This is a good seal pup beach in autumn. Trail climbs slightly and then drops steeply to ruined copper mine, directly opposite The Bitches.

❸ Continue easily to **Pen Dal-aderyn** and then

swing eastwards to enter **St Brides Bay**. Path climbs above some magnificent cliffs and passes between a few rocky outcrops before veering north above broad bay of **Porth Henllys**. Drop down into shallow valley until you come to fingerpost at junction of paths.

❹ Turn **L** and cross stile on **R**, into field. Turn **L** to follow track along wall to another gate, where you enter courtyard. Keep **L** here and pass barn on L. When track opens out into field, keep **R** to pass through gate and on to waymarked track.

❺ Follow this waymarked track down between dry-stone walls to reach another gate, which leads back out to coast path. Turn **R** and retrace your outward route along grassy clifftop path back to **St Justinian's**. While you're here it is worth taking a boat trip to Ramsey Island. As well as getting a close-up look at the seal colonies on the western flanks, you'll also get views of the rushing waters of The Bitches but you'll need waterproofs as it can get pretty wet.

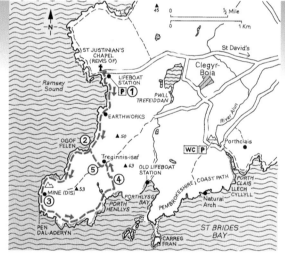

St Non's Bay *A Pilgrimage*

3½ miles (5.7km) 1hr 30min Ascent: 262ft (80m)
Paths: Coast path and clear footpaths over farmland, 6 stiles
Suggested map: aqua3 OS Explorer OL35 North Pembrokeshire
Grid reference: SM 757252
Parking: Pay-and-display car park in St David's

Easy walking around the coastline that gave birth to the Welsh patron saint, St David.

❶ Turn **L** out of car park in St David's and walk down road, as if you were heading for **Caerfai Bay**. As houses thin out, you'll see turning on **R** that leads to more dwellings. Take this and then turn **L** on to waymarked bridleway. Follow this bridleway between hedges, past end of road and go on to junction with another road.

❷ Walk straight across and then take waymarked path down pleasant track to stile. Cross over and keep to **L** of field to another stile, where you keep straight ahead again. This leads to farmyard, which is also caravan park.

❸ Turn **R** and keep hedge on your **R**, where drive swings off to L. Continue across this field and at end drop down between gorse bushes to road at **Porth Clais**. Turn **L** to bottom of valley and then, before crossing bridge, turn **L** on to coast path.

❹ Climb up steeply on to cliff tops and bear around to **L** to walk towards **Porth y Ffynnon**. The next small headland is **Trwyn Cynddeiriog**, where there's a lovely grassy platform above the cliffs if you fancy a rest. This is where St Non and Sant, St David's parents, were said to have lived. Continue walking into **St Non's Bay** and look for footpath on **L** that leads to ruined chapel, where St David is believed to have been born in the 13th century.

❺ From chapel, head up to reach gate that leads to **St Non's Well** and, from there, follow path beneath new chapel and back out on to coast path. Turn **L** to climb easily on to **Pen y Cyfrwy**, continue around this and drop down towards **Caerfai Bay**.

❻ You'll eventually come out beneath the Caerfai Bay car park where you turn **L** on to road. Follow this past the **Diving Centre** to **St David's** and start of walk. While you're in St David's Don't miss the opportunity to look around the **cathedral**.

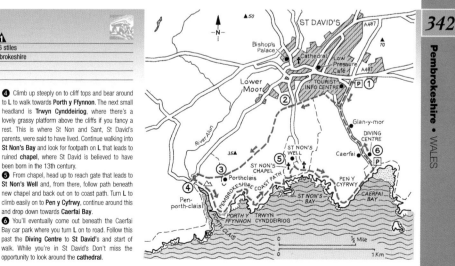

Pembrokeshire • WALES

343   BROAD HAVEN *THE HAROLDSTON WOODS*

3½ miles (5.7km) 1hr 30min **Ascent:** 290ft (88m) ▲

Paths: Woodland trail, country lanes and coast path, 1 stile
Suggested map: aqua3 OS Explorer OL36 South Pembrokeshire
Grid reference: SM 863140
Parking: Car park by tourist information centre in Broad Haven

A winding path through woodland then an easy stroll above the Haroldston cliffs.

❶ From anywhere in car park, walk towards National Park **information** centre and follow waymarked path ('Woodland Walk') that runs between information centre and coastguard rescue building. Go **R** and then **L** to bridge. Cross over bridge and continue straight ahead through kissing gate, with stream on your **L**.

❷ Ignore faint path forking to **R** and continue, on boardwalk, through wood. After ½ mile (800m) you'll come to waymarked path on **L**; ignore this and keep straight ahead until you arrive at junction of paths beneath small **chapel** on your **R**.

❸ Turn **L** to road and then **R** on to it to walk uphill, with church on your **R**. Keep ahead at T-junction, then take 1st **L**, towards Druidston Haven. Follow this over cattle grid to sharp **R-H** bend. (As you turn the bend note the good track running parallel to the road in a

field to your **L**. This is an ancient trade route, known as the Welsh Way, that runs from Monk's Haven or St Ishmael's, to Whitesands Beach.) Continue for another 300yds (274m) to reach small parking area and gate on your **L**.

❹ Go through this and follow well-surfaced track down towards coast. On reaching cliff tops, bear around to **L** and continue past the crumbled remains of an Iron-Age fort on **Black Point**.

❺ After passing **Harold Stone** on your **L** (the stone is believed to mark the spot where Harold, the Earl of Wessex, defeated the Welsh in the 11th century), path starts to drop, generally quite easily but there is one steep step. Follow path down to meet road and keep **R** to drop to walkway above beach.

❻ Cross over bridge and then, just before road you are on merges into main road, turn **L** on to tarmac footpath that leads through green and back to car park at start.

344   MARLOES *ISLAND VIEWS*

6 miles (9.7km) 2hrs 30min **Ascent:** 420ft (128m) ▲

Paths: Coast path and clear footpaths, short section on tarmac, 10 stiles
Suggested map: aqua3 OS Explorer OL36 South Pembrokeshire
Grid reference: SM 761089
Parking: National Trust car park above Martin's Haven, near Marloes village

Around a windswept headland overlooking two islands and a marine nature reserve.

❶ From car park turn **L** on to road and walk down to bottom of hill. Bear around to **L** and then go through gate straight ahead into Deer Park. Turn **L** and follow path along to stile and out on to coast.

❷ With sea to your **R**, continue easily along over **Deadman's Bay** to another stile. Next section crosses along easily, passing earthworks of Iron-Age **fort** on **L** and crosses another stile as you approach **Gateholm Island**.

❸ It is possible to get across to the island at low tide, but care is needed to scramble over the slippery rocks. To continue walk, follow coast path, above western end of beautiful **Marloes Sands** until you drop easily to main beach access path. If you are walking in the spring or summer you'll be impressed by the small white and pink flowers that carpet the cliff tops. These are sea campion (white) and thrift (pink)

and both are common along the Pembrokeshire coast.

❹ Turn **L** and climb up to road; turn **R** here. Follow road along for around ¾ mile (1.2km) to bridleway on **L**. Follow this down and turn **L** into **Marloes** village.

❺ Pass **Lobster Pot** on **L** and continue ahead to leave village. Ignore few tracks on **R**, as road bends around to **L**, and continue out into open countryside where you'll meet footpath on **R**.

❻ Walk down edge of field and bear around to **L** to drop back down on to coast path above **Musselwick Sands**. Turn **L** and follow path west for over 1½ miles (2.4km) to **Martin's Haven**. The Dale Princess, a 50-seat passenger boat, departs from Martin's Haven to Skomer Island regularly every morning during the summer and returns during the afternoon. As well as the wildlife and relics of ancient civilizations, there's also some fine walking. Please note that dogs are not allowed on the island. Meet road and climb past **information centre** back to car park.

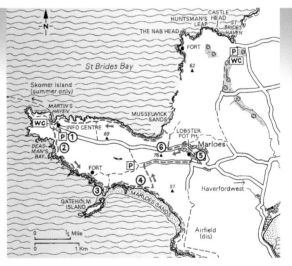

345   MILFORD HAVEN *ITS TWO FACES*

8 miles (12.9km) 3hrs 30min **Ascent:** 1,017ft (310m) ▲

Paths: Coast path and easy tracks over agricultural land, short road section, 37 stiles
Suggested map: aqua3 OS Explorer OL36 South Pembrokeshire
Grid reference: SM 854031
Parking: Car park at West Angle Bay

The waters of Milford Haven and the coastline that forms its entrance.

❶ Facing sea, walk **L** out of car park and pass between café and public toilets to waymarked stile. Follow field edge along, crossing further stiles to narrow, hedged track that leads to set of stone steps.

❷ Follow good track for a few paces and then fork **R** to drop towards ruined **tower** on headland. Continue back up, cross more stiles and then go down to footbridge. Climb up from this and pass **Sheep Island** on your **R**.

❸ Continue along coast, dropping steeply into succession of valleys and climbing back up each time. As you reach northern end of **Freshwater West**, keep your eye open for footpath waymarker to **L**.

❹ Cross stile and walk up floor of valley, swinging **L** to stile at top. Cross next field, and stile, and continue to road (**B4320**). Turn **L** on to road and walk past cluster of **houses** to **R-H** turn. Follow this down to

coast, turn **L** on to coast path and merge on to drive.

❺ Take drive to footpath sign on **R**. If tide is low, you can cross estuary here and continue along bank of pebbles to road on other side. If it's not, carry on along road into **Angle** village and bear **R** by church to follow dirt track along other side.

❻ Continue around, pass **Old Point House Inn** on your **L** and follow field edges to gravel turning point above **lifeboat station** on your **R**. Keep straight ahead, over stile, and follow bottom of field system into wooded area.

❼ You'll join broad track that runs around **Chapel Bay cottages** and **fort**. Keep **R**, to cross stile and follow narrow path back above coast. This rounds headland by **Thorn Island**.

❽ As you descend into **West Angle Bay**, path diverts briefly into field to avoid landslide. Continue downwards and bear **R** on to drive that drops you back to car park.

Pembrokeshire

MILFORD HAVEN A STROLL AROUND ST ANN'S HEAD

6½ miles (10.4km) 3hrs Ascent: 590ft (180m)
Paths: Coast path and clear paths across farmland, 20 stiles
Suggested map: aqua3 OS Explorer OL36 South Pembrokeshire
Grid reference: SM 812058
Parking: Large car park next to the beach in Dale

Easy navigation and superb coastal scenery at the mouth of Milford Haven.

❶ Leave car park by exit at the rear and follow drive to road. Turn **L** and walk to sharp **L** turn, by **Dale Castle**, where footpath leads straight ahead. Follow this up through 2 fields to stile that leads on to **Coast Path** above **Westdale Bay**. Turn **L** and climb steps up on to **Great Castle Head**, occupied by Iron-Age **fort**.

❷ For next 2 miles (3.2km), continue easily along **Coast Path** with sea to your **R** and farmland to your **L**. Despite spectacular scenery, there are no real drops or climbs and no real opportunities to get lost. Relax and enjoy ambience until you arrive at **Coastguard Headquarters** on St Ann's Head. The blockhouses and fort along this stretch of coast show how much strategic military importance was placed on **Milford Haven** in the past.

❸ At road, turn **R** and walk along drive, past lookout tower, to gate. Here, coast path veers **L** and then **R**, to follow series of marker posts along fence towards lighthouse and bank of cottages on **R**. At cottages, turn sharp **L** to cross green to track that leads behind walled enclosure. This then drops to join coast again above **Mill Bay**.

❹ Drop down to cross head of bay and climb up again to follow field edges around to Beacon on **West Blockhouse Point**. You'll pass pair of dew ponds and then come to crossroads, where you keep ahead.

❺ Path again swings inland, this time to drop down to **Watwick Bay**. Climb away from beach and follow path to **beacon** on **Watwick Point**. After following along edge of another 2 fields, cross stile and drop to **R** to start descent to **Castle Beach**. Cross footbridge and climb up steps towards narrow peninsula of **Dale Fort**. As ground levels, you'll meet junction of paths where you keep straight ahead to road. Turn **L** and follow it down, through woodland, to **Dale** and car park.

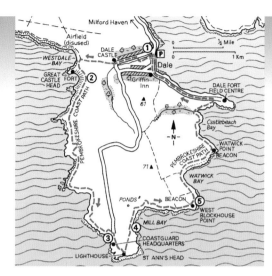

STACKPOLE BEACHES AND LAKES

6 miles (9.7km) 2hrs 30min Ascent: 390ft (119m)
Paths: Easy coast path, quiet lanes and well trodden waterside walkways, 1 stile
Suggested map: aqua3 OS Explorer OL36 South Pembrokeshire
Grid reference: SR 976938
Parking: National Trust car park above Broad Haven Beach

An undemanding tour of the clifftops, beaches and lakes at the southernmost point of the Pembrokeshire Coast National Park.

❶ From car park, head back to National Trust building at head of lane and bear **R**, down set of steps, to beach. Cross beach and keep **L** to walk up creek to footbridge.

❷ Go over this and bear **R** to walk above rocky outcrops, above beach, to gate. Follow grassy path around headland and back inland to stile above **Saddle Bay**. Continue around large blowhole and up to gate above deeply cloven zawn (cleft), known as **Raming Hole**.

❸ Go through gate and hug coastline on your **R** to walk around **Stackpole Head**. As you turn back inland, pass blowhole and then go through gate to drop down to **Barafundle Bay**. Cross back of beach and climb up steps on other side to archway in wall. Continue around to **Stackpole Quay**.

❹ Turn **L**, above tiny harbour, to pass Old Boathouse Tearoom on your **L** before turning sharp **R** on to road. Follow this past some buildings on **R** and up to T-junction, where you turn **L**.

❺ Drop down into **Stackpole** village, pass **Stackpole Inn** on **R**, and continue around a series of bends until you come to road on **L**, over bridge.

❻ Cross bridge and bear **L** to follow good path along side of lake. This leads through 1 kissing gate to 2nd, where you bear **R**, up short steep section. At top, bear **L**, on to broad path with wooden handrail. Follow this to bridge.

❼ Don't cross over bridge, but drop down on to path and follow it, keeping lake on your **L**. Continue straight ahead to another bridge, cross it, then carry on with lake now on your **R-H** side. This path leads to footbridge that you crossed at Point ❷. Retrace your steps across beach and up steps back to car park above **Broad Haven Beach**.

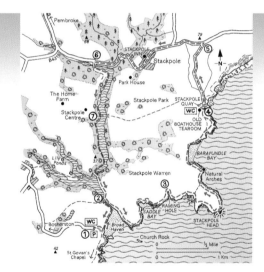

MANORBIER SWANLAKE BAY

3 miles (4.8km) 1hr 30min Ascent: 290ft (88m)
Paths: Coast path, clear paths across farmland, 6 stiles.
Suggested map: aqua3 OS Explorer OL36 South Pembrokeshire
Grid reference: SS 063976
Parking: Pay-and-display car park by beach below castle
Note: Not suitable for dogs due to difficult stiles

A short stroll across open farmland before taking in a remote cove and some breathtaking coastal scenery.

❶ Visit the impressive 11th-century **Manorbier Castle** either before or after your walk. Walk out of car park entrance and turn **L** on to narrow lane. Follow lane steeply upwards and bearing around to **R**. You'll continue to climb above coastline and pass impressively situated and well-named **Atlantic View** cottage on your **R** before reaching double gate and stile on your **L**.

❷ Cross stile and walk along field edge, with bank and fence on your **R**, to reach stone step stile. Cross stile and continue heading in same direction to wooden stile, which you also cross. Continue to stone step stile by farmhouse, which brings you into small enclosure, then to wooden stile that leads you away from buildings.

❸ Continue again along edge of field to another stone stile. Cross this stile and turn **L** to drop down field edge to yet another stile that leads on to **coast path**. Access to beach is more or less directly beneath you and this remote and beautiful cove is an excellent spot for a picnic on a sunny day.

❹ Turn **L** on to coast path and follow it over stile and steeply uphill. You'll eventually reach top on a lovely airy ridge that swings east and then north to drop steeply down into narrow dip above **Manorbier Bay**.

❺ Cross over another stile and climb out of dip to continue walking easily above rocky beach. This path leads to drive, beneath large house.

❻ Continue beneath The Dak and uphill slightly, where coast path drops off to **R**. Follow this as it skirts small car park then winds down through gorse and bracken to beach. Cross stream and turn **L** to follow sandy track back to car park.

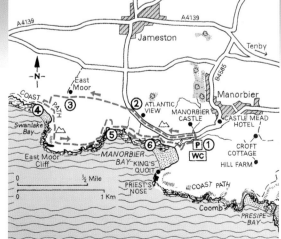

349 NEWPORT *WALK WITH ANGELS*

5½ miles (8.8km) 3hrs 30min Ascent: 1,080ft (329m)
Paths: Coast footpaths, boggy tracks, rough paths over bracken and heather-covered hillsides, 2 stiles
Suggested map: aqua3 OS Explorer OL35 North Pembrokeshire
Grid reference: SN 057392
Parking: Free car park opposite information centre, Long Street

Explore Newport then a stiff climb to Carn Ingli, one of Britain's most sacred hilltops.
❶ Turn R out of car park and L on to High Street. Fork L in Pen y Bont and continue to bridge, where waymarked footpath leads off to L. Follow this along banks of estuary to small road.
❷ Turn R; walk past toilets to its end, where path follows sea wall. Continue to another lane; turn L to follow it to A487. Turn R on to this road then L to continue up drive of Hendre farm.
❸ Go through gate, to L of buildings, and follow track across small stream. Path hugs L edge of field to reach another gate. Maintain direction along hedged section (boggy). Keep straight ahead at stile to climb up to road.
❹ Turn R on to road then fork L to continue past houses to pair of huge **stones** on L. Pass through these stones and follow faint track up to rocky tor. From here, head up towards larger tor of **Carn Ffoi**.

From here you'll be able to pick up clearer path that leads on to broken wall.
❺ Pass through it and follow clear footpath across hillside, aiming towards obvious top of **Carn Ingli**, which rises ahead of you. Pass beneath highpoint of **Carningli** Common, where you'll see faint footpath on R-H side heading up towards shallow saddle. Take this footpath then, as ground levels off, bear L to follow any of faint tracks that lead up on to ridge.
❻ Follow ridge line northwards and drop down, again on faint footpaths, to join good, clear track that runs straight down hillside. Continue on this, keeping ahead at 2 crossroads. Turn L then R when you get to next junction. This drops down to gate in corner, which leads on to lane.
❼ Take lane to crossroads and keep ahead to walk past house to obvious sunken track. Follow this down to drive; turn L, then R, on to Church Street. Continue into centre and cross main road into Long Street.

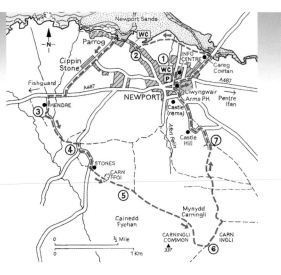

350 PRESELI HILLS *ROMANCING THE STONES*

5½ miles (8.8km) 2hrs 30min Ascent: 560ft (170m)
Paths: Mainly clear paths across open moorland, no stiles
Suggested map: aqua3 OS Explorer OL35 North Pembrokeshire
Grid reference: SO 165331
Parking: Small lay-by on lane beneath Foeldrygarn
Note: Not advisable in poor visibility as navigation is very difficult

A walk to find some of the planet's most mystical rocks.
❶ Walk to R out of lay-by on lane from Crymych, then turn R up stony track. When you reach gate, keep going straight ahead for another 100yds (91m) or so, and then fork L on to grassy track, which soon becomes clearer as it wends its way up hillside. Follow this all the way to rocky cairns and trig point on **Foeldrygarn**.
❷ Bear L at summit and locate grassy track that drops to south. Cross heather-clad plateau beneath, aiming for L-H corner of wood. When you meet main track, turn R to walk with edge of wood on your L.
❸ Leaving wood, path climbs slightly to some rocky tors. The 2nd of these, one that's closest to the wall, has sheepfold at its base. Shortly after this, path forks and you follow L-H track down to nearest of group of outcrops to your L, **Carn Gyfrwy**.

❹ Continue on faint paths to larger outcrops ahead, then curve R and drop slightly to **Carn Menyn**, lowest of bunch, perched precariously on escarpment edge. It was from here that the bluestones that form the inner circle of Stonehenge were believed to have been transported over 200 miles (320km) to Wiltshire. Path becomes clearer here and drops slightly into marshy saddle that can be seen ahead.
❺ In saddle you'll meet main track. Turn L and follow it steadily up towards **Carn Bica**, which is visible on hillside ahead of you. Just before this, you'll cross over circle made by stones of **Beddarthur**.
❻ Turn around and retrace your steps back to saddle. Climb slightly to pass tor with sheepfold and stay on this main path to walk beyond plantation once more, now on your R. At end of this path, drop on to grassy track, down to gate. Turn R on to lane and continue back to car park.

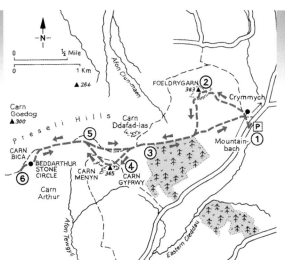

351 CARMARTHEN FAN *THE BLACK MOUNTAIN*

7½ miles (12.1km) 4hrs 30min Ascent: 2,000ft (610m)
Paths: Faint paths, trackless sections over open moorland, no stiles
Suggested map: aqua3 OS Explorer OL12 Brecon Beacons National Park Western & Central areas
Grid reference: SN 798238 **Parking:** At end of small unclassified road, southeast of Llanddeusant
Note: Best not undertaken in poor visibility

A walk in spectacular and remote scenery.
❶ From car park at end of unclassified road, head back towards Llanddeusant and after about 100yds (91m) turn sharp R, almost doubling back on yourself, to continue on faint track that contours eastwards around hillside. Follow track as it then veers northeast into small valley carved out by **Sychnant Brook**.
❷ Track becomes clear for short period, but don't be drawn uphill to north, instead remain true to course of stream, keeping L at confluence with another distinct valley, this one belonging to **Nant Melyn**.
❸ Track is faint but the going is reasonably easy as you continue up valley, crossing small tributary and following bank above **Sychnant**. Numerous paths and sheep tracks cross your way, but continue unhindered upwards, aiming for shallow saddle on blunt ridge above. Stream eventually swings to R and peters out. At this stage, bear R and head along ridge.
❹ You're now aiming for steep and obvious spur of

Fan Foel, which lies southeast of you, approximately 1½ miles (2.4km) away. Follow whatever tracks you can find over **Waun Lwyd** and, as ridge starts to narrow, keep to crest where you'll meet path coming up from northeast.
❺ Climb steeply up narrow path on to escarpment and keep R to follow escarpment along. Path becomes clearer as it drops steeply into **Bwlch Blaen-Twrch**. From here, climb up on to **Bannau Sir Gaer** and continue to summit cairn.
❻ Stay with footpath and follow edge of escarpment above precipitous cliffs into small saddle or col and up again above **Llyn y Fan Fach**. Continue around lake, with steep drop to your R-H side, and you'll see path dropping down grassy spur to outflow of lake.
❼ Follow this obvious footpath and then, when you reach dam, pick up well-surfaced track that heads back downhill. This will lead you to R of waterworks **filter beds** and back to car park.

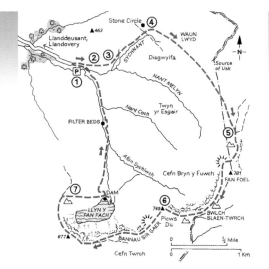

Carmarthenshire

RHANDIRMWYN *DINAS CIRCUIT*

2 miles (3.2km) 1hr Ascent: 230ft (70m)
Paths: Clearly defined tracks and boardwalks, a few steps
Suggested map: Aqua3 OS Explorer 187 Llandovery
Grid reference: SN 787471
Parking: RSPB Dinas and Gwenffrwd Nature Reserve Visitor Centre, 4 miles (6.4km) north of Rhandirmwyn

An easy saunter around the rugged scenery of the RSPB Dinas and Gwenffrwd Nature Reserve.
❶ Walk through kissing gate at far end of car park and follow boardwalk easily across open ground. It dips slightly to cross over boggy forest floor, where trees are home to countless nest boxes, and then rises again to enter woodland properly. Boardwalk comes to end at fork at bottom of wood.
❷ Turn **L** and follow slightly higher of 2 obvious tracks. This contours through oak trees, dropping close to fence on L. Another track comes in from road on L but keep above this and continue through forest, trending rightwards all the time.
❸ You're now walking parallel to **Afon Tywi**. Continue beneath some impressive crags to bench at great vantage point above its turbulent confluence with Afon Doethie. Path drops to bank of river, where

it offers great views over rapids. Continue upstream, path winds contorted route around and over few large boulders. As you reach distinct meander of river, you'll notice birch and rowan trees as well as oak. There's another bench above meander and this offers great views of crags on opposing hillside.
❹ Path then drops again to follow river to open ground, where you keep slightly **R**. The going eases now as you follow grassy path towards small stand of birch trees, where there's another bench – this one uniquely hewn out of twisted branches. Climb easily up for few yards (metres) and then continue to end of boardwalk. Turn **L** to follow this back to car park.

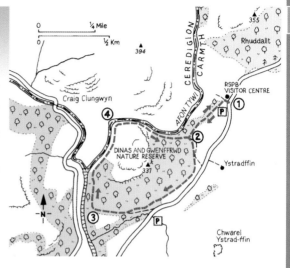

PUMLUMON *REMOTE LAKE*

5½ miles (8.8km) 3hrs Ascent: 623ft (190m)
Paths: Good track up, sketchy return path
Suggested map: aqua3 OS Explorer 213 Aberystwyth & Cwm Rheidol
Grid reference: SN 762861
Parking: Off-road parking – there is room for several cars by woods at start of walk, alternatively use car park by Nant-y-moch dam

Discover a tarn set among the rocks of the Rheidol's dark northern corrie.
❶ From car parking spaces beneath woods east of Nant-y-moch dam (near spot height 392m on OS Explorer maps), walk north along road and take **R-H** fork. The road descends to cross streams of **Nant Maesnant-fach** and **Nant-y-moch** before traversing rough moorland along east shores of **Nant-y-moch Reservoir**. The reservoir, stocked with native brown trout, is popular with anglers during season.
❷ Beneath quarried rocks of **Bryn y Beddau**, rubble track on **R-H** side of road doubles back up hillside then swings round to **L**. The steep sides of **Pumlumon** now soar away to skyline on your R, with little stream of Maesnant tumbling down them. The track climbs further, then levels out to pass some shallow lakes, which lie above rocks of **Fainc Ddu uchaf**. Now high above bare valleys of Hyddgen and Hengwm, track

swings south beneath crags of **Pumlumon Fach** to arrive at Llyn Llygad Rheidol's dam.
❸ To get to footpath along other side you'll have to ford stream short way downhill – take care if stream is in spate. Path, which runs parallel to eastern banks of stream, is sketchy in places, especially where you ford side stream. It descends peaty terrain where mosses and moor grasses proliferate.
❹ When you reach small stand of conifers in Hengwm Valley, turn **L** to follow old cart track which fords Afon Rheidol, close to its confluence with Afon Hengwm. Track heads west and soon Hengwm Valley meets that of Afon Hyddgen. Track swings southwest and passes between squat cliffs of **Fainc Ddu uchaf** and western shores of **Nant-y-moch Reservoir**.
❺ Go through gate above outdoor adventure centre at **Maesnant** and continue along tarmac lane used in outward route, to return to car park.

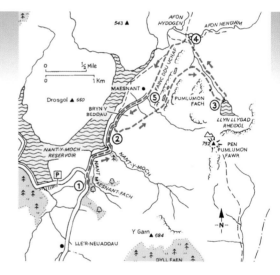

DEVIL'S BRIDGE *MYNACH RIVER RAMBLE*

5½ miles (8.8km) 2hrs 30min Ascent: 525ft (160m)
Paths: Mainly clearly defined tracks across open ground and through forests – riverside sections can be boggy, 8 stiles
Suggested map: aqua3 OS Explorer 213 Aberystwyth & Cwm Rheidol
Grid reference: SN 742768
Parking: Large car park on the B4574, Cwm Ystwyth road, out of Devil's Bridge

An easy riverside circuit from the enchanting village of Devil's Bridge. The bridge dates from the 12th century and together with the spectacular waterfalls is one of the most popular tourist attractions in Wales.
❶ Turn **R** out of car park and walk along road to waymarked bridleway on your **L**. Go through gate and turn immediately **L** on to narrow footpath that drops down to river. Cross over bridge and walk up other side to stile.
❷ Keep straight ahead, with some rocky hills to your R, to another stile. Cross this and follow track to waymark post. Turn **R** and climb past another post to good track. Cross this and turn **R** to traverse hillside, in wood, to another post on grassy shoulder.
❸ Keep straight ahead to another post and then drop to contour around gorse-covered hillside. Continue to stream and stile, which you cross to enter

plantation. Continue to another stile and drop to meet good track. Keep **L** on to this and follow it above grand-looking house to fork above some ruined buildings.
❹ Fork **R** and follow good track along above **Mynach** river. Eventually it bends leftwards to follow above banks of tributary. Shortly after this, waymark directs you **R**, down some steps and over tributary. Keep straight ahead to post by small bank. Turn **R** here and drop down to bridge over **Mynach**.
❺ Turn **R** to follow path downstream. Continue, through succession of gates, to gate on **L** that leads on to clear track. Follow this, away from river and up to join another good track. Turn **R** on to this and follow it to fork where you turn **R** through gate. Continue around hillside and over footbridge. Climb up past house and continue to **B4574**. Turn **R** to drop down to car park.

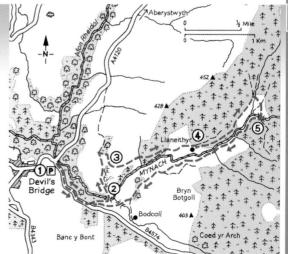

Ceredigion

355 TEIFI POOLS *A LAKELAND CIRCUIT*

4½ miles (7.2km) 2hrs 30min **Ascent:** 180ft (55m) ▲
Paths: Two good tracks and a short but tricky stretch across trackless moorland
Suggested map: aqua3 OS Explorer 187 Llandovery & 213 Aberystwyth & Cwm Rheidol
Grid reference: SN 777682 (on Explorer 213)
Parking: Small car park east of the bridge on double bend
Note: Navigation would be extremely difficult in poor visibility. It is recommended that you also carry OS Explorer 187 with you to aid navigation

You'll need good navigation skills for this short but rugged circuit across remote hillsides and moorland studded with lakes.

❶ Turn **R** on to narrow, winding road and follow it past a track on **R**, which heads down to **Llyn Teifi**, your return route, and then another that leads to **Llyn Hir**. After 1½ miles (2.4km), you'll reach 3rd track on **R**, to **Llyn Egnant**.

❷ Take this track and follow it around western shores of lake to reach gate, just beyond **dam**. Go through gate and turn **R** to follow fence up hillside. Stay with fence as it swings **R** and then **L**, and then, as it swings **R** again, leave it behind to head up shallow pass between 2 small hilltops, which are directly ahead of you.

❸ Navigation becomes difficult for short while from here but, if you are in any doubt at all, keep heading

R (north) and you will soon pick out one of lakes, which are distinctive enough in shape to help you pinpoint your position. Drop down from this shallow pass to **R** and cross over wet ground at bottom to climb back up on to another grassy ridge, above **Llyn y Gorlan**.

❹ Continue heading west, with lakes to your **R**, linking together as much of high ground as possible by crossing wetter patches in between. After another ½ mile (800m), you'll spot largest of Lakes, **Llyn Teifi**. Drop down on to concrete wall at water's edge and follow it easily around its southern and western shores to **dam** and small building.

❺ Follow steps up from building to gate that then leads on to good track. Follow this along western shore and around hillside to road. Turn **L** and retrace your outward steps back to car park.

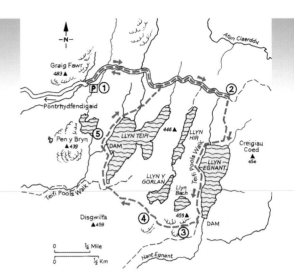

---

356 NEUADD RESERVOIRS *IN THE BRECON BEACONS*

7½ miles (12.1km) 4hrs **Ascent:** 2,000ft (610m) ▲▲
Paths: Clear well-trodden paths, small boggy patches, broad rocky track; 1 stile
Suggested map: aqua3 OS Explorer OL12 Brecon Beacons National Park Western & Central areas
Grid reference: SO 032179
Parking: At end of small lane leading north from Pontsticill

A magical tour of reservoirs, high ridges and mountains.

❶ Continue up lane to small gate, which leads into grounds of **reservoir**. Keep walking ahead to drop down narrow path to concrete bridge across outflow. Cross bridge and climb up on to bank opposite where you bear **L** to walk along top of bank. This will take you to gate that leads out on to open moorland.

❷ Go through this and keep ahead, taking **L-H** of 2 tracks, which leads easily uphill towards edge of mainly felled forest. Follow clear track up, with forest to your **L**, and then climb steeply up stony gully to top of escarpment.

❸ Once there, turn **R** on to obvious path and follow escarpment for over 2½ miles (4km). You'll eventually drop into distinct saddle with flat-topped summit of **Corn Du** directly ahead. Where path forks, keep ahead and climb easily up on to summit. Follow escarpment edge along then drop down into another saddle, where

you take path up on to next peak, **Pen y Fan**.

❹ Again, from summit cairn, follow escarpment around and drop steeply, on rocky path, down into deep col beneath **Cribyn**. Keep ahead to climb steeply up to cairn on narrow summit. Note: this climb can be avoided by forking **R** and following another clear path that contours **R** around southern flanks of mountain and brings you out at Point ❻.

❺ From top, bear slightly **R** and follow escarpment around to southeast. After long flat stretch, drop steeply down into deep col, **Bwlch ar y Fan**.

❻ Cross stile and turn **R** on to well-made track that leads easily down mountain. Follow this for over 1½ miles (2.4km), until it starts to swing slightly to **L** and drops steeply into rocky ravine. Turn **R** here on to track and take it down to gate. Go through this, turn **L** and follow track to its end. Turn **R** on to another track that leads back to head of lane. Go through gate and follow lane back to your car.

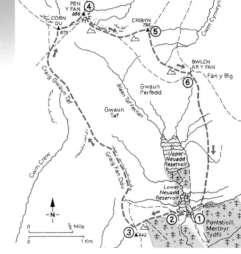

---

357 CAERFANELL VALLEY *SKYLINE WALKING*

5½ miles (8.8km) 3hrs 30min **Ascent:** 1,542ft (470m) ▲▲
Paths: Clear tracks across mountain tops, river and forest paths, some mud and wet peat, 3 stiles
Suggested map: aqua3 OS Explorer OL12 Brecon Beacons National Park Western & Central areas
Grid reference: SO 056175
Parking: Large car park at start, 3 miles (4.8km) west of Talybont Reservoir

Spectacular escarpments above a wild and remote valley.

❶ Walk back out of car park, either crossing cattle grid or stile to **L**. Turn immediately **R** on to stone track that heads uphill, with stream on your **L**. Follow this track steeply up to top of escarpment and keep ahead to cross narrow spur, where you bear around, slightly **L**, to follow escarpment.

❷ Stay on clear path, with escarpment to your **R**, for about 1½ miles (2.4km), until you meet a number of paths at head of valley.

❸ Turn **R** to follow narrow track slightly downwards, around head of valley, towards cliffs that can be seen on opposite hillside. Keep **L** at fork and continue to **memorial**, which marks where a Wellington bomber R1645 crashed, killing its Canadian crew, in 1942.

❹ Almost directly above **memorial**, you'll see rocky gully leading up on to ridge. Take this

to top; turn **R** on to narrow but clear track. Follow this track above crag, to distinctive cairn at southern end of ridge. Just north of cairn you'll see small stream.

❺ Follow this down for 10ft (3m) to join clear grassy track that trends towards **L** at first, then follows clear grove down spur. This becomes easy footpath that crosses broad plateau then leads to junction at a wall. Turn **R** here and drop down to **Caerfanell river**.

❻ Cross stile on your **L** at bottom and follow narrow footpath downstream, past **waterfalls**. Eventually you'll pass largest of them and come to footbridge.

❼ Cross footbridge then stile to follow track into forest. Pass ruined buildings on your **R**, and before you cross small bridge, turn **R** on to clear path that leads uphill into forest with **waterfalls** on your **L**.

❽ Continue uphill on main track, taking optional detours to **L** and **R** to see other waterfalls. Eventually you'll meet broader forest track where you turn **L** then **R** to return to car park.

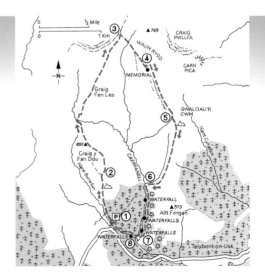

Powys

WAUN FACH *FROM THE GRWYNE FAWR VALLEY*

9¼ miles (14.9km) **4hrs** **Ascent:** 1,608ft (490m)
Paths: Clear tracks over open moorland, indistinct path over boggy ground, steep descent, 1 stile
Suggested map: aqua3 OS Explorer OL13 Brecon Beacons National Park Eastern area
Grid reference: SO 252284
Parking: Car park at head of lane at start

The easiest way on to the Black Mountains.

1 Take broad track at far end of car park and follow it out on to road. Turn **R** to continue up valley. After about 300yds (274m), fork **R** on to stony track that runs along bottom of forest. Follow this track and continue through 2 gates to 3rd, by stand of trees, situated above **Grwyne Fawr Reservoir**.

2 Keeping trees to your **L**, carry on past reservoir and up valley. Go through another gate; continue until track finally fords the **Grwyne Fawr** stream. Stay on stony track, which now peters out to become grassy before deepening into obvious rut. Continue on to flat ground above steep northern escarpment, where path meets fence by stile on your **R**.

3 Turn **L** on to clear track. After 200yds (183m), turn **L** on to faint grassy track that leads up front of blunt spur. Follow this over numerous peaty hollows to summit plateau of **Waun Fach**, identified by large concrete block.

4 Continue in same direction (southeast) across large expanse of boggy ground. There's no clear path on this section, but there are usually plenty of footprints in wet ground leading towards obvious cairn-topped peak of **Pen y Gadair Fawr**, at far end of ridge. In saddle between 2 summits, you'll pick up faint path that initially follows eroded line of stream.

5 Path improves as it continues, eventually leaving stream behind and making beeline for peak ahead. Climb to **cairn** then continue in same direction to drop steeply for 10yds (9m). As it levels, path splits. Fork **L** on to faint grassy track that drops slightly then turns to **R**, to edge of forest, by gate.

6 Don't go through gate; instead turn **L** to head down steep hillside, with forest on your **R**. Follow this path all the way down to river at bottom where you turn **R**, over stile. Continue along river bank for about 400yds (366m) then cross bridge to the road. Turn **R** on to this to return to car park.

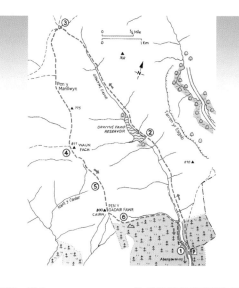

PORTH YR OGOF *ALONG THE WATERFALLS*

4 miles (6.4km) **2hrs** **Ascent:** 360ft (110m)
Paths: Riverside paths, some rough sections and steps, no stiles
Suggested map: aqua3 OS Explorer OL12 Brecon Beacons National Park Western & Central areas
Grid reference: SN 928124
Parking: Park car park at Porth yr ogof, near Ystradfellte

Riverside scenery and four waterfalls.

1 Cross over road at entrance to car park and head down **L-H** of 2 paths, waymarked with yellow arrow. Follow this path on to river bank, then keep river to your **R** to follow rough footpath through 2 kissing gates to reach footbridge.

2 Continue ahead, drop into dip and climb steeply out. Keep **L** to climb to broken wall where path forks. Take **L** fork here (bottom R-H path has fence along it) and follow edge of wood. When you see odd green-banded marker posts, follow them to waymarked crossroads where you turn **R**, now following red-banded posts.

3 Continue through dark tunnel of trees and out into more evenly spaced deciduous woodland. Carry on following waymarked trail to post directing you downhill. Follow this track and then bear around to **R** when you reach edge of forest. This leads to top of set of wooden steps, on **L**.

4 Go down steps to **Sgwd yr Eira** (Waterfall of the Snow) and then, having edged along bank and walked behind falls (waterproofs are recommended), retrace your steps back to edge of the wood. Turn **L** and continue, still following red-banded posts, to fork marked with green-banded post.

5 Turn **L** and descend to riverside. Turn **L** again to **Sgwd y Pannwr** (Fullers Falls) and then turn around to walk upstream to **Sgwd Isaf Clun-Gwyn** (Lower Waterfall of the White Meadow). Take care here, as ground is very steep and rough around best viewpoint.

6 Retrace your steps downstream to your descent path and turn **L** to climb back up to fork at top. Turn **L** and follow red-banded waymarkers along to **Sgwd Clun-gwyn**, where there's a fenced-off viewing area. From here, continue along main trail to place where you split off earlier.

7 Keep to **L-H** side to drop into dip and retrace your steps past footbridge and back to **Porth yr ogof**.

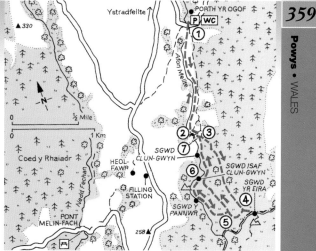

CWM GWESYN *WALK ON THE WILD SIDE*

9½ miles (15.3km) **6hrs** **Ascent:** 2,000ft (610m)
Paths: Riverside path, faint or non-existent paths over moorland, some good tracks, 4 stiles.
Suggested map: aqua3 OS Explorer 200 Llandrindod Wells & Elan Valley
Grid reference: SN 863533 **Parking:** Lay-by on minor road by bridge over Afon Gwesyn
Note: A tough trek, which you should avoid in poor visibility

1 Head up track west of lay-by; turn **R**, through gate. Follow track across fields and down to **Afon Gwesyn**; ford. Continue to gate and up towards wood where track splits. Choose top option here, as this bends around to **L** and heads downhill, fork **R**, to traverse clearing to gap in wood.

2 Follow path down to ford. Climb to open ground; bear **R** to farm track by buildings. Turn **L**; go through gate and under crags. Ignore fork to **L** and continue to open ground. Follow east side of valley for 1½ miles (2.4km) to **waterfall**.

3 Pass it on **R**; continue until path almost disappears. Follow stream until you reach ridge coming in from **R**. Take this for 100yds (91m); bear **L** on narrow path, around boggy patches until **Drygarn Fawr's** summit is visible.

4 Climb slope to trig point; follow ridge east past 2 **cairns**. You'll see 2 summits, 1½ miles (2.4km) away; one with **cairn** on top, **Carnau**, is your next objective. Grassy track descends east from cairn. Follow this until it levels out and rounds **L-H** bend, where you'll see faint path forking **R**. This is start of careful navigation. If you're in any doubt

about visibility turn round and retrace your tracks.

5 Follow track, which links boundary stones for 200yds (183m), until you see 1 stone offset to **R** of path. Turn **R** here (south), away from path, and cross wet ground to climb slightly on to broad rounded ridge. You'll see head of valley ahead and, as you drop into this, bear slightly **L** to follow high ground with valley to **R**. Continue on sheep tracks to cross 2 hollows, until you reach hilltop. From here, you'll see cairn ahead. Take path that leads to it.

6 From **Carnau** you'll see start of gorge to southwest. Walk towards it and pick up track across river. Follow bank to **L** to reach fork; take **R-H** path to descend hillsides and drop into bottom of valley, where it meets wood.

7 Go through gate; follow track over stream and up to 5-way junction. Turn **R**; go through gate then another on **L**. Drop down through field on to track; follow this to junction above **houses** on **L**. Keep **R**, cross stream. Take track over field to path junction. Keep ahead and descend past **Glangwesyn** to road. Turn **R** on road to return to start.

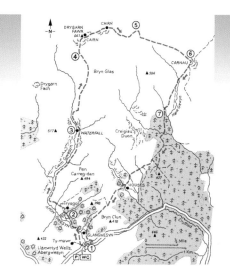

Powys

361 CRAIG CERRIG-GLEISIAD *BACK TO NATURE*

4 miles (6.4km) 2hrs **Ascent:** 1,050ft (320m) ⚠
Paths: Clear footpaths and broad stony tracks, 4 stiles
Suggested map: aqua3 OS Explorer OL12 Brecon Beacons National Park Western & Central areas
Grid reference: SN 972221
Parking: Pull-in by small picnic area on A470, 2 miles (3.2km) north of Storey Arms

The formidable crags of one of the Beacon's best-known nature reserves.

❶ This is one of many possible walks in the large 156-acre (63ha) National Nature reserve but it is the closest (in this collection) to the National Park Visitor Centre on Mynydd Illtud Common, near Libanus. It is a great source of information about the National Park and hosts some great displays and has a programme of guided walks. There is a bridge and a small picnic area at southern end of lay-by. Walk towards this and go through adjacent signposted kissing gate ('Twyn Dylluan-ddu and Forest Lodge'). Head towards crags, following clear footpath, until you come to gap in next wall.

❷ Pass through this and turn **R** to follow dry-stone wall north. Head down into small valley, cross stream, then stile to continue in same direction. Drop into another, steeper, valley and climb out, still following track. Continue through bracken to stile.

❸ Cross and turn **L** on to stony track. Follow this up to gate and stile and continue through rough ground, churned up by mining, until it levels on dished plateau. Bear **R** here to whitewashed trig point of **Fan Frynych**, then turn sharp **L** to return to main track above escarpment.

❹ Turn **R** on to main track again and continue past more rough ground before dropping slightly into broad but shallow valley. At bottom, go over stile by gate.

❺ Cross another stile on your **L** and turn **R** to continue in same direction, this time with fence to your **R**. Climb up to highest point, then follow obvious path around top of cliffs. Path starts to drop, easily at first but getting steeper as you go.

❻ Continue carefully down steep section and follow path around to **L** when you reach easier ground. This leads you to stream, which you can ford or jump (it's narrower a few paces downstream). Turn **R**, through gap in wall, and follow outward path back to car park.

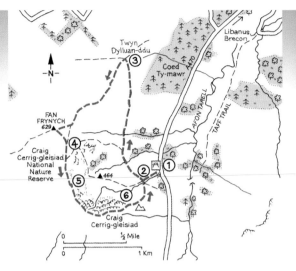

362 PEN Y FAN *THE BEACONS HORSESHOE*

7 miles (11.3km) 4hrs **Ascent:** 2,100ft (640m) ⚠
Paths: Well-defined paths and tracks, short distance on quiet lanes, 4 stiles
Suggested map: aqua3 OS Explorer OL12 Brecon Beacons National Park Western & Central areas
Grid reference: SO 025248
Parking: Car park at end of small lane, 3 miles (4.8km) south of Brecon

The connoisseur's way up to the high ground.

❶ Walk uphill from car park and pass information plinth before crossing stile. Walk along **R-H** side of field to top **R-H** corner and then bear **L** to continue along fence to another stile.

❷ Follow broad but faint grassy track straight on. It gradually becomes a better-defined stony track that swings slightly **L** and climbs hillside. Continue ahead, up towards head of **Cwm Gwdi**, and keep ahead, ignoring few **R** forks, until path eventually levels out on **Cefn Cwm Llwch**.

❸ Continue along ridge towards summit ahead. As you reach foot of peak, track steepens considerably, offering views over a perilous gully that drops into **Cwm Sere** on **L**. Continue to climb steeply over few rocky steps to reach summit cairn on **Pen y Fan**.

❹ Bear **R** to follow escarpment edge along and drop into shallow saddle beneath rising crest of **Corn Du**. Continue up on to this summit, then bear **L** to drop down through rocky outcrops on to easier ground below. Bear sharp **R** once you reach grassy hillside to walk north beneath peak.

❺ Continue down hill and pass Tommy Jones **obelisk** with steep crags of **Craig Cwm Llwch** on your **R-H** side. Above lake, path forks; take **R-H** option and drop steeply, around dog-leg and over moraine banks to lake shore.

❻ A clear track leads north from lake; follow it over easy ground to cross wall that leads on to broad farm track. Take this down to gate in front of building and climb stile on **L**. Cross compound and climb another stile to follow waymarker posts around to **R** on to another track, beyond building.

❼ Bear **L** on to this track and follow it down, over footbridge, to parking area. Keep ahead, through gate to T-junction, where you turn **R**. Cross over bridge and continue for over 1 mile (1.6km) to another T-junction. Turn **R** and walk uphill back to car park.

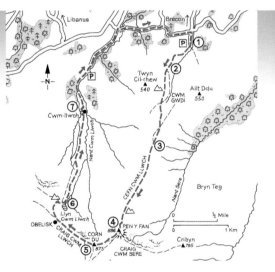

363 Y GRIB *AN AIRY STROLL*

8 miles (12.9km) 4hrs 30min **Ascent:** 1,960ft (597m) ⚠
Paths: Clear tracks over farmland, rolling moorland and narrow ridge, quiet lane, 3 stiles
Suggested map: aqua3 OS Explorer OL13 Brecon Beacons National Park Eastern area
Grid reference: SO 175295
Parking: Castle Inn, Pengenffordd, allows parking for small fee

A strenuous climb on to the Black Mountains via one of the Beacon's finest ridges.

❶ Wooden steps go down from back of car park on eastern edge of road. These lead on to rough track where you turn **R** then immediately **L** over stile. Follow permissive path down side of wood to stream, cross it and clamber over another stile.

❷ Keep to **L** edge of field, with wood on your **L**, and climb steeply to top of field. Leave wood behind and follow fence line upwards to another stile. This leads on to flanks of **Castell Dinas**.

❸ Keep ahead here to cross over ruins and descend steeply into deep saddle. Cross over broad track and then climb directly up steep spur ahead. You are now on **Y Grib** and it's possible to follow faint track all the way up to **cairn** then down to small notch where your route is crossed by bridleway.

❹ Climb steeply back out of this and hug crest up to another **cairn**, where ridge joins main escarpment. Don't be drawn off to **L**; instead keep ahead to climb short steep wall on to broad spur of **Pen y Manllwyn**, where you'll meet clear track.

❺ Turn **R** on to this track; follow it up to boggy plateau on top of **Waun Fach**. Summit is marked by concrete block that used to act as base for trig point. Turn **R**; follow obvious path down on to ever-narrowing spur of **Pen Trumau**.

❻ Cross narrow summit and, as ground steepens, follow path through rocky outcrops to broad saddle. Turn sharp **R** here; follow main track as it descends, easily at first. This steepens and becomes rocky for a while before it reaches gate above walled track.

❼ Follow track down to road; turn **R**, then immediately **L**. Drop to bottom of valley and climb out again on other side. As road turns sharply to **L**, bear **R** on to stony farm track that runs between hedgerows. Follow this track past stile you crossed earlier, on **R-H** side, then take steps on your **L**, back to car park.

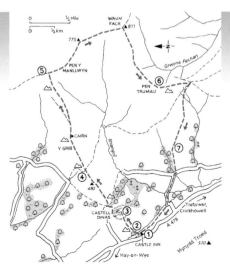

PEN CERRIG-CALCH *THE CRICKHOWELL SKYLINE*

8½ miles (13.7km) 4hrs 30min Ascent: 1,700ft (518m) ⚠

Paths: Waymarked footpaths, clear tracks, 8 stiles

Suggested map: aqua3 OS Explorer OL13 Brecon Beacons National Park Eastern area

Grid reference: SO 234228

Parking: Car park beneath small crag and next to bridge, in narrow lane running north from Crickhowell

Views of Crickhowell and the remote valleys of the central Black Mountains.

1 Walk back over bridge and up ramp that leads to 2nd gate on **R**. Cross stile and walk up edge of field to another stile that leads on to lane. Cross this and climb over another stile to continue, with wood on your **L**, up to yet another stile in dry-stone wall.

2 Cross this and turn **L** to follow faint path around hillside through bracken. Walk alongside wall, at one stage dropping slightly, and then, as wall drops to **L** in open area, turn **R** to climb slightly to another fork beneath steep bank. Keep **L** here to join wall again.

3 Continue for about 500yds (457m) to another open spot where wall dips to **L** and turn **R** on to track that leads up on to summit of **Table Mountain**.

4 Turn off plateau at its narrowest northern point and cross saddle on obvious track. This climbs steeply up on to **Pen Cerrig-calch**. As path levels, ignore track to **L** and keep ahead until you reach trig point.

5 Continue ahead to drop slightly down small crag to meet escarpment edge. Continue along ridge, which narrows slightly, then climb again to narrow summit of **Pen Allt-mawr**.

6 A path leads down steep northern spur. Take this and cross flat, open and often wet ground towards small hump ahead. As you start to climb, you'll come to parting of paths.

7 Fork **R** here and continue to small **cairn** on top of narrow ridge that leads southwest. Follow ridge easily down until you cross some quarried ground and come to large **cairn**. Walk down to stile at top of plantation. Cross this and then follow rutted track down to another stile.

8 This leads on to sunken track, which you follow downhill to junction of paths. Keep half **R** to cross stile and head along top of field to marker post that sends you **L**, downhill. Bear **L** at bottom to stile by gate. This leads back to car park.

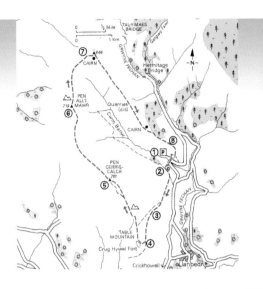

CAPEL-Y-FFIN *LLANTHONY AND ITS HILLS*

9½ miles (15.3km) 5hrs 30min Ascent: 2,460ft (750m) ⚠

Paths: Easy-to-follow paths, steep slopes, open moorland, muddy lowland trails, 15 stiles

Suggested map: aqua3 OS Explorer OL13 Brecon Beacons National Park Eastern area

Grid reference: SO 255314

Parking: Narrow pull-in at southern edge of Capel-y-ffin, close to bridge

A demanding trek.

1 Walk towards bridge, but before you cross it bear **L** up narrow lane ('The Grange Pony Trekking Centre'). Follow this past footpath on **L**, marked by stone archway, to drive on **L**. Follow this up to barns.

2 Keep **R**; continue to large house on **R** with gate. Bear **L**; climb to another gate. Go through and scale eroded grassy bank before turning **R** on to clear path through bracken. This then backs **L** and crosses easier ground, and source of stream, to foot of zig-zagging track that climbs steeply up escarpment.

3 Follow this track, bearing both **R** and **L** and then, as the gradient eases, continue ahead on broad and often boggy track. Continue past small cairns to large one, **Blacksmith's Anvil**, on top of ridge. Turn **L**; continue to follow track south over **Chwarel y Fan**.

4 Continue along ridge, to reach summit of **Bal-mawr**. Go down to **L** and pass good track on your **L**-H side. Keep ahead to **cairn** then descend to **L**. Drop

to fork; keep **R** to follow brook to crossroads of paths. Maintain your direction ('Cwm Bwchel').

5 Continue through 2 fields, past house, and on towards 2 stiles. Take **L** stile; follow marker posts and arrows to footbridge. Keep ahead to gate. Follow stream to footbridge. Cross and take lane to road. Turn **L**, then **R** to visit **Llanthony Priory**.

6 Cross stile on **L**, in front of priory ('Hatterrall Hill') and follow track to stream; turn **L** to stile. Continue through succession of fields and small copse to reach interpretation board. Follow path up to ridge. Continue to crossroads; turn **L** at **Offa's Dyke**.

7 Go along dyke, pass **trig point**, for 1 mile (1.6km) to **cairn** and marker stone at crossroads of paths. Turn **L**; follow path around **L–R** zig-zag to wall. Turn **R** then **L** over stile. Walk down to lane; turn **R**. Follow lane to **L-H** bend and keep ahead, up steps and over stile. Continue through fields to join lane and follow this past 2 chapels to road. Turn **L** to turn to start.

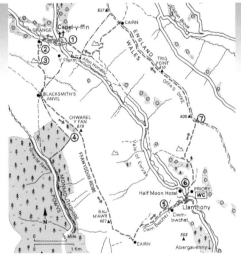

CAPEL-Y-FFIN *TACKLING THE VALE OF EWYAS*

9 miles (14.5km) 4hrs Ascent: 1,560ft (475m) ⚠

Paths: Easy-to-follow tracks, steep slopes, open moorland, no stile

Suggested map: aqua3 OS Explorer OL13 Brecon Beacons National Park Eastern area

Grid reference: SO 255314

Parking: Narrow pull-in at southern edge of village, close to bridge

A variation on the previous walk as you trek around the head of the Ewyas Valley.

1 Walk towards bridge, but before you cross it, bear **L** up narrow lane ('The Grange Pony Trekking Centre'). Follow this along side of stream and past footpath on **L**, marked by stone archway. Continue to drive on **L**, again leading to **trekking centre**, and follow this up to barns.

2 Keep **R**; continue uphill to large house on **R**, with gate blocking progress ahead. Bear around to **L** and climb on loose rocky track that leads up to another gate. Pass through this and scale eroded grassy bank ahead before turning **R** on to clear path that leads through bracken. This then backs **L** and crosses easier ground, and source of small stream, to foot of steep zig-zag track that climbs steeply up escarpment.

3 Follow this, bearing both **R** and **L** and then, as gradient eases, continue ahead on broad and often boggy track. Take this past small cairns to large one

that sits on top of rounded ridge. Turn **R**; follow track easily over **Twyn Talycefn** to trig point on **Pen Rhos Dirion**. (Summit can be avoided by clear path that traverses **R** before final climb.) Turn **R** and drop steeply down through heather into broad saddle.

4 Keep ahead over flat section then climb steeply up on to **Twmpa**. Turn **R** and then, for maximum effect, bear **L** on to narrower track that follows line of east-facing escarpment. Stay with this track until ridge narrows and drops steeply away.

5 Descend directly to large **cairn**, then zig-zag, **L** then **R**, to cut steep line through bracken to junction with broad contouring bridleway. Turn **R** on to this then fork **L**, down steep bank to pick up narrow stony track that runs along side of wood.

6 Follow this down to gate; keep ahead to pass between 2 houses. When you reach drive, bear **L** and walk down to the road, where you turn **R** to return past small whitewashed **chapel**, to start.

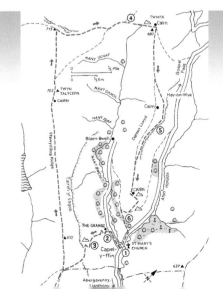

367 MONTGOMERY *MARCHER LORDS LAND*

4½ miles (7.2km) 2hrs 30min **Ascent:** 853ft (260m) ▲
Paths: Well-defined paths, farm tracks and country lanes, 3 stiles
Suggested map: aqua3 OS Explorer 216 Welshpool & Montgomery
Grid reference: SJ 224963
Parking: Car park on Bishops Castle Street on B4385 at south end of town

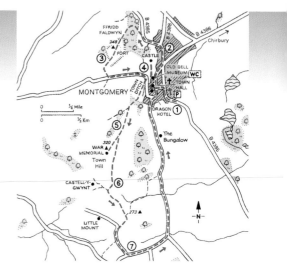

Iron-Age and medieval castles and views across a wide landscape.

❶ Montgomery is a fine country town with its origins in medieval times. Tucked beneath a castle-topped crag, many of the houses have Georgian façades but these are additions to older dwellings and the town is definitely worth exploring. From car park head north, then **L** along Broad Street, where you'll see **Dragon Hotel** and **town hall**. A signpost points to lane up to **castle** – a must see and free. Retrace your steps to **town hall** and head north up Arthur Street, past **Old Bell Museum**, and join main road, Princes Street.

❷ Continue north, ignoring turn for Chirbury, then turn **L** out of town along Station Road, B4385. Ignore 1st footpath on **L** side of road, but go over stile and cross field at 2nd stile. Path climbs through woodland, then swings **L** (southwest) to reach old hilltop fort above Ffridd Faldwyn.

❸ Go over stile at far side of fort and descend across more fields to roadside gate. Turn **L** down road, which takes you back towards **Montgomery**.

❹ As road turns sharp **R** just above town, leave it for footpath on **R** ('Montgomeryshire War Memorial') beginning beyond kissing gate. Footpath climbs steadily up hill to join farm track, which runs parallel to **Town Ditch** at first.

❺ As it enters high pastures, track begins to level out and traverse eastern hillside. Here you can detour to **war memorial** that lies clearly ahead at top of hill. Return to track and follow it through gate and past some pens with gorse and hawthorn lining way on L.

❻ In field above **Castell-y-gwynt farm**, on R-H side of path, footpath turns **R** to follow hedge. Go over stile at far side of field and turn **L** along a farm lane that descends to join narrow tarmac country lane southwest of **Little Mount** farm. Turn **L** along this.

❼ Turn **L** at 1st T-junction and **L** at 2nd. Follow lane back into **Montgomery**.

368 POWIS CASTLE *THE MONTGOMERY CANAL*

4 miles (6.4km) 2hrs **Ascent:** 262ft (80m) ▲
Paths: Tarmac drive, field path, canal tow path, 2 stiles
Suggested map: aqua3 OS Explorer 216 Welshpool & Montgomery
Grid reference: SJ 226075
Parking: Large pay car park off Church Street, Welshpool

See how the Earls of Powis lived as you walk through their deer park and past their huge red palace on the hill.

❶ From main car park, pass **tourist information centre** then go **L** along Church Street. At crossroads in centre of town turn **R** up Broad Street, which later becomes High Street.

❷ Just beyond **town hall** turn **L** past small car parking area and then pass through impressive wrought iron gates of **Powis Castle Estate**. Now follow tarmac drive through park grounds and past **Llyn Du** (black lake).

❸ Take **R** fork, high road, which leads to north side of castle. You can detour from the walk here to visit the world-famous gardens and castle with its fine paintings and furniture and works of Indian art collected by Robert Clive. Continue on walk on high road and follow it past 2 more pools on L and **Ladies Pool** on R to reach country lane.

❹ Turn **L** along lane. Opposite next estate entrance leave lane for path on **R** which follows dirt track across field. Track turns **L** over bridge and into another field. Here you follow fence on R and cut diagonally across fields to step stile in far corner. Over this, clear sunken grass track continues across another field to reach country lane close to **Montgomery Canal**. It was built by three different companies and was opened in stages from 1796. The canal is gradually being restored and you may see narrowboats cruising along this section.

❺ Turn **L** along lane before taking a path on **L** which descends to canal tow path at **Belan Locks**. Head north along canal, passing close to some half-timbered cottages. Pass **Powysland Museum and Canal Centre**, with its exhibits of local agriculture and crafts and canal and railway systems, to reach wharf and aqueduct at Welshpool. Turn **L** here along tarred path to return to car park.

369 PISTYLL RHAEADR *AND CADAIR BERWYN*

5 miles (8km) 3hrs **Ascent:** 1,870ft (570m) ▲
Paths: Well-defined paths and tracks, 6 stiles
Suggested map: aqua3 OS Explorer 255 Llangollen & Berwyn
Grid reference: SJ 076293
Parking: Car park 220yds (201m) before Tan-y-pistyll farm/café, where there's another pay car park

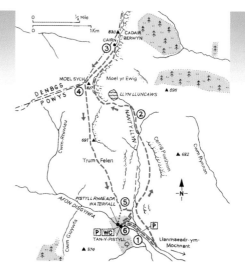

This demanding, but short, walk brings magnificent views and spectacular falls.

❶ From more easterly, and smaller, of 2 car parks turn **R** along road for 400yds (366m), then go through farm gate to follow wide grassy track that climbs northwest to enter cwm of **Nant y Llyn**. Here track heads north towards crags of **Cerrig Poethion**. Ignore path down to sheepfold by banks of stream below.

❷ The track degenerates into path that traverses hillsides scattered with gorse. Higher up it fords 2 outlet streams of **Llyn Lluncaws** before reaching moss and heather cwm of tarn. Now path climbs south of lake and up shale and grass spur to base of **Moel Sych's** crags. Follow path along edge of crags on **R** to reach col between **Moel Sych** and **Cadair Berwyn**. From here climb to rocky south top of latter peak. The trip to trig point on Cadair Berwyn's lower north summit is straightforward but offers no advantages as a viewpoint.

❸ From south top retrace your footsteps to col, but this time instead of tracing cliff edge follow ridge fence to cairn on Moel Sych summit plateau.

❹ Waymarker by summit ladder stile points way south, descending across wide, peaty spur with moor grass, mosses and heather. Note path follows west side of fence, not east shown on current maps. Halfway down cross stile and follow east side of fence. Beyond 2nd stile path descends southeast into high moorland cwm of **Disgynfa**, where path is met by stony track that has climbed from base of falls.

❺ To make there-and-back detour to top of falls, ignore stony track, and instead go through gate into forest and follow path to river. If not, descend along previously mentioned track, which zig-zags way down before turning **R** to head for **Tan-y-pistyll** complex. Path to bottom of falls starting from café leads to footbridge across Afon Rhaeadr for best views.

❻ From café walk along road to car park.

Powys

CENTRAL BRECON BEACONS *Cwm Cynwyn*

9½ miles (15.3km) 5hrs 30min **Ascent:** 2,360ft (719m)
Paths: Mostly clear paths along broad grassy ridges, 3 stiles
Suggested map: aqua3 OS Outdoor Leisure 12 Brecon Beacons National Park
Grid reference: SH 039244
Parking: At Pont y Caniedydd and a few spaces at the head of the road

This walks follows airy ridges to some of the lesser-visited peaks of the Brecon Beacons.
❶ Cross bridge and climb steeply up road past **Bailea** on your L. Keep straight ahead at junction where road levels and follow stony track up to gate that leads on to open ground by a National Trust sign.
❷ Continue straight up track and then fork **R**, over stile, to climb more steeply on to crest of grassy ridge. Follow ridge along and then climb steeply up sharp snout of **Cribyn**. Bear **L** at summit and follow escarpment edge along, dropping steeply down into **Bwlch ar y Fan**.
❸ Cross track in saddle and climb steeply up hillside opposite. Bear around to **L** at top and continue up summit of **Fan y Big**. Keep ahead in same direction to drop steeply down broad grassy ridge. The going eases for a while, steepens for a short distance and then eases again. Continue until path drops steeply once more, to edge of open ground.

❹ Bear **L**, towards bottom, and follow path as it contours around hillside above wall. After short spell of walking alongside wall, it drops away to your R. Continue traversing until you see **ruined building** down to your R. Cross stile here and follow track down around bend by ruin. Continue to stream, which you ford.
❺ Climb up other side and turn **R** on to good track. Follow this into farmyard and turn **L**, through gate, on to grassy track. Continue upward to another gate, which leads out on to open ground at foot of **Cwmcynwyn**. Turn **R** and follow track back down to start and parking place.

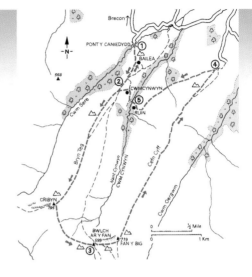

CENTRAL BRECON BEACONS *Pen Y Fan Pilgrimage*

5 miles (8km) 2hrs 30min **Ascent:** 1,610ft (491m)
Paths: Clearly defined tracks
Suggested map: aqua3 OS Outdoor Leisure 12 Brecon Beacons National Park
Grid reference: SN 983203
Parking: Huge lay-by on the A470, opposite the Storey Arms and a public telephone box

A straightforward circuit that follows the main trade routes up on to the roof of the National Park.
❶ Cross over road and hop over stile next to telephone box. Follow clear, in places man-made, path up hillside, leaving plantation behind and crossing open moorland on southern flanks of **Y Gyrn** – rounded peak to your L. You'll soon gain ridge where you cross stile to drop easily down to infant **Taf Fawr river**.
❷ Continue up other side of valley and keep straight ahead until you reach escarpment edge above **Cwm Llwch**. Turn **R** to follow clear path upward to rocky summit plateau of **Corn Du**. Path slips easily around craggy outcrops on your L and leads you up to huge summit cairn.
❸ Route to **Pen Y Fan** is obvious from here. Drop into shallow saddle to east and continue easily on to summit. From here, you should have fine views of the

Malvern Hills, the Bristol Channel and South Wales. From huge cairn, retrace your steps back across Corn Du to **Bwlch Duwynt**, obvious saddle between summit of Corn Du and long ridge that runs south.
❹ Take main track downhill to **R**, ignoring another track that comes in from R. Follow track easily down for just over 1 mile (1.6km) until you see **Taf Fawr river** to your R. A short diversion will expose a great rocky picnic spot above a small **waterfall**. Continue down to ford river and go through kissing gate into main car park.
❺ Turn **R** into car park and follow it to its end where gravel footpath (signposted with **Taff Trail** waymark) takes over. Continue along side of plantation and cross road to return to start.

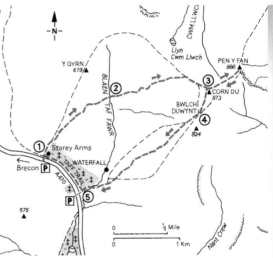

RHAYADER *Elan Valley Explorer*

5½ miles (8.8km) 2hrs 30min **Ascent:** 1,050ft (320m)
Paths: A mixture of good tracks and faint paths over featureless moorland that can be boggy, 1stile
Suggested map: aqua3 OS Explorer 200 Llandrindod Wells & Elan Valley
Grid reference: SN 899720
Parking: Small car park by the bridge at the start
Note: Navigation would be difficult in poor visibility

A simple circuit that explores some of the remote hillsides above the Elan Valley – a beautiful area around a chain of lakes.
❶ Turn **R** out of car park and cross over bridge. Turn **R** on to stony track and then follow it easily up into valley. As main track bears sharp L, keep straight ahead on very faint path that continues up valley. As you reach shallow pass at top, cross over to other side of valley.
❷ Here you'll locate good track that contours around to east and drops easily down into **Wye Valley**. At junction with another track, turn **L** and go through gate to drop into bottom **L-H** corner of field. Turn **R** here and continue into farmyard.
❸ Bear **L** and then **R** and continue along drive to 2nd turning on R, waymarked Wye Valley Walk. Turn **R** here and continue to drive of **Tymawr** on R. Walk up drive and past house to fork where you keep **L**.

Continue along this clear track, above small plantation, to stile.
❹ Go across this and then keep **L** to climb up towards obvious plateau at head of valley. Don't follow more obvious track, which clearly contours around head of valley. When you reach top, keep heading in same direction until you meet faint track and bank that run across hilltops.
❺ Turn **R** for few yards (metres) and then bear diagonally **L**, down open hillside, aiming for lowest point of road that you can see on opposite hillside. Contour around slightly and cross small stream. Continue in same direction, keeping to grassy hillside just above boggy hollow to your left.
❻ Turn **R** on to road and then fork **L** on to narrow path that runs parallel to road but below it. Follow this to Elan Valley Road and turn **R**, to climb up to junction, and then **L** to continue back to car park.

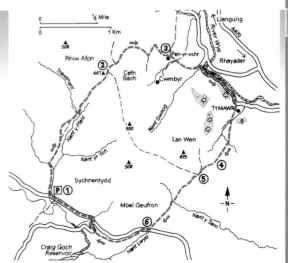

Gwynedd

373 ARAN FAWDDWY *To The Summit*

7½ miles (12.1km) 4hrs 30min **Ascent:** 2,625ft (800m)
Paths: Mostly clear paths, some crossing rough and boggy ground, 12 stiles
Suggested map: aqua3 OS Outdoor Leisure 23 Snowdonia
Grid reference: SH 854184
Parking: Grass verges at the top of Cwm Cywarch
Note: Do not tackle in poor visibility and due to the challenging nature of the ground, this walk should not be undertaken by inexperienced walkers as good navigation skills are required

Head for the summit on this rough and ready tramp on to the highest Welsh mountain south of Snowdon.

1 From your parking place walk along road, towards head of valley, and pass footbridge on your R (note that this is your return route). Keep R to walk beneath farm buildings on your L and then continue, in same direction, with wall now on your L. Follow wall around to L and then follow waymarks R to climb towards stream in apex of valley.
2 Cross over stream and turn L to follow it up on to boggy plateau. Continue with fence on your L to **pond** and then turn R to follow waymarked permissive path. Keep fence to your L and continue upward, over railway sleepers, which make easy work of boggy ground. Cross over stile directly ahead and then ignore next one to keep fence to your L. Go across another

stile and then continue over rocky ground to reach summit of **Aran Fawddwy** – enjoy the magnificient views and the opportunity to rest for a while.
3 Retrace your steps to stile and then bear **L** to descend on to obvious grassy spur of **Drysgol**. Pass the **memorial** stone to Mike Aspain – a member of the RAF St Athan mountain rescue team who was killed by lightning at this spot – on your R and then bear **R**, away from fence, to traverse slightly before dropping down steeply on grassy slope. This leads on to broad boggy saddle with waymarked footpath dropping down to **R**.
4 Follow this down, around hillside, with stunning views across valley, and then cross 2 stiles at bottom. Swing **R** and then **L** and continue to footbridge you passed on outward leg. Cross this and turn **L** on to road to return to start.

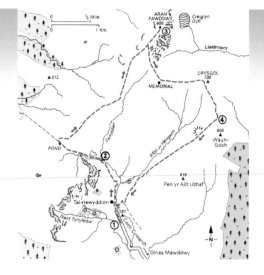

374 CADAIR IDRIS *Cwm Cau Horseshoe*

6½ miles (10.4km) 4hrs 30min **Ascent:** 3,120ft (950m)
Paths: Mostly clear rocky tracks, some are quite exposed. 6 stiles
Suggested map: aqua3 OS Outdoor Leisure 23 Snowdonia; Cadair Idris
Grid reference: SH 732115
Parking: Large car park at the start

A rocky ramble to the summit of Cadair Idris via one of Wales's most beautiful cwms.

1 Turn R out of car park on to road, and walk for 300 yards (274m) to gates of **Minffordd Estate**. Turn R through these and follow tree-lined path upwards to gate that leads into **Nature Reserve**. Continue steeply up through wood, with gushing **Nant Cadair** to your R. Eventually you'll pass through another gate and out on to open ground by banks of stream.
2 Don't cross over stream, but instead continue up its west bank and follow path around to **L**, beneath rocky ridge. When path splits, fork **L** (straight ahead to lake shore) and then climb steeply up on to ridge. Bear around to **R** at top and follow cliff line upward to step stile on summit of **Mynydd Pencoed**.
3 Cross over stile and drop down, still following cliff line, into broad saddle. Continue upwards again, on well cairned path that leads directly to trig point atop **Penygadair's** summit. Drop down from summit to

east (effectively straight ahead) and follow northern escarpment along, over 1 small summit, to 2nd highpoint of **Mynydd Moel**, where you will find small stone shelter.
4 Turn **R** here (path's quite faint) and drop down grassy spur. As gradient increases, path becomes clearer, crossing stile and winding easily down heather-covered hillside. This eventually leads to **Nant Cadair**, which you cross to rejoin outward path.
5 Turn **L** and retrace your earlier footsteps back down through wood. Instead of returning all way to road, as you leave woods turn **L**, and follow waymarked track back to car park.

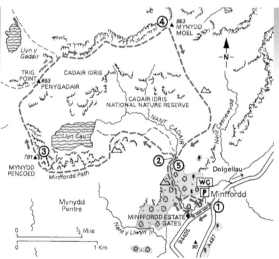

375 LLANBERIS *The Long Way*

10 miles (16.1km) 6hrs 30min **Ascent:** 3,839ft (1,170m)
Paths: Well-defined paths and tracks
Suggested map: aqua3 OS Explorer OL17 Snowdon
Grid reference: SH 577604 **Parking:** Several car parks throughout Llanberis

A route on one of Snowdon's quieter ridges.

1 From **Tourist Information Centre** in **Llanberis**, head south along High Street (Stryd Fawr) before turning R up Capel Coch Road. Go ahead at junction, where road changes name to Stryd Ceunant, and continue past **youth hostel** climbing towards **Brych y Foel**, northeast spur of **Moel Eilio**.
2 Where tarmac ends at foot of **Moel Eilio**, continue along track, which swings **L** (southeast) into wild cwm of **Afon Arddu**.
3 At base of **Foel Goch's** northern spur, Cefn Drum, track swings **R** into Maesgwm and climbs to pass named **Bwlch Maesgwm**, between Foel Goch and **Moel Cynghorion**. Go through gate then turn **L** for steep climb by fence and up latter-mentioned peak.
4 From Cynghorion's summit route descends along top of cliffs of **Clogwyn Llechwedd Llo** to another pass, Bwlch Cwm Brwynog, overlooking small reservoir of Llyn Ffynnon-y-gwas. Here join **Snowdon Ranger Path**.

5 Follow zig-zag route up **Clogwyn Du'r Arddu**, whose cliffs, on L, plummet to little tarn, Llyn Du'r Arddu, in dark stony cwm. Near top wide path veers **R**, away from edge, meets **Snowdon Mountain Railway**, and follows line to monolith at **Bwlch Glas**. Here you are met by both Llanberis Path and Pyg Track and look down on huge cwms of Glaslyn and Llyn Llydaw.
6 The path follows line of railway to summit. Retrace your steps to Bwlch Glas, but this time follow wide **Llanberis Path** on western slopes of **Carnedd Ugain** and above railway. (Don't mistake this for higher ridge path to Carnedd Ugain's summit.)
7 Near **Clogwyn Station** come to Cwm Hetiau, where cliffs fall away into chasm of Pass of Llanberis. Path goes under railway and passes below Clogwyn Station before recrossing line near **Halfway Station**.
8 Path meets lane beyond **Hebron**, and descends back into **Llanberis** near Royal Victoria Hotel. Turn **L** on main road, then **L** fork, to High Street and start .

Gwynedd

LLANSTUMDWY *LLOYD GEORGE COUNTRY*

6 miles (9.7km) 4hrs Ascent: Negligible ⚠

Paths: Generally well-defined paths and tracks, 6 stiles

Suggested map: aqua3 OS Explorer 254 Lleyn Peninsular East

Grid reference: SH 476383

Parking: Large car park at east end of village

Note: Small section of coast path is engulfed by high tides. Check times of tides before setting off

Following the last Liberal Prime Minister.

① Turn **R** out of car park and go through Llanystumdwy, past **museum** to bridge over **Afon Dwyfor**. Turn **R** along lane, then follow footpath on **L** past **memorial** and down to wooded river banks.

② After 2 miles (3.2km) path turns **R**, then tucks under stone archway to meet tarred drive to **Trefan** Hall. Turn **L** along this, continue to **B4411** and turn **R**.

③ Turn **R** down enclosed drive ('To Criccieth'). As another drive merges from L, turn half **L** along path shaded by rhododendrons. After few paces, go through kissing gate, then cross field guided by fence on L. Go through another kissing gate path veers half **R**, following fence now on R.

④ Beyond another gate, now sketchy route cuts diagonally (southeast) across 2 fields to rejoin **B4411**, just 1 mile (1.6km) north of **Criccieth**. Follow **B4411** into town. Keep straight on at crossroads, with main street, to reach promenade east of **castle**.

⑤ Follow coast road as it climbs past **castle** and bears **R** towards railway line. Take bridleway parallel to railway past **Muriau**, followed by footpath to track north of **Cefn Castell**. Here turn **R**, nearly to railway, then **L** back to coast, east of **Ynysgain Fawr** farm. Follow coast path west along grasslands and gorse scrub to estuary of **Dwyfor**, past crumbled sea defences. Alternatively, if open, pick up coast path from **Criccieth**, without diversions inland. At low tide you can go along sands.

⑥ At ladder stile follow wall back towards **Llanystumdwy**. The route becomes farm track that cuts under railway and passes through yard of **Aberkin** farm before reaching main road.

⑦ Cross main road with care and go through gate opposite. Short path leads to unsurfaced lane to village centre. Turn **R** for car park.

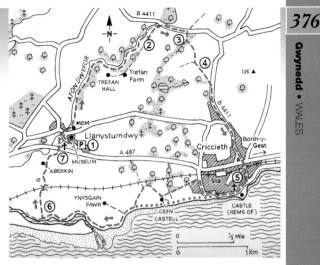

CNICHT *TACKLING THE KNIGHT*

6½ miles (10.4km) 4hrs Ascent: 2,297ft (700m) ⚠

Paths: Mostly well-defined, but sketchy by Bwlch y Battel, 9 stiles

Suggested map: aqua3 OS Explorer OL17 Snowdon

Grid reference: SH 631484

Parking: Limited roadside parking at Gelli-lago; car park 1 mile (1.6km) to south (grid ref SH 620467)

An exhilarating climb to one of the peaks.

① If you couldn't park at start of walk, you'll need to walk north from car park for about 1 mile (1.6km) up road before turning **R**, along track to **Gelli-lago** (cottage). Go through gate to **R** of farmhouse, then go through another gate on to footbridge across stream. Gravel path winds up hillside with stream on L and **Cnicht** on horizon ahead.

② Beyond ladder stile in cross-wall, path veers to **R**, climbing to wild pass of **Bwlch y Battel**. Path peters out, but stay on marshy route between high rocky hillsides. Keep to **L** of tarn, which lies just other side of pass. Soon well-defined track begins and runs alongside foot of **Cnicht's** south ridge to reach and join main Croesor to **Cnicht** route.

③ Here double-back along path climbing along crest of **Cnicht's** south ridge. On nearing top path divides, both routes reach summit after weaving between rocks.

④ Continue, passing **Llyn Biswail** on L and **Llyn Cwm-y-foel** on R, to reach cairn on col overlooking **Llyn yr Adar**.

⑤ Descend **L** (north) to traverse marshy grasslands to east of large tarn, **Llyn yr Adar**. Path veers northwest beyond northern shores before veering north and following grassy shelf in rocks of Y Cyrniau.

⑥ At natural grassy dry hollow, path turns sharp **L** to descend westwards towards **Llyn Llagi** – almost circular tarn. Beyond it path traverses rough pastures studded with heather, rock, crumbling walls and occasional tree. It stays roughly parallel to outflow stream of Llyn Llagi.

⑦ After going over stile and passing to **R** of **Llwynyrhwch** farm, which is surrounded by oak and rhododendron, take path leading across fields to Nantmor road. Turn **L** along road, and pass old converted chapel. If you couldn't park near Gelli-lago, you'll have to continue for 1 mile (1.6km) to car park.

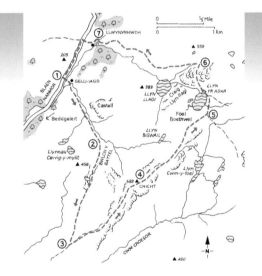

ABERGLASLYN *COPPER IN THE HILLS*

4 miles (6.4km) 2hrs 30min Ascent: 1,181ft (360m) ⚠

Paths: Well-maintained paths and tracks, 2 stiles

Suggested map: aqua3 OS Explorer OL17 Snowdon

Grid reference: SH 597462

Parking: National Trust pay car park, Aberglaslyn

Note: Short section of riverside path in Aberglaslyn gorge is difficult and requires use of handholds

A walk up to the old copper mines.

① Path starts to **L** of toilet block and goes under old railway bridge, before climbing through **Cwm Bychan**. After short climb path continues past iron pylons of aerial cableway.

② Beyond pylons, keep to **R** of cwm, ignoring paths forking L. Grassy corridor leads to col and stile in fence that is not shown on current maps. Turn **L** beyond stile and head for 3-way footpath signpost by rocks of **Grib Ddu**.

③ Follow path on **L** ('To Beddgelert and Sygun') and go over another ladder stile. After veering **L**, around small rocky knoll, path winds steeply down hillside to cairn at **Bwlch-y-Sygun**. Here you'll see a shallow peaty pool in green hollow to L.

④ Path now heads southwest along mountain's northwestern 'edge', overlooking **Beddgelert**. Take **L** fork to pass signpost; follow 'Beddgelert' direction.

⑤ Watch out for large cairn, highlighting turn-off **R** for **Beddgelert**. Clear stony path weaves through rhododendron and rock, goes through kissing gate in wall half-way down, then descends further to edge of **Beddgelert**, where little lane passing cottage of Penlan leads to **Afon Glaslyn**.

⑥ Turn **L** to follow river for short way. Don't cross footbridge over river but turn **L** through kissing gate to follow Glaslyn's east bank. The path joins and follows trackbed of old Welsh Highland Railway.

⑦ Just before 1st tunnel, descend **R** to follow rough path down to river. Handholds screwed into rocks allow passage on difficult but short section. Path continues through riverside woodland and over boulders to **Pont Aberglaslyn**.

⑧ Here, turn **L** up steps and follow dirt path through woods. After crossing railway trackbed turn **R**, then **R** again to go under old railway bridge back to car park.

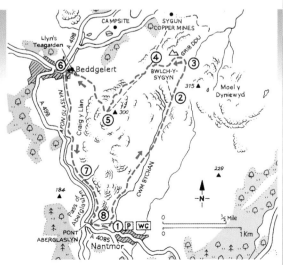

Gwynedd

379 ROMAN STEPS WITH THE DROVERS

7 miles (11.3km) 4hrs Ascent: 1,575ft (480m)

Paths: Peaty paths through heather and farm tracks, 11 stiles
Suggested map: aqua3 OS Explorer OL18 Harlech, Porthmadog & Bala
Grid reference: SH 646314
Parking: Llyn Cwm Bychan

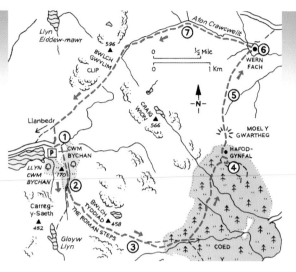

Along one of Snowdonia's oldest highways.

❶ Go through gate at back of car park at **Llyn Cwm Bychan**, and over paved causeway across stream. Beyond stile path climbs up through woodland.

❷ Over stile leave woodland behind and cross stream on small bridge. Path nicks **R** to go through gap in wall, then **L** again, heading towards Rhinog rocks. It slowly veers **L** and, now slabbed with '**steps**', climbs through heather-clad rocky ravine to enter nature reserve. Steps continue to climb to cairn marking highest point along rocky pass of **Bwlch Tyddiad**.

❸ Over col, continue along path which descends into grassy moorland basin beneath **Rhinog Fawr** then, beyond a stile, enter conifers of **Coed y Brenin** plantation. Well-defined footpath tucks away under trees and eventually comes to wide flinted forestry road, along which you turn **L**.

❹ After about 1 mile (1.6km) road swings **R** to head east, watch out for waymarked path on **L** that will

eventually take you out of forest. After a short way along this path, waymark guides route **L**, then another to **R** to pass ruins of **Hafod-Gynfal**. Beyond this head north to go over ladder stile and out of forest.

❺ There's no path across grassy moor of **Moel y Gwartheg**. Just head north here, with cliffs of **Craig Wion** well to your **L** and bridge across huge expanse of **Llyn Trawsfynydd** at 5 minutes past hour.

❻ Further downhill fence on L-H side guides you down towards isolated cottage of **Wern Fach**. Cross over stile just short of cottage, then turn **L** uphill, following clear waymarks which will guide you over 1st of many ladder stiles.

❼ Wet moorland footpath climbs up to lonely col of **Bwlch Gwylim**, narrow pass between **Clip** and **Craig Wion**. Here **Cwm Bychan** and start of walk come back into view. Footpath now descends to southwest, through heather, before turning **R** to head down slopes back to car park.

380 NANTCOL HIGH LAKES AND HIGHWAYMEN

5½ miles (8.8km) 3hrs 30min Ascent: 1,378ft (420m)

Paths: Peaty paths through heather and farm tracks, 1 stile
Suggested map: aqua3 OS Explorer OL18 Harlech, Porthmadog & Bala
Grid reference: SH 633259
Parking: Small fee for parking at Cil-cychwyn farm

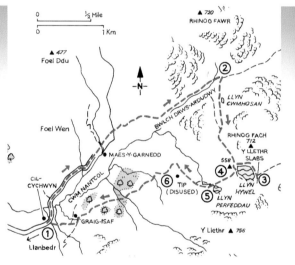

Wild Nantcol and a lake between two peaks.

❶ From farm at **Cil-cychwyn**, follow narrow lane, which bends **L** to cross Afon Cwmnantcol at Pont Cerrig (bridge) before resuming its course up valley. At road's terminus near **Maes-y-garnedd** farm, continue climb on wallside path through upper Nantcol. It traverses lower south flanks of **Rhinog Fawr** before entering dark pass of **Bwlch Drws-Ardudwy**. This was a drovers' route along which cattle would have been driven to markets in the Marches and the Midlands, and consequently the haunt of highwaymen.

❷ On reaching marshy basin beneath **Rhinog Fawr** and **Rhinog Fach** go over ladder stile in wall on **R**. Follow narrow path climbing through heather and passing west shores of **Llyn Cwmhosan**, and beneath boulder and screes of Rhinog Fach's west face. Beyond this, route comes to shores of **Llyn Hywel**.

❸ For best views follow path, bouldery in places, around north and east sides of tarn to reach top of

huge **Y Llethr Slabs**, that plummet into lake. You could do a complete circuit of Llyn Hywel, but this would mean climbing much higher up the slopes of Y Llethr. It is much easier to retrace your steps to the lake's outlet point, then continue along west shores.

❹ Turn **R** to follow sketchy narrow path down to Llyn **Perfeddau** which is visible from top. Intermittent peat path descends through heather, which is mixed with tussocky grass little further down, to reach north shores of lake.

❺ Follow wall running behind lake then, after ½ mile (800m), go through gap in wall to follow grassy path that rounds rocky knoll high above **Nantcol** before passing old mine. Here path becomes prominent track that winds past mine workings before veering **L** (west southwest) to descend gradually into Nantcol's valley.

❻ Through woodland and high pasture, track passes **Graig-Isaf** farm before reaching valley road at Cil-cychwyn.

381 BARMOUTH THE SUBLIME MAWDDACH

6 miles (9.7km) 4hrs Ascent: 656ft (200m)

Paths: A bridge, good tracks and woodland paths, 5 stiles
Suggested map: aqua3 OS Explorer OL23 Cadair Idris & Llyn Tegid
Grid reference: SH 613155
Parking: Car park on seafront

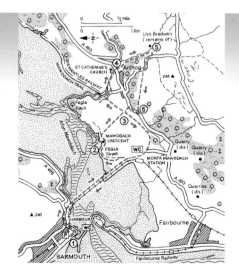

Follow in the illustrious footsteps of Wordsworth, Darwin and Ruskin on this lovely watery walk.

❶ Follow promenade round **harbour**, then go over footbridge across estuary (toll). On reaching path along south shore of estuary, turn **L** to follow grassy embankment that leads to track rounding wooded knoll of **Fegla Fawr**.

❷ When it comes to terraced houses of **Mawddach Crescent**, follow track that passes to rear of houses. Ignore tarmac lane going **R**, but continue along shoreline until you reach gate on **R** marking start of a good path heading across marshes of Arthog.

❸ Turn **L** along old railway track, then leave it just before crossing of little Arthog Estuary and turn **R** along tarmac lane that passes small car park. Turn **L** over ladder stile and follow raised embankment to wall, which now leads path to main Dolgellau road next to **St Catherine's Church**.

❹ Turn **L** along road past church, then cross road for footpath beginning with some steps into woodland. A good waymarked path now climbs by **Arthog**. Here you are presented with an elevated view of all that you have seen so far, the estuary, the sandbars, the mountains and the yawning bridge. This is the landscape that inspired artists like JMW Turner and Richard Wilson who came to capture the beauty and changing light of the area.

❺ Beyond stile at top of woods, turn **R** to reach lane. Turn **R** along descending lane, then **L** along stony track passing cottage of **Merddyn**. Path leaves track on **L** and descends into more woodland, beneath boulders of old quarry and down to Dolgellau road by Arthog Village Hall.

❻ Turn **R** along road, then **L** along path back to railway track and Mawddach Trail. Turn **L** along trail and follow it past **Morfa Mawddach Station** and back across **Barmouth's** bridge.

Gwynedd

PRECIPICE WALK *ON THE EDGE*

3 miles (4.8km) 2hrs **Ascent:** Negligible
Paths: Stony tracks and good paths, 8 stiles
Suggested map: aqua3 OS Explorer OL18 Harlech, Porthmadog & Bala
Grid reference: SH 745211 **Parking:** Coed y Groes car park on Dolgellau–Llanfachreth road
Note: Wear strong footwear as part of route follows narrow path with big drops down to Mawddach Valley. Not a walk for vertigo sufferers.

A balcony route with spectacular views of valley, mountain and estuary.
1 To begin walk, turn **L** out of car park on to **L-H** fork, Tyn y Groes road. Turn **L** again, along track ('**The Precipice Walk**'), and follow it through trees. The Precipice Walk is a private path around Nannau Estate, but its use has been authorised by the estate owners since 1890, on the basis that all walkers observe the country code. It has been one of Dolgellau's most famous attractions since the Victorian tourists came for their constitutional perambulations. Track swings **R** at the edge of fields. Across is the 18th-century mansion of **Nannau**.
2 Where track comes to estate cottage, Gwern-offeiriad, turn **L** off it and follow clear path with several stiles leading to hillside north of **Llyn Cynwch**.
3 Footpath signpost highlights hill path on **R**. This doubles back to climb hillside northwards by side of

dry-stone wall.
4 Beyond stile footpath climbs over crag-studded hill, with open slopes that give fine views across green valley below to village of Llanfachreth and rugged mountainsides of Rhobell Fawr and Dduallt that lie behind. The footpath edges round **Foel Cynwch** and passes Sitka spruce woodlands of **Coed Dol-y-clochydd**. Over another stile the route continues, now as dramatic, but even, ledge path traversing the high hill slopes above the **Mawddach Valley**. After scaling another ladder stile, footpath veers **L** to finally leave precipices behind. It heads and arcs round to southern side of **Foel Faner**, where it crosses high fields, straddles another stile, then descends **L** along a well-defined path that traces western shores of **lake**.
5 The path meets outward route by hill footpath sign. Retrace outward route past estate cottage of Gwern-offeiriad and through woods back to car park.

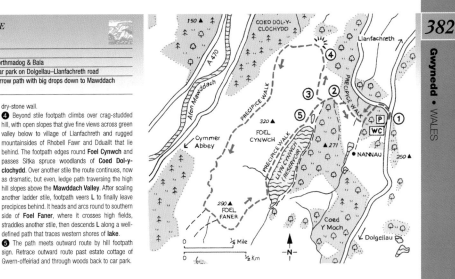

BALA *A VIEW OF BALA'S LAKE*

5 miles (8km) 3hrs **Ascent:** 656ft (200m)
Paths: Woodland and field paths, 8 stiles
Suggested map: aqua3 OS Explorer OL23 Cadair Idris & Llyn Tegid
Grid reference: SH 929361 **Parking:** Car park at entrance to Bala town from east

The best view of Wales' largest natural lake.
1 Go to northeast side of car park in **Bala** to access riverside path, where you turn **R** to follow raised embankment along west bank of **Tryweryn**. After dog-leg to **R**, which passes through 2 kissing gates, footpath continues, first by banks of **Tryweryn**, then by north banks of **Dee**.
2 At road by Bala's lake, **Llyn Tegid**, turn **L** then **R** along Llangower road. Go through kissing gate to cross small field to **Bala Station** on **Bala Lake Railway**. Footbridge allows you to cross track before traversing 2 small fields.
3 Turn **R** along cart track, and pass behind **Bala Lake Hotel**. Waymarker points direction up grassy bank on **L**, and path continues southwest, accompanied by fence on **R**.
4 After crossing stream, next to little cottage on R-H side, route comes upon area of rough pastureland interspersed with outcrops of rock, rushes and bracken. Here footpath on ground all but disappears.

Ascend half **L** (roughly southwards) to reach fenceline at top, then aim for ladder stile in middle distance.
5 Turn **L** along tarred lane just before that ladder stile. Where road ends take **R** fork track that ploughs through recently felled conifer plantation.
6 At whitewashed house of **Encil y Coed**, turn **L** off track to climb **L-H** of 2 ladder stiles, then follow grooved grass track heading north across high pastures. Where track bends to **R** leave it to descend steeply to another ladder stile. Well-waymarked path continues north, with **Bala** town below.
7 Go over partially hidden step stile into commercial forestry plantations of **Coed Pen-y-Bont**. Narrow footpath descends to bottom edge of woods (ignore forestry track you meet on way down).
8 At bottom of woods turn **R** along track to road by **Pen-y-Bont Campsite**. Turn **L** along road, walking back towards town, then turn **L** again to follow lakeside footpath past **information centre**. At main road, turn **R** to explore town centre.

THE DYSYNNI VALLEY *CASTELL Y BERE*

5 miles (8km) 3hrs **Ascent:** 656ft (200m)
Paths: Field paths and tracks, 16 stiles
Suggested map: aqua3 OS Explorer OL23 Cadair Idris & Llyn Tegid
Grid reference: SH 677069
Parking: Car park in Pandy Square, Abergynolwyn village centre

Exploring the valleys where the Welsh princes held out against the might of Edward I.
1 Cross road to **Railway Inn** and take lane ('**Llanfihangel**'). At far side of bridge over **Dysynni** river, turn **R** through kissing gate and trace north banks. Beyond 2nd step stile, path turns **L** before climbing steps beside tall leylandii to reach lane.
2 Turn **R** along lane which heads east through Dysynni Valley and beneath woodlands of **Coed Meriafel**. At junction with B4405 turn **L**, over stile and climb northwest across field. Continue over 2 more stiles to woodland path. Climb along this to reach forestry track near top edge of woods.
3 Turn **L** along track which climbs out of woods before veering **R** to gate and stile. Over stile, follow wall on **L**. Ignore faint grass track that goes ahead and across field. The route stays low and veers **L** through high grassy cwm with stream developing on **L**.
4 After traversing several fields, path joins flinted

track but leaves it after 200yds (183m) for streamside path on **L**. This descends into woods and stays close to stream. After passing several cascades it comes out of woods to reach track leading to road at Llanfihangel-y-pennant just opposite **chapel**.
5 Turn **L** past chapel and **Castell y Bere** (detour through gates on **R** for closer look). Just beyond castle, take path on **L** that climbs to gate at top R-H corner of field. Beyond gate turn **R** along barn track passing **Caerberllan** farm to road. Turn **R** along road, **L** at crossroads and cross **Pont Ystumanner** (bridge).
6 On other side, footpath highlights track continues on **L** to pass **Rhiwlas** farm then continues as green path high above river. Path crosses slopes of **Gamallt** and swings gradually **L** with valley.
7 Beyond river gorge, path approaches back of **Abergynolwyn** village and turns **L** to cross old iron bridge across river. Beyond it, turn **R** along unsurfaced street to return to village centre.

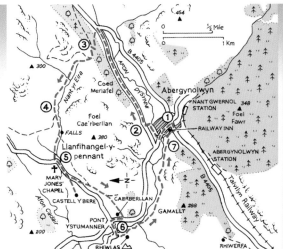

Gwynedd

385 DOLGELLAU *THE KING'S FOREST*

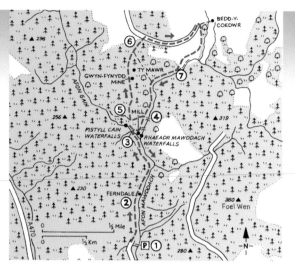

4 miles (6.4km) 2hrs **Ascent:** 660ft (200m) ⚠

Paths: Forest tracks and paths, 2 stiles

Suggested map: aqua3 OS Explorer OL18 Harlech, Porthmadog & Bala

Grid reference: SH 735263

Parking: Tyddyn Gwladys forest Car Park near Ganllwyd

Two waterfalls, hidden deep in the forest.

❶ Turn **R** out of car park and follow flinted forestry track with **Afon Mawddach** below **R**. Track passes beneath terraced Mostyn cottages.

❷ Take higher track to **L** of **Ferndale** holiday cottages – once gold mine workshops and blasting plant. Gold has been mined throughout Wales for centuries, but there were large finds of good quality gold in the 19th century, when Dolgellau became another Klondyke. Track eventually swings **R** to cross **Afon Gain**, close to its confluence with **Mawddach**.

❸ On reaching other side, detour **L** along rough path to take a closer look at **Pistyll Cain** waterfalls. The impressive cascades splash 150ft (45m) against dark rocks into a deep pool below. Return to main track, and turn **L** to old mine's **mill** buildings.

❹ Just beyond mill are **Rhaeadr Mawddach falls**. Ignore footbridges here and double back **L** on slaty path climbing through conifer plantation – ignore

cycle route on **R**, near beginning of this path.

❺ After winding up hillside, path comes to junction. Ignore signed footpath going straight ahead, but turn **R** on track with white-topped post (no 30). This soon becomes grassy path that comes out of forest at small gate, and continues as enclosed track through high pastures in area that was once main **Gwynfynydd Mine**. Track passes above **Ty Mawr** farm, and becomes tarred lane.

❻ Turn **R** on meeting country lane and follow it almost to **Bedd y Coedwr** farm. Footpath signpost points way downhill on field path that stays to R of some attractive birchwoods. Path veers **R** through heather-cloaked scrub and becomes rough and overgrown in places until it reaches old mine track by banks of Mawddach.

❼ Follow track past shafts of gold mines to reach outward route by **Rhaeadr Mawddach**. Retrace your steps to car park.

386 TANYGRISIAU *TACKLING THE BIG MOELWYN*

6 miles (9.7km) 4hrs 30mins **Ascent:** 2100ft (640m) ⚠

Paths: Mountain paths lanes, and quarry tracks, 5 stiles

Suggested map: aqua3 OS Explorers OL17 Snowdon & OL18 Harlech, Porthmadog & Bala

Grid reference: SH 682453 (on Explorer OL17) **Parking:** Small car park near start of Stwlan Dam road

Above the Glaslyn Estuary and Ffestiniog.

❶ Turn **R** out of car park then **L** across road bridge over river. Turn **L** at junction on other side. Where lane ends, continue along quarry road, climbing alongside stream to shores of **Llyn Cwmorthin**.

❷ Cross slate bridge spanning stream to pass beneath Cwmorthin Barracks and continue past derelict chapel. Track passes to **R** of more quarry buildings before arcing **L** past mountains of slag to reach high pass and vast quarry complex of **Rhosydd**.

❸ Climb on quarry incline behind ruined terrace building (barracks) to reach top pulley house. Here slaty track bends half **L** past more quarry buildings before heading for 2 huge pits.

❹ On approach to nearer pit at small cairn, turn **L** on grassy path heading for pass between **Moel-yr-Hydd** and **Moelwyn Mawr**. At pass climb **R** up grassy spur to summit of **Moelwyn Mawr**.

❺ From summit descend south on steep grassy slopes; continue with care on rough path over rocky

quartz-streaked ridge of **Craigysgafn** to reach **Bwlch Stwlan**, a grassy col beneath **Moelwyn Bach**.

❻ At col rake half **L** (NE) for 50yds/m, then descend **R** on faint path past south shores of **Llyn Stwlan** to dam. Path squeezes between wall-end of dam and rocky bluff. Turn **L**; follow steep path beneath dam.

❼ Turn **R** to follow fence by Stwlan's outlet stream, aiming for top of tramway. Wall on **L** leads route down hillside, through gap in wall corner and past bracken-infested ruins. Wall on **R** leads over rocky knoll down to footbridge over **Nant Ddu** stream. Do not cross, but turn **L** through tunnel in an old railway abutment. Beyond this path swings **L**, high above **Tanygrisiau Reservoir**, before crossing **Ffestiniog Railway** line (take care!). Stony track now follows shoreline towards **power station**.

❽ Turn **L** by power station on signposted path that re-crosses railway before climbing to metalled lane. Follow this and take **L** fork at road junction just above **visitor centre** before turning **L** back to car park.

387 TALSARNAU *THE TECWYN LAKES*

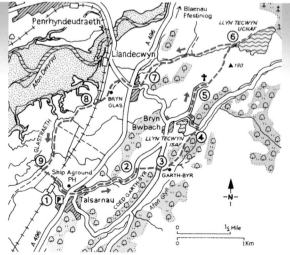

5 miles (8km) 3hrs **Ascent:** 800ft (244m) ⚠

Paths: Well-defined paths, lanes, 9 stiles

Suggested map: aqua3 OS Outdoor Leisure 18 Harlech, Porthmadog & Bala

Grid reference: SH 612360

Parking: Car park just off main road at Talsarnau

Unknown lakes and the breezy salt marshes.

❶ Turn **R** out of car park, then cross road. Climb lane opposite, then take **L** 'Llandecwyn' fork. Lane climbs hillsides and beneath **Coed Garth-byr** (woods).

❷ After about ¾ mile (1200m) go through small gate on signposted path that climbs hillside pasture with fence to **L**. Go through gate at top, into oakwoods. Through 3rd gate path descends to country lane.

❸ Across lane follow signposted track towards **Garth-byr** farm. Don't enter farm complex but turn **L** along grass path. Take higher **L** fork path 200yds (182m) beyond farmhouse, then take **R** of 2 gates. Path heads northeast through scrub. Crumbled wall joins from **L** and path follows it via thicker woodland. You can see **Llyn Tecwyn Isaf** through trees.

❹ Go over stile in wall and follow path to lane. Turn **L** along lane, round north shores of Llyn Tecwyn Isaf, then take lane on **R**, which climbs to Llandecwyn **church**, where tarmac ends.

❺ Continue along stony track, and go through gate to reach west shores of **Llyn Tecwyn uchaf**.

❻ Turn **L** along gated track that descends beneath pylons through narrow rocky valley. On nearing main road at bottom ignore grassy track to **R**, but climb ahead on grass path which passes **R** of outbuilding and **L** of cottage to reach lane in **Llandecwyn**.

❼ Turn **R** along this, cross main road and follow lane towards railway station. Turn **L** along lane with footpath sign, then climb ladder stile in front of **Bryn Glas** (cottage) and skirt base of rocky knoll beyond. Climb ladder stile, and cross railway (take care).

❽ Over another stile path follows flood embankment on edge of coastal marshes of **Glastraeth**. Across the wide estuary you can see Portmeirion and the mountains of Snowdonia, including Snowdon itself.

❾ Leave embankment on reaching stony track, which heads directly for houses of **Talsarnau**. Again cross railway with care and follow lane back to village.

ABERGWYNGREGYN *TWIN FALLS*

5 miles (8km) 3hrs **Ascent:** 820ft (250m) ⚠
Paths: Well-defined paths and farm tracks; 9 stiles
Suggested map: Aqua3 OS Explorer OL17 Snowdon
Grid reference: SH 783774
Parking: Small car park at entrance to glen. Large pay car park over bridge beyond

A fine mountain glen with two waterfalls
❶ Go through gate at south end of lower car park, and follow path through woods surrounding **Afon Rhaeadr**. Cross river on footbridge, go through gate at other side, and turn **R** to follow wide track heading south through pastures of valley.
❷ After passing under rows of pylons you reach visitor centre, which is housed in old farmstead of Nant Rhaeadr (marked Nant on maps). The glen is now part of the Coedydd Aber National Nature Reserve, which was set up in 1975 by the Nature Conservancy Council (now English Nature) as an example of a broad-leaved woodland habitat. The visitor centre explains the workings of the valley, past and present. Beyond Nant Rhaeadr path climbs steadily through valley with the top of the **Aber Falls** visible ahead.
❸ Path climbs up stone steps on last knoll before base of falls. Here continuing path turns **R**, over ladder stile, but first you will want to get nearer to falls. Short

detour descends into wooded hollow. Here the thunderous falls plummet hundreds of feet down cliffs of quartz-streaked Cambrian granophyre. Scrub birch trees eke out an existence high on the rock-ledges, as do liverworts, rare mosses and lichens, primroses and anemones. Return to ladder stile. On other side follow path marked 'North Wales Path only: no short return to Aber', which heads west beneath cliffs to pass beneath Rhaeadr Bach. (falls).
❹ Path swings N along western valley slopes and becomes track on slopes of Cae'r Mynydd. After rounding strip of conifer woods and passing sheep pens track veers **L**.
❺ Just before entering another conifer plantation turn **R** at junction of tracks to descend northwest towards northern tip of those same woods.
❻ Turn **R** on waymarked narrow path descending northeast down to Abergwyngregyn. On reaching lane turn **R** for short riverside walk to car park.

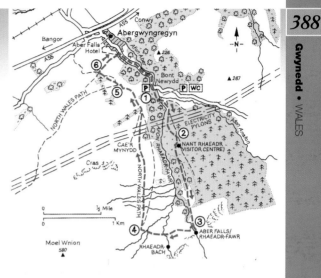

HOLYHEAD MOUNTAIN *LAST STOP BEFORE IRELAND*

4½ miles (7.2km) 2hrs 30min **Ascent:** 886ft (270m) ⚠
Paths: Well-maintained paths and tracks. Heathland, coastal cliffs and rocky hills
Suggested map: aqua3 OS Explorer 262 Anglesey West
Grid reference: SH 210818
Parking: RSPB car park

Rugged and rocky Holy Island offers some of the best walking in Anglesey.
❶ Take path signed for RSPB centre, past **Ellin's Tower**, small castellated building, then climb along path back to road which should be followed to its end.
❷ If you're not visiting **South Stack Lighthouse**, climb **R** on path passing concrete shelter. The path detours up to round BT aerials and dishes. At crossroads go **L**, heading back to coast, then take **L** fork. Ignore next **L**, dead end path. The footpath required works its way over north shoulder of **Holyhead Mountain**.
❸ Ignore paths to summit, but keep **L** on good path heading north towards **North Stack**.
❹ After passing through grassy walled enclosure path descends in zig-zags down some steep slopes before coming to rocky platform, where **Fog Signal Station** and island of **North Stack** come into full view. Retrace your steps back up zig-zags and towards

Holyhead Mountain.
❺ With summit path in sight, take a narrow path heading sharp **L** across heath. This joins another narrow path contouring round east side of mountain. Turn **R** along it, later ignoring another summit path coming in from **L**. Beyond mountain, take a **R** fork as path comes to a wall. Follow path downhill towards rough pastureland.
❻ Go down grassy walled track before turning **R** along another, similar one. This soon becomes rough path traversing more heathland, now to south of **Holyhead Mountain**.
❼ Near to **quarry** with lake, take path veering **R** alongside rocks of **Holyhead Mountain**. The BT aerials and dishes can be seen again on horizon by now. Follow paths towards them then, at crossroads, turn **L** and **L** again, along a concrete footpath leading back to road.
❽ Turn **L** along road to car park.

MOELFRE *THE ANCIENT VILLAGE*

3 miles (4.8km) 1hr 30min **Ascent:** Negligible ⚠
Paths: Well-defined coastal and field paths, 4 stiles
Suggested map: aqua3 OS Explorer 263 Anglesey East
Grid reference: SH 511862
Parking: Car park at entrance to village

Walk along Anglesey's beautiful east coast to discover a remarkably intact ancient village.
❶ From car park, follow main road down to shore. Here, main road swings **L** and uphill for village centre, leave it for shoreline path on **R**.
❷ Pass Seawatch Centre and lifeboat station and ignore footpath signs pointing inland. Instead follow a clear coast path that looks across to island of **Ynys Moelfre**. After passing to **R** of some terraced cottages and going through couple of kissing gates, path crosses **caravan site**. It then goes through another kissing gate and climbs past **Royal Charter** memorial to those who died when the British cutter was dashed on the rocks in a storm in 1859.
❸ After swinging **L** into **Porth Forllwyd**, go through gate and then through a narrow ginnel that rounds bay, past cottage of **Moryn** into bay of **Traeth Lligwy**.
❹ On reaching beach car park, turn **L** along narrow lane before going straight ahead at next crossroads.

❺ Take next path on **R** ('Din Lligwy'). Before visiting village you turn half **R** across field to old chapel, then half **L** towards woods, where you'll find **Din Lligwy**, a wonderfully preserved Celtic settlement dating back to the last years of the Roman Empire in the 4th century. Enter the foundations through thick rubble walls which would have been added as protection against the Romans. The circular huts inside were the living quarters, while the large rectangular hut you can see in the top R-H corner was the smelting workshop. Return to lane and turn **R** along it.
❻ After 275yds (251m), turn **L** along a signed footpath which, after an initial dog-leg to **R**, follows a field edge to roadside **quarry** at Aberstrecht.
❼ Turn **R** along lane, then **L** along a farm lane at Caeau-gleision. This brings you back to shoreline **caravan site** met earlier in walk.
❽ Turn **R** beyond it and follow shoreline path back to start.

391 CAPEL CURIG AN ALPINE JOURNEY

4 miles (6.4km) 2hrs **Ascent:** 295ft (90m) (doesn't include pinnacle scramble) ▲
Paths: Generally clear and surfaced, 9 stiles
Suggested map: aqua3 OS Explorer OL17 Snowdon
Grid reference: SJ 720582
Parking: Behind Joe Brown's shop at Capel Curig

Discovering the valley where the rocks and mountains provide challenging ground for today's climbers and mountaineers.

❶ The path begins at ladder stile by war memorial on A5 and climbs towards **Y Pincin** – large craggy outcrop cloaked in wood and bracken. Go over another stile and keep to north of outcrop. Those who want to go to top should do so from the northeast, where gradients are easier. It's fun, but take care! You'll need to retrace your steps.

❷ Continue east across woods and marshy ground, keeping to south of great crags of **Clogwyn Mawr**. On reaching couple of ladder stiles, ignore path back down to road, but maintain your direction across hillside.

❸ Just beyond footbridge over **Nant y Geuallt**, leave main footpath and follow less well-defined path across marshy ground. This veers southeast to cross another stream before coming to prominent track.

❹ Turn **R** along track, but leave it beyond ladder stile and at 4-way meeting of paths. Go **L** here and follow path down into some woods. Take **R-H** fork descending to road near **Ty'n y Coed Inn**.

❺ Turn **L** down road, then **R**, along lane over **Pont-Cyfyng**. Go **R** again beyond bridge to follow footpath that traces **Llugwy** to another bridge opposite Cobdens Hotel. Don't cross this time, but scramble **L** over some rocks before continuing through woods of **Coed Bryn-engan**, where path soon becomes wide track.

❻ After passing cottage of **Bryn-engan**, track comes to bridge at head of **Mymbyr** lakes. Turn **R** across it, then **L** along road for short way.

❼ Go over next ladder stile on **R-H** side of road and take higher of 2 tracks swinging round to **R**. This hugs foot of southern Glyder slopes.

❽ When you get beyond **Gelli** farm turn **R** to follow cart track back to car park.

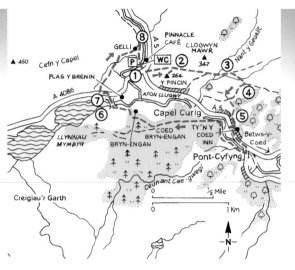

392 CAPEL CURIG Y FOEL GOCH

8 miles (12.8km) 5hrs **Ascent:** 2100ft (640m) ▲
Paths: Faint mountain paths and farm tracks, 5 stiles
Suggested map: aqua3 OS Explorer OL17
Grid reference: SJ 720582
Parking: Car park behind Joe Brown's in centre of Capel Curig

Superb panoramas unfold on this skyline walk along the quiet eastern end of the Glyder ridge.

❶ Turn **R** out of car park and follow gated stony track north past **Gelli** farm. Track bends **L** into widening valley of **Llugwy**. Pass beneath crags and cavernous cwm of **Gallt yr Ogof**. This stony track was the main route to Holyhead until the 19th century when engineer Thomas Telford built the A5. Beyond east buttress of Gallt yr Ogof track comes to campsite and farm of **Gwern Gof-isaf**.

❷ Just beyond farmhouse turn **L** over ladder stile and climb up rock and grass spur of **Braich y Ddeugwm**. Don't be enticed onto grassy shelves to west of spur – it's easy to do but you'll pay with a big climb back to crest later. If it's dry the rocks themselves make most pleasant walking surface on a fairly steep but spectacular climb.

❸ At top of spur, path arrives at shallow lakes of Llyn y Caseg-fraith, which lie at foot of bouldery slopes of **Glyder Fach**. However it's Tryfan that will capture your attention, with its grand buttresses and serrated summit crest. Beyond lakes turn **L** on faint path climbing grassy ridge to **Y Foel Goch** (summit).

❹ Path continues along ridge, then cuts across south side of **Gallt Yr Ogof**. Alternatively, stay on pathless ridge to summit (for views over **cwm**) then down easy grass slopes to rejoin main path.

❺ Go over ladder stile in dry-stone wall and continue along ridge (mostly on south side), then over another ladder stile in fence.

❻ Path weaves through rocky knolls of **Cafn y Capel** and becomes faint as it descends into valley. Farm of Gelli, passed on outward route, appears. Path on ground has disappeared now – just aim for junction of stony tracks just to north of farmhouse. Turn **R** along track heading south and on east side of farm to return to car park.

393 OGWEN THE DEVIL'S KITCHEN

3 miles (4.8km) 2hrs 30min **Ascent:** 1,706ft (520m) ▲
Paths: Well-defined paths, 2 stiles
Suggested map: aqua3 OS Explorer OL17 Snowdon
Grid reference: SH 649603
Parking: Small car park at Ogwen

Explore the most perfect hanging valley in Snowdonia – its rock ledges and Hanging Gardens.

❶ The Cwm Idwal nature trail starts to **L** of toilet block at Ogwen and climbs up hillside to pass some impressive waterfalls before turning **R** and continuing up hill.

❷ Go through a gate in a fence, which marks boundary of **National Nature Reserve**, and turn **L** along side of **Llyn Idwal's** eastern shores. The clear footpath climbs into dark shadows of Cwm Idwal.

❸ Now leave nature trail, which turns R to complete circuit around lake. Instead ascend beneath rock-climbing grounds of Idwal Slabs and across stream of Nant Ifan, beyond which footpath zig-zags up rough boulder ground to foot of **Twll Du** – Devil's Kitchen. If weather, and preferably forecast too, are fine, climb to **Llyn y Cwn** at top of this impressive defile, if not, skip this bit and turn **R** to Point ❻. The rich soils on the

crags around Twll Du allow many species of Arctic plants to flourish free from animal grazing. Collectively the foliage seems to flow down the rocks and you can see why it is called the Hanging Gardens.

❹ To ascend Twll Du climb engineered path as it angles **L** up rock face, which will now be on your **R-H** side, above an extensive area of scree and boulder. At top you come to a relatively gentle (by comparison) grassy hollow between rising summits of **Y Garn**, to R, and **Glyder Fawr**, to L.

❺ Just beyond first grassy mounds you come across small tarn of Llyn y Cwn, which makes a great picnic spot. Now retrace your steps to bottom of Twll Du.

❻ From here descend rocky ground down to western side of **Llyn Idwal**. The path reaches, then rounds, northern shoreline to meet outward route at gate near outflow stream, Point ❷. Now follow route of your outward journey back to car park at **Ogwen**.

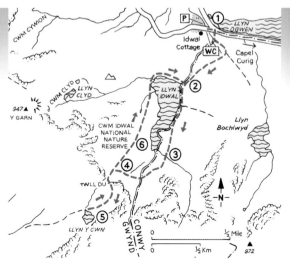

Conwy

LLYN CRAFNANT *THE TWIN LAKES*

5 miles (8km) Ascent: 3hrs Ascent: 656ft (200m)	

Paths: Clear paths and forestry tracks, 7 stiles
Suggested map: aqua3 OS Explorer OL17 Snowdon
Grid reference: SH 756618
Parking: Forestry car park, north of Llyn Crafnant

Discover two lakes, one to inspire poets present and one that inspired bards past.

1 Turn **R** out of car park and follow lane to north end of **Llyn Crafnant**, a lake surrounded by woodland, pasture and hills. Turn **R** and follow forestry track along northwest shores of lake, then take lower **L** fork.

2 Ignore 1st stile on **L**, and instead climb with forestry track. Keep watch for waymarked footpath on which you should descend **L** to pass beneath cottage of **Hendre**. Go over footbridge on **R**, then turn **L** down track past modern chalets.

3 Turn **L** along road which heads back towards lake. Leave this at **telephone box** for path ('Llyn Geirionydd') and waymarked with blue-capped posts. This climbs through conifer forests and over shoulder of **Mynydd Deulyn**.

4 Descend on winding forestry track, still following obvious blue-capped posts. Ignore track forking to **R** – that leads to Llyn Bychan.

5 On reaching valley floor, leave track to go over step stile on **L**. The path crosses a field beneath **Ty-newydd** cottage before tracing **Llyn Geirionydd's** shoreline. At northern end of lake, path keeps to **R** of a wall and meets farm track.

6 Turn **L** along this, then **R** to **Taliesin Monument** erected in 1850 to commemorate the 6th-century bard who is known to have lived here at the northern end of Geirionydd. Many of Taliesin's poems recall tales of magic and mystery, and many of them relate to the heroics of King Arthur, who some believe was his one-time master. Descend to green path heading northwest, then north, descending towards Crafnant Valley.

7 Veer **L** to cross ladder stile and follow undulating path over rock and heather knolls.

8 Path eventually swings **L** to reach old **mine**. Here, take lower track on **R** which descends back to valley road and forest car park.

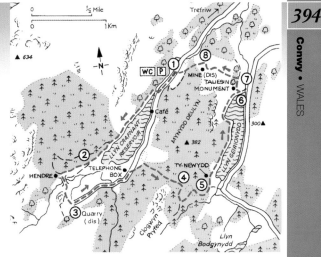

DOLGARROG *TRAGIC DISASTER AREA*

7 miles (11.3km) Ascent: 3hrs 30min Ascent: 328ft (100m)
Paths: Tracks and country lanes, 4 stiles
Suggested map: aqua3 OS Explorer OL17 Snowdon
Grid reference: SH 731663
Parking: Car park at the end of road

Discovering grim secrets, high in one of the Carneddau's loneliest valleys.

1 Follow track heading roughly southwest from car park into jaws of **Eigiau**. This track turns **L** below main dam and goes over a bridge across reservoir's outflow stream. One November night in 1925 the Eigiau dam disintegrated and the waters came thundering into the upper Afon Porth-Llwyd towards the Coedty Reservoir. That dam also broke, the waters carrying huge boulders down towards the hapless village of Dolgarrog, which was devastated and 16 lives were lost. It is said that the death toll would have been higher were it not for the fact that many of the villagers were at the cinema, which was situated on higher ground. The dam was never rebuilt.

2 Turn **L** along greener track that traces river's southeast banks, ignoring path on **R** beneath **Eilio**. The gated track passes **Coedty Reservoir** and leads to a country lane by dam. From the reservoir you can

see the boulders, by the oak-shaded river banks, deposited there on that fateful night.

3 Follow lane as it descends to cross river, then climbs out on to hillside high above Conwy Valley.

4 Turn **L** at T-junction to pass **Rowlyn Isaf** farm on your **R**. The quickest and recommended route follows this quiet country lane back to car park.

An Alternative Route

It is possible to get back by using path south of **Waen Bryn-gwenith**. However it's very rough in early stages where path is lost in thick bracken. For purist walker a signposted path from woods, Point A, beyond farm climbs beside a wall and fades near top end of woods. Here look out for small gate on **L**, Point B. Now you have to fight through thick bracken to go through to next field where you turn **R** to get to open hillside, Point C. Stay above wall/fence. As path nears road go over ladder stile in fence then turn **R** to another one at roadside. Turn **L** along road to get back to car park.

CONWY *CASTLE STRONGHOLD*

6½ miles (10.4km) Ascent: 4hrs Ascent: 1,214ft (370m)
Paths: Good paths and easy-to-follow moorland tracks, 6 stiles
Suggested map: aqua3 OS Explorer OL17 Snowdon
Grid reference: SH 782776
Parking: Large car park on Llanrwst Road behind Conwy Castle

Conwy's castle and a remote Celtic fort.

1 From Conwy Quay head northwest along waterfront, past Smallest House and under town walls. Fork **R** along tarmac waterside footpath that rounds **Bodlondeb Wood**. Turn **L** along road, past school and on to **A547**. Cross road, then railway line by footbridge. Lane beyond skirts wood to another lane where you turn **R**.

2 Another waymarker guides you on to a footpath on **R** that, beyond stile, ascends wooded hillsides to **Conwy Mountain**. Follow undulating crest of Conwy Mountain past **Castell Caer**.

3 Several tracks converge in fields of **Pen-pyra**. Here, follow signposts for **North Wales Path** along track heading southwest over **L** shoulder of **Alltwen** and down to metalled road traversing **Sychnant Pass**.

4 Follow footpath from other side of road, skirting woods on your **L**. Pass **Gwern Engen** on your **L-H** side and continue to pass to **L** of **Lodge**, to reach a lane.

Turn **R** along lane then turn **L**, when you reach next junction, into **Groesffordd** village. Cross road, then take road ahead that swings to **R** past a telephone box, then **L** (southeast) towards **Plas Iolyn**.

5 Turn **L** at next junction, then **R** at signposted enclosed footpath crossing fields to B5106. Turn **L** along road, then **R** at entrance to **caravan park**, following frequent waymarkers through scrubland and over several stiles. After crossing surfaced vehicle track, and descending into little hollow, path climbs **L** (north) along pastured ridge, with telephone mast ahead.

6 Turn **L** at road then go **R** to pass to **R-H** side of telephone mast and **Bryn-iocyn** farm. At **Coed Benarth** wood, turn **L** then follow narrow path northwards through woods.

7 Cross ladder stile on **L-H** side and descend field to roadside gate at bottom. Turn **R** on to B5106 to return to quayside, or turn **L** to return to main car park.

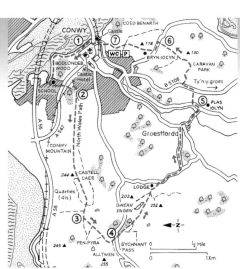

Conwy

397 TAL Y FAN STONES AND SETTLEMENTS

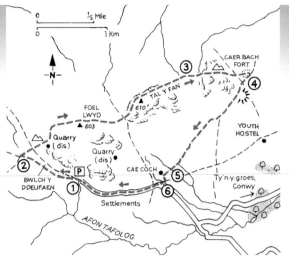

5 miles (8km) 3hrs **Ascent:** 984ft (300m) ⚠
Paths: Cart tracks and narrow mountain paths, 7 stiles
Suggested map: aqua3 OS Explorer OL17 Snowdon
Grid reference: SH 720715
Parking: Car park at end of Bwlch y Ddeufaen road, off B5106 Conwy–Llanrwst road

Visit the most northerly 2,000ft (610m) hill in Wales and see what remains from ancient settlers.

1 From car park at top of metalled section of road to **Bwlch y Ddeufaen**, continue along road, which is now unsurfaced, and follow it past ancient standing stones to high pass itself, where you go though a gate in crossing wall.

2 Turn **R** and follow course of wall, which traverses pass, goes under 3 lines of electricity pylons, and climbs steep rocky slopes of **Foel Lwyd**. A narrow footpath continues, first descending to a little saddle, or col, then climbing to even rockier summit of **Tal y Fan**. You should be able to pick out the field systems of the Bronze-Age farmers below the road in the valley of the Tafolog and in the pastures to the north of the youth hostel.

3 The descending footpath still follows line of dry-stone wall, but it stays with more even ground on L-H side. The wall turns **R** by particularly steep ground. Here you leave it to follow a pathless but smooth grassy ride, aiming for **Caer Bach** fort, to east, and prominent rocky knoll beyond.

4 Reach the remains of **Caer Bach** fort lying beneath the turf and gorse, but with its earth ramparts and a circle of stones still visible. Turn **R** to follow a tumbled down wall heading southwest across high pastureland overlooking Conwy Valley. Except for short stretch this wall now acts as your guide, as do frequent ladder stiles and locked gates sited in all intervening cross-walls.

5 The footpath eventually becomes a cart track, which passes beneath whitewashed cottage of **Cae Coch** before turning **L** to join stony vehicle track that has come from **Rowen Youth Hostel**.

6 Turn **R** along track, which soon joins **Bwlch y Ddeufaen** road at sharp corner. Go straight ahead along road and follow it back to car park.

398 NANT-Y-COED PASS OF THE TWO STONES

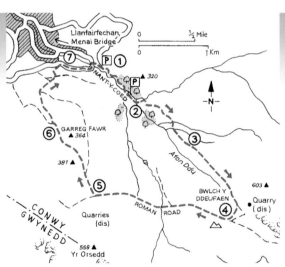

5 miles (8km) 3hrs **Ascent:** 1,214ft (370m) ⚠
Paths: Woodland, field and moorland paths, cart tracks, 5 stiles
Suggested map: aqua3 OS Explorer OL17 Snowdon
Grid reference: SH 694739
Parking: Small car park on Newry Drive, Nant-y-Coed, Llanfairfechan

A walk through one of the prettiest woods in Wales, to a high mountain pass.

1 Go through gate beyond car park and follow stony path through woods of **Nant-y-Coed** and by north bank of stream. This valley, part of the Newry Estate, was a popular tourist attraction in the 1900s. Take more prominent **L** fork to pass pond, then cross stream using stepping stones. More stepping stones are used to cross a side stream before climbing to 2nd car park.

2 Follow signpost up valley and cross a footbridge over river to continue. Keep a sharp eye open for waymarks, which guide you along zig-zagging path in a complex series of criss-crossing tracks.

3 Path enters open moorland, starting as a grooved rush-filled track before deteriorating into sheep tracks through gorse fields. Aim for col between **Foel Lwyd** and **Drosgl**, to point where 3 lines of pylons straddle fells.

4 At **Bwlch y Ddeufaen** (pass of the two stones) faint path arcs **R**, to other side of col, where it joins **Roman road**. Turn **R** along track and follow it across rough moor.

5 On reaching crossroads of tracks, turn **R** ('Llanfairfechan'). You're now following waymarked course of North Wales Path over **Garreg Fawr**. After going over top of 1st grassy summit path veers **L** to rake down west side of hill, from where you can see the coastal sands and the Isle of Anglesey.

6 Take waymarked **R-H** fork rather than track following wall on **L**. This trends to **R**, goes through kissing gate in crossing wall, then descends to high pasture land overlooking **Nant-y-Coed**. Turn **L** down little enclosed ginnel that descends to road.

7 Turn **R** along road, which descends further to cross a bridge over Afon Llanfairfechan. At other side take narrow lane back to car park.

399 MYNYDD Y GAER WITH THE POET

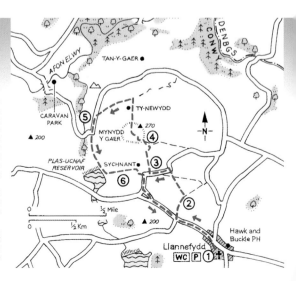

2½ miles (4km) 1hr 30min **Ascent:** 886ft (270m) ⚠
Paths: Field paths and tracks, 2 stiles
Suggested map: aqua3 OS Explorer 264 Vale of Clwyd
Grid reference: SH 981706
Parking: Llannefydd village car park

Visit an Iron-Age fort and look down on the magnificent land- and seascapes that inspired the 19th-century Jesuit priest and poet Gerard Manley Hopkins.

1 Turn **L** out of car park and follow lane ('Llanfair TH', TH standing for Talhaiarn). Where road comes in from **L**, go though gate on **R-H** side and traverse fields with hedge and fence on your **L**.

2 After going through 2nd gate turn **L** and follow hedge and fence, which is still on your **L**, uphill. Go through gate in small enclosure for caravan, turn **R**, then pass through another gate out on to metalled road. Turn **L** along road.

3 Where road turns sharply to **L**, leave it and double-back to **R** on tarmac track climbing up to Bryn Hwylfa. Just past whitewashed cottage, turn **L** to walk along enclosed grass track climbing hill. Beyond gate grassy footpath winds through gorse and scrub before veering **L** beneath outer ring defences of Iron-Age fort.

4 Where gorse bushes become more sparse, climb **R** to reach brow of hill. Go through farm gate to reach cairn which marks summit. Below and to the north you can see the **Afon Elwy** twisting and turning between low wooded hills. This is the landscape that inspired the 19th-century poet and Jesuit priest Gerard Manley Hopkins to write *In the Valley of the Elwy*. Descend north from here, to pick up track that passes a hilltop farm, **Ty-newydd**, before descending **L** to meet another lane.

5 Turn **L** to walk along lane, but leave it at **R-H** bend for a lovely grass track continuing straight ahead to pass above shores of **Plas-uchaf Reservoir**. Once you are past lake, track swings **L** towards **Sychnant**.

6 Beyond gate, follow track as it becomes path, winding through woodland before coming to lane that you left on outward route. Turn **R** along this lane and then take 1st **L**, continue straight ahead to return to **Llannefydd** village.

Conwy

BETWS-Y-COED *LLYN ELSI*

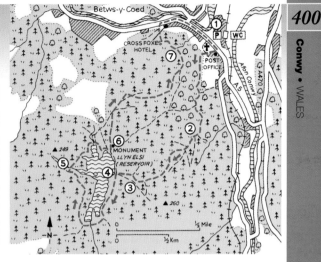

4 miles (6.4km) 2hrs 30mins **Ascent:** 840ft (256m)
Paths: Well-defined forest tracks and paths
Suggested map: aqua3 OS Explorers OL17 Snowdon & OL18 Harlech, Porthmadog & Bala
Grid reference: SH 795565 (on Explorer OL17)
Parking: Car park by railway station

A high lake with views to Snowdonian peaks.
1 From car park go to main road, turn **L**, then **R** along road between **post office** and **church**. Road veers **R** behind church. Here, take 'Llyn Elsi' forestry track on **L**. This swings **L** and climbs through forest. It bends **R** to cross lively stream, then **L** again to resume steady climb through trees. Ignore narrow path on **R** (direct but steep path to lake).
2 Take **R** fork with one of many white waymarks (these will guide you to and around Llyn Elsi). Take **L** fork at next junction, then **R** as track climbs steadily through conifers.
3 Take **L** fork as the gradient eases to arrive at lakeshore. At various points around the lake you will be able to pick out many of the Snowdonian peaks. Moel Siabod is the nearest and most prominent, while others include the jagged crest of Glyder Fach, and Tryfan, whose ruffled top just peeps out from behind the Glyder ridge. Heather, birch and rowan add

variation to the dark backdrop of conifers surrounding the lake. In autumn their mottled rusty colours make this a very pleasing place to be.
4 Follow track **L** along lakeshore then leave it beyond south dam for a path climbing **R** into woods. This becomes a track that winds along west shore of lake.
5 Leave the track for path on **R** (still waymarked with white posts), which winds through scrub, then beneath north dam to arrive at the **monument** that was erected in 1914 to celebrate the enlargement of the lake.
6 With your back to memorial plaque take narrow path straight ahead (slightly **R** of one you just used). Follow this north to cross two forestry roads. Soon rooftops of **Betws y Coed** flicker through trees on **R**.
7 Path gradually veers **L**, descends beneath wooden electricity pylons down to join another forestry track taking route to A5 near Cross Foxes Hotel. Turn **R** along road, back into village.

LLANDUDNO *ALICE'S WONDERLAND*

5 miles (8km) 2hrs 30min **Ascent:** 890ft (270m)
Paths: Well-defined paths and tracks
Suggested map: aqua3 OS Explorer OL17 Snowdon
Grid reference: SH 783829 Snowdon
Parking: In any of the town car parks.

The limestone sea-cliffs of Great Orme.
1 It has been said that Lewis Carroll was inspired to write his *Alice's Adventures in Wonderland* after a visit to Llandudno, and seeing the caves, rabbit warrens and captivating scenery you can realise why. From Llandudno Pier walk along Marine Drive to Happy Valley Gardens and follow waymarks for Great Orme summit, along zig-zag surfaced path. At top of park go through gate and follow path into limestone ravine with dry-ski slope and toboggan run.
2 Continue uphill and **R** to pass beneath limestone scars on to grassy slopes of **Great Orme**.
3 Further uphill and inland take middle of 3 paths signed 'summit'. Turn **R** at electric tramway's **Halfway Station**, following grassy path on nearside of track. After crossing St Tudno's road, climb along continuing path to summit. The **visitor centre** is open between Easter and October. Ex champion middleweight boxer Randolph Turpin used to be the landlord at the pub

next door, but tragically, after slipping into financial difficulties in 1966, he shot himself.
4 Go round north side of summit pub and follow waymarked path descending grassy hillside in direction of **St Tudno's church** and graveyard. Turn **L** along stony track near to its junction with tarmac road, and follow it round field-edges of **Parc Farm**.
5 Past rocks of **Free Trade Loaf**, path turns **L**, still following field-edge. Turn **L** again at cairn. You have now rounded Great Orme on to south side. It's worth detouring from wall to see cliff-edge and view across to Conwy Bay and Carneddau Mountains.
6 When cliff path runs out, return to wall and follow track, now high above cliffs. Ignore well-used path going **L** for summit complex, but instead take path bearing half **L**. Turn **R** on meeting summit road. On reaching Bronze-Age Copper Mines and Halfway Station, retrace steps of outward route across high fields, back through Happy Valley.

HORSESHOE FALLS *THE VELVET HILL*

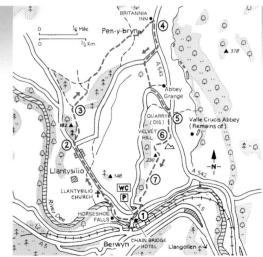

4 miles (6.4km) 2hrs 30min **Ascent:** 853ft (260m)
Paths: Field paths in valley and on hillside, 7 stiles
Suggested map: aqua3 OS Explorer 255 Llangollen & Berwyn
Grid reference: SJ 198433
Parking: Picnic site and car park at Llantysilio Green on minor road north of Berwyn Station

This walk on the Velvet Hill is probably one of the prettiest walks in North Wales.
1 From car park walk down to road, turn **R** for few paces then descend some steps to back of **Chain Bridge Hotel**. Turn **R** to follow path between river and canal. Once through kissing gate at end of canal you traverse riverside fields past **Horseshoe Falls**. The falls are in fact a weir created by Thomas Telford to harness the waters of the Dee to feed and control the levels of the Llangollen and Ellesmere canals. Climb to **Llantysilio church** and on reaching road, turn **L** through hamlet of **Llantysilio** to junction.
2 Go though 5-bar gate few paces along side road and climb along rutted track, with forest to your **L**, then climb north on high pastured hillside.
3 Through gateway at top of field, path swings **R**, keeping parallel to top edge of another wood. The now narrow path descends to complex of cottages at **Pen-y-bryn**. After squeezing through ginnel to **R** of 1st

cottage, route follows tarmac drive out to Horseshoe Pass road at **Britannia Inn**.
4 Turn **R** along road, then **R** again when you get to 1st junction. Go over stile on **L** to head south across 3 fields. Turn **R** along farm track then **L** past large stone-built house to arrive at narrow lane. Go **L** along this to meet Horseshoe Pass road again.
5 Go over stile on **R-H** side of road ('Velvet Hill') and ascend by quarry workings.
6 Turn **R** along wide grassy track climbing steeply through bracken to reach ridge, where you turn **L** for summit. The view from here takes in the meandering Dee, the Afon Eglwyseg flowing beneath limestone terraces and **Valle Crucis abbey**.
7 Descend southwards on narrow footpath to reach fence above some woods. Do not be tempted to cross (as many have done), but follow this fence down **L** to stile. Across stile go **R**, along path that leads back to car park and picnic site.

Denbighshire

403 VALLE CRUCIS *IDYLLIC VALLE*

6 miles (9.7km) 3hrs **Ascent:** 885ft (270m)
Paths: Tow path, farm tracks and field paths, 4 stiles
Suggested map: aqua3 OS Explorer 255 Llangollen and Berwyn
Grid reference: SJ 216421
Parking: Small car park on A542 just to east of town centre

From the Dee to the Eglwyseg, this walk discovers a fascinating tapestry of history and landscape.

1 Turn **L** out of car park to follow road to crossroads by Llangollen Bridge. Here turn **R**, then **L**, to café and on to canal tow path. Follow tow path westwards.

2 After about 1 mile (1.6km) canal veers **L**. Leave tow path to cross canal on an ivy-clad bridge. Turn **R** along pavement of main road (A542). Cross road and take a farm track ('FP to **Valle Crucis**'). The track heads north past old abbey, where track ends. Continue on footpath, keeping fence to L.

3 After crossing stile at **Abbey Cottage** turn **R** for few paces, then **L** to follow well-defined track through woodland. When you get to **Hendre** take **R-H** fork leading to minor road at **Tan-y-Fron**.

4 Turn **R** along road, heading towards prominent cliffs of **Eglwyseg**, then **R** again, along lane that hugs foot of cliffs.

5 A short stretch of tarmac to **Rock Farm** can be avoided by taking waymarked path that starts beyond gate and follows western edge of several fields before rejoining lane. Take **L-H** fork and stay with lane beneath cliffs.

6 When you reach 2nd junction take **R-H** fork for few paces, then go through gate on **R**, on to waymarked footpath leading to **Castell Dinas Bran**. From crumbling west walls of castle descend on zig-zag path. Go around **R-H** side of little knoll at bottom of hill to reach high lane near house called Tirionfa.

7 Follow lane southwards and then cross over stile into field. Trace **L-H** edge of field down to reach another high road.

8 Across this, route continues down narrow enclosed ginnel, passing **school** before crossing road and then **Llangollen Canal** close to start of walk. Descend road down to Llangollen Bridge before turning **L**, back to car park.

404 PRESTATYN *MOUNTAINS MEET SEA*

3 miles (4.8km) 1hr 30min **Ascent:** 558ft (170m)
Paths: Well-defined woodland paths and tracks
Suggested map: aqua3 OS Explorer 264 Vale of Clwyd or 265 Clwydian Range
Grid reference: SJ 071821
Parking: Picnic site at foot of hill

A nature walk through wooded hillsides and limestone knolls and a coastal panorama from Prestatyn to Llandudno's Great Orme.

1 Turn **R** out of car park and climb a few paces up steep lane. Turn **R** along public footpath marked with **Offa's Dyke National Trail** acorn sign. This enters an area of scrubby woodland with a wire fence to R, before climbing above some quarry workings. As footpath reaches high fields, ignore all paths off to L.

2 The footpath continues along top edge of woods to **Tan-yr-Allt**, where it swings **L** to follow a footpath signposted to **Bryniau**. This rounds a little cove with some buildings in bottom, then swings to **L** again with Graig Fawr now prominent across another hollow.

3 Go through a kissing gate on to a metalled lane and pass a house called Red Roofs. Turn **L** when you reach next junction, then **R** a few paces further on, to follow a lane rounding south side of **Graig Fawr**.

4 Turn **R** through a gate on to **Graig Fawr Estate** and follow a footpath leading to **trig point** on summit. Graig Fawr is an ideal place to picnic, either on the lush lawns or its gleaming white rock outcrops. Distant views from take in the North Wales coastline, the Vale of Clwyd and Carneddau mountains.

5 Descend eastwards along a grassy path that weaves through bracken to a place where a line of wooden electricity pylons meets a stone wall bordering woodland. Locate stepped path that descends through woodland. Turn **L** at path junction and follow that through woods.

6 Turn **R** along a **disused railway** track, before taking 2nd footpath on **R**, that crosses a field back towards **Prestatyn Hillside**. Turn **L** and follow a footpath into **Coed yr Esgob**, woods at foot of Prestatyn Hillside.

7 Where path divides, take upper fork that joins Bishopwood Lane. Follow this back to car park and start of walk.

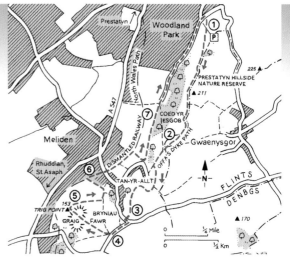

405 MOEL FAMAU *THE MOTHER MOUNTAIN*

8 miles (12.9km) 5hrs **Ascent:** 1,608ft (490m)
Paths: Well-defined paths and forestry tracks, 9 stiles
Suggested map: aqua3 OS Explorer 265 Clwydian Range
Grid reference: SJ 198625 **Parking:** Pay car park by Loggerheads Country Park Visitor Centre
Note: Route can be shortened by taking Moel Famau shuttle bus, which runs on Sundays (July to September) and bank holidays, from forestry car park to Loggerheads.

Walk to the highest of the Clwydian Hills.

1 Go past front of **Loggerheads Country Park Information Centre**, cross bridge over **Alun** and turn **L** along surfaced path through valley. Where path splits, follow route on **L** ('Leete Path').

2 Look out for small and slippery-when-wet path on **L** beyond Alyn Kennels that takes you down to footbridge across river. Across this, path heads west, then staggers to **R** across a farm lane and climbs past farmhouse. Enclosed by thickets, it climbs to **R** of **Bryn Alyn** (cottage) to reach T-junction of country lanes. Go ahead and follow lane uphill, then turn **R** to follow track that passes **Ffrith** farm before swinging **L** to climb round pastured slopes of **Ffrith Mountain**. Take **L** fork in tracks (grid ref 177637).

3 The route skirts spruce plantation and climbs to crossroads of tracks, marked by a tall waymarker post. Turn **L** here on wide path over undulating heather slopes towards tower on top of **Moel Famau**.

4 From summit, head southeast and go over stile at end of wall to follow wide track, marked with red-tipped waymarker posts, southeast along forest's edge. The track continues its descent from trees to meet roadside car park/picnic area ¾ mile (1.2km) east of **Bwlch Penbarra's** summit.

5 Turn **L** along road, then turning **R** when at 1st junction, quiet lane leading to busy A494. Cross main road (care) and continue along hedge-lined lane staggered to **R**.

6 A waymarked path on **L** heads northeast across fields towards banks of Alun. Don't cross river at bridge, but head north, through gateway and across more fields, keeping to **R** and above substantial stone-built house to meet **A494**. It's ½ mile (800m) to **Loggerheads Country Park** entrance, walk on verges and paths.

CEIRIOG VALLEY *IN THE BEAUTIFUL VALLEY*

4½ miles (7.2km) 2hrs 30min **Ascent:** 575ft (175m) ▲
Paths: Sketchy paths and farm tracks, 3 stiles
Suggested map: aqua3 OS Explorer 255 Llangollen & Berwyn
Grid reference: SJ 157328
Parking: Roadside parking in village

Discover an earthly heaven in one of ancient Clwyd's truly green and pleasant valleys.
❶ From **Hand Hotel**, take eastbound lane past church and uphill with conifer plantation on R and pastures of **Ceiriog** below L.
❷ At far end of plantation leave road for farm track on L. This ends at barn. Keep to **R** of barn and aim for gate beyond it. Through gate maintain your direction, over shoulder of grassy knoll, then aim for stile in fence ahead. Beyond this, route bends **L** very slightly, before going over another step stile.
❸ After crossing 2 streamlets, keep to field edge and to **R** of **Ty'n-y-fedw** farm. The track now enters woods. Take lower **L** fork, staying parallel to river.
❹ At far end of woods cross field, keeping roughly parallel with river, then aim for gate at top of field. Through gate, turn **R** to climb roughly southwest along enclosed farm road, which crosses country lane before continuing uphill through high pastures.

❺ At crossroads, turn **R** along green track – part of **Upper Ceiriog Way**. This heads southwest towards green hill known as Cefn Hir-fynydd.
❻ After about 300yds (274m) leave this track through gate on **R**. If you head west by R edge of rushy area and towards **Pen y Glog's** sparse crags, it will be easy to find small stile in next fence and then wooden gate on **L** soon afterwards. Go through gate then descend past rocks on **L**. The sheep track then levels out through bracken to pass beneath more rocks.
❼ A solitary wooden marker post acts as your guide to locate wide grassy track, which runs through valley of **Nant y Glog** and along low slopes of hill, **Pen y Glog**.
❽ After swinging **R** with lively stream, track terminates by lane to south of **Llanarmon Dyffryn Ceiriog**. Follow lane past several attractive cottages and village **school** to arrive by **Hand Hotel** in village square.

ERDDIG *A MAGNIFICIENT ESTATE*

4 miles (6.4 km) 2hrs **Ascent:** 150ft (46m) ▲
Paths: Waymarked field and woodland paths and tracks 3 stiles
Suggested map: aqua3 OS Explorer 265 Clwydian Range
Grid reference: SJ 346491
Parking: Small car park behind Kings Mill (on A525)

Discover the Errdig Estate and a haven of tranquillity just outside bustling centre of Wrexham.
❶ From car park head west, following **River Clywedog** as it goes under road bridge. At other side turn **R** on grass path, then **L** alongside woods cloaking north slopes of valley. Go over stile and follow path into woods. This section is marked on maps as **Clywedog Trail**.
❷ Go through kissing gate and **L** along road. Turn **R** through gate at back of small car park and follow **L** of 2 paths to riverbank. Follow riverside path across fields, to south of bulrush-ringed lake.
❸ Go through gate to **R** of stone bridge, then turn **L** along track over bridge, keeping woods of Erddig to R. Near John Blakes Patent Hydraulic Ram go over stile on **L** and follow track south into woods. On reaching **Erddig Hall's** perimeter fence ignore path doubling back L, but follow path heading east by fence.

❹ Path ends at T-junction on far side of woods. Detour **R** for 50yds (46m) to get view of hall. This can be seen beyond some ornate wrought iron gates and long park-like gardens. (N.B. for those who want to pay to see the fine 17th-century hall continue to the south side entrance.) Return to T-junction. Head north along inside perimeter of woods then turn **R**. Go through kissing gate on to lane.
❺ Turn **L** along lane for a few paces and then cross over stile on R-H side of lane. Trace L-H field-edge to waymarker post and descend to another post at edge of woodland. Follow narrow path through woods, go over stile, down some steps to cross stream, then climb far banks to path overlooking bend in **River Clywedog**. Stay on path to continue above river, then, out of woods, turn **L** to cross over footbridge.
❻ Turn right along river banks to meet outward route at path going under road bridge and into grounds of Kings Mill.

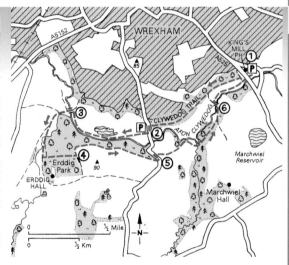

GREENFIELD VALLEY *GREY VALLEY*

5 miles (8km) 3hrs **Ascent:** 558ft (170m) ▲
Paths: Woodland paths and tracks, lanes, field paths and coastal embankment, 12 stiles
Suggested map: aqua3 OS Explorer 265 Clwydian Range
Grid reference: SJ 196774
Parking: Just off A548 at Greenfield

Following monks, martyrs and merchants.
❶ Take footpath from back of car park on L-H side and follow it around **abbey**.
❷ Turn **L** between **information centre** and old schoolhouse on track passing Abbey Farm. Take **L** fork by brick walls of Abbey Wire Mill, following sign to Fishing Pool, a lily-covered pond.
❸ Beyond **Victoria Mill** take lower R-H fork, then turn **R** through iron gates to pass remains of Meadow Mill. Beyond mill turn **L** up steps, climbing up by weir and back on to main track.
❹ Turn **R** along track to pass above Hall's soft drinks factory and brick chimney. Go through kissing gate; turn **R** to road. Turn **L** to view **St Winefride's Chapel and Well**, then go back down road to **Royal Oak Inn**.
❺ Climb lane, called Green Bank, that begins from opposite side of road. At end of lane go over stile by gate and follow scrub-enshrouded footpath. At new housing estate path is dog-legged to **L** and continues

through trees to large open field.
❻ Go over stile and head diagonally, northwest, across field. Go through gap in far hedge and then over stile in bottom corner of next field. Continue ahead (still going northwest) through several more fields to join cart track, just short of tree-filled hollow of **Afon Marsiandwr**.
❼ Leave cart track where it swings to **R** for 2nd time and follow signed footpath through trees and down to banks of **Afon Marsiandwr**. After crossing stream, path climbs out of woods and crosses field to lane.
❽ Turn **R** along lane following it down to coast road. Cross busy road with care. The continuing footpath to seashore is immediately opposite, over step stile. Cross railway track, again with care, and continue to inner flood embankments and turn **R**.
❾ The footpath comes out by Greenfield Harbour. Turn **R** along lane back in to **Greenfield**. Turn **L** to return to car park.

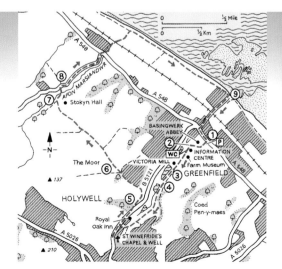

409 DUMBLETON HILL *CHURCH VIEWS*

8 miles (12.9km) 3hrs 15min **Ascent:** 427ft (130m)
Paths: Mostly good paths, field tracks and village roads, 6 stiles
Suggested map: aqua3 OS Explorer OL45 The Cotswolds
Grid reference: SP 039363 **Parking:** On street near church in Wormington

See several centuries of church building.

❶ Walk westwards to reach power lines. Just after, take footpath on L. Pass through gate, maintaining direction for 450yds (412m).

❷ Turn away from **Mill Farm**, to cross river. Cross field. Go diagonally across another field, under power lines, turning **R** beside fence that soon becomes hedgerow. In 120yds (110m) turn **L** through gate then along R-H field edge. Within 200yds (183m) turn **R**.

❸ Follow mud track – later green lane then tarmac – for nearly 1¼ miles (2km), to road junction. Turn **R**, passing entrance to **Toddington Manor**, to junction.

❹ Sign points to **Toddington's church**. Visit **church** and **Toddington House** ruin. Retrace your steps. Walk through **Toddington**. Turn **R**. Just after pavement ends (before **Buttermilk Farm**), cross to fingerpost and stile. Walk behind trees for 760yds (695m).

❺ Re-cross road. Take minor road past **Orchard Industrial Estate**. At T-junction turn **R**. Go **L**, before **farm shop**, up driveway, passing farmhouse

(**Evergreen**). At next T-junction turn **L** along grassy tarmac way, contouring hill. Reach broken tree just before track bends **L** to **Frampton Farm**.

❻ Continue for about 30 paces, then turn hard **R**, uphill, heading for gate near trees. Once through, way soon steepens. On brow join stony track coming in from **R**. Now on level, continue for 600yds (549m) to signposts at junction of tracks. Follow 'Public Bridleway **Dumbleton** 1¼ miles', soon into big field. Good track now leads all the way down to minor road, then driveway to **Dumbleton Hall** (hotel).

❼ Cross to crucifix-style war memorial. Turn **L**. Visit **church**. About 30yds (27m) beyond Dairy Lane on L, turn **R** along residential cul-de-sac. Enter field to skirt 2 field edges. Cross B4078. When drive to **Lane Farm Cottages** is reached, continue to find field path, crossing 2 fields. Cross service road to **College Farm**. Cross river on bridge. Pass under power lines and over stile into pasture. Walk to end of breeze-block barn wall. Turn **R** to gate, rejoining road in **Wormington**.

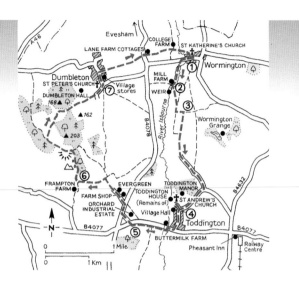

410 THE DITCHFORDS *THE LOST VILLAGES*

5 miles (8km) 1hr 45min **Ascent:** 130ft (40m)
Paths: Track and field, quiet lanes, ford or bridge, 2 stiles
Suggested map: aqua3 OS Explorer OL45 The Cotswolds
Grid reference: SP 240362
Parking: Lay-bys on Todenham's main street, south of village hall

Walk among the ghosts of abandoned medieval agricultural communities.

❶ From lay-by below **Todenham village hall** walk up towards hall. Turn **L** just before it, along track that runs to R of house.

❷ After few paces go **R** up bank to gate. Go into field then straight across. Go through gate on far side, into field of undulations (medieval ploughing). Keep ahead to stile – cross into next field and, staying in its upper part, go ahead, in direction of house.

❸ Cross another stile and soon join farm track. Where track goes into field on R, keep ahead. At bottom of field path may become indistinct – look for small bridge, with gates at either end, amid undergrowth 50yds (46m) to **L**.

❹ Cross bridge then keep ahead, crossing field (site of **Ditchford Frary**) with farmhouse before you to **R**. On other side, go through gate, cross field and through gate to farm track.

❺ To see site of **Lower Ditchford**, turn **L** here and keep going over former railway line until you approach road – remains are to your **L**. Then return along track. Otherwise turn **R** on track and pass behind farmhouse. Track becomes metalled lane.

❻ Just before **High Furze Farm** turn **R** through gate into field. Follow its **L** margin until it dips down to **ford** across **Knee Brook**. Turn **R** here and after few paces find bridge on **L**.

❼ Cross then return to faint, grassy track that rises from ford. Stay on this line, with brook now to R, to reach gate in top corner. Go through to track that rises between 2 hedges. Parts of this may be boggy but soon track will become firmer and eventually take you to junction opposite entrance to **Todenham Manor**.

❽ Turn **R** here. Follow this track as it curves **L**, around manor, and finally brings you back to village with **village hall** on **R**. Turn **L** for **church** and **Farriers Arms** pub, **R** to return to car park.

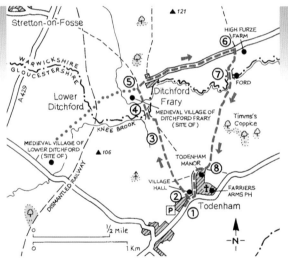

411 WINDRUSH *STONE SECRETS*

6 miles (9.7km) 2hs 30min **Ascent:** 120ft (37m)
Paths: Fields, tracks and pavement, 11 stiles
Suggested map: aqua3 OS Explorer OL45 The Cotswolds
Grid reference: SP 192130
Parking: Windrush village

An insight into Cotswold stone, the building blocks of the region's beauty.

❶ Walk out of village, keeping to L of **church**. After 100yds (91m), go **R**, through gate into field. Cross field to other side, keeping to **L**.

❷ Go through **R-H** gate; continue across series of stiles until you emerge in large field at wide grass strip (careful here, as it is used for 'galloping' horses) with houses of Little Barrington opposite. Cross two thirds of field then turn **L** and head for hedge at bottom.

❸ Go through gap to road. Ahead is **Fox Inn**. Turn **R**, enter **Little Barrington**. Turn **L** on 'No Through Road', which narrows to path. Where path becomes lane, go **L** over bridge and continue, to eventually emerge in **Great Barrington** at cross. Take road ahead.

❹ Where wall on L ends, go **L** on to track and immediately **R**. Stay on this track for little over 1 mile (1.6km) until you reach junction of tracks with large hedges ahead.

❺ Turn **L**. Follow track until you enter scrubby woodland. Cross over river; follow grassy track until, just before **Century Wood**, turn **L** into field. Follow margin of woods. Cross bridge into field and turn half **R** to far corner. Cross bridge then stile and go half **L** to another stile.

❻ Take track ahead then turn **L** over stile. Cross field then go through gate; walk along **R-H** margin on same line for several fields.

❼ Come to stile at corner. Go over into next field and cross it on **R** diagonal, in general direction of distant village. On far side go through gap into another field, with stone wall on **R**. Continue for several fields and pass stone barn to **R**, at which point **River Windrush** will appear to your **L-H** side. Finally, pass tin barn on your L-H side, just as you arrive at gate by lane.

❽ Opposite, go up to stile. In next field follow its perimeter as it goes **R** to reach stile. Cross to reach path; follow it into **Windrush**.

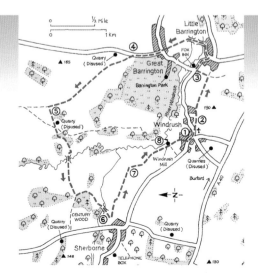

SEZINCOTE *A Taste of India*

3 miles (4.8km) 1hr 15min Ascent: 85ft (25m)
Paths: Tracks, fields and lanes, 7 stiles
Suggested map: aqua3 OS Explorer OL45 The Cotswolds
Grid reference: SP 175324
Parking: Street below Bourton-on-the-Hill church, parallel with main road

Discovering the influences of India through the Cotswold home of Sir Charles Cockerell.

1 Walk up road from **telephone box** with church to your R. Turn **L** down signposted track between walls. Go through gate into field and then continue forward to pass through 2 more gates.

2 Cross stile, followed by 2 kissing gates among trees. This is the **Sezincote Estate**. Its architecture and design was inspired, like many other buildings in the early 19th century, by the colourful aqua-tints brought to England from India by returning artists, such as William and Thomas Daniell. Built on the plan of a typical large country house, in every other respect it is thoroughly unconventional and owes a lot to Eastern influence, not least the large copper onion dome that crowns the house and the garden buildings. Go straight ahead, following markers and crossing drive. Dip down to gate among trees, with ponds on either side. Go ahead into field, from where **Sezincote**

House is visible to R.

3 Walk into next field and go right to end, aiming for top, **R-H** corner. Pass through gate to reach narrow road and turn **L**. Walk down this road, passing **keepers' cottages** to your **L**, and through series of gates. Road will bottom out, curve **L** and **R** and then bring you to **Upper Rye Farm**. Pass to R of farmhouse, go through gate and, immediately before barn, turn **L** along track and road.

4 After 2nd cattle grid, go **L** over stile. Follow edge of field to footbridge. Go over it and turn **R**. Now follow **R-H** margin of field to stile in far corner. Cross this to follow path through woodland until you come to stile and field and continue on same line to another stile.

5 Cross track to another stile and walk on. After few paces, with **Bourton-on-the-Hill** plainly visible before you, turn **R** and follow path to next corner. Turn **L** and pass through 3 gates. After 3rd one, walk on for few paces and turn **R** through gate to return to start.

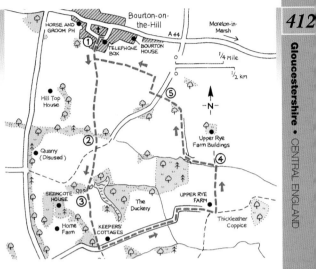

BOURTON-ON-THE-WATER *A Wildlife Walk*

4¾ miles (7.7km) 2hrs Ascent: 230ft (70m)
Paths: Track and field, can be muddy and wet in places, 26 stiles
Suggested map: aqua3 OS Explorer OL45 The Cotswolds
Grid reference: SP 169208
Parking: Pay-and-display car park on Station Road

A walk on the wilder side.

1 **Bourton-on-the-Water** can be very crowded during the summer with its river banks strewn with people picnicking and paddling – so arrive early or late to avoid the crowds. Opposite entrance to main pay-and-display car park in **Bourton-on-the-Water** locate public footpath and continue to junction opposite **cemetery**. Bear **R** to follow lane all the way to its end. There are 2 gates ahead. Take **R-H** gate, with stile beside it, on to grassy track.

2 Follow track between lakes to where it curves R. Leave track to cross bridge and stile into field. Go across field, curving **R**, to come to stile at road.

3 Cross road, turn **R** and immediately **L** on to track. After 100yds (91m) go **L** over stile into field. Turn **R**. Cross stile and return to track, with lake to L. Just before gate turn **R** over bridge and **L** over stile on to path alongside **River Windrush**. Continue until you reach stile at field. Turn **L**, cross another stile and go

L over bridge before turning **R** beside another lake.

4 Where 2nd, smaller lake ends bear **R** to stile, followed by bridge and stile at field. Keep to **R** side of fields until you reach track. At house leave track and continue to stile. In next field, after 25yds (23m), turn **L** over stile then sharp **R**. Continue to stile then go half **L** across field. Continue on same line across next field to stile. Cross this; follow **R** margin of field, to climb slowly to junction of tracks. Turn **L** to visit **Clapton-on-the-Hill**, or turn **R** to continue.

5 Follow track to field. Keep ahead then half **R** to pass R of woodland. Continue to stile, followed by 2 stiles together at field. Go half **L** to stile then follow succession of stiles, stream appearing to L.

6 Cross bridge then go half **R** across field to bridge. Continue to more stiles then walk along grassy track towards houses. Cross one more stile and follow path to road in **Bourton**. Walk ahead to cross river. Turn **L**, then **R**, to return to start.

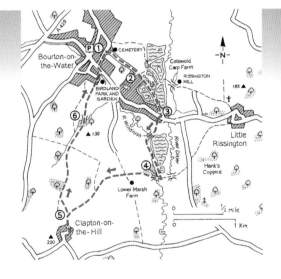

BLOCKLEY *The Arboretum*

4½ miles (7.2km) 2hrs Ascent: 410ft (125m)
Paths: Lanes, tracks and fields, 8 stiles
Suggested map: aqua3 OS Explorer OL45 The Cotswolds
Grid reference: SP 165348
Parking: On B4479 below Blockley church

The exotic legacy of a 19th-century diplomat adorns this part of the Cotswold escarpment.

1 Walk along road with church above you to your R. Continue ahead, pass **Brook House Cottage**, then turn **L** immediately, up lane. Follow this as it ascends for ¼ mile (400m) until it bears **L**.

2 Continue ahead to pass **R-H** side of barn. Pass through gate and in next field follow its **R-H** boundary to another gate. Pass through this to stay on **L** side of next field. Pass into yet another field and then go half **R** to gate leading out to road.

3 Turn **L** and follow road down to crossroads. Turn **R** to pass through **Batsford** village to junction (from where you can visit **church** on R). Bear **L**, and, at next junction, turn **R**.

4 After few paces turn **R** on to footpath and follow this through succession of fields, negotiating stiles and gates where they arise. **Batsford House** will be visible above you to R.

5 Finally, go through gate into ribbed field and turn **R** to stile just L of house at drive. This is the entrance to **Batsford Arboretum**, which offers 50 acres (20.3ha) of woodland containing over 1,000 species of trees and shrubs from all over the world, particularly from China, Japan and North America. Continue through this entrance, pass through gate and follow path up field to stile. Cross and continue to track. Follow this up until where it bends L. Turn **R** on to path and almost immediately **L** at wall, to contune ascent. Keep going until you reach road.

6 Cross road to go through gate and pass through 2 fields until you reach path among trees. Turn **L**, go through another gate, and, after a few paces, turn **R** over stile into field with **Blockley** below you. Continue down to stile at bottom. Cross into next field and pass beneath **Park Farm** on your R. Bear gently **L**, crossing stiles, along **Duck Paddle**, until you come to road. Turn **R** and return to your starting point in **Blockley**.

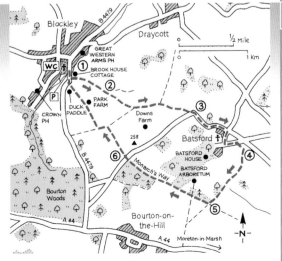

Gloucestershire

415 CHIPPING CAMPDEN *OLIMPICK PLAYGROUND*

5 miles (8km) 2hrs **Ascent:** 280ft (85m)
Paths: Fields, roads and tracks, 8 stiles
Suggested map: aqua3 OS Explorer OL45 The Cotswolds
Grid reference: SP 151391
Parking: Chipping Campden High Street or main square

From the Cotswolds' most beautiful wool town to Dover's Hill, the spectacular site of centuries-old Whitsuntide festivities.

❶ Turn **L** from Noel Arms, continue to Catholic **church**. Turn **R** into **West End Terrace**. Where this bears R, keep ahead on **Hoo Lane**. Follow this up to R turn, with farm buildings on L. Continue uphill over stile to path; keep going to a road.

❷ Turn **L** for few paces then **R** to cross to path. Follow this along field edge to stile. Go over to **Dover's Hill**. Follow hedge to stile with extensive views ahead. Turn **L** along escarpment edge, which drops away to your R. Pass **trig point** then **topograph**. Now go **R**, down slope, to kissing gate on **L**. Go through to road. Turn **R**.

❸ After 150yds (137m) turn **L** over stile into field. Cross and find gate in bottom R-H corner. Head straight down next field. At stile go into another field and, keeping to **L** of fence, continue to another stile.

Head down next field, cross track then find adjacent stiles in bottom **L** corner.

❹ Cross over 1st stile. Walk along bottom of field. Keep stream and fence to R and look for stile in far corner. Go over, crossing stream, then turn **L**, following rising woodland path alongside stream. Enter field through gate and continue to meet track. Stay on this, passing through gateposts, until you reach country lane. Turn **L**.

❺ After 400yds (366m) reach busier road. Turn **L** for 450yds (411m). Shortly before road curves L, drop down **R** on to field path parallel with road. About 200yds (183m) before next corner go half **R** down field to road.

❻ Turn **R**, down road. Shortly after cottage on R, go **L** into field. Turn **R** over stile and go half **L** to corner. Pass through kissing gate, cross road among houses and continue ahead to meet **West End Terrace**. Turn **R** to return to centre of **Chipping Campden**.

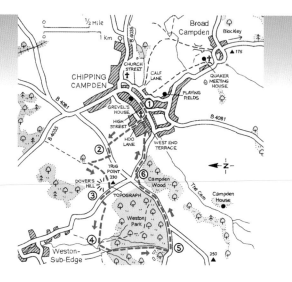

416 GUITING POWER *A SAXON VILLAGE*

5 miles (8km) 2hrs **Ascent:** 295ft (90m)
Paths: Fields, tracks and country lanes, 10 stiles
Suggested map: aqua3 OS Explorer OL45 The Cotswolds
Grid reference: SP 094245
Parking: Car park outside village hall (small fee)

A gentle ramble in from a typical village in quintessential Gloucestershire.

❶ From car park walk down road to village green. Cross road to walk down lane. At bottom go over stile into field. Turn **R**. Walk up bank, up to another stile. Don't cross one ahead but clamber over one to your **R** into field.

❷ Turn **L**. Walk straight across this field to another stile. Cross this and 2 more to pass farmhouse in **Barton** below. Follow lane down to larger road. Turn **R**. Cross bridge. Turn **L** up track and, after 100yds (91m), turn **R** up another track.

❸ After a few paces bear **L** and then walk along track for 1 mile (1.6km), until you reach another road. Turn **R**, walk along for 250yds (229m). Turn **L** on to track.

❹ Follow this all the way to road, past **quarry**. Cross road and then enter lane descending past house. This lane will bring you all the way into **Naunton**.

❺ At junction turn **R**. Walk through Naunton village and cross stone bridge by old mill, passing rectory to L and church concealed to R. (To get to **Black Horse Inn**, turn **L** and walk along street for 400yds (366m). Return by entering drive opposite pub, turning sharp R over stile, and walking back along side of river to emerge at road near church, where you turn **L**.) Continue up, out of village.

❻ After ¼ mile (400m) turn **R** over stile into field. Turn **L**, walk to stile and go into next field. Cross this field, enter next one. Follow path to **R** of trees to gate at road.

❼ Turn **R** along road. Continue to junction at bottom. Cross road to enter field and walk straight across. At end go down steps and pass to **R** of pond. Walk across next field then cross stile to walk to **L** of **church**. Before returning to the start take a look at the Norman doorway in **Guiting church**, it is an exceptionally rich golden hue.

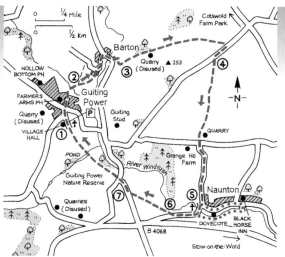

417 BIBURY *WOVEN CHARM*

6¼ miles (10.1km) 2hrs 30min **Ascent:** 165ft (50m)
Paths: Fields, tracks and lane, may be muddy in places, 6 stiles
Suggested map: aqua3 OS Explorer OL45 The Cotswolds
Grid reference: SP 113068
Parking: Bibury village

Enjoy the charm of a weaver's village.

❶ From parking area opposite mill, walk along **Cirencester** road. Immediately after **Catherine Wheel** pub turn **R** along lane then keep **L** at fork. Pass cottages then go through gates and stiles into field. Walk on same line across several stiles and fields until you pass to **R** of house to road.

❷ Turn **R**. Walk down to junction. Turn **R** into Ablington; cross bridge. After few paces, where road goes to R, turn **L** along track with houses on R and stream to L. Continue to gate then follow track as it traverses open countryside, arriving at another gate after just over ½ mile (800m).

❸ Go into field. Turn sharp **R** along valley bottom. Follow twisting route along bottom of valley. At next gate continue into field, still following contours of valley. Route will eventually take you through gate just before barn and another immediately after.

❹ Keep to track as it bears **R** and gently ascends

long slope, with woodland to L. When track goes sharp R, with gate ahead, turn **L** through gate on to track. Follow it all way to road.

❺ Turn **R**. After 250yds (229m), where road goes R, continue ahead, to enter track ('**Salt Way**'). Continue for ½ mile (800m), until you reach remains of **Saltway Barn**.

❻ Do not walk ahead but, immediately after barns, turn **L** into field then **R** along its R-H margin. Walk for just under ¾ mile (1.2km), passing hedge and woodland and, where track breaks to R, turn **R** through gate into field with wall on R.

❼ Continue to pass to **L** of Hale Barn. Enter track, with buildings of Bibury Farm away to your L. Keep on same line through gates where they arise. Eventually descend to drive which will lead to road in Bibury. Cross road to walk between row of cottages. At end, near church and school, turn **R**. Walk along pavement into village, passing **Arlington Row** and river on L.

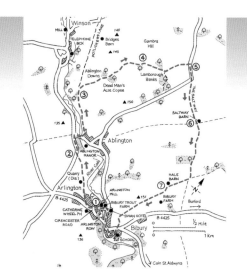

Gloucestershire

SOUTH CERNEY *THE COTSWOLD WATER PARK*

418

5 miles (8km) 2hrs Ascent: Negligible
Paths: Track, tow path and lanes, 10 stiles
Suggested map: aqua3 OS Explorer 169 Cirencester & Swindon
Grid reference: SU 048974
Parking: Silver Street, South Cerney

Ramble through an evolving landscape.

❶ From Silver Street walk north out of village. Immediately before turning to Driffield and Cricklade, turn **R** over stile on to bank. Stay on this for 800yds (732m), to reach brick bridge across path. Turn **R** up steps to reach narrow road.

❷ Turn **L**. Walk along for 200yds (183m) until you reach footpaths to R and L. Turn **R** along farm track, following signpost ('Cerney Wick'). Almost immediately remains of **Thames and Severn Canal** appear to L. When track veers R in farm, walk ahead over stile to follow path beneath trees – old canal tow path. At bridge keep ahead across stiles. Continue until you reach busy road.

❸ Cross with care. On far side you have 2 choices: continue on tow path or take path that skirts lakes. If you take lakeside path, you eventually rejoin tow path by going **L** at bridge after 600yds (549m). Continue until, after just under ½ mile (800m), you pass canal

roundhouse across canal to L and, soon after, reach lane at **Cerney Wick**.

❹ Turn **R**. Walk to junction at end of road, beside **Crown** pub. Cross to stile and enter field. Walk ahead to reach stile. Cross this aiming to L of cottage. Cross lane, go over another stile and enter field. Walk ahead and follow path as it leads across stile on to grass by lake. Walk around lake, going **R** then **L**. In corner before you, cross into field, walk ahead towards trees and cross stile to track.

❺ Turn **R**, rejoin old **railway line** and follow it all way to road. Cross this into car park. Go through gate on to track. Stay on this all the way to another road and follow path that runs to its L.

❻ Where path ends at beginning of **South Cerney**, continue along Station Road. Ignore footpath on R but turn **R** at 2nd one, which takes you across bridge and brings you to lane ('Bow Wow'). Turn **L** here between streams and return to **Silver Street**.

HAILES ABBEY *THOMAS CROMWELL AND THE ABBEY*

419

5 miles (8km) 2hrs Ascent: 605ft (185m)
Paths: Fields, tracks, farmyard and lanes, 7 stiles
Suggested map: aqua3 OS Explorer OL45 The Cotswolds
Grid reference: SP 050301
Parking: Beside Hailes church

A walk exploring the countryside around Hailes Abbey, an important abbey destroyed by the King's Commissioner.

❶ From **Hailes church** turn **R**. Follow this lane to reach T-junction. Turn **R**. After 200yds (183m) turn **R** on to footpath. Cross area of concrete. Follow track as it goes R and L, becoming grassy path beside field. Go through gate, followed by stile. After 75yds (69m) turn **L**, through gate, and cross field to gate at road.

❷ Turn **R**. Follow road as it meanders through pretty village of **Didbrook** then stretch of countryside. At junction turn **R** for **Wood Stanway**. Walk through village into yard of **Glebe Farm**.

❸ At gate and stile cross into field. Walk ahead, looking for stile on L. You are now on **Cotswold Way**, well marked by arrows with white dot or acorn. Cross into field. Go half **R**, keeping to L of telegraph poles, to gap in hedge. Bear half **L** across next field, heading towards house. Cross stile. Turn sharp **R**, up slope, to

stile on your **R**. Cross this and turn immediately **L** up field. Go **L** over ladder stile by gate. Follow footpath as it wends its way gently up slope. At top keep ahead to gate at road.

❹ Turn **R** and **R** again through gate to track. Follow track, passing through gate, until at top (just before trees), you turn **R** to follow another track for 50yds (46m). Turn **L** through gate into field. Turn **R** to follow perimeter of field as it goes L and passes through gate beside Iron-Age fort, **Beckbury Camp**. Continue ahead to pass through gate (leading to **stone monument** with a niche).

❺ Turn **R** to follow steep path through trees. At bottom go straight across down field to gate. Pass through, continue down to another gate and, in field beyond, head down to stile beside signpost.

❻ Cross this and turn **R** down lane, all the way to road. To L is **Hayles Fruit Farm** (café). Continue ahead along road to return to **Hailes Abbey** and start.

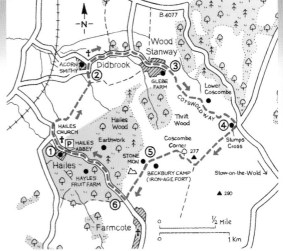

WINCHCOMBE *TO SUDELEY CASTLE*

420

4 miles (6.4km) 2hrs Ascent: 490ft (150m)
Paths: Fields and lanes, 10 stiles
Suggested map: aqua3 OS Explorer OL45 The Cotswolds
Grid reference: SP 024282
Parking: Free on Abbey Terrace; also car park on Back Lane

A walk above the burial place of Henry VIII's sixth queen – Catherine Parr.

❶ Walk towards village centre. Turn **R** on **Castle Street**. Where it levels out cross bridge. After few paces turn **L** on path between cottages. Pass into field and go half **R** to gate on other side.

❷ Turn **R** along lane. At end of stone wall, turn **L** into field. Go half **R** across field to find well-concealed gap in hedge, 50yds (46m) **L** of gateway, with plank across ditch. Cross then turn **L** to gate. Go through. Continue half **R** to another gap in hedge. Go through and keep ahead to protruding corner. Once you are round it, keep close to fence on L and continue into next corner to find (possibly overgrown) path leading to stile.

❸ Cross next field to another stile. Continue up following path to gate. Go through then go half **R** to far corner to stile (possibly concealed). Cross this then another stile almost immediately. Continue until you reach stile beside gate with stone barn above to R.

❹ Don't go over stile but turn **R** to head downhill to gate (at first hidden) in hedge 250yds (229m) below barn. Go through this on to track. Follow it as it curves towards house. Cross stile.

❺ Just before house turn **R**, cross field and go over stile. In next field go to bottom **L-H** corner to emerge on to road. Turn **L**. After few paces, turn **R** along lane, towards **Sudeley Lodge Parks Farm**.

❻ Opposite **cottage** turn **R** on to footpath across field. At bottom, cross stile. Turn **R**. At next corner turn **L**, remaining in same field. Cross another stile, continue for few paces then turn **R** over stile. Walk half **L**, following waymarkers to fence, with **Sudeley Castle** on R-H side.

❼ Go through 2 kissing gates to enter park area. Cross drive then field to another gate. Go through and bear half **R** to farthest corner. You will emerge on **Castle Street, Winchcombe**. Turn **L** to return to start in village centre.

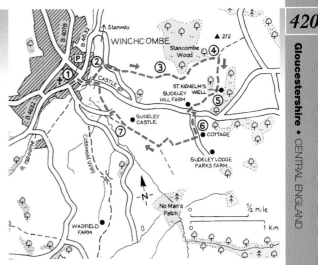

Gloucestershire

421 PRESTBURY A GHOSTLY TRAIL

3½ miles (5.7km) 1hr 30min Ascent: 100ft (30m)
Paths: Fields (could be muddy in places) and pavement, 10 stiles
Suggested map: aqua3 OS Explorer 179 Gloucester, Cheltenham & Stroud
Grid reference: SO 972238
Parking: Free car park near war memorial

Around Britain's most haunted village.

❶ Leave car park, turn **R** into The Bank and **R** into **Mill Street**. At main road turn **L**. After 100yds (91m) cross road to reach stile. Go into field then diagonally **L** to stile.

❷ Cross and follow track that is ahead and slightly to your **L**. Where it goes **R**, cross stile ahead. Cross field, heading slightly to **R**, to stile. Cross this into field and head for **Queen's Wood**.

❸ Stay to **L** of woods. Eventually cross track and enter another field. Where woods sweep uphill, continue through bushes to bridle gate. Go through on to woodland path. Turn **L** downhill, to reach main road.

❹ Ahead are medieval buildings of **De La Bere Hotel**. Cross road. Turn **R**. Follow pavement as it bears **L** into **Southam Lane**. After 200yds (183m) turn **L** along track to gate. Go through this and kissing gate to field.

❺ Head across, bearing slightly **R**, with De La Bere

on **L**. Follow path across series of paddocks and fields via stiles and gates. At stile, amid bushes in corner, cross on to track. Follow this to bridge stile.

❻ Cross and continue ahead into field with hedge on **R**. Go over brow of slope and down to gate in hedge to your **R**. Go through to track. Follow this to road.

❼ Turn **L** along **Shaw Green Lane**. After 400yds (366m) turn **R** along footpath passing between houses. Eventually this brings you out on to **Mill Street**, opposite **church**. Turn **R**, to walk past **Priory** and brick wall (site of haunted Grotto) until you reach **The Burgage**. Turn **L**, passing **Royal Oak**, **Prestbury House** and Sundial Cottage.

❽ At junction with Tatchley Lane turn **L** then **L** again into **Deep Street**, passing Three Queens and stone cottages. Just before Kings Arms turn **L** on footpath leading to **church**. Turn **R** just before church and pass through churchyard to return to **Mill Street**, opposite **Plough Inn**. Turn **R** and return to car park.

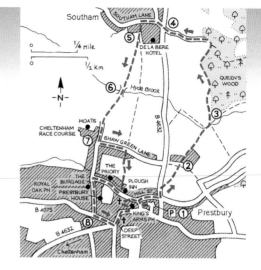

422 BRIMPSFIELD THE MEDIEVAL LOOTERS

4 miles (6.4km) 2hrs Ascent: 180ft (55m)
Paths: Fields, tracks and pavement, 9 stiles
Suggested map: aqua3 OS Explorer 179 Gloucester, Cheltenham & Stroud
Grid reference: SO 938124
Parking: Brimpsfield village; lay-bys on Cranham road

A walk through a vanished castle and secluded valleys, taking in the charming Syde and tiny Caundle Green.

❶ Go to end of road towards village centre. Turn **L**. Walk through village and, at corner, turn **R** through gate on to track towards **church**. Before church bear **L** across meadow (**site of castle**) to stile. In next field go half **R** to corner and road.

❷ Turn **R**. Follow road down to just before cottage near bottom. Turn **R** on to drive. After few paces drop down to **L** on to parallel path which will bring you back on to drive. Next, just before cottage, turn **L** and go down into woodland to follow path with stream on **L**. Follow this for 550yds (503m), ignoring bridge on **L**, to cross 2 stiles and emerge on to track.

❸ Turn **L**. Follow track as it rises to **R**. After 100yds (91m) go forward over stile into field with **Brimpsfield House** to **R**. Go half **R** to another stile, pass gate on **R** and cross another stile at next corner. Follow path to

cross bridge. Bear **L** up to track. Follow this for 250yds (229m), until you reach crossways.

❹ Turn **R** to follow footpath along bottom of valley. After ¾ mile (1.2km) track becomes grassy. Where houses appear above you to **L** you can go **L** up slope to visit church at **Syde**. Otherwise remain on valley floor and continue until you reach stiles. Take one furthest to **R**. Go ahead to pass to **L** of cottage. Follow drive up to road.

❺ Turn **L**. Follow road as it turns sharp **L**. At this point turn **R** over stile into field and walk up steep bank to arrive in **Caundle Green**.

❻ Turn **R**. At green, just before large house ahead, bear **R** to stile. Follow winding path down to valley bottom. Turn **L**, through bridle gate. Follow path along valley bottom on same line for ¾ mile (1.2km) until you reach stile at field.

❼ Once in field, continue up slope until you reach gate at road. Turn **L** to re-enter **Brimpsfield**.

423 SLAD VALLEY WALKING WITH ROSIE

4 miles (6.4km) 2hrs Ascent: 425ft (130m)
Paths: Tracks, fields and quiet lanes, 13 stiles
Suggested map: aqua3 OS Explorer 179 Gloucester, Cheltenham & Stroud
Grid reference: SO 878087
Parking: Lay-by at Bull's Cross

Around Slad, backcloth to Laurie Lee's most popular novel, Cider with Rosie.

❶ From **Bull's Cross** walk to end of lay-by (going south). Turn **L** on to tarmac drive. Follow it down and, immediately before buildings, turn **L** over stile into field. Go half **R**, down field and up other side, to gate at top. Turn **L** along track. Where it joins another track stay **R** and continue to lane.

❷ Turn **R** and walk to bottom. Pass between **pond** and Steanbridge Mill. To visit Slad, follow lane into village. To continue, turn **L** immediately after **pond**. Continue to stile. Cross into field, with hedge on **R**. Continue to stile at top.

❸ Cross and follow path to another stile. Cross next field and another stile then continue as path curves **R** towards farm. Pass through gate on to track, stay to **R** of **Furners Farm** and curve **L**. About 30yds (27m) after curve turn **R** over stile on to wooded path then, after few paces, go **R** again over stile into field. Walk

ahead, with farm above you to **R**. Cross another stile then keep to **R** of pond.

❹ At top of pond cross stile into field. Go half **L** across it to gate and stile. In next field, head straight across its lower part. At point where telegraph pole almost meets hedge, turn **R** over stile on to track. Turn **L** to reach lane.

❺ Turn **R**. Follow lane to valley bottom. Start to climb other side and at corner go over stile on **R**. Ascend steeply to another stile at road. Turn **R** along pavement. After 150yds (137m) cross to footpath and climb steeply. At junction of paths bear **L** and continue to field. Follow margin of field up then follow path as it weaves in and out of woodland.

❻ At top turn **R** on to **Folly Lane** and continue to junction. If you want to go into **Slad**, turn **R** otherwise continue on to path that will soon take you into woodland. Walk through woods, finally emerging at **Bull's Cross**.

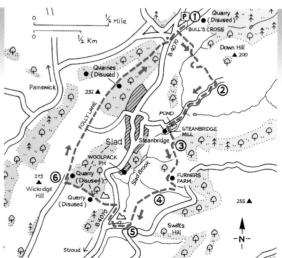

CHALFORD *WEAVING IN THE STROUD VALLEY*

6 miles (9.7km) 3hrs Ascent: 495ft (150m)
Paths: Fields, lanes, canal path and tracks, 3 stiles
Suggested map: aqua3 OS Explorer 168 Stroud, Tetbury and Malmesbury
Grid reference: SO 892025
Parking: Lay-by east of Chalford church

See the impact of the Industrial Revolution in the steep-sided Cotswold valleys.

❶ Walk towards **church**. Immediately before it, cross road and locate path going **R**, towards canal roundhouse. Note the **Belvedere Mill** on **L**. Follow tow path alongside **Thames and Severn Canal** (**R**).

❷ Cross road. Continue along tow path as it descends steps. Now follow path for about 2 miles (3.2km). It shortly disappears under railway line via culvert. Old mills and small factories line route.

❸ Shortly before reaching **Brimscombe**, path passes under railway again. Soon after, it becomes road into industrial estate. At road opposite mill turn **L**, to reach junction. Cross and turn **R**. Immediately after **Ship Inn** turn **L** along road among offices and workshops. Continue along path, with factory walls to **R**. Canal reappears (**L**). As you continue into country pass beneath 3 bridges and footbridge.

❹ At next bridge, with hamlet high on **L**, turn **R** to

follow path to road. Cross this and turn **L**. After few paces turn **R** up short path to meet **Thrupp Lane**. Turn **R**. At top, turn **L** into **Claypits Lane**, turn **R** just before **Thrupp Farm** and climb steeply.

❺ After long climb, as road levels out, you will see **Nether Lypiatt Manor** ahead. Turn **R**, beside tree, over stile into field. Go half **L** to far corner. Cross stone stile. Follow narrow path beside trees to road. Descend lane opposite. Where it appears to fork, go ahead, to descend past a **house**. Enter woodland and fork **R** near bottom. Keep pond on **L** and cross road to climb **Bussage Hill**. After 100yds (91m) pass lane on **L**. At top turn **L**. Opposite **Ram Inn** turn **R**.

❻ After telephone box and bus shelter turn **L** to follow path among houses into woodland. Go ahead until you reach road. Turn **L** and immediately **R** down path beside **cemetery**. Descend to another road. Turn **R** for 50yds (46m); turn **L** down steep lane, leading back to **Chalford**. At bottom turn **L** to return to start.

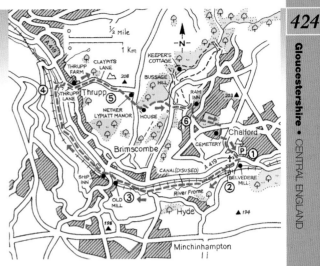

DEERHURST *SAXONS AND THE SEVERN*

3¼ miles (5.3km) 1hr 30min Ascent: 115ft (35m)
Paths: Fields, pavement and river bank, 11 stiles
Suggested map: aqua3 OS Explorer 179 Gloucester, Cheltenham & Stroud
Grid reference: SO 868298
Parking: Car park (small fee) outside Odda's Chapel

An easy walk to discover a rare Saxon chapel on the banks of the River Severn.

❶ With **Odda's Chapel** behind you, turn **L** then **R** through gate to walk along track as far as river bank. Here, turn **L** to follow **Severn Way**. Continue through number of gates and over stiles, following obvious path (sometimes overgrown), with river always close by on **R**. Eventually you reach **Coalhouse Inn**, set back a little to **L**.

❷ Turn **L** after pub to follow road. Once behind pub turn **R** through kissing gate on to area of rough grass. Go half **R** to stile and cross into field. Continue to another stile. In following field go uphill to find another stile at top, beside gate. Go over and follow **R-H** margin of field to another gate. Go through, and continue to road at **Apperley**.

❸ Turn **L** to walk through village. Opposite **post office** (which will be on your **L**) turn **R** down road with houses on your **L**.

❹ Just before **village hall** turn **L** and then walk across playing fields to stile. Cross it, and stay on same line to arrive at another stile. Now follow **R-H** margin of field as it eventually curves **R** and brings you to stile to lane.

❺ Go over stile on to lane and then turn sharp **R** to gate. Once in field turn **L** to come swiftly to another stile. Cross this to enter another field then walk down, crossing another stile and passing to **R** of house. Cross another stile (if there is one – it may only be a temporary measure) and then go half **L** to stile in hedge, well before **farm** ahead. Go over to road and then turn **R**.

❻ Continue until you come to concrete block on your **L**. Go up this and walk along ridge alongside private garden. Cross stile into meadow and continue diagonally **R** heading for stile and gate beside **Odda's Chapel** and timbered building next to it. This will bring you to gate by your starting point.

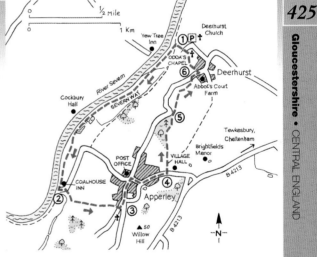

ASHLEWORTH *MEDIEVAL TITHES*

7 miles (11.3km) 3hrs 15min Ascent: 65ft (20m)
Paths: Tracks, fields, lanes and riverbank, 16 stiles
Suggested map: aqua3 OS Explorer 179 Gloucester, Cheltenham & Stroud
Grid reference: SO 818251
Parking: Grass verges in vicinity of tithe barn

Along the banks of the Severn, visiting a huge, and beautifully preserved, tithe barn.

❶ From **tithe barn** walk along road towards **River Severn**, passing **Boat Inn** on **L-H** side.

❷ Turn **L** over stile to walk along river bank. Follow it for just over 3 miles (4.8km). In general path is obvious, but where it sometimes appears to pass through gates, you may find gates are locked and that you should instead be using stile closer to river. **Sandhurst Hill** will come and go, followed by **Red Lion** pub (both across river). Eventually pass house. Immediately after it follow track that leads **L**, away from river then passes to **L** of houses and cottages. Track becomes lane and **Haw Bridge** will appear ahead.

❸ Eventually pass house. Immediately after it follow track that leads **L**, away from river then passes to **L** of houses and cottages. Track becomes lane and **Haw Bridge** will appear ahead.

❹ Just before lane goes **L** turn **L** over stile into field. Walk ahead then, as field opens up at corner, bear half **L** to reach stile. In next field, after few paces, turn **R** to cross bridge. Continue across 2 fields.

❺ This will bring you to lane. Cross it to walk down road opposite then, after 150yds (46m), look for bridge and stile concealed in hedge (**L**). Cross to field and aim half **R** to gateway in hedge. Continue on same line in next field and pass through gateway in corner to road.

❻ Turn **R** and pass **Great House**. Stay on lane as it bears **L**. After passing 2 houses, cross **L** into field. Head downhill, half **R**, to corner and rejoin lane.

❼ Turn **L**. Keep ahead into **Hasfield**, keeping **L** for **Ashleworth**. Turn **L** to see **church** then return to continue, via village, heading towards **Ashleworth**.

❽ Before cottages on **R**, turn **R** at footpath sign. Where path divides, take far **L** one across several fields on same line, passing **L** of **Colways Farm**. This will bring you to lane opposite turning for **Ashleworth Quay**. Just **L** of road opposite is stile in field. Cross it, then field to reach stile. Follow path on **R** side of fields all the way back to just before **tithe barn**.

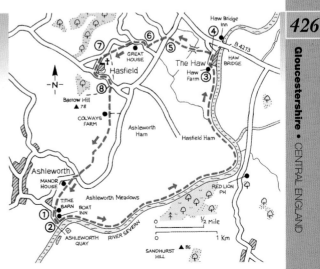

Gloucestershire

427 ULEY *MAGNIFICENT FORT ON THE HILL*

3 miles (4.8km) 1hr 30min **Ascent:** 345ft (105m)

Paths: Tracks and fields

Suggested map: aqua3 OS Explorer 168 Stroud, Tetbury and Malmesbury

Grid reference: ST 789984

Parking: Main street of Uley

The vast bulk of the ancient fort of Uley Bury forms the centrepiece for this walk along the Cotswold escarpment.

❶ From main street of Uley locate **post office** (on your **L** as you walk up street). Walk along narrow lane (to **R**, as you look at it). Pass between houses as lane dwindles to become track. Immediately before stile turn **R** along enclosed path towards **church**.

❷ When churchyard can be seen on R, turn **L** up narrow path beside cottage. This rises fairly sharply and brings you to kissing gate. Pass through into meadow. Climb steeply up grassland towards woodland.

❸ At tree-line keep **L** of woods. At corner go through gate and then follow winding woodland path, climbing among trees. When you come to fence stay on path as it bears **L**. Go over stile and then continue ascending, to emerge from woods. Stay on path as it rises across grassland to junction.

❹ Turn **R** to follow contour of hill – edge of ancient fort, **Uley Bury**. You are following perimeter of fort in anti-clockwise direction, with steep drops to your **R**. When you meet another junction of paths go **L** along edge of hill, with views to west.

❺ At next corner continue to follow edge of fort, disregarding stile that invites you to descend. At next corner, at fort's southeastern point, bear **R** on path that descends through hillocks and then quite steeply through bushes, keeping **L**. This will bring you to stile into meadow and tarmac path.

❻ Walk along path, all the way to cottage then kissing gate. Go through then pass beside cottage to arrive at lane. Turn **L** and follow it, soon passing **Uley Brewery**, which produces some fine beers including Uley Bitter and Uley Old Spot, to reach main road. Turn **L**, passing South Street, to return to start. If you want to sample the local beers, stop at the Old Crown pub on the main street opposite the **church**.

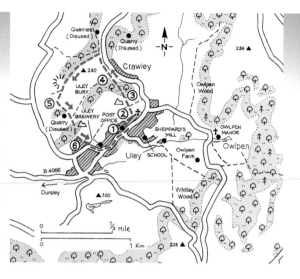

428 DYMOCK *THE WARTIME POETS*

8 miles (12.9km) 3hrs 45min **Ascent:** 100ft (30m)

Paths: Fields and lanes, 27 stiles

Suggested map: aqua3 OS Outdoor Leisure 14 Wye Valley & Forest of Dean; Explorers 189 Hereford & Ross-on-Wye; 190 Malvern Hills & Bredon Hill

Grid reference: SO 677288 (on Outdoor Leisure 14)

Parking: Main road of Kempley Green; near its southeastern end

One-time home to the Dymock Poets.

❶ Walk southeast out of **Kempley Green**. Turn **L** before **Knapp Cottage**. Take **R-H** of 2 paths. Cross stiles and pass barn. Go through gate into orchard. Enter **Dymock Wood** to follow path to road.

❷ Turn **R** then **L** before motorway bridge. Where road bears **L**, proceed through gate into fields. Follow route, alongside motorway, to reach stream. Turn **L** before it. Cross track and stiles, pass through gate and ahead along track, aiming to **R** of **Boyce Court**.

❸ Pass to **L** of lake. Go through woodland to lane. Turn **R** over bridge and **L** on to path by stream. Continue, staying first **R** then **L** of stream, to **Dymock**.

❹ Cross churchyard then go through gate into field. Turn half **L**; take 2nd bridge on **R**. Bear half **L** to stile. Turn **R** along disused road. Cross B4215. Follow track, leaving it to keep to **R** of **Allum's Farm**. Pass barn. Go half **L** across field to gate. Enter orchard, turn **R**.

Follow its **L** margin then that of field, to road.

❺ Turn **R**. After 600yds (549m) turn **R** into field alongside woodland. After 120yds (110m) go half **R** over mound to enter woods. Turn **R**. Follow boundary to stile. Turn **L** and re-enter woodland. Follow obvious path, eventually emerging at stile. Cross field, keeping to **L** of chimney then **R** into field. Look for stile on **L**, cross into adjacent field; turn **R** to find bridge across stream. Go half **L** across fields to road.

❻ Turn **L**. Continue past **St Mary's Church**. At next T-junction, go into field ahead. Proceed into next field. Continue with stream on **L** across fields to lane. Turn **L** to junction at **Fishpool**.

❼ Turn **R**. After 50yds (46m), turn **L** over stile. Curve **R**; pass series of stiles to aim eventually just to **R** of cottage. Follow path through poultry enclosures. Bear **L** over stiles so that house is on **R**. Pass house; go **R** into field. Turn **L**. Follow same line to **Kempley Green**.

429 BROCKWEIR *ALONG OFFA'S DYKE*

4½ miles (7.2km) 2hrs 15min **Ascent:** 740ft (225m)

Paths: Tracks, fields, lanes, stony paths and riverbank, 5 stiles

Suggested map: aqua3 OS Outdoor Leisure 14 Wye Valley & Forest of Dean

Grid reference: ST 540011

Parking: Lay-by near telephone box in Brockweir; Tintern Old Railway Station, on other side of river (fee)

Exploring the Saxon King's earthwork.

❶ Walk uphill out of **Brockweir** until you reach junction on **L** ('Coldharbour'). Turn **L** along narrow lane for 160yds (146m). At corner beside **Rock Farm** turn **L** on to track ('Offa's Dyke Path'), which soon narrows markedly and climbs fairly steeply. Continue walking up to reach lane.

❷ Cross this. Continue ascent until you reach another lane. Turn **L**. Follow lane for 200yds (183m), to pass cottage on **R**, followed by ruined stone buildings. Turn **R** along lane.

❸ Keep to **R** of **Chapel Cottage** on to path, still ascending. When you reach wider track, fork **L**. This dwindles to path, continuing to climb, until it brings you to another track, beside stone stile. Turn **L** again.

❹ After few paces, before gate and house, fork **R** to stile at field. Cross this to another pair of stiles, to **L** of house. In next field, stay to **L** of farm and come to stile at lane. Turn **R** and follow gently climbing lane. It levels

out then where it starts to climb again at corner, turn **L** on to **R-H** path, heading towards Oak Cottage, Bigs Weir and Monmouth. Descend until you arrive at lane before house.

❺ Turn **L** here to follow track that descends to **R** of another house. Track will continue down into woodland. Stay on main, obvious track, watching out for loose stones, as it meanders down hillside. This will bring you to cottage at corner. Go **L** with track, which later becomes narrow path. Stay on this. Follow it down hillside among trees, still keeping eye on loose pebbles. Soon **River Wye** will appear below you, to **R**. At bottom pass through gap in fence, and bear **R** towards grassy river bank, where you will meet stile.

❻ Turn **L** through stile. Follow river back to **Brockweir**, passing through gates and crossing bridges where they arise. As you approach the village keep close to river to enter path that will bring you on to lane leading up to road at Brockweir Bridge.

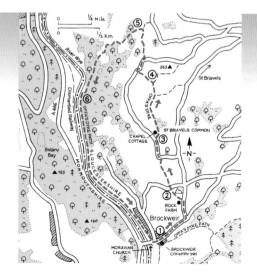

Gloucestershire

ADLESTROP EMPIRES AND POETS

5 miles (8km) 2hrs **Ascent:** 230ft (70m)
Paths: Track, field and road, 6 stiles
Suggested map: aqua3 OS Explorer OL45 The Cotswolds
Grid reference: SP 241272 **Parking:** Car park (donations requested) outside village hall

In the footsteps of imperialist Warren Hastings and the poet Edward Thomas.

❶ From car park turn **L** along road. Pass road on R, bus shelter (**Adlestrop**) and houses. 200yds (183m) after another road, turn **R** over stile. Follow woodland path to **L**. Continue on path until it meets stile at road.
❷ Cross road with care. Turn **L** along verge. Before road on R, turn **R** through gate to path in **Daylesford Estate**. Path curves **L** towards fence. Stay to **L** of fence until you reach stile. Go over and cross paddock. Pass through gate, turn **R** then **L** between fences.
❸ Cross bridge. Follow avenue towards buildings. Traverse farmyard; turn **R**, passing estate office.
❹ Walk along drive between paddocks, soon following estate wall. Pass gateway to offices then, as it goes sharp R, stay on drive, eventually reaching road. Turn **R**.
❺ Walk along road, with estate R, until **Daylesford** estate village. Opposite **Daylesford House** drive is footpath leading to **Daylesford church**. After visiting

church, return to road, turn **R** and retrace your steps. Before pavement ends, turn **R** over stile.
❻ Cross field to railway footbridge. Go over it and ahead into field (not field on L) then head, bearing slightly **R**, for another footbridge. Cross into field, turn **R** then **L** at corner. Follow field margin as it passes into another field. At next corner, enter field in front of you. Turn **R** then **L**. At next corner, go **R** to track.
❼ Turn **R** and pass **Oddington church**. Continue to junction. Turn **R**. Pass **Fox** pub and continue to next junction. Turn **R** and walk along pavement. Where this ends, cross road carefully to pavement opposite.
❽ Beyond bridge, turn **L** along Adlestrop road then turn immediately **R** over 2 stiles. Walk towards **Adlestrop Park**. As you draw level with **cricket pitch** go diagonally **L** to gate about 100yds (91m) to R of pavilion.
❾ Follow track past **Adlestrop church**. At next junction turn **L** through village until you reach bus stop. Turn **L** to car park.

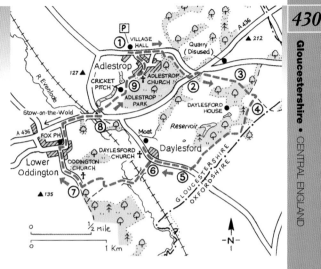

CHASTLETON A TIMELESS VILLAGE

4 miles (6.4km) 2hrs **Ascent:** 427ft (130m)
Paths: Meadows, lanes, woodland, 8 stiles
Suggested map: aqua3 OS Explorer OL45 The Cotswolds
Grid reference: SP 241271
Parking: Car park (donations) beside village hall, Adlestrop

Another shorter walk from this classic village to an age-old house.

❶ From car park turn **L** on to road and **L** again up broad track ('**Macmillan Way**'). Climb stile by gate; enter meadow. Bear **L** (yellow waymarker). Walk up field, with **Fern Farm** up to R. Cross stile in top **L** corner and continue up fence. Soon cross stile to **L**. Continue, pass bulging oak tree on R. Cross another stile. Continue ahead up field. Hill gets steeper.
❷ Cross stile by wooden gate. Walk up through line of trees. Continue straight across next field. Go over crest of hill and through iron gate into **Chastleton Estate**. Continue ahead up avenue of trees. Go through 2 gates to reach road.
❸ Turn **R** and along road, pass **Chastleton House** then **St Mary's Church**. Pass dovecote on R. Stay on road, which bends up **R**, and pass car park on R.
❹ Where road bends sharply R, turn **L** into private road. Cross cattle grid and immediately turn **R**. Go

through gate. Take bridleway diagonally **L** up field, parallel with road. On level with **Barrow House farm**, go through small gate, cross drive and take L of 2 gates opposite. Go through 2 more gates to enter tree circle of **Chastleton Barrow**.
❺ Now, retrace your route to drive. Turn **L**. At road turn **L**. After short distance turn **R** across stile. Walk ahead through trees and follow path, which leads diagonally **L** across field. Keep straight down, passing barns to L. Cross track and walk ahead down edge of woodland. At bottom corner bear **R** into woods. Follow winding path, cross stile and emerge at field.
❻ Turn **L** on track. Turn **R** before gateway, and walk down field edge. Go through gate into **Long Drive**. Follow path via trees and emerge on to road. Cross and go through gateway on other side. Soon turn **R** along narrow footpath. Follow this through trees; cross stile. Turn **L** on road. Take 1st turning **L**. Walk through **Adlestrop**, keeping **R** to return to car park.

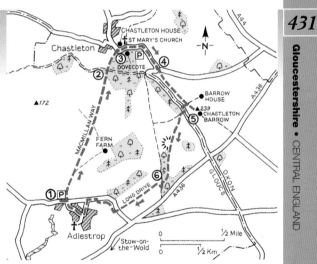

THE CAMPDENS ARTS AND CRAFTS

2½ miles (4km) 1hr 15min **Ascent:** 83ft (25m)
Paths: Fields, road and track, 8 stiles
Suggested map: aqua3 OS Explorer OL45 The Cotswolds
Grid reference: SP 151391
Parking: Campden High Street or parking area on main square

A walk between two lovely Cotswold villages, following the rise and fall of the Guild of Handicraft.

❶ This walk starts in **Chipping Campden**, perhaps the finest of all the Cotswold villages and extends to **Broad Campden**. Broad Campden has exceptionally pretty houses and it was in this idyllic rural setting that Charles Ashbee set up his Guild of Handicraft. From the High Street, walk through arch next to **Noel Arms Hotel** and continue ahead to join path. Pass **playing fields** and at junction with road go **L** into field then immediately **R** to follow field edge parallel with road.
❷ After 600yds (549m), fork **R** and come to gate. Follow drive, walk past house and then leave drive to walk ahead to gate. Pass through alley and follow it to pass **Quaker Meeting House**.
❸ Emerge at green with **church** to your L. At junction, continue ahead to walk through village. Road bears **L** and straightens. After turning for Blockley, go

L down road ('Unsuitable for Motors'). After 70yds (64m) turn **R** along drive of 'Hollybush'. Pass through gate and then another and continue along **L**, lower margin of orchard.
❹ Cross stile, then bridge and turn sharp **R** to walk along **R** edge of field, with stream on R. Go **R** to end of field to cross stream and in next field go straight across, bearing little **R**, to gap. Go up next field to stile and cross into field.
❺ Turn **L** and then go half **R** to pass to R of house. Cross stile and then go half **R** to gate. Go through and go quarter **R** down to another stile in corner. In next field go half **R**, with **Campden church** away R, to approach stream near stone arch.
❻ Don't cross stream but, 70yds (64m) after arch, turn **R** through gate and follow path as it turns **L** to drive. Turn **R**; follow drive to road (**Calf Lane**). At road turn **R** and at top turn **L** into Church Street (turn **R** to visit **church**) to return to junction with main street.

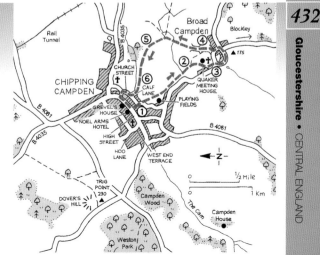

Herefordshire

(sidebar) Herefordshire • CENTRAL ENGLAND

433 ASHPERTON *Hereford's Lost Canal*

7¾ miles (12.5km) 3hrs 30min Ascent: 260ft (79m)
Paths: Field and woodland paths, minor roads, at least 35 stiles
Suggested map: aqua3 OS Explorer 202 Leominster & Bromyard
Grid reference: SO 642415
Parking: St Bartholomew's Church, Ashperton

Along an old waterway, now being restored.

❶ From car park take 'forty shillings' gate, behind houses. (For 10 paces path is in a garden.) Join track to A417. Turn L, then R, beside driveway. Follow fingerpost across meadows for 600yds (549m). Find gate by cricket net. Veer R. Cross driveway down field. Join Haywood Lane near house. Turn L. Follow this for 1 mile (1.6km). Find stile on L just beyond gate, 100yds (91m) after driveway to **Upleadon Court**.
❷ Cross arable fields and ditch, then **Upleadon Farm's** driveway. Aim for far **L-H** corner. Skirt woodland to L, later striking L (waymarked) up huge field. At Gold Hill Farm go R of tall shed. Behind this, turn L then briefly up and R. Follow boundary to road.
❸ Turn L for ¼ mile (400m). Where road turns L continue for ½ mile (800m), initially beside wood. Over rotting plank turn L but in 25yds (23m) turn R. After 500yds (457m) enter trees. On leaving them strike half R for **White House.**

❹ Turn R along road. At junction, take footpath opposite (ditch on R). (Beware of hitting your head on horizontal tree trunk just after single-plank footbridge.) Walk 700yds (640m) across fields, over 3 footbridges and under power lines, passing through gap in stile, but do not cross – note 3 waymarkers on its far side. Turn L, heading towards old orchards. Just beyond **Homend** find stile in far L-H corner, shielded by ash and elder. Turn L, soon moving R to double gates flanking wide concrete bridge. After avenue keep ahead, eventually veering R. Go 550yds (503m), crossing driveway to **Canon Frome Court**, then another track, finally reaching road by spinney.
❺ Cross road; walk to canal. Turn L. In 140yds (128m) turn R, over canal. Veer L and uphill, finding large oak in top L-H corner. Keep this line despite field boundary shortly curving away. At copse turn R, later moving L into indistinct lane. Village hall heralds **A417.** Turn L, along pavement then R to **church.**

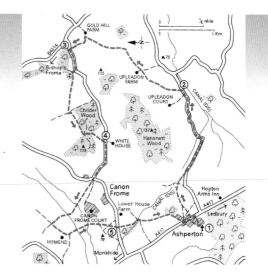

434 FROME VALLEY *Two Churches*

4¾ miles (7.7km) 2hrs 30min Ascent: 475ft (145m)
Paths: Field paths, dirt tracks, lanes and minor roads, 14 stiles
Suggested map: aqua3 OS Explorer 202 Leominster & Bromyard
Grid reference: SO 679502
Parking: Roadside just before grassy lane to Acton Beauchamp's church – please tuck in tightly

You'll discover secluded churches and special wild service trees set amid pastures on this easy ramble.

❶ Leave churchyard by iron gate in top corner. Soon enter orchard. Skirt round to R, passing outbuildings of **Church House Farm** and then down to pass behind tall barns. Now orchard track ascends. When 110yds (100m) beyond power lines, at corner of plantation, turn L (blue waymarker), to walk between orchard rows. At end turn L. In roughly 160yds (146m), well before power lines and just before trees shielding pond, go R. Soon you'll have hedge on your L; reach gate and stile of 3 railway sleepers.
❷ Once through **Halteshill Coppice** drop straight down to footbridge. Now go straight up bank, swapping hedge sides, to minor road. Turn R. Take the opportunity to visit the **church.** You will notice that the stonework is of a similar vintage to that in **Acton Beauchamp** – Norman and 13th-century. Return to

road and turn R. At entrance to **The Hawkins** take stile, then follow waymarkers across track to skirt this farm. Now head down pastures to cross footbridge over **Linton Brook.**
❸ Turn L, walking beside **Linton Brook** for ⅝ mile (1km), to road. Turn L for 160yds (146m). Turn R. Now driveway to **Upper Venn Farm** runs for ½ mile (800m). Just before farm buildings move L, to stile roughly 70yds (64m) along edge of field from farm.
❹ Cross field diagonally, to gate in L hedge. Turn L across field, aiming slightly uphill, beside residual mature oaks. You'll find stile beyond electricity pole. Pick up rough track to **The Venn.** Admire its cream walls and exposed timbers and then turn away, along drive. Follow this down to minor road.
❺ Turn L, passing **Frome Valley Vineyard** on a sharp bend. At crossroads go straight over. Climbing this quite steep lane, **Church of St Giles** comes into view. Take 1st turning on L to return to your car.

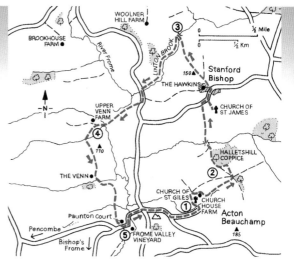

435 HEREFORD *Historic Streets*

2¾ miles (4.4km) 1hr 45min Ascent: Negligible
Paths: City streets, riverside path and tracks
Suggested map: aqua3 OS Explorer 189 Hereford & Ross-on-Wye
Grid reference: SO 510403
Parking: Garrick House long-stay, pay-and-display multi-storey car park, Widemarsh Street
Note: Several busy junctions without subways – care needed

Around a charming medieval city.

❶ Turn L out of car park. After 150yds (137m) is Coningsby Hospital, now **Coningsby Museum**. Go back short way to walk along Coningsby Street, to T-junction. Turn R on Monkmoor Street. Turn R into **Commercial Road.** At Blueschool Street junction is city wall, while on near side are magistrates' courts.
❷ Cross Commercial Road then Bath Street. Follow Union Street. Go R to High Town. Go L down Church Street, to **Hereford Cathedral** (TIC on R).
❸ Go L, beside cathedral, passing stonemasons' workshop. Go along Castle Street. Shortly before **Castle House Hotel** turn R to **Castle Green.** Hug railings on L, beside Castle Pool (part of original moat), to walk above green and Nelson Column (1809). Zig-zag down to cross **Victoria Footbridge.**
❹ Turn R (or L for extended riverside stroll) passing putting green, tennis courts and wood carving.

Keeping on south side of river – opposite **Left Bank** complex – cross St Martin's Street to go under **Greyfriars Bridge**, continuing to **Hunderton Bridge.**
❺ Cross old railway bridge. When **River Wye** floods, this footway/cycleway provides emergency vehicular access. Take steps down back towards city. Skirt **rowing club**, then walk up Greyfriars Avenue. Just before junction go half R across car park to go through pedestrian subway. (But go R, through car subway, to see city wall.) Brick building ahead is built on city wall. Go up steps. Cross St Nicholas' Street (take care).
❻ As you begin along Victoria Street, you'll see single tree. A few paces beyond it, 10ft (3m) up in wall, is a cannon ball, which was probably embedded there during the siege of **Hereford** in 1645. Go along West Street to Broad Street. Turn L. Walk towards **All Saints Church.** Turn R then L, down **Widemarsh Street** to car park.

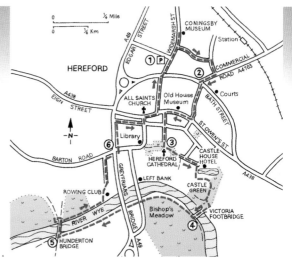

COPPET HILL *BESIDE THE RIVER WYE*

6¾ miles (10.9km) 3hrs **Ascent:** 855t (260m)
Paths: Quiet lanes, riverside meadows, woodland paths, 2 stiles
Suggested map: aqua3 OS Explorer OL14 Wye Valley & Forest of Dean
Grid reference: SO 575196
Parking: Goodrich Castle car park open daily 9:30am to 7pm

A peaceful walk with fine views.
❶ Walk back to castle access road junction; turn **L**. In 125yds (114m) cross bridge over **B4229**.
❷ Go up further 400yds (366m). Ignore another road branching off to R, and go on just a few paces – there are 3 low wooden posts to your L.
❸ Opposite, between 2 roads, sign ('Coppet Hill Nature Reserve') indicates return route. Go ½ mile (800m) up this dead end, to cattle grid. Here, at brow, woods give way to parkland. Go ahead for 275yds (251m) to single horse chestnut tree at **R** turn.
❹ Continue for 400yds (366m), bending **L** and dipping down, along road. It curves **R** slightly, while gravel track goes up ramp and slightly **L**.
❺ Curve **R**. Ignore pillared driveway but go down **youth hostel's** driveway. At its entrance gate take footpath that runs initially parallel to it. Go down wooden steps and along sometimes muddy path to reach T-junction beside **River Wye**.

❻ Turn **R**, following Wye Valley Walk (turn **L** to visit **church** first). Within ¼ mile (400m) you'll reach old, iron girder railway bridge, which now carries Wye Valley Walk across river, but stay this side, passing underneath bridge. After walking 125yds (114m) look out for 6 wooden steps down to **L** at fork.
❼ Take steps, to remain close to river. Continue for about 1¼ miles (2km). Enter **Coldwell Wood** to walk beside river for further ¼ mile (400m). On leaving, keep by river in preference to path that follows woodland's edge. In about 350yds (320m) you'll reach stile beside fallen willow.
❽ Turn **R** ('Coppet Hill'). Soon begin arduous woodland ascent. Eventually you'll have some fine views. Path levels, later rising to **The Folly**, then goes down (not up!) to triangulation point. Follow clear green sward ahead, becoming narrow rut then stepped path, down to road, close to Point ❸. Retrace your steps to castle car park.

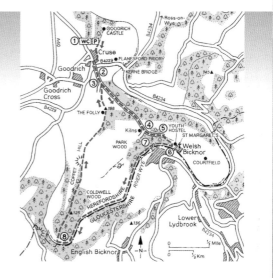

AYMESTREY *ROCKS OF AGES*

4¾ miles (7.7km) 2hrs 30min **Ascent:** 525ft (160m)
Paths: Good tracks, field paths, minor roads, steep woodland sections, 11 stiles
Suggested map: aqua3 OS Explorer 203 Ludlow
Grid reference: SO426658
Parking: At old quarry entrance, on east side of A4110, ¼ mile (400m) north of Aymestrey Bridge

Around a redeveloped quarry now used for grazing and woodland.
❶ Walk up access road for almost ½ mile (800m), until beyond garden of house and just before junction of tracks. Note stile on R – your route returns over this.
❷ Go 30yds (27m) further and turn **L**, passing house with stone wall relic in its garden. Continue, through **Yatton**, to T-junction. Turn **L** to **A4110**. Cross to stile, walking along L–H field edge. Through gate go forward then skirt round **R** edge of oak and ash embankment, to find corner stile. Walk up **L** edge of field but, at brow, where it bends for 70yds (64m) to corner, slip **L** through gap in hedge to walk along its other side. Within 60yds (55m) you will be on clear path, steeply down through woodland, ravine on your **L**. Join driveway of **River Bow**, to minor road.
❸ Turn **L** here, joining **Mortimer Trail**. Continue along riverside lane for nearly ¾ mile (1.2km), to reach **A4110**. Cross then walk for 25yds (23m) to **R**.

(**Riverside Inn** is 175yds/160m further.) Take raised green track, heading for hills. Then go diagonally across 2 fields, to stile and wooden steps.
❹ Ascend steeply through trees. Leave by stile, to cross 2 meadows diagonally. Take stile on **R** to walk along L–H edge of field, still heading downhill. At trees turn **L**. Soon reach tarmac road. Turn **L** along road, now going back uphill. Beyond **Hill Farm**, enter Croft Estate. Walk along gravel track. After 110yds (100m) ignore R fork but, 550yds (503m) further on, you must leave it. This spot is identified by end to deciduous trees on L and **Mortimer Trail** marker post on wide ride between larches and evergreens on R.
❺ Turn **L** (no signpost). Within 110yds (100m) go half **R** and more steeply down. Within 250yds (229m) look out for modern wooden gate, waymarked, leading out of woods. Walk along its **R–H** edge (and beside small plantation). At far corner, within field, turn **L** to Point ❷. Retrace your steps to start.

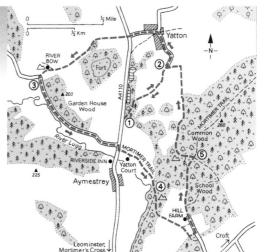

DOWNTON ON THE ROCK *PICTURESQUE CASTLE*

10 miles (16.1km) 4hrs 30min **Ascent:** 1,200ft (100m)
Paths: Pastures, leafy paths, grass tracks, dirt tracks, tarmac lanes, 13 stiles
Suggested map: aqua3 OS Explorer 203 Ludlow
Grid reference: SO 403741 **Parking:** Community centre and village hall car park, Leintwardine

A landscape designed to please the eye.
❶ Walk to Watling Street. At **school** turn **R**. Go half **L** at stile, in orchard, curve **L**. Avoid private drive. At road go **R**, along tarmac. In 300yds (274m) turn **L**, to **A4113**. Cross, then turn **R** up lane for 1 mile (1.6km). Soon after skew junction go forward. Cross 3 fields, into woodland. At **A4113** turn **L** then **R**, beside wire fence. At end follow field edge to **L** for 70yds (64m). Go down bank in trees to pass stables on R, then along dirt road for ½ mile (800m) to **Brakes Farm**.
❷ Keep ahead (waymarker). Cross minor road diagonally. Cross fields to lane beside houses Nos 20 and 19. Turn **L**. Soon turn **R**, downhill. Turn **R**, along river, just before **Forge Bridge**. Skirt 2 houses. Up bank, join track. Follow this to **Castle Bridge**. Ascend but within 110yds (100m) of leaving woodland go half **R**. Rejoin track into forest for perhaps 60yds (55m). Scramble up bank (waymarker). Traverse steep meadow to gate in top, among oaks. Keep this line to go down meadow then locate stile into trees.

❸ Turn **L** and descend. At meadow, curve round dry valley. At **L** bend go through gate on **R**. Go **L** of specimen oak to hidden stile in bottom corner. Cross over footbridge; turn **R**. Cross meadow to gate, and soon reach minor road. Turn **R**. Descend through **Burrington**, to its **church**. Behind church, cross meadows to **Burrington Bridge**. Cross **River Teme**. After 650yds (594m) take **R** turn. At **Downton**, head towards **Old Downton House**, but then turn **L**. Beyond wall take **R**-most gate (waymarker), along lane. Ascend **R–H** field edge, later following beech-lined avenue to reach junction with dirt track.
❹ Over stile, descend, initially steeply. Past small pond veer **L** along **R–H** field edge. Turn **R**. After 120yds (110m) of road go through difficult gate. In bottom **L–H** corner of field find stile just beyond power lines. Veer **R** (but cross drainage ditch) to stile. Aim for houses ahead. Pass through 2 gates. On residential road turn **R**, then **L**. Back in **Leintwardine**, turn **R** at **Lion Hotel** and from here return to start.

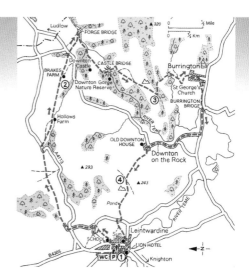

Herefordshire

439 KILPECK ORCOP HILL

4¾ miles (7.7km) 2hrs 45min Ascent: 590ft (180m) ▲
Paths: Field paths, tracks and minor lanes, 21 stiles
Suggested map: aqua3 OS Explorer 189 Hereford & Ross-on-Wye
Grid reference: SO 445304
Parking: Spaces beside St Mary's and St David's Church, Kilpeck

A walk once enjoyed by Violette Szabo, a wartime heroine.

❶ Walk down to **Red Lion**. Turn **R**. At junction follow 'Garway Hill'. Take 2nd fingerpost. Find another stile behind **The Knoll** (house). Strike diagonally across pasture. Cross another stile, now with field boundary on your **R**. Veer **L** to reach lane at bend. Turn **L**. Follow waymarkers through trees then go straight down field to near junction.

❷ Turn **L**, past **Two Brooks**. After 500yds (457m) turn **L**, through gate by **Grafton Oak**, tucked behind. Soon in meadow, follow fence until crossing stile. Now keep ahead but drift down, guided by gigantic oak. The stile you need is ahead, not another, further down, that crosses brook. Contour with trees on your **L** for 2 fields. In 3rd find footbridge down and **L**.

❸ Follow waymarkers, diagonally up field. Walk with wire fence on your **R**. Leave this long field at its top end (but, to observe rights of way, first cross and re-cross wire fence on your **R**, via wooded area). Go diagonally to opening beside hollow oak, not more easily seen, 3-bar stile. Move **L** to walk along **L-H** field edge. Ignore waymarker into **L-H** field – any way out has completely disappeared. Instead keep ahead, to tarmac road. Turn **L**. After 650yds (594m) fingerpost slants **L**.

❹ Take this path through bracken to track. Turn **R** for 25yds (23m), then **L**, to pass to **R** of **Saddlebow Farm**. Avenue below leads into field. Walk along this **R** edge, to just before gate. Join good track, following it for 650yds (594m), until 3 gates in corner.

❺ Take 2nd on **L**. Beyond **New House Farm** go over ¼ mile (400m) to junction. Don't turn down to Kilpeck yet! Go 160yds (146m) further. Here go **L**, around old farm buildings. Descend to unseen gap not 50yds (46m) **L** of bottom R-H corner. Out of this copse, cross 2 fields to pass between buildings of **The Priory**. Avenue of horse chestnuts leads to **Red Lion**.

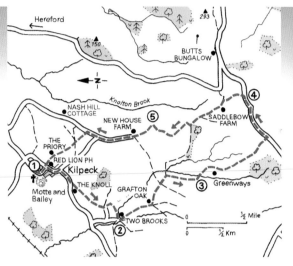

440 ABBEY DORE GOLDEN VALLEY

8 miles (12.9km) 3hrs 45min Ascent: 540ft (165m) ▲
Paths: Meadows, tracks and woodland paths (one stony, awkward descent), 24 stiles
Suggested map: aqua3 OS Explorer OL13 Brecon Beacons (East)
Grid reference: SO 386302 **Parking:** On east side of B4347, south of lychgate, facing south

In search of a 19th-century workhouse.

❶ Cross B4347 at lychgate. Slant **L** up fields. Beside dwelling go up path, to 3rd field. In 20yds (18m) turn **R** up hedged lane to **Ewyas Harold Common**.

❷ This is the prescribed route but dozens of paths and tracks criss-cross here. Across concrete track take **L** diagonal ride. In 65yds (60m) take slightly **L** option. After 45yds (41m) bear **R**. In 325yds (297m) take **R-H** option. After 70yds (64m) move **L** slightly to resume your line. In 160yds (146m) move 10yds (9m) **L** on wide track; turn **R**. In 55yds (50m) turn **L** on big gravel track. Just beyond seat fork **R**, down rutted track. After 3 houses swing **R**, over cattle grid.

❸ In village, turn **R** then **R** again. At bend go up steps. Aim **L** of spinney. After buildings ascend 3 fields to corner stile. When trees end swing up and **L** to boundary corner. Keep field edge **R**, to **Plash Farm**.

❹ Get behind farmhouse by turning **R** twice. Descend to bottom corner. Sunken lane leads to road.

Turn **R**, then **L** to **Dulas Court**. Cross **brook** by bridge beside buildings. Turn **R** in 30yds (27m). Go diagonally up meadow into conifers. Walk uphill for 50yds (46m) to track, but, within 30yds (27m), clear path bears **R**, uphill. Out of woodland, aim for pole. Pass between buildings of **Cot Farm**.

❺ Walk with hedge **L**. Keep this line across fields, to regain common. In 70yds (64m) join track (**L** part of hairpin); 70yds (64m) further continue on green sward, soon joining another track. Some 50yds (46m) before house, which you saw earlier, turn **L**. Stiles over deer fences lead to lane by **Cwm Farm**. Turn **R**. Before **Abbey Dore Court Garden** find stile at bridge. In 3rd field after 300yds (274m) move **R** to cross bridge.

❻ Waymarked stiles lead to **Riverdale** (Dore workhouse buildings). Retrace your steps to Point ❻. Now keep on east side of river. Turn **L** at road. In 60yds (55m) take well-waymarked route between military fence and gardens. Finally, concrete footbridge, meadow and agricultural graveyard lead to **abbey**.

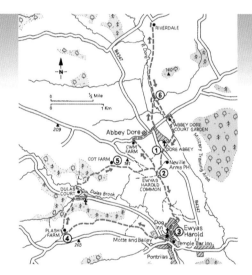

441 HERGEST RIDGE OVERLOOKING WALES

7½ miles (12.1km) 3hrs 30min Ascent: 1,115ft (340m) ▲
Paths: Meadows, field paths, excellent tracks, 14 stiles
Suggested map: aqua3 OS Explorer 201 Knighton & Presteigne
Grid reference: SO 295565
Parking: Mill Street car park (east and west sides of Crabtree Street)

Up to a glorious ridge overlooking Wales.

❶ Walk down High Street. Take alley on **R**, between hairdresser and shop. Zig-zag to Bridge Street. Turn **R**. Cross **River Arrow**. Take driveway to **Newburn Farm**.

❷ Walk through farmyard. Go round 3 sides then take gate into field. After area planted with trees, take stile to **R-H** field edge, under huge oak limbs. Walk for over ½ mile (800m) through meadows, curving **L** to stile and steps down to road.

❸ Turn **R**, and **R** again to cross Hergest Bridge. After 100yds (91m) take **L** fingerpost. Along **R** field edge, cross stile into trees. On track, bend **L**. Cross meadow to line of sweet chestnuts. Over difficult stile, turn **R**, along awkward path across steep, wooded bank. After 325yds (297m) stile puts you onto another meadow. Cross footbridge. Drop slightly to skirt woodland and reach marker post. Cross 2 more stiles in this pasture. Go ahead and fractionally **R** for 80yds (73m) to single-plank stile and waymarker (possibly obscured).

Another, more substantial, double-stiled footbridge stands 40yds (37m) ahead. Bear **L**, to find, in 100yds (91m), steps down to metal footbridge.

❹ At road on caravan site turn **R**. Just 30yds (27m) after gates find stile (perhaps overgrown), **R**. Almost immediately, take 2nd stile beside huge oak. At track beside **Mahollam Farm** bear **R**, downhill. Do not stay on green lane, but go **R**, finding another metal footbridge. Ascend steeply, soon in farmland. Cross fields to road. Turn **R**. Go **L** for 400yds (366m) to gate. Now go straight up to trig point on **Hergest Ridge**.

❺ Path leads to pool. Continue for 1½ miles (2.4km). Once on road again, 30yds (27m) after sign, 'Kington – centre for walking', turn **R**. Round **Haywood Farm**, continue to cattle grid. Along road look for fingerpost by 'No 31'. Go down this field. Turn away from **Kington** for 120yds (110m); turn sharply **L**, '16 Tatty Moor'. Cross meadows to recreation ground. Join Park Avenue, which becomes Mill Street.

Herefordshire

HARLEY'S MOUNTAIN *BRACING AIR*

3¾ miles (6km) 2hrs 15min **Ascent:** 755ft (230m)
Paths: Meadows, field paths, woodland tracks with roots, 10 stiles
Suggested map: aqua3 OS Explorer 201 Knighton & Presteigne
Grid reference: SO 364672
Parking: At St Michael's Church, Lingen (tuck in well)

A brisk walk in farming country.
❶ Walk away from **church**; cross to take minor road ('Willey'). At 1st bend, follow fingerpost directly ahead. Climb over difficult gate beside small corrugated shed; walk by paddock edge, reaching lane in trees.
❷ Strike up field, passing dead oak. Follow waymarker up and slightly **R**. In corner, negotiate rusty gate between better ones. At derelict **Mynde Farm** skirt **L**, around 2 collapsed buildings. Find gate on **R** behind low building.
❸ Go down and up meadow to stile. Veer **L**, passing beside **Mountain Buildings** on rutted, rocky track. After 160yds (146m) enter field. Take line diagonally across field (but if ridged with potatoes, or other crop, follow 2 field edges **L**) then keep that line, now with hedge **L**. Take track along ridge to gate with pool to **R** (dry in summer). Above and behind is trig point.
❹ Turn **L**, initially preferring L-H field edge to lane (overgrown). Descend for 650yds (594m). At bottom

move **L**, to small gate. Through trees, shortly emerge close to **The Red House**. Keep ahead, finding narrow path within trees, **R** of garage and beside hedge. Within 40yds (37m) negotiate metal gate. Don't be tempted down; instead move **L**, beside wire fence for just a few paces, then, maintaining fence's line, proceed to walk below narrow ridge on faint tractor track for 100yds (91m). When ground ahead drops steeply into dell turn half **L**, to walk down woody edge of meadow. In 2nd meadow, where trees bulge out to **L**, dive back into woodland – (waymarker on oak).
❺ Go ahead, sometimes boggy, in woodland then pasture, for ½ mile (800m). At wobbly silver-grey gate drop **L** 10ft (3m) to waymarked stile into once pollarded, streamside lane. Reach road.
❻ Turn **L**. After 450yds (411m), on bend, go straight down field to hedge beside farm buildings. Find stile in **L** corner. Go ahead, to stile that gives on to village road – take care! Turn **R** to see **church** before reaching car.

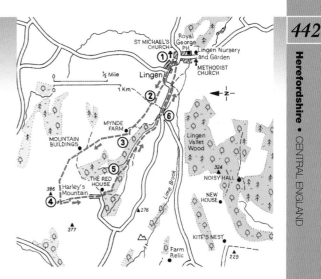

BLACK HILL *A HARSH LIFE*

8¾ miles (14.1km) 4hrs **Ascent:** 1,475ft (450m)
Paths: Muddy patches, stony descent, lanes, minor roads, 7 stiles
Suggested map: aqua3 OS Explorer OL13 Brecon Beacons (East)
Grid reference: SO 288328
Parking: Black Hill car park (signposted)

Visit the highest point in the two counties, where the harsh life was portrayed in Bruce Chatwin's 1938 book On the Black Hill.
❶ From car park go straight and steeply up clear track. Just keep going, enjoying airy path, or, if wind is strong, walk in lee on eastern side when terrain permits. The gradient varies over 1½ miles (2.4km) to trig point.
❷ Continue along what is now easy, broad ridge for 1¾ miles (2.8km), to low, concrete slab. Turn **L** here, joining both **Offa's Dyke Path** and border between England and Wales. In just over ½ mile (800m) is very indistinct top – at 2,305ft (703m), the highest point of all the Herefordshire walks in this book.
❸ Now carry on for 2½ miles (4km) along this gorgeous ridge: point where you turn off is indicated by pile of stones and similar concrete slab indicating **Offa's Dyke Path** again – this point is approximately perpendicular to sharp end of **Black Hill**. You may be

able to see your car from here, and re-ascent necessary to return to it.
❹ Turn **L**. Descent begins with L-H traverse. After 650yds (594m) be sure to swing round to **R**, heading down valley. When 140yds (128m) beyond this sharp bend, note, but do not take, waymarker, which indicates **L** turn option (in late summer waymarker may be concealed by bracken). After 30yds (27m) come to very finely forked junction.
❺ Be sure to take lower, L-H option; do not go 'straight on', that is, R fork. Descend to gate and stile. Walk along sunken track to 2nd stile. Turn **L** down old sunken lane. Later ignore stile on L and then reach minor road.
❻ Descend to junction. Turn **L**. Within 60yds (55m) take footpath on **R**, down into trees to cross **Olchon Brook**, then re-ascend. Go round buildings at **Blackhill Farm** and continue up through fields to road you came in on. Turn **L** then **R** to return to your car.

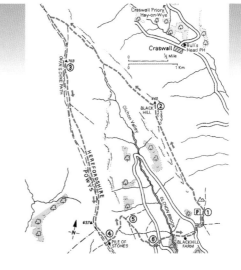

CLIFFORD *ORIGINAL SETTLEMENT*

5½ miles (8.8km) 2hrs 30min **Ascent:** 560ft (171m)
Paths: Field paths and lanes, awkward embankment, over 30 stiles
Suggested map: aqua3 OS Explorer 201 Knighton & Presteigne
Grid reference: SO 251450 **Parking:** Roadside parking at St Mary's Church, Llanfair

A 'backwater' of the River Wye.
❶ Just after road junction at corner of churchyard, take steps on **R**. Yellow arrows indicate route. Leave **Ton Wood** by gate on **L**, beside wire game-breeding enclosure. More arrows lead across old railway towards **Clifford**. Leave last meadow beside house.
❷ Walk to road. Turn **L** then **R** for **castle**. Retrace your steps to Point ❷. Take arrow pointing to oaks. At tarmac beyond follow 'Unsuitable for heavy goods vehicles'. On **R**, after 440yds (402m) find stile (hidden) and go up steep steps – easier is metal gate 30yds (27m) before stile. Across this green strip scramble down and up railway embankment. Halfway up field switch hedge from your **L** to **R**. Find stile behind derelict harvester. Wooded path soon reaches lane.
❸ Turn **L**. In 230yds (210m), before sheds, strike **R**, to stile behind 6 hawthorns in dip. Through garden, take rough track joining 2 tarmac lanes. Turn **R** for 30 paces. Waymarker points towards stile in trees. Go down this field to meet lane.

❹ Turn **L**; continue for ½ mile (800m) to B4352. Turn **R**. In 70yds (64m) cross to stile into meadow. Aim to **R** of trees on skyline then stile by house.
❺ Walk through garden. Take bridleway, **R**. After leafy interlude join stony track, but within 160yds (146m), where footpath crosses, turn **R**, to reach **Holy Trinity Church**.
❻ Retrace your steps to Point ❺. Go diagonally **L** to stile hidden by hedge. Turn **R**, around 2 sides of field. In next turn **R**, along field edge. Take driveway near by. At **Hardwicke Court** step around wall to walk **R** beside building, down path on lawn. At bottom, through small gate, maintain line, although 'Road Used as a Public Path' is obliterated. At farm gate keep ahead, past gigantic oak, to find wicket gate – 'RUPP' becomes more defined. Don't take waymarked stile 40yds (37m) to **R**. At **Hardwicke Mill** go into garden. Leave by stile on **R**. Ascend field edge, striking **L** at trees. Having skirted to **R** of house, you'll see **St Mary's Church** across fields ahead. Head for church.

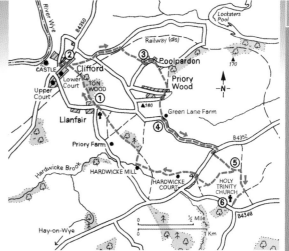

Herefordshire · CENTRAL ENGLAND

445 GOLDEN VALLEY HONEY COUNTRY

6 miles (9.7km) 3hrs Ascent: 1,165ft (355m)
Paths: Minor lanes, good tracks, meadows, couple of short but severe descents over grass, 24 stiles
Suggested map: aqua3 OS Explorer 201 Knighton & Presteigne or OL13 Brecon Beacons (East)
Grid reference: SO 313416 (on Explorer 201) **Parking:** Car park beside Dorstone Post Office

Across a heavenly landscape.

❶ Go down near side village green but turn **R** (not to church), passing houses. At lane end turn **L**, passing D'Or Produce Ltd. At **B4348** care is required. Continue, bridging **River Dore**. Be sure to switch sides before road bends severely **R**. Follow driveway towards **Fayre Way Stud Farm**. Clearly waymarked route across pastures leads up to **Arthur's Stone**.

❷ Beyond **Arthur's Stone** take route signed by fingerpost. Cross 2nd field diagonally. Follow **L** side of fence to stile **L** of the corner. After 2 fields descend very steeply on grass beside larches. Keep beside hedge to find awkward stile. Take lane but skirt **R** of **Finestreet Farm** using several stiles. In another steep meadow find stile below and **L** of massive oak with fallen one beside it. Cross field diagonally, pass beside timber-framed house. Beyond is **Bredwardine**.

❸ Cross road carefully. In 80yds (73m) avenue leads to **St Andrew's Church**. At very end, stile and waymarkers lead to Bredwardine's bridge.

❹ Go back to Point ❸. Take '25%' gradient road beside **Red Lion Hotel**. Go 700yds (640m) up lane, including steepest section, to just before **Hill Cottage**. Fingerpost points **R**, and behind you is '1 in 4' sign.

❺ Keep ahead, ignoring R turn after 160yds (146m). When road rises sharply after stream, find gate **R**, just past house ('**Finestreet Dingle**'). Now ascend dell (also called Finestreet Dingle) guided by blue arrows. In front of house turn **L** then **L** again, to skirt plantation. Row of hawthorns points to stile near brow. Tackle awkward gate near scrawny pines, keeping this line to minor road. Turn **R**. In 325yds (297m) turn **L** ('20%'). After another 325yds (297m) find fingerpost, hidden behind holly tree.

❻ Soon join track visible ahead. Continue to and through **Llan Farm**. However, 250yds (201m) beyond it, take diagonal footpath (not old lane, R). Cross sunken lane, old **railway**, then village playing fields to reach road near church. Cross then skirt **R** of churchyard, along fenced path, to village green.

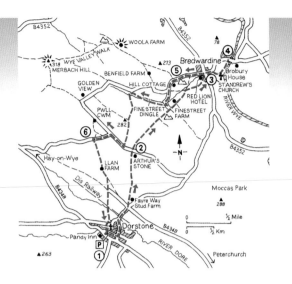

Worcestershire · CENTRAL ENGLAND

446 CLEEVE HILL A FRUITY ROUTE

4½ miles (7.2km) 2hrs Ascent: 225ft (69m)
Paths: Paths across fields, stony tracks and village roads, 8 stiles
Suggested map: aqua3 OS Explorer 205 Stratford-upon-Avon & Evesham
Grid reference: SP 077469
Parking: Outside Littleton Village Hall, School Lane, Middle Littleton (tithe barn parking for visitors only)

Walking in Victoria plum country.

❶ Walk westwards up School Lane to B4085, here called Cleeve Road. Cross diagonally **L** to take rutted, stony track, screened by hedgerow from **Kanes Foods**. At junction of tracks turn **R** to pass beside gate, following blue arrow. After 328yds (300m) reach opening **R** and line of plum trees making field boundary; on **L** is stile.

❷ Cross it, entering Worcestershire Wildlife Trust's **Windmill Hill Nature Reserve**. Descend, ignoring crossing tracks, to another stile and across 1 field to B4510. Follow footpath ('Cleeve Prior') through **caravan site**. (Keep on road for 220yds/201m for **Fish and Anchor**.) Take stile out of caravan park to walk on stone track beside river.

❸ At fenced log cabin with lanterns and basketball net, move to **R** to take double-stiled footbridge – don't be deterred by sign 'OPAC Private Fishing' – and resume riverside stroll. Continue through mostly ungated pastures. Go through small iron gate, leave river by taking R-H fork. Ascend through trees to clearing and path junction.

❹ Turn **R**, back on yourself, soon walking into trees again, to follow bridleway. In just under 1 mile (1.6km) B4510 cuts through hill, beside **The Hills**. Cross to fingerpost, but follow path for just 75yds (69m).

❺ Climb stile into nature reserve here, and follow waymarked, contouring path. After 440yds (402m) you'll recognise your outward route. Turn **L** here, up bank, retracing your steps for just 30yds (27m), to Point ❷. Once at top go straight across, walking with line of plum trees on your **L**. When this ends, maintain this direction to B4085, **tithe barn** making your objective ahead.

❻ Cross road and go straight ahead. Before young trees take stile or gate to **R**. In 15yds (14m) turn **L** to visit tithe barn, or turn **R** to reach village road. Turn **R** again, shortly to start.

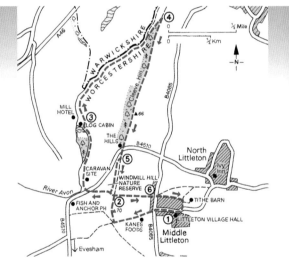

Worcestershire · CENTRAL ENGLAND

447 TARDEBIGGE THE UPS AND DOWNS

5½ miles (8.8km) 2hrs 30min Ascent: 295ft (90m)
Paths: Tow path, pastures, field paths and minor lanes, 21 stiles
Suggested map: aqua3 OS Explorer 204 Worcester & Droitwich Spa
Grid reference: SO 974682
Parking: Limited space, so park tightly and considerately, on north and east side of road bridge

Visit Worcestershire's famous big wet steps.

❶ Cross bridge No 51 and turn **L**, taking tow path on south side. Follow this until about 15yds (14m) before next bridge – No 52.

❷ Turn **R** here, into trees, then down field. Cross double-stiled footbridge among trees then keep ahead, over driveway to **Patchetts Farm**. Skirt copse to **L**, then another stile and 2-plank bridge. Cross 2 fields, keeping hedge on your **L**. You will reach gate on your **L**, close to broken oak tree with substantial girth.

❸ Turn **R**. Within 110yds (100m) go through gate ahead (no waymarker), ignoring gate to **L**. Go a quarter **R** (or skirt crops) to find stile. Retain this diagonal line to cross footbridge of 3 planks, then find rickety, narrow stile in next field's corner. Walk with hedge on your **L** to reach minor road junction. Turn **R** for 55yds (50m). Turn **L** to walk across 3 more fields to dilapidated metal gate. Now take R-H field edge to reach minor road.

❹ Turn **R**. Follow this for ½ mile (800m) to **Lower Bentley Farm**'s driveway. Go 140yds (128m) further, to fingerpost on **R**. Cross pastures by gaps in hedgerows, later with hedge on your **L**, but veer to stile in R-H corner at end. Cross this, then double stile, go three-quarters **L** to road.

❺ Turn **R**, and in 75yds (69m) turn **L**. Here, beyond awkward ditch, is new kissing gate with latch. Cross pastures easily towards **Orchard Farm**, but then turn **R**, away from it. Over corner stile go straight ahead. At double stile (across ditch) go half **L**, and at gap in hedge turn **R**. Now turn **L** without gaining height for 650yds (594m), aiming to **L** of black-and-white house, for stile and gate. In 80yds (73m) reach road.

❻ Turn **R**. At T-junction turn **L**. Join canal tow path this side of Stoke Pound Bridge. (The **Queen's Head** is on other side.) Now you have over ¾ mile (1.2km) to return to your car at road bridge, approximately mid-way up **Tardebigge Flight**.

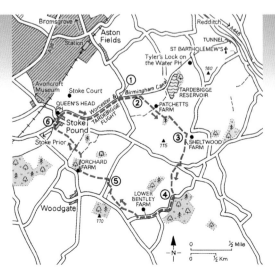

HANBURY HALL *THE ICE HOUSES*

4¾ miles (7.7km) 2hrs 15min Ascent: 250ft (76m) 🚶

Paths: Meadows, tracks and easy woodland paths, 17 stiles
Suggested map: aqua3 OS Explorer 204 Worcester & Droitwich Spa
Grid reference: SO 957652
Parking: Piper's Hill car park, on B4091 between Stoke Works and Hanbury (fast road and no sign)

A stroll around an estate park.

❶ From bottom of car park, follow driveway to **Knotts Farm**. Go ahead on **L-H** (1 of 2 parallel paths). 350yds (320m) after farm reach track at fingerpost.

❷ Keep ahead, with field boundary on **L**. Ascending towards **church**, reach stake with 2 waymarkers.

❸ Fork **L**, soon passing spinney, then losing height across meadow. Take care as stile and steps here spill you straight on to minor but fast road. Cross then go beside **school**. Ahead, when 20yds (18m) before exit out of 3rd field, turn **R**, aiming just to **L** of young, fenced oak. Cross wobbly stile. In 70yds (64m) cross footbridge on **L**. Cross 2 stiles to Pumphouse Lane.

❹ Turn **R**. Take stile and gate close to black-and-white **Grumbleground Cottage**. In 40yds (37m) cross 3-plank footbridge. Ascend slightly, in line with electricity poles. After 2 fields turn **R**, alongside wire fence. Reach road.

❺ Cross road to footpath opposite. At stile go half **L**, guided by solitary, fenced conifer. Pass close to **Hanbury Hall's** entrance, easing away from perimeter wall to cross large field to corner.

❻ Ignore minor road, turning immediately **R**. Hug boundary fence of coppice. Continue down **R-H** field edge. At junction turn **R** at National Trust sign, into this former deer park. After just 50yds (46m), at small drainage ditch, edge **R**, along slight green hollow. After another 110yds (100m), where it curves **R**, leave hollow to keep line. Aim for stile about 300yds (274m) away, to **L** of clump of fenced trees, which hides round pond. Maintain this line going up incline – **Hanbury church** is seen on **L** – to reach tarmac driveway.

❼ Turn **L**. When it curves **R** go straight ahead to walk in oak avenue. Keep this line for 700yds (640m), to minor road. Turn **R**, then **L** up to church. In churchyard walk round perimeter, down to kissing gate. Shortly rejoin outward route at Point ❸. Remember to go **L**, into woods, at Point ❷.

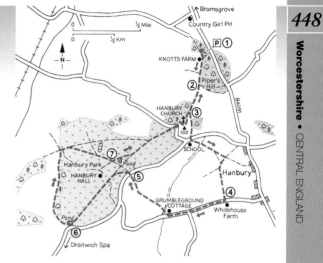

CLENT HILLS *A TREAT IN SPRINGTIME*

3½ miles (5.7km) 2hrs Ascent: 660ft (200m) 🚶

Paths: Woodland paths (sometimes muddy), tracks, 8 stiles
Suggested map: aqua3 OS Explorer 219 Wolverhampton & Dudley
Grid reference: SO 938808
Parking: National Trust pay-and-display car park, Nimmings Wood

A brief circuit of the most visited hills in Worcestershire and where, in spring, fields of oilseed rape flood the landscape with colour.

❶ Return to car park entrance and turn **R** for few paces. Cross road to stile and take **L-H** of 2 options. Immediately you'll see striking urban panorama. Descend steadily but, at cylindrical wooden post, turn **R** (with waymarker). Continue across fields, probably populated with horses, until kissing gate. Here take forward option (not **R** fork), to reach churchyard of **St Kenelm's** in Romsley parish. It may appear to be 'overgrown' since it is managed like a traditional hay meadow.

❷ Leave by lychgate. Turn **L** along road for short distance, then **R** at T-junction. In about 125yds (114m) take waymarked path at driveway to **The Wesleys** to ascend gently. Turn **L** on to tarmac road. Ignore **L** turn but, just 30yds (27m) beyond it, take muddy, narrow path into woodland up on **R**, angled away from road and not signposted. Emerge from trees to trig point on **Walton Hill**. Turn **L**, taking **R-H** of 2 options. Follow this for ¾ mile (1.2km) until just 10yds (9m) beyond National Trust marker post. Here take **R-H** fork to stile. Go steeply down 2 meadows to road beside **Church of St Leonard's** in Clent.

❸ Turn **R** then **R** again. At Church View Cottage, opposite church's driveway, turn **L**. In 125yds (114m) take upper, **L** fork. In 90yds (82m), at crossing, go **L**. After further 100yds (91m) ignore options to turn **R** or half **R**. Proceed for further 120yds (110m). Do not climb stile on your **L** but go straight on, soon ascending steeply up wooden steps. After another 100yds (91m) you'll emerge from trees. Now cross track then turn **R**.

❹ Keep on this broad, open path, passing close to (or viewing) a toposcope beside four standing stones. Maintain this line to descend in woodland to road. Just on **L** is car park.

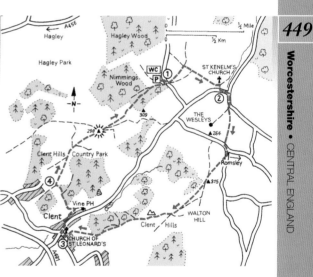

BREDON HILL *PERRY COUNTRY*

7½ miles (12.1km) 3hrs 30min Ascent: 1,115ft (340m) 🚶

Paths: Tracks, woodland paths, bridleways, minor lanes, 11 stiles
Suggested map: aqua3 OS Explorer 190 Malvern Hills & Bredon Hill
Grid reference: SO 955423 **Parking:** Roadside parking, Great Comberton village

A walk through perry country.

❶ Begin by **telephone box** in **Great Comberton**. Follow Church Street. Go through churchyard; leave by gate. At road go down stem of T-junction. In dip find stile. Ascend 2 fields, with stream on your **L**. After 100yds (91m) in 3rd field there is a signpost.

❷ Turn **R**, initially beside trees. Soon good farm track strikes across meadow. Follow waymarkers for next 1½ miles (2.4km), taking gravel driveway beside **Woollas Hall** and skirting **St Catherine's Farm**. Take hard track, later tarmac, down into **Bredon's Norton**. After first few houses reach junction.

❸ Keep ahead for 100yds (91m) to junction. Turn **R** if visiting **St Giles' Church**; otherwise go ahead again, then round **L** bend. Go into field, to **R** of 2 buildings – waymarker on telegraph pole. Now follow track steadily upwards, through several gates, eventually swinging southeast, for at least ¾ mile (1.2km). Less than 100yds (91m) beyond single marker post reach T-junction with 'no right of way' ahead.

❹ Turn **L**. Soon go half **R** along field edge, then **R** to walk along wooded escarpment ridge, before open field leads to **triangulation pillar**. Continue through fortifications and past 18th-century tower, **Parson's Folly**. Follow escarpment eastwards. Pass small plantation, then follow wire fence, slightly descending, for over ¼ mile (400m), to wood.

❺ Don't enter wood; turn **L**, beside it. Within 150yds (137m), bend **R** to junction. Turn **L**, down green hollow. At **Doctor's Wood** veer **L** to cross oddly level field (note absence of stiles on suggested map). Descend steeply through **Cames Coomb**, along wide, well-horsed path. Briefly follow level forestry road, then leave trees, descending on scalpings track for 400yds (366m) to path junction.

❻ Walk a further 375yds (343m) on good track to find path on **L**, initially between 2 hedges. When it ends keep ahead. Keep this general line – later hard track – back into **Great Comberton**. Turn **R** to telephone box.

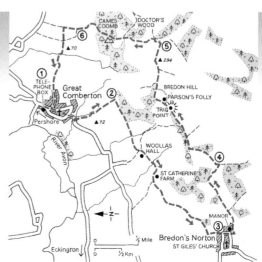

Worcestershire

451 DROITWICH SPA SALT INTO SILVER

5¾ miles (9.2km) 2hrs 30min **Ascent:** 230ft (70m)
Paths: Pavements, field paths, stony tracks, 6 stiles
Suggested map: aqua3 OS Explorer 204 Worcester & Droitwich Spa
Grid reference: SO 898631
Parking: Long-stay pay-and-display between Heritage Way and Saltway (follow signs for 'Brine Baths')

An historic salt-making town.

❶ From **TIC**, go along Victoria Square. Cross Heritage Way into Ombersley Street East. When it bends keep ahead, passing magistrates' court. After underpass proceed to St Nicholas's Church. Go round churchyard to take another underpass. Turn **L**. Take road over railway to mini-roundabout, filtering **R** to go through 3rd underpass. Walk for 65yds (60m) to fence corner, near lamppost. Turn **L**. In 30yds (27m) turn **R**. At bottom of this cul-de-sac, Westmead Close, turn **L**. Soon take Ledwych Close, on **R**. At canal you have left Droitwich Spa.

❷ Turn **L**. At bridge turn **R**; continue. Turn **L** just after A38 bridge. In 110yds (100m) reach **Westwood House** slip road. Facing allotments, take kissing gate to **L**. Beyond woodland go across several fields. Within 500yds (457m) of 2nd driveway is junction.

❸ Turn sharply **R**. Electric fencing leads between paddocks then veer **L** to walk briefly through **Nunnery**

Wood. Aim for 2 gateposts beside tree. Keep ahead for ½ mile (800m), beside big **dairy** on **L**, then curving **L** past **industrial estate** to reach Doverdale Lane.

❹ Turn **R** on lane. Just before '30' speed-limit sign, fork **L**. Cross A442. Go through **Hampton Lovett** to **St Mary's Church**. Take meadow path under railway. In 140yds (128m), at footbridge, bear **R**, along field edge. Maintain direction for over ½ mile (800m), walking in trees beside **Highstank Pool** when fence allows. Track leads to evergreens shielding golf tee.

❺ Cross vast field, then aim slightly **L** to metal gate. Follow road under A38 into housing estate. Find path running between Nos 49 and 53. Go through 2 kissing gates flanking level crossing. Turn **L** to pass Gardeners Arms. In 20yds (18m) turn **R** over **River Salwarpe**, into Vines Park. Veer **L** to cross the Droitwich Canal. Over B4090, follow Gurney Lane to High Street – ahead is **Spats Coffee House**. Turn **R**, passing Tower Hill, then **L** into St Andrew's Street.

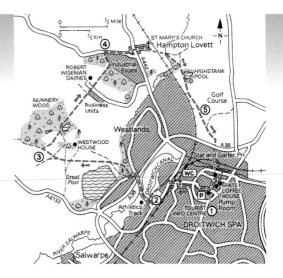

452 WORCESTER CITY SIGHTS AND SMELLS

2½ miles (4km) 1hr 30min **Ascent:** Negligible
Paths: City streets and tarmac riverside path
Suggested map: aqua3 OS Explorer 204 Worcester & Droitwich Spa
Grid reference: SO 846548
Parking: Long-stay pay-and-display car parks at New Road, Tybridge Street and Croft Road

A town walk in Worcester, known for Sir Edward Elgar, its battle, its porcelain, its racecourse and its sauce.

❶ The described route begins at the city side of the road bridge, but you can pick it up anywhere – at The Commandery or the Guildhall, for example – depending on where you have parked. Turn **L**, along North Parade, passing **Old Rectifying House** (wine bar). Turn **R** up Dolday, then **L**, in front of **bus station**, along **The Butts**. Turn **L** along **Farrier Street**, **R** into **Castle Street**, reaching northern extremity of route at its junction with Foregate Street.

❷ Go **R** along **Foregate Street**, passing **Shire Hall** and **City Museum and Art Gallery**, continuing along The Cross and into pedestrianised area called **High Street**. Turn **L** into Pump Street. (Elgar's statue stands close to his father's piano shop, at the southern end of High Street.) Turn **L** again, into **The Shambles**. At junction turn **R** into Mealcheapen Street. Another **R**

turn and you are in **New Street** (which later becomes Friar Street).

❸ Head down this street (look out for King Charles' House where he stayed during the battle of Worcester in 1651). At end of street is dual carriageway (College Street). Turn **R** then cross carefully, to visit **cathedral**.

❹ Leave cathedral along College Precincts to fortified gateway known as **Edgar Tower**. (It is named after the 10th-century King Edgar, but was actually built in the 14th century. Go through this gateway to see College Green.) Continue, along what is now **Severn Street**, which, unsurprisingly, leads to **River Severn**. Turn **R**, to complete your circuit, by following Kleve Walk, leafy waterside avenue; this section floods at some time most winters, and the **cricket ground** opposite was under several feet of water in 2000. For a more studied insight into the city's rich history, take a guided walk (on weekdays only) with a Green Badge Guide.

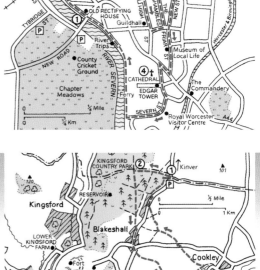

453 KINGSFORD COUNTRY PARK AND VILLAGES

5½ miles (8.8km) 2hrs 30min **Ascent:** 410ft (125m)
Paths: Forest rides, meadows, minor roads, village greens, canal tow path, 9 stiles
Suggested map: aqua3 OS Explorer 218 Wyre Forest & Kidderminster or 219 Wolverhampton & Dudley
Grid reference: SO 835820 (on OS Explorer 218)
Parking: Blakeshall Lane car park, Kingsford Country Park

A backwater that once knew busier times.

❶ Take track inside northern edge of **country park** for 550yds (503m), to point about 50yds (46m) beyond end of extensive garden. To **L** is wide glade, falling gently; ahead rises woodland track.

❷ Turn **L**, down ride. In 275yds (251m), at 5-way junction, go ahead (not along slight **R** fork). Join farm track. At road turn **R**, through **Blakeshall**. After 300yds (274m), at R-H bend near power lines, take stile into muddy and brick-strewn field. Keep hedge on your **R**, following yellow waymarkers into small valley. Reach, but don't go through, 7-bar metal gate before **Debdale Farm**. Turn sharply to **R**, uphill, following vague track. Enter **Gloucester Coppice** at gate and broken stile. Follow this track, soon more defined, all the way to southern end of Blakeshall Lane.

❸ Turn **L**, descending through street, The Holloway, into **Wolverley**. After village stores take 2nd footbridge on **R**. Reach Church of St John the Baptist

by zig-zagging up concreted footpath through deep cutting. Leave churchyard to **L**, by steps. Go down meadow opposite (with fingerpost) to minor road.

❹ Turn **R**. At B4189 turn **L**. In front of **The Lock** pub turn **L**, along tow path. After about 1¼ miles (2km) is Debdale Lock, partly hewn into rock. Some 220yds (201m) further, just before small wheel factory, is stile.

❺ Turn **L** along track. At T-junction after coniferous avenue turn **R** on broad gravel track. After about 440yds (402m) turn **L** (waymarker), up new wooden steps surfaced with scalpings, into trees. Go up **L-H** edge of one field and centre of another to road. Turn **L** for just 15yds (14m), then **R**. Some 400yds (366m) along this hedged lane take yellow option to **R** (to reduce road walking). At next stile wiggle **L** then **R**. Proceed ahead at junction to road. Turn **R**. In 150yds (137m), walk round wooden barrier to re-enter **country park**. Here, 2 paths run parallel to road – both lead back to car park.

Worcestershire

OMBERSLEY ALONG THE RIVER SEVERN

5¾ miles (9.2km) 2hrs 30min **Ascent:** 200ft (61m) ⚠
Paths: Riverside paths, field paths and tracks, village street, 9 stiles
Suggested map: aqua3 OS Explorer 204 Worcester & Droitwich Spa
Grid reference: SO 845630
Parking: Towards southern end of road through Ombersley on eastern side (southbound exit from village)

Explore an estate park.
❶ To south of village, and beyond cricket ground, take path on R. This is **Wychavon Way**. Briefly in trees, walk across meadow to stile beside willow. Go along L-H field edge, and briefly by water's edge. At corner of **fish pond** waymarker leads out to track. Turn **L**, following this track **R** in 80yds (73m). It becomes sunken path through delicious woodland. Cross meadow to river.
❷ Turn **R**. In 1 mile (1.6km) you'll pass 2 fishing pools to reach **Holt Fleet Bridge**. Go under this, continuing for another mile (1.6km), passing staffed **Holt Lock**. When opposite **Letchford Inn** you'll come to riverside stile.
❸ Don't go over it; instead, turn **R**. In field corner join access road. At junction keep ahead on public road. In 650yds (594m), at R-H bend, keep this line by moving **L**, on to farm track. The large area on the R was formerly an orchard, but it has gone completely.

It's over ¼ mile (400m) to top of this field. When you are 30yds (27m) before rusty shed, turn **R**. Now, in about 75yds (69m), go **L**, over stile.
❹ What could be a golf course fairway turns out to be an enormous garden. Aim to pass to **R** of house, by children's wooden watchtower. Cross gravel in front of house, **Greenfields**, to go down its private driveway. Turn **R** for 275yds (251m), passing several black-and-white houses, to T-junction – **Uphampton House** is in front of you.
❺ Turn **L** for 110yds (100m), then turn **R**, uphill. In 150yds (137m) don't bend R but go straight ahead, on shingly track. About 220yds (201m) further, main track bends R, rough track goes ahead and public footpath goes half **L**.
❻ Take public footpath option, along field edge. Continue through small area of market garden, reaching cul-de-sac. Shortly turn **R**, along village street to return to your car.

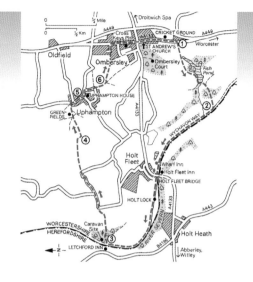

STOURPORT-ON-SEVERN HARTLEBURY COMMON

3¼ miles (5.3km) 1hr 30min **Ascent:** 328ft (100m) ⚠
Paths: Tow path, tracks, good paths, some streets
Suggested map: aqua3 OS Explorer 218 Wyre Forest & Kidderminster or 219 Wolverhampton & Dudley
Grid reference: SO 820704 (on Explorer 218)
Parking: Worcester Road car park on A4025 (poorly signed; height restriction bar spans narrow entrance)

A Georgian 'new town' and a common.
❶ Cross A4025. Turn **L** for 25yds (23m) to take footpath. Strike across bottom part of **Hartlebury Common**: you'll see buildings in far distance. Veer **R**, through silver birches, to find sandy track at back of houses. At housing estate join tarmac briefly, aiming for dirt track beyond 2nd 'Britannia Gardens' sign in front of Globe House. Shortly turn **L** down tarmac footpath, initially with wooden paling on L, to **river**.
❷ Turn **R**. In 650yds (594m) reach lock and Stourport's canal basins. Now, your route is neither across 2-plank walkway at upper lock gate, nor upper brick bridge with timber-and-metal railings; instead take neat brick-paved path to circumnavigate boarded-up **Tontine** public house. Now skirt Upper Basin, passing Severn Valley Boat Centre. Across York Street join tow path. Follow this for just under ¾ mile (1.2km), leaving it at **Bird in Hand** pub, before defunct brick railway bridge.

❸ Go down Holly Road, then half **L** into Mill Road, going under railway then meet **River Stour** to B4193. Cross and go to **L** of Myday Windows to take narrow, sandy, uphill path back on to common. Soon, at fork, go **L**, keeping direction as ground levels. Less than 50 paces after joining motor vehicle track reach trig point.
❹ Retrace your 50 paces and go another 30yds (27m), passing waymarker, to junction. Here turn **L**, away from car park. In just 40yds (37m) take **R** fork. In 100yds (91m) take **L** fork (not straight on). At corner of conifer plantation, 275yds (251m) further. After 110yds (100m) turn **L**, then in 220yds (201m), just after far end of plantation, enjoy views. Now 65yds (60m) beyond this viewpoint take **R** option at subtle fork. Go forward for another 250yds (229m), until opening. Here step very carefully over pair of exposed and disused (and not actually hazardous) pipes. Follow sandy track slanting downhill for (110yds) 100m, then swing **R**, now head for car park.

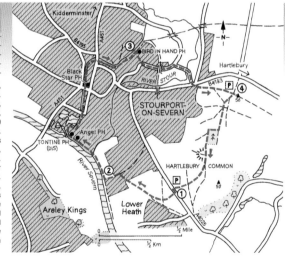

GREAT WITLEY AMONG THE TREES

4¾ miles (7.7km) 2hrs 45min **Ascent:** 1,150ft (350m) ⚠
Paths: Woodland paths, field paths, tracks, 9 stiles
Suggested map: aqua3 OS Explorer 204 Worcester & Droitwich Spa
Grid reference: SO 752662
Parking: Car park of Hundred House Hotel (please phone beforehand, tel 01299 896888)
Note: Lots of wild geese on route so please keep dogs under control.

A woodland walk up and down some hills.
❶ Cross A451 (take care). Through opening, strike sharply **R**, aiming for hedge end by last house. Step over fence; turn **L** on lane. Walk for ½ mile (800m) soon passing **Walsgrove Farm** and thousands of geese. Don't turn R up lane but go half **R**, taking path that becomes avenue of conifers, to top of **Woodbury Hill**. At marker post cross on to narrower track. In 130yds (119m) reach track above **Lippetts Farm**.
❷ Turn **R**, descending. At hairpin bend, aim away from farm to walk along inside edge of wood. Skirt to **L** of buildings at **Birch Berrow**, resuming on service road. As this goes up, R, to horse ring, take **R-H** of 2 gates. Go steeply down, taking stile into pines. Very soon, cross stile, turn **R** along road for 100yds (91m), so that you're past **1 Hillside Cottages**, but not before it.
❸ Turn **R** again, back uphill. Continue north for nearly 1 mile (1.6km), over several stiles, walking

mostly in trees but later enjoying fine views westwards. Then, on top of **Walsgrove Hill**, you'll see the magnificent **clock tower** (1883) of **Abberley Hall**. Now go steeply down this meadow, to take stile into lane. Turn **R** for 80yds (73m) to B4203.
❹ Cross carefully. Turn **L**, along verge. Take driveway to **Abberley Hall School**. Leave driveway as it swings R, keeping this direction close to **clock tower** and all the way, on track, to A443. Take road opposite ('Wynniatts Way') up to brow of hill.
❺ Turn **R**. In about 400yds (366m) reach **trig point**. Walk along ridge path another 650yds (594m) to Worcestershire Way sign at path junction, just beyond which are 4 trees growing in a line across path.
❻ Take path down to **R**, initially quite steeply then contouring as it veers **R**, later descending again. Emerge from woods over stile to walk 2 large fields, meeting road beside **Hundred House Hotel**.

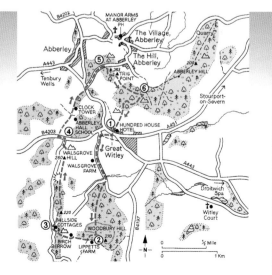

Worcestershire

457 MARTLEY *THROUGH THE CIDER ORCHARDS*

6¾ miles (10.9km) 3hrs **Ascent:** 720ft (219m)

Paths: Field paths, lanes, orchard paths, tracks, river meadows, minor roads, 20 stiles
Suggested map: aqua3 OS Explorer 204 Worcester & Droitwich Spa
Grid reference: SO 766597 **Parking:** St Peter's Church, Martley

A marvellous, airy stretch of countryside.

❶ Go through churchyard to B4204. Cross to track. In 100yds (91m) enter **school's** grounds briefly then walk in trees, parallel. Turn **R** at stile, then another, to re-enter grounds. Briefly follow **L** edge of playing fields. Another stile gives on to field. At road turn **L**. Turn **R** ('Highfields'). Beside **Lingen Farm** go down track. At bend take stile, across field. Cross stream; ascend, taking R-H gates. Reach minor road.

❷ Turn **L**. At **Larkins** go ahead. At **The Peak** walk behind **Ross Green's** gardens. Cross fields to reach road. Go straight over, to partially concealed stile, not diagonally to fingerpost. Walk beside barn, then on, to another lane. Turn **L** to reach fingerpost pointing into apple orchard before **Pear Tree Cottage**.

❸ Follow waymarkers through trees. Emerge at bridge over ditch, beside apple-sorting equipment. Go 220yds (201m) up track, to gap in evergreens. Turn **L**, down orchard ride. At T-junction turn **R**, up to just before gate beside small house. Turn **L**, almost back

on yourself. Go through orchard, following faded yellow splodges about 1½ft (45cm) up on tree trunks. Leave by footbridge, crossing fields to B4197.

❹ Turn **R** for 60yds (55m). Take track for ½ mile (800m) to **Rodge Hill's** top. Turn sharp **L**, 'Worcs Way South'. Follow this for 1 mile (1.6km). Steps lead down to road's hairpin bend.

❺ Turn **R**. In 20yds (18m) turn **L**, but in 15yds (14m) turn **R** again, into conifers. Emerge to drop down steeply. At B4204 turn **R** for 200yds (183m). Turn **L**, skirt barn to **L**; go diagonally to **River Teme**. Follow riverside walk, later in **Kingswood Nature Reserve**, for over ½ mile (800m). Leave river when wire fence requires it. Ascend path, later driveway, to road.

❻ Turn **R**, uphill; this soon bends **L**. Near brow move **R** (waymarker) to walk in field, not on road. At end turn **L** but, in 275yds (251m), cross 2 stiles beside caravan. Beside fields and allotments, emerge between **Crown** and garage. Pass telephone box into village. Turn **R** to church and start.

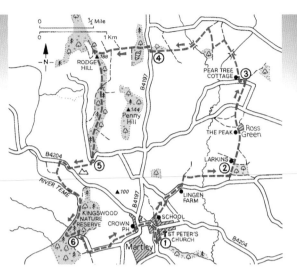

458 RAVENSHILL *A WILDLIFE RESERVE*

2¾ miles (4.4km) 1hr 30min **Ascent:** 475ft (145m)

Paths: Firm or muddy tracks, meadows, some very short but steep, slippery sections, very little road, 8 stiles. Woodlands and rolling green fields
Suggested map: aqua3 OS Explorer 204 Worcester & Droitwich Spa
Grid reference: SO 739539 **Parking:** Ravenshill Woodland Reserve (donation)

Elizabeth Barling's woodland dream.

❶ Walk towards **Lulsley** for 150yds (137m). Turn **L** on green track beside Hill Orchard's private drive. Soon in woods, go 500yds (457m), joining another track beside wire enclosures. When stile and nearby gate lead into field on **R**, go 20yds (18m) further. In 120yds (110m) climb rustic stile to turn partially **R**. Note well this point, where path joins obliquely from **L**, since you'll be returning this way – junction is easily missed! Go on for 100yds (91m) to driveway. Walk for 30yds (27m) away from house, to follow sign ('bridleway') down to **R**. Soon, at line of laurel bushes, reach tree-lined Worcestershire Way.

❷ Turn **R**. After 650yds (594m) go through gate. Peel **L**, hugging trees but not going under them. A narrow gap would lead into 2nd meadow but on **R** is fenced area. Climb waymarked stile beside padlocked gate. After another gate ascend diagonally **R**, veering

L as it levels. Maintain this line through metal gates across fields, then wooden gate into woodland. Eventually **The Steps** comes into view. Reach road by descending beside paddock fence, then through more gates, including red one.

❸ Turn **L**. Beyond Threshers Barn and Wain House is Crews Court. Beside fingerpost, go up steps to stile ('Beware butting sheep'). Go ahead, crossing private garden, to paddock. Go ahead but slightly **R**, to padlocked 7-bar gate; climb over this. Now move 20yds (18m) **R** to find your path up – proper stile, rendered obsolete by new fence. Go up quite steeply – you may need to scramble up last bit or find easier part. Now at ridge, don't fall off wobbly stile.

❹ Turn **L**. After 275yds (251m) fork down to **L**, not ahead. At road cross it before turning **R** to walk round The Crest then move **L** for Worcestershire Way again. Follow this to Point ❷. Retrace your steps to start.

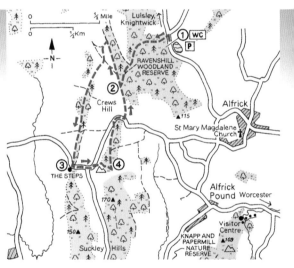

459 MAMBLE *A LONG AMBLE*

10½ miles (16.8km) 5hrs **Ascent:** 690ft (210m)

Paths: Minor roads, field and woodland paths, tow path, 18 stiles
Suggested map: aqua3 OS Explorer 203 Ludlow
Grid reference: SO 685712 **Parking:** Lay-by (bend in old road) west of Mamble on A456

Beside the Leominster Canal.

❶ Towards Tenbury, take minor road. Down **High Point Farm's** driveway, gate marks indistinct green lane to **Tetstill**. Turn **R**. Soon cross railway bridge.

❷ Through 2 fields, reach stile. Follow **L** field edge. Turn **L**. Just before **Sturts'** private bridge go down and **R** – flagstones lead to footbridge. Ascend track **L** of Sturts. At brow move **R**, taking **L** of 2 gates. Go to **R** edge of conifers. In 220yds (201m), at next corner, turn **L**. Aim **L** of massive oak, to gate into conifers.

❸ Descend to cross footbridge. Continue (not over bridge) soon into pasture. In 325yds (297m) go **L**. Take stile via **The Great House's** gardens. Follow minor roads to **St Michael's Church**. Take waymarked route, following pylons. In 600yds (549m), when descending, cross 1 stile; turn **L** at 2nd (don't cross).

❹ Follow tow path for 275yds (251m). Cross canal bed via exposed earth. Find gate to **R**. Reach track, Tavern Lane. Where drive to **Oxnall Farm** bends, go ahead. Of 2 gates lower, **R-H** one. In 60yds (55m)

keep **L**. Leave plantation at stile;, take gate immediately **R**. Strike diagonally to opening. In 10yds (9m) turn **R** along track briefly then to corner stile into trees. Cross old railway. Ditch on **L** marks canal. Brick lining is evident at next stile (**Rea Aqueduct**).

❺ Follow canal for 1¼ miles (2km). At A456 turn **R**. Cross to old canal bend, taking public footpath. Leave driveway at **Broombank Farm's** gate. Walk along **L** edge of several fields. At corner strike half-**R** to pylon. Around dry valley head, keep on brow, by hedgerow. Move **L**, to trees shielding pond (possibly dry). Ease away from fencing (now R) to 2-bar stile through plantation. Go to woodland corner. Veer **R** for 75yds (69m); cross stile, go down to cross dam.

❻ Go up to gate in fence's **L** corner. Walk 80yds (73m) to 2nd (not 1st) stile. Go forward to road, turning **L** then **R** then **L**, into **Mamble**. Turn **R**, then **L**. Before craft centre take fingerpost, beside Tudor Cottage's garage. After 2-plank brook bridge go up and **L**, across fields to Neen Sollars road junction and lay-by.

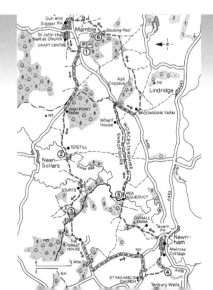

Worcestershire

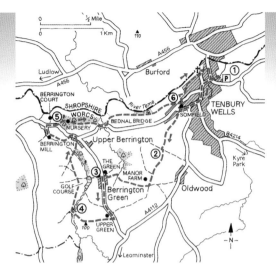

TENBURY WELLS *BERRINGTON COURT*

5¾ miles (9.2km) 2hrs 30min **Ascent:** 280ft (85m)
Paths: Town streets, field paths, minor lanes, 15 stiles
Suggested map: aqua3 OS Explorer 203 Ludlow
Grid reference: SO 598682 **Parking:** Long-stay car park, beside swimming pool, Tenbury Wells

A moderate stroll around a rural backwater.

❶ Leave car park by 'no exit' sign. Over bridge turn L. At Crow Hotel turn L then L. Walk through **Tenbury Wells**. Cross beyond Pembroke House, soon taking 'Berrington'. Opposite bungalow, '**Somfield**', cross stile. Go up and down to another, then walk on following power poles. Cross ditch over planks behind fallen trees. Go to field top.

❷ Turn L then R. Cross fields to join driveway of **Manor Farm**. 50yds (46m) beyond bridge turn R at triple waymarker to close stile. Cross fields for 440yds (402m). Veer down and R, through gap, then back up L; through **The Green's** several gates to lane.

❸ Go L for 750yds (686m). Just past '30mph' follow unsigned driveway of **Upper Green**. Through gates, head for far L field corner. Start up L edge. Over brow, at old tree line, strike diagonally, to footbridge.

❹ Turn R, soon on Cadmore Lodge Hotel's **golf course**. Go straight and level, leaving course when just beyond hotel. Walk round R field edge, then down

farm track. Join minor road between imposing dwellings. Turn L. In 100yds (91m) take fingerpost, up steps. Cross field diagonally. Path leads to **Berrington Mill**. Turn R, up lane, then R to Frank P Matthews' nurseries at **Berrington Court**.

❺ Take track behind house. Enter **nursery**. Walk beside potted trees under glass. Leave gravel track where it cuts down through woodland. Meadows lead to **Bednal Bridge**. Just beyond it take double gates into trees. Keep your line when this ample track runs out. It's now straightforward to outskirts of **Tenbury**. (Yellow arrow pointing R eases sharp slope.) Round backs of gardens, emerge through gate.

❻ Turn L for 15yds (14m). Take kissing gate on L. Continue across flood plain, for 90yds (82m). Turn R (gate aperture is now behind you) to hit suburbia again. Turn L. Move L at 'No cycling'. Keep on tarmac footpath, L of No 14, soon beside garden fences. Emerging at **church**, turn L. Opposite church turn R, down Church Walk, to Teme Street.

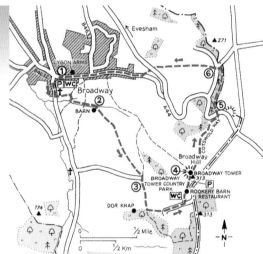

BROADWAY *WILLIAM MORRIS*

5 miles (8km) 2hrs 30min **Ascent:** 755ft (230m)
Paths: Pasture, rough, tree-root path, pavements, 8 stiles
Suggested map: aqua3 OS Explorer OL45 The Cotswolds
Grid reference: Grid reference: SP 094374
Parking: Pay-and-display, short stay (4hrs max) in Church Close, Broadway; long stay options signposted

A haunt of the Arts and Crafts pioneer.

❶ Walk down Church Close. Turn L. At far end of wall turn L, soon passing orchard. At gate before grass turn R, to reach bridge over rivulet. Turn half L, across pasture. Go to R-H field corner. In 40yds (37m) reach bridge beside stone **barn**.

❷ Cross this to waymarker through boggy patch to 2 stiles. Continue to reach gate. Cross field. On joining vague, sunken lane bear R, to descend briefly to gate. Tree-lined track reaches 2nd gate within 60yds (55m).

❸ Slant uphill, passing in front of stone building. At woodland turn L. Join tarmac road, steadily uphill. At brow turn L, into **country park**. Pass **Rookery Barn Restaurant**. Take kissing gate into **Broadway Tower**.

❹ Beyond tower go through gate then take gate immediately on L. Move down L, 20yds (18m) to walk in hollow, through pasture, to gate in dry-stone wall. Soon cross track and walk parallel to it in hollow, guided by **Cotswold Way** acorn waymarkers. Aim for

gates amongst trees. Beyond, keep ahead. In 45yds (41m), at next marker, bear R, walking above road. Soon cross it carefully, to footpath signs opposite.

❺ Leave **Cotswold Way** here. Care is needed in following these next instructions: descend, initially using steps. Ignore path on L after 50yds (46m). After another 50yds (46m) take yellow waymarker pointing up to R, over more steps. About 25 paces beyond steps use handrail to descend more steps. After 50yds (46m) you'll see orange Badger Trail on this for 10yds (9m). Here orange disc points L, but follow yellow marker ahead. Follow path (beware of exposed tree roots) near top of wood. Eventually take steps on L, down to cross road junction.

❻ Take field path ('**Broadway**') through pastures. Swing L then R under new road. Emerge and turn R, on to dead end of Broadway's main street. In centre, 50yds (46m) beyond 3 red telephone boxes, turn L, through arcade, to Church Close car park.

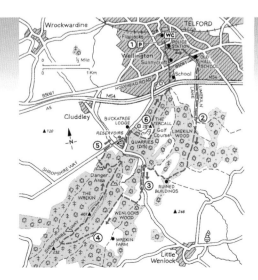

WELLINGTON *ALL AROUND THE WREKIN*

8½ miles (13.7km) 3hrs **Ascent:** 1,585ft (485m)
Paths: Woodland footpaths, urban streets, quiet lanes, 2 stiles
Suggested map: aqua3 OS Explorer 242 Telford, Ironbridge & The Wrekin
Grid reference: SJ 651113
Parking: Belmont or Swimming Pool East car parks, both on Tan Bank, off Victoria Road, Wellington
Note: Rifle range on The Wrekin – warning notices posted, but take care on firing days

A Shropshire classic.

❶ Walk along Tan Bank away from town centre. Cross Victoria Road and continue on Tan Bank then turn L on path just after police station. Walk to New Church Road; turn R. At **Holyhead Road**, turn L, then cross to **Limekiln Lane**. Don't miss **Old Hall School** (1480) on corner. Soon you see slopes of **The Wrekin**, as Limekiln Lane heads under **M54** into countryside.

❷ At end of lane, go ahead into **Limekiln Wood**; path leads along edge of wood at first. At junction, go to L, but few paces further fork R into wood. Ignore branching paths, sticking to well-trodden main route. At T-junction by ruined buildings, turn R, descend to junction and turn L, then L again at road.

❸ Turn R on access road to **Wrekin Farm**. At **Wenlocks Wood**, leave road. Turn R on field-edge path heading towards **The Wrekin**. Cross stile on to its eastern slopes. Continue for a few paces then turn L.

❹ Branch R where signpost indicates permissive path. Follow this round hill to cross path; turn R, to join **Shropshire Way** over summit ridge. Approaching northern end, keep L when path forks, then L again by prominent beech tree, descending through woods. At edge of woods, leave **Shropshire Way**; turn R to lane.

❺ Turn R to T-junction, join footpath opposite and go between 2 **reservoirs** before meeting lane; go L. When almost level with **Buckatree Lodge**, turn R into nature reserve. Go ahead along bridleway, past former **quarries** and pool. At junction, ignore path back towards quarries and continue for few paces to find that main track swings L and climbs to top of **Ercall**.

❻ As Wellington comes into view, turn R on ridge-top path. As you descend, path forks. Go to R and join track under M54. Keep ahead along Golf Links Lane to **Holyhead Road**. Cross to footpath opposite. At road (Roseway) turn R, then L on to Tan Bank

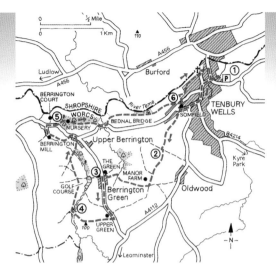

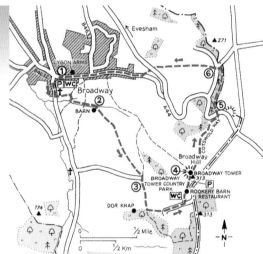

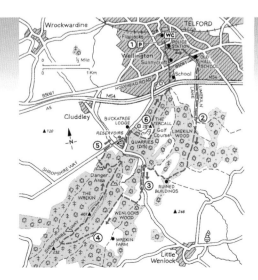

463 MARKET DRAYTON *A Sweet-toothed Town*

5¼ miles (8.4km) 2hrs **Ascent:** 165ft (50m)
Paths: Streets, tow path, sandy track and quiet lanes
Suggested map: aqua3 OS Explorer 243 Market Drayton
Grid reference: SJ 674344
Parking: Car park on Towers Lawn, next to bus station

Enjoy a veritable feast of gingerbread men and Cheshire cheese.

① Walk past bus station, cross at zebra crossing, then turn **L** down Queen Street to Buttercross and **L** on Stafford Street. Go straight on at 1st junction, **R** at next on to Great Hales Street and then **L** on Berrisford Road (use easily missed footway on **L** until forced to join road).

② You'll soon come to **Berrisford Bridge**, also known as 40 Steps Aqueduct, which carries Shropshire Union Canal over road. Go up steps and turn **R** on tow path. This part of Shroppie system was originally Birmingham and Liverpool Junction Canal, which went from Autherley to Nantwich. Thomas Telford was the engineer and the boldness of his design is apparent along this stretch, with its massive cuttings and embankments. The deep cutting on the approach to Tyrley Locks has its own microclimate, and positively drips with ferns, mosses and liverworts.

The tow path marks the county boundary – this stretch of the canal is in Staffordshire.

③ At bridge 60 by **Tyrley Wharf** go up to lane (**Tyrley Road**) and then turn **L**. This leads to main road (A529) and pub called Four Alls. Cross over road with care to Sandy Lane.

④ Sandy Lane comes to T-junction with track. Turn **R** here; it's still Sandy Lane, but this part is private road and dogs must be kept on leads. It heads north towards **Drayton**, overlooked by **Salisbury Hill**, where a Yorkist army under the Earl of Salisbury camped in 1459 before heavily defeating a Lancastrian force twice the size.

⑤ When you meet road, turn **R** to cross River Tern at **Walkmill Bridge** (a packhorse bridge). Cross Walkmill Road and go up Kilnbank Road opposite. This leads to Shropshire Street; turn **R**. After passing **Sandbrook Vaults**, turn **L** past Buttercross to Cheshire Street, which leads back to Towers Lawn.

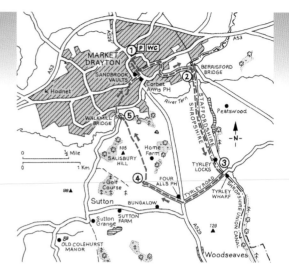

464 COALPORT *Shropshire's China Town*

5 miles (8km) 2hrs **Ascent:** 295ft (90m)
Paths: Mostly excellent, path through Lee Dingle is rough and may be muddy, 1 stile
Suggested map: aqua3 OS Explorer 242 Telford, Ironbridge & The Wrekin
Grid reference: SJ 677033 **Parking:** Next to Bedlam Furnaces on Waterloo Street, Ironbridge

A superb walk in Ironbridge Gorge.

① To **L** of furnaces (as you face them) ascend into parkland, zig-zagging through pergolas and steps. Turn **R** at top, then **L** on Newbridge Road to junction.

② Pass to **L** of **Golden Ball Inn**, cross **L** at junction with Jockey Bank, past Victoria Cottage. Go **L** at junction and through gate into wood (**The Crostan**). Stepped climbs to junction, take R-H path, climbing by woodland edge to waymarked junction.

③ Turn **R** on bridleway, cross 2 meadows and continue through woodland. Fork **L** at 2 junctions; at 2nd bridleway proceed between wood and houses.

④ Cross stile on **R** into **Lee Dingle** then descend to road. Cross Legges Way, turn **L** under 2 bridges, then **R** on footpath by entrance to **Blists Hill Museum**.

⑤ Ignore path **L**, carry on past wooden posts. Turn **R** on footpath by last post, skirting Blists Hill slope, soon entering woodland. Ignore paths **L** and keep close to museum. When path enters grassland take **L** fork, with trees between path and canal. At junction turn **R**.

⑥ Following signs for Coalport, descend to junction by bridge. Turn **L** on **Silkin Way**, then **R** and **R** again past **Shakespeare Inn** and Tunnel Tea Rooms. Cross road bridge, turn **L** over canal and **L** on tow path. Re-cross canal at footbridge, walk past **China Museum**, youth hostel and Slip Room Café. Join High Street and continue, rejoining **Silkin Way** opposite **Brewery Inn**. Follow track to **Coalport Bridge**, cross river.

⑦ Turn **R** on **Severn Way**, go through Preen's Eddy picnic area, climb away from river to continue along old railway trackbed. Turn **R** at signs for **Silkin Way** via **Jackfield Bridge** to reach Boat Inn. Head towards **Ironbridge** past cottages and Maws Craft Centre.

⑧ As you approach black-and-white former pub, path leads to access track, bending **L** into woodland. Turn **R** towards **Ironbridge**, soon joining Church Road. Pass **Jackfield Tile Museum** and Calcutts House, carry on at Jackfield Sidings, pass Black Swan. When bridge crosses path, access river. Cross **Jackfield Bridge**, turn **L** past Bird in Hand pub to return to start.

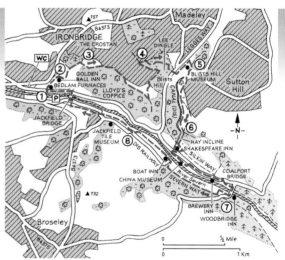

465 COALBROOKDALE *An Industrial Forerunner*

5 miles (8km) 2hrs **Ascent:** 770ft (235m)
Paths: Woodland paths, lots of steps (mostly descending), may be fallen trees at Strethill, 2 stiles
Suggested map: aqua3 OS Explorer 242 Telford, Ironbridge & The Wrekin
Grid reference: SJ 664037 **Parking:** Dale End Riverside Park, just west of Museum of the Gorge

A walk in wooded hills and valleys.

① Follow Severn upstream, on Severn Way, pass under 2 bridges. After 2nd, bear away from river towards **Buildwas Road**. Turn **L** for few paces, cross to footpath that ascends through woodland. Keep close to edge until waymarker directs you obliquely **R**.

② Cross stile and continue in same direction over pastureland. Pass under pylon, join farm track, turn **L** through gate. Follow hawthorn hedge on **R** to junction, turn **L** on bridleway, continue along field edges, then across middle of meadow to lane. Turn **L**.

③ Leave lane when it bridges road; turn **R** on farm access track (Shropshire Way). Go through gate on **R**, just before **Leasows Farm**, then downfield into **Lydebrook Dingle**. Descend through wood, continue along path (**Rope Walk**).

④ Descend steps **L** into **Loamhole Dingle**. Cross **Loamhole Brook** at footbridge, climb steps on other side to T-junction. Turn **R** on boardwalk and, at Upper Furnace Pool, cross it on footbridge to road.

⑤ Onward route is **L**, short detour **R** to Quaker Burial Ground. Resuming walk, go down to Darby Road; turn **R** beside **viaduct** and **Museum of Iron**. Turn **L** under viaduct at junction with Coach Road. Follow road past museum and Coalbrookdale Works to junction.

⑥ Cross to Church Road, turn **L** after chapel on corner and enter **Dale Coppice**. Follow signs for Church Road at first 2 junctions, at 3rd keep straight on. Leave wood to enter grassland, go forward to track. Turn **L**, shortly fork **R**, staying on track. Go **L** at junction, **R** at next 2. Dale Coppice is **R**, cemetery **L**.

⑦ A gate accesses Dale Coppice. Turn **R**, then **L**, descend to junction by bench. Turn **R**, then **L** when sign indicates Church Road, **L** again beside road.

⑧ Turn **R** into **Lincoln Hill Wood**, follow signs for Rotunda to viewpoint. Descend steep steps to junction. Turn **R**, **L** down steps, **L** again, signposted 'Lincoln Hill Road'. Cross to footpath opposite, descend to Wharfage. Turn **R** past Lincoln Hill lime kilns and **Swan** to Dale End Riverside Park.

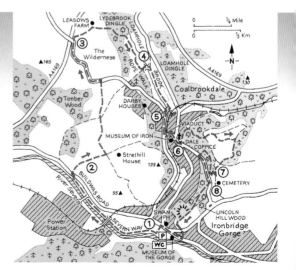

Shropshire

RINDLEFORD UP JACOB'S LADDER

6½ miles (10.4km) 2hrs 30min **Ascent:** 540ft (165m)
Paths: Steep and eroded in parts (beware landslips), 2 stiles
Suggested map: aqua3 OS Explorer 218 Wyre Forest & Kidderminster
Grid reference: SO 720934
Parking: Severn Park, off A442 on east bank of Severn at Bridgnorth

Sheer cliffs and secluded valleys.

❶ Cross A442, turn L, then R ('cemetery'). Here, take adjacent footpath, climbing steeply. When gradient eases, turn R on fenced path into woodland, then climb again, to cliff top. At wood's edge, turn L to waymarked junction at top of High Rock.

❷ Fork L, descending at first before path (Jacob's Ladder) levels out to contour round High Rock then Pendlestone Rock. At junction, keep to higher path which soon swings R. Leaving trees behind, it passes Woodside farm, then merges with farm access track.

❸ At lane, turn R for few paces, then L on footpath. Pass house, go through gate into field and keep along edge until waymarker directs you diagonally to far corner. Go through gate; turn L through field. Cross stile at far side; keep ahead through valley.

❹ Meet track at far side, opposite sandstone building; turn R along steep-sided valley. At junction, go ahead along grassy path through bracken, leaving main path, which bends R. Eventually you come to junction with sandy track beside River Worfe.

❺ Your onward route is to R, but first detour to L to explore Rindleford. Resuming walk, return to junction and follow River Worfe on sandy track which soon swings R, then climbs gently out of valley.

❻ Turn R when you reach lane, heading towards Bridgnorth, until signpost on L indicates footpath along field edge. This leads to A454 and continues on other side, past housing estate called The Hobbins.

❼ Turn R on another road, past Stanmore Country Park, to A454. Cross to footpath opposite, by Hermitage Farm. It runs to top of Hermitage Hill, where you turn R through Hermitage Hill Coppice. As you approach B4363, descend to lower path to visit The Hermitage, then walk to road and cross to footpath opposite. Follow this along cliff top to rejoin path which descends past cemetery to A442 and Severn Park.

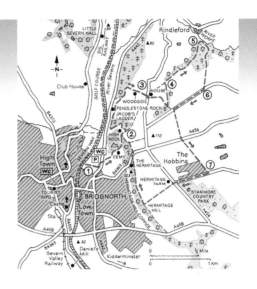

ALVELEY REGENERATION ROUTE

5 miles (8km) 2hrs 30min **Ascent:** 425ft (130m)
Paths: Riverside paths, green lanes, can be slippery in places and shallow streams in winter, 12 stiles
Suggested map: aqua3 OS Explorer 218 Wyre Forest & Kidderminster
Grid reference: SO 753840
Parking: Visitor centre at Severn Valley Country Park, Alveley

A great day out in the Severn Valley.

❶ Walk to river from visitor centre, using whichever route you prefer (History Trail, waymarked by red arrows, takes you directly to Miners' Bridge). Don't cross bridge, but descend steps to river bank and walk upstream for nearly 2 miles (3.2km).

❷ Follow short track to car park of Lion Inn. Turn L past Old Forge Cottage to Hampton Loade, then turn R past house called The Haywain (just before River and Rail pub). Waymarked path leads up through garden into wood, then along edge of field bordering wood. Go along two sides of field to reach top L corner, cross stile, turn R and cross another stile in next corner. Proceed to track and turn R.

❸ After few paces, look for waymarker indicating path on R. It descends through woodland to Lakehouse Dingle. Pass former watermill, cross footbridge and keep going along pebbly track. When you meet concrete track, turn R to junction with lane.

❹ Turn left, staying on lane until you've passed Yewtree Cottage and its neighbour. Take L turn after 2nd cottage. There is no signpost or waymarker here, but it's well-defined field-edge bridleway. At bottom of field look for gap in hedge, where way descends through trees to dingle.

❺ Turn R, climb up to meet lane and turn R again. After 100yds (91m), join track on R. When it bends R, keep straight on instead, along tree-lined green lane. Before long it becomes narrower and deeply rutted as it descends to brook. Cross at stepping stones, or at nearby footbridge. Track then swings L beside brook for while before turning sharp R.

❻ Turn L when you meet lane and walk into Alveley. Go through village centre, passing cottages, church, pub, shop and bus stop, then turning R on footpath next to premises of IGM. Path descends to junction where you turn L until you reach field through which well-trodden paths descend to country park.

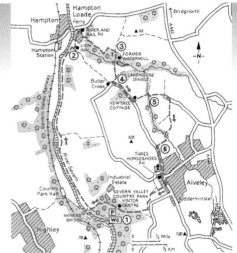

WYRE FOREST THE KING'S WOOD

5 miles (8km) 2hrs 30min **Ascent:** 575ft (175m)
Paths: Woodland and field paths, 2 stiles
Suggested map: aqua3 OS Explorer 218 Wyre Forest & Kidderminster
Grid reference: SO 743784
Parking: Forestry Commission car park at Earnwood Copse, on south side of B4194, west of Buttonoak

A leafy walk in Wyre Forest.

❶ Walk through gate on to forest road and immediately turn R on footpath (no signpost or waymarker) into Earnwood Copse. Keep straight on at all junctions, eventually joining sunken path not far from edge of forest. If you shortly pass under an overhanging yew tree you will know that you're on right path.

❷ Path descends to meet route of Elan Valley pipeline, bringing Welsh water to Birmingham. Turn R here and cross footbridge on edge of forest, to R of pipeline. Walk up bank into arable fields and then follow waymarked field-edge footpath uphill. At top, go through hedge gap and turn L towards Kingswood.

❸ Soon after passing timber-framed cottage (Manor Holding), come to T-junction at edge of forest. Go few paces to L towards Kingswood Farm and see track that swings R to enter forest. Keep straight on at all junctions, walking through Brand Wood.

❹ Soon reach Dowles Brook. Don't cross, turn L on bridleway that runs beside it. Follow bridleway for 1¼ miles (2km), with Wimperhill Wood on L.

❺ Turn L on another bridleway, which first passes through marshy area, then climbs through scrub and young woodland. It's waymarked and easily followed. After crossing forest road, go straight on, but turn R at next waymarked junction before swinging L to resume original heading. After crossing stream, bridleway turns R as it climbs above rim of steep valley.

❻ Turn sharp L (still on bridleway) through gap between 2 fenced areas when approaching Longdon Orchard (conservation area, dogs must be under control). At next junction go L, into conifers, then soon turn R.

❼ Turn R when you meet Elan Valley pipeline again, then very soon L, still on bridleway. Follow it up to edge of forest near Buttonoak, then turn L to return to Earnwood Copse.

469 BROWN CLEE HILLS *HIGH HILL*

7 miles (11.3km) 3hrs 30min **Ascent:** 1,460ft (445m)
Paths: Generally good, but can be very boggy in places, 5 stiles
Suggested map: aqua3 OS Explorer 217 The Long Mynd & Wenlock Edge
Grid reference: SO 607871
Parking: Cleobury North picnic site, on unclassified road west of Cleobury North

On Brown Clee's upland commons.

❶ Cross stile and walk uphill. Intercept path by bench, turn **L**; soon have plantation on **L**, woodland on **R**. When track forks, go **R** to another track, then **R** again. Soon you're by edge of woodland, with field **R**.

❷ There are 2 houses below and, as you draw level with 2nd, see small clearing on **L**. On edge of it faint path rises diagonally through plantation. It soon becomes clearer and leads to steep straight track. Join this, shortly crossing cattle grid on to pasture.

❸ Track turns sharp **L**, leaving tramway incline. Continue to **Abdon Burf**. Stand next to trig pillar (**radio masts** on your **R**) and look south west to see path descending hill. Follow it down to line of posts. Go through line, keep descending by fence. Path swings **R**, becoming hollow way.

❹ Turn **R** at lane, **L** at junction and **L** again at stile. Go along **L-H** edges of meadows, and keep ahead as path merges with remains of old green lane.

❺ Approaching **Abdon**, stile leads into garden. Go through, with signs directing you past house and down hollow way to lane. Turn **L** past farm buildings and continue to barns. There's stony track opposite – walk few paces along it to bridleway on **L**. Follow it uphill to **Lane Cottage**.

❻ Bear **R** to lane and cross to stile opposite. Go up steep pasture towards fence/hedge on skyline. Cross at stile and continue to top **L** corner of next field. Turn **L** on track, which becomes hollow way at **Highcroft**.

❼ Go through gate into pasture and follow **R-H** fence to top corner. Pass through gate and continue to beeches on ridge. Go forward through beeches, straight on along track, which descends through woodland, plantation and bracken to junction. Turn **R**.

❽ Where track crosses stream leave it to head downhill, following stream. At track, turn **L**. After 600yds (549m) reach junction. Branch **R** for pub or bus stop at **Burwarton**. If not, keep **L** to start.

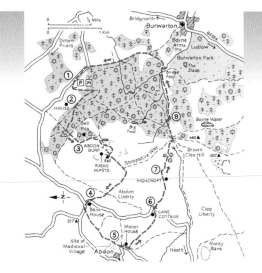

470 CLEE HILL *THE REAL BEDLAM*

8¼ miles (13.3km) 3hrs 30min **Ascent:** 1,330ft (405m)
Paths: Good but rough, uneven and/or boggy in places, 2 stiles
Suggested map: aqua3 OS Explorer 203 Ludlow
Grid reference: SO 595753
Parking: Car park/picnic site opposite turning for Kremlin Inn on A4117 on eastern edge of Cleehill village

In Shropshire's high and charismatic hills.

❶ Walk up track opposite picnic area, towards **Kremlin Inn**. Before you **inn**, go through bridle gate on **L** and along track. After 220yds (201m), right of way to **L** of it can be difficult – most walkers use track.

❷ At radar station access road by Hedgehog House, go **R**. Walk to end of **Rouse Boughton Terrace**, go through gate (**L**) to track. Don't follow it but turn **R** along edge of pasture. Go along edge of next field and through gate in corner to **Shropshire Way**, which goes **R**. Ignore it and keep ahead, cutting corner of field, to meet then follow **L-H** boundary after 300yds (274m).

❸ Continue through next field to **L** corner. Follow track to cross **Benson's Brook** at bridge. Climb out of valley on track which passes abutments of old tramway bridge (**Bitterley Incline** is called Titterstone Incline on OS maps), before arriving at **Bedlam**.

❹ Turn **L** into hamlet, then fork **R** past Old Shop House and Hullabaloo House towards **Titterstone**

Clee Hill. Gate gives access and path takes you **R**. After passing house, it cuts through bracken.

❺ Leave path when reach **Bitterley Incline** again. Climb embankment, joining **Shropshire Way**. Continue uphill towards ruined buildings ahead. Pass to **R** of main **quarry**, then go **L** to top.

❻ To north of trig pillar is cairn, **Giant's Chair**. Look north towards Brown Clee Hill to see **Callowgate**, red-roofed farm at edge of moorland. Aim for this, picking best way down slope then across moorland.

❼ At **Callowgate**, leave **Shropshire Way** and turn **R** by moorland edge. Joining lane at **Cleetongate**, turn **R** to **Cleeton St Mary**. Turn **R** past church, **R** past almshouses, **L** on to **Random bridleway** along moorland edge. Keep just to **R** of fence, except where you need to cut corner – obvious when you come to it.

❽ When fence makes sharp **L** turn, keep ahead to **radar station** access road. Turn **L** to **Rouse Boughton Terrace** then retrace your steps to start.

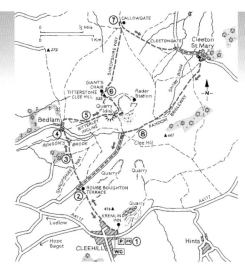

471 WENLOCK EDGE *CLOSE TO THE EDGE*

6¼ miles (10.1km) 3hrs **Ascent:** 689ft (210m)
Paths: Mostly good but ford on Dunstan's Lane can be deep after rain, 10 stiles
Suggested map: aqua3 OS Explorer 217 The Long Mynd & Wenlock Edge
Grid reference: SO 479875
Parking: Car park/picnic site on east side of unclassified road between Middlehope and Westhope

Along former drovers' roads to Corve Dale.

❶ Turn **L** out of car park along lane. At junction, turn **L** ('Middlehope'). Keep on at next ('Upper Westhope') where road becomes track and bends **L** towards house. Go through gate on **R** instead and along grassy bridleway that enters woodland. Keep straight on at 2 cross paths.

❷ Bridleway emerges into pasture; keep straight on along **L-H** edge to cross field. Turn **R** on field-edge path, which soon becomes wide track.

❸ Pass cottage and, with barns ahead, look for blue arrows directing sharp **R**. Keep **L** above **Corfton Bache**, deep valley, until blue arrows send you down into valley. Follow it to road at **Corfton** and cross to lane opposite.

❹ As lane degenerates into track, look on **L** for footpath starting at kissing gate. Go diagonally **L** across pasture to prominent stile at far side. Cross farm track and walk to far **R** corner of arable field.

❺ Go through gate, then little way along **L-H** edge of another field until gate gives access to parkland. Follow waymarker. **St Peter's Church** at Diddlebury comes into view, providing guide.

❻ Cross 2 stiles at far side of park; descend slope, to **R** of fence. Cross bridge to **Diddlebury**. Turn **R**, then **L** by church. Join footpath: pass to **R** of village hall, then diagonally **R** past **school**, over 2 stiles and across fields to road. Cross to lane; fork **R** after few paces.

❼ Footpath leaves lane on **R**, almost opposite **Chapel Cottage**. Turn **R** to visit **Swan Inn** or continue.

❽ At junction with bridle sign by sign ('Aston Top') keep **L** on lane. After ¾ mile (1.2km), branch **L** on byway, **Dunstan's Lane** (no signpost or waymarker). Follow it to Middlehope village. Turn **L**. Keep on at Y-junction. When footpath crosses road, turn **L** into woodland. Path is signposted on **R**, but not **L** – **L** branch is few paces further on. Go through woods back to picnic site.

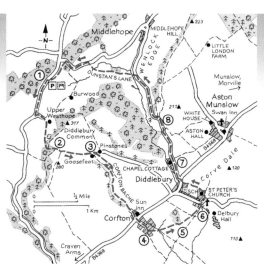

Shropshire

MUCH WENLOCK *PAYING HOMAGE TO ST MILBURGA*

6¼ miles (10.1km) 2hrs 30min **Ascent:** 426ft (130m)
Paths: Field paths, couple of boggy patches, 16 stiles
Suggested map: aqua3 OS Explorers 217 The Long Mynd & Wenlock Edge; 242 Telford, Ironbridge & The Wrekin
Grid reference: SO 623998 (on Explorer 217) **Parking:** Car park off St Mary's Lane in Much Wenlock

A walk in the countryside.

❶ Go down Burgage Way, **L** on Mutton Shut to High Street, **R** to Barrow Street, then **L**. Pass church, then turn 1st **R** on Bull Ring. Continue past **priory** and along lane (**Shropshire Way**).

❷ Turn **R** along track to footpath junction. Leave Shropshire Way here, follow **R-H** path. Cross brook and continue along **L-H** hedge to waymarker directing you diagonally towards stile.

❸ Cross stile, turn **R** along field edge. Ignore gate and stile in corner; turn **L**, until another stile gives access to adjacent field. Turn **L** to far corner, climb over low fence and along narrow path.

❹ Go through gate at end of field and over stile ahead, then on through wood into field. Keep by **L-H** hedge before joining track to **L** of holly hedge. When track bends **R**, keep ahead towards **Arlescott Farm**.

❺ Two stiles give access to pasture to **R** of farm. Turn **L**, passing to **L** of pool and then to **R** of Arlescott

Cottage to intercept **Jack Mytton Way**. Turn **L** to pasture. Approaching far side, veer away from hedge to gap in lower hedge. Turn **R**, following bridleway to lane at **Wyke**.

❻ Turn **R**, then **L** at road junction. Back on **Shropshire Way**, pass **Audience Wood** then turn **L** through woodland to fields. Path waymarked along field edges, then diagonally towards **Bradley Farm**.

❼ Pass through farmyard, turn **L** by house, then **R**. Cross lane to fields, going ahead to pastureland. Head for far **R** corner, cross footbridge and turn **L** to path junction near **Much Wenlock**, encountered earlier. Turn **R** to rejoin lane from **Much Wenlock**.

❽ Turn **R** to **dismantled railway**, go **L** for few paces, then **R** again at sign for **Jack Mytton Way**. Join footpath on **L** along edge of **Gaskell Recreation Ground**. After passing green shed, recross old railway line and turn **R** on fenced path. Pass **former station house**, turn **L** and emerge near **priory**. Turn **R** to start.

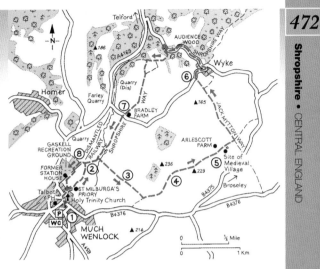

CLIVE *DRAMA ON HIGH*

5¼ miles (8.4km) 2hrs **Ascent:** 540ft (165m)
Paths: Rocky, woodland and field paths, mostly well used, 5 stiles
Suggested map: aqua3 OS Explorer 241 Shrewsbury
Grid reference: SJ 525237 **Parking:** Car park in Corbet Wood, next to Grinshill Quarry

Dramatic cliffs and views.

❶ Join bridleway near stone building on east side of car park, fork **R** to pass below car park. Go on at junction, passing sycamore tree, then slab of rock.

❷ At junction by another slab, keep to bridleway (blue arrow), descending to where wall rises on **R**, at right angles to bridleway. Follow wall up to **Shropshire Way**. Don't join it, instead turn **L** by post with carvings of butterfly, ascend to viewpoint.

❸ With view behind you, ascend to path. Follow this to **L**, keep **L** at fork. Continue to summit. With view behind you take **L-H** path. Keep **L** at fork. Path joins walled track (**Glat**), to All Saints' Church at **Clive**. You could turn **L** here, but to see **Clive**, turn **R** instead, then **L** on main street and **L** again on Back Lane.

❹ Turn **R** on footpath, which begins as green lane, then crosses sheep pasture to road. Turn **R** past **Yorton Station**, **L** under railway and **L** again. Soon after passing house (**Fox Fields**) join footpath on **L**, cross field then railway.

❺ Push through trees to track. Turn **R** for a few paces, then **L** between 2 pools to parkland. Follow **L-H** boundary, pass **Sansaw**. Go through iron kissing gate next to wooden field gate. Where Sansaw's garden wall turns **L**, keep straight on to another wooden field gate. Cross driveway and continue across parkland to road.

❻ Turn **L**, then immediately **R**, towards **Clive**. Turn **R** opposite Back Lane on walled bridleway, go below churchyard and round Grinshill Hill to Jubilee Oak and **village hall**.

❼ Turn **R** along track, passing church to main street. Turn **L**, then **L** again on Gooseberry Lane. Pass other side of village hall, rejoin walled bridleway and continue to walled grassy track. Turn **R** past houses.

❽ At fork, go **L** then up steps to cross stone step stile. Ascend through woodland, soon bearing **R** and climbing steeply to fenced area. Turn **R** on broad path to junction, turn **L** on track, **L** at road, past **Grinshill Quarry** to car park.

MERRINGTON GREEN *HERE BE DRAGONS*

5½ miles (8.8km) 2hrs 15min **Ascent:** 344ft (105m)
Paths: Field paths and bridleway, can be muddy, 6 stiles
Suggested map: aqua3 OS Explorer 241 Shrewsbury
Grid reference: SJ 465208
Parking: Car park on north side of road at Merrington Green nature reserve

Explore a common and a sandstone ridge.

❶ There is a map of the **reserve** on one side of the car park and, on the other side, 2 footpaths: you can take either as they soon merge into 1. Follow path through grassland, then fork **L** into woodland. Turn **R** at pool. After passing one side of pool, path moves briefly away from it, then turns **L** to pass end of it, with another pool on **R-H** side and boardwalk underfoot.

❷ Turn **L** on tree-bordered bridleway, which continues for nearly 2 miles (3.2km). As you approach road, look for stile on **R** (at bend) and walk across fields to meet road on edge of **Myddle**. Turn **R** into village.

❸ After passing **church**, turn **R** on walled lane, then through black gate on **L**. Pass to **L** of farm buildings, then cross 2 fields – you can see path stretching ahead of you to lane.

❹ Turn **R** along lane for 400yds (366m) until you can join footpath on **L**, which climbs wooded slope. At top well-trodden path turns **R** by woodland edge.

However, right of way goes diagonally across field to gate to road.

❺ Turn your back on gate and go straight across field, meeting wood again at corner. Go through gate and descend through trees, then through garden (dogs on leads) and past **cottage** towards lane. Just before you reach it, join another path on **L** that climbs back up slope. As you approach stile at top, turn **R**, then **L**, descending through former **quarry** and past house built into rock. Turn **R** along lane.

❻ Join footpath on **L** and cross narrow pasture. Right of way runs diagonally across next field, but is currently impassable at far side. If this may still be case (new waymarkers might indicate improvements), take another path, which follows **R-H** field edge.

❼ Turn **L** along **Merrington Lane**, and eventually **R** at T-junction at **Merrington**. When road bends **L**, go straight on along bridleway used earlier to join path that crosses **nature reserve** to car park.

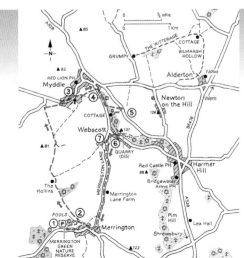

475 LYTH HILL *INSPIRATIONAL VIEWS*

8 miles (12.9km) 3hrs **Ascent:** 548ft (167m) ▲
Paths: Cross-field paths, mostly well-maintained, about 30 stiles
Suggested map: aqua3 OS Explorer 241 Shrewsbury
Grid reference: SJ 473069
Parking: Car park in country park at top of Lyth Hill: OS map shows bus turning area, not car park

A walk offering panoramic views.

❶ Head south on **Shropshire Way**. Ignore path branching R into Spring Coppice. Way descends to lane; turn L, then 1st R, on track to **Exfords Green**.
❷ Cross 2 stiles to skirt former **Primitive Methodist chapel**. Leave **Shropshire Way**, going diagonally R across field. Cross stile close to far R corner and go through copse to lane. Cross to path almost opposite, following L–H field edge. Cross stile into another. Head diagonally across to point near far R corner. Cross wobbly stile and continue across another field, past 2 oak trees. Worn path goes obliquely R across next 2 fields to lane.
❸ Turn R, then R again at main road, to pass through **Longden**, and R again on School Lane. Descend to cross brook, then go through gate on L and diagonally R across field corner to stile.
❺ Follow yellow arrow diagonally across next field to stile under oak tree to L of telegraph post. Cross

another field to road. Path continues opposite, crossing 2 fields to meet lane at **Great Lyth**. Turn R, keeping straight on at junction, turn L at next.
❻ Turn R on access track to **Lower Lythwood Hall** and **Holly Ash**. At latter, turn L as track becomes green lane leading to field. Cross field, pass row of 3 oaks, then keep to R of pond to reach stile by 2 oaks at far side. In next field go diagonally R, then through gate and continue along track for few paces to cross stile on R.
❼ Walk straight up sloping field and turn L at top. Cross stile in corner and keep on along worn path to waymarker, which directs you L, descending beside brook to meet road at **Hook-a-gate**.
❽ Turn R for 200yds (183m), R again on footpath that climbs to Hanley Lane at **Bayston Hill**. Continue to Overdale Road; turn R until you intercept Shropshire Way at Lythwood Road. Turn R, following Way to **Lythwood Farm**, across fields to Lyth Hill, and start.

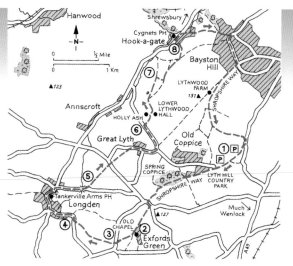

476 ELLESMERE *MERES, MOSSES AND MORAINES*

7¼ miles (11.7km) 3hrs **Ascent:** 180ft (55m) ▲
Paths: Field paths and canal tow path, 8 stiles
Suggested map: aqua3 OS Explorer 241 Shrewsbury
Grid reference: SJ 407344
Parking: Castlefields car park opposite The Mere

A wonderful watery walk.

❶ Cross to **The Mere**; turn L. Pass **The Boathouse** and **visitor centre** and walk towards town, until you reach Cremorne Gardens. Join path that runs through trees close by water's edge for ¾ mile (1.2km).
❷ Leave trees for field and turn L, signposted 'Welshampton'. Path soon joins track to **Crimps Farm**. Turn R past farm buildings to cross stile on R of track. Continue along another track.
❸ Track leads into sheep pasture then go straight on, guided by waymarkers and stiles. When you come to field with trig pillar, waymarker is slightly misleading – ignore it and go straight across. In next field aim for 3 prominent trees close together at far side. As you approach them, turn L into field corner.
❹ Go through gate and descend by R–H hedge. When it turns corner, go with it, to R. Skirt **pool** and keep going in same direction on grassy track, passing another pool. Track soon becomes much better

defined and leads to farm where you join road.
❺ Turn L and keep ahead at junction into **Welshampton**. Turn R on Lyneal Lane and follow it to bridge over **Llangollen Canal**. Descend steps to tow path. Turn R, passing under bridge. Pass **Lyneal Wharf**, **Cole Mere**, **Yell Wood** and **Blake Mere**, then through **Ellesmere Tunnel**. Beyond this are 3 footpaths signposted 'The Mere'. Take any of these short cuts, but to see bit more of canal, including visitor moorings and **marina**, stay on tow path.
❻ Arriving at **bridge 58**, further choices present themselves. You could extend this walk to include signposted Wharf Circular Walk or to explore town: just follow signs. To return directly to The Mere, however, go up to road and turn L.
❼ Fork R on road by **Blackwater Cottage**. Turn R at top, then soon L at Rose Bank, up steps. Walk across earthworks of long-gone **Ellesmere Castle** and follow signs for The Mere or car park.

477 WHITTINGTON *FROM CASTLE TO CANAL*

6 miles (9.7km) 2hrs 30min **Ascent:** Negligible ▲
Paths: Tow path, lanes and field paths, very overgrown, 19 stiles
Suggested map: aqua3 OS Explorer 240 Oswestry
Grid reference: SJ 325312
Parking: Car park next to Whittington Castle – honesty box

Follow the Llangollen branch of the Shroppie through pastoral countryside.

❶ Turn R by Shrewsbury road (B5009), using footway on left. After about ½ mile (800m), cross stile and follow waymarked path across 3 fields to far R corner of 3rd field.
❷ Walk along edge of next field, with wood on your L. Cross stile in corner, then go obliquely across another field as indicated by waymarker. prominent oak tree is useful guide. There is stile near tree, but you may have to wade through nettles to get to it. Continue in same direction across next field to lane and turn L.
❸ Keep L when you come to fork and continue to A495. Turn R for few paces, then cross to other side. Join footpath that runs along L–H edge of field to stile and footbridge. Beyond these, keep going along field edge until gap in hedge. Go through, but continue in same direction as before, soon going up bank.

❹ Meet canal at **Pollett's Bridge** (No 6). Don't cross it – go under to join tow path. Follow this to **Hindford Bridge** (No 11), then go up to join lane. Turn R past **Jack Mytton Inn**, then R again, signposted 'Iron Mills and Gobowen'.
❺ Take footpath on left. Walk down long, narrow paddock to far end, then cross stile on right. Follow fence to footbridge, then continue across next pasture to another footbridge and keep straight on to stile ahead. Go up to far R corner of next field, through gate and then L by field edge.
❻ Join track that soon bends R beside course of **dismantled railway**. Look out for stile giving access to railway. Turn R on former trackbed for few paces, then up bank on L – watch for steps concealed in undergrowth here. Cross stile to field, turn R to far side and cross another stile. Bear L to large oak tree, then continue to lane. Follow it to Top Street and turn right, then L to **Whittington Castle**.

Shropshire

STIPERSTONES *BACK TO PURPLE*

4½ miles (7.2km) 2hrs **Ascent:** 951ft (290m) ▲

Paths: Good paths across pasture, moorland and woodland, 1 stile
Suggested map: aqua3 OS Explorer 216 Welshpool & Montgomery
Grid reference: SJ 373022
Parking: Car park at Snailbeach

From the mining village of Snailbeach to the dragon's crest of Stiperstones.

1 Take Lordshill lane opposite car park, then join parallel footpath on **L**. Rejoining lane, cross to site of locomotive shed, then continue up lane, noticing green arrows directing you to main sites.

2 Turn **R** on track between **crusher house** and **compressor house**. Few paces past compressor house, turn **L** up steps. At top, turn **R**, then soon **L** up more steps. Turn **L** to Cornish engine house, then **R** and continue through woodland. Short detour leads to smelter **chimney**, otherwise it's uphill all way.

3 Sign indicates that you're entering **Stiperstones National Nature Reserve** (NNR). Woods give way to bracken, broom and bramble before you cross over stile on to open hill. Path climbs slope ahead to stile/gate at top.

4 Two paths are waymarked. Take **L-H** one, which runs between fence and rim of spectacular dingle on

your **R**. Path then climbs away from dingle and meets rutted track. Turn **R**. As path climbs you can see rock tors on summit. There's also one much closer to hand, isolated from rest. This is **Shepherd's Rock**.

5 Just beyond **Shepherd's Rock** is junction marked by cairn. Turn **R** here, then fork **L** to go round other side of rock. Leave NNR at gate/stile. The path runs to **L**, shortly bordered by hawthorn hedge. You'll soon see that this is an old green lane, lined at various points by either hedges/trees on both sides, one line of trees or tumbledown stone wall.

6 At junction take **L-H** path back into NNR. At next junction, fork **R** to leave NNR at gate by plantation. Go diagonally across field to track; turn **R**, going back across field, through plantation, then across pasture on bridleway.

7 Fork **L** at bridleway junction and continue past **Lordshill chapel** to lane. Turn **R** and stay with it as it swings **L** to **Snailbeach**.

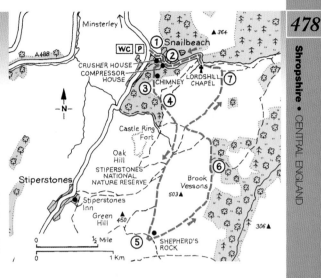

BISHOP'S CASTLE *LIFE AND DEATH*

7 miles (11.3km) 2hrs 30min **Ascent:** 738ft (225m) ▲

Paths: Waymarking can be patchy, path near Woodbatch cropped over, gates to climb, about 10 stiles
Suggested map: aqua3 OS Explorer 216 Welshpool & Montgomery
Grid reference: SO 324886
Parking: Car park off Station Street

A colourful border town.

1 Walk up Church Street, High Street and Bull Street, go **L** on Bull Lane to **Castlegreen**. Turn **R**, then **L** after No 11 on footpath to reach stile. Take **L-H** path, cross 2 fields, go ahead along green lane. At end, go through gate and along field edge to stile.

2 Turn **R** in next field, cross stile at top and go obliquely **L** over field to fence corner. Follow fence/hedge past **pond** to stile. Go obliquely **L** across highest point of next field, then down to gate halfway along far hedge. Go diagonally **R** across another field to hedge, next to crab apple trees. Follow hedge to track and turn **L** to road.

3 Turn **R**, immediately **R** again and **L** on to lane, which soon becomes track. Descend into woodland, cross into Wales and eventually meet lane.

4 Turn **L** and walk up to meet road, Kerry Ridgeway, at Bishop's Moat, where you cross back into England. Turn **R**, then through 1st gate on **L** (it

hangs from one hinge). Go diagonally **L** to end of line of hawthorn trees, continue in same direction over another field to kink in far hedge.

5 Go diagonally across 3rd field to line of trees which leads to gate. Continue down next field to far **R** corner, walking through scrap-metal collection.

6 Meeting farm lane, turn **R** through farmyard at **Upper Woodbatch**, passing barns. Approaching final group, see track descending by fence. Right of way is on other side of fence, so go through gate to join it and follow it down through 2 fields towards brook.

7 About 120yds (110m) before brook, turn **L** across field. Go through gate and continue across 2 fields to lane. Join **Shropshire Way** opposite, following it along bottom of several fields, quite close to brook.

8 Pass abandoned **quarry**, turn **L** uphill and head for **Bishop's Castle**, soon joining track leading to Field Lane. Follow this to Church Lane, which leads to Church Street and start.

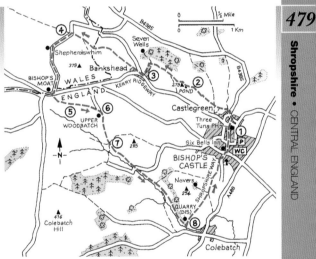

THE LONG MYND *AN ANCIENT SETTLEMENT*

7½ miles (12.1km) 3hrs **Ascent:** 1,545ft (471m) ▲

Paths: Mostly moorland paths and tracks, 3 stiles
Suggested map: aqua3 OS Explorer 217 The Long Mynd & Wenlock Edge
Grid reference: SO 453936
Parking: Easthope Road car park, Church Stretton

Prehistoric remains and magnificent views.

1 Walk up Lion Meadow to High Street and turn **R**. Turn **L** at The Square, go past church and straight on into Rectory Field. Walk to top **L** corner, turn **R** by edge, soon entering **Old Rectory Wood**. Path descends to junction. Turn **L**, soon crossing Town Brook, then climb again to gate on to Long Mynd.

2 Go forward beside brook to railings, continue with brook **L**. After slight height gain, path begins to climb more steeply and heads away from brook. Eventually path and brook meet up again near head of latter.

3 Path crosses brook. Go 50yds (46m) to junction marked by 1st in succession of pink-banded posts. Follow these posts, gaining height gradually again. Ignore branching paths and, after slight rise, you'll see summit ahead on **L**.

4 Meet unfenced road about 100yds (91m) **L** of junction. Turn **L**, ignore path to Little Stretton and go straight on when road bends **L**, joining bridleway. At

next junction, turn **L** to summit, then keep straight on to **Port Way**. Turn **R** past site of Pole Cottage.

5 Turn **L** on footpath, signposted to **Little Stretton**. When wide rutted track forks go **L** – you can see path ahead, cutting green swath over shoulder of **Round Hill**. Go straight on at junction, then descend to **Cross Dyke** (Bronze-Age earthwork). After dyke, path ascends briefly but soon levels out, then descends, eventually following brook to Little Stretton.

6 Cross at footbridge by ford and turn **R** on lane for few paces. Look for footpath **L**. It climbs by field edge to top corner, then turns **L**, following top of steep slope to pasture. Follow **R-H** edge of this until path enters woodland. Descend to **Ludlow Road**.

7 Here join bridleway next to footpath. It climbs into woodland, emerging at far side to meet track, which becomes road. As it bends **R** there's access **L** to **Rectory Field**. Descend to The Square, turn **R** on High Street and **L** on Lion Meadow to car park.

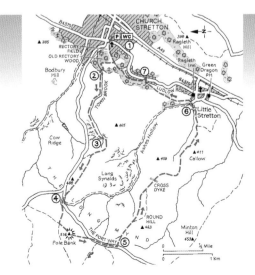

481 THE STRETTONS *THE SHAPELIEST HILLS*

6 miles (9.7km) 3hrs **Ascent:** 1,060ft (323m)
Paths: Good paths through pasture and woodland, 14 stiles
Suggested map: aqua3 OS Explorer 217 The Long Mynd & Wenlock Edge
Grid reference: SO 453936
Parking: Easthope Road car park, Church Stretton

Quality walking along the Strettons.

❶ Walk along Easthope Road to Sandford Avenue, turn **R** past station. Cross A49, go along Sandford Avenue, turn **R** on Watling Street South. Turn **L** by postbox, fork **R** on Clive Avenue, and **L** on Ragleth Road.

❷ Turn **R** into Woodland Trust reserve, Philla's Grove. Keep **L** at fork, climbing by edge of wood, and **L** at next junction. Leave wood at stile and turn **R** on footpath. After level section, path climbs steeply to stile. Turn **R** for few paces, then fork **L** to higher path, which goes by L-H fence through woodland.

❸ When path emerges on hillside, keep ahead to stile, but don't cross it. Turn your back on it and follow path up **Ragleth Hill**, then walk along spine of hill.

❹ Pole marks southern summit (smaller of 2), but descent isn't obvious. Go **L**, across rocky area to far fence, then follow it down to corner where stile leads into field. Turn **L** across field corner, cross stile and climb to top **L** corner of next field. Go ahead to far **L**

corner of field to lane.

❺ Turn **L**, then 1st **R** to **Ragdon Manor**. Take footpath on **L** through farmyard. Cross stile then field to gap at far side. Keep on along edges of 2 fields.

❻ Turn **L** on lane, cross junction to footpath on **R**. Go diagonally across field to far corner, cross lane and continue opposite. Walk through gorse and bracken to gate. Path continues through woodland.

❼ Approaching 2nd gate, don't go through, but turn **R** round **Hazler Hill**. Turn **R** at lane, walk to junction and cross to bridleway opposite, which passes **Gaerstones Farm**. After Caer Caradoc comes into view, look for bridleway, **L**, to gate/stile 40yds (37m) away. Descend past **Helmeth Hill** to another bridleway at point where this is crossed by brook.

❽ Turn **L**, emerge from woodland into pasture. Continue with fence **L**. Path leads to lane, turn **L** to **Church Stretton**. Turn **R** at Sandford Avenue, cross road, pass station then **L** on Easthope Road to start.

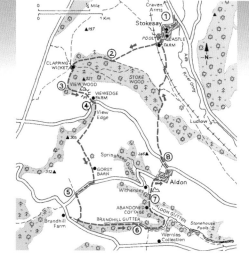

482 STOKESAY *OVER THE EDGE*

6¼ miles (10.1km) 2hrs 30min **Ascent:** 909ft (277m)
Paths: Mostly excellent, short stretch eroded and uneven, byway from Aldon to Stoke Wood occasionally floods, 12 stiles
Suggested map: aqua3 OS Explorers 203 Ludlow; 217 The Long Mynd & Wenlock Edge
Grid reference: SO 437819 (on Explorer 217) **Parking:** Lay-by on A49 north of Stokesay turn

A 13th-century house set in gorgeous hills.

❶ Take footway from lay-by to lane that leads to **Stokesay Castle**. Walk past castle; take 2nd footpath on **R**, at far side of **pool**. It skirts farm, then crosses railway. Keep ahead through 3 meadows on worn path, with series of stiles providing further guidance.

❷ Turn for **Stoke Wood**, proceed to track; turn **R**. Leave wood at stile at far end and walk past house, **Clapping Wicket**, then turn sharp **L** up field in front of house. Turn **R** at top, walking by edge of **View Wood**.

❸ Join track that leads into wood, then emerges from it to run alongside edge. It soon plunges back into trees, climbing quite steeply, then levelling out to reach lane by **Viewedge Farm**.

❹ Turn **L** for few paces, then join footpath on **R**. Turn **R** by field edge and walk to top of knoll, continuing in same direction across fields to waymarker that sends you sharp **L** across adjacent field. Join track at far side and continue past **Gorst Barn** to lane. Turn **R**.

❺ Turn **L** on footpath, crossing 3 pastures to concealed stile, which gives on to bridleway. Turn **L** down **Brandhill Gutter**. Eventually go through gate on **R**, but immediately turn **L** to continue in same direction. Keep close to stream (or, very often, dry streambed) on **L**.

❻ After passing through gate, bridleway becomes narrow, uneven and eroded for while but soon improves. It eventually crosses stream (next to stile) and starts to swing northwards, into **Aldon Gutter**. Beyond **abandoned cottage**, bridleway passes to **R** of pheasant pens – watch carefully for waymarkers here.

❼ 200yds (183m) after cottage, bridleway bears **R**, climbing steep valley side to meet lane at top. Turn **R** to pass through hamlet of **Aldon**, then **L** at T-junction. Join byway on **R** at slight bend in lane (no sign or waymarker). This lovely hedged track leads between fields, then through **Stoke Wood**, beyond which it descends to **Stokesay** and start.

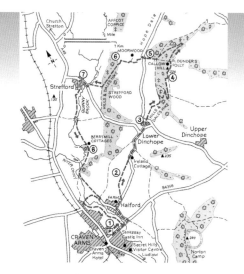

483 CALLOW HILL *SPOTTING BUZZARDS*

6½ miles (10.4km) 2hrs 30min **Ascent:** 817ft (249m)
Paths: Mostly good, not always clear between Quinny Brook and Halford, muddy in places, 18 stiles
Suggested map: aqua3 OS Explorer 217 The Long Mynd & Wenlock Edge
Grid reference: SO 433828
Parking: Car park off B4368 Corvedale Road, Craven Arms

Tackle steep Callow Hill.

❶ Walk down Corvedale Road, cross **River Onny** and turn **L** towards **Halford**. At hamlet, turn **R** towards **Dinchope**. Pass **farm**, take footpath on **L**. It climbs to far corner of field, then along L-H edge of another.

❷ When hedge turns corner, continue across field to stile by telegraph pole, then up next field to concealed stile, near top **L** corner. Turn **L** along lane and ignore all turnings, following signs for **Lower Dinchope** and **Westhope**. Pass through **Lower Dinchope** to junction.

❸ Take path almost opposite, where sign indicates that you're joining **Hills and Dales Hike**. Follow frequent waymarkers across fields and into woodland, before zig-zagging up paths to top of **Callow Hill**.

❹ Turn **L** at top, skirting round Flounder's Folly, then returning to edge until you descend sharp **L** into conifers. Path plunges steeply down to clearing. Join track which continues more gently, soon passing barrier to meet Dinchope–Westhope road.

❺ Turn **R**, then immediately **L** on track, where road bends sharply **R**. Go **L** at turning for **Moorwood** farm.

❻ Enter **Strefford Wood** and descend **L** on bridleway. At bottom of wood Hills and Dales Hike goes to **L**. Stay with bridleway, which leaves Strefford Wood and descends to lane. Turn **L**, then **R**, crossing **Quinny Brook** into **Strefford**.

❼ Turn first **L** on through road, which becomes footpath running through fields to footbridge over Quinny Brook. Cross bridge and proceed to another. Cross this too and keep going to stile just beyond 3 large oaks. Again, keep straight on, past **Berrymill Cottages** and through copse into field.

❽ Walk length of field to stile at far side, close to top **L** corner. Go through wood, then across fields towards **Halford**. Watch for concealed stile as you reach village. Go along track to junction, then turn **R** on another track which crosses River Onny. Permissive path on **L** runs into **Craven Arms** pub.

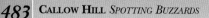

Shropshire

SUNNYHILL TO BURY DITCHES

484

5½ miles (8.8km) 2hrs Ascent: 804ft (245m)
Paths: Field and woodland paths, one boggy and overgrown; fence and gates to climb; 8 stiles
Suggested map: aqua3 OS Explorer 216 Welshpool & Montgomery
Grid reference: SO 334839
Parking: Forestry Commission car park at Sunnyhill off minor road north from Clunton

Magnificent views from a dramatic hill fort.

❶ From car park, walk back to lane; turn **L**. Descend through hamlet of **Lower Down** and continue to **Brockton**. Turn **L** on track shortly before you come to ford. Pass collection of semi-derelict buses behind **farm**, then go through gate on **L** and walk along **R-H** edges of three fields, parallel with track.

❷ Climb over fence into wood and continue in same direction, contouring round base of **Acton Bank**. After leaving wood path continues through scrub, then through pasture below some old quarries, before it meets lane at hamlet of **Acton**.

❸ Turn **L**, pass to **R** of triangular green and join path running past **White House Farm**. Frequent waymarkers guide you past house, across field, then **L** over stile and along **R-H** edge of another field.

❹ Cross footbridge and continue straight across ensuing field towards building at far side. Cross stile in hedge, turn **L** for few paces and then **R** on track

which passes by house called **Brookbatch** and rises into woodland. When track eventually bends to L, go forward over stile instead and continue climbing.

❺ Emerging on to track, turn **L** past **pond**. Cross cattle grid into Forestry Commission property and leave track, turning **R** on footpath leading through beechwoods. It winds through trees to meet **Shropshire Way** (waymarked with buzzard logo). Turn **L**, then soon **R** at junction. Ignoring R turn, stay on Shropshire Way, which soon forks **L** off main track.

❻ You now have choice of 2 buzzards to follow: main route of Shropshire Way goes straight on, but you should choose alternative route which branches **R**. Path leads to **Bury Ditches** hill fort, then cuts through gap in ramparts and crosses interior. At colour-banded post (red, blue and green), path branches **L** to allow visit to summit, with its toposcope and incredible views. Bear **R** to return to main path and turn **L** to follow it to car park.

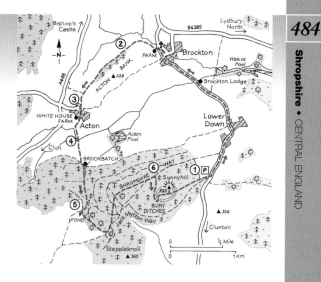

OFFA'S DYKE WALKING WITH OFFA

485

8 miles (12.9km) 3hrs Ascent: 1,542ft (470m)
Paths: Excellent, mostly across short turf, 8 stiles
Suggested map: aqua3 OS Explorer 201 Knighton & Presteigne
Grid reference: SO 287734
Parking: Informal parking in Kinsley Wood, accessed by forest road from A488 (or park in Knighton, next to bus station or near Offa's Dyke Centre)

Offa's Dyke on the Welsh border.

❶ Adjacent to car park, at northern end of **Kinsley Wood**, is meadow with barn. Join bridleway which runs along **L-H** edge of this meadow. After 200yds (183m), veer slightly away from field edge and descend through trees to **Offa's Dyke Path** (ODP).

❷ Turn **R**; follow ODP for 2½ miles (4km). Path runs just above steep slope falling away to west and just below top of **Panpunton Hill**, and follows dyke all way. After climbing around head of combe, it gains top of **Cwm-sanaham Hill** (1,328ft/406m), then continues northwards, soon descending past house, **Brynorgan**.

❸ Meeting road, leave ODP, turning **L**, then **L** again at **Selley Cross**. After ½ mile (800m), just beyond **Selley Hall Cottage**, join footpath on **R**. Follow path to far side of field, then turn **R**, heading to top **R** corner. Cross stile, then continue straight across several fields, to meet lane at **Monaughty Poeth**.

❹ Turn **L** for ¾ mile (1.2km) to junction at **Skyborry Green**. Turn **L**, then immediately **R**, joining bridleway to **Bryney** farm. Turn **R** on footpath (waymarked at regular intervals as it contours round hill), before descending to road again at **Nether Skyborry**.

❺ Turn **L** for ½ mile (800m), then **R** on to ODP just before **Panpwnton** farm. Cross railway and River Teme, then follow Teme towards **Knighton**. Still on path cross border and turn **R** to **Offa's Dyke Centre**.

❻ Leaving **centre**, turn **L** through Knighton, then **L** again on Station Road. After passing **station**, turn **L** on Kinsley Road. Join 1st path on **R** into **Kinsley Wood**, opposite Kinsley Villa and Gillow. Fork **L** after few paces, then embark on almost vertical climb. Gradient eases before path emerges from trees to continue through scrub and across forest road. Keep ahead to top of ridge; turn **L** to walk across summit. Path descends to track. Turn **R** to return to parking area.

CLUN UNDER THE SUN

486

5½ miles (8.8km) 2hrs 30min Ascent: 1,066ft (325m)
Paths: Excellent, through mixed farmland (mainly pasture) and woodland, 3 stiles
Suggested map: aqua3 OS Explorer 201 Knighton & Presteigne
Grid reference: SO 302811
Parking: Car park at Clun community area, signed from High Street

From the tranquil Clun Valley into the hills.

❶ Walk down Hospital Lane to High Street and turn **R** to The Square. Pass **Buffalo Inn**, turn **L** on Buffalo Lane and cross **Clun Bridge**. Go up Church Street, turn **R** on Knighton road, then **L** on Hand Causeway, signposted to **Churchbank** and **Hobarris**.

❷ After ¾ mile (1.2km), take bridleway on **R**, which leaves lane on bend by **Glebe Cottage** and immediately goes **L** into field. Walk up field, through gate at top, then on through 2 more fields to lane running across top of **Clun Hill** (part of prehistoric Clun–Clee Ridgeway).

❸ Path continues opposite, along **R-H** edges of 2 fields. At end of 2nd, go through gate on **R** and diagonally to far corner of another field, then in same direction down next – towards pool in valley below.

❹ Go through gate; turn **L** on byway, then **R** at T-junction. At **Hobarris** go **L** on to track, just before main farm buildings. Soon after crossing brook, branch **L**

along hollow way. When this bends R, go straight on, over stile into field. Go straight uphill, joining field-edge track. To your **L**, 3 Scots pines and prehistoric cairn mark summit of **Pen-y-wern Hill**. Turn **L** at lane.

❺ At crossroads, keep ahead, descending to 2nd of 2 bends in lane. Ignore signposted path on R; instead take unsignposted path few paces further on. It leads into plantation and soon bends **R**. About 200yds (183m) after this, branch **L** on descending path.

❻ After 200yds (183m) branch **L**, down through oakwood. Continue to meet path at bottom of wood.

❼ Turn **L** on path, which almost immediately swings **L**, back into wood and winds through trees to meet lane. Turn **R** towards **Clun**.

❽ Turn **L** at junction with 2 tracks. Keep along lane until stile on **R** gives access to field. Go diagonally **L** towards Clun. Join lane, then turn **R** and cross footbridge by ford. Turn **R** to High Street and Hospital Lane.

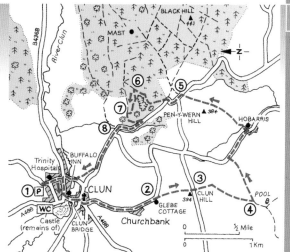

Oxfordshire

487 CORNWELL TO CHURCHILL

5½ miles (8.8km) 2hrs 30min **Ascent:** 459ft (140m) ▲
Paths: Open farmland, village lanes, quiet roads, 12 stiles
Suggested map: aqua3 OS Explorer OL45 The Cotswolds
Grid reference: SP 270270
Parking: Lay-by beside phone box at Cornwell

A walk linking two intriguing villages.

❶ Turn **L**. Walk down and up through **Cornwell**. Pass farm, R. Turn **R** ('D'Arcy Dalton Way'). Where track veers L, continue, by fingerpost. Walk down orchard; bear **L**. Go **R** at corner through hedge. Soon go through gate on **L**. Turn **R** and walk downhill. Cross stile, R; follow path down towards **St Peter's Church**.

❷ Go through gate into churchyard. Pass church, and leave via gate. Walk down hill, cross bridge at bottom and go up to gate. Turn **R** along drive, passing **Cornwell Glebe**. Bear **L**. Pass turning to Salford.

❸ Turn **R** along bridleway ('Kingham'). Follow this for ½ mile (800m); cross stile on **L**. Continue down field edge. Cross footbridge. Follow path diagonally **R**. Cross footbridge. Bear **R** along stream. Soon bear **L** and cross stile. Cross track. Cross footbridge opposite. Bear diagonally **R** up field. Cross footbridge in hedge. Maintain direction through another hedge.

❹ Cross stile into woods. Follow path down, over footbridge and up other side. Go through gate and ahead towards **Churchill**. Cross stile. Bear **R** beside house. Cross stile. Turn **L** up road. Pass post-box; turn **R** along path. At next road turn **L**. At top turn **R**.

❺ Turn **R** before *church*. Follow path round back of pub. Cross stile, pass barn and maintain direction into field. Soon turn **R** over stile and along lane. When you reach road turn **L**. Turn **R** at next junction, then **L** at end. Follow road out of village, passing old **chapel**. Continue through **Sarsden Halt**.

❻ Follow road **R**, then keep ahead along green lane. After ½ mile (800m) climb stile on **L**; bear diagonally up field. Walk up hedge and turn **R** along road.

❼ Continue through **Kingham Hill Farm**. Pass through gate at other side and around 2 fields. Cross stile, then footbridge and stile; keep ahead. Pass gate and continue up field. Cross another stile and continue, bearing slightly **L** over hillcrest. Take gate to **L** of main gate. Turn **L** up road to return to your car.

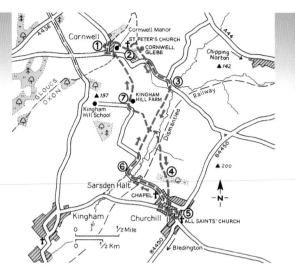

488 CHIPPING NORTON THE ROLLRIGHT STONES

8 miles (12.9km) 4hrs **Ascent:** 295ft (90m) ▲
Paths: Field paths and tracks, country roads, 9 stiles
Suggested map: aqua3 OS Explorer 191 Banbury, Bicester & Chipping Norton
Grid reference: SP 312270
Parking: Free car park off A44, in centre of Chipping Norton

An ancient and mythical site.

❶ Follow A44 downhill. Pass Penhurst School, then veer **R**, through kissing gate. Skirt L-H edge of recreation ground and aim for gate. Descend to bridge and, when path forks, keep **R**. Go up slope to 3 stiles and keep ahead along **R** edge of field. Make for gate and drop down to double gates in corner.

❷ Cross track just beyond gates. Walk towards **Salford**, keeping hedge L. Continue into village. Turn **R** by patch of grass ('Trout Lakes – Rectory Farm').

❸ Follow track to **R-H** bend. Go ahead here, following field edge. Make for gate ahead. Turn **R** in next field. About 100yds (91m) before field corner, turn **L**. Follow path across to opening in boundary. Veer **L**, then **R** to skirt field. Cross stream. Maintain direction in next field to reach road.

❹ Turn **L**, then **L** again for **Little Rollright**. Visit **church** then retrace route to D'Arcy Dalton Way on **L**. Follow path up field slope to road. Cross over.

Continue between fields. Head for trees and approach stile. Don't cross it; instead, turn **L** and skirt field, passing close to **Whispering Knights**.

❺ At road, turn **L** to visit **Rollright Stones**. Return to Whispering Knights, head down field to further stile and cross it to another. Continue along grassy path. Turn **R** at stile towards **Brighthill Farm**. Pass beside buildings to stile. Head diagonally **R** down field to further stile. Keep boundary on R and head for stile in bottom **R** corner of field. Make for bottom **R** corner of next field. Go through gate and skirt field; turn **L** at road.

❻ Keep **R** at fork and head towards **Over Norton**. Walk through village to T-junction. Turn **R**. When road swings to **L** by Cleeves Corner, join track ('Salford'). When hedges gives way, look for waymark on **L**. Follow path down slope, make for 2 kissing gates; follow path alongside wall to reach **church**. Join Church Lane. Follow it as far as T-junction. Turn **R** and return to town centre.

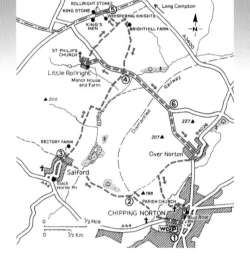

489 BURFORD A CLASSIC COTSWOLD TOWN

5 miles (8km) 2hrs 30min **Ascent:** 250ft (76m) ▲
Paths: Field and riverside paths, tracks, country roads, 7 stiles
Suggested map: aqua3 OS Explorer OL45 The Cotswolds
Grid reference: SP 252123
Parking: Large car park to east of Windrush, near parish church

Discover the delights of an ancient settlement with a long history on this attractive walk through the Windrush Valley.

❶ Head north along High Street to **Windrush**. Cross over river and turn **R** at mini-roundabout towards **Fulbrook**. Pass **Carpenters Arms** and continue along road. Avoid turning for Swinbrook and pass **Masons Arms**. Keep ahead, passing Upper End on L, and look for footpath on **R** by Masons Arms sign.

❷ Follow steps cut into side of slope up to field edge and then swing **R**. Follow boundary to waymark just before slope and curve **L** to cross field. Go through gap in hedge on far side and cross field to opening in hedgerow. Cross next field towards curtain of woodland and head for track.

❸ Keep **R** and follow track through woodland. Break cover from trees and pass row of cottages. Continue down track to **Paynes Farm**, and just beyond it, turn **R** to join signposted right of way. Head for gate and follow unfenced track towards trees. Descend slope to gate and continue ahead between hedges up hill to road.

❹ Turn **R** and follow road down into dip. Swing **L** at stone stile and sign for **Widford** and follow grassy ride through verdant **Dean Bottom**. Make for stile, turn **R** when you reach T-junction and visit Widford's **St Oswald's Church**.

❺ On leaving church, veer **R** and follow grassy track, passing lake on L. Turn **L** at road, recross Windrush and turn **R** at junction. Keep to road until you reach footpath sign and cross on **R**. Follow riverside path across series of stiles, to eventually reach road. Turn **R** towards **Burford**, pass **Great House** and **Royal Oak** and return to High Street. Leave plenty of time either at the start or finish of the walk to explore Burford. Take a leisurely stroll through the town and you'll stumble across a host of treasures – especially in the little roads leading off the High Street.

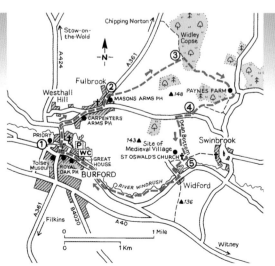

Oxfordshire

MINSTER LOVELL *A DOMESDAY VILLAGE*

490

4 miles (6.4km) 1hr 30min **Ascent:** 180ft (55m)
Paths: Meadows, tracks, pavement and lane, woodland, 17 stiles
Suggested map: aqua3 OS Explorer 180 Oxford, Witney & Woodstock
Grid reference: SP 321114
Parking: Car park (free) at eastern end of Minster Lovell, above church and hall

A gentle stroll through meadows and woods beside the Windrush.

❶ Walk up lane ('Crawley'). At end of village cross stile, **R**. Take footpath diagonally **L** across field ('Crawley'). Cross stile and keep ahead along path, with stone wall to **L**. Mill chimney on horizon belongs to **Crawley Mill**.

❷ Cross stile and ahead up slight incline. Cross another stile, go through gate and continue on path, walking up green tunnel of lane. Pass above **Crawley Mill**. At road turn **R**. Go through gate and continue past **Manor Farm**. Turn **L** through gate ('Witney'). Follow bridleway beside stream, marked by line of willows.

❸ Turn **R**. Follow pavement past **Manor Farm**, with its huge pond. Cross humpback bridge over **Windrush**. At other side of bridge cross road. Turn **L** through gate ('Witney'). Follow bridleway beside stream, marked by line of willows.

❹ At junction of paths by gate look ahead and **L** to see **New Mill**. Turn **R** through gate and walk up field

edge. Pass gate and cross road. Climb stile, go straight on to 2nd stile, and follow path down through woods.

❺ At bottom cross stile and follow path along fence. Wildflower meadows of **Maggots Grove** lie to **R**. Continue over 3 more stiles and bear **L** beside trees. Cross stile by meander of river.

❻ Cross further stile and enter woods. At gate bear **R**, following arrows, and cross 2 footbridges. After short distance cross bridge over river. Go through squeeze gate towards **Minster Lovell Hall**. Climb stile and go through gate to explore ruins.

❼ Leave by top entrance and walk through **churchyard**. Cross slab stile, continue along grassy path with village up to your **R**. Cross footbridge and stile and veer to **R**. Cross 1 stile then another into Wash Meadow recreation ground. Keep **R** and go through gate on to high street, with **Old Swan** pub to **L**. Turn **R**. Walk through village to car park.

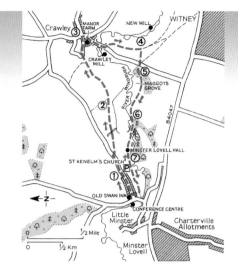

BUSCOT *TO KELMSCOTT*

491

4¾ miles (7.7km) 2hrs **Ascent:** 82ft (25m)
Paths: Riverside paths, fields, village lanes, 7 stiles
Suggested map: aqua3 OS Explorer 170 Abingdon, Wantage & Vale of White Horse
Grid reference: SU 231976
Parking: National Trust car park (free) in Buscot, signed 'Buscot Weir'

To the home of William Morris.

❶ Turn **L**. Walk back into **Buscot** to admire arcaded pump. Retrace your steps and continue on road, signed to weir. Road becomes track. Follow it round edge of **Village Field** and cross bridge. Keep **R**, to pass **Lock Cottage**. Follow footpath over weir. Bear **L** and cross lock gate.

❷ Turn **R**, cross stile and follow path beside river. Soon bear **L** and cross bridge, with view **L** to main weir. Turn **R**; follow Thames Path beside meandering river. Cross stile, and continue past 2 wartime **pill boxes** and gate. Go through pair of gates. Roofs of **Kelmscott** appear ahead. Go through gateway and continue towards bridge, passing through trees.

❸ Pass bridge, go through gate. Turn **L** up field. At far side, cross stile and 2 footbridges. Bear **L** and ahead up hedge (yellow waymarker). At end turn **R** along path (possibly overgrown). Follow this into **Kelmscott** village.

❹ Turn **R** to pass **Plough Inn**. Bear **L** along road, passing Memorial Cottages and Manor Cottages. Keep **R** to reach **Kelmscott Manor**. Keep ahead on track, pass World War II **pill box**. Turn **R** just before river.

❺ Cross bridge. Go through gate to join **Thames Path National Trail**. Cross stile and continue, passing **pill box** on **L**. Go through gate by footbridge; turn **L** over bridge. Bear **L** then **R** over 2nd bridge. Cross stile and walk up track. Soon cross ditch; now head diagonally **R** across field. At corner cross stile and footbridge by fingerpost. Turn **R**. Keep ahead up edge of field, with views of **Buscot House**, **L**. Follow track downhill and bend **R**. Turn **L** over footbridge. Continue on path diagonally **R** across next 2 fields.

❻ Go through gate by road. Turn **R** up drive. Look out for yellow waymarker and take footpath off **L**. Soon cross stile and veer **L** along edge of field. Cross stile and footbridge at other end, walk across Village Field. Turn **L** to retrace your route back to start in **Buscot**.

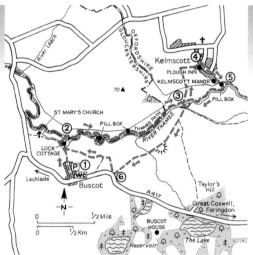

BROUGHTON *A MOATED CASTLE*

492

2¾ miles (4.4km) 1hr 30min **Ascent:** 82ft (25m)
Paths: Field and parkland paths and tracks, some roads, 6 stiles
Suggested map: aqua3 OS Explorer 191 Banbury, Bicester & Chipping Norton
Grid reference: SP 421384
Parking: Limited spaces in Broughton village

To a splendid Tudor pile.

❶ Keep **Wykeham Lane** **R** and parkland **L** and walk through **Broughton**. Pass Danvers Road on **R-H** side, followed by **Danvers Cottage** on **L**. When road curves **R** just beyond cottage, swing **L** over stile ('North Newington'). Keep ahead across field to reach stile in next boundary, then continue in next field to cross footbridge in trees (maybe obscured by foliage during summer). Continue ahead, keeping line of trees on your **R-H** side, and three-quarters of way along field boundary, look for footbridge on **R**.

❷ Cross footbridge, followed by concrete track, to reach stile. Head diagonally **R** across field to road. Take right of way on opposite side and follow stretch of **Macmillan Way** between fields to reach stile. Cross stile to lane; turn **L**. Walk towards **North Newington**, passing entrance to **Park Farm** on your **R-H** side. Pass **Blinking Owl** pub and Wheelwright Cottage then turn **L** into The Pound, opposite old village pump.

❸ Walk past **Pound Cottage** and look for footpath which starts about 30yds (27m) beyond it on **R-H** side. Follow footpath diagonally **R** across field to reach wide, obvious gap in hedgerow on far side. Turn **L** to reach another gap in hedge, then head obliquely **R** in field, making for top corner, which is defined by trees and hedgerow. Pass through gate and keep ahead, with field boundary on your immediate **L**. Walk along to next gate and then down field to rear.

❹ Cross road to galvanised gate and follow track towards **barns**. Keep to **L** of barns and look for stile and footpath branching off to **L**, running hard by fence on **R-H** side. Follow path to reach stile in far boundary and cross over into parkland of **Broughton Castle**. Soon **Broughton** church spire and castle come into sight ahead. Continue across parkland and down to meet castle drive. Head for gate into churchyard then follow path to reach **B4035** on outskirts of **Broughton**. Turn **L** along road and return to start.

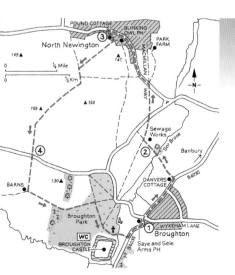

493 OTMOOR *THE FORGOTTEN LAND*

4 miles (6.4km) 1hr 30min Ascent: Negligible ⚠

Paths: Country road, tracks and paths
Suggested map: aqua3 OS Explorer 180 Oxford
Grid reference: SP 563157
Parking: Spaces near church at Charlton-on-Otmoor
Note: There's a military firing range on Otmoor. Look for written information about the range at the side of the path and follow the advice carefully.

Explore a desolate landscape which is a wildlife paradise.

❶ Keep church on R and walk through village. Pass Blacksmiths Lane and College Court and continue on road. Follow lane between hedgerows and fields. Soon reach sign for **Oddington**. When road bends R, branch off to **L** by telephone box ('Horton-cum-Studley').

❷ Take track out of village, crossing concrete bridge after short walk. At next junction, just beyond it, avoid galvanised gates on your R, and follow parallel bridleway, cutting between ditches and hedges. Pass stile on your L, leading to linking path, which provides an alternative route to the wetlands of Otmoor. There are a number of rare insects that are found on the moor including the Emperor moth, marsh fritillary butterflies and Black Hairstreak. In fact the whole area is a paradise for birdwatchers and botanists, and there

are many rare species of birds and plants here. The tower of **Charlton-on-Otmoor** church can be seen at intervals along the track. Continue to signs for Otmoor's military firing range (please heed any warning signs). Keep ahead until you reach gate on L and several gates on R.

❸ Turn **L** here and follow old Roman road north. The track is broad and can be wet in winter. When it curves R, branch off to **L** and begin last leg of walk.

❹ Follow path through trees and soon it broadens to track cutting between fields and hedgerows. There are good views across a broad expanse of Otmoor to the south. Cross over wooden footbridge and continue on track. Turn **R** by some corrugated barns and make for **Charlton-on-Otmoor**. The church tower is clearly visible now. Cross **New River Ray** and climb slope to junction. Turn **L** by the **Crown** and return to church.

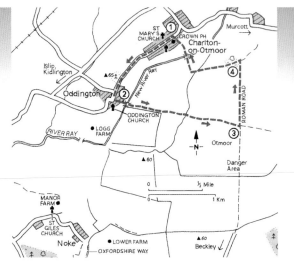

494 HOOK NORTON *A TOWERING SUCCESS*

4½ miles (7.2km) 2hrs Ascent: 164ft (50m) ⚠

Paths: Field paths, tracks and bridleways, quiet roads
Suggested map: aqua3 OS Explorer 191 Banbury, Bicester & Chipping Norton
Grid reference: SP 355330
Parking: Spaces in Hook Norton village centre

Explore delightful ironstone country before visiting Hook Norton Brewery.

❶ With **church** on your L, turn **R** into Middle Hill. Follow it down to next road and keep ahead to bridge. Turn **L** into Park Road and follow it to next junction. Continue ahead, keeping row of bungalows on L. When road bends sharp L, join waymarked bridleway and follow it out of Hook Norton. Pass remains of old **railway viaduct** and walk along to **Park Farm**.

❷ Cross cattle grid and continue for about 50yds (46m). When track forks, keep **L** and follow path to gate. Continue along field edge to next gate and follow obvious track as it curves to **R**. Cross ford at footbridge and make for next gate. Follow field boundary and cross into next field, keeping trees and hedgerow on L. Head for galvanised gate and swing **R** at bridleway sign. Head diagonally across field and look for gate in trees in top boundary. Follow grassy path alongside fence to reach drive.

❸ Turn **R** here, away from **Cradle Farm**, and walk along to outbuildings at point where drive bends sharp L. Keep **R** here and follow track alongside pair of semi-detached **houses** on R. Emerge from trees to 3 tracks; take middle track up slope between fences to reach road. Cross over to galvanised gate and follow bridleway between fences, trees and paddocks. On reaching gate turn **R** to wrought iron gate leading into field. Turn **L** and make for further gate into next field. Pass to R-H side of fencing and make for gate in field boundary.

❹ Turn **R** to join avenue of lime trees. At length, drive reaches road. Turn **L** then take 1st **R** for **Hook Norton**. At 1st junction, turn **R** at sign for Swerford and walk along to **Hook Norton Cutting**. Retrace your steps to junction and continue ahead towards Hook Norton. Pass speed restriction sign and keep ahead into village. Pass Park Road on R and take Middle Hill back up to church and pubs.

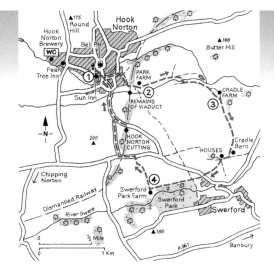

495 GREAT TEW *A RARE PLOT*

4 miles (6.4km) 1hr 45min Ascent: 150ft (46m) ⚠

Paths: Field paths and tracks, stretches of quiet road, 3 stiles
Suggested map: aqua3 OS Explorer 191 Banbury, Bicester & Chipping Norton
Grid reference: SP 395293
Parking: Free car park in Great Tew

A lovely village and undulating countryside.

❶ From car park turn **L**, pass turning to Great Tew, follow road as it bends **R** and as it straightens out turn **R** at footpath sign ('Little Tew'). Go diagonally across field, heading for farm outbuildings on brow of hill. Cross stile in front of them to gate and stile and keep field boundary on R. Follow it along to pair of galvanised gates and stile leading out to road at junction.

❷ Cross over and take path ('Little Tew'). Head diagonally across field, passing to R of **transmitter**. On reaching road, turn **R** and walk down hill into **Little Tew**. Pass through village and turn **L** at turning for Enstone. On corner is **Church of St John the Evangelist**.

❸ Follow road out of Little Tew and look for entrance to **The Lodge** on L. Continue for few paces to some white railings, then turn immediately **L** at opening in hedge leading into field. Keep along **L** boundary and

make for galvanised gate in field corner. Continue ahead on grassy path, passing house over on L. Keep ahead on clear track to kissing gate leading out to road.

❹ Cross over and follow track ('Sandford'). Keep alongside trees and then round to **L** towards house. As you approach it, turn **R** and join another track heading southeast. Keep fence on R and make for gate by trees. Continue for few paces to gate and waymark on **L**. Take path, keeping belt of woodland and field edge on your L. Beyond some trees, continue ahead into next field, again beside tongue of woodland. Pass into next field and continue alongside trees. Approach **lodge** and keep to L of it.

❺ Follow drive to meet road, cross over to junction and take turning ('Great Tew'). Pass entrance to **St Michael's Church** (a fine medieval church) on R. Look for village **school**, also on R, and then, just beyond turning to **Great Tew**, return to car park.

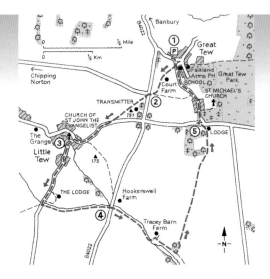

Oxfordshire

OXFORD *HEAVENLY JERUSALEM*

2¼ miles (3.6km) 1hr 15min **Ascent:** Negligible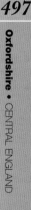
Paths: Pavements, field and riverside paths, 2 stiles
Suggested map: aqua3 OS Explorer 180 Oxford
Grid reference: SP 513062
Parking: Parking in city centre, or use park-and-ride, or travel by train

Discover Oxford's quiet corners and hidden backwaters.
❶ Start at **Carfax**, where 4 streets converge. Charles II was proclaimed King at **Carfax Tower** in 1660. Walk ahead into St Aldates and head for entrance to **Christ Church**, Oxford's largest college, founded in 1525 by Cardinal Wolsey. When he was disgraced it was refounded as King Henry VIII's College. Later it became known as **Christ Church** when the college and the cathedral became one. Leave by south exit and walk ahead down tree-lined New Walk. On L is Christ Church Meadow.
❷ On reaching **Thames** tow path, swing **L** and follow river bank. Keep ahead until you reach confluence of Thames and **River Cherwell**. Avoid steeply arched footbridge and keep alongside Cherwell. River meanders between meadows and sports fields. Leave river bank and pass through wrought-iron gates to walk up Rose Lane.

❸ With Magdalen Bridge and **Magdalen College** bell tower on your R, turn **L** at **High Street** or 'the High', as it is known in Oxford. Cross Longwall Street and turn R into Queen's Lane. Continue into New College Lane and on R, beyond arch, is entrance to **New College**. Keep along New College Lane to Bridge of Sighs, a 1913 replica of its Venice namesake, and ahead of you now is **Sheldonian Theatre**, designed by Sir Christopher Wren and completed in 1669.
❹ Turn **L** here for Radcliffe Camera and cross Radcliffe Square towards Brasenose College, which probably took its name from a door-knocker in the shape of a nose. Turn **R** into Brasenose Lane, then **R** again into Turl Street, cutting between Jesus College and Exeter College. Make for Broad Street and on R is St Giles, where Charles I drilled his men during the Civil War. Turn **L** into Cornmarket Street, passing Church of St Michael at North Gate. Its Saxon tower is the oldest building in Oxford. Return to **Carfax**.

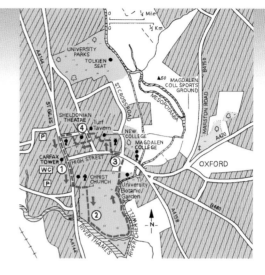

CUMNOR PLACE *A ROYAL SCANDAL*

6 miles (9.7km) 2hrs 30min **Ascent:** Negligible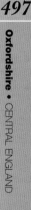
Paths: Field paths, quiet lanes and tracks, 1 stile
Suggested map: aqua3 OS Explorer 180 Oxford
Grid reference: SP 458044 **Parking:** Spaces by village hall in Cumnor

A centuries-old mystery.
❶ Sadly, a stone fireplace set in a bank in the churchyard is all that remains of Cumnor Place. This is where Dudley's, the Earl of Leicester, estranged wife died of a broken neck. Dudley was believed to have been Elizabeth I's lover and apparently showed no outward sign of grief on hearing of his wife's mysterious death – suicide, accident or murder? Turn **R** from parking area and walk to mini-roundabout. Turn **R** into Appleton Road and pass **Bear and Ragged Staff** pub on R. Veer half **L** a few paces beyond and keep **L** at junction ('Bessels Leigh'). Pass **cricket club** on L then continue on track. When it peters out continue in field, keeping ditch R. Pass alongside line of trees on far side of field, turn **L**, then **R** and make for opening in corner, concealed by vegetation in summer. Continue to reach galvanised gate and keep houses over to L beyond pasture. Cross footbridge to galvanised gate, swing **L** and cross field towards road. Keep in line with telephone wires and

make for waymark in field corner. Follow drive to road.
❷ To visit **Greyhound** pub, turn L. To continue turn **R** and follow road through **Bessels Leigh** and out into countryside, cutting between farmland. On reaching junction, keep **L** to next junction. Go straight on into **Eaton** and pass **Eight Bells** pub.
❸ Follow lane out of Eaton and through flat countryside. When lane becomes enclosed by trees, look for view of Thames on L. Continue to **Bablock Hythe**. Across river is **Ferryman Inn**. Walk back along lane for few paces and turn **L** at bridleway ('Cumnor').
❹ Pass through gate and when, some time later, path curves to **L**, look for **Physic Well** in trees to L. This is a muddy spring, once valued for its healing waters. Emerge from trees and cut between fields towards pylons. Go through gate, join drive and walk ahead. Ignore turning to **Upper Whitley Farm** and continue into Cumnor, passing **Leys Farm** on R. Look for United Reformed church and return to village hall and start.

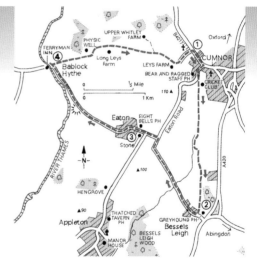

BLENHEIM PALACE *A SWEET HOUSE*

7 miles (11.3km) 3hrs **Ascent:** 150ft (46m) ▲
Paths: Field paths and tracks, parkland paths and estate drives. Some quiet road walking, 3 stiles
Suggested map: aqua3 OS Explorer 180 Oxford
Grid reference: SP 411158
Parking: Spaces in centre of Combe

To one of Britain's top country houses.
❶ From village green, take road ('East End'). Swing **R** by village pump into churchyard and keep to **L** of **church**. Exit through gap in boundary wall, flanked by 2 gravestones, and begin skirting **R-H** edge of sports field. After 50yds (46m), branch off into trees, then head diagonally across field. Cross into next field and keep to **R** edge of wood. In next field, turn **L**, still with trees L, and go up slope to woodland corner. Pass through gap in hedge; cross field.
❷ Exit to road, turn **L** and keep **R** at next junction. Walk to **Combe Gate**. Go through kissing gate into **Blenheim Palace** grounds, keep **L** at junction; follow drive through parkland. As it sweeps L to cattle grid, veer off to **R** by sign ('visitors are welcome to walk in the park'). Follow path to stile. Keep **R** when path divides and walk beside western arm of **The Lake**.
❸ Eventually reach tarmac drive. Turn **R** and walk towards **Grand Bridge**. As you approach it, turn sharp

L, passing between mature trees with **Queen Pool** on R. Cross over cattle grid and keep ahead through park. With **Column of Victory** on your L, follow drive as it sweeps to **R**.
❹ Turn **L** at cattle grid, in line with buildings of Furze Platt on R. Join **Oxfordshire Way**, cross stile and follow grassy track alongside trees, then between fields. At length cross track and continue towards woodland. Enter trees and turn **L** after few paces to join clear track running through wood.
❺ After 150yds (137m) take 1st **L** turning, crossing footbridge to reach edge of field. Turn **R** here, following obvious path across fields. When you reach track, turn **R**. Keep alongside trees to junction. Turn **R** and follow track down through wood and diagonally **L** across strip of pasture to opening in trees. Go up to track; cross it to ladder stile.
❻ Turn **L** to hedge; turn **R**, keeping it and ditch on R. Skirt field to road, turn **R** and walk into **Combe**.

499 BLADON *CHURCHILL'S GRAVE*

5 miles (8km) 2hrs 15min **Ascent:** 90ft (27m) ⚠
Paths: Field and woodland paths and tracks, quiet roads, 7 stiles
Suggested map: aqua3 OS Explorer 180 Oxford
Grid reference: SP 468138
Parking: Limited spaces outside Begbroke church, St Michael's Lane

The final resting place of Winston Churchill.
1 Keep **church** behind you, walk to Spring Hill Road. Turn **R**. Follow lane through 2 sharp bends, passing **Hall Farm**. Avoid path on **R**; continue to stile and galvanised gates. Follow track up gentle slope to next stile and cattle grid. Keep ahead, passing house on **L**, then swing **R** across field, passing under telegraph wires. Pass into next field; turn **R**.
2 Follow obvious boundary across several fields, eventually turning **L** in corner. Continue for 50yds (46m) and look for stile and footbridge on **R**. Continue in next field, with hedge on **L**. At field corner, continue for few paces; turn **R** through opening in hedge into adjoining field. Maintain direction, with boundary **L**. Make for stile and oak in field corner. Continue across next field, keeping to **L** edge of woodland. With trees by you on **R**, follow path towards **Burleigh Lodge**. Swing **L** for few paces to stile leading out to road.
3 Turn **R** by millennium stone, pass lodge and walk

to footpath sign on **R** ('Bladon'). Cross stile and keep hedge on **L**. Make for footbridge in field corner, turn **L** and follow hedgerow. Look for hedge running diagonally **R**; keep it **L** and head towards Bladon. Make for stile on to road on bend. Go forward, keep entrance to **Lamb** pub car park on **L**, continue to next junction; cross to Church Street. Walk to **Church of St Martin**; head through churchyard to gate on far side.
4 Turn **R**; follow tarmac lane to wooden gates. Continue on field path to corner; turn **R** at waymark. With hedgerow **L**, pass to **L** of woodland and head for white gate, with road beyond. Turn **L** by lock-up garages and follow path ('Begbroke').
5 Cross rectangular pasture and, at far end, follow path into trees and through gate. Emerge at length from wood at another gate and continue ahead along field boundary towards **Begbroke**. Go through gate in corner; follow path alongside drive to road. Turn **L** and **L** again into St Michael's Lane, returning to church.

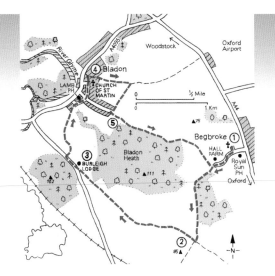

500 WANTAGE *ALFRED'S GREATNESS REMEMBERED*

6 miles (9.7km) 2hrs 45min **Ascent:** 150ft (46m) ⚠
Paths: Pavements, tow path, field paths and tracks, 1 stile
Suggested map: aqua3 OS Explorer 170 Abingdon, Wantage
Grid reference: SU 397881
Parking: Long-stay car park off Mill Street

Visit the statue of a revered British king before heading for downland country.
1 Keep to **R** edge of car park and look for pedestrian exit. Turn **L** into Mill Street and walk up into Market Place. Make for **statue of King Alfred** then follow signs for museum. Approach parish **Church of St Peter and St Paul**; turn **L** into Church Street. The **museum** is opposite you at next junction. Turn **R** here, avoid Locks Lane and follow Priory Road to **L**. Head for Portway and cross to footpath to **L** of The Croft.
2 Follow clear tarmac path as it runs between fences and playing fields. At length you reach housing estate; continue ahead into **Letcombe Regis** and make for junction with Courthill Road. Keep it on your **L** and go straight ahead through village, passing **Greyhound** pub and thatched cottage dated 1698.
3 Turn **R** by **church** ('Letcombe Bassett and Lambourn') and, when road bends sharp **L**, go straight ahead. After a few paces drive bends **R**. Keep ahead

along path between banks of vegetation, following it as it curves **R**, then swings **L**. Pass **Antwicks Stud** over to **R** and climb gently between trees and bushes.
4 Turn **R** at next intersection and follow tree-lined track to road. Turn **L** and make for junction. Cross, pass alongside house and follow **Cornhill Lane**. Begin gentle descent, cross track and continue down slope. Avoid **R** turning and keep ahead to footbridge crossing **Wilts and Berks Canal**. Turn **R** and follow tow path.
5 Cross A417 road and then continue towards Wantage. Follow drive then take parallel path on **R**, running alongside section of restored canal. On reaching tarmac drive, then after lock-up garages, **L** into Wasborough Avenue, then, after lock-up garages, **L** into St Mary's Way. Turn **R** and swing **L** into Belmont. Keep **R** at fork and make for Mill Street. Keep **L** and car park is on **L**.

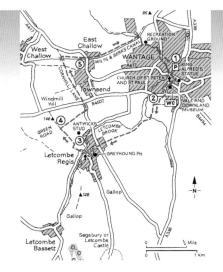

501 WITNEY *TOWN TO COUNTRY*

3½ miles (5.7km) 1hr 30min **Ascent:** Negligible ⚠
Paths: Pavements, meadow and waterside paths, 1 stile
Suggested map: aqua3 OS Explorer 180 Oxford
Grid reference: SP 357096
Parking: Public car park by Woolgate Shopping Centre, off Witan Way

Head out of town to a country park.
1 Turn **R** into Langdale Gate. Walk towards Butter Cross. Turn **L** immediately before it and walk down **L** side of Church Green. (Don't miss remains of **Bishop's Palace**, and **St Mary's Church**.) With your back to church, walk along **L** side of Church Green; turn **L** at Butter Cross into Corn Street. Keep ahead and, when street becomes tree-lined, cutting between houses, turn **L** just beyond **Three Horseshoes** pub into The Crofts. Follow road between terraced houses.
2 Follow The Crofts to **L**; turn **R** at end. Keep stone wall **L** and walk to St Mary's Court. Continue along alleyway, with school and spire of St Mary's on **L** and, when you reach corner of recreation ground, keep to its **R** edge, passing toilet block. Turn **R** at road then 1st **L** at pedestrian lights into Station Lane.
3 Follow road through **industrial estate**; take path at end, beneath A40. Avoid footbridge **R** and proceed through kissing gate. Route now cuts between Witney

Lake and surrounding meadows (country park). Continue along lakeside path, with Ducklington to **R** beyond area of scrub. Keep **Emma's Dike L** and curve to **L**. Witney church spire is seen at intervals in the distance. On **R** is **River Windrush**. Make for concrete bridge; cross it, branching **L** to kissing gate.
4 Keep field boundary over to **L** and look for kissing gate by A40. Pass under it to kissing gate; head north to stile, keeping your back to road. Cross over to gate and continue with offices **L**. Pass under power lines to 2 kissing gates and notice board. Keep ahead, passing to **R** of dilapidated **mill**. Follow path between margins of vegetation and eventually reach spur path to **Cogges Manor Farm Museum**.
5 To visit museum, turn **R** and follow path to Priory and **St Mary's Church**. Museum is next door. Retrace your steps, heading for town centre. Pass electricity sub station on **R** and walk to road. Cross into Langdale Gate and return to car park.

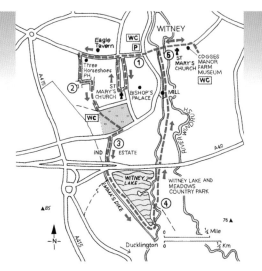

Oxfordshire

ABINGDON *A CLASSIC PATH*

7 miles (11.3km) 2hrs 45min **Ascent:** Negligible
Paths: Field paths, tracks, road and Thames Path. Town and village streets (roads can be busy), 4 stiles
Suggested map: aqua3 OS Explorer 170 Abingdon, Wantage
Grid reference: SU 503941
Parking: Small car park south of the church at Sutton Courtenay

Enjoy views of the town from the riverside.

❶ From car park, turn **L** to road, joining adjacent tree-lined path. Take turning for Milton and follow road to **former pub**. Turn immediately **R** to join footpath. Cross footbridge to cottages and swing **L** to kissing gate. Keep **L** at immediate fork and follow path alongside **Mill Brook**. Cross double stile and footbridge and continue to next stile and footbridge.

❷ Turn **R** to join track, following it between fields. Further on it narrows to muddy path running between hedges. Make for road, turn **R** then bear **L** at next junction, following **Drayton Road**. Take 2nd signposted right of way on **R**.

❸ Keep ahead when path merges with wide track and, when it curves **L** by 2 cottages, look for stile on **R**. Go diagonally across field, briefly cutting through undergrowth into next pasture. Keep quite close to **L** boundary and aim for tall trees and houses in distance. Make for footbridge in top **R-H** corner of

field. Walk ahead towards outskirts of Abingdon and join tarmac path. This is Overmead.

❹ Turn **R** at road and walk through housing estate to T-junction. Turn **L**; keep beside Thames to Old Anchor Inn. Pass pub then turn **L** by almshouses. Keep Church of St Helen on **R** and head for road. Cross into East St Helen Street and make for **Old County Hall**.

❺ Turn **R** to reach Bridge Street, pass Broad Face pub and cross **River Thames** to far bank. Go down steps on **L** to tow path, go under road bridge and walk along riverside. Pass Abingdon map, go through gate and cross meadows beside Thames, passing **Culham Bridge** on **L**. Follow line of **Culham Reach** and keep by water until you reach sign for Sutton Courtenay.

❻ Once over cut follow path across fields and back to Thames. Cross several bridges and weirs at **Sutton Pools** and keep ahead at road, passing The Wharf on **R**. Follow village street to parish **church** and return to car park.

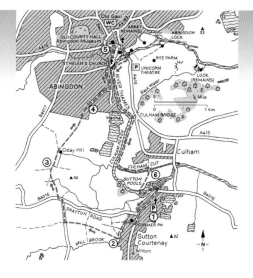

GARSINGTON *AGRICULTURE AND ARISTOCRACY*

3 miles (4.8km) 1hr 15min **Ascent:** 165ft (50m)
Paths: Field paths and roads (can be busy in Garsington), 11 stiles
Suggested map: aqua3 OS Explorer 180 Oxford
Grid reference: SP 580024
Parking: Spaces near Red Lion in Garsington village

Pass a manor house, which was once used as a sanctuary by some of Britain's most famous writers and artists, including Virginia Woolf and Bertrand Russell.

❶ Facing **Red Lion**, turn **L** and walk through **Garsington**. Veer half **L** at The Hill, leading to Sadlers Croft. Keep **R** and climb bank to bollards by war memorial. Cross over to The Green, keeping **Three Horseshoes** on **L** and historic cross on **R**.

❷ Continue along road to **St Mary's Church** and pass **Manor House**. Keep on road and, just as it descends quite steeply, branch **L** at sign ('Denton'). Strike out across field and pass between 2 trees. Ahead on horizon is hilltop church at Cuddesdon, with trees behind. Make for gap in boundary and continue in next field. Look for waymark in wide gap in next boundary and aim to **R** of copse. Pass through gap in field corner, avoid path on **L** and head diagonally **L** across field to far corner. Cross 2 stiles to reach road.

❸ Turn **R** and pass alongside stone wall on **L**. Walk along to **R-H** bend and bear **L** at sign ('Brookside only'). **Denton House** is on **L** and dovecote can be seen on **R**. Pass stile and footpath on **R** and keep along lane for few paces, turning **L** at public footpath.

❹ Head for stile and pass ornamental wall enclosing Denton House. Cross over paddock to next stile then go diagonally **R** across field to stile. Then head diagonally **L** in next field, keeping **farm** over to **R**. Cross 2 stiles and begin approaching houses of Garsington. Make for stile in **R-H** corner of field, keeping boundary on **R** in next pasture. Climb gently and look for stile on **R**. Cross it, turn **L** and make for 2 stiles in field corner. Join drive and follow it up to road.

❺ Turn **L** towards **Garsington**, pass houses of North Manor Estate and primary **school** before turning **R**, opposite **Denton Lane**, to join footpath. Follow it to lane, keep **R** and make for road. Turn **R** and return to parking area by **Red Lion**.

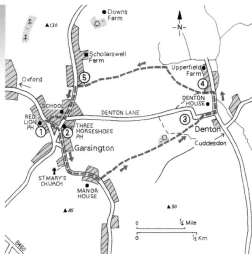

WATLINGTON *A CIVIL WAR BATTLEFIELD*

5½ miles (8.8km) 2hrs **Ascent:** 200ft (60m)
Paths: Field paths and tracks, stretches of road (busy), 9 stiles
Suggested map: aqua3 OS Explorer 171 Chiltern Hills West
Grid reference: SU 690943
Parking: Town car park in Watlington

From a quaint small town climb into spectacular Chiltern country and enjoy views towards a famous battleground, where Royalist and Parliamentarian armies engaged in bitter conflict.

❶ Turn **L** out of car park towards town centre. Turn **L** at junction, by **Town Hall**, and follow Couching Street to junction with Brook Street. Turn **R** and walk along to No 23. Take footpath opposite and climb **L** between walls. Make for kissing gate, keep **R** at immediate fork and cross field. Keep to **L** of tree and head for 2nd kissing gate. Veer **L** at fork and cut between trees and fencing.

❷ Turn **L** at track and follow it round to **R**. Swing **L** at 'private – no access' sign. Further on, follow path round to **R** and make for junction with concrete farm track. As you reach it, turn **L** to join path running along field edge. Keep hedge and trees on **R** and follow it along to stile in corner.

❸ Turn **L** here and walk along **Ridgeway** to road. Turn **R** towards Nettlebed and then take 1st **L** turning. Follow track for about 70yds (64m) and, when it forks at wooden post-and-brick pillar, keep **L** and follow enclosed path through trees to 2 stiles. Continue on path, climbing gently to kissing gate. Keep **L** at fork and keep climbing. Break cover from trees and then enter woodland again. Go through kissing gate and pass between beech trees to next gate. Follow path to **R** of **Watlington Hill** car park and turn **R** at road.

❹ Head for **Christmas Common** and turn **L** at next junction. Follow road for about 50yds (46m) and turn **L** at **Oxfordshire Way** sign. Cross stile and keep along field perimeter to 2nd stile. Keep ahead for about 70yds (64m) to stile and leave Oxfordshire Way at this point. Follow sunken path, looking for white arrows on trees, and descend gradually to fork. Keep **L** alongside chalk pit, go through kissing gate and turn **R** at road. Follow it back to car park.

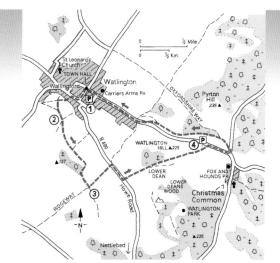

Oxfordshire

Oxfordshire • CENTRAL ENGLAND

505 · UFFINGTON *THE WHITE HORSE*

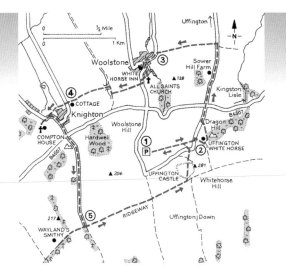

7 miles (11.3km) 3hrs **Ascent:** 415ft (126m)
Paths: Ancient tracks and field paths, road (can be busy), 13 stiles
Suggested map: aqua3 OS Explorer 170 Abingdon, Wantage
Grid reference: SU 293865
Parking: Large free car park near Uffington White Horse

Legends and magic on this downlands walk.

❶ From car park go through gate and follow outline of grassy path along lower slopes towards hill. Make for gate and cross lane to join bridleway. Keep **L** at fork, by bridleway waymark, and walk along to head of Uffington's **White Horse**.

❷ Descend steeply on path to tarmac access road, keeping chalk figure on your immediate **L**. If you prefer to avoid dramatic descent, retrace your steps to lane, turn **R** and continue to junction with **B4507**. Cross and take road towards **Uffington**, turning **L** at path ('Woolstone'). Cross stile and keep hedge on **R**. Make for 2 stiles in field corner. Continue across next field to stile and cut through trees to next stile. Keep ahead with hedgerow on your **L**.

❸ Cross stile, turn **L** at road and walk through **Woolstone**. Turn **L** by **White Horse Inn** and follow road to **All Saints Church**. As you approach it, veer **R** across churchyard to stile and gate. Cross paddock to further gate and stile. Turn **L** up road. Turn **R** at footpath sign. Follow edge of field, keeping hedge on your **L-H** side, eventually reaching stile. Turn **R** and walk through trees to footbridge. Cross footbridge to field, head diagonally **L** to stile; turn **R**. Follow field edge to stile within sight of thatched **cottage**. Cross it and continue to another stile leading out to road. Cottage is now level with you on **L**.

❹ Cross road; follow D'Arcy Dalton Way, signposted on opposite side. Make for stile, cross paddock and head for road by sign ('Compton Beauchamp'). Cross and take drive to **church**, next to **manor**. Retrace your steps to sign and walk up to meet junction with B4507. Cross and climb quite steeply to **Ridgeway**.

❺ Turn **R** to visit **Wayland's Smithy** or **L** to continue. Follow track to crossroads ('Woolstone') and continue on **Ridgeway** uphill to reach ramparts of **Uffington Castle** on **L**. Leave track here, cut through remains of fort to access road and return to car park.

---

506 · STONOR *RELIGIOUS REFUGE*

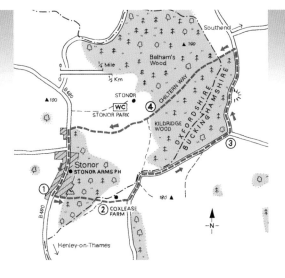

3½ miles (5.7km) 1hr 15min **Ascent:** 150ft (46m)
Paths: Wood and parkland paths and tracks, country lanes, 2 stiles
Suggested map: aqua3 OS Explorer 171 Chiltern Hills West
Grid reference: SU 735883
Parking: Off-road at southern end of Stonor, by barns of Upper Assendon Farm, which straddle road

Across a beautiful deer park.

❶ The chief attraction is **Stonor Park** and the Elizabethan house. **Stonor** has a 14th-century Chapel of the Holy Trinity. During the 16th and 17th centuries it was used as refuge for Catholics and the family endured persecution and imprisonment as a result of their devotion to the faith. Make for 30mph speed restriction sign at southern end of **Stonor**. Turn **L** at stile just beyond it to join footpath. Keep farm outbuildings on **L** and go up slope towards trees. Cross stile into woodland and begin climbing very steeply into Chilterns. Look for white arrows on tree trunks and further up reach clear track on bend. Keep ahead, cross track and pass beside **Coxlease Farm**.

❷ Keep to **R** of outbuildings and join track leading to farmhouse. Make for road; turn **L**. Pass several houses and follow lane between hedges. Avoid path on **R** and, further on, road bends sharp **R**. Ignore bridleway on **L** for **Stonor** and keep on road, which curves **L** and runs alongside **Kildridge Wood**. Pass some double wooden gates on **R** and keep to road as it curves **R**. Turn **L** after a few paces, signposted towards Southend.

❸ Keep Kildridge Wood on **L** still, with views over fields and rolling countryside on **R**. Follow lane until you reach turning on **L** – the **Chiltern Way**. Follow path beside pair of brick-and-flint cottages, following the way towards **Stonor Park**. Cross junction of tracks and descend between trees. Some of the trunks carry CW symbol for **Chiltern Way**. Keep **L** at fork, passing between laurel bushes and trees, and eventually you reach deer fence and gate.

❹ Pass alongside tall wire fence and gradually view of Stonor house edges into view. Head down towards road and look for kissing gate in deer fence. Turn **L** and head for Stonor. Pass footpath and turning to Maidensgrove and keep ahead to **Stonor Arms**. Continue through village and return to parking area.

---

507 · WALLINGFORD *THE CONQUEROR'S CASTLE*

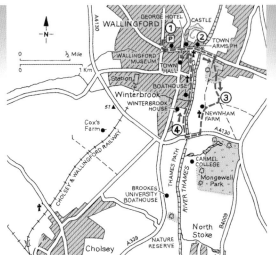

3 miles (4.8km) 1hr 30min **Ascent:** Negligible
Paths: Bridleways, pavements, Thames Path, 11 stiles
Suggested map: Aqua3 OS Explorer 70 Abingdon, Wantage
Grid reference: SU 604895
Parking: Long-stay car park in St George's Road, Wallingford

Discover an historic town beside the Thames.

❶ Turn **L** out of car park and walk along St George's Road. Turn **L** into High Street and head towards town centre. Wallingford is one of those towns that can hold your attention for hours. Its churches are well worth a look, its museum and Town Hall attract lots of visitors, and the grass-covered remains of its ruined castle serve as a reminder of the bitter struggle for supremacy during the Civil War. Continue past library and **Wallingford Museum** and keep ahead to junction with St Martin's Street and Castle Street. **Town Hall** is on **R** and remains of **castle** on **L**. Continue over junction and pass Lamb Arcade and **George Hotel**. On **R** is spire of St Peter's Church in Thames Street.

❷ Pass **Town Arms** and cross bridge over **Thames**. Continue along road and, about 80yds (73m) beyond traffic lights, turn **R** at bridleway ('Ridgeway and Grim's Ditch'). Follow enclosed track between fences, keeping river and adjacent meadows to your **R**. Keep **L** at waymark and stay on bridleway. Cross footpath and now woodland gives way to open fields.

❸ At junction with concrete farm track, turn **R** and head towards buildings of **Newnham Farm**. Keep **L** and walk along track to **St Mary's Church** at Newnham Murren. With church on your **R**, continue on tree-lined bridleway. Approaching **A4130**, veer **R** at sign ('cyclists dismount') then follow pavement along to bridge over Thames. Once over bridge, veer **R** and follow tarmac path down bank to riverside.

❹ Turn **L** and head upstream towards Wallingford, passing boathouse. Continue on Thames Path to tarmac drive running between houses. Just beyond property, '**The Boathouse**', turn **R** by flood marker (1894). Follow path to road by St Leonard's Church. Turn **R**; follow road along to St Peter's Street. Turn **L** then **L** again into Wood Street. After 70yds (64m) turn **R** into Mousey Lane and make for **Town Hall**. Retrace your steps along High Street to reach car park.

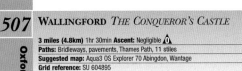

Oxfordshire

DORCHESTER *A VERY SPECIAL ABBEY*

4½ miles (7.2km) 1hr 45min **Ascent:** 115ft (35m)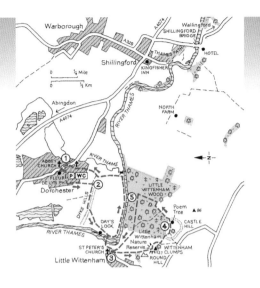
Paths: Field and woodland paths and tracks, stretch of Thames Path and main road with pavement
Suggested map: aqua3 OS Explorer 170 Abingdon, Wantage
Grid reference: SU 578939
Parking: Parking area in Bridge End at southern end of Dorchester

An ancient settlement with superb views.

❶ From parking area walk towards centre of **Dorchester**, keeping **abbey church** on R. As you approach **Fleur de Lys**, turn **L** into Rotten Row and walk to Mayflower Cottage and Pilgrims. Take path between the 2 properties and pass beside allotments. At row of cottages, veer **L** to follow track. Swing **R** after 60yds (55m) at sign for Day's Lock. Pass between fencing and out across large field. Ahead is outline of **Wittenham Clumps**. At low embankment of **Dyke Hills**, turn **R** in front of fence.

❷ Follow path along field edge, pass over track and continue. Path, enclosed by hedge and fencing, heads south towards **Thames** river bank. Go through gate and follow path, now unfenced, to footbridge at **Day's Lock**. Cross river to Lock House Island and head for **St Peter's Church** at **Little Wittenham**.

❸ Turn **L** just beyond it, at entrance to manor. Keep **R** at immediate fork, go through gate and begin steep climb to viewpoint on **Round Hill** at top. Veer **L** as you approach seat, pass 2nd seat and keep **L** at next fork, heading for **Castle Hill**. Head towards gates at foot of hill, avoid stile and go through gate, up flight of steps and into trees. At T-junction, turn **L**.

❹ Emerge from trees and pass commemorative stone, keeping it on R. Descend grassy slope to gate and pass through trees to field. Continue along perimeter, with woodland L. Pass stile, continue along field edge and round to **R** in corner. Swing **L** to join nature trail; follow it through **Little Wittenham Wood**.

❺ At a barrier and T-junction in heart of wood, turn **L** and follow path back to Little Wittenham. Recross Thames then turn **R** to follow river downstream. On reaching confluence of Thames and **Thame**, swing **L** and head north towards Dorchester. As Thame bends R, keep ahead to gate. Keep to **R** of Dyke Hills to another gate and skirt field to track (Wittenham Lane). Pass Catholic Church of St Birinus to reach car park.

JARN MOUND *THE OXFORD SPIRES*

5 miles (8km) 2hrs **Ascent:** 150ft (46m)
Paths: Field paths and tracks, roads (can be busy), 11 stiles
Suggested map: aqua3 OS Explorer 180 Oxford
Grid reference: SP 496005
Parking: Limited spaces in Sunningwell

A view preserved by Sir Arthur Evans.

❶ Walk along street towards **Abingdon**. Pass pond on R and **church** on L. As road bends L, turn **R** into Dark Lane. Keep cricket ground on R and soon lane becomes concrete track. When it curves R, keep **L**, following track between hedgerows then across fields.

❷ Take track running to **R** towards **farm** outbuildings and cut between them. Continue on track between trees to road; turn **R**. Follow verge to sign, '**Old Boars Hill**'; take path. Cross field, go through boundary hedge; continue towards house. Look for stile in field corner beside it and cross lane to stile and gate.

❸ Follow metalled lane to **The Linnings** (riding school). Keep to **R** of buildings, crossing 3 stiles. Go diagonally across paddock, passing under power lines, to reach boundary hedge. Cross 2 stiles, avoiding stiles in L and R boundary of field, and follow path beside high wire fence enclosing reservoir. Keep ahead at fence corner to gate and stile on **R**. Follow enclosed path beside paddock towards houses of **Wootton**. Cross stile and turn **R**, passing entrance to **Stones Farm**.

❹ At entrance to **Wootton End** on your L, keep **R**, following track. Go through gate and keep to **R** of pond. Head up slope to stile. Cross Matthew Arnold's Field to stile on to lane. Turn **L**; walk to junction with Jarn Way. Climb to **Jarn Mound**. Descend steps; turn **L** by seat, keeping memorial stone L. Keep parallel with road, veer **L** at fork and follow path to road. Turn **R**, pass house 'Holly Dene'; continue to junction.

❺ Continue into Berkeley Road, passing former Open University building on your R-H side. Walk on to T-junction; turn **R**. Head for Lincombe Lane and sign for **Sunningwell**. Follow road round to **R**, pass footpath and continue all the way to white gate and kissing gate. Follow field path towards Sunningwell church. Go through gate at bottom of field, emerge at road opposite church, and return to start.

GREYS COURT *A HOUSE AND HOME*

4 miles (6.4km) 1hr 45min **Ascent:** 150ft (45m)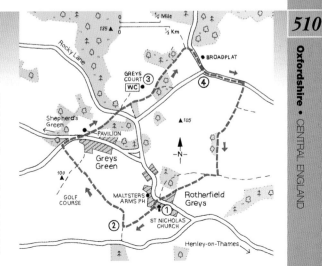
Paths: Field and parkland paths, drives and tracks, stretches of road (can be busy), 12 stiles
Suggested map: aqua3 OS Explorer 171 Chiltern Hills West
Grid reference: SU 726823
Parking: Spaces by church at Rotherfield Greys

A National Trust property in the Chilterns.

❶ With church lychgate on L-H side, walk towards **Maltsters Arms** pub. Turn immediately **L** before William's Cottage to join gravel drive. Follow footpath alongside churchyard and make for stile ahead. Head obliquely **R**, across field to another stile, pass through gap in hedgerow then veer half-**R** in next field. Make for stile, cross and join path.

❷ Turn **R**; pass between trees, hedges and margins of bracken. Path graduates to a track and passes alongside **golf course** before crossing drive to gate. Continue ahead to road; turn **R**. Pass turning for **Shepherd's Green** on L and follow road along to **Greys Green**. Veer **L** on to green and aim to **R** of **pavilion**. Join footpath, cross stile and descend very steeply to next stile. Pass under power lines in pasture and keep fence on L. Make for stile, cross lane to footpath and after a few steps reach stile. Continue towards Greys Court.

❸ Walk to admission kiosk and swing **L**, following footpath to next boundary. Continue on path to pond and along section of boardwalk. Pass alongside fence and woodland, avoiding gate and steps to reach stile on L just beyond them by corrugated barn. Cross stile and keep to R-H side, with fence and field on R. Turn **R** at drive and make for road ahead. Turn **R** at this junction and continue, passing **Broadplat**.

❹ Keep **L** at next junction and continue along road to reach track on **R** ('Rotherfield Greys'). Continue ahead when track bends to L, and follow rough track ahead. Pass footpath sign and look for stile on **L**. Follow path down hillside, keeping belt of woodland on R. Beyond it, continue on grassy path with fence on R. Turn **R**, across stile in field corner and follow path alongside fencing. After 60yds (55m), look for stile on **L**. Cross it and maintain same direction. Make for stile ahead then swing **L** and follow path up slope and back to road opposite **church** at Rotherfield Greys.

Oxfordshire

511 STOKE ROW *A Maharajah's Gift*

5 miles (8km) 2hrs **Ascent:** 164ft (50m)
Paths: Field and woodland paths and tracks, road (busy), 8 stiles
Suggested map: aqua3 OS Explorer 171 Chiltern Hills West
Grid reference: SU 678840
Parking: Roadside parking in Stoke Row; two spaces in village hall car park when hall not in use

Discover the link between India and a quiet village in the Chilterns.

❶ From car park turn **R** and walk past village stores. Enclosed in an exotic cupola you'll see the **Maharajah's Well**, which was a gift to the village from the Maharajah of Benares in 1863. Turn **L** into **Cox's Lane** and follow it as it curves to **L**. Soon it dwindles to a track. Continue to waymark, avoid footpath on **R** and keep ahead on right of way. The track narrows to a path now, running between trees and hedgerows. Pass stile and footpath and eventually you reach outbuildings of **Hundridge Farm**. Join track running through woodland and make for road.

❷ Turn **R** along road for several paces, then swing **R** at footpath sign into wood. Follow path between trees and cross drive. Make for stile ahead and then go diagonally **R** in field, using waymark posts to guide you. Look for stile in corner and cross lane to further stile on opposite side. Head diagonally **R** in field and

look for stile by hard tennis court. Pass alongside beech hedge to drive; turn **L**. As drive sweeps **L** to house, go forward over cattle grid to field. Continue with boundary on your **L** and on reaching corner, go straight on along track.

❸ Turn **R** at **English Farm** and follow narrow track known as **English Lane**. Go past footpath and stile on R-H side. Follow track along edge of woodland. Continue to junction and keep ahead through trees. Pass timber-framed cottage on L-H side and house on R called **Forrigan**. Keep ahead for about 100yds (91m) and swing **R** at sign ('Stoke Row').

❹ Cross stile and cut through wood to 2nd stile. Emerge from woodland at gate and cross pasture to further patch of woodland. Negotiate next stile within sight of **Crooked Billet** and go up gentle slope towards pub. Turn **R** at road, pass footpath on R, followed by Rose Cottage, and head for crossroads in centre of **Stoke Row**. Turn **R** and return to start.

---

512 WIGHTWICK *Along the Canal*

4½ miles (7.2km) 1hr 30min **Ascent:** 59ft (18m)
Paths: Canal tow path, disused railway track and field paths, 1 stile
Suggested map: aqua3 OS Explorer 219 Wolverhampton & Dudley
Grid reference: SP 870982
Parking: Near Mermaid pub, Wightwick

An easy family walk.

❶ From car park, cross A454 at pedestrian crossing to enter Windmill Lane. Bear **R** and descend to tow path of **Staffordshire and Worcestershire Canal**, heading in southwesterly direction. Initially tow path leads along back of private residences. After passing Cee-Ders Club (on far side of canal), you reach open countryside, with ducks, coots and moorhens for company. This stretch of the canal is similar to a river and you are likely to see anglers fishing for perch, roach, chub, bream or carp. You may even see a colourful narrowboat pass by. Continue beneath bridge No 55 (**Castlecroft Bridge**) and along tow path until you come to bridge No 54 (**Mops Farm Bridge**).

❷ Leave tow path and cross bridge. Go **R** past Pool Hall Cottages and follow waymarkers of **Monarch's Way**, heading generally southeast. At first, path is to **R** of field hedge then, later, it crosses over to L-H side until you come to stile to reach Langley Road.

❸ Go **L** along road to junction and then bear **R** through small gateway to descend to dismantled railway. Head **L** and follow **Kingswinford (South Staffordshire) Railway Walk**. This is easy walking and you are likely to meet a number of other walkers and possibly cyclists. Continue for about 2 miles (3.2km). You will eventually pass beneath road bridge near **Castlecroft**; following this there are moments when the scene opens up to give lovely views. After passing **Wolverhampton Environment Centre** you come to **Compton**. Leave disused railway line and climb up to **A454**, going **L**.

❹ Go **L** again and descend by side of **Bridge No 59** restaurant on to tow path and take it back to bridge No 56, passing couple of lock gates and number of moored narrowboats. Go beneath Bridge No 56 and leave canal on to pavement of Windmill Lane. Continue towards main A454 road and cross over to return to **Mermaid** pub in **Wightwick**.

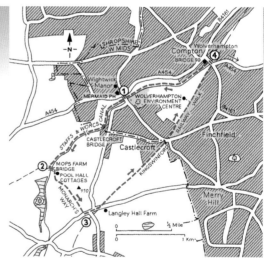

---

513 WOODGATE *Valley Country Park*

3½ miles (5.7km) 1hr 30min **Ascent:** 49ft (15m)
Paths: Grassy footpaths and tracks, 2 stiles
Suggested map: aqua3 OS Explorers 219 Wolverhampton & Dudley; 220 Birmingham
Grid reference: SP 995829 (on Explorer 219)
Parking: Woodgate Valley Country Park

A short, easy excursion showing the West Midlands' urban countryside at its best.

❶ Walk from car park down to **Woodgate Valley Urban Farm**. Go **L** past animal enclosures and follow waymarker ('Footpaths and Bridlepaths').

❷ When you reach lane, go **R** along tarmac footpath by side of stream – the **Bourn Brook** – with bridlepath up to your **L**. This path arcs **R**, around edge of park until you reach footbridge over brook. At footbridge, bear **L** past large oak tree and bench seat and walk along footpath that arcs away from stream towards area of young trees. This is easy, pleasant walking and in about 150yds (137m) you will come to junction of footpaths. Continue **L** ahead (if you go **R** you will return to **Bourn Brook**), keeping to **R** of young trees as you progress in generally easterly direction on grass path that meanders along edge of trees.

❸ Another footpath comes in from **L** and then, at junction of footpaths, bear **R** towards rather high

footbridge over stream. Do not cross it, instead bear **L** and follow footpath on **L** side of **Bourn Brook**. This leads into trees and there follows a very pleasant stroll through the park, always close to the bank of the stream.

❹ All too soon you will hear noise of traffic on **B4121** ahead. Just before you reach road, go **R** over footbridge and follow footpath down other side of stream. Path passes close to housing, but this is barely visible and country feel is maintained until you reach high footbridge once again.

❺ Do not cross over footbridge but leave **Bourn Brook** behind and bear **L** to take footpath that crosses open land diagonally with houses to your **L** (do not go **L** towards houses). Maintain your direction over 2nd open area, passing close to hedgerow of blackberry bushes. At end, bear **R** on to main track passing beside football pitch to arrive back at **visitor centre** and car park.

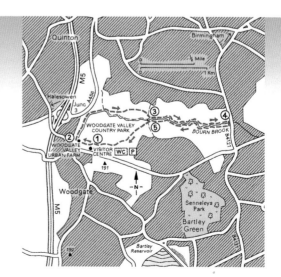

West Midlands

SANDWELL VALLEY *MINES AND MONASTERIES*

4 miles (6.4km) 1hr 30min **Ascent:** 66ft (20m)

Paths: Lakeside paths and tracks, no stiles
Suggested map: aqua3 OS Explorer 220 Birmingham
Grid reference: SP 035927
Parking: RSPB visitor centre

An RSPB nature reserve and country park reveals a spiritual and industrial legacy.

❶ Leave RSPB car park by going **L** of **visitor centre** building on to footpath. This leads down to strip of land between **River Tame** and **Forge Mill Lake**. Continue along footpath, which arcs gently **R**. As you work your way around lake you reach gateway where you go **L** over bridge across River Tame and continue on tarmac path/cycleway that leads down to Forge Lane.

❷ Cross busy lane with great care and walk to **R** of **Sandwell Sailing Club** premises, then bear **L** until you come to **Swan Pool**.

❸ Head **L** and stroll around side of pool for 150yds (137m), then bear **L** again on to footpath that leads across meadowland away from water's edge. Soon you enter hedged footpath heading generally southwest. At junction of paths go **L** and proceed through trees, then go **R** to follow path to north of **Cypress** and **Ice House** pools. You will emerge on to

tarmac lane by side of noisy M5. (If you had continued ahead at junction of paths instead of going **L** you would have arrived at same position.) Go **L** and stroll along this wide lane. At junction, bear **R** and take footbridge over M5.

❹ Follow tarmac path up to **Sandwell Park Farm** where there are toilets and you can get refreshments.

❺ Go **R** opposite to farm buildings and walk along signed public footpath heading northeastwards into trees. (To **L** you will see golf practice area.) When you reach end of hedged area bear **L** and proceed along tarmac path until you reach junction.

❻ Go **R** here along Salters Lane and return over M5 via 2nd footbridge. Take tarmac path that goes to **L** of **Swan Pool** and continue past **sailing club** premises to busy Forge Lane. Cross lane and take footbridge back over **River Tame** to reach junction of footpaths by edge of **Forge Mill Lake**.

❼ Go **L**; walk around lake back to **visitor centre**.

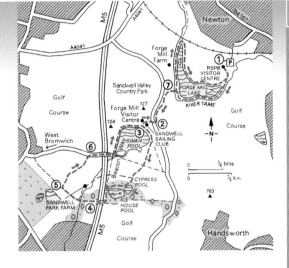

WALSALL *WOODLAND AND THE WATERFRONT*

3¾ miles (6km) 1hr 15min **Ascent:** 66ft (20m)

Paths: Field paths and tow paths, 2 stiles
Suggested map: aqua3 OS Explorer 220 Birmingham
Grid reference: SK 041910
Parking: Hay Head Wood Nature Reserve car park

Along the canal tow paths to Park Lime Pits.

❶ From car park proceed over **Longwood Lane** through parking area on to **Longwood Bridge** and descend to tow path of Rushall Canal. Go **L** (southwest) and walk along side of very straight part of canal.

❷ After 650yds (594m) you reach bridge, which crosses over canal. Don't cross it but go off to **R** and join footpath that leads around bottom end of **golf course**. Follow blue-topped white posts and continue past rear of gardens, with golf course to your **R**, and along back of **playing fields**. After passing exit area to **B4151**, continue ahead on tarmac driveway that leads to municipal golf course's main car park and large recreational area. Leave car park at its rear and continue along tarmac path by **L** side of stream. After about 700yds (640m), turn **R**, over stone footbridge, and walk to **R-H** side of play area up to tarmac driveway.

❸ Head **R**, up driveway to leave park area, then cross over Buchannan Road and continue up footpath until you reach Argyle Road. Go **R** along Argyle Road which arcs **L**, and look out for footpath sign. Go **R** and take hedged/fenced footpath along back of houses in Fernleigh Road. This emerges on to **A454** (Aldridge Road).

❹ Cross over **A454** and go **R** along its grass verge for 220yds (201m), then go **L** over stile by footpath sign ('Riddian Bridge'). Continue along footpath following series of fingerposts until you come to **Riddian Bridge on Wyrley and Essington Canal**.

❺ Descend to tow path (part of the **Beacon Way**) turn **R** and walk along it. This is easy walking, with just a few ducks and perhaps a heron or two for company and you may see fishermen on the banks of the canal. In about ½ mile (800m) you come to **Longwood Bridge**. Exit here on to A454. Cross canal and bear **R** to return to car park.

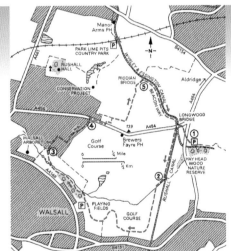

SUTTON PARK *A WILD EXPERIENCE*

7¼ miles (11.7km) 2hrs 30min **Ascent:** 230ft (70m)

Paths: Footpaths, tracks and road in parkland
Suggested map: aqua3 OS Explorer 220 Birmingham
Grid reference: SP 112961
Parking: Visitor centre car park, Sutton Park

A longer walk visiting the largest National Nature Reserve in the West Midlands.

❶ Walk from car park to entrance road and go **L** up to Keeper's Pool. At bottom of pool, bear **R** through gate and follow edge of pool, then go northwards through trees on path until you reach **Blackroot Pool**. Walk along **L** edge of pool for about 220yds (201m), then bear **L** (northwest) and take track through woodland of **Upper Nut Hurst**. In about ½ mile (800m), turn **R** and then cross railway track to arrive at **Bracebridge Pool**.

❷ Turn **R**, along edge of pool, and at end bear **R** along track. Go through car park and then **L** along park road for about 100yds (91m) on to track leading into woodland of **Gum Slade**. Continue to junction of paths, then go **L** across grassy clearing. Proceed into woodland on track that arcs **L** and gently descends to cross footbridge at end of Bracebridge Pool.

❸ Follow track as it arcs **L** and then **R** to cross

railway line again. Continue along track until you reach road, then go **R** for 750yds (686m) up to wide straight track.

❹ Head **L** and walk along this track for 1 mile (1.6km). Cross small brook and walk beside **golf course** to road exit from park. Don't leave park; instead cross road and bear **L** along pathway through trees of **Westwood Coppice** until you come to car park by **Banners Gate**.

❺ Bear **L** up road, passing to **R** of **Longmoor Pool**. About 90yds (82m) beyond end of pool, head **R** along track. After passing to **R** of trees, cross open grass area close to **Powell's Pool** to reach roadway near **Boldmere Gate**.

❻ Go **L** along road for 130yds (121m), then **R**, through edge of **Wyndley Wood**. In 220yds (201m) bear **R** on to straight road that leads to cattle grid and ford at end of **Wyndley Pool**. Continue ahead to return to **visitor centre**.

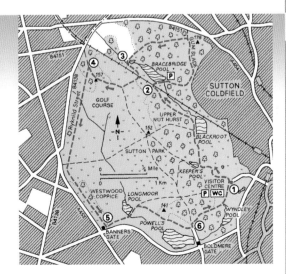

West Midlands

517 BERKSWELL AN ANCIENT PARISH

4½ miles (7.2km) 1hr 30min **Ascent:** 115ft (35m) ▲

Paths: Field paths and parkland footpaths, 13 stiles

Suggested map: aqua3 OS Explorer 221 Coventry & Warwick

Grid reference: SP 244791

Parking: Free car park near church in Berkswell

A walk around Berkswell, an ancient Saxon town with an intriguing five-holed stocks and two historic pubs.

❶ From car park, near **church** in Berkswell, follow **Heart of England Way** to Meriden Road. Go **L** along this road for 300yds (274m), then cross over and go **R** up farm lane, passing **Blind Hall Farm**.

❷ At end of lane/track cross stile by farm gate, bear **L** and walk along field edge to its **L** corner. Go **L** over 2 stiles and continue ahead by hedge. Waymarked footpath weaves in and out of hedge. After going through wide hedge gap, walk to field corner and go **L** past small pond until you come to some houses in **Four Oaks**. Bear **L**, cross over large cultivated field diagonally and exit on to Meriden Road. Cross road and continue down driveway to **R** of **Wilmot Cottage** opposite, going through gateway on to farmland. Path goes to **R** of hedge, offering clear view of Home Farm to **L**, then crosses field diagonally. In about 625yds

(571m) you will reach corner of Mercote Hall Lane.

❸ Go **L** along lane for about ½ mile (800m), passing Park Farm complex. Walk along lane past large enclosed **sand and gravel pits**.

❹ At end of pit area go **L** along footpath and over footbridges, ascending to **L** of hedge on approach to **Marsh Farm**.

❺ Just beyond farm, turn **L** and follow farm track towards **Sixteen Acre Wood**. Cross stile into wood and take track along wood edge for some 700yds (640m). Continue by hedge and go through strip of trees into parkland. Follow path for some 650yds (594m) and then enjoy a magnificent view of **Berkswell Hall Lake** before entering trees and going through kissing gate to rejoin **Heart of England Way**. Cross track and stile on to planked area with **Berkswell Hall** to your **L**. Continue through gates back into Berkswell. Just after going through church gate, bear **L** to return to car park.

---

518 BEDWORTH THE CANALS

4½ miles (7.2km) 1hr 30min **Ascent:** 56ft (17m) ▲

Paths: Lanes, field paths, woodland tracks and tow paths, 3 stiles

Suggested map: aqua3 OS Explorer 221 Coventry & Warwick

Grid reference: SP 364839

Parking: Near Elephant and Castle in Hawkesbury

An easy walk to see Hawkesbury Junction where the Coventry and Oxford canals meet.

❶ From **Elephant and Castle** pub ascend to Coventry Road. Go **L**, crossing bridge over **Oxford Canal**, and follow road past **Old Crown** pub.

❷ In about 250yds (229m), just before large sign for Bedworth and Nuneaton, go **R** and take footpath into meadowland. Continue along footpath to stile and then go **L** over stile into large field. Cross over field, heading towards double stile at end, but don't go over it.

❸ Go **L** again and head towards another stile in field corner. Cross this and continue in northeasterly direction. Your route passes by **Trossachs Farm** (on **L**) and you continue along path by field edge. After going over footbridge, walk diagonally over large hay field, aiming to **L** of oak tree in far corner.

❹ Cross stile near this tree, then **L** to join **Coventry Way**. Take footpath by field edge over several fields until you exit on to Coventry road once again, near to

Mile Tree Farm. Cross road and continue ahead on footpath heading generally towards **Hollyhurst Farm**. Path arcs **L** and you go through hedge gap into area being prepared as nature reserve – this is called **Coalpit Fields Woodlands**. Keep to **L** and go over stile on to farm track. Follow this track as it arcs **L** to reach bridge over **Coventry Canal**.

❺ Just before reaching bridge, go **L** and descend to tow path along this pleasant stretch of canal. Head south along tow path – this is part of **Centenary Way**. Path arcs gently **R** (southwest) and soon you reach **Hawkesbury Junction**. The junction was also known as Sutton Stop, after the name of the first lock keeper, and it became a famous resting place for bargees on this part of the canal system. Today you'll see lots of narrowboats and find the **Greyhound** pub.

❻ Leave Coventry Canal and go **L** along **Oxford Canal** tow path. Walk beneath electricity pylons and make your way back to **Elephant and Castle** pub.

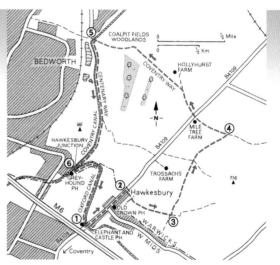

---

519 COMPTON WYNYATES PERFECT MANSION

6 miles (9.7km) 2hrs 30min **Ascent:** 298ft (90m) ▲

Paths: Field paths, tracks and roads, 10 stiles

Suggested map: aqua3 OS Explorer 206 Edge Hill & Fenny Compton

Grid reference: SP 338437

Parking: Spaces in Tysoe

Enjoy spectacular views of a fine house on this scenic walk over high ground.

❶ Make for southern end of **Upper Tysoe** and look for turning ('Shenington and Banbury'). Follow road, keeping Middleton Close on **L**. Turn **R** just before speed de-restriction signs at gate and footpath sign. Keep alongside field boundary to stile in corner and continue across field to next stile. Keep ahead in next field, passing under power lines, and make for plank bridge and stile in boundary hedge ahead. Go straight on up field slope and, on reaching brow of hill, look for stile and plank bridge in hedge by road.

❷ Turn **L**. Follow road as it curves **R** and up hill. Pass **Broomhill Farm** and continue ahead to 1st crossroads. Turn **R** here ('Compton Wynyates') and pass turning on **L** to **Winderton**. Follow lane along to main entrance to **Compton Wynyates** on **R**.

❸ Keep ahead, passing house on **L**-H side and, as road begins to curve **L**, look for galvanised gate and

stile on **R**. Join green lane and follow it to next gate and stile. Continue ahead and, when track curves to **L**, go straight ahead over stile and up edge of field. Pass ruined stone-built barn and make for top corner of field. Take some steps up bank before climbing steeply but briefly up to stile. Keep stone wall and restored **windmill** on your **L**-H side and look over to **R** for view of **Compton Wynyates** house. It was described by Pevsner as 'the most perfect picture-book house of the Early Tudor decade'. It was built on the site of Compton-in-the-Hole, which was demolished to make way for the house and parkland in the 15th century.

❹ Make for stile few paces ahead then follow path over high ground, keeping to **R** of windmill. Make for hedge corner ahead, pass through gap then descend field slope, keeping hedge on your **R**. Pass into next field and keep close to **R**-H boundary. Aim slightly to **L** of bottom **R** corner of field and make for stile leading out to road. Turn **R** and return to centre of **Tysoe**.

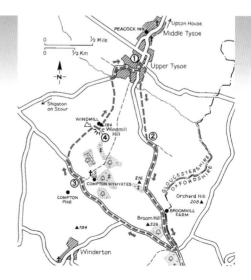

Warwickshire

EDGE HILL *THEATRE OF WAR*

3½ miles (5.7km) 1hr 30min **Ascent:** 280ft (85m) ▲
Paths: Field and woodland paths, country road, 6 stiles
Suggested map: aqua3 OS Explorer 206 Edge Hill & Fenny Compton
Grid reference: SP 370481
Parking: Radway village

Climb a wooded escarpment and enjoy fine views over a Civil War battleground.

❶ Walk through **Radway** to **church**. Veer **L** into West End and pass alongside grounds of **The Grange** on your **L**. Curve **L** by pond and thatched cottages. **Methodist chapel** can be seen here. Follow lane as it becomes stony track and go through kissing gate in field. Walk ahead to stile and continue ahead across sloping field towards Radway Tower, now **Castle Inn**. Look for gap in hedge by inspection cover and maintain direction, climbing steeply towards wooded escarpment.

❷ Make for stile and enter wood. Continue straight over junction and follow markers for Macmillan Way up slope to road. With Castle Inn on your **R**, turn **L** for several paces to **R-H** path running between Cavalier Cottage and Rupert House. Make for stile, turn **L** at road and walk along to **Ratley**. When road bends **L** by copper beech tree, turn **R** to fork. Veer **R** and follow

High Street down and round to **L**. Pass **church** and keep **L** at triangular junction.

❸ With **Rose and Crown** to **R**, follow Chapel Lane and, when it bends **L**, keep ahead up steps to stile. Keep fence on **L** initially before striking out across field to stone stile in boundary hedge. Turn **R** and follow **Centenary Way** across field to line of trees. Swing **L** and now skirt field to gap in corner. Follow path down to galvanised kissing gate, cut across field to footbridge then head up slope to gap in field boundary.

❹ Turn **L** and follow road past bungalows. Pass **Battle Lodge** and make for junction. Cross over and join woodland path running along top of escarpment. On reaching steps on **L**, turn **R** and descend steeply via staircase known as **Jacobs Ladder**. Drop down to gate then follow path straight down field to a stile at bottom. Go through kissing gate beyond it then pass alongside private garden to reach drive. Follow it to road and turn **L** for centre of **Radway**.

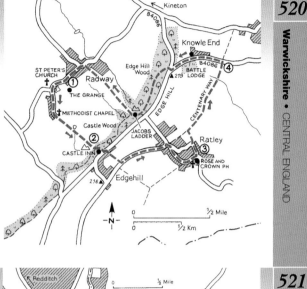

STUDLEY *A PRIORY APPOINTMENT*

4¾ miles (7.7km) 1hr 15min **Ascent:** 49ft (15m) ▲
Paths: Field paths and parkland, 9 stiles
Suggested map: aqua3 OS Explorer 220 Birmingham
Grid reference: SP 072637
Parking: Atcheson Close car park, Studley

A walk past a former castle and the site of a 12th-century priory.

❶ Walk down Needle Close to Alcester road; go **L** to traffic island. Cross and go to Priory Court on footpath to **L** of houses. Cross footbridge; bear **R** to stile into field, aiming towards 2nd stile at corner of field opposite. Head **L**; follow waymarker, going **L** alongside field hedge for about ½ mile (800m). Turn **R** at **The Dairy** and continue in northeasterly direction.

❷ Go **R** between buildings of **Field Farm** and walk along farm drive. In 100yds (91m), go **R** over stile crossing corner of field on to Hardwick Lane. Cross lane, keep between **Spinney Cottages**, then over parkland until you reach driveway near glasshouses. Cross over driveway, go through handgate and walk to **R** of cottage to enter wood. Follow footpath through trees and continue ahead by field edge until you reach end of woodland. Turn **L** and walk up farm track past duck pond and farm building.

❸ Go **R** to corner and cross next field diagonally to footbridge, then ascend to **L** of **Morton Common Farm**. Follow farm drive to road. Go **R** along road for 150yds (137m), then **R** again over footbridge and cross over cultivated field. At farm gate, bear **R** and walk by field hedge on to farm track.

❹ Continue **R** along track. In about ½ mile (800m), it arcs **R**; turn **L** here across middle of field towards Studley's **Church of the Nativity of the Blessed Virgin Mary**. Go through overflow graveyard and enter main churchyard, passing church and leaving via lychgate on to lane.

❺ Go **L** and cross lane and stile. Descend through pastureland, cross footbridge over **River Arrow**, then bear **R** and walk along river bank towards **Studley**. A handgate leads into end of Wickham Road. Head **L** along side of housing estate; bear **R** into Gunners Lane. Go **L** up Castle Road to Alcester road, cross and ascend Needle Close to car park.

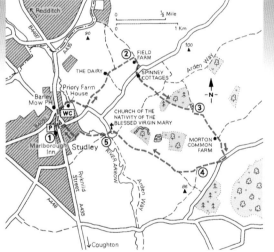

ALCESTER *A ROMAN TOWN*

5 miles (8km) 1hr 30min **Ascent:** 269ft (82m) ▲
Paths: Road pavements, field paths, woodland tracks and farm lanes, 6 stiles
Suggested map: aqua3 OS Explorer 205 Stratford-upon-Avon & Evesham
Grid reference: SP 088573
Parking: Bleachfield car park, Alcester

An easy walk through an old Roman town, woodland and attractive villages.

❶ From car park enter Bleachfield Street and go **L** to old Stratford Road. Cross over road and wander up High Street. Bear **R** past impressive St Nicholas Church and, at corner of road, turn **R** down Malt Mill Lane. At bottom of lane, go **L** through public gardens and follow tarmac footpath by side of River Arrow to reach old Stratford Road again. Cross road and go down lane opposite into Oversley Green village, passing by Alcester football club's ground, then crossing bridge over **River Arrow**.

❷ At road junction bear **L** and in 80yds (73m) go **R** along hedged footpath behind row of houses and past golf driving range. Soon you will bear **R** and then **L** to reach junction of paths. Go **R** here across pastureland close to **Oversley Hill Farm** before coming to Severn Trent sub station.

❸ Go **R**, under A46 road bridge, and bear **R** through

gateway into **Oversley Wood**. Take stone track into wood for about 400yds (366m) and then go **L**. In further 400yds (366m) track arcs **R** and continues westwards, descending back to main track. Now go **L** for 650yds (594m), then **R** to leave wood over stile.

❹ Go **R** and walk along edge of Oversley Wood to its corner. Continue ahead along hedged track until you reach farm lane, with **Oversley Castle** on hillock to **L**.

❺ Go **R** along lane and join **Heart of England Way**. Walk up lane towards some large grain silos by side of **Lower Oversley Lodge Farm**. From farm complex go down to footbridge, which crosses over busy A46. Cross and walk down Primrose Lane, passing beautiful thatched house. At T-junction go **L** along Mill Lane for about 650yds (594m).

❻ Just before reaching mobile home site, go **R**, down path and cross over footbridge over **River Arrow**. Path becomes lane by houses, with allotments to **R**. Walk up Bleachfield Street back to car park.

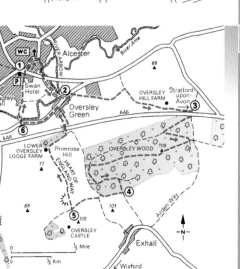

523 WELFORD-ON-AVON BLACK AND WHITE

3 miles (4.8km) 1hr **Ascent:** 49ft (15m)
Paths: Village footpaths and field paths, 3 stiles
Suggested map: aqua3 OS Explorer 205 Stratford-upon-Avon & Evesham
Grid reference: SP 148522
Parking: Near Bell Inn, Welford-on-Avon

A lovely village walk where black-and-white thatched cottages line the streets.

1 From your parking place, come out on to main road in Welford and go **L** down footpath at side of parking area. At end of path, near Daffodil Cottage, go **R** along footpath past back of houses until you come to end of Church Lane, by Applegarth House. Continue through gate and follow green path at back of more houses to reach main road once again, then go **L** along pavement for about 100yds (91m).

2 Go **L** again into entrance gate of **Synder Meadow Sports Ground**. Walk along track then go over 2 stiles to continue along footpath down to **River Avon**. At river, go **L**; follow bank for 500yds (457m).

3 Go over stile at end of field and **L** up Boat Lane, lined with beautiful old thatched black-and-white cottages. Look out for **Ten Penny Cottage**. Near top of lane is St Peter's Church; go **R** here along Headland Road. When you are opposite Mill Lane, turn **L** along

footpath at back of houses. You will pass by extension to graveyard of St Peter's Church and in about 400yds (366m) come to junction of paths. Go **L** and walk up to High Street to emerge opposite Maypole Wine Stores, near the famous maypole. There has been a maypole on the village green since the 14th century and the village children still dance around it each year.

4 Turn **R** along pavement for few paces, then cross and go down another waymarked footpath, past more thatched cottages. Walk through Pool Close to Chapel Street (chapel is on L). Go **R** along Chapel Street, then **R** again down Millers Close towards **Weston-on-Avon**.

5 At crossroads bear **L** to descend bridlepath set just above **River Avon**. Follow it as it arcs **L** then on to Duck Lane by another thatched house, 'Pear Tree Close'. At next residential drive, go **R** up hedged path and walk up to High Street, where you will emerge at junction with Church Street. Bell Inn is on **R**.

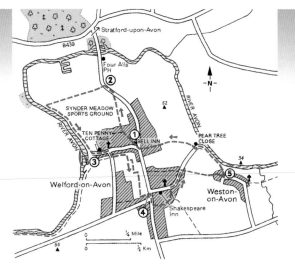

524 HENLEY-IN-ARDEN STRATFORD-UPON-AVON CANAL

5 miles (8km) 2hrs **Ascent:** 180ft (55m)
Paths: Field paths, farm tracks and tow path, 11 stiles
Suggested map: aqua3 OS Explorer 220 Birmingham
Grid reference: SP 152658
Parking: Prince Harry Road car park, Henley-in-Arden

A gentle walk around picturesque Henley-in-Arden, The Mount and the Stratford-upon-Avon Canal.

1 After leaving car park at rear, walk through gardens until you come to Beaudesert Lane, opposite Beaudesert Church. Go **R** through kissing gate by church wall and follow waymarkers of **Heart of England Way** for steep but short ascent to top of **The Mount**. Enjoy the fine views over Henley-in-Arden. Continue over old earthworks of the former **castle** of the de Montfort family until you reach corner of top far field. Go over stile and continue along footpath, which runs to **L** of hedge.

2 In about 220yds (201m), leave Heart of England Way by going **R** and diagonally crossing next field to come to lane in **Kite Green**. Go **L** along lane for about ¼ mile (400m) and then turn **R** over stile on to footpath, which arcs gently to **R**. In middle of next field bear **L** and proceed in easterly direction towards

Church Farm.

3 Go through gate to **R** of farm buildings on to lane. Turn **R** and follow lane, passing by **Manor Farm** to reach A4189 Henley to Warwick road. Go **L** along road for about 220yds (201m), then cross it.

4 Immediately after passing canal bridge, descend on to tow path of **Stratford-upon-Avon Canal** via gate and take this back towards **Henley-in-Arden**. Cross canal bridge and tarmac track/lane opposite. In 180yds (165m), this bends sharp **L**, bringing you to road near Pettiford Bridge. Turn **R** over bridge.

5 In 50yds (46m), go **L** into pastureland. Path arcs **R**, diagonally over field. Cross stile in far **L** corner to reach banks of **River Alne**. Take riverside path then, at junction, bear **R** and proceed ahead, passing to **R** of **Blackford Mill Farm** buildings. Continue on field paths to **L** of **Blackford Hill** to reach A4189 road in **Henley-in-Arden**. Cross road going **L**, then **R** on to Prince Harry Road which leads back to car park.

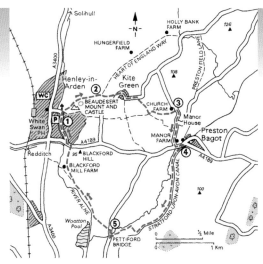

525 KINGSBURY A WATER PARK

3 miles (4.8km) 1hr **Ascent:** 33ft (10m)
Paths: Reservoir paths and footpaths, 1 stile
Suggested map: aqua3 OS Explorer 232 Nuneaton & Tamworth
Grid reference: SP 217962
Parking: Pear Tree Avenue car park (free)

A lovely stroll through old Kingsbury and around the pools of its water park.

1 From car park, go **L** along Pear Tree Avenue to reach A51. Go **R** along pavement then cross road passing in front of White Swan pub. About 20yds (18m) just before pub, cross road and go **L** along footpath by side of churchyard. Follow **Heart of England** waymarkers past church and descend steps to reach footbridge over **River Tame**. Cross bridge and walk along raised footway planks to enter **Kingsbury Water Park**. The water park was once 620 acres (251ha) of sand and gravel pits, but has been developed into a major leisure facility with more than 30 lakes attracting 200,000 visitors each year. With **Hemlingford Water** close on your **L**, by side of **Bodymoor Heath Water**, leaving **Heart of England** behind keep ahead to reach **visitor centre**.

2 From visitor centre follow signs to sailing club along lanes and footpaths. As you veer to **L**, walk by

side of **Bodymoor Heath Water** then pass by entrance gate to **Tamworth Sailing Club**. Continue to **R-H** side of **Bodymoor Heath Water**, along mixture of tarmac lane and grass footpaths.

3 At end of stretch of water bear **L**, then **R** and follow waymarkers for **Centenary Way**. These take you near to Swann Pool and then between **Mill Pool** and **Hemlingford Water** as your route veers northeast. Shortly you will pass another gateway and then cross over **Hemlingford Bridge**.

4 Walk along tarmac lane towards busy **A51**, but just before reaching it go **L** over stile and cross edge of field to final stile on to pavement of **A51**, near middle of **Kingsbury**. Go **L** along pavement until you reach area of open land on other side of road. Cross over road and go **R**, through kissing gate on to clear footpath that goes along back of some houses. In about 220yds (201m), turn **L** into Meadow Close, then **L** again into Pear Tree Avenue to return to car park.

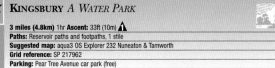

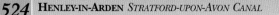

BADDESLEY CLINTON *A Medieval Manor House*

526

5 miles (8km) 2hrs **Ascent:** 16ft (5m)
Paths: Field paths and woodland tracks, 3 stiles
Suggested map: aqua3 OS Explorer 221 Coventry & Warwick
Grid reference: SP 204713
Parking: Lane near church at Baddesley Clinton Manor

A fine church, woodland and the opportunity to visit a superb National Trust property.

1 Take the short detour to visit **Baddesley Clinton Manor** – a fine medieval moated manor house. From driveway to church, walk to Hay Wood Lane. Cross lane, turn **L**, then **R** and walk down track opposite, passing by **Old Keeper's Lodge** on way into **Hay Wood**. Follow track through wood to emerge via gate. Head for another gate to **L** of **Wood Corner Farm**. Go through yet another gate to arrive on farm drive. Go **L** along drive, passing close to farmhouse building. This soon brings you to **A4141**.

2 Go **L** along grass verge of **A4141** for about 220yds (201m), then cross it and go **R** along bridlepath between buildings of **Abbey Farm**. Continue until you reach School Lane and walk **R** along it towards **A4141**. About 100yds (91m) before you reach end of lane, go **R** over stile and cross corner of field to reach **A4141** near Ducklings Day Nursery.

3 Cross **A4141**, enter **Wroxall Abbey park** through pair of gates. Benedictine nuns founded the abbey in 1135 and it was purchased in 1710 by Sir Christopher Wren as his retreat. Follow track through grounds. In 500yds (457m) you go fairly close to old abbey building. Where track veers L, continue towards gate set to **L** of small area of enclosed woodland. Follow path as it goes to **R** of **Gilbert's Coppice** and continue in southwesterly direction to stile. Cross stile; take path to **L** of hedge to Quarry Lane.

4 Go **R** along lane. Bear **L** at junction; keep along Rowington Green Lane for almost ½ mile (800m).

5 Pass by former **windmill** on L and just before reaching **Lyons Farm**, go **R** through gate on to track which is part of **Heart of England Way**. Route takes you to **R** of farm complex along path/track going over stile and through several gates. After passing **Rowington Coppice** you come to handgate on to entrance driveway of the church and start.

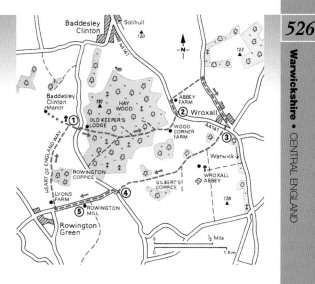

STRATFORD-UPON-AVON *In the Bard's Footsteps*

527

2½ miles (4km) 1hr **Ascent:** Negligible
Paths: Riverside paths and street pavements, no stiles
Suggested map: aqua3 OS Explorer 205 Stratford-upon-Avon & Evesham
Grid reference: SP 205547
Parking: Recreation Ground pay-and-display car park

A tour of theatrical Stratford-upon-Avon to see the sights.

1 From car park, walk along banks of **River Avon** opposite the famous **Royal Shakespeare Theatre**. Pass weir until you come to footbridge over river, just in front of A4390 road bridge.

2 Go **R** over footbridge and bear **R** past old mill building into Mill Lane. Continue up Mill Lane and go through churchyard of **Holy Trinity Church**, walking around church to see river view. Leave churchyard through main gate into Old Town and follow pavement. Just before reaching turn into Southern Lane, go **R** into New Place Gardens and walk up to **Brass Rubbing Centre**. Continue past ferry and stroll through attractive Theatre Gardens by side of Avon, exiting into Waterside and passing by frontage of old theatre building.

3 Go **L** up Chapel Lane, taking time to wander through Knot Gardens on your way up to Chapel Street. At top of lane is Guild Chapel to Shakespeare's Grammar School, with New Place Gardens to your R.

4 Go **R** along Chapel Street, passing Shakespeare Hotel and **Town Hall** into High Street. Harvard House is on L, near black-and-white **Garrick Inn**. At end of High Street, bear **L** around traffic island into Henley Street and walk along pedestrianised area that takes you past **Shakespeare's Birthplace** and the Museum. At top of Henley Street, bear **R** and then **L** into Birmingham Road. Cross road at pedestrian crossing and go **L** up to traffic-lights.

5 Head **R** up Clopton Road for 100yds (91m), then descend to tow path of **Stratford-upon-Avon Canal**. Follow this, going southeast. Cross over canal at bridge No 68 and continue along tow path into Bancroft Gardens by canal basin where you will see an array of colourful narrowboats and the Royal Shakespeare Theatre. Cross old Tram Bridge to car park on R.

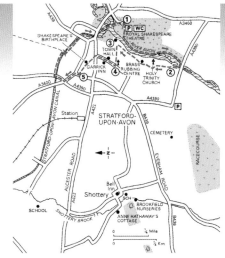

POLESWORTH *Monastic Lines*

528

4 miles (6.4km) 1hr 30min **Ascent:** 115ft (35m)
Paths: Canal tow paths, field paths and residential areas, 3 stiles
Suggested map: aqua3 OS Explorer 232 Nuneaton & Tamworth
Grid reference: SK 262024
Parking: Hall Court car park (free)

Polesworth and its ancient abbey church.

1 From car park at Hall Court, walk into Bridge Street and bear **L** towards bridge. After walking 25yds (23m), turn **L** into alleyway that leads to public footpath ('River Anker'). Cross footbridge over river, then bear **L** through gardens by riverside on footpath that arcs gently **R** towards bridge No 51 over **Coventry Canal**. Descend to canal; turn **L** along tow path, which you follow for 1½ miles (2.4km). Before walking beneath railway line look up to **R** and on far bank you will see **obelisk** on **Hoo Hill**. **Stiper's Hill** is to L. Continue beneath main electrified railway line.

2 Leave Coventry Canal's tow path at bridge No 49 and ascend on to road going generally northwest past **Kitchens Bridge Cottage**. Soon after passing cottage look out for hedge gap on **L-H** side and proceed through this to cross footbridge over railway line. Now climb hill passing through farm gate close to buildings of **Dordon Hall** farm and continue up to road. Go **L**

along road; turn **R** at junction, following signpost to Dordon. Continue along Dunne Lane into village.

3 Immediately after passing house, '**Lyndon Lea**', turn to **R** down track that leads to stile on to footpath over open farmland. Follow this footpath, heading generally northwards, towards prominent trees of **The Hollies**. Continue past trees, crossing couple of stiles and soon you will find yourself walking along stone track that becomes Common Lane on approach to **Polesworth**. Take pavement of lane through residential estate until you reach B5000 Tamworth to Grendon Road. Cross road (take care, it can be busy) and stroll down to park area by **River Anker**; cross back over footbridge. Public footpath now leads up to junction of paths where you go **R**, towards **abbey**. Bear **L** and leave through Old Nunnery Gateway on to High Street. Now turn **L** and continue along High Street, past **Nethersole Centre** and turn **L** again into Bridge Street to return to Hall Court car park.

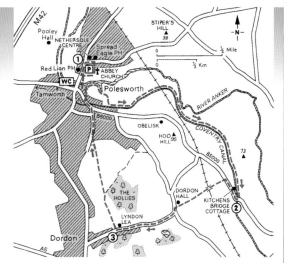

Warwickshire

Warwickshire • CENTRAL ENGLAND

529 CHARLECOTE PARK *An Elizabethan Jewel*

5 miles (8km) 1hr 30min **Ascent:** 33ft (10m)
Paths: Field paths and farm tracks, 2 stiles
Suggested map: aqua3 OS Explorer 205 Stratford-upon-Avon
Grid reference: SP 262564
Parking: National Trust visitors car park for Charlecote Park

An easy walk into open countryside.

1 From **Charlecote Park** car park, go **L** along grass verge and cross over **River Dene**. In about 100yds (91m), go **L** along wide track that arcs **L** on to clear fenced path by side of river and walk along for this 1½ miles (2.4km) into **Wellesbourne**. It was recorded in the Domesday Book as Walesbore. You will pass **weir** before you reach footbridge near St Peter's Church.

2 Go **L** over footbridge and up fenced path to **L** of church until you reach village. Continue up road to **L** of house No 21 – **Kings Head** pub is on **L**. Cross main road in village and walk up Warwick Road opposite.

3 In about 300yds (274m), just after passing Daniell Road, go **R** along tarmac path at back of houses. Cross footbridge and continue over several fields. Take footpath to **L** of copse of trees then go **R** into woodland. Turn **L** along track at top of hedge of trees. You will emerge from trees for short distance and then re-enter again. After you emerge for second

time, look for hedge gap to **L**.

4 Go through gap and then along footpaths to **Middle Hill Farm**.

5 Continue **L**, between farm buildings then go to **R** of farmhouse and walk along farm drive for about ¾ mile (1.2km), passing entrance to **Coppington Farm** on way to **A429**. Cross road with care then stile opposite on to fenced footpath. After crossing minor road continue along driveway past farm building.

6 In 100yds (91m), go **L** through kissing gate into pastureland. A 2nd kissing gate leads into large field that you walk around by field hedge. Go **R**, through further kissing gate, and continue to **R** of field hedge until you go through final kissing gate on to Charlecote Road. Go **L** along footway past thatched cottage into centre of **Charlecote**, then turn **R** along grass verge of main street past half-timbered houses and **Charlecote Pheasant Hotel**, with St Leonard's Church opposite, to reach **Charlecote Park** car park.

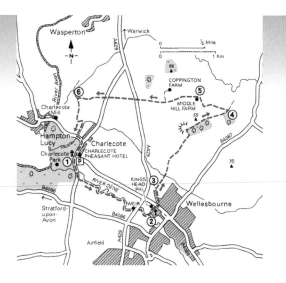

530 WARWICK *The Kingmaker Plot*

5 miles (8km) 2hrs **Ascent:** 33ft (10m)
Paths: Canal and riverside paths, street pavements, 2 stiles
Suggested map: aqua3 OS Explorer 221 Coventry & Warwick
Grid reference: SP 277647
Parking: Racecourse car park

Along the canal to Warwick Castle.

1 Walk to end of racecourse car park and go **L** towards golf **clubhouse**.

2 Go **R** and take wide green track between golf course and driving range. In 300yds (274m), cross over racetrack and go over stile on to footpath by small factory. Continue ahead and, at corner of common land, go **R** over another stile on to lane and descend to road. Go **L** along pavement beneath railway bridge, then **L** again over stile on to grassland by Saltisford Canal. Follow grassy area to tow path, passing large narrowboat mooring area, and climb steps up to canal bridge on to pavement beside road. Go **R** along pavement and in 50yds (46m) you reach canal bridge over Grand Union Canal and busy A425.

3 Cross road with care. Go **L** over canal bridge and descend to take tow path into **Warwick**, about 1½ miles (2.4km) away, passing by lock gate with **Cape of Good Hope** pub opposite and then going along

back of houses. Shortly after passing by Tesco store and just before **aqueduct** over **River Avon**, go **L** down steps to join 'Waterside Walk'.

4 Proceed **R** under aqueduct and follow river bank footpath. At **Castle Bridge**, climb steps on to pavement of A425 (Banbury) road; cross with care.

5 Stroll on to bridge for views of the castle, then turn around and follow pavement towards Warwick.

6 In 220yds (201m) go **L** and go down Mill Street for another view of castle. Return to main road and go **L** through main entrance gate to **Warwick Castle** grounds. Bear **R** and leave grounds via wall gate into Castle Street. Stroll up Castle Street passing by **Oken's House** until you reach tourist information centre on corner of High Street. St Mary's Church is ahead if you wish to visit. Turn **L** and walk along High Street, going under archway of **Lord Leycester's Hotel**. Go **R** into Bowling Green Street and, in 50yds (46m), turn **L** down Friars Street to reach racecourse.

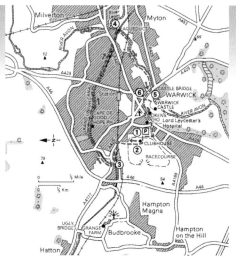

531 BRAILES *Over the Hills*

5 miles (8km) 1hr 30min **Ascent:** 476ft (145m)
Paths: Field paths and country lanes, 7 stiles
Suggested map: aqua3 OS Explorer 191 Banbury, Bicester & Chipping Norton
Grid reference: SP 308394
Parking: Village Hall car park in Lower Brailes – donation to hall funds expected

A fine hill walk with outstanding views.

1 Leave car park by village hall in **Lower Brailes** to join B4035. Turn **L** to stroll up through village for ½ mile (800m), first passing post office then **George Hotel** (popular with local ramblers).

2 Turn **R** and walk down waymarked public footpath by side of George Hotel. This runs beside small Cotswold dry-stone wall then crosses Cow Lane into pastureland. Continue ahead and, at junction of public footpaths, bear **L** to begin climb towards **New Barn Farm**. Footpath goes to **L** of farm and you should continue up hill, crossing several fields and stiles – there is a fine retrospective view over Lower Brailes. Walk up path, then go through hedge gap and bear **R**, walking above trees surrounding **Rectory Farm**.

3 Bear **R** at end of trees and now begin gentle descent on farm track, enjoying view ahead over the valley as you proceed towards **Sutton-under-Brailes**. When you reach road at bottom of hill, turn **L** and

wander through another beautiful Cotswold village, going to **R**, past fine village green, and heading for stile to **L-H** side of parish church.

4 Clamber over stile and walk past church, then across field by **Church Farm** on to farm lane/track. Go **R** up this track, passing to **R-H** side of **Oaken Covert** as you ascend Cherington Hill.

5 At junction of public footpaths, go **R** through metal bridle gate and follow tractor track heading generally eastwards. Route goes to **L-H** side of **New House Barn**, then veers roughly northeast along top of several farm fields, with more good views over Brailes Valley to **R**. After going through farm gate descend hedged track, High Lane, to Tommy's Turn.

6 Turn **L** and walk down lane, continuing your descent into Henbrook Lane. Soon you will come back out on to High Street in **Lower Brailes** (B4035). Turn **R** along road for about 100yds (91m) to car park on corner of Castle Hill Lane.

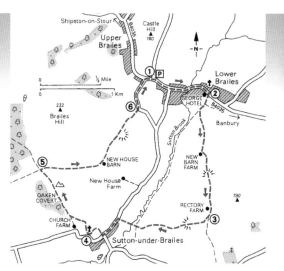

Warwickshire

HARTSHILL HAYES FINE VIEWS

4½ miles (7.2km) 1hr 30min **Ascent:** 295ft (90m)
Paths: Lanes, field paths, woodland tracks and tow paths, 3 stiles
Suggested map: aqua3 OS Explorer 232 Nuneaton & Tamworth
Grid reference: SP 317943
Parking: Hartshill Hayes Country Park

A walk in a country park and along a canal.
❶ From car park enter **Hartshill Hayes Country Park** at back of visitor centre. Take path which arcs **L** (northwest) along top of Hartshill and enjoy view over the surrounding area. Continue ahead on path that descends gently into woodland. At bottom of woodland go over footbridge then bear **L** to walk along open path as you continue. In about ¼ mile (400m) path bends to **R** and you will ascend northeast to brow of hill from where you can overlook the **Coventry Canal**. Now path becomes hedged as you progress northwards towards **Quarry Farm**. Go through handgate to **L** of farm buildings on to Quarry Lane.
❷ Turn **R** and stroll down lane, bearing **R** at junction to reach bridge No 36 over Coventry Canal. Cross bridge and descend on to tow path, walking in northwesterly direction and under bridge No 37.
❸ Leave tow path at bridge No 38 and cross canal on to quiet lane. Walk up lane for 150yds (137m) then,

just before private house, go **L** through tall kissing gate into meadowland and on into pastureland. Cross over footbridge at bottom of field, then walk across next field and on to 2nd tall kissing gate and enter woodland of **Purley Park**. Follow footpath up **R** edge of woodland. Path arcs **L** into trees and you will exit on to Quarry Lane again.
❹ Go **R**; head up lane, past entrance to **Mancetter Quarry**. In further 600yds (549m), go **L** over stile.
❺ Walk to **R** of **Oldbury Farm** on good bridlepath going southeast. This path crosses pastureland, but soon you will be following white marker posts across **golf course**.
❻ Exit on to road then go **L**. Road passes by **Oldbury Grange** and Adbury Gardens. Where there is sharp R-H bend in road, go **L** up towards rear entrance to gardens and enter **Hartshill Hayes Country Park** via gate. Once you are in park bear **R** and join park path back to visitor centre.

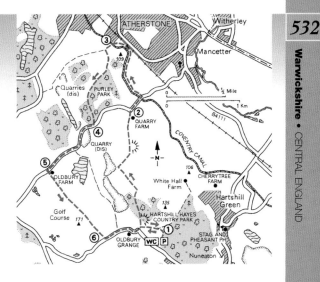

DASSETT INTO FENNY COMPTON

7¼ miles (11.7km) 2hrs 30min **Ascent:** 656ft (200m)
Paths: Field paths and farm tracks, 15 stiles Hilly countryside
Suggested map: aqua3 OS Explorer 206 Edge Hill & Fenny Compton
Grid reference: SP 394523
Parking: Burton Dassett Hills Country Park car park – small charge

A walk in the Burton Dassett Hills.
❶ From car park in **country park** descend on footpath to **R** of **Bonfire Hill** into **Northend** to arrive at Hampden Court.
❷ Go **R** along main street for 300yds (274m), then **R** again through pair of kissing gates. Follow footpath heading generally eastwards towards Fenny Compton, crossing mixture of pastureland, fields and stiles.
❸ Enter **Fenny Compton** over stile, then head along Grant's Close into Avon Dassett road. Walk past Duckett Cottage and go through handgate to **R** of village church. Now bear **R** and cross over pastureland to road known as The Slade. Go **L** along road past large farm barn, then **R** over footbridge into large cultivated field. Follow footpath signs and cross this field to 2nd footbridge, then walk up next field, aiming for marker post in hedge ahead. Here go **L** and walk along field edge – from the top of the hill there is a fine view of the landmark four-sail windmill at Chesterton

and the Post Office Communication towers near Daventry. Follow direction of waymarkers, climb **Windmill Hill**, then descend over farm fields and hedged footpath into **Farnborough**, emerging on main street near **Butchers Arms** pub.
❹ Head **R**, along main street, and bear **R** past entrance gates to National Trust's **Farnborough Hall**. Continue up road to **L**, past lake, walking along footpath inside trees. At end of woodland continue along road for 500yds (457m) then go **R** over stile and cross 2 cultivated fields into pastureland. Descend to **L** of large barn, which brings you to **Avon Dassett**.
❺ Go **L** past church and in 75yds (69m) go **R** up track to **R** of **Avon Inn** into open countryside. Up to **R** is the impressive **Bitham Hall**. Waymarked footpath hugs top of fields until you arrive in **Burton Dassett**, passing by its lovely Norman church. Continue up road to return to car park near Beacon viewing point on **Magpie Hill** (630ft/192m).

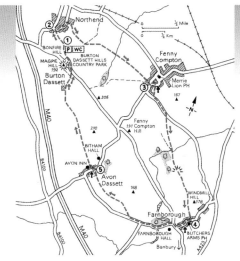

DRAYCOTE WATER TWO HISTORIC VILLAGES

6½ miles (10.4km) 2hrs **Ascent:** 164ft (50m)
Paths: Reservoir paths and field paths, 7 stiles
Suggested map: aqua3 OS Explorer 222 Rugby & Daventry
Grid reference: SP 462690
Parking: Pay-and-display car park at Draycote Water

Around Warwickshire's largest reservoir and into Dunchurch and Thurlaston.
❶ From **Draycote Water** car park proceed up to reservoir then bear **R** following tarmac lane along top of **Farnborough Dam** wall to reach **Toft Bay**.
❷ At end of Toft Bay go **R** and leave reservoir grounds via handgate. Continue ahead then go **R** and follow waymarker signs to footpath that climbs past llama pens up towards **Toft House**. Continue along hedged footpath to **L** of house. This bends **L** on to lane where you go **R** up to A426 Rugby to Dunchurch road. Go **L** along road, cross road bridge and enter **Dunchurch**, passing thatched houses. Village Square and St Peter's Church are **R** of crossroads, with **Dun Cow**, an old coaching inn, immediately opposite.
❸ At crossroads, go **L** along pavement of B4429 past the Dunchurch & Thurlaston WMC. Bear **L** along School Street and follow footpath past more thatched houses and infant **school** down to Dunchurch Scout

Group Hall. Here, go **R** then **L** along footpath to **R** of playing fields. Continue along hedged path and proceed to **R** of **Ryefield Farm**. Go ahead over pastureland then pass under M45 road bridge then diagonally crossing next field to 2 stiles to **Thurlaston**.
❹ Go to **L** by St Edmund's Church and down concrete farm track to handgate and footbridge to enter perimeter of **Draycote Water**.
❺ Go **R** along walkway by side of reservoir around **Biggin Bay**. To your **R** **Thurlaston Grange** can be seen, then you pass **golf course**. Continue around end of reservoir, passing by **treatment works**, and then stroll along **Draycote Bank**. To your **R** is spire of **Bourton-on-Dunsmore** church about 1 mile (1.6km) away; to its **R** is Bourton Hall. After passing by picnic area and just before reaching yachting area go **R** on footpath that leads up on to **Hensborough Hill** for a fine view. Meander past trig point, some 371ft (113m) above sea level, and return to car park.

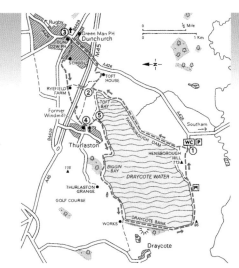

535   FLASH *HIGHEST VILLAGE*

6 miles (9.7km) 4hrs **Ascent:** 656ft (200m) ▲

Paths: Some on road but mostly footpaths which can be boggy in wet weather

Suggested map: aqua3 OS Explorer OL24 White Peak

Grid reference: SK 026672

Parking: On roadside near school

A walk from England's highest village.

❶ Walk through village, pass pub and an old chapel. Turn **R** at footpath sign and head towards last house. Go over stile, turn **R** and follow path over 2 walls. Veer **L** towards gate in corner of field to lane between walls. Cross another stile then turn **L** at waymarker.

❷ Continue through gate then follow waymarker **R** and uphill to **Wolf Edge**. Pass rocks, veer **L** downhill over stile and across heather moorland. Cross stile on **R** and continue downhill to marker post. Cross wall, then bridge and turn **L** on to road. Follow this road through **Knotbury** then, after last house on **L**, take path on **L**, crossing several stiles. Turn **L** at waymarker and **R** at next.

❸ Follow this path downhill, across fields, through an open gate and **L** on to farm road. Go through another gate, veer **R** of road at next waymarker, cross stile then keep straight ahead at next signpost. Follow this track until it crosses bridge, then heads uphill.

❹ Go through farmyard and then turn **R** on to road. Continue to junction and turn **R** then **L** through gap stile. Go downhill, over bridge, then uphill following path, **L** across field, through gap stile and then turn **L** along road.

❺ Go **L** at next signpost, following waymarked path to farm track. At farm buildings go through gate then fork **R**. Continue to road, cross it then continue on path through **Little Hillend**. Follow this waymarked path to **Adders Green Farm**.

❻ Turn **L**, through gate and along wall. At end of wall turn **L**, follow wall, cross gate then follow path round foot of hill and through gate to **Flash Bottom**. Go through small gate, turn **L** and over stile to road.

❼ Cross stile opposite, follow path over field and up steps to road. Turn **R**, then **R** again at next sign. Cross several fields on well waymarked path towards farm buildings. Cross stream then head uphill to **L** to rejoin road. Turn **R** to **Flash**.

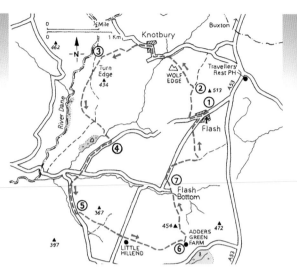

536   LONGNOR *PEAK PRACTICE*

6 miles (9.7km) 4hrs **Ascent:** 459ft (140m) ▲

Paths: Some on road, otherwise good footpaths, can be muddy

Suggested map: aqua3 OS Explorer OL24 White Peak

Grid reference: SK 089649

Parking: Longnor village square

The TV location of a popular medical drama.

❶ From square take road towards Buxton. Take 1st **R** into Church Street and go up lane, then **R**, up steps, to footpath. Follow waymarkers, behind some houses, over stile and along wall. Cross another stile, go downhill and turn **L** on to farm road.

❷ At fork go **L** then turn **R** on to road. After **Yewtree Grange** take farm road on **L**. At end of road continue through gate on to footpath, through gap stile, downhill, across bridge and continue straight ahead. Eventually cross stile and turn **L** on to road.

❸ Fork **L** on to farm road, following waymarked path. Cross bridge by ford and follow path, by stream, to road. Turn **R** through **Hollinsclough**, following road to **R** and uphill. Turn **R** on to footpath, through gate and downhill.

❹ Fork **L** by 2 stones and continue along flank of hill. Cross stile then, at stone wall, fork **L** and uphill. At top turn **L** at stone gatepost, through **Moorside Farm**, through kissing gate on to road. Turn **R** then cross stile to public footpath on **L**.

❺ Go downhill to stream and cross stile to **L** of ditch. Head uphill, under wire fence, through gap in wall and round field to gap stile. Turn back towards farm, then **L** on to well-signposted footpath to **Hill Top Farm**.

❻ Follow path over stiles and past farm to road. Cross it and take farm road to **L**. By small quarry, go **L** downhill, over stile and follow path along wall. Just before stream, cross stile on **L** and head uphill to **L** of some trees.

❼ Continue walking uphill, through gate in stone wall to some ruined buildings. Follow track to next farm, bear **L** after barn, then go **L** on to footpath uphill.

❽ Go through stile, follow wall uphill, over 2 stiles to road. Turn **L** then **R** towards **Longnor**. Just before road bends **L**, cross stile on **R**, go downhill and over several stiles to farm road. Turn **R** and follow this back to village.

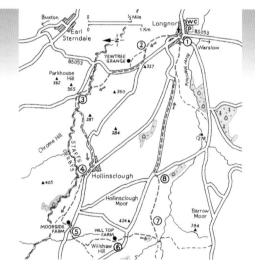

537   THE ROACHES *LUD'S CHURCH*

6¾ miles (10.9km) 4hrs **Ascent:** 1,020ft (311m) ▲

Paths: Rocky moorland paths, forest tracks and road

Suggested map: aqua3 OS Explorer OL24 White Peak

Grid reference: SK 006618

Parking: In lay-by opposite Windygates Farm; in summer park at Tittesworth Reservoir and catch bus

Follow in the footsteps of Sir Gawain, a Knight of the Round Table, and find the chapel of the Green Knight near the Roaches.

❶ From car park area go through gap stile and gate then continue uphill with wall on your **R**. At gate in wall turn **L** and cross over field. Go through another gate then uphill on rocky track. Go **L** through pair of stone gateposts and then continue **R** along this well-defined track.

❷ Path is flanked by rocks on **R** and woodland to **L** and below. Follow it to **R** and uphill through gap in rocks. Turn **L** and continue uphill. Continue following this ridge path. Pass to **L** of **Doxey Pool** and on towards trig point.

❸ From here descend on to paved path, past **Bearstone Rock** to join road at **Roach End**. Go through gap in wall, over stile and follow path uphill keeping wall on **L**. At signpost fork **R** on to concessionary path to **Danebridge**.

❹ Follow this path keeping straight ahead at crossroads, go over stile and up towards an outcrop. Carry on along ridge then head down to signpost by stile. Turn **R** and follow bridleway signed 'Gradbach'. At next signpost fork **R** towards Lud's Church. According to the 14th-century poem, *Sir Gawain and the Green Knight*, a knight on horseback gatecrashed a feast at Camelot and challenged the Knights of the Round Table. Sir Gawain rose to the challenge and beheaded the Green Knight. The latter retrieved his head and, laughing, he challenged Sir Gawain to meet with him again in a year's time at the Green Chapel – which has been identified as Lud's Chapel.

❺ After exploring Lud's Church continue along path, through woodland, following signs for Roach End, eventually taking paved path uphill. Cross stile and continue walking with wall on your L-H side. When path reaches road, cross stile on to it and follow this road back to car park.

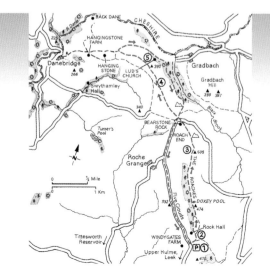

TITTESWORTH RESERVOIR *BIRDS AND BUTTERFLIES*

4¼ miles (6.8km) 3hrs **Ascent:** 131ft (40m)
Paths: Good well-made footpaths, forest tracks and roads
Suggested map: aqua3 OS Explorer OL24 White Peak
Grid reference: SK 999603
Parking: Near Middle Hulme Farm

Reservoir biodiversity provides drinking water for the Potteries and a valuable wildlife habitat.

1 Go through gate on to footpath and turn **R**. Cross 1st bridge, turn **L** then cross 2nd bridge and follow Long Trail/Short Trail direction signs along well-surfaced path. At junction beside picnic table turn **L** on to forest trail.

2 Follow waymarked Long Trail through wood crossing bridge and some duckboarding then turn **L** at T-junction again following Long Trail. Follow path as it leaves wood and on to grassy area where it is less well defined but still visible.

3 Continue along bank of reservoir then re-enter woodland, cross duckboards and continue once more on well-defined footpath. Cross bridge by picnic table, ascend steps and continue along duckboards. Skirt edge of wood, keeping fence on your **L**, then go downhill through wood and along reservoir bank.

4 Go through some more woodland, cross bridge, walk up some steps then leave wood and continue on gravel path. Cross stile then follow path downhill towards dam. Go over stile and cross dam head. Cross stile at far end, go uphill on series of steps and turn **R** on to footpath.

5 Cross stile and turn **R** at T-junction on to metalled lane. Continue ahead on this lane through farm, following signs for **Meerbrook**, straight ahead. At road junction cross over stile and turn **R** at Long Trail sign. Turn **R** again following road to **Tittesworth Reservoir**. When this turns to R, bear **L** on footpath beside reservoir.

6 Cross stile on to road then turn **R** into public entrance to reservoir. Turn **L** at entrance to **visitor centre**, cross car park then go **L** at Nature Trail sign. Continue across grass then turn **R** on to concrete path. Follow this to 1st bridge and turn **L** to return to car park.

MANIFOLD VALLEY *A RAILWAY ROUTE*

5½ miles (8.8km) 3hrs 30min **Ascent:** 518ft (158m)
Paths: Hard surface on Manifold Way, other footpaths can be muddy in wet weather
Suggested map: aqua3 OS Explorer OL24 White Peak
Grid reference: SK 095561 **Parking:** On Manifold Way near Wetton Mill

Follow the former route of a small railway.

1 From car park by bridge at **Wetton Mill**, turn **L** on to road and continue past bridge. When road bends sharply R near ford, go through gate on **R** and walk along track. In 100yds (91m) cross stile at gate on **R** on to public bridleway.

2 Go through another gate, follow stream on your **L**, then turn **R** across next stile. Leave bridleway and follow signposted footpath to **Butterton**, along course of stream until it ends at lane just beyond ford. Turn **L** and continue to main road.

3 Turn **R** on to road opposite **Brookside Stables** and head uphill, past church and **Black Lion Inn**. Turn **R** at T-junction, go **L** at public footpath sign, cross 2 stiles then head along spur, through trees and down steep hill to cross stream by wooden bridge.

4 Head uphill, keeping hedge on your **L**, cross 2 stiles and turn **R** on to road. Turn **L** towards Eckstone then **R** across stile on to footpath. Cross 2 stiles, turn **R** behind small derelict building and follow line of wall.

Cross stile then stream and head uphill keeping fence on your **L**.

5 At junction where fence meets stone wall, turn right, cross field and nip over stile by large tree. Follow path across field through gate then veer **L** to corner of next field. Veer **R** from derelict stone building, cross stile and bear **L** across marshy ground to 2 stone markers.

6 Cross to further 2 stones at end of hedgerow, go along hedgerow to waymark pole then **R** over stile, cross field and go through gate to road. Turn **L** and continue to **Warslow**. Turn **L** into Quarter Lane, pass church and, at T-junction, turn **R**.

7 Turn **R** again at next junction, cross road and walk down School Lane. Turn **L** through gap stile on to public footpath. Clamber through 3 more gap stiles, following course of stream. Enter wooded area, go downhill, cross stile and turn **R** to join **Manifold Way**. Follow this well-defined trail through old railway tunnel, back to car park.

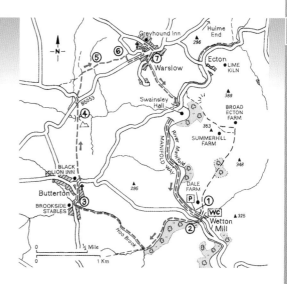

ENDON *WELL DRESSED*

3½ miles (5.7km) 1hr 30min **Ascent:** 269ft (82m)
Paths: Easy meadow paths and some roads, 11 stiles
Suggested map: aqua3 OS Explorer 258 Stoke-on-Trent
Grid reference: SJ 928537
Parking: Ample parking in St Luke's Church car park

A pleasant walk exploring a village that practises the ancient and colourful tradition of well dressing.

1 From **St Luke's Church** car park turn **R** up hill. At top, go straight through farm to gate and slot in wall to **L**. Follow track round to **L** and, 50yds (46m) after barn on R, go through slot in wall. Cut off corner of field to reach stile, making straight for another stile. Bear **R** towards another double stile.

2 Continue in same direction, keeping hedge just to your **L**. Cross stile at far side of field and proceed to another stile straight ahead. Keep following dry-stone wall to your **L** to reach well-hidden slot in top **L** corner of wall. After slot carry on up slope, now with hedge to your **R**.

3 At top **R** corner of field, cross stile and continue along rough track to road. Go straight over and cross pair of stiles, following hedge on L. Cross next stile to small slot in far **L** corner of field.

4 Turn **L** down road and, at junction with B5051, go **R** then 1st **L** along signed footpath, over residential road and up wide track to gate. After gate come to fork: head **L** to corner of wall then continue along bridleway that skirts bottom of **Tinster Wood**. As soon as path enters wood proper head sharp **L** down narrow track, following it to bottom **L-H** corner.

5 Go through slot in wall to your **L**. Continue straight across field, keeping wall to your **R**, through pair of wall slots. Cross small footbridge beneath tree before cutting off corner of field. At gap in wall go **L** up muddy track and **L** along road. After 50yds (46m) go **R** following footpath sign.

6 At bottom of this field cross stile to surfaced road, following it round to **L**. When you reach proper residential road, go hard **L** along rougher track to surfaced road. Head **R** and, shortly after, turn **L** along A53. Just before you get to **Plough** on R, head **L** up road signed to St Luke's Church.

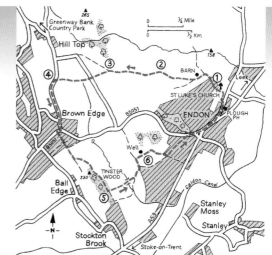

Staffordshire

541 CHEDDLETON *FLINT MILL AND DEEP HAYES*

3¼ miles (5.3km) 1hr 30min Ascent: 272ft (83m)
Paths: Tow path, tracks, grass paths and roads, 11 stiles
Suggested map: aqua3 OS Explorer 258 Stoke-on-Trent
Grid reference: SJ 961533
Parking: Deep Hayes Country Park visitors' centre

Water, flint and the Staffordshire potteries.
❶ From **visitors' centre** in Deep Hayes Country
Park go down to bottom of car park and cross stream
before following shore of reservoir along wooded
track. Path gains height above reservoir, but continues
along shoreline. At fork of 2 obvious footpaths take L-
H option down steep steps and across concrete
stepping stones.
❷ Once across stream head **R** through stile with
sign that says 'Keep dogs on leads'. After short while
this track runs alongside small stream that fills pools
of reservoir. When you cross back over stream,
continue to follow stream to L through an aluminium
kissing gate and along boardwalk.
❸ At junction of 3 paths (marked by signpost) head
sharp **L**, back over stream for final time, before
following footpath ('**Cheddleton**'). After crossing stile,
go **R** for 30yds (27m) before heading up hill along
wooded trail. At top of wood cross stile and go across

field, aiming for **L** of farm buildings, **Shaffalong**.
❹ In far corner of field, cross stile and go along
muddy farm track to gate. After gate, continue ahead
(rather than round to farm) to stile in wooden fence.
Head diagonally **R** to stile, and again to another. From
here go immediately **L**, keeping hedge to your **L**,
before crossing stile.
❺ At obvious wooden public footpath sign, head
across field following line of trees to your **L**. Cross
small stile over dry-stone wall and cross to far side of
next field. Just to **L** of clump of trees is stile followed
in quick succession by another stile and slot in wall,
bringing you out on to road into **Cheddleton**.
❻ At end of road, head **L**, with care, along A520
and, after 150yds (137m), turn **L** following signposts
to **flint mill**. After exploring mill museum, keep going
along canal tow path for 1 mile (1.6km) to bridge over
canal. Cross bridge, before turning **R**, along driveway,
to return to **visitors' centre**.

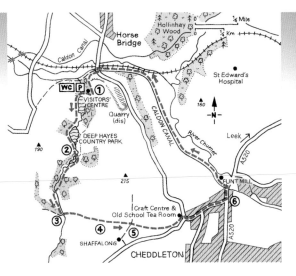

542 GRINDON *IN THE LAIR OF THE WHITE WORM*

5 miles (8km) 2hrs 30 min Ascent: 423ft (129m)
Paths: Forest tracks, grass and mud, hard footpath
Suggested map: aqua3 OS Explorer OL24 White Peak
Grid reference: SK 085545
Parking: At Grindon church

*A limestone trail to the film location of Bram
Stoker's last nightmare.*
❶ From car park turn **L**, then **R** at **Old Rectory** and
descend. Go **L** on to public footpath, go through gap
stile, cross field and descend, keeping **R**. Cross
bridge, go through gate then gap stile and follow
waymarkers downhill, keeping stream and wood on
your **R**.
❷ When wall heads **L** go through gap stile on your
R continuing downhill into National Trust land at
Ladyside. Cross stile, go through wood then leave it
via another stile. Turn **R**, still continuing downhill to
stile leading on to **Manifold Way**.
❸ Cross **Manifold Way**, then bridge and take path
uphill following signs for **Thor's Cave**. Anyone who
has seen Ken Russell's film, *The Lair of the White
Worm* (1988), may feel slightly apprehensive when
climbing up the hillside towards Thor's Cave. Fiction
apart, Thor's Cave was formed over thousands of

years from the combined effecs of wind and rain on
the soft limestone. Excavations have revealed it to be
the site of a Bronze-Age burial. At mouth of cave turn
L, continue on track uphill, curve right at stile and
follow path to summit for views over **Manifold Valley**.
❹ Retrace your steps to **Manifold Way** and turn **L**.
Continue past **caravan park** and then cross 2
bridges. At beginning of 3rd bridge cross stile on **R**
and follow path back, parallel to road and then curving
L and uphill.
❺ Go across stile by dried up pond and follow path
uphill with wall on your **R**. Go through gap stile
adjacent to barn. Keep on, go through next gap stile
and church spire at Grindon should be visible ahead.
❻ Continue on this path across fields, cross stile, go
through 4 gap stiles then turn **L** over final stile on to
farm road. Follow this road, keeping on when it
becomes lane then turn **R** on to road opposite
Chestnut Cottage, take 1st **L** back to car park.

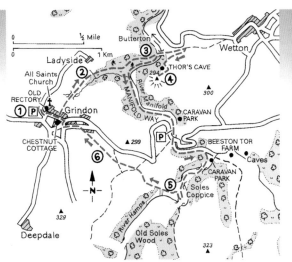

543 APEDALE *A MINING TRADITION*

4¾ miles (7.7km) 2hrs Ascent: 300ft (91m)
Paths: Wide gravel tracks, roads and dirt trails, 10 stiles
Suggested map: aqua3 OS Explorer 258 Stoke-on-Trent
Grid reference: SJ 822483
Parking: Ample parking opposite Heritage Centre

Exploring a wasteland returned to nature.
❶ From **Heritage Centre** in Apedale Country Park
take path to go **R**, through gate. After 400yds (366m)
turn **R** down to corner of park, then continue straight
ahead, passing to **L** of **sawmill**. At fork, head **R** down
short hill to corner of lake.
❷ Ignoring stile, turn **L** along narrow path into
woods. Follow most obvious trail to emerge into Fern
Bank, exotic landscape of giant ferns. Follow path to
junction of many paths, with clearing to your **L**. Walk
through clearing to main gravel track.
❸ Turn **L** and continue for 600yds (549m) to gate
and turn-off for lake (Point ❷). About 30 paces after
gate, head **R** up signed footpath along edge of small
copse, keeping fence to your **R**. At top of this wood, 30
paces off route to your **L**, is **disused mineshaft**.
❹ From top of wood continue up tree-lined track to
village of **Apedale**, former mining community. On **R**,
just after track veers to **L**, is **Gamekeeper's Cottage**.

❺ About 100yds (91m) beyond cottage turn **L** along
track to gate; bear **L** after gate down well-trodden
meadow path to stile. After stile, head **R** following
fence to bottom of hill, then skirt **L** to stile.
❻ Cross into **Watermills Wood** and follow trail to
stile, then junction of 2 paths. Head **R** here and, after
10 paces, fork **R** again. Shortly you cross series of
stiles before continuing up to **Watermills Farm**.
❼ Go through gate and continue for 100yds (91m)
before following footpath **L** over series of fields and
stiles to farm buildings on your **R**. When fence veers
round to **L**, follow it to edge of sapling plantation. At
wide gravel track, head **R** and at fork go **L**. At next fork
go **R** along tarmac to summit.
❽ From summit drop down other side, continue over
crossroads to pair of swing gates and T-junction. Head
R here, and then take 1st **L** down hill. At tarmac road
head **L** and continue back towards **Heritage Centre**
and start.

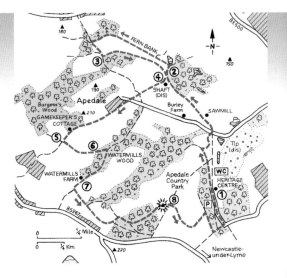

Staffordshire

ILAM *THE COMPLEAT ANGLER*

4¾ miles (7.7km) 2hrs 30min **Ascent:** 607ft (185m)
Paths: Metalled roads, parkland, open hillside, meadows and forest tracks, boggy in wet weather
Suggested map: aqua3 OS Explorer OL24 White Peak
Grid reference: SK 131507
Parking: At Ilam Hall (National Trust)

Explore the countryside once walked by Izaak Walton, the 'Father of Angling'.

1 Exit car park from top, turn **R** then **R** again through gate; follow track through **park**. Cross stile and turn **L** on to road through **Ilam**. Go uphill, turn **L** at Park Cottage on to Castern to Throwley road. At Y-junction go **L**, following road across Rushley Bridge.

2 Go through Rushley Farm steading. Turn **R**, over ladder stile on to public footpath. Cross another ladder stile, walk along side of fence and cross gate on **L**. Continue following waymarked path beside stone wall and then fence. At next ladder stile keep ahead.

3 Go over another 4 stiles then, when you get to 5th, turn **L** on to road. At crossroads turn **L** towards Ashbourne. Go **L** through gap stile at next public footpath sign and cross field. Cross stile, go through another field to stile to **L** of farm then head diagonally **L** across next field.

4 Cross wall by stone steps, head diagonally **R** to gap stile to **R** of some buildings. Continue on this line to another stile in hedge to **R** of **Fieldhead** farm and turn **L** on to road. Follow this round boundary of farm and go over stile on **R**.

5 Follow well-defined path uphill past derelict building. Cross stile, cross field to where 2 walls meet at corner and follow wall to **R**. Join farm road, pass derelict steading, then cross diagonally **R** across field and through gap stile in wall at far corner.

6 Follow direction pointer past 2 marker stones to next public footpath sign. Go **R**, through gap in wall and follow sign for **Ilam**. Follow wall on your **R**, go through gap, follow waymarker downhill, through gap stile and into **park**. Continue downhill and through another gap stile.

7 Go across field, stile then bridge and another stile, cross path and head uphill to **L** of path. At top of hill turn **R**, cross to caravan park and retrace your steps to car park.

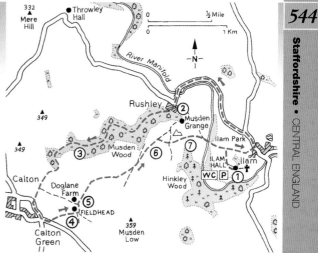

CALDONLOW *PEAK GEOLOGY*

6 miles (9.7km) 2hrs 30min **Ascent:** 480ft (146m)
Paths: Gravel tracks, grassy trails and roads, 5 stiles
Suggested map: aqua3 OS Explorer 259 Derby; OL24 White Peak
Grid reference: SK 086493 (on Explorer 259)
Parking: Ample parking at start point

The geology of this region provides a backdrop to a spectacular walk.

1 From road corner head east along gravel track, walking away from **Cauldon**. Go through gate and continue up small valley. Pass barn on your **R** and go through slot or swing gate then take **R** fork along wide dirt track. At another gate ahead go **R** through gate then follow field round to **L**. After 30 paces go through gap in dry-stone wall and carry on straight up hill.

2 At top **R-H** corner of field go through gate and head across next field to gap in dry-stone wall. Head for bottom **L-H** corner of next field and cross stile on to A52. Bear **L** for 100yds (91m) then turn **R** along narrow metalled road up to **Weaver Farm**. As road veers **L** there are 2 footpath signs on **R**: at 1st of these go back on yourself, up hill towards gate in dry-stone wall.

3 After crossing stile here keep following dry-stone wall to your **R** and at next gate continue in same direction, with wall to your **L**. At end of this wall bear slightly **R** to join another wall on **R** and follow it to gate.

4 Before crossing dry-stone wall ahead of you, go **L** for 100yds (91m) and then **R** over stile, before making straight for **trig point**. From trig point retrace your steps to stile, but instead of crossing it, head **L** across field, making for dry-stone wall at bottom. Follow this wall to **Wardlow**.

5 Continue to **A52** and go straight across, following public footpath sign. Continue over thistly plateau of this field to stile. Across stile head straight through next field, making for **L-H** corner.

6 Go **R** along base of field. Continue to bottom of hill and then bear slightly **L**, heading up and then downhill through succession of fields with trees to your **L**. At far end of fields, turn **L** for some 100yds (91m) and then **R** along trail through narrow valley. At bottom of valley rejoin main track to retrace your steps to start.

FROGHALL *STAFFORDSHIRE'S STEEPEST RAILWAY*

4½ miles (7.2km) 2hrs **Ascent:** 650ft (201m)
Paths: Grass paths and dirt tracks may be muddy and slippery in very wet weather; 9 stiles
Suggested map: aqua3 OS Explorer 259 Derby
Grid reference: SK 027486
Parking: Ample parking at Froghall Wharf

To Froghall's well-preserved wharf.

1 From car park go up ramp and along gravel track. At fork head **R** and, just after Harston Rock, go **L** on trail ('Moorlands Walk'). At bottom cross footbridge.

2 After footbridge, cross over stile and bottom of field. Back in woods, cross footbridge and go through narrow stone slot. Continue across field to stile and footbridge. Cross stile and then follow dry-stone wall up hill.

3 At top bear **R** and continue round, following curve of wall. After slot, go down gravel track to surfaced road then head **R** to wide fork. Go **R** through **Foxt** and after **church** go hard **L** down rough road.

4 Just before private drive go **L** and then across stile on **R**, following path along fence. After crossing stile continue through wood to stream. Shortly after go through kissing gate and follow path to farm road.

5 Turn **R** to **Ipstones**. At end, follow footpath round to **L** then immediately up stone steps to road. Follow road **R** then round to **L** and, at next corner, continue between houses and along road. At main road go **R** then **L** along footpath (signed) to **Stones Farm**.

6 Bear slightly to **L** of farm and, just past it, go through gate on **R** then continue **L** along track. Go through gate and carry on to gap in wall ahead. In next field cross diagonally **L** to gap in hedge. Keep going straight down field to cross stile in far **R** corner. Keep on down **L-H** edge of this field to track to **Booth's Wood Farm**.

7 Cross stile and head **L** following **Moorlands Walk**. Cross stile into **Booth's Wood** and follow steepish footpath down to footbridge and stile. At top of wood go through gate and across field to corner of dry-stone wall. Follow wall and track to **Hermitage**.

8 Go **R** on main road and, after 400yds (366m), follow footpath sign into woods on **L**. Follow this steep path down to T-junction, then turn **R** to canal. At canal turn **L** towards bridge, then cross it to car park.

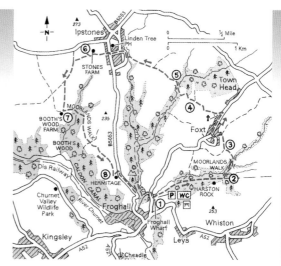

547 ELLASTONE A FICTIONAL PAST

3½ miles (5.7km) 1hr 30min **Ascent:** 360ft (110m)
Paths: Gravel tracks, roads and grass trails, 11 stiles
Suggested map: aqua3 OS Explorer 259 Derby
Grid reference: SK 118426
Parking: Ample parking along roads

Discover the area that was the source of inspiration for author George Eliot and composer George Handel.

① Ellastone, the start of the walk, inspired the setting of *Adam Bede*. From **post office** go **L** and then take 1st **L** down obvious gravel track. At junction of 2 bridleways, keep going straight to **Calwich Abbey**, where Handel composed *The Messiah* while staying with friends. Follow track **L** of abbey and along metalled road as far as **Calwich Home Farm**.

② Pass farm and follow track round to **L** of **The Grove** and through gate. At fork follow yellow footpath arrows to your **L** and, after 50yds (46m), veer **L** off track up short hill to stile in front of **Cockley** farm. Cross stile and head just to **R** of **Cockley**, following dirt and grass track all way to B5032.

③ At road go **L** and then 1st **R**, through **Calwichbank Farm** and up gravel track. When track bears round to **R**, keep going straight into field,

making for gap in hedge at top **R-H** corner. Shortly after this gap, go through gate on **R** and then follow hedge **L**, down field.

④ At bottom follow hedge round to **L** and cut diagonally **R** across field to stile. After crossing stile, skirt round top of wood to another stile and continue as far as **Hutts Farm**. After stile take gravel track up hill to gate into farmyard and head straight on to another stile into field.

⑤ Continue straight across this field making for corner of **Aldercarr Wood**. Keep going to stile in bottom **R-H** corner of field and carry on along **R-H** edge of next field. At far end is another stile, cross this and continue straight to B5032. Turn **L** along road and, after 100yds (91m), take path to **L**. Head diagonally **R** across field to gate and then **L** round bottom of small mound with trees. Keep going as far as junction of 2 bridleways, at Point **①**, and from here retrace your steps back to post office.

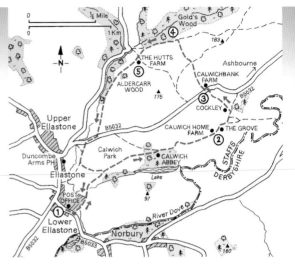

548 ALTON ON THE QUIETER SIDE

4¾ miles (7.7km) 1hr 30min **Ascent:** 361ft (110m)
Paths: Roads, gravel tracks and dirt trails
Suggested map: aqua3 OS Explorer 259 Derby
Grid reference: SK 072423
Parking: Ample parking on Alton village roads

A tranquil walk from the village made famous by its theme park.

① At **castle** gate, head straight down track to **R** of **St Peter's Church**. At main road, head **R**, down hill to river and **Alton Bridge Hotel**. Head **L** along metalled road, past hotel, going straight ahead where road goes round to **L**, along base of **Toothill Wood**. Just after road goes round an obvious hairpin bend, follow wide track into woods on **L** ('Smelting Mill and **Dimmings Dale**'). After 400yds (366m) go **R** off track down less obvious trail which will bring you out at Dimmings Dale car park and **Rambler's Rest** pub.

② Go through car park to **R** of pub and then continue straight on following signs for **Staffordshire Way**. Pass the **smelting mill**, now a private residence and although it's hard to see any detail the original waterwheel is still there and you can't miss the necklace of pools that stretches up the valley. The mill was built in 1741 and was used for forging lead ore.

Next pass lake on your **L**, and continue straight on at end of lake, staying to **R** of impressive stone house.

③ When you climb up to path coming in from **R**, go briefly **L**. Where path turns back on itself, carry straight on. At top of hill go **R** along metalled road, over cattle grid and follow this road all way to T-junction.

④ Go **L** at junction and, after 400yds (366m), go **L** again just before **Old Furnace House**. When you get to fork in track, head **R**, close to stream and past series of pools, until you get to picnic table and causeway between 2 **pools**.

⑤ Continue to **L** of stream after final pool, staying on **L** at 1st wooden footbridge. When you get to dry-stone wall barring way straight ahead, go **R** over wooden footbridge and continue to follow river **L**. This path will shortly bring you back to smelting mill and Rambler's Rest. From there head along road back to hotel and then retrace your steps back to St Peter's Church.

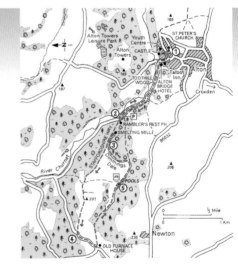

549 LOGGERHEADS THE BATTLE OF BLOREHEATH

5½ miles (8.8km) 2hrs **Ascent:** 240ft (73m)
Paths: Gravel tracks, roads and grass trails, 8 stiles
Suggested map: aqua3 OS Explorer 243 Market Drayton
Grid reference: SJ 738359
Parking: Ample parking in Loggerheads village

A gentle walk around a famous battleground.

① Head along A53 towards Market Drayton and take 1st **L** along Kestrel Drive. Just after The Robins head **L** along gravel track down back of houses. Follow this to end of fence then go **L** along metalled track. This becomes gravel track leading to clearing; bear **R** past iron bar across wide track and, at fork, go **R** to clearing.

② From clearing take 3rd path on **L**. When this runs out, after 400yds (366m), veer slightly **R** on to narrower track to join gravel track. Turn **R** and continue for ½ mile (800m), until main track goes **R**.

③ Head straight through gate and along footpath, hedge to **R-H** side. At bottom of field bear **R** towards **R-H** corner of trees. Go through gate and head up towards **Knowleswood** farm (derelict) and gate.

④ Continue straight ahead and, at bottom of field, go **R** over stile and descend through small dip. At bottom of dip go through gate and head **R** along

concrete track. At fork go **L** to **The Nook Farm** and, after 1 mile (1.6km), to **Home Farm**. Turn **R** along **Flash Lane** and up hill to **Blore Farm**. At junction keep going straight ahead and, after 200yds (183m), head **L** through hedge over stile. Follow hedge **R** to stile in **R-H** corner of field – a vantage point from which to view the main battlefield, now private farm land. At time of writing it was overrun by pigs.

⑤ Continue to bottom **R-H** corner of next field before bearing diagonally **R** across another field to **R-H** end of trees. Cross stile and follow faint track across middle of next field to stile.

⑥ Follow path to fence ahead then cross stile to **L**. Keep following faint track alongside wood to your **R** and, at clearing, head diagonally across field to **L-H** end of trees. At corner of this field cross stile and footbridge to wide dirt track, which you follow **R** and up hill to large oak at top. Turn **L** to cross stile back on to **A53**.

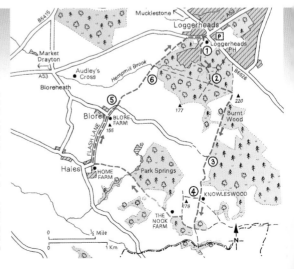

BARLASTON *IN WEDGWOOD COUNTRY*

3¼ miles (5.3km) 1hr 15min **Ascent:** 180ft (55m)
Paths: Roads, gravel tracks and tow paths, 1 stile
Suggested map: aqua3 OS Explorer 258 Stoke-on-Trent
Grid reference: SJ 889395
Parking: Ample parking along road at starting point

A gentle, short walk exploring the life and times of the Staffordshire Potteries' most famous son, Josiah Wedgwood.
❶ From **visitors' centre** drive head **L** across river and then **R** up drive towards **Barlaston Hall**. Go past this hall and continue along metalled road as far as crossroads in **Barlaston**. Josiah set up his first pottery factory in Burslem in 1759 and revolutionised what up until that point had been a cottage industry. Rather than rely on family members he paid people to work in the factory. A decade later and with business booming Josiah built a bigger factory in Burslem and this became a model for other pottery manufacturers. At crossroads turn **R** and after 250yds (229m), just past St John's Church on your **L**, head **L** along wide gravel track. This track passes through broad expanse of open farmland, with sweeping (if not altogether dramatic) views of Trent and Mersey canal to **R** and, beyond, flood plain of Trent Valley.

❷ After about 800yds (732m), you get to gate ahead of you: from here follow less obvious track **R**, around to stile where another track comes in on **L**. After crossing stile head **R** along track, straight over railway, before bearing **R** to bridge over canal. Go over bridge and take steps down to **L**.
❸ At bottom of steps head **L** and then follow canal all way to 1st bridge (at Barlaston) and then 2nd (at Wedgwood Station). The **Trent and Mersey Canal**, completed in 1777, linked the River Trent at Derwent Mouth near Derby with the Bridgewater Canal at Preston Brook, near the mouth of the Mersey. This effectively meant that the country could be navigated all the way from the west coast to the east and that fine clay from the West Country could be shipped to the doorstep of Josiah Wedgwood's factories. Head **L** here, up to metalled road, and then **R**, back towards visitors' centre. To find out more about Wedgwood, visit The Wedgwood Story **visitors' centre**.

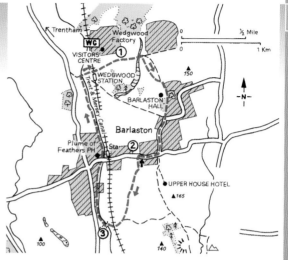

HANBURY *THE CRATER*

4¼ miles (6.8km) 2hrs **Ascent:** 240ft (73m)
Paths: Meadow tracks and bridleways, 27 stiles
Suggested map: aqua3 OS Explorer 245 The National Forest
Grid reference: SK 170279
Parking: St Werburgh's Church car park

The site of the biggest non-nuclear explosion of World War II.
❶ From car park, go back along Church Lane and after 150yds (137m), go **R** through car park and over stile. Cross field to pair of stiles over road and continue across field to gate, then to corner of hedge. With hedge to your **R**, head for **Knightsfield Farm**.
❷ Go through farm courtyard and along rough surfaced track. As it bears **R**, follow footpath sign, **L**, across stiles, keeping hedge to **L**. At turning circle, go across to stile and footbridge before continuing, with hedge to **L**, to stile before road.
❸ Turn **R**, then 1st **L** before **Crown Inn**, across car park. Cross into field ahead to stile at bottom. Continue up next field, crossing stile under tree at top.
❹ Where hedge goes **L**, follow it across stile and aim for **R** of **Hanbury Park**. In top **R-H** corner of field, go through gate to road. Turn **L**, going through gate into farm courtyard, then through gate to **R**.

Continue on bridleway to **Woodend**.
❺ At road head **R** for 100yds (91m) then **L** through gate, to stile in fence to **R**. Head diagonally **L** across field to stile, continue across next field to stile. Cross **Capertition Wood** to open field, continuing with hedge to **L**, up hill, across stile, then down to stile. At end of field go through gate.
❻ Skirting to **L** of **farm**, climb over succession of stiles before turning **L** through iron gate. Head across field keeping hedge to **L**. At end cross stile on **L** and go **R** towards **R-H** end of trees.
❼ Head **R** up short hill to stile, continue to stile amongst trees. Head round to **L** to **crater**. Follow path round to **L**, past **memorial** stone, to bridleway leading away.
❽ At end of bridleway head **L** across field, keeping hedge to **R**. Go through gap in hedge ahead and continue ahead to gate at top. At end of hedge on **L** go through gate and stile to return to **Hanbury**.

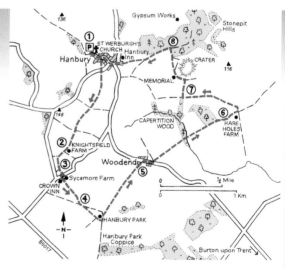

STAFFORD CASTLE *HILLTOP HOME*

3½ miles (5.7km) 1hr 30min **Ascent:** 240ft (73m)
Paths: Pavement, gravel tracks and grass trails, 2 stiles
Suggested map: aqua3 OS Explorer 244 Cannock Chase
Grid reference: SJ 918232
Parking: Ample paid parking near start point

A short walk from Stafford town around one of the county's oldest monuments.
❶ From roundabout head away from town, over river. After 100yds (91m) go **L** along Castle Street and over railway bridge to main road with roundabout. Cross and walk along path to next road.
❷ Bear **R** here, heading diagonally across road and through avenue of trees on other side, following public footpath signs to **L** of houses. Follow gravel track all way up through middle of **golf course** and, at top of this track, keep going straight across field ahead of you, following faint grass trail to stile and, shortly after, to path into wood, signed to **castle visitor centre**. Visitor centre makes an ideal starting point for any visit, packed as it is with information on the Norman Conquest and featuring a short film on history of castle itself. There's also shop selling snacks, souvenirs and guides, not just on the castle, but on other castles, churches and historical buildings

throughout Staffordshire.
❸ After following castle's self-guided walk (¾ mile/1.2km) go back way you came, along bottom of wood to stile, and skirt **L** around outside of wood. At corner of wood go through hedge and head **R**. Continue down through fields following footpath signs to Doxey. Descending through these fields also serves to illustrate how tough it must have been for the Saxon forces to charge in the opposite direction; even assuming they survived the onslaught of arrows from Norman long-bows, by time they got anywhere near the castle they'd have been absolutely spent.
❹ When you come to junction and road ahead, go **L** to T-junction and then **R** towards Doxey and **Burleyfields**. Follow track round to **R** and back towards **Stafford**. When track runs out, bear **R** on to road and then **L** across roundabout. Just before next roundabout (Point ❶) head **L**, retracing your steps back into Stafford.

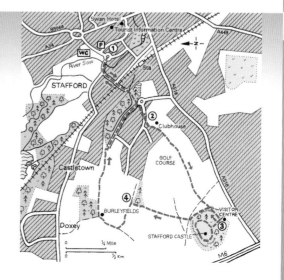

Staffordshire

553 SHUGBOROUGH *THROUGH THE ESTATE*

4¾ miles (7.7km) 2hrs **Ascent:** 180ft (55m) ▲
Paths: Gravel tracks, roads and tow paths
Suggested map: aqua3 OS Explorer 244 Cannock Chase
Grid reference: SK 004205
Parking: Ample parking at start point

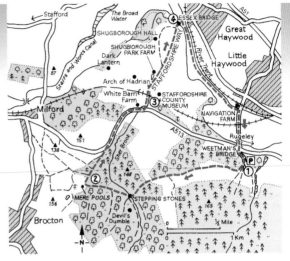

To Staffordshire's greatest country house.

❶ Take **R-H** path at end of Seven Springs car park and continue **R** at fork shortly after. Follow wide gravel track, ignoring all paths to **L** or **R**, and continue as far as **Stepping Stones**. Ford stream here and head **R** as far as major T-junction.

❷ Head **R** here, following **Staffordshire Way** footpath sign. Continue along wide gravel track, again ignoring less obvious paths to **L** or **R**, as far as A513. Cross road carefully and follow it **R** for 400yds (366m) before turning **L**, again following **Staffordshire Way** footpath signs.

❸ Follow metalled road past **Staffordshire County Museum** and **Shugborough Park Farm**. Shortly after Park Farm, continue along Staffordshire Way, ignoring more direct path **L** to house itself. Follow bridleway all way to **Essex Bridge**. If you do want closer look at façade, head **L** instead and follow path round past front of house; it's signed as private drive but this is meant more for cars, and it is open to public when grounds are open. If you continue all way round you'll eventually rejoin main route just before **Essex Bridge**. From close range it's also interesting to note that the columns aren't made of stone at all, but wood that has been clad with slate and painted to look like stone, a solution that would have been considerably cheaper.

❹ By way of short diversion, just 350yds (320m) to north of **Essex Bridge**, heading **L** along tow path, is junction of Trent and Mersey and Staffordshire and Worcestershire canals. Toll-keeper's cottage has disappeared, but toll-house with arched windows and kiosk still remain on south side of latter. Go across bridge and head **R** along canal (cross **Essex Bridge** and canal to reach Lockhouse Restaurant on **L**). Follow tow path for 1 mile (1.6km) and, at **Navigation Farm**, head **R** on metalled road. Carry on over **Weetman's Bridge**, cross A513 carefully, and continue up short drive back to car park.

554 ABBOTS BROMLEY *HORN DANCING*

5 miles (8km) 2hrs **Ascent:** 525ft (160m) ▲
Paths: Roads, grass trails and gravel tracks, 10 stiles
Suggested map: aqua3 OS Explorer 244 Cannock Chase
Grid reference: SK 079245
Parking: Ample street parking in Abbots Bromley

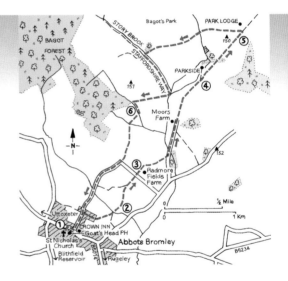

A colourful and ancient tradition in one of the county's charming villages.

❶ From Church Lane go **R**, along B5014 and **L** just before **Crown Inn**. At top of hill turn **R** along Swan Lane and at end head **R** along path to stile. Head diagonally **L** across field to gap in hedge. Go through gap and continue across next field to footbridge. After footbridge keep following faint grassy trail to stile near top **R-H** corner of field.

❷ Bear slightly **L** across middle of field to stile. Carry on straight up next field, keeping hedge just to your **L**. across series of stiles and fields until you get to road. Head across road, following footpath sign and, just as track heads hard **R**, go straight on over concrete stile and across next field.

❸ After another stile, follow curve of field to **R** as far as metalled road. Go **L** here, following road and track to **Parkside** farm gate. Just before this gate, go through gate on **R** and then **L** through series of gates.

❹ Continue across field, with hedge to **L**, before crossing funnel-shaped section of meadow to hedge on far side. Follow this hedge to stile and wood. Bear diagonally **R** through band of trees to pair of footbridges and stile. Leaving wood behind, head for far **R-H** corner of field.

❺ At road opposite **Park Lodge** turn **L**. Just after crossing **Story Brook** head **L**. At far **L-H** corner of field, follow hedge round to **R** and cross small copse with help of pair of stiles. Continue to follow fence to corner of **Bagot Forest** then go **L** through hedge. Follow another hedge just to your **R** for about 200yds (183m) and then go **R**, through gate.

❻ Follow **Staffordshire Way** footpath sign through next field, keeping hedge just to your **R**. At far **R-H** corner of field go through gap in fence and follow hedge to your **L** to gate at top of field. Carry on along track as far as metalled road. Go straight on to get back to start.

555 CANNOCK CHASE *MEMORIALS TO THE BRAVE*

4 miles (6.4km) 1hr 30min **Ascent:** 361ft (110m) ▲
Paths: Gravel tracks and roads
Suggested map: aqua3 OS Explorer 244 Cannock Chase
Grid reference: SK 980181
Parking: Ample parking at start point
Note: Beware of cyclists

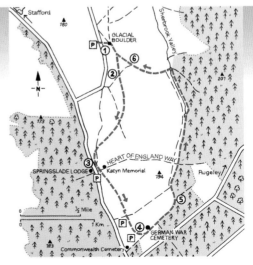

This heathland walk around the wartime cemeteries serves as a poignant reminder of less peaceful times.

❶ From **Glacial Boulder**, walk away from road along narrow dirt trail for about 40 paces and then turn **R** along wide gravel track. When you get to fork, go **R**, following **Heart of England Way** footpath sign.

❷ At next major fork, continue in same direction (ignoring footpath off to **R**). At next path crossroads, again carry straight on as path curves gradually around to **R**. Continue along this track across 2 more path crossroads until your path curves round to **L** alongside road. At point where another wide track comes in from **L**, go straight on rather than taking shortcut down to road.

❸ After crossing narrow surfaced road opposite **Springslade Lodge**, continue up dirt track and across path crossroads. After about 500yds (457m) you come to T-junction in path that requires dog-leg **R** then **L** to keep going in same direction through car park. Continue in this direction to 2nd car park and, as track curves around to **L**, another metalled road.

❹ Turn **L** past **German War Cemetery** until road becomes wide gravel track. Continue along this track, down into woods, and when you get to fork go **L** down hill, ignoring path heading uphill to **R**.

❺ Continue along bottom of valley for 1 mile (1.6km), staying to **R** of stream, until you get to obvious ford. Cross stream using stepping stones. At junction on other side head away from stream following track **L** around bottom of hill ahead, rather than **R**, straight over top of it. Follow this track as it curves round to **R**, all way to top of hill.

❻ Continue across plateau until path starts to descend other side, at which point you rejoin path, heading **R**, back towards start and car park.

Staffordshire

LICHFIELD *SOARING HEAVEN ON EARTH*

2½ miles (4km) 1hr **Ascent:** Negligible

Paths: Roads, surfaced paths and dirt trails
Suggested map: aqua3 OS Explorers 232 Nuneaton & Tamworth; 244 Cannock Chase
Grid reference: SK 118095 (on Explorer 232)
Parking: Ample paid parking in Lichfield town centre

A town walk and a magnificent cathedral.
1 From **tourist information centre** head **R** along Bore Street and then **L** along Conduit Street, leading to Market Square. Pass Market Square on your **L** and carry straight along Dam Street, past tea shops and cafés, until you get to Pool Walk. Go **L** here, keeping pool on your R-H side, until you get to Beacon Street.
2 Go diagonally **R** over Beacon Street to public toilets and entrance to park. Skirt around **L-H** edge of park, keeping first bowling lawn and then tennis courts to your **R**. After tennis courts follow path round to **R** and, at next path junction, walk **L**, continuing around edge of park.
3 At car park bear slightly **R**, following path to far end of playing fields. After path has entered narrow band of trees, and just before **A51**, turn **R** along narrow dirt trail and carry on to **golf course**. Just before golf course, turn **R** and follow small brook back along edge of playing fields to little duck pond.

(Canoes for hire in summer.) Continue on past pond before crossing over footbridge to **L** to Shaw Lane.
4 Follow Shaw Lane to **Beacon Street**, then go **R** for 150yds (137m) and then **L** along The Close to cathedral. If you're not in any rush, visit cathedral before continuing. There's an excellent shop with leaflets and guides and free leaflet is also available, which describes the cathedral's highlights. Bear to **R** of cathedral and, at end of The Close, just after Cathedral Coffee Shop, go **R** down Dam Street and then immediately **L** along footpath to **Stowe Pool**. From far end of Stowe Pool you can look back at cathedral's towers and see through windows from one side to the other, giving the impression that they're lighter and more delicate than stone.
5 When path divides into 2 parallel tracks, follow cycle path sign. Continue around pool and back to Dam Street, before retracing your steps to tourist information centre at start.

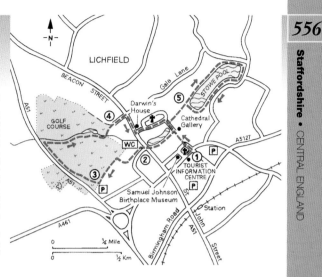

TRYSULL *WINE-LOVER'S DELIGHT*

5¼ miles (8.4km) 1hr 45min **Ascent:** 270ft (82m)

Paths: Roads, grass and dirt trails, gravel tracks, 3 stiles
Suggested map: aqua3 OS Explorer 219 Wolverhampton & Dudley
Grid reference: SJ 852942
Parking: Ample street parking in Trysull

An escarpment walk taking in a vineyard.
1 From **All Saints' Church**, head north along **Trysull Holloway** for 100yds (91m) and, after crossing small brook, go **L** along Church Lane as far as Seisdon (this might be muddy after heavy rain, so suitable footwear is recommended). Turn **L** on to road (there is no pavement here, so exercise caution) and then take first **R** towards **Lea Farm**.
2 Follow this road to T-junction with **Fox Road**, heading **L** then immediately **R** towards **Woodcote**. Stay on this track round to **R**, following signs for **Staffordshire Way** and, at top of lane, go through swing gate to continue along narrower dirt trail. At corner of field follow path **L** around edge of field and then immediately **R** up to Wolmore Lane.
3 Head **L** along this metalled road and then **R** along **Tinker's Castle Road**. At top of hill, just before **cottage** on **L**, head **L** up path between wall and fence. Continue along edge of escarpment for 1¼ miles

(2km), until it joins B4176. Just after junction, head **R** along track down to **vineyard**. Just after coming from here, keep going along B4176 for 50yds (46m), and turn off **L** over stile (there's no pavement, but plenty of grass on L-H side of road).
4 Go across middle of field to stile then follow hedge just to your **R** in same direction. At far **R-H** corner of this field keep ahead, aiming for tree in hedge ahead. Go through wide gap in hedge and bear slightly **L** to cross this next field all way to **Crockington Lane**. (If this field is impassable because of crops, it may be easier to bear **R** along hedge to **Fiershill Farm**, but this means longer walk along road into Trysull.)
5 Cross stile to Crockington Lane then go **R** for 100yds (91m), before turning **L** through kissing gate. Go straight on across this field to another gate and then down track between houses to **Seisdon Road**. Turn **R** here, back to start.

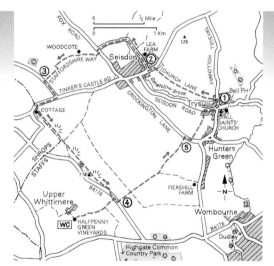

KINVER *ROCK HOUSES*

2¾ miles (4.4km) 1hr **Ascent:** 374ft (114m)

Paths: Wide gravel tracks
Suggested map: aqua3 OS Explorer 219 Wolverhampton & Dudley
Grid reference: SJ 835836
Parking: Ample parking in car park at start

A short walk combining curious cave dwellings with some of the best views in Staffordshire.
1 From National Trust car park, head back along road towards **Kinver** village. Within 100yds (91m), after going **R** at fork in road, follow public footpath signs to **R**, up into woods. Once you're in woods proper, take obvious stepped path **L** to small clearing and then turn 90 degrees to **R** to follow short, steep path to viewpoint.
2 Enjoy the lovely views before continuing along top of escarpment, following wide, gravel track running more or less alongside western edge of ancient rectangular earthworks to your **L**, with glimpsed views across Severn Valley through trees to your **R**. After 400yds (366m) you will come to end of clearing. Take fork to your **L** here, up slight rise at corner of earthworks, before carrying on along escarpment top and past trig point.

3 Staying on highest path, continue as far as National Trust boundary gate and then continue straight along main track avoiding smaller trails off to **L** and **R**. Path descends gradually to picnic spot with benches, an information board and signs for **Staffordshire Way** and **Worcestershire Way**. Narrow track to **R** leads back down to road and public toilet if required, although it criss-crosses other paths and it's very easy to lose your bearings!
4 For this reason, it's easiest to return way you came. From path junction, head back along escarpment to viewpoint. At end, head **R** then **L**, back down to clearing, and then **L** again down wooden steps, through trees to road. Follow road **L** as far as car park. For those armed with more detailed OS map, there is suitable alternative which returns via forested slopes to west of ridge top, but because of number of little tracks that cross back and forth, it's difficult to give adequate directions here.

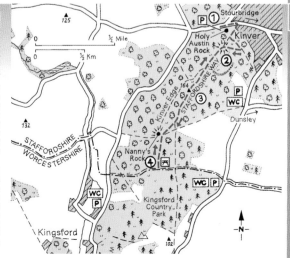

Hertfordshire

559 THERFIELD *FAIR ON THE DEWEY DOWNS*

3½ miles (5.7km) 1hr 30min Ascent: 120ft (36m) ⚠
Paths: Green lanes, tracks, field paths, village lanes, 1 stile
Suggested map: aqua3 OS Explorer 194 Hertford & Bishop's Stortford
Grid reference: TL 335370
Parking: Around Therfield village green

A walk between Therfield and Kelshall along winding green lanes.

❶ From **Therfield** village green walk down Church Lane and into parish churchyard. Go through gap in railings to south of southern porch on to green lane, with vicarage garden on L and field on R. At footpath post keep straight on along grassy margin L of field, then go across field to kissing gate. Cross pasture to stile and over this turn **R** into green lane, **Duck's Green**. Ignoring footpaths to R and L, track bears **L**, now following parish boundary. Where path meets track, turn **R** into green lane.

❷ Follow green lane, which soon turns **R**, climbing gently between ancient hedges. At track junction go **L** and continue climbing, passing footpath junction before reaching crest of hill. Ignore track turning **L** – carry straight on along loosely metalled track.

❸ At crest turn **R** on to bridleway, with fence and paddocks to L, arable land to your R. This becomes

track through arable land. At bridleway post, where hedge reappears, turn **R** into green lane, soon hedged only on L. At post-and-railed sheep enclosure go **L**. Then, through gate, turn **L** to another gate into lane and cross to church lychgate.

❹ Visit **Church of St Faith**, entering through 15th-century door. Leave churchyard from behind chancel on to path between fence and walls ('Hertfordshire Way'). At lane turn **L**. At road junction jink **R** then **L** to walk past telephone box and village hall.

❺ Continue past **Fox Hall farm** and **pond**. Turn **R** at footpath sign, just before thatched cottage, on to track initially between hedges, then beside patchy hedge. At end of field go through hedge and over footbridge. Turn sharp **L** to walk round 2 sides of small field. At track go **L** to walk past tall **water tower**. At road turn **R** and follow it past **Tuthill Farm** and Victorian estate cottages. Turn **R** past Bell House into Pedlars Lane, which winds back to **Therfield** village green.

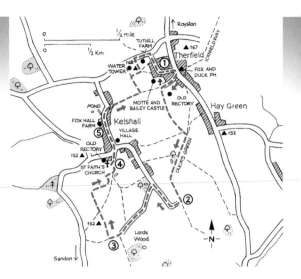

560 BUNTINGFORD *A MEDIEVAL MARKET*

8 miles (12.9km) 3hrs Ascent: 120ft (37m) ⚠
Paths: Tracks, lanes, field paths, village roads, 2 stiles
Suggested map: aqua3 OS Explorer 194 Hertford & Bishop's Stortford
Grid reference: TL 360295
Parking: Buntingford High Street car park

Visit the old parish church, Wyddial village and return past manor houses.

❶ From High Street car park cross road; turn into Church Street. Descend past Fox and Duck pub. Go **L** into Wyddial Road, then **R** over **River Rib** ford into **The Causeway**. Lane becomes winding and rural. At public bridleway sign go **L** to visit the remains of **St Bartholomew's Church**.

❷ From churchyard keep along green lane downhill to road. Turn **R**; follow road uphill. At bend go **L** at bridleway sign, following grassy path between arable fields. At road go ahead through **Wyddial** to **church**.

❸ From churchyard continue along road to bend. Turn **R**, by footpath sign, to walk along **R** side of hedge. Turn **L** at end of field, over footbridge. Continue east, first on R-H side of hedge, then on **L**, to farm access road. Turn **R** along this to **Beauchamps**.

❹ Pass to L of **Beauchamps**, initially alongside neat hedge, then bear **L** off concrete track on to grassy

track, poplars on R. Continue to track at brow of hill; turn **R**. Past **Beauchamp's Wood** track descends to valley floor before turning **L** and ascending to next crest. Turn **R** by concrete hardstanding. Descending gradually, follow metalled track to **L**.

❺ At road cross on to drive to **Alswick Hall**. Passing **pond** and farm buildings, then hall itself, route follows green lane to **Owles Hall**.

❻ Beyond **Owles Hall** turn **R** on to lane. Descend westwards, to cross valley of **Haley Hill Ditch**. Ascend towards **Buntingford**, **Sainsbury's distribution centre** to L. At end of Owles Lane turn **R** to walk along Roman **Ermine Street**.

❼ Turn **L** past **Railway pub** into Aspenden Road, **R** into Luynes Rise. At footpath sign go **R**, the tarmac path winding along beside **River Rib**, with modern housing on L. Beyond cottages emerge into High Street. Turn **L**, passing **St Peter's Church** and Seth Ward Almshouses, to start.

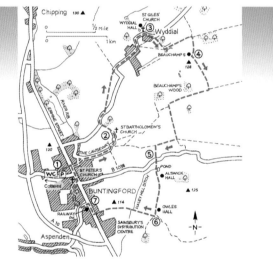

561 GREAT HORMEAD *RICH WITH CORN*

4 miles (6.4km) 2hrs Ascent: 85ft (26m) ⚠
Paths: Field paths, tracks, quiet country lanes, village road, 5 stiles
Suggested map: aqua3 OS Explorer 194 Hertford & Bishop's Stortford
Grid reference: TL 402298
Parking: Horseshoe Hill, Great Hormead

A walk round Great and Little Hormead, east of the young River Quin.

❶ Start on Horseshoe Hill, turning just west of **Three Tuns** pub. Uphill, you bear **R** at war memorial, and follow lane to St Nicholas', the parish church of **Great Hormead**. From churchyard continue along lane, turning **L** at junction ('**Little Hormead** and Furneux Pelham'). Eventually passing **Little Hormead Bury Farm**, its barns now converted to houses, reach Norman parish **church of Little Hormead**.

❷ Continue along lane. Opposite **Bulls Farm** go **L** at footpath sign into cultivated land, initially following hedges north through 2 fields, then turn **L** and **R** alongside hedge to junction. Carry straight on along track. At first following this becomes footpath, leading to main street of **Great Hormead**.

❸ Turn **R** on to road. Go beyond L turn, **Hall Lane**. When opposite thatched barn, go to L of chevron-style bend sign to inconspicuous start of footpath. This

follows course of **Black Ditch** stream, sometimes on L side, sometimes on R, the stream and hedge eventually bearing **L**. Cross stream on bridge into pasture and head for footpath post at lane.

❹ Turn **L** to walk along lane, initially with hedge on L only, then on both sides. The lane continues winding gently downhill – you will see electricity pylon on your L. Pass beneath its cables to go **L** at footpath sign on to track, with hedge to your R. Over brow descend towards **Hormead Hall**. Go to **R** of cattle grid to stile and then head diagonally **L** across pasture to reach another stile.

❺ Once over this go **L** along edge of arable field. Look to L here, through hedge, to see the remains of **Hormead Hall's** medieval moat. Turn **L** out of field on to lane and then turn **R** along another, Hall Lane, to road junction. Turn **R** into **Hormead Road**, main street of **Great Hormead**. A **L** turn past **Three Tuns** pub returns you to Horseshoe Hill.

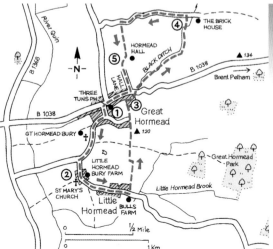

Hertfordshire

MUCH HADHAM *GORGEOUS PALACE, SOLEMN TEMPLE*

4½ miles (7.2km) 2hrs 30min Ascent: 115ft (35m)
Paths: Field paths and tracks, 4 stiles
Suggested map: aqua3 OS Explorer 194 Hertford & Bishop's Stortford
Grid reference: TL 428197
Parking: North end of High Street, just south of B1004 L turn

A walk through Much Hadham.

1 Walk along High Street into village, going **R** just before **war memorial**, over stile beside ball-finialled gate piers. Follow drive, then go **L** to stile at corner of tennis courts. Now in parkland of **Moor Place**, head diagonally to skirt to **L** of farm buildings. Go to **R-H** corner of wood and join farm access track. Cross drive on to metalled track, bear **L** along granite slabway to kissing gate beside **Dell Cottage**.

2 Cross road to footpath ('Windmill Way') and cross arable field, heading **L** of rendered cottage. Follow track behind gardens to road which bears **R** past telephone box, becoming metalled lane and later hedgeless track in cultivated land. Where this swings **L**, carry straight on to valley floor, bearing **R** at cottages, still along field edge. Head towards **Camwell Hall**, attractive 15th-century house.

3 At farm bear **L** on to its access drive, which becomes lane, passing **Wynches** on **L**. Turn **R** on to

B1004 to descend to **Hadham Mill**. Turn **L** at lane after crossing bridge over **River Ash**.

4 Follow lane and go **L** through gate with bridleway and **Hertfordshire Way** signs. Turn **R** along track and then bear **L**, not uphill to **R**. Follow delightful, waymarked path, with steeply sloping woods to **R** and river to **L**. Eventually reach lane.

5 Go **L** here and follow it to turn **L** at T-junction by **Sidehill House**. At kissing gate go **R** ('Hertfordshire Way'), to walk along floor of valley, **River Ash** to **L**. At lane go straight on, then go **R** ('Public Footpath 21') over **River Ash**. Climb steeply through copse. Turn **L** on to metalled lane, wooded river cliff now on **L**.

6 Just before road junction go **L** at public footpath sign. Bear **L** (not straight on) to descend steeply on hollow way track through woods down to river. Cross footbridge and follow path to churchyard.

7 Visit **St Andrew's Church**. Continue westwards, back to High Street.

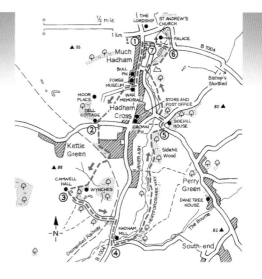

LITTLE HADHAM *A ROYAL SLEEPOVER*

4 miles (6.4km) 1hr 45min Ascent: 125ft (100m)
Paths: Field paths, tracks, roads and village pavements, 2 stiles
Suggested map: aqua3 OS Explorer 194 Hertford & Bishop's Stortford
Grid reference: TL 440228
Parking: Albury Road, Little Hadham (north of traffic lights at A120 crossroads)

To the picturesque 'ends' and hamlets of Little Hadham and to Hadham Hall.

1 Walk uphill on **Albury Road**, to footpath sign on **R** ('To Church ½ and Bishop's Stortford 2¾'). Take this path alongside arable field, descending to **River Ash**. Cross footbridge to climb on to grassy baulk between fields. This leads to church, whose tower peeps from churchyard surrounded by trees.

2 Leave churchyard with gabled rear of **Church End** farmhouse on your **R** to enter lane. Go **L**, past old church hall (now bungalow). Follow track round to **R** of farm buildings to climb to brow of hill. At public bridleway junction-post turn **L**. Modern little development of houses called **Baud Close** stands behind brick-built barn, now converted into house.

3 From central courtyard of **Hadham Hall**, pass gatehouse to walk down lime avenue to main road, **A120** (**Roman Road**). Turn **R**; shortly turn **L** down Millfield Lane. Junction is highest point on walk.

4 Beyond **Millfield Cottage** go **R**, on to metalled green lane by public byway sign where lane turns **L**. At fork go **R**, still on hedged green lane. Passing **Muggins Wood**, climb to lane, path overhung by trees. Turn **R**; follow lane, descending into **Hadham Ford**.

5 At junction, with **war memorial** in small triangular green, turn **R** along main street. The lane crosses river. At public footpath sign opposite **Nag's Head pub** turn **R**, across footbridge leading to stile.

6 Over stile turn **L** and head for **L-H** corner of wood, **river** on your **L**. Continue uphill to stile by gate, joining track which curves **R**, past trees, and then goes **L** between arable fields with **St Celia's Church** in **Little Hadham** ahead. The path passes paddocks on **L**, then jinks past **primary school**, emerging on to **A120** past single-storey thatched cottage.

7 Turn **L** along pavement, past school, to traffic lights. Cross river bridge to buildings at staggered central crossroads. Turn **R**, back into **Albury Road**.

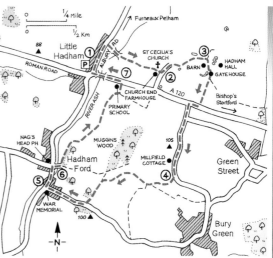

STANDON *ROMANS IN THE RIB VALLEY*

5 miles (8km) 2hrs 30min Ascent: 190ft (57m)
Paths: Tracks, paths, some roads and former railway line, 5 stiles
Suggested map: aqua3 OS Explorer 194 Hertford & Bishop's Stortford
Grid reference: TL 396223
Parking: High Street, Standon (off A120)

Along the Rib Valley.

1 Walk south along **Standon** High Street to church. At junction with Paper Mill Lane go **L** into **Hadham Road**. Beyond village turn **L** at public footpath ('Frogshall Cottages'). Go **L** along edge of cultivated field and continue as path becomes green lane descending to **A120**. Turn **R**, uphill. Before bend, go **L** at public bridleway sign.

2 Follow green lane, eventually descend into valley, bear **R**, keeping stream on **R**. At end of arable field cross parish boundary to climb away from stream, with oak woods on **R**. Pass old farm buildings on your **L** to reach road.

3 Cross to bridleway sign by post box. Keep by metal park fence to skirt **Upp Hall**. Cross to corner of field into green lane, initially with woods away to your **L**, to ascend to lane.

4 Go **L** on to lane and follow this until, passing cottages, go to **L** of No 28, on to path that passes

behind gardens to your **R** and descends to road.

5 Here, in **Braughing**, turn **L**, then turn **R** at Square into **St Mary's** churchyard. From church descend to lane junction with Church End. Turn **R** down Fleece Lane. This becomes footpath, which crosses **River Quin** on an iron bridge and climbs to road.

6 Turn **L** briefly on to **B1368**, then **L** again down Malting Lane. A footbridge bypasses **River Quin** ford. Turn **R** into **Ford Street**. Once out of village turn **L** on to **B1368**, shortly crossing **River Rib**.

7 Go **L** at footpath sign just before old railway bridge. Bear **R** to former trackbed to turn **L** on to it – **Roman town site** is on **R**. Follow track, sometimes beside it, with river to **L**. Eventually pass **school** on your **R** and bear **R** at signpost to cross trackbed. At cul-de-sac, Meadow Walk, turn **R** to **Station Road**.

8 Turn **L** along **Station Road** and **L** on to road, **A120**. Pass former **Standon Flour Mills**. Cross road at crossing; cross bridge. Turn **R** into High Street.

565 ASHWELL *PLAGUE STRIKES*

6½ miles (10.4km) 2hrs 30min Ascent: 140ft (43m)
Paths: Tracks and paths, some lanes around Ashwell, 1 stile
Suggested map: aqua3 OS Explorers 193 Luton & Stevenage; 208 Bedford & St Neots
Grid reference: TL 268396 (on Explorer 193)
Parking: East end of High Street, outside United Reformed church

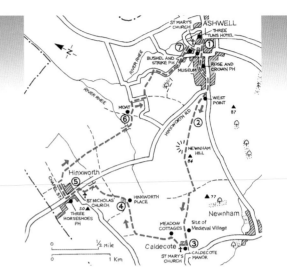

See evidence of the bubonic plague before strolling along the chalky downs.

❶ Walk west down **Ashwell** High Street, curving **L** to ascend to junction. Turn **R** into **Hinxworth Road**. Shortly after passing gates to **West Point**, go straight on to track at bridleway sign, road bearing **R**.

❷ Ascend **Newnham Hill** with views back to **Ashwell church** tower. Descend to bridleway junction. Turn **R** alongside hedge, turn **L** at footpath post to go through hedge and continue westward.

❸ Beyond former farm cottages turn **R** on to road to walk past **Caldecote Manor** and **St Mary's Church** (not open). Follow road until just before **Meadow Cottages**. Here go **L** to skirt copse, then keep along track between fields. At deep ditch, go **L** few paces to cross it. Continue ahead, aiming for **L** end of hedge, turning **R** to walk beside it, and then through pasture.

❹ At lane keep ahead past medieval **Hinxworth Place** to skirt to **R** of scrub. Go diagonally over arable land, heading for **Hinxworth** church. Go through hedge, beside deep ditch, then **L** over footbridge. Go along field edge before turning **R** into churchyard via kissing gate.

❺ Leave churchyard along short lime avenue, turning **L** up High Street, past war memorial clock tower. Turn **R** into **Chapel Street**. At footpath sign go **R** on to cinder track which curves **L** to pass between 2 cottages, then through arable fields. At crossroads pass farm buildings to descend over arable land. Cross footbridge over **River Rhee**, go diagonally **L** in pasture to cross 2nd bridge. Turn **L** along field edge.

❻ At lane go **L** past cottage and opposite go **R**, with **moat** in field on **L**. Turn **R** on to lane and, where this turns **R**, go **L**, path curving **R** through farmland to stile. Over stile turn **R**; stay on lane into Rollys Lane.

❼ At T-junction go **R** into Mill Street, visit **church**. Cross Swan Street to path beside **Ashwell Village Museum**, and back to High Street.

566 BALDOCK *ON THE GREAT NORTH ROAD*

4½ miles (7.2km) 2hrs Ascent: 95ft (29m)
Paths: Pavements, lanes and field paths, stretch of old Great North Road, 1 stile
Suggested map: aqua3 OS Explorer 193 Luton & Stevenage
Grid reference: TL 099666
Parking: In High Street, Baldock

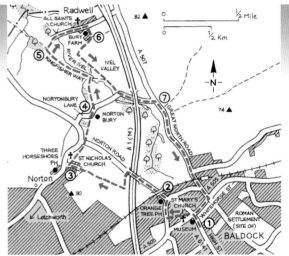

From a Roman and medieval town into water-meadows by the river bank.

❶ Head north along **High Street** to crossroads and into Church Street, then **L** into **St Mary's** churchyard. Pass church and go **L** by church hall, alongside narrow extension to churchyard. Turn **R** on **Norton Road**. Beyond **Orange Tree pub**, turn **L**.

❷ Follow **Norton Road** under railway. Immediately after road crosses A1(M) in its cutting go **L** to stile with footpath sign. Turn **L** along edge of farmland, with A1(M) down on **L**, and go **R** on to grassy path across arable ground to **R** of pylon. Cross brow of hill, descend to hedge with 2 cottages to **R** of opening. Through opening reach lane leading into old **Norton**.

❸ Turn **R** through war memorial lychgate. Go to **R** of **St Nicholas' Church** to gate into paddock. Follow hollow trackway and ignore via kissing gate. Cross lane towards **Nortonbury Lane**, but go to its **R**, to footpath climbing between overgrown hedges to edge of field. Descend and turn **R** on to lane to **Norton Bury farm**.

❹ Opposite stable buildings go to kissing gate to path running diagonally **R**, through horse paddocks. Leave through kissing gate and turn **L**, ignoring iron footbridge over **River Ivel**. Route follows waymarked **Kingfisher Way** through pasture and water-meadows by side of **River Ivel**.

❺ Keep on **Kingfisher Way**, turning **R** to pass pink-washed cottage to lane. Cross **Ivel** into **Radwell**. As lane climbs ignore **Kingfisher Way**, which turns **L**. Pass Victorian **All Saints Church** and go **R** at footpath sign by post box. Walk through yard of **Bury Farm**.

❻ At far end of farmyard turn **R**, path descending past horse chestnuts to **Ivel valley**. Turn **L** at public footpath sign and walk along grass path, river on **R**, arable fields on **L**. At road turn **L**; pass under A1(M).

❼ At old **Great North Road**, turn **R** and follow this south into **Baldock**. At traffic-light crossroads turn **R** into **Whitehorse Street** and back to **High Street**.

567 DEACON HILL *GREAT VIEWS*

6½ miles (10.4km) 2hrs 30min Ascent: 360ft (110m)
Paths: Mix of green lanes, tracks and field paths, 1 stile
Suggested map: aqua3 OS Explorer 193 Luton & Stevenage
Grid reference: TL 146317
Parking: On village roads in Pirton

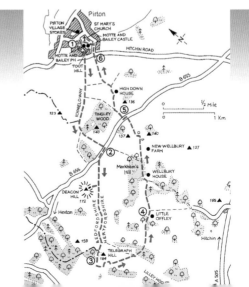

Ascend the chalk downs to Deacon Hill and descend via High Down House.

❶ Start at **St Mary's** churchyard in centre of **Pirton**. Turn **L** into Crabtree Lane, then Great Green with **Motte and Bailey pub**, to cross Hitchin Road on to bridleway, **Icknield Way**. The track climbs steadily between fields, eventually curving **L** to pass edge of **Tingley Wood**, now following county boundary. Past wood, fork **L** and continue southwards to road.

❷ Turn **R**, leaving road at lay-by on **L**, on to green lane, here ancient **Icknield Way**. At stile go **R** to climb **Deacon Hill** through chalk downland and enjoy wonderful views. Track levels out with woods to **R** then descends with **Telegraph Hill** downland on **L**.

❸ Turn **L** by information board. The track climbs downland, emerging in open fields. At crest head in direction of solitary oak, then go **R**, on to track, turning sharp **L** on grass track. Head into woodland beside waymarker following hedge.

❹ Passing **Little Offley** go between 2 outbuildings, and straight on to track. Where this bears **R**, go straight on, heading for **Wellbury House**, to lane. Turn **L** round **Wellbury House** grounds. Follow track past drive to **New Wellbury Farm** and **Park View Stables**, going **R** at waymarker into copse. Cross stables' yard to follow grassy track uphill. Once through kissing gate, bear **R** across meadow to main road (B655).

❺ Cross road, go **L** within tree belt, then **R** ('**Pirton**'). Cross field and, through gate, bear **R** into pasture, heading towards chimneystacks of picturesque **High Down House** set in remnants of parkland. Follow signs downhill then, through gate, turn sharp **L** alongside hedge. Turn **R** to follow another hedge to **Hitchin Road**.

❻ Cross road into Walnut Tree Road, then go **L** through kissing gate into pasture. Walk diagonally **R** to Pirton's **St Mary's Church** (mostly Norman) and its 12th-century **motte-and-bailey castle**.

KINGSWALDEN PARK *MANNERS AND MANSIONS*

5 miles (8km) 2hrs 30min **Ascent:** 115ft (35m)
Paths: Mix of field paths, green lanes and village lanes, 5 stiles
Suggested map: aqua3 OS Explorer 193 Luton & Stevenage
Grid reference: TL 180247
Parking: Preston village green, near the Red Lion pub

A walk in rolling hills between Preston and Kingswalden with its former deer park.

❶ From **Preston** village green walk down Hitchin Road, turn **L** into Chequers Lane. Beyond **Chequers Cottages** go **L** at footpath sign. At lane go briefly **L**, then **R** at another footpath sign, to head diagonally **R** through pasture. Passing between shelter shed and **Pond Farm**, bear **L** and follow field path to kissing gate. Turn **R** on to green lane, **Dead Woman's Lane**. Ascend then turn **L** on to another green lane, which curves **L**. Descend and at tarmac lane turn **R**.

❷ Near **Wantsend Farm** turn **L** into Plough Lane, which curves uphill. Just before **Plough pub** go **R**, over stile. Path reaches lane through playground. Out of this turn **R** to road, then **L** past **School House** and **L** again, ('Offley, **King's Walden**'). At road junction bear **R** to footpath sign beside de-restriction sign.

❸ Turn **L** on to footpath, descending beside winding hedge. Turn sharp **L** to pass farm building. Follow track until it turns **L** – here turn **R**, along edge of wood. Turn **L** at next footpath post. At end of field turn **R**, over stile, into lane to descend to **King's Walden church**.

❹ From churchyard you can glimpse **Kingswalden Bury**. Retrace your steps uphill, past yew hedge; turn **R** ('Frogmore Bottom 1') into **Kingswalden Park** with views of Kingswalden Bury house. Cross lime avenue to deer park. Go diagonally **R**. Just beyond oak, at footpath post, bear **L** towards gabled house, outside park. Leave park through kissing gate. Turn **R** on to lane. Turn **L** at junction past **Whitehall Farm**.

❺ At footpath sign go **R** by farm building, then diagonally **L**, descending across arable land and keeping to **R** of Whitehall Wood. Across lane footpath climbs on grassy track, then runs alongside hedges and through horse paddock to lane. Here turn **L**. At junction turn **R**. At boundary wall of **Temple Dinsley** park, now **Princess Helena College**, turn **L**, back to **Preston** village green.

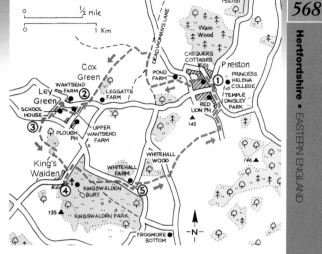

TEWIN *ALONG WATER-MEADOWS*

6 miles (9.7km) 2hrs 45min **Ascent:** 225ft (69m)
Paths: Bridleways, field paths through water-meadows, lanes, 2 stiles
Suggested map: aqua3 OS Explorer 182 St Albans & Hatfield
Grid reference: TL 271156
Parking: On roadside around Lower Green, Tewin, opposite Tewin Memorial Hall

The Mimram valley and Queen Hoo Hall.

❶ From **Lower Green** turn **L** into School Lane, then **R** at footpath ('Digswell'). Across fields track merges from **R**. Ignore footpath crossroads, go next **L** into lane. Turn **L** at junction; shortly go **R** to **St Peter's Church**.

❷ From churchyard descend to valley floor and turn **R**. Path bears **R** then turn **L** on to track. Where it veers **L** carry straight on, along field edge to merge with lane. Continue to **River Mimram** bridge.

❸ Cross bridge; climb stile on **L** to permissive path in water-meadows beside river. At footbridge cross river. Leave water-meadows via kissing gate.

❹ Cross farmland, enter scrub becoming parkland, to reach **Marden Hill**. Cross lime avenue; follow drive to road.

❺ Cross road walk alongside oak woods. Where track curves **R** go straight over stile into paddocks and out via kissing gate. Cross more cultivated ground to track. Follow this past derelict barn of **Westend Farm** to hornbeams of **Park Wood**; turn **R** along its edge.

❻ Path passes **Bramfieldbury** (not visible), then cuts across fields to its access lane. Follow this into **Bramfield**, turn **R** to church.

❼ From churchyard turn **R** into recreation ground then **L** to retrace your steps past **Grandison Arms pub** to valley floor. Turn **R** ('Beal's Wood'). Cross arable ground to corner of wood. Path goes through woods with occasional waymarker posts. At track junction briefly join it, then pass T-junction before bearing **R** to skirt pheasant enclosure. At more tracks go 2nd **R**, on to wide track. At pole barrier go **R**. Emerge from woods on to track across more cultivated land.

❽ Pass 16th-century **Queen Hoo Hall**. At lane turn **L** and go down **Tewin Hill** into **Tewin**.

❾ At main road turn **R**. Pass **Plume of Feathers pub** to **Upper Green**; go **L** to walk along edge of green to footpath behind scrub. Pass pond to metalled green lane. Follow this, eventually curving **L** to **Lower Green**.

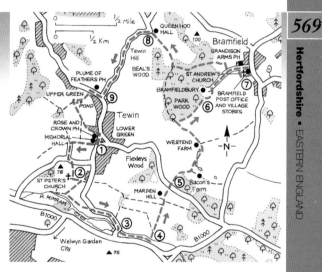

BEANE VALLEY *WALKING THE VALLEY*

6 miles (9.7km) 2hrs 45min **Ascent:** 165ft (50m)
Paths: Field paths, bridleways, village roads, 10 stiles
Suggested map: aqua3 OS Explorers 193 Luton & Stevenage; 194 Hertford & Bishop's Stortford
Grid reference: TL 297235 (on Explorer 193)
Parking: On roadside near Benington's parish church

To Walkern and its castle.

❶ Walk past entrance to **Lordship Gardens**. At green turn **L**, passing Old School Green. Before bend go **R** on to Bridleway 78. Go **L** of gates to **Walkern Hall**. Passing horse paddocks to your **L** and stucco hall to **R**, reach lane and turn **R**.

❷ Immediately past **Walkern Hall Farm** turn **L** to leave lane for bridleway ('Bassus Green'). Continue past some farm buildings on track to stream. Ascend, with woods to your **R**, curving **R** to lane. At lane go **L** to **Bassus Green** and straight on at crossroads, on to farm access lane.

❸ At **Walkern Bury Farm** turn **L**. At public bridleway sign go **R** on to green lane to descend into valley bottom. Here you turn **L** on to green lane. Follow this muddy green lane into **Walkern** village.

❹ From **church** cross **River Beane** on footbridge, then turn **L** through kissing gate into pasture. Beyond some farm buildings head diagonally to kissing gate and then to road. Turn **L** into **Walkern High Street** to walk through village, passing **school**, former brewery and **flour mills**.

❺ Once out of village, where road bears **L**, go over stile. Immediately go **L** to gate along track. Through kissing gate is start of 1-mile (1.6km) walk along Beane Valley, river winding on **L**. At footpath junction, where river swings **R**, cross it on modern footbridge.

❻ Now head between arable fields towards woodlands on ridge ahead. Cross road to footpath ('Benington 1') and climb to woods. After these you pass through **Lordship Farm** – follow waymarker arrows painted on buildings – on to an often very muddy track. Continue into cattle-grazed pasture. Across footbridge path bears **R** in more pasture to bypass **Benington Bury**, large Victorian house, to stile in far corner. The path skirts **Lordship Gardens** on your **R** and sheep pasture on your **L** to Walkern Road. Turn **R**, back to green and **St Peter's Church**.

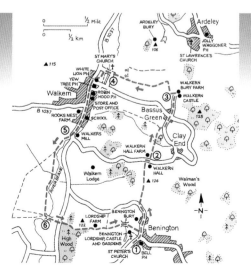

Hertfordshire • EASTERN ENGLAND

571 HUNSDON ROYAL HUNTING DAYS

6 miles (9.7km) 2hrs 30min Ascent: 150ft (46m)
Paths: Trackless arable ground, paths, canal tow path, verges and pavements
Suggested map: aqua3 OS Explorer 194 Hertford & Bishop's Stortford
Grid reference: TL 417140
Parking: Along High Street, Hunsdon, near and west of Crown pub

Through the former parkland of Hunsdon House, a royal estate, to the Stort Valley.

❶ Walk east along High Street. At parish pump bear **R** into **Drury Lane**. At its end go through gates to Gilston Park Estate, then straight ahead on farm access track between arable fields and remnants of lime avenue. Path skirts to **L** of **Hunsdon Lodge Farm**, then runs through more cultivated fields, bearing **R** to cross track and enter woodland. Out of woods cross concrete road (copse to your **R**), then go straight on across more cloying ground.

❷ Halfway across this field, at a waymarker post marking T-junction of footpaths, turn **R** and descend arable prairie to track. Cross and head for **R-H** end of vestigial hedgerow. Here join track which becomes green lane. Descend, with stream shortly appearing alongside. At lane turn **R** by footpath sign to **Acorn Street** and **Hunsdon**. Just before **Eastwick Hall Farm** turn **L** over stile by footpath post.

❸ Descend alongside hedge. By pylon bear **L** on track that winds to road. Horse-grazed paddocks on each side contain earthworks of **Eastwick Manor**.

❹ At lane turn **R** and descend to crossroads, by pub and church, in **Eastwick** village. Go along Eastwick Road, **Lion pub** on R. Follow lane to **A414**; cross with care. Take lane that crosses **River Stort** on ford bypass footbridge. Continue to **Lee and Stort Navigation**.

❺ At **Parndon Mill Lock** cross lock bridge; turn **R** on to canal tow path. Follow this for 1 mile (1.6km). Cross canal again at **Hunsdon Lock**, then double back to gate to cross single-arch bridge over mill leet.

❻ Follow lane uphill to cross **A414** dual carriageway again. Follow Hunsdon road (verges mostly on R-H side). Trees in grounds of **Hunsdon House** appear on R and then **St Dunstan's Church**.

❼ Continue along road, pavement soon appearing on R-H side. Main road bears **R** into **Acorn Street**. Follow this back into **Hunsdon** village.

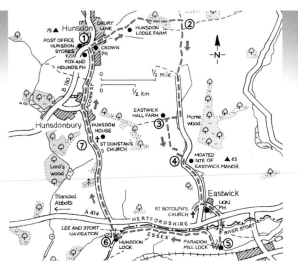

572 THUNDRIDGE HEROES AND PIONEERS

4 miles (6.4km) 2hrs Ascent: 140ft (43m)
Paths: Good paths and tracks with only one large arable field to cross, no stiles
Suggested map: aqua3 OS Explorer 194 Hertford & Bishop's Stortford
Grid reference: TL 359172
Parking: Ermine Street, Thundridge (to east of A10)

Explore a pagan settlement at Thundridge.

❶ At bend in **Ermine Street** there are 2 footpath signs: follow footpath ('Ware') steeply uphill to Victorian parish churchyard, for good views northwards and westwards. Retrace your steps downhill to **Ermine Street** and follow other footpath, ('Thundridge Old Church'). After kissing gate go straight on across pasture, now on **Hertfordshire Way**, then cross arable land to descend to Rib Valley. Turn **R** on to lane. Where it goes R carry straight on to metalled track. Ruined **church tower** is visible ahead and to **L**, beyond river, are grounds of **Youngsbury**.

❷ Continue along metalled track, between pastures. Where goes R, continue straight ahead, now on footpath. Cross access road. At footpath crossroads go **L** over footbridge that bypasses River Rib ford.

❸ Climb out of valley with arable fields to your R, **Youngsbury's** picturesque parkland to your L. At brow, track skirts an **arboretum**. Carry straight on, ignoring track bearing R. Go straight on, past farm buildings. Track, now metalled, curves **L** and downhill.

❹ By some white-painted, iron gates go sharp **R** across cultivated land, heading for footpath post in front of some houses. Turn **L** here and head west towards tower and spirelet of **High Cross church**.

❺ From churchyard turn **L** down A10, Roman **Ermine Street**. Near **White Horse pub** turn **R** into Marshall's Lane. Pass houses, then **Marshall's Farm** and **Marshall's**, to descend into valley by winding holloway lane.

❻ Cross **The Bourne**; go **L** by footpath ('Wadesmill'). Footpath is to **L**, don't take field track on R. Path keeps alongside **The Bourne** almost into **Wadesmill** where it crosses to other bank on footbridge. Path becomes gravelled access lane and continues to A10 road.

❼ Turn **R**, cross over River Rib bridge. Turn **L** at Post Office Stores, back into **Ermine Street, Thundridge**.

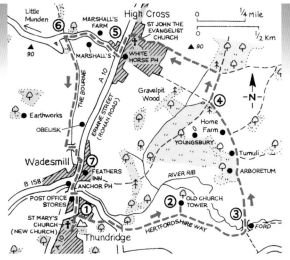

573 HERTFORD A COUNTY TOWN

6 miles (9.7km) 2hrs 45min Ascent: 100ft (30m)
Paths: Town streets, field and riverside paths, 1 stile
Suggested map: aqua3 OS Explorer 194 Hertford & Bishop's Stortford
Grid reference: TL 360142
Parking: Kibes Lane car park, off High Street, Ware

From Ware to the county town of Hertford.

❶ From car park walk down East Street, past entrance to **Bluecoat Yard**, to merge with High Street. Past Town Hall and church, road curves **R** into Baldock Street. At roundabout turn **L** into Watton Road, then ahead along **Park Road** past GSK. Keep ahead at fork.

❷ Cross **A10** bridge to lane. At gap by waymarker go **L**, parallel to lane in lime avenue remnants. Across pasture carry straight on, into woodland, shortly bearing **L** to descend to valley.

❸ At lane go **L** across bridge and bear **R** along lane, river to your **L**. Once across river bridge go immediately **L** over stile, heading for **River Lea** bridge. Do not cross bridge but turn **R**, climbing from valley towards house in **Bengeo**.

❹ After visiting **Bengeo's** Norman church, continue westwards, downhill, past cottage called The Vineyard. Keep on this path to ornamental gates, then turn **L** on to **Port Hill**, now in **Hertford**.

❺ Go downhill, then bear **L** into Cowbridge. Cross river, pass **McMullen's Brewery**, and turn **R** into St Andrew Street. Past church go **L** on footpath. Cross footbridge then turn **L** through gate by playground, into grounds of **Hertford Castle**.

❻ Cross over stream and turn **L** to walk past **gatehouse** and go out between gate piers. Turn **L** into Parliament Square. Turn **L** into Fore Street, then **L** again into Market Street. Next, turn **R** past Duncombe Arms pub. Go straight on across Bircherley Green towards store through Bluecoat Yard. Turn **L** to pass **station** forecourt.

❼ Carry on into Dicker Mill. Go **R** before bridge to tow path. Follow this to **Hertford Lock 1**.

❽ Go through gate; head **L** towards bridge. Cross it and go **L** to **New Gauge** building. Through gate turn **R** to follow **Lea Navigation** under A10 and into **Ware**.

❾ Passing **gazebos**, ascend to modern road bridge and turn **L** back into town.

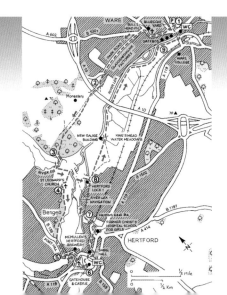

Hertfordshire

BERKHAMSTED *TWO RIDGE VILLAGES*

4 miles (6.4km) 2hrs Ascent: 195ft (59m) ▲
Paths: Bridleways, field paths and golf course, 7 stiles
Suggested map: aqua3 OS Explorer 182 St Albans & Hatfield
Grid reference: TL 291077 **Parking:** Lay-by opposite Five Horseshoes pub, Little Berkhamsted

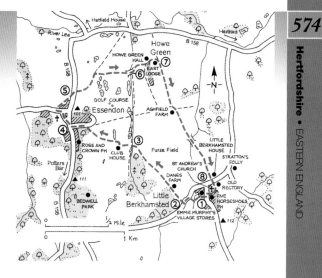

A walk from Little Berkhamsted to Essendon.

❶ From Church Road go through recreation ground. At gate turn **R** into paddock. Go out through gate and turn **L**, descending to bridleway sign.

❷ Turn **R** through gates, past white estate lodge. Beyond **Danes Farm** tarmac track becomes green lane bridleway. Later descend into woodland, bearing **R** and emerging past another lodge.

❸ Curve **L** to gates and ahead on metalled track, past golf club estate's yard. Now, on **golf course**, continue towards barn-like **club house**. Here turn **R**, then **L** and straight on, path now narrow green lane. Merging with access drive, turn **L** at School Lane.

❹ Now in **Essendon**, turn **R** at main road and head to **L** of war memorial to churchyard, entering through war memorial lychgate. Leave churchyard near 15th-century tower, turning **L** on to lane to descend to footpath ('Lower Hertford Road'). Go **R**, over stile, by garden of former Wheatsheaf pub. Head across paddock towards L-H house.

❺ Go over stile, cross road to footpath sign. Go through kissing gate to follow field path parallel to **L** fence. Through gap in hedge, re-emerge on **golf course**. Cross fairway and keep ahead. Cross another fairway and descend, metalled path becoming grassy.

❻ Cross footbridge, turning **L** on to access road. After 100 paces turn **R** to stile behind field-shelter. Ascend paddock, heading for oak tree. Over stile turn **L** on to lane, which curves **R** past Howe Green Hall.

❼ Turn sharp **R** immediately past East Lodge. Over another stile, walk beside hedge; cross footbridge. Keep on across pasture, aiming for thick hedge. Cross stile on to bridleway to **L** of **Ashfield Farm**. Cross stream on footbridge; head diagonally **L** up long pasture field. At top go through gate on to lane into **Little Berkhamsted.**

❽ At road cross to churchyard path, to **R** of **Old Rectory.** Pass **church** and go through lychgate, back into Church Road.

HERTFORD HEATH *GREAT WELLS AT GREAT AMWELL*

6½ miles (10.4km) 2hrs 30min Ascent: 200ft (61m) ▲
Paths: Bridleways, field paths and canal tow path, 4 stiles
Suggested map: aqua3 OS Explorer 174 Epping Forest & Lee Valley
Grid reference: TL 350116
Parking: Green at Church Hill or Mount Pleasant Road, Hertford Heath, off B1197

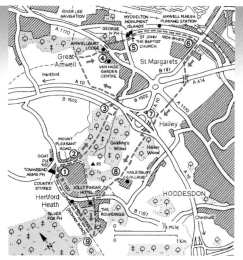

From Hertford Heath.

❶ Walk east along **Mount Pleasant Road**, by Mount Pleasant sign take **L** fork along metalled track.

❷ At end bridleway bears **R** on to wooded heath, then **L** at bridleway post. Descend through woods, marked by waymarkers. As it becomes sunken lane, bear **R** out of wood, then **L**. Cross access lane and descend beside embankment of A10.

❸ Go under A10, turning immediately **L** up to stile, ('Ware Road'). Proceed beside A10 to chain-link gate. Ascend paddock beside conifers to meet metalled lane at crest.

❹ Turn **R**. At next road with **Van Hage Garden Centre**, turn **L** by **Amwellbury Lodge**. Shortly turn **R** into Church Path; follow footpath to **Great Amwell**.

❺ Pass **George IV pub** and turn **R** into churchyard. Descend steps, cross lane and descend to **New River**. Turn **R** to follow **New River** footpath, shortly passing **Amwell Marsh Pumping Station.**

❻ Leave **New River** at road, turning **R**, uphill. Past Hillside Lane go **L** to 'Road Used as a Public Path' sign. Continue between fields, over **A414** and **A1170**. Cross; go over stile into pasture. Climb to crest, go over stile then another. Turn **R** to descend to A10 roundabout.

❼ Turn **L** under **A10**, cross to footpath sign and go **L** up bank. At top turn **R** to walk alongside woods, now in grounds of **Haileybury College**. Continue ahead on track past end of woods.

❽ At crossroads continue on tarmac drive, with **Haileybury College** on **L**. College road merges with **B1197**. Turn **L** at **Jolly Pindar Hotel**, soon with heathland of **The Roundings** on **R**. Where road bears **L**, fork **R** on to heath, through trees, to bear **L** into wide greensward. Follow this to road; turn **R** on to track.

❾ Now on **Roman Road, Ermine Street**, follow it northwards to merge with **B1197** through **Hertford Heath**. At **Country Stores** shop turn **R** into Church Hill and back to green.

CHESHUNT *A PEACEFUL OASIS*

6 miles (9.7km) 2hrs 45min Ascent: 130ft (40m) ◐
Paths: Lanes, footpaths, field and river paths, 7 stiles
Suggested map: aqua3 OS Explorer 174 Epping Forest & Lee Valley
Grid reference: TL 349023
Parking: Churchgate, Cheshunt, east of church near Green Dragon pub

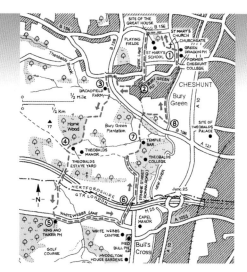

A walk from the centre of Cheshunt, taking in construction, demolition and removal.

❶ From **Churchgate** cross over churchyard; leave by its far corner. Pass to **R** of **St Mary's School**, on path initially between fences, then playing fields. At road go **L**, then **L** again into **Dark Lane**. Beyond Cromwell Avenue, pass between cemeteries into **Bury Green Road**.

❷ Just past No 104 turn **R**, on to footpath. Go along cul-de-sac and turn **L** at T-junction, almost immediately turning **R**, on footpath ('Barrow Lane'). At bypass path goes **R**, to road bridge.

❸ Over bridge turn **L** by footpath ('Whitewebbs') along **Broadfield Farm's** access road. Turn **L** at farmyard gate, skirt some farm buildings and descend to cross Theobalds Brook. Now ascend **R** side of paddock. Once over stile go **R**, along edge of fields towards woods. Skirt these **L**, then **R**, to join track by **Theobalds Estate Yard** and turn **L** to lane.

❹ Turn **L** and, just before **Theobalds Manor**, go **R** ('Whitewebbs Road'). At some woods path goes along their **L** side and crosses **M25**. Descending to stile and footbridge, follow line of oaks to climb another stile into pasture. At its corner go **R** over bridge, path then skirting stables towards **King and Tinker pub.**

❺ Turn **L** along **Whitewebbs Lane** and turn **L** opposite **White Webbs Centre** on to Bulls Cross Ride ('Theobalds College').

❻ Across **M25** follow lane past Western Cemetery, bearing **L** at gates to **Theobalds**. At T-junction go **R**, on to bridleway, initially alongside walls of Theobalds' kitchen gardens, then along green lane curving **L**.

❼ Past **Temple Bar**, continue to **Cheshunt** bypass. Across it, go **R** over stile into road. Continue into paddocks, then through gate by bridge over **New River**.

❽ Turn **L** along tow path. Walk past housing estates and leave **New River** at road bridge. Turn **L** then **R** into **Churchgate**, passing borough offices to church.

Hertfordshire • EASTERN ENGLAND

577 WHEATHAMPSTEAD *WHERE JULIUS CAESAR MARCHED*

5 miles (8km) 2hrs **Ascent:** 155ft (47m) ▲

Paths: Field paths, bridleway tracks and lanes, 1 stile
Suggested map: aqua3 OS Explorer 182 St Albans & Hatfield
Grid reference: TL 178141
Parking: East Lane car park, Wheathampstead

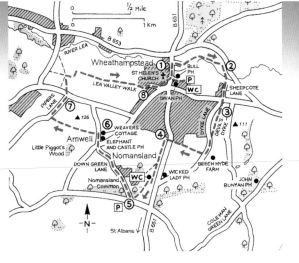

In the footsteps of the Roman legions.

❶ Turn **R** past **Bull pub**, cross **River Lea**; turn **R** into Mount Road. At bridleway sign follow track ('**Lea Valley Walk**'). Emerge in countryside to wind by river.

❷ Go through gate with bypass embankment ahead; turn **R**. Go between fences and through gate, bear **R** on to metalled track, recrossing **Lea**. Now on **Sheepcote Lane**, go uphill, over main road into **Dyke Lane**.

❸ By Tudor Road go **L** on to footpath along deep ditch of **Devil's Dyke**. Emerging at lane, turn **L**. Go **R** at footpath sign opposite **Beech Hyde Farm**. Now on grass track amid arable fields, pass modern housing to **R**, to reach road.

❹ Cross road to footpath ('**Nomansland**'), turn **L** on to tarmac track – road runs parallel, to your **L**. Descend to **Wicked Lady pub** and turn **R** on to access drive to Wheathampstead Cricket Club. Pass behind pavilion to footpath. Turn **L** past cricket nets, path now winding through trees. Across clearing, ignore path to

R and continue through trees to another clearing. Head towards bench in oak copse, then to another bench where path bears **R** to road.

❺ At **Nomansland** car park turn **R** into **Down Green Lane**, which leads off common. At crossroads carry straight on, past **Elephant and Castle pub**.

❻ Shortly, opposite **Weavers Cottage**, go **L** at footpath sign and up few steps. Path passes golf course, then crosses cultivated land to reach road, **Pipers Lane**. Turn **R**.

❼ At T-junction go straight on and cross stile, heading diagonally **L** across pasture to stile and **R** on to track. Turn immediately **R** on to muddy track which shortly turns **L** downhill between horse fences, then **R** over stile. After about 1 mile (1.6km) housing appears on **L**, path becomes tarmac and jinks to road.

❽ Go **L** into High Meads then **R** to descend into **Wheathampstead**. At Bury Green go **L** to **church**. From churchyard go **L** into High Street.

578 AYOT ST LAWRENCE *SHAW CORNER*

5 miles (8km) 2hrs **Ascent:** 120ft (37m) ▲

Paths: Bridleways, former railway line and field paths, 2 stiles
Suggested map: aqua3 OS Explorer 182 St Albans & Hatfield
Grid reference: TL 195168
Parking: Roadside parking in Ayot St Lawrence near Brocket Arms pub

Past the home of George Bernard Shaw.

❶ From **Brocket Arms pub** head west past ruined Church of St Lawrence. At bend go to **R** of telephone box through kissing gate. Portico of old church is straight ahead. In pasture, take R-H fork, with post-and-wire fence to **R**. Go through kissing gate and cross pasture grazed by sheep to **St Lawrence's church**, entering churchyard via kissing gate.

❷ Exit churchyard from behind church, along access drive. At lane go **R** ('**Hertfordshire Way**'), then **L** past **Priors Holt** at stile and footpath sign into pasture. At stile descend steps to path along edge of wood. Turn **L**, passing grounds of **Shaw Corner**, to road.

❸ Turn **R**. Soon, where road swings **L**, keep ahead at public bridleway sign. Follow bridleway – narrow, high-hedged and often muddy green lane for much of its length. At summit bypass footpath through scrub avoids muddiest sections. Go through wooded kissing gate; follow path as it winds to road via kissing gate.

❹ At road, jink **L** then **R** to public bridleway sign. Walk alongside oak and hornbeam coppiced woodland. Path emerges through conifer copse into arable field, hedge to **L**. Ahead is embankment of old Hatters Line railway.

❺ Go **R** at railway bridge, climb embankment and **L**, back across bridge. Follow old trackbed until just before woods. Go **L** over stile. Bear **R**, ignore L-H path, skirt woods, later enter them on old hollow track.

❻ At road go **R** to **Ayot St Peter church**. Retrace your steps past former school and continue along lane until it turns sharp **L** at cemetery. Go straight on to grassy track to **L** of **Tamarisk Cottage**. Follow bridleway, mostly hedgeless track between arable fields, cross road and continue on bridleway.

❼ Pass through hedge to lane opposite Stocking Lane Cottage and turn **R** uphill to road junction. At Lord Mead Lane go **L** ('**Shaw Corner**') and bear **L** back to **Brocket Arms pub** and start.

579 WELWYN GARDEN CITY *EBENEZER'S VISION*

4 miles (6.4km) 2hrs **Ascent:** 120ft (37m) ▲

Paths: Town roads, parkland paths and woodland tracks, 3 stiles
Suggested map: aqua3 OS Explorer 182 St Albans & Hatfield
Grid reference: TL 235133
Parking: Campus West Long Term car park (free on Sunday) off B195 in Welwyn Garden City

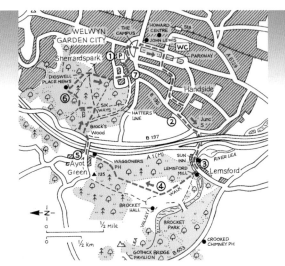

A walk around the first garden city.

❶ Cross **The Campus**; pass to **R** of **John Lewis** department store, along **Parkway**. At traffic lights cross **R** into Church Road. At end turn **L** into Guessens Road. Cross Handside Lane into Youngs Rise and then **L** into Elm Gardens. At end turn **R** into Applecroft Road.

❷ Turn **L** into Valley Road. Leaving **Welwyn**, go under **A1(M)** bridge and straight on into **Lemsford** village, with **River Lea** to **L**.

❸ At **Lemsford Mill** turn **R** to cross river on modern bridge. Follow footpath and bear **R** at junction, now on Lea Valley Walk. Soon enter Brocket Park, this part golf course. Carry straight on where R-H fence ends. Cross tarmac path to footpath post – thatched tennis pavilion behind here.

❹ Turn **R**, follow drive for 20 paces, then carry on across golf course, follow waymarkers. Footpath climbs **R**, out of dry valley. Pass cottage, climb stile out

of Brocket Park. Over another stile turn **L** into Brickwall Close, **Waggoners pub** on **R**. At Ayot Green turn **R** and cross over **A1(M)**.

❺ At T-junction turn **L** and almost immediately **R**, down to stile leading into woods. Go diagonally **L**, not sharp **R**. At bridleway junction bear **R**, path descending to cross course of old railway line. At **Six Ways** (carved totem poles) turn sharp **L** on to bridleway. Pass through car park to lane. Turn **R**, with parkland beside to **Digswell Place** on **L**.

❻ At **Digswell Place Mews** turn **R** by waymarker post, to return to woods. At bridleway post bear **R** uphill through woods. Ignore turns **L** and **R** until you near gardens of houses. Turn **R** to walk beside fences, eventually bearing **L** to merge with track and leave woods. Go straight over Reddings into Roundwood Drive and on to tarmac path between gardens.

❼ Turn **L** on to old railway (**Hatters Line**). Turn **R** up fenced ramp, out of cutting and into car park.

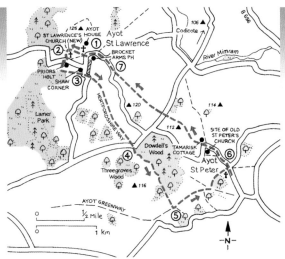
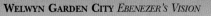

Hertfordshire

RICKMANSWORTH CHESS AND COLNE MEETING

7½ miles (12.1km) 3hrs **Ascent:** 210ft (64m) ⚠
Paths: Field paths, footpaths, canal tow path and some town pavements, no stiles
Suggested map: aqua3 OS Explorer 172 Chiltern Hills East
Grid reference: TQ 033966
Parking: Car park off A404 Rickmansworth Road on Chorleywood Common

Across Chorleywood Common.
① From car park head along ride cut through trees of **Chorleywood Common**. Ignoring cross-track, turn **L** at next crossroad of rides. Keep straight on, merging with lane close to **Black Horse pub**.
② Turn **R**. At T-junction turn **R**, into Berry Lane. Go under railway bridge then turn **L** on to woodland footpath ('Mill End'). Shortly take **R** fork to climb out of valley, then alongside **M25**, crossing it on **footbridge**.
③ Turn **R** on to path behind garden fences, then turn **L** through barrier to housing estate. Turn **R** then, at T-junction, go **L** into Chiltern Drive. Turn **R** into Coombe Hill Road, go straight on along path to cul-de-sac. Turn **R** by No 13 then cross another green and path between gardens. At road go **R** and at T-junction go **L** along Church Lane to main road.
④ Turn **L** and, past bus stop, go **R** at footpath sign. Over **footbridge** turn **L**, then **R**, over **River Colne** on bigger bridge. Follow footpath between large lakes.

⑤ Turn **L** on to **Grand Union Canal** tow path, continue to **Rickmansworth**. Under bypass bridge turn **L** up steps to road. Go **R** to roundabout, carrying straight on into **Church Street**.
⑥ Go straight over Rickmansworth's High Street's crossroads into Northway. Turn **R** into Solomon's Hill between blocks of flats, then **R** again on to footpath by railway. Turn **L** at road. Cross **A412** on footbridge.
⑦ Go to path ('Chess Valley Walk'), to **L** of **Catholic church**, to banks of **River Chess**. Continue on west bank to skirt wood.
⑧ Beyond paddocks cross road, continuing on Chess Valley Walk. Bear **R** at path fork, cross road and go through pony paddocks to walk alongside **M25**.
⑨ At road turn **L**, over **M25**, going **R** at footpath sign just before houses, still on Chess Valley Walk. Where tarmac track bears **R** go **L**, to path within edge of woods. Follow path uphill. At T-junction go **L** into wood and follow road past cemetery to gates and car park.

SARRATT AROUND THE VALLEY

7 miles (11.3km) 2hrs 45min **Ascent:** 245ft (75m) ⚠
Paths: Paths, tracks, village roads and country lanes, 5 stiles
Suggested map: aqua3 OS Explorers 172 Chiltern Hills East; 182 St Albans & Hatfield
Grid reference: TQ 042994 (on Explorer 172)
Parking: On west side of Sarratt Green

Walk through Flaunden, Sarratt and the water-meadows of the Chess Valley.
① From **Sarratt** green walk north. Beyond **Great Sarratt Farm** go **L** ('Rose Hall'). Bear **R** over pastures. Go along lane, beside some woods, now on **Chiltern Way**. Take **L** fork to skirt Rose Hall Farm to path. Over stile skirt **R** of barns of **Bragman's Farm** to lane.
② Turn **L** uphill and go **R** at **Chiltern Way** sign. Head **L** to stile, then by hedge to lane. Turn **R**. Past **Newhouse Farm** turn **L** on to path. At stile go diagonally **L** across field and, at hedge, bear **R** to lane.
③ Turn **L** and walk through **Flaunden**. At church turn **L** on to bridleway. Follow this to T-junction by 2 small observatories and turn **R**.
④ As lane goes **L**, continue on bridleway into woods. Go **L**, ignoring path to **R**. Fork **R** and descend steeply. Emerging from wood descend between fences to road.
⑤ Turn **L**, pass **Latimer** green, and turn **L** again on **Chess Valley Walk**. Descend to an information board

about **Flaunden** old church. Rejoin path and, passing **Liberty's tomb**, follow waymarks through **Mill Farm** and turn **L** on to lane.
⑥ After about 150yds (137m) leave lane on **R** and carry on over stile, on **Chess Valley Walk**. Through wood follow path between fences. At concrete access road keep ahead, with working cress beds on your **R**.
⑦ At lane turn **R**, turning **L** uphill at T-junction, leaving **Chess Valley Walk**. Beyond **Cakebread Cottage** go **R**, through gate. Ascend beside hedge, go over stile and cross pasture to join sycamore and beech avenue, then walk beside holly hedge to **Sarratt** churchyard.
⑧ Retrace your steps out of churchyard; bear diagonally **R** towards woods – reach them at **Chiltern Way** signpost. Continue along wood edge, then cross drive to kissing gate. Follow path through copse, then alongside hedge through cattle pasture to emerge between houses into **Sarratt**.

HARPENDEN IN ROTHAMSTED PARK

5½ miles (8.8km) 2hrs 30min **Ascent:** 110ft (34m) ⚠
Paths: Field tracks, former railway line, pavements, 4 stiles
Suggested map: aqua3 OS Explorer 182 St Albans & Hatfield
Grid reference: TL 132140
Parking: Amenbury Lane car park, Harpenden

A stroll through Rothamsted Park.
① From Amenbury Lane car park, go **R** into Hay Lane. Past **Harpenden Leisure Centre** enter park and follow path to lime avenue. Turn **R** and continue along lime avenue to T-junction.
② Turn **R** into another lime avenue. After 4 trees go **R**, through gate at bridleway sign, and head diagonally **R** to gate in far corner.
③ Look **L** for views of **Rothamsted Park's** chimneys and gables before turning **R** to join lane. When road turns **R** towards **Rothamsted Experimental Farm** go **L** on tarmac track then **R** at bridleway sign, path now grassy margin. Continue across lane on to path between arable fields and follow it as it curves **L** down to **Knott Wood**. Walk alongside it and, out of field, turn **L** on to **Nicky Line** path.
④ Path follows course of this former railway line to Harpenden Road. Cross road, skirt to **L** of roundabout and go up **R-H** side of A5183 ('Nicky Line'). Path

regains trackbed. Just past gates to gypsy site go **L** over stile to cross **A5183**.
⑤ Over main road climb steps to stile. Continue across arable field, with electricity poles to your **L**. Go through hedge gap and straight on, then bear **R**. Path goes into overgrown green lane, shortly with **golf course** to your **L**. Pass behind 8th tee and turn **L** along **golf course** side of hedge. Past 9th tee turn **R**, path winding through scrub. Beyond this cross stile and pasture, bypassing **Hammonds End Farm**.
⑥ Turn **L** on lane then **R** on to **Redbourn Lane**. At **White Horse pub** go **L** by Flowton Grove, turn **R** on to footpath (L of **Flowton Grove**). Beyond cottage reach road on west-side of Harpenden Common.
⑦ Turn **L**; walk past Institute of Arable Crop Research. Continue alongside West Common into **Harpenden**. Go along High Street to Church Green and parish church. From here walk south to Leyton Green. Turn **R** into Amenbury Road and car park.

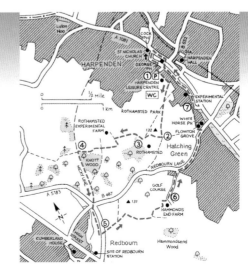

583 MARKYATE *THE LONG AND STRAIGHT ROAD*

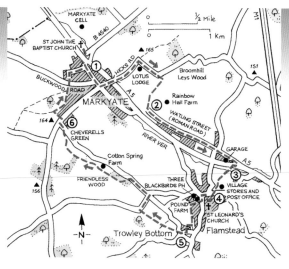

7 miles (11.3km) 3hrs **Ascent:** 175ft (53m) ⚠
Paths: Chalk ridges on either side of young Ver's valley
Suggested map: aqua3 OS Explorer 182 St Albans & Hatfield
Grid reference: TL 059166
Parking: On Markyate High Street

Along Watling Street and the chalky ridge.

❶ From north end of **Markyate** High Street walk southwards. Turn **L** into **Hicks Road**, crossing A5 on footbridge. Past **Lotus Lodge** turn **R**. Where lane turns **L**, go straight on along green lane which shortly turns **R** to descend, through mud, to valley road.

❷ Turn **L** on to course of **Watling Street (Roman road)**. Continue for over 1 mile (1.6km), at **garage** turn **R** to cross **A5**.

❸ Over stile head diagonally **R**, across stream to stile. Follow field edge before heading into copse that climbs valley side. From copse, climb stile to go **L** alongside hedge. Cross stile and head to lane, River Hill, which leads into **Flamstead**.

❹ At junction turn **L** along High Street, **R** into Church Lane and then **R** again, into parish churchyard. Leave via gate by war memorial cross. Turn **L** along High Street and then **L** into Trowley Hill Road. Beyond number 30, **Pound Farm**, turn **R** on to tarmac path

('The Chiltern Way'). At footpath post turn **L** and descend along edge of arable field. At bottom of field go **L** between gardens to lane and round to footpath **R**.

❺ At **Trowley Bottom** go straight on, then immediately **R** on to bridleway, behind cottages then along valley. At lane turn **R** to climb out of valley. At crest turn **L** at footpath ('Cheverells Green'), bear **L** into **Friendless Wood**. Out of wood go **R** and follow ridge along edge of this and another wood before heading through kissing gates and sheep pasture to rejoin lane.

❻ Go **L** to junction, turn **R**, then **L** to footpath ('Buckwood Road'). At footpath junction turn **R** and walk alongside arable field and gardens to road. Across it path climbs between gardens. Go along Cowper Road to Cavendish Road junction. Turn **R**, descending to **Markyate** High Street. Turn **L** and, just before White Hart Inn, go **R** to subway under A5. Turn **L** to visit church. Retrace your steps to High Street.

584 GREAT GADDESDEN *A RICH PARISH*

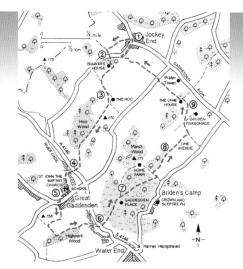

6 miles (9.7km) 3hrs **Ascent:** 240ft (73m) ⚠
Paths: Field paths and bridleways, lots of stiles
Suggested map: aqua3 OS Explorer 182 St Albans & Hatfield
Grid reference: TL 030137
Parking: The Green, Jockey End

A walk within the parish of Great Gaddesden.

❶ From The Green pass bus shelter and turn **L** at footpath sign into paddocks. Walk alongside hedge. Where it ends cross to another hedge. Turn **L**, pass through oak and thorn scrub to road.

❷ Cross road on to **Bunkers House** drive; bear **L** at gates. Cross stile. walk alongside garden hedge, cross cultivated field to stile. Go through hedge and turn **L**.

❸ Cross stile by large oak, head diagonally to **R** of **The Hoo** (house). Follow fence towards woods. From woods descend across arable land to hedge, following field edge as it curves **R** to road by houses.

❹ Cross into water-meadows. Walk across long footbridge, bear **L** towards **church**. Beyond **school** turn **R** into churchyard.

❺ From southwest corner of churchyard, cross pasture to road. Turn **R**, go **L** at footpath sign by cottages. In field, head to stile, cross it and follow grass margin to arable land. Turn **R** at crest. At

footpath T-junction turn **L** to head for woods. In woods turn immediately **L**, descending to valley. At stile bear **R** to footbridge and go between buildings to road.

❻ Go through gate beside cottages, climb stile, and turn **L**, uphill, across cultivated land towards **Gaddesden Place**. Go into parkland, climb 2 stiles, and head uphill, to **L** of oak and then to waymarker post to **L** of mansion.

❼ Past **Gaddesden Place** and through field gate, head to drinking trough. Bear **R** to stile by woods, then head to gate. Turn **L** on to track to **Home Farm**. At wood edge go **R** at footpath sign to walk beside wood.

❽ Path enters **Golden Parsonage's** lime avenue. Leave this at valley bottom by turning **L** on to track. At track junction go **R** then diagonally **L** towards stile, passing sweet chestnuts. Cross it.

❾ Go through paddocks and stiles, passing **The Lane House**, crossing road and continuing northwest, passing copse. At road, turn **R** back to **Jockey End**.

585 ASHRIDGE PARK *A WEDDING CAKE*

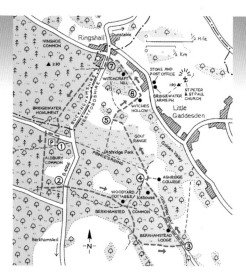

6½ miles (10.4km) 3hrs **Ascent:** 225ft (69m) ⚠
Paths: Mostly tracks through woodland or parkland, 1 stile
Suggested map: aqua3 OS Explorer 181 Chiltern Hills North
Grid reference: SP 976128 **Parking:** Car park on Aldbury Common, on road to Bridgewater Monument

A walk in Ashridge Park and wooded commons of Chiltern plateau.

❶ From car park on **Aldbury Common** head towards column of **Bridgewater Monument**, turning **L** at footpath sign behind young beech tree. Keep straight on along track until, just before pond, go **L** by footpath post at track crossroads.

❷ At road, cross on to byway. Woodland gives way on **L** to parkland with cattle. Track bears **R** into woodland, skirting paddock and **Woodyard Cottages**, to reach metalled track. Follow it to **R**, still in woodland. At footpath crossroads, before gate to farm buildings, go **L** on to track. At fork, bear **L** and at field, follow path that descends along **R-H** edge of woods to tree belt and then runs through it to road.

❸ Turn **L** on road and, past ornate **Berkhamstead Lodge**, bear **R** at footpath sign, to climb through woodland and, at crest walk alongside wire fencing and grounds of **Ashridge College**.

❹ Turn **R**. With an oak copse on your **L**, head for

footpath sign to **L** of large oak. Follow drive and cross white-topped posts across **Prince's Riding**, vista terminated by **Bridgewater Monument**. Continue through copse and follow more white posts. Cross dry valley then **golf practice range**. Beyond practice tees path winds through copse to road.

❺ Turn **R** on road, now **Chiltern Way**. Where it turns **L**, footpath bears **R** between garden hedges, across fairway (watch for flying golf balls), then between gardens and past gate to **Witches Hollow**. At footpath crossroads turn **L** on to metalled track.

❻ Follow lane downhill. Past drive to **Witchcraft Hill** it becomes path through woods. Over stile path bears **L** by clearing, then into woods to road at Ringshall.

❼ Turn **L**; immediately past garden walls, turn **R** into woods of **Ivinghoe Common**. At bridleway post bear **L** and **L** again to walk along ride, ignoring tracks and paths to **L** and **R**. Eventually cross dry valley; at bridleway post where track bears **R**, go almost straight on winding through wood to **Prince's Riding** and start.

TRING *DELIGHTS AND SURPRISES*

5½ miles (8.8km) 2hrs 30min **Ascent:** 335ft (102m)
Paths: Pavements, footpaths, 3 stiles
Suggested map: aqua3 OS Explorer 181 Chiltern Hills North
Grid reference: SP 925114 **Parking:** Car park, east end of Tring High Street (except market day, Friday)

From Tring up into the wooded Chilterns and back through Tring Park.

1 Go along High Street from car park, pass **church**, turn **L** at crossroads to **Akeman Street** and **Zoological Museum**. At Park Street turn **R**, then **L**, up Hastoe Lane, to climb out of Tring and under **A41**.

2 Just beyond bridge turn **R** at footpath ('Hastoe'). Beyond A41 cutting, at gate and stile, bear **L** to climb ridge, with hedge on **L**. At **Stubbing's Wood**, follow its edge then enter it. At path fork bear **R** – route marked by arrows on trees. Pass footpath ('Shire Lane Pavis Wood'), then descend to sunken way and turn **L** along it. Climb towards gateway and out of woodland. Continue on metalled lane. At junction turn **L**, briefly on to Ridgeway National Trail along Gadmore Lane. Leave Trail at crossroads, turn **R** on to Browns Lane, metalled bridleway.

3 Turn **L** at footpath crossroads on to Chiltern Way. Follow **Grim's Ditch**. After about 1¼ miles (2km) go through kissing gate on to **Chesham Road**.

4 Turn **R** at road, then **L** through kissing gate, still on Chiltern Way. At lane turn **L**. At electricity substation turn **R**. Where Chiltern Way veers **R**, leave it following **L-H** hedge, to hedge gap and waymarker post. Cross dry valley – church belfry visible opposite. At hedge line head diagonally **L** into cattle pasture. Through kissing gate turn **R** on to **Chesham Road** and go to **Wigginton church**.

5 From church head north along Twist, winding downhill to Ridgeway National Trail signs. Turn **L** to follow this Trail to just beyond pair of Rothschild estate cottages (**Ladderstile and Westwood**). Here Trail turns **L** but go straight on, into woods of **Tring Park**.

6 At cross path turn **R** to **Temple** or Summer Pavilion. Head west to **Obelisk**. Still in woodland, continue downhill to kissing gate. Bear **R** here, into cattle-grazed parkland, to head for footbridge over **A41**. Across bridge follow footpath back into **Tring** – route is clear, near town being mainly between high walls – emerging in High Street.

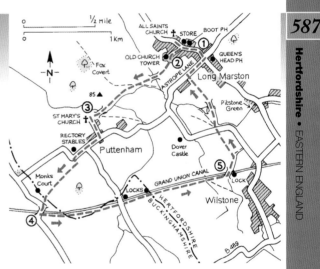

LONG MARSTON *ADVANCING ON THE TRING SALIENT*

4 miles (6.4km) 2hrs **Ascent:** Negligible
Paths: Field paths alongside hedges, some roads, canal tow path, lots of stiles
Suggested map: aqua3 OS Explorer 181 Chiltern Hills North
Grid reference: SP 898156
Parking: Along village roads in Long Marston

A walk on lowlands of the Vale of Aylesbury around Long Marston and Puttenham.

1 From crossroads by **Queen's Head pub** walk north along Station Road which curves past **Boot pub**. Continue past war memorial to visit **All Saints Church**. Return to war memorial. Turn **R**, down Chapel Lane, towards medieval tower of old church, set amid trees beyond thatched Old Church Cottage.

2 Opposite, go through 5-bar gate and walk diagonally across field to stile. Cross track and climb stile to walk along **R-H** side of stream and hedge through 2 large fields. At end follow hedge on **R** to gate. Cross footbridge and stile then head for footbridge in far **L** corner of next field, ignoring stile away to **R**. Over footbridge, turn **R** to another one and, once over this, cross pasture to **Puttenham church**.

3 Follow lane, past Cecilia Hall, to road junction. Turn **R** to walk along road but, where it turns **L**, carry straight on, past **Rectory Stables**. At modern farm cottages go **L** over stile by footpath sign to follow hedge south then west, around 2 sides of field. Over stile and through another field, next hedge and stile is Buckinghamshire county boundary. Crossing track, path passes alongside corrugated iron sheds. At track head for canal bridge beyond 10-ton limit signs.

4 Cross bridge No 8, descend to canal tow path; follow this through bridge No 7, past 2 **locks** to bridge No 5.

5 Leave tow path and cross bridge No 5. Bear **R** to follow **L-H** side of hedge and stream. Over stile by gate, follow path through 2 fields, then cross lane and head north along green lane, ignoring stile to **L**. Shortly, climb stile to follow overgrown lane by stream. Emerging from scrub, cross corner of field. Exit via stile to **L** of electricity pole. Path crosses arable field to footbridge. Cross 2 stiles to reach lane (**Astrope Lane**) and public footpath ('Wilstone 1 mile'). Turn **R** to return to crossroads in **Long Marston**.

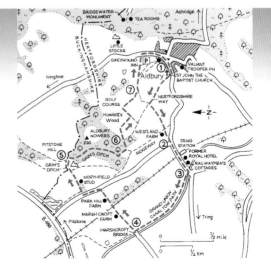

ALDBURY *TRANSPORT ARTERIES*

5 miles (8km) 2hrs **Ascent:** 230ft (70m)
Paths: Bridleways, field paths, canal tow path, woods, 1 stile
Suggested map: aqua3 OS Explorer 181 Chiltern Hills North
Grid reference: SP 965124
Parking: Around green in centre of Aldbury or in public car park up Stocks Lane at north end of village

Across the railway to the Grand Union Canal and the woods of Aldbury Nowers.

1 From village green, visit **St John the Baptist Church**. Leave via lychgate. Turn **R** to kissing gate ('Pitstone Hill'). Turn **R** on to **Hertfordshire Way**. Past farm buildings and across track, path climbs between hedge and fence. At crest turn **L** on to bridleway, with **golf course** on **R**. Descend to join Ridgeway National Trail to reach road via drive to **Westland Farm**.

2 Follow road, cross Northfield Road junction and then railway in its cutting. Passing **Tring Station** and former **Royal Hotel** and **cottages**, on **R** of bridge descend steps to **Grand Union Canal** tow path.

3 This canal bridge is No 135. Follow tow path beside canal in its cutting as far as next bridge, unnumbered **Marshcroft Bridge**, and climb up to lane.

4 Turn **R** on to lane to **Marsh Croft Farm**. Go across railway and through gate on to concrete road. Pass **Park Hill Farm**, then horse paddocks. At road turn **L** and pass gates to **Northfield Stud** and copse. Turn **R** beyond, to footpath sign set back from road, ('Pitstone and Pitstone Hill'). Go through gate on to path skirting old chalk pits. Go across footpath junction to climb steeply alongside woodland, with downland on **L**, to reach **Pitstone Hill**.

5 Turn **R** through kissing gate into woods of **Aldbury Nowers**. Here path follows section of **Grim's Ditch** along ridge until, descending, you veer **L** down steps. At footpath junction, where Ridgeway turns **R**, go **L**. At guidepost go straight on, initially in woods, ignoring path to **R**.

6 Go through kissing gate and across track. Path, now on **golf course**, curves downhill through young trees, then turns **L** at hedge. At sign go **R** and keep on metalled track, with hedge **R**. At next hedge go through kissing gate, path now between high hedges.

7 Turn **L** on to bridleway to road. Turn **R** to follow Stocks Lane back to **Aldbury** village.

Bedfordshire

589 HARROLD ODELL Working Up an Appetite

4¼ miles (6.8km) 2hrs **Ascent:** 197ft (60m)
Paths: Park tracks, field edges and woodland paths, can get boggy
Suggested map: aqua3 OS Explorer 208 Bedford & St Neots
Grid reference: SP 956566
Parking: Country park car park, near Harrold

Enjoy a day out at a country park.

❶ Leave car park by **visitor centre** and walk to far end of park beyond main lake – either along semi-surfaced path between 2 lakes or across long meadow by side of **River Great Ouse** (this may be difficult after heavy rain). Go through gate at far end of main track and along lane to **pub** at Odell, with its riverside garden. Beyond this join pavement of main road on rising bend and cross over at top, before you reach church.

❷ Go through double gate on **L** for public bridleway – not footpath further on beside church. Follow wide grassy track uphill between fields, ignoring all paths and tracks off L and R, and follow this broad and direct route into **Odell Great Wood**. After ¼ mile (400m) of woodland walking you reach major junction of routes.

❸ Turn 1st **L**, almost back on yourself, for public footpath (indicated on nearby waymarked post) through trees to southwest edge of wood. Turn **L** and walk along perimeter to end, then don't go through inviting gap in hedge but turn **R** to follow field-edge to far corner.

❹ Go over high stile. Turn **L** to follow series of field edges gradually downhill to road at bottom – admire views over country park and river valley. **St Nicholas's Church**, isolated on the hilltop on the far side of river, is prominent, and to the west is the 14th-century tower of St Peter's Church at **Harrold**. Final field is narrow, enclosed grassy strip used by local stables.

❺ Cross road and turn **L** to walk along pavement. In 150yds (137m) go **R**, down through wide field opening, and follow **R-H** side of field as it zig-zags around to far corner.

❻ Re-enter **country park** and turn **R** on to semi-surfaced path that skirts northern side of main lake. At far end either walk along grassy strip back to **visitor centre** or follow path into woodland by road, and turn **L** for short and shady track back to start.

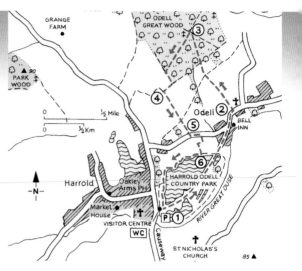

---

590 AMPTHILL A Pilgrim's Progress

7 miles (11.3km) 3hrs 30min **Ascent:** 607ft (185m)
Paths: Variety of field paths, farm tracks and lanes, 12 stiles
Suggested map: aqua3 OS Explorer 193 Luton & Stevenage
Grid reference: TL 03438 **Parking:** Car parks in Ampthill (Church and Bedford streets)

Step out in John Bunyan's Bedfordshire.

❶ From Market Square go along Church Street and **L** to **Church of St Andrew**. Walk along Rectory Lane, to its **L**. At end, go **L** through gate by **Rectory Cottage** for **Holly Walk**. At far end cross road. Turn **R**. Walk up pavement. At top of bend, cross over to lane opposite.

❷ To visit **Houghton House** fork **L** by houses, otherwise proceed to reservoir gates then switch to farm track on other side of hedge. Walk along hilltop track to **King's Wood**. Go through stile to **R**; follow path around edge of wood (or parallel path through trees).

❸ After ¼ mile (400m) turn **R** for wide track that crosses first open fields then **Brickhill Pastures** farmyard, then follows its drive to lane at end. Go **L** and, just before turning for **South Limbersey House**, turn **R** on public footpath across field just to **R** of buildings. Follow this across and down to kissing gate, then along field-edge path to go through another gate.

❹ To shorten walk by 1½ miles (2.4km) go ahead to Maulden church, otherwise turn **L** through gate for path to **Maulden Wood**. At junction of tracks by its entrance turn 1st **R** for bridleway (to R of ditch) that ends up skirting edge of woodland on fenced route.

❺ At **octagonal lodge** (private) turn **R**. Walk along track via picnic area with sculptures, down to join lane at bottom by Green End Farm. After 220yds (201m) go up steps in embankment on **R** for waymarked route around **R-H** side of **Old Farm**. Continue through fields, end of drive, then short field to Maulden church.

❻ Follow path out of far side of churchyard (black gate) to road. Turn **R** on George Street via **Maulden**.

❼ After 300yds (274m), just before Cobbitts Road, turn **R** on walkway between houses. Where it veers L, go ahead past end of house to reach road. Cross over.

❽ Continue through fields, to L of **King's Farm**. At end of fenced enclosure, go along green lane. Turn **L** at junction of routes at end. After following successive field edges bend **L** on track. Just before ruined barn, turn **R** for path that eventually leads to Gas House Lane. Go **L**, then **R** to follow main road to **Ampthill**.

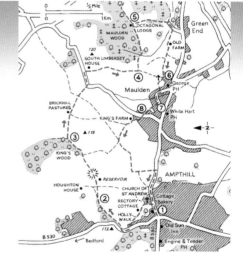

---

591 ROCKINGHAM FOREST Flying Kites

6½ miles (10.4km) 3hrs **Ascent:** 426ft (130m)
Paths: Firm forest tracks throughout except one ploughed field
Suggested map: aqua3 OS Explorers 224 Corby, Kettering & Wellingborough or 234 Rutland Water
Grid reference: SP 978983
Parking: Forestry Commission car park, Fineshade Wood (off A43)

An ancient forest, now home to red kites.

❶ From car park walk up lane past **Forestry Commission office**, and just past what were originally forest workers' houses it becomes wide and semi-surfaced forest drive. Go out along this route.

❷ Just before 2nd of 2 semi-detached cottages (Nos 2 and 4 Top Lodge), you can detour to gravel track on **L** that leads through trees to **bird hide** (free) overlooking artificial pond and area of open ground. Continue along main track through open woodland until, just after 1 mile (1.6km) from start, you turn **R** at crossroads of paths, signed ('**Jurassic Way**').

❸ Walk along track through trees, with field soon opening up to L. When field ends, keep ahead over junction of paths into **Westhay Wood**. In few paces, join main forest track to proceed south via woodland.

❹ At junction at very far end, where main track turns abruptly R, go **L** and walk through small timber yard to **Wood Lane**. Walk down to old railway bridge.

❺ To visit village of **King's Cliffe** continue to bottom of lane, cross over and turn **L** – pub and church are at far end of West Street. Otherwise turn **R** before railway cutting for field-edge footpath. At border of **Westhay Wood** continue through fields alongside woodland, until in very far corner path disappears into trees.

❻ Follow well-waymarked route (direction arrows attached to some trees), which at one point crosses former railway by remains of old footbridge. After following old fence, eventually emerge into fields. Walk around **R-H** edge, beside trees, until clear path cuts across corner to woodland on far side.

❼ Continue along path through conifers, then turn **R** on to wide farm track that drops down via gate on to open hillside above **Fineshade Abbey** (private).

❽ Turn **R** along fenced path above buildings and onward across tree-covered hillside. Go over wide and dipping field and then turn **R** on to lane at far side to car park at top.

Northamptonshire

CASTLE ASHBY *A Fine State of Affairs*

6½ miles (10.4km) 3hrs 15min **Ascent:** 557ft (170m)
Paths: Field paths, farm tracks and river bank, potentially muddy
Suggested map: aqua3 OS Explorer 207 Newport Pagnell & Northampton South
Grid reference: SP 860594
Parking: Roadside in Castle Ashby; car park for visitors to gardens and farm shops

A varied walk that takes in a leisurely river and a grandiose mansion.

❶ Walk out of **Castle Ashby** along road heading southwestwards, with house (and visitors' car park) over to **L**. Where pavement ends turn **R** for hamlet of **Chadstone**. Descend lane past cottages and converted barns to farm of **Chadstone Lodge**.

❷ Turn **L** for bridleway alongside hedge and, at end, go on through trees to continue route alongside next field and down to road. Cross over for footpath down to **Whiston Spinney**, then via footbridge in shady dell to junction of tracks on far side. Here go straight on ('Footpath via Jerusalem Steps'), and cross field to trees on far side.

❸ Follow path up steps and out along field edge with woodland (**The Firs**) on your **R**. Beyond gate go down sharp flight of steps to **R** and across field to turn **L** on far side and descend to road below.

❹ Route continues up through field opposite. Head

half-**L**, then follow bridleway waymarks to **R**, through long narrow field with houses of Cogenhoe on your **L**. At far side join lane and descend to **Cogenhoe Mill**.

❺ Just before old mill buildings and sluice, with caravan park beyond, turn **R** for path alongside River Nene ('Nene Way'). Follow this waterside walk for 1 mile (1.6km) as far as **Whiston Lock**, then turn **R** for straight farm track across fields to main road, heading towards **Whiston church** sitting astride hilltop.

❻ Go across junction and walk along lane into **Whiston**, branching **L** at triangular green. Take gated passageway beside outbuildings of **Manor Farm** up to church. There are good views over Nene Valley.

❼ Walk past **church** to far side of churchyard, go over metal rung in wall and turn **R** on to an obvious field-edge path. This continues along grassy strip between further fields and emerges on to bend of lane. Go straight on/**L** and continue all the way back to **Castle Ashby**.

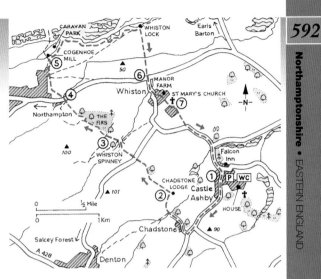

BADBY *A Village Trail*

6¾ miles (10.9km) 3hrs 30min **Ascent:** 787ft (240m)
Paths: Mostly pasture, muddy where cows congregate, 22 stiles
Suggested map: aqua3 OS Explorer 207 Newport Pagnell & Northampton South
Grid reference: SP 560590
Parking: On Main Street, Badby

Three lovely villages west of Northampton.

❶ Walk up to Badby church via Vicarage Hill (off which is Britain's only thatched **youth hostel**). Take alleyway path ('Fawsley'), opposite south side of church, then half-**R** up sloping field for path around western edge of **Badby Wood**, famous for its springtime bluebells.

❷ After ¼ mile (400m) take **R** fork (upper path), and follow waymarks for **Knightley Way** out across open hilltop of **Fawsley Park** and down towards lakes near **Fawsley Hall**.

❸ Go ahead along lane at bottom to inspect church, otherwise turn **L**, and in few paces **L** again (before cattle grid) for footpath up and across large sloping field. Go through gate and down track to road, then resume opposite climbing steadily through field, passing **Westcombe Farm** on **L**. Continue across **Everdon Hill** and down to village of **Everdon** below, joining lane via stile to **R** as you near bottom.

❹ Walk through village, following road as it bends **L** past church and **pub**. Turn **L** for lane to **Little Everdon**. When road appears to split go ahead/**L** for path via stiles to **L** of farm buildings. Continue across open fields, with **Everdon Hall** to **R**. On far side, pass end of strip of trees and maintain northwesterly direction to carry on through 4 more fields to river (aim just to **R** of Newnham's church spire when in view).

❺ Cross **Nene** via footbridge and walk uphill through 1st field, then veer **L** in 2nd to cross 3rd, and drop down to pick up farm drive which, beyond gate, becomes Manor Lane. Walk on to main street.

❻ Turn **L**; drop down past **pub** by green. Continue along **Badby Road** out of village. In 150yds (137m) go **L** for field-edge paths alongside infant **River Nene**.

❼ Go over footbridge at end and walk half-**L** through field ahead, keeping **L** of clump of trees in middle and aiming for Badby church. At far corner turn **R** into Chapel Lane to return to centre of **Badby**.

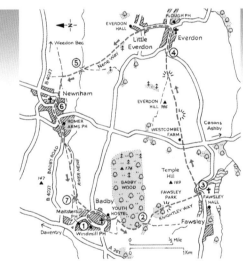

OUNDLE *The Banks of the Nene*

6¾ miles (10.9km) 3hrs 30min **Ascent:** 115ft (35m)
Paths: Waterside meadows and farmland tracks. Small weir near Cotterstock may be impassable after very heavy rain
Suggested map: aqua3 OS Explorer 227 Peterborough
Grid reference: TL 042881 **Parking:** Oundle town centre (long-stay car park off East Road)

A riverside meander around Oundle.

❶ From end of Market Place, in centre of **Oundle**, walk down St Osyth's Lane past supermarket until it curves **R**, then go straight on into Bassett Ford Road. Where this bends **L** into Riverside Close go ahead to gate at end. There are 2 riverside walks indicated – go half-**L** across field and follow bank downstream (not over footbridge ahead).

❷ For next 2¼ miles (3.6km) route follows bank of **Nene** as it completes giant loop. Go underneath Oundle bypass and eventually out by open meadows.

❸ Eventually, beyond **weir**, reach long, high footbridge where you can cross river to visit picturesque village of **Ashton**, round trip of ¾ mile (1.2km). Otherwise continue straight ahead and back under bypass to reach old bridge.

❹ Cross road and turn **R**. On far side of river turn **L** at Riverside Walk sign, past boat sheds, and strike out along flat eastern bank of **Nene** via 2 **weirs**. Second

can be tricky if water level is very high, in which case retrace your steps to road bridge and take field path and then lane further to east.

❺ Cross river via **'guillotine' lock**; continue to lane at far end by converted **corn mill**. Turn **L**. Walk through **Cotterstock**. After 550yds (503m) turn **L** before telephone box for path between fence and hedge.

❻ Head out along **L-H** side of an open field, then beside narrow plantation with river on far side. Continue past small **sewage works** and directly down through 2 more fields before reaching playing field.

❼ Half-way along pitch turn **L** for gap in hedge and boardwalk out to **Nene** – permissive route through Snipe Meadow nature reserve. Turn **R** and walk along river bank until just before bridge, then head **R** for **Oundle Wharf**. Go through field beside buildings to reach New Road.

❽ Turn **L** and walk to end, then **R** into Station Road/North Street to return to town centre.

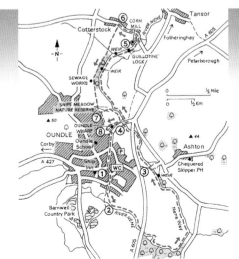

Cambridgeshire

595 WICKEN FEN THE LAST SURVIVOR

4¾ miles (7.7km) 2hrs **Ascent:** Negligible
Paths: Mostly river banks and farm tracks, potentially slippery
Suggested map: aqua3 OS Explorer 226 Ely & Newmarket
Grid reference: TL 564706
Parking: Wicken Fen nature reserve car park if visiting the reserve, otherwise off Wicken High Street

A walk through an authentic fen.

1 From **nature reserve** walk up Lode Lane towards **Wicken**. Before main road turn **R** on to Back Lane. Follow route, behind houses (including windmill), which soon becomes track. At far end of lane, turn **R** on to wide track through fields. (If you have parked in **Wicken** take signposted public footpath via Cross Green, just along from and opposite pub, out to fields.)

2 Follow route to cross 2 footbridges. Don't take path off to **L** but continue straight ahead (beyond green-painted 2nd footbridge) along bank of **Monk's Lode**, with **St Edmund's Fen** opposite.

3 After 550yds (503m) branch **L** by new fence and gate for long and straight track, out across fields to **Priory Farm**. Join surfaced lane and continue to end.

4 By Environment Agency's private raised bridge turn **R** along bank of **Burwell Lode** (ignore footbridge). Continue on this path for 1½ miles (2.4km) past **Adventurer's Fen**.

5 At high-arched footbridge over **Wicken Lode** turn **R** and, once over stile, walk along this bank back towards **Wicken Fen** past National Trust sign. If you continue across footbridge and walk for another ¼ mile (400m) you come to Upware, with pub and picnic area. Ignoring paths off into open fen and fields on your **R**, continue along bank until its junction with **Monk's Lode**.

6 Cross short bridge by **Goba Moorings** and continue alongside **Wicken Lode**, not along **Monk's Lode** (to R). Lush vegetation of **Wicken Fen** now on either side, and across water you will pass lofty tower hide, one of several dotted around **reserve**.

7 When you get to end turn **L** to explore **visitor centre** (open Tuesday to Sunday). There is a small admission charge to **reserve** itself, which is open daily from dawn to dusk. Near by is the restored Fen Cottage, and thatched boathouse. To return to car park and **Wicken**, simply walk back up lane past houses.

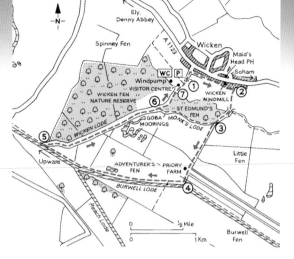

---

596 MANEA FENLAND'S BIG SKIES

6¼ miles (10.1km) 3hrs **Ascent:** Negligible
Paths: Lanes and hard farm tracks
Suggested map: aqua3 OS Explorer 228 March & Ely
Grid reference: TL 478893
Parking: Roadside parking in centre of Manea

An enigmatic landscape links remote Manea with an historic drainage cut.

1 Walk eastwards along High Street (which becomes Station Road), past **post office** and fish and chip shop, then turn **R** for public footpath alongside primary **school**. At football pitch at far end turn **R** and go past **Manea Wood**. Continue along path as it bears **R** and approaches **Bearts Farm**.

2 Turn **L** by old barns and sheds for wide track out into fields, with farm on your **R**, to reach attractive reedy lake known locally as '**The Pit**'. This was originally dug for clay, which was then transported across fields on a light railway to shore up the banks of nearby **Old and New Bedford rivers. The Pit** is now a popular place for fishermen and wildlife.

3 At end of track turn **R** on to lane, with lake still on your **R**, then when you reach junction at corner of road turn **L**, on to **Straight Road**, and follow this through fields to end.

4 Turn **L** on to **Purl's Bridge Drove** ('Welches Dam and RSPB reserve'). Follow this open lane to **Purl's Bridge**, by **Old Bedford River**. Continue along bank to reach **Ouse Washes Nature Reserve** (visitor centre and public toilets).

5 Return along lane for 440yds (402m) and turn **L** for signposted public bridleway by dark wooden sheds. Known as **Old Mill Drove**, this runs directly across open fields as far as rusting farm machinery and outbuildings of **Boon's Farm**. Turn **R** and walk along dead-straight **Barnes's Drove** for 1¼ miles (2km) to road at far end.

6 Turn **L** and after 80yds (73m) turn off **R** over stile for public footpath across fields back into **Manea** (aim for **fire station** tower). Route veers one way then other as it skirts series of pig enclosures – just follow clear yellow waymarks past enormous porkers. At far side cross successive stiles and turn **R**, past village stores, to follow main road back to centre.

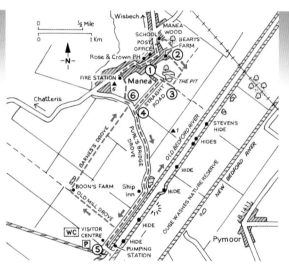

---

597 EXTON THE MINIATURE CHARM OF RUTLAND

6½ miles (10.4km) 3hrs **Ascent:** 425ft (130m)
Paths: Mainly field paths and firm farm tracks, 12 stiles
Suggested map: aqua3 OS Explorer 234 Rutland Water
Grid reference: SK 924112
Parking: Roadside parking in centre of Exton

Explore the open countryside and parkland around Exton.

1 With your back to **pub** leave Green on far R-H side on Stamford Road and, at end, turn **R**. This becomes Empingham Road and, when houses finish, continue over stream and turn **L** on public footpath.

2 Just before fence at end go over stile on **R** (not one ahead). Drop down across end of field. Turn **L** to stile in fence ahead. Cross it then follow wide, grassy track along shallow valley for 1 mile (1.6km), at one point climbing into field on **L** to avoid **Cuckoo Farm**. Finally it clambers up through fields on **R** to lane.

3 Turn **L** and walk on verge until just beyond bend, then go **L** on footpath ('Fort Henry and Greetham'). Follow this above **trout hatchery**, then head diagonally **R** via small concrete bridge to fence at top. Turn **L** to **Lower Lake**, then go ahead/**R** on surfaced drive for few paces, over stile to **L** of old bar gate, and out across pasture above water.

4 At far side turn **R** on to lane and then, in a few paces, turn **L** for footpath signposted 'Greetham'. Follow this alongside **Fort Henry Lake** and then on along corridor between woodland. At far end climb stairs to lane.

5 Turn **L** and walk up through woods and, when semi-surfaced drive bears **L**, go straight on through newly planted trees. Wide, unmade track now heads out across open fields for 1 mile (1.6km).

6 At trees on far side turn **L** on to track that descends and bears **L**. Here go straight on via stile and wooden plank footbridge and head up diagonally **L** towards top of field. Go over stile and turn **L** on to farm track.

7 At junction turn **R** on to straight, metalled lane. Bear **L** at fork before woods and follow this back to **Exton**. Follow signs around Home Farm, then turn **L** at end of West End and **R** by stone shelter into High Street and return to Green.

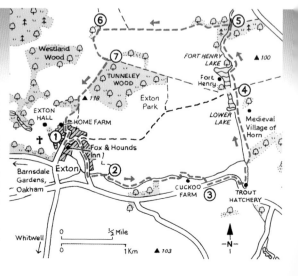

Rutland

RUTLAND WATER *A Waterside Walk*

4½ miles (7.2km) 2hrs 30min **Ascent:** 311ft (95m)
Paths: Wide and firm the whole distance
Suggested map: aqua3 OS Explorer 234 Rutland Water
Grid reference: SK 900075
Parking: Roadside parking in Upper Hambleton

A short but scenic introduction to the aquatic charms of Rutland Water.

❶ From **St Andrew's Church** in centre of **Upper Hambleton**, walk east on long and level main street as far as red pillar box. Turn **L** through gate for grassy lane ('public footpath') that leads straight through gate and down middle of sloping field.

❷ Go through gate at bottom and turn **R** on to wide track that runs just above shore. This popular and peaceful route around Hambleton peninsula is also shared by cyclists, so be alert. Follow it from field to field, and through **Armley Wood**, with views across **Rutland Water**. You gradually swing around tip of Hambleton peninsula with views towards dam at eastern end.

❸ When you arrive at tarmac lane (gated to traffic at this point, as it simply disappears into water a little further on!), go straight across to continue on same unmade track. It turns **R** and for short distance runs

parallel with road before heading **L** and back towards water's edge and mixed woodland.

❹ Approaching **Old Hall**, handsome building perched just above shore, turn **L** to reach its surfaced drive, then go **R** and walk along it for 160yds (146m) to reach cattle grid.

❺ At this point you can return directly to **Upper Hambleton** by following lane back uphill; otherwise veer **L** to continue along waterside track, with views across to Egleton Bay and corner of **Rutland Water** reserved for wildlife (out of bounds to sailing boats).

❻ After 500yds (457m) look for easily missed stile in hedge on your **R**, and public footpath that heads straight up field. (If you overshoot, or want to extend walk by ½ mile/800m, carry on along track to far end and return along lane to village.) Aim for apex of field, where successive stiles lead to narrow passageway between hedge and fence that eventually brings you out in churchyard in centre of village.

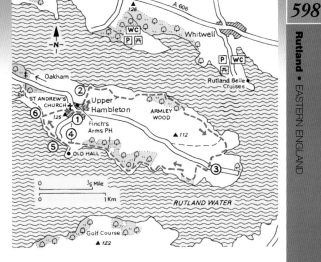

FRISBY ON THE WREAKE *A Village Ramble*

3¾ miles (6km) 1hr 45min **Ascent:** 150ft (40m)
Paths: Pasture, ploughed fields heavy if wet, around 20 stiles
Suggested map: aqua3 OS Explorer 246 Loughborough
Grid reference: SK 694176
Parking: Roadside parking on Main Street or Water Street, Frisby

Wander through the Wreake Valley.

❶ Go along **Frisby's** Main Street, past **post office**. Turn **L** into Mill Lane. After 50yds (46m) turn **R** between houses on public footpath (fingerpost bearing footprint). Walk over field, dropping slightly downhill. Cross double stile and ahead through 2nd field.

❷ Ignore turning down to railway (L), instead continue across further wide fields, with **Ash Tree Farm** away to your **R**. Despite lack of well-walked path, route is clearly indicated by yellow-topped signposts. Continue to road.

❸ Go across and continue through 2 smaller fields, 2nd in which horses are usually kept, and via kissing gate in corner to reach houses of **Kirby Bellars**. Turn **L** and walk down lane to **church**.

❹ Continue down narrowing lane, which twists and then **R**, past **nursery**. Track emerges into open field where you turn **L** and walk beside top fence. Where fence juts out before The Hollies go **R**, across

pasture, and over stile by lifebuoy for leafy path along causeway across **Priory Water** (nature reserve). At end go ahead over more stiles, as path veers **L** and follows bank of **River Wreake**. It then winds through copse to end at road bridge into **Asfordby**.

❺ To visit **Asfordby** turn **R** and take surfaced pathway off to **R** on far side of bridge. Otherwise cross road (but not bridge) for path opposite, which initially shadows river then strikes out diagonally **L** across 2 fields. Aim for far corner of 2nd, with spire of Frisby church just in view above treetops ahead.

❻ Turn **R** and walk along narrow, grassy field parallel with railway, then cross railway via pedestrian crossing ('stop, look and listen', as sign directs). Follow lane on far side until it bends **L**. Here go **R** into Carrfields Lane, then **L** via short alleyway and another quiet back street to reach Church Lane. Turn **L** and follow this back to Main Street. Entrance to church is via side of old school building on Church Street.

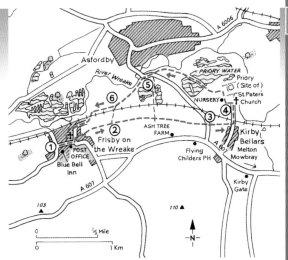

MEDBOURNE *Curious Customs*

7½ miles (12.1km) 4hrs **Ascent:** 787ft (240m)
Paths: Farm paths, tracks, some rough and muddy, over 16 stiles
Suggested map: aqua3 OS Explorer 233 Leicester & Hinckley (224 Corby, Kettering & Wellingborough, also useful)
Grid reference: SP 799929
Parking: Roadside parking near village hall, Main Street, Medbourne

Unusual Eastertide goings-on in two villages.

❶ Walk up Rectory Road, opposite church, which becomes path. Cross road at end and through fields opposite (veer slightly **R**). Turn **L**. Walk across to and through yard of **Nut Bush**. Just before entrance, take path from field on **R** to road. Turn **R** to **Nevill Holt**.

❷ Turn **L** at end. Where brick wall finishes go **L** through gate to cross wide field. Follow direction of finger sign and aim to **L** of **Hallaton** (in middle distance). Go through gate and drop down through 2 fields, separated by **Uppingham Road**. Beyond woodland strip go left, then up **R-H** side of next field along before veering half-L across top one – aim for solitary tree on skyline. At far corner drop down ahead to join track. Turn **R** and walk farm track into **Blaston**.

❸ At Church of St Giles turn **L** and follow **Hallaton Road** to junction at end. Go over. After 2nd stile turn **R** to walk through open pasture towards **Hallaton**.

Follow yellow-topped waymark posts, aiming initially for spire of **Hallaton** church, then veer to **R** of isolated clump of trees in middle of field. Cross footbridge.

❹ Go **L** then **R** beyond stile. Follow signs through modern housing development. Eventually turn **L** on to Medbourne Road. Keep ahead to centre of **Hallaton**.

❺ Leave village via passageway underneath house, just along from **Bewicke Arms** pub and almost opposite butter cross. Cross footbridge. Go directly up gently sloping field, aiming just to **R** of wooden fence beneath trees. Go through gate. Turn **L** for wide track ('**Macmillan Way**'). Continue along edge of 2 gated fields, then **L** into lane. Turn **R** at 1st bend. Follow this long, semi-surfaced lane below **Slawston Hill**.

❻ At road junction cross over and go down lane. 500yds (457m) beyond former railway bridge turn **L** for bridleway along foot of successive fields. At far end, turn **L** to follow road back into **Medbourne**.

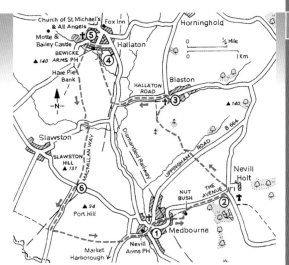

Leicestershire

601 FOXTON LOCKS *FLIGHTS OF FANCY*

5 miles (8km) 2hrs 30min Ascent: 213ft (65m) ▲
Paths: Canal tow path and open fields (mostly pasture), 12 stiles
Suggested map: aqua3 OS Explorer 223 Northampton & Market Harborough
Grid reference: SP 691891
Parking: Foxton Locks Country Park (pay-and-display)

Discover a staircase of locks.

❶ Turn **L** out of car park and along signposted path parallel with road to reach canal. Go **R**, under road bridge, then over footbridge, in order to turn **R** on far bank and along tow path to **Foxton Locks**. Descend lock staircase to basin at bottom.

❷ Go ahead past former lock-keepers' cottages and switch banks via high-arched brick footbridge (**Rainbow Bridge**). Walk along tow path beyond. Continue along this route for 1¾ miles (2.8km), following **Grand Union Canal** as it swings **L** beyond **Debdale Wharf**. Notice the boats moored in the marina, some for repairs and renovation, others are kept here permanently. There are lovely views towards **Kibworth Beauchamp** to the north.

❸ At bridge No 68 go over stile on **R** to cross metal footbridge via 2 more stiles. On far side go up **L-H** edge of wide, sloping field to pass **Debdale Grange**. Continue through top field to lane on far side.

❹ Turn **R** and walk along road for ¼ mile (400m) then, approaching road junction, cross stile on **L** for signposted public footpath across field, aiming for far edge of **Gumley Wood**. Follow track around side of plantation until 2nd stile, by section of fence used as horse jump.

❺ From here strike out across deeply undulating grassy field towards stile below trees on far side. To visit pub in village of **Gumley**, go **R** before stile for short uphill path, otherwise aim half-**L** through next field. Go over stile and directly out across more fields, separated by farm drive, to return to canal on very far side. Cross high, thin footbridge and turn **R** to return to basin and locks. Walk back up beside staircase, crossing over half-way up to visit **museum**.

❻ From **museum** follow path along its side (don't recross main canal again) and on along canal arm through trees. Go over lock and continue back to road bridge. Go under this. Turn **L** to return to car park.

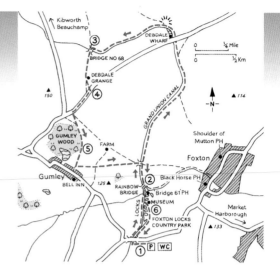

602 MARKET BOSWORTH *DOING BATTLE*

8¼ miles (13.2km) 4hrs 30min Ascent: 279ft (85m) ▲
Paths: Easy lanes and tow path, other paths may be muddy
Suggested map: aqua3 OS Explorers 232 Nuneaton & Tamworth; 233 Leicester & Hinckley
Grid reference: SK 412031 (on Explorer 232)
Parking: Market Bosworth Country Park (main car park), off B585

Visit England's most famous battlefield site.

❶ Facing playground and spinney in **Market Bosworth Country Park** (far end of large car park), turn **R** along grassy track through wildflower meadow to woods beyond. Follow gravel path through trees and bear **L** at fork. Look for wide kissing gate on **L**.

❷ Go through. Follow path for ½ mile (800m) along edge of woodland and past **Looking Glass Pond**.

❸ Go over stile and pass to **R** of **Woodhouse Farm**. Path continues along **L-H** side of field and then climbs **R-H** side of next.

❹ As hedge falls away well-walked path heads across middle of field before turning **R** approaching (but not quite at) top. It keeps to top of next field, then turns **L** across another to reach **Royal Arms Hotel** car park. Turn **R**. Walk through **Sutton Cheney** until, just past **church** entrance, turn **R** at junction ('**Shenton**').

❺ Follow lane as it forks **L**. In 550yds (503m) turn **L**, via Cheney Lane Battlefield car park, to **visitor centre**.

❻ Follow waymarked Battle Trail across **Ambion Hill** and down past Richard's and Henry's standards (bare flagpoles if they're not flying) to **Shenton Station**. Cross over railway line by gate and then turn **L** out of car park entrance on to lane. Continue to canal bridge.

❼ Cross over bridge to double back and turn **L** on to canal tow path, which is signposted '**Market Bosworth**'.

❽ After 2½ miles (4km) leave canal at **King's Bridge** (No 43), one after **Bosworth Wharf Bridge**. Cross this and then railway bridge beyond for field-edge path across stiles. Head half-**R** across 2 large open fields – aim to **L** of house in front of hilltop woodland. Go over another stile and along top of field before joining unmade lane into **Market Bosworth**.

❾ At end of lane, join narrowing road (Back Lane), **L** and ahead, that comes out in market place. Cross and walk past **Old Black Horse Inn**, then turn **L** into Rectory Lane, at end of which is a **country park**.

603 BRADGATE PARK *AMONG THE DEER*

3¾ miles (6km) 1hr 45min Ascent: 558ft (170m) ▲
Paths: Easy surfaced tracks and undulating grassy paths
Suggested map: aqua3 OS Explorer 246 Loughborough
Grid reference: SK 522098
Parking: Car park at Newtown Linford (pay-and-display)

In Leicester's scenic Bradgate Country Park.

❶ Enter grounds from large car park at **Newtown Linford** and turn sharply **L** on wide track. Go through open gateway and, ignoring paths off to **R**, stick on main route uphill (2 parallel tracks), keeping park's boundary wall in sight on your **L**.

❷ When level with wooden swing gate in wall, fork **R**. Go steadily uphill on wide grassy ride through banks of bracken, past small plantation known as **Tyburn** and soon see prominent hilltop **war memorial** up ahead on your **L**. Follow obvious grassy track to 'summit', then go round to **R** of walled plantation behind it to reach folly, **Old John Tower**. Although Leicester is only a few miles away, extensive views from this viewpoint (695ft/212m) are predominantly rural, with large tracts of woodland.

❸ Turn **R**, straight down hillside, to small circular pond in bracken below. Take **L** of 3 paths on far side and continue on to reach track around walled plantation, **Sliding Stone Enclosure**. Turn **L** and walk along this track for 100yds (91m).

❹ Ignore path down to gate in wall on **L**. Instead go straight on. Grassy track gradually descends to park boundary wall and then continues downhill on short tarmac strip past small underground reservoir.

❺ After 125yds (114m) take track off to **R**, by wooden bench and 2 drainage covers. This long, straight grassy track heads across middle of country park and is easy to follow. It passes between **Coppice Plantation** and **Dale Spinney**, from where there are good views across **Cropston Reservoir**. Continue to surfaced drive at bottom and turn **R** to visitor centre.

❻ Continue along this easy, tarmac route past **ruins** of house and restored **chapel**, then on alongside pools and waterfalls of small valley, **Little Matlock**. Look out for monkey puzzle tree and cedar of Lebanon, introduced to park in 19th century. Continue all way back to car park at **Newtown Linford**.

Leicestershire

WEST LEAKE HILLS *PANORAMIC HILLS*

4¼ miles (6.8km) 2hrs **Ascent:** 246ft (75m)

Paths: Field-edge paths, farm lanes and forest tracks
Suggested map: aqua3 OS Explorer 246 Loughborough
Grid reference: SK 527264
Parking: Roadside parking near West Leake church

An enjoyable walk with great views.

❶ Walk across road from **church**, half-way along **West Leake's** main street, to cross stile opposite. Go between houses and directly across open field. Cross stile at far side. Turn **R** to follow field-edge path to end.

❷ Go through to next field. Turn **L**. Now follow route alongside hedge, past vegetation-choked pond (often dry in summer), and out across middle of subsequent fields on obvious farm track. Far away to **L** are cooling towers of Ratcliffe-on-Soar power station.

❸ When you arrive at wide gravel track, turn **R** and follow this as far as dilapidated open barn, called **Grange Farm** on map, with hedge behind.

❹ Go **L** before hedge and after 275yds (251m) turn **R** for bridleway route (waymarked with blue arrows) up steep hillside between trees. At top this becomes clear, straight path through attractive mixed woodland of **Leake New Wood**. When you reach far side go through gate and across to far side of field.

❺ Turn **R**. Walk along initially open hilltop, with views **L** over Trent Valley. Continue along this easy, panoramic route via **Court Hill** for almost 1 mile (1.6km). Beyond trees of **Shiddock's Spinney**, golf course appears on your **L**. At fork of paths keep **R** so that you end up alongside arable field on your **R** and not fairway on your **L**.

❻ At **Crow Wood Hill** you reach bend of semi-surfaced lane. Turn **R** and follow its southwesterly route across open fields of **Fox Hill**, with wide views over to red tile roofs of **East Leake**.

❼ When drive turns into **Fox Hill Farm** go straight on along clear field-edge track ahead, and ignoring path off to **L** follow this long, straight route all way back down to **West Leake**. Vista now stretches out southwards, where wooded ridges of Charnwood Forest (especially Beacon Hill and Bradgate Park) dominate the skyline. At road junction at bottom go straight on for centre of village.

LAMBLEY *DEEP IN THE DUMBLES*

6¼ miles (10.1km) 3hrs 30min **Ascent:** 508ft (155m)

Paths: Undulating paths and green lanes, over 20 stiles
Suggested map: aqua3 OS Explorer 260 Nottingham
Grid reference: SK 627452
Parking: Recreation ground car park behind school (opposite Nags Head, on Catfoot Lane)

The hidden dells of Lambley's Dumbles.

❶ From **Nags Head pub** walk down Main Street into village. In 220yds (210m) go **R** for public footpath between houses and around edge of fenced field. Turn **L** at end. Cross successive stiles (at 2nd take **L-H** choice of 2) for path behind houses. Turn **L**, via gate, to descend, cross road, and enter **nature reserve**.

❷ Veer **L** to gate in far **L** corner. Turn **R** and out along bottom of several large fields, cutting across lower part of 2nd. At opening to large field (straight ahead) by copse, turn **L**.

❸ Follow wide track uphill to **L** of hedge. In far corner of 3rd field, with grassy airstrip along its middle, turn **L** (not footpath straight on) and walk along field edge.

❹ Just before it ends go **R** and, following direction of footpath post (not bridleway), aim half-**L** across next field then bear **L** across pasture. Drop down hillside, to stile beyond wooden enclosure in far corner by road.

❺ Turn **R** and walk along verge past **Wood Barn Farm** to sharp R-H bend. Go **L** across top of fields to reach wooded track on far side, here turn **L** and follow it back to junction with **Lingwood Lane**.

❻ Turn **R**, cross field (aiming half-L), then follow waymarks down through 3 fields into woodland at bottom. Go straight on via footbridge, **L** into field on far side, then almost immediately **R** and walk up through field to top. Turn **L** on to road for 100yds (91m), then go **R** beside bungalow to descend diagonally **R** across ridged fields to football pitch.

❼ At far corner continue on path to walk through newly planted woodland area, **Bonney Doles**. Go over footbridge, turn **L**, and follow field edge to corner.

❽ Here path with handrail leads into wooded dell for short way. Ignore this. Continue to cross footbridge. Turn **L**. Follow path through woods then field bottom along south side of **Lambley Dumble**. Eventually turn **L** on to Spring Lane to return to car park.

EASTWOOD *IN THE FOOTSTEPS OF DH LAWRENCE*

5¾ miles (9.2km) 2hrs 30min **Ascent:** 360ft (110m)

Paths: Rough field and woodland tracks, heavy-going after rain
Suggested map: aqua3 OS Explorer 260 Nottingham
Grid reference: SK 481481
Parking: Colliers Wood car park, Engine Lane, off B600

Explore the countryside that provided inspiration for much of the writer's work.

❶ Walk out of entrance of **Colliers Wood** car park. Turn **R** then **L** along pavement of B600. At bend turn **R** by **Beauvale Lodge** and take track to **L** (signposted 'Felly Mill'). Walk this fenced route through **High Park Wood**, above **Moorgreen Reservoir**, branching **L** after ¼ mile (400m) at footpath sign. Continue on main track until open field appears on R.

❷ Continue for 150yds (137m). Turn **R** at stile. Walk up **L-H** side of line of trees separating 2 fields. At far side turn **L**; follow woodland edge. Go around corner and, joining wide farm track, continue alongside forest. (Site of Felly Mill is to **L**.) After ½ mile (800m) turn **R** beyond bench for public footpath through trees.

❸ Where this emerges at junction of 3 forest rides keep ahead. Turn **L** after bend on clearly indicated footpath into woods. This emerges to follow field edge, swinging **R** on far side and eventually reaching lay-by.

❹ Turn **R** to see remains of **Beauvale Priory**, otherwise go **L** and walk down lane to bend by **Brooksbreasting Farm**. Go sharply **R**, along **L-H** edge of field. Turn **L**. Descend through 2 fields. Look for gap in undergrowth to **R**, and go over footbridge.

❺ Turn **L** and follow direction of sign across lower part of field. Continue along top edge of successive fields, going **R** to skirt final sloping field before descending to road.

❻ Cross over and turn **R** to enter churchyard of **St Mary** at Greasley, next to **Minton's Tea Rooms**. At far side exit churchyard on footpath ('Moorgreen'). Go across field and continue up through stables to reach road at top.

❼ Turn **L** and almost immediately **R** for enclosed path between houses. Follow waymarks across and down through fields, and at bottom go **R** for path back into **Colliers Wood**. Turn 1st **L** to reach ponds, and car park beyond.

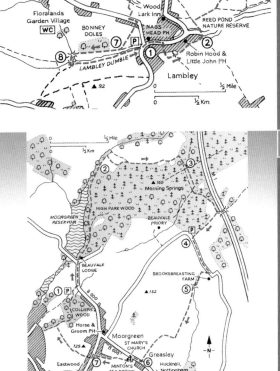

607 NEWSTEAD ABBEY *BYRON'S ROMANTIC HOME*

5¾ miles (9.2km) 3hrs Ascent: 460ft (140m)
Paths: Firm, uncomplicated paths and tracks, well-signposted
Suggested map: aqua3 OS Explorer 270 Sherwood Forest
Grid reference: SK 541540
Parking: Newstead Abbey car park (small charge), access from A60

Explore Byron's beautiful mansion.

❶ From main car park walk down drive short distance to **abbey**, then on along tarmac lane below large **Upper Lake**. Follow this route for 1¼ miles (2km) until you exit perimeter of park after 2nd lodge.

❷ Immediately turn **L** and go through gate to reach small hill with young trees (**Freckland Wood**). Quite easy path runs up and across its panoramic top, or may skirt its R-H foot on waymarked **National Cycle Network Route 6**. Both routes meet up on far corner for direct 1¼-mile (2km) track all way to **Linby**.

❸ Turn **L** when you emerge close to roundabout, and **L** again to walk through **Linby** as far as **pub**. Cross over to read notice board by bus stop detailing village's history. Continue out of village on pavement opposite 2nd of 2 medieval road-side crosses.

❹ When pavement ends cross over once more and take popular footpath on **L** across **Church Plantation**. Continue across **River Leen**, then half-

way up next field go through archway in hedge on **L** to reach tiny Papplewick church. Leave churchyard via main gate and go down surfaced drive to main road. Turn **L** and walk along pavement for 550yds (503m) until entrance for **Papplewick Hall**.

❺ Turn **L**, not to enter hall's gated driveway but for wide, semi-surfaced Hall Lane that runs via green gate past **Top Farm**. Where lane bends sharply **L**, around brick wall, go straight on via gate along hedged farm track across fields. Where farm track turns **R** to **Newstead Grange**, go straight on along main grassy track towards wooded perimeter of park.

❻ Follow waymarks around lodge and continue along surfaced drive through trees – look out for ancient beech and oak along way. About ¾ mile (1.2km) beyond lodge, lane bends **L** and path branches off ahead/**R**, clearly indicated. Soon it drops down to reach main drive to **abbey**.

❼ Turn **L** and walk along road to car park.

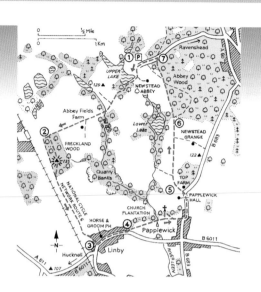

608 SHERWOOD FOREST *A MERRIE TALE*

5½ miles (8.8km) 2hrs 30min Ascent: 278ft (85m)
Paths: Easy woodland tracks and wide forest rides
Suggested map: aqua3 OS Explorer 270 Sherwood Forest
Grid reference: SK 626676 **Parking:** Sherwood Forest Visitor Centre (pay-and-display)

Walk among the oaks of this legendary forest.

❶ Facing main entrance to **Sherwood Forest Visitor Centre** from car park, turn **L** and follow signposted route to **Major Oak**.

❷ Go along curving path as it completes semi-circle around impressive old tree and continue as far as junction with public bridleway (signposted). Turn **L** here and walk this straight route for ¼ mile (400m), ignoring all paths off.

❸ At green notice board, warning of nearby military training area, main path bears **L**. Instead go ahead, past metal bar gate, for path that continues over crossroads to become wide, fenced track through pleasant open country of heather and bracken known as **Budby South Forest**.

❹ At very far side go through gate and turn **L** on to unmade lane, and continue for ¾ mile (1.2km).

❺ At major junction just before plantation, turn **L** ('Centre Tree'). With rows of conifers on **R**, and good views across **Budby South Forest** on **L**, keep to this

track. Where track divides into 2 parallel trails, gravelly track on **R** is cycle route, while more leafy and grassy ride to **L** is bridleway, but either can be used.

❻ When you reach **Centre Tree** – huge spreading oak – 2 routes converge to continue past bench down wide avenue among trees. Don't go down this but instead turn **L** and, ignoring paths off, carry straight on along main track back into heart of forest.

❼ After almost ¾ mile (1.2km) pass metal bar gate on **R** and meet bridleway coming in from **L**. Ignoring path straight ahead (which returns to **Major Oak**) bear **R** on main track, past bare holes and dips hollowed out by children's bikes. At large junction of criss-crossing routes go straight on ('Fairground') so that open field and distant housing becomes visible to your **R**. Wide sandy track descends to field by **Edwinstowe** cricket ground. **Art and Craft Centre** and **youth hostel** are on far side, and village centre beyond.

❽ To return to **visitor centre** and car park, follow signposted track back up past **cricket ground**.

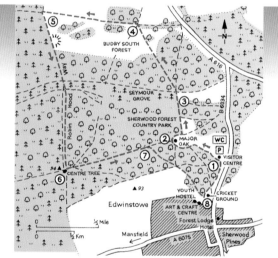

609 CLUMBER PARK *ENJOYING COUNTRY LIFE*

3¾ miles (6km) 2hrs 15min Ascent: 131ft (40m)
Paths: Clear, level paths and tracks throughout
Suggested map: aqua3 OS Explorer 270 Sherwood Forest
Grid reference: SK 625745
Parking: Main car park in Clumber Park near tea rooms (pay)

Clumber Park provides an enjoyable day out for all ages.

❶ From tea room, shop and information point near main car park, walk across site of former mansion down to lakeside. Turn **R** along clear path along shore and through area of patchy woodland. Continue on path, which curves **L** then **R**, to **Clumber Bridge**.

❷ Cross bridge and turn **L** past car park to resume route by shore. If path by water's edge below trees is boggy then switch to wider, firmer track further back. As you draw opposite site of former house, there are paths off across parkland to your **R** – detailed map available from NT shop. At far corner of lake swing **L** on embankment path. To **R** is area of wetland popular for birdwatching. Carry on past toilet block at **Hardwick** to surfaced road beyond car park.

❸ Go **L** on to road and in 50yds (46m) turn **R**, before causeway begins, for narrow, sandy path up through dense vegetation. Follow this twisting route through

The Lings. Trees include beech, sweet chestnut, silver birch, yew and pines. When you drop down and emerge into open, flat area beyond end of lake, walk ahead to turn **L** on to wide, curving gravel track.

❹ In few paces, where narrowing route veers **L** towards shore, keep ahead to **L** of 2 grassy paths. At end turn **L** on to wide track that crosses road and continues past wooden barrier into **Ash Tree Hill Wood**.

❺ Go over crossroads of tracks and on along this popular and direct route through trees, ignoring **R** turn. When you emerge in open ground on far side, continue ahead to ornate gateway into wooded **Pleasure Ground** ahead.

❻ Go through this and veer **L** on any minor path through undergrowth to reach main lakeside route. Turn **R**. Follow this along **Lincoln Terrace** back to start. Just beyond lawned terrace looping track to **R**, across lawns, leads to church and car park.

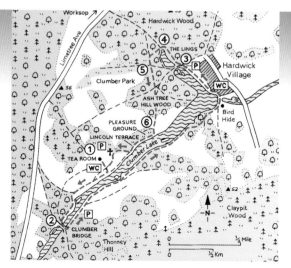

610

DANESHILL LAKES *WILDLIFE EXCURSION*

3 miles (4.8km) 1hr 30min **Ascent:** Negligible
Paths: Firm gravel tracks and woodland paths
Suggested map: aqua3 OS Explorer 279 Doncaster
Grid reference: SK 668865
Parking: Nature reserve car park, Daneshill Road, signed from A638

An easy stroll around a watery nature reserve near Retford.

❶ From car park go through main gate and ahead past notice board on wide gravel track. At junction swing **R**, large lake opens up on **L**. Go past **warden's office** and sailing club hut along water's edge.

❷ Approaching railway look for 2 large track-side signs 'Edinburgh 350 miles'. First **L** turn is continuation of lakeside path, and 2nd **L** is via dog-run next to railway. Both join up 350yds (320m) later and resume easy tour around main lake, past large bushes of rose hip. Second, smaller lake opens up on right.

❸ When you meet fence at end, with open field beyond, turn **L**. As this bears **L** after 300yds (274m) take small grassy path into woods half-**R**, as indicated by small wooden post bearing letters 'MM'. This wildlife trail wanders through bushes and trees and beside stream (look out for pond-dipping platform). When it finally emerges from undergrowth turn **R** and

R again to return to car park. Continue via small path through trees to **L** of road entrance and cross road.

❹ Go through gateway on opposite side and turn **L** on to wide track ('Easy Access to Reserve') – ignore footpath to right. Follow this track to wooden footbridge. Go across, then turn **R** and walk along to notice board by woodland pond.

❺ Continue to follow this easy and obvious track through reserve, keeping ditch and stream on your R-H side and ignoring turning to R across footbridge.

❻ Unless you want to make diversion to visit Ranskill, ignore R turn for Millennium Pathway. Instead stick to main path as it completes giant loop around nature reserve. Look out for pools and scrapes among the undergrowth, which, unless they've dried out in hot weather, are a focus for frogs and beetles. After about 1 mile (1.6km) you arrive back at wooden footbridge. Turn **R** here to cross it, go through gateway to road and cross over to return to car park.

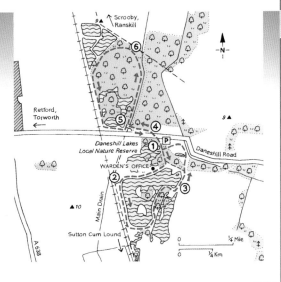

611

WOOLSTHORPE BY BELVOIR *KING OF THE CASTLE*

4¾ miles (7.7km) 2hrs 30min **Ascent:** 558ft (170m)
Paths: Tow path, field and woodland tracks and country lane
Suggested map: aqua3 OS Explorer 247 Grantham
Grid reference: SK 837342
Parking: Main Street in Woolsthorpe by Belvoir

A fairy-tale castle and a lost canal.

❶ Walk northwards out of **Woolsthorpe by Belvoir** on the pavement of **Sedgebrook Road**, continuation of Main Street, towards **Bottesford**. Turn **R** into wide-verged lane for the Rutland Arms pub (signposted) and go over canal bridge at **Woolsthorpe Wharf**.

❷ Turn **L**. Follow straight, grassy bank of **Grantham Canal** until **Stenwith Bridge** (No 60). Go underneath and **R**, for short path up and on to road. Turn **L**. Follow this over old railway bridge and out along wide lane of oak trees. At far end it bends **L**, and here turn **R**.

❸ Follow initially hedged and unmade Longmoor Lane for ¾ mile (1.2km). At far end turn **L** before bridge, to join gravel tow path, and walk along this to wooden arched bridge ('Bridle Bridge').

❹ Cross bridge. Head across middle of arable field. Go over course of old railway again and continue up L-H side of sloping field. At top turn **L** on to well-walked track.

❺ Follow track with views towards hills surrounding **Grantham**. Where track kinks L, after focced section, go straight on/**R** across wide field – follow direction of public footpath signpost and aim for hedge opening at very far side of field. Go across **Cliff Road** for track into woodland.

❻ Just before private tip, turn **L** to enter field via stile. Turn **R** and follow field edge along and then down grassy slope back to **Woolsthorpe**. Excellent views across head of Vale of Belvoir to Belvoir Castle opposite. At bottom go over stile behind cricket scorebox, along edge of pitch (football ground to L), and down drive of **pub** to reach village centre.

❼ To extend walk to **Belvoir Castle**, turn **L** into Main Street then **R** into Belvoir Lane. At end of cul-de-sac go over small brick bridge and continue straight ahead across fields towards hilltop fortification. Using same route to return, complete journey is further 2 miles (3.2km) and involves further 100ft (30m) of ascent.

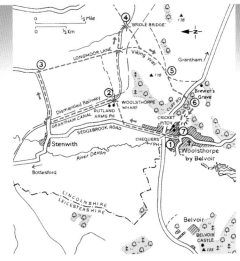

612

GEDNEY DROVE END *WILDLIFE IN THE WASH*

5¾ miles (9.2km) 2hrs 30min **Ascent:** Negligible
Paths: Field edges, firm tracks and sea banks
Suggested map: aqua3 OS Explorer 249 Spalding & Holbeach
Grid reference: TF 463292
Parking: Roadside parking in centre of Gedney Drove End (off A17 east of Holbeach)

A wander on the South Lincolnshire coast.

❶ With your back to **Rising Sun pub**, turn **L**. Walk along **Dawsmere Road** past junction and take signposted public footpath on **R**, between bungalows, opposite playground sign. At far side of field cross footbridge and up steps then turn **L** into wide field.

❷ For 1 mile (1.6km) walk along field edge (former sea wall) keeping more or less parallel with present, higher sea bank to **R**. And as sign indicates, continue ahead where old sea bank veers invitingly away to R.

❸ When field ends near woodland turn **R** for 50yds (46m) then, faced with small thicket, descend to join wide farm track on **L**. Turn **R**. Follow main, higher route (ignore lower track) alongside belt of woodland. This wide, gravel track heads out towards sea bank then bends **L** and continues past Browns Farm.

❹ Stay on main track for ¾ mile (1.2km) beyond farm, then go **R** by old wartime pill box for short path over to sea wall.

❺ Turn **R** and follow either grassy top of **sea bank** (public right of way) or surfaced lane just below it past succession of military observation towers. Bombing range is spread out before you, with low Norfolk coast over to R and Lincolnshire seaboard towards Boston and Skegness leftwards.

❻ After 3rd tower ignore gated road that heads off inland (short cut back to **Gedney**) but instead continue along grass-topped sea bank past final building until you reach stile.

❼ In sight ahead is public footpath sign that points **R**, down steps, for direct path along field edge to junction of open lane. Here continue straight ahead into **Gedney**, turning **R** at end back on to **Dawsmere Road**. If you want to prolong your Wash-side wander continue beyond stile for 1¼ miles (2km) until sea bank divides. Bend **R**, on inland arm, and join small lane before turning **R** on to Marsh Road back into **Gedney Drove End**.

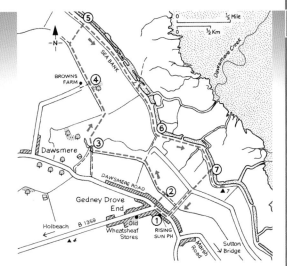

Lincolnshire

Lincolnshire • EASTERN ENGLAND

613 BARDNEY *SAINTLY PATHS*

7¾ miles (12.5km) 4hrs Ascent: Negligible **0**
Paths: Easy field paths and bridleways
Suggested map: aqua3 OS Explorer 273 Lincolnshire Wolds South
Grid reference: TF 120694
Parking: Horncastle Road, centre of Bardney

A walk to the ruined abbeys around Bardney.
1 From **RAF memorial** opposite **Bardney** post office, walk along adjacent Church Lane. Just beyond **St Lawrence Church** take public footpath indicated on **L**, which squeezes between two fences and turns **R** along end of gardens. (This path can be overgrown in summer, in which case follow road around to **R**, past Methodist chapel, and then **L** on to main road, turning off **L** at sign for **Viking Way**.)
2 At end of path turn **L** on to wide track through fields, with huge sugar **factory** away to your **R**. Ignore permissive bridleways into **Southrey Wood** (**L**).
3 When wood ends proceed on main track, which despite kink maintains its southeasterly direction. When it reaches buildings of **Southrey** it swings **L** past **Poplars Farm**. Take 1st road on **R**. At end of road go **R** again to reach **pub** at far end of **Ferry Road**.
4 Turn **L** on to raised river bank. The overgrown platforms and signs of the former waterside railway

station make a strange spectacle. Follow old trackbed alongside anglers by river for 650yds (594m).
5 Go **L** at public footpath sign and across footbridge over drainage dyke for track across field. Continue straight on as it turns into firmer track and then surfaced **Campney Lane**.
6 At road junction at end turn **L**. After sharp **L** bend, turn **R** on to signposted public bridleway. Follow this wide grassy ride between hedges. Go through gate and past **farm** to reach **remains of Tupholme Abbey**.
7 Beyond **abbey** turn **R** on to road and then almost immediately **L** on to lane. About 750yds (686m) after **Low Road Farm** take public footpath indicated between two fields on **L**. Fence is first on your **R**, but when small dividing dyke appears keep both it and fence on your **L**. Go across small wooden bridge and then through another field to turn **R** on to cross track all way to road.
8 Turn **L** for verge then pavement back to **Bardney**.

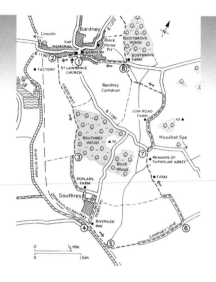

614 BELCHFORD *VILLAGE LIFE*

7½ miles (12.1km) 4hrs Ascent: 672ft (205m) **3**
Paths: Variety of up-and-down field paths and tracks, over 15 stiles
Suggested map: aqua3 OS Explorer 273 Lincolnshire Wolds South
Grid reference: TF 293754
Parking: Lay-by near church on Belchford's main street

An undulating walk through a trio of villages.
1 From **Belchford church** walk west along Main Road. Turn **L** into Dams Lane, opposite post office. At end continue through kissing gate and along fenced path, then uphill beside fields. At top go **R**. After 100yds (91m), go **L** through wide gap in hedge for path directly uphill.
2 Continue on waymarked field-edge route across hilltop before heading south towards **Fulletby** via undulating pasture. Turn **L** into lane then, at top, **L** again to main road.
3 Cross stile opposite, by private drive, for view over southern Wolds. Route now continues east for 1½ miles (2.4km) down pasture then along bottom of ploughed fields by woodland. Near far end go over stile on **R** and, skirting **R**-**H** edge of fishing lake at **Salmonby**, walk along drive of **Beck House** to road.
4 Turn **L** and follow road uphill, going **L** at junction. After ¼ mile (400m) turn **R** for field-edge route across

to another lane. Turn **R** then **L** on to path via newly planted hedge, ponds and woodland. On far side of woodland turn **R** for path to **Tetford**.
5 Turn **L** along West Street for 100yds (91m) then go **R**, before holly hedge, for well-walked path across wide ploughed field. Cross 2 stiles on far side and turn **L** along East Street past **pub** and church. Follow road around into North Street and along to triangular junction with West Street at far end.
6 Go **R** by **Wood Farm** for road out of village. Where this bends sharply **R**, keep ahead past **Platts Lane**, wide farm track across fields. Where main track swings up to ruined **Glebe Farm**, proceed along field edge down to small bridge.
7 On far side turn **R** and follow track up alongside ditch across open fields. Route is signposted **L** and, after zig-zagging to north of **Glebe Farm Low Yard**, it turns **R** on to surfaced farm drive to road.
8 Turn **L**. Follow this back to centre of **Belchford**.

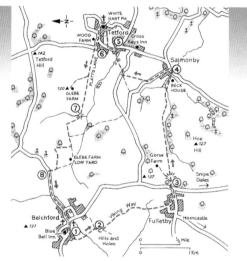

615 SALTFLEET *ON THE DUNES*

4¾ miles (7.7km) 2hrs 30min Ascent: Negligible **0**
Paths: Coastal tracks and field paths, some muddy after rain
Suggested map: aqua3 OS Explorer 283 Louth & Mablethorpe
Grid reference: TF 467917
Parking: Nature reserve car park at Rimac, off corner of A1031

A wander along the wildlife-rich salt marshes of North Lincolnshire.
1 Walk out of far (seaward) end of car park. Turn **L**, through gate (or over stile) and up steps, then out along top of dunes with sea to your **R**. Go past **Sea View Farm** and small parking area and continue beyond white barred gate, forking **R** to marshes. Go **L** and follow clear track along edge of marshes.
2 At far end join rough lane across 2 bridges, then turn **R** on to pavement of coast road. After 100yds (91m) cross small bridge and turn **R** for wide, bumpy lane ('**Saltfleet Haven**'). Continue to small car park among dunes – and bit further if you want to view sandy bay and river mouth (tide permitting).
3 At back of marsh and, with all your back to **Haven**, go up steps and take one of several faint paths through dunes to pick up wide track that runs just seawards of vegetation-topped dunes (not along actual water's edge). Strip of marshes is to your **R**.

4 In under ½ mile (800m), turn **L** up concrete ramp by evergreen trees and walk down **Sea Lane** past **caravan parks**. Turn **L** at end, then **R** after **Crown Inn** into Pump Lane. At far end follow unmade track as it curves **L**, between houses and, at gap in hedge, take footbridge on **R** for path across fields.
5 Emerging on bend of Louth Road, turn **L** and just after **Hilltop Farm** turn **R**, across footbridge, for long field-edge public footpath.
6 At junction of tracks at far side go straight on, over small stone bridge across ditch near house. Go over 1st of several wooden footbridges and continue alongside **Mar Dike** until you switch banks nearing far end, to reach road.
7 Turn **L** and descend to crossroads. Go straight over and along drive opposite as far as **Sea View Farm**. Turn **R** on waymarked public footpath through farmyard and field beyond, and continue on clear path along landward edge of dunes to return to car park.

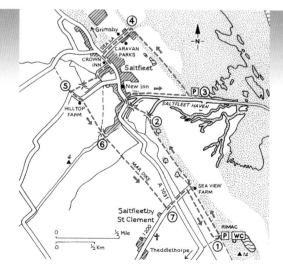

Lincolnshire

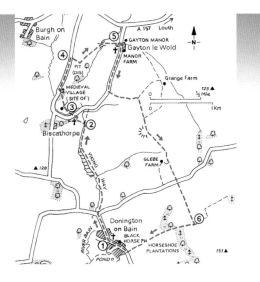

DONINGTON ON BAIN *A Taste for Lincolnshire*

616

6 miles (9.7km) 3hrs **Ascent:** 410ft (125m)

Paths: Bridleways and lanes, field paths, may be boggy, 17 stiles
Suggested map: aqua3 OS Explorer 282 Lincolnshire Wolds North
Grid reference: TF 236829
Parking: Main Road, Donington on Bain

A scenic walk through the Wolds.

1 Walk out of village northwards, past Norman church and post office, on to Mill Road. At 1st junction turn **R** ('Hallington and Louth'), then in a few paces go **L**, over stile. Walk along bottom of successive fields, with **River Bain** on **L** and Belmont Transmitting Station dominating skyline further west. After ¾ mile (1.2km), and having passed fishing lake, reach footbridge.

2 Cross over to **Biscathorpe's** isolated little church, rebuilt in the mid-1800s in medieval Gothic style. Walk around perimeter wall and continue past house and on across another footbridge ahead.

3 Head half-**L** across site of deserted **medieval village**. Ditches, ridges and mounds indicate its layout, and there are more abandoned settlements to the north of the A157. Head towards top of pathless, low hill and cross stile for path through small plantation. Turn **R** on to lane. Walk along this for 550yds (503m).

4 Go over stile on **R** for signposted public footpath down side of disused workings, then **L** across wide field, aiming for far corner down by stream. Go over footbridge and half-**L** through 2 more fields to reach lane at **Gayton le Wold**, with **Gayton Manor** beyond.

5 Turn **R**. Take lane past **Manor Farm's** whitewashed buildings, another miniature church, and out across hilltop fields. In ½ mile (800m), where lane bends R, go **L** on broad track ('public bridleway'). Veer **R** into field at top and follow this waymarked route alongside huge ploughed fields. Continue around and above back of **Glebe Farm**, by thick hedge, and go straight over lane.

6 In just under ½ mile (800m) from road crossing, turn **R** where signpost points to public footpath downhill behind hedge. Follow this wide track gradually down via **Horseshoe Plantations**, then hedge by fields of horses. Turn **R** on to road at bottom to return to centre of **Donington on Bain**.

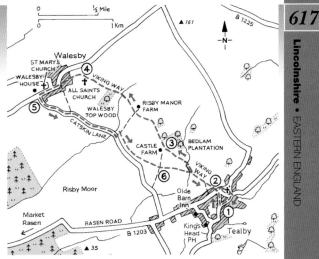

TEALBY *Churches of the Wolds*

617

4¼ miles (6.8km) 2hrs **Ascent:** 721ft (220m)

Paths: Field paths, some steep and others muddy, 16 stiles
Suggested map: aqua3 OS Explorer 282 Lincolnshire Wolds North
Grid reference: TF 157907
Parking: Front Street, Tealby, near tea rooms

A quiet ramble through two beautiful Lincolnshire villages.

1 From **Tealby** Tea Rooms walk down Front Street as far as B Leaning & Sons, butchers. Turn **R** into Church Lane, which becomes walkway. At top, turn **L** and cross over **Rasen Road** to follow public footpath that runs between houses on opposite side. As far as **Walesby** you will be following Norse helmet waymarks of **Viking Way**.

2 Cross rough pasture, aiming for stile in far bottom corner. Go over this and along path ahead, ignoring footbridge to **L**. Walk up hillside ahead to reach corner of **Bedlam Plantation** above **Castle Farm**.

3 Turn **R**. Cross stile for fenced path beside woods. At far end strike out diagonally **L** and down undulating grassy field to pass below **Risby Manor Farm**. Keep ahead, crossing deep valley, to reach R-H edge of **Walesby Top Wood**. Beyond stile path leads out across field to **All Saints Church, Walesby**.

4 From church, continue along **Viking Way** as it drops down wide track then lane into village. At Rasen Road at bottom go straight on, past **St Mary's Church**, to junction with Catskin Lane.

5 If you need refreshment, cross road to **Walesby House**. Otherwise turn **L** and walk along **Catskin Lane** for ¾ mile (1.2km) until just past R-H curve, then turn **L** at entrance of farm drive and go over cattle grid. This public bridleway leads back up to hilltop, but you should turn **R** in few paces and join footpath route (not defined) across rough pasture, initially parallel with road. At large ploughed field go along its L-H side to meet drive to **Castle Farm**.

6 Public footpath continues east over field beyond. Path is waymarked at either end (at time of writing it had been ploughed; line of path indicated by sticks). At far side of field, cross stile and descend to cross footbridge. Turn **R** to rejoin route back to **Tealby**. This time turn **L** up **Rasen Road** to visit **All Saints Church**.

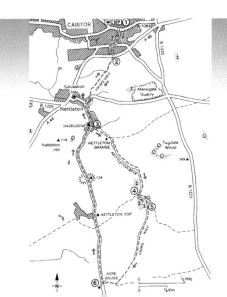

CAISTOR *North Wolds' Geology*

618

6¾ miles (10.9km) 3hrs 30min **Ascent:** 640ft (195m)

Paths: Field paths (mainly pasture) and firm tracks, over 20 stiles
Suggested map: aqua3 OS Explorer 282 Lincolnshire Wolds North
Grid reference: TA 118014
Parking: Public car park behind town hall, Caistor (follow signs)

Walk to the top of the Wolds to unearth the origins of Lincolnshire's gentle hills.

1 From car park walk through to Market Place, then leave down Plough Hill (signposts for **A46** and **Viking Way**). Turn corner at bottom by Pigeon Spring. At end, cross over Nettleton Road for public footpath along passageway. Thread your way (**L**) through small estate, following waymarks for **Viking Way** (Viking helmet).

2 Cross over Caistor bypass and go directly ahead through 6 fields towards **Nettleton**, veering diagonally **L** in last to skirt bungalow. Turn **R** into lane below and walk to junction in middle of village. Go **L** on Normanby Road. In little over ¼ mile (400m), leave lane for private drive on **L** ('public bridleway') by house called **Hazeldene**.

3 Follow this route as far as **Nettleton Grange**, then veer **L** with track as it goes through gate. On far side of gate turn **R** (main track goes straight on) and for ½ mile (800m) follow public footpath alongside **Nettleton Beck**, keeping stream and ponds on R. Ignore side valley to L, and eventually route climbs rough grassy hillside to emerge on surfaced lane.

4 Turn **L** and walk along lane uphill for 150yds (137m) until sign points **R** for track into woodland. Follow undulating path bricked-up tunnel entrances, remains of former ironstone workings.

5 Go out across stiles for more open pasture and route that keeps to **L** of **Nettleton Beck**. When stream disappears into spring, continue uphill beyond stile to reach final, upper part of valley. Turn **R** at top on to farm track (bridleway) and along to lane at end near **Acre House**.

6 Turn **R**. Follow lane, via **Nettleton Top**, all the way back to village of **Nettleton**. There are superb views over the flat plain of North Lincolnshire to South Yorkshire and Humber, with the towers of the Humber Bridge visible on a clear day. At **Nettleton** retrace your steps back to **Caistor**.

Lincolnshire • EASTERN ENGLAND

Essex

619 HARWICH SEAFARERS AND WANDERERS

4 miles (6.4km) 1hr 30min Ascent: Negligible
Paths: Town streets and promenade with gentle cliffs
Suggested map: aqua3 OS Explorer 197 Ipswich, Felixstowe & Harwich
Grid reference: TM 259328
Parking: Free car parks at Ha'penny Pier and informal street parking

An exciting maritime past.

❶ With your back to **Ha'penny Pier** turn **L** along The Quay and follow road into **Kings Quay Street**. Turn **L** just before colourful mural of local buildings and ships. Follow road, with sea on your **L**, until it turns inland. Take path by sea, which is start of **Essex Way**, a long distance path of 81 miles (130km) connecting **Harwich** with Epping. Pass **Harwich Town Sailing Club** and keep ahead along Esplanade where at low tide you can walk along shingle beach.

❷ Pass **Treadwheel Crane** on your **R** and continue along seafront taking care along sloping concrete walkway. Keep raised, fenced area of **Beacon Hill Fort** and gun emplacements to your **R**. As you pass breakwaters there are views of **Dovercourt**. Ignore steps to **R**; continue along **Essex Way**, walking parallel with upper road of **Marine Parade** on your **R**.

❸ Turn **R** into **Lower Marine Parade** and pass **War Memorial and Gardens** at junction with Fronk's

Road and **Marine Parade**. Continue, passing Cliff Hotel on **L** and then go **L** into **Kingsway**, opposite statue of **Queen Victoria**. Turn **R** into **High Street** and bear **L** into **Main Road**, passing **police station** on your **L**. Walk for 250yds (229m) and turn **R** up track to see **Redoubt** – Martello-style fort, part of defences against Napoleonic invasion. Continue to pass **Cox's Pond**, once owned by local bankers of same name.

❹ Pass **High Lighthouse** on **R**, turn **R** into **Wellington Road** and **L** into Church Street passing **St Nicholas' Church**. Turn **R** into Market Street and **L** into **Kings Head Street**, passing timber-framed Elizabethan houses including No 21, home of Christopher Jones, captain of the *Mayflower*.

❺ Turn **R** into The Quay. Facing the sea is Quayside Court, now apartments, but built in the 19th century as a hotel for travellers from the Continent who would arrive by steamer at what is now Trinity Quay, before continuing to London by rail.

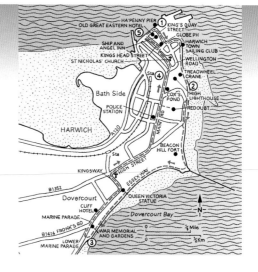

620 MANNINGTREE ENGLAND'S SMALLEST TOWN

7 miles (11.3km) 3hrs 30min Ascent: 98ft (30m)
Paths: Field paths, footpaths, tracks and sections of road, may be boggy, 5 stiles
Suggested map: aqua3 OS Explorer 184 Colchester, Harwich & Clacton-on-Sea
Grid reference: TM 093322
Parking: Pay-and-display at Manningtree Station; free at weekends

Where the Witchfinder General was born and buried.

❶ From car park turn **R** at Dedham following fingerpost ('Lawford') on steep, grassy path to **St Mary's Church**. Go through black gate, keep church on your **R**, cross stile over church wall. Turn **L** and, at wooden post, follow yellow waymark half **R** across meadow. Cross earth bridge over Wignell Brook, go **L** uphill keeping line of trees on your **R**. Just before house at top of hill, cross stile and bear **L** to **Cox's Hill**, on to **A137**.

❷ Cross **Cox's Hill**, turn **L** and after 40yds (37m), at fingerpost ('Essex Way'), turn **R**. Walk downhill with trees on **L** and pond on **R**. Pass housing estate on **L** and cross plank bridge over stream. Follow gravel path through Owl Conservation Area. Ignoring concrete path on **L**, turn half **R** on to cross-field path towards playing fields. Cross **Colchester Road**, and at T-junction turn **R** into Trinity Road, ignoring signs for

Essex Way. At Evangelical church turn **L** between houses to New Road, **Wagon and Horses pub** is on **L**.

❸ Cross **New Road** and follow yellow waymarked footpath between backs of houses. At T-junction turn **L** on to wide bridleway. After 70yds (64m) follow waymark half **R** and rejoin Essex Way. Continue, crossing earth bridge over brook and 2 stiles. Just after 2nd stile, follow track between 2 concrete posts into wooded slopes of **Furze Hill**. Emerge from woods, go ahead keeping to field-edge path to **Church Farm**. Turn **L** on to Heath Road.

❹ Cross road to low wall to **remains of St Mary's Church**. Continue north and turn **L** on to B1352 and into **Shrubland Road** which becomes green lane. Cross 1st stile on **R** and walk under railway. Turn **L** into Mistley Green which joins **High Street**.

❺ Turn **L** at **High Street**; follow The Walls by **River Stour** to **Manningtree**. Turn **L** into **High Street**. Walk 1 mile (1.6km) along **Station Road** to car park.

621 WALTON-ON-THE-NAZE WALTZING AROUND

4¼ miles (6.8km) 2hrs Ascent: Negligible
Paths: Grassy cliff paths, tidal salt marsh and some town streets
Suggested map: aqua3 OS Explorer 184 Colchester, Harwich & Clacton-on-Sea
Grid reference: TM 253218
Parking: Pay-and-display at Mill Lane and Naze Tower

A day beside the Essex coast exploring a town with two seasides.

❶ From Mill Lane car park turn **R** into High Street then **L** into Martello Street. Bear **L** along New Pier Street and go on to Pier Approach. To your **R** is the pier, at ½ mile (800m) the 2nd longest in England, after Southend. From here there are good views of the beaches of **Walton-on-the-Naze** and Frinton.

❷ Turn **L** and, with sea on your **R**, walk along Princes Esplanade through East Terrace at end of which is **Maritime Museum**. Continue walking along Cliff Parade and cliff tops to **Naze Tower**. Built by Trinity House in 1720 as a navigational aid, it was one of many **Martello** towers constructed along the east and southeast coasts of England to fend off Napoleonic invasion. Nowadays, the grassy area with wooden tables is a good place for a picnic.

❸ From car park café walk inland to Old Hall Lane, turn **L** and then **R** into Naze Park Road. At end of Naze

Park Road, where it bears sharp **L**, turn **R** on to narrow path and **L** on to field-edge path passing 2 small ponds filled with wildlife.

❹ After 100yds (91m), turn **L** on to cross path, go through gate and on to permissive path which follows sea wall, keeping caravan site on your **L** and Walton Channel on your **R**. This wide expanse of mudflats, islands, channels and small boats is a paradise for seabirds and is a Site of Special Scientific Interest. Skippers Island, an Essex Wildlife Trust nature reserve, is the habitat of rare seabirds and wildlife. Follow sea wall for ¾ mile (1.2km) then bear half **L** down embankment and into field.

❺ Walk 70yds (64m) to path between primary school playing field and houses and enter Saville Street past row of old cottages on your **R**. Take first **R** into North Street, continue to High Street and turn **R**. Turn **R** again into Mill Lane and return to car park.

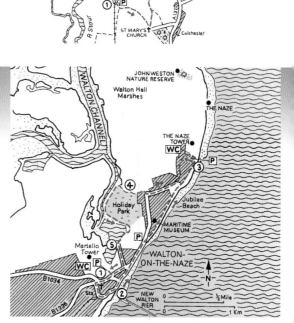

Essex

Bradwell-on-Sea *Smugglers and Sea Walls*

6 miles (9.7km) 3hrs **Ascent:** Negligible
Paths: Stony and grassy paths with some road walking
Suggested map: aqua3 OS Explorer 176 Blackwater Estuary, Maldon
Grid reference: TM 024078
Parking: Informal parking at the footpath at East Hall Farm entrance; free car park at Bradwell Nuclear Power Station

Sea air and a dying nuclear power station.
❶ Take wide grassy path from car park towards sea. In ½ mile (800m) reach **Chapel of St Peter's-on-the-Wall**. Continue walking towards sea for another 30yds (27m) and turn **L** at T-junction. After 100yds (91m) climb wooden steps to sea defence wall.
❷ At fingerpost ('Othona Community') turn **R**. Walk along wall with sea on your R. For next 2 miles (3.2km) stay on top of sea wall, mainly firm, grassy path punctuated with areas of concrete. On your L is private farmland. On your R, salt marsh gives way to white sand and shingle and mudflats at low tide. The seashore makes a lovely detour but at high tide you must remain on the concrete path. On seaward side there are concrete pill boxes. The 2nd pill box marks **Sales Point**, from where there are views of the mooring area used by Thames sailing barges. Follow path for 1 mile (1.6km).

❸ In 1½ miles (2.4km) reach **Bradwell Nuclear Power Station**. Either continue on the route by the coast or make a detour to the nature trail around the station and Visitor Centre. Route continues along sea wall to **Bradwell Waterside**.
❹ At jetty, turn **L** on to Waterside Road keeping yacht club and **Green Man pub** on your R. Continue along Waterside Road with marina on your R. Continue past marina and turn **L** into Trusses Road. At T-junction, turn **R** towards **Bradwell-on-Sea** (turn **L** here towards **Bradwell Nuclear Power Station** to **RAF memorial** at Bradwell Bay Airfield).
❺ At **Bradwell-on-Sea** follow High Street to its junction with East End Road where, on corner, is **St Thomas' Church** opposite **Kings Head pub**. Pass Caidge Cottages on L, village school on R and continue for about 1 mile (1.6km) along **Roman Road**, past **Cricketers pub**, before reaching car park.

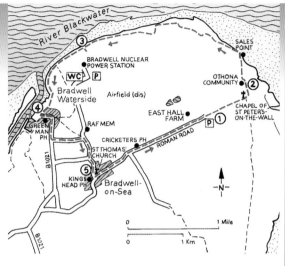

Paglesham *Paddling up the Creek*

6¼ miles (10.1km) 2hrs 45min **Ascent:** Negligible
Paths: Grassy sea wall, field edge, unmade tracks, 5 stiles
Suggested map: aqua3 OS Explorer 176 Blackwater Estuary, Maldon
Grid reference: TQ 943922
Parking: Informal street parking at Paglesham Eastend beside Plough and Sail Inn

A stroll along the sea wall.
❶ Walk to **L** of **Plough and Sail Inn** along driveable track. After 100yds (91m) follow fingerpost ahead to **L** of house ('Cobblers Row'). Keep along field-edge path, with arable fields either side, until path narrows and you approach houses in distance. Keeping red-brick wall on your L, go through white wicket gate, with brook on your R, and along lawn of **Well House**. Go through another wicket gate and turn **L** on to permissive path which becomes unmade road.
❷ At corrugated barn of **East Hall**, follow **Roach Valley** waymark, **R** and then **L**, and continue along good, grassy field edge. Walk by paddock fencing, with Church Hall on your R and pond on your L, to **St Peter's Church** at **Paglesham Churchend**.
❸ Keeping church on your R, continue along Churchend High Street to **Punch Bowl Inn**. Continue for 50yds (46m), take concrete path to your **R** and after few paces follow **Roach Valley** waymark, **L**,

which soon becomes grassy field-edge path running parallel with waterway on your L.
❹ Clamber up grassy embankment and, leaving **Roach Valley Way**, turn **R** on to sea wall of **Paglesham Creek**. Keep to path meandering by **creek**, which widens as you approach **River Roach**. To your L salt marshes stretch towards **River Crouch**. Much of landward side of embankment is given over to sheep grazing which makes this walk difficult for larger dogs as enclosures are often divided by wooden stiles and low-voltage electric fencing.
❺ As path bears **R**, with river on your L, maintain direction past oyster beds until you reach boatyard. Go down steps from sea wall and pick your way through boats and machinery to gate. Squeeze through gate. Follow unmade track until you pass row of cottages on L, followed by Cobblers Row and fingerpost on your R that was direction for outward journey. Turn **L**. Return to **Plough and Sail Inn** at **Paglesham Eastend**.

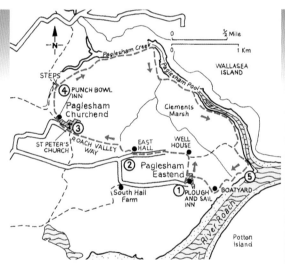

Maldon *A Historic Route*

4¼ miles (6.8km) 2hrs **Ascent:** 113ft (35m)
Paths: Mainly grassy paths, narrow in parts and prone to mud after rain, some roads, 5 stiles
Suggested map: aqua3 OS Explorer 183 Chelmsford & The Rodings, Maldon & Witham
Grid reference: TL 853070
Parking: Pay-and-display car park at Butts Lane

Combine historic Maldon, home of salt making, with a network of waterways.
❶ From car park turn **L** and walk towards Downs Road, keeping houses on your L. Footpath drops quite steeply and soon you have views of **River Chelmer** and salt works. At riverside turn **L**, cross Fullbridge with care, and follow grassy embankment keeping river on your R. Maintain direction and cross 2 stiles separated by concrete cross path. Follow often muddy path, going uphill through sloping meadow usually occupied by horses.
❷ At top of hill turn **R** over stile. Turn immediate **R**, descending through woodland and pass under **A414** Maldon bypass. Continue on rising concrete path, and at end turn **R** with field (often with horses) on your L.
❸ Continue along green lane bounded by hedgerows, keeping **L** to cross stile. Follow yellow waymark along grassy path keeping L to emerge on to gravel path via timber gate.

❹ Continue past **Beeleigh Abbey** on your R. At end of road turn **R**. Ignore footpath on L and pass **Beeleigh Grange** on L, and **Beeleigh Falls House** on R. Go through kissing gate; soon hear **Beeleigh Falls**.
❺ Cross timber bridge over weir. At end of bridge turn **R**, keeping river on your R. Stop at 2nd weir for river views. Continue, keeping river on your R, and go through wooden kissing gate. At canal lock turn **R** and walk, with canal on your L, towards red-brick bridge. Do not cross bridge, instead turn **R** on to concrete path and then **L** on to grassy path. Continue with canal on L and golf course on R. Cross next bridge and turn **R**, keeping canal on R. Continue under Maldon bypass on to grassy bridleway running parallel with canal.
❻ At next bridge take steps up to Heybridge Street. At top turn **R** and join **B1018** towards **Maldon**. Continue to cross River Chelmer via Fullbridge, bear **L** into Market Hill, turn **L** into High Street and return to car park via Butt Lane on your L.

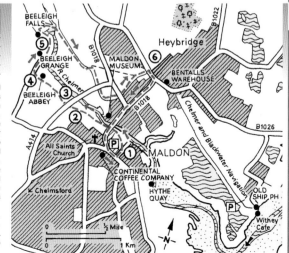

Essex

Essex • EASTERN ENGLAND

625 ROCHFORD *PLACE OF THE PECULIAR PEOPLE*

8 miles (12.9km) 3hrs **Ascent:** Negligible ⚠️
Paths: Grassy sea wall, field-edge paths and town streets
Suggested map: aqua3 OS Explorer 176 Blackwater Estuary, Maldon
Grid reference: TQ 875904
Parking: Pay-and-display at Back Lane

Discover a tiny medieval town.

❶ From car park walk north between houses into Market Square. Turn **R** into South Street, passing police station on your **L**. By **Horse and Groom** pub, turn **L** into Watts Lane following Roach Valley Way through industrial installations and keeping River Roach on your **L** for 1 mile (1.6km).

❷ Follow path over bridge, with **Stambridge Mill** straight ahead. Follow concrete path around mill to Mill Lane. Turn **L**. After 50yds (46m), turn **R** on to cross-field path to footbridge over fishing lake. Go through kissing gate and on to gravel path. Continue through trees and across meadow, passing **Broomhills** house on your **R**.

❸ Follow waymark through kissing gate and join river-bank path. With river mudflats and salt marsh on your **R**, continue ahead along grassy sea wall. Look left to see the distinctive Saxon tower of the church at **Great Stambridge**. Continue around peninsula of

Bartonhall Creek, mudflats popular with migrating birds. At northwestern tip, walk **L** down embankment to fingerpost, leaving Roach Valley Way, and turn **L** towards **Great Stambridge** to pass old Essex barns converted into modern housing. Continue along field-edge path towards houses and after ½ mile (800m) pass Ash Tree Court and emerge on Stambridge Road. Turn **R** into **Great Stambridge** past **Royal Oak** pub.

❹ Just before post office, turn **L** into Stewards Elm Farm Lane and follow waymark over footbridge. Continue between paddocks until you reach kissing gate. Turn **L** to follow field-edge path keeping **Ragstone Lodge** and **Rectory** on your **L**. Continue on cross-field path following waymarks **R**, **L**, then half-**R** past houses on **R**, until you meet Stambridge Road.

❺ Turn **R** at **Cherry Tree** pub. After 200yds (183m), turn **L** into Mill Lane, then **R** on to cross-field path to join Rocheway into East Street and pass **New Ship Inn** on **R**. Turn **L** into South Street; return to car park.

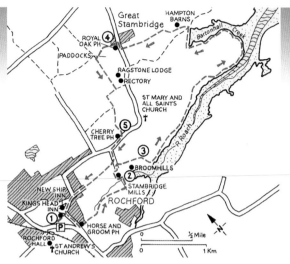

626 HANNINGFIELD RESERVOIR *A RESERVOIR TRAIL*

3½ miles (5.7km) 1hr 30min **Ascent:** Negligible ⚠️
Paths: Grassy and gravel forest tracks, prone to mud after rains, some boardwalk
Suggested map: aqua3 OS Explorer 175 Southend-on-Sea & Basildon
Grid reference: TQ 725971
Parking: Free parking at the visitor centre, Hawkswood Road entrance. Gates close at 5pm

Birds, wildlife, and a nature walk through meadows and woodlands.

❶ From **visitor centre**, take path to waymark C1 and detour **L** for views of reservoir from **Lyster Hide**. Return to C1 and continue along path through **Chestnut Wood** for 100yds (91m). At waymark C2, bear **R** towards clearing then go ahead towards oaks and waymark C4. Bear **R**, over wooden footbridge, passing pond on your **L**, and continue to waymark C5 on edge of wood. Turn **L** along gravel path, keeping meadow on your **R**, and follow boardwalk to clearing with ponds and seating.

❷ Walk **L** past waymark 7 to **Rawl Hide**, for views of reservoir and reed covered embankment on **L**. Return to waymark 7, turn **L** on to grassy path to enter **Peninsular Wood** and continue to waymark 6. Bear half-**L** for 100yds (91m), pass **Oak Hide** and continue to tip of peninsula, waymark 5, and **Point Hide**. Return to waymark 4, walk ahead with reservoir on **L**.

Continue through thick forest passing waymarks 3 and 2, turn **L** and cross bridge over ditch.

❸ Ignore stile across to **Hawkswood**, turn **L** through forest for 200yds (183m) to waymark B and enter **Well Wood**. Turn **L** and then **R** for 200yds (183m) to waymark A, with **Fishing Lodge** and **Water's Edge** to **L**. Swing **R**, continue between trees with embankment on your **L** to waymark C. Turn **L**, keeping meadows on your **R**, to waymark D. Turn **L** to waymark K and **R** to waymark H. Turn **R** into less-dense woodland with **South Hanningfield Road** on **L**.

❹ At waymark F, continue along wide bridleway to clearing of coppiced hornbeams. Descend steps, pass several small ponds to waymark E to enter **Hawks Wood** passing waymarks H1, H2 and H3 in quick succession. At H3 bear **R** over an earth bridge to H10, with meadow on your **R**, and bear **L** towards H9 and H11. Path leads through hedgerows and double set of kissing gates. Return to car park.

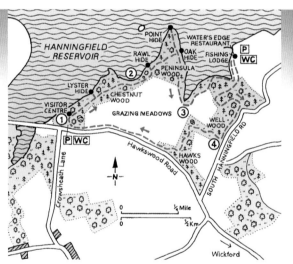

627 DANBURY *PLACES AND PALACES*

4 miles (6.4km) 2hrs **Ascent:** 164ft (50m) ⚠️
Paths: Grass and woodland paths, field paths, some road
Suggested map: aqua3 OS Explorer 183 Chelmsford & The Rodings, Maldon & Witham
Grid reference: TL 781050
Parking: Free car park off Main Road opposite library and inside Danbury Country Park

Ancient woodland, meadows and lakes.

❶ Leave car park via grassy path to **R** of leisure centre. Walk downhill, with playing fields **L** and hedgerows **R**. In 100yds (91m) after **Armada beacon**, turn **L** at cross path for panoramic views.

❷ Turn **R** into Pennyroyal Road past **Cricketers Arms** pub. Cross Bicknacre Road into Sporehams Lane. Follow path ('Butts Green'). At signpost, take path through oaks and gorse, to cross bridge. After 25yds (23m), turn **R**, past houses in Fitzwalter Lane.

❸ At last house, called Dane View, keep **L** and follow footpath through woodland to Woodhill Road, and turn **L** to sign marking entrance to **Danbury Country Park** on **R**. In car park take kissing gate on **L** and go **L** again on to path just before information board.

❹ Maintain direction past another car park and 2nd lake, until you reach toilets. Turn **R** between lakes, and continue ahead to red-brick perimeter wall of Danbury Conference Centre and Palace.

❺ Turn **R** through formal gardens and, with lake on your **R**, follow path half-**L** through woods. Maintain direction uphill, diagonally across meadow and through kissing gate. From kissing gate, walk half-**L** uphill towards copse. Follow boardwalk around small water-filled gravel pit, then take path uphill between red-and-white painted posts and continue ahead, passing yellow waymark. Cross meadow towards oak trees, keeping white metal posts to your **R**.

❻ At last white post, turn **L** and cross over stile carefully on to busy **A414**. Cross road into Riffhams Lane, and walk uphill to Elm Green Lane. Turn **R**, uphill, to A414 by **war memorial** on green. Cross **A414**, turn **L** along verge and **R** along footpath beside **Rectory Farmhouse**.

❼ At T-junction turn **L** for views of **St John the Baptist Church**. At 2nd T-junction, turn **L** to visit church. Turn **R** to rejoin outward path past radio mast and return to car park.

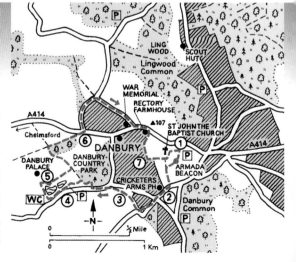

Essex

EARLS COLNE *ALONG THE RIVER VALLEY*

6½ miles (10.4km) 3hrs 30min **Ascent:** 78ft (24m)
Paths: Grassy with some muddy tracks, forest and field-edge paths, 3 stiles
Suggested map: aqua3 OS Explorer 195 Braintree & Saffron Walden
Grid reference: TL 855290
Parking: Free parking at Queens Road car park in Earls Colne

Walk along a disused railway track, now a nature reserve, and through woodland.

① From car park, turn **L** and **L** again into Burrows Road. Cross Hilly Bunnies Road and continue to Wildside waymark. Bear slightly **R**, then **L** on to cross-field path, downhill across golf course. Cross footbridge following yellow waymark over **River Colne**. Follow path for 70yds (64m), bear **L** on lesser path towards trees to waymarked stile and information board at entrance to railway nature reserve. Turn **R** on to railway embankment and continue, river and golf course on your **R**. Cross footbridge over River Peb and continue for 600yds (549m).

② Leave reserve by turning **R** at waymarks. Keep fence of sewage works on **L** and follow grassy path to Colne Ford Road. Turn **L**, cross road, and follow footpath and waymark between house Nos 20 and 22 through wooden gate. Cross meadow with **River Colne** down on your **R** and climb stile No 2.

③ Turn **R**, cross bridge, passing **Chalkney Mill** on **R**. Continue into **Chalkney Wood**. Walk for 300yds (274m), take 2nd path on **R** and go along bridleway, with Corsican pine on **L**. Proceed for 500yds (457m), bear **R** to parking area. Take downhill track for 300yds (274m). Turn **L** into Tey Road at **Peek's Corner**.

④ After 300yds (274m) turn **R** at fingerpost and go along field-edge path keeping hedgerows on your **R**. Cross earth bridge through trees, continue uphill, and pass **Tilekiln Farm**, on your **R**, to **Coggeshall Road**.

⑤ Turn **R**. After 200yds (183m) turn **L** at fingerpost ('Park Lane'). Follow path through kissing gate. Turn immediately **R** along path. Follow path **L** and downhill, woods on your **R**, to reach Wildside waymarked stile. Cross stile and walk along field-edge path, hedgerow on your **R**, to an earth bridge, turn **R** over stream.

⑥ Take path past Brickfields information board on **R**. Turn **R** into Park Lane, St Andrews Church on **L**. Turn **L** into **Coggeshall Road** and High Street and car park.

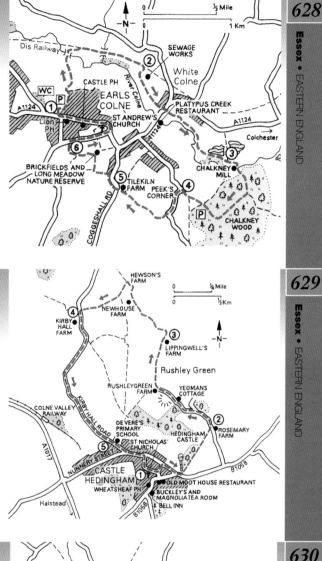

CASTLE AT HEDINGHAM *SIX FARMS AND A CASTLE*

3½ miles (5.7km) 1hr 30min **Ascent:** 64ft (20m)
Paths: Grassy, field-edge and farm tracks, some woodland and town streets
Suggested map: aqua3 OS Explorer 195 Braintree & Saffron Walden
Grid reference: TL 784356
Parking: Informal street parking in Castle Hedingham village

Explore a wealth of history in this tiny area.

① With church on your **R**, walk along Church Ponds into Falcon Square with its medieval houses. Turn **L** into Castle Lane with 17th-century Youth Hostel building on your **R** and walk uphill to Bayley Street. Cross road and, at castle entrance, turn **R** and walk to T-junction. Turn **L** into Sudbury Road and, just after New Park Road on your **R**, turn **L** at narrow track to **Rosemary Farm**.

② Turn **L**, follow track to Y-junction and bear **L** passing red-brick, thatched Keepers Cottage on **L**. Pass houses and admire view of rolling countryside beyond stile on your **L**, opposite **Yeoman's Cottage**. After 200yds (183m) track bears **R** with converted barns of **Rushleygreen Farm** on your **L**. Ignore timber footbridge immediately after farm and continue along main farm track with arable fields to your **L**.

③ Pass **Lippingwell's Farm** on your **R**, bear **L** across meandering field-edge path passing front of

Newhouse Farm, with pond on your **L**, and continue to **Hewson's Farm** and brick-built tower on your **R**. Turn sharp **L** at fingerpost along field-edge path to small row of trees at rear of **Newhouse Farm**. At waymark bear **R** across another field-edge path to **Kirby Hall Farm**.

④ Turn **L** at crossroads to Kirby Hall Road and, ignoring all footpaths **L** and **R**, follow wide farm track to return to **Castle Hedingham**. Along the way, you will pass through high embankments of hedgerows and an impressive row of oak trees. Before rising towards village of **Castle Hedingham** you can see top of castle keep above trees to your half-**L**.

⑤ Walking into **Castle Hedingham**, you will pass **de Vere's Primary School** and modern housing estate on your **L**. At T-junction, turn **L** into Nunnery Street and then **R** into Crown Street, where jettied buildings and medieval cottages mark your return to old village and church.

HALSTEAD *COURTAULDS CONNECTION*

3 miles (4.8km) 1hr 15min **Ascent:** 90ft (27m)
Paths: Town streets and grassy tracks
Suggested map: aqua3 OS Explorer 195 Braintree & Saffron Walden
Grid reference: TL 812306
Parking: Pay-and-display in Chapel Street and Mill Bridge

Discovering the influence of the Courtauld textile family.

① Turn **R** into Chapel Street then **L** into High Street by post office. Walk up Market Hill to Jubilee Fountain for panoramic views of town and distant Mount Hill.

② Turn **L** into Hedingham Road (**A1124**) passing Halstead **Hospital** and Courtauld Homes of Rest on your **R**. Turn **L** into Box Mill Lane where several cottages and larger dwellings attest to further building by Courtaulds.

③ At end of Box Mill Lane, maintain direction into **Box Mill Meadow**, a fine picnic spot, and cross footbridge over **River Colne** as it flows south into town. Along river bank, traces of rubble are all that remain of 2 mills, one a watermill and the other wind powered. Take footpath to **L**.

④ At edge of Halstead Town Football Ground, cross stile and continue along footpath which becomes grassy track, former route of Halstead and Colne

Valley Railway. Go straight ahead into Butler Road, named after R A Butler (1902–82), better known as Rab, Conservative politician and Member of Parliament for Saffron Walden. At the T-junction with Trinity Street notice the redevelopment across the road, where flats and a park area called Trinity Court now stand on the site of the old railway station.

⑤ Turn **R** and walk to **Holy Trinity Church** on your **R**. Close by are some of the oldest houses in town. Retrace your steps for few paces and turn **R** just after police station into New Street. Note public gardens opposite Methodist church, turn **L** into Martin Street, then **L** again and **R** into Factory Lane West by tourist information office.

⑥ Turn **L** into The Causeway, Courtaulds old **Townsford Mill** on **R**, and walk ahead into Bridge Street. Turn **R** to cross bridge and go into High Street to post office. Pause here to note varied architecture. Walk along Chapel Street and car park.

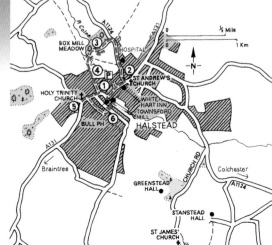

631 LANGDON *An Old Plot for Eastenders*

3¾ miles (6km) 1hr 30min Ascent: 230ft (70m) ▲
Paths: Forest, field and horse tracks
Suggested map: aqua3 OS Explorer 175 Southend-on-Sea & Basildon
Grid reference: TQ 599873
Parking: Free parking at the visitor centre at Dunton

Explore ancient woodland and grassy meadows where Eastenders fulfilled a dream.

1 From car park, walk up wide avenue of Plotlands, passing **museum** on your L. After 500 yards (457m) go ahead at red waymark No 1, on wide tarmac bridle path, with fields on your R, and occasional views of south Essex between trees. Ignoring other paths continue along bridlepath, passing Val's Gate on your R, then look L for the **recreation ground**, full of orchids in spring. Continue for 100yds (91m) to wide cross paths.

2 Turn R at red waymark No 2, now in **Lincewood**. Path undulates through high trees and open woodland, passing behind houses on your L, with glimpses of pond on your R at red waymark No 3.

3 At waymark No 4 there are 4 steep wooden steps. Ignore these and turn R along path, keeping wooden fencing enclosing **Hall Wood** on your L. Walk for 20yds (18m), to break in trees, for views of London

skyline. Retrace your steps and descend 1st path on your L towards wooden kissing gate.

4 Follow this narrow track downhill through ferns, and after 200yds (183m) reach duckboard skirting pond. Continue ahead through kissing gate and walk downhill through open woodland, with ferns and patches of meadow. Continue to wooden bench beneath large oak tree, where there are views of rolling farmland and London in distance.

5 At Y-junction, take L-H path downhill keeping arable field on your L. Go through pair of timber posts and turn L on to wide grassy bridleway. At kissing gate, turn R and after 10yds (9m) turn L on to another grassy path. Maintain direction through 2 meadows, keeping houses on your R. At end of 2nd meadow is red waymark No 1. Here, turn R keeping Plotland ruins on your L. Pass Plotland Trail waymarks 5 and 6, turn L at next bridlepath and follow waymarks to return to car park.

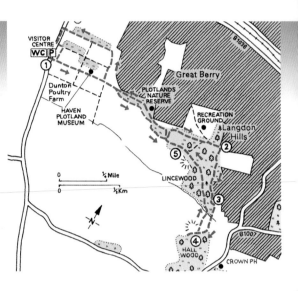

632 WEALD COUNTRY PARK *A Royal Deer Park*

5 miles (8km) 2hrs 45min Ascent: 117ft (35m) ▲
Paths: Open parkland, forest tracks and some cross-field footpaths
Suggested map: aqua3 OS Explorer 175 Southend-on-Sea & Basildon
Grid reference: TQ 568940
Parking: Free car parks at visitor centre, Belvedere and Cricket Green on Weald Road and Lincolns Lane

A fairly strenuous walk taking in a great Tudor mansion and a royal deer park.

1 With your back to **Weald** Road, turn R out of car park past golden willow tree. Keep red-brick wall on your R and continue to **Belvedere car park** – site of the foundations of Weald Hall. An information board (L) tells the story of **Weald Hall**. Walk into car park and take earth path uphill. Turn L, keeping church on your R. At end of church wall, turn L through trees and go on to grassy knoll overlooking original gardens.

2 Keeping gardens to your L, walk up steps to site of **Belvedere Hill** where, in Tudor times, spectators would watch hunting and enjoy banquets. Walk down steps, turn R and take path downhill, between conifers, to open parkland. Maintain direction and turn L through gap in fence keeping **Bluebell** Pond and cricket field on your R.

3 Turn R through kissing gate and follow grassy path uphill, passing bridleway waymarks on your R. At

top of hill, pass through thickly wooded area of ancient hornbeam and silver birch, and continue along bridleway, which runs parallel with Sandpit Lane.

4 As path veers away from road, note steep embankment to your R – remains of an **Iron-Age settlement**. You are now walking around what was a moat. Keep to path through meadow and parkland and, at tree-clad embankment rising to your R, continue clockwise to join hard track.

5 Turn L through gap in fence on L and continue downhill through **Langton's Wood**. Follow this hard bridleway, which hugs edge of woods, to pass avenue of sweet chestnut trees by **Shepherd's Spinney**.

6 At fingerpost turn L on to public footpath. After 400yds (366m), at cross path, turn L and then R between wide avenue of chestnut trees. After 500yds (457m), turn R before kissing gate to walk with lake on your L. At end of lake, turn L over footbridge and return to car park passing deer paddock.

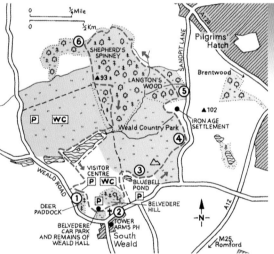

633 EAST TILBURY *Riverside Ramble*

8½ miles (13.7km) 3hrs Ascent: 34ft (10m) ⚠
Paths: Riverside path, field paths, sections of road, 1 stile
Suggested map: aqua3 OS Explorer 163 Gravesend & Rochester
Grid reference: TQ 689768
Parking: Free parking at Coalhouse Fort

A riverside walk from the home of the Bata Shoe Company to Tilbury Fort.

1 From visitor centre, turn L keeping moat bank. Bear R; walk along disused railway track to grassy embankment with river on L. Follow footpath above shingle of river, towards radar tower. Near by are the remains of the jetty used to transport ammunition from Purfleet and the site of a 1540 **blockhouse**.

2 After 1 mile (1.6km) with **East Tilbury marshes** on your R, which are popular with migrant wading birds, cross metal gate beyond which are remains of concrete jetties surrounded by grassy banks. Path is mainly concrete and **power station** looms large ahead. On both sides of path, earth has been dug up by treasure hunters foraging for discarded bottles, ceramics and other paraphernalia. Keep on concrete path following high sea wall fronting power station and Bill McRoy Creek to reach metal steps leading to car park at **Tilbury Fort**.

3 Turn R into **Fort Road** and after 1 mile (1.6km) you can see houses at southern end of **West Tilbury** village. Looking ahead, to R, is a church, originally built by the Normans, strategically placed on the escarpment for views across the estuary. Turn R into Cooper Shaw Road. To R, across **Tilbury Marshes**, twin chimneys of **power station** dominate landscape.

4 At T-junction, turn L into Church Road and walk about 500yds (457m) into **West Tilbury** with its picturesque green overlooked by **Kings Head pub**. Walk past pub and about 100yds (91m) on R, take cross-field footpath to Low Street Lane where you turn L. Walk along Low Street Lane for 300yds (274m) and take footpath on R. Walk towards houses of **East Tilbury** on cross-field path and emerge at Beechcroft Avenue. Cross this road into Stenning Way and, after about 200yds (183m), take path on R to Princess Margaret Road. Turn R, passing East Tilbury railway station, and return to car park at Coalhouse Fort.

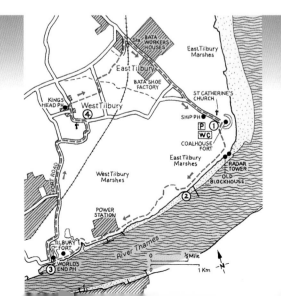

Essex

WILLINGALE A PINT-SIZED PARISH

3¾ miles (6km) 1hr 30min **Ascent:** 33ft (11m)

Paths: Field-edge paths, riverside meadows and green lane
Suggested map: aqua3 OS Explorer 183 Chelmsford & The Rodings, Maldon & Witham
Grid reference: TL 597076
Parking: Car park at Willingale village hall (call 01277 896340 to request permission to park here)

An easy stroll along the Essex Way to a lovely rural village.

1 Turn **R** outside **village hall**. Follow road around to **L** and turn **R** at footpath sign by former village school, now a private residence. At end of gardens, turn **R** along grassy path on to field-edge path and continue to bear **R** for 500yds (457m) to Dukes Lane. To your **L** are panoramic views of Roding Valley.

2 Turn **L** into **Dukes Lane** and walk for 200yds (183m). After passing **Dukes Farm** outbuildings, turn **R** at fingerpost. Walk up embankment and continue along field-edge path with stream on your **R** for about 400yds (366m). Turn **L** on to uphill cross-field path through gap in hedge and go across another field to cross wooden footbridge. Maintain direction along 2 field-edge paths until you reach junction with Elms Farm Road on **L** and **Elm Cottage** on **R**.

3 Turn **R** on to bridleway, pass **Elm Cottage** and, at T-junction where bridleway bears **L**, turn **R** on to path.

Continue for 200yds (183m) then follow field-edge path for 300yds (274m) until you meet **Essex Way**. Follow this wide byway south, passing **Windmill Farm** on **L** and cross footbridge towards Shellow Road.

4 Cross Shellow Road and continue along **Essex Way**, with views of **Shellow Hall** to your **L**. After 300yds (274m), bear **R** and then **L**, keeping hedgerow to your **R**. After another 100yds (91m), turn **R** through gap in hedge, then continue with hedgerow on your **L**.

5 In front of cottages at **Spains Wood**, cross footbridge over ditch and turn **R**, continuing along **Essex Way**. After another bridge, maintain direction keeping hedgerow on your **L**. Follow path through cricket field and into **Willingale** where **Essex Way** continues past Bell on your **R** (now private house) and crosses churchyard between **St Christopher's** and **St Andrew's churches**. Retrace your steps to The Street, which becomes Beech Road and return to **village hall** car park.

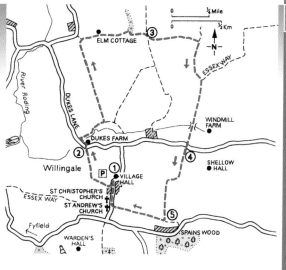

PLESHEY A CROWNING CASTLE

3 miles (4.8km) 1hr 30min **Ascent:** 56ft (17m)

Paths: Grassy tracks, field and woodland paths prone to muddiness, some roads, 1 stile
Suggested map: aqua3 OS Explorer 183 Chelmsford & The Rodings, Maldon & Witham
Grid reference: TL 662142
Parking: Free car park at the village hall

A gentle walk combining rolling countryside and a fine motte and bailey castle.

1 From car park at **village hall**, walk to The Street and turn **R** passing **Holy Trinity Church** on your **R** and **White Horse pub** on your **L**. After the church you will see the 16th-century gatehouse, behind which is the convent, collectively they are known as the House of Retreat. Just after restored water pump turn **R** into Pump Lane. After 100yds (91m), on your **L** you will see a bridge over a moat – the entrance into earthworks of the motte and bailey castle.

2 With your back to **castle**, and keeping church to your **R**, walk across cricket field to waymark beside wooden gate. Turn **R** along concrete path keeping field on your **L**. Maintain direction, ignoring 2 footpaths on **R** and one on **L** by reservoir.

3 At 2nd fingerpost, **L**, follow bridleway bounded by trees. This path, may be very muddy after rain, passes **Fitzjohn's Wood** with good views of the countryside.

4 When level with old house on **R**, which was **Fitzjohn's Farm**, walk a few paces to line of trees on your **L** and turn **L** on to field-edge path, downhill. At bottom of hill, ignore wooden footbridge over **brook** to your **L** and follow path which bears **L** over earth bridge. After 100yds (91m) turn **R** over another earth bridge at **Walthambury Brook** and climb over stile fence and up embankment, brook is now on your **L**. You are now on grassy path of Essex Way, which follows **Walthambury Brook** to The Street at **Pleshey**.

5 Turn **L** at The Street then **R** into Back Lane, passing **Pleshey Hall Cottages** on your **L**. At fingerpost ('Pleshey Grange'), turn **R** into Vicarage Lane, passing **Pleshey Forge** on your **L**. At next fingerpost, turn **L** on to grassy path which follows Town Enclosure, with ditch on your **L**. Cross footbridge and continue until you reach **White Horse pub** on your **L** and emerge into The Street. Turn **R** to car park.

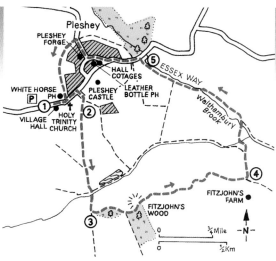

CHIPPING ONGAR DAVID LIVINGSTONE

6½ miles (10.4km) 3hrs 30min **Ascent:** 151ft (46m)

Paths: Track and field paths prone to muddiness, stretches of road, 6 stiles
Suggested map: aqua3 OS Explorer 183 Chelmsford & The Rodings, Maldon & Witham
Grid reference: TL 552031
Parking: Pay-and-display car parks at rear of Sainsbury's, police station and library in Chipping Ongar High Street

Home of missionary David Livingstone.

1 From rear of car park take Essex Way towards Greensted. As path narrows, walk between dwarf oaks, over cross path and through kissing gate. Bear **R**, then **L** towards 2nd kissing gate, passing pond of Greensted Hall on your **R**. Walk past many Church Lodge on your **L**; **Greensted church** is on **R**.

2 Keeping church on your **R**, bear **R** past terraced cottages and go through gate. After 100yds (91m), turn **L** across footbridge and follow field-edge path keeping hedgerow on your **R**. Maintain direction through 3 fields, passing **Greensted Wood** on your **R**, to reach Greensted Road. Turn **L** and pick up footpath on your **R**. Continue along field-edge path keeping hedgerows on your **L** for about 100yds (91m), where you cross stile so that hedgerow is now on your **R**. Climb series of 5 stiles.

3 At 5th stile turn **R**. After 100yds (91m), cross

another stile. Turn **R**, passing low wall of **Widow's Farm** on **L**; follow path **R**. After 25yds (23m), take footpath **L**; follow field-edge path to Toot Hill Road. Turn **L** for Clatterford End. At T-junction maintain direction for **Coleman's Farm**, following lane.

4 As lane bears **R** into Coleman's Farm, maintain direction on bridleway for ½ mile (800m), ignoring paths **L** and **R** until you reach tarmac lane. Just before T-junction, turn **R** on to cross-field path to **Stanford Rivers**. At barn dwellings, turn **R** on to gravel path and **L** on to School Road with **St Margaret's Church** (**L**).

5 Walk to crossroads; turn **L**. After 400yds (366m) follow **R** turn next to house, 'Ambermead'. Continue on uphill path and pass oak stile at **Kettlebury Spring**. Follow path past school; turn **R** on to The Borough. Continue to T-junction passing **Two Brewers pub** on **R**. Turn **L** into High Street. Return to car park.

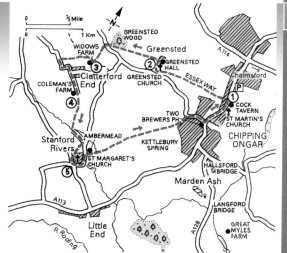

Essex

637 GREAT BARDFIELD *A Windmill called Gibraltar*

4½ miles (7.2km) 2hrs Ascent: 100ft (30m)
Paths: Field-edge paths, river bank, grassy tracks and some town streets, 4 stiles
Suggested map: aqua3 OS Explorer 195 Braintree & Saffron Walden
Grid reference: TL 677305
Parking: Informal parking in Great Bardfield village

An easy stroll combining gentle hills, a windmill and a lovely village.

❶ From village green take fingerpost **L** off Mill Road and follow path by stream on your **L** with houses on your **R**. After 200yds (183m) at field, take **L** fork still following stream. Look over your **R** shoulder for good view of **Gibraltar windmill**.

❷ Cross stile through hedge, turn **R** and continue with hedge on your **R** to lane at **Great Bardfield Watermill**. Cross lane, keep mill pond and River Pant on your **L** for 200yds (183m) to **pump station**. Turn **R** then **L** around perimeter, and take cross-field path, keeping river and **Champions Farm** and **Robjohns Farm** on your **L**. Near lake in front of **Robjohns Farm**, path is indistinct, while river meanders south and east. Stay on grassy strip, keeping river on your **L-H** side, to stile at Daw Street, south of **Sculpins Bridge**.

❸ Turn **R**. After 400yds (366m) pass **Whinbush Farm**. At junction of Bardfield–Waltham road, bear

half-**R** following green fingerpost ('Great Saling and **Great Bardfield**'). Cross 2 stiles; continue along path skirting edge of **Lodge Wood**. Keep wood **L**; proceed to its southwestern extremity where path turns **R**.

❹ Follow path by hedge under row of poplar and larch trees and, as **Great Bardfield** and **Gibraltar windmill** come into view, turn **L**. Follow track with hedgerows on your **L** for 300yds (274m) and then turn **R** into green lane.

❺ Pass recreation ground on your **R**, cross residential street, follow footpath into Braintree Road and turn **R**. On **L** is **Church of St Mary the Virgin**.

❻ Next to the church is the 16th-century manor house of **Bardfield Hall**. Follow road **L** through Brook Street, passing starting point of walk into High Street. After seeing the 15th-century **Gobions**, one of the oldest houses in Great Bardfield, **Place House**, the **Cottage Museum** and the **Town Hall** retrace your steps to the green.

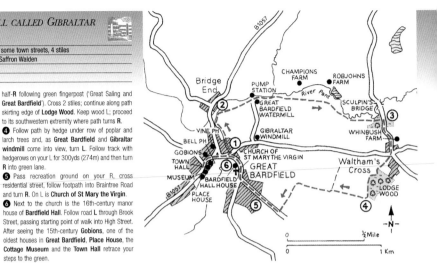

638 THAXTED *The Sound of Music*

3 miles (4.8km) 1hr 30min Ascent: 92ft (28m)
Paths: Field-edge paths, bridleway prone to muddiness, river bank and some town streets
Suggested map: aqua3 OS Explorer 195 Braintree & Saffron Walden
Grid reference: TL 610311
Parking: Free car park at Margaret Street

In the footsteps of composer Gustav Holst.

❶ From car park turn **L** into Margaret Street, **R** into Weaverhead Lane and **L** into Copthall Lane, passing cottages called **Bridgefoot**. After houses on **L**, pass through gap between trees by gate ('Walnut Tree Meadow'). Turn **R** along grassy path and keep parallel with **Copthall Lane** on your **R**. After 400yds (366m) bear **L** along waymark through trees, cross 2 footbridges at **R** angles, in quick succession, and turn **R** keeping stream and hedgerows on your **R**.

❷ Continue along field-edge path through 2 fields. After line of trees on your **L**, turn **L** at waymark over footbridge and follow another field-edge path keeping hedgerow on your **L**, to **B1051**, Sampford road. In distance, to your **L**, spire of **St John the Baptist Church** dominates skyline. Turn **R**, cross road with care, and take 1st turning **L** along farm track ('Boynton End'). The track zig-zags **L** and **R** past **Sorrel's Farm House** and **Golden's Farm**. At the

farm bear **R** on to canopied bridleway between buildings, keeping paddock fence on **L**. Proceed downhill to waymarks outside **Goddard's Farm**, turn **L** then **R**; follow path uphill with farm on **R-H** side.

❸ Descend short steep embankment and cross farm track to follow fingerpost through hedge. Turn half-**L** across field and follow path with **River Chelmer** on your **R** to **Walden Road**.

❹ At Walden Road turn **R** across **Armitage Bridge** and immediately **L** at fingerpost. Follow field-edge path with river on your **L** passing conifers and, after 300yds (274m) where river veers away, turn **L** at waymark concealed in hedgerows. You are now on **Harcamlow Way**. Turn **L** downhill past house called **Haslemere**, over bridge across river. Ignore paths **L** and **R** and keep on tarmac road, past modern housing.

❺ Continue along Watling Lane passing cottages and Piggots Mill to emerge opposite **Swan Hotel**. Turn **L** and **R** into Margaret Street and return to car park.

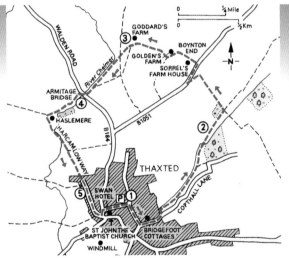

639 SAFFRON WALDEN *To Audley End*

5½ miles (8.8km) 2hrs 30min Ascent: 180ft (55m)
Paths: Urban, field-edge paths, grassy tracks
Suggested map: aqua3 OS Explorer 195 Braintree & Saffron Walden
Grid reference: TL 534384
Parking: Pay-and-display at Swan Meadows, Common Hill and Fairycroft Road, or free parking at Catons Hill

A challenging walk to Audley End.

❶ From car park turn **R** into Park Lane and first **R** into Primes Close. Go through arch under almshouses and go **R** into Abbey Lane through wrought iron gates of **Audley Park**. Continue along grassy path to top of hill, passing Ice House on your **L** by more wrought iron gates, to **Audley End Road**.

❷ Turn **R** along embankment and go downhill for 600yds (549m), keeping red-brick wall of **Audley Park** on your **R**, to fingerpost ('College of St Mark'). Cross road and turn **L** to **Audley** village.

❸ Cross bridge and turn **L** at lane ('Abbey Farm private') and continue along this footpath keeping St Mark's College, followed by farm, to your **R**. Continue through arable fields, cross Wenden Road and go through trees to join **Beechy Ride** (track). Keep stream and line of beech trees to your **R** for 200yds (183m), cross earth bridge between trees, and

continue with stream and trees to your **L** to **B1052**. Cross road with care, turn **R** and continue to footpath on your **L**. Turn **L** along field-edge path with hedgerow and stream on your **L**. At earth bridge turn **L** and immediately **R** (stream now on your **R**).

❹ Follow field-edge path to **Brakey Ley Wood** and ignore 3 sets of waymarks indicating **R** turns. At 4th waymark, **Thieves' Corner**, turn **L** just before footbridge and follow grassy field-edge path steeply uphill to **Debden Road**.

❺ Turn **R** at Debden Road and opposite **The Roos**, turn **L** on to uphill path. Bear **L** at **Herberts Farm** and **L** again to rejoin **Debden Road**. Turn **R** towards Claypits Plantation; continue into Seven Devil's Lane.

❻ After ½ mile (800m) turn **R** on B1052 towards Saffron Walden. At roundabout bear **L** across road; follow footpath between houses passing deep ditch on **L**. At end of path turn **R** into Abbey Lane and car park.

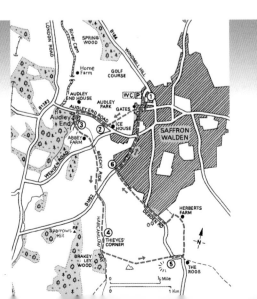

Essex

CHIGWELL *A DICKENS OF A WALK*

9 miles (14.5km) 3hrs 30 min **Ascent:** 148ft (45m)
Paths: Forest tracks, field-edge paths, green lanes, some streets, 9 stiles
Suggested map: aqua3 OS Explorer 174 Epping Forest & Lee Valley
Grid reference: TQ 478943
Parking: Three free car parks along Manor Road in Hainault Forest

A challenging walk combining an ancient forest, a village immortalised by Dickens and views of the London skyline.

❶ From car park walk along bridleway between trees. After 350yds (320m) at 3-way fingerpost, turn R on to footpath No 43 towards **Hainault**. At 2nd fingerpost go R for Retreat Path. After 300yds (320m), bear L to pass backs of houses on your L. Continue through kissing gate to **Retreat pub** car park.

❷ Turn L into **Manor Road** and, at traffic lights, turn L for **All Saints Parish Church**. Cross **Romford Road** and bear R on cross-field path through recreation ground. Cross **Manor Road** and into **Chapel Lane** passing **United Reformed Church** on your L. Take narrow path between houses into small meadow.

❸ Continue across 4 stiles and at iron fence turn L along path, keeping **waterworks** behind fencing to your R. At concrete path at **waterworks** gate, bear half-L. Keep hedgerow on your L and follow field-edge path downhill, keeping hedgerow on your R, to fingerpost. Turn L and continue along field-edge path. Turn R on to green lane and walk uphill with **Old Farm** buildings to R. Just before **Old Farm** turn L across field, turn R; cross Vicarage Lane. After 150yds (146m) turn L on path emerging on Chigwell High Road.

❹ Turn R and R again, back into Vicarage Lane. Turn immediately L on to cross-field path. Bear R passing primary **school** on your R. Follow fingerpost diagonally across 2 fields, and continue downhill crossing 2 stiles and footbridge. Turn L and L again through hedgerow then R, on to field-edge path uphill.

❺ At top, cross **Pudding Lane**. Follow fingerpost on field-edge path keeping **Pudding Lane** on L. Take cross-field path R and emerge by **Taylors Farm**. Cross **Gravel Lane** beside **Taylors Farm** gate. Continue uphill towards dead tree, passing through gap in hedge to R. Continue to **Hoe Lane**. Turn R to return to car park.

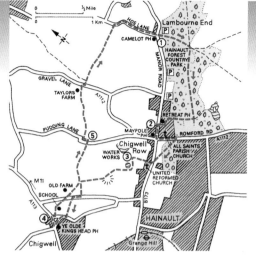

HARLOW *OLD AND NEW*

4 miles (6.4km) 1hr 30min **Ascent:** 67ft (20m)
Paths: Cycle tracks, footpaths, sections of road, 1 stile
Suggested map: aqua3 OS Explorer 174 Epping Forest & Lee Valley
Grid reference: TL 465109
Parking: Plenty of on-street parking

A leisurely stroll exploring town and country from Mark Hall to Old Harlow.

❶ Turn R outside **Harlow Museum**, take 1st L into Muskham Road; follow fingerpost to join cycle path ('Netteswell Road'). Turn R and follow cycle path under **A414** into **Old Harlow**. Continue along Market Street to T-junction and turn L at **Chequers pub** into Station Road. After 300yds (274m), turn R into Swallows Estate, take 1st L and follow footpath through **recreational park** to Manor Road. Turn L then R into **Priory Avenue** passing a row of corporation houses, the first to be built in the early days of Harlow new town, to crossroads with Old Road.

❷ Turn R. To your L you can just see **Harlowbury Chapel**; for better views walk 150yds (137m) along **Old Road** to kissing gate. Maintain direction until you reach T-junction opposite **Green Man Hotel**. Turn R; take footpath between old ambulance and fire station and walk field-edge path. Just before main road, turn L between concrete posts on footpath to B183. Bear half-L; cross road. Follow footpath through trees; bear L on to field-edge path. After 200yds (183m), cross stile and footbridge. Walk towards spire of **St Mary's and St Hugh's Church** and arrive at graveyard.

❸ Turn R into **Churchgate Street** passing 17th-century Widow's House, **Queen's Head** pub and other timber-framed houses. Continue downhill for 200yds (183m) to footpath on R just before Churchgate Manor Hotel. Keeping church and stream on your R, follow field-edge path to kissing gate. Bear half-L across meadow through break in fence opposite and, keeping trees on your R, continue to kissing gate at top of hill.

❹ Pass outbuildings of **Old Harlow Kennels and Cattery** on L. Follow tarmac road to **London Road**. Turn R into **London Road**; cross just before roundabout on to B183 to next roundabout on A414. Follow underpass into **First Avenue/Mandela Avenue**, turn L. Take 1st R back to **Harlow Museum**.

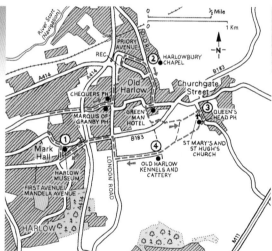

MATCHING *TWO TRAILS*

3½ miles (5.7km) 1hr 30min **Ascent:** Negligible
Paths: Bridleways, grass and field-edge paths, 3 stiles
Suggested map: aqua3 OS Explorer 183 Chelmsford & The Rodings, Maldon & Witham
Grid reference: TL 515112
Parking: Free parking at Matching Tye village hall

A walk between Matching Tye and Matching Green with a church to match.

❶ From **Matching Tye village hall** turn R. Directly opposite **Fox Inn** take lane ('Sheering and Hatfield Heath'). After 200yds (183m), turn R at fingerpost ('**Forest Way**') and follow grassy field-edge path. Go through wooden gate and maintain direction along bridleway to **Matching church**.

❷ Pass Marriage Feast House on your L and continue to metalled road to R of church. Take footpath on your R, opposite church, through kissing gate and skirt moat on your R. After 100yds (91m), cross stile and walk half-L on cross-field path towards edge of line of trees. At yellow waymark, turn L along cross-field path.

❸ At mid-field fingerpost, turn R and walk to line of trees (boundary of **Brick House**). Turn L at fingerpost, keeping house and paddock on your R. After paddock turn R across field towards houses, maintain direction along field-edge path. After playing field on your L, walk between houses into **Harlow Road** at **Matching Green**.

❹ Turn L and immediately R ('Epping'), and take 1st R into **Colvers**. After 200yds (183m), turn R at break in hedge and go over 2 stiles in quick succession. Cross meadow and maintain direction over footbridge. Take cross-field path half-L towards line of trees. Keep trees on your R passing yellow waymark to another copse of trees.

❺ Maintain southwesterly direction and, soon after footpath appears on L, bear R on field-edge path keeping ditch and trees on R-H side. After 100yds (91m), turn L then R through trees and walk for 300yds (274m) with trees on R until you reach **Harlow Road**. Turn L; walk with care along busy **Harlow Road** for ½ mile (800m) to return to village hall at **Matching Tye**. Here you can finish off with a well-earned rest at nearby comfortable **Fox Inn**.

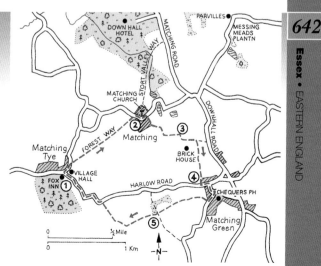

Essex

643 UGLEY *Ugga the Viking*

5½ miles (8.8km) 2hrs 15min Ascent: 75ft (23m) ⚠

Paths: Woodland and grassy tracks, field edge, some road walking, 5 stiles

Suggested map: aqua3 OS Explorer 195 Braintree & Saffron Walden

Grid reference: TL 513288

Parking: Park in field behind the Chequers pub, Cambridge Road (please ask the landlord's permission)

An easy walk along the Harcamlow Way.

❶ Cross B1383 (take care) and follow fingerpost opposite **Chequers pub** through **Broom Wood**. Cross stile and follow yellow waymarks through conifers, via plank bridge and another stile. After stile, turn **L** and follow field-edge path to **R**. Continue following field-edge path **R** and **L** to cross path.

❷ Turn **L** on to wide cross-field path towards conifers. Go through gap in hedgerow and **L** on wide bridlepath, **Harcamlow Way**. Ignore path L and bear **R** along **Harcamlow Way** south, with fields on your R and conifer wood to your L. Continue, passing dilapidated farm buildings of **Wade's Hall**, and isolated farmstead of **Bollington Hall**. Now path is tarmac, with arable fields on either side and clear view of **Ugley**. The village was named after Ugga the Viking who set up home in what was once a huge forest.

❸ Turn **L** in front of **Bollington Hall Cottages** and take straight road towards **B1383**, with skyline of **Ugley** ahead. Cross road (take care) and follow narrow, overgrown path ahead through **Gaul's Croft**. Well-defined path crosses stile and meanders through small thick forest bounded by bramble. At next waymark, bear half-**L** along field-edge path and continue via waymarks **R** and **L** between houses to peaceful **Ugley Green**.

❹ Turn **L** on to tarmac road ('Fieldgate Lane no-through road'). Continue past some houses and **Fieldgate Farm** on R. Road becomes wide muddy track bisecting arable fields with good views of **Bollington Hall**.

❺ Track bisects outbuildings of **Ugley Hall Farm** where you maintain direction on to road and turn **L** immediately after large corrugated barn and into **St Peter's Church** at Ugley. Go through churchyard and follow tarmac road through grazing fields, passing **The Lodge**, where you turn **L** and return via Patmore End to car park.

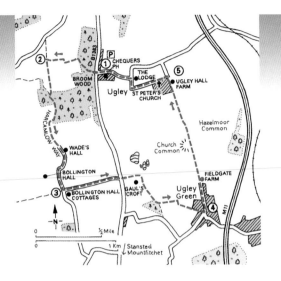

644 STANSTED *Taking Off*

3¼ miles (5.3km) 1hr 30min Ascent: 54ft (16m) ⚠

Paths: Grass and gravel tracks, grassy verge, field edge and some road walking

Suggested map: aqua3 OS Explorer 195 Braintree & Saffron Walden

Grid reference: TL 528239

Parking: Informal street parking at Burton End village

You don't have to be a plane spotter to enjoy this rural walk beside the runway of London's third international airport.

❶ Follow fingerpost opposite **poultry farm** at **Burton End** and walk between houses to arable field. Ignore fingerpost on L and follow field-edge path with ditch and hedgerows to your **R**. At waymark, cross between bushes and maintain direction half-**L** with ditch and hedgerow on your L.

❷ Continue, turning **R** and **L** at waymarks, to waymark on edge of copse of trees and footbridge. Turn **R** and after 300yds (274m) take footbridge **L** over railway cutting (spur line to **Stansted Airport** so you can plane and train spot at same time). Over bridge, turn **L** with railway on L and, at waymark, turn **R** on to cross-field path to emerge at Tye Green Road.

❸ Turn **R** on to **Tye Green Road**. At houses, turn **L** to explore old cottages and moated farm at Tye Green. Follow track around **The Green** back to Tye Green Road and turn **L** along road which changes its name to **Claypit Hill**. Road bears sharply **R**, opposite is emergency gate set in perimeter fence of **Stansted Airport**. From here, if there is room, you can jostle for position with plane spotters to watch aircraft landing.

❹ In front of fence, turn **R** to walk along verge between airport perimeter fence and road. Continue following path around control tower and fire service training centre. At grassy mound, possibly earthworks from runway, there is some parking used by plane spotters.

❺ Turn **R** on to farm track between **Riders Farm** and **Monks Farm** to 3-way junction at Belmer Road and then turn **L**. Call in at **Ash public house** on your **L**. Here there is a large car park and garden area, popular with aircraft workers from the nearby hangars. From pub, turn **L** passing **Warmans Farm** on your R and return to your car at Burton End.

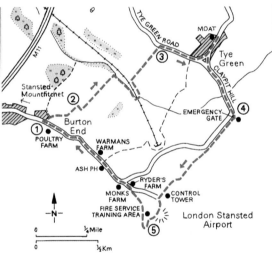

645 STANSTED MOUNTFITCHET *On the Ground*

5¾ miles (9.2km) 2hrs 15min Ascent: 101ft (34m) ⚠

Paths: Grassy and forest tracks, field edge and some street walking

Suggested map: aqua3 OS Explorer 195 Braintree & Saffron Walden

Grid reference: TL 515248

Parking: Pay-and-display at Lower Street

A rural saunter around the ancient and modern sights of Stansted Mountfitchet.

❶ From car park turn **L** into Lower Street and cross **Chapel Hill**. At top of hill turn **L** at traffic lights on to B1383. Take next **L** into Millside. Pass **windmill** on L; turn **R** into Brook Road. After 100yds (91m) walk between houses to footbridge over **Stansted Brook**.

❷ Cross **Stansted Brook**, turn **L** so that brook is on your **L**. Take slope up at railway footbridge on your **R** to cross line. Turn **L** and bear **R** uphill into Park Road through housing estate to T-junction. Turn **R** into **Church Road** and, a few paces after Churchfields, bear **L** on to concrete track ('**Manor House**').

❸ Continue along track keeping to **L** of **Manor House** where it becomes a narrow path. Pass line of trees and arable field to your **L**. Keep church to your **L** and follow path to **Church Road**. Turn **L** and after gate for **Stansted Hall**, cross over M11 and at T-junction turn **R**. After 250yds (229m) follow fingerpost through hedgerow on to track running parallel with **M11**. Continue for 1,000yds (914m).

❹ Turn **R** into tunnel under **M11**. Turn **L** along field-edge path following ditch. After 200yds (183m), turn **L** over concrete bridge, **L** again on to path and after a few paces turn **R** keeping pond on your **R**. Follow field-edge path for 100yds (91m), turn **R** over 2nd bridge, then **L** and **R** to maintain direction keeping hedgerow on your R. After 200yds (183m), cross wooden bridge and continue across field to waymark and turn half-**R** with woods on your R. At next waymark **L**, follow field-edge path. After 150yds (137m), turn **L** with backs of houses on your R and emerge into Birchanger Lane next to **Three Willows pub**.

❺ Turn **R** at Birchanger Lane and **R** into Wood Lane. Continue along track, with **Digby Wood** on your R, to **Parsonage Lane**. Turn **L** along road to cross Foresthall Road on to footpath. After 300yds (274m) turn **L** into **Church Road** and return to car park.

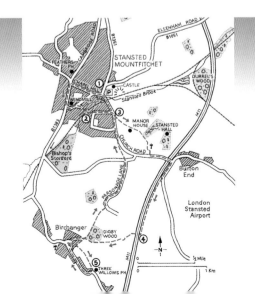

Essex

EPPING FOREST *FOREST RETREAT*

7¼ miles (11.7km) 3hrs 30min **Ascent:** 227ft (70m)
Paths: Woodland paths and bridleways, some road
Suggested map: aqua3 OS Explorer 174 Epping Forest & Lee Valley
Grid reference: TQ 404950
Parking: Free car park on A1069 at Connaught Water

Follow Queen Victoria's path to the opening of the forest to Londoners.

1 From car park walk between wooden posts and bear **L** on gravel path which hugs **Connaught Water**. Walk around lake for 800yds (732m), turn **L** over footbridge and along path with trees to **Fairmead Bottom**. This low-lying area may flood after heavy rain.

2 After 400yds (366m), turn **L** on to disused tarmac road and after a few paces cross **Palmer's Bridge** and bear **R** on to grassy track, which continues ahead close to **A104** on your **R**. Path crosses meadows to **Fairmead Pond** on your **L**. After 750yds (686m), turn **L** on to road uphill and into car park (tea hut).

3 Continue up tarmac road for 100yds (91m) and turn **R** by metal gate on to wide hoggin bridleway, through high woods and pollarded beech trees. Continue for ½ mile (800m) and take path **L**, which leads into wooden fenced enclosure of **Epping Forest Conservation Centre**.

4 Leave **Conservation Centre** by front path, turn **L** and walk past **Kings Oak** pub. After 300yds (274m), with **Paul's Nursery** on your **L**, take path on **R**. Walk under high trees for 250yds (229m) to reach tarmac road and secluded location of **High Beach church**. With church behind you, turn **L** downhill and after 300yds (274m), turn **R** on to path between high pollarded trees.

5 This is **Centenary Walk**, which continues through woodland for ½ mile (800m) to deep cutting of small brook. Walk downhill southwest, keeping brook on **R**. After 400yds (366m), at grassy cross path, turn **L**.

6 After 300yds (274m), turn **R** on to **Green Ride** bridleway. This popular horse ride bisects **North Long Hills** and **White House Plain**. At confluence of paths keep ahead through **Bury Wood** and at cross paths walk half-**R** taking uphill track. Ahead is Butlers Retreat, next to **Queen Elizabeth's Hunting Lodge**. Turn **L** downhill by A1069 and return to car park.

GILWELL PARK *SCOUTING AROUND*

6 miles (9.7km) 2hrs 30min **Ascent:** 231ft (70m)
Paths: Grassy paths, forest tracks, green lanes, some stretches of road, 9 stiles
Suggested map: aqua3 OS Explorer 174 Epping Forest & Lee Valley
Grid reference: TQ 387963
Parking: Free car park in Gilwell Lane

The woodland HQ of the Scout Association.

1 From car park turn **R** and pass through gates of **Gilwell Park** following yellow waymark. Keep to wide grassy path between trees and Scout Association buildings. At the top of the hill there are panoramic views of the reservoir. Follow steep downhill path with wood and pond on your **R** and go over stile to village hall at Sewardstone.

2 Turn **L** into Daws Hill and **L** again into Sewardstone Road. Turn **R** into Mill Lane passing houses and continue on downhill track towards **King George's Reservoir**. Turn **R** and follow track, with reservoir and Horsemill Stream on your **L**, to footbridge over stream.

3 Do not cross bridge. Go straight through kissing gate and turn **R** on to waymarked London Loop path, walking east to **Sewardstone Road**. Turn **R** and after 100yds (91m), turn **L** over stile and ignore London Loop path **R**. Walk up steep north flank of **Barn Hill**,

where there are views over reservoirs, Epping Forest and **Waltham Abbey**.

4 After crossing gravel path and 7th stile, turn **R** on to wide **Green Lane**. Maintain direction and turn **L** at 2nd fingerpost ('Lippitts Hill'). Bear **L** past **police firearms training camp** fence on your **R** (marksmen are well away from you).

5 At **Lippitts Hill**, turn **R** passing **training camp** and **Owl pub**. 50 yards (46m) after pub turn **R** at fingerpost, go up wooden steps and on to steep grassy downhill path. Maintain your direction between horse paddocks and cross stile, followed by footbridge and another stile. Follow path over meadow across flank of hill, then downhill to houses on your **L**. At double fingerpost, ignore direction to Hornbeam Lane, but turn **R** to Sewardstonebury, following line of oak trees across West Essex **Golf Course**. Continue across fairways and past houses to emerge into **Bury Road**. Turn **R** then 1st **L** to return to car park.

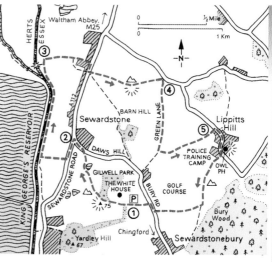

WALTHAM ABBEY *LEE VALLEY PARK*

7½ miles (12.1km) 4hrs 30min **Ascent:** 269ft (82m)
Paths: Grassy riverside, steep field paths, green lanes prone to mud after rain, short stretches of road, 5 stiles
Suggested map: aqua3 OS Explorer 174 Epping Forest & Lee Valley
Grid reference: TL 384015
Parking: Free car park at Cornmill Meadows, closes at 6pm

Gunpowder mills, woodland and waterways.

1 From rear of car park at Cornmill Meadows, take gravel path to fingerpost and go ahead through woodland. At **Cornmill Stream** turn **R** with stream down on your L-H side and views across Cornmill Meadow. At footbridge turn **R** following fence of **Waltham Abbey Royal Gunpowder Mills**.

2 Keep fence on **L** until you reach cross-field path towards alder woodland. Follow field-edge path with brook on your **L**, ('Hook Marsh'). Turn **L** on to Fishers Green Lane, to car park and information board.

3 Cross 2 footbridges over streams and go through kissing gate on **R** ('Ware'). Follow gravel path and picnic area by **Seventy Acres Lake** on **L**.

4 After 600yds (549m) at fingerpost ('Lea Valley Park farms and Nazeing'), cross footbridge and turn **L** passing Bittern Watchpoint. Cross access road to **electricity substation** and follow riverside path to

tarmac road. Turn **R** and then **L** through kissing gate and continue. On your **L** is birdwatching stand.

5 Proceed to **sailing club** entrance. Cross 2 stiles on **R**; walk along field-edge path (keep **sailing club** **L**). Keep to path as it bears **R** uphill to another stile.

6 Follow fingerpost for Clayton Hill through kissing gate, cross bridge and emerge at **Coleman's Shaw**. Turn **R** on to **B194** and follow road as it goes downhill.

7 At T-junction, turn **L** at **Coach and Horses pub** into **Waltham Road**. Cross carefully; walk uphill past **Denver Lodge Farm** on **R**. Cross stile on **R**. Follow field-edge path to **Galleyhill Wood**. Cross next stile. Continue, with woods on **R**, to break in trees. Go through. At cross path turn **R** and continue to **Aimes Green**. Turn **R**. After 100yds (91m), turn **L** in front of houses on to **Claygate Lane** to emerge beside **Eagle Lodge**. Cross Crooked Mile Road to meadow. Turn **L** through kissing gate. Return to car park.

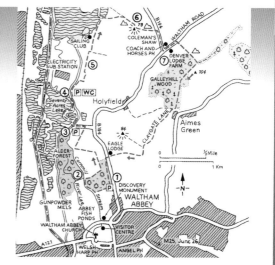

Suffolk

649 SOMERLEYTON *GREAT VICTORIAN ENTREPRENEUR*

6¼ miles (10.1km) 2hrs 30min **Ascent:** 131ft (40m)
Paths: Farm tracks, field-edge paths, country lanes, 2 stiles
Suggested map: aqua3 OS Explorer OL40 The Broads
Grid reference: TM 484972 **Parking:** On-street parking outside Somerleyton post office

Around the delightful estate village designed by a flamboyant Victorian railway magnate.
❶ With **post office** behind you, turn **L**. Walk past estate cottages towards green. Turn **L** around it and around school. Return to road, turn **L** on pavement opposite red-brick wall of **Somerleyton Park**.
❷ Follow road round to **L** and turn **R** on lane ('Ashby') with glimpses of **Somerleyton Hall** across parkland to your **R**. After 300yds (274m), turn **R** past thatched lodge at pedestrian entrance to **Somerleyton Hall**. Go through gates. Keep on lane for 400yds (366m), then turn **L** on to field-edge path.
❸ After 300yds (274m), turn **R** on to farm track. Stay on this waymarked path as it swings **L** through farmyard and then alongside 2 fields, then turns sharp **R** towards wood. Turn **L** along edge of wood; keep to path as it bends around pond and enters woodland. Keep **R** through woods, cross stile, look for gap in hedge on **R**. Bear half-**L** on cross-field path to lane.
❹ Turn **R** and continue for 1 mile (1.6km). Just

before road junction, take meadow-edge path to your **L** to gap in wall. Cross **B1074**, climb stile and keep ahead on field-edge path for ¾ mile (1.2km).
❺ Turn **R** at end of track along Waddling Lane. Path descends towards water-meadows with railway and **River Waveney** to **L**. When path divides, fork **L** to climb around **Wadding Wood**. Keep **R** when track joins from **L** to head uphill away from marsh.
❻ Turn **L** opposite **Waveney Grange Farm** and walk down towards station. Turn **R** opposite station entrance on wide track. When track bends **R**, keep **L** on grassy path to descend to **boatyard**. Turn **L** around boatyard buildings to marina and swing bridge over river, turn **R** past marina; climb access drive to road.
❼ Turn **L** at telephone box and walk along pavement to **Duke's Head pub**. Continue on road as it bends **R** with views of Herringfleet church to your **L**. At next bend, by black railings of cottage, turn **R** on waymarked path, continue along field edge and turn **R** beyond telegraph pole to return to start of walk.

650 COVEHITHE *THE CRUMBLING CLIFFS*

4½ miles (7.2km) 1hr 45min **Ascent:** 131ft (40m)
Paths: Cliff top, shingle beach, farm track and country lanes, 1 stile
Suggested map: aqua3 OS Explorer 231 Southwold & Bungay
Grid reference: TM 522818 **Parking:** On street near Covehithe church

See the effects of coastal erosion on a walk along a rapidly disappearing cliff top.
❶ Take tarmac lane from St Andrew's Church down towards sea to barrier ('Danger') and sign warning that there is no public right of way. Although this is strictly true, this is well-established and popular path stretching north towards Kessingland beach and you are likely to meet many other walkers. The warnings are serious but it is quite safe to walk here so long as you keep away from the cliff edge.
❷ Walk through gap to **R** of road barrier and continue towards cliffs. Turn **L** along wide farm track with pig farm to your **L**. Path follows cliff top then descends towards beach to enter **Benacre** nature reserve. On **L** is **Benacre Broad**, once an estuary, now a marshy lagoon. The shingle beach attracts little terns in spring and summer and you should keep to the path to avoid their nesting sites.
❸ Climb back on to cliffs at end of Benacre Broad. The way cuts through pine trees and bracken on

constantly changing path before running alongside field and swinging **R** to descend to beach level, where you take wide grass track on your **L** across dunes.
❹ At concrete track, with tower of Kessingland church in distance, turn **L** following waymarks of **Suffolk Coast and Heaths Path**. Cross stile and keep straight ahead, passing **Beach Farm** on **R**. Stay straight ahead for 1 mile (1.6km) on wide track between fields with views of Benacre church ahead.
❺ Go through white gates and turn **L** on to quiet country lane. Stay on lane for ¾ mile (1.2km) as it passes between hedges with arable farmland to either side and swings **L** at entrance to **Hall Farm**.
❻ When road bends **R**, turn **L** past gate with an English Nature 'No Entry' sign for cars. Stay on this permissive path as it swings **R** around meadow and continues into woodland of **Holly Grove**. Pass through another gate and turn **L** along road for ¾ mile (1.2km) back into **Covehithe**. Turn **L** at junction to return to **St Andrew's Church**.

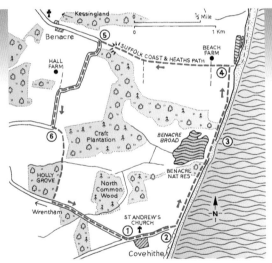

651 SOUTHWOLD *FROM THE PIER*

4 miles (6.4km) 1hr 30min **Ascent:** Negligible
Paths: Riverside paths, seaside promenade, town streets, 2 stiles
Suggested map: aqua3 OS Explorer 231 Southwold & Bungay
Grid reference: TM 511766
Parking: Beach pay-and-display car park or free in nearby streets

A walk around this old-fashioned holiday resort on an island surrounded by river, creek and sea.
❶ Leave **Southwold Pier**, recently rebuilt after years of storms and neglect and now providing a focus for good, old-fashioned fun, and turn **L** along seafront, either following promenade past brightly coloured beach huts and climbing some steps or walking along clifftop path with views over beach. After passing **St James' Green**, where a pair of cannon stand either side of a mast, continue along clifftop path to **Gun Hill**, where you can see six more cannon, captured at the Battle of Culloden near Inverness in 1746.
❷ From **Gun Hill**, head inland alongside large South Green. Turn **L** along Queen's Road to junction with Gardner Road. Cross this road and look for Ferry Path footpath, that follows stream beside **marshes** as it heads towards river. Alternatively, stay on clifftop path and walk across sand dunes to mouth of **River Blyth**.

❸ Turn **R** and walk beside river, passing **Walberswick ferry**, group of fishing huts where fresh fish is sold, and **Harbour Inn**. After about ¾ mile (1.2km) you reach iron bridge on site of old Southwold-to-Halesworth railway line.
❹ Keep straight ahead at bridge, crossing stile and following path round to **R** alongside **Buss Creek** to make a complete circuit of island. There are good views across the common to **Southwold**, dominated by the lighthouse and tower of **St Edmund's Church**. Horses and cattle can often be seen grazing on the marshes. Keep straight ahead at 4-finger signpost and keep walking along raised path until you reach white-painted bridge.
❺ Climb up to road and cross over bridge, then continue on path beside **Buss Creek** with views of colourful beach huts in distance. The path skirts **boating lake** on its way down to sea. Turn **R** back across car park to return to **pier** to start of walk.

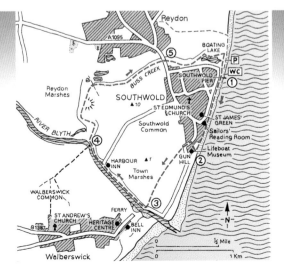

Suffolk

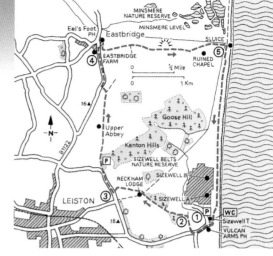

SIZEWELL *NUCLEAR POWERED*

6¾ miles (10.9km) 3hrs **Ascent:** 164ft (50m)
Paths: Footpaths, coast path, short stretches of road, 6 stiles
Suggested map: aqua3 OS Explorer 212 Woodbridge & Saxmundham
Grid reference: TM 474628
Parking: Sizewell Beach free car park

The unexpected delights of a circuit around a controversial nuclear plant.

① Walk along road heading away from beach or cross meadow behind car park and cross stile to reach Vulcan Arms pub. Continue along road past entrance to power stations. Turn **R** after 400yds (366m) on to track at Sandy Lane and stay on this track for 300yds (274m).

② Turn **L** just before cottage and follow path beneath power lines and alongside small wood on **L**. Cross stile beside gate and continue across open meadow with views of **Sizewell B** to your **R**. Path on **R** leads into **Sizewell Belts nature reserve** (no dogs). Keep straight ahead on wide bridlepath. When path swings **L**, turn **R** and immediately **L** beside **Reckham Lodge**. Path crosses heathland and heads half-**L** across meadow to road.

③ Turn **R** and walk carefully uphill along road. When road bends **L**, keep ahead on gravel track, passing old

laboratory and car park for permissive walks. Stay on this track between hedges for ¾ mile (1.2km) until it bends **L** at derelict cottage to road. Turn **R** to walk into **Eastbridge**.

④ After passing **Eastbridge Farm** on your **L**, look for footpath on **R**, ('**Minsmere Sluice**'). After 50yds (46m) path swings sharp **R** then turns **L** beside hedge and continues alongside field. Pass through belt of trees and stay on narrow footpath across fields with views over **Minsmere Level** to your **L**. Pass through 2 gates to cross to far side of ditch and continue on grassy lane. The path eventually swings **L** to run alongside New Cut, with views of Minsmere Nature Reserve to your **L** and **Sizewell B** behind **ruined chapel** to your **R**.

⑤ Turn **R** at Minsmere Sluice to return to Sizewell along wide grass track or scramble up to top of cliffs. Turn **R** just beyond power stations to return to car park and start.

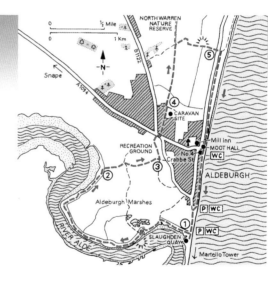

ALDEBURGH *BENJAMIN BRITTEN*

5¾ miles (9.2km) 2hrs 30min **Ascent:** Negligible
Paths: River and sea wall, meadows, old railway track, 6 stiles. Note: Dogs not allowed on beach between May and September
Suggested map: aqua3 OS Explorer 212 Woodbridge & Saxmundham
Grid reference: TM 463555
Parking: Slaughden Quay free car park

On the trail of Benjamin Britten.

① Start at **Slaughden Quay** (yacht club). Walk back briefly in direction of **Aldeburgh** and turn **L** along river wall on north bank of **River Alde** – views to your **L** of the Martello tower. Stay on river wall for 2 miles (3.2km) as river swings **R** towards Aldeburgh.

② When river bends **L** at stile, go down wooden staircase to your **R** and keep straight ahead across meadow with water tower ahead. Go through gate and bear half-**R**, then keep straight ahead across next field to another footbridge. After crossing 3rd footbridge, path runs alongside allotments and goes through gate to lane.

③ Turn **L** by brick wall; cross **recreation ground**. Continue past fire station to road. Turn **R** for 75yds (69m) then go **L** on signposted footpath almost opposite hospital entrance. Follow path via housing

estate, cross road. Continue with caravan site on **R**.

④ When you see stile on **R**, leading to track across **caravan site**, turn **L** and immediately **R** on permissive path that follows old railway trackbed. Stay on this path for ½ mile (800m) climbing steadily between farmland to **L** and woodland and marshes to **R**. Turn **R** at junction of paths and cross stile to open meadows. Stay on this path, crossing **North Warren nature reserve** with Sizewell power station to your **L**.

⑤ Cross road and turn **R** along concrete path running parallel to beach. As you approach **Aldeburgh**, pass fishermen's huts and fishing boats on shingle. Pass **Moot Hall** and continue along Crag Path past model yacht pond, lifeboat station and pair of lookout towers. Stay on this esplanade between houses and beach with Martello tower ahead. At end of Crag Path, bear **R** across car park and walk around old mill to return to **Slaughden Quay**.

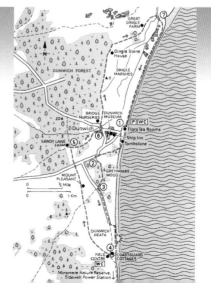

DUNWICH *LOST CITY*

8 miles (12.9km) 4hrs **Ascent:** 262ft (80m)
Paths: Farm tracks, heathland paths, quiet roads, shingle beach
Suggested map: aqua3 OS Explorers 212 Woodbridge & Saxmundham; 231 Southwold & Bungay
Grid reference: TM 478706 (on Explorer 231)
Parking: Dunwich Beach free car park

Conjure up visions of a lost city as you stand on the cliffs gazing out to sea.

① Walk up road from beach car park and keep **L** at junction. When road bends, turn **L** on to footpath that climbs through woods to ruins of Greyfriars Friary. Turn **L** along cliff top, go over set of wooden steps and bear **R** through trees on waymarked path. At end of path, turn **R** along track to road.

② Turn **L** off road after 100yds (91m) on track to Dairy House. Keep straight ahead as it enters **Greyfriars Wood** and continues to road.

③ Turn **L** along road for ½ mile (800m), passing 2 caravan sites on **L**. As soon as you enter National Trust land, turn **L** on to path waymarked with white arrows.

④ Walk around National Trust's **Coastguard Cottages** and take track beside Heath Barn field centre, then bear **R** on to sandy path that climbs through heather. Keep on path, bearing **L** and **R** at crossing track to follow Sandlings Walk nightjar

waymarks. At bridleway, keep ahead on farm track passing Mount Pleasant farm. Cross road and keep ahead on concrete lane to **Sandy Lane Farm**.

⑤ Turn **R** for ½ mile (800m) on shady lane to St James's Church, built in 19th century when Dunwich's other churches were falling into sea. For short cut, keep straight ahead here to return to **Dunwich**.

⑥ Turn **L** at road and, in 100yds (91m), go **R** at **Bridge Nurseries**. Keep to **R** around farm buildings and stay on this track for 1½ miles (2.4km) beside **Dunwich Forest** before turning seawards. Pass through gate to enter covert and fork **R** at junction around **Great Dingle Farm**, then follow path through reed beds towards sea.

⑦ Turn **R** at junction, with old drainage mill to your **L**, and follow flood bank across **Dingle Marshes**. Turn **R** to return to **Dunwich** along beach or take path behind shingle bank.

Suffolk

655 SOUTH ELMHAM THROUGH SAINTS COUNTRY

8¾ miles (14.1km) 4hrs Ascent: 295ft (90m) ▲
Paths: Field paths, meadows and country lanes, 3 stiles
Suggested map: aqua3 OS Explorer 231 Southwold & Bungay
Grid reference: TM 306833
Parking: South Elmham Hall free car park

Wide views and huge expanses of farmland on a walk through scattered parishes.

❶ From car park, walk between trees and cross moat on permissive path. Take footbridge over stream and keep straight ahead across meadow. Go through gate and turn **L** along green lane enclosed by hedges. At junction of tracks, turn **L** and walk across meadows to site of **minster**, a romantic ruin enclosed by trees.

❷ After visiting **minster**, continue ahead along line of hedge; turn **L** at end of next meadow to cross footbridge and climb on to field-edge path. Turn **R** at road. After 300yds (274m) turn **L** on to lane. Stay on this lane as it bends to **R** for ¾ mile (1.2km).

❸ Cross main road and keep ahead on field-edge path. Pass through hedge, cross next field; turn **R** beyond hedge. Walk beside hedge for ½ mile (800m) to junction; turn **R** on to cross-field path that becomes wide track. Turn **L** at crossroads and walk across fields, water tower to R, to **St Michael's Church**.

❹ Turn **L** along road. After ½ mile (800m), cross humpback bridge and continue to **St Peter's Church**. Follow road round to **R** past entrance to **St Peter's Hall**, then turn **L** across plank bridge to walk beside moat. The path swings **R** then **L**, following line of hedge between open fields.

❺ At junction of paths, go **L** along field-edge, ('**Angles Way**'). This becomes grassy lane then pebbled road. Cross road; proceed on concrete track.

❻ Turn **L** at next road to pass **Mushroom Farm** and, in 300yds (274m), go **R** on field-edge path. After ½ mile (800m), at junction of paths with half-white, half-weatherboarded farmhouse visible to R, turn **L** to climb towards small wood and continue through woods. Go through gate, cross stream and climb green lane to road.

❼ Turn **L** then **R** in 300yds (274m) on to lane ('**South Elmham Hall**'). Follow lane round to **R** to return to start.

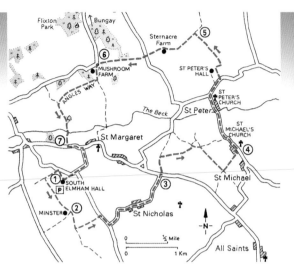

656 LAXFIELD WALKING UP A THIRST

3½ miles (5.7km) 1hr 30min Ascent: 98ft (30m) ▲
Paths: Field-edge paths and country lanes
Suggested map: aqua3 OS Explorer 231 Southwold & Bungay
Grid reference: TM 295723
Parking: Church Plain, Laxfield

What better way to enjoy a summer evening than a country stroll to a Victorian pub – the King's Head at Laxfield?

❶ Laxfield is a historic village whose former market square is edged by All Saints Church, the **Guildhall** and the 15th-century **Royal Oak pub**. From Church Plain with **Royal Oak pub** behind you, walk along High Street. After passing Baptist chapel on your R, look for footpath on same side of street which runs between hedge and cemetery. Stay on this path as it passes beneath green canopy and crosses footbridge over **River Blyth**. The river rises just outside **Laxfield** and is little more than a stream at this point.

❷ Keep straight ahead to reach open countryside and take field-edge path with hedge to R. Ignore all paths leading off and stay on this path to climb around field towards distant farmhouse. Eventually path turns **L** beside ditch and then **R** along outer wall of farmhouse to reach road.

❸ Turn **R** and stay on this road for 1 mile (1.6km), keeping to **R** when road divides. This is a lovely quiet country lane and there are good views towards **Laxfield** across huge fields to your right.

❹ Turn **L** at **Corner Farm** and fork **R** along lane, ('Ubbeston'). After passing stud farm, road bends **R**, then narrows and starts to descend into valley. When you see cream-coloured **cottage** ahead, turn **R** on to footpath. As you pass through hedge you will once again see tower of All Saints Church up ahead. Keep straight ahead towards line of willow trees and continue along edge of field. Turn **R** then **L** to join farm track that leads to tarmac lane, where you should keep staright ahead.

❺ When you reach road, turn **L** to return to **Laxfield**. Take first **R** to arrive at Low House (**King's Head pub**) and that well-earned pint. When you are ready, turn **R** outside pub and **L** along Church Walk, or walk through churchyard to return to Church Plain.

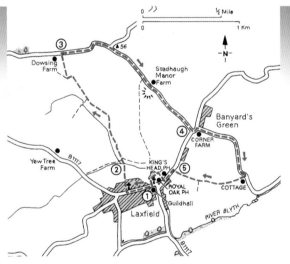

657 DEBENHAM HISTORIC COUNTY TOWN

6 miles (9.7km) 2hrs 30min Ascent: 197ft (60m) ▲
Paths: Field-edge and cross-field paths, country lanes
Suggested map: aqua3 OS Explorer 211 Bury St Edmunds & Stowmarket
Grid reference: TM 174631
Parking: Cross Green free car park, High Street, Debenham

Exploring the green lanes and pathways around a historic county town.

❶ Walk away from High Street past butcher and fork **R** at Priory Lane to cross **River Deben**. Turn **R** at road and, after 100yds (91m), turn **L** on sloping cross-field path. Pass through hedge and continue around edge of field before turning **L** along country lane.

❷ At junction of bridleways, ignore 'Circular Walk' signs and keep straight ahead on oak-lined drive to **Crows Hall**, which takes its name from Debenham family crest. Follow waymarks around to **R** of farm, pass bungalow and turn **L** beside hedge on to field-edge path. Go **L** again at end of field and stay on this path as it turns to **R** around **Great Wood**. After another 250yds (229m), turn **L** across fields to come to wide track. Turn **R** here and turn **R** along lane to pass large farm buildings of **Crowborough Farm**.

❸ At start of line of telegraph poles, turn **L** alongside hedge on to grassy path. Stay on this path for ½ mile (800m), passing **wind pump** and pair of water towers before descending to cottage with wooden barns.

❹ Turn **L** along **Waddlegoose Lane**. Stay on this green lane for about 1¾ miles (2.8km). When track joins from L, keep straight ahead to return to circular walk. The path is now enclosed by tall hedges, obscuring your view of fields.

❺ At next junction, turn **R** along farm track and stay on this track past converted barn and brick farmhouse. Turn **L** along road for about 400yds (366m) then turn **R** on to bridlepath ('Circular Walk'). After passing through gate, path goes around **Hoggs Kiss Wood**, one of 200 community woodlands created for the millennium. You have a choice between staying on the path or walking through woods and meadows.

❻ When you reach end of **Hoggs Kiss Wood**, turn **R** around group of allotments and fork **R** along Water Lane to reach High Street. Turn **L** along High Street to return to start.

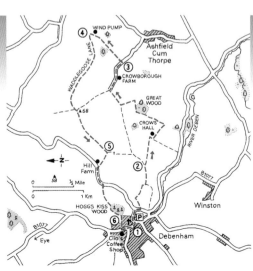

Suffolk

CHARSFIELD DISCOVERING 'AKENFIELD'

5 miles (8km) 2hrs **Ascent:** 262ft (80m)
Paths: Field paths, farm tracks, meadows, lanes, 2 stiles
Suggested map: aqua3 OS Explorer 212 Woodbridge & Saxmundham
Grid reference: TM 254564
Parking: Charsfield village hall

Read the book then walk the landscape around a village immortalised in literature.
1 Walk along The Street from **village hall**, passing **Three Horseshoes pub**. At Baptist chapel, turn **L** and walk up Chapel Lane. The road bends **L** and climbs to summit with good views over village and tower of St Peter's Church.
2 Turn **R** at end of lane. After 100yds (91m), turn **L** on to Magpie Street and continue for ¾ mile (1.2km) passing apple orchards on **L**. Just after **Pear Tree Farm**, go **L** through hedge on to field-edge path. Keep to **L**-**H** side of field and turn **R** on grassy track that runs through an orchard where blackcurrants are grown. Bear **R** around hedge and keep ahead on paved track that passes between apple, pear and plum trees before descending to **The Hall**.
3 Turn **L** along road. Turn **R** in 150yds (137m) on to cross-field path. At far side of field, keep ahead on grassy track to climb towards distant line of poplar

trees, then continue ahead along side of next field.
4 Turn **L** past old barn and fork **L** by pond to walk past **Moat Hall** and along Martins Lane. After 600yds (549m), turn **L** across meadow that runs behind white house. The path turns **R**, bears **L** around field, then turns sharply **R** as it approaches line of trees. Look for gap in hedge and scramble across ditch to reach field with huge oak tree at its centre. Turn **R** here along edge of field. In corner of field, take overgrown path through hedge and turn **L** on to wide orchard track. At end of orchard, turn **L** and immediately **R** to cross plank bridge through hedgerow and bear diagonally **R** across 3 meadows to road.
5 Turn **R** along road, ('Charsfield Street'). After 400yds (366m), turn **L** on to wide track climbing between fields. Turn **R** at path junction and continue across fields, passing small primary school before reaching St Peter's Church. Turn **R** and walk downhill to return to start of walk.

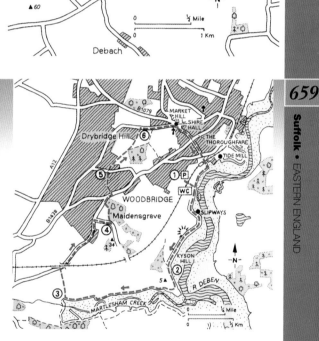

WOODBRIDGE DOWN BY THE RIVER

4 miles (6.4km) 1hr 30min **Ascent:** 164ft (50m)
Paths: River wall, riverside paths, town streets, some steps
Suggested map: aqua3 OS Explorer 197 Ipswich, Felixstowe & Harwich or 212 Woodbridge & Saxmundham
Grid reference: TM 271485
Parking: The Avenue car park, Woodbridge

Along the River Deben from a riverside town, with views of a working tide mill.
1 Leave car park on The Avenue and cross railway line to boatyard at end of lane. Turn **R** along river wall, passing **slipways** of Deben Yacht Club. Continue on easy section of walk, on tarmac path with views over meadows to **R**, to enter National Trust's **Kyson Hill**.
2 Turn **L** at 3-way junction; descend to beach. Walk along foreshore under oak trees. (At high tide you may have to turn **R** instead, picking up route at Point **4**.) Keep **R** at railings, follow path to **Martlesham Creek**, scramble up embankment and follow riverside path.
3 Turn **R** at end of creek and walk around sewage works to Sandy Lane. Turn **R** beneath railway bridge and stay on this road as it climbs for 700yds (640m). At top of rise, turn **R** on to Broom Heath.
4 When road bends round to **R**, turn **L** past gate leading to Woodland Trust woods (short cut rejoins

from **R** here). Stay on path on outside of woods to return to Sandy Lane by telephone box. Turn **R** here and **R** at main road, then cross road and climb steps on far side after 50yds (46m). Keep ahead to end of footpath and cross road to Portland Crescent.
5 Continue to descend hill and climb up other side. Continue on Fen Walk, enclosed by black railings with graveyards either side. Fork **L** at junction of paths to descend grassy slope with views of church tower ahead. Keep ahead and climb steps to Seckford Street.
6 Turn **R** and continue to **Market Hill**. Alleyway on **R-H** side leads to churchyard. Turn **L** through churchyard on to Church Street, emerging alongside site of old abbey, now private school. Walk down Church Street and cross over **The Thoroughfare**, pedestrian street, on **L-H** side. Continue along Quay Street and cross station yard to footbridge over railway line. Turn **L** to visit **Tide Mill** or **R** to return to start.

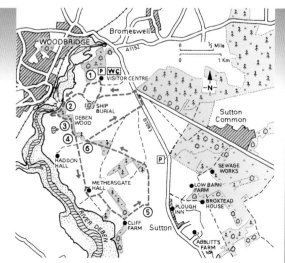

SUTTON HOO A WARRIOR'S GRAVE

7 miles (11.3km) 3hrs **Ascent:** 262ft (80m)
Paths: Field-edge and riverside paths, farm lanes, short section of busy road, 3 stiles
Suggested map: aqua3 OS Explorer 197 Ipswich, Felixstowe & Harwich
Grid reference: TM 289492
Parking: National Trust car park – included in entry price for exhibition, or pay-and-display when exhibition closed

By the site of a pagan burial ground.
1 Take signposted blue trail from National Trust **visitor centre**, descending towards river on gravel track. Turn **L** opposite entrance to Little Haugh and turn **R** by map of Sutton Hoo Estate. Path narrows and turns **L** along fence on its way to river. Keep **L** around meadow then cross footbridge and climb steps to river bank with **Woodbridge** visible on opposite bank.
2 Turn **L**; walk along river bank (overgrown in places, plank bridges can be slippery.) After 400yds (366m), turn **L** to leave river and turn **L** around turf field. Keep to field edge as it swings **R** and climbs between woodland to **L** and reservoir to **R**.
3 Turn **R** at top of rise to follow bridleway along field edge with **Deben Wood** to **L**. At end of wood, path swings half-**L** across field then passes through hedge on to lane. Turn **L** here for short cut, picking up walk in 300yds (274m) at Point **6**.

4 Keep ahead for ¾ mile (1.2km), crossing drive to **Haddon Hall**. Bear **R** around farm buildings then **L** on footpath beside brick wall. Pass cannon on lawn of **Methersgate Hall**. Continue with **River Deben** opening out in front. Cross stile; cross access field. Cross another stile and turn **R** along lane. Continue for 1 mile (1.6km) as lane bends **L** past **Cliff Farm**.
5 Turn **L** at 3-finger signpost along field-edge track, passing embankment on **R**. Keep to public bridleway as it swings **L** around woodland. At end, keep ahead between fields and continue as path becomes broad grass track, passing cottages to reach minor lane.
6 Turn **R** and stay on lane for 1 mile (1.6km) to main road (**B1083**). Turn **L** and walk carefully along verge for 400yds (366m). Turn **L** opposite road junction past National Trust sign. When you see burial mounds to your **L-H** side, turn **R** to return to visitor centre on National Trust permissive path.

Suffolk

661 EAST BERGHOLT *CONSTABLE COUNTRY*

3¾ miles (6km) 1hr 30min Ascent: 246ft (75m) ▲
Paths: Roads, field paths and riverside meadows, 9 stiles
Suggested map: aqua3 OS Explorer 196 Sudbury, Hadleigh & Dedham Vale
Grid reference: TM 069346
Parking: Free car park next to Red Lion, East Bergholt

A gentle walk through the landscape that inspired one of England's greatest artists.

① Turn **R** out of car park, past **Red Lion** pub and post office. Turn **R** along lane, note **Constable's studio** on L. Continue past chapel and cemetery, through gate and down **L-H** side of meadow to cross footbridge. Climb path on far side for views of Stour Valley, church towers at **Dedham** and **Stratford St Mary**.

② Turn **L** at junction of paths to walk down **Dead Lane**, sunken footpath ('Dedham Road'). At foot of hill, turn **L** on to field-edge path. The path goes **R** then **L** to cross stile on edge of **Fishpond Wood**. Walk beside wood for few paces, then climb stile into field and walk beside hedge to your **R**. Path switches to other side of hedge and back again before bending **L** around woodland to Fen Lane.

③ Turn **R** along lane, crossing cart bridge and ignoring footpaths to L and to R as you continue towards wooden-arched **Fen Bridge**. Cross bridge

and turn **L** beside **River Stour** towards **Flatford** on wide open pasture of flood plain.

④ Cross bridge to return to north bank of river beside **Bridge Cottage**. Turn **R** here, passing restored dry dock on way to **Flatford Mill**.

⑤ Pass **Willy Lott's House** and turn **L** past car park. An optional loop, on National Trust permissive path, leads **R** around outside of Gibbonsgate Field beside newly planted hedge. Otherwise, keep **L** on wide track and go through gate to join another National Trust path through Miller's Field. Stay on this path as it swings **L** and climbs to top of field, then go ahead through kissing gate, crossing 2 stiles to T-junction of footpaths. Turn **L** along edge of meadow and continue down drive of **Clapper Farm** to Flatford Road.

⑥ Turn **R** along road. At crossroads, turn **L** passing **King's Head** pub and **Haywain Tea Rooms** on way back to **East Bergholt**. Stay on pavement on **R** side of road to walk through churchyard and return to start.

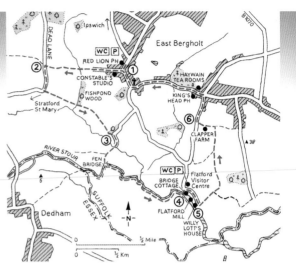

662 SHOTLEY *BETWEEN TWO RIVERS*

6½ miles (10.4km) 3hrs Ascent: 262ft (80m) ▲
Paths: Field and riverside paths, country lanes, 2 stiles
Suggested map: aqua3 OS Explorer 197 Ipswich, Felixstowe & Harwich
Grid reference: TM 246335
Parking: Opposite Bristol Arms at Shotley Gate

Views of Harwich and Felixstowe from a spit between the Stour and Orwell estuaries.

① From **Bristol Arms** pub, looking across to Harwich; head **L** along waterfront to **Shotley Marina**. Pass to R of **HMS Ganges Museum** (open summer weekends) and keep **R** to walk across lock gates to **Shotley Point**. Path follows headland around marina basin, with views of Felixstowe Docks. Turn **R** to continue along flood bank between marshes and mudflats. After 1 mile (1.6km) pass old oyster beds and swing **L** by salt marshes at **Crane's Hill Creek**.

② Halfway around creek, at sign ('Suffolk Coast and Heaths Path') pointing ahead, descend bank to **L** and pass through gate to join meadow-edge path. Cross stile and bear **L** along track to climb past vineyards at **St Mary's Church**.

③ Walk ahead past church on tarmac lane leading to **Shotley Hall**, then turn **L** on to cross-field path opposite drive. Follow this path diagonally across field

and bear **R** at far corner, following line of telegraph poles towards road where you turn **L**.

④ After 50yds (46m), turn **R** along lane ('Erwarton Walk'). At end turn **R**, passing Tudor gatehouse of **Erwarton Hall**. Stay on this quiet country road as it bends towards **Erwarton** village. Just after R-H bend, turn **L** beside churchyard on to wide track. Pass to R of cottage and turn **L** along field-edge path.

⑤ Riverside footpath, shown on maps, has been eroded so turn **L** at end of field. Climb hill, pass reservoir. Turn **R** through trees, then cross stile and go half-**R** over fields with cranes of Felixstowe visible up ahead. At gap in hedge just before houses, turn **R** then **L** at telegraph pole to reach **Shotley Cottage**.

⑥ Keep ahead on wide track and turn **R** along road to **Shotley Gate**. Turn **L** at post office along Caledonia Road to see mast of **HMS Ganges**. Turn **R** along School Lane to return to main road. The **Bristol Arms** is just down hill to your **L**.

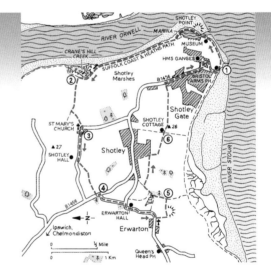

663 FELIXSTOWE FERRY *FISH AND SHIPS*

6½ miles (10.4km) 3hrs Ascent: 164ft (50m) ▲
Paths: Field and riverside paths, country lanes, farm tracks, sea wall, 4 stiles
Suggested map: aqua3 OS Explorer 197 Ipswich, Felixstowe & Harwich
Grid reference: TM 328376
Parking: Ferry Café car park, Felixstowe Ferry

A pleasant walk along the Deben Estuary reveals another side to Felixstowe.

① Take tarmac path along embankment behind **Ferry Café** car park. The path passes boatyard and follows river wall as you look down on abandoned boats lying moored in muddy flats. Turn **R** across stile to walk beside Deben Estuary. After ½ mile (800m) path swings **L** and then **R** across inlet at entrance to **King's Fleet**.

② Turn **L** to descend embankment and walk along broad track. Pass old wind pump and stay on this track as it winds between farmland and King's Fleet. After 1 mile (1.6km) track bends **R** and climbs to farm where it becomes tarmac lane. Continue to T-junction.

③ Turn across field to climb to ridge then drop down through next field to The Wilderness (belt of trees beside Falkenham Brook). Turn **L** through trees and follow path alongside stream, then bend **R** to cross meadow. Make for corner of hedge opposite and

bear **R** alongside fence to cross footbridge and continue on grassy path between fields. At end of field, turn **L** and continue to end of hedge, then turn **R** to climb track to **Brick Kiln Cottages**.

④ At top of track, turn **L** along lane and stay on this lane past **Gulpher Hall** and duck pond. As road bends **R**, walk past entrance to The Brook and turn **L** on field-edge path. Path ascends then turns **R** around field and cuts straight across next field, unless it's diverted by crops. Pass through gate and keep straight on along lane, then turn **L** in 150yds (137m) on another path that runs between fields.

⑤ At pill box, turn **R** on to Ferry Road down to sea. Cross Cliff Road and turn **L**, walking past clubhouse and turning half-**R** across signposted path to sea wall. Turn **L** and walk along wall, passing two **Martello** towers and row of beach huts. Continue to mouth of estuary and turn **L** just before jetty to return to **Ferry Café**.

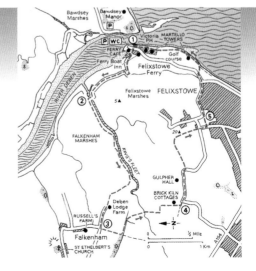

Suffolk

KERSEY AN ARCHITECTURAL STROLL

6½ miles (10.4km) 3hrs **Ascent:** 525ft (160m) ▲3
Paths: Field paths, country roads, town streets, 1 stile
Suggested map: aqua3 OS Explorer 196 Sudbury, Hadleigh & Dedham Vale
Grid reference: TM 001440
Parking: The Street, Kersey (between church and The Splash)

Suffolk architecture on a country walk.

❶ Walk down main street and cross **The Splash** (ford). Pass 1st house, turn **L** along path, **R** through allotments and climb field-edge path to road. Walk **L** for 150yds (137m), turn **R** on fenced-off path. At end of meadow, turn **R** by ditch. Cross footbridge to road.

❷ Turn **L**. In 75yds (69m) go **R** on bridleway between trees. Path bends **R** and descends to farm. Turn **R** on farm track and briefly **R** along road, then **L** by shed to cross field. Turn **L** by stream, cross footbridge, climb steps. Continue uphill towards road.

❸ Turn **R** for 100yds (91m) then **L** on to farm drive. Go **L** of farm buildings to narrow path between fence and hedge. At track, turn **R** and go **L** at telegraph pole to cross fields. Cross footbridge, continue ahead and bear half-**L** to A1071. If path diverted by crops follow obvious route, not right of way.

❹ Cross road, bear **L** across field, turn **L** along green lane. Turn **R** on to **Castle Road**. At end of road

cross Friars Hill and pass cricket ground, cemetery wall to **R**. Through gate turn **L** across recreation ground to meadows. Cross footbridge, walk through car park to Bridge Street.

❺ Turn **R** and **R** again to High Street. After 400yds (366m), turn **R** along Church Street to St Mary's Church. **Guildhall** is on **L**. Walk through gate to **R** of **Guildhall** (if closed, walk around building to **L**). Continue to road, turn **R** to cross Toppesfield Bridge.

❻ Ignore Riverside Walk, turn **R** on field-edge path behind riverside park. When path divides, keep **L** to climb to Broom Hill nature reserve and up **Constitution Hill**. Turn **R** at track, proceed to road, go **L**.

❼ Cross **A1071**; look for wide track ('Kersey Vale'). At field corner, keep **R**, descend to cottage. Cross footbridge and stile to **R** of cottage. Turn **R** on lane to **Kersey**. Pass green, follow road round to **R**. Turn **L** past school to St Mary's Church. Steep footpath by churchyard leads to main street.

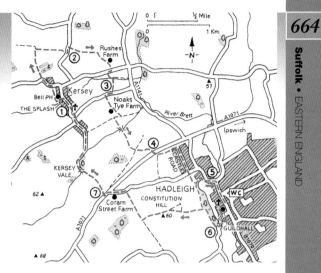

POLSTEAD MURDER MOST FOUL

4 miles (6.4km) 2hrs **Ascent:** 394ft (120m) ▲2
Paths: Field-edge paths, meadows, country lanes, short section of busy road, 8 stiles
Suggested map: aqua3 OS Explorer 196 Sudbury, Hadleigh & Dedham Vale
Grid reference: TL 990381
Parking: Lay-by beside duck pond at Polstead

On the trail of a grisly Victorian murder.

❶ Walk up lane opposite the **duck pond** towards **St Mary's Church**. From churchyard there are views across the valley to **Stoke-by-Nayland**. Leave **St Mary's** churchyard through gate on **L-H** side to enter area of pasture called The Horsecroft. Cross meadow and bear **R** towards white house. Pass house, go through gate and continue along road for ¼ mile (400m). Cross bridge, turn **L** on to footpath through meadow with hedge on R-H side.

❷ Turn **R** at junction of paths and climb over gate to enter field on **L**. Path climbs steadily around edge of field before turning **R** through small wood to road. Turn **R** and stay on lane to **Stoke-by-Nayland**. If you don't want to visit village, take short cut between houses to your left after 200yds (183m).

❸ Turn **L** at crossroads and walk along B1068 for 350yds (320m), then turn **L** at **Stour Valley Path** waymark. Descend alongside tall hedge to meet up

with short cut, then cross undulating farmland and head diagonally **L** across field. At far corner of field, turn sharp **L** and walk along edge of crops before crossing stile to road.

❹ Turn **R** to cross **River Box**. Turn **L** over footbridge and go through kissing gate. Follow path across meadows, then fork **R** over stile and immediately **L** to enter woodland. Leaving woods, cross stile and turn **R** along wide track towards **Marten's Lane**.

❺ Turn **L** on **Marten's Lane**. Opposite entrance to **Cherry Tree Farm**, turn **R** on to footpath across parkland and around meadow. This is the Red Barn Path that leads to the site where the local molecatcher's daughter was murdered. Instead, turn **L** through kissing gate on edge of meadow, passing pond on **R**. Stay on enclosed path, through kissing gate and cross meadow where horses graze. Turn **R** at end of meadow; go between houses to reach green. Turn **L** to walk downhill and return to **duck pond**.

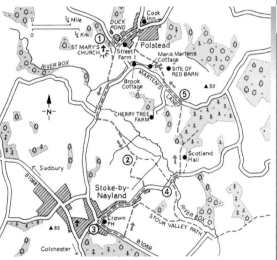

GIPPING VALLEY WILDLIFE WANDER

5 miles (8km) 2hrs **Ascent:** 213ft (65m) ▲2
Paths: Riverside, field-edge and cross-field paths, 12 stiles
Suggested map: aqua3 OS Explorer 211 Bury St Edmunds & Stowmarket
Grid reference: TM 123512
Parking: Gipping Valley Centre

A walk along a peaceful valley, looking out for herons, kingfishers and otters.

❶ Follow signs from **Gipping Valley Centre** to river. Path crosses play area, climbs embankment, crosses road and descends on far side. Turn **L** beside fence. Bear **R** between 2 fishing lakes. Turn **R** under railway bridge. Proceed on **Gipping Valley River Path**.

❷ Turn **L** to cross bridge at Great Blakenham Lock. Follow **Gipping Valley River Path** markers to turn **R** between houses and take narrow passage beside Mill Cottage to return to river. Stay on riverside path for 1½ miles (2.4km). Pass beneath railway line and cross quarry access road to wider stretch of river with water-meadows to **L**. Pass lock and keep ahead at **Causeway Lake**. Continue around edge of meadow, ignoring footbridge to **R**. Soon cross stile and bear **R**, following river. Walk around another meadow with views of **rare breeds farm**, cross footbridge and follow narrow path to **Baylham Mill**.

❸ Turn **L** across bridge. Cross railway line and turn **R** at road. After 200yds (183m), cross road and walk through hedge to pass behind **Moat Farm**. Keep ahead on wide track. Turn **L** then **R** to climb between fields to reach plateau with sweeping views.

❹ Turn **L** on field-edge path to descend to **Upper Street** village. Path swings **L** through hedge and **R** across meadow. Go through gate and down lane past church and old school.

❺ At foot of Church Lane, turn **L** and then **R** by sign ('No horses please'). Path crosses farmland and briefly enters Devil's Grove before emerging opposite **Walnut Tree Farm**. Turn **L** along lane and **R** by pond to pass through gate and cross meadow. Go through gate and keep ahead on cross-field path, then follow signs ('circular walk') past rusting farm machinery and keep **R** on farm track. Turn **L** to **Great Blakenham**.

❻ Cross B1113. Walk along Mill Lane. Road bends **L** to return to Point ❷. Retrace route to car park.

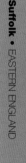

Suffolk

667 HOXNE A THOUSAND-YEAR TREE

3½ miles (5.7km) 1hr 30min Ascent: 197ft (60m)
Paths: Country lanes, field and woodland paths, 2 stiles
Suggested map: aqua3 OS Explorer 230 Diss & Harleston
Grid reference: TM 179769
Parking: Hoxne village hall

Around the village where the last King of East Anglia met his untimely death.

1 Turn **L** out of car park to cross **Goldbrook Bridge**, noting inscription on bridge: 'King Edmund taken prisoner here, AD 870'. Turn **R** to cross tributary of **River Dove** and pass **Swan Inn** on **L**. Fork **R** to climb past post office, alongside village green, to top of lane and Church of St Peter and St Paul.

2 Turn **R** along road and take 2nd **L**, Watermill Lane. Bear **R** along concrete lane ('To the **watermill**'). Lane descends into valley beside water-meadows of River Waveney. At entrance drive to mill, turn **R** on to concrete track that swings **L** past huts to become green lane bordered by hedges. Turn **R** alongside fence. Path swings **L** and **R** across fields then becomes tarmac lane. Turn **R** at end of lane to return to main road.

3 Turn **L**, walk around bend; turn **R** on to country lane ('Hoxne, Cross Street'). Cross stream, turn **R** to enter **Brakey Wood**, created to commemorate millennium. Keep to **R** beside stream, walk around edge of woods; cross stile to arrive at sewage works.

4 Continue on footpath along field edge. **St Edmund's Monument** is in R-H field, where a thousand-year-old oak tree once stood. It is usually possible to reach it on permissive footpath. Cross plank footbridge; stay on footpath as it bends to **R** around 2nd field and enters narrow woodland before arriving at **Cross Street** by side of garage and shop.

5 Walk straight ahead for another 60yds (55m). When road bends sharply **R**, continue ahead on public footpath between houses which then turns **L** around field. Path turns **R** and **L** to cross ditch and descends steeply beside next field with tall hedge on L-H side. Cross stile, turn **R** and in 50yds (46m) go **L** over footbridge. Pass through gate and keep ahead on sloping cross-field path to road.

6 Turn **R** and return to start at **Goldbrook Bridge**.

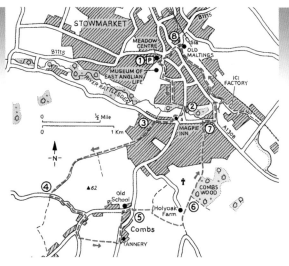

668 STOWMARKET HEART OF SUFFOLK

6 miles (9.7km) 2hrs 30min Ascent: 213ft (65m)
Paths: Town streets and footpaths, country lanes, field-edge and riverside paths, 1 stile
Suggested map: aqua3 OS Explorer 211 Bury St Edmunds & Stowmarket
Grid reference: TM 046585
Parking: Meadow Centre pay-and-display car park or follow signs to Museum of East Anglian Life

Rural, urban and industrial landscapes.

1 From car park, take path past museum and gates of Abbot's Hall. When path divides, fork **R** beside high brick wall then turn **R** on lane. At end turn **L** and find narrow path between houses on R, just before No 19. Stay on path as it descends to river, turn **L** along wide lane between houses and **River Rattlesden**.

2 At road, turn **R** over bridge; fork **R** when road divides. Just before **Magpie Inn**, turn **R** through shopping precinct to Combs Lane. Cross road, walk along pavement to cross stream just beyond Edgecomb Road.

3 Turn **L** at stream by telegraph pole with circular sign ('Charcoal and Churches'). Path follows stream then heads through wood into open countryside. Cross footbridge and turn **R** along field-edge path.

4 At metal barrier, turn **L** along Jack's Lane. Turn **R** at T-junction, then fork **L** along Mill Lane. After 70yds (64m), turn **L** on path between parkland and fields.

Turn **L** at road to pass old **tannery**, head **L** on tarmac path at Webb's Close to climb to centre of **Combs**. Turn **R** at road and walk past **old school**.

5 At junction, turn **R** and immediately left, descending between fields. Cross footbridge and follow field-edge path to **R**. Cross stile and bear diagonally across field to junction and turn **L**, passing thatched farmhouse on your way to **Combs Wood**.

6 Stay on path as it runs alongside wood and into housing estate. Continue ahead on paved path, crossing Lavenham Way and diverting around school.

7 Turn **R** on Needham Road, then **L** along Gipping Way and **R** towards paint **factory**. At **factory**, turn **L** across bridge and **L** again ('Gipping Valley River Path'). Follow path to **old maltings**.

8 Climb steps to bridge. Turn **L** along Station Road. Keep ahead at crossroads, go **L** through churchyard. Narrow Buttermarket leads to Market Place. Cross square. Walk through **Meadow Centre** to car park.

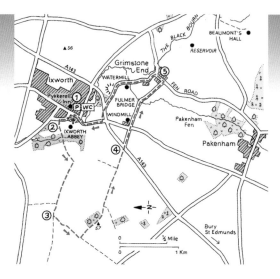

669 PAKENHAM A WATERMILL WALK

4½ miles (7.2km) 1hr 45min Ascent: 164ft (50m)
Paths: Bridleways, field-edge paths and quiet country lanes
Suggested map: aqua3 OS Explorers 211 Bury St Edmunds & Stowmarket; 229 Thetford Forest in the Brecks
Grid reference: TL 932703 (on Explorer 229)
Parking: Ixworth village hall free car park

Visit a working watermill on an easy walk around gentle farmland.

1 Leaving village hall car park, cross High Street and take path that leads through churchyard around **R** of parish church. Turn **L** on to Commister Lane and follow road as it bends round to **R**.

2 Turn **L** on to bridlepath opposite Abbey Close. Looking **L**, there are good views of **Ixworth Abbey**, a Georgian manor built around the ruins of a 12th-century Augustinian priory. Stay on this path as it crosses Black Bourn and continues towards small wood, where it swings **R**. A footpath on your **L** after 600yds (549m) is a short cut across fields. For full walk, keep straight on towards point **3**.

3 Turn **L** at end of hedgerow and follow field-edge path to metal gate ahead. Turn **L** here on to farm track that passes around wood. Soon after wood, short cut rejoins main walk from your **L** and you glimpse

Pakenham Windmill ahead. Stay on this track to reach main road, **A143**.

4 Cross road carefully and go ahead to another crossroads, where you keep straight ahead to **windmill**. Stay on this narrow road, Thieves Lane, as it descends to **Fulmer Bridge**, bucolic spot of meadows and streams. Continue towards T-junction, then turn **L** along **Fen Road**, passing council houses and bungalows before reaching junction at foot of hill.

5 Stay on **Fen Road** as it bends round to **L** into small hamlet of **Grimstone End** and soon reach **Pakenham Watermill**. Just beyond **watermill**, there are views of Mickle Mere, a popular birdwatching spot, to your **R**. Stay on this road to return to **A143**, turn **L** along pavement before crossing main road at white post to quiet lane on far side. Turn **L** where you see house with dovecote in garden. At end of lane, turn **R**. Follow road into **Ixworth** to return to car park.

Suffolk

SUDBURY *OIL ON CANVAS*

4¾ miles (7.7km) 2hrs **Ascent:** Negligible

Paths: Old railway track, meadows and town streets
Suggested map: aqua3 OS Explorer 196 Sudbury, Hadleigh & Dedham Vale
Grid reference: TL 875409
Parking: Kingfisher Leisure Centre

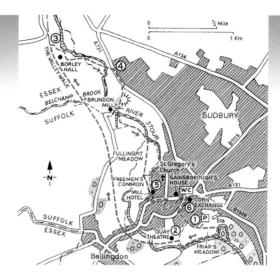

On the trail of Thomas Gainsborough.

❶ Leave car park through gate at start of **Valley Walk**, turn **L** to walk around **Friar's Meadow**. Cross meadow. Turn **R** to follow bank of **Stour**, turn **R** beside tributary and climb steps to rejoin **Valley Walk**.

❷ Turn **L** and cross footbridge, noting **Quay Theatre** in town's old maltings, to your **R**. Stay on **Valley Walk** for 2 miles (3.2km). Path is enclosed between tall embankments but, after passing sign ('Stour Valley Path') and crossing **Belchamp Brook**, it opens out to views of farmland and meadows.

❸ Before road junction, climb steps of embankment on **R**, cross paddock and turn **R** along driveway to **Borley Hall**. Look for narrow footpath between high garden wall of hall and Borley Mill, 1st of 3 former watermills on route. Go through gate to cross small meadow, turn **L** beside stream. Cross footbridge and meadow to road at end of enclosed path.

❹ Turn **R** along pavement for 250yds (229m). Pass hotel, turn **R** on to gravel lane with views of North Meadow Common to **L**. Cross bridge to pass **Brundon Mill** and turn **L** alongside pink cottages. Soon you are on Sudbury Common Lands among horses and cattle. Cross meadow, passing pill box, then cross footbridge and bear half-**R** across **Fullingpit Meadow**. Metal bridge leads into **Freemen's Common**, where you bear **L** towards old mill, now converted into **Mill Hotel**.

❺ Go through gate to walk around mill, turn **R** and **L** along Stour Street, passing half-timbered buildings. Turn **R** along School Street past old grammar school, then **L** along Christopher Lane to emerge on Gainsborough Street opposite **Gainsborough's House**. Turn **R** to reach Market Hill and statue of Thomas Gainsborough in front of St Peter's Church.

❻ Turn **R** past **Corn Exchange**, now library, along Friars Street. After passing half-timbered Buzzards Hall, once owned by Gainsborough's uncle, look for passage on **L** leading back to start.

LONG MELFORD *A TUDOR MANSION*

6 miles (9.7km) 2hrs 45min **Ascent:** 213ft (65m)

Paths: Farm tracks, field and woodland paths, 8 stiles
Suggested map: aqua3 OS Explorer 196 Sudbury, Hadleigh & Dedham Vale
Grid reference: TL 864465
Parking: Church Walk, Long Melford

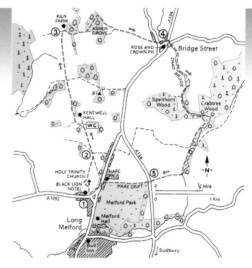

A walk through farmland and woods, by a Tudor mansion and a fine church.

❶ Starting from **Black Lion Hotel**, walk up west side of green towards church, passing almshouses of Trinity Hospital on way. Bear **L** around church and walk through rectory garden. Cross stile, then turn **R** across paddock and head for corner behind stables. Cross 2 more stiles to reach meadow and continue straight ahead until you reach long drive to **Kentwell Hall**.

❷ Turn **L** and walk beside avenue of lime trees towards **Kentwell Hall**. At main gate, turn **L** to walk through grounds with good views of hall. Follow waymarks to turn **R** beside hedge and continue straight ahead on wide track that crosses farmland with sweeping views to both sides. Ignore tracks leading off to **R** and **L**; continue towards **Kiln Farm**.

❸ Just before derelict farm buildings, turn **R** on to track running between fields and woods. At 2nd wood, **Ashen Grove**, turn **L** on to shady woodland path that crosses 2 areas of grassland and swings **R** through trees to emerge on to field-edge path. Continue ahead on cross-field path, that cuts through hedge and makes its way across fields towards **Bridge Street**. Cross lane and walk past recreation ground, go over pair of stiles to reach **A134** by **Rose and Crown pub**.

❹ Cross main road carefully and take **L** fork opposite. Almost immediately, turn **R** on to path alongside **Chad Brook**. Stay on path for about 1¾ miles (2.8km) as it crosses footbridge to west side of brook, then clings to stream between farmland to **R** and woodland to **L**. Ignore 1st path off to **R**. At end of woods, path suddenly swings **R** to climb around edge of field and return to **A134**.

❺ Cross road again and keep straight ahead along **Hare Drift**, now tarmac lane. Reach **Long Melford** between garden centre and pub. Cross road, turn **L** and walk back down towards green.

LAVENHAM *WOOL TOWN*

5½ miles (8.8km) 2hrs 30min **Ascent:** 197ft (60m)

Paths: Field-edge paths and tracks, some stretches of road
Suggested map: aqua3 OS Explorers 196 Sudbury, Hadleigh & Dedham Vale; 211 Bury St Edmonds & Stowmarket
Grid reference: TL 914489 (on Explorer 196)
Parking: Church Street car park, Lavenham

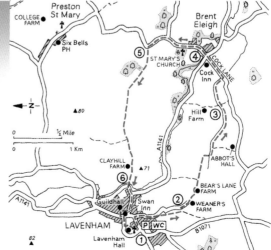

A walk through picturesque medieval streets.

❶ Turn **R** out of car park and walk down hill into town. At 1st junction, turn **R** along Bear's Lane. Continue for ¼ mile (400m) until last house, then take footpath to **R** across fields. After ¼ mile (400m) reach field boundary. Turn **L** across small footbridge and follow ditch to rejoin road.

❷ Turn **R**, walk past **Weaner's Farm**, then turn **L** at footpath sign just before barn. Stay on this path as it swings around **Bear's Lane Farm**, then turn **L** on to wide track beside hedge. Walk along this track as it descends to valley bottom. When track bends **R** towards **Abbot's Hall**, keep straight ahead and fork to **R** on grassy path beside stream.

❸ Emerging from poplar grove, arrive at concrete drive and turn **R** and immediately **L**. Path swings round to **R** to road, **Cock Lane**. Turn **L** and stay on road as it climbs and then descends to crossroads.

❹ Cross **A1141** into **Brent Eleigh**. When road bends, with village hall and half-timbered Corner Farm to **R**, keep ahead to climb to **St Mary's Church**. Visit church to see 13th-century wall paintings and 17th-century box pews. Proceed climbing up same road.

❺ When road swings sharp **R**, look for path on **L**. Stay on path for 1¼ miles (2km) as it winds between tall hedges. Pass **Clayhill Farm** and descend into valley, crossing white-painted bridge.

❻ Turn **L** at junction and walk into **Lavenham** along Water Street, with its fine timber-framed houses. After De Vere House, turn **R** up Lady Street, passing tourist office on way to market place. Turn **L** down narrow Market Lane to arrive at High Street opposite picturesque Crooked House. Turn briefly **L** and then **R** along Hall Road. Before road bends, look for footpath on **L**, then walk through meadow to reach **Lavenham church**. Car park is across road.

Suffolk

673 HARTEST *PICTURE-BOOK VILLAGE*

5 miles (8km) 2hrs **Ascent:** 394ft (120m) ▲
Paths: Quiet country roads, footpaths and bridleways
Suggested map: aqua3 OS Explorer 211 Bury St Edmunds & Stowmarket
Grid reference: TL 833525
Parking: Hartest village hall

Discover a link with a well-known nursery rhyme on the rooftop of Suffolk.

❶ Turn **L** out of **village hall** car park and cross road to village sign. Continue along south side of green, passing **Crown Inn** and All Saints Church. Keep on this road as it bends **R**, leaving village behind to climb **Hartest Hill**. Along way pass a peaceful burial ground.

❷ At public footpath leading off to **R**, pause at summit of **Hartest Hill** to admire extensive views over High Suffolk and **Hartest** nestling in its own little valley. Stay on this road for further ¾ mile (1.2km). Turn **R** at junction to reach **Gifford's Hall** and continue until you reach next bend in road.

❸ When road swings **L** at **Dales Farm**, keep straight ahead on bridleway, which clings to hedges and field edges as it descends towards **Boxted**. At road, turn **R** to walk into village itself.

❹ Turn **L** when you see sign ('Boxted church'). Cross bridge over **River Glem** and stay on this road as

it climbs out of village. When road divides, keep **L**. About ½ mile (800m) after leaving **Boxted**, you reach church, hidden among trees, with views over **Boxted Hall** from churchyard. Retrace your steps into **Boxted** (for short cut, you could leave this section out, but you would be missing one of high points of walk). Returning to start of Point ❹, turn **L**, pass electricity sub station and keep **L** towards Hawkedon when road divides.

❺ Approaching 1st house on **L**, look for public footpath, half-hidden between tall hedges to your **R**. This path is known as **Roger's Lane**. At times it can become very muddy and overgrown, in which case to go back to junction and return to **Hartest** by road. Otherwise, keep on this path as it ascends hill.

❻ At the top of **Roger's Lane**, turn **R** along road to descend into Hartest village, with more wonderful views. The road ends at the **village hall**, which was erected by Thomas Weller-Poley in 1888.

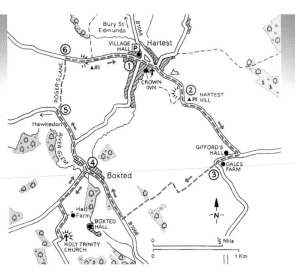

674 WEST STOW COUNTRY PARK *SAXON SETTLERS*

4¼ miles (6.8km) 1hr 45min **Ascent:** Negligible ⓪
Paths: Country park, riverside and forest paths
Suggested map: aqua3 OS Explorer 229 Thetford Forest in the Brecks, and map of country park available from visitor centre
Grid reference: TL 800714 **Parking:** West Stow Country Park car park

In the footsteps of the Anglo-Saxons.

❶ From car park, follow signposted nature trail between toilets and **visitor centre**. Path is waymarked with yellow arrows. There are interpretation boards describing flora and fauna. After walking through woody glade, reach open space of **West Stow Heath**. Go through 2 gates; continue to river.

❷ Turn **R** at junction of paths to walk around lake with ducks and Canada geese. Returning to start of Point ❷, keep **R** along river bank. When nature trail turns **L**, keep straight ahead on riverside path. Stay on path as it swings **L**, then climb embankment and turn **R** towards an old pump house. A diversion to **R** leads to a **bird hide** overlooking **Lackford Wildfowl Nature Reserve**.

❸ Turn **R** at pump house and follow **Lark Valley Path** through pine woods and turning sharp **R** to return to river with views over lake. Turn **L** here and stay close to river as you pass behind sewage works.

❹ When you see small weir ahead, turn **L** on wide Forestry Commission track leading into **West Stow** village. Track doubles back on itself, then swings **R** alongside pine woods, past barrier and behind group of houses to road. Turn **R**, passing 30mph sign, then go **L** along concrete lane marked by red Forestry Commission sign (No 205). Walk along this lane to **Forest Lodge**.

❺ Turn **L** across car park and take path behind notice board to enter forest. Follow path round to **L**, then turn **R** where it joins wide track. Stay on this track as it crosses clearing and continues through forest. Between March and July herons breed here and it is essential to stick to the path to avoid disturbing nesting birds.

❻ When you see derelict barn at corner of field (just before red Forestry Commission sign No 209), turn **L** along narrow footpath on edge of woods to return to road directly opposite car park.

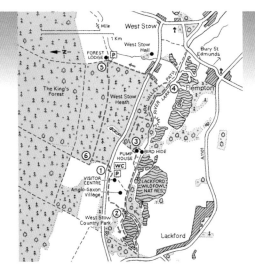

675 CAVENDISH *A CHOCOLATE-BOX VILLAGE*

6 miles (9.7km) 2hrs 30min **Ascent:** 311ft (95m) ▲
Paths: Field paths, bridleways, short stretches of road, 3 stiles
Suggested map: aqua3 OS Explorers 196 Sudbury, Hadleigh & Dedham Vale; 210 Newmarket & Haverhill
Grid reference: TL 805464 (on Explorer 196)
Parking: Cavendish High Street, opposite Sue Ryder Museum

Fine views in the Stour Valley.

❶ Take path on far side of **Cavendish** village green past **Five Bells pub** and school, then cross stile by cemetery to join **Stour Valley Path**. Continue around meadow and through hedge, then turn **L** along field-edge path that crosses plank bridge and swings round to **R** between fields and hedgerows to road.

❷ Turn **L**. Walk uphill for ¼ mile (400m). Pass single house, turn **L** on to path along edge of field path. Path descends, then bends **R** and crosses wooden bridge to huge field. Turn **R** beside hedge, then **L** between fields, following **Stour Valley Path** waymarks to **Houghton Hall**. Keep ahead and stay on path as it turns **L** and then half-**R** to drop to **Hermitage Farm**.

❸ Keep to **Stour Valley Path** as it bends **L**, entering trees before reaching lane and passing playing field on its way to A0192.

❹ Cross road carefully, walk across bridge and turn **L** on narrow path beside small graveyard ('Clare

Castle Country Park'). Enter park and keep **L**, beside stream to old railway bridge. Cross bridge and immediately ascend path to your **L** to housing estate. Turn **R** and cross old bridge over railway to **Mill House** and footbridge by old mill.

❺ Cross bridge and walk diagonally **L** across field, taking footbridge over **River Stour**. Keep ahead across field. At road, go **L** for 200yds (183m) before turning **L** on wide bridleway leading back down to river. At T-junction of paths, turn **R** across field. The track swings **L**, passes poplar grove and enters muddy section of woodland as it meets river.

❻ At lane, turn **L** passing half-timbered **Bower Hall**. Keep on public bridleway for 1 mile (1.6km) as it crosses farmland towards **Pentlow Hall**.

❼ Turn **L** on to road and cross bridge. Cross stile on L-H side to walk beside river. Climb bank on **R**, cross stile and walk through gardens to main road by **Sue Ryder Museum**.

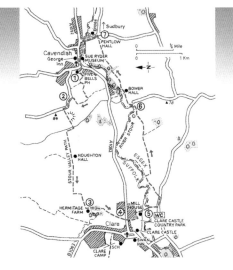

Suffolk

MILDENHALL *THE SKIES ABOVE*

5½ miles (8.8km) 2hrs **Ascent:** Negligible
Paths: Bridleway and riverside footpath, town streets, 2 stiles
Suggested map: aqua3 OS Explorer 226 Ely & Newmarket
Grid reference: TL 713745
Parking: Jubilee car park, Mildenhall

American aircraft can be seen overhead on this peaceful walk in the Lark Valley.
① Walk up King Street to **Mildenhall Museum**, an old flint-faced building on L. Turn **L** along Market Street to enter Market Place, with its parish pump and Market Cross. Cross High Street, turn **L** and immediately **R** along Church Walk to walk through churchyard and continue along narrow road.
② At end of road, turn **L** and follow bridleway signs to **R** past cricket ground. Path is shady and tree-lined at first, then passes behind cottage and continues across fields on track leading to **Wamil Hall Farm**. After passing farm buildings, keep ahead on concrete lane that bends **L** and **R** towards large house enclosed by brick wall. Views across river to Worlington church and **Mildenhall airfield** to your **R**.
③ Keep ahead on grassy field-edge path and continue for ¾ mile (1.2km) until path turns sharply **R** to road at **West Row**. Turn **L**, passing bungalows.

When road bends **R**, take 2nd **L** into Ferry Lane down to River Lark at **Jude's Ferry** pub.
④ Walk past pub and take steps down to river to turn **L** on to riverside path beneath bridge to return to **Mildenhall**. The walk back is completely different even though you not far from your outward route and you are more likely to see herons than military planes. Keep to river bank, passing through kissing gates either side of garden and climbing to bridge behind **Wamil Hall Farm**. Eventually path turns away from river to briefly rejoin outward route.
⑤ Turn **R** at cottage. When path divides after 300yds (274m), keep **R** by river, passing behind **cricket ground**. When river divides, cross bridge to reach island by small lock. Climb to road bridge and cross to south bank. Turn **L** on gravel drive that soon becomes riverside path. Cross river over pair of arched bridges and bear **L** at playing fields to return to start.

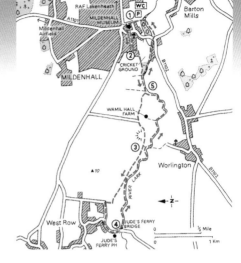

THURLOW *ESTATE VILLAGES*

3½ miles (5.7km) 1hr 30min **Ascent:** 164ft (50m)
Paths: Country roads, meadows and field-edge paths, 6 stiles
Suggested map: aqua3 OS Explorer 210 Newmarket & Haverhill
Grid reference: TL 678502
Parking: Great Thurlow Reading Room or village hall

An easy walk across the high farmland of a large agricultural estate.
① Walk north from **Reading Room** along main street, passing post office and **village hall**. Turn **R** on narrow path between houses. Cross stile and bear **L** across meadow to reach stile. At junction of paths, go ahead across wide track and keep **L** to cross 2 more meadows. Walk behind **school** and bear **R** to pass through gate. Cross concrete footbridge and stay on fenced-off path to St Peter's Church, **Little Thurlow**.
② Walk through churchyard. Turn **L** to cross road and continue on footpath beside **River Stour**. The path is lined with hedges at first but you soon reach open fields. Keep to **R** to walk beside river. Although it rises only a short distance away, the **Stour** has already gathered pace, though it is nothing like the river you will see at Sudbury, Flatford or Shotley Gate.
③ At weir, turn **R** along road into **Little Bradley** and follow it round to **L** to All Saints Church, whose round

tower dates to early 11th century. The road now bends **R** and climbs gently between farmland to L and meadows to R. Turn **R** at footpath sign along farm drive. Walk past stables and barns of **Hall Farm** then go through gate to cross meadow. Leaving meadow, keep straight ahead alongside hedge to road.
④ Turn **R** to walk along Broad Road into hamlet of **Little Thurlow Green**. After passing green, walk downhill past modern houses and thatched **Old Inn**. Turn **L** on to concrete farm track with thatched pink farmhouse behind hedge to your **R**. The path passes sewage works then turns **R** and **L** around field to enter woodland beside **River Stour**.
⑤ Keep straight ahead when you see an arched footbridge across river to your **R**. Cross stile and bear **R** around meadow then pass through gate to enter small graveyard opposite **Great Thurlow church**. Turn **R** at road, alongside high brick wall of **Great Thurlow Hall**, and cross river to return to start.

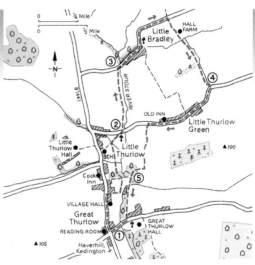

MOULTON *A BORDER WALK*

6½ miles (10.4km) 3hrs **Ascent:** 295ft (90m)
Paths: Field-edge, cross-field and woodland paths, 9 stiles
Suggested map: aqua3 OS Explorer 210 Newmarket & Haverhill
Grid reference: TL 696644
Parking: Moulton village hall

An enjoyable walk in rolling downland.
① Turn **R** out of village hall car park along Bridge Street, passing **King's Head pub** on your way to packhorse bridge. Cross bridge and turn **R** along Brookside, beside **River Kennett**. Just before **Old Flint Bridge**, notice the old rectory school on your L, dating from 1849. Keep on this road to churchyard.
② Go through gate to churchyard and pass **St Peter's Church**. Cross stile behind church and walk up through trees to stile at top. Bear **R** across fields. On clear days, Ely Cathedral is visible on horizon to L.
③ At road, turn **R**. Keep straight ahead when road bends, walking between hedges of **Gazeley Stud**, where mares and foals can be seen. Continue to **All Saints Church** and walk around rear of church to emerge by **Gazeley** village sign and **Chequers pub**.
④ Walk down Higham Road, opposite church, and bear **R** following **Icknield Way** waymarks at Tithe Close. Walk between houses and follow path across

fields and into Bluebutton Wood. Where path turns sharply **R**, look for footbridge in hedge to your **L**.
⑤ Keep on **Icknield Way Path** as it winds through 2 more woods, emerging by wide field. Walk along field edge, up, via trees, to crossroads. Turn **R** and climb to **St Mary's Church**, with **Dalham Hall** visible behind.
⑥ Pass through metal gate opposite church and walk down through an avenue of chestnut trees to **Dalham** village. Go through kissing gate and turn **L**, noting large conical red-brick **malt kiln** standing beside road. For lunch, a short walk along this road leads to the **Affleck Arms pub**.
⑦ Cross white footbridge to your **R** and follow path beside **River Kennett**. At road, turn **R** across Catford Bridge. Now turn **L** on wide bridleway to return to Moulton at **St Peter's Church**.
⑧ Cross **Old Flint Bridge**. Walk across green to reach Dalham Road; turn **R**. Gate opposite post office leads to recreation ground and back to village hall.

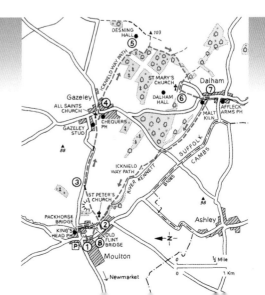

679 HORSEY MERE *SILENT WINDMILLS*

3½ miles (5.7km) 1hr 30min **Ascent:** Negligible
Paths: Marked trails along dykes, walk quietly to avoid disturbing nesting birds, 5 stiles
Suggested map: aqua3 OS Explorer OL40 The Broads
Grid reference: TG 456223
Parking: National Trust pay-and-display at Horsey Drainage Mill

Explore whispering reed beds and windmills and finish at a National Trust pub.

❶ From car park walk towards toilets and take footpath to **R** to footbridge. Cross bridge, turn immediately **R** and follow path along side of **Horsey Mere** through reeds and alder copses. Cross stile and wooden bridge across dyke to enter grassy water-meadow. Cross 2nd stile and bridge, with sign asking visitors to keep to footpaths.

❷ Turn **R** when path meets brown-watered dyke (Waxham New Cut). Eventually see derelict **Brograve Drainage Mill** ahead.

❸ Turn **R** immediately adjacent to mill and walk along edge of field and dyke. Reed beds give way to water-meadow. Continue straight ahead. The path bends **L**, then **R**, then crosses stile and plank bridge and then small lane and continues through field opposite. At end of field, make sharp **L**, eventually coming to another lane.

❹ Go **R** at lane, bearing **R** where it meets track, and walk past **Delph Farm** and Poppylands Café. At junction by telephone box, turn **L**, following signs for **Nelson Head pub**. Pass pub on your **L**, then look for marked National Trust footpath to **R**.

❺ Walk through gate and continue along wide sward ahead, with narrow dyke to your **R**. When sward divides, bear **L** and head for stile at end of footpath. Climb this and immediately turn **R** along spacious field. This area is used for grazing breeding stock and you should look for prominently displayed signs warning about presence of bulls. As this part of walk is permissive, and not a public footpath, the National Trust can graze bulls here. If this is case, walk back to lane and turn **L**, back to car park at start of walk.

❻ If there are no bulls, climb stile between field and road, and cross road. Car park where walk began is ahead of you and slightly to your **R**. Explore restored **Horsey Drainage Mill** to your **L**.

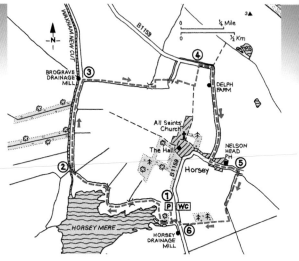

680 BREYDON WATER *BURGH CASTLE*

8½ miles (13.7km) 3hrs **Ascent:** 49ft (15m)
Paths: Riverside paths, footpaths, some roads, several steps, 1 stile
Suggested map: aqua3 OS Explorer OL40 The Broads
Grid reference: TG 476050
Parking: Car park near Church Farm Freehouse

Vast skies and endless reed-choked marshes.

❶ Leave car park and walk towards church. Take path to **L** of church, through kissing gate ('Castle'). After few steps and another kissing gate, take well-trodden path cutting diagonally across fields to reach walls of **Roman fort**. Aim for gap in middle.

❷ Go through gap, explore castle then aim for 28 steps in northwest corner. Descend steps, walk through field, and look for 40 steps leading down to river bank. Turn **R** along Angles Way and continue to junction. Go **R** and continue to T-junction.

❸ Turn **L** towards double gates, which will take you on long (3½-mile/5.7km) uninterrupted trail along edge of **Breydon Water**. Path occasionally swings away from river, but mostly sticks close by it, giving views across flat marshes and mudflats. Eventually, you will see struts of **Breydon Bridge** in distance.

❹ When path divides take **R-H** option, away from river. This winds across meadow into **Herbert Barnes**

Riverside Park. At rugby club, head **L** until you see stile. Cross this, then go **R**, then **L** to main road.

❺ Turn **R** on to road, keeping to wider **R-H** verge. Continue to roundabout, keeping **R** past more marshes. Before you reach **industrial estate**, look for footpath on your **R**.

❻ Turn down footpath between estate and marshes. After ¾ mile (1.2km), it turns sharp **L** and, after few paces, divides. Take track to **R**, past farm buildings of **Bradwell Hall**, to crossroads.

❼ At crossroads go through rusty gate and past derelict house, then skirt edges of fields, where nettles can be problem. Go through gate and down short track before turning **L** to lane. Then turn **R** again on to Back Lane. Bear **L** past houses and an Anglian Water station, until quiet lane emerges on to larger road at **Queen's Head pub**.

❽ Turn **R** and keep walking past chapel until you see church. Turn **R** into car park.

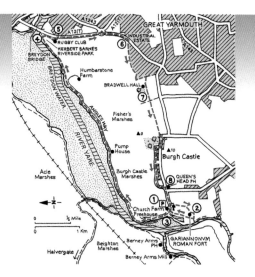

681 LUDHAM *THE BROADS*

5 miles (8km) 2hrs **Ascent:** 33ft (10m)
Paths: Quiet country lanes and grassy footpaths
Suggested map: aqua3 OS Explorer OL40 The Broads
Grid reference: TG 391180
Parking: Free car park in Horsefen Road, Ludham

Enjoy the windmill-studded skyline in this lovely stroll to the River Ant.

❶ Leave car park and busy **marina**; walk up Horsefen Road, going same way that you came in.

❷ Turn **L** at end of Horsefen Road, walking along footpath that runs inside hedge and parallel to lane. When you see **King's Arms pub** and 14th-century **St Margaret's Church** on your **L**, turn **R** up road ('Catfield'). After few paces turn **L** up School Road ('How Hill'). Houses soon give way to countryside and at junction go straight ahead.

❸ Turn **R** on 1st road after house called **The Laurels**, along lane ('How Hill'). The lane winds and twists, and is fairly narrow, which makes for pleasant walking. Soon reach **How Hill House** and sail-less windmill and How Hill nature reserve. There are marked trails through reserve, if you feel like a pleasant diversion. When you have finished, continue down **How Hill Road** with **River Ant** and its reedy

marshes to **L**. Pass **Grove Farm Gallery and Studio** on your **R**, and look for red-brick barn followed by lane, also on **R**.

❹ Turn **R** down Wateringpiece Lane, where sign warns you that this road is liable to flood. Pass modern **water tower** on your **L** and walk past 2 large fields. At end of 2nd field, look for public footpath sign on your **L**. Take path that runs along edge of field until it ends at lane. This path can sometimes be overgrown, and nettles can occasionally be a problem.

❺ Turn **R** on Catfield Road and walk along footpath on verge on **R**. This road can be busy in summer, when visitors flock to Ludham and How Hill. Ignore lane on your **L**, heading to Potter Heigham, and continue walking to crossroads by chapel.

❻ Go straight across, walking few paces until you reach next junction with Ludham church ahead of you. Turn **L** along Yarmouth Road, then turn **R** into Horsefen Road. This will take you back to car park.

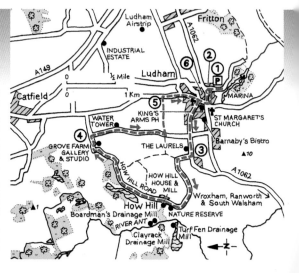

Norfolk

LODDON *BOATS AND BULRUSHES*

5¼ miles (8.4km) 2hr 15min **Ascent:** 98ft (30m)
Paths: Footpaths along waterways, farm tracks and some paved roads, 2 stiles
Suggested map: aqua3 OS Explorer OL40 The Broads
Grid reference: TM 362986
Parking: Free car park on Church Plain in Loddon (opposite Holy Trinity Church); or car park near river

High reeds rustle all around between the River Chet and Hardley Flood.

❶ Turn **R** past **library** on to Bridge Street and walk down hill to cross river into **Chedgrave**. At **White Horse pub** go **R**, then look for public footpath sign on **R** just after row of terraced houses. Meet residential street, cross it to footpath opposite, that runs between hedges, and continue to Chedgrave church.

❷ Turn **R** at end of graveyard, passing meadow on your **L** before going through small gate at public footpath sign on your **R**. Nettles can grow in abundance here. Go through 2nd small gate to path along north bank of **River Chet**. Cross 2 wooden footbridges, pass Norfolk Wildlife Trust sign and continue to stile.

❸ Cross stile and continue along river path. Depending on growth of reeds you may be able to see that you are on causeway here, with Chet on your **R** and meres of **Hardley Flood** on your **L**. Cross 2nd

stile, and see tantalising glimpses of **Hardley Flood** and its abundant birdlife. It is well worth pausing here if you are interested in birdwatching, since the Trust has erected nesting areas in the water. Continue along this path until broad gives way to farmland and you can see **Hardley Hall** off to your **L**. Path then meets wide farm track.

❹ Turn **L** on farm track. Go up hill, passing **Hill Cottage** on your R-H side. After 1 mile (1.6km) farm track ends at lane. Turn **L** towards woodland. Continue to line of ancient oak trees and sign to your **L** stating 'Loddon 1¼'. Don't take L-H footpath here, which heads to **Chedgrave Common**. Ignore 1st turning on L ('No Through Road'), and continue walking to 2nd.

❺ Take this turning ('Church'). When you reach church, look for grassy footpath to **R** which takes you back to Point ❷, passed earlier in walk. Retrace your steps along footpath, go **L** on main road, across river and up hill to car park.

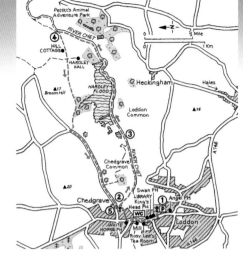

WORSTEAD *LIGHT AND DURABLE WORSTED*

4 miles (6.4km) 1hr 45min **Ascent:** 33ft (10m)
Paths: Easy public footpaths and some paved country lanes
Suggested map: aqua3 OS Explorer OL40 The Broads
Grid reference: TG 301260
Parking: On Church Plain

In the footsteps of medieval weavers.

❶ From Church Plain, in centre of **Worstead**, turn **R** into Front Street with 14th-century **St Mary's Church** behind you. Bend to **L**, then immediately **R**, by house called Woodview, and continue out of village. The road veers **L**, then **R**. The mixed deciduous plantation to your **L** is **Worstead Belt**. Pass **Worstead Hall Farm** (originally 16th century) on your **R** before plunging into shady woodland.

❷ At house called **White Orchard**, turn **L**. Ignore 2 lanes off R, but follow road round to **L** when it bends sharply through woods and up hill. At T-junction turn **L** on to unmarked lane and continue down to 'Private Road' sign.

❸ Turn **R** and walk along wide track (marked as public footpath) that leads through tunnel of mixed woodland. This is **Carman's Lane**, and it emerges out to quiet country lane after ½ mile (800m). Cross lane, heading for footpath opposite. There is hedge right in

front of you, with fields on either side, and footpath sign that is bit vague about where to go. However, keep to **L** of hedge and walk along edge of field to signs for footpath off to **L**.

❹ Turn **L** along this path, walking until decaying red roofs of **Dairyhouse Barn** come into view. Just after this, there is T-junction of footpaths. Take footpath to **R**, farm track called Green Lane, and continue to paved road.

❺ Go **L**, along lane bordered by tall hedgerows filled with nesting birds in spring. Pass few neat houses on your **L** before lane ends in T-junction.

❻ Turn **R** opposite Rose Cottage and Windy Ridge on to Honing Row, and walk for few paces to **Geofferey the Dyer's House** on your **R**. This dates from the 16th century, and has unusually tall ceilings in order to accommodate the merchant's looms. The site of the old manor house lies up this lane, too.

❼ Turn **L** opposite **Geofferey's** house to car park.

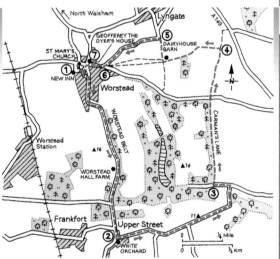

OVERSTRAND *TO NORTHREPPS*

4 miles (6.4km) 2hrs **Ascent:** 295ft (90m)
Paths: Farm tracks, footpaths, quiet lanes
Suggested map: aqua3 OS Explorer 252 Norfolk Coast East
Grid reference: TG 246410
Parking: Pay-and-display car park on Coast Road, Overstrand

From the coast to the Poppylands.

❶ Go **R**, out of car park on to Paul's Lane. Pass Old Rectory, then continue on pavement on **L**. When you see Arden Close, look for public footpath sign on **L**. Follow this alley to road.

❷ Cross road, aiming for sign 'Private Drive Please Drive Slowly'. To **L** is footpath. Go up this track, then take path to **L** of gate to **Stanton Farm**. Climb hill, taking path to **R** when main track bears **L**. At brow of hill follow path towards line of trees. The track becomes sandy as you go downhill, eventually reaching **Toll Cottage**.

❸ Take lane ahead. After Broadgate Close there's pavement on your **R**. At **Northrepps** village sign and T-junction, turn **L** towards Church Street, keeping **L**. Pass **Foundry Arms pub** and look for phone box and bus stop, beyond which lies Craft Lane.

❹ Turn **R** along Craft Lane, using pavement on sign marks this as 'quiet lane' for walkers. After about

700yds (640m) there is **Paston Way** sign on your **L**. Take this through woods, and bear **L** when it becomes track to **Hungry Hill** farm.

❺ At lane next to farm, turn **L**. After few paces go **R** ('Circular Walk **Paston Way**'). Follow this gravel track towards **radar** installation.

❻ Keep **L** where track bends towards radar tower, following footpath signs. Path descends through woods, passing under disused railway bridge before meeting main road. Cross, then turn **L** along pavement for few paces before turning **R** along Coast Road. When road bends, look for signs to **Overstrand Promenade**.

❼ Go down steep ramp to your **R** to arrive at concrete walkway. Up to your **L** are remains of fallen houses in crumbling cliffs. Follow walkway (or walk on sand, if you prefer) to slipway for boats. To **L** of slipway is zig-zag pathway.

❽ Follow this upwards to top of cliffs. Car park is **R**.

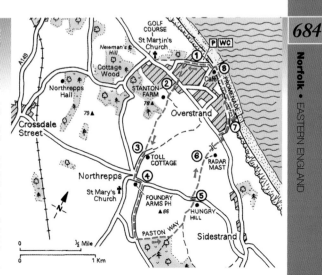

Norfolk

685 CAISTOR ST EDMUND *A REVOLTING QUEEN*

6¼ miles (10.1km) 3hrs **Ascent:** 279ft (85m)
Paths: Paved road and public footpaths, several sets of steps
Suggested map: aqua3 OS Explorer 237 Norwich
Grid reference: TG 232032
Parking: South Norfolk Council and Norfolk Archaeological Trust car park at Roman fort

Walk in the footsteps of Boudica in the countryside around a Roman fortress.

1 Follow marked circular trail (marked by red and white circles) around **Venta Icenorum** through gate next to notice board at car park. Climb 36 steps, then descend 6 to huge bank that protected the town, with deep ditch to your **L**. Head west, towards **River Tas**.
2 Turn **R** by bench, past fragments of old walls, then **R** again at longer section of wall, still following trail markers. Go through gate, then along side of bank with more wall to your **R**. Go up 39 steps, then descend again to ditch on eastern edge of town. Go past 11th-century **St Edmund's Church** and then continue through car park to lane and turn **R** on to **Boudica's Way**.
3 Just after brick cottages take tiny unmarked lane to your **L**, still following **Boudica's Way**. Go up hill, keep straight at next junction and continue until you see **Whiteford Hall**.

4 Turn **L** up Valley Farm Lane, following yellow **Boudica's Way** markers. After farm, look for footpath sign to your **R**. Take this and keep to your **R**, along side of hedge. Jig **R**, then immediately **L** and continue to paved lane. Turn **L** and then look for another footpath sign to your **R**.
5 Take footpath, and follow markers down hill and up other side. Keep to footpaths here, because there are plenty of signs indicating private property. At top of field, take **R-H** path ('Arminghall'). This narrow track leads you past several houses to eventually meet paved lane by **St Mary's Church, Arminghall**. Lane is used by cyclists, so take care. Follow it for about 1¼ miles (2km), using intermittent gravel track on **L**.
6 At T-junction go **L**, using gravel path and verges. Descend hill into village of **Caistor St Edmund**, and follow signs for **Roman town**, passing 17th-century **Caistor Hall** to your **L**. Keep walking until you reach signs for **Venta Icenorum**, then turn **R** into car park.

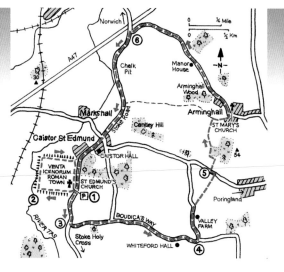

686 PULHAM MARKET *PULHAM PIGS*

5½ miles (8.8km) 2hrs 30min **Ascent:** 98ft (30m)
Paths: Country lanes and paths, nettles a problem, 2 stiles
Suggested map: aqua3 OS Explorer 230 Diss & Harleston
Grid reference: TM 196862
Parking: Pulham Market, at car park on Falcon Street

From Pulham Market to Pulham St Mary with lunch at the King's Head.

1 Go **L** out of car park and walk up main street to **Barnes Road** and turn **R**. Take waymarked footpath to **L**. Cross field, and take **R-H** route when path forks to come out on **Barnes Road** again. If this path is closed, stay on **Barnes Road**. Either way, **Barnes Road** eventually reaches junction with **Poppy's Lane** and Duck's Foot Road.
2 Take **Poppy's Lane**. After few paces look for wooden public footpath sign to your **L**. Path runs by ditch, with wide, open fields on either side. Larks breed here. Path bears **R** and you head to outbuildings of **North Farm**.
3 At farm, walk down lane to your **R**, North Green Road, with views of stocky tower of **Pulham St Mary**. Pass thatched cottages and barn conversions then take 1st turning to your **L**. This is Kemps Road and takes you towards **Church Farm**. Before farm, take

public footpath to **R**, which hugs hedge for short distance then goes through centre of field. Go through hedge and across stile, keeping to **L-H** side of meadow that occasionally contains over-friendly horses. At end of meadow you may have to don long trousers, because this is nettle country. Cross another stile (may be difficult to locate in nettles), and continue along backs of houses to **Church of St Mary the Virgin** with fine carvings on its porch.
4 Turn **R**, when you emerge from church, and fork **L** by village sign, **King's Head pub** (good place to stop for refreshments) and Pennoyer School. This leads down lane with modern houses. Continue straight on past Dirty Lane.
5 At **Semere Lane**, go **R** on narrow lane to Station Road (different from the one in **Pulham St Mary**).
6 Go **R** at Station Road; cross **dismantled railway**. You are now in **Pulham Market**, where you will see tower of **St Mary Magdalene**. Return to car park.

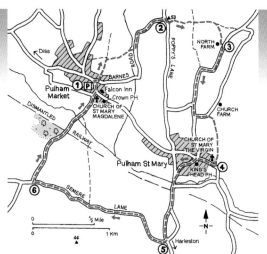

687 BLICKLING *THE WEAVERS' WAY*

6½ miles (10.4km) 3hrs **Ascent:** 98ft (30m)
Paths: Public footpaths and some paved lanes
Suggested map: aqua3 OS Explorer 252 Norfolk Coast East
Grid reference: TG 175285
Parking: Blickling Hall car park on Aylsham Road (fee)

Stroll through the grounds of Blickling Hall.

1 Go towards **National Trust** visitor centre and take gravel path to its **L**, past restaurant and shop. Look for purple Mausoleum trail markers and follow them to The Beeches, where path veers off to **L**. Continue walking straight ahead across open countryside and then by **R-H** side of hedge. Keep to **R** near Moorgate to avoid trespassing on private land.
2 Turn **L** at lane, following winding path past **Mill Cottage**, with mill pond, on your **R** and **Mill Farm** on your **L**. The mixed deciduous **Great Wood** on your **L** belongs to National Trust. Leave woods and walk through pretty Bure Valley for about 700yds (640m) to footpath on your **L** (sign is on **R**).
3 Turn **L** down this overgrown track, with hedgerows to **R** and trees to **L**. Go up slope to **Bunker's Hill Plantation** (also National Trust), skirting around edge of this before footpath merges with farm track. It eventually comes out on **B1354**.

4 Turn **L** and then **R**, on to **New Road** ('Cawston and **Oulton Street**'). Continue on this wide lane for about ¾ mile (1.2km) to crossroads at village sign for Oulton Street.
5 Turn **L** by **RAF memorial** and its bench. Lane starts off wide, but soon narrows by village of Oulton Street. Continue for 1½ miles (2.4km), passing through line of trees known as **Oulton Belt** and eventually arriving at **Abel Heath**, small National Trust conservation area.
6 Turn **L** by oak tree, then **L** at T-junction towards **Abel Heath Farm**. The lane winds downhill to red-brick cottages of little hamlet of **Silvergate**. You are now on **Weavers' Way** long distance footpath. Pass cemetery on your **R** and continue until you see **St Andrew's Church** (partly 14th century, but mostly Victorian). Continue on to main road (**B1354**).
7 Turn **L**, passing **Buckinghamshire Arms** and estate cottages at park gates on your **R**. Continue to signs for car park, where you turn **R**.

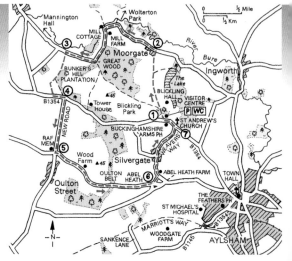

Norfolk

WYMONDHAM *A FIGURE OF EIGHT*

5½ miles (8.8km) 2hrs 15min **Ascent:** 98ft (30m)
Paths: Town pavements, meadows, steps and 1 stile
Suggested map: aqua3 OS Explorer 237 Norwich
Grid reference: TG 109014
Parking: Free car park off Market Street, Wymondham

Explore a lovely market town.

❶ From car park on Market Street turn **L**. To your R is Market Cross (built in 1616) now a tourist information office. At bottom of road is Church Street, leading past chapel of Thomas Becket, founded in 1174. It is now a public library. Go past **Green Dragon pub** and Abbey Hotel to **abbey** churchyard.

❷ Exit **abbey** churchyard through gate by north porch and turn **R** on to Becketwell Road, which becomes Vicar Street. Pass Feathers Inn and walk along Cock Street, then straight across roundabout and up Chapel Lane. In few paces reach track on **L**, **Frogshall Lane** (may not be marked). This gravel track leads past backs of gardens, then narrows to path, eventually reaching stile.

❸ Cross stile. This is part of the Tiffey Valley Project, grazing pastures restored and managed using traditional methods. Walk over meadow to kissing gate and wooden footbridge across river. Turn **L** and walk

along stream bank. Eventually, you reach area known as **Kett's Country**, then Becketwell nature reserve, and on to White Horse Street and Damgate.

❹ Turn **R** at Damgate, past cottages. Cross B1172 and head for Cemetery Lane, and Wymondham Abbey **railway station**. Lane ends at **industrial estate**.

❺ Cross main road; head **L** of Railway pub. After passing under railway bridge, you will see cars on L-H side of road.

❻ Take path to **L** leading to **Lizard nature reserve**. Boardwalk takes you across meadow to where steps lead up to **dismantled railway** embankment. Turn **R**, descend more steps, and walk towards gate.

❼ Go through gate; cross meadow, turning **R** after 2nd gate. Path leads along hedge, crosses meadow and back past **Lizard** entrance. Retrace route under railway bridge until you reach main road. Turn **R** up Station Road to traffic lights, then aim for Fairland Street, which leads to Market Street and car park.

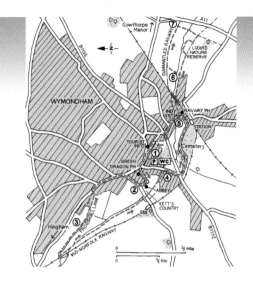

BUCKENHAM *A 12TH-CENTURY CASTLE*

3¾ miles (6km) 1hr 30min **Ascent:** Negligible
Paths: Mostly country lanes
Suggested map: aqua3 OS Explorer 237 Norwich
Grid reference: TM 088904
Parking: On village green opposite Market House, New Buckenham

Stroll along peaceful country lanes around a medieval planned town and its castle.

❶ The timbered Market House dates back to the 16th century and was raised on columnar legs in 1754. William d'Albini established a market here to attract local traders and farmers, and tolls they paid were used to finance his new castle. From green, walk along **Queen Street**. Turn **R** on King Street to **castle**.

❷ Explore remains of **castle**, then retrace your steps and return to village green. The Old Vicarage on way claims to be a 15th-century guildhall.

❸ From village green, head towards post office and then turn into Church Street, past **St Martin's Church**, mainly 15th and 16th century. At end of street, you will see long, narrow **cemetery** in front of you, along with sign for **Cuffer Lane**. Walk through **cemetery**, keeping lane on your L-H side. When you reach last of graves, pass through gap in hedgerow to emerge on to **Cuffer Lane**. Turn **R**, past village

allotments, and continue in same direction to sign for **Harlingwood Lane**.

❹ Turn **R**, down unnamed branch (maps tell you it becomes **Folly Lane**). There is grass growing in the middle of the lane, indicating that it is seldom used by traffic. However, it can be busy during harvest and you should watch for agricultural vehicles in late summer.

❺ At T-junction, turn **R**, then take next **R-H** turn down single-track lane. You can sometimes see waterfowl on **Spittle Mere** in scrubby meadow to your **L**. The water table is often high here, making the land very boggy and an ideal habitat for water-loving bog plants – you will see marsh mallows, rushes and many other wetland wild flowers in season.

❻ When you see cricket pitch on R-H side, you are nearing village. Pass playground on R to T-junction. Turn **R** on street ('Norwich Road') and enter village. After few paces, road forks. Take **R-H** lane, past Crawford's and Corner Cottage, to green.

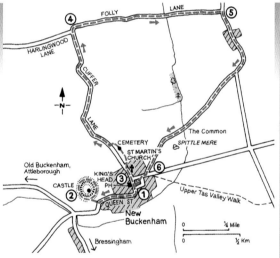

REEPHAM *CHURCH TRILOGY*

5¼ miles (8.4km) 2hrs 30min **Ascent:** 82ft (25m)
Paths: Field paths and trackways, beware poor signposting, 3 stiles
Suggested map: aqua3 OS Explorer 238 East Dereham & Aylsham
Grid reference: TG 099229
Parking: Town car park on Station Road, Reepham

Around an ancient market town.

❶ From car park turn **R** towards Methodist church and turn **L** up Kerdiston Road ('Byway to Guestwick'). At next junction, take path **L** into CaSu Park. Take footpath ahead, then bear **R** each time paths meet, to emerge through trees to lane again. Turn **L** and walk under bridge.

❷ Immediately after bridge, look for stile on **R** and follow blue-and-white trail marker across meadow ahead. There is ditch to your R. Keep ahead at junction of paths near water trough, then go through gate marked with Norfolk County Council footpath sign. Go through 2nd gate, over stile, and then ahead towards **plantation** not marked on OS map.

❸ At plantation, turn **R** and walk around it to other side. Signposting is poor here and, at beginning, footpath is often lost under crops, but walk towards about 10:30 on clock face and path becomes more obvious. Continue for about ¾ mile (1.2km) until

footpath emerges on to wide track.

❹ Turn **R** along track and take next turning to **R**, with tower of **Salle** church ahead. Stay on track, with occasional circular walk markers. When track ends at lane, turn **L** and continue to next junction.

❺ At junction, turn **R** by **Gatehouse Farm** and walk up **Salle's** High Street to church. On leaving church, cross road and walk behind 2 buildings opposite church to far **L-H** corner of village green, to footpath sign. Walk along edge of field with fir trees on your **R**, ignoring footpath to your **L**, to end of plantation.

❻ The path is now signposted **R**, towards road, and then **L**, along side of hedge. Continue until path emerges on to lane and turn **L** to junction.

❼ At junction, take path that leads under old railway bridge on to **Marriott's Way**. Walk along this cycle route past **Reepham Station**. Continue to steps to your **R**. Walk down them, cross stile, and turn **R** under bridge. Walk along this lane to fork. Bear **R** to car park.

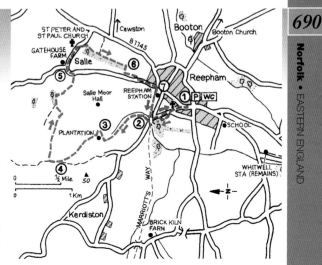

Norfolk

691 MATTISHALL PARSON WOODFORDE

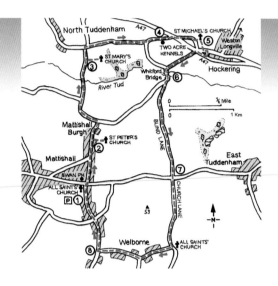

8 miles (12.9km) 3hrs 30min **Ascent:** 131ft (40m) ▲
Paths: Mostly paved country lanes and public footpaths
Suggested map: aqua3 OS Explorer 238 East Dereham & Aylsham
Grid reference: TG 053110
Parking: At village square behind Mattishall church on Church Plain

Wander in the steps of the diarist to five churches that he knew and loved.

❶ Leave car park and walk towards **All Saints' Church**. Cross Dereham Road and head for Burgh Lane opposite. Walk up this, past cemetery and through residential area to Church Lane on your R. Continue to **Mattishall Burgh's St Peter's Church**.
❷ Leave church and retrace your steps to Burgh Lane. Turn **R** and continue to T-junction. Turn **L** ('North Tuddenham'). The lane narrows, and winds down a hill and up other side. Keep ahead to an unpaved lane on your **R** after about ¾ mile (1.2km).
❸ Turn **R** and follow track to **St Mary's Church, North Tuddenham**. Retrace your steps to paved lane, turn **R** through village and continue to another T-junction. Go **R**, along lane ('Hockering and Honingham'). When lane bends to R, keep walking straight ahead, past High Grove Farm and **Two Acre Kennels**, to crossroads.

❹ Go straight across to tiny lane opposite, aiming for battlemented tower of **Hockering's St Michael's Church**. Cross **A47** carefully, and aim for lane opposite. There is a notice board outside church giving details of Parson Woodforde.
❺ Walk through churchyard and look for 2 brick buttresses. Opposite these is a gate. Go through it, and walk through field ahead to lane. Turn **L**, then **R** and re-cross **A47**, aiming for Mattishall Lane opposite and to your **R**. Turn **L** at 1st junction.
❻ Cross over bridge, and keep **L** at following junction, **Blind Lane** (not signed). Walk for 1 mile (1.6km) to crossroads.
❼ Go straight over, walking down **Church Lane** to **Welborne**. At junction, proceed past village hall to **All Saints' Church**. Retrace route. Turn **L** along Church Road, then **R** at next junction towards **Mattishall**.
❽ Turn **R** towards **Mattishall** at end of Welborne Road, and continue to Church Plain again.

692 NORTH ELMHAM THE SAXON CATHEDRAL

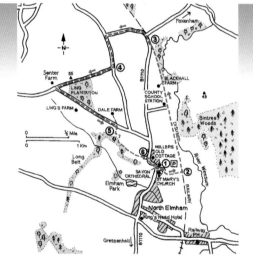

5½ miles (8.8km) 2hrs **Ascent:** 115ft (35m) ▲
Paths: Disused railway line and paved roads, 1 stile
Suggested map: aqua3 OS Explorer 238 East Dereham & Aylsham
Grid reference: TF 987216
Parking: Car park near Saxon cathedral North Elmham

Walk where Saxons prayed and Victorians built their railways.

❶ Explore site of **Saxon cathedral**, then leave way you entered. Turn **L** along gravel track with North Elmham's parish church of **St Mary** to your **R**. Path winds downhill with hedges on either side to old brick bridge with **disused railway** running underneath it. Cross bridge and look for stile immediately to your **L**.
❷ Cross stile and descend 14 steps to **disused railway** line. Turn **R**, and then continue along path until functional railway tracks appear. At this point path moves away to **R**, safely tucked to one side. After about ¾ mile (1.2km) you reach **County School Station** (refurbished in 1999) and a good place for a break. Walk through white gates marking level crossing, and follow Wensum Valley Walks sign (blue arrows) ahead. Continue for ¾ mile (1.2km), past **Blackhall Farm**, until footpath leaves railway track and emerges on to **B1110**.

❸ Turn **R** and, at remains of a Victorian railway bridge, keep **L**, following blue cycle-way signs to King's Lynn and Fakenham. Walk on this quiet lane to T-junction. Turn **L** and continue to next junction.
❹ Bear **R**, passing **Ling Plantation** on your **L**. Turn sharp **L** along Great Heath Road ('North Elmham'), following rustic wooden fences surrounding **Ling's Farm** to other edge of **Ling Plantation**. Walk along this lovely lane for just over ¾ mile (1.2km), to scattered houses. Look for footpath to your **R**, opposite track leading to **Dale Farm** on your **L**.
❺ Take footpath to **R**, mostly wide track. Follow it around to **L** behind houses then **R**, towards small plantation. Footpath hugs edge of woods for short distance and becomes access point for houses. Path eventually emerges on to **B1110**, **North Elmham's** High Street. Opposite is **Millers Old Cottage**.
❻ Turn **R** on High Street. Walk until you see signs for **Saxon cathedral** to your **L**. Follow them to car park.

693 BLAKENEY MAGICAL MARSHES

4½ miles (7.2km) 2hrs **Ascent:** 98ft (30m) ▲
Paths: Footpaths with some paved lanes, can flood in winter
Suggested map: aqua3 OS Explorer 251 Norfolk Coast Central
Grid reference: TG 028441
Parking: Carnser (pay) car park, on seafront opposite Blakeney Guildhall and Manor Hotel

Walk along the sea defences to some of the finest bird reserves in the country.

❶ From car park head for **wildfowl conservation project**, fenced-off area with ducks, geese and widgeon. A species list has been mounted on one side, so you can see how many you can spot. Take path ('Norfolk Coast Path') out towards marshes. This raised bank is part of the sea defences, and is managed by the Environment Agency. Eventually, you have salt marshes on both sides.
❷ At turning, head east. Carmelite friars once lived around here, although there is little to see of their **chapel**, remains of which are located just after you turn by wooden staithe (landing stage) to head south again. This part of the walk is excellent for spotting kittiwakes and terns in late summer. Also, look for Sabine's gull, manx and sooty shearwaters, godwits, turnstones and curlews. The path leads past **Cley Windmill** (1810) which last operated in 1919. It is

open to visitors and you can climb to the top for a view across the marshes. Follow signs for **Norfolk Coast Path** until you reach **A149**.
❸ Cross **A149** to pavement opposite, turn **R**. Take 1st **L** after crossing little creek. Eventually reach cobblestone houses of **Wiveton** and a crossroads; go straight ahead.
❹ Take grassy track opposite **Primrose Farm**, and continue to T-junction. This is **Blakeney Road**, turn **R** along it. However, if you want refreshments, turn **L** and walk a short way to **Wiveton Bell pub**. Lane is wide and ahead is 13th-century **St Nicholas Church**. Its 2 towers served as navigation beacons for sailors, and east one is floodlit at night.
❺ At **A149** there are 2 lanes opposite you. Take High Street fork on **L** to walk through centre of **Blakeney** village. Don't miss the 14th-century **Guildhall** undercroft at the bottom of Mariner's Hill. Keep ahead into car park.

Norfolk

WALSINGHAM A MEDIEVAL SHRINE

7¾ miles (12.5km) 3hrs 45min **Ascent:** 164ft (50m)
Paths: Mostly country lanes
Suggested map: aqua3 OS Explorer 251 Norfolk Coast Central
Grid reference: TF 933368
Parking: Pay-and-display car park, Little Walsingham

A walk to one of the most important medieval shrines in England.

① From car park head for exit sign, and turn **L** down hill. Go straight across at junction, down narrow Coker's Hill. The remains of a Franciscan **friary** are off to your L, incorporated into a private house. When you reach open fields, go **L** and down a hill, then turn **R** and continue down road.

② Take **R-H** fork, with stream on **L-H** side. This is part of the old pilgrim route, when folk left their shoes in **Houghton St Giles** in order to walk the last stretch barefoot as a mark of their sincerity. Pass **Slipper Chapel** on your L (built in the 1300s and partly destroyed during the Reformation), and then walk past remains of now **dismantled railway** to enter **North Barsham**.

③ At junction, keep **L**; take lane ("West Barsham") to junction in copse. Take lane to **L**, up hill with fir plantation on R. Descend hill, past more of

dismantled railway eventually reaching **East Barsham**.

④ Turn **L** at T-junction and walk past **White Horse Inn**. Just after red-brick **manor house**, turn **R** into Water Lane ('Great Snoring'). Look for partridges, yellowhammers and finches in the hedgerows.

⑤ At junction, take **R-H** turn towards **Thursford**. (It is possible to take **The Greenway** to Walsingham shortly after this point, but be warned that it can be extremely boggy.) Continue ahead into **Great Snoring**, and turn **L** by large red-brick house, then quickly reach open fields again. After a little more than 1 mile (1.6 km), bear **L** towards **Little Walsingham** and continue to a patch of shady woodland.

⑥ At crossroads, continue straight ahead, and ahead again at next crossroads, to pass Anglican **shrine**. Go up hill to pumphouse topped by a brazier that is lit on state occasions. Turn **R** by Shrine Shop, and then immediately **L** to reach car park.

EAST WRETHAM COMMON BIRDS AND BUNNIES

2¾ miles (4.4km) 1hr **Ascent:** Negligible
Paths: Gravel track and waymarked trails across heath
Suggested map: aqua3 OS Explorer 229 Thetford Forest in the Brecks
Grid reference: TL 913885
Parking: Norfolk Wildlife Trust car park off A1075. Open 8am to dusk.

Once shaken by roaring war planes, this is now a peaceful nature reserve.

① From car park go through gate and follow trail marked by green-and-white arrows. This will take you over sandy Breckland heath that is pitted with rabbit warrens, so watch your step. Rabbits can nearly always be seen here. At kissing gate, follow green arrow trail that takes you to **R** through a pine plantation. You might notice traces of tarmac underfoot, a relic of the airbase.

② At electric fence with a bench on other side, inspect area beyond. You may see the crumbling remains of the **airfield's** concrete and tarmac 'panhandle' dispersal point. Make a sharp **L**, ignoring green arrow that will take you on a shorter route, and continue on.

③ Go **R** at bend in this path, passing more ruins before reaching grassy track. Turn **R**, so that **Langmere** is on your **L**. A little way down this path is

a sign pointing to a bird **hide** (excellent for watching resident waterfowl). However, because water level in mere is dependent on water table the hide is often flooded, and therefore closed. Continue along path, following white arrows. Eventually reach another kissing gate.

④ Go through kissing gate on to old Drove Road. This is part of **Hereward Way** and is wide gravel track with fences on either side. The Norfolk Wildlife Trust opens and closes parts of the reserve depending on the season and weather conditions, so it is sometimes possible to extend the walk to **Ringmere**. In which case turn **R** off Drove Road and, after reaching **Ringmere**, return same way. Look for notices to see if path is open. Drove Road then takes you past **memorial** to Sydney Herbert Long, who founded Norfolk Naturalists' Trust in 1926.

⑤ At A1075, turn **L** and follow marker posts back to car park.

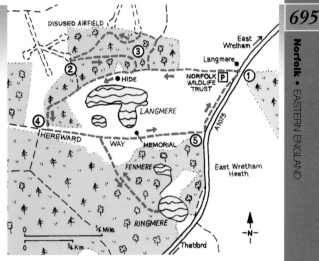

GREAT EASTERN PINGO TRAIL FULL STEAM AHEAD

5¾ miles (9.2km) 2hrs 30min **Ascent:** 33ft (10m)
Paths: Wide grassy footpaths to narrow muddy ones, some steps
Suggested map: aqua3 OS Explorer 229 Thetford Forest in the Brecks
Grid reference: TL 940965
Parking: Great Eastern Pingo Trail car park off A1075

A walk along an old railway course that has remnants of the ice age.

① Take straight path in front of you – disused railway line that gives walk part of its name. Pass Stow Bedon Station, opened in 1869 and now a private house. Continue through mixed woodland and in just over 1 mile (1.6km) reach farm track, with **Crow Farm** on your R.

② Turn **R** where track meets Peddars Way Circular Walk, heading towards **Breckles and Stow heaths**, which have been under conifers since Stow Bedon Enclosure Act of 1813. At **Watering Farm**, continue straight ahead.

③ Turn **R** along gravelled footpath of main north–south Peddars Way trail. Soon you'll see **Thompson Water** on your R. On your L note signs warning that this is an area used by Ministry of Defence. Once lake is to your R, look out for a sign for Great Eastern Pingo Trail.

④ Turn **R** into Thompson Common nature reserve. This part of walk can be muddy, and may necessitate some acrobatics across fallen trees and through sticky bogs. There are trails to the lake if you want to see teals, shovellers, reed warblers and crested grebes. Main path can be hard to follow, so look out for waymarkers. Head for bridge crossing sluggish stream.

⑤ Turn **L** after you cross bridge and walk next to stream along path lined by nettles.

⑥ Cross another bridge, going away from stream and out into open area of **Thompson Carr**, a meadow grazed by Shetland ponies. In the next meadow there are a large number of pingos, shallow depressions, often water-filled, that were formed during the last ice age. Once through meadow you will see **Thompson** village on horizon. Follow track to paved lane.

⑦ At lane, continue into outskirts of village. Pass houses, until you see Pingo Trail sign to your **R**. Follow it through woodland to arrive back at car park.

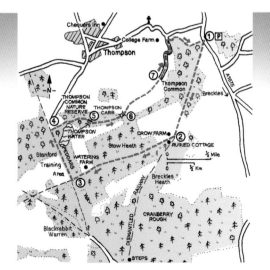

697 · GREAT CRESSINGHAM *Ploughs and Pheasants*

5¾ miles (9.2km) 2hrs 30min Ascent: 164ft (50m) ▲
Paths: Paved country lanes
Suggested map: aqua3 OS Explorer 236 King's Lynn, Downham Market & Swaffham
Grid reference: TF 845018
Parking: Car park opposite Windmill pub, Great Cressingham

Stroll in quiet lanes around Pickenham Hall.

❶ Park opposite **Windmill pub** in **Great Cressingham**. Turn **L** along peaceful country lane. The grassy verges and hawthorn hedges here are a joy in spring, with nesting thrushes, wrens, blackbirds and robins. After 350yds (320m) reach crossroads.

❷ Turn **R** along lane ('South Pickenham') that runs parallel to **River Wissey**. Some of trees on this lane – oaks, chestnuts and beeches – were planted in 19th century. There is marshy meadow to R then lane plunges into shady wood where pheasants nest. After woods look for meadow with mature trees on your R. Due to modern agricultural methods trees are seldom tolerated in the middle of fields, so when you see them, it means the landscape must be fairly ancient.

❸ Turn **R** at crossroads, and join **Peddars Way** bridle route towards Ashill. This is another wooded lane, with sturdy walls of **Pickenham Hall** estate to R. The Hall, which you may glimpse through trees, is

known for its shooting – hence the number of pheasants in the surrounding fields. Before long, you will see distinctive round tower of **South Pickenham's All Saints' Church**. Go straight over next junction towards Ashill. Lane can be plagued by fast cars, so walk with care. Cross brick bridge over **River Wissey** and continue to next junction.

❹ Turn **R** along narrow track, part of long distance National Trail, **Peddars Way and Norfolk Coast Path**, and continue along it for about 2 miles (3.2km), to junction with main road.

❺ Turn **R** and continue to **Great Cressingham**. You pass **St Michael's Church**, which has flint walls and large Gothic windows. There are interesting carvings above the tower door – each shield is crowned with the letter 'M', standing for **St Michael's**. Inside, you'll see 15th-century stained glass and brasses.

❻ Leave church and follow main road as it bears **L** into village. Turn **R** at T-junction to return to car park.

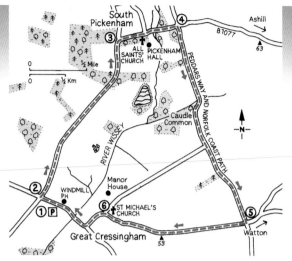

698 · WEETING *To Grimes Graves*

7½ miles (12.1km) 3hrs Ascent: 148ft (45m) ▲
Paths: Farm tracks and gravel tracks through forest, 1 stile
Suggested map: aqua3 OS Explorer 229 Thetford Forest in the Brecks
Grid reference: TL 776891
Parking: Lay-by at Weeting Castle, next to church. Note: Entrance fee for Grimes Graves, even to park

Travel back in time from a 12th-century moated house to a prehistoric flint mine.

❶ Park in sandy lay-by at sign for **Weeting Castle**. Walk across meadow to look at remains of this fortified manor house, then follow farm track past St Mary's Church with its round tower, originally 12th century, but rebuilt by the Victorians in 1868. Go through **Home Farm**, then jig **L** then **R**, passing curious sows in their pens to your L. After pig enclosures, turn **R**.

❷ At junction by **Sunnyside Cottage**, take L–H turn, following track with woodland on L and field on R. After 1 mile (1.6km) cross A1065 (very carefully), turn **R** and walk for about 350yds (320m) on verge.

❸ Go **L** up paved lane ('Grimes Graves'). Stay on this road for about 1¼ miles (2km), to sign on your **R** for **Grimes Graves**. You will need to pay an entrance fee to visit the site. With its shop and exhibition area it is a good place to take a break. When you have looked

around mines, take southerly track across heath that leads to perimeter fence.

❹ Turn **R** at fence and walk along it to stile at corner of site. Climb over and walk few paces to sunken water butt with corrugated-iron roof, looking like house that has half-disappeared into ground. Go straight across this junction and walk along sandy track to A1065 again. Despite the proximity of the main road, you're in depths of prime forest here, where you can hear nothing more than birdsong.

❺ Cross **A1065**; take sandy track directly opposite, near sign for **Emily's Wood**. After short walk, woods give way to farmland again. Pass **Brickkiln Farm** and ignore track going off to R. At end of field, turn **R** and walk beside **Shadwell's Plantation**, planted in memory of the poet Thomas Shadwell, resident of Weeting who died in 1691. Track turns slightly **L**, and rejoins outward path by **Sunnyside Cottage**. Retrace your steps past pig farm back to car park.

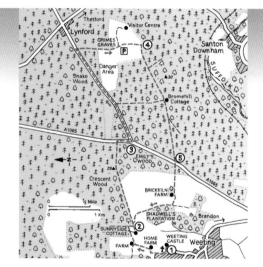

699 · THE BURNHAMS *Lord Admiral Nelson*

4 miles (6.4km) 2hrs Ascent: 49ft (15m) ▲
Paths: Waymarked paths and some paved lanes, 1 stile
Suggested map: aqua3 OS Explorer 251 Norfolk Coast Central
Grid reference: TF 844441
Parking: On-street parking on main road in Burnham Overy Staithe

In the footsteps of Nelson around the marshes.

❶ From **The Hero pub**, turn **R**, then immediately **L** down East Harbour Way to **Overy Creek**. Turn R next to black-painted house, go through gate and bear **L** along waterfront. Eventually, path reaches T-junction.

❷ At junction, turn **R**, around gate, into marshy meadow of long grass. This area is an English Nature reserve (part of **Holkham National Nature Reserve**) and sand dunes, salt marshes and mudflats are home to wide variety of birds and plants, including sea aster and plovers. Cross stile, then follow grass track to A149. Cross to track opposite, and follow this until you have passed 2 fields on your right.

❸ Go through gap at entrance to 3rd field, which may or may not be marked as footpath. Keep to **R** to waymarker pointing **L**, across middle of field. Keep ahead, through gaps in hedges, to dirt lane. Cross this and go down track opposite, towards Norman tower of **Burnham Overy's Church of St Clement**.

❹ Turn **L** at end of track on to Mill Road, then **R** up track called Marsh Lane. Go through gate and into field, so that **River Burn** is off to your L, with round Saxon tower of **Burnham Norton** in distance to your L and **Burnham Overy windmill** straight ahead. Go through gate by **Mill House**, complete with mill pond and mill race (1820).

❺ Cross A149, with pond on your L, then take public footpath into next field. If stile is too choked by brambles, use main gate, but keep hedge not too far from your **R**. In distance you will see **Burnham Overy windmill** (privately owned and not open to public).

❻ At junction of paths, take small one that leads straight ahead (ignore sign 'Marshes only no access to village'). This will take you across marshes again, until path leads you back to East Harbour Way. (If you want to avoid the marshes turn **R** at the junction and head towards the road and thence to start.) Turn **R**, up lane, and return to **The Hero pub**.

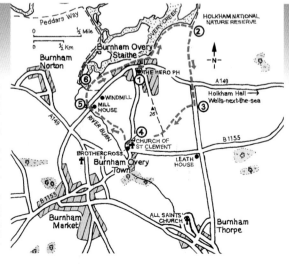

Norfolk

THETFORD FOREST *An Arboretum Trail*

4½ miles (7.2km) 2hrs **Ascent:** 66ft (20m) ▲

Paths: Wide grassy trackways and small paths
Suggested map: aqua3 OS Explorer 229 Thetford Forest in the Brecks
Grid reference: TL 813917
Parking: Lynford Stag picnic site off A134

Walk along the paths of Thetford Forest, from a stag to a mock-Jacobean hall.

❶ Leave car park and follow blue marker posts into trees. Jig slightly to **R** and follow markers heading north. The path then turns **L**. Take next wide track to your **R**, next to bench, leaving blue trail to walk along edge of Christmas tree plantation. Eventually reach paved road.

❷ Cross road and continue ahead on what was once part of driveway leading to **Lynford Hall**. There is notice board giving information about **arboretum** and its 'lost' Victorian gardens. Go past it to **Pumphouse Plantation** along gravel path, picking up next set of blue and green trails. **The Church of Our Lady of Consolation** is behind trees to your **R**. It was designed by Pugin in the 1870s for the owner of the hall who was a Catholic, but the next owner, a Protestant, planted trees to shield the unattractive building from view. After few minutes, you reach stone bridge.

❸ At stone bridge across **Lynford Lakes**, sign gives information about history of **Lynford Hall**, now hotel. Cross bridge and walk until **Lynford Hall** comes into view. Continue walking past the **hall**.

❹ At T-junction, turn **R** and walk along road to visit **arboretum**. When you have finished, retrace your steps along lane, then turn **L** so that the **hall** is on your **L**.

❺ Turn **R** on to wide grassy sward called Sequoia Avenue. Walk almost to end of it, then follow blue markers to **L** into wood. After few paces come to lake. This is a good place to look for frogs and newts. The blue trail bears to **L** at end of lake, but our walk continues straight ahead on bridleway. Path jigs **L**, then **R**, but keep to bridleway.

❻ Cross paved lane and continue straight on, towards Christmas trees. Turn **L** at end of track, then almost immediately **R**, where you will pick up blue trail markers again. Follow these until you reach car park.

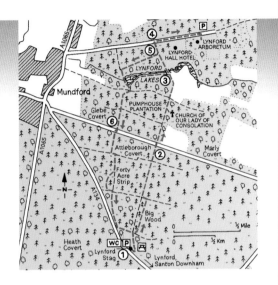

CASTLE ACRE *The Priories*

6½ miles (10.4km) 2hrs 45min **Ascent:** 230ft (70m) ▲

Paths: Footpaths, trackways and some tiny country lanes, can be very muddy, nettles, 2 stiles
Suggested map: aqua3 OS Explorer 236 King's Lynn, Downham Market & Swaffham
Grid reference: TF 817151
Parking: On road by village green, Castle Acre

A walk between Castle Acre and West Acre.

❶ From village green, go along lane past **St James' Church** to reach **priory** entrance. Turn **R** and then **L**, after a few paces, on footpath ('**Nar Valley Way**'). Proceed to pond.

❷ At pond, turn **L** and go through kissing gate along trail waymarked with white disk. Walk through meadow, with **River Nar** to your **L** and enter wood. Keep to this grassy track, going ahead through several junctions, to stile. Cross, walk across footbridge, cross stile at other end. At another bridge over **Nar** keep ahead to gate. At lane with ford on your **R**, go straight across to path opposite and walk along woodland track, with glimpses of **West Acre priory** ruins ahead.

❸ Turn **L** by circular waymarker sign. Follow footpath for ¼ mile (400m) to lane. Cross lane and take footpath opposite (not bridleway on your **L**). Go up hill, under power lines and past wood. At crest of hill reach crossroads.

❹ Turn **L** on to bridleway and continue straight ahead at 2 crossroads.

❺ Turn **L** at 3rd crossroads, on to drove road, passing **Bartholomew's Hills Plantation** on R. Keep uphill along this sandy track until you see **Castle Acre priory** and **St James' Church** ahead. Descend, go under power lines again, and meet lane at foot of hill.

❻ Proceed on lane, part of Peddars Way. At junction go straight on, down lane ('Unsuitable for Motors'). Pass **Church Farm** on R to river and **ford**. Cross river. Continue to acorn sign marking Peddars Way.

❼ Turn **R** along Peddars Way and keep straight ahead to sign for Blind Lane. Turn **R** into Cuckstool Lane with **castle** to your **L**. The track peters out into grassy path that skirts around **castle** bailey. Keep **R** to walk around edge of **castle**, then follow track to **L** when it reaches steep hill. This will bring you to lane.

❽ Turn **L**. Walk along lane, past old **castle** gate, to village green.

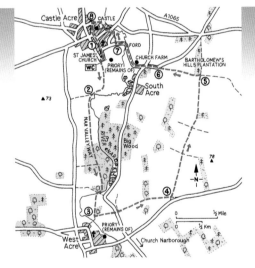

BRANCASTER *To Branodunum*

4½ miles (7.2km) 2hrs 15min **Ascent:** 148ft (45m) ▲

Paths: Winding paths and tracks, with some paved lanes, 2 stiles
Suggested map: aqua3 OS Explorer 250 Norfolk Coast West
Grid reference: TF 793443
Parking: Near National Trust's Dial House or in lay-by on A149 on edge of Brancaster Staithe

Enjoy the scent of the sea as you walk from Brancaster to its Roman fort.

❶ Walk into area owned by **Sailing Club** and, just before slipway, see National Trail marker on your **L**. Go through kissing gate and along boardwalk edging marshes. You can sit on one of the benches here to admire the view across the marshes, littered with masts of countless tiny sailing vessels. Continue walking for ¾ mile (1.2km).

❷ Turn **L** and leave coastal path, crossing stile to enter large field. This is Rack Hill, the site of the Roman fort of Branodunum. Built in about AD 240, at that time right on the estuary, the fort was protected by a wide ditch. Today there is little to see except the earthworks. Follow **L-H** side of field to top, then turn **R** and continue to 5-bar gate on your **L**. Cross it, and walk up small lane ahead. Cross A149 and turn **L**, staying on pavement to Green Common Lane. Turn **R** and pass felled tree stumps blocking vehicular access

and go uphill. Track bends twice, follow it into gated field. Take grassy track to your **R** between hedges.

❸ At waymarked gate further up hill, enter **Barrow Common nature reserve**. The footpaths wind all over the place, but walk straight ahead for few paces and take one slightly to your **L**. Eventually exit on to peaceful paved lane. Turn **L**, and follow lane down fairly steep hill. Turn **L** at junction and continue straight on to wood.

❹ Head **L** at footpath through copse to another paved lane. At lane, turn **L** to eventually reach A149.

❺ Cross over **A149** with care and turn **R**. After few paces take first **L**, opposite garage and post office. At end of lane is sign for coast path. Follow it down narrow, tree-lined track to marshes and main **Norfolk Coast Path**.

❻ Turn **L** along path to small boatyard and follow trail through some wooden huts. The next set of buildings is home to **Sailing Club** and car park.

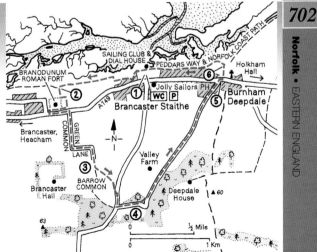

703 | SANDRINGHAM *A ROYAL VISIT*

6¼ miles (10.1km) 2hrs 45min **Ascent:** 131ft (40m) ▲
Paths: Marked forest trails and country lanes
Suggested map: aqua3 OS Explorer 250 Norfolk Coast West
Grid reference: TF 666279
Parking: Car park on road to Wolferton, or Scissors Cross car park

A stately home, country park and nature reserves on a forest stroll.

❶ From **Wolferton** road car park turn **L** towards **Wolferton**. The walled gardens of **Old Rectory** mark end of mixed woodland. Continue ahead at junction, past **St Peter's Church**. The road bends to **R** and here you will see cottages (1881) bearing motto 'Ich Dien' and fleur-de-lis. Just after **Manor Farm** is **Wolferton Station** on **L**, not currently open to public.

❷ After **Wolferton Station**, follow road to **L** and go up a hill to car park for Dersingham Nature Reserve and a gate beyond.

❸ Go through gate and take track to your **L**, ('Wolferton Cliff and wood walk'). This reserve comprises valley mire and heath, as well as some fairly recent woodland. Follow track to 330yd (302m) circular boardwalk around bog. When you have finished bog walk, continue along track, into woods again, to **Scissors Cross** car park.

❹ Turn **L** out of car park, then take **L-H** fork, crossing **A149** and passing a house named **The Folly**. After a few paces you will see lane to your **L** ('scenic drive'). Just beyond this is footpath running parallel to scenic drive.

❺ Take this footpath through **Sandringham Country Park**. There are lots of picnic places. Follow yellow trail when it leaves lane and winds towards **Jocelyn's Wood**, then continue to visitor centre. If you want to visit **Sandringham House** this is time to do it.

❻ From **visitor centre**, head for lower car park and pick up yellow trail again, which follows main road, but is tucked away behind trees of Scotch Belt. Eventually cross lane and find path again on opposite side as it passes through **Brickkiln Covert**.

❼ At crossroads, where footpath ends, turn **R** down a quiet lane with wide verges, still in woodland. Cross **A149** to reach **Scissors Cross**. Take fork on your **L** and you will be back at your car.

704 | OLD HUNSTANTON *DUNE WALK*

8 miles (12.9km) 3hrs 15min **Ascent:** 164ft (50m) ▲
Paths: Country tracks, lanes, muddy paths and sand dunes, 1 stile
Suggested map: aqua3 OS Explorer 250 Norfolk Coast West
Grid reference: TF 697438
Parking: Beach car park at Holme next the Sea

From the coast's wide-open magnificence to a peaceful nature reserve.

❶ Walk towards sea and turn **L** to head across **dunes**. This is Norfolk at its best, with miles of flat sandy beaches, and **dunes**. You may find some areas fenced off to protect breeding birds. After about 1 mile (1.6km) you will see a notice board and outskirts of **Old Hunstanton**.

❷ Take path that leads past **golf course** and into Smugglers' Lane, to a T-junction. Turn **R** and walk past **Caley Hall Motel**. Cross **A149** and aim for road ('To **St Mary's Church**'), where you can see grave of William Green.

❸ Turn **R** up Chapel Bank Green, through a tunnel of shade before reaching open farmland. When road forks, go down a grassy track with views of Norfolk's countryside. At **Lodge Farm**, follow track around farm buildings to T-junction.

❹ Turn **R** along route ('Norfolk County Council Ringstead Rides') along avenue of mature oaks and ashes. In the field to your **R** are the stark ruins of 13th-century St Andrew's Chapel.

❺ Bear **L** at **Downs Farm**; head for gate and notice telling you what to expect in **Ringstead Downs Nature Reserve**. It belongs to the Norfolk Wildlife Trust and the area is grazed by traditional hill sheep. This is one of the most beautiful parts of the walk. Follow path **R** through reserve until you reach lane.

❻ Turn **L** into **Ringstead**. Pass **Gin Trap Inn**, continue through village, then take **R** fork. This is part of Peddars Way. It jigs **L** again after a few paces, but is clearly marked. Follow it along lane towards sailless windmill.

❼ At last house, look for waymarked path to **L**. This cuts across field, then turns **R** into tunnel of hedges. Note Norfolk Songline sculpture halfway along path.

❽ Cross **A149**. Walk through **Holme**, with its long village green until you reach car park.

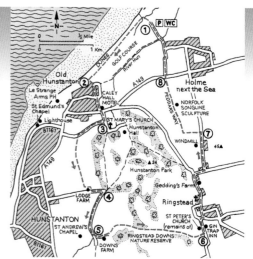

705 | CASTLE RISING *A QUEEN'S PRISON*

7 miles (11.3km) 3hrs **Ascent:** 131ft (40m) ▲
Paths: Some country lanes, but mostly footpaths, 3 stiles
Suggested map: aqua3 OS Explorer 250 Norfolk Coast West
Grid reference: TF 666244
Parking: English Heritage Castle Rising car park opens at 10am, or on lane outside church

From the medieval splendour of Castle Rising to lovely ancient woodlands.

❶ Leave car park, turn **L**, then go ahead at crossroads. Follow lane past Norman church and **Trinity Hospital**, then past point where gates close it to vehicles. Continue to bridge with white railings.

❷ Take path to **R** through a grassy meadow, with **Babingley River** to your **L**. Cross **A149** to stile opposite. Path passes ancient beech before heading for gate. Follow gravel road in front of you to **Mill House Cottage**, then take track (not footpath) to your **R**, just past ruined barn.

❸ Cross bright orange stream (stained by dissolved iron-rich rocks). Head across meadow in front of you by aiming slightly to your **L** until you reach another stream. Turn **R**, following stream. Nettles can be a problem, although these do not deter geese and pheasants. At gate, turn **R**, away from stream. Pass through gate and go **L** at track. Turn **R** to reach lane.

❹ Turn **R** at **A148**, then walk along verge on opposite side until you reach first lane on your **L**. Go down it. Enter **Roydon** and turn into Church Lane. The church has a Romanesque south door. Continue out of village until you see **Hall Farm**. Church Lane bends to **R**, reaching a green-gated lane.

❺ Turn **L** on to green-gated lane (marked as footpath) and follow signs for Sunnyside Veterinary Clinic. On your **R** is a farm track leading ahead. Follow this for 700yds (640m) to meet another public footpath on **R**.

❻ Follow this sandy track to **A148**. Take minor road opposite, which has oak trees that grow progressively larger as you walk further from main road. By time you reach **Fowler's Plantation**, they tower above you. To **R** is a **conservation area** with native wild species – excellent for a detour, but keep dogs on a lead.

❼ Cross **A149** to lane opposite. Turn **L** up lane marked towards castle and then **R**, into car park.

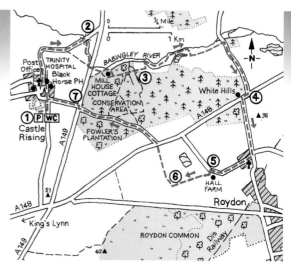

Norfolk

KING'S LYNN *PORT ON A RIVER*

4¼ miles (6.8km) 2hrs (allow longer for museums) **Ascent:** Negligible △
Paths: Pavements, cobbled streets, grassy river path and steps to ferry (operates all year)
Suggested map: aqua3 OS Explorer 250 Norfolk Coast West
Grid reference: TF 620199
Parking: Clough Lane pay-and-display car park

Cobbled lanes to King's Lynn's museums, the river and a ferry ride.

❶ Walk towards **King's Lynn** Auction Rooms. Pass fitness centre and cross road to park. Take path towards **chapel** of St John the Evangelist.

❷ Turn **R** by **pond**. On a little knoll to your L is **Red Mount Chapel** (1485) for pilgrims travelling to Walsingham. At ruinous walls of town's defences, continue along Seven Sisters Walk with football ground to L.

❸ Pass Beeches Guest House into Guanock Terrace, past Lord Napier pub and statue. Bear **L** at London Road and, when you see 15th-century **South Gate**, cross to Honest Lawyer pub. Turn **L** along Saddlebow Road, to footpath sign on R after you cross **Nar River**.

❹ Turn **R** on to **Nar Valley Way**, a grassy footpath between scrub and terraced houses. Path follows **Nar** to Nar Outfall **Sluice** then turns south to follow **Great Ouse**. At bridge, turn **R** on road and cross bridge.

❺ Turn **R** at sign ('**Fen Rivers Way**'). Continue with views across river to **King's Lynn**. Initially, path is grassy, then becomes boardwalk passing factories on west bank of river to **ferry station**.

❻ Take ferry (every 20 mins) back to **King's Lynn**. Walk up Ferry Lane to King Street. Turn **L** to **Tuesday Market Place** and Corn Exchange concert hall.

❼ Retrace your steps and head for Purfleet Quay, which houses **Custom House** and a statue of explorer George Vancouver. Cut through Purfleet Place into Queen Street, then back down King's Staithe Lane and up College Lane to Thorseby College (1500). Go round corner to Saturday Market Place, looking at Town House Museum and **Town Hall** (1421) before bearing **R** to Priory Lane to see **Priory Cottages**. Turn **L** on Church Street to St Margaret's Church (c1100).

❽ Turn **R** on to pedestrian High Street and town, **R** into New Conduit Street, then along Tower Street to car park.

THE WALPOLES *IN THE MARSHES*

7¼ miles (11.7km) 3hrs **Ascent:** Negligible △
Paths: Footpaths in fields and housing estates, country lanes
Suggested map: aqua3 OS Explorer 236 King's Lynn, Downham Market & Swaffham
Grid reference: TF 520199
Parking: Near war memorial and Woolpack Inn, Walpole Cross Keys

Walk through the edge of the Fens, near where King John lost his treasure.

❶ With village sign behind you, turn **L** along Little Holme Road, on pavement on R-H side. After about ¾ mile (1.2km) see track ('No Through Road') on **L**. Follow it, cross A17 with care, and head down lane opposite, ('No access to the Walpoles'). Lane follows ancient sea defences; proceed for 350yds (320m).

❷ Turn **L** on to unmarked footpath that cuts diagonally across field. Follow this until it meets another path, and turn **R** along track towards farm buildings. Track ends at crossroads.

❸ Go **R** down lane, past 30mph sign and into **Walpole St Andrew**. Use pavement on **R** to **Princess Victoria** pub; cross and use pavement **L**, continuing along Wisbech Road to **St Andrew's Church**.

❹ Bear **L** at crossroads at **St Andrew's Church**. Take 1st **L** down Church Close towards Anthony Curton Church of England Primary **School**. Take

footpath down side of school and through housing estate before emerging near **St Peter's Church** in **Walpole St Peter**. Turn **R**, using pavement on R to junction.

❺ Turn **L** across from house called **Quantum** and walk past farmland to more houses. Look for Chalk Road and turn **L**. After a few paces turn **R** into Bustard's Lane and continue to junction.

❻ Turn **L**. Walk until you see **communications tower** on R. Keep **L** again. After ½ mile (800m) reach junction you made earlier at Point ❸. Go **R**, greenhouses to **L**, to another junction. Turn **L**. Follow lane until you see tall fence and conifer hedge.

❼ Turn **L** in front of hedge, past Old Railway Inn house to A17. Follow pavement to **L**. Cross over at end of railings, using central island. On other side, walk to **L** of piled pallets and up lane past scattered houses and fruit farm. At T-junction turn **R** along Station Road back to car park.

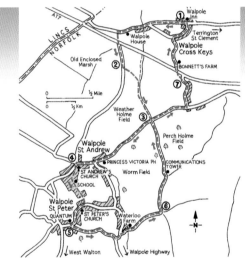

DOWNHAM MARKET *DEEP IN THE FENS*

5¾ miles (9.2km) 2hrs **Ascent:** 98ft (30m) ▲
Paths: Riverside footpaths and country lanes, several stiles
Suggested map: aqua3 OS Explorer 236 King's Lynn, Downham Market & Swaffham
Grid reference: TF 610033
Parking: Pay-and-display Town Council car park in Paradise Road

Visit a working mill and a floodgate protecting the Fens from tidal surges.

❶ Leave car park and turn **R**. When you reach Somerfield on your L, cut through car park to road running parallel to Paradise Road and turn **R**. The road winds downhill, passing White Horse pub and Cosy Corner restaurant, before reaching a level crossing and **station**. Continue towards Heygates **Flour factory** on L, and cross Hythe Bridge. On **R** you will see a stile. Cross this, and walk up track to T-junction.

❷ Take L-H fork, and cross 2nd stile to reach **Fen Rivers Way** walking east bank of **River Great Ouse**. The banks have been raised to prevent flooding. After about ¼ mile (400m) reach stile.

❸ Cross stile, then **A1122** and, climb a 3rd stile to reach footpath again. The path continues until you reach **lock** at **Salters Lode**. Proceed until **Denver Sluice** comes into sight. Cross stile and descend track to lane to explore **sluice**.

❹ Return to lane, and follow it past footpath entrance to bridge over **Relief Channel**. Keep to lane as it winds through farmland and across level crossing. After passing a huge field on your R and then **West Hall Farm** with its elegant clock tower, look for sails of **Denver Windmill**. Turn to **R** to visit windmill.

❺ Return to lane and continue along it, then turn **L** up Sandy Lane. The lane becomes track, which you follow until it ends at junction with B1507.

❻ Turn **L** and then, after a few paces, you reach A1122. Turn **L**, then immediately **R** down lane called London Road ('Town centre'). Use pavement on L-H side, passing police station on your R. Eventually you reach junction.

❼ Aim for war memorial and turn **L**. Then aim for clock tower, walking along High Street and through market square to **Castle Hotel**. Turn **L** at hotel and walk down Paradise Road a few paces until you reach car park.

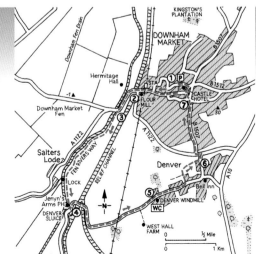

709   Mow Cop *Down and Up Again*

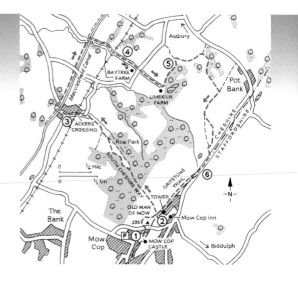

5¼ miles (8.4km) 2hrs **Ascent:** 720ft (219m) ▲

Paths: Open fields and woodland paths, canal tow path, quiet lanes, short sections where path indistinct, 10 stiles

Suggested map: aqua3 OS Explorer 268 Wilmslow, Macclesfield & Congleton

Grid reference: SJ 857573

Parking: National Trust car park directly below Mow Cop castle

The lush plains and some wilder ridges.

❶ Head towards castle. Before reaching it take narrower path **L**, to road. Go **R**, then **L** ('**Old Man**' and '**South Cheshire Way**'). Swing **L**, then **R**, then fork **R** on narrow path past Old Man. Rejoin wider track, heading towards communications mast.

❷ At junction of footpaths go **L**. Follow field edges downhill into wood. Where footpath splits at holly bushes go **L** and into field; bear **R**. Skirt farm then join rough track. Keep descending to join surfaced lane. Bear **L**; cross railway at Ackers Crossing.

❸ Follow lane to wider road and turn **R**. Cross canal bridge, then go down steps and **L**, along tow path. At bridge No 81 go up to lane and turn **L**, over bridge.

❹ Follow lane to crossroads by **Baytree Farm** and continue up track to **Limekiln Farm**. Take track on **L** just beyond buildings. Keep low, along edge of wood, until track bends **R** by post marked with yellow arrows.

❺ Go **L**, through undergrowth to duckboards and stile. Turn **R** along field edge. After 100yds (91m) there's another post. Descend sharp **R**; cross several, sometimes slippery, plank bridges. Narrow path heads uphill to wider track, then tarmac near house. Before track starts to descend, go **R** to stile. Follow **L** edge of field alongside wood. After another stile go up narrower field until it opens out. Above signpost, go **R** on green track to stile amid holly trees. Continue to another boundary; beyond is rougher ground with rushes and gorse. Firm track curves across this, though last bit to stile remains rough and rushy. Bear **L** up drive to road, then follow it **R** for 300yds (274m).

❻ By gateway on **R-H** side **Gritstone Trail** sign under tree points way into wood. Footpath roughly follows its upper margin and emerges on level floor of old quarry workings. Bear **L**, below communications **tower**, to rejoin outward route near **Old Man of Mow**.

---

710   Little Budworth *Woods and Heaths*

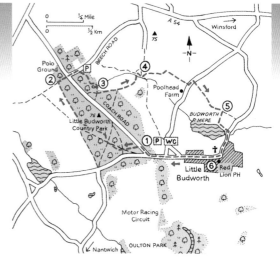

3½ miles (5.7km) 1hr 15min **Ascent:** 98ft (30m) ▲

Paths: Easy tracks at first, field and farm paths and some (usually quiet) road walking, 14 stiles

Suggested map: aqua3 OS Explorer 267 Northwich & Delamere Forest

Grid reference: SJ 590654

Parking: Main car park for Little Budworth Country Park

An easy walk centred around the distinctive heathland of Little Budworth Country Park.

❶ Cross **Coach Road** to path; turn **R** on wider path. Fork **L**; follow main path, keeping ahead at crossroads, with Heathland Trail sign, and again at next crossing. When field appears ahead, follow path alongside to its **R**. This veers away **R**. Go back **L** just before cleared area, by Heathland Trail marker.

❷ Go **R** on track to **Coach Road** and over into **Beech Road**. After 230yds (210m) enter small car park. Go through gap in fence near far end beside signboard with map. Path skirts depression with boggy pool, then curves round larger pool.

❸ Cross causeway/dam by pool and gently climb sunken track beyond. As it levels out, fork **L** by Heathland Trail sign then turn **L**, with an open field not far away to **L**. Bear **L** on wider surfaced track, swinging down past ornamental pool in dip. Immediately after this turn **R** on sandy track.

❹ Where another path crosses, most people evidently go through gate ahead into corner of field. Strictly speaking, however, right of way goes over stile to its **R** then across (very wet and smelly) corner of wood to 2nd stile. From here bear **R** under power line, to stile in far corner. Follow narrow path (beware nettles), then go over stile on **R** and straight across large field. Aim just **L** of farm to gate and stile. Go **L** on lane for 60yds (55m) then **R** down track. This becomes narrower, then descends slightly.

❺ As track levels out, fork **R**, with sign for **Budworth Mere**. Go down towards water then **L** on path skirting mere. At end go **R** up road, swinging further **R** into centre of **Little Budworth**.

❻ Keep straight on ahead along road, through village then past open fields. Opposite entrance gates of **Oulton Park** is start of **Coach Road**. Follow this road, or parallel footpath to its **L** for 125yds (114m), to car park at **Little Budworth Country Park**.

---

711   Buwardsley *Views of Beeston Castle*

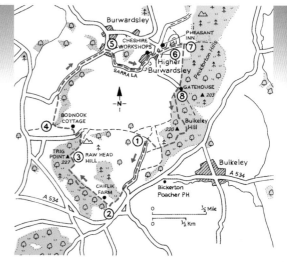

5½ miles (8.8km) 2hrs **Ascent:** 919ft (280m) ▲

Paths: Field and woodland paths, plus some lane walking, 9 stiles (currently being replaced by gates)

Suggested map: aqua3 OS Explorer 257 Crewe & Nantwich

Grid reference: SJ 520550

Parking: Verges at end of tarmac on Coppermines Lane, off A534

A walk on a prominent sandstone ridge.

❶ Walk down Coppermines Lane to a sharp **L-H** bend then over stile beside arched sandstone overhang. Cross field then ascend edge of wooded area. Cross fields to edge of another wood. Go up **R** joining track towards **Chiflik Farm**.

❷ Go through kissing gate by farm and up fenced path. Path generally runs below top of steep slope, gradually climbing to trig point on Raw Head Hill.

❸ Path goes **R** and into slight dip. Go **L** down steps then back **R**, slanting through steep plantation. Go **L** down narrow track for 300yds (274m). Opposite track and footpath sign, descend **R** on clear ground under tall trees. At bottom cross stile and go up towards **Bodnook Cottage**. Just below this bear **L** and into wood. Follow much clearer path, roughly level then slightly **L** and downhill among spindly beech trees.

❹ Cross stile at edge of wood, then another to its **R**. There's no path, so aim directly for stile below large tree, 50yds (46m) **L** of house. Path is clearer through next field. At end cross stile and follow road ahead.

❺ On edge of **Burwardsley** village turn **R** up 1st lane. Go **R** again up Sarra Lane, then fork **L** at 'Unsuitable for Motor Vehicles' sign. Follow lane through narrow section then past **Cheshire Workshops**. Just beyond this road forks.

❻ Go **R** then up hill. Keep **R** at fork. Lane becomes unsurfaced at Crewe and Nantwich boundary.

❼ Just before boundary sign go **R** over stile and follow clear path down edge of field. Keep straight on to meet narrow lane and go up **L**. On crest, opposite **gatehouse**, go **R** on track.

❽ Go **L** up steps into wood; continue less steeply. Where path splits, **L** branch follows brink of steep slope. Keep fairly close to this edge as path levels. Go through gap in fence then descend ahead, through plantation, to kissing gate by iron gate. Go diagonally **R** on clear track across field to Coppermines Lane.

Cheshire

THE CLOUD *VIEWS FROM THE CREST*

7 miles (11.3km) 2hrs 30min **Ascent:** 804ft (245m)
Paths: Field paths, canal tow path, some lanes, rougher and steeper on The Cloud, 11 stiles. Meadows and fields along canal, craggy summit
Suggested map: aqua3 OS Explorer 268 Wilmslow, Macclesfield & Congleton
Grid reference: SJ 894627
Parking: Car park on outskirts of small village of Timbersbrook

An exhilarating walk to a superb viewpoint.
1 From car park, turn **R** on road for 500yds (457m). Just past houses, go **L** over stile and down track. After 600yds (549m) go **R** over stile. Follow trodden line to cross stream in dip. Continue diagonally across meadow. A short embankment leads to a canal bridge.
2 Cross and loop round **L**, under bridge and along tow path. Follow this for 3¼ miles (5.3km) to bridge 57. Go up steps and over bridge. Vague track bears **L** then **R** through gorse along edge of hollow. Descend to stile under sycamore and down slope (muddy) to footbridge. Cross stile, go down to **River Dane** and step round tree on its side. Turn **R** up edge of field.
3 Cross stile to road. Turn **R** and climb steadily. As it levels out, go **L** on narrower lane. Opposite house, cross stile on **R**, then up fields over series of stiles, bearing slightly **L**. Join lane and go **L**, past **Hillside Farm**, then right, up track to stile.

4 Here is National Trust sign ('The Cloud'). Path is narrow but clear, directly uphill then slanting **R**. It passes below crags then levels out and dips slightly to start of broad shelf. Path now goes straight up hillside, through highest band of crags, to summit ridge. Trig point is about 100yds (91m) to **L**.
5 Retrace this short section of summit ridge then follow edge down, gently descending and swinging slowly **L**. Lower down path runs through pine plantations. Below gap in wall, broader track runs through more open woods. As track starts to curve **L**, clear path continues straight ahead. Stick to crest of ridge until you rejoin gravel track near sharp bend. Just below bend is footpath sign and steeply descending line of steps. Turn **L** on road, into edge of **Timbersbrook**. Just after 1st house on **R** go through gap in fence, down few more steps and across field with picnic tables. Car park is at its far end.

FRODSHAM HILL *SANDSTONE TRAILS*

3 miles (4.8km) 1hr **Ascent:** 375ft (114m)
Paths: Clear woodland paths, golf course, 4 stiles
Suggested map: aqua3 OS Explorer 267 Northwich & Delamere Forest
Grid reference: SJ 518766
Parking: Small car park on Beacon Hill, near Mersey View

A short walk on the crest and the flanks of a red sandstone escarpment.
1 Go **R** along lane for 100yds (91m), then **L** down sunken footpath and over stile to **golf course**. The path is much older than the golf course and officially walkers have priority, but don't take it for granted! Head straight across to 17th tee and arrow on post. Drop down slightly to **R**, crossing sandy patch, to footpath in trees **R** of green below. Bear **L** at sign for **Woodhouse Hill**, down steps. Keep to **L**, passing above crags; go down steps into **Dunsdale Hollow**.
2 Go **R**, rising gently, below more crags. Go past stile on **L** then up scratched steps on corner of rocks ahead. Follow level path through trees, near edge of golf course. Soon after this ends, path rises slightly and passes bench. After 20yds (18m), path forks. Keep straight on along level path, soon passing Woodland Trust sign, to wider clearing with signpost on **L** near corner of field beyond.

3 Just before corner of field, at break in overgrown old wall on **R**, narrow path slants steeply down slope. Bare rock on path can be slippery when wet, take care. Near bottom, path turns directly downhill to bottom corner of wood. Go **R** along base of hill. After 800yds (732m) path twists and descends into base of **Dunsdale Hollow**. Cross it and go up other side alongside stone wall and up steps. Go **R** on sandy track, climbing steadily and then passing below steep rock face.
4 Go **L** up steps, briefly rejoining outward route. **Jacob's Ladder** is just to **L** here, up R-H edge of crags. At top, bear **L** ('Mersey View'), and follow sandy track, with occasional Sandstone Trail markers, along brink of steeper slope. Pass below small steep crags before emerging near summit obelisk.
5 Turn **R** before **memorial** on footpath, aiming for telecommunications towers ahead. Go through ornate iron gates on to lane and turn **R**, back to car park.

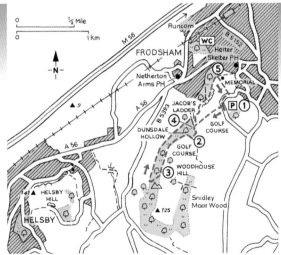

ALDERLEY EDGE *WIZARDLY WANDERINGS*

3 miles (4.8km) 1hr **Ascent:** 445ft (136m)
Paths: Woodland tracks and paths, some field paths, 7 stiles
Suggested map: aqua3 OS Explorer 268 Wilmslow, Macclesfield & Congleton
Grid reference: SJ 860772
Parking: Large National Trust car park off B5087

Layers of history and legend surround this famous Cheshire landmark.
1 From large National Trust car park, off B5087, walk towards tea room and information tower. Go **R** on wide track past **National Trust works yard**, then **L**. Cross open area past **Engine Vein**. At crossroads of paths turn **L** and come out by Beacon Lodge.
2 Go straight across road into **Windmill Wood**. Follow descending track to clearing, bear **L** and continue. About 140yds (128m) beyond National Trust sign, in more open terrain, with bare sand hills ahead, bear **R** across grass to crossroads with field ahead. Turn **R**, skirting damp ground then pool. Just before another open field, go **R**, along edge of wood. Continue in strip of trees, with fields either side. Cross road again and follow track to crest of **Castle Rock**.
3 Descend steps to level path. Go **L** 120yds (110m) to **Wizard's Well**. Return to steps and continue below crags on terrace path, then up steps to join higher

path. Go **L** and almost immediately start descending, with more steps in places. At bottom cross footbridge and climb, levelling out briefly by **Holy Well**. Few paces to **L** of well go up over tree roots to where path resumes. Climb shallow steps to wider path, go **L** then turn **R** on to crest of **Stormy Point**.
4 Follow wide level track to crossroads; go **L**. Follow signs ('Hare Hill'), descend with small ravine at bottom. Turn **R** and ascend. Climb steps past beech trees, then descend through **Clock House Wood**. Climb again to National Trust sign and out into open.
5 Go **R**, over stile, across waist of field to stile near pond. Go **L** along hedge to stile hidden in curve, then up fenced path. Join wider track and at top go over stile on **R**. Go **L** over next stile and up to stile and grassy track. Cross gravel track into narrow fenced path and at end turn **L**. Opposite **National Trust works yard** go **L** through gate for short cut to car park or continue straight on to tea room.

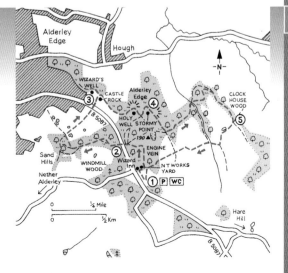

715 SHUTLINGSLOE *MINI MOUNTAIN*

5 miles (8km) 2hrs **Ascent:** 1,129ft (344m)
Paths: Farm and forest tracks, field paths, lane, moorland, 11 stiles
Suggested map: aqua3 OS Explorer OL24 White Peak
Grid reference: SJ 984706
Parking: Car park at Vicarage Quarry, Wildboarclough (alternative at Clough House, lower down valley)

From valleys and forest to a stark peak.
❶ From car park at **Vicarage Quarry**, turn **L** up road, away from **Wildboarclough** village. Just past **Dingers Hollow Farm**, go over stile on **L** and up to iron gate. Go **R** through another gate and follow green track across hillside to 3rd gate. Cross field near power line, down to stream then up **L** to stile by gate. Cross lane and walk few paces to stile. Narrow path rises gently, but our route rises steeply, above large trees. Continue on this line to stile into another lane. Go **R** to junction.
❷ Turn **L**, on lane ('Macc Forest Chapel), over top and down, past chapel. Follow road for 250yds (229m) to dip. At corner of wood go **L** on footpath, down hill. At bottom, near small dam, take newly made permissive footpath on **R**, over bridge. When gate blocks way, drop to **L**, down steps to stile and road.
❸ Cross to gap in wall almost opposite. Continuation path parallels road; when it rejoins it by gate, bear **L**

on wider path, swinging back **R**. Go up flight of steps on **L** and sharply back **L** on path climbing alongside stone wall. When gradient eases near kissing gate, bear **L** on established footpath. At next junction, after 300yds (274m), go **R**, with sign ('Shutlingsloe'), and up to kissing gate.
❹ Footpath, partly surfaced with large gritstone flags, crosses open moorland. At shoulder, path levels out and **Shutlingsloe** rears up ahead. Descend slightly, cross duckboards to stile and then follow obvious, flagged path alongside wall. Final steep staircase leads to trig point.
❺ Descend ahead, winding down steeply between low outcrops. Keep ahead as gradient eases. After 2 stiles follow wall to tarmac track. Go **R** on track to cattle grid. Take another track sharply back to **L**. This runs more or less level along hillside, then gently descending green track interrupted by stile and small stream leads down to road. Go **L** up this back to start.

---

716 LYME PARK *MR DARCY!*

5½ miles (8.8km) 3hrs 30min **Ascent:** 950ft (290m)
Paths: Generally firm, field tracks can be slippery if wet, 12 stiles
Suggested map: aqua3 OS Explorer OL1 Dark Peak
Grid reference: SJ 964823
Parking: Lyme Park, off A6 (free to National Trust members)

Around Lyme Park – Mr Darcy's home in the BBC's serialisation of Pride and Prejudice.
❶ With lake on **R** and house on **L** leave car park by drive and, as it begins to bend away to **R**, turn **L** for wide track through gate ('Gritstone Trail'). Follow through **Knightslow Wood**, negotiating several ladder stiles, until you reach moorland.
❷ Keep ahead/**L** on main track as it climbs moorland, aiming for small TV masts on skyline. At top, cross stile and field to reach end of surfaced lane by **Bow Stones**.
❸ Turn **L**; follow lane downhill until you reach junction, opposite hotel driveway. Turn **L**; walk up drive of **Cock Knoll Farm**. At buildings, head **R** across farmyard, following footpath signs. At far side go through gate and down **L-H** side of field.
❹ As you draw level with small thicket in shallow valley on **L**, go across stile and through trees. On other side head **R**, across bottom of field. Clear waymark

posts now point you through several rough fields to walled lane on far side.
❺ Once on lane, turn **R** and continue over **Bollinhurst Bridge**. (Turn **L** for short cut back to house via **East Lodge**.) Beyond Macclesfield Borough's newly planted Millennium Wood you reach junction of tracks. Go through gate on **L**; take grassy track, half **L**, signposted to North Lodge.
❻ Descend **R-H** side of field to woodlands at bottom. Path goes over several stiles as it skirts round **Bollinhurst Reservoir** – keep close to wall on **L**. Gated gravel path leads around side of Cockhead Farm, across another field and down grassy lane. At end of lane go **R** on to surfaced drive to **North Lodge**.
❼ Go through pedestrian gate at lodge; turn **L**. Walk along main drive for 250yds (229m). Take footpath up hillside on **L**, between short avenue of trees, to reach top of open, grassy ridge. Head for hilltop folly, 'The Cage'. Continue straight on to return to car park.

---

717 BOLLINGTON *A WALK TO WHITE NANCY*

3½ miles (5.7km) 2hrs **Ascent:** 1,180ft (360m)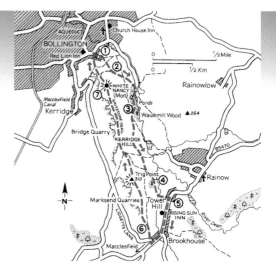
Paths: Easy field paths and farm tracks, one short, sharp descent
Suggested map: aqua3 OS Explorer OL24 White Peak
Grid reference: SJ 937775
Parking: Kerbside parking on Church Street or Lord Street, Bollington

A short but scenic ridge above Bollington.
❶ Walk starts towards top of Lord Street (which Church Street leads into) where it turns sharply **R** at top of steep hill. Walk along Cow Lane, cul-de-sac, then through gate at far end. Take upper of 2 field paths, quickly passing into larger sloping field on **R**. Aim for gate and cattle grid at far **L** top corner.
❷ Turn **L** on to open farm track; follow this all way down to lane in bottom of valley. Turn **R**, then almost immediately fork **R** again past some terraced cottages. Weir and pond below on your **L** are the remains of former silk mill. Follow path through Woodland Trust's **Waulkmill Wood**.
❸ Leave wood via stile and go across lower part of sloping field, then in 2nd aim for buildings on **R**. Follow gated path around to **R**, and on through successive fields.
❹ Go over stile with Gritstone Trail waymark (footprint with letter 'G') and along bottom edge of very

new, mixed plantation, then down walled track through woodland to reach main road at **Tower Hill**.
❺ Turn **R**; walk along pavement, past **Rising Sun Inn**, for ½ mile (800m). Turn **R** into **Lidgetts Lane** then as it bends almost immediately go **R** over high stile ahead and on to gated track, past row of hawthorn trees. Swinging **L**, follow grassy path up to ridge above – ignore lower route by **R-H** fence.
❻ Follow obvious hilltop track all way along spine of **Kerridge Hill**, ignoring tracks off **L** and **R**.
❼ Admire views at monument (**White Nancy**) at far end. This rather strange, bell-shaped monument was built in 1820 to commemorate the Battle of Waterloo – it was originally an open shelter but gradual decay and vandalism led to it being bricked up. Drop down sharply on to eroded path beyond, with **Bollington** spread out below; cross sunken farm lane and continue across 2 more steep fields to reach stile back into Cow Lane/Lord Street.

ROSSEN CLOUGH *HIDDEN VALLEY*

4 miles (6.4km) 2hrs 30min **Ascent:** 1,377ft (420m) ⚠
Paths: Sloping field paths and tracks, occasionally boggy, 15 stiles
Suggested map: aqua3 OS Explorer OL24 White Peak
Grid reference: SJ 938697 **Parking:** Limited spaces on Hollin Lane, near Lowerhouse Farm

A walk via a well-known radio tower.

❶ Walk up narrow, sloping driveway almost opposite **Lowerhouse** farm entrance (within few paces there is half-hidden public bridleway sign); continue past **Kinderfields Farm** with hilltop communications tower ahead. Ignore occasional turnings L, and continue along wide lane up valley bottom for ¾ mile (1.2km).

❷ After crossing cattle grid, rising lane approaches **Civit Hills Farm**. Go through gate on L and, drop down slightly to rough field through scrub towards far fence, with farm above (R) and brook below.

❸ After pond go through gate; continue along valley bottom following blue bridleway waymarks through successive gates. Keep brook on L and, ignoring footbridge to Lower Pethills, veer slightly uphill towards gate; cross field to reach **Higher Pethills Farm**.

❹ In middle of buildings turn L; walk down main drive. As you approach lane at bottom, turn R through gate. Keep ahead across high grassy bank. At gate, where bridleway is indicated ahead, turn R for footpath (yellow arrow) up short sunken track. After swinging half L, walk across field beside line of hawthorn trees and via fence stiles, cross 2 more fields to reach road at top.

❺ Turn R; walk along verge for 160yds (146m), before turning R on rough farm track. Now follow Gritstone Trail waymarks for several short field paths to reach telecommunications tower, making for top L corner of final field by **Lingerds Farm**.

❻ Turn R; walk along ridge-top track for almost 1½ miles (2.4km), ignoring paths off to L, and passing just to L of small summit (**Hill of Rossenclowes**).

❼ Finally route drops down through field with trees on R. At end go R, over extraordinary stile/bridge across wall, then down through sloping field. Keep to R of shallow valley, towards **Foxbank Farm** below.

❽ At wall, at bottom, go through gate by plantation for grassy path around R-H side of buildings; drop down steeply to stile in far corner of field (ahead) to return to lane.

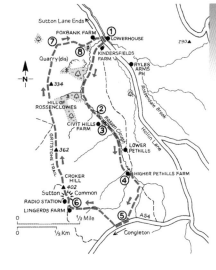

MACCLESFIELD FOREST *ROYAL FOREST*

7 miles (11.3km) 3hrs 30min **Ascent:** 2,820ft (860m) ⚠
Paths: Sloping field paths, lanes and easy forest tracks, steep hillside, 20 stiles
Suggested map: aqua3 OS Explorer OL24 White Peak
Grid reference: SJ 980681
Parking: Lay-by at Brookside, on lane 1 mile (1.6km) south of Wildboarclough

Another route around old and new Macclesfield Forest, then up Shutlingsloe.

❶ Walk along road for 440yds (402m) to **Crag Inn**, then at foot of its drive cross stile on L for path across sloping field. This maintains its direction through successive fields (each with ladder stile) until finally you reach farm drive at very top. Turn L and then walk along to lane.

❷ Turn R; walk along lane as far as **Greenway Bridge**. Go over stile on R; follow path beside stream, until it crosses it to veer L, up Oaken Clough. Keep to bottom of little valley, past ruined stone shelter, and as it rises from its far head, near small **pond**. Turn R on to private drive; then go almost immediately L for wall-side path uphill.

❸ At top, go over stile and across moorland on clear grassy track. Keep ahead until you reach stile on far side. Cross, and descend sunken, fenced track to emerge opposite **Hanging Gate pub**.

❹ Turn R; follow road for 1 mile (1.6km), keeping ahead at junction where road bends sharply L. Ignore another turning on L, until finally lane turns R, into **Macclesfield Forest**, where there is wide gate on R.

❺ Don't go through gate, but cross stile to L ('Shutlingsloe/Trentabank'); follow footpath, which runs parallel with lane. Drop down to newly planted area; cross footbridge; at junction of tracks, near wood sculpture, keep ahead ('Shutlingsloe'). At far end turn R, or for **visitor centre**/toilets at Trentabank turn L.

❻ Walk up wide forest drive; go L at fork; at far end turn R for long but quite easy gravel track through trees. At top go through gate, then continue ahead; turn R to leave forest for stone-flagged path across open moorland to distinctive top of **Shutlingsloe**.

❼ From summit descend eroded track down steep eastern slope of hill, until eventually turn R on to open farm drive. Follow this all the way down to road at bottom; turn R to return to car park.

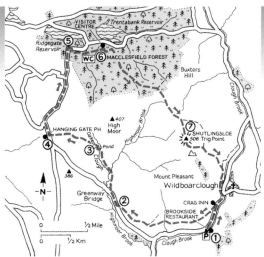

LONGDENDALE *MANCHESTER'S BIT OF DERBYSHIRE*

7½ miles (12km) 4hrs **Ascent:** 1,180ft (360m) ⚠
Paths: Good paths and tracks, a few stiles
Suggested map: aqua3 OS Outdoor Leisure 1 Dark Peak
Grid reference: SK 073994
Parking: Crowden pay car park

The wild Pennines meet the metropolis.

❶ Leave car park; cross **A628**. Take permissive footpath east; cross footbridge over Etherow beneath Woodhead **dam**. Passing through wood, path meets road. Across it, follow path to **Longdendale Trail**.

❷ Turn R along trackbed, following **Longdendale Trail** westwards above south shore of **Torside Reservoir**. Leave track where it crosses road, then follow lane opposite, crossing **dam** to north shore. At apex of R-H bend leave lane for permissive footpath but heading west above **Rhodeswood Reservoir**.

❸ After going through L of 2 gates follow path through scrub woodland to Rhodeswood **dam**, where tarmac lane takes you back to main road.

❹ Turn L along road for few paces, then cross it to climb on track **R** of intake wall. Turn **R** to follow old quarry track that zig-zags up heather and grass slopes before delving into woods of **Didsbury Intake**. Track passes between cliffs and bouldery landslip area of Tintwistle Knarr Quarry.

❺ After leaving woods behind, you reach brim of moor by **Rawkins Brook**. Go over stile in fence and trace peaty path known as Black Gutter. This heads roughly northeast across heathland towards gritstone 'edge' of **Millstone Rocks**.

❻ Follow edge to **Lad's Leap**, where you descend to ford **Hollins Clough** stream before climbing back on to moors. Dilapidated wall comes in from R, and path descends with it into Crowden valley.

❼ Halfway down slope it meets Pennine Way route, where you turn R, descending towards **Torside Reservoir**.

❽ Turn L along prominent, unsurfaced lane that descends parallel to northern shore of reservoir and then to bottom of Crowden valley. Walk across bridge over Crowden Brook; follow walled lane as it curves **R** to reach crossroads. Turn **R**, passing campsite and toilet block, to return to car park.

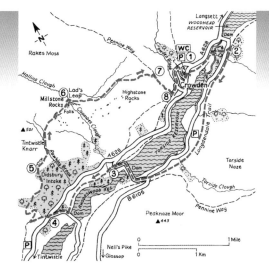

Derbyshire

721 GLOSSOP AVOIDING THE BLACK STUFF

7 miles (11.3km) 4hrs Ascent: 1,500ft (460m)
Paths: Unsurfaced tracks and moorland paths, a few stiles
Suggested map: aqua3 OS Outdoor Leisure 1 Dark Peak
Grid reference: SK 043947 **Parking:** Glossop High Street car park

Walking the dark peatlands of Bleaklow.

1 From High Street turn **L** on Manor Park Road into **Old Glossop**. Turn **R** on Shepley Street, passing factory to bus turning circle. Farm track continues east, leading into glen with partially wooded dome of **Shire Hill** on R and slopes of **Edge Plantation** on L.

2 Leave track at ladder stile. Path, confined at first by fence and drystone wall, climbs on pastured spur overlooking **Shittern Clough**. In upper reaches and beyond 2nd ladder stile, path climbs through bilberries, then over heather of upper Lightside.

3 Narrow stony path switches to spur's southern brow high above **Yellowslacks Brook**. Dilapidated wire fence comes in from R; path goes along **R** side of it before joining cliff edges of **Yellowslacks** and **Dog Rock**. Crags close in, to form rugged channel of **Dowstone Clough**. Path, now intermittent, stays close to stream and away from peat hags.

4 As clough shallows and stream divides among bed of rushes (grid ref 089954), aim for **Higher Shelf**

Stones by crossing main stream and following its southbound tributary – just follow bootprints along its sandy bed. Near summit of channel shallows and widens then, suddenly, trig point rises from grassy plinth ahead.

5 From Higher Shelf Stones, trace brow of **Shelf Moor** towards **Lower Shelf Stones**, but avoid naked peat that proliferates on L. Prominent grassy channel descends just north of west and forms reasonably dry course over Shelf Moor to boulder-strewn edge above **Ferny Hole**.

6 There's no path from here to **Doctor's Gate path** but it's quite easy as you'll see track quite early on descent. Just head to grassy shelf west of James's Thorn rocks, passing small pool before descending steep grassy flanks parallel to Little Clough.

7 **Doctor's Gate** meanders through moorland clough of **Shelf Brook** before passing through fields of **Mossy Lea Farm**. It joins outward route at foot of **Lightside** and return to **Old Glossop**.

722 LADYBOWER RESERVOIR LOST VILLAGE

6 miles (9.7km) 4hrs Ascent: 1,200ft (365m)
Paths: Well-defined moorland paths and a reservoir road
Suggested map: aqua3 OS Outdoor Leisure 1 Dark Peak
Grid reference: SK 195864
Parking: Ladybower Reservoir pay car park

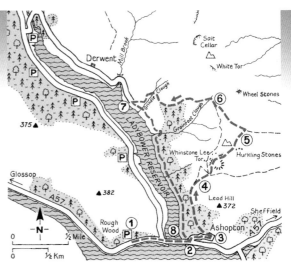

Beneath Ladybower Reservoir lies the remains of the old village of Ashopton.

1 Turn **L** out of car park and follow road beneath **Rough Wood** and across Ashopton Viaduct.

2 On other side, take 1st track on **L**, private road that zig-zags past few of **Ashopton's** remaining cottages.

3 Where road ends at turning point, double back **L** on forestry track climbing through pines and larches. This track can be muddy after periods of heavy rain. Track emerges from shade of forest out on to **Lead Hill**, where **Ladybower Reservoir** and sombre sprawl of Bleaklow come into view.

4 Path keeps intake wall to L as it rakes up bracken slopes of **Lead Hill**. However, at the time of writing, zig-zag path to **Whinstone Lee** Tor shown on OS maps has been replaced by well-worn path that diverts from wall to climb directly to summit rocks.

5 Path continues along peaty ridge past **Hurkling**

Stones to summit. Beyond it meets signposted path heading from Ladybower over to Moscar. Descend **L** until you reach gate at edge of open hillside.

6 Go through gate, then path descends westwards and alongside top wall of conifer plantation. It fords **Grindle Clough's** stream beyond another gate and turns **L** over stile to pass several stone-built barns. Path, now paved, descends further to join track running along east shores of **Ladybower Reservoir**.

7 It's worth detouring to see **Derwent** village remains. It lies 400yds (366m) northeast along track at foot of Mill Brook clough. Afterwards, retrace your steps along well-graded track, heading southwards along shores of reservoir. After rounding **Grainfoot Clough** track passes beneath woodlands with rocks of **Whinstone Lee Tor** crowning hilltop.

8 It meets outward route at gate above **Ashopton** viaduct. Turn **R** along road over viaduct and back to car park.

723 HAYFIELD ON THE MOORLAND'S EDGE

7 miles (11.3km) 4hrs Ascent: 1,640ft (500m)
Paths: Good paths and tracks, plenty of stiles
Suggested map: aqua3 OS Outdoor Leisure 1 Dark Peak
Grid reference: SK 036869
Parking: Sett Valley Trail pay car park, Hayfield

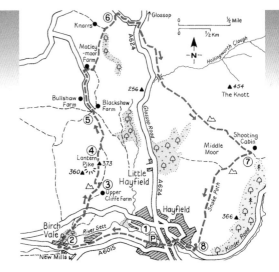

To Lantern Pike and Middle Moor.

1 Follow old railway trackbed ('The Sett Valley Trail') from western end of car park. It heads west down valley, above River Sett to meet **A6015** New Mills road at **Birch Vale**.

2 Turn **R** along road, then **R** again along cobbled track behind cottages of Crescent into woods. Beyond gate, track meets tarred farm lane at hairpin bend. Follow hedge-row course to reach country lane. Staggered to **R** across it, tarred bridleway climbs further up hillside. Take **L** fork near **Upper Cliffe Farm** to gate at edge of National Trust's **Lantern Pike** site.

3 Leave bridleway here; turn **L** along grassy wallside path climbing heather and bracken slopes to rock-fringed ridge. Turn **R**; climb airy crest to **Lantern Pike's** summit (topped by view indicator).

4 Path continues northwards from top of **Lantern Pike**, descending to gate at northern boundary of National Trust estate, where it rejoins track that you

left earlier. Follow this across high pastures to 5-way footpath signpost to west of **Blackshaw Farm**.

5 Turn **L** along walled farm lane past **Bullshaw Farm**, then **R** on track passing **Matley-moor Farm** buildings. Where track swings R leave it for grassy track **L**. Cross stile at its end; continue northwards on grooved path, which joins surfaced track from Knarrs.

6 Turn **R** to **A624**. Cross with care; go over stile at far side. Turn immediately **R**, following faint track with wall on **R**. This crosses **Hollingworth Clough** on footbridge before climbing slopes of **Middle Moor**.

7 By white **shooting cabin**, turn **R** on stony **Snake Path**, which descends through heather, then kissing gate, across fields to reach stony walled track. Follow it down to Kinder Road near centre of **Hayfield**.

8 Turn **R** down lane, then **L** down steps to Church Street. Turn **L** to St Matthew's Church, then **R** down side street ('Sett Valley Trail'). This leads to busy main road. Cross with care back to car park.

Derbyshire

HAYFIELD *The Trespass*

8 miles (12.9km) 5hrs Ascent: 1,450ft (440m)
Paths: Well-defined tracks and paths, quite a few stiles
Suggested map: aqua3 OS Outdoor Leisure 1 Dark Peak
Grid reference: SK 048869 **Parking:** Bowden Bridge pay car park

A dramatic route to Kinder Downfall.

❶ Turn **L** out of car park; walk up lane that winds by **River Kinder**. After 550yds (503m), leave lane at signposted footpath that crosses bridge. Follow path as it traces east bank of river before turning **L** to rejoin road at point just short of **treatment plant** buildings.

❷ Fork **L** through gate, on to cobbled bridleway, climbing above buildings. Continue by reservoir's north shore, turning sharp **L** on **White Brow**. Beyond gate and signpost ('To open country') path climbs beside **William Clough**, where **Snake Path** joins from **L**.

❸ Path crosses and re-crosses stream as it works its way up grass and heather clough. In upper stages narrowing clough stream becomes trickle. Clough divides. Go **L** here; climb to **Ashop Head** to meet **Pennine Way** at crossroads of paths.

❹ Turn **R** along slabbed **Pennine Way** path across moor towards Kinder Scout's northwest edge, then climb gritstone slopes on pitched path to gain summit plateau. Now it's easy walking along edge.

❺ After turning **L** into rocky combe of River Kinder, **Mermaid's Pool** and **Kinder Downfall** (waterfalls) come into view. Descend to cross Kinder's shallow rocky channel about 100yds (91m) back from edge before turning **R** and continuing along edge.

❻ Beyond **Red Brook**, leave plateau by taking **R** fork, which descends southwestwards, contouring round grassy slopes beneath rocky edge.

❼ After passing **Three Knolls** rocks and swinging **L** beneath slopes of **Kinder Low End**, go through gate in fence (grid ref 066867). Take **R** fork in paths along boundary of moor and farmland. Go over stile in wall to **R** by crumbling sheep pens; turn **L** through gateway at nearby field corner. Descend trackless pastured spur, passing through several gates and stiles at field boundaries to pass to **L** of **Tunstead Clough Farm**.

❽ Turn **R** beyond farmhouse to follow winding track that descends into upper Sett Valley. Turn **R** down tarmac lane at bottom, then **L** along Kinder Reservoir road to return to Bowden Bridge.

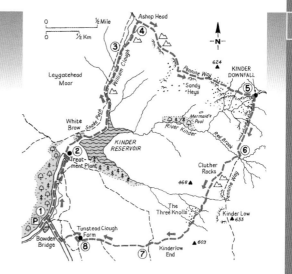

EDALE *Pennine Ways on Kinder Scout*

5 miles (8km) 3hrs Ascent: 1,650ft (500m)
Paths: Rock and peat paths
Suggested map: aqua3 OS Outdoor Leisure 1 Dark Peak
Grid reference: SK 125853
Parking: Edale pay car park

A walk along a section of the Pennine Way as it ascends to the craggy outcrops of the Kinder Plateau.

❶ Turn **R** out of car park and head north into **Edale** village, under railway and past **Old Nags Head** pub. Turn **R** by footpath signpost and follow path across footbridge over **Grinds Brook**.

❷ Leave main **Grindsbrook Clough** path by side of small barn, taking **R** fork that climbs up lower hillslope to stile on edge of open country. Beyond stile, path zig-zags above **Fred Heardman's Plantation** then climbs up nose of **Nab** to skyline rocks. Where path divides, take **R** fork, which leads to summit of **Ringing Roger**.

❸ Follow edge path **L**, rounding cavernous hollow of Grindsbrook past **Nether Tor**. Old Pennine Way route is met on east side, at place marked by large cairn.

❹ Ignoring **L** fork heading for outlier of **Grindslow Knoll**, follow well-worn footpath westwards to head of another deep hollow, clough of **Crowden Brook**.

❺ Cross over **Crowden Brook** and then leave edge to follow narrow level path traversing slopes on your **L** beneath imposing outcrop of **Crowden Tower**. This meets path from **Crowden Tower** before descending steep grassy hillslopes to banks of **Crowden Brook**. Path now follows brook, fording it on several occasions.

❻ Go through gate at edge of open country, then cross over footbridge shaded by tall rowans to change to west bank. From here, path threads through woodland before descending in steps to road at **Upper Booth**. You now need to follow Pennine Way path back on to Edale.

❼ Turn **L** along road and then **L** again into farmyard before crossing stile at top **R** corner. After following track to gateway, bear **L** uphill to reach stile by old barn. Here track traverses fields at foot of **Broadlee Bank** before joining tree-lined track into village. Turn **R** along road back to car park.

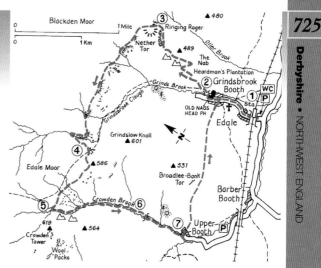

CHINLEY *Edge of the Moors*

5 miles (8km) 3hrs Ascent: 950ft (290m)
Paths: Field paths, quarry and farm tracks, a few stiles
Suggested map: aqua3 OS Outdoor Leisure 1 Dark Peak
Grid reference: SK 041827
Parking: Roadside parking by Chinley War Memorial, Maynestone Road, or village car park

The green hills above Chinley.

❶ From **war memorial**, head northeast up **Maynestone Road**. Leave it for signposted path (grid ref 042828) through narrow ginnel on **L**. Go over stile; climb northwest across fields towards **Cracken Edge**. At cart track turn **R**, then **L** on path passing between 2 hillside farmhouses. Go through gate, past farm on **R** before climbing to lower edge of quarry.

❷ Swing **R** on sketchy path, passing hawthorn tree at base of hillslope. Join quarry track that zig-zags up slope before heading beneath quarry cliffs. Go over stile in fence over track; climb by this fence to clifftop.

❸ Turn **R** along narrow edge path, then **R** again on grassy ramp bridging 2 quarried pits. Now descend **L** to prominent grassy track running beneath brow of hill and past **Whiterakes** cottage.

❹ Turn **R** on track from **Hills Farm** then descend to tarred lane which passes **Peep-O-Day** to A624.

❺ Turn **L** on pavement. After 150yds (137m) cart track (**R**) takes your route past quarry crater. Turn **R** at T-junction of tracks to traverse lower slopes of **Mount Famine** to reach col beneath **South Head** peak.

❻ To detour to **South Head** follow obvious route which leaves track to climb to summit. Back at col, go through gate by more easterly of 2 access notices. Go over stile by pole and descend southwestwards to walled track.

❼ Follow this down to crossroads of routes north of **Andrews Farm**. Keep ahead into muddy field. Path soon develops into track and joins descending cart track from **Andrews Farm**.

❽ On reaching A624 turn **R** for 50yds (46m) then cross to signposted footpath, which cuts diagonally to **R** corner of 1st field before following wall towards **Otter Brook**. As old field boundary comes in from **R**, path turns half-**L** to cross brook on slabbed bridge.

❾ Muddy path climbs out through scrubby woodland to **Maynestone Road**. Turn **L**; follow it to **Chinley**.

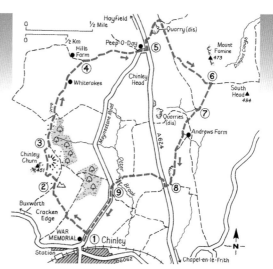

Derbyshire

727 ALPORT CASTLES *In the Clouds*

8 miles (12.9km) 5hrs 30min **Ascent:** 2,000ft (610m)
Paths: Well-defined paths and tracks in forests and on moorland
Suggested map: aqua3 OS Outdoor Leisure 1 Dark Peak
Grid reference: SK 173893 **Parking:** Fairholmes pay car park

Up to the rocky pinnacles of Alport Castles.

① Leave car park for road, then follow permissive forestry track ('Lockerbrook'). Track climbs through **Hagg Side** Wood, crossing bridge over water leat before steepening on higher slopes. Near top, waymarked path swings R, then L to leave forest.

② Obvious footpath, guided by stone wall, traverses fields of **Lockerbrook Heights**. Go L at public footpath signpost; follow track past **Lockerbrook Farm**.

③ At ridgetop by **Woodcock Coppice**, turn R along permissive path climbing to moor at **Bellhag Tor**.

④ Continue over **Rowlee Pasture** and along ridgetop path climbing to **Alport Castles**.

⑤ Descend on good path at southern end of Castles. Initially path follows old wall. On lower slopes it traces perimeter of **Castles Wood**.

⑥ Cross footbridge over **River Alport**, where path turns R to traverse riverside meadows. At **Alport Castles Farm**, follow track swinging round to nearby **Alport Farm** before heading southwards down valley.

⑦ Where track veers R for **Hayridge Farm**, leave it for signposted footpath descending to southeast towards edge of small riverside wood. Path stays above riverbanks to exit on busy **A57 Snake Road**. Across road follow stony track to **River Ashop** then cross footbridge to R of ford. Rejoin track, which skirts hill slopes beneath **Upper Ashop Farm** before climbing steadily across rough grassy slopes of **Blackley Hey**. Ignore L fork descending to **Rowlee Bridge**, but continue on same track as far as path intersection to east of **Crookstone Barn**.

⑧ Turn L here on rutted track along top edge of pine woods before entering them. Leave track just beyond R-H bend; follow narrow path to **Haggwater Bridge**.

⑨ Beyond bridge, path climbs up again to **A57 Snake Road**. Cross road; join track opposite. It climbs out of Woodlands Valley; zig-zags across upper slopes at edge of **Woodcock Coppice** before skirting **Hagg Side** conifer plantations. Here, retrace outward route to car park.

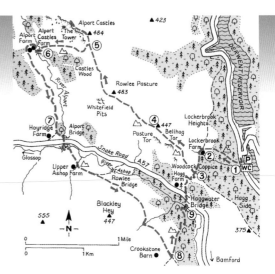

728 GOYT VALLEY *Errwood Reservoir*

3½ miles (5.7km) 2hrs 30min **Ascent:** 984ft (300m)
Paths: Good paths and tracks, a few stiles
Suggested map: aqua3 OS Outdoor Leisure 24 White Peak
Grid reference: SK 012748
Parking: Errwood car park

Around Errwood Hall.

① Take path signposted to **Stakeside** and the Cat and Fiddle pub, which begins from roadside just south of car park. Climb through copse of trees, go straight across cart track, then climb grassy spur separating **Shooter's Clough** and **Goyt Valley**.

② Go through gate in wall that runs along spur; follow grassy path that zig-zags through pleasant woodland of **Shooter's Clough** before fording stream. Path heads north (R), threading through rhododendron bushes before continuing across fields to signposted junction of footpaths.

③ Turn R here on good path skirting near side of wooded knoll, then fork L, along path ('To Errwood Hall'). Path continues past ruins, and rounds other side of knoll before descending steps to ford stream.

④ Climb steps up far bank to reach another footpath signpost. Turn L along path ('Pym Chair'). This gradually swings north on hillsides beneath **Foxlow Edge**. There is short detour down and L to see **Spanish Shrine** – built in memory of Dolores de Bergrin, a governess of the Grimshawes family.

⑤ Just before reaching road, path reaches more open moorland. Turn R along waymarked path ('2a') that climbs to top of **Foxlow Edge**. On reaching old quarry workings near top, path is joined by tumbledown drystone wall. Keep to L of wall, except for one short stretch where path goes the other side to avoid crosswalls. Ignore waymark pointing into woods on R. That route isn't often used and is too rough. Instead, stay with ridge route. Wall (R) and fence (L) soon confine path as it descends to woods.

⑥ At fence corner, by woodland's edge, path becomes faint groove on grass slope. Follow it down for 100yds (91m) to where it meets narrow dirt path. Turn L along this, back into woodland, from where path descends to roadside at **Shooter's Clough Bridge** just 100yds (91m) north of car park.

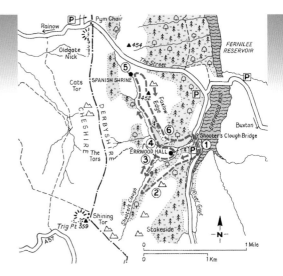

729 COMBS RESERVOIR *A Quiet Corner*

3 miles (4.8km) 2hrs 30min **Ascent:** 164ft (50m)
Paths: Can be muddy, quite a few stiles
Suggested map: aqua3 OS Outdoor Leisure 24 White Peak
Grid reference: SK 033797 **Parking:** Combs reservoir car park

Around Combs Reservoir.

① Follow path from dam along reservoir's western shore, ignoring 1st footbridge over **Meveril Brook**.

② As reservoir narrows, path traverses small fields, then comes to another footbridge over brook. This time cross it and head south across another field. Beyond foot tunnel under Buxton line railway, path reaches narrow hedge-lined country lane. Turn L along lane into **Combs** village.

③ Past **The Beehive** pub in village centre, take lane straight ahead, then L fork ('Dove Holes'). This climbs out of village towards **Combs Edge**.

④ Take 2nd footpath on L, which begins at muddy clearing just beyond Millway Cottage. Go through stile; climb on partially slabbed path through narrow grassy enclosure. After 200yds (183m) path emerges on pastured slope overlooking huge comb of **Pygreave Brook**. Climb pathless spur; go through gateways in next 2 boundary walls before following wall on R. Ignore gate in this wall – path to **Bank Hall Farm** –

stay with narrow path raking across rough grassy hill slopes with railway line and reservoir below L.

⑤ Path comes down to rutted vehicle track running alongside railway. This joins narrow lane just short of **Lodge** (grid ref 053794). Turn L to go under railway and north to **Down Lea Farm**.

⑥ Turn L through kissing gate 200yds (183m) beyond farmhouse. Signposted path follows overgrown hedge towards **Marsh Hall Farm**. Fields are very boggy on final approaches. On reaching farm turn R over stile; follow track heading northwest.

⑦ After 200yds (183m) turn L on field path that heads west to stile at edge of **Chapel-en-le-Frith golf course**. Waymarking arrows show way across fairway. Stile marking exit from golf course is 300yds (274m) short of clubhouse. Cross field to **B5470**.

⑧ Turn L along road (pavement on far side); follow it past **Hanging Gate** pub at **Cockyard**. After passing sailing club entrance, turn L across reservoir's dam and back to car park.

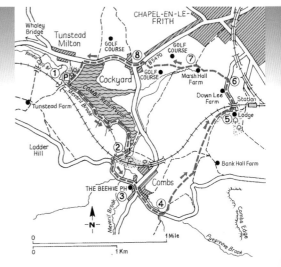

Derbyshire

CASTLETON CASTLES AND CAVERNS

5 miles (8km) 3hrs Ascent: 820ft (250m)
Paths: Path below Blue John Mines can be tricky in wintry conditions, a few stiles
Suggested map: aqua3 OS Outdoor Leisure 1 Dark Peak
Grid reference: SK 149829 **Parking:** Main Castleton pay car park

Where the White and the Dark peaks collide.

1 From car park, turn **L** down main street then has along Castle Street, passing church and youth hostel.

2 On reaching Market Place, turn **L** to Bar Gate, where signpost points to **Cavedale**. Through gate, path enters limestone gorge with ruined keep of **Peveril Castle** perched on cliffs to R.

3 As you gain height, gorge shallows. Go over stile in dry-stone wall on R; follow well-defined track across high pastureland. It passes through gate in another wall before being joined by path that has descended grassy hillside on R. Track divides soon after junction. Take **L** fork, which climbs uphill, slightly away from wall on R, to top corner of field. Go through gate; follow short stretch of walled track to crossroads of routes near old **Hazard Mine**.

4 Turn **R** beyond gate, along stony walled lane, which swings **R** to reach B6061 near **Oxlow House farm**. Take path across road to disused quarry on **Windy Knoll**.

5 At quarry turn **R** on footpath to B road. After turning **L** to junction, take old **Mam Tor** Road (ahead).

6 After 400yds (366m) turn **R** on tarmac approach road to **Blue John Cavern**, then **L** by ticket office. Cross stile in fence; trace path as it crosses several fields. Beyond stile path arcs to **R**, traversing, now precipitous, grassy hill slopes. It passes **Treak Cliff Cavern** ticket office. Go **L** down concrete steps by ticket office, then **R** on concrete path with handrails.

7 Just before reaching road, cross step-stile on **R**; follow narrow cross-field path by collapsed wall. On approach to **Speedwell Cavern** path becomes indistinct, but there is obvious stile straight ahead, which leads on to Winnats road.

8 Path on far side of road takes route through National Trust's Longcliff Estate. It roughly follows line of wall and veers **L** beneath hill slopes of **Cow Low** to reach **Goosehill Hall**. Here, follow Goosehill (lane), back into **Castleton**. Beyond Goosehill Bridge, turn **L** down surfaced streamside path back to car park.

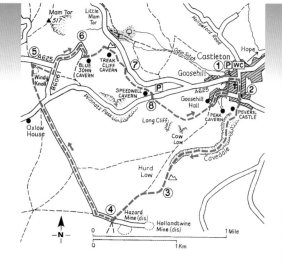

HOPE MARCHING ROADS

8¾ miles (14km) 5hrs Ascent: 1,050ft (320m)
Paths: Paths can be slippery after rain, quite a few stiles
Suggested map: aqua3 OS Outdoor Leisure 1 Dark Peak
Grid reference: SK 149829
Parking: Main Castleton pay car park

Over Win Hill to the Roman Fort at Navio.

1 Turn **L** out of car park along main street. At far end of village turn **R** on walled lane; continue along well-defined path accompanying Peakshole Water. Cross railway with care; continue along path to its end at Pindale Road.

2 Turn **L**, then **R** at next junction. After about 100yds (91m), cross stile by gate; follow path running roughly parallel to lane at first, then River Noe to reach **Roman fort**. Beyond earthworks cross stile in fence; bear half **R** across field to reach B6409 at **Brough**.

3 Turn **L** through village; cross footbridge. Go **L** over stile; head northwest to A625. Turn **L** along road for 200yds (183m) to small gate, just beyond cottage. Follow hedge and dyke on R to pass to R of houses.

4 Turn **L** towards railway station; go **R** along narrow path which leads to footbridge over line. Cross bridge; turn **R** at its far end, then **L** over stile to cross more fields, keeping fence on R.

5 At Aston turn **L**, then almost immediately turn **R** along narrow, surfaced lane ('To Win Hill').

6 Beyond **Edge Farm**, unsurfaced track on **L** leads along top edge of woods to path junction above **Twitchill Farm**. Now, climb **R** on well-used path to summit.

7 From summit retrace route back to junction above **Twitchill Farm** but descend **L** past farm, to railway.

8 Turn **L** under tunnel, where lane doubles back **L** and winds its way to **Kilhill Bridge**, then **Edale Road**. Turn **R**, pass under railway bridge; turn **L** on field path.

9 By cottage turn **R** on path climbing towards **Lose Hill**. Take **L** fork at signposted junction of paths to follow waymarked route to **Spring House Farm**.

10 Beyond farmhouse, turn **R** on stony track heading west behind **Losehill Hall**. Where lane swings **L**, leave it; follow cross-field path, which joins unsurfaced lane. After passing outdoor activity centre, turn **L** along Hollowford Road, back into **Castleton**.

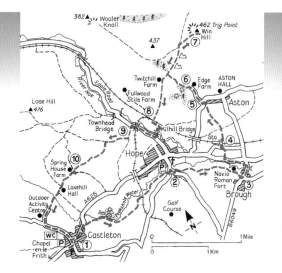

HATHERSAGE ON THE EDGE AT STANAGE

9 miles (14.5km) 5hrs 30min Ascent: 1,150ft (350m)
Paths: Well-defined paths and tracks, a few stiles
Suggested map: aqua3 OS Outdoor Leisure 1 Dark Peak
Grid reference: SK 232814 **Parking:** Hathersage car park

Skirting Sheffield's moorland edge.

1 From car park, head up Oddfellows Road to Main Road. Continue up **Baulk Lane**, which begins on opposite side of road by **Hathersage Inn**. Lane climbs steadily north, passing cricket ground. Beyond buildings it becomes unsurfaced track.

2 Just short of **Cowclose Farm** take signposted **L** fork, which passes to R of **Brookfield Manor** to reach country lane. Turn **R**, then **L** along drive to **North Lees Hall**. After rounding hall, turn **R**, climbing steps that cut corner to another track. This crosses hillside pastures before continuing through woodland.

3 Stepped path on **L** makes short cut to roadside toilets and mountain rescue post. Turn **L** along road for short distance; turn **R** on grassy path heading for rocks of **Stanage Edge**. After 200yds (183m), join path from nearby car park. Paved path now climbs through **Stanage Plantation** then arcs **L** to cliff top.

4 Follow firm edge path northwestwards (**R**) to see summit of **High Neb** and **Crow Chin**.

5 At Crow Chin, where edge veers north, descend to lower path that doubles back beneath cliffs. This eventually joins track from R, which returns route to top of cliffs. Continue walking southeast along edge to bouldery east summit (marked on OS maps by spot height of 457m), which is capped by trig point.

6 Stay on track to road at **Upper Burbage Bridge**. Proceed **L** for 150yds (137m), to higher of 2 paths, which head south to summit of **Higger Tor**.

7 From rocky top, double back (roughly north of north west) to **Fiddler's Elbow** road. Heading slightly uphill, take path on **L**. This descends **Callow Bank** to walled track leading to **Dale Bottom** road. Follow road for 300yds (274m) to track on **R** that descends hill slopes to **Toothill Farm**. Turn **L** by farmhouse on drive that soon joins tarred lane taking route to **Hathersage's** spired **church** and **Roman fort**.

8 Turn **R** down School Lane to reach Main Road, which leads to centre of **Hathersage**. Go **L** down Oddfellows Road to reach car park.

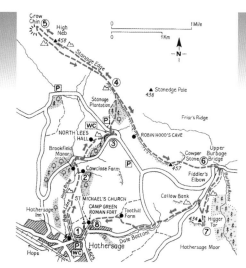

Derbyshire

---

733 AXE EDGE *FROM DARK TO WHITE*

7½ miles (12km) 4hrs 30min **Ascent:** 980ft (300m)
Paths: Good paths except between Hollinsclough and Brand End, can be slippery after rain, lots of stiles
Suggested map: aqua3 OS Outdoor Leisure 24 White Peak
Grid reference: SK 034697 **Parking:** Axe Edge car park

From limestone to gritstone.

❶ From car park cross main road; descend lane opposite. At 1st R-H bend turn **L** to take **L** of 2 farm tracks, descending to cross Cistern's Clough bridge before raking across to **Fairthorn Farm**. Past house swing **L** up to road at Thirkelow Rocks.

❷ Turn **R** along road for 200yds (183m), then take 2nd track on **R**, heading south past **Thirkelow Farm**. Take **R** fork into clough.

❸ Where track ends, veer slightly **R** to waymarks highlighting bridge; continue towards **Booth Farm**.

❹ Keep to **L** of farm; go over steps in wall ahead. After crossing small field, turn **L** along farm road; fork **R** for **Stoop Farm**. Turn **L** along waymarked field path, bypassing farmhouse and climbing to footpath intersection at top wall. Take path ('**Chrome Hill**'). It follows wall before descending **R** to foot of hill.

❺ Cross stile; follow wallside path that eventually climbs **L** to crest, continues over summit then descends to lane beneath **Parkhouse Hill**.

❻ Turn **R** along lane, then **R** again to follow farm track. Take **L** fork to reach surfaced road, just short of **Hollinsclough**. Walk through village; cross stile on **R** to follow field path. Take higher **L** fork traversing **Hollinsclough Rake**.

❼ On reaching green zig-zag track at **Moor Side**, descend **R** to pass ruin and continue up narrow valley. Go across stream, then over stile to reach old packhorse bridge. Across bridge take stony track climbing towards farm buildings at **Leycote**. Beyond sharp R-H bend go **L** through gate; follow narrow path heading northwest into wooded clough.

❽ Clough divides below **Howe Green**. Follow path across slab bridge; ascend through bracken towards **Brand End**. Path becomes more obvious track, passing Brand End Cottage before eventually descending to ruins of **Brand End Farm**.

❾ Turn **L** up bank by wall here, passing to **L** of another farm. Turn **L** along farm track to **Brand Top**. Here, road leads you to **Axe Edge** and car park.

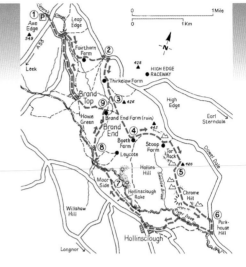

---

734 TIDESWELL *GHOSTS OF MILLER'S DALE*

6 miles (9.7km) 4hrs **Ascent:** 690ft (210m)
Paths: Well-defined paths and tracks, path in Water-cum-Jolly Dale liable to flooding, quite a few stiles
Suggested map: aqua3 OS Outdoor Leisure 24 White Peak
Grid reference: SK 154743 **Parking:** Tideswell Dale pay car park

Enjoying the rural serenity of Miller's Dale.

❶ Follow path southwards (beside toilet block) into **Tideswell Dale**, taking R-H fork to cross bridge.

❷ On entering **Miller's Dale**, go **L** on tarmac lane to **Litton Mill**. Go through gateposts on to concessionary path through mill yard. Beyond mill, path follows River Wye, as it meanders through tight, steep-sided dale.

❸ River widens in **Water-cum-Jolly Dale**; path, liable to flooding here, traces wall of limestone cliffs before reaching **Cressbrook**. Don't cross bridge on R, but turn **L** to pass in front of **Cressbrook Mill** and out to road.

❹ Turn **L** along road then take **R** fork which climbs steadily into **Cressbrook Dale**. Where road doubles back uphill, leave it for track going straight ahead into woods. Track degenerates into narrow path that emerges in clearing high above stream. Follow it downhill to footbridge over stream; take **R** fork path, which climbs high up valley side to stile in top wall.

❺ Do not cross stile, but take downhill path to dale bottom, where there is junction of paths. Take path that recrosses stream on stepping stones, and climbs into Tansley Dale.

❻ Path turns **R** at top of dale, follows tumbledown wall before crossing it on step stile. Head for wall corner in next field, then veer **R** through narrow enclosure to reach walled track just south of **Litton**.

❼ Turn **L** along track, which comes out on to country lane at crown of sharp bend. Keep ahead on lane but leave it at next bend for well-defined cross-field path to Bottomhill. Across road, further field path descends to lane at **Dale House Farm**. Turn **L** along this lane, then **R** on narrow lane marked unsuitable for motor traffic. Follow road into **Tideswell**.

❽ Head south down main street, then **R** on to Gordon Road, which heads south.

❾ Where this ends, continue down track ahead, which runs parallel with main road. Watch for stile on **L**, which gives access to path, down to road into **Tideswell Dale**. Turn **R** along road to reach car park.

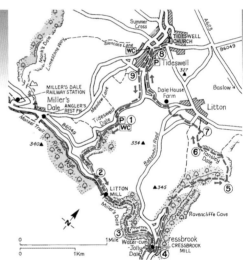

---

735 CHESTERFIELD *LINACRE'S PEACEFUL RETREAT*

5 miles (8km) 3hrs **Ascent:** 820ft (250m)
Paths: Generally good paths and farm lanes. Field paths can be muddy at times of high rainfall
Suggested map: aqua3 OS Outdoor Leisure 24 White Peak
Grid reference: SK 336727
Parking: Linacre Woods car park

A walk around three reservoirs.

❶ From bottom of lowest car park go down steps into woods. After about 100yds (91m) turn **R** along waymarked bridleway heading westwards, high above lower reservoir. Ignore path going off to L, which goes to dam of middle reservoir, but continue on wide bridleway along north shore of middle reservoir.

❷ Take **R** fork on footpath raking up to top end of woods, high above upper reservoir's dam. Path continues westwards, dipping to one of reservoir's inlets. Cross bridge; follow well-defined concessionary footpath along shoreline.

❸ At end of reservoir, ignore **L** turn over **Birley Brook**, but head west on waymarked footpath. Shortly exit wood via stile and enter first scrub woodland then fields with woods to L of wall and gorse bushes to R.

❹ Cross stone slab across brook (grid ref 317727), then stile beyond it. Muddy path now climbs through more woods before emerging in fields north of Wigley

Hall Farm. It passes to **R** of farm to tarmac lane in **Wigley**. Follow lane to crossroads.

❺ Turn **L** towards **Old Brampton**. Just beyond **Royal Oak** pub turn **R** down tarmac bridleway, **Bagthorpe Lane**, following it past **Bagthorpe Farm**. Lane, now unsurfaced, descends into valley of **River Hipper**, passing through farmyard of **Frith Hall**, down to river bridge. Winding surfaced track climbs to **Westwick Lane**, where you should turn **L**.

❻ Just before **Broomhall Farm**, descend **L** on another track down to river, then up other side of valley into **Old Brampton**.

❼ Turn **L** on lane, passing **George and Dragon** pub and church. Turn **R** by telephone box. Track descends to top edge of **Linacre Wood**, and swings **R**.

❽ At junction of paths turn **L** through gate before descending to dam. At far side of dam turn **L** on metalled lane, passing toilets and ranger's office; climb back to car park.

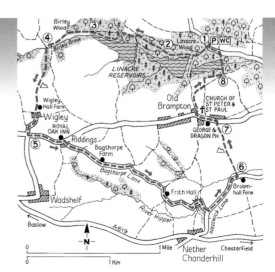

Derbyshire

ASHFORD-IN-THE-WATER *THE VALLEY OF THE GODS*

5½ miles (9km) 3hrs 30min **Ascent:** 656ft (200m)
Paths: Well-defined paths and tracks throughout, lots of stiles
Suggested map: aqua3 OS Outdoor Leisure 24 White Peak
Grid reference: SK 194696
Parking: Ashford-in-the-Water car park

Through lovely Monsal Dale.

1 From car park, turn **R** up Court Lane and **R** again along Vicarage Lane. Footpath on **L** ('To Monsal Dale') doubles back **L** then swings sharp **R** to proceed along ginnel behind houses. Beyond stile path enters field.

2 Head for stile in top **L** corner then veer slightly **R** to locate stile leading on to **Pennyunk Lane**. Walled stony track winds among high pastures. At its end, footpath signpost directs you **L** along field edge. In 400yds (366m) it joins track, heading north towards rim of **Monsal Dale**. Path runs along top edge of deep wooded dale to reach **Monsal Head** car park.

3 Take path marked **Monsal Trail** here – this way you get to walk across **viaduct**. On other side go through gate on **L**. Ignore path climbing west up hillside, but descend southwest on grassy path raking through scrub woods down into valley. This shouldn't be confused with steep eroded path plummeting straight down to foot of viaduct.

4 Now walk down valley. Right of way is well away from river at first but most walkers trace riverbank to emerge at **Lees Bottom** and roadside stile.

5 Cross A6 with care; go through White Lodge car park on other side to stile, where path back to Ashford begins. Paths are numbered here – this route uses number 3. Beyond another stile there's a path junction. Take **L** fork, which veers **L** across rough fields. Ignore next path into **Deepdale** and swing **L** (south) into **Great Shacklow Wood**.

6 Climb through trees and stony ground to footpath sign. Turn **L** here, following path ('Ashford and Sheldon'). After 200yds (183m) Sheldon path climbs **R**, but keep ahead, following ledge path along steep wooded slopes. Eventually path comes down to river, before joining minor road at bottom of **Kirkdale**.

7 Turn **L** along road to A6; turn **R** towards Ashford. Leave road to cross **Sheepwash Bridge**. Turn **R** on Church Street, then **L** on Court Lane to car park.

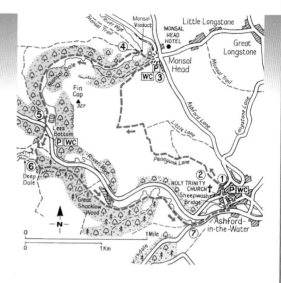

WOLFSCOTE DALE *A RAILWAY TRAIL*

7½ miles (12.1km) 5hrs **Ascent:** 557ft (170m)
Paths: Generally well-defined paths, limestone dale sides can be slippery after rain, quite a few stiles
Suggested map: aqua3 OS Outdoor Leisure 24 White Peak
Grid reference: SK 156549
Parking: Tissington Trail pay car park (by Stonepit Plantation)

Wind through the heart of upland limestone country.

1 From car park by **Stonepit Plantation**, cross busy A515 road and follow Milldale road immediately opposite. After short way you are offered parallel footpath, keeping you safe from traffic.

2 On reaching bottom of dale by **Lode Mill**, turn **R** along footpath, tracing river's east bank through winding, partially wooded valley.

3 Ignore footpath on R at **Coldeaton Bridge**, but instead stay with **Wolfscote Dale** beneath thickly wooded slopes on R. Beyond stile, woods cease and dale becomes bare and rock-fringed, with cave on R and bold pinnacles of **Peaseland Rocks** ahead. Here valley sides open out into dry valley of **Biggin Dale**, where this route goes next.

4 Unsignposted path into **Biggin Dale** begins beyond stile in cross-wall and climbs by that wall. It continues through scrub woodland and beneath limestone screes. Beyond gate you enter nature reserve.

5 There's another gate at far end of nature reserve. Beyond it, dale curves **L**, then **R**, before dividing again beneath hill pastures of **Biggin Grange**. We divert **L** here, over stile to follow footpath ('Hartington'). On other side of wall there is concrete dewpond.

6 After 200yds (183m) there's another junction of paths. This time ignore path ('Hartington') and keep walking ahead, following path to **Biggin**. It stays with valley round to **R**, passing small sewage works (on **L**) before climbing out of dale to reach road at **Dale End**.

7 Turn **R** along road for few paces then **L**, following road past **Waterloo Inn** and through **Biggin** village.

8 Turn **R** again 500yds (457m) from village centre on short path that climbs to **Tissington Trail** bridleway. Follow old railway trackbed southwards across pastures of **Biggin** and Alport moors. After 2 miles (3.2km) you will reach car park.

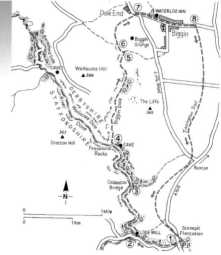

CROMFORD *THE BLACK ROCKS*

5 miles (8km) 3hrs **Ascent:** 720ft (220m)
Paths: Well-graded – canal towpaths, lanes, forest paths and a railway trackbed, quite a few stiles
Suggested map: aqua3 OS Outdoor Leisure 24 White Peak
Grid reference: SK 300571
Parking: Cromford Wharf pay car park

Walking through a valley, which changed forever in the Industrial Revolution.

1 Turn **L** out of car park on to Mill Road. Cross A6 to Market Place. Turn **R** down Scarthin, passing Boat Inn and old millpond before doubling back **L** along Water Lane to Cromford Hill.

2 Turn **R**, past shops and Bell Inn, then turn **L** up Bedehouse Lane, which turns into narrow tarmac tunnel after rounding some almshouses (otherwise known as bedehouses).

3 At top of lane by street of 70s housing, signpost for Black Rocks points uphill. Path continues its climb southwards to meet lane. Turn **L** along winding lane, which soon divides. Take **R** fork, limestone track leads to stone-built house with woods behind. On reaching house, turn **R** through gate, and follow top field edge.

4 After climbing up steps, climb **L** through woods of Dimons Dale up to **Black Rocks** car park and picnic site. This track is former trackbed of Cromford and

High Peak Railway. Immediately opposite is there-and-back waymarked detour to rocks.

5 Returning to car park, turn **R** along **High Peak Trail**, which traverses hillside high above Cromford.

6 After about ¾ mile (1.2km) watch out for path on **R** leaving Trail for **Intake Lane**. At lane, turn **R** and follow it to sharp L-H bend. Here, keep ahead following path heading southeast along top edge of some woodland. (Note: neither path nor wood is shown on current OS Outdoor Leisure map.)

7 On nearing **Birchwood Farm**, watch out for 2 paths coming up from **L**. Take path descending more directly downhill (northwest, then north). At bottom of woods path swings **L** across fields, coming out to A6 road by **Oak Farm**.

8 Cross road and follow little ginnel opposite, over Matlock railway and **Cromford Canal**. Go past High **Peak Junction** information centre, and then turn **L** along canal towpath. Follow this back to car park.

Derbyshire

Derbyshire • NORTH-WEST ENGLAND

---

739 MATLOCK BATH *SCALING THE HEIGHTS*

8 miles (12.9km) 5hrs Ascent: 1,200ft (365m)
Paths: Narrow woodland paths, field paths and unsurfaced lanes, lots of stiles
Suggested map: aqua3 OS Outdoor Leisure 24 White Peak
Grid reference: SK 297595 **Parking:** Pay car park at Artists Corner

A steady climb to a Peakland landscape.

❶ Cross A6 then take St John's Road up slopes opposite. It passes under **St John's Chapel** to reach gates of **Cliffe House**. Take path on **R** ('To the Heights of Abraham'). Path climbs steeply through woods before veering **L** across fields above **Masson Farm**.

❷ By farmhouse, waymarked path rakes up to gateway with **Victoria Prospect Tower** ahead. Turn **R** beyond gateway; climb to stile at top of field. Keep on path through hawthorn thickets before passing entrance to **Heights of Abraham** complex.

❸ Ignore engineered path; continue uphill along perimeter of complex, then turn **L**, over stile. After crossing wide track narrow path re-enters woodland.

❹ At far side of woods, turn **R** on green lane, passing close to **Ember Farm**. Lane winds down pastured hillslopes into **Bonsall** village.

❺ Turn **L** by church along lane that becomes unsurfaced beyond **Town Head Farm**. Lane comes to abrupt end by high fences of quarry. Turn **L** here;

follow wide track around quarry perimeters.

❻ Track bends **R** and ends at large gate. Turn **L** on narrow path through woodland above Via Gellia (in valley below). Take **L** fork after about 200yds (183m).

❼ Turn **L** at next junction, following waymarked path, Derwent Valley Walks ('DVW'). This climbs further up wooded bank. It then turns **L**, tracing mossy wall on **R**. It rakes across wooded hillside, passes large complex of buildings then climbs away past cave entrances to lane at **Upperwood**. Ignore next DVW sign and continue along lane between cottages, and past entrance to **Heights of Abraham** showcave.

❽ Road, now surfaced, descends towards **Matlock Bath**. Just beyond sharp corner, leave it for stepped path through woods. Climb steps to high wooden footbridge. Cross and continue on woodland path. You'll pass under **Heights of Abraham** cable cars before joining track that comes in from **L**.

❾ This joins St John's Lane and outward route at **Cliffe House**.

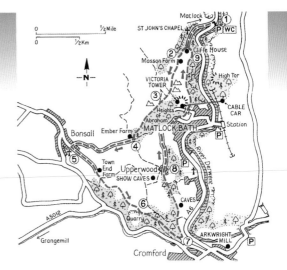

---

740 TISSINGTON *A TRAIL OF TWO VILLAGES*

4¼ miles (7km) 2hrs 30min Ascent: 525ft (160m)
Paths: Field paths, lanes and an old railway trackbed, lots of stiles
Suggested map: aqua3 OS Outdoor Leisure 24 White Peak
Grid reference: SK 177522
Parking: The Tissington Trail pay car and coach park

Along a famous trackbed, the Tissington Trail, between two very different villages – Parwich and Tissington.

❶ From car park follow trackbed of northeast bound **Tissington Trail**. After 800yds (732m) leave trail and turn **R**, over bridge and along cart track.

❷ Just past 1st bend descend on waymarked but trackless path into valley of **Bletch Brook**, going through several stiles at field boundaries and across footbridge spanning brook itself. More definite path establishes itself on climb out of valley. It reaches top of pastured spur, well to **R** of small cottage.

❸ In next high field, path follows hedge on **L** to stile in field corner. It then descends to footpath signpost, which points short way across last field to western edge of village.

❹ To explore village of Parwich turn **R**, otherwise turn **L** down lane to Brook Close Farm. A signposted footpath on your **L** follows tractor tracks climbing to

ruined stone barn, beyond which lies stile into next field. Path now heads southwestwards to top **R-H** corner of field then follows muddy tree-lined track for few paces.

❺ On entering next field turn **L**. This first follows hedge on **L**, then descends to recross **Bletch Brook** footbridge. It climbs up middle of next long field before zig-zagging up steep upper slopes to reach bridge over **Tissington Trail**. Go down to trail and follow it northwestwards through Crakelow cutting.

❻ After 500yds (457m) turn **L**, following Tissington footpath over stile to **R-H** corner of field. Now follow wall on **R** to Rakes Lane at edge of Tissington.

❼ Maintain your direction along lane to reach **Chapel Lane**. You can walk either way around village square. Hall and church are straight ahead, while Methodist **chapel** and **Coffin Well** are on Chapel Lane to **L**. Car park lies to southeast of square; take **L** turn just beyond **Coffin Well**.

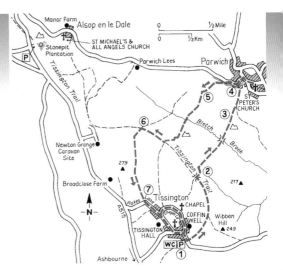

---

741 CARSINGTON RESERVOIR *SKELETONS FROM THE PAST*

5½ miles (8.8km) 3hrs 30min Ascent: 1,148ft (350m)
Paths: Hill paths, some hard to follow and railway trackbed, numerous stiles
Suggested map: aqua3 OS Outdoor Leisure 24 White Peak
Grid reference: SK 249528
Parking: Sheepwash pay car park by Carsington Reservoir

Following the lead miners' tracks.

❶ Take signposted path northwards towards **Carsington**. It winds through scrub woods and rounds finger of lake before reaching B5035. Path continues on other side, meeting lane by **Wash Farm**; follow it to enter village by Miners Arms pub.

❷ Turn **L** on lane to reach Hopton road. Where road turns **L** keep ahead along lane, passing cottages. Beyond gate lane becomes fine green track beneath limestone-studded slopes of **Carsington Pasture**.

❸ Where track swings **L**, leave it for path climbing slopes to west. At top, aim **R** of copse; go through gap in broken wall before descending into little valley.

❹ Go over 2 stiles to cross country lane, then follow miners' track for 200yds (183m) towards old mine workings. Here footpath sign directs you around limestone outcrops before arcing **R** towards **Brassington**. Turn **L** at footpath signpost; follow waymarked route across fields into village.

❺ Turn **L**, then **R** up Miners Hill. Go **R** up Jasper Lane, **L** up Red Lion Hill, and **L** along Hillside Lane. After 200yds (183m) leave lane for footpath on **R**, which climbs past outcrops. Faint waymarked path gradually veers **R**, and passes head of green lane.

❻ Climb **R** to waymarking post. Through next 3 fields path climbs parallel to, and to **R** of, line of electricity pylons. In 4th field bear half **R** above outcrops; go through top gate. Aim for buildings of **Longcliffe Dale Farm**. Cross next stile, turn **L** up road, passing farm. Footpath on **R** cuts corner to High Peak Trail, passing electricity sub station and Peak Quarry Farm.

❼ Turn **R** along trackbed of **High Peak Trail** passing **Harborough Rocks**.

❽ Go **R** at footpath ('Carsington'). Go down field to cross **Manystones Lane**. Follow wall over **Carsington Pasture**; descend by woods to gate by cottage.

❾ Turn **L** down little ginnel leading to road and **L** again to retrace earlier route to Sheepwash car park.

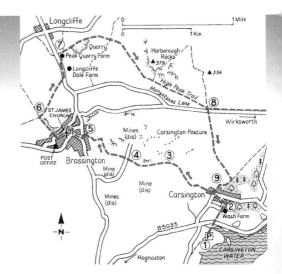

CRICH *In Search of Cardale*

7½ miles (12.1km) 5hrs **Ascent:** 721ft (220m)
Paths: Woodland and field paths and canal tow path, many stiles
Suggested map: aqua3 OS Outdoor Leisure 24 White Peak
Grid reference: SK 349517 **Parking:** Ambergate, car park by station

On the old hunting grounds of Crich Chase.
❶ Leave car park at **Ambergate Station**. Walk down zig-zag lane; turn **R** on busy **A6**. Turn **R** down Chase Lane and under railway bridge to **Cromford Canal**. Follow tow path northwards to next bridge.
❷ Cross bridge; follow footpath climbing into woodland of **Crich Chase**. In upper reaches of wood, waymarked path swings **L**; follow it through clearings. Then follow wall (**R**) at top edge of wood. Turn **R** over stile; cross 2 fields to reach Chadwick Nick Road.
❸ Turn **R** along road. After 300yds (274m) path on **L** begins with steps and stile, and continues climb northwards across numerous fields with stiles and gates – and by rock outcrops of Tors.
❹ Path becomes enclosed ginnel, which emerges on Sandy Lane. Follow this to Market Square; turn **L**, then **R** along Coasthill. Coasthill leads to unsurfaced lane. Where lane ends, follow path in same direction across fields to join another lane by houses. Follow this to Carr Lane; turn **R** passing entrance to **National Tramway Museum**.
❺ Continue along road to sharp R-H bend; turn **L** along approach road to **Crich Stand**, topped by **Sherwood Foresters Monument**. Pay small fee to visit viewing platform on monument otherwise, continue along right of way on **R**. Footpath ('Wakebridge and Plaistow') veers half **R** via shrubs and bramble, before circumnavigating **Cliff Quarry**.
❻ Path then crosses museum's tram track near its terminus, before winding down hillside through scrub woodland. It joins wide track descending past Wakebridge and Cliff farms before coming to road.
❼ Turn **R** along road for few paces; turn **L** on footpath ('To the Cromford Canal'). This descends across fields before swinging **R** to enter wood. Well-defined path passes beneath rock faces, and crosses minor road before reaching canal at **Whatstandwell**.
❽ Turn **L**; follow tow path for 2 miles (3.2km) through shade of tree boughs. At Chase Bridge you meet outward route; retrace your steps to car park.

DOVEDALE *Ivory Spires and Wooded Splendour*

5 miles (8km) 3hrs 30min **Ascent:** 557ft (170m)
Paths: Good paths, field paths and lanes, a few stiles
Suggested map: aqua3 OS Outdoor Leisure 24 White Peak
Grid reference: SK 146509 **Parking:** Dovedale car park, near Thorpe

Through the Peak's most famous dale.
❶ Turn **R** out of car park and follow road along west bank of Dove. Cross footbridge to opposite bank; turn **L** along footpath. It twists and turns through narrow dale, between **Bunster Hill** and **Thorpe Cloud**.
❷ Follow path as it climbs some steps up through woods on to justifiably famous rocky outcrop of **Lover's Leap**, then descends past magnificent **Tissington Spires** and **Reynard's Cave**. Here, a huge natural arch surrounds much smaller entrance to the cave. As dale narrows path climbs above river.
❸ Dale widens again. Leave main path for route signposted('To Stanshope') and cross footbridge over Dove. Narrow woodland path turns **R** beneath huge spire of **Ilam Rock**. Beyond stile, path eases **L** into **Hall Dale**. Following valley bottom and wall on **R**, it climbs out of woods into limestone-cragged gorge.
❹ As gorge shallows, path enters pastureland – village of **Stanshope** is on skyline. At crossroads of paths (grid ref 130541) turn **L** through squeeze stile in wall and head south with wall on **R**. Where wall turns **R**, keep straight ahead to another stile, and then veer half **R** by wall in next field. Path cuts diagonally to **L** across last 2 fields to reach **Ilam-Moor Lane**, 250yds (229m) south of **Damgate Farm**.
❺ Turn **L** along quiet country lane with great views.
❻ After 800yds (732m) take footpath on **L**, following drive for a few paces before turning **R** over stile. Field path now heads southeast, crossing low grassy fell sides to top of **Moor Plantation** woods.
❼ Here path cuts across steep sides of **Bunster Hill**, before straddling its south spur and descending to step-stile in intake wall. Take great care on this section over **Bunster Hill** as the path is quite narrow and you may have to scramble in places over exposed limestone rock where the path has fallen away. Sturdy footwear is advised. Clear path now descends across sloping pastures to back of **Izaak Walton Hotel**.
❽ Turn **L** by hotel across 2 more fields and back to car park.

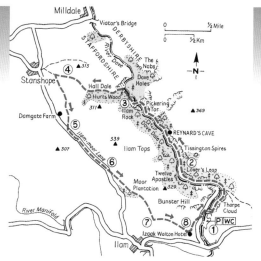

OSMASTON *Among the Aristocracy*

4½ miles (7.2km) 4hrs **Ascent:** 295ft (90m)
Paths: Estate tracks and field paths, quite a few stiles
Suggested map: aqua3 OS Explorer 259 Derby
Grid reference: SK 200435
Parking: Osmaston village hall car park

A gentle walk in aristocratic parklands.
❶ Turn **R** out of car park; follow road past **Shoulder of Mutton** to green and duck pond. Turn **L**. Take middle of 3 rights of way ('Bridleway to Shirley'). Wide track descends among fields and through woodland.
❷ Continue as track reaches beyond **Home Farm** (**L**), then follow it as it separates 2 narrow lakes.
❸ After water mill keep to track ahead, which climbs through woodlands of **Shirley Park**. Track eventually becomes tarmac lane, continuing towards **Shirley**.
❹ Return path to **Osmaston**, highlighted by **Centenary Way** (CW) waymarker, begins on **R**, just before village. Look around centre.
❺ Return to previous footpath, which begins in steps. Beyond stile, it crosses fenced-off section of lawn. Beyond 2nd stile, path follows hedge on **L** round edge of 3 fields. It cuts diagonally across 4th to stile; beyond turn **L** to descend towards wood, southern extremity of Shirley Park.
❻ Cross footbridge over **Shirley Brook**; follow muddy streamside path to another footbridge. Cross it then turn **R** into woods on path with CW marker.
❼ Beyond gate at edge of woods, ignore CW path on **R**. Instead, leave woods and follow sunken track heading west of northwest across fields and alongside lake, southernmost of **Osmaston Park** lakes.
❽ Where sunken track fades, keep ahead beside southern edge of narrow strip of woodland (valley of **Wyaston Brook**) although, although path is invisible, stiles in cross-fences are all in place.
❾ Bridleway from Wyaston Grove joins route just beyond one of these stiles (grid ref 196423). Double-back **R** along it, passing railings on **R** and entering woods. Bridleway track now climbs northeast out of valley and back into **Osmaston Park** estate. Follow it through park, ignoring private tracks to lodge. After passing through avenue of lime trees it emerges by village green. Turn **L** by **duck pond** then **R** to car park.

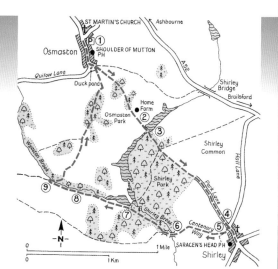

Derbyshire

745 MACKWORTH *A Rural Idyll*

6 miles (9.7km) 4hrs Ascent: 197ft (60m)
Paths: Farm tracks and field paths (can be muddy after rain), quite a few stiles
Suggested map: aqua3 OS Explorer 259 Derby
Grid reference: SK 333379
Parking: Markeaton Park car park

This slice of South Derbyshire belongs much more to the Midlands than the North.
❶ Leave car park at Markeaton Park; cross road to follow surfaced lane to **Markeaton Stones Farm**. Once past farm, track becomes stony, climbing gently up crop fields towards stand of trees on hilltop.
❷ At trees turn **L** at T-junction; follow crumbling tarmac lane alongside trees until you reach buildings of **Upper Vicarwood Farm**.
❸ At farm buildings continue through gate on **L-H** side of stable block; follow grassy hilltop track.
❹ Through gate, track reaches **Lodge Lane**. Turn **L** along lane to gardens of **Meynell Langley**, then **L** into field next to drive. Path heads southeast, following hedge on **R**. Through small, wooded enclosure lake appears in hollow to **R**. Beyond next stile, route enters large field and hedge wanders off to **R**.
❺ Aim for large lime tree at far side of field to locate next stile. Cross footbridge spanning **Mackworth**

Brook. Path now goes parallel to hedge on **R**, aiming for large barn on hillside ahead.
❻ At gateway, path divides. Take path on **R**, whose direction is highlighted by waymarking arrow. Go through next gate; follow **R** field edge, passing to **L** of red-bricked **Bowbridge Fields Farm**. Now head south across fields following hedge on **L**.
❼ Cross stile in tall hedge; turn **L** along pavement of busy **A52** (take care), passing garage and Little Chef. After 600yds (549m) go **L** along **Jarveys Lane**, passing through **Mackworth** village.
❽ Where lane turns sharp **R**, leave it for path passing in front of **church**. Bonnie Prince Charlie waymarks show well-defined route eastwards across fields to **Markeaton**.
❾ At road you can either turn **L** to car park or continue through **Markeaton Park**. For latter go through gateway, turn **L** over twin-arched bridge, **L** by children's playground, and **L** again past boating lake.

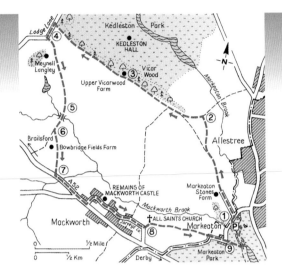

746 CALKE ABBEY *The House that Time Forgot*

3¾ miles (6km) 2hrs Ascent: 197ft (60m)
Paths: Estate roads and field paths, a few stiles
Suggested map: aqua3 OS Explorer 245 The National Forest
Grid reference: SK 352241
Parking: Village Hall car park, Ticknall

Around Sir John Harpur's forgotten baroque mansion, Calke Abbey, on Derbyshire's southern border.
❶ Turn **R** out of car park and follow road to its junction with A road through village. Turn **L** by **Wheel** public house, then **R** by bridge to go through gates **Calke Abbey** Estate. Tarmac estate road goes between avenue of mature lime trees and through **Middle Lodge** Gates. If you want to go inside **abbey** you'll have to go here.
❷ Continue southeast along road, past **Betty's Pond** (L) then, as road swings **L**, carry on along grassy track that climbs to south end of park.
❸ Take **L** fork, which doubles back **L**, descending beneath hilltop church towards **abbey**, which appears in dip to **R**. After viewing fine house, continue along track past red-brick stables and offices. Cross car park and go through its exit on far **R**. Where exit road swings **L**, leave it and descend north, down to **Mere**

Pond, narrow strip of water surrounded by trees.
❹ Turn **R** along water's-edge path, then **L** between end of mere and western extremities of another one, to climb through woodland to north.
❺ On meeting lane at top edge of woodlands, turn **L** for few paces then **R** through gate. After tracing wall on **L**, go over stile in hedge ahead to enter next field. Path now heads north of northwest along **L** edge of crop fields, passing close to **White Leys Farm**. Just past large ash tree, go over stile on **L** and follow clear field edge track downhill through more crop-growing fields.
❻ On meeting flinted works road turn **L**, following it through area of woodland and old gravel pits (now transformed into pretty wildlife ponds). Winding track passes several cottages and meets **A514** about 500yds (457m) to east of village.
❼ Turn **L** along road through village, then **R** by side of **Wheel** pub to get back to car park.

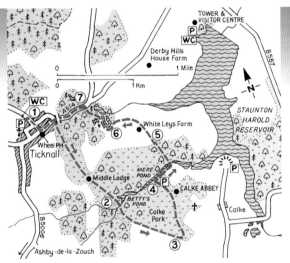

747 CHATSWORTH *Park and Gardens*

7 miles (11.3km) 3hrs Ascent: 459ft (140m)
Paths: Good paths and forest trails
Suggested map: aqua3 OS Explorer OL24 White Peak
Grid reference: SK 251699
Parking: Endsor village

Past gardens and through parkland created by gardening guru, 'Capability' Brown.
❶ From Edensor village cross B6012; take footpath at R-H side of large tree. Walk across parkland to join main drive to **Chatsworth House** near bridge. Cross over road; continue on footpath, walking downhill on other side to river bank.
❷ Follow **River Derwent** past couple of **weirs** and remains of old mill to next bridge that carries B6012 over river. To **L** of bridge, metal kissing gate allows access to road. Cross bridge.
❸ Ignore **L** turn into drive past gatehouse to estate and take next **L** along side of gatehouse. Continue up hill, past house on **R** and then farm. Cross stile on **L** to footpath ('Robin Hood and Hunting Tower').
❹ Cross field and over next stile; go diagonally **L**, uphill following waymarkers on well-defined path. When this meets made-up track turn **L**, cross wall into estate by high stile and continue to crossroads.

❺ Keep ahead, following track as it passes **Swiss Lake** on **R** and then loops round **Emperor Lake** on **L**. Path will come to another, faint, crossroads. On **L** is **Hunting Tower**.
❻ Continue on path as it loops **L** around tower, ignoring turn off to **R**. Path heads downhill, past what appears to be remains of old viaduct with water cascading from end, then doubles back, still going downhill, eventually reaching car park at **Chatsworth House**.
❼ Go past wooden hut at car park entrance; turn **R** on to estate road heading north. Follow road past several wooden sculptures until you are within sight of gates at end of estate.
❽ Near here turn **L** across park to gate that leads eventually to **Baslow**. Don't go through gate but turn **L** on to trail that follows river back to Chatsworth. Turn **R** on to road, cross bridge then go immediately **R** on track, which leads back to **Edensor** village.

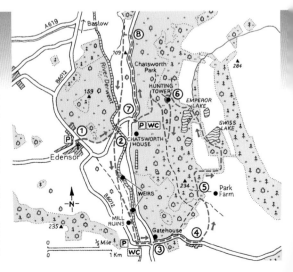

Derbyshire

ARBOR LOW ANCIENT CIRCLES

6 miles (9.7km) 4hrs **Ascent:** 492ft (150m)
Paths: Mostly well-defined paths, some road walking
Suggested map: aqua3 OS Explorer OL24 White Peak
Grid reference: SK 194645
Parking: Pay car park at start

Around Arbor Low – the 'Stonehenge of the North' and an ancient trade centre.

1 Exit car park, turn **L** and follow road to Y-junction. Cross road, go through gap in wall, through kissing gate and follow well-defined path across field to stand of trees.

2 Cross wall by stile, go through gate and continue following path. Cross fence by another stile and continue to wall at edge of wood. Go through kissing gate into **Low Moor Wood**.

3 Follow path through wood, cross wall via stile and follow well-defined path across parkland. Take diverted path round **Calling Low Farm** via 2 kissing gates, go through wood and 2 more kissing gates to get back on to open meadow.

4 Follow this path diagonally downhill and go through another kissing gate. Continue on path still downhill, through another gate into **Lathkill Dale National Nature Reserve**. Head downhill on limestone path and steps. Cross stile at bottom then head uphill on path to your **L**.

5 Look out for **cave** in rocks on **L** as you reach top. Continue uphill, through gate and on to farm. Enter farmstead via some stone steps and continue on road until you see signpost, pointing **L**.

6 Turn on to this farm road and follow it until it joins main road. Turn **R** and continue for ½ mile (800m) then turn **L** on to farm road following signs for henge.

7 Go through farmstead following signs, cross stile, turn **L** along path then cross another stile to reach **Arbor Low**. The henge is probably one of the most important prehistoric sites in Britain but its purpose remains a mystery. Across the field from Arbor Low lies a long barrow with a round one built on top of it. The name **Gib Hill** indicates that it was used as a gibbet, probably in the Middle Ages. Retrace your steps to main road, turn **R** and walk about 2½ miles (4km) back to car park.

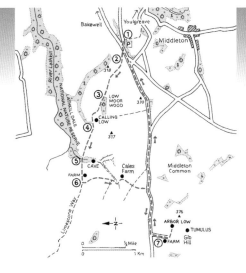

EDALE MYSTERIOUS MAM TOR

6 miles (9.7km) 3hrs 30min **Ascent:** 984ft (300m)
Paths: Mainly good but can be boggy in wet weather
Suggested map: aqua3 OS Explorer OL24 White Peak
Grid reference: SK 124853
Parking: Good public car park at Edale

Approaching from the Edale side, discover the ancient secrets of the great 'Shivering Mountain'.

1 Exit car park at **Edale** and turn **R** on to road. Look out for public footpath sign on your **L** and turn on to farm road. Just before this road turns sharply **L**, take public footpath that forks off to **R** and goes uphill through wood.

2 At end of wooded area, cross over stile and continue uphill. Cross another stile, follow path across open hillside and cross yet another stile and turn **L** on to road. Just before road bends sharply **L**, cross over road, go over stile and then follow this path towards hill.

3 Near foot of hill, cross over stile to **L** and then turn **R** on to road. Continue to find some steps on **L** leading through ramparts of Iron-Age fort to summit of **Mam Tor**, enjoy the views. From here retrace your steps back to road.

4 Cross road, go over stile and continue on this footpath uphill and on to **Rushup Edge**. Follow this well-defined path along ridge, crossing 5 stiles. Where another path intersects, turn **R**. This is **Chapel Gate** track, badly eroded by off-road motorbikes. Go through kissing gate then head downhill.

5 Near bottom of hill go through gap stile on **L**. Go across another stile, pass through gate, then across another stile on **L**. This leads to some tumbledown buildings. Cross over stile by corner of one building then veer **R** and cross another stile on to farm road.

6 Cross road, go over stile and follow path until it joins road. Turn **R** then **L** at junction and continue towards **Barber Booth**. Take 2nd road on **L** then, near outskirts of village, go **L** on road ('Edale Station').

7 Follow path across series of meadows, going through several gates and 3 stiles to join road to **Edale Station** next to **Champion House**. Turn **R** on to road then, near junction, turn **L** into car park.

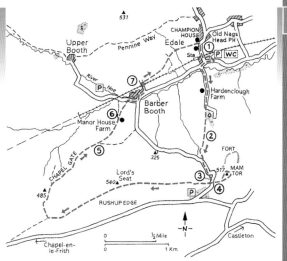

THURSTASTON UNCOMMON DELIGHTS

5¼ miles (8.4km) 1hr 45min **Ascent:** 345ft (105m)
Paths: Some road walking, sandy tracks and bare rock, then field paths, 2 stiles
Suggested map: aqua3 OS Explorer 266 Wirral & Chester
Grid reference: SJ 238834 **Parking:** Wirral Country Park at bottom of Station Road, Thurstaston

Panoramic views from a heathland crest.

1 From car park, loop round past **visitor centre** and wildlife pond, go to **Station Road** then continue up for ½ mile (800m). At top swing **R**.

2 Turn **L** before **church** to A540. Go **L**, past **Cottage Loaf**, go **R** through kissing gate. Follow track ahead to end of cul-de-sac.

3 Go through kissing gate to broad path; go **R** on smaller path. Cross track near cattle grid and take **L** of 2 paths, swing **L** and cross clearing. Go **R** to meet clearer path just inside edge of wood. Go **L**, following **Greasby Brook**.

4 Turn **L** alongside boundary wall ahead. Where it ends keep straight on, passing **model railway**. Alongside **Royden Park** wall resumes. Where it ends again turn **L** by sign and map. Cross clearing to junction.

5 20yds (18m) further turn **R** on narrow path before kissing gate. Cross another path and go through gorse for 20yds (18m) to broader path. Go **L** then up past marker stone, over tree roots and bare rock. Descend steps, pass small pool, then ascend to larger area of bare rock. Go **R** and when path forks, go **L**, then **R**, through trees. Go **L** on broad path to sandstone pillar with map/view indicator and then trig point. Descend broad path that rejoins outward route. Retrace your steps past **Cottage Loaf** and down top section of **Station Road**.

6 Turn **L** past church. When road swings to **L**, lane continues ahead. Cross stile and follow well-marked footpath. In dip cross stream and turn **R** at footpath sign. After recrossing stream, zig-zag down steeper slope into The Dungeon.

7 Cross stream again and follow it down. Climb on to old railway embankment and go **R**. When green gates bar way, sidestep **L**. Continue for another 220yds (201m) to gap in hedge. Follow path, winding past ponds then out to cliff tops above estuary. Go **R** for 240yds (219m), then bear **R** across grass towards visitor centre and car park.

751 FORMBY POINT *SQUIRRELS AND SAND*

3½ miles (5.7km) 1hr 30min **Ascent:** 50ft (15m)

Paths: Well-worn paths through woods and salt marsh, plus long stretch of sand

Suggested map: aqua3 OS Explorer 285 Southport & Chorley

Grid reference: SD 278082

Parking: Either side of access road just beyond kiosk

An exhilarating walk through an area of great significance for wildlife.

1 Start just **L** of large notice-board. Follow 'Squirrel Walk', with its wooden fencing, to **L** and then round to **R**. Keep straight on at crossroads, where there's sign for **Blundell Avenue**. There are many subsidiary paths but the main line runs virtually straight ahead to **Blundell Avenue**. Cross avenue to fainter path almost opposite, with 'No Cycling' sign and traces of bricks in its surface. Follow this, skirting around edge of field (brick traces still useful guide). Go up slight rise then across more open sand hills to line of pines on rise ahead. Skirt **L** round hollow and see houses ahead.

2 Just before houses turn **R** on straight track. This swings **L** slightly then forks. Go **R**, down steps, then straight on down side of reed-fringed pool. Beyond this keep fairly straight on, towards sand hills. When you reach them swing **L** then **R**, picking up boardwalk, to skirt highest dunes and out to beach.

3 Turn **R** along open and virtually level sand. The firmest walking surface is usually some way out from the base of the dunes. Walk parallel to these (north) for over 1¼ miles (2km). The shoreline curves very gently to **R** but there are few distinctive landmarks apart from signs to various approach paths. Watch for sign for Gipsy Wood Path.

4 Distinct track winds through sand hills then swings more decisively to **R** near **pools**, where there's sign board about natterjack toads. Follow track back into woods and, at junction, go **R**. The track curves round between woods and sand hills then joins wider track by Sefton Coastal Footpath sign. Go through patch of willows then bear **L** to line of pines on rise. From these drop down to broad path with gravelly surface and follow it **L** into woods again. Stay on main path, with timber edgings and white-topped posts, bear **R** by large 'xylophone', and it leads quickly back to the start.

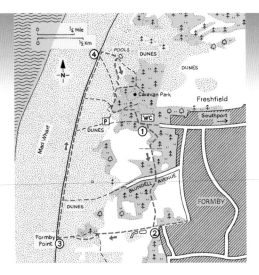

752 HEALEY DELL *A HIDDEN GEM*

2½ miles (4km) 4hrs **Ascent:** 640ft (195m)

Paths: Field paths, old railway line and surfaced tracks, 5 stiles

Suggested map: aqua3 OS Explorer OL21 South Pennines

Grid reference: SD 879155

Parking: Parking by Healey Dell Nature Reserve Visitor Centre

Around a gem of a nature reserve.

1 With your back to **visitor centre**, turn **L** and walk past 1st range of buildings. Cross bridge; turn **R**. Take lower path, along river, past more overgrown ruins. Near green footbridge, go sharp **L** up bank then **R** along edge of clearing, and back into woods. Go **L** just before stream on narrow path, climbing steeply in places. Stone flags help you over wet patch before path dips to cross stream. Climb again on other side and join broader green track. Where this narrows, continue over stile up **L** edge of field to **Smallshaw Farm**.

2 Go **L** before 1st building then through gate into yard. Go **L** on track to road. Go **R** and up to bus turning circle. Turn **R** opposite this, along track. Follow this for about 400yds (366m) to **Knack's Farm**.

3 Continue over cattle grid and down lane between high banks, then fork **R** on track. After slight dog-leg track becomes greener. Follow it round **L** and back **R**, then over stile ahead and down field by ruined wall. Go

over stile at bottom, down to reach lane and then go **L** for a few paces.

4 Go down ramp and steps to **old railway** line. Turn **R** along it for 500yds (457m), then cross viaduct high above **Healey Dell**. Go **L** down steps to access lane, down under viaduct then sharply back **R** on broad path. Where this starts to level out there is stile on **L**. But first go a short way upstream, until path starts to climb again, to see **cascades**.

5 Return to stile and cross it. Follow stone setts (which are often slippery) down to sharp bend, with more remains just down and **R**. From bend, footpath follows tops of some old walls then curls down steeply to weir. Step across water-cut on stone slabs and follow it down. When it enters tunnel carved in solid rock, footpath goes to **R**. Almost opposite tall pillar it swings away from river and out past terrace of houses to lane. Go down this below to tall brick retaining wall and back to start at **visitor centre**.

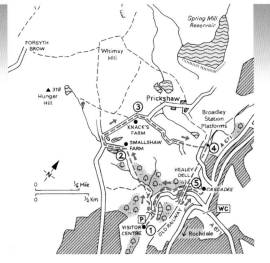

753 DOVE STONES *ANOTHER PEAK EXPERIENCE*

8 miles (12.9km) 3hrs **Ascent:** 1,296ft (395m)

Paths: Mostly on good tracks but with some rocky sections, occasionally very steep, 2 stiles

Suggested map: aqua3 OS Explorer OL1 Dark Peak

Grid reference: SE 013034 **Parking:** Dovestone Reservoir dam (pay-and-display at weekends)

Along the edge of the moors.

1 Cross dam and continue just above shoreline. Climb up near end then drop down again to **Yeoman Hey Dam**.

2 Follow **L** side of reservoir. At fork keep to higher path, rising gently to next dam. Follow **L** side of **Greenfield Reservoir** then wind up narrowing valley. Climb more steeply to waterworks where valley forks.

3 Skirt **R** above tunnel entrance, then take rough path up **R** branch, **Birchen Clough**. Cross stream when steep little crag blocks way. Path is steep and rough, with one awkward step just below 20ft (6m) cascade. Above this clough is shallower and less steep. After some wet patches clough opens out, with nearly level ground on **R**.

4 Cross stream and go up **R** to marshy terrace. Keep climbing to **R** where slope is less steep. Path materialises just below plateau edge, rising gently towards crags. Cross stile then follow top of crags past **Trinnacle**. After about 440yds (402m) path forks.

5 Go **L** to stile, with cairn just beyond, and near-level path across moor. Above ruin, bear **L** up short stony slope, reaching plateau near **Ashway Cross**. Continue along edge of moor; path keeps generally level, swinging **L** to cross stream then back **R**. Where path is unclear follow boundary between peat and rock. The main path keeps discreet distance from edge of **Dove Stones**. Beyond isolated **Fox Stone** route bears little **L**, passing remains of stone hut below crag, **Bramley's Cot**.

6 Continue along moor edge, crossing **Charnel Clough**. Path still keeps generally level, swinging **L** above **Chew Valley** until dam of **Chew Reservoir** appears ahead. Watch out for unfenced edge of small quarry. Skirt round this and down grass slope beyond to reservoir road.

7 Descend road until gradient eases. Just before gate, drop down **L** to ridge. Take obvious rising path beyond. Slant down **R** before plantation, past some boulders. Rejoin road past sailing club to car park.

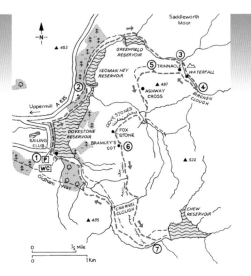

BLACKSTONE EDGE *ROMAN WAYS*

6½ miles (10.4km) 2hrs 30min **Ascent:** 1,066ft (325m) 🏔

Paths: Field paths, rough tracks and faint paths across open moorland, 2 stiles

Suggested map: aqua3 OS Explorer OL21 South Pennines

Grid reference: SD 939153

Parking: Hollingworth Lake Visitor Centre

A steady climb to a rocky ridge.

❶ From far end of car park well-made path runs past picnic tables then crosses and follows small beck. At track go **L** 200yds (183m) then up **R** with yellow arrows. Zig-zag up slope then **L** and down to stream and footbridge. Where path forks keep to lower one, just above stream, through birch woods then up to wider path and round to **Owlet Hall**.

❷ Go through lychgate and **L** alongside house to stile. Cross stream, then another stile. Ignore path on **L** and keep **R**, just above stream, along line of thorn trees. Cross decrepit fence and follow neglected path alongside wall. Go up to trees flanking drive to **Shore Lane Farm**. Turn **L**, then **L** again on lane.

❸ Just before road, turn **R** on track past houses. Continue on narrower but clear path. Meet farm track just below A58, go **R** few paces, then **L** up well-worn path ('**Roman Road**'). Cross water-cut and keep climbing. Slope eases near **Aggin Stone**.

❹ Turn **R**, through kissing gate; follow path across rock-strewn moor to trig point. Follow main edge south for 400yds (366m) to break in line of rocks.

❺ Slant down **R** across rough moor to old water-cut. Go **L** alongside this until path veers off **R**. It soon rises again, across shoulder of moor, then levels off by small cairn. Keep **R**, along edge, descend more steeply then swing **R**, joining old grooved track. Continue down green track, past **cairn**, then back **L** descending towards **Dry Mere**.

❻ Where ground steepens, just beyond tarn, path splits. Take lower path, towards pylon. Go straight across well-used track to another track just below. Go **L**, fording small stream, then swing **R**. Drop down to shale track in small valley and go **R** down it.

❼ At **Syke** farm join old lane. At **Hollingworth Fold**, with its multicoloured signpost, keep straight on down lane to join road along lake side. Entrance to **visitor centre** is just across 1st embankment.

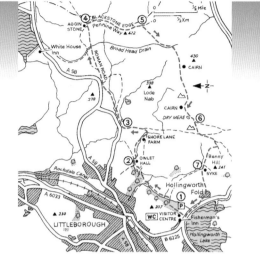

RIVER DOUGLAS *VALLEY DELIGHTS*

4 miles (6.4km) 1hr 45min **Ascent:** 410ft (125m) 🔺

Paths: Field paths and canal tow path, 7 stiles

Suggested map: aqua3 OS Explorer 285 Southport & Chorley

Grid reference: SD 517109 **Parking:** Large lay-by on A5209

A gentle yet surprising corner of Lancashire.

❶ At end of lay-by there's stile into corner of field. Go up side of field and **L** along top, then into wood. Cross small footbridge and continue up footpath, then alongside tiny stream. Follow side of conifer plantation until it bends away, then bear **R** to **L**-**H** side of trees enclosing pool. Continue up to **R** into enclosed track below power lines and up to meet junction with tarmac track.

❷ Go **L**, then bear **L** again down earthy track. (If you want to visit **Rigbye Arms** pub first, go **R** at this point, then **L** along **High Moor Lane**.) At end of earthy track go slightly **R**, across field, to corner of wood then down its **L**-**H** edge. Keep following this, which eventually becomes narrow strip of woodland, to stile in bottom corner of field. Follow footpath down through wood then up to A5209.

❸ Cross road and go **L** to stile where pavement ends. Go straight down field and over another stile into lane. Go **R** on this then immediately **L** down another lane. Cross railway at level crossing and continue to bridge over canal. Drop down to tow path and follow it eastwards for about ½ mile (800m) to next canal bridge (No 40).

❹ Cross bridge and follow obvious track, taking you back over railway and up to gate and stile. Turn **R** on another track. In places there's separate footpath alongside, but it's always obvious. Where track finally parts company, go ahead over stile and along bottom edge of field beside area of new plantings. Cross next field to post and then stile.

❺ Descend steep steps down into wood and bear **L** into **Fairy Glen**. Cross footbridge, climb some steps, then go **L** up good track. Cross another footbridge below waterfall and ascend steps. Keep to principal footpath, straight on up glen as it becomes shallower, until path crosses tiny footbridge. Soon after this footpath leaves side of brook and briefly joins track before it emerges on to **A5209**. Cross and go **R**, back to lay-by.

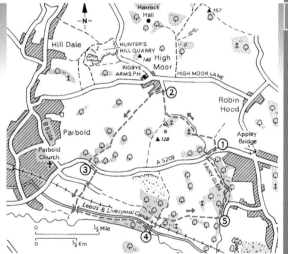

MARTIN MERE *LANCASHIRE'S 'FENS'*

5 miles (8km) 2hrs **Ascent:** 50ft (15m) 🔺

Paths: Canal tow paths, lanes, farm tracks and field paths, 2 stiles

Suggested map: aqua3 OS Explorer 285 Southport & Chorley

Grid reference: SD 423126

Parking: Several small lay-bys near mid-point of Gorst Lane

An easy walk around a superb bird centre.

❶ Near mid-point of **Gorst Lane** at timber yard, follow short track via yard to meet canal by swing bridge. Go **R** along tow path for ¾ mile (1.2km) to **Gregson's Bridge**. Go under bridge then up to lane.

❷ Join wider road (Martin Lane) and follow itfrom canal for 350yds (320m). At bend, by **Martin Inn**, bear **R** down narrow lane. Follow this for 700yds (640m), past farm, to open section. Opposite glasshouses find footpath sign on **R**. Follow track to railway line.

❸ Cross line and descend track to green shed. Go **R**, alongside drainage ditch, to another ditch. Go **L**. Continue to stile by gate then go **R** alongside reed-lined channel. Follow over 2 bridges, 2nd bridge is close to southern corner of **Martin Mere Reserve**. Continue down green track, following edge of reserve, to road (**Tarlscough Lane**).

❹ Turn **R** and follow road for 500yds (457m). Immediately past **Brandreth Farm** find footpath sign.

Go down side of large shed, go **R** then **L** round pool and on down obvious track.

❺ At end, just before lane, turn **R** on track. Turn **R** before house and follow fence round to **L**. Keep almost straight on, past signpost, and follow footpath through crops towards 2 trees. These act as signposts join track to and through **Crabtree Bridge Farm**.

❻ Swing **R** on tow path and continue for 200yds (183m) to swing bridge by **Farmers Arms** pub and 500yds (457m) to smaller one above timber yard. Drop back down through this to **Gorst Lane**.

Important note: During bird migration season (1 Oct–1 Apr) avoid path immediately beside reserve and use alternative route: turn **R** just before 1st railway crossing (Point ❸). Walk alongside line to New Lane Station. Turn **L** up Marsh Moss Lane to junction with Tarlscough Lane and rejoin main route.

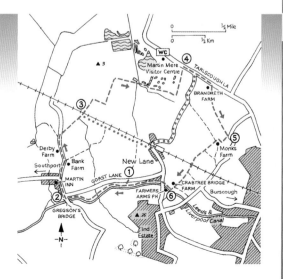

Lancashire

757 ANGLEZARKE *ROCKS AND WATER*

7 miles (11.3km) 2hrs 30min **Ascent:** 689ft (210m) ⚠
Paths: Mostly good tracks with some field paths, 20 stiles
Suggested map: aqua3 OS Explorer 287 West Pennine Moors
Grid reference: SD 621161
Parking: Large car park at Anglezarke

Walking in a landscape shaped by reservoirs and quarries.

❶ Leave car park by kissing gate and follow track near water. Fork R, via Lester Mill **Quarry**; go R, and straight on at next junction. Track climbs steep rise.

❷ Go through gap on L, on bend. Path traverses wooded slope. Descend steps, join wider track and go L. Beyond stile follow narrower path to road.

❸ Go L 50yds (46m) to kissing gate. Follow track up valley below **Stronstrey Bank**. Cross bridge then go through kissing gate and over another bridge to **White Coppice cricket ground**.

❹ Bear L up lane, then follow tarmac into White Coppice hamlet. Cross bridge by post-box. Follow stream then go up L by reservoir. Bear L to stile. Cross next field to top R corner and go R on lane. Where it bends R go L up track.

❺ Skirt **Higher Healey**, follow field edges, then angle up L into dark plantations. Fork L just inside, and ascend to an old **quarry**. Follow its rim for three-quarters of way round then bear away L through larch plantation.

❻ Go L on clear path then R to large cairn on **Grey Heights**. Descend slightly R, winding down past small plantation, and join wider green track. Bear L over small rise; follow track to lane by **White House farm**.

❼ Cross stile on L, below farmyard wall; bear L to corner of field. Cross stile on L then go up field edge and join confined path. From stile on R follow trees along field edge to rough track. Go R and ahead to **Kays Farm**.

❽ Go R down track then L on lane below reservoir wall. As lane angles away, go L over stile then skirt reservoir until pushed away from water by wood. Join road across dam. Go through gap and up steep track. Go L at top round **Yarrow Reservoir** to road.

❾ Go L, passing entrance to **Anglezarke Quarry**, to junction. Go R, and car park entrance is on 1st bend.

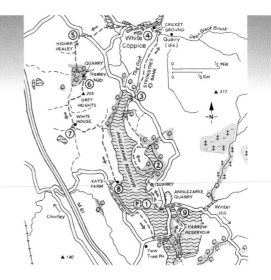

758 HASLINGDEN GRANE *THE DESERTED VALLEY*

3½ miles (5.7km) 1hrs 30min **Ascent:** 426ft (130m) ⚠
Paths: Good tracks, a few steep and rough sections, 11 stiles
Suggested map: aqua3 OS Explorer 287 West Pennine Moors
Grid reference: SD 750231
Parking: At Clough Head Information Centre, on A6177

A walk that lays bare the past.

❶ Footpath starts immediately L of information centre. Go through small plantation then climb alongside wall. Cross stile by **Rossendale Way** sign then go immediately L over stone slab stile and follow path along fine wall. After 100yds (91m) past plantation, go L over stile by **Rossendale Way** sign and down to road.

❷ Go L down road for 90yds (82m), then R on track, swinging R to pass ruins. After 440yds (402m) track swings L near spoil heaps. Keep ahead, past more ruins then dip into small valley beside old water-cut.

❸ Go R 50yds (46m) on walled track, then L again across short wet patch. Follow old walled track past ruined houses and into another small valley, just above extensive ruins. Skirt rightwards round these, descend to stream then climb up alongside plantation. Cross into this at stile. Path starts level but soon descends quite steeply, winding past Rossendale Way signs, to meet clearer path just before footbridge at bottom.

❹ Cross bridge and go up steps then across hillside below beech wood. Cross another small stream, go up few paces then go L and follow path through pine plantation. Continue along bilberry-covered hillside above **Calf Hey Reservoir**, passing ruin on L and through dip with small stream. Another 90yds (82m) further, you'll see solitary, large sycamore tree.

❺ Cross stile just below tree then descend slightly R to stile by dam. Cross it and go up tarmac path past some valve gear to gate.

❻ Go through another gate on R, then through gap in wall and up path. This runs alongside road to car park. Where this path ends there's another up to L, ('**Clough Head**'). Go up this, meeting access road again, then continue up steps and through small plantation just below main road. Go L up road for 50yds (46m) then cross it by footpath sign to kissing gate opposite. Short footpath leads back to start.

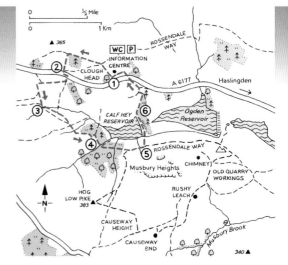

759 DARWEN TOWER *FREEDOM OF THE MOORS*

4 miles (6.4km) 1hr 30min **Ascent:** 705ft (215m) ⚠
Paths: Well-defined tracks throughout, 3 stiles
Suggested map: aqua3 OS Explorer 287 West Pennine Moors
Grid reference: SD 665215
Parking: Car park near Royal Arms

A simple walk, if moderately steep in parts, to a great landmark on the moors.

❶ From car park cross bus turning area and then road. Go through gates and reach footpath sign in 30yds (27m). Go R ('Woods and Water Trail'). Path descends to crossroads. Turn R on broad path – still 'Woods and Water Trail' – then after 200yds (183m) go R at fork on gently rising path. Gradually curve to R and climb little more steeply, with open fields on L, out to road. Go L for 200yds (183m).

❷ Go R up walled track, part of **Witton Weavers' Way**. Go straight on at crossroads then descend steeply, with section of old paving, towards **Earnsdale Reservoir**. Cross dam and swing L at its end then follow lane up R until it swings L out over cattle grid. Go straight up steep grass slope ahead, skirting fenced area with regenerating trees.

❸ Go L on track then, just above house, bear R up concrete track. At gap in aluminium barrier bear L on level path towards old quarry. Here go up R on stony track then keep L where it forks. A gate on L, flanked by flagstones, gives a superb view of town of **Darwen**, dominated by the India Mill chimney. Continue along main track for another 100yds (91m). As gradient eases and **tower** comes into view bear R, past marker stone with its likeness of tower, and then go straight up to real thing.

❹ From tower bear L past **trig point** and the go along broad path above steeper slope that falls to **Sunnyhurst Hey Reservoir**. Path swings L past bench. Go over stile on R overlooking valley of **Stepback Brook** and down zig-zag path. Don't cross next stile but go back L, towards stream then over stile at bottom. Go L on track to cross over stream.

❺ Track swings back R and up through wood. As it levels out pass to R of gates and continue down towards row of houses. Lane just L of these leads to road. Go back past bus turning area to car park.

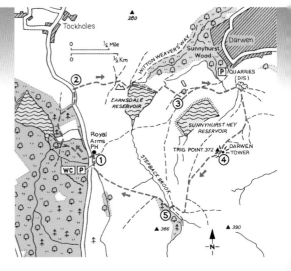

Lancashire

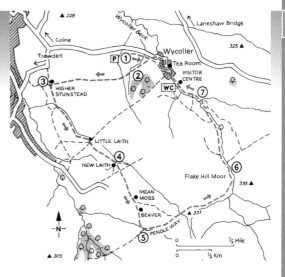

WYCOLLER WEAVING WAYS

5¼ miles (8.4km) 2hrs Ascent: 538ft (165m)
Paths: Field paths, some rough tracks and quiet lanes, 19 stiles
Suggested map: aqua3 OS Explorer OL21 South Pennines
Grid reference: SD 926395
Parking: Car park just above Wycoller village (no general access for vehicles to village itself)

Around a district steeped in the history of the textile industry.

1 At top of car park are notice-board and sign 'Wycoller 500m'. Follow footpath indicated, just above road, until it joins it on bend. Cross stile on **R** and slant **R** across field to stile, then up to gate and into garden. Follow arrow through trees up **L** side to stile.

2 Bear **R**, cross stream, then bear **L**, up towards house on skyline, until footbridge and stile appear in dip. Follow hedge and then wall in same line. When it ends at open, rushy pasture bear slightly **R**, towards Pendle Hill. Cresting rise, see stile and signpost by corner of walls. Sign for Trawden points too far **R**. Aim slightly **L**, between 2 power line poles and again, once over rise, see stile and signpost by end of fine wall. Follow wall and then walled track to **Higher Stunstead**. Go past 1st buildings and into yard.

3 Go **L** up walled track to cattle grid then ahead to stile and follow course of stream up to **Little Laith**.

Continue to pass house on your **L** then go straight ahead, along field edges, to large barn on skyline by **New Laith**. Follow arrows round farm.

4 Continue virtually straight ahead to stile by gate and over more stiles to **Mean Moss**. Go few paces **L** up track then follow wall on **R** and more stiles to **Beaver**. Go slightly **R** down field to stile near corner then up by stream to track.

5 Go **L**, then keep straight on above wall following rougher continuation (**Pendle Way** sign). When wall turns sharp **L**, track bends more gradually, above stream, down to signpost.

6 Go slightly **L** to stile by gate then take lower path, down towards stream then up round wood. From kissing gate drop down to cross stream, then follow it down and out to lane.

7 Go **L** down lane to reach **visitor centre** and **Wycoller**. Go **L** up lane and join outward part of route back to car park.

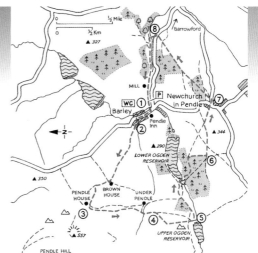

PENDLE HILL WITCHING WAYS

4¾ miles (7.7km) 2hrs Ascent: 738ft (225m)
Paths: Field paths and rough moorland, surfaced track, 10 stiles
Suggested map: aqua3 OS Explorer OL21 South Pennines or OL41 Forest of Bowland & Ribblesdale
Grid reference: SD 823403 **Parking:** Public car park in Barley village

A grand loop around the flanks and ridges of Pendle Hill.

1 From toilets follow path **R** across green then over footbridge. Go **R** then up street. Just past Meadow Bank Farm go **L** up footpath alongside stream.

2 Keep straight on up then cross footbridge and join lane. Follow this, with signs, to kissing gate and well-marked path that leads to **Brown House**. Go into yard, **R** on track for 60yds (55m) then **L** through kissing gate. Go down and **R**, then up through new plantings and up to gate **L** of **Pendle House**.

3 Go **L** to meet path just above wall. After another gate, climb away from wall. Path undulates, then dips more definitely and meets wall again. From stile (don't cross it) just above **Under Pendle**, bear **R** and follow fence. Cross stream then go straight on up clearer track to rejoin wall.

4 Bear **R** on trackway climbing alongside obvious groove. Pass old wooden gateposts. There's another gate and stile just ahead, go **L** through gate and

straight down by wall. Cross track and descend to gate just below **Upper Ogden Reservoir**.

5 Follow reservoir road until just above **Lower Ogden Reservoir**. Go **R** over bridge, down steps then round **R** to footbridge. Climb steps; go **L** and climb steps through plantation. At its end go up **R** to ridge.

6 Turn **L** following fence then wall. At signpost bear **R**, keeping roughly level until rooftops of **Newchurch** appear. Aim for water trough, then stile and signpost. Descend short path to road.

7 Go down road opposite ('Roughlee'). After 100yds (91m) cross stile on **L-H** side; follow rising footpath. Fork **L** just inside plantation. At far end of plantation keep descending gradually converging with wall on **L-H** side. Follow wall, changing sides halfway along, to join sunken track. Cross it and descend to road.

8 Go down tarmac track opposite, cross Pendle Water then go **L** alongside it. Continue on stonier track past cottages and old mill. Finally short path on **R** leads back to car park.

HODDER VALLEY THE FOREST OF BOWLAND

7 miles (11.3km) 2hrs 30min Ascent: 853ft (260m)
Paths: Field paths, farm tracks and quiet lane, 8 stiles
Suggested map: aqua3 OS Explorer OL41 Forest of Bowland & Ribblesdale
Grid reference: SD 658468
Parking: Roadside parking near Inn at Whitewell or below church

Around the heart of the Forest of Bowland.

1 From lower parking area follow river bank **L** to stepping stones. Climb just **R** of woods and straight through farmyard of **New Laund**. By old cheese press go **L** on curving track below slopes, then up field. Bear **L** to gate into lane. Go few paces **L** to stile on **R**.

2 Cross rough pasture, aiming just **L** of house, then go **R** on surfaced track, swinging round into another little valley. Go **L** to **farm**, then **R**, through farmyard and down to footbridge.

3 Turn **L**, past chicken coops, to stile on **R**. Cross field corner to 2nd stile thenahead to **Dinkling Green Farm**. Gap to **R** of cow shed leads into farmyard.

4 Halfway down yard go **R**, between buildings, to ford. Keep **L** past plantation, follow next field edge then go through gate in dip. Follow hedge round then cross it and go over rise. Bear **R**, down to beck, then up lane to **Lickhurst Farm**.

5 Turn **L** into farmyard then bear **R** and straight on

down track. When it swings **R**, go **L** before next gate then straight ahead on intermittent track.

6 Just before **Knot Hill Quarry**, turn **L**, past limekiln, to junction. Go **R** and down to lane. Go **L** then **L** again, round bend and down. Cross bridge on **R** and head towards **Stakes** farm, crossing river on stepping stones.

7 Turn **L** and climb above river. At next junction go **L**, descend steeply, then swing **R**, slightly above **River Hodder**, to stile. Follow fence to stile, then bear **L** to ford. Go up rough track and keep climbing past **R** edge of plantation. Keep straight on across open field to stile in furthest corner.

8 Across road, few paces **L**, is gate. Bear **L** to iron gates. Contour round hill, just above fence, to more gates. After 100yds (91m) go down through aluminium gate. Track swings **R**. Just past Seed Hill turn **L** and descend steps by graveyard. Short steep lane descends back to start.

Lancashire

763 DUNSOP BRIDGE *MOORS AT THE CENTRE*

9¼ miles (14.9km) 3hrs 30min **Ascent:** 1,247ft (380m) ▲

Paths: Field paths, rougher moorland paths, surfaced road, 9 stiles

Suggested map: aqua3 OS Explorer OL41 Forest of Bowland & Ribblesdale

Grid reference: SD 660501

Parking: Public car park at Dunsop Bridge

This is a tough walk on the high moors.
❶ From car park, go up surfaced track, just to **L** of **post office** and tea room, for about 800yds (732m). At end of track, by houses, follow public footpath for 100yds (91m) then go **R**, up steep bank.
❷ Cross large field, bearing slightly **L** to power lines. Continue to stile before **Beatrix** farm. Follow track round farm until it swings back **R** again. Go **L**, through 2nd of 2 gates. Climb slope **R** of stream, cross stile. Follow wire fence across hillside. Drop into **Oxenhurst Clough**; climb out through plantation, rejoining fence as gradient eases. Continue to join another track.
❸ Follow track for ¾ mile (1.2km) to **Burn House**, where it swings **R**. Bear **L**, across open field, towards middle of young plantation. Follow path through it, bearing **R** to stile. Aim **R** of another young plantation in dip, then across field towards houses (Laythams). Go **L** on lane for 300yds (274m).
❹ Turn **L** up metalled track. Clearly marked gates

guide you round house. About 50yds (46m) above this, drop to stream and continue up to its **L**. From top of enclosure, path rises to **R** alongside obvious groove, then swings back **L**. Climb ridge then swing **R** above upper reaches of **Dunsop Brook**. Cross plateau, parallel to old wall, to circular patch of stones.
❺ Turn **L** and cross wall at stile. Path ahead is rough but clear. After slight rise descend, gently at first but gradually getting steeper. As ground steepens, descend in zig-zags, with gate halfway down. Just above farm at **Whitendale** go **L**.
❻ Follow level track for ¾ mile (1.2km) until it swings round little side valley, over footbridges. Cross stile and wind down to track by river. Follow this down to bridge by **waterworks**.
❼ Cross bridge, join road and follow it down valley for 1½ miles (2.4km), past **Bishop's House**.
❽ Just after cattle grid, cross river on substantial footbridge. Just beyond this rejoin outward route.

---

764 HURST GREEN *MAYBE MIDDLE-EARTH*

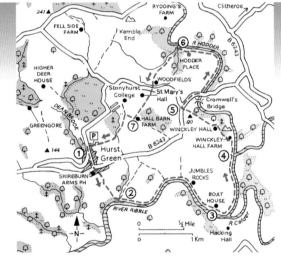

6½ miles (10.4km) 2hrs **Ascent:** 459ft (14m) ▲

Paths: Grassy riverside paths, woodland and farm tracks, 11 stiles

Suggested map: aqua3 OS Explorer 287 West Pennine Moors

Grid reference: SD 684382

Parking: By Hurst Green village hall or on roadside adjacent

Did these rivers, fields and woods inspire Tolkien's creation of The Shire?
❶ Walk down road to centre of **Hurst Green** village. Cross main road and go down **L** of **Shireburn Arms** pub to stile below main car park. Go down edge of field then follow small stream to duckboards and footbridge. After slight rise, wooden steps wind down to River **Ribble**. Bear **L** just above river.
❷ Skirt aqueduct and return to river bank. Gravel track swings **R** past **Jumbles Rocks**. Go through gate alongside small stone building with mast to rejoin river bank and follow it, towards **Boat House**.
❸ After rounding big bend, go up slightly to track. Follow it for about ½ mile (800m). Opposite confluence of Ribble and Hodder, go over stile by bench.
❹ Narrow path quickly rejoins track. At **Winckley Hall** Farm go **L** to houses, **R** between barns then **L** past pond and out into lane. This climbs steeply then levels out, swinging **L** past **Winckley Hall**. Go through

kissing gate on **R** and across field to another. Keep straight on across large field, just **L** of wood, then down past pond and up to road.
❺ Turn **R** down pavement to river. Immediately before bridge, turn **L** along track. Follow river round, climb up past **Hodder Place** then descend again to bridge over stream.
❻ Go up track on **L**, cross footbridge then climb long flight of wooden steps. Follow top edge of plantation then cross stile into field. Keep to its edge and at end cross stile on to stony track. Keep **L**, past **Woodfields** and out to road. Go down track by post-box to **Hall Barn Farm** and along **R** side of buildings.
❼ Turn **R** on tarmac track for 200yds (183m). Go **L** through gate by end of wall and along narrow field. At its end go **R** to track alongside wood then up to kissing gate. Follow field edge to another kissing gate. At top of final field, through gate, narrow path leads to short lane. At its end turn **L** back to start.

---

765 KNOTT END *BREEZY BRINE FIELDS*

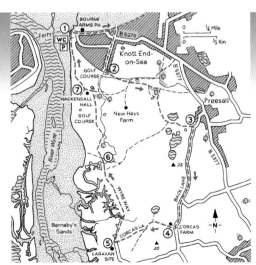

5½ miles (8.8km) 1hr 45min **Ascent:** 115ft (35m) ▲

Paths: Quiet streets and lanes, farm tracks and sea wall, 3 stiles

Suggested map: aqua3 OS Explorer 296 Lancaster, Morecambe & Fleetwood

Grid reference: SD 347485

Parking: Free car park by end of B5270 at Knott End

An easy walk exploring an unexpected corner of Lancashire's coastal plain.
❶ Go out to sea wall, turn **R** past ferry, along road past **Bourne Arms** and then along Esplanade. Where main road swings away, keep on along seafront, down private road then short stretch of footpath. Where this ends, before grassy stretch of seafront, go **R** down short side-street then straight across main road into Hackensall Road. Go down this almost to its end.
❷ Just before last house on **L** there's footpath (sign high up on lamppost) that wriggles round and then becomes clear straight track. Follow this through narrow belt of woodland, across open fields and then alongside wooded slope. Where wood ends go through iron kissing gate on **R** then up edge of wood and over stile into farmyard. Go straight through this and down stony track, which swings **L** between pools. It then becomes surfaced lane past some cottages.
❸ Join wider road (**Back Lane**) and go **R**. It

becomes narrow again. Follow this lane for about 1 mile (1.6km), over slight rise and down again, to **Corcas Farm**.
❹ Turn **R** on Corcas Lane ('Private Road Bridle Path Only'). Follow lane through brine fields. After ½ mile (800m) it swings **L** by caravan site.
❺ Go **R**, past **Wyre Way** sign and over stile on to embankment. Follow its winding course for 1 mile (1.6km) to stile with signpost just beyond.
❻ Go ahead on tractor track (sign 'Public Footpath to **Hackensall Hall** 1m'). When it meets **golf course**, track first follows its **L** side then angles across – heed danger signs! Follow track to **R** of Hackensall Hall. Just past its main gates go **L** on track with Wyre Way sign. This skirts round behind outlying buildings.
❼ Path swings **R** and then crosses **golf course** again. Aim for green shelter on skyline then bear **R** along edge of course. Skirt round white cottages, then go **L** to sea wall. Turn **R** along it back to car park.

Lancashire • NORTHWEST ENGLAND

Lancashire

BROCK BOTTOM *THE BOTTOM AND THE TOP*

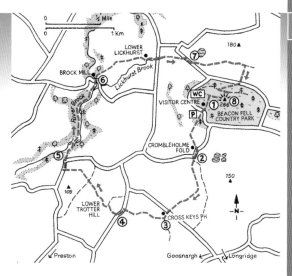

6 miles (9.7km) 2hrs Ascent: 689ft (210m)
Paths: Field paths, in places indistinct, clear tracks, 19 stiles
Suggested map: aqua3 OS Explorer OL41 Forest of Bowland & Ribblesdale
Grid reference: SD 565426
Parking: By Beacon Fell visitor centre

Upland Lancashire countryside, by turns both expansive and intimate.
❶ Look for public footpath sign in L-H corner of car park by **visitor centre**. Go down broad track, then through field. Bear **L** towards **Crombleholme Fold**. Walk, via farmyard, to country lane. Turn **R** to bend.
❷ Go **L**, cross stream then up track swinging **R**. After 50yds (46m) go **L**, down to stile just before field ends. From stile, 15yds (14m) further on, go down field then angle **R** to low bridge and straight up track beyond.
❸ Go through **Cross Keys** car park, through farmyard and into field. Go **R** to stile then straight on to corner of hedge. Follow it to tree then **L** to stile. Go **R** then straight ahead to lane and go **L**.
❹ Go **R** to **Lower Trotter Hill**. Cross cattle grid, go **L**, then round to **R** and past house. Go through L-H gate and up to stile. Follow field edge, eventually bending **L**. Go down stony track and **R** on road.

❺ As road bears **R** keep ahead. Descend on sunken track through woods; cross footbridge. Go up few paces then **R**. Follow path near river to **Brock Mill**.
❻ Cross bridge then go through gateway on **L**. Bear **R** up track then go **R**, through rhododendrons. Follow edge of wood, then go **R**, crossing stream. Go up field edge and straight on towards **Lower Lickhurst**. Go round into drive and up to road. Then go **R**, up drive. Keep straight on as it bends **L**, up fields to lane. Go **R** for 140yds (128m).
❼ Go **L** over stile and diagonally to isolated thorn tree. Continue to gateway and then to stile and footbridge. Follow old boundary, now muddy depression, then bear **L** to power lines. Follow these to marker post. Go **R**, directly uphill. Cross road to track rising through forest. At junction go **L** for 200m (183m) then **R** up narrow path to summit trig point.
❽ Bear **R** along edge of forest then **L** across boardwalk. Keep straight on to **visitor centre**.

CLOUGHA PIKE *DOWN TO THE SUMMIT*

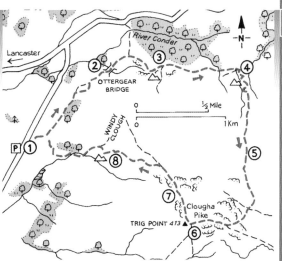

5¼ miles (8.4km) 2hrs Ascent: 1,050ft (320m)
Paths: Mostly very rough moorland, sometimes rocky, 5 stiles
Suggested map: aqua3 OS Explorer OL41 Forest of Bowland & Ribblesdale
Grid reference: SD 526604 **Parking:** Access Area car park at Birk Bank

A wild walk to an unrivalled viewpoint.
❶ Follow track above car park, then fork **L**. It becomes green path to **Ottergear Bridge**.
❷ Turn **L** along level track, then bear **R** at next junction. Track climbs slightly, descends into narrow valley, then climbs steeply up far side before it finally eases and swings round to **R**.
❸ Go **L** on narrow path, running almost level above steeper slope. After 500yds (457m), it angles back down into valley. Follow base of steep slope and cross stream. After 30yds (27m) green track climbs to **R**.
❹ Ascend steeply to near-level moor. Path follows slight groove, then skirts **L** around boggy patch. Grassy path ahead is initially very faint. Keep just **L** of continuous heather and it soon becomes clearer. There's another grooved section then clear stony path rises **L** across steeper ground.
❺ As slope eases path remains clear, passing sketchy cairns, then 'Limit of Access Area' sign. Follow groove, through or past tumbledown shooting butts.

As ground levels, trend **R** past cairns and marker stakes to ugly new track. Cross and follow thin grassy path with more marker stakes. Bear **R** up slight rise and join wider path at cairn. Go **R** on broad ridge, crossing fence, to summit **trig point**.
❻ Descend clear path on **R** past large cairn. There's steep drop near by on **L**, with small crags. Fence converges from **R**, eventually meeting well-built wall.
❼ Scramble down rocks by end of wall. Continue down its **L** side for 300yds (274m). Bear **L** at levelling above boulders. Descend through gap flanked by rocks and then cross gentler slopes to gate by corner of wall.
❽ Head straight down until ground steepens, then swing **R** and descend towards **Windy Clough**. From stile go **L** down grooved path to area of young trees. Fork **L**, closer to stream, rejoining wetter alternative routes above larger oaks. Descend through gorse then follow duckboards skirting bog. Turn **R** along track then keep **L** over slight rise to car park.

LECK BECK *OVER THE UNDERGROUND*

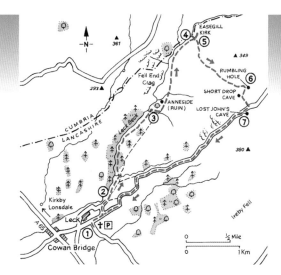

7½ miles (12.1km) 3hrs Ascent: 968ft (295m)
Paths: Field paths, indefinite moorland paths, quiet road, 3 stiles
Suggested map: aqua3 OS Explorer OL2 Yorkshire Dales – Southern & Western
Grid reference: SD 643767
Parking: Park by Leck church (honesty box)

The subterranean mysteries of limestone.
❶ Turn **R** on road then **R** again. Turn **L** by post-box and go down lane, bearing **R** at bottom.
❷ At end of tarmac take lower **L** track to stile then continue on good tractor track. Just after crossing stream track divides. Go **L** through gate into wood then continue through pasture, passing wooden house. Cross stile at end. Descend almost to river level then climb away.
❸ Climb steeply for 300yds (274m) then go **L** in slight dip past ruins of **Anneside**. Path, now sheep track, runs level and straight to ruined wall. Cross dip of small stream then bear **L** out of it, crossing damp ground on to grassy shoulder. Follow crest of steeper slopes dropping towards beck to tree-filled gorge.
❹ Go ahead on narrow path across slope – not difficult, but don't slip. Continue to upper reaches of **Easegill Kirk**. Look around, then retrace to crossroads and descend to level area below small outcrops. Cross

steep grass slope into gorge. After exploring this return to crossroads.
❺ Take uphill footpath. Where it levels go sharp **R** on narrow track to ruined wall. Follow this up to **L** then along, above rocky outcrops to green conical pit. Continue up and to **R**, on sheep tracks, to long, straight, dry-stone wall. Follow this up to **L** to clearer path. Fenced holes now appear in shallow dip in moor. Bear **L** to nearest, then follow narrow footpath past 2nd and 3rd. Follow shallow valley with no permanent stream, past small sink holes to deep shaft (**Rumbling Hole**).
❻ Turn **R** on faint footpath across level moorland to 2nd fenced hole, 200yds (183m) away (**Short Drop Cave**). From this head back towards dry-stone wall and, just before it, head up to **L** to road. Turn **R**. After 150yds (137m) **Lost John's Cave** can be seen to **L**.
❼ Continue down road for 2½ miles (4km) to **Leck**. Turn **L** near church to return to start of walk.

769 SILVERDALE *A QUART IN A PINT POT*

5½ miles (8.8km) 2hrs Ascent: 426ft (130m)
Paths: Little bit of everything, 10 stiles
Suggested map: aqua3 OS Explorer OL7 The English Lakes (SE)
Grid reference: SD 471759
Parking: Small National Trust car park for Eaves Wood

Enjoy continuous changes of scenery.

❶ From end of National Trust car park at **Eaves Wood**, follow footpath to T-junction. Go **R** few paces then **L**, climbing gently. Keep **L** to beech ring, then straight on. Descend through complex junction to high wall and continue on this line to lane.

❷ Cross on to track ('Cove Road'). Keep ahead down narrow path (Wallings Lane), drive, another track and another narrow path to wider road. After 200yds (183m) go **L** down Cove Road.

❸ From Cove walk **L**, below cliffs, to shore. Walk up road to Beach Garage then take footpath alongside.

❹ At next road turn **R** for 600yds (549m) then bear **R** down Gibraltar Lane for 350yds (320m). Enter National Trust property of **Jack Scout**.

❺ Descend **L** to limekiln then follow narrowing path directly away from it. This swings **L** above steep drop and descends. Follow broad green path to gate. After 100yds (91m), another gate leads into lane. At end

bear **L** below **Brown's Houses**. Follow edge of salt marsh to stile, go up slightly, then along to signpost.

❻ Turn **L**. Climb steeply to awkward squeeze stile. Gradient eases, over rock and through lightly wooded area into open. Go **L** to stile; follow wall down and into small wood. Follow track down **R**. Cross road to gap in wall, descend then walk below crags to **Woodwell**.

❼ Path ('The Green via cliff path') leads to rocky staircase. At top go ahead to join broader path. Follow it **L**, slant **R**; continue into woodland. Stile on **R** and narrow section lead to road. Go **R** 100yds (91m), then **L** into The Green. Keep **R** at junction; join wider road.

❽ Go **L** for 75yds (69m) then **R** ('Burton Well **Lambert's Meadow**'). Track soon descends then swings **L**, passing Burton Well on **R**. Cross stile into **Lambert's Meadow**, then go **R**, over footbridge to gate. Climb up, with steps, and continue more easily to fork. Go **L** alongside pool (**Bank Well**) into lane. Go **L** and at end car park is virtually opposite.

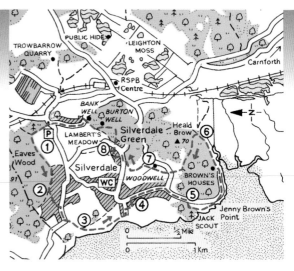

770 KENDAL *TWO CASTLES*

3 miles (4.8km) 1hr 30min Ascent: 300ft (91m)
Paths: Pavements, surfaced and grassy paths with steps, no stiles
Suggested map: aqua3 OS Explorer OL7 The English Lakes (SE)
Grid reference: SD 518928
Parking: Free parking area by river (occasionally occupied by fairground), plenty of pay car parks near by

Visit two ancient castles.

❶ Walk upstream along riverside parking area to footbridge. Cross and bear **L** to follow surfaced walkway, through **Gooseholme**. At junction of roads by **Church of St George** turn **R** down Castle Street. Pass **Castle Inn** and join Ann Street. Turn **R**; continue up hill to **Castle Road**. Ascend **Castle Road** to where kissing gate on **R** leads on to Castle Hill. Follow broad path ascending shoulder to **Kendal Castle**.

❷ Round castle ruins until, beneath its southern end, you find path dropping down to **R**. Descend steeply to pass through iron kissing gate on to Sunnyside. Follow Sunnyside, which becomes Parr Street; exit on to **Aynam Road**.

❸ Turn **R** along Aynam Road to crossing. Cross footbridge over **River Kent**. Bear **L**, downstream, and walk short distance to narrow, surfaced path leading **R**. Continue along path, lined by yew trees and limestone coping stones, to pass between parish

church and **Abbot Hall Art Gallery**. Emerge on to Kirkland Road by church gates with **Ring O'Bells** pub to **L**. Turn **R** along road; continue for 300yds (274m) to crossing. Cross it; bear **R** to cross **Gillingate Road** and keep along main road, now called Highgate. At chemist shop go **L** up **Captain French Lane** for 300yds (274m). Go **R** up Garth Heads Lane. Follow this until steep path ascends to **L**. Steps lead to terrace and view over Kendal. Cross grass terrace towards mound and its distinct bodkin-shaped obelisk. Climb steps then spiral **L** until, as path levels, steps lead up **R** to obelisk and top of **Castle Howe**.

❹ Return to path and go **R**. Find gap on **L** and emerge on road at top of Beast Banks. Descend hill, which becomes Allhallows Lane, to traffic lights and pedestrian crossing opposite **Town Hall**. Cross road and go **L**, then immediately turn **R** down Lowther Street. Go **L** at bottom to zebra crossing beyond Holy Trinity of St George, which leads to riverside.

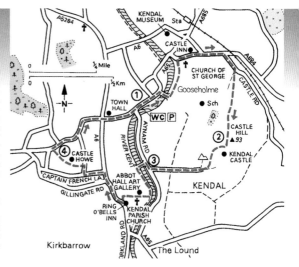

771 SEDGWICK *THE LANCASTER CANAL*

5½ miles (8.8km) 2hrs 30min Ascent: 600ft (183m)
Paths: Field paths, tow paths and some quiet lanes, 10 stiles
Suggested map: aqua3 OS Explorer OL7 The English Lakes (SE)
Grid reference: SD 513870
Parking: Roadside parking in Sedgwick

Walking by the Lancaster Canal.

❶ From canal aqueduct, follow Natland lane as far as 2nd junction and turn **R**. At Crosscrake church, go **R** again ('Stainton Cross').

❷ Leave through 1st gate on **L**; cross to stile in far **R** corner of field. Follow **L-H** hedge, continuing over 2nd stile. Beyond crest, drop to **Skettlegill Farm**, cross **Stainton Beck**; walk out to lane beyond.

❸ Cross to gate opposite then pass through another gate ahead. Climb again to stile, and maintain your direction across next field. Over another stile, walk to far wall and turn **R** to corner before emerging on to track by **Summerlands**.

❹ Walk ahead, passing through gate by Eskrigg Wood. Your way shortly broadens into meadow, but keep going to further of 2 gates at **L** corner. Waymark confirms route along hedged track into rough woodland. Soon path bends **L** to stile near a gate. Walk away across field to track at far side.

❺ Follow track to **R**, leading through farmyard at **High Commonmire**, and continuing as metalled way. Bear **R** at junction and proceed to **Field End Bridge**.

❻ Cross canal, drop **L** on to tow path; walk beneath bridge. Presently, beyond aqueduct built to take waterway over **Stainton Beck**, canal ends, onward section to Kendal has been filled in, de-watered or lost beneath road construction. However, its course remains clear, eventually leading to lane below **A591**.

❼ Pass under bridge and rejoin canal through gate on **R**. Cutting leads to mouth of **Hincaster Tunnel**, where path to **L** carries walkers, as it once did horses, over **Tunnel Hill**. At far side, turn **R** behind cottages to regain tow path. Remain by canal until forced on to lane and continue eventually to cross A591.

❽ Beyond bridge, steps rise to field on **R**. Walk ahead by fence, shortly passing under bridge. Beyond, canal cutting is evident, accompanying you to Sedgwick, where steps beside aqueduct drop to road.

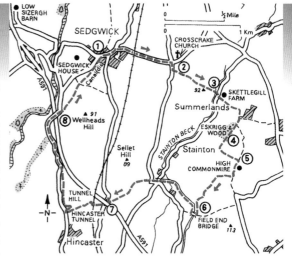

Cumbria

CUNSWICK SCAR *ALONG THE LIMESTONE*

3 miles (4.8km) 1hr 30min **Ascent:** 250ft (79m)
Paths: Paths and tracks, can be muddy, take care as edge of scar is unguarded in places, 2 stiles
Suggested map: aqua3 OS Explorer OL7 The English Lakes (SE)
Grid reference: SD 489923
Parking: Beneath radio mast near top of hill

The freedom of the heights, extensive views and varied flora, fauna and fossils make this an intriguing and liberating outing.

1 Walk away from road and cross sloping limestone bed, which forms car park; take track leading to communications **mast**. Pass low barrier then bear **R** to follow narrow path through wood. Leave wood by kissing gate at junction of stone walls. Look for footpath ('**Cunswick Fell**'). Enter field; continue along by stone wall. On reaching corner of field go **R** and follow path parallel to wall. Continue over humpback of field and descend to pass gate, beyond which wall turns sharp corner.

2 Bear **L** and follow grassy path, making slight descent before ascending to follow raised shoulder. Continue to intercept grassy track, with stone wall on R, and either cross stile or take gate through wire fence. Follow track along by stone wall to bear **R** beyond bottom of dip. As wall bends to R track rises

off to **L**. Follow track for 50yds (46m) until grass path bears off **L** in direction of top of hill. Ascend directly to summit cairn of **Cunswick Scar**. look out for fossils in the limestone of **Cunswick Scar** and **Cunswick Fell**. The corals are particularly attractive.

3 Continue beyond cairn and drop to lower terrace edged by scar. Take care here, cliff face of scar is unfenced at this point and reaches vertical height of around 40ft (12m). Turn **L**, facing out, and bear south along edge of scar. Fence now runs along edge of crag. Keep along rim of scar through avenue of gorse and hazel to edge of wall. Take narrow path alongside wall to find stile, crossing fence.

4 Cross stile and continue along by wall before bearing **L** to merge with original footpath at end of raised shoulder. Retrace your steps to join dry-stone wall at its corner, with gate just beyond. Pass gate and follow path along by walls to kissing gate at edge of wood. Follow path **L** through wood.

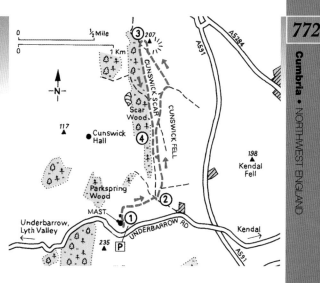

KENTMERE *A REMOTE VALLEY*

6¾ miles (10.9km) 2hrs 15min **Ascent:** 689ft (210m)
Paths: Generally good tracks and paths, some open fields, 7 stiles
Suggested map: aqua3 OS Explorer OL7 The English Lakes (SE)
Grid reference: SD 456040
Parking: Very limited in Kentmere, but small field by Low Bridge is occasionally available

Once ravaged by Scottish rivers, this lovely remote valley now basks in tranquillity.

1 Begin on bridleway ('**Kentmere Hall**') opposite St Cuthbert's Church. Approach farmyard and bear **R** behind cattle pens, then **R** again through side gate. Signpost ('**Kentmere Reservoir**') directs you up field. Leave at top and continue to gate. Pass barn and go through gap to another gate, where track leads past **Nook House**.

2 Ignore turn-off to Garburn, and immediately after next house, Greenhead, go **L**. Still following signs to reservoir, turn **R** through gate then **R** again at 2nd fork to join metalled track up valley.

3 Valley bottom here is wide and flat. Turn **L** past entrance to **Hartrigg Farm** and continue on track through valley, now progressively squeezed between craggy breasts of **Yoke** and **Kentmere Pike**. Eventually dam appears, rising above spoil heaps of abandoned slate quarries.

4 Continue to dam.

5 Bridges below dam take return route across outflows to path just above, which then follows Kent downstream. Beyond quarries, cross ladder stile into enclosure by barn and leave by gate on **L**.

6 Track continues through successive valley bottom fields, eventually leading to **Overend Farm**. Ignore tarmac lane and bear **R** through gate on to grass track. Where track later drops from Hallow Bank, keep ahead along **Low Lane**.

7 This old track ultimately emerges on to lane. Carry on, at next junction, to waymarked stile on **R** little further along. Route now lies across field but, for snack, continue along lane to 2nd junction and turn **L** to **Maggs Howe**, above lane on R.

8 Retrace your steps to stile and walk down to far bottom corner of field. Steep path drops beside stream through larch to emerge on to lane. Turn **L** and, at end, go **R**, back to church.

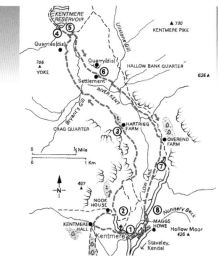

GRANGE-OVER-SANDS *ABOVE HAMPSFELL*

4 miles (6.4km) 2hrs **Ascent:** 790ft (241m)
Paths: Paths and tracks, can be muddy in places, 7 stiles
Suggested map: aqua3 OS Explorer OL7 The English Lakes (SE)
Grid reference: SD 410780 **Parking:** Car park below road and tourist office in central Grange

A walk above a charming seaside resort.

1 Join main road through Grange; go **R** (north), to pass **ornamental gardens**. Cross road; continue to roundabout. Go **L** along **Windermere Road** rising to round bend; find steps up to squeeze stile on **L** ('Routen Well/Hampsfield').

2 Take path rising above Eggerslack Wood. Cross over surfaced track; keep ahead, passing house on L. Steps lead to track. Cross this diagonally to follow track ('Hampsfell'). Track zig-zags to follow (house to L) and ascends through woods to stile over wall.

3 Cross stile to leave wood; follow path directly up hillside. Pass sections of limestone pavement and little craggy outcrops until path levels and bears **L** to stile over stone wall. Cross stile; go **R** along wall. Continue ahead, following grassy track, to pass stone cairns and up to square tower of **Hospice of Hampsfell**.

4 Leave tower heading south and following path over edge of limestone escarpment (take care). Continue over 2nd escarpment. Descend to stile over

wall, then to bottom of dip; rise directly up hill beyond. Cross over top; descend to find stile over wall. Path bears diagonally **L** but it is usual to continue to cairn marking **Fell End**. Go down **L**, picking up grassy track, which leads **L** round valley to gate leading on to road.

5 Cross road, take squeeze stile; descend diagonally **L** across field to gate or to road by **Springbank Cottage**. Descend surfaced track to enter farmyard; continue **L** over stone stile. Go over hill, following path (parallel to wall); take stile into narrow ginnel. Follow this down, with high wall to **R**, round corner; descend to junction of roads. Go **L** on private road/public footpath; bear **R** at fork. At next junction, turn **R** to descend track. At following junction go **L** down **Charney Well Lane**. At next junction, turn **L** below woods of **Eden Mount** to junction with Hampsfield Road near bottom of hill. At junction with larger road go **L** (toilets to R); pass church before descending past clock tower and junction with road (B5277). Go **L** then **R** to car park.

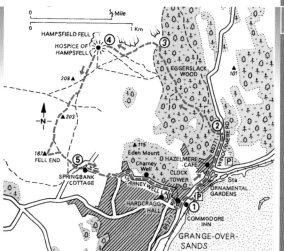

Cumbria

Cumbria • NORTHWEST ENGLAND

775 POOLEY BRIDGE *A ROMAN ROAD*

4½ miles (7.2km) 2hrs **Ascent:** 740ft (225m)
Paths: Surfaced roads, stony tracks, grassy tracks and hillside
Suggested map: aqua3 OS Explorer OL5 The English Lakes (NE)
Grid reference: NY 470244
Parking: Pay car parks either side of bridge

Enjoy views over the lake, cross a Roman road and spot the prehistoric artefacts.

❶ From bridge over **River Eamont** follow main street (B5320) through **Pooley Bridge**. Pass church; turn **R** to follow pavement along Howtown Road.

❷ At junction continue over crossroads. Road rises and becomes pleasantly tree-lined before ending at unsurfaced track beneath **Roehead**. Gate and kissing gate lead out on to open moor.

❸ Go through kissing gate and climb broad track, continuing to where going levels and track intercepts route of **High Street Roman road**.

❹ Bear **R** along now very boggy stretch of Roman road to reach low circular ancient wall of earth and stone. This, the **Cockpit**, is the largest of the many prehistoric antiquities found on **Moor Divock**.

❺ Way leads back diagonally north to shallow shake holes (sinkholes) to original track at **Ketley Gate**. (Little to R, **White Raise** burial cairn is worthy of

attention.) Either follow track (route marked on map), which leads off north ascending to walled wood high on hillside and then bear **L** to find top of **Heughscar Hill**, or go **L** up well-worn path through bracken, starting by stone parish boundary marker. Flat summit of hill offers rewarding views.

❻ Proceed north along high shoulder to pass broken little limestone crag of **Heugh Scar** below to **L**. At end of scar make steep descent of grassy hillside to point where track and grassy lane of **High Street Roman** road cross each other. Descend to **L** taking track that passes under Roman road; head in general direction of **Ullswater**. Note lime kiln and little **quarry** to L. Continue descent to corner of stone wall marked by sycamore tree. Follow route, which falls steeply down beside stone wall and beneath trees. Bear **L** near bottom of incline and gain original track just above gate and kissing gate situated beneath **Roehead**. Return by same road back to **Pooley Bridge**.

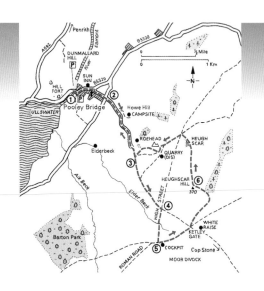

776 PATTERDALE *ULLSWATER'S SHORE*

4 miles (6.4km) 1hr 30min **Ascent:** 490ft (150m)
Paths: Stony tracks and paths, no stiles
Suggested map: aqua3 OS Explorer OL5 The English Lakes (NE)
Grid reference: NY 396159 **Parking:** Pay-and-display car park opposite Patterdale Hotel

From the shores of Ullswater to one of its most spectacular viewpoints.

❶ From car park walk to road; turn **R** towards **Ullswater** shore. Pass **school** to track leading off **R**, through buildings. Follow unsurfaced track over bridge; continue to pass stone buildings of **Side Farm** to join another unsurfaced track.

❷ Turn **L** along track, with stone wall **L**; pass through woodland before open fell side appears above. Proceed along path above **campsite** to pass larch, then descend to cross stream above buildings of **Blowick**, seen through trees below. Path ascends again to crest craggy knoll above woods of **Devil's Chimney**. Make steep descent following path through rocks (take care) before it levels to traverse beneath craggy heights of **Silver Crag**. Caution is needed as steep ground falls directly to lake below. Slight ascent, passing holly trees, gains shoulder of **Silver Point**.

❸ Follow path, which sweeps beneath end of **Silver Crag**, and continue to pass small stream before steep

stony path, eroded in places, breaks off to **R**. Ascend this, climbing diagonally **R**, through juniper bushes. Gain narrow gap, which separates **Silver Crag** to **R** from main hillside of **Birk Fell** to **L**. Little valley is quite boggy and holds small **tarnlet**.

❹ To avoid steep, exposed ground, follow high narrow path to make gradual descent south in direction of **Patterdale**. But if you have a head for heights, take short steep scramble, which leads to top of **Silver Crag**. Care must be exercised for steep ground lies in all directions. Descend back to ravine and main path by same route. Path is easy though it traverses open fell side and may be boggy. Pass open **quarry** workings, where there is a large unfenced hole next to path (take care); continue on, to cross over slate scree of larger **quarry**. Bear **R** to descend by stream; cross footbridge leading to gate at end of track.

❺ Go **L** through gate; follow lane through meadows. Cross bridge; join road. Bear **R** through **Patterdale** to return to car park.

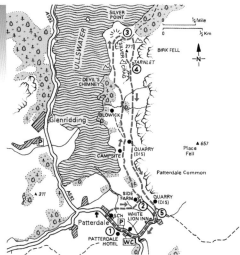

777 BOWNESS-ON-WINDERMERE *BRANT FELL*

3½ miles (5.7km) 1hr 15min **Ascent:** 525ft (160m)
Paths: Pavement, road, stony tracks, grassy paths, 2 stiles
Suggested map: aqua3 OS Explorer OL7 The English Lakes (SE)
Grid reference: SD 398966
Parking: Fee car park on Glebe Road above Windermere lake

Enjoy woodlands and breathtaking views.

❶ Take Glebe Road into Bowness. Swing **L** and, opposite steamer pier, go **R** over main road; turn **L**. Opposite **Church of St Martin**, turn **R** to go up St Martins Hill. Cross Kendal Road to climb **Brantfell Road** directly above. At head of road, iron gate leads to **Dales Way**, which climbs up hillside. Proceed to kissing gate by wood, leading on to lane.

❷ Pass through kissing gate; turn **R** ('**Post Knott**') to follow lane. Proceed ahead, rising through woods until lane crests height near flat circular top of **Post Knott**. Bear **L**; make final short ascent to summit. Retrace steps to track; bear **R** to kissing gate, leaving wood on to open hillside.

❸ Beyond kissing gate take grassy path, rising to rocky shoulder. Cross shoulder and first descend, then ascend to ladder stile in top corner of field by fir trees. Cross stile; bear **R** to ascend up open grassy flanks of **Brant Fell** to rocky summit.

❹ Go **L** (north) from top of fell, descending grassy path intercepted by grassy track. Bear **R** here; follow track to stone stile and gate on to road. Turn **L** on road; continue **L** at junction to pass stone buildings and entrance drive to **Matson Ground**. Immediately beyond is kissing gate on **L**, waymarked **Dales Way**.

❺ Go through kissing gate; continue down field to cross track; pass through kissing gate into another field. Keep on grassy track until path swings **L** to emerge through kissing gate on to surfaced drive. Go **R** along drive for 30yds (27m) until path veers off **L** through trees to follow fence. Iron kissing gate leads into field. Follow grassy path, first descending and then rising to iron gate in field corner. Continue to join grassy track; go through kissing gate. Cross **Brantfell Farm's** surfaced drive; keep ahead to another kissing gate leading into field. Follow path, parallel to wall, descending hill to intercept track, via kissing gate; regain Point ❷. Retrace route back to **Glebe Road**.

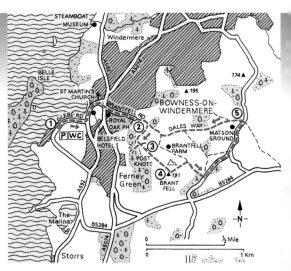

Cumbria

AMBLESIDE *LILIES AND LAKES*

3¼ miles (5.3km) 1hr 45min **Ascent:** 575ft (175m)

Paths: Road, paths and tracks, can be muddy in places, 3 stiles

Suggested map: aqua3 OS Explorer OL7 The English Lakes (SE)

Grid reference: NY 375047

Parking: Ambleside central car park

Above little Ambleside.

❶ Take wooden footbridge from car park; go **R** along Rydal road to pass waterwheel and Bridge House. At junction bear **R** along Compston Road. Continue to next junction (cinema on corner); bear **R** to cross side road and enter Vicarage Road alongside chip shop. Pass school; enter Rothay Park. Follow main path through park to emerge by flat bridge over **Stock Ghyll Beck**. Cross beck, then go **L** to cross over stone arched **Miller Bridge** spanning **River Rothay**.

❷ Bear **R** along road over cattle grid until, in few paces, steep surfaced road rises to **L**. Climb road, which becomes unsurfaced, by buildings of **Brow Head**. At S-bend, beyond buildings, stone stile leads up and off **L**. Pass through wall; in few dozen paces, stone squeeze stile. Pass through; climb open hillside above. Paths are well worn and there are various possible routes. For best views keep diagonally **L**. Rising steeply at first, path levels before

rising again to ascend 1st rocky knoll. Higher, larger knoll follows and offers good views.

❸ Beyond this, way descends to **R**, dropping to well-defined path. Follow path to pass little pond before cresting rise and falling to little pocket-handkerchief **Lily Tarn** (flowers bloom late June to September). Path skirts **R** edge of tarn, roughly following crest of **Loughrigg Fell**. Gate/stile leads to base of further knoll and this is ascended to another viewpoint.

❹ Take path descending to **R** to track below. Bear **R** to gate, which leads through stone wall boundary of open fell and into field. Continue to descend track, passing **old golf clubhouse** on **L**. Intercept original route just above buildings of Brow Head.

❺ Continue to cross **Miller Bridge** then, before flat bridge, bear **L** to follow track by side of **Stock Ghyll Beck**. Beyond meadows, lane through houses leads to main Rydal road. Bear **R** along road to car park beyond fire station.

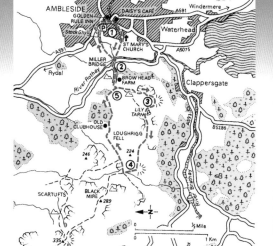

SOUTHER FELL *A BONNIE TRAIL*

6 miles (9.7km) 3hrs **Ascent:** 985ft (300m)

Paths: Grassy and stony paths, open fellside, 4 stiles

Suggested map: aqua3 OS Explorer OL5 The English Lakes (NE)

Grid reference: NY 364300

Parking: Wide verge above river in Mungrisdale

Rolling grassy fells offer quiet solitude.

❶ Head north on road, following **Glenderamackin** upstream. Bear **R** where road crosses bridge and continue to hairpin bend. Go **L** to leave road, pass telephone box; follow lane between cottages. Go through gate; continue on track above north bank of river. Bear **L**; cross little **Bullfell Beck** by footbridge.

❷ Bear **L** off steeply ascending track; follow lesser stony track, which traces route along **R** bank (true **L**) of **River Glenderamackin**. Route is straightforward although path is eroded in places and there is a steep drop into little river. Continue along track (very boggy in places) to ford **Bannerdale Beck**. Quite easy if you keep dry by balancing on stones. Round shoulder of **Bannerdale Fell** (**White Horse Bent**). Continue ascent until path falls **L** to wooden footbridge to cross **River Glenderamackin**.

❸ Path ascends hillside striking diagonally **L** to climb to top of high grassy shoulder. Mousthwaite

Comb lies down below to R. Bear **L** following path; ascend long shoulder of **Souther Fell**. Pass large circular cairn and continue along level shoulder, heading north to summit (little rocky knoll).

❹ Keep north and continue to descend grassy nose of fell. Easy at first, angle steepens progressively until nearing base. Little craggy outcrops are best avoided by following path to their **L**. Path is well defined and soon leads to stone wall near bottom of fell. Go **R** alongside wall. Path is extremely boggy in places. Continue along by wall until it bends **L** and steep short descent leads to surfaced road.

❺ Go **L** on road, through gate until, at bottom of hill, grassy lane continues to **River Glenderamackin**, just upstream of buildings of **Beckside**. Before reaching ford that crosses river, stone steps over wall on **R** give access to footbridge. Cross bridge; go **L** to exit field via squeeze stile. Turn **R**, climb grassy bank to road. Head **L**; go upstream to return to parking area.

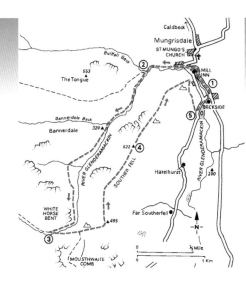

ST JOHN'S IN THE VALE *A WILD FELL*

5 miles (8km) 2hrs 45min **Ascent:** 1,115ft (340m)

Paths: Grassy paths and track, 8 stiles

Suggested map: aqua3 OS Explorer OL5 The English Lakes (NE)

Grid reference: NY 318195

Parking: Car park at Legburthwaite, head of St John's in the Vale

Exploring a compact valley.

❶ Pass through head of car park to small gate leading on to old road. Turn **L**; go down lane to kissing gate that opens on to verge of busy **A591**. Turn **R** and cross **Smaithwaite Bridge** to stile climbing wall to **R**. Cross stile; take path that rises to **L**. This leads through stand of Scots pine and climbs to top of **Wren Crag** with fine views.

❷ Descend steeply into dip; take gap in wall. Climb again to follow along above rocky outcrops of **Long Band**. Grassy incline leads to stile over wire fence to **L**. Cross this then go **R**, first rising then falling to pass little **tarn** in hollow. Path descends to **L**, dipping to reach stile over stone wall. Beyond stile, path runs along wall, climbing to pass through corridor formed by rocky knoll of **Moss Crag**. Immediately beyond, turn **L**. (Small tarn to **R**.) Make steep ascent to top of **High Rigg**. High grassy ridge leads above shining tarns of Paper Moss to hollow and pond. Ascend to

summit of **Naddle Fell** (unnamed on Ordnance Survey maps), highest point of walk, which offers views to high fells of Blencathra and Skiddaw.

❸ Wide path falls down steepening hillside to buildings by road above **St John's Church**. Turn **R** down road, past church, to gate and stile leading to grassy track. Skirt foot of fell along track. Below **Rake How** pass ruined farm.

❹ Keep along track, taking high route **R** of and above **Sosgill**, to pass through 3 gates/stiles followed by kissing gate into larch and conifer plantation. Exit trees via kissing gate; continue to take path to **R** side of **Low Bridge End Farm**. Continue along track through another series of gates and stiles to point where track meets bank of **St John's Beck**, beneath **Wren Crag**. Here track ends and footpath continues above river, rising through trees to grassy shoulder above stile that leads back on to A591. Turn **L** and Lagain to return to car park.

Cumbria • NORTHWEST ENGLAND

781 · CONISTON *To Tarn Hows*

6¾ miles (10.9km) 3hrs 30min Ascent: 885ft (270m) ②
Paths: Road, grassy paths and tracks, 4 stiles
Suggested map: aqua3 OS Explorer OL7 The English Lakes (SE)
Grid reference: SD 303975 **Parking:** Coniston car park

Explore Yewdale before reaching Tarn Hows.
❶ Exit car park on to Tilberthwaite Avenue; turn **R**. Continue until road leads off **L**. Follow this beyond football field to **Shepherd Bridge**. Cross; go immediately **L** over stone stile. Path leads to kissing gate into field. Bear diagonally **R** towards rocky outcrop and oaks; continue along to **R** of stone wall. Shortly, path leads to stone building.
❷ Pass building on **L**. Ascend through gate. Bear **R**, following wall, then rise to gate through stone wall (**High Guards Wood** perimeter). Climb steeply to top of hill. Cross ruined stone wall; follow waymarked path to descend through wood. Exit wood; continue on track, muddy in places, to gate and stile leading to lane.
❸ Go **L** up lane. Shortly, go **R** through gate. Rise with grassy track until it swings **R** to pass through gate/stile. Vague grassy track intercepts fence with larch plantation of **Tarn Hows Wood** below. Keep **R** along track; continue to steep, surfaced track. **Tarn Hows Cottage** is below to **L**. Go **R** to Tarn Hows road.

Go **L**, ascending road, past car park, to track bearing **L** above Tarn Hows.
❹ Follow track in anticlockwise circumnavigation of **The Tarns**. At end is little dam.
❺ Turn **R** here; descend path to **R** of beck. At bottom, go **L** over footbridge, then **R** through Tom Gill car park out on to Coniston road. Cross and go **L**. Turn **R** at Yewtree Farm; go **R** through gate. Rise to pass through another gate, then **L** above fence. Follow grassy track around **High Yewdale Farm**, until gate leads to Hodge Close road. Turn **L** over **Shepherd's Bridge**; join Coniston road.
❻ Cross and go **L** until, opposite **High Yewdale Farm**, path leads **R**, passing yew trees. Go **R** across fields. Enter farmyard of **Low Yewdale**. Go **L** along lane, over bridge; continue to round sharp bend. Go **R** ('Cumbria Way') through field. Beyond stone wall, track ascends then bears **R**. Continue to enter **Back Guards Plantation**. Follow track through wood. Pass through yew trees; descend to join outward route.

782 · SATTERTHWAITE *Medieval Industry*

4¾ miles (7.7km) 2hrs Ascent: 1,017ft (310m) ▲
Paths: Mainly good paths and tracks throughout, 3 stiles
Suggested map: aqua3 OS Explorer OL7 The English Lakes (SE)
Grid reference: SD 344912
Parking: Forest car park at Blind Lane

Follow paths once trodden by charcoal burners, iron smelters and coppicers.
❶ Path from back of car park, marked by green-and-white-topped posts, heads **R**, over rise to forest trail. Walk **L** and, after 400yds (366m), turn **L** on to path through birch wood. Go ahead over junction at top and descend to join metalled track into Satterthwaite.
❷ Turn **L** by church; walk through village. After ¼ mile (400m), at **L-H** bend, go **R** on to track, **Moor Lane**, and then at marker post, head **L** on to rising path into trees. Bear **L** in front of reconstructed charcoal burner's **hut** and then shortly drop down on to broader track.
❸ Go **R**, over another hill and **R** again where you eventually reach broad forest trail. Pass **waterfall**. Beyond, track bends across stream before rising to junction. Turn **L** for 220yds (201m) and branch **L** again on to unmarked, descending grass track.

❹ Emerging on to lane at bottom, go **R**, then turn in between cottages at **Force Forge**. Through gate on **R**, go **L** by tall beech hedge and across **Force Beck**. Continue along winding path into **Brewer Wood**, bearing **R** when you shortly reach crossing path.
❺ After about ¼ mile (400m), at fork, bear **L** to gap in wall and continue through trees. Reach indistinct fork beyond crest of the hill and take **R-H** branch, which descends to **Rusland Reading Rooms**. Cross out to lane in front of church and walk **L**.
❻ After little way along, leave lane for byway opposite junction. Climb over top of **Strickely** beside wooded pastures and eventually drop to lane at **Force Mills**. Go **R** and then **L** to ascend beside **Force Falls**.
❼ At green-and-white post, part-way up hill, turn **R** on to path climbing steeply into larch plantation. Keep **R** where path forks, shortly passing through gap in wall. Go through another gap few paces on; descend through trees back to car park.

783 · ELTERWATER *Four Seasons Walk*

4 miles (6.4km) 2hrs Ascent: 328ft (100m) ②
Paths: Grassy and stony paths and tracks, surfaced lane, 4 stiles
Suggested map: aqua3 OS Explorer OL7 The English Lakes (SE)
Grid reference: NY 328048
Parking: National Trust pay-and-display car park at Elterwater village

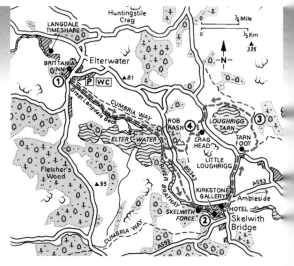

Bluebell woods, a lake and Little Loughrigg.
❶ Pass through small gate to walk downsteam above **Great Langdale Beck**. Continue to enter mixed woods of **Rob Rash**. Gate leads through stone wall (open foot of **Elter Water** lies to **R**). Continue through meadows above river. (Lane can be wet and is prone to flooding.) Pass through gate and enter mixed woods. Keep along path to pass **Skelwith Force** waterfall down to **R**. A little bridge leads across channel to viewing point above falls. Keep along path to pass through buildings (Kirkstone Quarry).
❷ **Kirkstone Gallery** is on **R**, as path becomes surfaced road. Continue to intercept **A593** by bridge over river. Turn **L** to pass **hotel**. At road junction cross over Great Langdale road to lane, which passes by end of cottages. Follow lane, ascending to intercept another road. Turn **R** for short distance, then **L** towards **Tarn Foot** farm. Bear **R** along track, in front of cottages. Where track splits, bear **L**. Through gate

continue on track to overlook **Loughrigg Tarn**. At point halfway along tarn cross stile over iron railings on **L**.
❸ Follow footpath down meadow to traverse **R**, just above tarn. Footpath swings **R** to climb ladder stile over stone wall. Follow grassy track leading **R**, up hill, to gate and stile on to road. Turn **L** along road, until surfaced drive leads up to **R** ('Public Footpath Skelwith Bridge'). Pass small cottage and keep on track to pass higher cottage, **Crag Head**. Little way above this, narrow grassy footpath leads off **R**, up hillside, to gain level shoulder between outcrops of **Little Loughrigg**.
❹ Continue down and descend path, passing little tamlet to **R**, to intercept stone wall. Keep **L** along wall descending to find, in a few hundred paces, ladder stile leading over stone wall into upper woods of **Rob Rash**. Steep descent leads to road. Cross this, and go over little stone stile/broken wall next to large double gates. Descend track to meet with outward route. Bear **R** to return to **Elterwater**.

Cumbria

STONETHWAITE *HERRIES FAMILY SAGA*

4½ miles (7.2km) 3hrs 30min **Ascent:** 1,102ft (336m)
Paths: Bridleways, fairly good paths and some rough walking
Suggested map: aqua3 OS Explorer OL4 The English Lakes (NW)
Grid reference: NY 262137
Parking: By telephone box in Stonethwaite

Through Walpole's Herries country – from Stonethwaite to Rosthwaite.

❶ From parking area, turn **R** and walk down track to **Stonethwaite Bridge**. Cross it and go through gate then turn **R** on to bridleway to Grasmere. Go through another gate. After about 150yds (137m), look for path off to **L**, through gap in low wall.

❷ Follow path uphill, through wood, then cross stile and continue uphill on well-paved path through trees. Path emerges from trees still climbing. Cross stile beside **Willygrass Gill** and follow path to **Dock Tarn**.

❸ Ignore track going R, over beck, and continue on obvious path around **L** side of tarn. There are rocky sections but going isn't difficult. If lower path is flooded, there are higher paths available to your **L**, which lead in same direction.

❹ At north end of tarn broad path continues above boggy ground in direction of gap between 2 low crags. Ahead, view opens up. Just past small rock pinnacle

on **L**, **Watendlath** comes into view and path descends steep rocky staircase to kissing gate.

❺ Go through gate, cross beck; follow green-topped wooden posts on stone path across bog. Turn **R** at junction ('**Watendlath**'); descend to sheep pen. Go through gap in wall and descend to kissing gate.

❻ Go through gate, follow stream downhill, cross it then follow line of wall round field before turning **L** on to farm track. Go through 2 gates and turn **R** across old pack bridge into **Watendlath**.

❼ From Watendlath re-cross little bridge and follow public bridleway sign to **Rosthwaite**. Walk uphill on well-used route; go through kissing gate and head downhill, passing gate on R. At bottom of hill, sign on wall indicates that path continues to **Stonethwaite**.

❽ Ignore sign and instead turn **R** through gate in wall, go downhill, pass through another gate beside **Hazel Bank hotel**; turn **L** on to public bridleway and follow it to **Stonethwaite Bridge**.

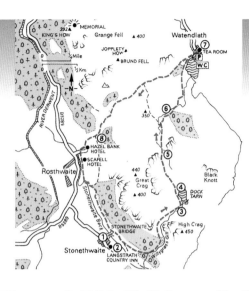

LATRIGG *TAKING THE LINE*

5 miles (8km) 2hrs **Ascent:** 902ft (275m)
Paths: Railway trackbed, country lane, grassy fell paths, 3 stiles
Suggested map: aqua3 OS Explorer OL4 The English Lakes (NW)
Grid reference: NY 270238
Parking: At former Keswick Station

A walk along a disused railway line leads to a fine viewpoint above Keswick.

❶ From old Keswick Station, head along trackbed, away from **Keswick**. Beyond A66 road, here cantilevered above trackbed, route covers boardwalk section high above **River Greta**, before continuing to site of bobbin mill at **Low Briery**, now **caravan site**.

❷ Beyond Low Briery, **River Greta** is agreeable companion as far as old railway building on R used as **information point** (with river bridge beyond) – but keep your binoculars handy. Greta's fast-flowing waters are a habitat for many young invertebrates, making it a popular hunting ground for dippers, kingfishers and grey heron. Before reaching building, turn **L** through gate and cross narrow pasture to back lane. Turn **L** and climb, steeply for short while, to reach footpath ('Skiddaw and Underscar') at gate and stile.

❸ Go over stile on to broad track, which swinging round gorse bushes then runs centrally up eastern

ridge of **Latrigg**. Look back here for spectacular views of Blencathra. Shortly, you reach plantation on R. Before plantation ends, climb **L** from metal gate towards top of ridge and walk along it to gate.

❹ After gate, lovely stroll leads across top of **Latrigg**, with great views of Vale of Keswick, Dodds, Borrowdale, Newlands Valley, and, to R, Skiddaw's massive bulk.

❺ Beyond highest point of **Latrigg**, bench is perfectly placed to admire view. From here take path descending gently northwards, later dropping in zig-zags to intercept track alongside another plantation.

❻ At track, turn **L**, and then continue down to **Spooney Green Lane**, which crosses high above **A66** and runs on to meet **Briar Rigg**, back lane. At this junction, turn **L** into **Briar Rigg**, and follow lane (enclosed path on L along **Briar Rigg** makes for safer passage), until you can branch **R** at pronounced **L** bend to return to station car park.

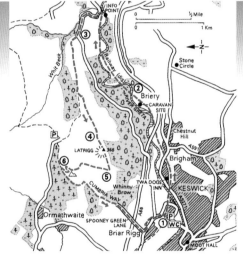

SWIRL HOW *AVOIDING THE OLD MAN*

8 miles (12.9km) 5hrs **Ascent:** 2,820ft (860m)
Paths: Well-defined mountain paths and tracks, no stiles
Suggested map: aqua3 OS Explorer OL6 The English Lakes (SW)
Grid reference: SD 303975
Parking: Pay-and-display near Coniston church
Note: Caution, this walk is not advised in poor visibility

A tough mountain route on Swirl How.

❶ While you are in **Coniston** it is worth visiting the Ruskin Museum. It is an interesting memorial to the artist and a useful guide to the area's heritage. Turn **L** out of main car park in **Coniston** to pass St Andrew's Church, then **L** again in village centre, before taking first **R** up Walna Scar Road. After passing **Sun Hotel** go **R** to follow path tracing **Church Beck** to old **Miners Bridge** above some dramatic waterfalls.

❷ Cross bridge before climbing alongside beck. Track comes to vast area of Coniston copper mines, and passes beneath some terraced cottages before swinging **L** behind **youth hostel**. At next junction, take **R** fork which zig-zags up slopes of **Tongue Brow** to reach shores of **Levers Water**.

❸ From here track becomes path, climbing steadily up to high pass of **Swirl Hawse**, which separates summits of **Swirl How** and **Wetherlam**.

❹ On reaching pass, turn **L** and climb up rough path that weaves and scrambles over rocks of **Prison Band** to reach cairn on **Swirl How's** summit.

❺ Continue along cairned ridge path, descending to saddle between **Swirl How** and grassy whaleback of **Brim Fell**. Keep watch for narrow path branching off to **R**. This takes you round high sides of **Brim Fell** for direct route to **Goat's Hawse** (pass overlooking **Goat's Water**).

❻ On reaching pass, descend towards tarn, passing beneath cliffs of **Dow Crag**. Rough and rocky route traces eastern shores of tarn before swinging **L** into grassy bowl known as **The Cove**.

❼ Path meets **Walna Scar Road** just above Cove Beck **packhorse bridge**. Turn **L** to follow ancient road round south sides of **Old Man**. In lower regions, road becomes tarmac, hedge-lined lane, descending to **Sun Hotel** and back into village centre.

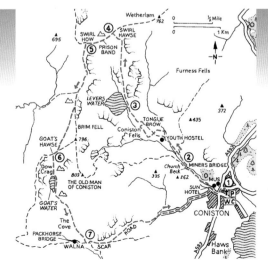

Cumbria

787 KESWICK *ABOVE DERWENT WATER*

5¼ miles (8.4km) 3hrs Ascent: 1,083ft (330m) ⚠️
Paths: Good paths and tracks, steep ascent and descent, 3 stiles; **Caution:** One steep, unfenced drop
Suggested map: aqua3 OS Explorer OL4 The English Lakes (NW)
Grid reference: NY 265229
Parking: Derwent Head car park

Wonderful panoramas, a lake and sylvan splendour are the delights of this walk.

❶ Proceed down road to **Derwent Bay**. Go **L** opposite landing stages, past toilets, to take track through Cockshot Wood. Walk through wood; exit on to fenced lane, which leads across field to **Borrowdale** road. Cross road; climb stone steps to enter **Castlehead Wood**. Take path, which bends **L** to ascend shoulder. Shortly, steeper path climbs up to **R**, to rocky summit of **Castle Head**.

❷ Descend by same route to reach shoulder; follow path **R** to find kissing gate. Exit wood; enter lane through field. Continue to Springs Road; go **R**. Ascend to cross bridge by **Springs Farm**. Take track up through **Springs** Wood. Bear **R** at junction; follow edge of wood to pass TV mast. Ascend until footbridge crosses **L** to Castlerigg Road. Bear **R** and continue to footbridge below **Rakefoot**.

❸ Cross footbridge. Turn **L**; follow path, ascending by stone wall. Cross stile; walk on to open shoulder of fell, ascending steep grassy nose. Going levels until you reach stile on **R** through fence, which leads to path following edge of crag. **Caution,** there is steep unfenced drop. To stay away from cliff edge, take higher stile. Follow path, which crosses head of gully, **Lady's Rake**, to climb on to polished rock cap of **Walla Crag** where views are superb.

❹ Return to boundary; follow wall down, taking lower stile. Path descends steeply above Cat Gill. Descend to track by bridge; bear **R** into **Great Wood**. Follow track then descend **L** into car park. Continue straight across, to path, which descends to gap in wall by **Borrowdale Road**. Take gap in wall opposite; follow the path to lake shore.

❺ Bear **R**, following round **Calfclose Bay**, by **Stable Hills**, around **Ings Wood** and **Strandshag Bay** to Scots pine on **Friar's Crag**. Continue to **Derwent Bay**; take footpath along roadside to car park.

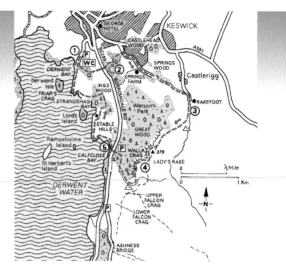

788 ARD CRAGS *ANCIENT OAKS*

5 miles (8km) 2hrs 30min Ascent: 1,306ft (398m) ⚠️
Paths: Road, narrow fell paths, one vague turning, no stiles
Suggested map: aqua3 OS Explorer OL4 The English Lakes (NW)
Grid reference: NY 229201
Parking: Small car park in old roadside quarry at Rigg Beck

Walking in the ancient Lakeland fells.

❶ Leave **quarry** car park at **Rigg Beck**; walk up road. Keep **R** at junction to rise gently past farms and fields. Pass **Birkrigg Farm B&B**, **Gillbrow Farm** and **Bawd Hall**. Road later descends gently across more rugged fellside and reaches sharply pronounced bend crossing beck of Ill Gill. Steep slope covered in ancient sessile **oaks** rises to **R**.

❷ Immediately after crossing beck, turn **R**; climb steeply uphill past **Keskadale Farm**. Follow wire fence until gradient eases. Look carefully at flank of fell to spot grassy path rising uphill (line is clear when path is flanked by bracken). Once located, follow path.

❸ Path is narrow as it crosses steep, heathery slope and there are stony patches. At higher level slope is boggy and path is vague. Look up to **R** and aim for rounded summit (topped by small pile of stones). This is **Knott Rigg** (1,824ft (556m), completely surrounded by higher fells.

❹ Clear path heads roughly northeast along hummocky ridge. Mosses, sedges and rushes indicate wet ground. Path drops to gap, then climbs uphill slightly to **R** of ridge. Ground cover is now heather. Gullies fall away to **R** before you reach summit cairn on **Ard Crags** (1,906ft (581m).

❺ Walk along heathery ridge, with superb views over Vale of Newlands. Your descent is in 2 stages: drop to heathery bump then drop more steeply past outcrops of rock.

❻ Heather gives way to bracken as gradient eases, then path runs level on to blunt, grassy ridge. Swing **L** to descend alongside wall and fence, where slope is wet and boggy. At **Rigg Beck**, ford flow. If narrower crossing point is needed, look short way upstream.

❼ Climb up from **Rigg Beck**; join clear path; turn **R** to follow it down valley. Slopes are covered in bracken with occasional clumps of gorse. Path leads back to car park.

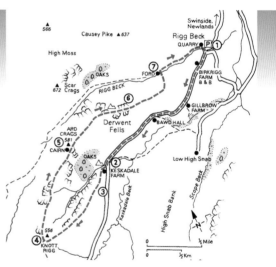

789 CAT BELLS *HIGH SPY*

9 miles (14.5km) 4hrs Ascent: 2,460ft (750m) ⚠️
Paths: Generally good paths, indistinct above Tongue Gill, 4 stiles (Not advised in poor visibility)
Suggested map: aqua3 OS Explorer OL4 The English Lakes (NW)
Grid reference: NY 247212 **Parking:** Wooded parking area at Hawes End

A delightful romp above two lovely valleys.

❶ At **Hawes End**, walk up road. At bend take stepped and rocky path rising steeply. Follow this, climbing steadily via rocky outcrops before reaching Brandlehow. Route keeps to middle of grassy ridge, before rising through more outcrops to **Cat Bells**.

❷ From **Cat Bells** descend to broad col of **Hause Gate**. Proceed across **Hause Gate** on grassy path and on to broad expanse of **Maiden Moor**, across which path leads to summit of **High Spy**.

❸ Head down path towards col housing **Dalehead Tarn**. Gradually ravine of **Tongue Gill** appears to **L**, but finding right moment to quit **Dalehead Tarn** path can prove difficult. Paths are indistinct and wet underfoot, but just keep heading for fence.

❹ Either of stiles across fence gives on to path leading to large cairn at start of path down to **Rigghead Quarries**. Take care descending steep slate paths until gradient eases alongside **Tongue Gill** itself. Keeping to **R** bank, follow gill to path T-junction; turn **L** to gate and stile, and footbridge.

❺ Path now climbs gently and soon crosses shallow col near **Castle Crag**. Pass crag, descending, shortly to enter woodland at gate. Cross narrow footbridge spanning Broadslack Gill; follow path down to banks of **River Derwent**. Just before river, cross footbridge on **L** and another little further on, keeping to path roughly parallel with river until you reach wall. Take broad track, following wall; eventually walk out to lane. Go **R**; walk up to **Grange** village. Go **L** and follow road.

❻ Just after **Manesty Cottages**, branch **L** on to path climbing gently above road to stile and gate. Go through this and continue on to gently rising broad track and, when it forks, bear **R**, heading for path above intake wall. Pressing on beyond **Brackenburn**, footpath soon dips to make brief acquaintance with road at small quarry car park. Beyond gap, immediately return to gently rising path. This old road, traversing lower slopes of **Cat Bells**, will ultimately bring you back to road at **Hawes End**.

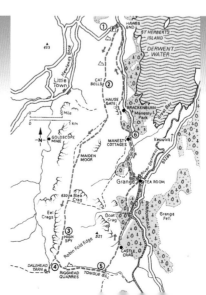

Cumbria

BARDSEA *DISTANT PAST*

8 miles (12.9km) 3hrs **Ascent:** 577ft (176m)
Paths: Paths and tracks, some field paths may be muddy, 10 stiles
Suggested map: aqua3 OS Explorer OL6 The English Lakes (SW); OL7 The English Lakes (SE)
Grid reference: SD 301742 (on Explorer OL7)
Parking: Small car parks between coast road and shore at Bardsea

A walk strewn with ancient remains.
❶ Follow shore to **Sea Wood**. Path runs parallel, turning **R** on inside edge of wood to reach road. Turn **L**, then **R** at gate into another part of wood. ❷ Turn **L** to follow path around top edge of wood, then **L** again to leave wood at gate. Cross road; follow grassy path across **Birkrigg Common**. Turn **L** to reach wall corner; walk few paces to **stone circle**. Follow any grassy path to skyline and trig point. ❸ Pass bench; take path to **R** to reach road. Cross then walk parallel to another road – common tapers out to cattle grid. Proceed on road; make sharp **R** along walled track. ❹ Cross stile at end; bear **R** past stone trough (ancient **homestead**). Keep **L** of wall to cross stile at gate. Bear **L** to take path down valley to gate. Turn **R** before gate; cross stile; follow hedgerow across slope to house. Cross stile leading down to road; turn **L** to pass farm buildings at **Holme Bank**.

❺ Turn **R** ('Public Footpath Church Road'). Cross ladder stile and footbridge; take path to **village hall** and road. Cross road; turn **R** to pass school. Pass church and shop. ❻ Turn **R** at **Coot on Tarn** to follow another road. At Clint Cottage on L and Tarn House on R, turn **L** up steep track. At 2 gates go through gate on **L**; proceed ahead, keeping **R** of low hill. ❼ Wall leads to gate, then keep straight on. Cross stile on **R**, other side of gate; cross stile on **L**. Walk ahead, crossing 2 stiles to reach road junction. Turn **R** to walk through crossroads to farm. ❽ Turn **R** at **Far Mount Barrow** ('Bardsea Green'). Cross stile by gate; keep **L** to cross road on **Birkrigg Common**. Turn **L** for **Bardsea Green**, along path parallel to road, then parallel to wall. ❾ At corner of wall, go through gate; follow track to road and cross dip. Turn **L** at junction into **Bardsea** then **R** at **Braddylls Arms** pub. Follow road to shore.

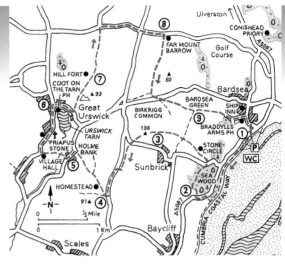

DUNNERDALE *IN WORDSWORTH'S FOOTSTEPS*

5 miles (8km) 3hrs **Ascent:** 850ft (260m)
Paths: Paths, tracks, can be muddy below Seathwaite Tarn, 9 stiles
Suggested map: aqua3 OS Explorer OL6 The English Lakes (SW)
Grid reference: SD 228960
Parking: Roadside pull-off at grid reference SD 231975, limited roadside parking near pub and church
Note: If River Duddon in spate, not advisable to cross at Fickle Steps Point ❺. Return to Seathwaite via road

Discover the landscape that inspired William Wordsworth on this walk through the Duddon Valley.
❶ From **Newfield Inn** at Seathwaite, Dunnerdale, follow main valley road past church. Turn **R** on tarmac lane towards **Turner Hall Farm**. Leave this and follow track on **L** through gate marked 'High Moss'. Where track ends, keep to **L-H** side of farm, go through top gate; follow field path to **Walna Scar Road**. ❷ Turn **R** along road, then **L** on to utility company's access road to **Seathwaite Tarn**. This is a pleasant green track that climbs steadily up the fell sides to the reservoir dam. ❸ Retrace your footsteps for a couple of hundred paces to waymarking post highlighting downhill path that weaves its way through rock and rough pasture. Mountain stream then leads path down into valley and **Tarn Beck**.

❹ Ladder stile on your **R-H** side gives access to footbridge across stream. On far bank turn **L** and then follow footpath along edge of narrow wood. After passing behind 2 cottages path turns uphill and across marshy fields to reach **Duddon Valley** road. ❺ Once you are across road follow signed bridleway to **Fickle Steps**, huge boulders, which allow you to cross **River Duddon**. (Caution: if river is in spate here and steps are under water, return by road.) ❻ To continue on route, turn **L**, go over footbridge across **Grassguards Gill** and then climb along waymarked path above tight wooded **Wallowbarrow Gorge**. Footpath descends again to cross boulder-strewn terrain on bank of **River Duddon**. ❼ At tall single-arched footbridge, cross to other side of river; turn **R** along path, now tracing eastern bank of **River Duddon**. Cross footbridge, before following path to road. Turn **L** to return to **Seathwaite**.

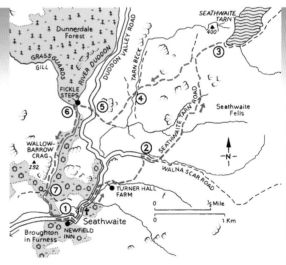

ESKDALE *TO MITERDALE*

6¾ miles (10.9km) 4hrs **Ascent:** 1,312ft (400m)
Paths: Good paths in valleys, but often indistinct on hills, 4 stiles (Not advised in poor visibility)
Suggested map: aqua3 OS Explorer OL6 The English Lakes (SW)
Grid reference: NY 173007 **Parking:** Car park beside Dalegarth Station (pay-and-display)

Discovering peaceful hills that were once a Norman hunting preserve.
❶ Follow lane down valley towards **Beckfoot Bridge**. Immediately before railway halt, cross line to gate from where zig-zag path to **Blea Tarn** is signed up hillside. Approaching tarn, go **L**, crossing stream emanating from its foot. ❷ Vague path maintains firm ground **R** of **Blind and Siney tarns**; at fork, bear **L**. Beyond lone tree, go **L** again. Although way is marshy, old sleepers span worst patch around Sineytarn Moss. Eventually, route joins wall, dropping beside it to level grass. ❸ Bear **R** to fence stile and continue along its edge below **Fell End**. Keep going near wall, eventually reaching its corner before another plantation. Short track **R** descends to junction, and another **R** turn takes you into Miterdale. ❹ Emerge on to tarmac lane at bottom; go through gate opposite into Miterdale Forest. Drop over river and then bear **R** on undulating, weaving path above its

far bank. Lateral wall shortly forces you uphill on to forest track. Turn **R** and follow it out of trees, joining track from R to continue up valley to **Low Place farm**. ❺ Walk past farmhouse and through 2nd yard, leaving by **R-H** gates ('Wasdale'). Follow river upstream before crossing bridge to track that continues along its opposite bank. Keep ahead for nearly ¾ mile (1.2km) until you cross stile at far end of plantation. Here, leave track and climb hill beside trees to another stile at top. ❻ Bear **L** above **Black Gill** and continue parallel to wall towards higher ground of **Low Longrigg**. After 400yds (366m) strike **R** on barely visible path, making for stone circles, which briefly break horizon. ❼ Bear **R** at 2nd circle; after passing beneath rocky outcrop, fork **L**. Way is still vague, but drops towards stone huts where clear path descends by them to **R**. ❽ Follow it down **Boot Bank** and into **Boot**, and cross Whillan Beck by **Eskdale Mill** to continue through village. At end turn **R** to Dalegarth Station.

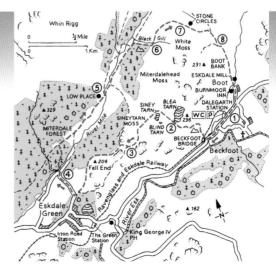

Cumbria

793 DUDDON BRIDGE SWINSIDE STONE CIRCLE

6 miles (9.7km) 2hrs 30min **Ascent:** 820ft (250m)
Paths: Good paths, some can be muddy, farm roads, 6 stiles
Suggested map: aqua3 OS Explorer OL6 The English Lakes (SW)
Grid reference: SD 197882
Parking: Parking space at Duddon Iron Furnace, near Duddon Bridge

Discover Swinside Stone Circle.
❶ **Duddon Iron Furnace** is on L of **Corney Fell road**, soon after turning from **Duddon Bridge**. Public bridleway sign points up track beside ruins. At last building, turn **L** up woodland path marked by bridleway sign hidden among brambles.
❷ Cross narrow access road; continue uphill. Turn **R** at junction of paths and keep climbing. Join track leading further up wooded slope. Go through gate in wall on L; follow deep, narrow path flanked by bracken, crossing low gap in thills.
❸ Turn **R** to reach gate. Go through and follow walled track. Go through next gate; turn **L**. Path running roughly parallel to tall wall passes old quarry near **Thwaite Yeat** farm. Path is vague on moorland slope, but look ahead to spot signpost at road junction.
❹ Turn **L** down narrow road ('Millom'); then turn **R** along farm track. It crosses dip and leads to gate ('**Fenwick**'). Go through; follow track almost to farm,

but turn **L**, following public footpath sign. Cross 3 stiles as path leads through fields to **Black Beck**.
❺ Cross footbridge; climb uphill, looking ahead to spot **Swinside** farm. Keep to R of buildings, but turn **L** to follow access road away from buildings. **Swinside Stone Circle** is in field on L.
❻ Walk down farm access road; continue on tarmac road to white building. Just before it there is stile and public footpath signpost. Field path and stile lead to **Black Beck** and **stepping stones** lead to **Beck Bank Farm**. Use L of 2 tracks, leading from farm to road
❼ Turn **L** and **L** again on busy main road. Walk to reach 2 farm roads signposted as public bridleways. Take 2nd one to **Ash House**. Narrow footpath leads away from buildings; stile leads into woods. Walk uphill, then down to reach marker post at junction.
❽ Turn **R**; walk downhill; turn **L** at junction. Keep **R** at next junction, following path of outward route. Cross narrow access road; walk to **Duddon Iron Furnace**.

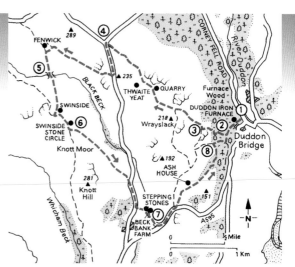

794 BUTTERMERE IN PARADISE

4½ miles (7.2km) 2hrs **Ascent:** 35ft (11m)
Paths: Good path, some road walking, 2 stiles
Suggested map: aqua3 OS Explorer OL4 The English Lakes (NW)
Grid reference: NY 173169
Parking: National Park car park beyond Fish Hotel (fee)

Walk through one of the Lakeland's most attractive valleys.
❶ Leave car park and turn **R**, passing **Fish Hotel** to follow broad track through gates. Ignore signposted route to Scale Force; continue along track towards edge of lake. Then follow line of hedgerow to bridge at **Buttermere Dubs**. Cross small footbridge; go through nearby gate in wall at foot of **Burtness Wood** and cascade of **Sourmilk Gill**. Turn **L** on track through woodland that roughly parallels lakeshore, just emerging from woodland near **Horse Close**, where bridge spans **Comb Beck**.
❷ Continue along path to reach wall leading to sheepfold and gate. Go **L** through gate, cross **Warnscale Beck** and walk out to **Gatesgarth Farm**. At farm, follow signs to reach valley road. Short stretch of road walking, **L** on B5289, now follows, along which there are no pathways. Take care against approaching traffic.

❸ As road bends L, leave it for footpath on L ('Buttermere via Lakeshore Path'). Path leads into field, beyond which it never strays far from shoreline; continue along stand of Scots pine, near **Crag Wood**.
❹ Beyond Hassnesshow Beck bridge, path enters grounds of **Hassness**, where rocky path, enclosed by trees, leads to gate. Here path has been cut across crag where it plunges into lake below, and shortly disappears into brief, low and damp tunnel. The tunnel was cut by employees of George Benson – 19th-century Manchester mill owner – so that he could walk around the lake without straying too far from its shore. After you emerge from tunnel, gate gives access to gravel path across wooded pasture of **Pike Rigg**, beyond which clear path leads to traditional Lakeland bridge of slate slabs.
❺ Short way on, through gate, path leads to **Wilkinsyke Farm**, and easy walk out to road, just short way above **Bridge Hotel**. Turn **L** to return to car park.

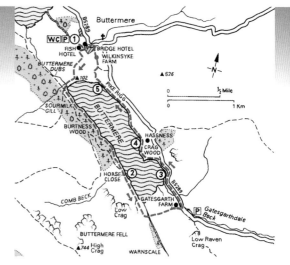

795 LOWESWATER GETTING HIGH

5 miles (8km) 3hrs **Ascent:** 650ft (200m)
Paths: Well-defined paths and tracks, all stiles have adjacent gates
Suggested map: aqua3 OS Explorer OL4 The English Lakes (NW)
Grid reference: NY 134210
Parking: Maggie's Bridge pay car park, Loweswater (get there early)

Discovering the Lakeland's finest balcony.
❶ Just opposite car park entrance at **Maggie's Bridge** go through gate ('High Nook Farm') and follow track through fields. After passing through farmyard continue on stony track that climbs into comb of **Highnook Beck** and beneath **Carling Knott**.
❷ Take **R** fork each time path divides. This will bring you down to footbridge across beck. Across bridge route continues as fine grassy track that doubles back **R** raking across hillside to top of **Holme Wood** plantations. Track follows top edge of woods before traversing breast of **Burnbank Fell**.
❸ Track swings **L** and climbs to ladder stile and gate to north of fell. Here it divides. Ignore L fork, which doubles back to an old mine. Instead go over stile and descend gradually northwest across high pastureland.
❹ Couple of hundred paces short of road at **Fangs Brow**, turn **R** over ladder stile and continue along rutted track past **Iredale Place** farm. Just beyond

house track joins tarmac lane.
❺ On reaching **Jenkinson Place** (farm) tarmac lane ends. Turn **L** here over stile and follow well-defined grass track across fields towards **Hudson Place** and lake. Signpost diverts way **L**, around farm complex. Path meets lane from **Waterend** then turn **R** and follow lane, which nears shores of **Loweswater** before entering National Trust's **Holme Wood**. Oak predominates near the lake, although the trees at the top of the wood largely consist of pine, larch and Sitka spruce. **Holme Wood** is one of the last strongholds of the red squirrel. You're very likely to see pied and spotted flycatchers here, and maybe, if you're lucky, a green woodpecker.
❻ Wide track now heads through woods, but by taking path to **L**, you can get nearer shoreline. This 2nd path rejoins original track just beyond stone built outhouse. At **Watergate Farm**, turn **L** to follow wide gravel road back to car park at **Maggie's Bridge**.

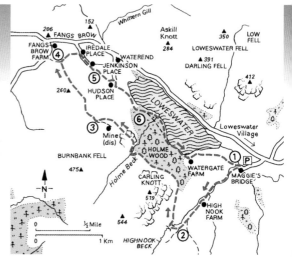

GARRIGILL *ASHGILL FORCE*

3 miles (5km) 1hr 30min **Ascent:** 328ft (100m)
Paths: Field paths, tracks and a quiet lane, 17 stiles
Suggested map: aqua3 OS Explorer OL31 North Pennines
Grid reference: NY 7444150 **Parking:** On green in front of post office

Through upland pasture to a waterfall.

❶ From green leave village on road ('**Alston, Nenthead**'). Cross bridge and walk up steep track opposite. Continue past cottages on R to lane.

❷ Turn R ('**Pasture Houses**') through gate. Go across field, aiming for stile far side. Cross and continue over field to stile below ruined farm buildings. Descend R across field towards buildings and trees. Aim for back of buildings and go through gate at end of barn. Bear L across yard through gates to lane. Follow to gate and stile leading out to road.

❸ Cross road and stile opposite ('**Ashgill**') below cottages L. Cross stile, large field and another stile. After another field and stile, aim for buildings ahead. Arrow on 1st barn directs you over stile into yard. Bear L, passing white building on L then cross stile at end of yard. Cross short field and stile on to track. Cross this, and stile into paddock. Leave by stile on far side. Bear R round back of buildings through gap into field.

❹ Turn L; follow track to 4-way fingerpost by bridge.

❺ Don't cross bridge but turn L ('**Ashgill Force**') over stile then follow track up L of beck. Go through gate and continue up to bridge with main falls ahead. Cross bridge and continue to falls, passing old mine workings R. Path behind falls can be very slippery.

❻ Retrace steps to level area. Ignore path L, but stay this side of beck and take level path away from bridge. Cross stile then continue towards **Bird's Nest**. Go through gate then turn R to gate on far side. Descend track in field. Follow downhill and bear R to bridge. Go through gate then cross bridge to 4-way fingerpost. Turn L ('**Low Crossgill**') with Ashgill Beck now L.

❼ Where beck meets **River South Tyne**, cross stile on to riverside path. Follow path, over stile and through gap in wall, maintaining direction when river loops L. Ignore bridge to **Mid Crossgill** and continue with river L to stile, then along field edge. Go through gate and continue to 4-way fingerpost.

❽ Turn L over bridge; walk up lane to gate by **Low Crossgill**. Turn R along road into **Garrigill**.

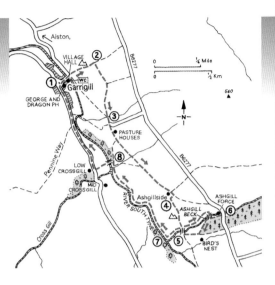

CASTLE CARROCK *LIME KILNS*

4½ miles (7.2km) 2 hours **Ascent:** 476ft (145m)
Paths: Field paths, farm tracks, metalled lanes, 7 stiles
Suggested map: aqua3 OS Explorer 315 Carlisle
Grid reference: NY 543553
Parking: On street between parish church and Watson Institute

Discovering fine industrial remains.

❶ Facing **church** turn L then R past school ('**Garth Head**'). Cross bridle gate into field by stile. Ascend L of hedge and maintain direction through trees up to gate on L. Keep hedge R and continue up hill, cutting corner of field. Continue with hedge R, up to stile in corner behind bush.

❷ Bear slightly L up bank and across field then go through gate in top R corner. Follow lane through **Garth Marr** farmyard then through 2 gates by **Garth Head** farmyard. Walk up track into field, then turn R, up to gate on to road.

❸ Go L for 20yds (18m) then R ('**Brackenthwaite**'). Walk along field edge to stile. Join track with wall on L. Follow until wall comes in R. Go through gap. Follow track with wall now R. After 350yds (320m) cross stile. Eventually, go through gap in wall and join track from L. Descend to bridge with **lime kiln** up to L. Continue to L of wall, ahead. Track leads through reeds then L of pond. Cross stile on far side. Bear R to fingerpost.

❹ Turn L up R edge of field to gate. Turn R alongside fence. Past **lime kiln** on L, path opens out and continues through gap in wall into boggy area. Keep L and continue along base of hillside. Cross beck and pass **lime kiln**. Continue along track following wall on R. Go through stile R and follow path with wall now L for 100yds (91m) to **lime kiln**.

❺ Turn R through gap in wall. Follow track down to L of tin-roofed shed. Cross stile and bear R down track. Go through gate on to road. Turn R, round back of farmyard, signposted to reservoir. At corner of yard, carry on through gateway, turning R in front of barn to gate on R. Walk up field for 10yds (9m), turn L and cross 4 fields to gate on to road, just past green shed.

❻ Turn L. Follow road for ½ mile (800m) to junction. Turn R and follow track by reservoir, ignoring turn to **Tottergill**. Pass dam and go through woods to gate on to road. Turn L; walk back into **Castle Carrock**.

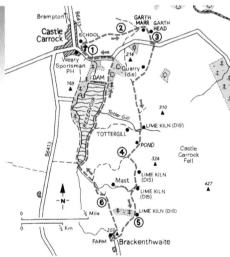

GREAT ASBY SCAR *AROUND ORTON*

8½ miles (13.7km) 4hrs **Ascent:** 951ft (290m)
Paths: Field paths, tracks and minor lanes, at least 11 stiles
Suggested map: aqua3 OS Explorer OL19 Howgill Fells & Upper Eden Valley
Grid reference: NY 622083 **Parking:** Village square at centre of Orton

Across the best limestone scenery in Cumbria.

❶ Head towards **church**. Cross road; follow track ('Shap'). Turn R in churchyard, down to road. Cross and follow road opposite. Turn L before bridge. Turn L after 100yds (91m), behind buildings to snicket and gate. In field turn R on to green lane. Cross beck and go ahead through gate. Follow hedgerow and swing L to gate. Cross bridge. Follow edge to gate on to track to road.

❷ Turn L for 500yds (457m). Past **Scar Side Farm**, by gate across road, climb stile L. Cross field to gate R. Follow wall line to cut corner to gap. Cross field to gate on top edge. Turn R, through gap; join track from R. After 50yds (46m) strike R towards stile by trough. Bear half L over field to gate. Bear half R to gate.

❸ Keep ahead through gate into **nature reserve**. Past **quarry** R, leave track for path R. Continue ahead for ½ mile (800m) to exit reserve by gate. Follow path R to gate. Proceed with wall R to **Sayle Lane**.

❹ Bear R for ¼ mile (400m). Turn R ('**Sunbiggin**'). Follow track for ½ mile (800m), crossing 4 cattle grids.

❺ Turn R ('**Sunbiggin**') to gate. Continue with wall L to another, then with wall R. Go through gate by marker. After 50yds (46m) signs directs through 2 gates to wall. Go through gate; follow path through notch in scar. Descend through gate then across fields towards **Sunbiggin Farm**. Follow path behind barns, through gate down to road.

❻ Turn R for 700yds (640m), to bridleway R. Follow track across 11 fields to **Knott Lane**. Cross to stile ('**Scarside**') and follow path to gate and stile. Turn R along road past farm, then L '**Street Lane**'.

❼ Follow track through gateway up field. Cross stile by gate into muddy area. Keep to L of hedge then bear R over bridge and through gap. Keep wall L to gate with stile. Follow R-H edge of field to stile; aim for stile in far L-H edge of next field. Turn L 200yds (183m) then take footpath R. Cross to stile at end of field. Walk down snicket to road. Cross to footbridge and gate by playing fields. Follow path to gate and bridge, back to village square.

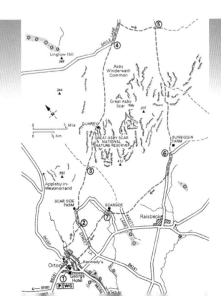

Cumbria

799 SEDBERGH *THE QUAKERS*

4½ miles (7.2km) 1hr 30min Ascent: 131ft (40m)
Paths: Mostly on field and riverside paths, 7 stiles
Suggested map: aqua3 OS Explorer OL19 Howgill Fells & Upper Eden Valley
Grid reference: SD 659921
Parking: Pay-and-display car park just off Sedbergh main street (which is one-way, from west)

A walk to the Quaker hamlet of Brigflatts.

❶ From car park, turn **R** along main street, continue to junction with main road; turn **L**. At churchyard turn **R** ('Cattle Market or Busk Lane'). At next signpost, go **L** behind pavilion; straight ahead through 2 kissing gates and out on to road. Cross and go through another metal kissing gate ('Birks'). Follow path through another gate to **Birks House**.

❷ Go through kissing gate beyond house; turn **L** along lane. Opposite Old Barn go **R**, through metal kissing gate. Follow **Brigflatts** sign roughly half **L** to waymarker. Go through 4 gates and under gated railway arch. Continue ahead and go through, in turn, gate in crossing wall, metal kissing gate and farm gate on to lane opposite Quaker Burial Ground.

❸ Turn **L** to visit **Meeting House**, then return to gate, continuing up lane to main road. Turn **L**. Just beyond bend sign, go through signed kissing gate in hedge on **L**. Follow riverside path through 2 gates to

another gate, to **L** of large railway bridge over river.

❹ Go through gate; over embankment to another gate. Continue along riverside, passing through gate near confluence of 2 rivers, then 2 more gates to reach metalled lane by old **mill**.

❺ Follow lane back into Birks. Go **R**, though kissing gate ('Rawthey Way') (you went through this gate on outward route). By hedge around **Birks House**, bear **R** towards river and over stile. Follow river to another stile; climb slightly **L** to stile by gateway; past **folly**, to **L** of wood, through kissing gate. Walk through wood to stile. Go across field to metal gate then stile on to road by bridge. Turn **L**. By ('30') sign, go **R**, though stile. Go across field to another stile; bear **L** alongside building to another kissing gate.

❻ Cross drive to another kissing gate. Continue downhill to another, and go straight on along lane to main road. Cross over road. Walk behind row of houses, along **Sedbergh's** main street to car park.

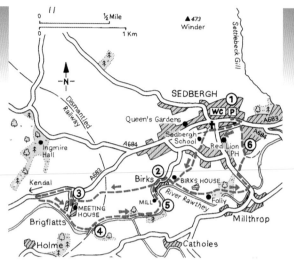

800 DENT *ADAM SEDGWICK'S LAND*

6 miles (9.7km) 2hrs 15min Ascent: 918ft (100m)
Paths: Tracks, field and riverside paths, some roads, 13 stiles
Suggested map: aqua3 OS Explorer OL2 Yorkshire Dales – Southern & Western
Grid reference: SD 70487 **Parking:** Pay-and-display car park at west end of Dent

From his birthplace through the countryside that inspired geologist Adam Sedgwick.

❶ Leave car park; turn **R**, then **L** by **Memorial Hall**. Pass green; keep ahead at signpost ('Flinter Gill'). Metalled lane becomes stony track that climbs steeply. Cross stile by gate. Continue uphill, through gate, to another gate by seat. Go through gate to T-junction of tracks.

❷ Turn **R** ('Keldishaw'). Follow walled track for 1½ miles (2.4km), through gate and over bridge, then downhill to metalled road. Turn **R**; follow road for ¼ mile (400m) to signpost to Underwood on **L**.

❸ Go through gate. Follow grassy track, to ladder stile. Continue with wall on **L** to reach track. It bends **R** and becomes path on ridge above valley, eventually descending through yard of **ruined farmhouse**.

❹ Bend **R** at end of farm buildings to follow track to **R** of ruined stone wall. Go through gap in wall, then downhill, bending **R** to another gateway. After gateway keep ahead, away from track, to waymarked post.

Turn **L** along stream bank for few paces, then go downhill to cross simple bridge of 2 stones. Climb other side of bank; go through 2 gates by buildings.

❺ Continue down track, until just before telephone lines, then cross it. Turn **L** by tree; go through waymarked gate. Walk ahead across field, around **R** of ruined farmhouse. Continue downhill to gate with handgate beside it, after which track bends **R**, descending to metalled lane by barn.

❻ Turn **L** along lane for few paces; keep ahead along track to **Dillicar** farm. In farmyard, bear **L** then **R** to gate; turn **R** to ladder stile by barn. Turn **L** along lane; turn **R** to plank bridge and stile ('Dales Way'). Cross field to river bank; follow river upstream through 7 gates and over 3 footbridges to arrive at gated stone steps up to squeeze stile and on to stone bridge.

❼ Cross bridge, go through stile and down steps, to continue on riverside path. Cross 4 stiles, plank bridge, then 3 more stiles to emerge to road. Turn **L**. Follow road to **Dent**.

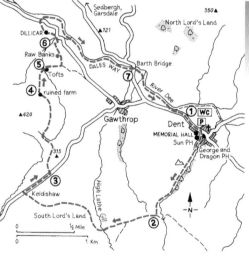

801 GRISEDALE *THE DALE THAT DIED*

5 miles (8km) 2hrs 15min Ascent: 722ft (220m)
Paths: Moorland paths and tracks, may be boggy, 19 stiles
Suggested map: aqua3 OS Explorer OL19 Howgill Fells & Upper Eden Valley
Grid reference: SD 786919
Parking: Roadside parking on road to Garsdale Station

The derelict farmsteads tell their own tale of the farmers' struggle and surrender to the climate, misfortune and lack of subsidies.

❶ Walk down hill to main road. Cross at junction; take stile ('Grisedale and Flust'). Bear gradually **R** to stile in wall. Follow sign ahead on track across field to signpost. Follow sign to gated stile, **R** of fieldbank.

❷ Go half **R** after stile, over 2 more stiles then downhill over bridge and on to stile and signpost by ruined building. Go over stile. Follow sign, through stile to **L** of barn and onwards to signpost **L** of farmhouse.

❸ Cross metalled lane to signposted stile. After 2 more stiles, follow wall towards ruined building, descending to walk beside stream. Go through gate; bear **R** to signposted stile. Continue with wall on **L** to gate, then to humpback bridge. Do not cross, but follow 2 signposts uphill and along ridge, bearing slightly **R** to tumbled farm buildings of **Round Ing**.

❹ Follow signpost towards **East House**. There's no

clear path, but look for waymarked post by end of wall. Proceed towards houses on hillside. Cross stream. Continue downhill to grassy track. Turn **L** towards barn. Just before it turn **R**, off track, to pass below barn to gate. Go through gate; bear **R** over stream.

❺ Pass ruined building; head across field towards houses. Go over wooden stile; then over ladder stile **R** of farm buildings. Follow track through 2 gates on to metalled road. Turn **L**, uphill, to T-junction, where metalled road ends. Turn **R**, along track, first following wall on **R** then continuing to stile beside gate. Walk downhill to railway buildings in valley bottom.

❻ Go over wooden stile by buildings, pass footbridge and, just by track over line, take gated stile on **L** corner. Walk half **R**, away from railway, pass through tumbled wall; follow path over 2 stiles; through another broken wall to pass beside barn and to stile on to main road. Turn **R**, back to road junction and parking place.

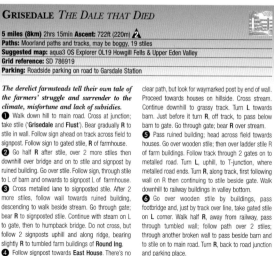

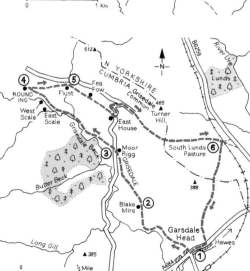

Cumbria

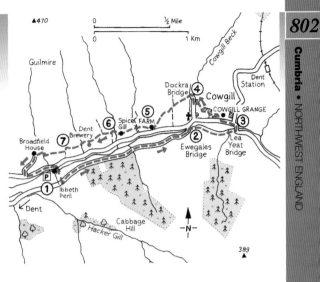

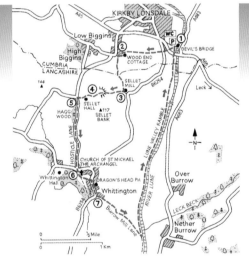

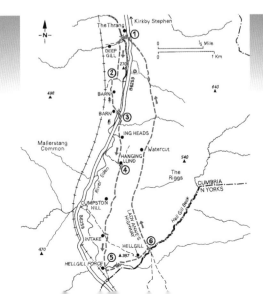

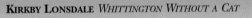

COWGILL ALONG RIVER DEE

802

3½ miles (5.7km) 1hr 30min Ascent: 131ft (40m)
Paths: Tracks, field and riverside paths, some roads, 17 stiles
Suggested map: aqua3 OS Explorer OL2 Yorkshire Dales – Southern & Western
Grid reference: SD 742864
Parking: Parking place at Ibbeth Peril

An easy walk beside the River Dee.

1 Leave back of car park on footpath going through woodland. Cross footbridge; head across field to gate. Turn **L** along road. Follow road for 1 mile (1.6km) until stone bridge.

2 Don't cross bridge, but continue along riverside over stile ('**Lea Yeat**'). Go through stone stile. Cross over 2 tributary streams to wooden stile on to **Lea Yeat Bridge**. Cross bridge; turn **L** at signpost towards Dent and Sedbergh.

3 Just beyond post-box on **L**, follow sign on **R** to **Dockra Bridge**. Go short way up drive for **Cowgill Grange**; bear **L** to gated stile. Go ahead, passing through 2 gates in front of cottage and on to track. Bear **R**. Path goes round **L** end of 2 houses, through 3 gates and stile. After last gate, turn **L** to reach track; go **R** to Dockra Bridge.

4 Cross bridge, bend **R**; take stile on **L**. Go half **L** to stile in crossing wall. Continue ahead to waymarked handgate. Go **R** of barn, through gateway in crossing wall to another gated stone stile, then half **L** across field towards farmhouse to signposted stile.

5 After stile go half **R** then through stile. Continue to another stile; head towards **farm** buildings; over stone stile by gateway beside barn and through gate. Pass farmhouse, bend **R** then **L** behind barn to bridge with steps and gated stile beyond.

6 Cross field to another stile. Just beyond, turn **R** along track. As it bends **R**, go ahead to pass house, through gate and behind another building to wooden stile. Go ahead across field to stone stile, go **L** of barn on to track over stream and uphill again.

7 Curve round **L** of next barn; follow wall. At next farm buildings, go through metal gate by barn; follow walled lane **R**. After another gate bear **L**, through stile, go to **R** of farm building and on to track. Turn **R**, then **L** through waymarked gate, pass farmhouse; follow track to road. Turn **L** to return to car park.

KIRKBY LONSDALE WHITTINGTON WITHOUT A CAT

803

4¾ miles (7.7km) 2hrs 30min Ascent: 197ft (60m)
Paths: A little overgrown and indistinct in patches, quiet lanes and tracks, plenty of stiles
Suggested map: aqua3 OS Explorer OL2 Yorkshire Dales – Southern & Western
Grid reference: SD 615782 **Parking:** Devil's Bridge car park, Kirkby Lonsdale (free of charge)

Along the banks of the River Lune.

1 From west bank of river, downstream from **Devil's Bridge**, take path ('**Whittington**') across to **A65**. Cross road, go through meadow and between houses; cross B6254. At meadow head uphill, keeping walled wooded area on **L**. Yellow markers and sign to **Wood End** help find route. Proceed over brow of hill and through 2 stiles. Turn **L** at gap stile into Wood End farmyard.

2 Turn **R** on track towards **Wood End Cottage**. Go **L** in front of cottage along walled path to **Sellet Mill**. Stream comes in **L**, but drier ground approaches. Path opens out by mill race.

3 Turn **R** by homesteads; walk up field, keeping fence **L**, until level with end of garden. Go **L** through yellow-marked gate; cross field to gate followed by stream. Bear **R** around **Sellet Bank**, aiming initially for corner of hedge under pylons. Continue with hedge **R**.

4 Go through yellow-marked stile on **R**; bear **L** round wooded area. Facing **Sellet Hall**, turn **R** next to driveway following marker arrows; cross over corner of field to cross stile; descend steps to road at T-junction. Turn **L** on **Hosticle Lane** towards **Whittington**.

5 Follow lane to Whittington with **Hagg Wood** on **R**, beech and hawthorn hedges beside you.

6 Go **L** at T-junction for few paces; cross road; turn **R** over mosaic at **Church of St Michael the Archangel**. Keep bell tower on **L** before descending steps to go through stile and graveyard. Proceed through gate in **L** corner. Cross over 2 fields to stone stile leading to walled lane leading to Main Street. Turn **R**, in front of building (1875). Continue past village hall and **pub**.

7 At sharp **R** bend on village edge turn **L** along sandy lane, passing farm and tennis courts. Follow lane between fields to reach pair of gates. Go through gates on **L**. Bear **L** to reach riverside walk – **Lune Valley Ramble** – back to **A65** bridge at **Kirkby Lonsdale**. Go through gate, up steps to **L** of parapet. Cross road then drop down other side to cross park.

MALLERSTANG LADY ANNE'S HIGHWAY

804

6 miles (9.7km) 2hrs 30min Ascent: (150m)
Paths: Field paths and upland tracks, can be very boggy, indistinct at times, 12 stiles
Suggested map: aqua3 OS Explorer OL19 Howgill Fells & Upper Eden Valley
Grid reference: NY 783004 **Parking:** On roadside on B6259, 50yds (46m) south of The Thrang

In the footsteps of Lady Anne Clifford.

1 Go through gate ('**Deep Gill**'). Follow track over bridge and for 60yds (55m) on other side. Strike **L**, cross beck aiming for dead tree **R**. Pass and aim for stile in crossing wall. Now head for stile opposite. Aim slightly **R** towards green post on wall by stile. Cross and aim for top **R-H** corner. Go through gate; continue with wall **R**. At corner, go through gate to lane.

2 Turn **R** then **L** in front of yard. Continue towards barn. Go through gate, pass barn and then through gateway. After 10yds (9m), dip **L** heading for barn 2 fields away. Go through gate below plantation and follow wall (R) towards gap opposite. Aim for gate in corner, **L** of barn. Go through gateway, cross bridge to gate on to road.

3 Turn **R** for 30yds (27m) to footpath **L** ('**Hellgill**'). Cross stile, walk half **R** to stile in wall **R**. Maintain direction to stile on far side. Aim half **L** to stile in front of **Ing Heads**. Cross yard, go through gate and turn **L**, to stile beyond trees. Aim for junction of walls far side.

Go through stile below barn. Cross pasture to stile in crossing wall. Aim for edge of plantation by **Hanging Lund**, crossing track to gate in corner. Go through gate, cross beck, then up through gateway and **L**. Round **R** of **Hanging Lund** then go through gate.

4 Turn **R**, up through gap and gate to barn **R**. After 50yds (46m) track leads **L** away from wall. Pass 2nd barn and through gate. Drop **R**, towards trees beyond wall above **Cumpston Hill**. Go through gap; follow wall **R** to gate. Aim **L** of wall enclosing field at **Intake**. Walk around to road. Follow for 500yds (457m) past sheds and through gate to ford above **Hellgill Force**.

5 Cross ford (if beck in spate retrace steps to Intake and follow footpath to **Hellgill**). Turn **L** up track. Cross bridge; continue through gate into yard. Continue up field above beck. Go through gate by bridge.

6 Turn **L**, follow track ('**Lady Anne's Highway**') with wall then fence **L**. Pass '**Watercut**' sculpture after 1 mile (1.6km). Track descends to valley. Go through gate on to road. Turn **R** back to your car.

East Riding

805 HUGGATE FRIDAYTHORPE

6½ miles (10.4km) 3hrs **Ascent:** 738ft (225m)

Paths: Field path, farm tracks, 1 stile

Suggested map: aqua3 OS Explorer 294 Market Weighton & Yorkshire Wolds Central

Grid reference: SE 882551

Parking: On street around village green

Open fields and hidden dales.

❶ From green, walk past play area and duck pond. Continue past cottages to junction. Turn **R**, down lane. Past last house, fork **L** ('Wolds Way'). Follow access road for ½ mile (800m) until it bends **R** into farmyard. Take path **L** between fences. Emerge on road on other side of farm. Continue up to fingerpost on horizon.

❷ Turn **R** along field-edge path ('Chalkland Way'). At end of field, go through gate and turn **L** along top of **Horse Dale**. Track descends to valley floor and gate. Go through gate and up side valley. Aim for **R-H** fence corner and go through **L-H** gate. Continue up enclosed track ignoring gate to R. After 300yds (274m) track continues along edge of open field. Eventually reach crossing track to **Wold House Farm**.

❸ Turn **R** along track into farmyard. Bear **L** across yard, through gate diagonally opposite. Bear **R**; continue on track across 3 fields. At end of 3rd field, turn **L** (don't follow right of way); turn **R** down side of field to gate. Bear **L** with rising track above **Holm Dale**; then dip to collection of fingerposts at gate.

❹ Go through gate. Cross to enclosed track ('Wolds Way'). Follow this to Huggate Lane into **Fridaythorpe**. Turn **R** along main road then **L** by **Manor House Inn** to the green and **St Mary's Church**.

❺ Return to Huggate Lane; follow lane back to gate by collection of fingerposts. Go through gate and follow **Wolds Way** down dale. Keep to **L** of fence as **Horse Dale** joins from R.

❻ Go through gate, ignore Wolds Way going off to R, but turn **L** over stile and continue down **Harper Dale**. Pass game breeding area on **L** then bear **R** with rising path to meet track on hill. Bear **R** to cattle grid. Turn **L** and follow track round to R. Turn **L** at end and follow track to **Northfield House**.

❼ Walk through yards; follow access road back towards **Huggate**. Continue up lane; turn **L** across green to return to car park.

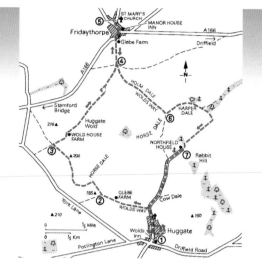

---

806 CARL WARK MOORLAND RAMPARTS

5½ miles (8.8km) 3hrs **Ascent:** 328ft (100m)

Paths: Generally good paths

Suggested map: aqua3 OS Explorer OL1 Dark Peak

Grid reference: SK 252801

Parking: Surprise View car park on A6187 beyond Hathersage

Along medieval packhorse trails in search of the dwelling place of ancient Britons.

❶ From car park at Surprise View go through kissing gate and uphill on well-worn path. At large group of stones path weaves **L** and continues uphill towards **Over Owler Tor**. Just before this, go **L** on smaller track, head downhill towards fence. Turn **R** at fence.

❷ Continue following track until it meets with dry-stone wall that has been running parallel with track. Follow path **R** towards sheepfold. At end of sheepfold, path veers slightly **R** across moorland. Rocky outcrop of **Higger Tor** is on **L** and **Carl Wark** in front. The fort is probably of Iron- or Bronze-Age construction and was re-fortified at the end of the Roman occupation.

❸ When path intersects another, turn **R**. Continue past Carl Wark, keeping it to R. Go downhill towards far **R** corner of wood. Cross stone bridge then wooden bridge, head uphill on well-worn path to join old green road; turn **L**.

❹ Continue along road with **Burbage Rocks** above you and to R. At **Upper Burbage Bridge** cross 2 streams via large stones, head uphill and follow upper of 2 paths to **L** and uphill. Continue across moorland then ascend **Higger Tor** on stone stepped path. Cross tor then descend other side near southeast corner.

❺ Follow track across moor towards **Carl Wark**. Ascend and turn **L** to reach summit then return to top of path and, keeping stone ramparts on **L**, continue past cairn and descend via path to southwest.

❻ From here, path heads across boggy section of moor, curves round small, rocky hill then heads downhill towards **A6187**. Cross on to this via stile, cross road and turn **R** on to pavement. Follow this to next stile on **L**, cross it and continue on path that runs parallel to road.

❼ When track nears car park go through kissing gate, cross road then continue on grass track back into car park.

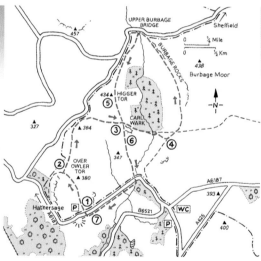

---

807 BRADFIELD DALE DIKE DAM DISASTER

5½ miles (8.8km) 3hrs 30min **Ascent:** 394ft (120m)

Paths: Minor roads, bridleways, forest paths

Suggested map: aqua3 OS Explorer OL1 Dark Peak

Grid reference: SK 262920 **Parking:** By cricket ground in Bradfield

A quiet waterside walk around the site of an horrific industrial tragedy.

❶ Walk out of car park and then turn **R** on to road. At Y-junction go **R** towards Midhopestones. Walk uphill, following road, passing **Walker House** farm and **Upper Thornseat** passing on R. At entrance to **Thomson House**, when road turns sharply R, turn **L** on to farm road.

❷ From here go through gate ahead and on to **Hall Lane**, public bridleway. Follow this along edge of wood then through another gate and continue **R** on farm road. Another gate at end of this road leads to entrance to **Hallfield**.

❸ Right of way goes through Hallfield's grounds but alternative permissive path leads **L** over stile, round perimeter of house and across another stile to re-join bridleway at rear of house. Follow bridleway crossing stile, gate and then past **Stubbin Farm**.

❹ The next gate leads you to **Brogging Farm** and dam at head of **Strines Reservoir**. Look out for sign near end of farmhouse and turn **L**. Go slightly downhill, over stile, follow path, then cross stile and go through wood.

❺ Cross stream by footbridge, keep to **R**, ignoring 2nd footbridge. Follow path along bank of **Dale Dike Reservoir** to dam head. Several hundred people were killed and many properties destroyed when the dam collapsed in 1864. It was rebuilt in 1875 but it was not brought into full use until 1887 – a very dry year. From here continue through woods, down several sets of steps and continue on path. Look out for **memorial** to those who were killed in the tragedy.

❻ Follow path until it reaches road. Cross stile, turn **R** on to road; proceed to Y-junction. Turn **R**, cross bridge then look for public footpath sign ('Low Bradfield') just before entrance to **Doe House**. Cross stile on **L** and follow path. Path crosses 2 stiles then terminates at T-junction with **Mill Lee Road** opposite **Plough Inn**. Turn **L** and follow road downhill, through village and back to car park.

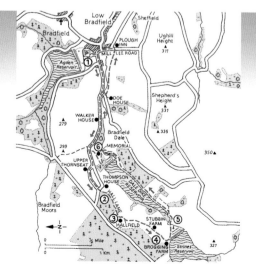

FAIRBURN INGS *LAKES AND BIRDS*

808

5 miles (8km) 2hrs 30min **Ascent:** 131ft (40m)
Paths: Good paths and tracks (some newly created from spoil heaps), 7 stiles
Suggested map: aqua3 OS Explorer 289 Leeds
Grid reference: SE 472278
Parking: Free parking in Cut Road, Fairburn. From A1, drive into village, turn L 100yds (91m) past Three Horseshoes pub

A visit to West Yorkshire's very own 'Lake District', now a bird reserve.

❶ Walk down Cut Road as it narrows to track. Soon you have main lake to R, and smaller stretch of water to L. When track forks, keep R (unless you want to visit 1st of bird hides, in which case detour to L). Path finishes at end of lake, on approaching **River Aire**.

❷ Go **R** here to join path along top of ridge (old spoil heap), with river to L and lake R. Look out for couple of other bird hides, before you lose sight of lake. Path crosses broader expanse of spoil heap, through scrubland, following river in broad arc to **R**, before descending to stile above another small mere. Bear **R** on broad track and drop down into car park of **Fairburn Ings visitor centre**.

❸ Meet road. Go **R** for 100yds (91m), then go **L** ('Ledston and Kippax') for just 100yds (91m), and pick up path on **R** that hugs **R-H** fringe of wood. Beyond

wood, take path between fields; it broadens to track as you approach **Ledsham**. At new housing estate, turn **R**, along Manor Garth.

❹ You arrive in village by **ancient church**. Walk **R**, along road (or, for refreshments, go **L** to **Chequers Inn**). Beyond village, where road bears L, take gate on **R**, leading to good track uphill. Where main track goes R, into fields, continue along track ahead, into woodland. Leave wood by stile, crossing pasture on grassy track. Cross 2 stiles taking you across narrow spur of woodland.

❺ Head slightly **L**, uphill, across next field, to follow fence and hedgerow. Continue – soon on better track – across stile. Beyond next stile track bears L, towards farm buildings: but keep straight on, with fence on R, along field path. Go through metal gate then join access track downhill. When you meet road, go **L** and back into **Fairburn**.

ACKWORTH *EAST OF WAKEFIELD*

809

5 miles (8km) 2hrs 30min **Ascent:** 131ft (40m)
Paths: Mostly field paths; take care with route finding, on first section to East Hardwick; 11 stiles
Suggested map: aqua3 OS Explorer 278 Sheffield & Barnsley
Grid reference: SE 441180
Parking: A few parking places in middle of High Ackworth, near church and village green

An easy stroll through rolling countryside.

❶ From top of village green, take ginnel to **R** of Manor House. Beyond stone stile, keep to **R-H** edge of field to reach stile. At Woodland Grove, go **L** then 1st **R** to **A628**, Pontefract Road. Go **L** for 100yds (91m). Watch for gap on **R** in hedgerow and footpath sign opposite house, Tall Trees. Cross field (follow sign) to footbridge. Continue along **R-H** edge of next field; cross bridge. Keep ahead between fields – going sharp **L** then **R** over footbridge – to follow hedgerow. At gap in hedge, cross 2 fields (houses ahead).

❷ Cross railway line, via bridge; continue between fields, towards **Hundhill Farm**. Keep **R** at farm's boundary wall, to stile. Bear **L** on lane; after 75yds (68m) and L-H bend, take stile on **R**, to enclosed path. Beyond next stile, bear **R** along minor road that meets **A639**. Cross road; walk into **East Hardwick**. Beyond **church**, where road bears **L**, look out for sign, 'Public Bridleway', on **R**, just before house, 'Bridleways'.

❸ Go **R**, between hedgerows. Shortly, track goes **L**; take gap in hedge to **R**. Follow field path uphill (keep hedgerow R). At top of field, continue on footpath between fields. Follow drainage channel to meet crossing track. Go **R** over **A639**. Take 'Rigg Lane' and, at farm, go **L**, between buildings, on to track.

❹ Pass **water treatment works**, to bridge and old packhorse bridge. Don't cross either, but bear **R**, along field edge, to accompany river. Cross plank bridge over side-beck, then under 6 railway viaduct arches.

❺ Continue by riverside. Pass, don't cross, stone bridge. Bear **R**, across corner of field, in front of barns of **Low Farm**, to join field-edge path. Follow hedge towards houses, to stile and road to **Low Ackworth**.

❻ Cross and take ginnel between houses. Beyond stile at far end, bear half-**L** across field to stile and across another field. Cross stile to another ginnel. Continue along Hill Drive, soon bearing **R**, into cul-de-sac. At bottom, take ginnel on **L**, to return to start.

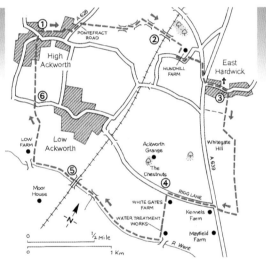

WETHERBY *THE RIVER WHARFE*

810

3½ miles (5.7km) 2hrs **Ascent:** 65ft (20m)
Paths: Field paths and good tracks, a little road walking, 1 stile
Suggested map: aqua3 OS Outdoor Leisure 289 Leeds
Grid reference: SE 405479
Parking: Free car parking in Wilderness car park, close to river, just over bridge as you drive into Wetherby from south

Walk around a handsome country market town with a long history and along a stretch of the mature River Wharfe.

❶ Walk to far end of car park, to follow path with River Wharfe on your R and cliffs to your L. You pass in quick succession beneath shallow arches of 2 modern bridges, carrying **A58** and **A1** roads across **River Wharfe**. Go through kissing gate to continue on riverside path, soon with open fields on L. Take another kissing gate to arrive at Wetherby's **water treatment works**.

❷ Go **L** here, up track around perimeter fence. After 150yds (138m) you meet metalled track at works' main entrance; go **L** here. At top of incline, where track bears slightly to **R**, you have choice of routes. Your path is sharp **R**, along grassy track between fields. You soon approach wooded slope that overlooks River Wharfe. Take stile, and follow line of trees to

farm, **Flint Mill Grange**. It was here where flints were ground for use in the pottery industry of Leeds. Enter farmyard and take farm access road to **L**.

❸ Meet **Walton Road** and walk **L** for 75yds (68m), then go **R**, along metalled drive (this is signed as a bridleway and the entrance to **Wetherby Racecourse**). After gate you have a choice of routes. Bear **L** here, downhill, to join the trackbed of the old Church **Fenton–to–Harrogate** railway line, which carried its last train in 1964.

❹ Go **L**, to enjoy level walking along railway trackbed, until you approach A1 road, raised up on embankment as it skirts around Wetherby. Take underpass beneath road, and bear **R** along Freemans Way, until you meet Hallfield Lane.

❺ Walk **L**, along Hallfield Lane, which bears **R** around **playing fields** of Wetherby **High School** and back into centre of Wetherby and start.

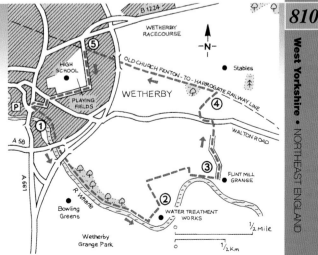

West Yorkshire

811 BARDSEY *LAND OF ROMANS*

3½ miles (5.7km) 2hrs Ascent: 164ft (50m)
Paths: Good paths and tracks (though some, being bridleways, may be muddy), 8 stiles
Suggested map: aqua3 OS Explorer 289 Leeds
Grid reference: SE 369430 **Parking:** Lay-by on A58, immediately south of Bardsey

A rolling landscape with Roman earthworks.
❶ From lay-by, walk past metal bollards into woods. Join railway trackbed going **R**, shortly, then **L** over stile on to woodland path. Soon reach field-edge path, (fence to **L** and hedgerow to **R**). Continue when fence ends. When hedge turns to **R**, follow it, and **Bardsey Beck**, downhill.

❷ Cross stile to enter **Hetchell Wood**. Keep **R** through woods, soon passing beneath **Hetchell Crags**. At meeting of paths, near stepping stones, don't cross beck, but go **L** briefly, through kissing gate, and join track (Roman origin) going uphill.

❸ Go **R** almost immediately then cross stile. Path goes **R** around earthworks (**Pompocali**). Pass between stream and overhanging rock; take stile next to gate. Walk uphill to pass **ruinous mill**, take stile and join track, passing under railway line. Immediately after crossing stream, go through gate; walk across field to another gate. Beyond main gate to **Moat Hall**, follow track for 20yds (18m); take step stile in wall **R**.

❹ Take field-edge path, with hedge to **R** (keep on **Leeds Country Way** back to **Bardsey**). Towards far end of field, path bears **R** into copse. Cross stile and beck on footbridge. Go **L** as you leave copse, then immediately **L** again on to hollow way between hedgerows. Follow path through scrub, past 2 lakes, to emerge at field. Continue up field-edge path, keeping hedge **R**. At top of hill, walk downhill for 75yds (68m). Where hedge ends you meet cross-track. Ignore track ahead; go **L** on track. Follow wall to A58.

❺ Walk **L** for 20yds (18m) and then bear **R** on to **Wayside Mount** (unsurfaced access road). Beyond last house, go through gate; follow track ahead, with tall hedge on **L**. When track bears **L** proceed down field-edge path, following hedge on **L**. Bear half **R**, near bottom of field, to join narrow path through scrubland, over beck, and to gate into churchyard. Keep **R** of church to meet road.

❻ Go **R** on Church Lane to A58. Go **R** for 100yds (91m) to lay-by.

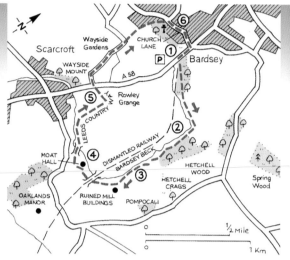

812 HAREWOOD *TREASURE HOUSE*

6½ miles (10.4km) 3hrs Ascent: 164ft (50m)
Paths: Good paths and parkland tracks all the way, 2 stiles
Suggested map: aqua3 OS Explorer 289 Leeds
Grid reference: SE 332450
Parking: Limited in Harewood village. From traffic lights, take A658, and park in first lay-by on left

Around a 'Capability' Brown parkland.
❶ From lay-by, walk 50yds (46m) away from **Harewood**, cross road and walk **R**, down access track to **New Laithe Farm**. Keep to **L** of farm buildings, on grassy track heading into valley bottom. Go through 2 gates and bear half **L** up a field, towards **Hollin Hall**. Keep **L** of buildings to pass **Hollin Hall Pond**.

❷ Beyond pond take gate and follow track to **L**, uphill, skirting woodland. Continue uphill on field-edge path with hedgerow to **L**. Pass through 2 gates, path is now enclosed between hedges.

❸ Bear **R** at top of hill to easy, level walking on enclosed sandy track (you are now joining **Leeds Country Way**). Keep straight ahead when track forks, through gate. Skirt woodland to emerge at road; bear **R** here to arrive at A61.

❹ Cross road to enter **Harewood Estate** (via R-H gate, between gateposts). Follow broad track ahead, through landscaped parkland, soon getting views of **Harewood House** to **R**. Enter woodland through gate, bearing immediately **L** after stone bridge.

❺ Bear **R** after 100yds (91m), as track forks. At crossing of tracks, bear **R**, downhill, still through woodland. At next 2 forks keep 1st **R**, then **L**, to pass farm. Follow good track down towards lake. Go through gate, keep **L** of wall and walk uphill to join metalled access road to **L**. Walk down past house and keep ahead at crossroads. Cross bridge; follow lane up to gate, soon pass **Home Farm** (business units).

❻ Follow road through pasture, keeping **R**, uphill, at choice of routes. Continue through woodland until you come to houses (Harewood estate village).

❼ Cross A61 road (take care); walk **R**, for just 50yds (46m), to take metalled drive immediately before **Harewood Arms**. Pass Maltkiln House, keeping ahead, through gate, as road becomes track. After stile by gate, take another stile in fence to **R** and follow field path back to A659 and start.

813 GOLDEN ACRE *GREEN SPACES OF LEEDS*

5 miles (8km) 2hrs 30min Ascent: 100ft (30m)
Paths: Good paths, tracks and quiet roads, 21 stiles
Suggested map: aqua3 OS Explorer 297 Lower Wharfedale
Grid reference: SE 266418
Parking: Golden Acre Park car park, across road from park itself, on A660 just south of Bramhope

A walk in the rolling countryside.
❶ From far **L** end of car park, take steps and underpass into **Golden Acre Park**. Walk round lake via **L** or **R** paths; at far **L** end of lake exit by gate ('Meanwood Valley Trail'). Go **L**, along tree-lined path, to T-junction. Take road ahead to '**Five Lane Ends**'.

❷ Turn **L** on Eccup Moor Road, past golf course on **R**. Ignore side turnings until you reach outbuildings of **Bank House Farm**; take track **L**. It soon narrows to become path between hedgerows. 50yds (46m) before footpath bears **R**, take stile in fence on **L**, to join field path to wall stile. Cross field to road.

❸ Go **L** for 20yds (18m). Cross stile **R** ('**Dales Way**') to field path. After another stile join track ahead over further stile and another (wall to **L**). Veer **R** across pasture to wall stile; continue towards Lineham Farm. Beyond 2 wall stiles, pass farm buildings to join track. When track goes **L** proceed between fences. After field-edge walking and 3 stiles, reach road.

❹ Go **R** along road for 150yds (138m); take waymarked stile on **L** by gate. Follow field-edge path (fence on **L**). Through 2 kissing gates; bear **L** across field, keeping **R** of **Breary Grange** Farm. Cross over ladder stile, then over field to bottom **R-H** corner and another stile. Head **L**, across next field, to stile, to meet A660 by roundabout.

❺ Cross road and take '**The Sycamores**' ahead. After 250yds (230m) take waymarked stile on **L** to join field-edge footpath (hedge on **L**). Cross 5 stiles and **Marsh Beck**; then skirt woodland on **R**. Beyond ladder stile join farm track, bearing **L** past farmhouse to enter **Fish Pond Plantation** via gate.

❻ Bear **R**, through wood, soon reaching retaining wall of '**Paul's Pond**'. Bear **L** on woodland path accompanying stream. Cross over stream via footbridge; shortly join duck-boarded walkway across **Breary Marsh**. Walkway meanders back towards underpass. Go **L**, in front of it, back into car park.

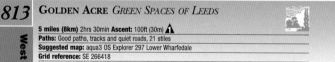

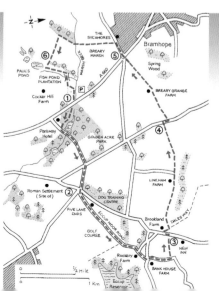

West Yorkshire

FULNECK MORAVIAN SETTLEMENT

4 miles (6.4km) 2hrs Ascent: 262ft (80m)
Paths: Ancient causeways, hollow ways and field paths, 12 stiles
Suggested map: aqua3 OS Explorer 288 Bradford & Huddersfield
Grid reference: SE 222306
Parking: Lay-by in Tong village, near church, or on edge of village

A little rural oasis.
1 From **Tong** village walk up **Keeper Lane** which, beyond gate, becomes sandy track. Walk steadily downhill, following line of old causey stones, into woodland. Cross **Pudsey Beck** on footbridge.
2 After bridge you have choice of tracks. As you approach waymarker post, continue ahead between stone posts ('**Leeds Country Way**'). Follow beck with **golf course** on R. Beyond stile follow field path to another stile, footbridge and meeting of paths. Don't cross bridge, but turn sharp **R** instead, up farm track. Meet road by **Bankhouse Inn**.
3 Follow road to **R** to see Georgian buildings that make up **Fulneck Moravian settlement**, on ridge with good valley views. 50yds (46m) beyond Fulneck Restaurant go **R**, down lane that soon bends to **R**. At bottom of large brick building look out for steps and footpath downhill. Follow delightful sunken path with hedgerows – and golf fairways – to either side. Come

out on to **golf course**, keeping half L across fairway, to rejoin path accompanying **Pudsey Beck**.
4 After 3 stiles reach ruined **mill**; bear **R** to continue on beckside path. You have easy walking, through fields and scrubland, punctuated by stiles. Leave beck via walled path out on to road.
5 Go **R** here, passing another mill, to T-junction. Cross over road and take waymarked footpath between gateposts into Sykes Wood. Go **R** through gate ('Leeds Countryside Way'). Follow path downhill, soon with **Tong Beck**. After walking about ½ mile (800m) through woodland, take footbridge over beck and walk across field, bearing **L** to stile. Follow path along field edge, then through woodland. Keep **L**, when track forks, to stile. Keep following track – ignoring bridges and side-paths – until you reach stile next to gate and broader track.
6 Go **R**, uphill, on good track. When you meet road go **L** to arrive back in **Tong** village.

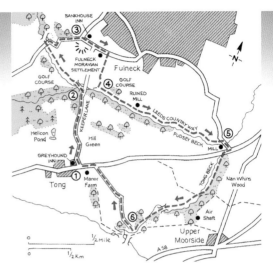

BURLEY IN WHARFEDALE GIANT FOOTSTEPS

4 miles (6.4km) 2hrs Ascent: 560ft (170m)
Paths: Good tracks and moorland paths, 5 stiles
Suggested map: aqua3 OS Explorer 297 Lower Wharfedale
Grid reference: SE 163457
Parking: Burley in Wharfedale Station car park

The moorland where a giant once lived.
1 From car park, cross line via footbridge and go **L** along lane. Follow it past houses and between fields up to **Hag Farm**.
2 When track wheels R, into farmyard, keep **L** on track to stile and gate. Accompany wall downhill; after 100yds (91m) take gap stile in wall. Bear off sharply to **R**, to follow stream up to another wall and gap stile. Follow fence uphill to take another stile, cross over stream via footbridge and join approach road to group of houses. Walk uphill to meet Guiseley–Ilkley road. Cross road and continue on stony track ahead. After 50yds (46m), ford stream and follow path uphill through woodland, on to path between hedges. Out on to open pasture you come to gate. Follow wall to **R**, soon leaving it to take indistinct path uphill.
3 Meet stony track; follow it to **R**, along moorland edge. Follow wall to stile by gate. Immediately after, keep **R** when track forks. Keep **R** again as you

approach small brick building. Route finding is now easy, as track wheels around farm. Keep **L** at next farm ('**York View**') to make slow descent, following wall on R. As you approach 3rd farm, watch for 2 barns and gate, on R. Take indistinct path to **L** here, passing small quarry. Enjoy level walking. Then, go steeply down little ravine and cross beck; continue up other side. Before reaching top, bear **R** and follow path downhill to meet road by sharp bend.
4 Walk 100yds (91m) down road, to another sharp R-H bend. Bear **L** here ('**Ilkley Moor Garden Centre**'). Keep **L** of garden centre, by continuing down stony track. Keep **L** of house, R of **The Lodge**; when track bears sharp L towards farm, your route is to **R**, through kissing gate, to follow field path downhill with woodland to L. After another kissing gate, follow fence – then wall – on **R**. Beyond 3rd kissing gate and another gate, join tree-lined track heading to **R**.
5 Meet road and walk downhill back to car park.

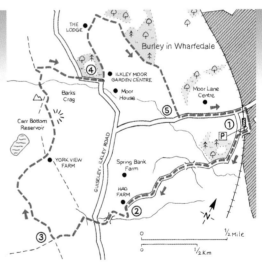

FARNLEY TYAS CASTLE HILL

4½ miles (7.2km) 2hrs 30min Ascent: 360ft (110m)
Paths: Field paths, a little road walking on quiet lanes, 18 stiles
Suggested map: aqua3 OS Explorer 288 Bradford & Huddersfield
Grid reference: SE 162125
Parking: 200yds (183m) along Butts Road by church in Farnley Tyas. Park in lay-by by recreation field

Huddersfield's most prominent landmark.
1 Enter recreation field; follow wall to R. Pass 2 gates, on to track. At road, turn **R**.
2 100yds (91m) past **farm** bear **R** on track. When track bends R, towards **Ludhill Farm**, take path on **L**. Take stile next to gate, keeping **L** across field, to stile, and descend towards houses. Keep **L** at fork of paths; walk between hedgerows, soon bear **L** to path to road.
3 Go **R**, downhill. Bear **R** after cottages on track into woodland. Bear **L**, after 50yds (46m), on path that descends to stile. Continue across field (aim towards farm); cross stream, then go through woodland. Cross another field (L of **High Royd Farm**). Go through gate and join track that leads to road by **High Royd Cottage**. Walk **R** for 100yds (91m). Where road bears R take gap stile on **L** by gate; follow path. Take stile by gate; bear **R**, uphill, along field edge; go through gap in wall; cross over another field. Follow edge of next field (hedge left). Path levels out until meets road.

4 Go **R** for 20yds (18m), then **L** through gap stile. Keeping hedge **R**, follow field-edge path. 150yds (138m) before wood, take waymarked gap in wall **L**. Follow it downhill, over stile; keep to **R-H** edge of next field. Keep ahead at next stile. Go through farmyard; join access track to meet road. Go **R**, downhill. After passing 2 cottages, go through gap stile **R**.
5 Descend into valley. Take stile and steps; cross **Lumb Dike** via plank bridge. Bear **L** uphill, then **L** to follow river and through **Molly Carr Wood**. Descend to where 2 streams meet (jump 2nd beck). Follow watercourse; cross side-beck. Take few steps to **R**, uphill, to shortly join track, via gate to road.
6 Go **R**, uphill; 75yds (68m) past sharp L-H bend, take track to **R** ('Farnley Bank'). Pass house; when track bears R, to **Farnley Bank Farm**, take stile ahead; follow field path uphill. Meet road; walk **R**, uphill and into **Farnley Tyas**. At T-junction bear **R**, then **L** by church on to **Butts Road**.

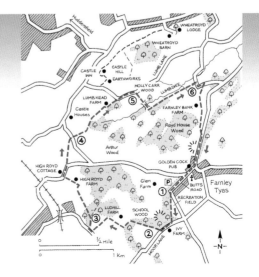

West Yorkshire

817 HOLMFIRTH *LAST OF THE SUMMER WINE*

4½ miles (7.2km) 2hrs **Ascent:** 558ft (170m)
Paths: Good paths and tracks, 8 stiles
Suggested map: aqua3 OS Explorer 288 Bradford & Huddersfield
Grid reference: SE 143084
Parking: Park in Crown Bottom car park (pay-and-display) on Huddersfield Road

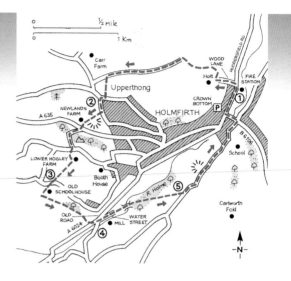

Land of Compo, Foggy and Clegg.

❶ From car park, walk to **R** along **Huddersfield Road** for 100yds (91m) then turn **L** up **Wood Lane**. Road soon narrows to steep track. Keep **L** of house, through gate, to continue on walled path. At top of hill, by bench, follow track to **R** and into valley. Shortly after nearing woodland, there's several tracks: keep **L** on walled path, uphill. Join farm track and, 100yds (91m) before cottage, look for wall stile on **L**. Follow field path to emerge, between houses, in **Upperthong**. Turn **R** into village, past pub to T-junction.

❷ Bear **L** along road, which wheels round to **R**. Walk downhill. After 150yds (138m), take cinder track on **R**. Descend past **Newlands Farm** to road. Cross and take lane ahead, down into valley and up other side. When road forks at top go **R** uphill. Immediately after 1st house, go **L** on sandy track. Follow track to **Lower Hogley Farm**; keep **R**, past houses, to gate and on to field path (wall to L). Cross stile and next field (wall to

R). Past next wall stile, veer half **L** across next field (aim for mast). After another field, descend to road.

❸ Go **R** for 50yds (46m) to bear **L** around **schoolhouse**. Follow walled path downhill, through gate. As path opens out into grassy area, bear **L** on track into valley. Follow high wall on **R**, over stile, on to enclosed path. On approaching houses, take stile and join metalled track at fork. Bear **R**, then immediately **L**, on path between houses. Follow field path through gate, pass houses and mill to meet **A6024**.

❹ Cross road; by cottages take **Old Road** to **L**. Keep ahead at junction down **Water Street**. Beyond **mill**, cross **River Holme** on footbridge; follow riverside path. Soon path veers **R** through pasture; when path forks, keep **R**, uphill, to enter woodland. Continue in same direction, uphill, emerging from wood on to field path. After 2 stiles join track by house. Pass more cottages to meet road.

❺ Go **L** on road to make long descent to **Holmfirth**.

818 ADDINGHAM *TO A VICTORIAN SPA TOWN*

5½ miles (8.8km) 2hrs 30min **Ascent:** 197ft (60m)
Paths: Riverside path and field paths, some road walking, 7 stiles
Suggested map: aqua3 OS Explorer 297 Lower Wharfedale
Grid reference: SE 084498
Parking: Lay-by at eastern end of Addingham, on bend where North Street becomes Bark Lane

Along a stretch of the lovely River Wharfe.

❶ Walk 50yds (46m) then descend steps down to **R** ('Dales Way'). Bear **R** again, and cross **River Wharfe**. Follow path along field edge. Cross stream and join track between walls that soon emerges at minor road by sharp bend. Turn **R**; after about ½ mile (800m) of road walking you reach **Nesfield**.

❷ 100yds (91m) beyond last house, and after road crosses stream, bear **L** up track ('High Austby'). Immediately take stile between 2 gates. Cross field ahead, keeping parallel to road (ignoring track going L, uphill). There is no obvious path; follow wall on **R**, over stile. Beyond conifer plantation, take ladder stile in fence ahead to keep **L** of **Low Austby Farm**.

❸ Cross footbridge; beyond stile you enter woodland. Follow path downhill, leaving wood by step stile. Follow fence uphill, then cross mid-field to stile at far end, to enter woodland. Follow path through trees, before reaching road via wall stile. Descend **R** to

road junction. Go **R** across **Nesfield Road**; take path to **L** of **electricity sub-station**. After few minutes of riverside walking, you reach **Ilkley's** old stone bridge.

❹ Cross bridge; turn **R** on to riverside path ('**Dales Way**'). Proceed, passing **tennis club**. Opposite clubhouse, take footpath to **L**, via kissing gate then pasture. Navigate 7 kissing gates to reach river. Cross footbridge and enter woodland. Cross stream to track. Go **R**, downhill, on track to river. Through kissing gate, follow path (woodland and fence L) before joining **A65**.

❺ Follow road by riverside. After almost ½ mile (800m), go **R**, just before terraced houses, on to **Old Lane**. Pass housing, 'Low Mill Village', to find riverside path at far side. Once past **Rectory** on L, and Old Rectory grounds on R, look for kissing gate on **R**. Take steps and follow path to arched bridge over **Town Beck**. Take path across pasture, in front of church, before crossing another bridge, between houses, to re-emerge on **North Street** in **Addingham**.

819 SHIPLEY GLEN *A RURAL PLAYGROUND*

4 miles (6.4km) 2hrs **Ascent:** 492ft (150m)
Paths: Moor and field paths, 1 stile
Suggested map: aqua3 OS Explorer 288 Bradford & Huddersfield
Grid reference: SE 132389
Parking: On Glen Road, between Bracken Hall Countryside Centre and Old Glen House pub

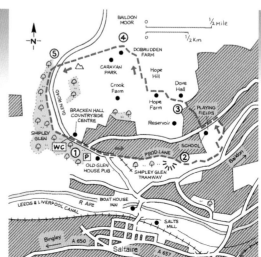

The playground of the millworkers.

❶ Walk down **Glen Road**, passing **Old Glen House** pub. Continue as road becomes **Prod Lane**, signed as cul-de-sac. Pass tiny funfair and entrance to **Shipley Glen Tramway**. Where road ends, keep ahead and locate enclosed path to **R** of house. Follow path, with houses on L, and woodland to R. As you reach metal barrier, ignore path to L. Keep straight on downhill. 100yds (91m) beyond barrier, you have choice of paths; bear **L** here, uphill, soon getting good views over Saltaire, **Shipley** and Aire Valley.

❷ Beyond woodland, walk beneath quarried sandstone cliff. At open area, with panoramic views, take steps, with handrails, up to top of cliff. Bear **R** on path between chain-link fences around **school playing fields**, to meet road. Walk **L** along road for 150yds (138m). When you are level with school on L, cross road and take narrow, enclosed path on **R**, between houses. Walk gradually uphill, crossing road

in housing estate and picking up enclosed path again. Soon, at stile, you emerge into pasture.

❸ Go half **L**, uphill, to kissing gate at top **L** corner of field. Before you reach farm ahead, join access track, walking past buildings on cinder track until metal gate bars your way. Go **R** here, through wooden gate, on path between walls. Beyond next gate you come out on to **Baildon Moor**. Your path is clear, following wall to L. Keep straight on, as wall curves to L, towards next farm (and **caravan park**). Cross over metalled farm track and curve **L** to follow boundary wall of **Dobrudden Farm**.

❹ Walk gradually downhill towards Bingley in valley. When well-trod bears **L**, keep straight ahead, through bracken, more steeply down. Cross over metalled track and carry on down to meet **Glen Road** again.

❺ Follow path along rocky edge of wooded **Shipley Glen** leading you back to **Bracken Hall Countryside Centre** and your car.

West Yorkshire

HALIFAX *THE SHIBDEN VALLEY*

4½ miles (7.2km) 2hrs 30min Ascent: 410ft (125m)
Paths: Old packhorse tracks and field paths, no stiles
Suggested map: aqua3 OS Explorer 288 Bradford & Huddersfield
Grid reference: SE 095254
Parking: In Halifax

An old packhorse track to a hidden valley.
❶ Walk downhill, past tall spire and down **Church Street**, past parish church. Bear **L** on to **Lower Kirkgate**, then **R** on to **Bank Bottom**. Cross **Hebble Brook** and walk uphill; where road bears sharp **L** keep ahead up steep cobbled lane. At road, go **R** for about 200yds (183m). Just after warehouse entrance (Aquaspersion), take cobbled path on **L** that makes steep ascent up **Beacon Hill**.
❷ This old packhorse track – known as **Magna Via** – joins another path and continues uphill to large retaining wall, where you have choice of tracks. Keep **L** on cinder track, slightly downhill. Keep **L**, when track forks again after further 100yds (91m), then take walled path on **L** ('**Stump Cross**'). Follow hedgerow downhill through small housing estate to road. Cross and take gated path immediately to **R** of farm entrance, which takes you downhill, under railway line and into **Shibden Park**, close to **boating lake**.

❸ Follow drive uphill. Near top of hill there's footpath on **L**, giving access to **Shibden Hall**. Otherwise, continue uphill; just before A58, bear **R**, down **Old Godley Lane**. Pass houses and take steps up to main road at busy junction of **Stump Cross**.
❹ Cross road. Take **Staups Lane**, to **L** of **Stump Cross Inn**. Walk up lane, which becomes cobbled, to meet surfaced road. Bear **L**, down metalled track, through gate, to join straight, double-paved track into Shibden Dale. When paving ends, continue via gate and open pasture. Turn **L**, at next gate, walking down lane that soon leads to **Shibden Mill Inn**.
❺ Walk to far end of pub's car park, to join track that crosses **Shibden Beck**. Beyond brick house, track narrows to walled path. You emerge from countryside, to walk past houses of **Claremont** and cross A58, as it goes through steep-sided Godley Cutting, on bridge. Take steps immediately after bridge and walk **L** along road. From here retrace your route into **Halifax**.

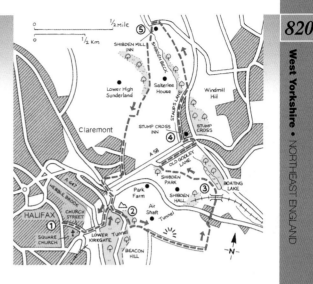

BINGLEY *THE DRUID'S ALTAR*

5½ miles (8.8km) 3hrs Ascent: 525ft (160m)
Paths: Good paths and tracks throughout, 2 stiles
Suggested map: aqua3 OS Explorer 288 Bradford & Huddersfield
Grid reference: SE 107393 **Parking:** Car parks in Bingley

Enjoy great views of Airedale.
❶ Walk downhill from town centre, towards church. Go **L** at traffic lights, passing Old White Horse pub, on to **Millgate**. Cross **River Aire** and take 1st **R**, Ireland Street, veering **R** past industrial buildings to join riverside track. Shortly town becomes country. Bear **R** in front of **Ravenroyd Farm**, to pass between farm buildings and continue on walled track. Pass house, '**Cophurst**', and through pasture (woodland on **L**).
❷ Skirt hillock and approach **Marley Farm**. Through gate on **L** and continue on field path that soon emerges on to more substantial track. Bear **L** by **Blakey Cottage**, on setted (paved) track uphill. Pass 2 more farms. Track bears **L** and, after 100yds (91m), **L** again. Look for stile ahead and take narrow path that climbs steeply through bracken. Keep **L** at fork of tracks to top of hill to enjoy level walking with wall on **R**. Cross track to arrive, just 100yds (91m) further on, at rocky outcrop, **Druid's Altar**.
❸ Bear **R**, after rocks, to come to meeting of tracks.

Go through gap in wall ahead, on to walled track that leads into **St Ives Estate**. Bear immediately to **R**, through gap stile in wall, to take path (woodland to **L** and open fields to **R**). After ½ mile (800m) you reach kissing gate on **R**. Turn **L** here, into woods and between fairways. At choice of paths ahead, take **R–H** option, soon having wall on **L** and heathland on **R**. Follow path downhill, passing **Lady Blantyre's Rock**.
❹ Ignoring side-tracks, follow path downhill to **Coppice Pond**. Join road to bear **L**, soon passing stable block, **golf clubhouse** and **St Ives house**.
❺ Bear **R** past house, to follow drive downhill. 100yds (91m) before road, bear **L** through woodland. Keep **R** where track forks, to reach B649, Bingley to Cullingworth road. Cross and continue downhill on **Beckfoot Lane**. After houses, lane becomes unmade track leading to **Beckfoot Farm**.
❻ Here, cross bridge and bear **L**, to find allotments on **L**. Where allotments end, take path to **L**. Cross footbridge and **Myrtle Park** to return to **Bingley**.

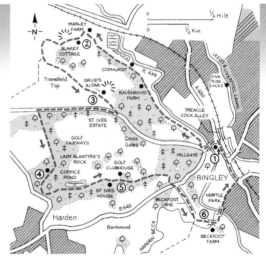

ILKLEY MOOR *TWELVE APOSTLES*

4½ miles (7.2km) 2hrs 30min Ascent: 425ft (130m)
Paths: Good moorland paths, some steep paths towards end of walk
Suggested map: aqua3 OS Explorer 297 Lower Wharfedale
Grid reference: SE 132467
Parking: Off-road parking on Hangingstone Road, opposite Cow and Calf rocks, pay-and-display car park

Discover some ancient standing stones and plenty of history on Ilkley Moor.
❶ Walk along road; 150yds (138m) beyond **Cow and Calf Hotel**, where road bears **L**, fork **R** up grassy path. Scramble up ridge to **Pancake Stone**, and enjoy extensive views back over **Ilkley** and Wharfedale. Bear **R** on path along edge of ridge, cross stony track and pass Haystack Rock. From here track slowly wheels **L**, to run parallel to **Backstone Beck**, uphill, on to open heather moorland.
❷ At top, meet **Bradford–Ilkley Dales Way** link path. Go **L** here; soon you are walking on section of duckboarding. Pass boundary stone at top of next rise, and continue to ring of Bronze-Age stones known as **Twelve Apostles**. These stones are the most visible evidence of 7,000 years of occupation of these moors. There are other smaller circles and Ilkley Moor is celebrated for its Bronze-Age rock carvings, many showing the familiar 'cup and rings' designs. The most

famous of the rocks features a sinuous swastika; a symbol of good luck until corrupted by the Nazi movement.
❸ Retrace your steps from **Twelve Apostles**, and continue along **Dales Way** link path. Having crossed **Backstone Beck**, you soon leave open moorland behind, and find yourself on top of ridge. Enjoy views across Ilkley and Wharfedale, before taking path (which is stepped in some places) steeply downhill. Beneath clump of trees you come to **White Wells**.
❹ Bear **R**, passing to **L** of ponds, on path, downhill. Aim for pyramid-shaped rock, after which you emerge on to metalled track. Walk either way around **tarn**. At far end take path, uphill, then down to cross **Backstone Beck** again on little footbridge, then final haul uphill to reach **Cow and Calf rocks**.
❺ It's worth taking a few minutes to investigate the rocks or watch climbers practising their belays and traverses. From here paved path leads to car park.

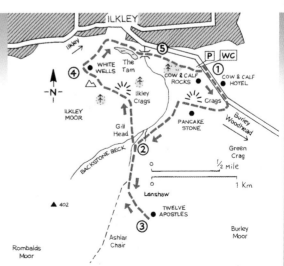

West Yorkshire

West Yorkshire • NORTHEAST ENGLAND

823 OXENHOPE AGE OF STEAM

6 miles (9.7km) 3hrs Ascent: 492ft (150m)
Paths: Good paths and tracks, 6 stiles
Suggested map: aqua3 OS Outdoor Leisure 21 South Pennines
Grid reference: SE 033354
Parking: Street parking in Oxenhope, near Keighley and Worth Valley Railway station

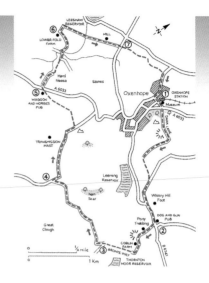

Moorland and the Worth Valley Railway.

❶ From **station** entrance take minor road to **L**, to A6033. Cross and take **Dark Lane** ahead, sunken lane that ascends steeply. Follow track to road. Go **R**, downhill, to join Denholme Road (**B6141**). Walk **L** to reach **Dog and Gun** pub then **R** on to Sawood Lane.

❷ At **Coblin Farm**, route becomes rough track. Go through gate to join metalled road to **R**, uphill ('**Brontë Way**'). After 100yds (91m), when road accesses **Thornton Moor Reservoir**, keep ahead on unmade track. Go through gate into rough pasture, ignoring **Brontë Way** sign to **R**.

❸ At fork, just 50yds (46m) further on, keep **R** as track goes downhill towards **transmission mast** on mid-horizon. Pass clump of trees, and cross watercourse before descending to minor road.

❹ Go **R** here to pass cattle grid and mast. 150yds (138m) beyond **mast**, as road begins steep descent, take wall stile on **L**. Go through another wall stile, to

walk **L**, uphill, on broad, walled track to **Waggon and Horses** pub.

❺ Cross road. Take track between gateposts, which bears **R**, steeply downhill. Where it bears sharp **R** again, after 300yds (274m), take stile to **L**, by gate. Follow wall downhill to take 3 stiles; at bottom meet walled path. Go **L** here; cross stream, and continue uphill to arrive at entrance to **Lower Fold Farm**.

❻ Follow farm track to **R**; turn **R** again, 20yds (18m) further on, at end of cottage, to join metalled track. Track soon bears **R** above **Leeshaw Reservoir** and makes gradual descent. Pass mill to meet road.

❼ Cross road and take track ahead ('Marsh'). Keep **R** of 1st house, on narrow walled path, then paved path. Pass through courtyard of house as path goes **L**, then **R** and through kissing gate. Follow path between wall and fence to meet walled lane. Go **R** here, passing houses, then on field path to meet road. Go **R** here and back down into **Oxenhope**.

---

824 SLAITHWAITE ALONG THE COLNE VALLEY

6 miles (9.7km) 2hrs 30min Ascent: 550ft (170m)
Paths: Field paths, good tracks and canal tow path, 12 stiles
Suggested map: aqua3 OS Outdoor Leisure 21 South Pennines
Grid reference: SE 079140
Parking: Plenty of street parking in Slaithwaite

The rural face of the valley.

❶ Walk along **Britannia Road** to A62. Cross, turn **R** and take **Varley Road** to **L**. Beyond last house go **R**, through stile. Join track across field to stile on **R-H** end of wall. Follow to **R**, cross stile, to minor road. Go **R**; follow road **L** to T-junction. Keep ahead on track then **L** on track between houses. Go through gate on to field path. Follow wall on **R**. Towards its end go through gap in wall; take steps to proceed in same direction. After step stile, keep to **R**, slightly downhill, following wall to stile.

❷ Go **R** at road, then **L** ('**Hollins Lane**'). Track becomes rougher; when it peters out, keep **L** of cottage and through gate. Follow field-edge path ahead, through pair of gates either side of beck. Pass ruined house to descend on walled path. When it bears **R** keep ahead through gate on to field path. Follow wall on **R**; where it ends keep ahead, slightly uphill across 2 fields to meet track. Go **L**, towards

farm; then **R**; through stile and pair of gates, on to another walled path. Path soon bears **R**; take stile to **L** to follow field-edge path. Cross another field and go **L**, uphill, at wall. Take stile and follow path to B6107.

❸ Go **R** for just 75yds (68m); take track to **L**. Keep **L** of house, via kissing gate. 150yds (138m) past house, turn **R** at fork, taking less obvious track. Soon follow wall. Across beck, track forks again; keep **L**, uphill, to skirt shoulder of **Hard Hill**. Track descends steeply, then up to stile, then down again to cross beck on stone retaining wall. After another climb, route levels. Bear **L**, steeply uphill, at stone building, cross 2 stiles and meet track. Follow it **R**, downhill, to road.

❹ Go **R**, passing terraced houses. Keep ahead at roundabout, down **Fall Lane**, soon bearing **L**, under main road, into **Marsden**. Take **Station Road**, far end of green, to meet **Huddersfield Narrow Canal**.

❺ Take path on **R**. Follow canal tow path for 3 miles (4.8km) back into **Slaithwaite**.

---

825 RISHWORTH MOOR ALONG BLACKSTONE EDGE

5½ miles (8.8km) 2hrs 30min Ascent: 328ft (100m)
Paths: Moorland paths; may be boggy after rain
Suggested map: aqua3 OS Outdoor Leisure 21 South Pennines
Grid reference: SE 010184
Parking: Small car park above Baitings Reservoir

A bracing ramble on old moorland tracks, with extensive views all the way.

❶ From car park, walk **L** down road. 50yds (46m) after crossing beck, take gate in wall on your **R** ('Booth Wood Reservoir').

❷ Follow tumbledown wall uphill towards **L-H** side of **Blackwood Farm**. Walk between farmhouse and outbuilding, to reach gate at top of farmyard. Walk up next field to stile and then continue steeply uphill, following wall to your **R**. Look for views of **Ryburn Valley**, as you crest hill and arrive at ladder stile, next to gate in wall.

❸ From here you strike off to **R**, across rough moorland; path is distinct but narrow. Keep straight ahead at yellow-topped post (you will see others en route). Walk roughly parallel to M62, heading just to **R** of tall mast on far side of motorway. At next waymarker stick, bear slightly **R**, on less-obvious path. As you start to walk downhill you have good views

down to **Green Withens Reservoir** ahead. Descend to cross side-beck on little plank bridge, to meet reservoir drainage channel.

❹ Take bridge over channel and walk **R**, following this watercourse towards reservoir. About 300yds (274m) before reservoir embankment, take bridge back over channel ('Blackstone Edge and Baitings'). Bear slightly **L** to follow path uphill – soon quite steeply – before it levels out and bears **L** around **Flint Hill**. The view behind you recedes; ahead is Upper **Ryburn Valley**. Descend to water channel on your **L** and fork of paths.

❺ Go **R** (sign indicates **Baitings Reservoir**), continuing to skirt hill on good, level path. Keep **L**, where path forks, to begin gradual descent towards **Baitings Reservoir**. When you come to wall corner, keep straight ahead, following wall on your **L**. Soon you are on walled track, passing through 2 gates and finally emerging at little car park above reservoir.

HARDCASTLE CRAGS TWO WOODED VALLEYS

5 miles (8km) 2hrs 30min **Ascent:** 787ft (240m)
Paths: Good paths and tracks, plus open pasture, no stiles
Suggested map: aqua3 OS Outdoor Leisure 21 South Pennines
Grid reference: SD 988291
Parking: National Trust pay-and-display car parks at Midgehole, near Hebden Bridge (accessible via A6033, Keighley Road)

Walk in a pair of beautiful wooded valleys, linked by a high level path.

❶ Walk along drive, passing **lodge**, and into woods. Take 1st path to **L**, which descends to **Hebden Water**. Follow good riverside path through delectable woodland, passing Hebden Hey – popular picnic site, with stepping stones – to reach **Gibson Mill**. Buildings and mill dam behind are worth investigating.

❷ Join track uphill, to **R** of **Gibson Mill**, soon passing crags that give woods their name. Keep on main track, ignoring side-paths, to leave woodland and meet metalled road. Keep **L** here, still uphill, across beck and approach **Walshaw**, knot of houses, enjoying terrific views.

❸ Just before you reach houses – when you are opposite some barns – bear sharp **R** through gate on to enclosed track ('Crimsworth Dean'). You are soon walking along grassy track crossing pasture,

descending to beck and through gate. Walk uphill, soon bearing to **R** as you follow wall around shoulder of **Shackleton Knoll**. Go through gate in wall on your **L**, and continue as path bears **R**, still following wall, but now it's on your **R**. Here you have level walking and great views. Take gate in wall on **R**, just above Coppy Farm, to join walled track downhill into valley of **Crimsworth Dean**. You meet more substantial track by another ruin of farm. This track is old road from Hebden Bridge to Haworth: a great walk to contemplate on another day.

❹ Bear **R**, along this elevated track, passing farm on **L**. Look out, by farm access track to **R**, for **Abel Cross**: not one but a pair of old waymarker stones. Continue down main track, into **National Trust woodland**, keeping **L**, after field, when track forks. Beyond pair of cottages track is metalled; you soon arrive back at car parks at **Midgehole**.

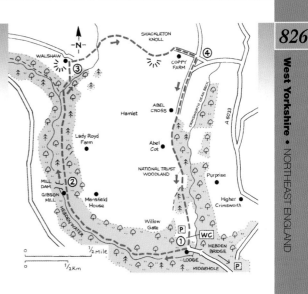

TODMORDEN ON THE PACKHORSE TRAIL

5 miles (8km) 2hrs 30min **Ascent:** 656ft (200m)
Paths: Good paths and tracks throughout, 2 stiles
Suggested map: aqua3 OS Outdoor Leisure 21 South Pennines
Grid reference: SD 945201 **Parking:** Roadside pull-in for cars, near Bird i' th' Hand pub on A6033, between Todmorden and Littleborough

A moorland walk, punctuated by reservoirs.

❶ Walk to **R** for 75yds (68m). Cross road; take track on **L**, Warland Gate End, past cottages. Cross **Rochdale Canal** via swing bridge; follow track uphill, between houses. At **R-H** bend, by houses, track becomes metalled. Continue uphill, passing house and stables, to gate above house. Now bear slightly **R**, up to another stile. Follow wall to **L** with a stream to **R**. Cross stream by gate. At retaining wall of **Warland Reservoir**, follow track on **R** or take steeper short cut on **L** to track that follows contours of reservoir.

❷ Walk **L** along track. Cross bridge at northern end of reservoir, and keep on track as it follows a drainage channel. When both track and channel wheel to **R**, go **L** at stone bridge, to follow path (not very distinct and may be boggy) in direction of another, smaller reservoir, with windfarm visible on horizon.

❸ Line of paving stones will help keep you dry-shod, before you walk along **L** edge of **Gaddings Dam**.

❹ Bear half **L** at far end of reservoir, by stone steps, on clear path that soon passes **Basin Stone** outcrop. Soon reach waymarked junction of paths.

❺ Bear **L**, on path (soon delineated by causeway stones). Gradually descend across moorland, then accompanying wall. On approaching houses, go through gate and between walls to join track past houses and downhill. After 75yds (68m) you have choice of routes. Keep **L** on metalled track to house. Through metal gate below house, follow causeway stones to **R**, accompanying wall (ignoring more obvious track to L). Descend, passing to **L** of white-painted house. Paved path leads across beck and up into houses, 'Bottomley'. Go **R** on metalled track, and bear immediately **R** again, through gate, and on to cobbled, walled path downhill towards **Rochdale Canal**.

❻ Cross canal by **Bottomley Lock**, and walk along tow path. At 4th bridge, go **R** to return to pub.

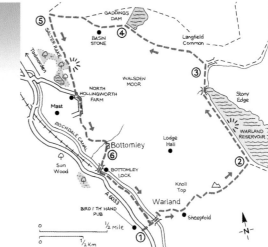

LYDGATE THE BRIDESTONE ROCKS

5 miles (8km) 2hrs 30min **Ascent:** 984ft (300m)
Paths: Moorland and packhorse paths, some quiet roads, 3 stiles
Suggested map: aqua3 OS Outdoor Leisure 21 South Pennines
Grid reference: SD 924256
Parking: Roadside parking, Lydgate, 1½ miles (2.4km) out of Todmorden, on A646, signposted to Burnley

Ancient tracks and gritstone outcrops.

❶ From **post office**, take **Church Road**. At end go **R**, down drive towards house. Look immediately for path that passes to **R** of house and soon goes beneath arch of railway viaduct. Join stony track, walking steeply uphill, where track is sunken, between walls. Where walls end, track gives on to moorland. Keep **R** on track towards **farm**. Keep **L** of farmhouse, continuing along walled track uphill. At another walled track, go **R** towards outcrop on 1st horizon. Beyond 2 gates you reach open moorland again: **Whirlaw Common**. Cross pasture on section of paved causeway to arrive, via gate, at **Whirlaw Stones**.

❷ Follow path that bears **R**, below stones. Leave **Whirlaw Common** by gate on to walled path. Bear **L** at farm, on track that follows wall uphill. Bear **R** around rocks, to join **Windy Harbour Lane**. Climb steeply, before road levels off to meet **Eastwood Road**. Go **L** here for 150yds (140m). Where walls end,

take stile on **L**. Grassy path leads to **Bridestones**.

❸ Continue past **Bridestones** passing boulders, before turning **R** to follow indistinct path across rough terrain. At road, you reach **Sportsman's Inn**.

❹ Go **L** along road; you have 1 mile (1.6km) of level walking, passing **Hawks Stones** on **R** and houses, until you reach minor road on **L**. This is **Mount Lane**, ('Shore and Todmorden'). Walk down road and beyond farm on **R**, take good track to **L**, slightly downhill. Look out for **Mount Cross** in field to **L**.

❺ Detour past **Lower Intake Farm** on path, soon enclosed by walls. 200yds (183m) beyond bridge cross stream and look out for stile on **R**, by gate between gateposts. Follow field path downhill, keeping wall to **L**. Grassy track leads under **Orchan Rocks**.

❻ Where wall bears **L**, beyond rocks, follow it downhill to stile. Now join farm track that takes serpentine route downhill, through woodland. Your way is clear: down into valley and back into **Lydgate**.

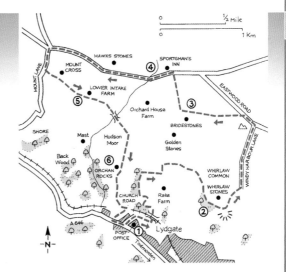

West Yorkshire

West Yorkshire • NORTHEAST ENGLAND

829 HEBDEN BRIDGE *JUMBLE HOLE AND COLDEN CLOUGH*

5½ miles (8.8km) 3hrs **Ascent:** 722ft (220m)
Paths: Good paths, 13 stiles
Suggested map: aqua3 OS Outdoor Leisure 21 South Pennines
Grid reference: SD 992272 **Parking:** Pay-and-display car parks in Hebden Bridge

A tour of textile country.

❶ From centre, walk to **Rochdale Canal**. Go **R**; follow tow path under 2 bridges. Beyond railway bridge, canal broadens; before next bridge, bear **R**; join track **R**, to **A646**.

❷ Cross; bear **R** then **L** on **Underbank Avenue**. Past houses, where another road comes through viaduct, turn **L**. Go **R** past **mill**; follow beck into woodland. Beyond ruined **mill**, leave track. Bear **L**; cross beck. Beyond hairpin bend, climb steeply, past dam. When track wheels **L**, keep ahead. Go through gate. Cross bottom of field; re-enter woodland. Continue uphill to gap in fence. Descend, past **mill** ruins. Ascend steeply to cross stile. Take steps. Cross field to waymark. Keep **L**; follow wall to gate before **Hippins**.

❸ Join **Calderdale Way**; bear **R** between farm buildings to stile. Follow path to next stile, then between fence and wall. Cross track to farm; follow causeway stones across 3 stiles, passing to **R** of cottage. Cross over field to gate (R corner); follow causeway over stile, then to **Blackshaw Head**.

❹ Go **R** for 20yds (18m), then **L** through gate. Bear half **R** across field to stile; follow **R**-edge of next field. Cross 4 fields, and stiles, to gate. Go **L** on path to **Shaw Bottom**. Keep **L** of house to metalled track.

❺ Go **R**. When track bears **L**, proceed on stony track. At marker post, go **L**, down steps; cross bridge. Follow causeway to **R**, at top of woodland. At 2nd stile bear slightly **L** to continue on causeway, through gates and stiles. Keep **R** at crossing of tracks, passing to **L** of house. Proceed on walled path, at next crossing of tracks, by bench. Keep **L** at fork to road.

❻ Go **L**, uphill; before road bears **L**, take gap in wall **R**. Continue through woodland (scrambling in places). Exit woodland; follow wall to **Hell Hole Rocks**.

❼ Bear **L** at wall-end; cross access road. At junction turn **R** to **bowling club**. Go **R**, on walled path; follow wall to **L**; through woodland and on to track round to **L**. Past houses, meet junction. Go **L** for 50yds (46m); take track **R**. Descend steeply on **Buttress** to start.

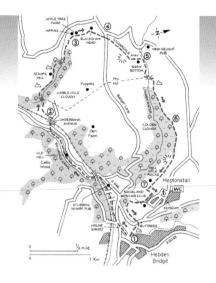

830 MUSTON *GRISTHORPE MAN*

North Yorkshire • NORTHEAST ENGLAND

5 miles (8km) 2hrs **Ascent:** 249ft (75m)
Paths: Field paths and tracks, muddy after rain, 11 stiles
Suggested map: aqua3 OS Explorer 301 Scarborough, Bridlington & Flamborough Head
Grid reference: TA 096796
Parking: Street parking in Muston, near the Ship Inn

Where prehistoric man lived and died.

❶ From **Ship Inn**, walk in direction of Folkton. Just before **Muston** village sign on R, take waymarked stile in hedge on **L** ('Wolds Way'). Go forward to meet track, and follow ('Wolds Way') signs uphill over 2 waymarked stiles. At top **R-H** corner of next field cross stile; continue ahead to next signpost.

❷ Turn **R** on track, following bridleway. Continue downhill, in hollow way. Cross 2 fields to main road.

❸ Cross road and walk through **farm** buildings, bearing **R** along track. Cross over river on concrete bridge.

❹ At end of bridge turn **R** along riverside. Follow track to next bridge. Turn **L** up waymarked track. Follow track along edge of **farm** buildings. At end, it swings **R** and, at crossroads of tracks turn **L** towards red-roofed houses. Track becomes metalled and goes over level crossing. Follow road as it bends **R** into main street of **Gristhorpe**.

❺ Opposite Briar Cottage take public footpath to **R**. Go through metal gate, beside farm buildings to stile by another gate. Follow track down field, over another stile, then half **L** across field towards railway crossing.

❻ Go through white kissing gates at crossing and then continue across field to 2 stiles at either end of footbridge. Continue ahead up ridge to reach stile in top **R-H** corner of field. After another small field go across plank bridge and over stile. Continue ahead with fence on **R**. On reaching telegraph pole, go through opening in hedge and continue with fence now on **L-H** side. Go over stile and continue ahead. Path becomes grassy track. Go through metal gate on to another track, continuing to meet crossing track.

❼ Turn **R**, following bridleway sign. Cross stile by metal gate. Follow hedge on **L** as it bends **L**. Follow path along field edge; through gateway, across bridge, through gateway and bend **L** on to track. Follow track to kissing gate on to main road. Turn **L** back to village.

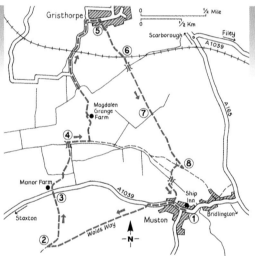

831 SCARBOROUGH *THROUGH RAINCLIFFE WOODS*

North Yorkshire • NORTHEAST ENGLAND

5 miles (8km) 2hrs **Ascent:** 584ft (175m)
Paths: Field tracks, woodland paths, some steep, 2 stiles
Suggested map: aqua3 OS Outdoor Leisure 27 North York Moors – Eastern
Grid reference: SE 984875
Parking: Hazelhead picnic site on Mowthorpe Road, near road junction

A woodland walk to a glacial lake.

❶ From picnic site, walk on to road; turn **L**, downhill. After woodland ends, pass houses on R, then opposite bungalow, No 5, turn **R** down track to **Thorn Park Farm**. Follow track, as it bends **L** by farm buildings then **R** past cottage to metal gate. Continue following track, which bends **L** then **R**, then through 2 gateways.

❷ Just before next gateway turn **R** and walk up field side to stile beside gateway, which takes you on short path to road. Turn **L**. Follow road to reach next car park on **R**.

❸ Go up through car park towards gate and uphill on path ahead. Where main path bends R, go straight ahead, more steeply, to reach crossing, grassy track. Turn **L** through gate and follow path. Where it forks, take **R-H** path.

❹ Look out for path on **L**, which immediately bends **R** over drainage runnel. Path goes down into small valley. Turn **L**, downhill, then follow path as it bends **R** again, past old quarry. Path descends to reach **Throxenby Mere**. Turn **R** along edge of Mere – part of path is on boardwalks.

❺ Just before you reach picnic place, turn **R** through area bare of undergrowth to take path which goes up steeply until it reaches grassy track at top of hill.

❻ Turn **R** and go through metal gate, then follow path for 1 mile (1.6km), parallel with wall. It passes through gateway with stile by it and eventually reaches gate with public bridleway sign.

❼ Do not go through gate out into fields, but turn **R** and continue in woodland. Where main path swings **L** and another goes **R**, go ahead, steeply downhill. When path joins another go **L**, down steps and along boardwalk to meet crossing path.

❽ Turn **R**; go down into car park. Turn **L** on to road, and **L** again to junction. Turn **R**, following Harwood Dale sign, for Hazelhead picnic site.

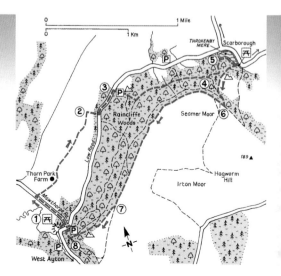

ROBIN HOOD'S BAY *ALONG THE COAST*

5½ miles (8.8km) 2hrs 30min Ascent: 466ft (142m)
Paths: Field and coastal paths, a little road walking, 14 stiles
Suggested map: aqua3 OS Outdoor Leisure 27 North York Moors – Eastern
Grid reference: NZ 950055
Parking: Car park at top of hill into Robin Hood's Bay, by the old railway station

Along part of the Cleveland Way.

❶ From car park, return via entry road to main road. Turn **L** up hill and, where road bears **L**, take signed footpath to **R** over stile. Walk up fields over 3 stiles to metalled lane.

❷ Turn **R**. Go **L** through signed metal gate. At end of field, path bends **R** to gate in hedge on **L**. Continue down next field, stone wall on **L**. Go **R** at end of field; over stile into green lane.

❸ Cross to another waymarked stile; continue along field edge with wall on **R**. At field end, go over stile on **R** then make for waymarked gate diagonally **L**.

❹ Walk towards farm, through gate; take waymarked track round **R** of buildings to another gate then to waymarked opening beside gate. Continue with stone wall on **R**, through another gate and on to track that eventually bends **L** to waymarked stile.

❺ Continue to another stile, then to footbridge over **beck**. At T-junction by telegraph pole, veer **R**; take

path to **R** of bank. After 50yds (46m), look for signpost ('Hawsker') in woodland; follow it **R**. As hedge to **R** curves **L**, go through gap on **R** and over signed stile, walking through field to another stile on to main road.

❻ Go **R** and **R** again, following footpath sign, up metalled lane towards **holiday parks**. Pass **Seaview Caravan Park**, cross old railway track and continue along metalled lane, which bends **R**, goes downhill, crosses stream and ascends to **holiday park**.

❼ Follow footpath sign **R**, then go **L**. Follow metalled track through caravans, eventually leaving track to go **L** to waymarked path. Follow path towards coastline, to reach signpost.

❽ Turn **R** along **Cleveland Way** for 2½ miles (4km). Footpath goes through kissing gate; over 3 stiles; through 2 more kissing gates; past Rocket Post Field to 3 gates by National Trust sign. Go **L** through field gate and past houses to reach main road. Car park is directly opposite.

FYLINGDALES *A FOREST TRAIL*

7½ miles (12.1km) 2hrs 30min Ascent: 642ft (196m)
Paths: Forest tracks and moorland paths, 3 stiles
Suggested map: aqua3 OS Outdoor Leisure 27 North York Moors – Eastern
Grid reference: SX 106836
Parking: May Beck car park, beside stream

Visit the early warning system at Fylingdales and Lilla Cross.

❶ Walk up wide track opposite approach road. Where track bends to **R**, go **L** down signed footpath and descend to go over bridge and continue along green track. Go through kissing gate and up valley, eventually swinging away from stream and into forest.

❷ On reaching forest road turn **R**, passing flooded quarry on **R**. At next junction of forest roads bear **R**. After about ½ mile (800m), look for broad ride to **L**, with white bicycle waymark by it.

❸ Go up ride, leaving forest and out on to moorland. Continue past base and shaft of **York Cross**. Pass track, going **L** and continue until you reach waymarked (bridleway) post, where you turn sharp **L**.

❹ Walk along track, past **Foster Howes**, and continue with fence on **R**. Pass **Ann's Cross** to **R** and ½ mile (800m) beyond you'll reach T-junction, where you turn **R** and continue along bridleway.

❺ When you reach crossroads with signpost, turn **R** along track to visit **Lilla Cross**, which can be seen little way away. It is the most impressive and ancient of the Moor's crosses and dates from AD 626. After visiting it, return to crossroads, and go straight ahead, following **Robin Hood's Bay** sign. Path goes parallel with forest edge.

❻ Go **R** when you reach post with number 9 on it. Pass posts 8 and 7, going **L** when you reach trail sign.

❼ Pass post 6 (by remains of **John Cross**) and go through gate, to continue walking downhill on track. When you reach yellow waymarker leave track and walk down to **L** until you get to waymarked stile near ruins of building.

❽ Go to **L** of ruined building and make for another stile. Follow obvious footpath downhill through bracken, passing 2 public footpath signs, and over another wooden stile to reach road. Turn **L** to return to car park at start.

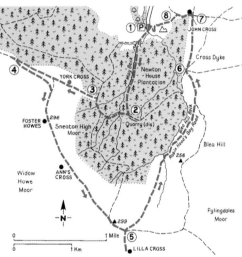

THIXENDALE *A WALK ON THE WOLDS*

4 miles (6.4km) 2hrs Ascent: 459ft (140m)
Paths: Clear tracks and field paths, 9 stiles
Suggested map: aqua3 OS Explorer 300 Howardian Hills & Malton
Grid reference: SE 842611
Parking: Thixendale village street near the church

From the hidden village of Thixendale over chalk hills and through typical dry valleys.

❶ From church, walk west along **Thixendale's** village street. Just beyond last house on **R**, go up track, following sign ('Wolds Way/Centenary Way'). Cross ladder stile in wire fence on your **R** and continue walking up track as it curves round past television aerial.

❷ As you approach top of hill, watch out on **L** for Wolds Way sign, which takes you **L** along grassy track. Go over ladder stile then along field side to meet track again. Continue straight ahead.

❸ At next Wolds Way sign go over stile. Continue with wire fence on **L**. At top of field go **R** by stile descends to reach wooden ladder stile and descends steeply into dry valley to another waymarked stile, then curves to descend to stile by gate.

❹ Follow blue public bridleway sign to **R**, winding **L** up side valley. Near top of valley is deep earthwork

ditch, cross over stile and continue along edge of field. Where footpath divides go **R** through patch of woodland on to track by signpost.

❺ Turn **R** and follow signs ('Wolds Way'). Follow clear track for ¾ mile (1.2km). At end of woodland on your **R**, look out for signpost. Turn **R** here, now following **Centenary Way**, going down edge of field and passing ruined building with tall chimney. Follow winding footpath past signpost.

❻ At next signpost turn **R** off track ('Centenary Way'). Walk down field side on grassy track. At field end leave track and go through waymarked gate. Path goes **L** and passes along hillside to descend to stile beside gate.

❼ Follow yellow waymark straight ahead across field, to pass over track up hillside **L** of row of trees. Path descends to village cricket field on valley floor. Go over stile by gate, on to lane by house. When you reach main road, turn **R** back to start.

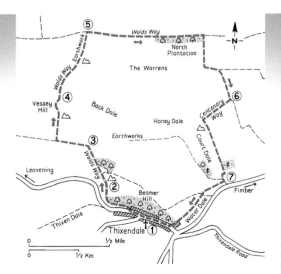

835 · GOATHLAND *MALLYAN SPOUT AND MOORLAND*

4½ miles (7.2km) 2hrs **Ascent:** 557ft (167m)

Paths: Streamside tracks, field and moorland paths, 2 stiles
Suggested map: aqua3 OS Outdoor Leisure 27 North York Moors – Eastern
Grid reference: NZ 827007
Parking: West end of Goathland village, near church

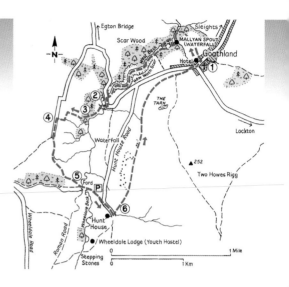

From the moorland village of Goathland, used as the setting for the popular television series Hartbeat, *through woodland and over the moor.*

❶ From opposite church go through kissing gate beside **Mallyan Spout Hotel** ('Mallyan Spout'). Follow path to streamside signpost and then turn **L**. Continue past **waterfall** (take care after heavy rain). Follow footpath signs and cross over 2 footbridges then over stile and up steps, to ascend to stile on to road beside bridge.

❷ Turn **L** along road and climb hill. Where road bends **L**, go **R** along bridleway through gate. Turn **L** down path to go over bridge, then ahead between buildings, through gate and across field.

❸ Part-way across field, go through gate to **R** into woodland. Ascend stony track; go through wooden gate to reach facing gate as you leave wood. Do not go through gate, but turn **R** up field, going **L** at top

through gateway. Continue with wall on your R and go through waymarked gateway in wall and up field, to emerge through gate on to metalled lane.

❹ Turn **L** along lane, go through gate and follow sign ('Roman Road'). Go through another gate, still following public bridleway signs as you join green lane. Continue through small handgate, to descend to another gate and then on until you reach **ford**.

❺ Cross ford and go straight ahead along track, eventually to reach road by farm buildings. Turn **R** up road and, just before wooden garage, turn **L** on green track up hillside.

❻ Go straight ahead at crossing track, passing small cairn and bending **L** along ridge. Path is obvious and is marked by series of little cairns. Eventually take **L** fork where path divides, to go down small gill and join clear track. **Goathland church** soon comes into sight. Pass bridleway sign and descend to road near church to return to start.

836 · LASTINGHAM *ST CEDD'S MONASTERY*

4½ miles (7.2km) 2hrs **Ascent:** 463ft (141m)

Paths: Farm tracks and field paths, 8 stiles
Suggested map: aqua3 OS Outdoor Leisure 26 North York Moors – Western
Grid reference: SE 729905
Parking: Village street in Lastingham. Alternative parking in car park at north end of Hutton-le-Hole

From the ancient site of St Cedd's monastery.

❶ Begin by Green and follow signs ('Cropton, Pickering and Rosedale'), past red telephone box. Where road swings **L**, go **R** to wind over small bridge and beside stream. Ascend to footpath sign, and go **R**, uphill, through gate and woodland to handgate on to road. Turn **R** ('Spaunton').

❷ Follow road through **Spaunton**, and bend **R** at end of village, then turn **L** by public footpath sign over cattle grid into farmyard. Waymarked track curves through **farm** to reach another footpath sign, where track bends **L**. At barn track bends **L** again.

❸ After about 200yds (183m), follow public footpath sign **R** and walk on to another sign as track bends **L**. After 100yds (91m) take footpath to **R**, down hill into woodland. Where path divides, take **L** fork down to stile on **R**, going off track and down steep grassy path into valley. Descend beside stream to stile by gate, which takes you on to road in **Hutton-le-Hole**.

❹ Turn **R** up main street. Turn **R** at yellow waymark by Beckside Gift Shop. Go through gate beside Barn Hotel car park entrance and ahead through garden and to **R** of sheds to stile. Go ahead over 3 stiles to kissing gate before footbridge. Follow path through woodland to gate and follow grassy track to road.

❺ Turn **R** and follow road for ½ mile (800m) and turn **L** at footpath sign just before road descends to stone bridge. Follow grassy path, going over stile, to footpath sign just before **farm**.

❻ Follow direction indicated by signpost to **L**, bending alongside clump of trees and descending into valley. Cross over stream to stile and kissing gate. Continue walking with wall on R-H side to another kissing gate and stile, which leads to carved stone with cross and 3-pointed sign.

❼ Take none of directions indicated by sign, but turn **R**, downhill through gate and on to metalled road. Follow road downhill back into **Lastingham**.

837 · CASTLE HOWARD *A FAMOUS STATELY HOME*

5¼ miles (8.4km) 2hrs **Ascent:** 256ft (68m)

Paths: Field paths and estate roads, 1 stile
Suggested map: aqua3 OS Explorer 300 Howardian Hills & Malton
Grid reference: SE 708710
Parking: Roadside car park near lake north west of Castle Howard, near crossroads

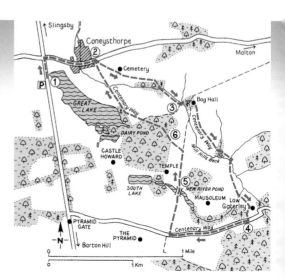

A charming walk around the well-ordered estate of Castle Howard, designed in 1699 by John Vanbrugh.

❶ From car park, walk to crossroads and then turn **R** towards **Coneysthorpe**. Walk all the way through village, and just beyond 'Slow' sign go **R** through tall white gate in wall, following sign ('Centenary Way').

❷ Go half **L**, crossing track and head towards further telegraph pole. Pass cemetery on your **L**, walking now along track. Through gateway, go **R** along edge of field and, when you reach double gate, turn **R** again along edge of wood. Continue along track to reach bridge.

❸ Do not cross bridge, instead turn **L** to walk along track, following track as it bends **R** through farm buildings, following **Centenary Way** sign. Track passes through wood and then winds **L** to cross over bridge and then **R**. At farm buildings follow **Centenary Way** sign off to **R**.

❹ At T-junction, turn **R** along metalled lane. The **Pyramid** comes into view on your L-H side. As you approach nearer to **The Pyramid**, you will reach staggered crossroads where **Centenary Way** is signed to your **L**. Turn **R** here and descend to bridge over dammed stream, with **Mausoleum** on your R and **Castle Howard** on your **L**.

❺ Cross bridge and continue up track, with **Temple of the Four Winds** on your **L**. Path goes over ridge, then turns **L** to park wall. Follow wall as it bends **L** and go over stile beside white gate and continue along track.

❻ After about 30yds (27m), just beyond gate on your **L** marked 'Private No Public Right of Way', go **L** off gravel track down grassy path. Follow this to another gravel track, where you turn **L** to reach signpost. Turn **R** here and follow track back to tall white gate in **Coneysthorpe**. Turn **L** here, and retrace your route back to car park.

North Yorkshire

ROSEDALE ABBEY *THE IRON VALLEY*

3½ miles (5.7km) 1hr 30min Ascent: 558ft (170m) ⚠

Paths: Mostly field paths and tracks, 11 stiles

Suggested map: aqua3 OS Outdoor Leisure 26 North York Moors – Western

Grid reference: SE 708964

Parking: Roadside parking, with care, in Thorgill

A walk with an industrial theme.

1 From your car in **Thorgill**, continue up lane, pass public bridleway sign and go through metal gate. Follow track, going through wooden gate and beginning to rise. Almost opposite farmhouse on L, go **R** over wooden stile beside gate.

2 Descend slope to cross stream on gated footbridge, then turn slightly **L** to go uphill on opposite bank by trees. Continue through gate into field and walk ahead, going over stile then through metal gate into yard of **Craven Garth Farm**. Go through gateway and pass between buildings to reach Daleside Road.

3 Turn **R**; just before reaching cottage, turn **L** up track by parish notice board. Little way up track look for stile beside gate to **Clough House**.

4 Go over stile and follow track downhill towards wood, passing around garden of **Clough House** and up to stile, where you turn **R** and follow waymarked path through wood to reach stile on to road.

5 Turn **R**, then go **L** through gate at bridleway sign. Go down grassy path to meet level track. Turn **L**. Just before gate, go **R**, following bridleway sign. Continue downhill to ladder stile and go straight ahead across field to reach gateway on to road by bridleway sign.

6 Cross road and continue. After passing through gateway, turn **R** at footpath sign before bridge. Track climbs steeply to road. Turn **L** along road to Thorgill.

7 Turn **L**. Opposite Bell End Farm sign turn **R** through gate, and continue down field to stile. Path bends and descends steeply. On reaching fence, turn sharp **R** to go over boardwalk and through waymarked gate. Follow path over 2 stiles. Turn **L** down track, which passes through gateway, and go straight on.

8 Just beyond gate, go **L**, following stream. Cross footbridge with stiles at each end. Follow footpath uphill towards **farm** buildings. Follow waymarks through buildings and up farm track to reach lane. Turn **R** and return to your car.

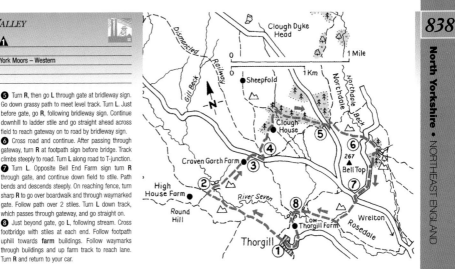

COCKAYNE *REMOTE LANDS*

4 miles (6.4km) 2hrs Ascent: 754ft (230m) ⚠

Paths: Field paths and moorland tracks, a little road walking, 1 stile

Suggested map: aqua3 OS Outdoor Leisure 26 North York Moors – Western

Grid reference: SE 620985

Parking: Roadside parking near cattle grid at T-junction in Cockayne

A walk in Bransdale from the remote hamlet of Cockayne along an ancient moorland track.

1 From your parking place in **Cockayne** cross over cattle grid and then turn **R** at T-junction towards Kirkbymoorside. Follow road uphill and, as it bends sharp **L**, go through gate ('Bransdale Base Camp') and follow track down hill to gate. Continue along track.

2 At signpost by crossroads of tracks next to Bransdale Mill carry straight on, continuing parallel with stream on your R. Go through 2 gates, following side of stream. Climb over slight ridge to reach another gate. Continue with wire fence on your R, keeping on top of ridge then descend to waymarked gate.

3 Cross stream and continue ahead. At top of rise go half **L** across the field, making for corner of wall. Go through 3 field gates and follow grassy track along field edge to another waymarked gate. At top of field,

go over stile beside wooden gate on to lane. Look out for the rough-legged buzzard, which is occasionally spotted in **Bransdale**.

4 Turn **L**. Pass farm buildings to road junction and turn **R**. Follow road uphill for ¼ mile (400m), passing bend sign. Where track joins road from R, turn **L** on to moorland.

5 Path through heather is indistinct, but bears half **R**, passing quarried area. You will eventually reach track, where you turn **L**. Follow track to reach metal barrier. Turn **R** at junction just beyond and follow track to crossroads.

6 Turn **L** and follow gravel track for ¾ mile (1.2km), past boundary stone and **Three Howes**. Where gravel track is crossed by grass track, turn **L**.

7 Follow track downhill. It passes end of wood and continues to wind downhill. Go through wooden gate and then bend **L** to another gate on to lane. Turn **R** and follow road back to start point in **Cockayne**.

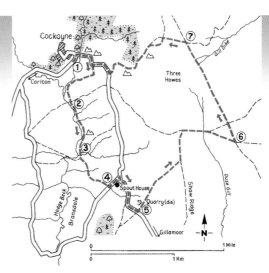

YORK *HIDDEN CITY*

3¼ miles (5.3km) 1hr 30min Ascent: 82ft (25m) ⚠

Paths: City pavements

Suggested map: AA York streetplan

Grid reference: SE 598523 **Parking:** Marygate Car Park, off Bootham

Through the historic walled city.

1 Walk to **Marygate**, turn **L**, cross road; enter **Museum Gardens** through archway. Follow path ahead, passing **Observatory**; leave by lodge.

2 Turn **L**, then **L** again towards **library**. Go **L** through gate, and alongside **library**. Ascend steps; go through gate. At bottom of slope, turn **R**. Follow Abbey Wall into **Exhibition Square**.

3 Cross at traffic lights; through **Bootham Bar**. Shortly on L, take passageway beside Hole in the Wall pub; turn **R** down Precentor's Court. By Minster go **L** through gate ('York Minster Library and Archives').

4 Follow path **L** to library. Bend **R** through gate on cobbled road. Turn **L** by post-box down Chapter House Street, bending **R** into Ogleforth. At crossroads turn **R** then **L** through archway opposite tea rooms.

5 Bear **R** into Bartle Garth. At T-junction go **R** then on Spen Lane. Opposite Hilary House go **R** on St Saviourgate. At T-junction turn **L** to crossroads, then Next to Jones's take passage, Lady Peckitt's Yard.

6 Go under building; turn **L** to Fossgate. Turn **R**, cross bridge. Turn **R** on Merchantgate. At T-junction, cross road; take passageway beside bridge ('Jorvik Viking Centre') into car park by **Clifford's Tower**.

7 Bend **R** and go to R of Hilton Hotel. Just before Job Centre, go **L** down Friargate, along Clifford Street, then **L** by **York Dungeon**. At riverside turn **R**, ascend steps by **Ouse Bridge**; turn **R**. At traffic lights turn **L** by **St Michael's Church**. By NatWest Bank, go **R**, forking **L** by The Link shop.

8 Cross Parliament Street and pass **St Sampson's Church**. Keep ahead at crossroads into Goodramgate. Opposite Bon Marche, go through gateway into **Holy Trinity** churchyard; leave by passage to **L**, to reach Low Petergate. Turn **R**; turn **L** into Grape Lane. Where it bends L, turn **R** down Coffee Yard into Stonegate.

9 Go **L** to **St Helen's Square**; turn **R** by TSB. Keep ahead at crossroads to Exhibition Square. At traffic lights turn **L** up **Bootham**. Turn **L** down **Marygate** by circular tower to start.

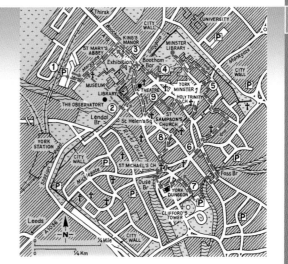

North Yorkshire • NORTHEAST ENGLAND

841 ROSEBERRY TOPPING *CAPTAIN COOK COUNTRY*

5½ miles (8.8km) 2hrs 30min **Ascent:** 1,214ft (370m) ▲
Paths: Hillside climb, then tracks and field paths, 3 stiles
Suggested map: aqua3 OS Outdoor Leisure 26 North York Moors – Western
Grid reference: NZ 570128
Parking: Car park on A173 just south of Newton under Roseberry

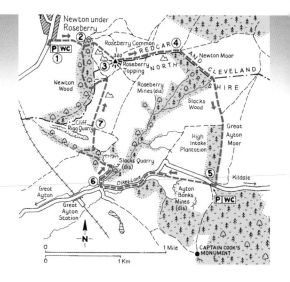

Climb Roseberry Topping for fine views.

❶ Take rough lane beside car park towards **Roseberry Topping**. Path goes through gateway then rises to 2nd gate at beginning of woodland.

❷ Go through gate into National Trust Land and turn **L**. There is well-worn path to summit, with several variations to route. Some are easier than others but whichever you take, it is a stiff climb to trig point on top of hill. **Roseberry Topping** attracts more than 100,000 visitors each year. As a result it is in constant danger of erosion. The National Trust needs to maintain a balance between access and conservation. You may find, therefore, that access is limited in some areas and you can help conservation of the area by staying on the tracks and observing warning signs.

❸ From summit, take Cleveland Way path on opposite side from ascent, going down track which rises through gate to corner of woodland. Go through another gate and turn **R** alongside wood.

❹ Follow this track as it follows edge of wood. It passes through another gate and goes past 2nd area of wood, descending hillside to reach road.

❺ Turn **R**, cross cattle grid and bear **L** past bench to gate. Turn **R** to go over stile, down field, over another stile and out into lane. Walk past cottages to reach road, where you go straight ahead.

❻ At crossroads go **R**, down Aireyholme Lane. Follow lane as it winds past houses; take signed footpath **L** through woodland. After ½ mile (800m), go **R** on path, ascending through woods, turning **L** at crossing path and continuing along edge of woodland. Continue bearing **R** to reach track to farm buildings, which goes **L** then **R**, to gate.

❼ Walk across 2 fields to stile, then continue uphill to tower. Beyond it, take grassy path **L** down gully, to gate into woodland. Follow path downhill through woods to return to gate at top of lane leading back to car park.

842 BYLAND ABBEY *MONKS AND ASTRONOMY*

5 miles (8km) 2hrs 30min **Ascent:** 623ft (190m) ▲
Paths: Woodland tracks, field paths, 11 stiles
Suggested map: aqua3 OS Outdoor Leisure 26 North York Moors – Western
Grid reference: SE 548789 **Parking:** Signed car park behind Abbey Inn in Byland

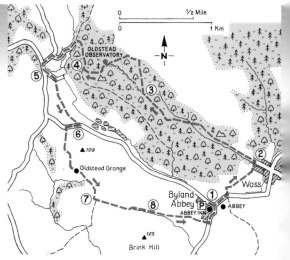

The romantic ruins of Byland Abbey.

❶ From car park, walk towards **abbey ruins**; turn **L** along abbey's north side. At public footpath sign, go **L** through gateway, then **R** through waymarked gate, just before 2nd set of gateposts. After 2nd gateway bear half **L** to waymarked gate behind bench. Through 2 more gates, then on to metalled lane.

❷ Turn **L**. At top of lane, go through gate ('Cam Farm, Observatory'). Path climbs then leaves wood edge to rise to terrace. After stile take **L-H** path, following Cam Farm. At junction of 3 paths, turn **R**, climbing up track, which levels out to big, open space.

❸ Turn **R** then, just before waymarked metal gate, turn **L** along wood edge. Follow path to **Oldstead Observatory**. Go to **L** of Observatory, down slope to track descending steeply to signpost.

❹ Turn **R** ('Oldstead'). Follow track as it curves **L** to become metalled lane. Turn **L** at T-junction, then **L** again on to road by seat. Just before road narrows sign, turn **L**.

❺ Go through gateposts and over cattle grid. As avenue of trees ends, take waymarked footpath to **R**, uphill. Climb to stile, bending to **L** beside woodland to stile, marked by fingerpost. Continue past waymarker and over waymarked stile. Footpath goes between hedge-and-wire fence, then over stile on to road.

❻ Turn **R** then, just beyond road sign, indicating bend, take track to **L** by **'Oldstead Grange'** sign. As you near house, turn **L** towards barns; wind your way through farmyard to stile by metal gate. Bear **R** downhill, then bend slightly **R** to waymarked stile.

❼ Over stile turn **L**; through wood to **'Byland Abbey'** signpost. Follow path as it bends **L** by another sign; go over stile; down field with hedge on **L** to another signpost. Go over stile beside metal gate and along field with hedge on **R**.

❽ Cross 2 stiles then bear slightly **L** to stile. Go half **L** to signpost by metal gate. Follow fence, then on to road by wooden stile. Turn **L**, then **L** again past **Abbey Inn** to start.

843 SWAINBY *INDUSTRIAL PAST*

6 miles (9.7km) 2hrs 30min **Ascent:** 1,098ft (335m) ▲
Paths: Tracks and moorland paths, lots of bracken, 11 stiles
Suggested map: aqua3 OS Outdoor Leisure 26 North York Moors – Western
Grid reference: NZ 477020
Parking: Roadside parking in Swainby village

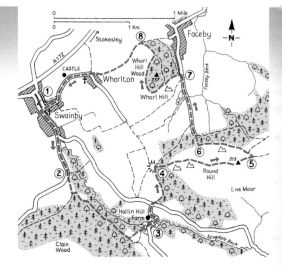

A walk with fine views from the Moors.

❶ With church on **L**, walk down village street to **R** of stream. Continue past sign 'Unsuitable for Coaches' and proceed uphill. As road bends to **R**, follow bridleway sign to Scugdale, up track ahead.

❷ Go through 2 gates, turning **L** after 2nd to join waymarks for Cleveland Way National Trail. Walk through woodland, turning **L** just after bench, down to stile. Footpath goes downhill across fields to another gate. Cross over stream on footbridge to reach lane, with another footbridge, over **Scugdale Beck**.

❸ Follow lane past **Hollin Hill Farm** to T-junction with telephone and post boxes. Cross lane and go through Cleveland Way signed gate. Walk up path beside woodland to gate with stile beside it.

❹ Path turns **R** to stile and goes on to paved track in wood. Keep ahead at crossing stile to another stile. Continue to follow paved path on to heather moorland. After 1st summit, path descends beyond cairn into dip. After paved path ends, look out for narrow path off to **L**, down through heather.

❺ After about 100yds (91m) you reach concrete post where path forks. Take **L** fork; follow path down gully to fence beside wall. Turn **L**, forking **L** again down another gully to signpost by wall and fence. Follow sign **L** and go over spoil heap to reach gate on **R**.

❻ Through gate, go down hill via woodland. At bottom cross stile by gate; go down lane. Just past drive, where wood begins, take footpath over 2 stiles.

❼ Walk through woodland on to grassy track. Turn **L**, and **L** again at another track. At T-junction, turn **L** again; follow track downhill to stile. Keep ahead through waymarked gateway.

❽ Cross stile beside gate; follow track along hillside. Over stile with steps beyond, turn **L** at bottom; follow field edge. Go over waymarked stile by gate and along field. At gate at end of field, follow metalled lane past **Whorlton church** and castle back to **Swainby**.

North Yorkshire

BOLTBY *OUT ON THE TILES*

5¼ miles (8.4km) 2hrs **Ascent:** 656ft (200m)
Paths: Mostly easy field and woodland paths; very steep and muddy climb up Thirlby Bank, 10 stiles
Suggested map: aqua3 OS Outdoor Leisure 26 North York – Western
Grid reference: SE 490866
Parking: Village

Village mosaics and distant views.

❶ From humped-back bridge in **Boltby** village centre, follow signed public footpath along stream to gate, and through 3 more gates to pass over small footbridge to stile. Continue following stream, going over another 3 stiles, to cross stone footbridge.

❷ Continue over 2 stiles, then turn **R** to another stile beside gateway. Continue ahead, crossing plank across drainage ditch. Cross over field to stile and stone bridge. At another stile in crossing fence, keep ahead through next field to reach waymarked gate. Continue along side of field to wooden stile, then through gate on to metalled track.

❸ Turn **L** and then at end of farm buildings, turn **R** by sign ('Southwoods') and through gate to go diagonally across field. Bend **L** at waymarked gate to continue with wire fence on R. Path veers **L** and descends to gate.

❹ Continue through another gateway and past house. Continue along metalled track, and across crossing track to gate. Confusingly this old track is named **Midge Holm Gate**. Follow track to reach another gate beside cottage, **Southwoods Lodge**; go on to metalled lane.

❺ Turn **L** here, following track, then turn **L** up public footpath ('Thirlby Bank'). This is steep and often muddy track that ascends ridge, past another public bridleway sign to reach **Cleveland Way** sign at top.

❻ Turn **L** and follow long distance footpath for about 1 mile (1.6km) along ridge, until you reach public bridleway sign to **L**, to **Boltby**. Descend to gate then follow woodland ride, crossing track to gate. Proceed down field, through gate. Follow track round to **R**.

❼ At signpost, turn **R** towards **Boltby**, to continue to gate. Pass tree stump with mosaic of toadstool and descend to gate on to lane. Cross over stream by footbridge then continue up metalled lane. At T-junction in village, turn **L** back to hump-backed bridge.

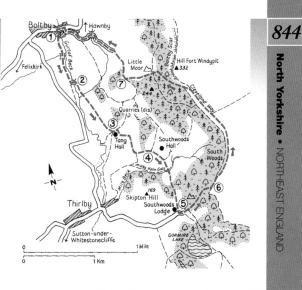

THIRSK *HERRIOT'S DARROWBY*

5 miles (8km) 2hrs **Ascent:** 66ft (20m)
Paths: Town paths, field paths and tracks, 6 stiles
Suggested map: aqua3 OS Explorer 302 Northallerton & Thirsk
Grid reference: SE 430813
Parking: Roadside parking in the main street of Sowerby village

James Herriot based his fictional home town on his real one – Thirsk.

❶ Walk down street, away from **Thirsk**. Just past Methodist Church on L, go **L** down Blakey Lane. After bridge turn **L** through kissing gate. Go through 4 kissing gates to reach footbridge.

❷ Continue along path, with stream on L, to stile. Go through 2 gates to car park, keeping ahead to road. Cross it and take path that curves **L** then **R** by bridge. At paved area turn **R**, to go alongside green to road.

❸ Cross and continue beside houses, going **L** at top of green. Cross metal bridge and continue beside beck opposite east end of church. Before reaching road take path to **R**, beside bench, to footbridge on **R**.

❹ Cross bridge, go through 2 gates and curve **L** to follow beck to gate by bridge. Go ahead (not over bridge). Go over fields, veering slightly **R** to stile on **R**.

❺ Go over stile; follow stream, crossing another 2 stiles to pass beside houses. Continue **L** over footbridge by mill buildings. Path winds **R** to 2nd footbridge. Follow bridleway sign across field through 2 more gates to reach main road.

❻ Cross road; go through signed gate opposite, to another gate beside wood. At open space, past wood, turn **L** through gap in hedge, opposite waymark to R.

❼ Walk down field with hedge on L. In 2nd field, go **L** over stile. Continue with hedge on R to another stile. Bear **L** to meet path that crosses field and becomes grassy lane between hedges, then track.

❽ At metalled road keep ahead, bearing **L** then **R** past church tower. Turn **R**; walk into town centre. In Market Place head half **L** towards Three Tuns Inn then down signed passageway by drycleaners.

❾ Cross road diagonally **R**; go towards **swimming pool** entrance. Turn **L**; bend round pool building to gate. Proceed to gate and alongside **beck**. At bridge turn **R** across field on grassy track to gate on to lane. Keep ahead to return to **Sowerby**.

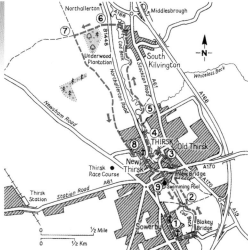

FOUNTAINS ABBEY *A MEDIEVAL WALK*

6½ miles (10.4km) 3hrs **Ascent:** 328ft (100m)
Paths: Field paths and tracks, a little road walking, 8 stiles
Suggested map: aqua3 OS Explorer 298 Nidderdale
Grid reference: SE 270681 **Parking:** Car park at west end of Abbey, or at visitor centre

From the ruins of Fountains Abbey to the medieval manor of Markenfield Hall.

❶ From car park turn **R** uphill ('Harrogate'). At fork go **L** ('Markington, Harrogate'). Just after road bends **L** cross stile beside gate with bridleway signs.

❷ Follow grassy path just inside ancient Abbey Wall, past small **pond**. Go through waymarked gate and follow track as it curves round to **R** through another gate then **L** round farm buildings of **Hill House Farm**. Go through small gate near farmhouse.

❸ Turn **R** then follow footpath signs to go **L** at end of large shed and then **R**. Go through metalled gate on to track. At end of hedge proceed down field to gate on to road. Follow track, passing ruined archway, to road to crossroads.

❹ Go straight on ('Ripon'). Track climbs to gate with [Ri]pon Rowel Walk sign. Follow track beside line of [tre]es to gate on to **Whitcliffe Lane**. Turn **R**. At top of [rise], keep ahead on metalled road.

Go over cattle grid by **Bland Close**, then straight ahead with hedge on R to reach stile. Continue along waymarked track, eventually with woodland to R. Go over stile near metal gate and follow track as it goes **R** to reach gate. Turn **R** to farm buildings by **Markenfield Hall**.

❺ Follow wall to **L**, going through metal gate and straight ahead down track, through gate. Follow track, then waymark sign, across field to stile by gate. Turn **R** up narrow **Strait Lane**, to emerge into field.

❻ Follow waymarked path beside field. Go through gate in field corner and continue ahead with hedge to R. Go **R** through 4 more gates and follow track as it curves towards farm buildings. Go over stile into farmyard of **Morcar Grange**. Keep ahead to metalled **Whitcliffe Lane**.

❼ Turn **L**; follow lane as it bends **L** then **R**. At next corner, look for stile on **R** by gate. Cross field half **L** and cross 3 stiles, following waymarked path towards buildings. Go over stile; pass between buildings to reach metalled road. Turn back to car park.

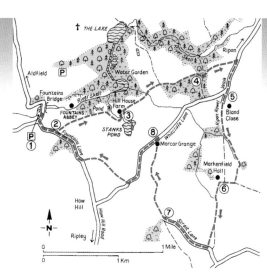

North Yorkshire

847 RICHMOND *THE DRUMMER BOY*

6 miles (9.7km) 2hrs 20min **Ascent:** 656ft (200m) ▲
Paths: Field and riverside paths, a little town walking, 20 stiles
Suggested map: aqua3 OS Explorer 304 Darlington & Richmond
Grid reference: NZ 168012
Parking: Friars Close long-stay car park

In search of the Richmond Drummer.

❶ Leave car park; turn **R**, then **L** at T-junction. At roundabout go **L** then **R** at roundabout down Dundas Street. Bear **R** into Frenchgate then **L** into Station Road. Just past church, take Lombards Wynd **L**.

❷ Turn **R** at next junction; follow track, passing to **R** of Drummer Boy Stone along path. The stone commemorates an 18th-century drummer boy who was sent down a tunnel beating his drum so that the soldiers could follow the sound above ground. The drumming stopped at this spot! Leaving Richmond behind, go over 2 stiles, then follow waymarks towards **Abbey** to another 2 stiles. Turn **R** along track and **R** again, this time down metalled lane, which leads to abbey in **Easby**.

❸ Go to **L** of car park along track. Where track divides, keep on higher path; go **R** by **Platelayers Cottage** over old railway bridge. Follow trackbed for 400yds (366m); go **L** over cattle grid, to follow track

R, to reach road.

❹ Turn **R**; follow road for ½ mile (800m). Turn **L** up Priory Villas, bearing **R** to go in front of houses and through 3 gates. Keeping parallel to river, cross playing fields and pass clubhouse to road.

❺ Cross road; take signed path opposite, to **L** of cottage. Climb steeply through woodland, through gate and stile, bending **R** at end of woodland to stile in crossing fence. Turn **R** over stile; follow signed path over 12 more stiles. Just before reaching gate, go **R** through wall gap; **L** to another stile.

❻ Turn **R**, to go through gate. Follow track as it bends downhill to bridge. Cross it and walk to lane. Go **L** and **L** again at main road. After 200yds (183m) go **R** up gravel track, to junction.

❼ Turn **R**. Follow track uphill, bearing **R** then **L** near farmhouse, to reach metalled lane. Turn **R**; follow lane back into **Richmond**. Go ahead at main road; follow it as it bends **L** to garage, where you turn **L** to car park.

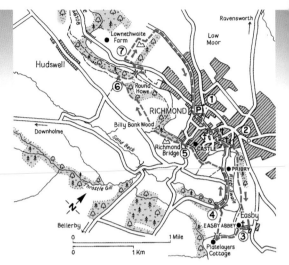

848 MIDDLEHAM *A KINGDOM FOR A HORSE*

7 miles (11.3km) 2hrs 30min **Ascent:** 475ft (145m) ▲
Paths: Field paths and tracks, with some road walking, 18 stiles
Suggested map: aqua3 OS Outdoor Leisure 30 Yorkshire Dales – Northern & Central
Grid reference: SE 127877 **Parking:** In square in centre of Middleham

From a castle and back via the gallops.

❶ From cross in Square, walk uphill past Black Swan Hotel. Just beyond, turn **L** up passage beside tea rooms. Continue over road and **L** of **castle** to gate.

❷ Go half **L** across field, following sign towards stepping stones. Cross next 3 fields, over waymarked stiles. After 3rd field, turn along side of field, ignoring track to **R**. Turn **R** at waymarked crossing walk down to bank of **River Cover** by stepping stones.

❸ Turn **R** (don't cross stepping stones); follow riverside path, going through gate and up steps. After returning to river bank, go **R** where path forks. Cross 2 more stiles, turning immediately **R** after 2nd stile. Follow waymark uphill to marker post.

❹ Turn **L**; follow line of wood. At end of field go **L** through waymarked stile, through trees to 2nd stile, then straight down field back to river bank. Cross waymarked stile and onward to bridge.

❺ Go through gate over bridge. Follow track as it winds **R** and uphill through 2 gates on to road,

opposite **Braithwaite Hall**. Turn **R** and follow road for 1 mile (1.6km) to **Coverham Bridge**. Turn **R** over bridge, then **R** again.

❻ Before gates, turn **L** through gate, walk beside waterfall and into churchyard. Leave by lychgate; turn **L** along road. After ¼ mile (400m) go through gate on **R**, opposite disused factory, bearing slightly **L**. Cross 3 stiles. Go through gate, pass between buildings, then cross 3 stiles through woodland.

❼ Cross field to gateway **R** of wood. After passing house, bend **L** to gate on to track. Turn **R**; go through gate; turn **R** again. Don't follow track, but go half **L** to meet bridleway across moor. Follow it for 1½ miles (2.4km) to road.

❽ Turn **L**. Just before sign ('Middleham') take signposted path on **R**. Turn **L** over stile. Follow path parallel to road. Go through 2 more stiles, then take another towards **Middleham Castle** (favourite home of King Richard III), passing through gate on to lane. Turn **L**. Return to square.

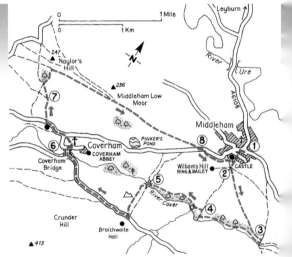

849 GREENHOWE *THE MINES*

6 miles (9.7km) 2hrs 45min **Ascent:** 1,181ft (360m) ▲
Paths: Field and moorland paths and tracks, 5 stiles
Suggested map: aqua3 OS Explorer 298 Nidderdale
Grid reference: SE 128643
Parking: Car park at Toft Gate Lime Kiln

Through an industrial landscape.

❶ Cross road from car park; go over stile opposite into field. Follow faint path downhill, over gate in wall and to **R** of barn. Cross another stile; descend to track. Turn **L**; walk up hill through 2 gates to road. Turn **L**; walk up to main road. Turn **R**; follow this past burial ground and **Miners Arms** pub. About 100yds (91m) on, just past converted chapel, take lane to **R**. At junction go **L**; follow lane to cattle grid and through gate. Curve **R**, round behind farmhouse.

❷ Follow track downhill into valley of **Gill Beck** and then **Brandstone Beck**. Where track swings **L**, go ahead down valley to reach main track near concrete building. Go **R** of building. Just beyond, proceed down valley to **ford**.

❸ Cross, then follow obvious track up hill. Cross stile beside gate by trees then, 100yds (91m) beyond, take another stile on **R**. Follow track towards farm, going **L** between stone walls. Descend to stile on to track.

❹ Turn **L**, through waymarked gateway. By spoil heap follow track to **R** and downhill. Veer slightly **L**, past iron cogwheel, to cross **Ashfold Side Beck** on concrete causeway to gate.

❺ Follow bridleway sign **R**. Climb hill to **Nidderdale Way** sign. Turn **R** along track to gate. Wind round valley head, via 2 gateways and 3 cattle grids. Just beyond 3rd, go through gate to **R**. Cross bridge.

❻ Go ahead; bear **L** to gate; follow track uphill and **L** to wall. Turn **R** at end of wall along lane between walls. Continue on track to gate; cross footbridge.

❼ Turn **R** through gate; follow track uphill, passing through another gate. Turn **L** at track, making towards farmhouse, but bear **R** across grass to meet metalled lane. Turn **R**; follow lane over cattle grid.

❽ About 100yds (91m) beyond farm on **R**, turn **L** up path. After cattle grid go **R**; follow track through gate. At **Coldstonesfold Farm** turn **R**; follow track uphill through gate. Go **L** over stile to retrace outward route.

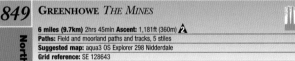

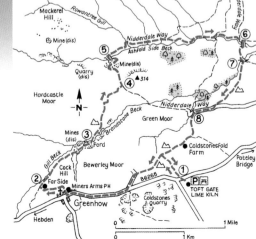

North Yorkshire

REETH *HEART OF SWALEDALE*

850

5½ miles (8.8km) 2hrs **Ascent:** 508ft (155m) ▲
Paths: Field and riverside paths, lanes and woodland, 14 stiles
Suggested map: aqua3 OS Outdoor Leisure 30 Yorkshire Dales – Northern & Central
Grid reference: SE 039993
Parking: In Reeth, behind fire station, or by the Green

Farmers, miners, knitters and nuns all played important roles in the history of this part of Swaledale.

❶ Spend some time exploring **Reeth** and perhaps visit the **Folk Museum**. For a long time, sheep were the basis of **Reeth's** prosperity and their wool was used in its knitting industry. It also had a vital lead mining industry. From Green, walk downhill, in direction of Leyburn, to **Reeth Bridge**. Over bridge, continue along road as it swings **R**. After 100yds (91m), turn **R** at footpath sign to **Grinton Bridge**.

❷ Follow path through gate and across fields to ascend steps and through gate on to bridge. Turn **L**, cross road and take track beside bridge.

❸ Follow riverside path over 4 stiles, on to metalled lane. Turn **L** and follow lane to **Marrick Abbey**. Walk past buildings, over cattle grid, and turn **L** through gate ('**Marrick**'). In the Middle Ages, it was one of the most important churches in the Dales and home to a group of Benedictine nuns.

❹ Walk up grassy track, through wooden gate and up paved path through woodland. Go through gate, up path and through 3 more gates. Opposite Harlands House turn **L** up metalled road, and **L** again at T-junction.

❺ Follow road for ¼ mile (400m), and turn **L** over stile at footpath sign. Walk up field, going **R** over waymarked, gated stile and follow wall, to go over another gated stile. Continue over further stile by metal gate, then through 2nd metal gate on to road.

❻ Turn **L** and follow road for ¾ mile (1.2km). Where road bends **L**, turn **R** through stile ('**Fremington**'). Follow path through fields, going through gate, to another stile, then along path to lane.

❼ Turn **L**. At houses turn **R**, and as lane bends **L**, go ahead to stile by gate. Keep by wall on **L**, and follow path through 4 stiles back to **Reeth Bridge**. Cross bridge and follow road back to Green.

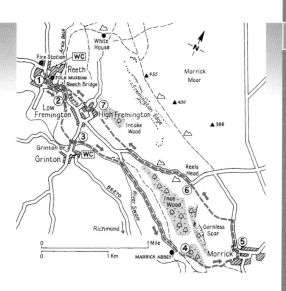

UPPER NIDDERDALE *SCAR HOUSE RESERVOIR*

851

8¼ miles (13.3km) 3hrs 30min **Ascent:** 886ft (270m) ▲
Paths: Moorland tracks, field paths and lanes, 16 stiles
Suggested map: aqua3 OS Explorer 298 Nidderdale; OS Outdoor Leisure 30 Yorkshire Dales
Grid reference: SE 070766 **Parking:** Signed car park at top of reservoir access road

Natural and artificial landscapes.

❶ Walk towards dam wall; continue along L-H side of **reservoir** to '**Nidderdale Way**' signpost, before gate. Follow track **L** uphill. Track levels and goes through gate. Just beyond, go **R** through gate in wall.

❷ Go diagonally towards wall **R**; follow faint path as it bends **L**. At track, turn **L**, cross 2 cattle grids; turn **R**, via field, to gate in crossing hedge. Go down field; go between farm buildings, following waymark, to gate.

❸ Cross field to handgate by barn. Pass to **R** of wall to stile. Go through woodland, go up **L** to waymark then along hillside to stile; down to riverside path.

❹ Go through squeeze stile; where path divides take **L-H** fork, away from wire fence. Ascend to ladder stile, then to stone stile by **Nidderdale Way** sign. Turn **R**; through gate, then cross footbridge. Ascend steps to 2 more stiles on to lane. Turn **L** down lane, passing How Stean Gorge entrance, to stone bridge.

❺ Go **L** over bridge, **R** at T-junction ('Lofthouse'). Where road bends R, go ahead to gate and to **R** of buildings. Go through gate, across road; keep ahead over bridge. Turn **R** between buildings to street.

❻ Turn **L**; climb hill. As road bends **R**, go **L** down grassy track to gate. Continue along lower track through 4 gates; follow waymarks to river bank. Cross river to another gate. Continue along bank, over 2 stiles to gate. Turn **R** towards **farm**.

❼ Just after 1st buildings **L**, go through gateway, then gate to riverside. Follow path over 2 stiles to footbridge with stile at its end. Cross; turn **L** to continue by riverside then go through gate and over stile to reach gate to track.

❽ Turn **L** over cattle grid, then **R** just before bridge. Where track bends **R**, go ahead through 4 stiles to gate. Cross stream to another gate; follow fence to field. Go through waymarked gate. Pass between buildings to another gate. Track climbs **R**; go through 5 gates, turning towards dam and descending to track. Turn **R**; go through gate. Track becomes metalled. Cross dam back to car park.

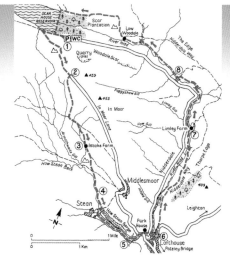

WEST BURTON *VILLAGES, FALLS AND FOLLIES*

852

4 miles (6.4km) 1hr 30min **Ascent:** 394ft (120m) ▲
Paths: Field and riverside paths and tracks, 35 stiles
Suggested map: aqua3 OS Outdoor Leisure 30 Yorkshire Dales – Northern & Central
Grid reference: SE 017867
Parking: Centre of West Burton, by (but not on) the Green

A diverse walk to the famous Aysgarth Falls.

❶ Leave Green near shop. Opposite ('Meadowcroft') go **L** ('Eshington Bridge'). Cross road, turn **R** then **L**, through gate and down steps. Pass barn, through gateway and across field. Go through gap in wall with stile beyond then bend **R** to stile on to road.

❷ Turn **L**, go over bridge and ahead up narrow lane. As it bends **L** go ahead through stile ('Aysgarth') then on through gated stile. Proceed to gap in fence near barn, then through gate. Bend **L** to gate in field corner then go through gateway and on to stile. Turn **R**; descend to signpost.

❸ Proceed to stile in field corner. Follow signpost uphill to gateway; go through stile on **R**. Cross field half **L** to go through gated stile to lane. Turn **L**, then almost immediately **R** through stile ('Aysgarth'). Go through 3 stiles to road.

❹ Turn **R** into village, past George and Dragon. At bend, go ahead toward **chapel**, then **R** at green; follow lane. Go through stile by Field House to another stile, turning **L** along track. Follow path through 8 stiles to road.

❺ Go ahead into churchyard, pass **R** of **church**; go through 2 stiles, waymarked, then over stile. Follow path downhill towards river, descending steps to gate, then stile. When footpath reaches river bank, take signed stile **R**.

❻ Follow path over 2 stiles to signpost, bending **R** across field to road. Turn **L** over bridge, turning **R** into woodland few paces beyond ('Edgley'). Cross stile and field to gate to road.

❼ Turn **R**. About 150yds (137m) along, go **L** over stile ('Flanders Hall'). Walk below follies on ridge to footpath sign, cross track; go uphill to stile with steps.

❽ Opposite stone barn go **R**, through gate; go downhill through 2 gates, then over 3 stiles to lane. Turn **R**. Go over bridge to join village road. Turn **L**, back to Green.

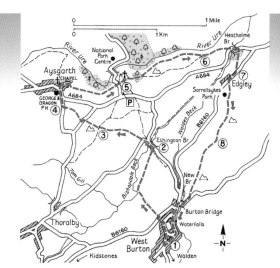

853   HUBBERHOLME *DALESFOLK TRADITIONS*

5 miles (8km) 2hrs **Ascent:** 394ft (120m)
Paths: Field paths and tracks, steep after Yockenthwaite, 11 stiles
Suggested map: aqua3 OS Outdoor Leisure 30 Yorkshire Dales – Northern & Central
Grid reference: SD 927782
Parking: Beside river in village, opposite church (not church parking)

From JB Priestley's favourite Dales village, along Langstrothdale.

1 Literary pilgrims should visit the George Inn in **Hubberholme**, where JB Priestley enjoyed the local ale, and the churchyard, the resting place for his ashes. To start, go through Dales Way signed gate near east end of church, bend **L** and then take lower path ('Yockenthwaite'). Walk beside river for 1¼ miles (2km) through 3 stiles, gate and 2 more stiles. Path eventually rises to another stone stile into **Yockenthwaite**.

2 Go through stile and bend **L** to wooden gate. Continue through farm gate by sign to Deepdale and Beckermonds. Before track reaches bridge go **R** and swing round to sign to **Cray** and **Hubberholme**.

3 Go up hill and, as track curves **R**, continue to follow **Cray** and **Hubberholme** sign. Partway up hill go **R** at footpath sign through wooden gate in fence.

4 Go through 2nd gate to footpath sign and ascend hillside. Go through gap in wall by another signpost and follow obvious path through several gaps in crossing walls. Go over 2 stone stiles and ascend again to footbridge between stiles.

5 Cross bridge and continue through woodland to another stile. Wind round head of valley and follow signpost to **Cray**. Go over footbridge. Footpath winds its way down valley side. Go through gate and straight ahead across meadowland to gateway on to track, and on to stone barn.

6 Bend to **R** beyond barn, down to public footpath sign to **Stubbing Bridge**. Go down path between stone walls and through wooden gate and on to grassy hillside. Pass another footpath sign and continue downhill to meet stream by **waterfall**.

7 Continue along streamside path through woodland. Go over wooden stile and on past barn to stone stile on to road. Turn **R** along road back to parking place in **Hubberholme**.

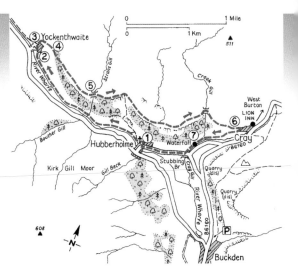

854   SEMERWATER *LEGENDARY GLACIAL LAKE*

5 miles (8km) 2hrs **Ascent:** 853ft (260m)
Paths: Field paths and tracks, steep ascent from Marsett, 19 stiles
Suggested map: aqua3 OS Outdoor Leisure 30 Yorkshire Dales – Northern & Central
Grid reference: SD 921875
Parking: Car park at the north end of the lake

Legends boast that an angel, disguised as a beggar, drowned the town when he was refused food – the only survivors were a poor couple, who had shown him kindness.

1 Turn **R** out of car park up road. Opposite farm buildings go **R** over ladder stile ('Stalling Busk'). Go through gated stile and ahead towards barn, then through 2 stone stiles. Just beyond 2nd stile is Wildlife Trust sign. Continue over 2 more stiles to gate.

2 Just beyond gate, follow **Marsett** sign to corner of field and over gated stone stile. Follow waymarked path as it curves beside river, to barn. Go over stile above barn to stile. Go across field to another stile. Proceed towards barn then go across stream bed.

3 Immediately afterwards, turn **R** down well-worn footpath, which curves towards roofless barn. Cross 3 stiles, then turn **R**, following path to trees, with stone wall on **R**. Continue over 2 stiles to footbridge; go straight on to track, then turn **R** to reach ford.

4 Before ford, veer **L** over footbridge and back on to track, which winds into **Marsett**. Just before village, follow stream as it goes **R**, and make for road by red telephone box. Turn **R** over bridge. 100yds (91m) beyond take track ('Burtersett and Hawes') and not path by river.

5 Walk uphill to gate on **R** at start of stone wall. Go over stile, then continue uphill, over 3 stiles. Soon after steep path flattens out, you reach track that crosses path, coming through gap in wall on **L**.

6 Turn **R** along track and then go through gate in wall. Where it divides, take **R** fork downhill to stile. Path descends steeply through 2 gates, to reach crossing track. Continue straight ahead. Follow track as it bends **L** to gate on to metalled road.

7 Turn **R** and then follow road downhill to staggered crossroads, turning **R**, then **L** ('Stalling Beck'). Go down hill, cross over bridge and then continue back to car park.

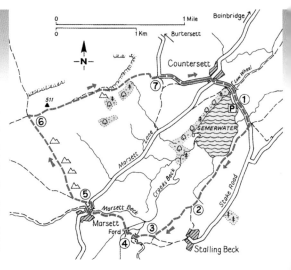

855   KELD *A RIVERSIDE CIRCUIT HIGH IN THE DALES*

6 miles (9.7km) 2hrs 30min **Ascent:** 820ft (250m)
Paths: Field and riverside paths and tracks, 10 stiles
Suggested map: aqua3 OS Outdoor Leisure 30 Yorkshire Dales – Northern & Central
Grid reference: NY 892012
Parking: Signed car park at west end of village near Park Lodge

A classic walk in Upper Swaledale from Keld to Muker along Kisdon Side, and back by the river.

1 Walk back down car park entrance road, and straight ahead down gravel track ('Muker'). Around **Muker**, you will see traditional hay meadows. They are an important part of the farmer's regime and help maintain the wide variety of wild flowers that grow in them, which is why signs ask you to keep to single file as you walk through them. Continue along at upper level, ignoring path downhill to **L**. Go through gate, pass sign to **Kisdon Force**, and continue along track to signpost.

2 Turn **R**, following **Pennine Way** National Trail. Path goes through gated stone stile, then through gap in wall to continue with wall on your **L**. Go on through gate and over 4 stiles to descend towards **Muker** to reach signpost where **Pennine Way** goes **R**.

3 Go straight on down track ('Muker'), between stone walls. Go through wooden gate, still following bridleway to **Muker**. Track becomes metalled, as it descends through 2 gates and into walled lane in village to T-junction.

4 Turn **L** and **L** again by sign to **Gunnerside** and **Keld**. Follow paved path from 5 stiles to reach river. Turn **R** and go over stile to footbridge.

5 Walk up steps beyond footbridge and turn **L** ('Keld'). Follow course of river along clear track, until it curves **R** around **Swinner Gill**, over footbridge by remains of lead workings, and through wooden gate.

6 Go straight ahead up hill and into woodland. Track eventually winds **L**, then **R** round stone barn, then downhill through wooden gate to reach another gate above **Kisdon Force**.

7 Go **L** by wooden seat, at sign to **Keld**. Follow stream down to footbridge. Go through gate and turn **R**, walk uphill to T-junction, where you turn **R** and proceed to follow path back to car park.

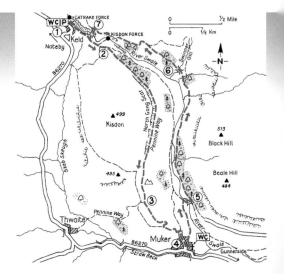

North Yorkshire

STAINFORTH *FORCES OF NATURE*

4¾ miles (7.7km) 2hrs **Ascent:** 525ft (160m) ▲
Paths: Green lanes, field and riverside paths, some road, 15 stiles
Suggested map: aqua3 OS Explorer OL2 Yorkshire Dales – Southern & Western
Grid reference: SD 821672
Parking: Pay-and-display car park in Stainforth, just off B6479

From an attractive, stone-built village in the heart of the Ribble Valley, with a visit to two impressive waterfalls.

❶ From car park turn **R**, then **R** again ('Settle'). Cross over bridge, go **L** through gap in wall. Follow beck to open area. Go through white posts and turn **L**. Go **R** of green then turn **R**. Go uphill on lane for ¾ mile (1.2km) to gate and ladder stile. (To visit **Catrigg Force**, take smaller gate to **L**. Return to same point.)

❷ Go over ladder stile. Track bends **R**. Go over stile to cross wall; turn **R** ('Winskill'). Path bears **L** to join track. Go over stile and continue to **farmhouses** then keep ahead over stile ('Stainforth and Langcliffe'). As track bends **R**, go **L** over stile ('Langcliffe').

❸ Cross field to stone stile, turning **R** immediately afterwards, to follow path downhill. After short walled section, path descends more steeply to handgate then bears **L** halfway down hill, to descend to handgate. Follow path beyond to another gate.

❹ After gate, lane becomes walled. At crossroads of paths near village, keep ahead. At **Langcliffe's** main street turn **R** and walk to main road.

❺ Cross road and go through gap in wall diagonally **R**. Follow footpath over railway footbridge. Where path ends go towards **mill**. Just before buildings take signed path **R**, behind mill and beside millpond. Go through gate and continue along pond side and through stone stile to reach gate on **L** by houses.

❻ Go through gate and turn **R** between rows of cottages. Where row ends, before post box, go **L** over footbridge over **River Ribble** and at end turn **R**, beside **weir**, to stone stile ('Stainforth'). Follow riverside path, going over 6 more stiles to **caravan site**.

❼ Go **R** of site, on riverside path, past Stainforth Force to humpback Stainforth Bridge. Go through stile on to lane, turn **L** over bridge and follow narrow lane as it bends and climbs to main road. Turn **R** and take 2nd turning **L** back to car park.

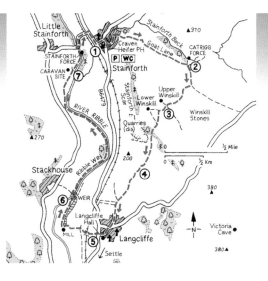

MALHAM *LIMESTONE COUNTRY*

6¼ miles (10.1km) 3hrs **Ascent:** 1,148ft (350m) ▲
Paths: Well-marked field and moorland paths, 400 plus steps in descent from Malham Cove, 5 stiles
Suggested map: aqua3 OS Outdoor Leisure 30 Yorkshire Dales – Northern & Central
Grid reference: SD 894658
Parking: At Water Sinks, near gateway across road
Note: Caution, sheer drops and gaps (grikes) in limestone pavement

Discover the noble Malham Cove.

❶ From car parking space, walk through gate, then turn **L** through kissing gate at **Malham Cove** sign. Walk parallel with dry-stone wall on your **L** and follow dry valley as it bends to reach stile at head of another dry valley.

❷ Turn **L** and follow footpath down valley to reach stile at end. Go over stile then walk ahead to limestone pavement at top of **Malham Cove**. Turn **R** and walk along pavement to reach steps. Take great care here, both of sheer drop down to your **L** and gaps in limestone pavement (known as grikes). Turn **L** to cautiously descend more than 400 steps to foot of Cove (take care).

❸ When you reach bottom turn **R** along track beside river. Go through 2 kissing gates to reach road. Turn **L** and follow road into centre of **Malham** village. Turn **L** to go over bridge.

❹ Turn **R** along riverside on track ('Janet's Foss'). Follow signposted, mostly gravelled, path through 8 gates. Eventually footpath climbs up through woodland and passes by waterfall (**Janet's Foss**) to kissing gate. Turn **R** on road, towards **Gordale Scar**.

❺ At bridge go through gate to **L**. (To visit **Gordale Scar**, continue straight ahead here. Take signed gate to **L** and follow path up through field into gorge. Keep going on obvious route as far as waterfall and then follow same route back to bridge.) On main route, follow signed public footpath uphill through 2 stiles and out on to lane.

❻ Turn **R** and walk uphill for ¼ mile (400m), to ladder stile over wall on your **L**. Follow track, going **L** at fork to reach another footpath fingerpost.

❼ Turn **L**, following sign, to reach small **tarn**. Turn **R** at sign for **Malham Tarn**, go over ladder stile and then take **L-H** path; follow it back to car park.

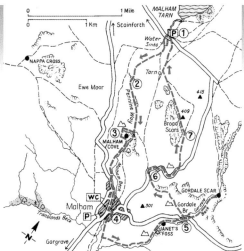

GARGRAVE *ALONG THE CANAL*

3½ miles (5.7km) 1hr 30min **Ascent:** 114ft (35m) ⚠
Paths: Field paths and tracks, then canal tow path, 4 stiles
Suggested map: aqua3 OS Outdoor Leisure 2 Yorkshire Dales – Southern & Western
Grid reference: SD 931539
Parking: Opposite church in Gargrave or in village centre

A lovely route following the Leeds and Liverpool Canal from Gargrave, which has long been a stopping-off point for travellers.

❶ Walk along wall with church tower on your **L**. Just past Church Close House on your **R**, turn **R**, following **Pennine Way** sign then cross over stone stile in wall on your **L**.

❷ Follow side of wall, along **Pennine Way** path, which is partly boarded and partly paved here. Go ahead across field to waymarked stile, then half **L** to another stile. Walk towards top **L-H** corner of field to stile that leads to Mosber Lane near railway bridge.

❸ Turn **L**, going over bridge over railway, then follow track through gateway and climb hill. After cattle grid, go half **L** off track and across field to meet another track, which leads to signpost.

❹ At post, turn **R**, soon to walk below wire fence, to reach waymarked gate in crossing fence. Go ahead across field to pair of gates. Take waymarked **L-H** one

and then continue ahead, at first with fence on your **R**. Follow track through 2 gateways into lane.

❺ Follow lane between wall and fence to descend to canal by **Bank Newton Locks**. Cross over bridge and turn **R** along tow path. Path passes through gate and goes on to road.

❻ Go ahead along roadside, cross bridge over canal and then turn **L** down winding path under bridge and continue along tow path. Pass over small aqueduct crossing river, then go under railway bridge to reach **Gargrave Lock**.

❼ Beyond lock, opposite Anchor Inn, go under road bridge and then continue along tow path to reach Bridge 170, at **Higherland Lock**. Go on to road by signpost.

❽ Turn **R** along road, and follow it through village, past **Gargrave** Village Hall. At main road turn **R**, cross over road and then go **L** over bridge back to church and your car.

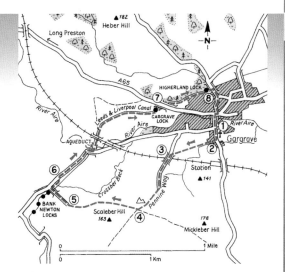

859   AUSTWICK *ERRATIC PROGRESS*

5½ miles (8.8km) 2hrs 30min **Ascent:** 558ft (170m) ▲

Paths: Field and moorland paths, tracks, lanes on return, 10 stiles

Suggested map: aqua3 OS Outdoor Leisure 2 Yorkshire Dales – Southern & Central

Grid reference: SD 767684

Parking: Roadside parking in Austwick village

Along ancient tracks to the Norber Erratics.

❶ From green in centre of **Austwick**, walk northwards out of village ('Horton in Ribblesdale'). Pass Gamecock Inn and, just past cottage, 'Hob's Gate', turn **L** up Town Head Lane. Just after road bends round to R, go **L** over waymarked ladder stile.

❷ Walk through field to another stile and on to another stile on to lane. Turn **R**. Just before reaching metalled road turn **L** over ladder stile. Follow line of track. As track veers L, go straight on, following line of stone wall to stone stile by gate.

❸ Go through gate; continue along rocky track. Where stone wall on L bends L, by very large boulder across path, go **R** on track to pass R-H edge of **scar**. At signpost, go **L** ('Norber').

❹ Follow path uphill, to plateau; explore **Norber Erratics**. Return same way, back to signpost. Turn **L** ('Crummack'). Follow track as it winds downhill then up beside wall by scar to stone stile on **R**.

❺ Descend to another stile; follow path beneath rocky outcrop, which goes downhill with wall to L to reach ladder stile on to metalled lane. Cross lane; go over another ladder stile opposite.

❻ Turn **L** across field. Go over 2 ladder stiles then cross farm track and ridge of rock to stone stile then ladder stile. Cross stile and on to track. Turn **R**. Cross **ford** on clapper bridge.

❼ Follow track between walls for ½ mile (800m) into **Wharfe**. Turn **L** by bridleway sign in village; follow road round to **R** and down village approach road to reach metalled road. Turn **R**. After 100yds (91m) turn **L** at bridleway sign to **Wood Lane**, down road to **Wood End Farm**.

❽ By farm buildings track goes **R**. Follow it, as it bends **L** and **R** to crossroads of tracks. Go straight ahead, following line of telegraph poles. Track winds to reach metalled lane into village. Turn **R** over bridge to village centre.

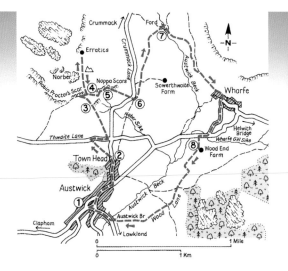

860   RIBBLEHEAD *A MAJESTIC VIADUCT*

5 miles (8km) 2hrs **Ascent:** 328ft (100m) ▲

Paths: Moorland and farm paths and tracks, 2 stiles

Suggested map: aqua3 OS Outdoor Leisure 2 Yorkshire Dales – Western

Grid reference: SD 765792

Parking: Parking space at junction of B6255 and B6479 near Ribblehead viaduct

Beside and beneath a great monument to Victorian engineering, opened in 1876 by the Midland Railway.

❶ From parking place, cross road and take boardwalk by sign towards **viaduct** to track. Turn **R** and follow track until it turns under **viaduct**; continue straight ahead.

❷ Continue walking, now parallel with railway line above you to your L. Go past Three Peaks signboard, following **Whernside** sign. Go over gated wooden stile and continue until you reach railway signal. Go **L** under railway arch, following public bridleway sign.

❸ Go through gate at end of arch and follow track downhill towards stream, then bear **L** towards farm buildings. Go through gate between buildings and on to humpback bridge by cottage.

❹ Follow lane over 2 cattle grids. Go through wooden gate by barn then through metal gate, to wind through farm buildings. Go through another metal gate and waymarked wooden gate.

❺ Walk along track through fields, going over small bridge of railway sleepers. By sign to **Scar End**, bear **R** to small gate. Go across 3 fields, through series of gates and continue ahead through next field, to reach farm buildings.

❻ Turn **L** by farm down farm track. Where it bends R, go over cattle grid and turn sharp **L** round fence and on to track, following bridleway sign to reach ladder stile.

❼ Track is obvious as it winds through fields to reach stream bed (dry in summer). Cross this, and continue along track to meet road near cattle grid. Turn **L** and walk down road and over bridge.

❽ Where road divides, go **R**, through gate, towards **viaduct**. At next gate go **R** again over footbridge by **farm** buildings. Continue through 2 more gates and follow track under viaduct. Continue towards road and parking place.

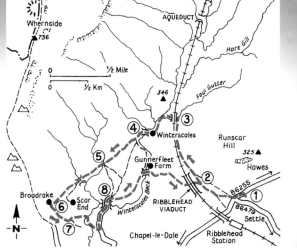

861   ARKENGARTHDALE *LEADEN LAND*

8 miles (12.9km) 3hrs 15min **Ascent:** 1,213ft (370m) ▲

Paths: Mostly clear tracks, some heather moor, 4 stiles

Suggested map: aqua3 OS Explorer OL30 Yorkshire Dales – Northern & Central

Grid reference: NZ 005024

Parking: Pay-and-display car park at south end of Langthwaite village

Around an austere valley where hundreds of lead workers once toiled.

❶ Leave car park, turn **R**, then **R** again into **Langthwaite**. Go over bridge; continue ahead between cottages. Climb hill; follow lane to hamlet of **Booze**. Pass farmhouse and stone barn and follow track to gate.

❷ After gate, where track bends L, go straight on next to broken wall. Bear **R** to go past ruined cottage, then follow path to stream. Walk upstream, go through gate then cross over stream on stepping stones.

❸ Walk slightly **L**, through moorland, to reach wooden **hut** near crossing track. Turn **L** along track. At crossing of tracks go straight ahead and then at T-junction turn **L**. Where wall on your R ends, leave track, bending **R** along path and down to gate in corner of 2 walls.

❹ Follow small gully downhill and then go through gate on to track. Turn **R** along track and continue through gateway and on to another track by barn. Follow track as it bends **L** by stone wall and then passes farm buildings. Go through 2 gates to reach a 3rd, white gate.

❺ Go through white gate to enter grounds of **Scar House**. Follow drive as it bears **R**, downhill. Go over bridge and cattle grid at bottom. Turn **R**. Follow track to road. Turn **L**, uphill, to T-junction. Turn **R** and follow road. After cattle grid, turn **L** along signed track.

❻ At gravelled area bear **R** and continue uphill on track. Where it divides, go **L** beside spoil heaps and pass junction of 2 flues. Follow track as it winds uphill, **R** then **L**, to reach T-junction of tracks. Turn **L** and follow track downhill to reach road.

❼ Turn **L** along road. Just after **farmhouse** turn **R** at bridleway sign, which takes you towards house; turn **L** before reaching it and follow signed track. Go through gate and continue downhill. Before small barn, turn **L**. Go over 4 stiles to reach road. Turn **L** back to car park.

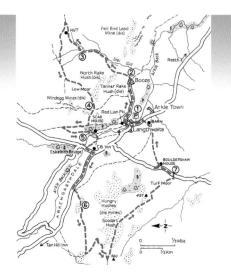

North Yorkshire

HAWES TO THE WATERFALL

862

5 miles (8km) 2hrs **Ascent:** 426ft (130m)
Paths: Field and moorland paths, may be muddy, 44 stiles
Suggested map: aqua3 OS Explorer OL30 Yorkshire Dales – Northern & Central
Grid reference: SD 870898 **Parking:** Pay-and-display car park off Gayle Lane at west of Hawes

A visit to the waterfall – Hardraw Force.

❶ From car park turn L; go R over stile ('**Youth Hostel**'). Follow track uphill to stile. Pass barn, cross 6 stiles and lane, to road. Turn L then R through gate ('**Thorney Mire House**'). Follow path for ½ mile (800m) to gate on to lane. Turn R. Follow for ¾ mile (1.2km), passing under **viaduct** to road at **Appersett**.

❷ Turn L across bridge. Follow road; cross next bridge, then bend L to junction. Go through stile, ('**Bluebell Hill**'). Go across field, through gate and over bridge; bear half L uphill. Go through gate; continue to crossroads signpost.

❸ Turn R and then follow valley to stile (Bob's Stile). Go across field beyond then cross over stile. Turn L to cross ladder stile over wall. Go across field towards **Hardraw**, crossing over wooden stile, then ladder stile into lane.

❹ Turn R then L at main road; cross bridge. **Hardraw** Force entrance is through **Green Dragon** pub. Immediately beyond pub, turn L; go R through

signed gap in wall, through courtyard and over stile. Follow flagged path over another stile, steeply uphill, over stile and up steps. By house, go through stile and R of stables, then through 2 more stiles on to lane by **Simonstone Hall Hotel**.

❺ Turn R then L along road. Almost immediately turn R through stile ('**Sedbusk**'). Follow track through metal gate, over 2 ladder stiles and another gateway then cross 14 stiles into **Sedbusk**.

❻ Turn R along road, bend L near post-box; go downhill. Go R, over stile ('**Haylands Bridge**'). Cross field, bend R to stile in crossing wall, then down to stile on to road. Cross to another stile and follow path; go across stream, over stile then bear R over humpback bridge. Go through gated stile on to road.

❼ Turn L. Cross **Haylands Bridge**; beyond go R through kissing gate ('**Hawes**'). Through field then go over stile. Turn L then R on to main road. Go across at junction; turn R past post office. Follow main road through Hawes, turning L after school, to car park.

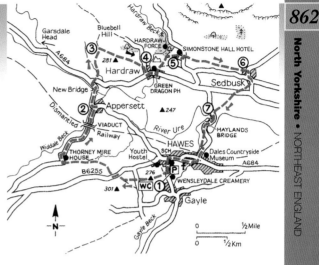

HORSEHOUSE MOOR AND RIVERSIDE

863

6½ miles (10.4km) 2hrs 30min **Ascent:** 459ft (140m)
Paths: Field, moorland and riverside paths and tracks, 31 stiles
Suggested map: aqua3 OS Explorer OL30 Yorkshire Dales – Northern & Central
Grid reference: SE 047813 **Parking:** Roadside parking below former school in Horsehouse

A moor and riverside walk.

❶ Walk past **Thwaite Arms**, then curve behind it on track. Turn R down signed track, go through 2 gates; bend L to 3rd gate. Beyond it bear half R to gate and footbridge.

❷ Cross bridge; bear L. Go over stile ('**Swineside**'), cross small field to another stile then bear half R. Cross track; follow wall to stile. Bear L, eventually on track, through 2 stiles. Go half L to signed stile. Climb grassy path to gap in wall. Take lower path towards buildings. Go through stile and gateway; bend R to gate, to R of buildings.

❸ After gate, follow track past farmhouse then R, uphill. At top, go over cattle grid; follow metalled lane for 1½ miles (2.4km) into **West Scrafton**. In village take track to L ('No Through Road'). Turn L ('Carlton'); turn R. After gate and walled section, turn L down field. Go through kissing gate and R of barn, towards **Caygill Bridge**. Bear R, following wooded valley, through gate and down to 2 footbridges.

❹ After bridges, go through gate; ascend steeply, past signpost. At top bear L beside wall; continue to gate. Follow footpath sign L, eventually reaching **Carlton**. Turn L along road, passing **Forester's Arms**. Where it widens, bear L between cottages following footpath sign to stile. Cross 6 more stiles to road.

❺ Turn L and immediately through gate. Descend to stile; bear R above barn to stile; follow wall to stile then road. Turn L. At L bend, go R, over stile ('**Gammersgill**'). Go across 2 stiles and stream to waymarked gate. Go over fields, crossing stile and wooden footbridge, through gate. Where walled lane bends R, cross stile. Turn R to stile to road.

❻ Turn L into **Gammersgill**, cross bridge, then turn L through gate ('**Swineside**'). Bear R to another gate; cross to stile beside gate. Bear half L to field corner; go over stile. Now follow river over 5 more stiles and past stone bridge. After another stile reach footbridge crossed near start of walk. Retrace your steps back to **Horsehouse**.

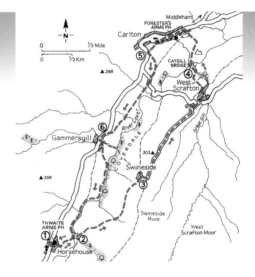

LEIGHTON A DRUIDIC DREAM

864

4¼ miles (6.8km) 2hrs **Ascent:** 426ft (130m)
Paths: Tracks and field paths, 7 stiles
Suggested map: aqua3 OS Explorer 298 Nidderdale
Grid reference: SE 177787
Parking: Car park by Druid's Temple

A rural ramble from a mock-druidic temple.

❶ Park in car park by **Druid's Temple**. To visit Temple, walk through wood then return to car park. Walk down road you drove up. Just after row of metal posts, cross stile on L marked with **Ripon Rowel Walk** symbol, opposite farm track. Walk ahead across field; go through gate surrounded by boulders. Bend L, along edge of wood; at farm track go L to gate.

❷ After gate turn R following track. It bends away from wood and down to ladder stile. After stile, bear half L across field towards trees to stile in crossing wire fence. Continue over ridge of hill, to descend by small wood to 2 waymarked wooden posts.

❸ At posts turn sharp R, uphill, on grassy track. Follow track through 5 gates. Near farmhouse go through another gate and walk to R of buildings. After gateway, track becomes metalled lane. At road junction continue ahead. As road begins to descend, turn R through metal gate towards **Stonefold** farm.

❹ Walk through farmyard, past buildings. Bear L through gateway into field. Go through gate on R, then half L towards row of trees to another gate. After gate, go half R across field through gateway in crossing fence; descend into valley. Turn R, beside stream, then half R through metal gate and over stile in wire fence to footbridge.

❺ Cross bridge and waymarked stile, then turn R, along track. Go through 2 gates, past barn and through another metal gate on to lane.

❻ Turn L, then turn R up next track. Go over stile beside gate, and along track. After gateway, turn R alongside wall toward farm on ridge. Climb hill on track. Go through metal gate then over stile in wire fence.

❼ After stile bend to L, following fence in front of farm building, then through metal gate on R-H side. Follow farm track, going through metal gate. Continue to meet metalled lane. Turn L back to car park.

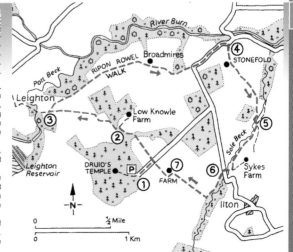

North Yorkshire

865 INGLETON *The Falls*

5 miles (8km) 2hrs Ascent: 689ft (210m)
Paths: Good paths and tracks, with some steps throughout
Suggested map: aqua3 OS Explorer OL2 Yorkshire Dales – Southern & Western
Grid reference: SD 693733
Parking: Pay-and-display car park in centre of Ingleton, or at start of Waterfalls Walk Ingleton. Admission charge for Waterfalls Walk

By the falls, on a route opened in 1885.

❶ Leave car park in centre of **Ingleton** at its western end. Turn **R** along road and follow signs ('Waterfalls Walk'), which take you downhill and across river to entrance to falls. Walk through car park, pay admission fee and go through 2 kissing gates. Path goes downwards then ascends steps. Cross **Manor Bridge** and continue upstream, now with river on your L, to **Pecca Bridge**.

❷ Cross bridge, and turn **R**, back on to L bank of stream. Continue to follow path as it climbs uphill to reach **Thornton Force**. Path winds slightly away from stream and up steps to pass waterfall, and then takes you over **Ravenray Bridge**, and up more steps, to kissing gate on to **Twisleton Lane**.

❸ Turn **R** along rough lane. Go through 2 gates, after which track becomes metalled. Walk past farm buildings, following signs for 'Waterfalls Walk'. Go over gated stone stile and along track, then through kissing gate and on to road.

❹ Go across road ('**Skirwith**'). Follow path as it bends **R**, still following 'Waterfall Walk' sign. Go through gate, then another into woodland. Path passes **Beezley Falls** and Rival Falls. Little further down, take path to **L** on to footbridge with good view of deep and narrow Baxenghyll Gorge. Continue to follow path, which takes you to another footbridge.

❺ Cross bridge, go through kissing gate. Follow path as it bends, at one point almost at water level, then going away from water into trees. Path eventually leads through former **quarry** workings. Continue through handgate on to lane.

❻ Beyond gate follow lane that soon enters **Ingleton**.

❼ Bear **R**, through houses and back into village, bearing **L** under railway viaduct and back to car park.

866 ARNCLIFFE *Over from Littondale*

6½ miles (10.4km) 3hrs 30min Ascent: 1,315ft (400m)
Paths: Mostly clear, some rocky sections; may be muddy, 23 stiles
Suggested map: aqua3 OS Explorer OL30 Yorkshire Dales – Northern & Central
Grid reference: SD 932719
Parking: In Arncliffe, near church

To Kettlewell, and back via River Skirfare.

❶ From car park, cross bridge. Turn **R** at its end, over gated stile. Walk parallel with river then ascend steps to cross road via 2 stiles. Bear **R**. Follow footpath steeply uphill over stile and through gate. Bear **R**. Climb through woods up **Park Scar** to stile.

❷ Beyond, follow footpath to **R** to another ladder stile. Pass signpost; go through gap in tumbled wall to another signpost. Continue to ladder stile then cross corner of field to another ladder stile at summit.

❸ Beyond stile, bear half **R**; descend to ladder stile. Follow path beyond towards **Kettlewell**, descending steeply to signpost. Cross track to reach limestone scar. Descend through narrow cleft (**The Slit**) then walk down to stile and, beyond it, footpath sign. Turn **R**; go through gate and on to road.

❹ Turn **R** for 300yds (274m); go **R** through gate ('Hawkswick'), bending **R** at another sign. Climb through woodland, through waymarked gate; bear **L** through gap in wall. Continue uphill, winding steeply to gap in wall by stile. Bear **L** to another stile then ascend grassy path, bearing **R** where path forks, to another stile. Beyond, continue downhill bending **R** by cairn.

❺ At junction of tracks proceed with wall L. Go through gated stile into **Hawkswick**. Bear **L** at junction, curve **R** between buildings; go through gate to bridge.

❻ Cross and follow road, bending **R**. Just before farm buildings on L, turn **R** towards footbridge. Don't cross but turn **L** at sign ('**Arncliffe**'). Follow river, cross 3 stiles, then footbridge and another ladder stile. Path leaves riverside and reaches gate. Go across field beyond to ladder stile, then another footbridge.

❼ Walk to **R** of barn; go through gate. Bear **L** to squeeze stile in crossing wall. Cross track. Go through 3 stiles, following river then through gate near house. Follow waymarked posts to kissing gate, past churchyard, to start.

867 BORDLEY *The Monks' Road*

5 miles (8km) 2hrs Ascent: 436ft (133m)
Paths: Tracks and field paths, 2 stiles
Suggested map: aqua3 OS Explorer OL2 Yorkshire Dales – Southern & Western
Grid reference: SD 951652
Parking: Roadside parking, before gate across lane from Skirethorns

A walk around remote farmsteads and on an old walled green lane, with monastic origins, between Malhamdale and Wharfedale.

❶ From parking place go through gate; follow metalled lane downhill to crossroad of tracks. Turn **R** here ('Kilnsey'). Follow track parallel with dry-stone wall on **R** to reach crossing track at another signpost at **Mastiles Gate**.

❷ Turn **L** along lane ('**Mastiles Lane**'). At next signpost continue ahead through gate and on to another gate. In 100yds (91m) beyond gate turn **L** through gate in wall and follow track with fence on L. Track eventually goes between walls to gate.

❸ Go through gate. Follow track, which bears **R** by large triangular **boulder**. After 200yds (183m), pass through gateway; turn **L**, going to **L** of bungalow down to large **standing stone** near **Middle Laithe**. Turn **L** through farmyard; go over cattle grid. Follow farm track, crossing 2nd cattle grid by National Trust sign for **New House** farm.

❹ Continue along walled lane into farmyard of **New House**. Go through gate then bear half **R** to go down field to gate in bottom L-H corner. Go through gate, turn **L**. Follow line of telegraph poles. Go over stile; descend across stream.

❺ Follow path on other side of stream, to **R** to telegraph poles. Path eventually follows wall on your **R**. Go through 1st gate on **R**; follow wall on L, bearing **R** to go through gap in tumbled wall.

❻ Bear **L** to go round angle of wall on L to stone stile in crossing wall. Follow wall on L up field, past tumbled wall, to join track.

❼ Turn **R** along track, going through 2 gates. After 2nd gate bend **R**; then go **L** at blue waymark sign and through **farm** buildings to double gates. Beyond gates turn **R**; follow track past farmhouse. Climb track, going through gate, then descend to another gate. Turn **R** to crossroads and ascend back to start.

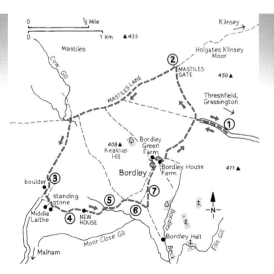

LOFTHOUSE *THREE NIDDERDALE VILLAGES*

7 miles (11.3km) 3hrs Ascent: 656ft (200m)
Paths: Mostly field paths and tracks; may be muddy, 20 stiles
Suggested map: aqua3 OS Explorer OL30 Yorkshire Dales – Northern & Central
Grid reference: SE 101734 **Parking:** Car park by Memorial Hall in Lofthouse

Walking in the valley.

❶ Walk down past **Crown Hotel** to main road; turn **L**. Just beyond farm go **R**, through stile. Follow track to waymarked stile; bear **L** to another stile. Beyond, head half **R** and through gate in field corner. Turn **L**, then **R** through gate. Follow fence to stile on to road.

❷ Cross road and through gate. Follow wire fence to stile; walk along track. Before next gateway, go **L** over stile, then **R** over another. Bear **L**; ascend, following path through 3 gates to track. Turn **R**, through gate. At junction take R-H track, go **L** of farmhouse, through gate to stile. Follow waymarkers to gate. Bear **R**. Cross bridge. Go through gate and ahead. Bear **R** past house to gravelled track and metalled road.

❸ Bear **R** to T-junction. Turn **L**, over bridge. Take next track **R**, by triangular green; bear **R** ('Stean'). Go through gate to track; cross 4 cattle grids to where track bends **L** to Grindstone Hill House.

❹ Proceed over 4 stiles. At **West House Farm** cross stile between farm and bungalow. Cross farm road.

Follow waymarked posts, through 2 gates and over ladder stile to descend to signpost near barn. Continue into valley. Cross small bridge.

❺ At T-junction of tracks, turn **L**, uphill. Follow walled track as it bends **R**. Beyond farm entrance track becomes grassy. In 100yds (91m), after track joins from **L**, turn **R**. At bottom, bend **L** above houses; descend into **Stean**.

❻ Track becomes metalled. Bear **R**, past telephone box, take stile on **L** ('**Middlesmoor**'). Go through stile, down steps, over bridge and up steps. After gate, at top, follow signs through 3 stiles to road. Turn **L** towards Middlesmoor. Near hilltop turn **R** beside Wesleyan chapel to gateway of church.

❼ Turn **R** before gate, through stile ('Lofthouse'). Descend steps, through stile and 2 gateways by **Halfway House**. Continue through stile, go diagonally **L** to gate in corner. In lay-by go **L** through gate, then **R** of buildings to another gate. Cross lane, then bridge; bear **R** to centre of **Lofthouse**. Turn **L** to car park.

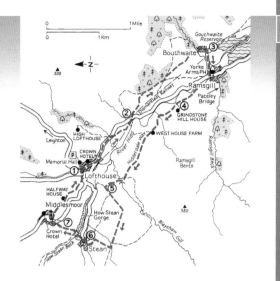

BOLTON ABBEY *RIVER AND WOODLAND*

6¾ miles (10.9km) 2hrs 30min Ascent: 870ft (265m)
Paths: Field and moorland paths, then riverside paths, 4 stiles
Suggested map: aqua3 OS Explorer OL2 Yorkshire Dales – Southern & Western
Grid reference: SE 071539
Parking: Main pay-and-display car park at Bolton Abbey

Over moorland and alongside the Strid to the romantic priory.

❶ Leave car park at its north end and go past **Village Store** and telephone box. Turn **R**, walk down **L** side of green; turn **L**. Pass under archway. Opposite battlemented **Bolton Hall**, turn **L** on to track through signed gate. At top of track, go through gate on **R** with bridleway sign. Walk half **L** to pass corner of some **pools**. Continue through gate beyond; turn **R** towards another gate into wood.

❷ Go through gate and follow signed track through wood to another gate out into field. Follow blue waymarks, many of them painted on rocks, across fields. Path eventually ascends small hill, with wide views. Descend to gate, and 20yds (18m) beyond, take path downhill to **R** to gated stone stile on to road.

❸ Turn **R** along road. After 200yds (183m) go **R** through gate by sign 'FP to **B6160**'. Follow path across fields, crossing stile to reach wall. Turn **R** here,

following wall and then yellow-waymarked posts. Eventually descend to stone stile on to road.

❹ Turn **L** and walk along road for 300yds (274m), then turn **R** into car park and pass beside **Strid Wood Nature Trails Kiosk**. Follow paths ('The Strid') down to river bank; turn **R** to reach narrowest part of river at **The Strid**.

❺ From **The Strid**, continue on riverside path until you reach information board and gateway near **Cavendish Pavilion**. Go through gate, turn **L** by café and go over footbridge.

❻ Immediately at end of the bridge turn **R** ('Bolton Abbey'). Follow path parallel with river, eventually descending to bridge beside stepping-stones and **priory**.

❼ Cross bridge and walk straight ahead up slope and steps to gateway – known as the Hole in the Wall. Go through gateway then keep ahead beside green to reach car park.

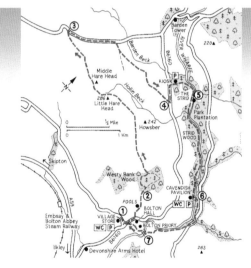

LOTHERSDALE *TUCKED AWAY VILLAGE*

4 miles (6.4km) 2hrs Ascent: 1,509t (100m)
Paths: Tracks and field paths, some steep sections, 8 stiles
Suggested map: aqua3 OS Explorer OL21 South Pennines
Grid reference: SD 939472
Parking: Roadside parking on Carleton to Colne road, north of Clogger Lane

A short walk with fine views and a glimpse of Lothersdale's industrial past.

❶ From car park walk downhill towards mast on hillside. Just before cattle grid turn **L** up signed track. At next signpost turn **R**, off track. Follow wall; bend **L** to go over stile in wall on **R**. Bear **L**, past small plantation, then go diagonally **R**. Go over stile and continue downhill with wall on **R**, which bends **L** to signed stile on to metalled drive.

❷ Turn **L** along drive. After cattle grid bear **R** along concrete road and over another cattle grid. Emerge on to metalled lane; turn **L**. Follow lane as it bends downwards over small stream then starts to rise again. Turn **R** over cattle grid by house sign 'The Knott'.

❸ Follow concrete road, which bends **L** round building, then **R** on to track. Follow track with wall on **L** and, at end, descend towards pool in valley. At bottom of field go across stile in crossing wall; over

another stile; then across dam at end of small pool and on to road. Turn **L**. Just beyond **Hare and Hounds**, turn **L** at Pennine Way sign.

❹ Follow track uphill. Leave track to go **R** of large farm building. Follow wire fence on **R** above wooded valley and continue straight ahead at top of valley, now with stone wall on **L**. Pass broken wall, then take stile in wall on **L**, signed with acorn. Go straight across field to stone stile on to lane.

❺ Cross lane and continue up track ahead ('Pennine Way'). Where concrete farm track bends **L**, keep ahead over stone stile on to walled track. Follow wall on **L** to stile; continue to follow wall on **L** to where it bends sharply **L**.

❻ Follow wall **L**, go over plank bridge; continue to **trig point** on hilltop. Follow either of 2 downhill paths, which converge, and continue past signpost (passed near start). Continue downhill to road; turn to **R** to car parking place.

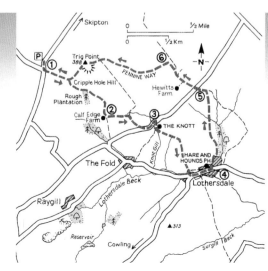

Durham

871   CAUSEY ARCH *The World's Oldest Railway*

4 miles (6.4km) 2hrs **Ascent:** 394ft (120m)

Paths: Mostly on tracks, one short stiff climb
Suggested map: aqua3 OS Explorer 308 Durham & Sunderland
Grid reference: NZ 205561
Parking: Causey Arch car park, off A6076

In the footsteps of the early railway pioneers.
1 From car park, walk through 'Exit' archway, L of toilets. Cross road. Take signed footpath, L of bus stop. Cross stile. Go up field to cross stile on to metalled road.

2 Turn L. After 200yds (184m) turn R ('Beamish Hall'). Where concrete track swings R, go straight ahead down footpath until you reach farm track. Go straight ahead. Where track forks, bend R. Eventually track goes through gateway and into woodland.

3 Descend between houses to road, opposite **Beamish Hall**. Turn R. Follow road for ½ mile (800m) to entrance, on L, to Beamishburn Picnic Area. Turn L. Follow lane through picnic site to footbridge.

4 Cross bridge. Follow footpath as it bends R. Where it forks, proceed by burn side. At waymarked post turn L, go up steps and R at wide crossing track to reach road. Turn L then go R, by **Mole Hill Farm** ('Great North Forest Trail and Causey Arch').

5 Go through wooden stile beside gate. Climb track to yellow waymark sign on post. Go L off track; follow path over wooden stile. Continue with hedge on R to another stile. Path beyond curves downhill to road.

6 Cross road; take footpath opposite. Ascend hill, cross over field and descend to another road. Turn R. Follow road for ½ mile (800m) to '**Tanfield Railway**' sign.

7 Turn R, up approach road, then go ahead through gap in fence. Follow wagon track alongside burn, above gorge. Eventually climb steps to bench by start of **Causey Arch**. To avoid descent into valley, cross arch and continue along path back to car park.

8 To view arch, turn L at bench and go downhill, crossing burn on footbridge. Follow path through woodland and over another footbridge. Go R at end, then cross another footbridge by quarry. Do not cross next footbridge, but bear R, up steps. Turn L at top. Follow embankment back to car park.

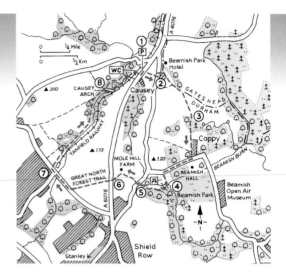

872   CONSETT *A Steel Walk*

3½ miles (5.7km) 1hr 30min **Ascent:** 311ft (95m)

Paths: River and streamside paths with some roadside walking
Suggested map: aqua3 OS Explorer 307 Consett & Derwent Reservoir
Grid reference: NZ 085518
Parking: Car park off Sandy Lane, off A691

A walk along the banks of the river that first brought steel making to Consett, with plenty of industrial relics.
1 From car park, walk beside house, following wall, and then bend R to cross river via footbridge. Turn L along river bank and follow it through woodland. Where path divides, stay by river. Eventually you'll reach area of beech woodland where path rises on to wider track.

2 Follow track, keeping L when it forks – there are waymarks on this section. This path follows alongside wire fence, and eventually bears R over tiny stone bridge skirting house to reach **A68**.

3 Turn L down hill. Go over road bridge, passing from Northumberland into Durham. Where road joins from L, go L through entrance into **Allensford Country Park**. Bear round to R, and walk through grassed riverside area to car park. Go through car park to reach road by entrance to **caravan site**.

4 Go ahead across road to waymarked stile in fence opposite. Follow path, which goes up 2 sets of steps. At top follow grassy path. Where it divides, bear to L and follow winding path into woodland and continue downhill. When you reach crossing path by marker post, turn L to road.

5 Turn R and follow the road (take care because it can be busy). It rises through woodland and then passes through a more open area. After ½ mile (800m), pass a road off to the R. In ¼ mile (400m) beyond, look for a footpath that descends on your R to meet the road, by trees.

6 Continue ahead to follow road for 400yds (366m). As roads rises, take signed footpath L, downhill into woodland. The path opens out into track and then becomes path again. Follow path for ½ mile (800m) to reach lane. Turn L here, downhill. At bottom of hill turn L again, following car park sign back to start of walk.

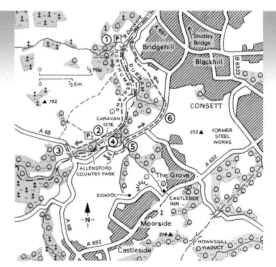

873   WESTGATE *Through Meadow and Woodland*

6¾ miles (10.9km) 4hrs **Ascent:** 525ft (160m)

Paths: Field paths, tracks and country lanes, 5 stiles
Suggested map: aqua3 OS Explorer OL31 North Pennines
Grid reference: NY 909380
Parking: By river at Westgate

Visit Weardale's prettiest village and stride high above the land of the Prince Bishops.
1 From car park walk out to road bridge that crosses over **River Wear**. Don't cross but follow path ahead, which goes across fields alongside river's south bank. This path crosses minor road close to ford and footbridge, then continues by some cottages and across riverside meadows, passing more cottages at Windyside.

2 On reaching main road at **Daddry Shield** turn R, then L, over crash barrier and down to Wear's south bank again. This new path stays closer to river than before. Turn L on meeting country lane and follow it into village of **St John's Chapel**. Turn R along its main street and pass through village.

3 At far side of village, turn R along signed footpath that tucks under old railway bridge and crosses footbridge over river. Beyond crossing turn L through gap stile to follow path close to north bank. Ignore next

footbridge, but instead head for farmhouse, which should be rounded on L.

4 Follow grassy enclosed path raking diagonally across hillside pasture to reach high country lane above hamlet of **New House**.

5 Turn R along lane then, after about ¾ mile (1.2km), take higher **L-H** fork which traverses southern side of **Carr Brow Moor** with its disused quarries and mine shafts.

6 At its terminus turn L up walled **Seeingsike Road** (track). Turn R at junction of tracks and descend into Middlehope Cleugh. Conveniently placed stones allow you to cross over river.

7 Turn R again to follow **Middlehope Burn's** east bank, past series of lead mines. The path enters **Slit Woods** and comes out by mill and some cottages on outskirts of **Westgate**.

8 The lane leads to main road where you turn L, then R past **Hare and Hounds** pub, back to car park.

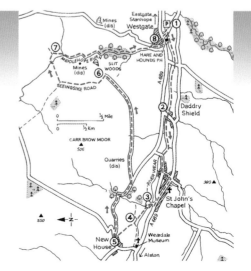

Durham

ROOKHOPE INDUSTRIAL LAND

5¼ miles (8.4km) 2hrs **Ascent:** 508ft (155m)
Paths: Tracks and field paths, one steep climb. Use former railway tracks as embankment may be unstable in places
Suggested map: aqua3 OS Explorer 307 Consett & Derwent Reservoir
Grid reference: NY 924430
Parking: Parking area beside Rookhope Arch, west of village

Among the relics of the lead-mining industry.
❶ Walk towards **Rookhope**. Opposite Blanchland road go **R**, over stile and footbridge. Go ahead, bending **L** past white building, then **R** on track. Go through gate, and **L**, uphill. After cattle grid bear **L** when track divides. Go through 2 gates to house.
❷ Just beyond, take path **L** then descend and go through gate in wall on your **R**. Cross field to stile, then on through gate towards stile by farm buildings. Pass in front of them to wooden stile. Head downhill towards village, to ladder stile.
❸ After stile walk past buildings and turn **R** along track for ¾ mile (1.2km), going through 3 gates, then through farmyard with 2 more. Follow track beyond, uphill, to where it bends **L**.
❹ Turn **L**. As track disappears continue downhill to stile. Turn **L** along road. Just after small lay-by go **R** over stile ('Weardale Way'). Cross footbridge and climb

path opposite, bearing **R**. Walk through field, go over stile then uphill to gate on ridge.
❺ Cross lane and go through gate opposite. Track curves **L** then disappears. Go towards **L** of buildings, then bear **L** keeping beside wall. At field end go **R**, over stile, then head **L** to gate by house.
❻ Go through gate and up steps on **R** to handgate into field. Turn **L**, behind house; go through gate and cross field bearing slightly **L** to gate. Walk behind buildings and at end take gate to **L** of metal gate. Pass large farm building then go downhill to stile on to lane. Turn **R**, then **R** again at junction into **Rookhope**.
❼ Pass **post office** and **Rookhope Inn**, then take signed path **L**. Cross bridge and turn **R** along track at 'Rookhope Trails' sign. Path ascends to higher track. Continue over stile and ahead, past nursery. After gate and wooden stile, turn **R** over footbridge, go over stile and turn **L** on road back to start.

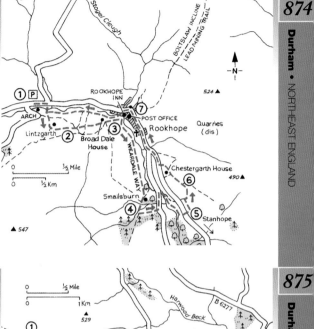

COW GREEN RESERVOIR AND THE TEES

8 miles (12.9km) 5hrs **Ascent:** 525ft (160m)
Paths: Roads tracks and well-defined paths, 2 stiles
Suggested map: aqua3 OS Explorer OL31 North Pennines
Grid reference: NY 810309 **Parking:** Car park at Cow Green
Note: Take note of any warning signs posted by army to keep you from straying on to their firing range.

The remote hillscapes of Widdybank Fell.
❶ From car park walk back along road across **Widdybank Fell** and over watershed, where the wide green sweep of **Harwood Beck's** valley comes into view. Go ahead at junction with Harwood road.
❷ As road approaches river, leave it for signposted path on **R**, which follows track to **Widdybank Farm**. The winding track heads for rocks of **Cronkley Scar** which lies on far banks of **River Tees**.
❸ Through farmyard of **Widdybank**, path goes over stile by gate and heads **L** across rough pasture to join **Pennine Way** by banks of **Tees**.
❹ Across grassy plains at first, path threads through tightening gorge, eventually to be squeezed by cliffs and boulders of **Falcon Clints** on to a bouldery course close to river. Briefly grassy plain develops and path, sometimes stony and traversing heather and sometimes crossing marshy areas using duckboards, continues into wild North Pennine recesses. Across

river you'll see warning signs posted by army to keep you from straying on to their firing range. Usually the guns are a long way off and all is calm.
❺ The valley of **Maize Beck** comes in from behind **Black Hill** in the west, and route comes to foot of the impressive cataract of **Cauldron Snout**. Here path becomes a bit of a scramble up rocks beside falls – take care.
❻ At top of falls you are confronted with huge **Cow Green dam**. Here Pennine Way turns **L** to cross footbridge over Tees but your route continues along lane, which climbs to top **R** of dam.
❼ The lane continues above eastern shores of **reservoir**. You're now on a nature trail and there are numbered attractions. There are no interpretation notices – annoying if you didn't bring the explanatory leaflet (available from local tourist information centres). Beyond gate across road leave tarmac and turn **L** along track, which returns to car park.

BARNARD CASTLE AROUND OLD BARNEY

4¼ miles (6.8km) 2hrs 30min **Ascent:** 165ft (50m)
Paths: Town streets and good paths, 6 stiles
Suggested map: aqua3 OS Explorer OL31 North Pennines
Grid reference: NZ 051163
Parking: Pay-and-display car park at end of Queen Street between Galgate and Newgate

A town and riverside walk with plenty of history.
❶ From car park go through passageway signposted for town. Go across Newgate Street and continue through little ginnel, which leads through churchyard of **St Mary's**, founded in the 12th century, then out on to riverside parkland of **Demesnes**.
❷ Here turn **L** along stony path, which angles down to river. It passes **Demesnes Mill** and then follows north bank of **Tees**, with river on your **R**.
❸ You pass (quickly if the wind is in the wrong direction) local sewage works. Ignore upper **L** fork of 2 paths and stay by river to enter pretty woodland, which allows glimpses of remains of **Egglestone Abbey** on far banks. Go through gate on to road and turn **R** over **Abbey Bridge**.
❹ Turn **R** at junction on far side of bridge, then go **L** up access track to view the 12th-century **abbey**. Return to road and follow it, **L**, to pass **Bow Bridge**.

Squeeze stile in hedge on **R** marks start of path along south bank of Tees. On approach to **caravan park** path crosses fields and veers slightly away from river.
❺ Turn **R** along surfaced track, down to **caravan park** and take 2nd drive on **L**, which eventually leads to continuation of riverside path.
❻ Turn **R** to cross over footbridge back into **Barnard Castle** and then go straight ahead into Thorngate. Turn **L** along Bridgegate. Where road crosses County Bridge go straight ahead, on to follow path that rounds **castle** walls to entrance. The **castle** was built in 1112 for Bernard de Balliol, whose father fought side by side with William the Conqueror at the Battle of Hastings. After visiting castle continue past Methodist church to start of Galgate.
❼ Turn **R** along Market Street and continue to Market Cross. Carry on down The Bank then, at top of Thorngate, go **L** to **Demesnes**. Retrace earlier footsteps back to car park.

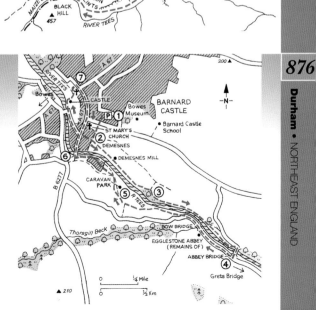

Durham

---

877 BALDERSDALE *WILD FLOWERS AND MOORS*

5½ miles (8.8km) 3hrs 15min Ascent: 750ft (229m)
Paths: Tracks, field and moor paths and lanes, no stiles
Suggested map: aqua3 OS Explorer OL31 North Pennines
Grid reference: NY 928187
Parking: Car park by Balderhead dam

The spartan home of Hannah Hauxwell.

1 Walk across **Balderhead Dam** causeway to south side of **reservoir**. Double back **L** on stony track descending past **Blackton Youth Hostel**. Beyond this, grass track leads down towards **Blackton Reservoir** where it meets **Pennine Way** track beyond gate. It's worth detouring **L** from here to visit the wetlands on the northwest shores before returning to this point. Turn **R** along track and climb past **Clove Lodge**.

2 Beyond this take tarmac lane to your **L**. On your **L** you pass pastures of several farms, while on your **R** are barren slopes of **Cotherstone Moor**.

3 Just beyond driveway of **East Friar House** take path climbing half **R** (southeast) towards rocks of **Goldsborough** (part of Bowes Loop Pennine Way).

4 By 1st of rocks take **L** fork to climb to summit. Return to this position then take narrow **R** fork path that descends northwards, back to road. Turn **R** along road and follow it down to **Hury Reservoir**.

5 Just beyond **Willoughby Hall**, double back **L** along Northumbrian Water access track, then turn **R** off it along grassy causeway to north of reservoir. A path veers **L** above north shore, climbs above **Blackton Dam** where it goes through gate on **R**.

6 Once through 2nd gate in northwest corner of field, path veers **R** alongside line of hawthorns, then turns **L** beside more hawthorn trees. Past barn, walls to **R** then to **L** guide route to footbridge across **Blind Beck**. Waymarking arrows now aid route finding.

7 Footpath now crosses 2 fields, parallel with reservoir's shoreline. In 3rd field, follow dry-stone wall half **L** down towards **Low Birk Hat**, then pass in front of farmhouse to reach stony track. House itself is now in private ownership and it is courteous not to pause too long here. Turn **R** along gated track and climb out of valley, past Hannah's Meadow and **High Birk Hat** to reach higher road. Turn **L** then take next turning on **L**, tarmac lane back to car park.

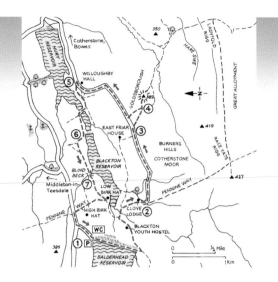

---

878 MARSDEN BAY *SMUGGLERS AND THE LIGHT*

5½ miles (8.8km) 2hrs Ascent: 246ft (75m)
Paths: Roads, tracks, field and coastal paths
Suggested map: aqua3 OS Explorer 316 Newcastle upon Tyne
Grid reference: NZ 412635
Parking: Whitburn Coastal Park car park, signed off A183 (southern end)

Along the coast then inland to the hills.

1 Leave car park at its southern end, following gravel track toward houses. Path winds and goes past sign for Whitburn Point Nature Reserve. Follow track ahead to go through gap in wall. Turn **R**. Path bends **R**, **L** and **R** again to join road into houses. Keep ahead to join main road.

2 Cross road; turn **L**. Walk until you reach **windmill**. Turn **R** to enter grounds. Go up slope on path then between houses. Bear **L** then **R** to T-junction.

3 Keep ahead on path that goes to **R** of house No 99. When you reach another road turn **L**. Just after 1st bungalow on **R**, turn **R** along signed track. Follow track towards farm. Go through farmyard over 2 stiles and follow lane beyond, with hedge to your **R**; where it ends, turn **R** over stile.

4 Follow path along field edge. Cross another stile, gradually ascending. Path bends **L** then **R**, still following field edge. Go over another 2 stiles. Path will

bring you to tower of **Cleadon Windmill**.

5 Go to **R** of windmill, following wall on your **R**. Go **R** through kissing gate, then bear slightly **R** (brick tower to **L**). Go parallel with wall on your **R**. Cross track and go through wire mesh fence at **R** angles to wall. Follow path through scrubland to emerge by yellow post by golf course.

6 Cross course, following yellow posts (watch out for golfers). Go over stone stile, turn **R** along signed footpath, following wall on your **R**. Path eventually descends beside houses to road.

7 Cross and take footpath almost opposite, to **R** of **caravan site**, heading towards sea. Carefully cross busy **A183** then turn **R**, following sea edge. **Marsden Rock** is near by, and **Marsden Grotto** to your **L** as you cross road. Follow coast as it bends **L** to **Lizard Point**. After visit to **Souter Lighthouse**, continue ahead on path slightly inland from coast, which returns you to car park.

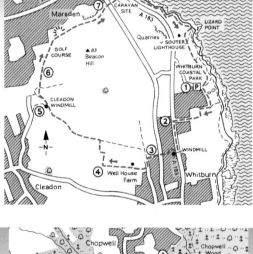

---

879 CHOPWELL *DERWENT VALLEY'S PAST*

7 miles (11.3km) 2hrs 30min Ascent: 541ft (165m)
Paths: Tracks, field paths and old railway line
Suggested map: aqua3 OS Explorer 307 Consett & Derwent Reservoir
Grid reference: NZ122579
Parking: Roadside parking in Chopwell; follow signs for 'Chopwell Park Car Park' (irregular opening)

Steel making and Roman remains.

1 Walk up entrance road to Chopwell Park. Turn **R** past barrier; bear **R**, past sign 'Chopwell Woodland Park'. Follow woodland track, turning **R** at crossing track. Pass barrier to metalled area. Turn **R**. Follow track downhill. Where woodland ends cross stile and continue on fenced path. Enter farmyard through gate.

2 Bear **R** and follow track to road in **Blackhall Mill**. Turn **L**, over bridge. Just after footpath sign, go **L** along field edge, **R** of hedge. Follow riverside path. At crossing path, turn **L**, uphill. At top go sharp **L**, following waymark signs. Go **L** of buildings, over stile and across field. Go over 2 stiles; turn **R**. Follow route uphill, passing **Derwentcote Ironworks**, to main road.

3 Cross and take signed footpath almost opposite. Go over stile and, at crossing path, turn **R** to another stile. Follow path through woodland to former railway track. Turn **R**; follow track, which crosses another track (barriers at each side) and eventually rises to

another barrier on to metalled lane.

4 Turn **R** and descend into **Ebchester**. Bend **R** by community centre to meet main road. Cross and turn **R** in front of **post office**. Turn **L** at footpath sign beyond. Follow fence on your **L**, bend **L** at end beside wall then follow footpath downhill to reach metalled lane. Turn **R** along lane to footbridge.

5 Cross bridge. Footpath bends **R** before going straight ahead across field to stile. Follow green lane uphill, pass **farmhouse** and follow track through 2 gates. Where main track bears **L**, keep ahead. Go through farm gate, and along field edge. Go through 2 gates to T-junction of tracks.

6 Turn **L** ('Whinney Leas'). About 300yds (274m) after farm go **R**, over stile; walk across field to another stile, hidden in hedge. Continue up field to stile **R** of houses, and along narrow lane. At end, turn **R** along tarmac lane. At main road turn **R** then **L**, following 'Chopwell Park Car Park' signs back to your car.

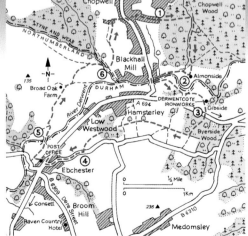

Northumberland

BERWICK-UPON-TWEED TOWN WALLS

6½ miles (10.4km) 2hrs 15min **Ascent:** Negligible
Paths: Paved pathways and field paths, flood-meadows may be wet, particularly around high tide, 4 stiles
Suggested map: aqua3 OS Explorer 346 Berwick-upon-Tweed
Grid reference: NT 998529 **Parking:** Below ramparts outside Scots Gate
Note: Sheer, unguarded drop from outer edge of town walls and bastions, keep to marked pathways

Exploring old Berwick.

❶ From old Town Hall, walk west along Marygate to Scots Gate. Just before it, turn **L** to gateway on **R**; climb on to walls by **Meg's Mount**. Follow wall back over Scots Gate and on past **Cumberland Bastion**.

❷ **Brass Bastion** lies at northern corner of town. 100yds (91m) beyond, path descends inside wall to meet The Parade by corner of parish church graveyard. Turn **R** past barracks to church.

❸ Return to walls. Continue, pass **Windmill Bastion** and site of earlier fort. Beyond **King's Mount**, walls rise above Tweed Estuary before turning upriver at **Coxon's Tower**, past terraces and on above old quay.

❹ Leave walls at Bridge End and cross Old Bridge. Turn **R** past war memorial, go beneath modern **Royal Tweed Bridge** and remain by river beyond, shortly passing below Stephenson's railway viaduct.

❺ Continue upstream along (muddy) path. Where bank widens to rough meadow, keep along **L** side to kissing gate in far corner and continue at edge of next field. Eventually, beyond gate, contained path skirts water treatment plant. Turning **L** through 2nd gate, it emerges on to tarmac track. Turn **R**.

❻ At bend 40yds (37m) on, bear **R** along field edge above steep river bank. Continue in next field but towards its far end look for stepped path, descending bank to stream. Rising to stile beyond, bear **R** to road.

❼ Cross **Tweed** and drop **R** on to path ('Berwick via Plantation'), which crosses 2 stiles to riverside pasture. Walk away beside **L** boundary for ½ mile (800m). After crossing head of stream, move away from hedge, aiming to meet river below wooded bank. Over side bridge, bear **R** to stile; continue through trees beyond to path at top of bank.

❽ Go **R**, eventually drop from wood by cottage, where riverside path leads back to **Berwick**. Just beyond **Royal Tweed Bridge**, turn **L**, climbing under it. Continue beside town walls to **Meg's Mount**.

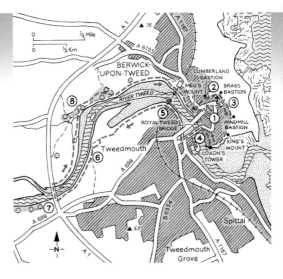

NORHAM THE TWEED VALLEY

4½ miles (7.2km) 1hr 30min **Ascent:** 205ft (62m)
Paths: Field and woodland paths, 4 stiles
Suggested map: aqua3 OS Explorer 339 Kelso & Coldstream
Grid reference: NT 899473
Parking: Roadside parking in Norham

A delightful wander along the Tweed, returning past Norham's former railway station and ancient castle.

❶ Leave village green by cross, heading along Pedwell Way to **St Cuthbert's Church**. In churchyard, walk along grassy path between graves to pass behind north side of church, where you will find stile, which marks head of enclosed path down to **Tweed**. Follow river bank upstream, shortly arriving at **Ladykirk** and Norham Bridge.

❷ Immediately beyond, go over ladder stile on **L**, turn **R** and continue at field edge. Towards its far end, approaching **Bow Well Farm**, look for stile, which takes path down tree-clad bank and out to lane. Walk **R** and, at end, pass through gate ('Twizell Bridge') to carry on across pasture in front of cottage and then through 2nd gate into wood. An undulating path continues above river.

❸ When you reach path junction by footbridge, go **L** through broken gate. Bear **L** again a little further on and climb to another junction at top of wood. Now turn **R** to walk above **Newbiggin Dean**, passing beneath stone arch of railway viaduct. Shortly, at fork beyond stile, take **R** branch ('East Biggin'), which eventually leads out on to lane.

❹ Turn **L**, climbing over hill to descend between piers of dismantled railway bridge. Just before here, to **L**, is former **Norham Station**, which closed in 1964. Its buildings are now restored and house railway museum. Continue to walk on to end of lane.

❺ Turn **R**, but then leave some 250yds (229m) further on, through opening on **L**, signed as bridleway to **Norham Castle**. Keep ahead along field edge to bottom corner, where raised track continues beside brook through trees. Shortly, go **L** over bridge into field, and there turn **R**, following its edge out to lane. Turn **L** and walk past entrance of **Norham Castle**, eventually returning to village.

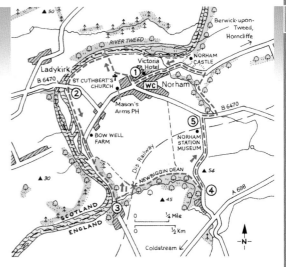

ETAL ESTATE VILLAGES

6 miles (9.7km) 2hrs **Ascent:** 525ft (160m)
Paths: Lanes, tracks and field paths
Suggested map: aqua3 OS Explorer 339 Kelso & Coldstream
Grid reference: NT 925392
Parking: Free car park by Etal Castle

Discover two very different estate villages.

❶ Walk to main road. Turn **R** towards Ford, shortly leaving along lane on L-H side to **Leathamhill**. At cottages, go **R** on track beside sawmill ('Heatherslaw and Hay Farm'), and keep on across fields beyond.

❷ At bottom, by **Shipton Dean**, go through gate on **R** into strip of wood. Beyond, head down edge of successive fields to main road opposite **Heatherslaw Station**. Cross to lane opposite, following it over bridge and around past **Heatherslaw Mill**.

❸ Keep going to **Heatherslaw** farm but, after R-H bend, leave through 5-bar gate on **L** ('Ford Bridge'). Pass shed and go through 2nd gate. Bear **R**, crossing to gate in far corner of field by river. Continue above **Till** to Ford Bridge, there following field edge away from river to gate leading out to lane. Head back along it, crossing bridge to junction.

❹ To **R**, road winds up to **Ford**. Go past entrance to church and Ford Castle before turning **L** into village. At bottom, opposite **Lady Waterford Gallery**, turn **R** to ascend to junction opposite Jubilee Cottage.

❺ Now go **L** but, where lane later bends sharply **R** beyond former stables, leave through gate on **L** into wood ('Hay Farm'). Ignore obvious track ahead; instead, bear **L** on path through trees to stream. Continue over bridge to emerge in field and follow its perimeter to **L** above wood.

❻ Don't go through corner gate, turn **R** up field edge to top of hill. There, pass **L** through gate and cross small field to track in front of **Hay Farm** cottages.

❼ Walk as far as another track on **R**, which leads past barns to junction. Turn **R** to enter gate 20yds (18m) along on **L** ('Heatherslaw and Leathamhill'). Follow field edge to power cable post; go **R**, following boundary and eventually pass wood to reach bottom corner. Drop through gate into trees to bridge over stream. Through 2nd gate, turn **L** along field edge to return to Point ❷. Retrace outward steps to **Etal**.

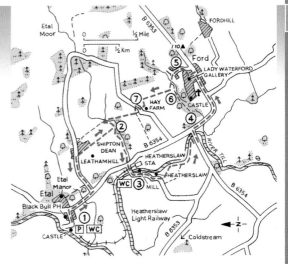

Northumberland

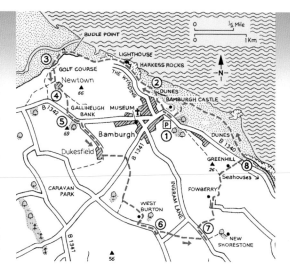

BAMBURGH *COAST AND CASTLE*

8½ miles (13.7km) 3hrs 15min Ascent: 450ft (137m) ▲
Paths: Field paths, dunes and beach, 10 stiles
Suggested map: aqua3 OS Explorer 340 Holy Island & Bamburgh
Grid reference: NU 183348 **Parking:** Pay-and-display parking by Bamburgh Castle

Enjoy views to a castle and the Farne Islands.
1 Walk towards **Bamburgh**; continue along beach, reached either across green below castle or follow **The Wynding**, just beyond then crossing **dunes** behind.
2 To **L**, sand gives way to **Harkess Rocks**. Carefully pick your way round to **lighthouse** at Blackrocks Point (more easily negotiated to landward side). Continue below dunes, shortly regaining sandy beach to pass around **Budle Point**.
3 Shortly before derelict pier, climb on to dunes towards World War II gun emplacement, behind which waymarked path rises to **golf course**. Continue past markers to gate, leaving along track above caravan park. At bend, go through gate on **L** ('Private'). Continue along field edge to cottages at **Newtown**.
4 Beyond, follow wall on **L** to regain **golf course** over stile at top field corner. Bear **R** to pass **L** of lookout and continue on grass track to main road.
5 Walk down **Galliheugh Bank** to bend; turn off to **Dukesfield**. Approaching lane's end, go **L** over stile to

field's far corner. Continue by hedge to road. Cross to follow green lane opposite and eventually, just after cottage, reach stile **L**. Make for **West Burton** farm, turn **R**, via farmyard, to lane. Turn **L**.
6 Beyond bend and over stile on **L** ('New Shorestone') bear half **R** across field. Emerging on quiet lane, cross another stile opposite and continue ahead to **Ingram Lane**.
7 300yds (274m) to **L**, gated track on **R** leads away then around to **L** towards **Fowberry**. Meeting lane, go **L** to farm then turn **R** immediately before entrance on to green track. In next field, follow **L** perimeter around corner to metal gate. Once through that, remain beside R-H wall to double gate, there turning **R** across final field to **Greenhill**. Keep ahead to main road.
8 Continue across to beach and head north to **Bamburgh**. Approaching **castle**, turn inland, over **dunes**, where cattle fence can be crossed by one of several gates or stiles. Work your way through to regain road by car park.

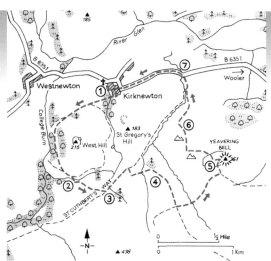

884

KIRKNEWTON *ANCIENT YEAVERING BELL*

5 miles (8km) 2hrs 15min Ascent: 1,115ft (340m) ▲
Paths: Tracks, field paths and moorland, steep ascent and descent
Suggested map: aqua3 OS Explorer OL16 The Cheviot Hills
Grid reference: NT 914302
Parking: In Kirknewton village, in wide area of road beyond school and church, off B6351

Views of the Cheviot Hills and the sea are the reward for climbing to this hilltop fort.
1 From parking place, walk towards village centre; turn **L**. Just before gate, bend **R** along lane, following 'Hillforts Trail' sign. Metalled lane bends **R** again and becomes grassy track. Go through metal gate and ahead at next waymarker. Go through 2 metal gates and gateway. At next marker post bear **R** ('Permissive Path') and go over stream and ladder stile.
2 Turn **L** after stile then cross another stile. Bear half **R** across field to handgate in crossing wall. Go through gate, and bear **R** to reach waymarked post beside track. This is part of **St Cuthbert's Way**.
3 Turn **L** along track and follow it through wooden waymarked gate, past farmhouse and over cattle grid. Just before next cattle grid turn **R** off track, following 'St Cuthbert's Way' sign. Bend **L** through gate and continue along grassy track uphill to ladder stile in wall on your **L**.

4 Go over stile and turn **R** to follow footpath uphill. At low-level signpost, turn **L** ('Yeavering Bell'). Follow waymarks down into valley, across stream then uphill. Path eventually passes through fort wall. Bend **R** to reach summit of **Yeavering Bell**.
5 After enjoying view, go downhill to valley between 2 peaks. Bear **R** and head downhill, on opposite side of hill to that which you came up. Go through wall and follow waymark just beyond. Path is waymarked all the way down steep hill, until you reach stile.
6 Go over stile then ladder stile on your **R** on to track. Follow track past marker post and, just after it, bend **L** towards another track, which leads towards farm buildings in valley bottom. Go over ladder stile by buildings. Turn **R** along track. Go through metal gate and past cottages to reach road.
7 Turn **L** along road and follow it back to **Kirknewton**. At 'Yetholm' sign at entrance to village keep ahead, through gate, then turn **R** back to start.

885

CHILLINGHAM *WILD CATTLE*

6 miles (9.7km) 3hrs Ascent: 754ft (230m) ▲
Paths: Hill track, surfaced road
Suggested map: aqua3 OS Explorer 340 Holy Island & Bamburgh
Grid reference: NU 071248 **Parking:** Forest car park at Hepburn Wood
Note: Dogs not allowed in Chillingham Wood, even on lead

A superb walk that encircles a haunted castle and the home of the only wild cattle left in Britain.
1 On leaving car park, turn **R** on to road. Go uphill for ½ mile (800m) and round bend to National Trust notice indicating **Ros Castle**. Follow track to gate in wall to **L** and go through gate into **Chillingham Wood**. Turn **R**, then **L**. Follow marker posts on to broader track after 100yds (90m). This leads you uphill, then across level stretch to fence. On your **L** is a view over **Chillingham Park**, where you might, on occasion, be able to see the wild cattle.
2 Turn **R** at fence and go uphill following signpost ('Chillingham'). When you reach wall, turn **L**. Follow track between wall and fence to picnic table. Continue to next forest, and walk between wall and forest for 250yds (229m) to next signpost to **Chillingham**.
3 Turn **L**. Descend through forest, following marker posts about 50yds (46m) apart. When small track

reaches junction with track ('Forest Way') turn **R** and continue to signpost pointing to **Amerside Moor** and **Chillingham**. Take **Chillingham** direction, through 2 tall kissing gates to picnic area with 2 tables.
4 Continue along track to forest road and turn **R** (path becomes metalled lower down). At sign pointing **L** over small bridge to Forest Walk, ignore this and instead go through gate and along road out of forest. This road now leads to entrance to **Chillingham Park**.
5 Follow road past **Church of St Peter**, on **L**, then past gate leading to **Chillingham Castle**. Cross Hollow Burn either by ford or footbridge and continue to T-junction with main road. Turn **L** and follow road, passing main castle gate after 550yds (500m).
6 At next fork in road, take **L** fork and go uphill to crossroads. This road is not very busy with traffic and has good grass verges for walking. Turn **L** on to road to **Hepburn Farm**. Follow this, past farm buildings, and continue to **Hepburn Wood** car park.

BREAMISH VALLEY *BURNED HAMLETS*

10 miles (16.1km) 5hrs 30min (add another 6hours for detours) **Ascent:** 590ft (180m) ⚠️

Paths:	Part metalled road, part hill tracks, 1 stile
Suggested map:	aqua3 OS Explorer OL16 The Cheviot Hills
Grid reference:	NT 976162
Parking:	Roadside parking at Hartside

Remains of an ancient settlement.

❶ From parking place, **Hartside**, take metalled road ('Alnhammoor') over cattle grid then turn sharp **R** and go downhill. At bottom of hill, road turns **L** and leads to wooden bridge. Cross bridge and continue steadily uphill, past farm and across 3 more cattle grids.

❷ Near top of 1st rise, another track joins main roadway from L. You are now on side of **Meggrim's Knowe.** (A relatively easy but trackless detour over hill to R and down to shoulder on other side, about ¼ mile/400m, to remains of Celtic settlement.) Continue on metalled road, which follows contour. Road swings **L**, descend gently to join river, then turns **L** again through narrow gorge to Low Bleakhope Farm. Beyond, valley opens out to High Bleakhope. Continue past this and 2 small woods beyond, to gate.

❸ Follow signposted public bridleway to **R**, steeply uphill to gate and stile. Go through gate and continue less steeply for 550 yards (500m) to 2nd gate. Go through this and across to 3rd gate, 220 yards (200m) farther. Beyond, 3 tracks diverge. Take middle track across open moorland. Continue past **Rig Cairn**, then downhill to fence that runs across broad saddle.

❹ Go through gate and down to side of forest, passing through another gate on way. **Linhope Spout** can be reached by following lower track along forest edge, through kissing gate and downhill for ¼ mile (400m). Back on main route, follow rubble track to **R** to reach **Linhope** village after ¼ mile (400m).

❺ Metalled road leads across bridge and uphill for 220yds (200m) to where broad track on **L** gives into field at side of forest. To visit **Grieve's Ash**, go on to this track then follow edge of forest steeply uphill for 110yds (100m). The extensive remains of the settlement occupy the area behind the forest. Main road leads you back to **Hartside** in ½ mile (800m).

ALWINTON *THE GORGE OF THE RIVER COQUET*

4½ miles (7.2km) 3hrs **Ascent:** 590ft (180m) ⚠️

Paths:	Mostly hill footpaths, 8 stiles
Suggested map:	aqua3 OS Explorer OL16 The Cheviot Hills
Grid reference:	NT 919063
Parking:	Car park at Alwinton
Note:	Close to MOD artillery range over Barrow Scar. When red flags flying, walk may be inadvisable. Contact Range Control Officer on 01830 520569 or 0191 239 4261 prior to setting off

A demanding but spectacular walk.

❶ Turn **R** out of car park and follow road for 700yds (640m) to gate on **L** leading to **Barrow Mill**. Go through gate and down to farm, passing remains of a corn-drying kiln (1812). Go through another gate into field, cross this and go through gate to river bank. Ford river. After rain, this will involve getting your feet wet.

❷ Enter field and follow fence to **R** to gate. Go through this or over stile about 20yds (18m) away to **L** and continue to derelict farm buildings. Follow track up hillside to **R-H** corner of conifer forest.

❸ About 50yds (46m) before reaching signpost marking edge of military firing range, follow less well-defined track across heather-covered hillside to **R**, rising slightly, until you come to wire fence. Follow this over top of **Barrow Scar**, keeping fence on your **R**. When you meet 2nd fence, follow this to stile. Cross stile and go down to obvious loop in river. In late summer, bracken may obscure track.

❹ At river bend, cross stile, then another after 100yds (91m). Cross field and stile into farmyard at **Linshiels**. Go through farmyard, across 2 bridges and join road. Turn **L** and follow road until just past farm buildings, to signpost ('Shillmoor').

❺ Go up hillside, over stile and follow track overlooking gorge and its waterfalls. For short distance, slopes below are quite precipitous and care is needed, though track is good. When track splits, keep to higher branch and go round hillside to join more prominent track leading up from L. Turn **R** and follow this track uphill.

❻ At top continue over level ground then descend to stile. Cross and follow track, over 2nd stile and down to road. Follow road for 1 mile (1.6km) back to **Alwinton**.

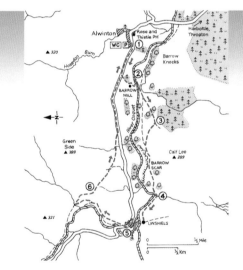

CRASTER *A RUINED CASTLE*

5 miles (8km) 1hr 45min **Ascent:** 275ft (84m) ⚠️

Paths:	Generally good tracks, some field paths tussocky, 1 stile
Suggested map:	aqua3 OS Explorer 332 Alnwick & Amble
Grid reference:	NU 256198
Parking:	Pay-and-display behind Craster tourist information centre

The castle that inspired artist JMW Turner.

❶ From car park, turn **R** towards village. Immediately before **harbour**, go **L** into Dunstanburgh Road ('Castle') and continue through gate at end above rocky shore towards **Dunstanburgh Castle**.

❷ After 2 more gates, if you want to visit castle, keep to main track, which leads to its entrance. Otherwise, bear **L** on less distinct path through gorge on landward side. Continue below castle, with ruins of Lilburn Tower, perched on top of rocky spur outcrop.

❸ Beyond, as you pass above bouldery beach, glance back to cliffs protecting Dunstanburgh Castle's northern aspect, which, in the early summer, echo the screams of seabirds, squabbling for nesting sites.

❹ Go through kissing gate at edge of **golf course**, bear **R** to remain above shore. Ahead is **Embleton Bay**; if tide permits, continue along beach.

❺ Shortly, look for prominent break in dunes, through which path leads across **golf course** to meet lane. Follow it up to **Dunstan Steads**, turning **L** immediately before on to drive ('Dunstan Square'). Where this bends behind buildings, bear **L** across open area to gate and continue over open fields on farm track.

❻ After 1 mile (1.6km), at **Dunstan Square**, pass through 2 successive gates by barn and turn **L** through 3rd gate ('Craster'). Walk down field edge and through gate at bottom then along track rising through break in cliffs ahead, **The Heughs**. Keep going across top to field corner and turn through gate on **R**.

❼ Walk away, initially beside L-H boundary, but after 150yds (137m), by gate, bear **R** to follow line of ridge higher up. Eventually meeting corner of wall, continue ahead beside it. Shortly after crossing track, go on over stile, beyond which path becomes more enclosed. Approaching village, path turns abruptly **L** behind house and emerges on to street. Follow it down to main lane and turn **R**, back to car park.

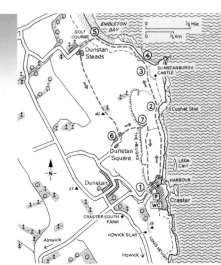

Northumberland

Northumberland • NORTHEAST ENGLAND

889 OTTERBURN *MEDIEVAL AND MODERN BATTLEFIELDS*

4½ miles (7.2km) 2hrs **Ascent:** 300ft (91m) ▲

Paths: Bridleway, moorland track and metalled road.
Suggested map: aqua3 OS Explorer OL42 Kielder Water & Forest
Grid reference: NY 889929 **Parking:** Roadside car park at eastern end of Otterburn village
Note: Close to MOD danger area. When red flags flying, walk may be inadvisable. Contact Range Control Officer on 01830 520569 or 0191 239 4261 before setting off

Skirt a medieval battlefield and a training ground for modern warriors.
① From car park, walk through **Otterburn**. About 100yds (91m) after passing Church of St John the Evangelist, turn **R** on to road to **Otterburn Hall**. At top of incline, go on to public bridleway on **L**, past farm buildings and into field. Follow bridleway alongside wall and through gate into next field. Continue, this time with wall, which gives way to wire fence on R.
② Go through next gate and, keeping in same direction, cross field to gate through opposite wall. Go through gate and across marshy ground past small plantation, now mostly cut down, to junction with metalled road. Follow this to **R**, across cattle grid and around bend to **L**, up gentle incline.
③ About 100yds (91m) after bend, follow grassy track across hillside to **R**, past **sheep pen**. This leads to gate, beyond which there is military warning notice.

Go through gate and continue across moorland, downhill. The ground is boggy and track indefinite in places, but it leads to better track, which follows fence on your R to join metalled road at **Hopefoot** farm.
④ Follow road to **R**, crossing bridge over stream, then through woods, to join main army camp to Otterburn road at **Hopefoot Cottages**. Turn **R** and follow road past **Doe Crag** cottages and across bridge to entrance to **Otterburn Hall**. Go through gate opposite this on to footpath, signposted to Otterburn and leading across field.
⑤ Follow track, passing **sports centre** on your R. At bend in wire fence, track forks. Follow **L** fork downhill, across 2 small footbridges, through kissing gate and along river bank. The track may be muddy and overgrown at times. After crossing stile, track brings you into Otterburn, just opposite **Percy Arms**. Turn **L** and return to car park.

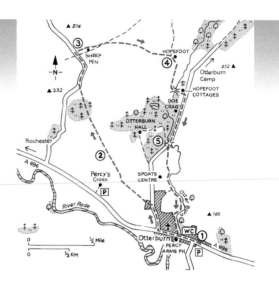

890 SIMONSIDE HILLS *ANCIENT SPIRIT*

5½ miles (8.8km) 3hrs **Ascent:** 820ft (250m) ▲

Paths: Generally good tracks, but steep and muddy in places
Suggested map: aqua3 OS Explorer OL42 Kielder Water & Forest
Grid reference: NZ 037997
Parking: Large car park at forest picnic area

A hill that had spiritual significance to early settlers and now popular with rock climbers.
① From notice board in picnic area, go through gate on to broad forest road. Follow this gently uphill, swinging to **R** round long hairpin bend, then back **L** at top of hill. When track splits, take **R-H** fork, past communications **mast** and go gently downhill. When you get to next junction, take **L-H** fork and follow road past sign indicating detour to **Little Church Rock**.
② When you come to marker post, where narrow track leads to L, ignore this and continue along broad track, which now becomes grassy. After passing huge, heavily overgrown boulder, continue to small **cairn** which marks start of subsidiary track on **L**. Follow this track uphill through forest and out on to heather-covered hillside. You will now see Simonside's crags ½ mile (800m) away to your **L**.
③ Continue up narrow track to join broader one at edge of upper forest and follow this for about 275yds

(251m) to corner of trees. A rough track, sometimes quite muddy in places, picks its way through boulders up the hillside. Follow this, keeping crags on your L-H side, on to plateau and walk along top of crags to large **cairn** on the summit, which is probably a burial mound, built around 350 BC.
④ Away from summit, track splits into 2. Follow **R** fork across boggy ground for ⅓ mile (530m). Climb short rise, keeping wonderfully wind-sculpted **Old Stell Crag** to your **L**. and move round on to summit and another large **cairn**.
⑤ Take narrow path down to join lower track. This leads, in ½ mile (800m), to **cairn** on **Dove Crag**. At Y-junction, ¼ mile (400m) further on, follow **R** fork gently uphill to **The Beacon cairn** and continue downhill for ½ mile (800m) to join road at **Lordenshaws** car park.
⑥ Turn **L** and follow road for 1 mile (1.6km) until you arrive back at forest picnic area.

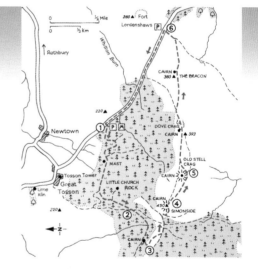

891 ELSDON *REIVER COUNTRY*

4 miles (6.4km) 1hr 45min **Ascent:** 623ft (190m) ▲

Paths: Field paths and tracks
Suggested map: aqua3 OS Explorer OL42 Keilder Water & Forest
Grid reference: NY 937932
Parking: Signed car park in Elsdon, by bridge on Rothbury road

A walk in the hills and valleys.
① Follow 'Toilets' sign past village hall and through gateway. Climb lane past **Mote Hills**, pass house and cross gravel to gate. Cross small field and go through next gate, then head half **R** to go through gate near trees. Follow path up sunken lane then along field edge to gate.
② Go through gate and turn **L** over cattle grid. Follow metalled lane through farm buildings and down to row of cottages. Opposite them, turn **R** in front of barn, cross stream and go through gate.
③ Walk ahead through field with bank on **L** and, at top of rise, bear **L** across bank, making for gate in crossing wire fence. After gate, bear half **L** again, towards L-H end of crossing wall.
④ Turn **R** and follow wall downhill. Go through gate in crossing wall and continue to follow wall on your **L** to reach waymarked post. Turn **R**, cross small bridge, then go uphill to gate beside barn. Go straight on then

take metal gate on your **L**. Curve **R** to another gate on to road. Turn **L** along road, crossing cattle grid and bridge, to 2nd cattle grid.
⑤ Cross it, then turn immediately **R** ('East Todholes'). Cross stream and go through gate, then cross 2nd stream. Follow wall on your L-H side to reach ladder stile by pine trees. After stile bear half **L** to go round R-H side of **East Todholes** farm and cross over stile on to lane.
⑥ Follow lane past next farm and up hill to join road. Turn **R**. Opposite 'bend' sign go **R** over stile. Follow old wall downhill towards **Elsdon**, bending **R**, then **L**, at fence to cross stile. After another stile bear **R** to footbridge, then **L** to another. Path eventually brings you to larger footbridge near village.
⑦ Cross footbridge, then turn **R** to stile beside gate. Go up track between houses to road that takes you to green. Bear **R**, along edge of green. Go over bridge and back to start.

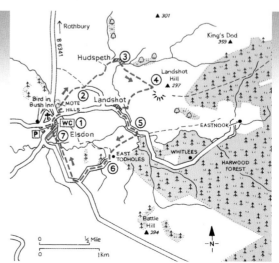

Northumberland

DRURIDGE BAY *A Beachy Nature Reserve*

5½ miles (8.8km) 1hr 45min **Ascent:** Negligible
Paths: Paths and tracks, with good walk on beach, no stiles
Suggested map: aqua3 OS Explorers 325 Morpeth & Blyth
Grid reference: 332 Alnwick & Amble NU 282024 (on Explorer 332)
Note: Close to MOD danger area. When red flags flying, walk may be inadvisable. Contact Range Control Officer on 01830 520569 or 0191 239 4261 before setting off

A nature reserve, country park and beach.

1 A waymarked footpath beside car park entrance winds between **nature reserve** and **caravan site** towards coast. Go through gate at bottom, turn **R** on to track. Shortly pass 2 gates to bird hides.

2 Leaving reserve, continue a little further on tarmac track to parking area on **L**, where there's access on to beach. Now, follow shore past **Togston Links**, across stream and on below **Hadston Links**.

3 After 1¼ miles (2km), wooden steps take path off sands on to dunes. Cross tarmac track and continue over marshy area into pinewood. Beyond trees, emerge by car park and walk across to **Druridge Bay Country Park visitor centre** (café and toilets).

4 A footway to **L** winds around **Ladyburn Lake**, soon passing boat launch area. Keep to lower path, which soon leads to stepping stones across upper neck of lake. If you would rather not cross there,

continue around upper edge of wooded nature sanctuary above water to footbridge higher up. Over bridge and through gate, turn **R** by field edge, soon drop around internal corner to kissing gate. Descend through trees to regain lake by stepping stones.

5 Path winds through trees to emerge beside lush shoreline. After crossing bridge over lake's outflow, carry on back to visitor centre.

6 Retrace your steps to beach and turn back towards **Hauxley**, but when you reach point at which you originally dropped on to sands, remain on shore towards **Bondi Carrs**. Seaweed can make rocks slippery, so be careful clambering over as you round point, where Coquet Island then comes into view ahead. Not far beyond there, after passing lookout post and approaching large rocks placed as storm defence, leave across dunes, retracing your outward path short distance back to car park.

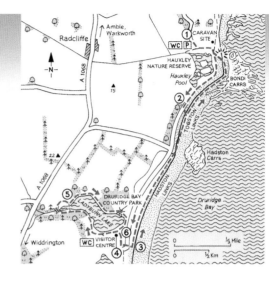

MORPETH *Along the River Wansbeck*

8½ miles (13.7km) 2hrs 45min **Ascent:** 420ft (128m)
Paths: Woodland paths (muddy after rain) and field paths, 9 stiles
Suggested map: aqua3 OS Explorer 325 Morpeth & Blyth
Grid reference: NZ 198859 **Parking:** Car parks within town

A fine woodland valley walk.

1 From **Town Hall**, walk east along Bridge Street to end, continuing around to **L** along main road towards **Pegswood**. Immediately after **Old Red Bull Inn**, take enclosed path on **R** that later rejoins main road. Cross to footpath rising through woodland opposite ('Whorral Bank and Cottingwood Common'). Bear **R** when you get to fork, past residential home, then go **R** at next junction to again meet main road.

2 On far side, path ('Bothal') descends into lushly wooded valley through which flows **River Wansbeck**. There follows delightful, undulating walk for 2¼ miles (3.6km), eventually ending over stile by sawmill. Walk to lane beyond and turn **R** across river.

3 After climbing from valley, lane continues above wood. Where it later bends sharply **L** at **Shadfen Cottage**, go ahead over stile into field corner, and continue at edge of series fields beside **R-H** boundary. Eventually pass **R** of deep excavation, before dropping to stile into woodland. Go through to bridge; cross.

4 Re-emerging into fields above far bank, follow path ahead between cultivation to gain track past **Parkhouse Banks**. After 120yds (110m), immediately beyond drive, turn through gap in **R-H** hedge ('Whorral Bank'), and walk away beside field edge. At corner, slip **R** through another gap and carry on along track past cottage and through fields to railway bridge.

5 Keep going over field beyond to stile, there dropping across rough pasture back into wood. Soon joined by track, continue down to junction by river and turn **L** above bank. Emerging from trees, bear **L** along field path that leads past cottage, ongoing track returning to river.

6 Over bridge, street leads around past ambulance station into town. Go ahead to St George's Church then turn **L** over Telford Bridge to Castle Square. Cross into **Carlisle Park** and, beyond flowerbeds, bear **R** following main drive to riverside promenade. Walk upstream past Elliott Bridge to top of park then turn **R** over Oldgate Bridge to return to town centre.

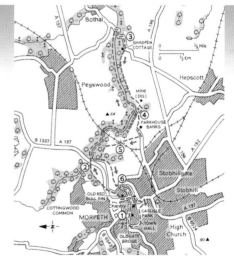

LANEHEAD *A Once-lawless Landscape*

7½ miles (12.1km) 3hrs **Ascent:** 1,083ft (330m)
Paths: Burnside and moorland paths and tracks – some wet areas
Suggested map: aqua3 OS Explorer OL42 Keilder Water & Forest
Grid reference: NY 793858 **Parking:** Beside Tarset Village Hall in Lanehead, on Greenhaugh road

Hills and valleys with an interesting village.

1 Walk to staggered crossroads in middle of Lanehead. Turn **R** ('Donkleywood'). At **Redmire cottages** turn **R**. Go through gate, over 2 stiles and through handgate. Bear **L** to stile in field corner. Bend **R**, following river bank; cross 5 stiles. Go through handgate to footbridge. Go through gate at end, then ahead to meet track. Turn **L** to farm buildings.

2 Go through 2 gates between buildings, then ascend lane. As it bears **L**, go ahead past waymarker and downhill to cross stream. Pass waymarked post and through gateway. Bend **R** after it; go through handgate. Turn **L** along fence. Cross stile on **R**, then go half **L** towards house and church. Keep **L** of ruined wall; bear **L** to follow wall downhill to stream.

3 Cross stream and stile beyond; climb hill. Bear **L** past church to gate. Turn **L** along lane. At T-junction turn **L**. Follow lane past **Redheugh** farm and 'Forestry Commission **Sidwood**' sign to Sidwood Picnic Area, near white-painted buildings.

4 Turn **L** ('Slaty Ford'). Go through wood for short distance, then take track to **R**. Go over crossing track; continue uphill. After track levels out, it goes beside woodland to gate. Continue, via field and plantations, to ford; cross, go past signpost to crossing track.

5 Turn **L**; cross another ford. Continue up track to gate. After ¼ mile (400m) look for stile in wall on **R**. Cross and bear half **R** down field. Go over stream, up to wire fence; follow it **L**. Go **R**, through gate, and cross field, through gate, into farmyard.

6 Take **R-H** of 2 gates to **L**. Go through another gate; bear **L** to follow track downhill. At bottom turn **L** along road. As it begins to rise, take footpath ('The Hott') over stile. Follow riverside path, through kissing gate, to **suspension bridge**.

7 Just after hut beyond bridge, bear **L**. Cross railway embankment and go through gate. Bear half **R** to tree in field corner and join road. Turn **R** then **L** on road. Continue over cattle grid. Cross bridge and continue to **Lanehead**, turning **L** at junction to start.

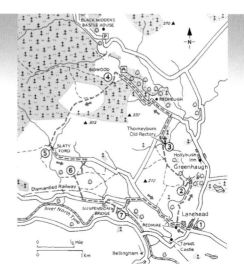

895 CORBRIDGE *ROMANS AND COUNTRYFOLK*

6 miles (9.7km) 3hrs 30min **Ascent:** 525ft (160m)
Paths: Village streets, riverside and farm paths and lanes, 8 stiles
Suggested map: aqua3 OS Explorer OL43 Hadrian's Wall
Grid reference: NY 992642 **Parking:** On town centre streets

Discover Corbridge, Catherine Cookson's home and a rich history.

1 Start at Low Hall Pele on eastern end of Main Street. Head west down Main Street. Turn **R** up Princes Street. At town hall turn **L** along Hill Street, then, just before church, turn **L** up narrow street to pass Vicar's Pele. Turn **R** at Market Place; head north up Watling Street, then Stagshaw Road, which is staggered to **L** beyond Wheatsheaf Inn.

2 Go **L** along Trinity Terrace then **L** again along footpath ('West Green'). This leads past Catherine Cookson's old house, Town Barns, to Orchard Vale. Here, turn **R**, then **L** along lane to river.

3 Turn **L** along Carelgate. Follow riverside path to town bridge. Cross bridge; follow south banks of Tyne on unsurfaced track that passes cricket ground at **Tynedale Park** before mounting grassy embankment running parallel to river.

4 Turn **R** up steps, cross ladder stile, then railway tracks (with care). Another stile and steps lead through

wood and across field to **A695**; turn **R** – footpath on nearside.

5 Just beyond cottages, turn **L** up lane, which zig-zags up **Prospect Hill**. Just after 1st bend leave lane for southbound path that climbs fields. Just before woods, path meets track; turn **R** for few paces to rejoin lane. continue to crossroads at top of hill; turn **R**.

6 After passing **Temperley Grange and West farms** leave road for path on **R** that follows first R-H side, then L-H side of dry-stone wall across high fields and down to **Snokoehill Plantations**.

7 Go through gate to enter wood. Turn **L** along track running along top edge. Track doubles back to **R**, soon to follow bottom edge of woods.

8 Turn **R** beyond gate above **High Town** farm; follow track, which becomes tarred beyond **West Fell**.

9 Beyond **Roecliff Lodge** path on **L** crosses field to reach **A695**. Cross, then continue into copse, The Scrogs, before joining **B6529** by Corbridge Railway Station. Follow this over bridge and into **Corbridge**.

896 HEXHAM *AN HISTORIC TOWN*

3¾ miles (6km) 2hrs **Ascent:** 590ft (180m)
Paths: Town streets, lanes and woodland paths, 4 stiles
Suggested map: aqua3 OS Explorer OL43 Hadrian's Wall
Grid reference: NY 939641
Parking: Pay-and-display car park, next to supermarket

A walk round the abbey and market town.

1 From car park (not supermarket end) take exit between **tourist information centre** and café to follow narrow street past Old Gaol. Go under arches of Moot Hall and enter Market Place. Take tour of The Sele, park grounds surrounding **Hexham Abbey**, before aiming roughly southwest across them to Queen Hall on Beaumont Street.

2 Turn **R** along here to reach Benson's Monument then continue straight ahead on unnamed street. After taking 1st turning on **R** ignore Elvaston Road on L, but instead go straight ahead on tarred lane that leads to foot of wooded Cowgarth Dene.

3 At bridge, turn into woodland where unsurfaced track crosses footbridge and climbs out to little park at edge of modern housing estate. Follow woodland edge, then track past water treatment works.

4 On nearing housing estate, go through gate on **L** then double-back **L** on path by houses. Where path

turns **R**, climb steps on to track that runs along north side of **Wydon Burn Reservoir**, filled with reeds and tall grasses, not water.

5 Turn **L** along lane then, at **Intake** farm, turn **R** along path that leads into thick woodland of **Wydon Burn's** upper reaches. A narrow path continues through woods to reach lane at Causey Hill where you turn **L** past campsite to junction with road, **The Yarridge**. The modern building you'll see here is part of the **Hexham Racecourse**.

6 Turn **L** along road and go ahead at crossroads.

7 Beyond **Black House**, stile on **L** marks start of downhill, cross-field path to **Hexham**. Beyond step stile path veers **R** to round gorse bushes before resuming its course alongside **L** field edge.

8 Just before reaching whitewashed cottage go over stile on **L** and follow road down into town. Turn **L** along shopping street at bottom, then **R** along St Mary's Chare, back to Market Place.

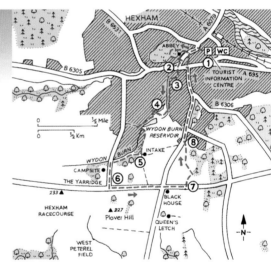

897 CRAG LOUGH *ALONG THE EMPEROR'S WALL*

8 miles (12.9km) 4hrs **Ascent:** 885ft (270m)
Paths: Mainly well walked National Trails, 16 stiles. Please don't damage wall by walking on it
Suggested map: aqua3 OS Explorer OL43 Hadrian's Wall
Grid reference: NY 750677 **Parking:** Steel Rigg (pay) car park

A moorland walk along Hadrian's Wall.

1 From car park descend to grassy depression beneath **Peel Crags**. Path arcs **L** and climbs back to ridge in series of steps before climbing cliff tops past **Turret 39A** and **Milecastle 39**.

2 After another dip, climb to **Highshield Crags**. Beyond lake, footpath climbs past **Hotbank** farm.

3 At next dip, **Rapishaw Gap**, turn **L** over ladder stile; follow faint but waymarked **Pennine Way** route across moorland. The 1st stile lies in far **R** corner of large rushy enclosure. Clear cart track develops beyond dyke and climbs to ridge on **Ridley Common**. Here, turn half **L** to descend grassy ramp.

4 Path arcs **R** to cross fenced track at **Cragend**. Grassy ridge zig-zags to moorland depression with **Greenlee Lough** to L. At bottom, ground can be marshy and path indistinct in places. Waymark points sharp **R** but path loses itself on bank above it. Head north, keeping farmhouse, **East Stonefolds**, at ten to the hour. Next stile lies in kink in cross wall.

5 Beyond, turn half **L** to traverse field. Cross ladder stile. Turn **L** along farm track, which passes through **East Stonefolds**. Track ends at . Right of way goes through farm and over stile on **R** past farmhouse. However you are encouraged to take the alternative route in field at back of the farm (on R) by 'dogs running free' sign and an Alsation in the yard.

6 Past house continue, with wall (L), along grassy ride, and cross step stile to reach signposted junction. Keep ahead on permissive path ('Greenlee Lough Birdhide'). Path follows fence to lake. Ignore stile (to hide) and continue alongside fence.

7 Cross next stile and wetlands north of lake on duckboard path, which soon swings **R** to gate. Beyond, continue on path, climbing northwest, guided by waymarker posts to farm beyond by conifers of **Greenlee Plantation**.

8 Turn **L** along track; follow it past **Gibbs Hill** farm. Past farmhouse, tarmac lane leads back towards wall. Turn **L** at T-junction to return to car park.

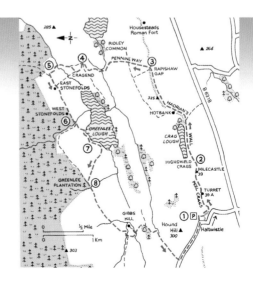

Northumberland

ALLEN BANKS *GORGEOUS GROUNDS*

5 miles (8km) 2hrs 45min **Ascent:** 420ft (128m)
Paths: Well-signposted woodland paths, 7 stiles
Suggested map: aqua3 OS Explorer OL43 Hadrian's Wall
Grid reference: NY 798640
Parking: Car park included in fee for walk
Note: Early part of walk is not right of way, National Trust makes small charge per adult to walk here

A walk through a wooded gorge.
❶ Follow riverside path from back of car park and stay with lower **L** fork where path divides. Stay on **Allen's** west banks rather than crossing suspension bridge. Beyond it path tucks beneath **Raven Crag**. River bends to **R** and you soon enter nature reserve at **Briarwood Banks**. Here the ancient woodland dates back to the end of the last ice age, some 10,000 years ago. With broadleaved trees like sessile oak, wych elm, ash, birch, rowan and alder flourishing, this is a haven for wildlife, and over 60 species of bird have been recorded in the valley.
❷ On Briarwood Banks, path uses footbridge across **Kingswood Burn**, then turns **L** to cross suspension bridge across Allen. You are now at **Plankey Mill**.
❸ Turn **R** along field-edge path close to river and go over either of 2 step stiles back into woodland. If you chose riverside stile, some steps will lead you back to

main track. You are now following green waymarks of Staward Pele path, which stays close to river, though it's often high above banks. Just beyond a footbridge path divides. Take **R** fork – **L** is your downhill return route.
❹ On reaching top eastern edge of woods, path turns **L**, where it first passes gatehouse of **Staward Pele** then ruins of fortified farm itself.
❺ Beyond pele track descends, steeply, sometimes in steps, back to previously mentioned footbridge. Retrace your steps to **Plankey Mill**.
❻ On reaching tarred lane by mill, turn **R**, go uphill along it, then, at sharp bend, turn off it on to enclosed footpath. This leads to another footpath that follows field edge alongside river's east bank.
❼ Turn **L** over suspension bridge opposite **Morralee Wood** turn off, then turn **R** along outward footpath back to car park.

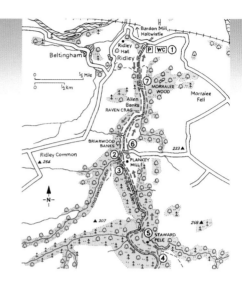

ALLENDALE TOWN *SHINING WATER*

3¾ miles (6km) 2hrs 15min **Ascent:** 590ft (180m)
Paths: Good river paths and faint field paths, 19 stiles
Suggested map: aqua3 OS Explorer OL43 Hadrian's Wall
Grid reference: NY 838558 **Parking:** Ample parking in village centre

Exploring an attractive river valley.
❶ From Market Place take Whitfield road down past Hare and Hounds and round **L-H** bend to old Mill Bridge across **River East Allen**.
❷ Immediately beyond bridge, turn **L** along tarred lane past cottages ('to Wooley Scar'). Where track swings **R**, leave it and go through gate ahead before following cross-field path, parallel to river.
❸ At narrow end of wedge-shaped field go over ladder stile on **R**. Here path veers away from river and enters area above Wooley Scar (overgrown with nettles and ragwort in summer). Route continues generally southwest across fields.
❹ Beyond **Black Cleugh** it swings southeast along short section of rutted track. Ignoring 1st stile on **R** follow **R** field edge. Waymark on broken fence points way down towards woods surrounding **Steel Burn**.
❺ Turn **L** along grass track running parallel to burn and go through gate behind little cottage. Turn **R** over footbridge crossing burn; follow banks of East Allen.

Clear route crosses riverside meadows and ignores 1st river footbridge near **Peckriding**.
❻ After meandering with river, path meets track near **Hagg Wood** and follows it across bridge over East Allen. Track zig-zags past farm at **Studdondene** to reach **B6295**. Turn **L**.
❼ At woods of **Parkgates Burn** take **L** of 2 waymarked paths. Over stile it climbs fields towards **L** of 2 farmhouses on skyline – **Low Scotch Hall**. It turns **R** then **L** to round farmhouse, now following **L** field edge high above valley.
❽ On reaching woods of **Prospect Hill**, turn **R** through animal pens then along enclosed path to farm of **Finney Hill Green**. Turn **L** beyond house and continue along **L** edge of 3 fields.
❾ Modern housing estate at edge of **Allendale Town** comes into view and path heads north, parallel to houses. In last field it descends towards more mature housing and enters estate through little ginnel. Go past playground and out on to main road in village.

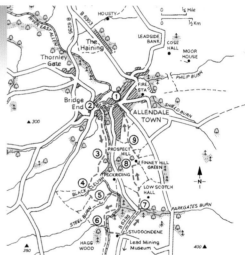

ALLENHEADS *HIGH ON BYERHOPE BANK*

5 miles (8km) 3hrs **Ascent:** 656ft (200m)
Paths: Stony tracks and generally well-defined paths, 3 stiles
Suggested map: aqua3 OS Explorer OL31 North Pennines
Grid reference: NY 860453
Parking: In Allenheads village centre

Taking to the high moors of Hexhamshire.
❶ From front of **heritage centre** head east to B6295. Cross to follow lane ('Rookhope'). This climbs steeply out of valley between spruce plantations. At sharp **L-H** bend beyond **Eastend Reservoir**, leave road and go over step stile on path ('Rookhope Road'). Trackless, but guided by wall on **R**, path climbs westwards across 2 fields of pasture and over 2 stiles.
❷ After cutting corner, path rejoins road and arrives at an old quarry high on moors. Turn **L** along road for a few paces, then follow stony track at **R-H** side. This traces moorland rim above **Allenheads**.
❸ After passing quarry and huge cairn, track turns **R** then meanders around **Middle Rigg** before turning sharp **L** to pass old ruins of **Byerhope** hamlet.
❹ Beyond **Byerhope Farm**, at **High Haddock Stones**, track swings **R** again, away from valley. Here you leave it. A waymaker post, 1st of many, signs your bridleway. This clear grooved grassy path makes

circuitous descent into Allendale, where you'll see quarries of Swinhope and **Coatenhill Reservoir**. After passing old quarry workings, bridleway descends to gate by terraced cottages on main valley road.
❺ Across road go ahead, down minor lane, which fords **River East Allen**; use footbridge on **R** to cross.
❻ Where road bends **R** uphill at **Peasmeadows**, leave it and go down cottage's drive, beyond which riverside path begins. Ignore 1st bridge across river and stay with path past **Burnfoot**. Go across footbridge over **Middlehope Burn**, then continue though pleasing little ravine of heather and bilberry. As it approaches lead mining spoil heaps, path gets sketchy. The easiest course is to climb to brow of bank on **R** and follow this to road near **Slag Hill**.
❼ Turn **L** down road to recross East Allen, then turn **R** at T-junction. This quiet lane leads back into **Allenheads**, past hamlet of **Dirt Pot** and old Presbyterian chapel.

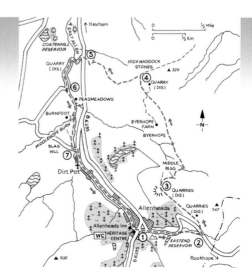

901 GLENTROOL *The Battle of Independence*

5 miles (8km) 2hrs **Ascent:** 151ft (46m)
Paths: Forest trails, metalled roads, 1 stile
Suggested map: aqua3 OS Explorer 318 Galloway Forest Park North
Grid reference: NX 396791
Parking: Entrance to Caldons Campsite

Forest trails lead to a famous battlefield.

❶ Leave car park and then follow obvious waymarkers for Loch Trool Trail. Cross bridge over Water of Trool to enter **Caldons Campsite**, then take **L** turn on to footpath that runs along banks of river. Cross over bridge and go past some toilet blocks.

❷ Follow this well waymarked trail through campsite picnic area, across green bridge and then head **R** across grassy area to pick up trail as it heads uphill and into forest.

❸ Keep on this path uphill and through clearing, then go through kissing gate and re-enter woodland. Continue along southern side of **Loch Trool** until you reach interpretation board near loch end. This marks the spot where Robert the Bruce and his army lured the superior English forces to a well-planned ambush and routed them. Using a small part of his force as bait, positioned here, he concealed the bulk of his men on the slopes above. The English were forced to

dismount and follow in single file and when they were at their most vulnerable the Scots blocked the path and hurled boulders down on them.

❹ Follow path from here, leaving woodland and heading downhill and turn to **L**, briefly joining **Southern Upland Way**. Turn **L** and go through two gates and over wooden bridge. Cross bridge over **Gairland Burn** and continue ahead. Eventually reaching bridge over **Buchan Burn**, cross over and take path to **L**, branching off uphill.

❺ Follow this to top and **Bruce's Stone**, which was raised to commemorate victory at the Battle of Glentrool, the first victory in the Independence Wars. From here, look across the clear waters of the loch to the tree-clad hills opposite, which is one of the finest views in Scotland. Follow track past stone then turn **L** on to narrow road, head through car park and keep going until you reach waymarker on **L** which leads to forest trail and take this to return to car park.

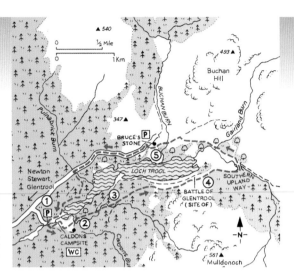

902 DEVIL'S BEEF TUB *A Hearty Walk*

4½ miles (7.2km) 2hrs **Ascent:** 1,076ft (328m)
Paths: Grassy moorlands and firm farm tracks
Suggested map: aqua3 OS Explorer 330 Moffat & St Mary's Loch
Grid reference: NT 055127
Parking: By forest access gate

Around Devil's Beef Tub near Moffat.

❶ From forest gateway on **A701**, go through wooden gate on R-H side, then climb wooden fence ahead. Ascend grassy slope of Annanhead Hill, keeping to R of 2 wire fences as you walk to **trig point** on summit.

❷ Bear **R** over Peat Knowe, keeping wall and fence to your **L**. Follow path down grassy slope to head of gully, where path meets wall. Walk to other side of gully, then turn **R** and pick your way to edge to enjoy views over **Devil's Beef Tub**.

❸ Follow narrow path as it continues to descend, walking over grass and bracken with valley views. Eventually reach area of pasture, in front of **plantation**. Walk to 2 gates; go through metal gate **R**.

❹ Continue downhill on grassy bank, then go through gate and along rough track, swinging **L** round wall of plantation. Go through gate behind red-brick house, then continue towards farm buildings. Walk

between buildings on to tarmac track and towards timber barn, continuing ahead to join farm road.

❺ Follow farm road along valley bottom. Keep an eye out for small area of undulating ground on your **R** – it's all that remains of an ancient settlement. Eventually reach **Ericstane** farm.

❻ Turn **R**, through gate, then head uphill on stony track, with woodland on **L**. Soon pass area of pronounced banks and ditches – another reminder of former settlement – then reach house. Shortly after farmhouse, go through gate; turn sharp **R**, following track as it runs by stone wall. Eventually reach main road, cross over (with care) and go through gate.

❼ Continue over **Ericstane Hill**. Bear **R** and follow track north round far side of hill. Track is indistinct in places, covered in grass and reeds. Keep to **L** of summit, walking around brow of hill to rejoin road. Turn **R** here to visit **Covenanter memorial**, or turn **L** to return to start.

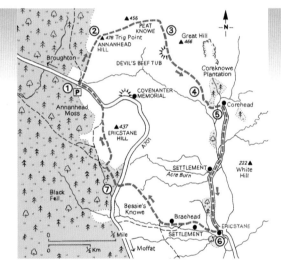

903 LANGHOLM *A Poet's Passions*

3 miles (4.8km) 1hr 30min **Ascent:** 919ft (280m)
Paths: Firm hill tracks and tarmac roads
Suggested map: aqua3 OS Explorer 323 Eskdale & Castle O'er Forest
Grid reference: NY 364845
Parking: On main street in Langholm

An exhilarating climb is followed by a gentle stroll past Hugh MacDiarmid's memorial.

❶ From **post office** on main street, turn **L** and take path next to it that runs uphill. Go through gate at top. Follow grassy track that continues ahead to green seat beside **Whita Well**, natural spring.

❷ Take track just to **L** of seat, running steeply up hill. Follow track as it runs under line of pylons and up to top of **Whita Hill**. Stone steps take you up to the monument, a 100ft (30m) obelisk commemorating Sir John Malcolm, a once-famous soldier, diplomat and scholar. From here you'll get great views – and on a clear day you can see the Lake District peaks.

❸ From monument, walk down few paces to join wide footpath that runs in front of it, then turn **R**. It's easy walking now, following clear track downhill with heather on slopes to either side. Eventually reach unusual metal sculpture on L-H side. The sculpture, which is meant to resemble an open book, was

created by Jake Harvey and is a **memorial** to Hugh MacDiarmid. There's a small cairn there too.

❹ Go through metal gate by sculpture and turn **L**. Now simply follow road as it winds downhill – it's quite a long stretch but it's fairly quiet. Go back under line of electricity pylons then, just after you pass copse on your R-H side, take track on **L**.

❺ Follow this footpath, which is lined with wild grasses and thistles – it's a good place to see butterflies in summer. Eventually footpath becomes less distinct and runs through small boggy patch. After this you soon return to gate that you reached on your outward journey.

❻ Turn **R**, through gate, walk downhill, past golf course and into town. It's a good place to see red clover lining the path, which really attracts bees. Eventually reach main street in **Langholm**, with **hotel** ahead.

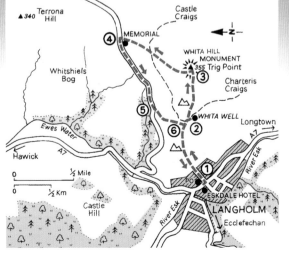

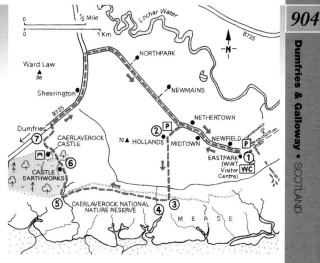

Dumfries & Galloway

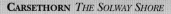

CAERLAVEROCK *THE SOLWAY MERSES*

5¼ miles (8.4km) 2hrs 30min **Ascent:** 82ft (25m) ⚠
Paths: Country lanes, farm tracks and salt marsh, 1 stile
Suggested map: aqua3 OS Explorer 314 Solway Firth
Grid reference: NY 051656 **Parking:** Car park at Wildfowl and Wetlands Trust Reserve

An ancient fortress and a nature reserve.

1 Exit car park and turn **R** on to farm road. Follow this past farms of **Newfield** and **Midtown** then turn **L** and go past bungalow and houses. Just before farm of **Hollands** there is waymarker pointing to car park, on **R**, and straight ahead for walks. Go straight ahead, continue to farm steading and turn **L**.

2 Go through gate and on to farm track. This stretches into distance and has high hedges on both sides. Continue along this track between hedges and on, over overgrown section, to fence. Cross by stile and turn **R** at signpost ('**Caerlaverock National Nature Reserve**').

3 Sign here informs visitors that regulated wildfowling (shooting) takes place between 1 September and 20 February. Follow rough track through grass along edge of **merse** in direction of arrow on footpath waymarker post. Path can be very boggy at all times and grass will be high in summer.

4 Cross small wooden bridge, electric fence covered with insulated piping and another small bridge. Path splits at several points and meanders back and forth, but all lines of path rejoin and you'll end up at same place which ever one you take.

5 Eventually tumbledown wire-and-post fence will appear on R-H side. Follow this fence towards wood, passing through overgrown area and then bear **R**, through gate and into field. Walk to **L** around perimeter of this field, past cottages, and then turn **L** through gate to emerge on to farm track, passing sign pointing way for **Caerlaverock Castle** and into castle grounds.

6 Follow road past old castle (don't miss information boards) and go through wood with nature trail information boards to **Caerlaverock Castle**.

7 At far end go through arch and then continue to T-junction with country lane. Turn **R** and continue for about 1 mile (1.6km) then turn **R** on to another lane ('Wildfowl and Wetlands Reserve'). Continue past farms of **Northpark**, **Newmains** and **Nethertown** and then back to car park at **Eastpark**.

CARSETHORN *THE SOLWAY SHORE*

5½ miles (8.8km) 2hrs 30min **Ascent:** 82ft (25m) ⚠
Paths: Rocky seashore, woodland tracks and country roads
Suggested map: aqua3 OS Explorer 313 Dumfries & Dalbeattie, New Abbey
Grid reference: NX 993598
Parking: Car park by beach at Carsethorn

Visit the birthplace of the 'father of the American Navy'.

1 From car park head down to beach and turn **R**. Continue along shore for 2 miles (3.2km). Beach here is sandy and may be strewn with driftwood, but if tide is in you will be walking over more rocky ground.

2 After you reach **The House on the Shore**, beside beach on your **R**, headland juts out and you should look for track heading uphill on **R**. At top of hill well-defined track heads alongside stone wall.

3 Look for fainter track leading off to **L**, which descends steeply to arrive at beach beside natural rock arch called **Thirl Stane**. You can go through the arch to the sea if the tide is in, although if the tide is out, the sea will be far off in the distance.

4 Continue along rocks on pebble shore and up grassy bank to car park. Exit car park on to lane. Continue on lane past **Powillimount**. Turn **R** at lodge house on R-H side and walk along estate road to

cottage birthplace of John Paul Jones.

5 There are picnic tables here and a **museum**. Continue along road past gates to **Arbigland** on to road ('No vehicular traffic'). Follow road as it turns **R** and along side of Arbigland Estate buildings.

6 When road turns **L** at cottage, go **R** on to dirt track. Continue until it emerges on to surfaced road next to **Tallowquhairn** to your **R**. Take road away from farm, turning sharply **L** around houses, then **R** and continue to T-junction.

7 Turn **R** and follow road round to **L**. Follow long straight road as far as **R** turn to **South Carse**. Go along farm road and straight through farm steading as far as you can, then turn **L**.

8 To return to shore again, walk along footpath passing brightly coloured caravan and rear of cottages. Look for narrow track heading downhill to **R** allowing access to beach. Turn **L** and walk along beach to car park.

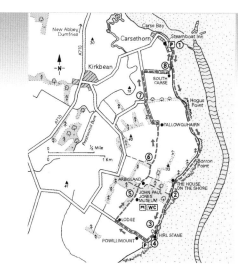

NEW ABBEY *TO CRIFFEL*

3¾ miles (6km) 3hrs **Ascent:** 1,686ft (514m) ⚠
Paths: Forest road, rough hill and wood tracks, 1 stile
Suggested map: aqua3 OS Explorer 313 Dumfries & Dalbeattie
Grid reference: NX 971634
Parking: Car park at Ardwall farm

The 13th-century love story of the Lady Devorgilla, set forever in stone.

1 From car park head towards **Ardwall** farm then go through gate on **L**. Turn **R** after 70yds (64m) then head towards hill on track between dry-stone walls. When road curves **L**, in front of wood, take track off to **R**. (Criffel Walk sign has fallen from its post.)

2 Follow well-trodden track uphill and through trees following course of **Craigrockall Burn**. Path narrows in places and ground is uneven with large boulders to climb over or around. Many trees have been felled here and it is not long before you emerge from woods on to open hillside.

3 At T-junction with forest road, keep ahead to pick up trail on other side and continue uphill. Ground can be boggy, even in summer, and care needs to be taken. Cross another forest road and eventually reach fence marking where tree line used to be. Cross stile here and veer to **L**, heading towards summit of **Criffel**.

4 From the OS triangulation pillar on the summit of Criffel are views across Solway to the south to England and the hills of the Lake District; a little to the right of that is the Isle of Man, while the coast of Ireland is visible to the west. On good day the summit is an ideal place for a picnic. When you've enjoyed view head roughly northwest from cairn, then go north crossing over rough ground towards broad ridge that runs from **Criffel** to neighbouring hill of **Knochendoch**. When you intersect narrow footpath turn **R**, head downhill on it then continue, ascending again now, to reach summit of **Knochendoch**.

5 From summit cairn head east and go downhill. In summer, when the heather is particularly thick, the going can be fairly tough and you'll have to proceed slowly and with caution. Make for fence that runs across hill in front of you. Turn **R** here and follow it back to stile. Cross stile and retrace your steps to bottom of hill.

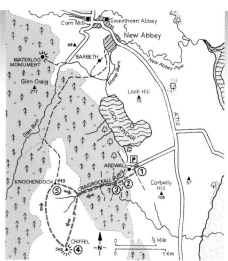

907 GLENKILN *Outdoor Sculptures*

4 miles (6.4km) 2hrs 30min **Ascent:** 312ft (95m)
Paths: Country roads, farm tracks, open hillside
Suggested map: aqua3 OS Explorer 321 Nithsdale & Dumfries
Grid reference: NX 839784
Parking: Car park in front of statue of John the Baptist

Discover works of art in this unique countryside setting.
1 From car park in front of statue *John the Baptist* return to main road and turn **R**. Cross cattle grid then turn **R** and go past statue to **Marglolly Burn**. Turn **L** and walk along bank towards **Cornlee Bridge**. Just before bridge turn **L** and head back to road. Henry Moore's *Standing Figure* is before you at junction with farm road.
2 Turn **L** and head back along main road. Just before entrance to **Margreig** farm on R is muddy track running across field to gate in dry-stone wall. Head up and through gate then keep straight ahead, uphill and towards telephone pole. At pole veer **L** and follow track uphill. **Glenkiln Cross** should now be visible ahead.
3 There are several footpaths and tracks available. Take one that is closest to large tree in front of you. Cross burn at tree then take path that skirts to **L** of it. Veer **R** and head for high ground. Once **cross** comes

into view again head directly towards it.
4 From **cross** turn to face **Glenkiln Reservoir** then head downhill towards telephone pole. Go through gate in fence at bottom of hill and turn **R** on to road. Short distance along here farm track leads uphill to **R**. Go through gate and on to it. To your R on hillside is Henry Moore's *King and Queen*.
5 Continue on this track. Go through gate, pass small wooded area on your R and then bare hillside until you spot small stand of Scots pine on your **L**. Leave road at this point and continue to trees and Epstein's *Visitation*. Return to road and continue to end where you go through gate, over bridge, then turn **L** on to road.
6 Go downhill for ½ mile (800m), crossing cattle grid. Just before end of conifer plantation on L, look out for Moore's *Two Piece Reclining Figure No 1* on your R. Follow road all way downhill from here, turn **L** at junction and continue to car park.

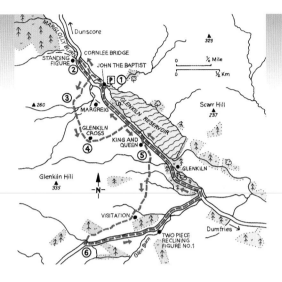

908 MONIAIVE *The Glasgow Boys*

5 miles (8km) 3hrs **Ascent:** 295ft (90m)
Paths: Dirt roads, hill tracks, forest road and country lane
Suggested map: aqua3 OS Explorers 321 Nithsdale & Dumfries, Thornhill; 328 Sanquhar & New Cumnock, Muirkirk
Grid reference: NX 780910 (on Explorer 328) **Parking:** Moniaive village car park

The village that inspired the Glasgow Boys.
1 Exit car park and turn **R**. At nearby T-junction turn **R** and go over pedestrian bridge, beside garage, to enter Moniaive High Street at **George Hotel**. Walk along High Street to Market Cross of Moniaive, pass it then turn **L** and cross road. Turn **R** at other side and head up Ayr Street, passing public toilets.
2 The imposing building on the right with a clock tower is the former village schoolmaster's house. Continue up Ayr Street passing park on R and wooden garages on L. Take next **R** on to narrow lane. Continue to end of lane and, at T-junction turn **R**.
3 Pass modern bungalow on L, then field, then turn **L** on to dirt road at end of field. Cross bridge and continue up road to **Bardennoch**. When road curves R to enter grounds of house, go straight on and follow road, which goes up side of wood and uphill.
4 At end of woodland section go through gate and continue uphill on road. Cross fence and then at top,

near ruin of **Upper Bardennoch**, go through another gate. From here continue to climb towards stand of Scots pine, circle them keeping them on your R and continue to summit of **Bardennoch Hill**.
5 From summit keep going in same direction towards woodland. Wall should be running beside you to R. Head slightly downhill to corner where this wall meets one running in front of woodland. Cross wall and go on to forest road.
6 Turn **R** and follow road downhill through several gates until it goes through final gate, at T-junction with country lane, where you turn **R**. At next T-junction, **L** turn will soon take you to hamlet of **Tynron** which is worth visiting. Otherwise turn **R** again.
7 Follow this road past **Dalmakerran** farm then uphill and through hazel wood. Continue uphill passing cottage on R then, further along, another house. Road starts to go downhill again on to **Dunreggan Brae**. At bottom of hill re-enter **Moniaive**; turn **R** into car park.

909 WANLOCKHEAD *Scotland's Highest Village*

3¾ miles (6km) 3hrs **Ascent:** 525ft (160m)
Paths: Footpaths, hill tracks, hillside and old railway lines, 1 stile
Suggested map: aqua3 OS Explorer 329 Lowther Hills, Sanquhar & Leadhills
Grid reference: NX 873129
Parking: Museum of Lead Mining car park

Discover the secrets of lead and gold mining.
1 With museum to your back turn **L** and join **Southern Upland Way**. Head uphill on steps then, at top, cross to stone building with large white door. Turn **R** on to rough road, cross main road and take public footpath to Enterkine Pass. Follow this until you reach the front of white house.
2 Turn **L** on to an old railway. Follow this, cross road then go through long cutting to reach **Glengonnar Station** then follow narrow path that runs along L side of railway tracks.
3 Eventually path runs on to rough road and in distance see 2 terraced houses. Where telephone wires intersect route turn **L** at pole on L-H side and follow line of fence down to sheep pens. Turn **R** at end of pens and walk out to main road.
4 Turn **R** then almost immediately **L** on to hill road. Walk until road bears sharp R and dirt track forks L. Turn **L** on to track and continue to gate. Cross

over then veer **L** on to faint track. Follow track downhill to where it comes close to corner of fence on your L.
5 Cross fence and go straight ahead on very faint track picking your way through heather. Eventually, as track begins to look more like recognisable path, reach fork. Go **R** and cross flank of hill passing through disused tips.
6 Path here is little more than series of sheep tracks and may disappear altogether, but don't worry. Ahead is large conical **spoil heap**, and provided you keep heading towards it, you know you will be going in right direction.
7 Towards end of hill track heads **L**, starts to descend, then passes behind row of cottages. Head downhill, after cottages to join road. Turn **L** and continue past **Glencrieff cottages** then turn **R**, leaving road and heading downhill again. Cross bridge and climb up on to **Southern Upland Way**. Turn **L** along it and follow this route back to car park.

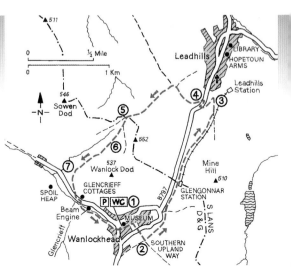

Loch Enoch *Cycling on the Merrick*

9 miles (14.5km) 5hrs **Ascent:** 2,339ft (713m)	

Paths: Hill tracks, section to Loch Enoch can be very boggy, 1 stile
Suggested map: aqua3 OS Explorer 318 Galloway Forest North
Grid reference: NX 415804
Parking: Bruce's Stone car park

Follow in the cycle tracks of Davie Bell.

1 From car park at **Bruce's Stone** head east along narrow road, and across **Buchan Bridge**. Continue short distance then turn **L** and go uphill to cross stile. Follow path along wall, then veer **R** and head uphill to rejoin wall. Go through gate and turn **R** on to path. Follow this up valley of **Gairland Burn** with **Buchan Hill** on your **L**.

2 To your **L** is ridge of **Buchan Hill** and to **R** is **White Brae** and to far side of that is **Rig of the Jarkness**. Do not cross the **Gairland** but keep going on path to reach **Loch Valley**, skirting it to west and then continue beside **Mid Burn** to reach **Loch Neldricken**.

3 Head for far west corner of loch to find infamous **Murder Hole** featured by S R Crockett in his novel *The Raiders* (1894). The story is based on a local legend that unwary travellers were robbed on these hills and their bodies disposed of in the loch.

4 From **Murder Hole** head north, crossing burn and then wall. Pass to east of **Ewe Rig** and tiny **Loch Arron** and eventually reach south side of **Loch Enoch**. Don't worry if the track vanishes or becomes indistinct, just keep heading northwards and you'll eventually reach the loch.

5 As you approach **Loch Enoch** you will see outline of Mullwharchar beyond it and to **R**. When you reach loch go **L** and then cross another wall. The slope, which is in front of you, is **Redstone Rig** and although you have 1,000ft (305m) to climb it is an enjoyable ascent and not particularly taxing.

6 From summit cairn of **Merrick** head downhill towards narrow ridge called **Neive of the Spit** to reach summit of **Benyellary**, Hill of the Eagle. From here follow footpath downhill beside dry-stone wall then turn **L** and keep going downhill, into forest, to reach bothy at **Culsharg**. From there continue downhill to return to car park.

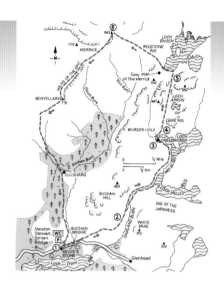

Wigtown *The Killing Times*

4 miles (6.4km) 3hrs **Ascent:** 98ft (30m)	

Paths: Roads, old railway tracks and pavements
Suggested map: aqua3 OS Explorer 311 Wigtown, Whithorn & The Machars
Grid reference: NX 439547
Parking: At Wigtown harbour

Visit the memorial to two women drowned at the stake for their religion.

1 Leave car park, turn **R** and head uphill on narrow country lane, Harbour Road. House on **L** near top of road was former station house for **Wigtown**. Just before it is farm gate on **L**. Go through it and on to farm track.

2 Follow track to where it goes through another gate then veer **R** and climb up old railway embankment. This has a good grassy surface. Proceed along embankment and through gate.

3 Wall across track will stop you where former railway bridge carried track across **River Bladnoch**. Turn **R** and go down side of embankment and cross fence into field. Veer **R** and head across field to far corner then go through gate on to main road.

4 Turn **L** and walk through **Bladnoch**. At junction by roundabout, cross road to enter **Bladnoch Distillery** car park. After visiting distillery head back out of car

park and turn **L** at roundabout. Continue along this road (B7005) for 1 mile (1.6km) to crossroads.

5 Turn **R** on to **B733** and walk along it to **Wigtown**. At centre of town bear **L** round square and head towards large and impressive former county buildings. Pass them on your **R**, then church and war memorial on your **L** and continue downhill. Eventually turn **R** into car park for **Martyrs' Memorial**.

6 Walk through car park; turn **L** and make your way to bird hide at end of path. From here retrace your steps to car park and continue on path leading to **Martyrs' Memorial**. Turn **L**; walk over sands of wooden causeway to reach the memorial erected to mark the spot where the two women were drowned.

7 Return to path and turn **L**. Go through kissing gate then another gate, which is slightly below level you are walking on and to **L**. At end of path go through another gate in front of old station house, turn **L** on to Harbour Road and return to car park.

Wells of the Rees *Ancient Stone Domes*

6¼ miles (10.1km) 3hrs 30min **Ascent:** 558ft (170m)	

Paths: Forest roads, forest track, very rough ground
Suggested map: aqua3 OS Explorer 310 Glenluce & Kirkcowan
Grid reference: NX 260735
Parking: Near Derry farm

A tough walk on the Southern Upland Way.

1 Cross cattle grid; head west along Southern Upland Way (SUW) on well-surfaced forest road. Pass **Loch Derry**, on **R** in just under 1 mile (1.6km) then continue on forest road, passing signpost on **L** to **Linn's Tomb**.

2 Follow road as it curves **R** and then, following SUW markerpost, turn **L**, leave road and head uphill. It's rather steep climb, on fairly well-trodden path with plenty of waymarkers.

3 Cross forest road and continue on uphill path heading to summit of **Craig Airie Fell**. Reach summit at Ordnance Survey trig point.

4 From trig point, continue on well-marked path towards waymarker on horizon. Turn **L** at waymarker and head downhill on footpath that twists and turns to waymarker near bottom. Turn **R** here on to another obvious trail and continue to edge of forest.

5 SUW now follows forest ride. Short distance

along reach clearing with **cairn** on your L-H side. Keep ahead following direction arrows on waymarkers to next clearing where sign points **L** to **Wells of the Rees**. Turn **L**; head downhill, through bracken, across ruined dry-stone wall, through bracken again and then gap in wall. It is more difficult to find wells in summer, when bracken is thick. First 2 wells are on **R** as you come through gap and other is off to **L**.

6 Retrace your steps from here to signpost and turn **R**. Retrace your steps to edge of forest and turn **R**, following edge of forest and burn, slightly downhill to fence. Cross this and head roughly west across rough and boggy ground towards **Craigmoddie Fell**.

7 Climb to highest point then look to your **L** to **Loch Derry** then, to **R** of it, **Derry** farm. Head in straight line for **Derry** farm then drop down off fell and pick up path heading towards **Loch Derry**.

8 Follow this to patch of trees, through gate and on to forest road. Turn **R** and return to **Derry** farm.

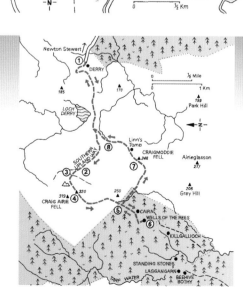

913 PORT LOGAN *FICTIONAL RONANSAY*

3 miles (4.8km) 2hrs Ascent: 492ft (150m)
Paths: Shoreline, country lanes and hill tracks, 1 stile
Suggested map: aqua3 OS Explorer 309 Stranraer & The Rhins
Grid reference: NX 097411
Parking: Public car park on road to Logan Fish Pond

A walk around a picturesque fishing village where everything is not as it seems.

❶ From car park go across wooden walkway, down some steps on to beach and turn **L** to walk along beach. When you reach start of village climb on to road in front of **Port Logan Inn**. Turn **R** and then continue along main street, passing war memorial to reach **village hall**. In the television series, *Two Thousand Acres of Sky*, the village hall features as a school, and has a school sign fixed to the front. There's also a timetable for Caledonian MacBrayne ferries displayed on the notice-board on the wall. Opposite the village hall is a small but picturesque harbour with a rather unusual lighthouse. Nowadays, when it is not in use as a film location, **Port Logan** harbour is used only by a few pleasure craft.

❷ This was a thriving fishing port in the past and the **pier** once again looks as though it is busy, festooned with fishing gear, gas bottles and sacks of coal.

Although they are all real, they are only there as props. Move away from harbour area and go along road to farm of **Muldaddie**.

❸ Just before farm turn **L** on to old hill track and head uphill. Near the top look back downhill for a magnificent view back to the village and across **Port Logan Bay** to the Mull of Logan. Track is heavily overgrown here, and is blocked by barrier made from gates, but this can easily be crossed by stile at side.

❹ Continue along track to T-junction. Turn **L**, go through gate and head along farm road to **Cowans farm**. Continue through farm steading and reach end of road at T-junction. Turn **L** on to **B7065** and then head downhill.

❺ Follow this winding road back to Port Logan then go back on to beach, turn **R** and retrace your steps to car park. From here you can continue along rough road to **Logan Fish Pond**. It's right at end on **L** and is by only building there.

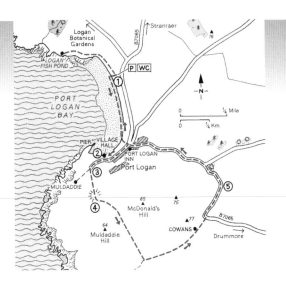

914 SELKIRK *TO THE WILDS OF AFRICA*

3 miles (4.8km) 1hr 40min Ascent: 131ft (40m)
Paths: Riverside paths and woodland tracks, town streets, 4 stiles
Suggested map: aqua3 OS Explorer 338 Galashiels, Selkirk & Montrose
Grid reference: NT 469286
Parking: West Port car park in Selkirk

A gentle walk by Ettrick Water, laced with memories of the great explorer Mungo Park.

❶ From Park's statue, walk to Market Place, go **L** down Ettrick Terrace, **L** at church, then sharp **R** down Forest Road. Follow this downhill, cutting off corners using steps, to Mill Street. Go **R**, then **L** on to Buccleuch Road. Turn **R** following signs for riverside walk. Go across **Victoria Park** to join tarmac track.

❷ Turn **L** and walk by river; join road and continue to cross bridge. Turn **L** along Ettrickhaugh Road, passing row of cottages on **L**. Just past them turn **L**. Cross tiny footbridge then take indistinct track on **L**. Walk to river bank. Turn **R**.

❸ Follow path along river margin; it's eroded in places so watch your feet. In spring and summer your way is sprinkled with wild flowers. Eventually join wider track and bear **L**. Follow this until you reach weir and salmon ladder. Turn **R** to cross tiny bridge.

❹ Immediately after this go **L** and continue walking

alongside river until you reach point at which Yarrow Water joins Ettrick Water. Retrace your steps for about 100yds (91m) then turn **L** at crossing of tracks.

❺ Your route now goes through woods, then cross bridge by weir again. Take footpath **L**; follow grassy track round meadow until you reach **mill** buildings.

❻ Bear **R** (but don't cross bridge) and continue, walking with mill lade (small canal) on **L**. Where path splits, take track on **L** to follow straight, concrete path beside water to reach **fish farm** (you'll smell it).

❼ Walk around buildings, then bear **L** to continue following mill lade. Go **L** over footbridge, then **R**, passing cottages again. At main road go **R** to reach bridge. Don't cross bridge but join footpath on **L**.

❽ Follow footpath as it goes past sports ground, then skirts housing estate. Continue until you reach pedestrian footbridge on your R-H side, where you cross over river, bear **R**, then retrace your footsteps back over **Victoria Park** and uphill to Market Place.

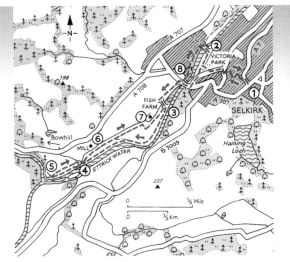

915 ETTRICK *GOING THE WHOLE HOGG*

4½ miles (7.2km) 2hrs 30min Ascent: 689ft (210m)
Paths: Narrow hill tracks, moorland and waymarked trail, 4 stiles
Suggested map: aqua3 OS Explorer 330 Moffat & St Mary's Loch
Grid reference: NT 265144
Parking: By village hall on minor road west of B709

In the footsteps of a local poet.

❶ From parking place by **village hall**, turn **L** along road past **monument to James Hogg** and up to **war memorial**. Turn **R** and walk past church, then take track that bears sharp **L** past farm buildings. Go through metal gate, then fork **L** at right of way sign.

❷ Walk uphill, following track through another gate and up grassy slope. Keep monument on hill above to your **L**. Follow narrow track, passing a circular **sheepfold** on your **L** and 2 on opposite hillside on **R**.

❸ Path now skirts **Craig Hill**, roughly above **Kirk Burn**. Look for another circular **sheepfold** on your **L**, then 2 more away to **R**. At this point track disappears and ground becomes boggy underfoot. Don't take track that bears **L** but maintain direction, heading for low ground ahead.

❹ Keep walking over moorland – passing lone fence post on your **L**, and circular, stone **sheepfold**, also on L-H side but further away. Continue towards **The**

Slunk, heavily eroded burn, from where you get great views back up Ettrick Valley.

❺ Scramble down banks of **The Slunk**, and cross over water – there are some rocks to help you across, but be careful. Your way then takes you over to meet wire fence. Bear **L** along line of fence to metal fingerpost ('Riskinhope').

❻ At fingerpost, cross stile and continue descending along other side of fence to meet **Southern Upland Way**. Cross back over fence at wooden stile, then bear **L** on wide path as it runs down into Ettrick Valley. Pass 2 well-maintained **sheepfolds** along way, and come to stone stile.

❼ Nip over this stile to enter pasture, then go down to meet road at bottom L-H corner. Cross another stone stile here and drop into lane opposite **Scabcleuch** farm. Turn **L** again over bridge and walk back to **war memorial**. Walk past **monument** and return to parking place at start.

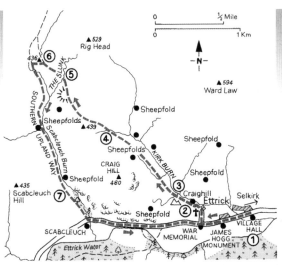

Borders

NEWCASTLETON *REMEMBERING THE REIVERS*

5 miles (8km) **2hrs** **Ascent:** 689ft (210m)
Paths: Quiet byroads and farm tracks, one rough climb
Suggested map: aqua3 OS Explorer 324 Liddesdale & Kershope Forest
Grid reference: NY 483875
Parking: Douglas Square

Through borderlands where cattle raiding was once a part of everyday life.

❶ From Douglas Square, with your back to **Grapes Hotel**, walk along Wyitchester Street (or any other street opposite) and go down to **Liddel Water**. Turn **R**, walk along riverbank and join path downstream to bridge. Turn **L** at top of steps and cross bridge.

❷ After 100yds (91m), turn **R** and follow **Brampton Road**, passing static caravans on either side. Eventually pass old **sawmill** with corrugated iron roof and reach **Tweeden Burn** bridge. Cross bridge and walk uphill, turn **R** and join metalled track that leads to **Mangerton** farm. Continue on this road until you near farm buildings.

❸ Turn **L**, then sharp **R**, and walk down on to bed of old railway line, which has joined you from **R**. Follow line as it leads past remains of **Mangerton Tower**, in a field to your **R**, and continue until you reach **Clerkleap** cottage.

❹ Turn **L** immediately after cottage, then go through wooden gate to join rough track. This leads through woodland and on, uphill, to join road by **Sorbietrees** farm. Turn **R** and walk along road, past farm, to small stand of conifers on **L**. Turn **L** through gate.

❺ Bear **R** now and head up **L-H** side of trees. Walk past top of wood and former **quarry**, to dry-stone wall. Turn **L** and follow wall uphill, crossing it about 437yds (400m) ahead at a convenient R-angle bend.

❻ It's a bit of a scramble now, over bracken and scree, to reach summit – great views. Known locally as Caerba Hill, this was once the site of a prehistoric settlement. Retrace your steps to reach road again, then turn **R** and walk back to **Sorbietrees** farm.

❼ At farm, continue on main road as it bears **R** and follow it back over Tweeden bridge and up to Holm Bridge. Cross bridge and walk straight on for 100yds (91m), then turn **R** on to B6357 and walk back to village square via little **heritage centre**.

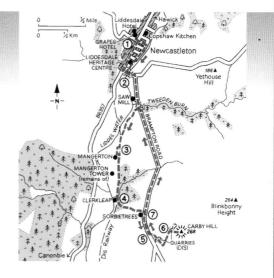

BROUGHTON *JOHN BUCHAN COUNTRY*

5 miles (8km) **2hrs 30min** **Ascent:** 1,575ft (480m)
Paths: Hill tracks and grassy paths, 1 stile
Suggested map: aqua3 OS Explorer 336 Biggar & Broughton
Grid reference: NT 119374
Parking: Parking in front of cottage past Broughton Place Art Gallery

A lovely walk through John Buchan country.

❶ From parking place, go through gate and follow obvious, grassy track that runs in front of **cottage**. Soon pass a copse on L-H side and then pass **Duck Pond Plantation**, also on L-H side. Track becomes slightly rougher now and you cross wooden rollers to help you over burn.

❷ Your track continues ahead, over larger burn and past feathery carpets of heather and bracken – listen for skylarks in summer. Continue walking and path will soon level out and lead you past deep gully on R-H side. Follow track until it bends, after which you come to meeting of tracks.

❸ Take track that bears **L** and head for dip that lies between 2 hills – **Clover Law** on L and **Broomy Side** in front. You should just be able to spot fence on skyline. Make for that fence and, as you near it, eventually spot gate, next to which is wooden stile.

❹ Cross stile, then turn **R** and follow fence line. You

soon get superb views to **L**. Continue following fence and walk up track until you reach **trig point** on **Broughton Heights** – final ascent's a bit of a puff – but it's thankfully not too long.

❺ Now retrace your steps to reach stile again, nip over it, but this time turn **R** and follow narrow track that climbs **Clover Law**. Continue walking in same direction, following fence line as it runs along top of ridge. When you near end of ridge, keep your eyes peeled for track that leads down to your **L**.

❻ Follow track as it runs down between 2 **plantations**, roughly in direction of **cottage**, in quite a steep descent. At bottom you come to old wall and burn, which you cross, then continue ahead to reach main track.

❼ Turn **R** here and walk past little **cottage** again, through gate and back to your car. If you want to visit **Broughton Place** and its **art gallery**, just continue walking down track to reach house on your **L**.

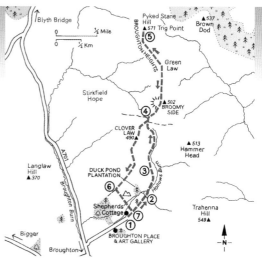

PEEBLES *BIRTHPLACE OF CHAMBERS*

3½ miles (5.7km) **1hr 20min** **Ascent:** 295ft (90m)
Paths: Waymarked riverside paths and metalled tracks
Suggested map: aqua3 OS Explorer 337 Peebles & Innerleithen
Grid reference: NT 250402 **Parking:** Kingsmeadows Road car park, Peebles

Discover the founders of an encyclopaedia on this lovely walk.

❶ From Kingsmeadows car park, turn **R** and cross bridge. Turn **L** at **Bridge Hotel** and walk down slope, past swimming pool, to river. Cross small footbridge, go up steps, turn **L** and follow riverside track to pass white bridge and children's play area.

❷ Continue following obvious path and cross burn via little bridge, after which path becomes a bit more rugged. Now enter woods, going through kissing gate and following signs ('Tweed Walk'). Eventually leave woods and reach **Neidpath Castle** on R-H side.

❸ From castle continue walking by river to go through another kissing gate. Soon come on to higher ground with great view of old railway bridge spanning water in front of you. After another kissing gate, maintain direction to reach red sandstone bridge.

❹ Go up to **R** of bridge to join old railway line. Maintain direction and continue following Tweed Walk. Follow this disused track to reach **Manor Bridge**.

❺ Turn **L** and cross bridge. Take turning on **L**, ('Tweed Walk'). You're now on metalled track that winds uphill – stop and look behind you for views of Borders landscape, with rolling hills and the busy Tweed. Continue to track on **L** that then leads into woods, ('public footpath to **Peebles** by **Southpark**').

❻ Follow this track for few paces, then take wide grassy path which you follow until you leave wood by ladder stile. Follow grassy path downhill, nip over another stile and follow enclosed path – good views of **Peebles** now. Follow obvious track until you join wide tarmac road.

❼ Follow road; go **L** into **Southpark Industrial Estate**. Walk to bottom R-H corner past units, then go down steps and bear **L** at bottom. Soon reach footbridge.

❽ Turn **R** and follow wide track beside river. This is a popular part of the walk and attracts lots of families on sunny days. Continue walking past weir, then go up steps at bridge and cross over to return to car park.

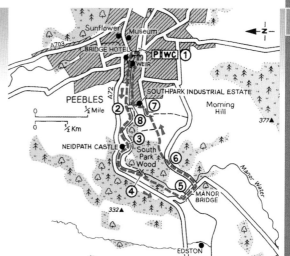

Borders

919 TRAQUAIR *THE JACOBITE REBELLION*

6½ miles (10.4km) 2hrs 45min Ascent: 1,378ft (420m) 3
Paths: Firm, wide moorland tracks, 1 stile
Suggested map: aqua3 OS Explorer 337 Peebles & Innerleithen
Grid reference: NT 331345
Parking: Southern Upland Way car park in Traquair

*Jacobite connections in an atmospheric old
house and a moorland fairy well.*

❶ From **Southern Upland Way** car park, join
tarmac road and walk L away from **Traquair**. Continue
ahead, passing a house called **The Riggs**, and join
gravel track following signs for **Minch Moor**. After you
go through kissing gate track becomes even grassier,
then cross stile and enter Forestry Commission land.
❷ Continue on obvious track to pass **bothy** on R. At
crossing of tracks maintain direction, crossing area
that has been clear felled. Route goes through gate,
just to R of cycle way, winds uphill, through kissing
gate and joins up with cycle way again.
❸ Maintain direction, with great views over
Walkerburn to L. It feels wilder and windier up here,
with large tracts of heather-covered moorland by your
path. At marker post, turn R and walk up to cairn on
Minch Moor – views should be great on a clear day.
❹ From cairn, retrace your steps back to main track.

Turn L and walk back downhill – stopping to leave
some food for the fairies when you pass **Cheese Well**
on L – it's by boggy part of path. Continue, to go
through gate again, to reach next crossing of tracks.
❺ Turn L and walk downhill. Landscape opens out
on R-H side giving pleasant views of valley and river
winding away. At apex of bend, turn R along grassy
track. Follow this downhill, go through gate and walk
in front of **Camp Shiel** cottage.
❻ Go through another gate, cross burn, then follow
grassy track and pass **Damhead Shiel** cottage. Go
through another gate and follow path across bridge
over burn. Pass expanse of scree on R-H side, and ox-
bow lake evolving on L. Cross bridge and continue to
Damhead farm.
❼ Walk past farm and down to road, turn R. Now
cross burn again and walk past cottages on R-H side.
When you reach war **memorial** on L, turn R and walk
up track to reach parking place at start of walk on L.

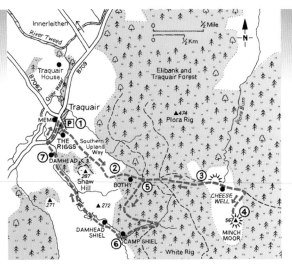

920 JEDBURGH *HOLY ORDERS*

4½ miles (7.2km) 3hrs Ascent: 295ft (90m) 2
Paths: Tracks, meadow paths and some sections of road, 2 stiles
Suggested map: aqua3 OS Explorer OL16 The Cheviot Hills
Grid reference: NT 651204
Parking: Main car park by tourist information centre

Pathways from a historic town.

❶ From car park, walk back to **A68**. Turn R, then
cross over before river. Take path on L to walk beside
river, under old bridge, then come on to road. Cross
and join road opposite. Take 1st R turn, then turn R at
fire station and cross bridge.
❷ Turn L, following sign for **Borders Abbeys Way**.
Where road divides, turn L and walk beside river again
– there's a small 'W' waymarker. At main road, cross
over and walk along tarmac road. Continue to large
building on your L (derelict at time of writing).
❸ Turn R here to walk in front of farmhouse,
Woodend. At another tarmac road, turn L. Route now
runs uphill, taking you past radio **mast** and in front of
Mount Ulston house. Maintain direction to join narrow
grassy track – can be very muddy, even in summer.
❹ Squelch along track to fingerpost at end, where
you turn L to join **St Cuthbert's Way** – wide, firm
track. At tarmac road, turn R and join main road. Turn

L, go over bridge, then cross road and go down steps
to continue following **St Cuthbert's Way**.
❺ You're now on narrow, grassy track beside river.
Cross couple of stiles before walking across meadow
frequently grazed by sheep. Walk past **weir**, then go
through gate to cross suspension bridge – take care
as it can get extremely slippery.
❻ Pass sign for **Monteviot House** and then walk
through woods to fingerpost, where you can turn R to
enjoy views over river. To extend your walk, continue
along **St Cuthbert's Way** until it joins road, then
retrace your steps. Whatever you choose, you then
retrace your steps back over suspension bridge, along
riverside and back to main road. Cross over and rejoin
tarmac track.
❼ Track almost immediately forks and you now turn
R, following road to join **A68** once again. Turn L and
follow road back into **Jedburgh**. Eventually you'll
come to car park on L-H side.

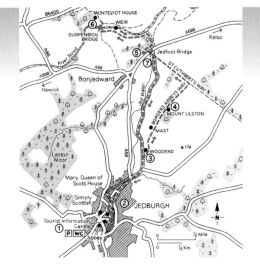

921 DRYBURGH *A GREAT SCOTT*

4½ miles (7.2km) 1hr 30min Ascent: 131ft (40m) 1
Paths: Firm woodland and riverside tracks, 3 stiles
Suggested map: aqua3 OS Explorer 338 Galashiels, Selkirk & Melrose
Grid reference: NT 592318
Parking: Dryburgh Abbey car park

*A gentle walk in the Borders countryside
much beloved by Sir Walter Scott.*

❶ From car park at **abbey** walk back to join road,
pass entrance to **Dryburgh Abbey Hotel**, then walk
down road in front of you. You'll soon see river and will
then pass small **temple** in trees on R-H side. Go L and
cross bridge over **River Tweed**.
❷ Turn L immediately and then join **St Cuthbert's
Way**. This waymarked trail now takes you along banks
of river. At some points there are steps, tiny
footbridges and patches of boardwalk to assist you.
Continue to follow this trail which eventually takes you
past 2 small islands in river, where it then leads away
from river bank.
❸ Follow trail on to a tarmac track, bear R and then
L. At main road in **St Boswells** go L again and
continue to follow trail signs, passing **post office** and
later Scott's View chippy on L. After house No 101,
turn L then go to your R along a tarmac track at end.

❹ Follow this, then turn L and walk past golf **club**
house. Continue few paces, then turn R and follow **St
Cuthbert's Way** as it hugs golf course. Continue by
golf course until your track eventually brings you back
down to river bank. Walk past **weir** and up to bridge.
❺ Go up steps and cross bridge, then turn sharp L
and walk towards cottages. Before cottages, go L,
over footbridge, then turn R along river bank to walk in
front of them. At **weir**, take steps that run up to R, nip
over stile and into field.
❻ Go L, through gate, and follow indistinct track
overgrown with high grasses in summer, but isn't hard
to follow. Where path divides, go L to keep to river,
now you'll be on short, springy grass.
❼ Follow river, keeping an eye out for fish leaping up
to feed from the water's surface. You'll cross stile, then
pass greenhouse on your L. Climb another stile here,
turn R, walk past toilets and, at house ahead, turn L
and walk back into car park.

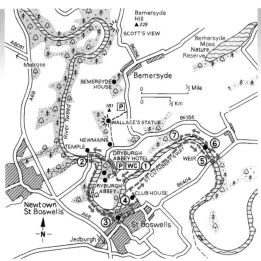

Borders

KIRK YETHOLM *OVER THE BORDER*

5 miles (8km) 3hrs 45min Ascent: 1,378ft (420m)
Paths: Wide tracks and waymarked paths, one short overgrown section, 3 stiles
Suggested map: aqua3 OS Explorer OL16 The Cheviot Hills
Grid reference: NT 839276
Parking: Car park outside Kirk Yetholm at junction of Pennine Way and St Cuthbert's Way

An energetic walk over the Scottish border.
① From car park cross bridge, following signs ('St Cuthbert's Way'). Follow track uphill, keeping **Shielknowe Burn** below on L. Eventually track crosses burn, then continues uphill, skirting edge of **Green Humbleton** hill, eventually reaching fingerpost.
② Here, **St Cuthbert's Way** splits from **Pennine Way**. Take L-H track, **St Cuthbert's Way**, narrow grassy sheep track. Continue uphill, to fingerpost by wall marking border between Scotland and England.
③ Follow track which eventually bears downhill to boggy area. Look out for waymarkers, then continue to wood. Cross stile and into trees. Maintain direction, turn **R** at fence and follow fence line. Soon walk down avenue of trees and leave wood by stile.
④ Keep ahead over field, then descend to cross burn and join wider track. Eventually reach **Elsdonburn** farm. Walk through farm and follow track as it bears **R**. Join track with wood L and burn **R**.

⑤ Continue, crossing cattle grid, then leave **St Cuthbert's Way**; join track on **R**. Continue, pass **sheepfold** then 2 conifer plantations. Finally, track winds upwards, skirts hill, then descends to **Trowupburn** farmhouse. Walk in front of farm buildings; bear **R** to fingerpost.
⑥ Go through gate and follow sign ('Border Ridge 1½'). Continue on this wide grassy track then cross **ford** next to very large **sheepfold**. Maintain direction, burn now on **R**, then cross burn again, cross stile and join sheep track that bears **L** through bracken.
⑦ Walk round hill and, when parallel with **sheepfold** on L, bear **R** so valley of **Wide Open** burn is on your L, **sheepfold** behind you. Continue uphill through bracken to head of burn to fence on higher ground.
⑧ Go through gate at corner; cross open ground. Descend to cross burn and keep ahead, crossing border. Bear **R** on **Pennine Way**. At fingerpost follow track downhill and cross burn to start.

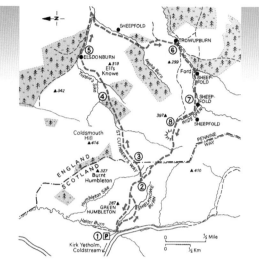

DUNS *STEPPING BACK IN TIME*

4½ miles (7.2km) 2hrs 30min Ascent: 230ft (70m)
Paths: Quiet roads and firm tracks
Suggested map: aqua3 OS Explorer 346 Berwick-upon-Tweed
Grid reference: NT 785539
Parking: Long-stay car park near Duns Market Square

Quiet lanes through gentle countryside and past a fine Edwardian mansion.
① From Market Square walk northeast, and turn **R** along Currie Street and then **L** at main road (A6105) and continue ahead for about 1½ miles (2km). Take care walking along this road as it can be busy. When the A6105 bears off **R** continue ahead following signs for **Manderston House**.
② After a short distance, you pass entrance to **Manderston House** on your R-H side. Continue walking ahead until your reach fork in road.
③ Take L-H fork and follow road downhill, then take track on **L** just after **Howdens Plantation**. Follow path, passing in front of **Broomhill** on R. Continue ahead to cross cattle grid and join another road.
④ Turn **L**; take track on **L** that runs between cottages. Follow it between fields and under pylons. At main road turn **L**, then take turning to **R** ('Abbey St Bathans, Cranshaw and Gifford').

⑤ Follow road, take turning on **L** that leads into wildlife **reserve**. Follow track ('Hen Poo', lake). Pass pond on R and come to head of **Hen Poo**. Turn **L**.
⑥ Keeping lake on your R, follow track as it bears to **R**, around water. Continue, to cross cattle grid and, after short distance, enjoy great view of **Duns Castle**. Continue to castle entrance on your **R**.
⑦ Turn **L**, walk past **memorial** to John Duns Scotus and continue. When you reach a signpost on your **L**, you can follow this to climb **Duns Law**. Otherwise just follow road, go through arch, walk down Castle Street and continue ahead to reach start of walk in Market Square in **Duns**.

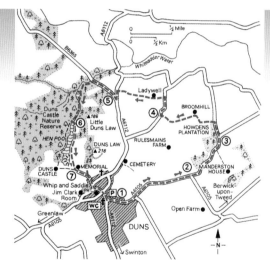

ST ABBS *A WINDY WALK*

4 miles (6.4km) 1hr 30min Ascent: 443ft (135m)
Paths: Clear footpaths and established tracks
Suggested map: aqua3 OS Explorer 346 Berwick-upon-Tweed
Grid reference: NT 913674
Parking: At visitor centre

A refreshing walk along the cliffs where there is plenty of wildlife.
① From car park, take path that runs past information board and play area. Continue past **visitor centre** and then take footpath on your **L**, parallel to main road. At end of path turn **L** and then go through kissing gate – you'll immediately get great views of the sea.
② Follow track, pass sign to **Starney Bay** and continue, passing fields on your L-H side. Your track now winds around edge of bay – to your R is little harbour at **St Abbs**. The track then winds around cliff edge, past dramatic rock formations and eventually reaching some steps.
③ Walk down steps, then follow grassy track as it bears **L**, with fence on L. Go up slope, over stile and maintain direction on obvious grassy track. Path soon veers away from cliff edge, past high ground on R, then runs up short, steep slope to crossing of tracks.

④ Maintain direction by taking L-H track which runs up slope. You'll soon get great views of **St Abb's Head** lighthouse ahead, dramatically situated on the cliff's edge. Continue to lighthouse and walk in front of lighthouse buildings and down to join tarmac road.
⑤ Follow this road which takes you away from cliff edge. Continue to obvious bend, from where you get your first views of **Mire Loch** below. You now follow path downhill to right, to reach cattle grid.
⑥ Turn **L** here to pick up narrow track by loch, with wall on your R-H side. It's pretty overgrown at start so it can be hard to find, but as you continue it becomes much more obvious. Walk beside loch and continue until you reach gate.
⑦ Turn **R** along wide track and walk up to road. Go **L** now and continue to cross cattle grid. When you reach a bend in road, follow tarmac track as it bears **L**. You'll soon go through a gate, then pass some cottages before reaching car park on L-H side.

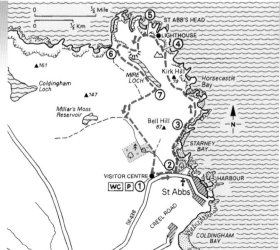

Midlothian

925 · ROSLIN ROMANTIC ROSLIN GLEN

5 miles (8km) 2hrs 30min **Ascent:** 279ft (85m)
Paths: Generally good, but can be muddy and slippery
Suggested map: aqua3 OS Explorer 344 Pentland Hills
Grid reference: NT 272627
Parking: Roslin Glen Country Park car park

Tree-lined paths take you beside a river to a special ancient chapel in this glorious glen.

❶ From **country park** car park, walk northeast on to track to reach river. Go up metal stairs, cross footbridge, then walk ahead, following path uphill. In summer, you'll smell wild garlic. At bottom of flight of steps, turn **R**, walk under old **castle** arch, down stone steps, then turn to your **L**.

❷ Your path now descends and you keep walking ahead, before climbing more steps. Path ascends again, until you reach crossing of paths where you turn **R** and follow path steeply downhill. Keep going down until you reach water's edge.

❸ Walk to your **L**, then follow path as it climbs again (handrail to assist you). At crossing of paths turn **R**, following direction of river. Your way now takes you high above river; continue ahead to cross stile. After you cross another stile view opens out to fields on your **L**, then takes you closer to river again. Cross burn and

another stile to point where river goes back on itself.

❹ Cross broken fence, then keep ahead, passing old pollarded tree on L-H side. Follow small sign pointing uphill to **Maiden Castle**. At top turn **L** ('caution, path erosion'). You now get great views over river valley as you cross over ridge and then keep walking to reach a metal gate.

❺ Turn **L** and follow wide path. Eventually pass buildings of **Animal Research Centre**, then pass **memorial** to Battle of Rosslyn on your R-H side. Keep ahead, through outskirts of **Roslin** and up to crossroads at village centre.

❻ Turn **L** and walk ahead. After short distance you see **Rosslyn Chapel** on R-H side. If you don't intend to visit chapel, take path that bears downhill to **R**, just in front of it. When you reach cemetery turn **L** ('Polton'), and walk between cemeteries to metal gate for **Rosslyn Castle**. Go down steps on R-H side, over bridge again and return to car park.

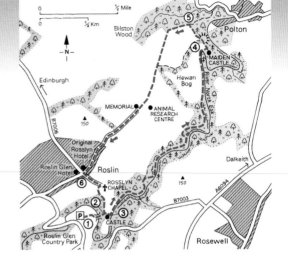

926 · EAST LINTON POPPY HARVEST

4½ miles (7.2km) 2hrs 30min **Ascent:** 295ft (90m)
Paths: Field paths, river margins and woodland tracks. Short section of busy road, 2 stiles
Suggested map: aqua3 OS Explorer 351 Dunbar & North Berwick
Grid reference: NT 591772
Parking: Main street in East Linton

A lovely walk past an old doo'cot and a mill.

❶ From Market Cross in centre of town, take path that runs to **L** of church. At main street bear **L**, cross over bridge and continue to garage on R-H side. Turn **L** into farm opposite garage ('Houston Mill and Mill House').

❷ Follow path round farm buildings to old doo'cot (dovecote) ahead. Turn **R** front of it and follow path along field edge. At footbridge, turn **L** to continue walking around field edge, with river on **R**. Cross next footbridge and go through metal gate.

❸ Take R-H path across field and go through kissing gate to old **mill**. Inspect **mill** – you can go inside when it's open – continue on to meet main road, then turn **L** back into town. Turn **R** along High Street, cross road and turn **L** to go down Langside.

❹ At recreation ground, maintain direction and walk towards railway. Go through underpass and walk ahead through fields. Continue in same direction,

crossing 3 walls with help of steps and 2 stiles. After you cross 3rd wall track becomes indistinct, but maintain direction to reach wooden sign. Turn **L** here to reach road.

❺ Turn **R**, cross over at parking place to continue along track running parallel to road. Walk to **Overhailes** farm, through yard, then bear **L** and follow wide track down to **Hailes Castle**. Ignore 1st path that joins from **L** and go a few paces further to turn **L** along another path that leads to bridge.

❻ Don't cross bridge but instead follow track that runs to **L** of steps. You're now walking along river's edge on narrow path. Follow path to cross stile, walk along field margin, then ascend. Ascend flight of stairs, go down steps, and continue following path to walk under road bridge.

❼ Path runs through garden and on to road, where you turn **R**. Walk under railway bridge, turn **L** and return to starting point of walk in town.

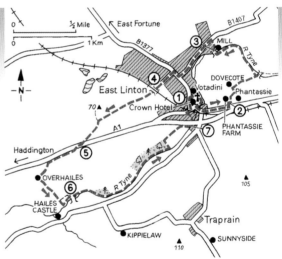

927 · BALLANTRAE ARDSTINCHAR CASTLE

3 miles (4.8km) 2hrs **Ascent:** 295ft (90m)
Paths: Country lanes and farm tracks
Suggested map: aqua3 OS Explorer 317 Ballantrae, Barr & Barrhill
Grid reference: NX 082824 **Parking:** Car park near school on Foreland, Ballantrae

The Ayrshire Tragedy, a murder most foul.

❶ Leave car park and then turn **L** on to Foreland. At T-junction with Main Street cross road and turn **R**. Near outskirts of village, just before bridge over **River Stinchar**, look to **L** to view ruins of **Ardstinchar Castle**. Walls are unstable, do not go closer.

❷ From here cross Stinchar Bridge and take 1st turning on **R**, heading uphill on narrow country lane and past cottages. At junction keep to **L** but look out for one of **Garleffin Standing Stones** in rear garden of bungalow at junction.

❸ Continue uphill passing **cemetery**, R, **Glenapp Castle gates** on **L** and further on **Big Park Civic Amenity Site**, on **L**.

❹ Continue past farm road to **Bigpark** on **L** and look out for next farmhouse on **R**. About 300yds (274m) before this house road dips; there's stream beside road here. Turn **R** on to farm track that heads downhill between 2 high hedges.

❺ Near bottom of hill, just past large barn on **L**, road

splits. Turn **R** and continue along road, through farm steading, past **Downan** farmhouse and uphill. When road levels out look to horizon ahead for distinctive outline of Knockdolian Hill, referred to by local mariners as 'false Craig'.

❻ Look over to your **L** at same time to see real Ailsa Craig away to northwest. Looking along beach towards **Ballantrae** is **Shellknowe**. Continue along this road, past farm of **Kinniegar** and through hamlet of **Garleffin**. Note that some houses have names like Druidslea and Glendruid.

❼ In front garden of Druidslea is another **standing stone**. Turn **L**, go downhill on country lane, turn **L** on to main road and return to **Ballantrae**. Go through gate on L-H side and into **kirkyard**. Kennedy crypt can be found by going up some steps on **R**. If door is locked look through small window on door. Return to Main Street and turn **R**, go along street and take 1st turning **L** past library. Walk along street to T-junction and turn **L** into Foreland and return to car park.

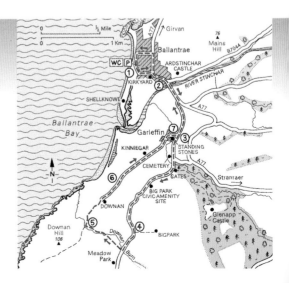

BYNE HILL *FIRTH OF CLYDE*

3¾ miles (6km) 3hrs Ascent: 571ft (174m)
Paths: Farm roads, dirt tracks and open hillside, 1 stile
Suggested map: aqua3 OS Explorer 317 Ballantrae, Barr & Barrhill
Grid reference: NX 187955
Parking: On road beside Girvan cemetery

Enjoy the views across the sea to Ailsa Craig.
❶ Go along road to **Brochneil** farm which runs along east side of **cemetery**. Continue through Brochneil steading, then cross wooden bridge. Go through gate, over stone bridge and follow road uphill, as it turns **R**, and then **L**.
❷ This is farm road to **Drumfairn**, formerly shepherd's house for Woodland farm, now part of wildlife reserve. Cross cattle grid, go through 2 gates then, at 3rd cattle grid, cross stile and go **L** towards **Drumfairn** steading.
❸ The house at Drumfairn has been damaged by fire, is derelict and in a dangerous condition. Turn **R** at steading and, keeping sheep pens on your **L**, walk ahead. Go through gate and then cross wire fence near another gate. Go through this gate and head **R**, across field. At fence turn **L** and follow it to reach junction with tumbledown wall. Cross here and, keeping fence on your **R**, head along edge of field.

Cross small burn near sheep pens and continue following line of fence to gate.
❹ Go through gate then go **R**, cross small burn and continue along faint track heading for saddle between **Mains Hill** on your L-H side and **Byne Hill** on your **R**. Retrace your steps short distance and turn **L** through gap in wall and head up side of **Byne Hill** to prominent commemorative **cairn** at summit. On a clear day you can see the Antrim coast of Northern Ireland, the island of Arran and the Mull of Kintyre to the north and west, and, about 8 miles (12.9km) out in the sea, the distinctive outline of Ailsa Craig, the plug of an extinct volcano and source of granite for curling stones.
❺ With **cairn** at your back, walk ahead. Cross saddle between summit and lower part of hill, keeping at first to higher ground then descending towards northeast side of hill where footpath ends at kissing gate. Go through this gate and turn **L** on to farm road. Retrace your steps from here to return to start.

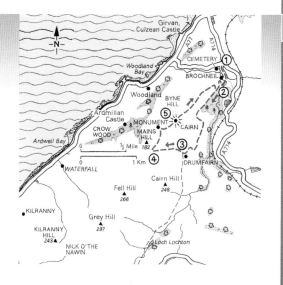

LOUDOUN *LADY FLORA*

7½ miles (12.1km) 4hrs Ascent: 187ft (57m)
Paths: Pavements, footpaths and farm roads
Suggested map: aqua3 OS Explorer 334 East Kilbride Galston & Darvel
Grid reference: NS 539373 **Parking:** On-street parking near Lady Flora's Institute

A tragic tale of jealousy and intrigue.
❶ From Lady Flora's Institute, go south along Main Street. Turn **L** into Craigview Road. Cross bridge, turn **R** and follow road to T-junction. Turn **L** then, where road forks, keep to **R**, go along side of factory, turn **L** into Stonygate Road. Continue to join Irvine Footpath.
❷ Continue, passing **Strath** and on to kennels. Turn **R** at gate; follow path round perimeter. Continue along river bank on muddy path. Keep on this, going through woodlands until you see white cottage.
❸ As path forks go **L** through gap stile on to surfaced footpath to **L** of **Barr Mill**, and uphill to main road. Continue, heading downhill and passing Galston library, Barr Castle Social Club and Masons Arms pub to crossroads –'Four Corners'.
❹ Turn **R**, cross road and continue, heading out of town, crossing 'Muckle Brig' and **Galston** bypass on pavement; continue along A719 towards **Loudoun Academy**. Pass **Waterside** farm on L, **academy** on R then entrance gates to **Loudoun Castle**.

❺ Turn **L** opposite gates and head along narrow country lane for ½ mile (800m) to **Loudoun Kirk** Bridge. Turn **L**; go into Loudoun kirkyard. Return from there, cross small bridge and turn **R** on to signposted footpath ('Galston'). After 100yds (91m) path bends **R** and narrow grassy footpath forks **L**. Go **L**.
❻ Keep on well-trodden path to T-junction at **Galston** bypass. Turn **R**. Head along pavement, over bridge then turn **R** and head downhill. Turn **L** at waymarker and go through underpass to other side of bypass. Turn **L**. Walk along footpath beside river.
❼ At end of path go **R** on lane then **L** into Titchfield Street. Turn **R** at next junction, cross road; take next **L**. Pass school and **cemetery** to reach staggered junction. Cross B7037. Continue on Clockstone Road.
❽ Turn **L** at T-junction. Take next **R** beside house. Follow road downhill, then back up to pass **Piersland** farm. Head downhill and cross gate where road turns **L** under railway bridge. Turn **R** after bridge; retrace your steps to start.

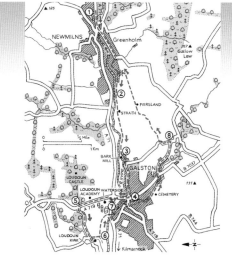

DUNASKIN *THE IRON WORKS*

4 miles (6.4km) 3hrs Ascent: 492ft (150m)
Paths: Old rail and tram beds and rough hillside
Suggested map: aqua3 OS Explorer 327 Cumnock & Dalmellington
Grid reference: NX 440084
Parking: Dunaskin Open Air Museum

A hill walk to a deserted village.
❶ Turn **R** in front of **visitor centre**. Follow road towards **playground**. Go uphill on track to **R** of playground and through woodland. Emerge at T-junction opposite railway bridge; turn **L** on grassy trail.
❷ At metal gate across trail, go through small wooden one at its side. Climb over next gate, turn **R** and head uphill following line of disused **tramway**, between ends of an old bridge. This is trackbed of former horse-drawn **tramway**.
❸ At top of hill, when path divides, keep **L** and follow path as it goes through 2 short sections of wall. Ground to your **R** in front of conifer plantation was once village football field. Where path is blocked by fence, turn **R**, then go **L** through gate and **R** on to metalled lane.
❹ Head along here, past remains of miners' houses of **Step Row**, which are clearly visible amongst trees. Stone **memorial** stands near site of former village

store. To **R** of this, and now within wood, is former village square and remains of more houses.
❺ From stone **memorial** turn back towards **war memorial**, then return to gate at corner of wood and continue along track beside wood. In trees are remains of **Low Row**. Go through another gate and continue along former railway. When it forks, keep **R**.
❻ Continue until route ahead is blocked by sheets of corrugated iron, near wall. Turn **R** and follow line of wall downhill. Cross wall and continue downhill towards **chimneys** of **Dunaskin**. At broken hedge, near end of **Green Hill**, turn **R** along front of it and continue until you are level with 2nd **chimney**.
❼ Turn **L**, heading downhill short way then though gate. Veer to **R** and head towards another gate. Go through wood and emerge at **Ardoon**. Go past house, turn **L** on to footpath and follow it downhill and under small, disused railway bridge. Cross track and carry on heading back downhill on footpath back to start.

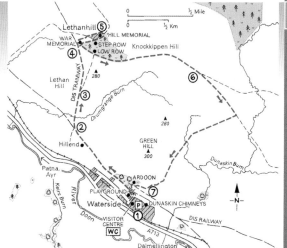

931 MUIRKIRK *ON OLD ROADS AND RAILS*

3½ miles (5.7km) 3hrs **Ascent:** 16ft (5m)

Paths: Old railway beds, farm tracks and country lanes, 1 stile
Suggested map: aqua3 OS Explorer 328 Sanquhar & New Cumnock
Grid reference: NX 696265
Parking: Walkers' car park, Furnace Road

Around a once prosperous moorland town that stood at an industrial crossroads.

❶ From car park follow blue waymarker and exit via gate on to rough track with high wall running along to R. This continues as fence and, once past end of it, look for waymarker pole on L.

❷ Turn L on to grass track. Follow this to steps, go downhill and through kissing gate. Turn R and walk along what may have been bank of 18th-century canal. Go through kissing gate then veer L on to rough track at next waymarker.

❸ Follow to duckboard and stile; cross here. Turn L on to gravel path; turn R at waymarker. Railway track here appears to fork. Keep L and continue along trackbed eventually reaching kissing gate.

❹ Go through gate and turn R on to quiet country road. Follow this past remains of old railway bridge, past farm entrance on R then go through gate to continue on farm road. At next gate turn R, go through

4 gates and return to car park.

❺ Turn R and exit car park on to Furnace Road then turn L. Continue past clock tower of derelict **Kames Institute** and along edge of **golf course**. Go through gate and continue, passing cottage on L, on to old drove road to Sanquhar. Go through another gate and continue to **McAdam memorial**.

❻ Just past this head along green track on R. When it forks L on to what may have been a tramline, keep R. Follow this track along side of stream until it joins dirt track just above **Tibbie's Brig**. Near here, in a small clay dwelling, lived local poetess, Tibbie Pagan, who eked out a living by singing, selling her poetry and possibly supplying illicit whisky. A volume of her poems was published in 1803.

❼ Go down to **Brig** and **monument** then return uphill keeping L on access for disabled route to McAdam's cairn. Follow this back to drove road where you turn L to return to car park.

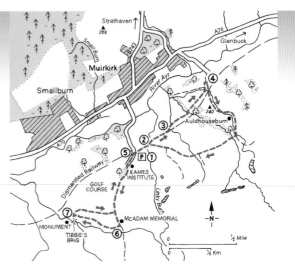

932 DARVEL *SIR ALEXANDER FLEMING*

7 miles (11.3km) 3hrs **Ascent:** 459ft (140m)

Paths: Country lanes and pavements
Suggested map: aqua3 OS Explorer 334 East Kilbride, Galston & Darvel
Grid reference: NX 563374
Parking: On-street parking at Hastings Square at start of walk

In the footsteps of Sir Alexander Fleming.

❶ From Alexander Fleming Memorial, cross square to pedestrian crossing, cross road, turn R and go along Main Street. Near outskirts of town cross Darvel Bridge and take 2nd turning on L just past **John Aird Factory**. Go uphill on this road and pass cemetery.

❷ Continue uphill to crossroads near **New Quarterhouse** farm. Follow waymark arrow pointing L. Road continues uphill, passing **Henryton** on R and **Byres** on L. Near **Byres** there is a bench if you want some respite on this steep climb.

❸ **Little Glen** is next farm on L-H side and shortly afterwards road forks. Take L turn. Next 2 farms passed on this road are **Meikleglen** and **Feoch**, which come in quick succession. Just before next farm on L, **Laigh Braidley**, farm road leads off to R. This is the entrance to Lochfield, Alexander Fleming's birthplace, which is not open to the public. Continue past Laigh Braidley.

❹ After Laigh Braidley road turns sharply L, then R and goes downhill to cross Glen Water at **Braidley Bridge**. As you descend hill look slightly to R and uphill and you will see steading of Lochfield, which is still farmed. Follow road uphill from bridge. There's another bench by the roadside at the T-junction near the top of hill. Enjoy a well-earned rest and the view.

❺ Ignore waymark and turn L, heading along lane and past **Gateside**. When road forks take L fork, cross **Mucks Bridge** and continue uphill. Lane now passes roads to **Low** then **High Carlingcraig**, then levels out. As you continue along top of this hill look to L for distinctive outline of Loudoun Hill.

❻ When you reach **Dyke**, road heads downhill again. Go over crossroads at **Intax** and continue short distance to bungalows on R. Just past here take **L** turn. After Hilltop road turns sharply **R** and downhill. As you approach town lane continues into Burn Street. At T-junction turn **L**; follow it back to Hastings Square.

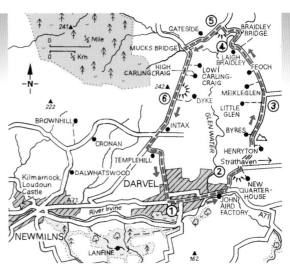

933 NEW LANARK *A REVOLUTIONARY UTOPIA*

6 miles (9.7km) 3hrs **Ascent:** 476ft (145m)

Paths: Clear riverside tracks and forest paths, a few steep steps
Suggested map: aqua3 OS Explorer 335 Lanark & Tinto Hills
Grid reference: NS 883426
Parking: Main car park above New Lanark

A rustic walk from a model community.

❶ From car park, walk downhill into **New Lanark**. Bear L and walk to Scottish Wildlife Trust **visitor centre**. Turn up stone steps on L ('Falls of Clyde'). Path soon goes down some steps to reach **weir**, where you'll find lookout point.

❷ Continue along path. You'll pass Bonnington **Power Station** on your R, where it divides. Take **R-H** path, which begins to climb and takes you into woodland and up some steps. You'll soon come to **Corra Linn** waterfall, with another lookout point.

❸ Your path continues to R ('Bonnington Linn', ¾ miles). Go up some more steps and follow track to go under double line of pylons. You'll pass an area that is often fenced to protect breeding peregrines. Follow path to reach large new bridge, cross it, then turn **R** into Falls of Clyde **Wildlife Reserve**.

❹ Walk through reserve, turn **R** at crossing and over small bridge. Pass underneath double line of pylons

again, then bear **R** at gate to reach **Corra Castle**. Continue walking by river, cross small footbridge, then follow wide path through woods. When you meet another path, turn **R**.

❺ Follow path to pass houses on your L. At road turn **R** (take care, no pavement), then **R** again to cross old bridge, which brings you into cul de sac. Go through gate on **R** – it looks like someone's drive but is signed ('**Clyde Walkway**').

❻ Walk past stables to river. Go through gate to water treatment works, up steps beside it, then pass stile on your L. Continue on main track ('**Clyde Walkway**'). Pass house on R and follow path leading down to R (you'll see broken fingerpost there).

❼ Your path zig-zags down to river. At water's edge turn **L**, cross footbridge and follow forest track. Go down some steps, close to river again, then up more steps and over bridge. Follow path to road, turn **R** and into **New Lanark**. Turn **L** at church for car park.

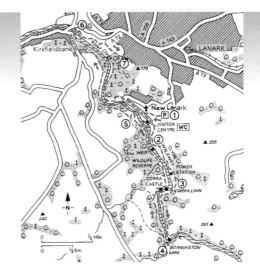

South Lanarkshire

934 · EAST KILBRIDE *KITTOCHSIDE FARM*

5 miles (8km) 3hrs **Ascent:** 262ft (80m)
Paths: Farm tracks and country roads
Suggested map: aqua3 OS Explorer 342 Glasgow
Grid reference: NS 608558
Parking: Car park at Museum of Scottish Country Life

An 18th-century time warp in a 20th-century new town.

❶ Exit car park and turn **R** on to road, heading past front of main Exhibition Building, then turn **R** on to farm road. Continue along this, keeping your eyes open for tractors ferrying visitors from Exhibition Building to farm. Take gated turn off to **L** and follow this path to go through another gate on to farm road.

❷ Turn **L** and, short distance further on, turn **R** on to another farm road. Follow this across field and into wooded area surrounding **Wester Kittochside**. Road turns sharply **R** then joins another road. Turn **L**, walk past bungalow then turn **L** again where farm road joins country road.

❸ Follow this quiet road for just over 1 mile (1.6km), past fields of **Wester Kittochside** farm, then fields of more modern farms and finally into **Carmunnock**. Road ends at T-junction. Turn **R** then, short distance further on, take next turning on **R** into **Cathkin Road**.

❹ Keep on **Cathkin Road** for about ½ mile (800m) then, when it bends sharply to **L**, turn **R** and continue straight ahead on minor road. Follow this as it twists and turns to reach **Highflat Farm** after about ½ mile (800m) and then continues for another ½ mile (800m) to end at T-junction opposite road leading to **West Rogerton** farm.

❺ Turn **R** and, in just over ½ mile (800m), you will come to crossroads. On **R** is farm track leading back to **Highflat**. Turn **L** here and proceed to next T-junction. Walk along this country lane passing farm of **East Kittochside** on **L**.

❻ Pass junction on your **R** and then continue ahead through **Kittochside**, pass drive to **Kittochside House** and you'll reach another T-junction. Cross over road here and continue along farm track ahead of you. Take 1st turning on **L** on to another farm track and, at end of this, you will be back in front of **museum** Exhibition Building.

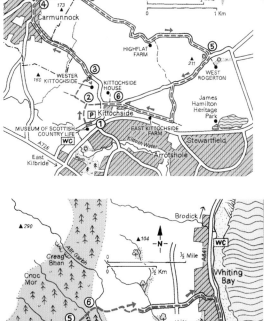

935 · WHITING BAY *THE SPECTACULAR FALLS*

2¾ miles (4.4km) 2hrs **Ascent:** 442ft (135m)
Paths: Forest paths and forest roads
Suggested map: aqua3 OS Explorer 361 Isle of Arran
Grid reference: NS 047252
Parking: Car park opposite youth hostel in Whiting Bay

Enjoy this short scenic woodland walk over the Isle of Arran's ancient bedrock.

❶ From car park turn **R** on to road, cross it and turn **L** on to footpath ('Giants' Graves and Glenashdale Falls'). Follow lane until it reaches rear of house, then continue on path along river bank. Go through gate, pass forest walks sign and continue until you reach signpost pointing in direction of **Giants' Graves**.

❷ Path forks here. Go **R**, following sign to **Glenashdale Falls**. Path continues, rising gently, through wooded area, where several trees are identified by small labels fixed to trunks. Continue uphill on this path, which is marked by occasional waymarkers, crossing several bridges and fording shallow section of burn.

❸ Eventually path starts to climb steeply uphill and continues to some steps and then forks. Keep **R** and follow this path to reach falls. Keep on path past falls and continue uphill to cross bridge. The picnic table situated on the river bank is a good spot to stop for some refreshment.

❹ From here follow path into area planted with Sitka spruce. Keep to track marked by green waymarkers as it heads through this dark part, going through gap in wall and eventually arriving at sign pointing to an Iron-Age **fort**. Turn off to look at remains of ramparts then retrace your steps to gate and continue on path.

❺ Cross bridge by another waterfall then follow more waymarkers to clearing and viewpoint – enjoy panoramic views across the glen. From here you can see the full extent of **Glenashdale Falls**. Waymarker points uphill through densely wooded area before ending at T-junction with forest road.

❻ Turn **R** on to forest road and continue, crossing water at ford and going through 3 kissing gates until route continues as metalled road. Continue along this road, go over crossroads and wind downhill. Turn **R** at T-junction and walk 200yds (183m) back to car park.

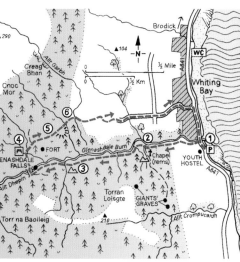

936 · MACHRIE MOOR *ARRAN'S STANDING STONES*

5½ miles (8.8km) 3hrs **Ascent:** 114ft (35m)
Paths: Footpaths, rough tracks, road, 3 stiles
Suggested map: aqua3 OS Explorer 361 Isle of Arran
Grid reference: NS 898314
Parking: King's Cave car park

Discover the ancient standing stones of one of Scotland's finest early settlements on the Isle of Arran.

❶ From car park take footpath ('King's Cave'). This goes through area of woodland, past site of some **hut circles** on **R** and continues along edge of woods until it starts to head downhill towards sea. Look out for waymarker on **R** pointing back in direction you have just walked.

❷ Turn **R** here on to faint path, which in summer will be very overgrown with bracken. Plough your way through this and, in short distance, you will come to wire fence, which you can easily climb through. Cross this field and go through gate, then head downhill aiming for **L** end of white **cottage** by shore.

❸ As you near end of cottage you will see gate at corner of garden wall. Turn **R** at gate and follow line of fence on your **R** until you reach stile. Cross stile and turn **L** on to farm road running between 2 fences.

Keep on this road passing another cottage on **R** and keeping **R** at fork.

❹ When road ends at T-junction with A841 turn **L**. Continue to signpost ('Machrie Moor Standing Stones'). Turn **R**, go over stile and follow access road. This rough track passes through 2 fields.

❺ In 2nd field, near far L-H corner, is the **megalithic site**, one of the oldest in the area. Nothing is to be seen above ground as the site was only identified when flints were found that were around 7,000 to 9,000 years old. Continue on road to **Moss Farm** road stone circle. Dating from approximately 2000 BC it has never been excavated.

❻ From here track continues, passing deserted **Moss Farm** then crossing stile to main stone circles of Machrie Moor. When you have finished wandering around them return to stile and take **Moss Farm** road back to A841. Turn **L** on to this and walk for approximately 1½ miles (2km) to return to car park.

City of Glasgow

City of Glasgow · SCOTLAND

937   GLASGOW *ALEXANDER 'GREEK' THOMSON*

6½ miles (10.4km) 3hrs 30min **Ascent:** 98ft (30m) **A**
Paths: Pavements
Suggested map: aqua3 OS Explorer 342 Glasgow; AA Street by Street
Grid reference: NS 587653 **Parking:** Sauchiehall Street multi-storey or on-street parking

An urban walk around a Victorian city.
1 Exit **Central Station**; turn **R**. At junction with Union Street turn **R**. The building on the opposite corner is **Ca' d'Oro**, 19th-century Italianate warehouse by John Honeyman. A little way down Union Street on the same side as **Ca' d'Oro** is Thomson's Egyptian Halls.
2 Cross over then head down Union Street turning **L** into **Argyle Street** at next junction. Cross **Argyle Street**, walk along to junction with Dunlop Street to **Buck's Head** building. Cross **Argyle Street** again, retrace your steps, turning **R** into Buchanan Street. Turn **L** into Mitchell Lane, pass Lighthouse, turn **R**.
3 Walk up Mitchell Street, continue along West Nile Street; turn **L** into **St Vincent Street**. Continue for just under ½ mile (800m), going uphill to junction with Pitt Street. You are now in front of 'Greek' Thomson's **St Vincent Street church**. Cross St Vincent Street here then head up Pitt Street to **Sauchiehall Street**.
4 On the opposite corner is Thomson's **Grecian Chamber** (1865) and to the R along Scott Street is

Rennie Mackintosh's Glasgow **School of Art**. From front of **Grecian Chamber** turn **L**, head down **Sauchiehall Street** to Charing Cross then take pedestrian bridge over motorway to **Woodlands Road**. Go along here until it ends at Park Road, turn **R**, then **L** again into **Great Western Road**.
5 Turn **R** into Belmont Street, **L** at Quad Gardens then **L** again at Queen Margaret Drive. Cross road and head down past **Botanic Gardens** to turn **R**, back into **Great Western Road**. Cross road and continue to Thomson's **Great Western Terrace**. Trace your steps back from here to top of **Byres Road** and turn **R** then, near bottom, turn **L** into University Avenue.
6 Turn **L** into Oakfield Avenue, pass Eton Terrace on corner with Great George Street. Turn **R** into Great George Street, **R** at Otago Street, **L** into Gibson Street and continue when it becomes Eldon Street. Turn **R** into **Woodlands Road** and return to **Sauchiehall Street**. Follow this to junction with Renfield Street, turn **R** and head downhill to **Central Station**.

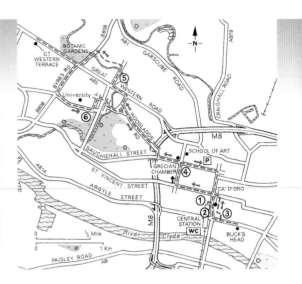

938   CLYDESIDE *HARBOUR'S TALL SHIP*

4¾ miles (7.7km) 3hrs 30min **Ascent:** 98ft (30m) **A**
Paths: Pavements and footpaths
Suggested map: aqua3 OS Explorer 342 Glasgow; AA Street by Street
Grid reference: NS 569652 **Parking:** SECC car park beside Clyde Auditorium (Armadillo)

The last of the Clyde-built sailing ships.
1 From Scottish Exhibition and Conference Centre (**SECC**) car park go on to Clyde Walkway; turn **R**, following signs to Pier 17, the **Tall Ship** and **Museum of Transport** (leave route to visit **Tall Ship**, *Glenlee*). At roundabout with **Tall Ship** on L, go over pedestrian bridge to cross **Clydeside Expressway**. Turn **L**; head west along pavement beside derelict building.
2 Follow footpath when it branches **R** and goes uphill, eventually reaching junction. Go **R** under railway bridge and continue on pavement beside stone wall. Go **R** at next junction and along Old Dumbarton Road ignoring signs pointing to Kelvin Walkway. Cross road then bridge; turn **L** into Bunhouse Road.
3 Pass **Museum of Transport** on R. At junction, cross road via pedestrian crossing and continue along lane around Kelvingrove **Museum and Art Gallery**, through car park and on to T-junction with **Kelvin Way**. Turn **L**, go over bridge and **R** through green gates on to Kelvin Walkway.

4 Route is waymarked through **Kelvingrove Park**. Cross bridge then pass memorial to the Highland Light Infantry. Shortly after, at large bridge on L, path forks. Take **L** path next to river.
5 This eventually goes uphill. Just before top of hill look for narrow path on **L** through bushes, easily missed. Go **L** here and under bridge. Turn **L** at next waymark, go over bridge and past café/bar then continue along walkway.
6 Cross bridge, go **L** at junction, still following river. Go through tunnel and then **L** across humpback bridge to **Botanic Gardens**. Head up steps to gardens. When path reaches 3-way junction take 2nd on **R**. Pass Kibble Palace, turn **L** and follow this drive to gates and exit gardens.
7 Cross **Great Western Road** at traffic lights and walk to end of **Byres Road**. Cross Dumbarton Road and take **R** fork. Take 2nd **L**, go along this street, cross bridge and continue past junction to end of street and under railway bridge, turning **L** to return to SECC.

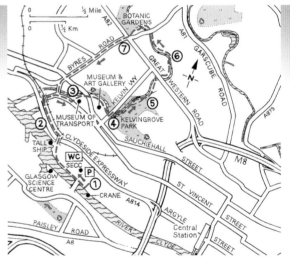

939   KILSYTH *ALONG THE WALL*

3½ miles (5.7km) 3hrs **Ascent:** 344ft (105m) **A**
Paths: Tow path, farm road, footpath and road
Suggested map: aqua3 OS Explorer 348 Campsie Fells
Grid reference: NS 719770
Parking: Car park near old quarry at Kilsyth

Travel back in time by walking along an 18th-century canal and then a section of the Antonine's Wall.
1 Leave car park on to main road and turn **R**. Cross over road and turn immediately **L** on to road ('Twechar and Kirkintilloch'). Continue along this road for a short while and, when it turns sharply **R**, veer off on footpath to **L** and on to tow path of the **Forth and Clyde Canal**.
2 Go round hairpin and keep on along tow path until it rejoins pavement beside main road. Take next turning on **L**, cross canal via bridge and enter **Twechar**. Continue on this road, heading uphill; near top look out for sign on **L** pointing to **Antonine Wall** and **Bar Hill**.
3 Take next turning on **L** on to access road. Continue along here past some houses and continue on farm tracks. Go through gate and uphill. Look back the way you have come for a grand view of the canal.

4 When you reach entrance to **Antonine Wall** go **L** through kissing gate and along lane, then through another kissing gate to access site. The wall spans Britain's narrowest land-crossing, running 40 miles (64km) from the Firth of the Forth to the Clyde. Unlike Hadrian's Wall it was built of turf, but was nonetheless substantial. Veer **L** and uphill to **Bar Hill Fort**. From top of **fort** you will see some woodland in front of you. Head for opening in trees and on to well-defined trail.
5 Follow this trail through trees and then up on to summit of **Castle Hill**. From here, head downhill with remains of **Antonine Wall** on your L-H side. Turn **R** when your path is blocked by dry-stone wall and follow it until you intersect farm track.
6 Turn **L** and follow this track, crossing gate, to reach T-junction with main road. Turn **L** and head downhill. Keep to **L** at roundabout, still heading downhill to reach another T-junction. From here cross road and re-enter car park.

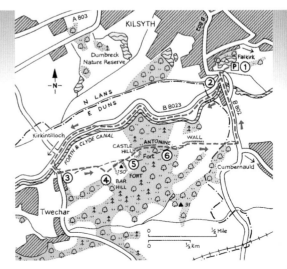

North Lanarkshire · SCOTLAND

PENTLAND HILLS *SOLDIERS AND SAINTS*

7 miles (11.3km) 3hrs Ascent: 837ft (255m)
Paths: Wide firm tracks, short stretches can be muddy, 3 stiles
Suggested map: aqua3 OS Explorer 344 Pentland Hills
Grid reference: NT 212679
Parking: Car park at end of Bonaly Road, by Edinburgh bypass

Across the hills near Edinburgh's reservoirs.
❶ From car park by bypass, follow signs to **Easter Kinleith** and walk along metalled track. Reach water treatment works on your L-H side. Continue past works to gate by East of Scotland Water sign.
❷ Go through kissing gate and continue, keeping **Torduff Reservoir** on L-H side. At top of **reservoir**, cross bridge and follow metalled track as it bends round to R. Walk under line of electricity pylons, and go over small bridge, passing artificial waterfall on L-H side, and continue past **Clubbiedean Reservoir**.
❸ Path bears R, with fields on both sides. Go under another line of pylons and walk to **Easter Kinleith** farm. Follow path as it bends back to L ('Harlaw'). Pass sign for Poets' Glen and continue over bridge and on to white house on L-H side called **Crossroads**.
❹ Turn L and follow sign for **Glencorse Reservoir**. Follow track, past conifer plantation on your L-H side, then cross stile next to metal gate. Continue ahead to

reach 2 more metal gates, where you cross a stile on L-H side signposted to Glencorse.
❺ Follow track, with hills either side; cross old stone stile. Continue in same direction to copse of conifers on R-H side, with Glencorse Reservoir ahead. Turn **L** here, following sign to Colinton by **Bonaly**.
❻ Walk uphill and maintain direction to go through gap in wire fence. Track narrows and takes you through hills, until it eventually opens out. Maintain direction to fence encircling conifers. Keep fence on L and walk down to cross stile on L-H side.
❼ Walk past **Bonaly Reservoir**, go through kissing gate and walk downhill, with good views over Edinburgh. Go through wooden gate and continue ahead, walking downhill, with trees on either side. Go through another kissing gate and follow tarmac path ahead, passing **Scout Centre** on R-H side followed by **Bonaly Tower**. Turn **L** at bridge over bypass and return to car park.

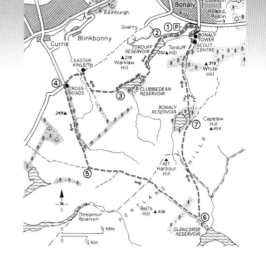

EDINBURGH OLD TOWN *MURKY SECRETS*

2 miles (3.2km) 1hr Ascent: 197ft (60m)
Paths: City streets, some hill tracks
Suggested map: AA Street by Street Edinburgh
Grid reference: NT 256739
Parking: Several NCP car parks in Edinburgh

Through Edinburgh's Old Town.
❶ From main entrance to **Waverley Station**, turn L, go to end of street, then cross and walk up Cockburn Street to **Royal Mile**. Turn **L** and walk downhill. Continue to black gates of **Holyroodhouse**. Turn **R** and walk to face new **Parliament visitor centre**.
❷ Turn **L** and follow road to R, then turn **R** again past **Dynamic Earth** (building looks like huge white woodlouse) and walk up into Holyrood Road. Turn **L**, walk past new buildings of *The Scotsman*, and walk up to St Mary's Street, where you turn **R** and rejoin **Royal Mile**.
❸ Turn **L**, stroll to main road, then turn **L** along South Bridge. At Chambers Street turn **R** and pass **museums**. At end of road, cross and turn **L** to see little statue of Greyfriars Bobby, a dog that refused to leave this spot after his master died.
❹ You can now cross road and make short detour into **Greyfriars Kirk** to see where Greyfriars Bobby is

buried close to his master. Or simply turn **R** and walk down Candlemaker Row. At bottom, turn **L** and wander into atmospheric **Grassmarket** – once a haunt of the body-snatchers Burke and Hare, it's now filled with shops and lively restaurants.
❺ When you've explored **Grassmarket**, walk up winding Victoria Street (it says West Bow at bottom). About two thirds of way up look out for flight of steps hidden away on L. Climb them and at top walk ahead to join **Royal Mile** again.
❻ Turn **L** to walk up and visit **castle**. Then walk down **Royal Mile** again, peeking into dark wynds (alleyways) that lead off it. Pass St Giles' **Cathedral** on your R – well worth a visit.
❼ Next on L pass City Chambers (under which lies the mysterious Mary King's Close). Continue to junction with Cockburn Street. Turn **L** and walk back down this winding street. At bottom, cross road and return to **Waverley Station**.

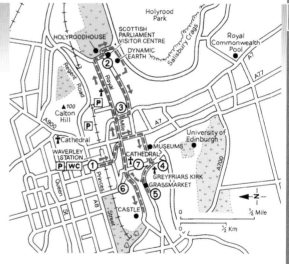

EDINBURGH NEW TOWN *LURING THE LITERATI*

3 miles (4.8km) 1hr 30min Ascent: 164ft (50m)
Paths: Busy city streets
Suggested map: AA Street by Street Edinburgh
Grid reference: NT 257739 **Parking:** Several large car parks in central Edinburgh

A walk in the footsteps of literary giants.
❶ From **TIC**, turn **L** and walk along **Princes Street**. Just after Scott Monument on L, cross road to Jenners department store. Continue along **Princes Street**, take **R** turn up Hanover Street.
❷ Take 2nd turning on L and walk along **George Street** to **Charlotte Square**. Turn **R** and **R** again to go along Young Street. At end, turn **L** and walk down North Castle Street to **Queen Street**.
❸ Cross road, turn **L**, then **R** down Wemyss Place and **R** into Heriot Row. At Howe Street turn **L** and, before church in middle of street, turn **L** and walk along South East Circus Place. Walk past Royal Circus and down into **Stockbridge**.
❹ Cross bridge, turn **L** along Dean Terrace. At end, turn **R** into Ann Street. At Dean Park Crescent turn **R** and follow road round into Leslie Place and into **Stockbridge** again. Cross road to walk down St Bernard's Row (almost opposite). Follow this then bear **L** into Arboretum Avenue.

❺ Follow road past **Water of Leith** and down to Inverleith Terrace. Cross over and walk up **Arboretum Place** to entrance to **Botanic Gardens** on R. Turn **L** after exploring gardens and retrace steps to **Stockbridge** again.
❻ Turn **L** at Hectors bar and walk uphill, then turn **L** along St Stephen Street. At church, follow road and turn **L** along Great King Street. At end, turn **R**, then immediately **L** to walk along Drummond Place, past Dublin Street and continue ahead into London Street.
❼ At roundabout turn **R** and walk up Broughton Street to Picardy Place. Turn **L**, pass statue of Sherlock Holmes, bear **L** towards **Playhouse Theatre**. Cross over, continue **L**, then turn **R** into Leopold Place and **R** again into Blenheim Place. At church turn **R**, walk up steps and turn **L** at meeting of paths.
❽ Go up steps on R, walk over **Calton Hill**, then turn **R** to pass cannon. Go downhill, take steps on your **L** and walk down into Regent Road. Turn **R** and walk back into **Princes Street** and start.

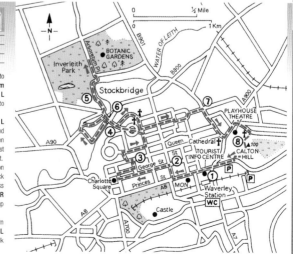

City of Edinburgh

City of Edinburgh • SCOTLAND

943 LEITH *INTOXICATING MEMORIES*

3½ miles (5.7km) 1hr 30min **Ascent:** Negligible

Paths: Wide riverside paths and city streets

Suggested map: aqua3 OS Explorer 350 Edinburgh

Grid reference: start NT 243739; finish NT 271766

Parking: Scottish National Gallery of Modern Art, Belford Road

Along the river to Edinburgh's ancient port.

❶ From junction of Dean Bridge and Queensferry Street, turn **L** to walk down Bell's Brae. You are now in **Dean Village**, which dates back to 1128. It was once a milling centre and had 11 water mills producing meal for Edinburgh. At bottom, turn **R** into Miller Row.

❷ Follow this to walk under impressive arches of Dean Bridge, designed by Thomas Telford and opened in 1832. Your path then runs along bottom of steeply sided gorge, beside **Water of Leith**, and feels extremely rural. Pass old well on your L, followed by impressive **St Bernard's Well**.

❸ **St Bernard's Well** was discovered by schoolboys in 1760. The mineral water was said to have healing properties and, in 1789, the present Roman Temple was built. From here continue along main path, then go up steps. Turn **L**, and go **R** on to Dean Terrace to reach **Stockbridge**.

❹ Cross road; go down steps ahead, immediately to R of building with clock tower. Continue to follow path beside river. Where path ends, climb on to road, turn **L** and then **R** to go down Arboretum Avenue.

❺ Walk along this road, then turn **R** along path marked Rocheid Path. This runs beside river and is popular cycleway and jogging path. Follow this, passing backs of Colonies – low-cost housing built by Edinburgh Co-operative for artisans in the late 19th century. Walk to Tanfield Bridge.

❻ Go **R**, over bridge, up steps, then turn **L**, walking towards clock tower. At end turn **L** along Warriston Place, cross road. Turn **R** down Warriston Crescent, lined with elegant town houses. Continue to **park**.

❼ Bear **R**, around edge of park, then follow path uphill between trees. Turn **L** at top and follow cycle track ('**Leith** 1¼'). Follow it into **Leith**, where it brings you out near old Custom House. Bear **R** then **L** to walk along **The Shore**, before returning to town by bus.

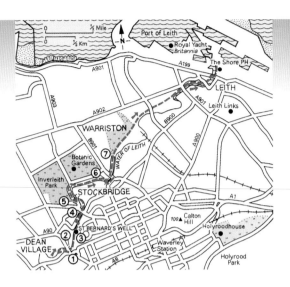

Falkirk • SCOTLAND

944 FALKIRK *REINVENTING THE WHEEL*

2 miles (3.2km); 4 miles (6.4km) with monument 1hr **Ascent:** 197ft (60m)

Paths: Canal tow paths and town streets

Suggested map: aqua3 OS Explorer 349 Falkirk, Cumbernauld & Livingston

Grid reference: NS 868800

Parking: Car park at Lock 16, by Union Inn

Along the canal to a 21st-century waterwheel.

❶ Start at **Union Inn** by **Lock 16**, once one of the best-known pubs in Scotland catering for canal passengers. Turn **R**, away from canal, then go **R** along road. Turn **R** along Tamfourhill Road and go through kissing gate on **L**-H side of road. Continue along this path (alternatively, don't turn up Tamfourhill Road yet, but continue uphill to go under viaduct. Continue to **monument** on L. This commemorates the Battle of Falkirk (1298) where William Wallace was beaten by Edward I's troops). Retrace your steps, under viaduct, turn **L** into Tamfourhill Road, and **L** through kissing gate on L-H side of road.

❷ This takes you on to section of Antonine Wall – there's a deep ditch and rampart behind it. Walk along parallel with Tamfourhill Road. At end go up bank on **R**-H side then down steps to join road by kissing gate.

❸ Go **L** to continue along road to another kissing gate on L leading you to another, shorter, section of wall. Leave wall, rejoin road and continue to mini-roundabout. Turn **L** along Maryfield Place. At end join public footpath signed to canal tow path and woodland walks. Follow this track as it winds up and over railway bridge, then on to **Union Canal**.

❹ Don't cross canal but turn **R** along tow path. This long straight stretch is popular with joggers. Eventually reach **Roughcastle** tunnel – it currently closes at 6PM to protect the Wheel from vandalism.

❺ Walk through tunnel – it's bright, clean and dry – to new **Falkirk Wheel** and another section of **Antonine Wall**. Walk on as far as **Wheel**, then continue to visitor centre at bottom. Bear **R** from here to cross bridge over **Forth and Clyde Canal**.

❻ Turn **R** and walk along tow path. Lots of dog walkers and cyclists come along here, while people frequently go canoeing along the canal. Continue to return to **Lock 16**, then turn **R** and cross canal again to return to start at **Union Inn**.

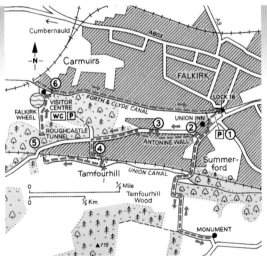

Argyll & Bute • SCOTLAND

945 BENMORE *A BOTANIC GARDEN*

4 miles (6.4km) 2hrs 30min **Ascent:** 459ft (140m)

Paths: Mainly forest roads and well-made footpaths, 1 stile

Suggested map: aqua3 OS Explorer 363 Cowal East

Grid reference: NS 142855

Parking: Car park at Benmore Botanic Garden

Discover the story of James Duncan, the man who altered the Cowal landscape.

❶ From car park cross A815 and follow footpath past a waymarker for Black Gates. Pass sign for Big Tree Walk and turn **R** on to surfaced lane. Continue along this lane for about 1 mile (1.6km) and just after parapet of bridge is first footpath to **Puck's Glen** on L.

❷ Milestone here points to Dunoon Pier 6 miles. Ignore this entrance and continue along lane until you reach car park. Turn **L** and along footpath past waymarker pole for **Puck's Glen**. Climb uphill on a steep path.

❸ At top of hill path levels out then starts to head back downhill, rather steeply on series of steps to bottom of gorge. Signpost at junction at bottom of steps points **L** for lower gorge and **R** for upper.

❹ Turn **R**, head downhill on another set of steps then cross bridge on **L** and turn **R** to head along footpath on opposite side of stream. Head uphill, cross another bridge then go past series of small waterfalls. Eventually reach yet another bridge to cross before coming to set of steps that takes you up steep part of hillside to another bridge at top. After crossing it, path levels out slightly and continues through trees to reach T-junction with forestry road.

❺ At junction there is waymarker and signpost. Turning **R** will lead you along forest road to Kilmun Arboretum. However, for this walk you must turn **L**, following signs for Black Gates. Because of ongoing forestry operations and renovations to several footpaths, diversions may be in place or footpaths may simply be closed.

❻ Follow signs to **L** and go on to path for Black Gates car park and, from there, return to **botanic garden**. Otherwise continue on forest road until you reach a gate near its end. Cross a stile then turn **L** at T-junction on to A815. Walk along here for ½ mile (800m) to return to start.

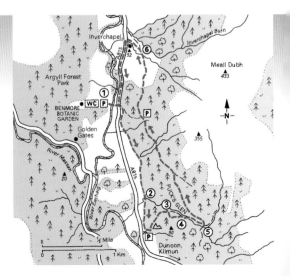

Argyll & Bute

DUNARDRY FOREST AROUND MHOINE MHOR

8¼ miles (13.3km) 5hrs **Ascent:** 176ft (55m)

Paths: Canal tow path, country roads and farm tracks
Suggested map: aqua3 OS Explorer 358 Lochgilphead & Knapdale North
Grid reference: NR 824908
Parking: Dunardry Forest car park

A canal and Scotland's last wild peat bog.

1 From car park descend steps, cross road and turn **L**. Continue to white cottage on **R**. Turn **R** and on to dirt track that runs behind cottage then go through gap between fence and wall. Cross canal over **Dunardry Lock** and turn **L** on to tow path.

2 Continue to **Bellanoch** Bridge; turn **R** on to road, cross **Islandadd Bridge** and on to B8025. This narrow, but quiet, road is long, straight and runs through **Moine Mhor**. Continue for nearly 2 miles (3.2km); turn **R** on to unclassified road ('Drimvore').

3 Continue for 1¾ miles (2.8km) as road runs through **National Nature Reserve** and passes farms of **Dalvore** and **Drimvore**. Finally reach T-junction with **A816** and turn **R**. After ½ mile (800m) Historic Scotland fingerpost points to **Dunadd Fort**.

4 Turn **R** here on to long straight farm road and continue, passing farm of **Dunadd**, to Historic Scotland car park. Make your way towards hill on well-trodden path, go past house on **L** and through kissing gate. Continue on path, following directions arrows, to emerge through gap in rocks within outer ramparts.

5 Continue to summit and then return by same route to car park. Leave it and turn **R** on to farm track. Go through gate then, almost immediately, go **L** through 2nd and follow it as it curves **L**.

6 Go through another just before road turns **R** and heads uphill. Continue following road going through another gate until you reach **Dunamuck** farm. Turn **L** through steading, go through gate and head downhill on farm road, continuing to T-junction with **A816**.

7 Turn **R** on to road and follow it for ½ mile (800m) then turn **R** on to unclassified road signposted from **Cairnbaan Hotel**. After ¼ mile (400m) turn **R** on to B841 towards Crinan. As road turns **L** across swing bridge keep straight ahead and on to canal tow path. Follow this back to **Dunardry Lock** and retrace your steps to car park.

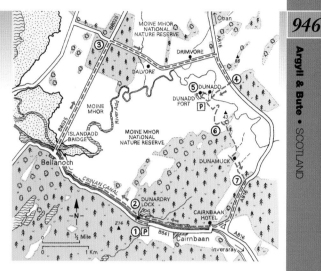

KILMARTIN GLEN NEOLITHIC MONUMENTS

3½ miles (5.7km) 3hrs **Ascent:** Negligible

Paths: Boggy fields, old coach road and country lanes, 3 stiles
Suggested map: aqua3 OS Explorer 358 Lochgilphead & Knapdale North
Grid reference: NR 835988
Parking: Car park outside Kilmartin church

A short walk to the stone shrines and monuments in the valley of the ghosts.

1 From car park visit Kilmartin church to view stones and Kilmartin Cross. Leave church, turn **L** and walk along road past **Kilmartin House**, exit village and head downhill towards garage on **L**. Just before garage turn **L**, go through kissing gate and head across field to **Glebe Cairn**.

2 From **cairn** head half **R**, across field; cross stile. In wet weather this can be very boggy. Cross stream by bridge. Go through gate and turn **L** on to old coach road. Follow this to next **cairn**. Go **L** over a stile and follow path to visit **cairn**.

3 Return to **cairn** and turn **L**, continuing to next **cairn**. After exploring this, follow coach road to **Kilmartin school**, where route becomes a metalled road. Go through crossroads, past **Nether Largie** farm and, ignoring **cairn** on **L**, continue short distance to **Temple Wood** ahead on **R**.

4 Go through gate on **R** into Temple Wood, then return by same route. Turn **R** on to road and continue until you reach a T-junction. Turn **L** and walk along this road until you come to sign on **R** for **Ri Cruin Cairn**. Cross wall via stile and proceed along well-defined path to ancient monument.

5 Return by same route and turn **R** on to road. Follow it to T-junction then turn **L** and keep straight ahead until you reach car park at Lady Glassary Wood. Opposite this take path to **L** ('Temple Wood'). Cross bridge, go through gate, cross another bridge and head towards **standing stones**.

6 Turn **R** and walk across field away from **stones** towards wood. Go through gate and follow fenced path to **Nether Largie Cairn**. From here continue along fenced path, go through another gate and turn **R** on to road. Continue past **Nether Largie** farm and **Kilmartin school** and then retrace your steps back to Kilmartin church and car park.

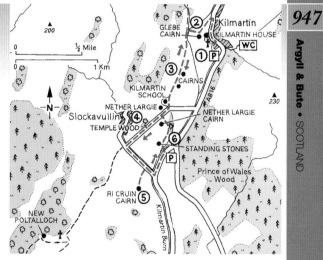

CRUACHAN THE HILL WITH THE HOLE

2 miles (3.2km) 1hr 45min **Ascent:** 1,200ft (365m)

Paths: Steep rugged paths, 2 ladder stiles
Suggested map: aqua3 OS Explorer 377 Loch Etive & Glen Orchy
Grid reference: NN 078268
Parking: Two pull-ins on north side of A85, opposite visitor centre; lay-by ½ mile (800m) west. Not visitor centre car park

Along Loch Awe from Cruachan Reservoir.

1 Two paths run up on either side of **Falls of Cruachan**. Both are initially rough and steep through woodland. The western one starts at tarred lane opposite entrance to **power station** (not visitor centre, slightly further to west). This diminishes to track, which becomes rough and crosses railway at level crossing. Path continues uphill in steep zig-zags through birch, rowan and oak. There are points to stop and look along **Loch Awe**, which disappears into distance. Path continues steeply to top of wood.

2 Here high ladder stile crosses deer fence. With stream on your **R**, continue uphill on small path to track below **Cruachan dam**. Turn **L**, up to base of dam. Because it's tucked back into corrie, it can't be seen from below. Hollows between 13 huge buttresses send back echoes. Steps on **L** lead up below base of **dam**, then iron steps take you to top.

3 From here look across **reservoir** and up to skyline that's slightly jagged at back **L** corner, where Ben Cruachan's ridge sharpens to rocky edge. In other direction, your tough ascent is rewarded by long view across low country. Turn **R** to **dam** end, where track leads down **R** to junction, then **R** for 50yds (46m).

4 At this point you could stay on track to cross stream just ahead, leading to top of path used for coming up. You might wish to do this if you are concerned about ladder stile on main route. There is no clear path as you go down to **L** of stream, to reach this high, steep and slightly wobbly ladder stile. Below this is clear path that descends grassy slopes and gives good view of some of **Falls of Cruachan**. Inside wood, path becomes steep and rough for rest of way down. Just above railway, it turns to **L**, then passes under line by low tunnel beside **Falls of Cruachan Station**, to reach A85 below.

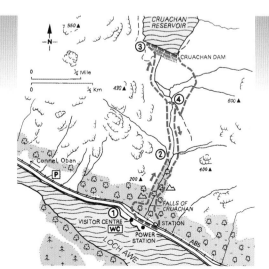

949 IONA HOLY ISLAND OF ST COLUMBA

5¼ miles (8.4km) 3hrs 30min **Ascent:** 650ft (198m) ▲
Paths: Tracks, sandy paths, some rugged rock and heather
Suggested map: aqua3 OS Explorer 373 Iona, Staffa & Ross of Mull
Grid reference: NM 286240
Parking: Ferry terminal at Fionnphort on Mull

A circuit of Iona to the marble quarry and Coracle Bay.

❶ Ferries cross to **Iona** about every hour. On island, take tarred road on L, passing **Martyr's Bay**. After 2nd larger bay, rejoin road as it bends R. Follow road across island to gate on to Iona **golf course** (please keep dogs on leads).

❷ Take sandy track ahead, then bear L past small cairn to shore. Turn L along shore to large beach. At end, bear L up narrow valley. After 100yds (91m) pass small concrete hut to join stony track. It passes fenced **reservoir** and drops to corner of **Loch Staoineig**. Walk along to L of lochan on path, improved in places, that runs gently down to **Coracle Bay**. Cross to L of area with furrows of lazybed cultivation – fields drained to improve crop yields – and reach shore just to L of rocky knoll.

❸ Route ahead is pathless and hard. If your ferry leaves in 2 hours' time or earlier, return by outward route. Otherwise, return inland for 200yds (183m) and bear R into little grassy valley. After 100yds (91m), go through broken wall and bear slightly L, past another inlet on R. Cross heather to eastern shoreline of island. Bear L, above small sea cliff, for ¼ mile (400m). Turn sharp R into little valley descending to remnants of **marble quarry**.

❹ Turn inland, back up valley to its head. Pass low walls of 2 ruined cottages and continue for about 200yds (183m) to fence corner. Keep fence on your L, picking way through heather, rock and bog on sheep paths. Dun I with its cairn appears ahead – aim directly for it to reach edge of fields, where fence runs across ahead. Turn R along it to small iron gate.

❺ This leads to track that passes **Ruannich** farm to tarred road of outward walk. Cross into farm track, which bends to R at **Maol**. It reaches **Baile Mor** (Iona village) at ruined **nunnery**. Just ahead is **abbey** with its squat square tower, or turn R directly to ferry pier.

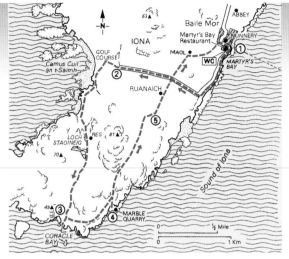

950 INVERARAY THE CASTLE OF CUPS

4 miles (6.4km) 2hrs 15min **Ascent:** 900ft (274m) ▲
Paths: Clear, mostly waymarked paths, no stiles
Suggested map: aqua3 OS Explorer 363 Cowal East
Grid reference: NN 096085
Parking: Pay-and-display, Inveraray Pier

Enjoy a fine view of Inveraray.

❶ Follow seafront past Argyll Hotel and bear L towards **Inveraray Castle**. At 1st junction, turn R past **football pitch** with **standing stone**. After coach park on L and end wall of castle on R, estate road on L is signed '**Dun na Cuaiche Walk**'. It passes a **memorial** to clansmen killed for religious reasons in 1685. Cross stone-arched **Garden Bridge** to junction.

❷ Turn R to riverside track and follow it to picnic table with view back to castle. Rough track runs up L, but turn off instead on to small path just to R of this, beside stone gatepost. It climbs quite steeply through area where attempts are currently being made to eradicate rhododendron.

❸ At green track above, turn L, slightly downhill, for 50yds (46m). Steps on R lead up to terraced path that goes slightly downhill around hillside for ¼ mile (400m). Turn sharp R up steep path with rope handrail. This works its way back around hill, passing below small crag. Where it crosses open screes, there are fine views to R over **Inveraray**. At path junction, turn L, following waymarker pole up through woods. As slope eases, path crosses grassy clearing to meet wider one. Turn L, in zig-zags, to reach summit of **Dun na Cuaiche. Tower** at top should be just seen from below, but also offers outstanding views.

❹ Return down path to clearing, but this time keep ahead. Path, rather muddy, bends L then enters plantation and becomes clear track. It passes between 2 dry-stone pillars where wall crosses, turns back sharp L, and passes between 2 more pillars lower down same wall. Continue down track, ignoring side-tracks on L, to **lime kiln** on R.

❺ Below **lime kiln**, gate leads out into field. Cross it diagonally L, going over track to kissing gate beyond. This leads into wood of sycamores. Path runs down to track junction before **Garden Bridge** (Point ❷). Return along castle driveway to **Inveraray**.

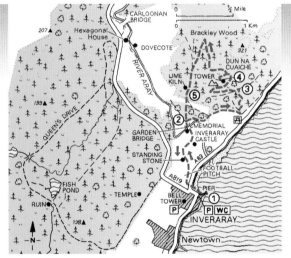

951 STIRLING A BRAVEHEART

4 miles (6.4km) 2hrs **Ascent:** 279ft (85m) ▲
Paths: Ancient city streets and some rough tracks
Suggested map: aqua3 OS Explorer 366 Stirling & Ochil Hills West
Grid reference: NS 795933
Parking: On streets near TIC or in multi-storey car parks

Discover the truth about William Wallace on this town trail.

❶ From **TIC** on Dumbarton Road, cross road and turn L. Walk past statue of Robert Burns then, just before Albert Halls, turn R and walk back on yourself. Just past statue of Rob Roy, turn L and join Back Walk.

❷ Follow path uphill, with old town wall on your R. Go up flight of steps that takes you on to Upper Back Wall. It's steady climb, up past Lady's Rock and on past Star Pyramid, triangular cone by graveyard.

❸ Continue following path uphill to Stirling Castle. Take path running downhill just to side of **visitor centre**, so **castle** is on your L. At bottom go L and walk to cemetery. Turn R and follow path to other side of cemetery. Bear R and go through gap in wall.

❹ Follow track downhill on to Gowan Hill. There are several branching tracks but continue on main path to – heading for cannons on hill ahead. Walk down to wider grassy track, then climb uphill to Beheading Stone.

Retrace your steps to wide track and follow it to road.

❺ Turn R along Lower Bridge Street, then fork R into Upper Bridge Street. Continue ahead, then turn R down Barn Road. Follow it uphill, then go L at top. Eventually pass Castle Esplanade, followed by Argyll's Lodging, to reach junction.

❻ Turn L, passing Hermann's Restaurant and Mercat Cross. Turn R at bottom down Bow Street, then L along Baker Street. When you reach pedestrianised Friars Street, turn L and walk down to end.

❼ Turn R, then 1st L to station. Turn L, then R over bridge, continuing to riverside. Continue to join Abbey Road. Bear L at end, go R over footbridge and continue along South Street, turning R at end to visit remains of Cambuskenneth Abbey.

❽ Retrace your steps, over footbridge and back to station. Turn R at station, then L at top to pass Thistle Shopping Centre. Continue along Port Street, then turn R and walk along Dumbarton Road to start.

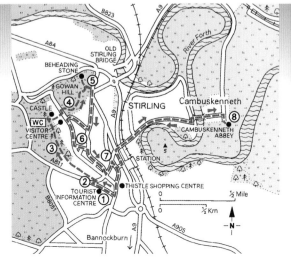

CALLANDER *ROMANCE OF ROB ROY*

3 miles (4.8km) 2hrs 15min **Ascent:** 896ft (273m) ▲
Paths: Forest tracks and some rocky paths
Suggested map: aqua3 OS Explorer 365 The Trossachs
Grid reference: NN 625079
Parking: Riverside car park

Steep wooded paths lead through the crags for views of the Trossachs.

❶ From car park, walk back to main road; turn **L**. Follow this, then turn **R** along Tulliepan Crescent. Just in front of new housing estate, turn **L** and follow wide track. Where track splits, take path on **L** ('The Crags').

❷ Path winds steeply uphill through trees and can get slippery after rain. Keep following path and cross footbridge. Climb to reach wall on L-H side, after which path narrows. Follow it to pass large boulder.

❸ Continue following path, which eventually bears **L**, up steps to fence. Cross footbridge, scramble over rocks and go through metal kissing gate. Eventually come to memorial **cairn**, created in 1897 for Queen Victoria's Diamond Jubilee. On a clear day there are panoramic views of the surrounding countryside.

❹ Leaving **cairn**, your path now begins to wind downhill. It is rocky in places and you'll need to take care as you descend. Eventually spot road through trees. Turn **R** into trees and walk down to join road.

❺ Turn **R** along road – you'll see Wallace Monument in distance. Soon pass sign on R-H side for Red Well, where water runs a distinctly reddish colour owing to iron traces in the local rock. Continue to car park on your **L**. Detour here to see Bracklyn Falls.

❻ After car park, stay on road for 100yds (91m), then turn **R** to climb wooden steps – they're signposted 'The Crags Upper Wood Walk', but sign faces away from you. Walk past small building, cross little footbridge and walk to crossing of footpaths.

❼ Turn **L** for few paces, then turn **R**. Continue through woods, cross footbridge and at wider, slate-covered track, turn **R** uphill. At end of track, turn **L** and walk downhill to wooden seat and footbridge.

❽ Take path that runs to **R** of seat (don't cross footbridge). Follow path downhill back to place where you entered woods. Turn **R**, then go **L** along main road back into **Callander** to car park.

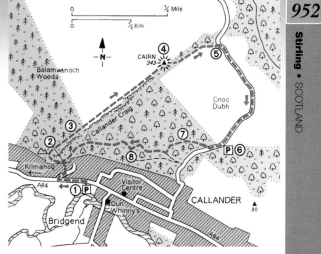

THE WHANGIE *A GASH IN THE ROCK*

2½ miles (4km) 3hrs **Ascent:** 515ft (157m) ▲
Paths: Hill tracks and well-trodden footpaths, 2 stiles
Suggested map: aqua3 OS Explorer 347 Loch Lomond South
Grid reference: NS 511808
Parking: Queen's View car park

The hidden training ground of generations of rock climbers.

❶ Head toward **L** of car park on to small hillock where Queen Victoria stood for her first view of Loch Lomond. Descend and cross stile over wall where well-defined path crosses duckboards and meanders uphill. Turn **R** to follow edge of wood. After duckboards this is pleasant grassy walk.

❷ As you get to top, near fence, admire view. Look away to your **R** for expanse of Loch Lomond and Ben Lomond towering over it to **R** and Arrochar Hills away to **L**. Cross ladder stile over fence; turn **R** on to narrow but well-trodden path. Follow this along side of hill.

❸ When path forks go **L** and head uphill. As you near top you will see Ordnance Survey pillar on summit of **Auchineden Hill**. Head towards this by any route you find. Ground round here is often boggy and several attempts may be required to find best way across it. To the south from here are the Kilpatrick Hills and, beyond

them, the River Clyde. Look for Burncrooks Reservoir to your **R** and Kilmannan Reservoir to your **L**. Beyond is Cochno Loch, another reservoir and popular excursion for Clydebank residents.

❹ Looking towards Ben Lomond, the area in front of you is Stockie Muir. Walk towards Ben on path leading away from OS pillar and go downhill into dip. Another path runs across this. Turn **L** on to it and follow it round side of small hill. Where path curves **R** look for crags on **R**.

❺ Here you'll find hidden opening to **The Whangie**. It's easy to miss so look out for spot on **R** for easy climb few steps up to crags and it's as if wall opens up in front of you. Climb into **The Whangie** and walk to other end on path.

❻ Exit **The Whangie** and head to **R** on another footpath. Continue on this until it rejoins path you took on uphill journey. Go back to stile then retrace your steps downhill and back to car park.

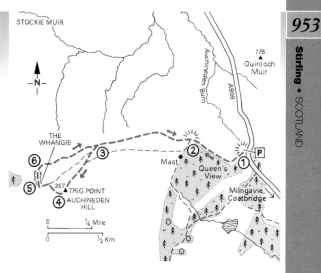

ABERFOYLE *QUEEN ELIZABETH FOREST PARK*

4 miles (6.4km) 3hrs **Ascent:** 446ft (136m) ▲
Paths: Forest roads and footpaths
Suggested map: aqua3 OS Explorer 365 The Trossachs
Grid reference: NN 519014
Parking: At visitor centre near Aberfoyle

The Highland Boundary Fault and along a 19th-century inclined railway.

❶ From front of **visitor centre** turn **L**, go down steps on to footpath and follow blue waymarkers on **Highland Boundary Fault Trail**. Continue on this trail to reach **Waterfall** of the Little Fawn with its 55ft (16.7m) drop. Shortly after this turn **L** to cross bridge then **R** following white arrow **L** again on to forest road.

❷ This is part of **National Cycle Route (NCN)** so look out for cyclists. Head uphill on this road following blue **Highland Boundary Fault** markers and **NCN** Route 7 signs. When road forks at junction, keep **L** continuing uphill until you reach crossroads.

❸ Turn **R**, at blue waymarker, on to smaller, rougher road. **Boundary Fault Trail** parts company with NCN Route 7 here. The going is easy along here. Continue until you eventually reach viewpoint and seat on **R**.

❹ From here road heads uphill until it reaches waymarker near path heading uphill towards **mast**.

Turn **R** then go through barrier and start descending. Although this is well-made path it is nevertheless very steep descent through woods and great care should be taken.

❺ This path follows line of **Limecraigs Railway** an early 19th-century inclined railway used for transporting limestone. It continues downhill to go through another barrier where path is intersected by forest road. Cross this road, go through another barrier and once again head downhill.

❻ At bottom of hill is set of steps leading to forest road. Turn **R** on to road and follow blue waymarkers. Stay on this road until you reach green signpost on **L** pointing to **visitor centre**. Turn **L** on to downhill track and head through woods.

❼ Eventually you will reach board announcing end of trail. From here route is signed back to **visitor centre**. When trail forks take R-H turning and head uphill beside handrail and return to start.

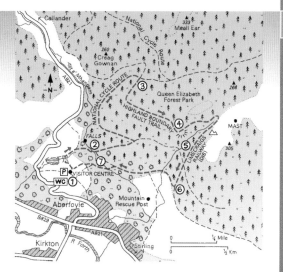

955 ABERFOYLE GREAT FOREST OF LOCH ARD

3½ miles (5.7km) 2hrs **Ascent:** 98ft (30m)
Paths: Roads, forest roads and trails
Suggested map: aqua3 OS Explorer 365 The Trossachs
Grid reference: NS 521009
Parking: Car park at Aberfoyle beside tourist office in centre of town

Discover the Stone of Destiny's hiding place and birthplace of the Scottish Parliament.
❶ Leave from west end of car park and turn **L** into Manse Road. Cross narrow bridge over **River Forth** (river has its source near here although it is more usually associated with Edinburgh) and continue along grass beside road until 1st junction on R. Turn **R** here and head uphill, passing **Covenanters Inn**. Short distance past here is open countryside and start of **Great Forest of Loch Ard**.
❷ Head straight on along forest road, keeping an ear open for heavy timber lorries. During week this can get fairly busy, as this is main forestry extraction route, so keep well into side. After approximately ½ mile (800m) you will reach staggered crossroads. Continue straight ahead along forest road until you come to turning on R with yellow waymarker. Turn **R** here.
❸ Follow waymarked trail through forest almost to banks of **Duchray Water**. This rises on the north face

of Ben Lomond and joins with **Avondhu** from **Loch Ard** to create the **River Forth** near Aberfoyle. Path curves R, continues to descend slightly to junction.
❹ Turn **R** and follow path through trees to north banks of **Lochan Spling**. Path then swings **L** and, at end of **Lochan**, turns **R** at waymarker pole, crosses small stream and heads slightly uphill.
❺ When path reaches T-junction, turn **L** and rejoin main forest access road continuing along it to **Covenanters Inn**. This takes its name not from the activities of the 17th-century Scottish Presbyterians, who were persecuted by the Stuart monarchy for refusing to give up their faith, but to the activities of 20th-century Scottish Nationalists.
❻ Continue past **inn**, where later a group of Nationalists temporarily hid Scotland's Stone of Destiny when it was liberated from Westminster Abbey in 1950, then turn **L** on to Manse Road at junction and return to start.

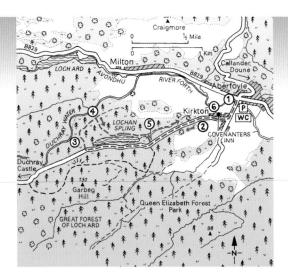

956 LOCH LOMOND THE SALLOCHY WOODS

2 miles (3.2km) 2hrs 30min **Ascent:** 131ft (40m)
Paths: West Highland Way, forest trail and forest road
Suggested map: aqua3 OS Explorer 364 Loch Lomond North
Grid reference: NS 380957
Parking: Sallochy Woods car park

A gentle stroll by the bonnie banks of Loch Lomond, Britain's largest fresh water lake.
❶ From car park head towards entrance on to main road. Go **R** on to track beside starting post to **Sallochy Trail**. Cross over road and then continue along trail on other side. This trail runs alongside some woodland which you should keep on your R-H side. Continue and, when path eventually forks, keep **R** and go into wood following obvious waymarker posts. The diverse woods here are part of the **Queen Elizabeth Forest Park** and contain a staggering variety of animals and plants. Over a quarter of the plants that flourish in Britain can be found here. You may spot a rare capercaillie (it's the size of a turkey), ptarmigan or even a golden eagle.
❷ Trail goes through wood and then passes into ruined 19th-century farm steading of **Wester Sallochy**, which Forestry Commission has now cleared of trees. Several buildings can be seen and it

is worth spending some time investigating these old ruins. When you have finished, circle buildings to **L** and follow well-worn trail until it ends at T-junction beside waymarker post. Turn **R** on to forest road here.
❸ Follow forest road for about ½ mile (800m) to reach gate just before junction with main road. Cross gate, then cross main road and turn **R**. Look carefully for faint track running through woods to your **L**.
❹ Follow faint track back towards **loch** (if you miss track then enter wood at any point and head west towards **loch**). When track intersects with well-surfaced footpath turn **R** on to **West Highland Way**. Follow waymarkers, keeping on main path and ignoring any subsidiary tracks branching off it.
❺ Follow path uphill through rocky section and then, as it levels off, through wood. There is some boggy ground here but strategically placed duckboards make going easier. Eventually trail passes through **Sallochy Woods** car park returning you to start.

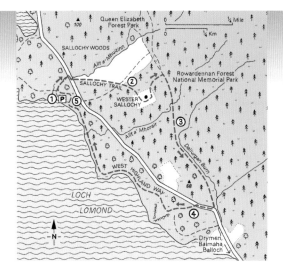

957 BALQUHIDDER ON THE TRAIL OF AN OUTLAW

2½ miles (4km) 2hrs **Ascent:** 328ft (100m)
Paths: Forest roads and hillside, 2 stiles
Suggested map: aqua3 OS Explorer 365 The Trossachs
Grid reference: NN 536209
Parking: At Balquhidder church

On the trail of the Highland outlaw, Rob Roy, and on to see his final resting place.
❶ From car park at **Balquhidder church**, walk along dirt track, go past shed and cross stile on **R-H** side which gives access to forest. Follow direction arrows on green signposts pointing to **Creag an Tuirc** along forest road and heading up hill.
❷ Continue on this obvious trail for about ½ mile (800m) then turn **R**, beside green building, again following clearly signposted route along forest road. After another ½ mile (800m) cross gate on R-H side, go slightly downhill on some stone steps and across small stream.
❸ Path now heads uphill on some stone steps, through old pine trees and on towards summit of knoll. Here is cairn erected by Clan Maclaren Society in 1987 to commemorate their 25th anniversary. The plaque proclaims that this place is the ancient rallying point of their clan.

❹ A seat below the cairn is a grand place to rest after the climb up here. Sit for a while and enjoy superb views over the meandering line of **River Balvag** and the length of **Loch Voil** with Braes of Balquhidder rising steeply above it. You can see the route that Rob Roy's funeral procession would have taken from Inverlochlarig down to the village itself, and the churchyard where his body lies. Now retrace your steps back down hill but before reaching top of stone steps which you came up, take path to **L** ('Forest Walk'). This continues downhill following waymarked poles, down some steps and across small bridge. Path goes through bracken, over small stream and across stile. Eventually it will pass through small wood of young native trees before emerging on to forest road.
❺ Turn **L** here and retrace your steps back downhill over stile and turn **L** to return to car park. From here enter churchyard and turn **L**. **Rob Roy's grave** is on **L** in front of ruins of pre-Reformation church.

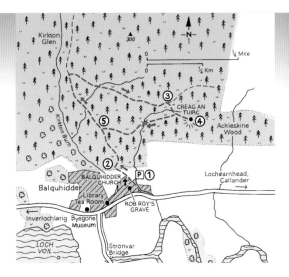

Stirling

LOCH KATRINE *ALONG THE SHORE*

6¾ miles (10.9km) 4hrs 30min Ascent: 420ft (128m)
Paths: Waterboard roads, hill tracks
Suggested map: aqua3 OS Explorers 364 Loch Lomond North; 365 The Trossachs
Grid reference: NN 404102 (on Explorer 364)
Parking: Car park at Stronachlachar Pier

A walk around Glasgow's water supply in the heart of the Trossachs.

❶ From car park follow road back towards B829 and take 2nd turning on **L**. This is access road for Scottish Water vehicles only. Continue along access road until you come to cattle grid with green gateposts at building known as **Royal Cottage**. Turn **R** just before this on to rough gravel track that heads through some dense bracken.

❷ As path emerges on to open hillside you will see 1st of several ventilation shafts and beyond it, on hill, strange **obelisk**. Follow path along this line. When you reach the **obelisk** be sure to look back for super views over **Loch Katrine** below and across to the hills with their narrow passes where Rob Roy and his men moved from **Loch Katrine** to Balquhidder and beyond, moving cattle or escaping from forces of law and order. Continue following line of ventilation shafts towards chimney-like structure on top of hill. From

here go **R** and downhill. Take great care on this section as path has eroded and is very steep. At bottom, go through gap at junction of two fences. From here go **L**.

❸ Follow well-defined track that goes through some pine trees and past another ventilation **shaft**. Keep **L** at **shaft**. It can be very muddy on this short stretch. Continue on path until it intersects forest road by stream. Cross road and look for faint track continuing downhill in same direction. In summer this path may be difficult to find because it's hidden by bracken. In this case follow line of telephone poles. Eventually after working downhill through more woodland track emerges on to B829.

❹ Turn **R** here and follow road. It will eventually emerge from **Loch Ard Forest** into open countryside. **Loch Arklet** can be seen on L; it is now connected to **Loch Katrine** by underground pipeline. When road reaches T-junction with Inversnaid road, turn **R**. When road forks, turn **R** and return to **Stronachlachar Pier**.

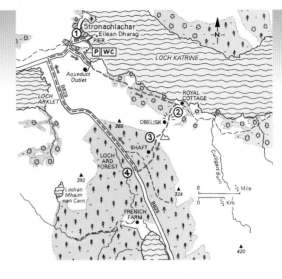

CARBETH *THE HUT COMMUNITY*

3 miles (4.8km) 2hrs 30min Ascent: 98ft (30m)
Paths: Roads, access tracks and footpaths, 1 stile
Suggested map: aqua3 OS Explorer 348 Campsie Fells
Grid reference: NX 524791
Parking: Carbeth Inn, check beforehand with landlord

Discover a working class Utopian dream.

❶ From car park at **Carbeth Inn** turn **R** on to A809. After ¼ mile (400m) take 1st turning **R** on to B821. Continue on this road for 1 mile (1.6km) passing huts on L and ignoring public footpath sign to R.

❷ Turn **R** at signpost for **West Highland Way**. There's also Scottish Rights of Way Society signpost beside this pointing to Khyber Pass Road to Mugdock Country Park – the favoured route of early walkers heading out of Glasgow to the Campsie Fells.

❸ Go through gate and continue along well-surfaced access road. Ignoring Kyber Pass turn-off, keep **R** and go over stile to follow **West Highland Way** along access road to more huts. After passing some huts on R and another hut on L look out for partially concealed public path signpost on **R** beside **West Highland Way** marker post.

❹ Turn **R** here on to narrow but well-surfaced footpath and continue along it, passing **Carbeth Loch**

on R-H side, to reach junction with drive leading to **Carbeth House**. This is a private house and is not open to the public. Turn **L**, pass house on R then take next turning on **L**.

❺ Continue along this lane ignoring public right of way sign pointing R, then head uphill to reach another grouping of **Carbeth huts**. At 1st hut, green one, road forks with narrow path branching to R. Ignore this and take wider road which passes to **L** of hut.

❻ Keep on this road as it passes through main part of **Carbeth huts**, extraordinary assortment of small dwellings, shanties and shacks. Ignore all smaller tracks branching off this road; they allow access to individual huts or other parts of the settlement.

❼ Eventually pass much larger hut on R, then smaller green one with fenced garden on L, and follow road as it curves to **L**. Continue downhill on this to reach T-junction with A809 beside **Carbeth Inn**. Turn **R** and return to car park.

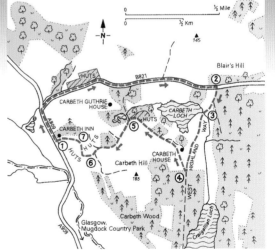

CULROSS *A LEISURELY CIRCUIT*

3 miles (4.8km) 1hr 30min Ascent: 180ft (55m)
Paths: Generally firm paths, some muddy woodland tracks
Suggested map: aqua3 OS Explorer 367 Dunfermline & Kirkcaldy
Grid reference: NS 983859 **Parking:** Culross West car park

An easy walk around an historic town.

❶ Turn **L** out of car park and walk along road, with bay to L and housing to R. Continue, past cottages, to edge of town. Take care of traffic now as there is no pavement. Pass entrance to **Dunimarle Castle** on R and continue to entrance to **Blair Castle** – now a memorial home for miners.

❷ Turn **R** and walk up tarmac drive ('private') which is lined with rhododendrons. Walk until you see **castle** on L. Before you reach it, take **R-H** turning in trees and follow it as it bears **R**. Continue to **Blair Mains** farmhouse on L.

❸ Continue on track, walking under line of pylons with fields on either side. Walk ahead towards trees and continue to gate on **L-H** side. Look carefully to spot wooden fence post on **R-H** side, with words 'West Kirk' and 'grave' painted on it in white. Take narrow **R-H** path immediately before it, through trees.

❹ Follow this path and then go through kissing gate and continue ahead, with trees on your L and fields on

your R. Go through another kissing gate, and continue as path opens out to wider, grassy track. At crossing of paths, continue ahead along narrow path and walk under a line of pylons. Soon pass remains of **church** on L.

❺ Continue ahead, past old cemetery, until track joins tarmac road. Walk in same direction to junction. Turn **R** and then head downhill – watch out for traffic now as road can be busy. Soon reach **Culross Abbey** on L-H side.

❻ Stop to visit **abbey**. Continue to walk on downhill, down Tanhouse Brae, to soon reach Mercat (old Market) Cross, with **The Study** on R-H side. Continue in same direction, down Back Causeway, to reach main road.

❼ Turn **R**, walk past tourist information centre, past Tron (old burgh weighing machine), then past large ochre-coloured building on R, **Culross Palace**. To reach starting point, continue in same direction – car park is on **L-H** side, just past children's play area.

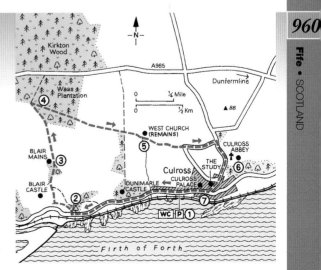

Fife

961 ST ANDREWS *ACADEMIC TRADITIONS*

4½ miles (7.2km) 2hrs **Ascent:** 33ft (10m)
Paths: Ancient streets and golden sands
Suggested map: aqua3 OS Explorer 371 St Andrews & East Fife
Grid reference: NO 506170
Parking: Free parking along The Scores, otherwise several car parks

A town trail to an ancient university.

1 With Martyrs **Monument** on The Scores in front of you, walk **L** past bandstand. At road turn **R**, walk to British Golf **Museum**, then turn **L**. Pass clubhouse of **Royal and Ancient Golf Club** on your **L**, then bear **R** at burn to reach beach.

2 Your route now takes you along **West Sands**. Walk as far as you choose, then either retrace your steps along beach or take any path through dunes to join tarmac road. Walk back to Golf **Museum**, then turn **R** and walk to main road.

3 Turn **L** and walk to St Salvator's College. Peek through archway at serene quadrangle – and look at initials PH in cobbles outside. They commemorate Patrick Hamilton, who was martyred here in 1528 – they say students who tread on the site will fail their exams. Cross over and walk to end of College Street.

4 Turn **R** and walk along Market Street. At corner turn **L** along Bell Street, then **L** again on South Street.

Just after you pass Church Street, cross over into quadrangle of St Mary's College. Join path on **R** and walk up to reach Queen's Terrace.

5 Turn **R** to reach red-brick house, then **L** down steeply sloping Dempster Terrace. At end cross burn, turn **L** and walk to main road. Cross and walk along Glebe Road. At park, take path that bears **L**, walk past play area and up to Woodburn Terrace.

6 Turn **L** to join St Mary Street, turn **L** again, then go **R** along Woodburn Place. Bear **L** beside beach. You'll get good views of **Long Pier**, where students traditionally walked on Sunday mornings. Cross footbridge and join road.

7 Bear **R** for few paces, then ascend steps on **L** to remains of church and on to famous ruined **cathedral**. Gate in wall on **L** gives access to site.

8 Your route then takes you past ancient **castle** on R, former palace/fortress. Pass Castle Visitor Centre, then continue along The Scores to return to start.

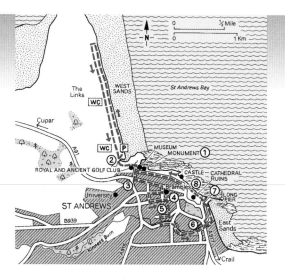

---

962 EAST NEUK *A FISHY TRAIL*

4 miles (6.4km) 1hr 30min **Ascent:** 49ft (15m)
Paths: Well-marked coastal path, 3 stiles
Suggested map: aqua3 OS Explorer 371 St Andrews & East Fife
Grid reference: start NO 613077; finish NO 569034
Parking: On street in Crail

A linear coastal walk through East Neuk.

1 From **tourist information centre** in Crail, walk down Tolbooth Wynd. At end turn **R**, continue to garage, bear **L** ('no vehicular access to harbour'). Walk by old castle wall to lookout point and view of harbour. Bear **R** to High Street.

2 Turn **L** along road, passing 2 white beacons, which help guide boats into harbour. Turn **L**, walk down West Braes ('Coast Path'). At Osbourne Terrace bear slightly **L**, go down steps, through kissing gate and on to grassy track by shore.

3 Follow path as it hugs shoreline. Soon see cormorants on rocks to your **L** and views of Isle of May. Go down steps, over slightly boggy area and continue to reach 2 derelict cottages – area known as **The Pans**.

4 Pass cottages and continue along shore, cross stone stile. Pass flat rocks on L covered with interesting little rock pools. Cross burn by footbridge –

see Bass Rock and Berwick Law on your L and village of **Anstruther** ahead. Soon reach **caves**.

5 Pass **caves**, cross stone stile on L-H side and then footbridge. Track is narrower now and passes fields R, then maritime grasses L. Big stepping stones take you to another stile; cross them to reach **Caiplie**.

6 Go through kissing gate by houses, follow wide grassy track, go through kissing gate to walk past field. Path now runs past free-range pig farm and up to **caravan park**.

7 Continue along shore, following track to play area and war memorial on R. Continue to enter Cellardyke and on to harbour. Pass it and **The Haven** restaurant; continue on John Street then on James Street.

8 At end of James Street maintain direction, then follow road as it bends down to **L**. Walk past guiding beacon and into **Anstruther's** busy little harbour. You can now either walk back to **Crail** or take bus which leaves from harbour.

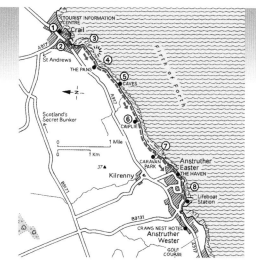

---

963 PERTH *ALONG THE TAY TO SCONE*

4 miles (6.4km) 1hr 30min **Ascent:** Negligible
Paths: City streets and wide firm tracks
Suggested map: aqua3 OS Explorer 369 Perth & Kinross
Grid reference: NO 114237
Parking: On street in Perth

A town trail around Perth with views over Scotland's ancient capital.

1 From **TIC** turn **R**, then take 1st **R** and walk around building. Turn **R** again and walk down to road. Cross and take R-H road ahead, passing bus stops. Walk down to Kinnoul Street, then cross and join Mill Street.

2 Continue down Mill Street, passing Perth **Theatre** on R-H side. Pass **Caffe Canto** on R-H side, and join Bridge Lane. Pass **museum and art gallery** on L-H side and reach Charlotte Street. Turn **L**.

3 At corner turn **L** to visit Fair Maid's House. Otherwise, cross road and turn **R** through park. Pass war memorial then bear **L** to join riverside path and good views of smart houses along opposite bank.

4 Continue ahead, passing **golf course**. At sign for 14th tee, turn **R** and follow track. At end there's wall on L. Here either go **L** of wall along enclosed cycle track (keeping ear open for cyclists), or go **R** of it to walk by water's edge.

5 Follow your chosen track until 2 tracks meet, just past electricity sub station. Walk by riverside now to enjoy great views of **Scone Palace** on opposite bank – there's a seat for a break.

6 Retrace your steps, walking back beside river or along cycle track and back to **golf course**. Turn **L** and walk back towards **Perth** until you reach cricket and football pitches on R-H side.

7 Turn **R** and walk between pitches to join Rose Terrace – John Ruskin once lived here. Turn **L**, then bear **L** at end into Charlotte Street and **R** into Bridge Lane again. Turn **L** along Skinner Gate, site of the oldest pub in Perth, and walk to end.

8 Cross over to pass **St John's Kirk**. Cross South Street and join Princes Street. At Marshall Place turn **L** and walk to **Fergusson Gallery** on L-H side. Then turn back along Marshall Place, walk up to King Street, then turn **R**. Maintain direction, then turn **L** into West Mill Street and return to start of walk.

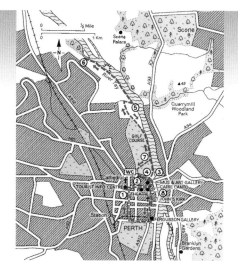

FORTINGALL *AN ANCIENT YEW*

3½ miles (5.6km) 2hrs Ascent: 33ft (10m)
Paths: Quiet roads and firm farm tracks, 1 stile
Suggested map: aqua3 OS Explorer 378 Ben Lawers & Glen Lyon
Grid reference: NN 741470
Parking: Fortingall village

An easy walk amidst mountain scenery.

1 With your back to **Fortingall Hotel**, turn **R** along road, passing several pretty thatched cottages (unusual in Scotland) on **R-H** side. Follow road over burn and then past entrance to Glen Lyon farm. Eventually reach fork in road.

2 Ignore **R-H** fork and keep ahead. Road soon crosses bridge over **River Lyon**.

3 Just over bridge turn **R** and follow road (it's tarmacked but very quiet), and walk past some little cottages on **R-H** side. Continue ahead until you reach sign for **Duneaves**.

4 Turn **L** and follow road – river is on your **L-H** side. You feel as if you're in a secret valley as you walk along here, and in late summer you can stop to pick wild raspberries that grow by the roadside. Continue past area of woodland, after which you get views across valley to Fortingall.

5 Continue to follow the road until you see a white

house on **R-H** side. Leave metalled track and turn **L** at the pylon just before the house – good views of surrounding hills.

6 Follow wide, stony track as it leads down to **Duneaves**. Just before you reach house go through the rusty gate in the wall on **R-H** side. Then walk across the field, maintaining your direction to go over a rather bouncy footbridge. Bear **R** after crossing the bridge, then go through the gate and join the road.

7 Turn **L** and walk back along road. You'll soon pass 2 sets of standing stones in the field on **L** – 6 stones in a ring near the road, and 3 further away. Walk back into **Fortingall** to reach the starting point. Note the ancient yew tree in the churchyard at Fortingall. It is generally reckoned to be about 5,000 years old and is the oldest living thing in Europe, and possibly the world. In 1769 the tree's girth was measured and found to be 56ft (17m).

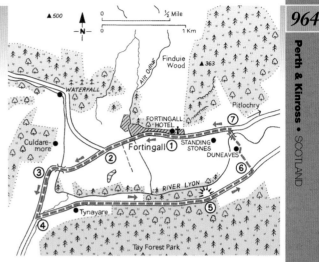

964

ALYTH *THE SWEET FRUITS*

5 miles (8km) 3hrs Ascent: 787ft (240m)
Paths: Wide grassy tracks, some rougher paths on hill
Suggested map: aqua3 OS Explorer 381 Blairgowrie, Kirriemuir & Glamis
Grid reference: NO 236486
Parking: Car park in Alyth Market Square

Through the fertile heart of Scotland.

1 From Market Square, cross burn, then turn **L** along Commercial Street, so river is on your **L-H** side. Turn **R** up Tootie Street, **R** again up Hill Street, then take Loyal Road on **L**. Continue uphill to reach sign ('Hill of Loyal Walk').

2 Walk uphill now, go through gate and continue in same direction, walking past wood on **R-H** side. Go through kissing gate, passing area that in summer is mass of purple foxgloves. Eventually path levels out and then starts to bear downhill. Maintain direction to go through kissing gate and over burn.

3 Here path becomes narrower and bears uphill, becoming rockier and more overgrown. Walk under trees, through gate and leave birch and oak woodland. Keep an eye out for deer here, as I spotted one bounding into the trees, just a few feet away from me. Maintain direction through grass, then go through kissing gate to road.

4 Turn **L**; walk along generally quiet road ('Hill of Alyth Walk'). Pass conifer plantation, house on **R-H** side and go over cattle grid. Soon turn **L** and follow signs ('Cateran Trail').

5 Walk uphill and, at crossing of tracks, turn to **R**. When ground flattens, turn **L** uphill. At another crossing of paths, turn **R**. There are lots of paths traversing hill, so choose your own route here, but essentially you must keep lakes on your **L** and don't walk as far as beacon. Make for small copse on your **R**, between 2 farmhouses. Then go through gate.

6 Walk downhill along enclosed track – you'll see the spire of the church below. When you reach another track turn **L** and then **R** to continue downhill on metalled track. Walk under line of pylons and come into village by church.

7 Path now bears **L** and downhill, past phone box on **L-H** side. Turn **R**, walking past crumbling old arches, and retrace your steps to Market Square.

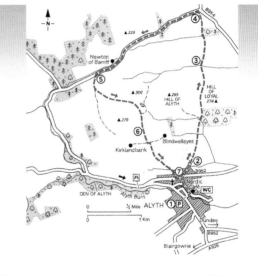

965

LOCH RANNOCH *THE BLACK WOOD*

3¾ miles (6km) 2hrs 30min Ascent: 1,150ft (350m)
Paths: Forest roads, rough woodland paths, no stiles
Suggested map: aqua3 OS Explorer 385 Rannoch Moor & Ben Alder
Grid reference: NN 590567
Parking: Small pull-in just west of Rannoch School

In the ancient Caledonian forest.

1 From pull-in, walk back along road with **Loch Rannoch** on your **L** and **Rannoch School** on **R**. Pass commando climbing tower on **R**, **sailing centre** on **L** and **golf course**. At school's goods entrance, Scottish Rights of Way Society (SRWS) signpost points up to **R** – this is old and unused route to Glen Lyon. Follow tarred driveway past tennis courts to 1st buildings and turn **L** at another SRWS signpost.

2 Sketchy path runs up under birch trees. At empty gateway in rotting fence it enters larch trees and becomes narrow track that's slightly damp in places. Avoid lesser path turning off to **L**; main one becomes green path contouring across slope with glimpses of **Loch Rannoch** on **R**. Path runs up to wide forest road.

3 Ignore path continuing opposite and turn **R**, contouring around hill. Clear-felling has opened up views to **Loch Rannoch** and the remote hills beyond. The highest of these, with a steep right edge, is Ben

Alder, the centre of the southern Highlands. This hill is glimpsed from many places but isn't easily reached from anywhere. After ½ mile (800m), keep ahead where another track joins from **L**. Joined tracks descend to triangle junction. Turn **L**, gently uphill and, after 220yds (201m), bear **R** on to little-used old track. This descends to bridge over **Dall Burn**.

4 Some 120yds (110m) after bridge, track bends **L** and here path descends on **R**. This is the **Black Wood of Rannoch**, now a forest reserve. Path runs under beautiful pines and birches. On **R**, **Dall Burn** is sometimes in your sight and can always be heard. Path is quite rough, but unmistakable as it cuts through deep bilberry and heather. After 1 mile (1.6km), path bends **L** to track. Turn **R** to leave Caledonian Reserve at notice board. At T-junction, turn **L**, away from bridge leading into **Rannoch School**. Track improves as it runs past school's indoor **swimming pool** to lochside road.

966

967 GLEN TILT *A ROYAL ROUTE*

6½ miles (10.4km) 3hrs 15min Ascent: 852ft (250m)
Paths: Estate tracks and smooth paths, 1 stile. Note: Track through firing range is closed a few days each year (mostly weekdays). Consult Atholl Estate Ranger service
Suggested map: aqua3 OS Explorers 386 Pitlochry & Loch Tummel; 394 Atholl
Grid reference: NN 866662 (on Explorer 386) **Parking:** Castle main car park

Following Queen Victoria's route through the Grampians.

❶ Turn R in front of **castle** to 4-way signpost, bear R for gate into Diana's Grove. Bear L on wide path to **Diana** herself. Turn R on path to giant redwood, bear L to cross **Banvie Burn** on footbridge alongside road bridge. Gate leads to road.

❷ Now at **Old Blair**, turn R and follow Minigaig Street uphill. It eventually becomes track and enters forest. Ignore track on L and, in ¼ mile (400m), fork R. In 60yds (55m) pass path down to R with green waymarker. This is return route if **firing range** is closed. Otherwise keep ahead to emerge from trees at **firing range** gate.

❸ Red flag flies here if **range** is in use, but read notice as on most firing days track route through **range** may be used. Follow main track downhill, below **firing range** targets, to riverside, then fork R to Gilbert's Bridge.

❹ Cross and turn R over cattle grid. Follow track for 220yds (201m). Turn L up steep path under trees to stile. Green track now runs down-valley. Once through gate into wood, keep on main track, uphill. After the gate out of the wood, there's a view to Schiehallion. Another gate leads on to gravel track then tarred road.

❺ Turn R, down long hill, crossing **waterfalls** on way down. At foot of hill turn R ('Old Blair'), to cross **Old Bridge of Tilt**, then turn L into car park.

❻ Just to R of signboard, yellow waymarkers indicate path that passes under trees to River Tilt. Turn R through exotic **grotto** until wooden steps on R lead up to corner of **caravan park**. Head away from river under pines. Ignore track on R and, at corner of **caravan park**, keep ahead under larch trees following faint path. Cross track to take clear path ahead towards Blair Castle. Bear L at statue of Hercules, passing Hercules Garden (which you may walk round) to front of **castle**.

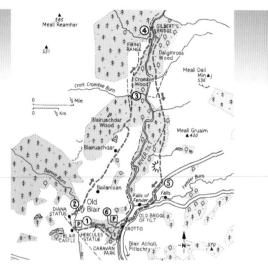

968 LOCH FASKALLY *THE BRAES O' KILLIECRANKIE*

8¾ miles (14.1km) 4hrs Ascent: 492ft (150m)
Paths: Wide riverside paths, minor road, no stiles
Suggested map: aqua3 OS Explorer 386 Pitlochry & Loch Tummel
Grid reference: NN 917626 **Parking:** Killiecrankie visitor centre

From the battlefield to Loch Faskally.

❶ Cross front of **visitor centre** to steps ('Soldier's Leap'), leading down into wooded gorge. Footbridge crosses waterfall of Troopers' Den. At next junction, turn L ('Soldier's Leap'). Ten steps down, spur path on R leads to viewpoint above **Soldier's Leap**.

❷ Return to main path ('Linn of Tummel'), which runs down to join **River Garry** below railway viaduct. After 1 mile (1.6km) it reaches footbridge.

❸ Don't cross footbridge, but continue ahead ('Pitlochry'), along riverside under tall South Garry road bridge. Path runs around huge river pool to tarred lane; turn R here. Lane leaves lochside, then passes track on R, blocked by vehicle barrier. Ignore this; shortly turn R ('Pitlochry').

❹ Immediately bear L to pass along R-H side of **Loch Dunmore**, following red-top posts. Footbridge crosses **loch**, but turn away from it, half-R, on to small path that becomes dirt track. After 110yds (100m) it reaches wider track. Turn L, with white/yellow

waymarker. After 220yds (201m) track starts to climb; here white/yellow markers indicate smaller path on R, which follows lochside. Where it rejoins wider path, bear R at green waymarker and cross footbridge to A9 road bridge.

❺ Cross **Loch Faskally** on Clunie footbridge below road's bridge; turn R, on to road around **loch**. In 1 mile (1.6km), at top of grass bank on L, is **Priest Stone**. After **Clunie power station**, reach car park on L. Here sign indicates steep path down to **Linn of Tummel**.

❻ Return to road above for ½ mile (800m), to cross grey suspension bridge on R. Turn R, downstream, to pass above **Linn**. Spur path back R returns to falls at lower level, but main path continues along riverside ('Killiecrankie'). It bends L and goes down wooden steps to **Garry**, then runs upstream and under high road bridge. Take side-path up on to bridge for view of river, then return to follow descending path ('Pitlochry via **Faskally**'). This runs down to bridge, Point ❸. Return upstream to start.

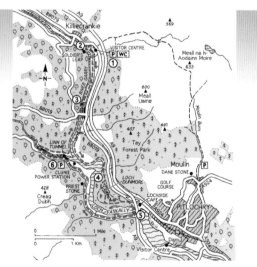

969 ABERLEMNO *THE MYSTERIOUS STONES*

5 miles (8km) 2hrs Ascent: 394ft (120m)
Paths: Mainly quiet roads but one extremely overgrown area
Suggested map: aqua3 OS Explorer 389 Forfar, Brechin & Edzell
Grid reference: NO 522558
Parking: Car park by school in Aberlemno

A lovely there-and-back route through a mysterious landscape once inhabited by the Picts.

❶ From car park turn R and walk along road, go 1st L ('Aberlemno church and stone'). Pass church – famous **Pictish stone** in churchyard – and follow road as it bends R. Follow road to T-junction.

❷ Turn R and follow road, passing entrance to **Woodside** on L. At corner, follow road as it bends R. Walk down to join B9134, turn R and follow this short distance to turning on L.

❸ Turn L along this road ('Finavon Hill'), passing house at bottom called Hillcrest. Road winds uphill, past several rocky outcrops, then under line of pylons. Continue as road skirts hill, with areas of new tree planting on L.

❹ Continue and soon see **mast**, followed by pond on L, and pass hill on R, once topped with ancient **fort**. Continue to padlocked gate on L. You can make a

diversion here. Climb gate and walk up track, passing 2 ponds to reach house.

❺ Turn R on grassy track and walk back on yourself, going through gate in deer fence, then past several pheasant feeders. Go through another gate at bottom, turn L and return to road.

❻ After completing the loop turn R and retrace your steps back to the start at Aberlemno.

Aberdeenshire

OLD ABERDEEN *STRIKING OIL IN THE NORTH SEA*

6 miles (9.6km) 2hrs 30min **Ascent:** Neglible 🅰
Paths: Exellent in all weathers
Suggested map: OS Explorer 406 Aberdeen & Banchory; AA Street by Street Aberdeen
Grid reference: NJ 954067
Parking: Outside Harry Ramsden's on the Esplanade or Queen Link Leisure Park

This walk around the old fishing port celebrates the prosperity and tragedy that oil has brought to Aberdeen.

❶ Head southwards on promenade beside shore with sea on R. Descend slipway on to beach and continue for short distance. Step over rocks to reach wooden steps on R and leave beach into children's play area.

❷ Walk past **Silver Darling restaurant** and into harbour area. Continue past **war memorial**, keeping blue storage tanks on your L and along **Pocra Quay**. Turn L into **York Street**. At **Neptune Bar**, turn L into **York Place**. Then, take 1st R, 1st L and 1st R again to emerge on **Waterloo Quay**.

❸ Where Waterloo Quay becomes **Commerce Street**, turn L into **Regent Quay**. At T-junction cross road at pedestrian lights. Turn L then 1st R to reach **Aberdeen Maritime Museum** and **John Ross's House**.

❹ From here, head along Exchequer Row, turn L into **Union Street** and turn R into **Broad Street**, where you will find **Provost Skene's House**, which dates from 1545, and **Tourist Information Office** on L, behind offices.

❺ Continue past **Marischal College**; turn R into Littlejohn Street, cross **North Street**. At end of Meal Market Street turn R into **King Street** then L into Frederick Street. At junction with **Park Street** turn L and keep walking until road crosses railway.

❻ Shortly after you reach roundabout. Head along **Park Road**, almost straight ahead. Follow it through **cemetery** and towards **Pittodrie Park** and its junction with **Golf Road**.

❼ Turn R into **Golf Road** and walk through **golf links**. Detour to top of Broad Hill, mound behind cemetery, for magnificent views. Road turns sharply L towards its junction with **Esplanade**. Cross **Esplanade**; turn R on to promenade, which you follow back to start.

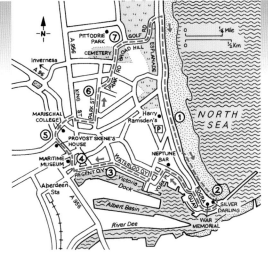

AUCHENBLAE *AN INSPIRATIONAL LANDSCAPE*

4½ miles (7.2km) 2hrs 20min **Ascent:** 459ft (140m) 🅰
Paths: Established footpaths, overgrown woodland tracks
Suggested map: aqua3 OS Explorer 396 Stonehaven, Inverbervie & Lawrencekirk
Grid reference: NO 727787
Parking: On street in Auchenblae

Walk through the Howe of Mearns.

❶ With your back to **post office** on main street, turn R and cross over to follow signs ('Woodland Walk'). Go down tarmac slope, past play area and over bridge. Follow track uphill, passing woodland on your R, continue to road.

❷ Turn R, walk along long, straight road, passing **cemetery**. Take 1st turning L, which runs between arable fields. Continue to wood ahead. Go through rusty gate and scramble through undergrowth to get into woods and join track.

❸ Turn R and follow track round margin of woods – thickly carpeted with vegetation. At wider gravel track, turn R and continue – fields still visible through trees on R-H side. Follow track to crossing of tracks.

❹ Take L-H fork. At pylon on R-H side of track, strike off on indistinct track that runs downhill to R under line of pylons. (If you go under pylons on main track, you've gone too far.)

❺ Scramble through undergrowth and follow indistinct track as it swings to L, in northwesterly direction. (I had to negotiate my way past fallen trees at this point, which had been damaged by a recent storm – so be careful, as some of them were large.) Eventually come down to meet main road.

❻ Turn R and follow road, pass the entrance to **Drumtochty Castle** ('Private Residence'). Continue along road until you reach fork in road.

❼ Take L-H fork and continue ahead.

❽ Turn R along road for few paces, then go L at junction and follow road back into **Auchenblae**. At main street, turn R and return to start.

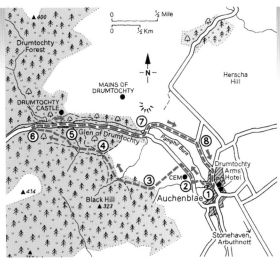

STONEHAVEN *HIDDEN TREASURE*

3½ miles (5.7km) 1hr 30min **Ascent:** 377ft (115m) 🅰
Paths: Cliff edges, metalled tracks, forest paths, 3 stiles
Suggested map: aqua3 OS Explorer 273 Stonehaven & Inverbervie
Grid reference: NO 874858
Parking: Market Square, Stonehaven

Along the cliffs to Dunnottar Castle, which once housed Scotland's crown jewels.

❶ From Market Square, walk back on to Allardyce Street, turn R and cross road. Turn L up Market Lane. At beach, turn R to cross footbridge. Turn R at signs to **Dunnottar Castle** to reach harbour. Cross here to continue down Shorehead, on east side of harbour. Pass **Marine Hotel**, then turn R into Wallis Wynd.

❷ Turn L into Castle Street. Emerge at main road then maintain direction walking along road until it bends. Continue ahead, following enclosed tarmac track, between arable fields and past war **memorial** on R-H side. Nip over stile at end of track.

❸ Make your way across middle of field, cross footbridge and 2 more stiles. You now pass track going down to **Castle Haven** and continue following main path around cliff edge. Cross another footbridge and bear uphill. You'll soon reach some steps on your L that run down to **Dunnottar Castle**.

❹ Route bears R here, past **waterfall**, through kissing gate and up to house. Pass house to reach road into **Stonehaven** by Mains of Dunnottar, turn R then take 1st turning on L, walking in direction of radio **masts**. Follow this wide, metalled track past **masts** and **East Newtonleys** on L-H side, to reach **A957**.

❺ Turn R and walk downhill. Take 1st turning on L. Follow track to sign on R ('Carron Gate'). Turn R and walk through woods, following lower path on R-H side that runs by burn. You'll soon reach **Shell House** on L.

❻ Pass it on L, continue along lower track then climb uphill to join wider track. Bear R here, to maintain direction and reach edge of woods. Go through housing estate to join Low Wood Road and river.

❼ Turn L, then R to cross footbridge with green railings. Turn R and walk beside the water. You'll soon pass art-deco **Carron Restaurant** on L-H side, and then come to cream-coloured iron bridge. Bear L here then turn 1st R to return to Market Square.

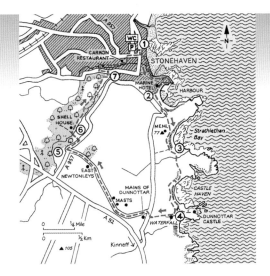

973 BRAEMAR *MOORLAND ON MORRONE*

6¾ miles (10.9km) 4hrs 15min Ascent: 2,000ft (610m)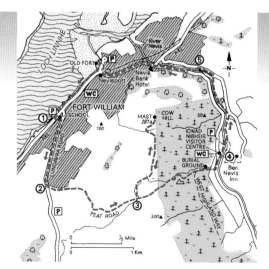
Paths: Well-made but fairly steep path, track, 1 stile
Suggested map: aqua3 OS Explorer 387 Glen Shee & Braemar
Grid reference: NO 143911
Parking: Duck Pond, at top of Chapel Brae, Braemar

The hill at the back of Braemar gives a taste of the Cairngorms.
❶ Take wide track uphill, to R of **duck pond** at top of Chapel Brae, bearing **L** twice to **Woodhill** house. House can be bypassed by taking small footpath on **R** which rejoins track just above. When track forks again, bear **L** to viewpoint indicator.
❷ Cross track diagonally to hill path ('Morrone') – rebuilt with rough stone steps. Higher up, it slants to **R** along line of rocky outcrops. At top of this it turns directly uphill, passing 5 sprawling **cairns**. These are the turning point in the Morrone Hill Race that is part of the Braemar Games. Wide, stony path runs up to **radio mast** and other ugly constructions on summit.
❸ The summit, with your back to buildings, has fine views across to the **Cairngorms**. On the main tops snow may show in summer. To the east are Loch Callater and White Mounth plateau. The notable hump is Cac Carn Beag, one of the summits of Lochnagar.

Morrone's summit area is bare stones, but if you go past buildings you'll find start of wide track. It runs down to shallow col and climbs to **cairn** on low summit beyond. Here it bends **L** towards lower col, but before reaching it, turns **L** again down hill. Gentle zig-zagging descent leads to road by **Clunie Water**.
❹ Turn **L**, alongside river, for 1½ miles (2.4km). Ben Avon with its row of summit tors fills the skyline ahead. After snow gate and golf **clubhouse** comes road sign warning of cattle grid (grid is round next bend). Here track, back up to **L**, has blue-topped waymarker pole.
❺ Go up between caravans to ladder stile with dog flap. Faint path leads up under birches, bearing **R** and becoming clearer. After gate in fence path becomes quite clear, leading to Scottish Natural Heritage signboard and blue waymarker at top of birchwood. Path becomes track with fence on **R** and, in 220yds (201m), reaches viewpoint indicator, Point ❷. Return to **duck pond**.

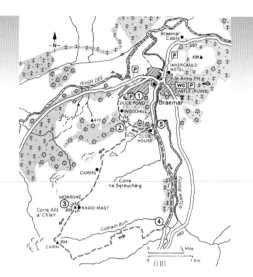

974 GLENLIVET *THE WHISKY HILLS*

6¼ miles (10.1km) 3hrs 15min Ascent: 1,000ft (305m)
Paths: Waymarked, muddy and indistinct in places, 11 stiles. Note: Grouse shooting in August/September – consult Glenlivet Ranger Service at Tomintoul
Suggested map: aqua3 OS Explorer 420 Correen Hills & Glenlivet
Grid reference: NJ 218257
Parking: Track opposite church at Tombae runs up to quarry car park

Through a green valley and heather moor.
❶ At **Tombae** church, turn **L** for 330yds (300m) to stile on **R** ('Walk 10'). Track leads down into birchwoods. Bear **R** at waymark and follow main track to bridge over **River Livet**. After 60yds (55m), turn **R** to bridge over **Crombie Water**. Turn half-**L**, up to stile beside field gate. Walk follows top of low wooded bank above **Crombie Water** to footbridge (grid ref 226245).
❷ Across footbridge, path runs across meadow into wood, slanting up to **R** to green track. Turn **R**; follow this through wood, then bend **L** on to moorland. Below abrupt hill of **The Bochel** track forks. Keep ahead, with waymark. Way becomes peaty path. At top of 1st rise is stile with gate alongside. Path, with waymarker, leads to gateway in another fence. Don't go through, but turn **R**, with fence on your **L**, to stile with signpost.
❸ For easier alternative, follow sign ahead. Just before house, turn **R** at signpost and follow rough

track towards **Bochel** farm. But main route goes over **The Bochel** itself. Across stile, turn uphill on small paths to summit cairn. Turn **L**, to descend towards large white **Braeval distillery** below Ladder Hills. As slope steepens, see **Bochel** farm below. Head down **L-H** edge of nearer pine wood to join rough track leading into farm.
❹ At once stile on **R** leads to faint path into plantation. This becomes green track running just above bottom edge of wood. It becomes more well-used and leads to road.
❺ Turn **R**, over bridge to waymarker stile on **R**. Track rises to open fields above river. At highest point, waymarker points down to **R**. Go down to fence, with waymarked stile on **L**, then through heather with fence on your **L**. Turn downhill to stile at bottom. Cross and turn **L**, ignoring another stile on **L**, to reach footbridge, Point ❷. Retrace 1st part of walk back to **Tombae**.

975 FORT WILLIAM *PEAT ROAD TO COW HILL*

7¼ miles (11.6km) 3hrs 30min Ascent: 1,000ft (300m)
Paths: Smooth tracks, 2 stiles
Suggested map: aqua3 OS Explorer 392 Ben Nevis & Fort William
Grid reference: NN 098736
Parking: Shore Car Park (pay-and-display)

A superb walk, looking down at Fort William and up at Ben Nevis and then home along the glen.
❶ From back corner of car park cross over **A82**, and go up to R of **school** to path under trees, and then up to **Lundavra Road**. Turn **R**, going uphill, to top of town. Cross over cattle grid to signed gate on **L** ('Keep Clear 24hr').
❷ The track ahead is the **Peat Road**, once used for hauling peat off the hill on wooden sledges. Follow track past waymarker ('Peat Road') to **Cow Hill** summit with radio **mast**. This is the destination of a mid-winter hill race straight up from the town. Return to waymarker.
❸ Turn **L** down path, into forest and head steeply downhill. Cross over track, with **West Highland Way** marker, and then leave forest. On **L** is burial ground, reached by short side path through gate. Continue on main path to Glen Nevis road. Turn **L** 100yds (91m)

and then bear **R** on path to **Ionad Nibheis** visitor centre, which has interesting displays on the geology and wildlife of the glen.
❹ Follow river bank past car park to footbridge ('Ben Path'). Cross and then turn **L**, downstream. With road ahead, riverside path forks off. This path is narrow and can sometimes be boggy, but alternatively you can follow road ahead instead. Path and road rejoin after ½ mile (800m) and then continue for 300yds (274m) to green footbridge on **L**.
❺ Cross and turn **R**, down track then road, to roundabout. Turn **L** along pavement into **Fort William**. In front of station, pass underpass entrance (or go **L** through underpass for shopping shortcut to walk start). Bear **R** past front of station and through Safeway car park, and cross roundabout to **Old Fort**. This is the original **Fort William**, and the start point of the Great Glen Way. Turn **L** on pavement above **Loch Linnhe**, to car park.

CORPACH *The Banks of the Caledonian Canal*

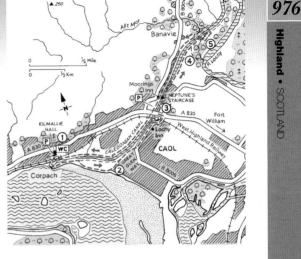

4½ miles (7.2km) 1hr 45min **Ascent:** 100ft (30m) ⚠
Paths: Wide tow paths, no stiles
Suggested map: aqua3 OS Explorer 392 Ben Nevis & Fort William
Grid reference: NN 097768
Parking: Kilmallie Hall, Corpach

A walk alongside and underneath Thomas Telford's masterpiece.

1 Go down past **Corpach** Station to canal and cross sea lock that separates salt water from fresh water. Follow **canal** (on **L**) up past another lock, where path on **R** has blue footpath sign and **Great Glen Way** marker. It passes under sycamores to shore. Turn **L**, across grass to road sign warning motorists of nearby playground. Path ahead leads up wooded bank to tow path.

2 Turn **R** along tow path, for ½ mile (800m). Just before **Banavie** swing bridge, path down to **R** has **Great Glen Way** marker. Follow waymarkers on street signs to level crossing then turn **L** towards other swing bridge, one with road on it.

3 Just before bridge, turn **R** at signs for **Great Glen Way** and the Great Glen Cycle Route and continue along tow path to **Neptune's Staircase**. The 60ft (18m) of ascent alongside 8 locks is the serious uphill

part of this walk, but more serious for boats. It takes about 90 minutes to work through the system.

4 Gate marks top of locks. About 200yds (183m) later, grey gate on **R** leads to dump for dead cars; ignore this one. Over next 100yds (91m) **canal** crosses little wooded valley, with black fence on **R**. Now comes 2nd grey gate. Go through, to track turning back sharp **R** and descending to cross stream.

5 On **R**, stream passes right under **canal** in arched tunnel, and alongside is 2nd tunnel which provides a walkers' way to other side. Water from the **canal** drips into the tunnel (it's a bit spooky) – try not to think of the large boats sailing directly over your head! At end, track runs up to join **canal's** northern tow path. Turn **R**, back down tow path. After passing **Neptune's Staircase**, cross **A830** to level crossing without warning lights. Continue ahead along **R-H** tow path. After 1 mile (1.6km) tow path track leads back to **Corpach** double lock.

GRANTOWN-ON-SPEY *Sir James Grant's Town*

7 miles (11.3km) 3hrs **Ascent:** 200ft (60m) ⚠
Paths: Tracks and smooth paths, 1 stile
Suggested map: aqua3 OS Explorer 419 Grantown-on-Spey
Grid reference: NJ 035280
Parking: Grantown-on-Spey Museum

Around an 18th-century planned town.

1 Go past **museum**. Turn **L** into South Street, then **R** into Golf Course Road. Tarred path crosses **golf course** to gate into **Anagach Wood**.

2 Wide path ahead has blue/red waymarker. At junction, blue trail departs to **R**; turn **L**, following **Spey Way** marker and red-top poles. Keep following red markers, turning **L** at 1st junction and bearing **L** at next. When track joins new fence and bend in stream is on **L**, keep ahead, following **Spey Way** marker.

3 Track emerges into open fields. After crossing small bridge, turn to **R** through chained gap stile. Path with pines on its **L** leads to track near **River Spey**. (**Bridge of Cromdale** is just ahead.)

4 Turn sharp **R** on track, alongside river. At fishers' hut it re-enters forest. About ¾ mile (1.2km) later it diminishes to open path and slants up past cottage of **Craigroy** to join its entrance track.

5 At **Easter Anagach**, grass track on **R** has red

waymarkers and runs into birchwood. With barrier ahead, follow marker poles to **L**, on to broad path beside falling fence. At next junction, turn **R**, following red poles, over slight rise. Descending, turn **L** just before blue-top post, on to smaller path with blue-and-red posts. This runs along top of ridge, to reach bench above lane. Down the lane is the stone bridge built as part of the military road system.

6 Path bends **R**, alongside road, to meet wide track (former military road). Turn **R**, to path on **R** with green-top posts. At small pool, main path bends **L** for 150yds (137m), with blue-and-green posts; take path ahead, with green posts. A very old tree in the middle of the path was once used for public hangings. At 5-way junction bear **L** to find next green post. At edge of **golf course** turn **L** to car park and information board.

7 Follow tarred street uphill, past end of **golf course**, to High Street. Turn **R** to The Square. Just past Grant Arms Hotel, sign points **R**, to **museum**.

SHIELDAIG *Loch-side Shores*

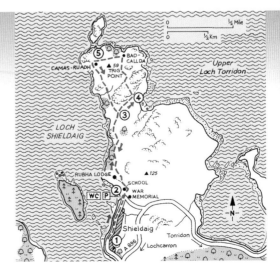

3¼ miles (5.3km) 1hr 45min **Ascent:** 500ft (152m) ⚠
Paths: Well-made old paths, 1 rough section
Suggested map: aqua3 OS Explorer 428 Kyle of Lochalsh
Grid reference: NG 814538
Parking: South end of Shieldaig village, opposite shop and hotel

In the footsteps of Bonnie Prince Charlie around the inlets of the Shieldaig peninsula.

1 Follow village street along shoreline. At village end it rises slightly, with another parking area, and **war memorial** above on **R**.

2 From front of **school**, turn **R** up rough track. Track passes 2 houses to left. In another 100yds (91m) it divides and here main track for **Rubha Lodge** forks off **L**, but your route bears **R**, passing to **R** of glacier-smoothed rock knoll. Terraced path runs through birch woods at first, with **Loch Shieldaig** below (**L**). It passes above 2 rocky bays then strikes across peat bog. In middle of this flat area it divides at cairn.

3 **R-H** path runs along **L** edge of peaty area, with rocky ground above on its **L**, then next to birch trees for 50yds (46m). Look out for point where its pink gravel surface becomes peaty, with rock formation like low ruin on **R**, because here there is easily-missed path junction.

4 What appears to be main footpath, ahead and slightly downhill, peters out eventually. Correct path forks off to **L**, slanting up on to higher ground just above. Path is now clear, crossing slabby ground in direction of peninsula's **trig point**, ¼ mile (400m) away. After 220yds (201m) it rises slightly to gateway in former fence. Aiming **R** of **trig point**, it crosses small heather moor. At broken wall, path turns down **R** through gap to top of grassy meadow. Shoreline cottage, **Bad-callda**, is just below. Rough paths lead to **L** across boggy top of meadow and above birchwood, with trig point just above on **L**. Keep going forward at same level to heather knoll, with pole on it. Just below you is 2nd cottage, **Camas-ruadh**.

5 Footpath zig-zags down between rocks. White paint spots lead round to **R** of cottage, to join clear path coming from cottage. Return path is easy to follow, with cottage's phone line always near by on **L**. After ½ mile (800m) it rejoins outward route at cairn.

979 GLEN COE *INTO THE LOST VALLEY*

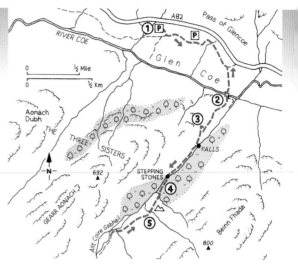

2¾ miles (4.4km) 2hrs 15min Ascent: 1,050ft (320m)
Paths: Rugged and stony, stream to wade through, 1 stile
Suggested map: aqua3 OS Explorer 384 Glen Coe & Glen Etive
Grid reference: NN 168569
Parking: Lower of two roadside parking places opposite Gearr Aonach (middle one of Three Sisters)

A rugged waterfall walk.

❶ From uphill corner of car park, faint path slants down to old road, which is now well-used track. Head up-valley for 650yds (594m). With old road continuing as green track ahead, your path now bends down to R. Path reaches gorge of **River Coe**. Descend on steep wooden step ladder to cross footbridge.

❷ Ascent out of gorge is on bare rock staircase. Above, path runs through regenerating birch wood which can be wet on legs. Cross high ladder stile over temporary fence. Path runs uphill for 60yds (55m). Here it bends L; inconspicuous alternative path continues uphill, which can be used to bypass narrow path of main route.

❸ Main route contours into gorge of **Allt Coire Gabhail**. It is narrow with steep drops below. Where there is alternative of rock slabs and narrow path just below, slabs are more secure. Two fine **waterfalls** come into view ahead. Pass these, continue between boulders to where main path bends L to cross stream below boulder size of small house. (Ignore small path which runs on up to R of stream.) River here is wide and fairly shallow, 5 or 6 **stepping stones** usually allow dry crossing. If water is above stones, it's safer to wade alongside them; if water is more than knee-deep crossing should not be attempted.

❹ Well-built path continues uphill, now with stream on R. After 100yds (91m) rock blocks way. Path follows slanting ramp up its R-H side. It continues uphill, passing above boulder pile that blocks valley. At top of rock pile path levels, giving view into Lost Valley.

❺ Drop gently to valley's gravel floor. Stream vanishes into gravel, to reappear below boulder pile on other side. Note where path arrives at gravel, as it becomes invisible at that point. Wander up valley to where stream vanishes, ¼ mile (400m) ahead. Beyond this point is more serious hillwalking. Return to path and follow it back to start.

980 GLEN COE *AROUND THE SMALL SHEPHERD*

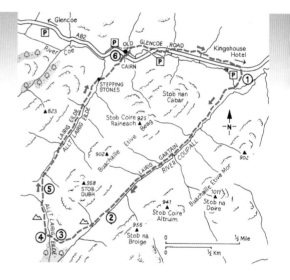

8 miles (12.9km) 4hrs 30min Ascent: 1,300ft (396m)
Paths: Rough, unmade paths, some boggy bits, no stiles. Note: Fords in Lairig Eilde can be impassible or dangerous after heavy rain
Suggested map: aqua3 OS Explorer 384 Glen Coe & Glen Etive
Grid reference: NN 213559
Parking: Large parking area on south side of A82, marked by yellow AA phone post

Through the mountains.

❶ Signpost to Glen Etive, at edge of car park, marks start of path into **Lairig Gartain**. Path, clear but boggy in places, heads up-valley with **River Coupall** down on L. Gradually it draws closer to river, but does not cross it. Large cairn marks top of path, which is slightly to R of lowest point of pass.

❷ Descending path is steeper, over boggy grass with new stream forming on L. After ½ mile (800m), ignore small path branching off L towards waterfall below, and stay on main, higher path. This slants along R-H wall of valley, ascending above stream. Eventually emerge on to steep south ridge of **Stob Dubh**.

❸ Here path runs down to gate in deer fence, but do not continue downhill. Follow faint path above deer fence, descending to cross **Allt Lairig Eilde**. If stream is too full to cross, return and go down through deer fence to wider, shallower crossing, 200yds (183m) downstream. Alternatively, head up on small path to R of stream, to find safer crossing higher up. Across stream, follow fence up to gate at its corner. Turn up wide path that rises out of Glen Etive.

❹ Path ascends to L of stream, passing waterfalls. Eventually cross stream, now smaller, then continue straight ahead, crossing col well to R of its lowest point. Large cairn marks top of path.

❺ New, descending stream is also, confusingly, **Allt Lairig Eilde**. Path crosses it by wide, shallow ford and goes down its L bank. 1 mile (1.6km) ahead, path recrosses via boulder **stepping stones**. It runs down to join A82 near **cairn** that marks entry into Glen Coe.

❻ Cross road, and river beyond, to join **old Glencoe road** at arched culvert. Turn R along firm track, which soon rejoins new road, then cross diagonally, on to damp path. This runs to R of new road, then recrosses. It soon rejoins **A82** opposite start.

981 KINLOCHLEVEN *GREY MARE'S TAIL*

3½ miles (5.7km) 2hrs 15min Ascent: 984ft (300m)
Paths: Well-made paths, one steep, rough ascent, no stiles
Suggested map: aqua3 OS Explorer 384 Glen Coe & Glen Etive or 392 Ben Nevis & Fort William
Grid reference: NN 187622 (on Explorer 384) **Parking:** Grey Mare's Tail car park, Kinlochleven

A ramble down the West Highland Way.

❶ Smooth gravel path leads up out of car park to multicoloured waymarks pointing L. Path rises to view through trees of **Grey Mare's Tail** waterfall, then descends to footbridge. Here turn L (blue waymarker) to visit foot of spectacular waterfall, then return to take path on R (white, yellow and green waymarker). Follow stream up for 100yds (91m), then turn L at waymarker. Path, steep and loose, zig-zags up through birches to more open ground.

❷ Where path forks take R-H branch, with yellow-and-green waymarker, to pass under power lines. Path follows crest of heathery spur, then bends L to cross 2 streams. Immediately after 2nd stream is another junction.

❸ Confusing waymarker has 8 arrows in 4 colours. Turn L, following white arrow slightly downhill, to cross footbridge above waterfall and red granite rocks. Path leads up under birches. Ground cover here includes the aromatic bog myrtle, which can be used to discourage midges, though it is less effective than chemical repellent. When path reaches track, turn L (white arrow). Below track is tin deer used by stalkers for target practice. Signed footpath bypasses **Keepers' Cottages** on L, then rejoins track beyond, to junction above **Mamore Lodge**.

❹ Keep ahead, above lodge, climbing gently past 2 tin huts, self-catering accommodation labelled 'stable' and 'bothy'. At high point of track there is TV **mast** on R and bench on L. Track descends gently, with slabs of quartzite above. Wide path of **West Highland Way (WHW)** can be seen below and gradually rises to join track, with large waymarker planted in slabs.

❺ Turn L down WHW path, which drops into woods below. Watch out for junction where main path seems to double back to R; take smaller path, continuing ahead with WHW waymarker. After crossing tarred access track of **Mamore Lodge**, path fords small stream to reach village. Turn L along pavement and fork L into Wades Road to regain car park.

Strontian *The Elements of Chemistry*

7 miles (11.3km) 3hrs 45min Ascent: 950ft (290m)
Paths: Good through woodland, sketchy on open hill, no stiles
Suggested map: aqua3 OS Explorer 391 Ardgour & Strontian
Grid reference: NM 826633
Parking: Nature Reserve car park at Ariundle

To the site of an old lead mine.

❶ From car park, go along track into oakwoods. After ½ mile (800m), footpath turns off at waymarker on **R**. It crosses **Strontian River** and heads upstream along it. After ¾ mile (1.2km) it recrosses **river**, following duckboard section to rejoin oakwood track.

❷ Turn **R**, away from car park, to reach high gate in deer fence. Track immediately forks. Take downward branch on **R** to emerge into open grazing at **river** level. Track ends at gate and stream.

❸ Ford stream on to rough path. This crosses 3 more small streams, then forks. The lower, R-H branch continues alongside **Strontian River**, but path, which is quite faint, slants up to **L** to solitary holly tree. Here it turns straight uphill for 50yds (46m), then bends **R** to slant up as before, passing 200yds (183m) below bare rock knoll. Remains of wooden steps are in path and few cairns stand beside it. It steepens slightly to pass below small crag with 3 different trees growing

out of it – rowan, hazel and oak. With large stream and **waterfalls** ahead, path turns uphill and reaches brink of small gorge. Above waterfalls, slope eases and there is footbridge down on **R** which you don't cross; it acts as useful landmark. Just above, path reaches broken dam wall of former reservoir.

❹ Green path runs across slope just above. You can turn **R** on this, heading up beside stream for about ¼ mile (400m). Here you will find spoil heap; heather bank marks entrance to an **adit** – mine tunnel.

❺ Return along green path past Point ❹, with remains of **Bellsgrove Lead Mines** above and below. Path improves into track, following stream down small and slantwise side valley. As this stream turns down to **L**, track contours forward, to cross wooded stream valley by high footbridge above **waterfall**.

❻ Wide, smooth track continues through gate. After ½ mile (800m) it rejoins outward route at edge of **nature reserve**. Follow track back to car park.

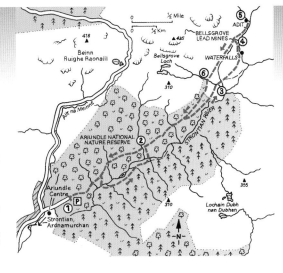

Nevis Gorge *Great Falls*

2½ miles (4km) 1hr 30min Ascent: 270ft (82m)
Paths: Well-built path with drops alongside, no stiles
Suggested map: aqua3 OS Explorer 392 Ben Nevis & Fort William
Grid reference: NN 168691
Parking: Walkers' car park at end of Glen Nevis road

A walk beside Scotland's Himalayan lookalike leading to an enormous waterfall.

❶ It should be noted that waterslide above car park is Allt Coire Eoghainn – if you mistake it for **Steall Fall** and set off towards it you are on difficult and potentially dangerous path. The path you will take on this walk is much easier, but even here there have been casualties, mostly caused by people wearing unsuitable shoes. At top end of car park you will see signpost that shows no destination closer than 13 miles (21km) to Kinlochleven – accordingly, this walk will be short out-and-back. The well-made path runs gently uphill under woods of birch and hazel, across what turns into very steep slope. For few steps it becomes rock-cut ledge, with step across waterfall side-stream. The path at this point is on clean pink granite, and you will see boulder of grey schist beside path just afterwards. Ahead, top of **Steall Fall** can now be seen through notch of valley.

❷ The path continues briefly downhill to cross 2nd stream; rock now is schist, with fine zig-zag stripes of grey and white. Short rock staircase leads to wooden balcony section. From here path is just above bed of **Nevis Gorge**. The river runs through huge boulders, some of which bridge it completely.

❸ Quite suddenly, path emerges on to level meadow above gorge. Ahead, **Steall Fall** fills your view. The best path runs along L-H edge of meadow to point opposite waterfall.

❹ The walk ends here, beside footbridge, which consists simply of 3 steel cables over a very deep pool. Those who wish to attempt crossing should note that it gets wobblier in middle and it is hard to turn around, but the return journey is rather easier. From wire bridge, driest path runs alongside main river round 1 bend before heading up to foot of waterfall. The view from directly beneath the waterfall is even more spectacular – enjoy.

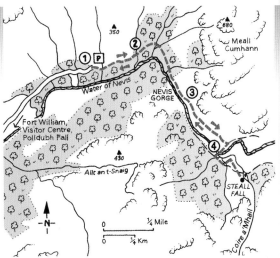

Ben Nevis *Half-way Up*

10 miles (16.1km) 6hrs 15min Ascent: 2,000ft (610m)
Paths: Hill paths, well-built, then very rough, 6 stiles
Suggested map: aqua3 OS Explorer 392 Ben Nevis & Fort William
Grid reference: NN 123731 **Parking:** Large car park at Glen Nevis Visitor Centre

The great north corrie of Nevis.

❶ At downstream corner of car park, bridge ('Ben Path') crosses **River Nevis**. Path turns upstream, crossing fields to join **Mountain Trail** (formerly Pony Track) to Ben Nevis. After long climb, notice points you to zig-zag up **L** on to half-way plateau. Path passes above **Lochan Meall an-t-Suidhe**, Halfway Lochan, down on **L**.

❷ Main path takes sharp turn back to **R**, heading for summit. Your smaller path descends ahead, behind wall-like cairn. Soon it climbs gently over peat bog to cairn on skyline. Here it becomes rough and rocky as it slants down across steep slide slope of valley of **Allt a' Mhuilinn**. Eventually it joins stream and runs up beside it to Charles Inglis Clark (**CIC**) **Hut**.

❸ Return for 100yds (91m); cross stream on **R** to join path downhill. This descends rocky step with waterslide and reaches ladder stile into plantations.

❹ Go down forest road and where it bends **L** over bridge, keep ahead down rough path. Stay beside

stream to ladder stile at railbed. Turn **L** for ½ mile (800m), when side-track joins from **L** and track passes under power lines. In 220yds (201m) take smaller track on **R** that rejoins **Allt a' Mhuilinn**. Keep to **R** of distillery buildings to reach A82.

❺ Cross River Lochy on **Victoria Bridge** opposite and turn **L** into fenced-off side road and **L** along street. It rises to railway bridge. Turn **L** on to long footbridge back across Lochy. At end, turn **R** over stile for riverside path. Pass to **R** of rugby ground, then enter woodland. After 2 footbridges, bear **L** on smaller path to edge of **Inverlochy**. Turn **R**, then **L** into street with copper beeches. This leads through Montrose Square to A82.

❻ Take street opposite ('Ben Nevis Footpath'). Shortly, take stone bridge to Glen Nevis road. Turn **L** for ¼ mile (400m) to track on **L**. Recross **Nevis** on green footbridge and turn **R** to lay-by ('No Overnight Parking'). Just beyond this small riverside footpath leads up-river to footbridge at **visitor centre**.

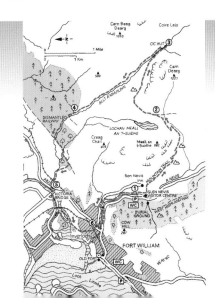

985 COIRE ARDAIR *HAPPY BIRCH-DAY*

8 miles (12.9km) 4hrs 15min **Ascent:** 1,400ft (427m)
Paths: Mostly good, wet and stony in places, no stiles
Suggested map: aqua3 OS Explorer 401 Loch Laggan & Creag Meagaidh
Grid reference: NN 483872
Parking: Nature reserve car park at Aberarder track end beside Loch Laggan

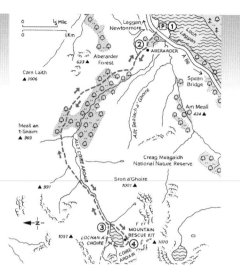

Regenerating woodlands lead to a high pass.

❶ Take gravel track to **Aberarder** farm. (Information area and covered picnic table.) Pass to **R** of buildings following footprint waymarker on to rebuilt path.
❷ Path rises through bracken, then crosses boggy area on old railway sleepers. It heads up valley of **Allt Coire Ardair**, keeping little way up **R-H** side, becoming fairly rocky and rugged as it ascends through area of regenerating birch trees. Crags of **Coire Ardair** come into sight ahead. Path crosses many streams then bends **L**, slightly downhill, to join main river. Peaty area, crossed on railway sleepers, leads up suddenly to outflow of **Lochan a' Choire**.
❸ Outflow is fine viewpoint for crag walls of **Coire Ardair**. These walls are too loose and overgrown for rock climbing, but when covered in snow and hoarfrost give excellent sport for winter mountaineers. The circuit of **lochan** is considerably more rugged than path up glen, and can be omitted if outflow

stream is too full, or if you just wish to picnic. Cross outflow stream near where it emerges from **lochan** and follow small path round shore to notable clump of boulders marked by stretcher box. (The stretcher is used for removing mountain casualties from the foot of the crags.) One of boulders forms small cave, with spring running through it. A vigorous rowan tree, seeded where deer can't get at it, shows that without grazing pressure this glen would be wooded even at this altitude of 2,000ft (610m).
❹ After boulder cave you must cross rocks and scree. This short section is awkward so take care. Once past head of **lochan**, slant up away from shore. Path descends from high on L, coming out of notch called Window. Join this path back to loch's outflow (Point ❸ again). Quite clearly there's no way out of this dead-end valley that doesn't involve serious mountain walking – or one of those winter climbs up icy gullies. Return down valley by outward path.

986 FORT AUGUSTUS *UP AND DOWN THE CORRIEYAIRACK*

7¼ miles (11.7km) 4hrs **Ascent:** 1,300ft (395m)
Paths: Tracks, one vanished pathless section, 2 stiles
Suggested map: aqua3 OS Explorer 400 Loch Lochy & Glen Roy
Grid reference: NH 378080
Parking: Southern edge of Fort Augustus, signed lane leads off A82 to burial ground

On the road the English built.

❶ Track leads round to **L** of **burial ground** to meet minor road. Turn **R** for ¼ mile (400m) to foot of rubbly track ('Corrieyairack Pass'). After 50yds (46m) track passes through gate, getting easier; soon, right of way joins smoother track coming up from **Culachy House**.
❷ After ¼ mile (400m), gate leads on to hill. 350yds (320m) further on, track passes under high-tension wires. Here bear **L** across meadow. As this drops towards stream, see green track slanting down to R. Bear **L** off track to pass corner of deer fence, where path continues to stream. Cross and turn downstream on grassy track. It recrosses stream and passes under high power line to bend with view across **Glen Tarff**.
❸ Turn **R** across stone bridge. Disused track climbs through birch woods then, as terraced shelf, across high side of **Glen Tarff**. A side stream forms wooded re-entrant ahead. Old track contours into this and crosses below waterfall (former bridge has gone).

❹ Contour out across steep slope to pick up old track as it restarts. It runs uphill to gateless gateway in fence. Turn up fence to another gateway, 150yds (137m) above. Turn **L** for 20yds (18m) to brink of stream hollow. Don't go into this, but turn uphill alongside it, through pathless bracken, to top. Deer fence is just above; turn **L** alongside it to go through nearby gate, then **L** beside fence. When it turns downhill, green path keeps ahead, uphill. Ahead and above, pylons crossing skyline mark Corrieyairack Pass. Path bends **R** to join Corrieyairack track just above.
❺ Turn **R**. Track passes knoll on **R** where cairn marks highest point. It descends for 1¼ miles (2km). Pass is technically road, and where it crosses stream, Highways Authority sign warns motorists coming up it of difficulties and dangers ahead. From here track climbs gently to rejoin upward route. At final bend, stile offers short cut through ancient **burial ground**.

987 LOCH AN EILEIN *CASTLE ON THE ISLAND*

4¼ miles (6.8km) 1hr 45min **Ascent:** 100ft (30m)
Paths: Wide smooth paths, optional steep hill with high ladder stile
Suggested map: aqua3 OS Explorer 403 Cairn Gorm & Aviemore
Grid reference: NH 897084
Parking: Estate car park near Loch an Eilein

The castle on the island in the loch is the heart of Rothiemurchus Forest.

❶ From end of car park at beginning of walk, made-up path leads to **visitor centre**. Turn **L** to cross end of **Loch an Eilein**, then turn **R** on smooth sandy track. Loch shore is near by on R. Small paths lead down to it if you wish to visit. Just past red-roofed house, **Forest Cottage**, deer fence runs across, with gate.
❷ Track becomes wide, smooth path, which runs close to loch side. After bridge, main track forks **R** to pass bench backed by flat boulder. Smaller path on **L** leads high into hills and through pass of Lairig Ghru, eventually to Braemar. After crossing stream at low concrete footbridge, path bends **R** for 120yds (110m) to junction. Just beyond is footbridge with handrails.
❸ To shorten walk, cross footbridge and continue along main track, passing Point ❹ in 170yds (155m). For longer walk, turn **L** before footbridge on to narrower path to pass around **Loch Gamhna**. This

2nd loch soon appears on your R-H side. Where path forks, keep **R** to pass along loch side, across its head (rather boggy) and back along its further side, to rejoin wider path around **Loch an Eilein**. Turn **L** here.
❹ Continue around **Loch an Eilein**, water on your **R**, to reedy corner of loch and bench. About 55yds (51m) further, path turns sharply **R** ('footpath'). After gate, turn **R** to loch side and **memorial** to Major General Brook Rice. Follow shore to point opposite **castle**, then back up to wide track above. Deer fence on L leads back to **visitor centre**.
❺ From here, stiff climb (around 500ft/152m) can be made on to rocky hill of **Ord Ban**, superb viewpoint. Cross ladder stile immediately to R of toilets and follow deer fence to R for 150yds (137m), to point behind car park. Just behind one of lowest birches on slope, small path zig-zags up steep slope. It slants up to **L** to avoid crags, then crosses small rock slab (take care if wet) and continues to summit. Descend by same path.

GLENMORE *THE THIEVES' ROAD*

5 miles (8km) 2hrs 15min **Ascent:** 400ft (122m)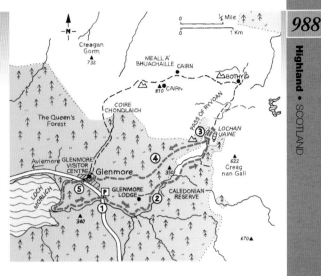
Paths: Smooth tracks, one steep ascent, no stiles
Suggested map: aqua3 OS Explorer 403 Cairn Gorm & Aviemore
Grid reference: NH 980095 **Parking:** Bridge just south of Glenmore village

To the lochan, once the haunt of fairy folk.
❶ Head upstream on sandy track to L of river. Interpretation signs explain the flowers of the forest – there are many ferns and mosses. After 550yds (503m), turn **L** on wide smooth path (blue/yellow waymarkers). Ahead is gate into **Glenmore Lodge** rifle range; here path bends **R**, to wide gravel track.
❷ Turn **R**, away from **Glenmore Lodge**, to cross over concrete bridge into **Caledonian Reserve**. Immediately keep straight ahead on smaller track (blue waymarker) as main one bends R. Track narrows as it heads into **Pass of Ryvoan** between steep wooded slopes of pine, birch and scree. At sign that warns of end of waymarking, path turns **L** (blue waymarker), which you take in a moment. Just beyond, steps on **R** lead down to **Lochan Uaine**. Walk round to L of water on beach. At head of loch small path leads back up to track. Turn sharp **L**, back to junction already visited and now turn off to **R** on to narrower path (blue waymarker).

❸ This small path crosses duckboard and heads back down valley. Very soon it starts to climb steeply to **R**, up rough stone steps. When it levels going is easier, although it's still narrow with tree roots. Path reaches forest road at bench and waymarker.
❹ Continue to **L** along track. After clear-felled area with views, track re-enters trees and slopes downhill into **Glenmore** village. Just above main road turn **R**, through green barrier, to reach **Glenmore Visitor Centre**. Pass through car park to main road.
❺ Cross to Glenmore shop (café). Behind red post-box, steps lead down to campsite. Pass along its R-H edge to wide path into birch woods (blue/brown waymarkers). Head **L** across footbridge to shore of **Loch Morlich** and follow beaches (or paths in woods on **L**) until another river blocks way. Turn **L** along river bank. Ignore footbridge, but continue on wide path (brown/blue waymarkers) with river on your **R**. Where path divides, smaller branch (blue waymarkers) continues beside river through bushes to car park.

GLENELG *OVER THE SEA TO SKYE*

7¼ miles (11.7km) 3hrs 30min **Ascent:** 750ft (228m)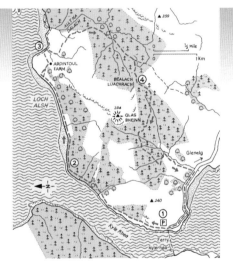
Paths: Tracks, grassy shoreline, minor road, no stiles
Suggested map: aqua3 OS Explorer 413 Knoydart, Loch Hourn & Loch Duich
Grid reference: NG 795213
Parking: Above pier of Glenelg ferry

Along the coast with views to Skye.
❶ Track runs out of car park ('Ardintoul and Totaig'), ascends gently through 2 gates, then through 3rd into plantation. With high power lines just above, track forks. Take **L-H** one, downhill, passing arrow painted on rock. Track runs between feet of pylon then climbs through birch wood. It runs in and out of tiny stream gorge, then descends towards shore. On other side of **Loch Alsh**, houses of Balmacara are directly ahead.
❷ At shoreline, track disappears into open field strip. Follow short-cropped grass next to shingle beach, passing salmon farm just offshore. When trees once more run down to sea, green track runs next to shore. It passes below small crag with birches to reach open flat ground near **Ardintoul Farm**. Keep along shore, outside field walls, sometimes taking to stripy schist shingle, towards square brick building on point ahead. Before reaching it you come to wall gap. Here track, pair of green ruts, runs directly inland. It

joins gravel track, where you turn **L** to pass sheds and house to regain shoreline at Ardintoul.
❸ Track runs along shoreline, then turns inland to climb hill. Steeper uphill sections are tarred. Below on L, **Allt na Dalach** runs into **Loch Alsh**, with clear example of gravel spit where river debris runs into tidal water. Track enters plantations, crosses stream and bends **R** to complete climb to **Bealach Luachrach**. You may see fresh peat workings on L.
❹ Divert here on to **Glas Bheinn** – a tough hill, but a fine viewpoint. (Grading and timing don't take account of side-trip.) From road's high point, turn **R** up wet tree gap to reach hillside. Follow remains of old fence up first rise. Where it bends R, continue uphill to summit, returning by same route. Use old fence to guide you back into tree gap. Continue downhill from Point ❹ on unsurfaced road, which reaches tarred public road 1 mile (1.6km) north of **Glenelg**. Grassy verge between road and sea leads back to ferry pier.

GLENBRITTLE *HEART OF THE CUILLINS*

5¾ miles (9.2km) 4hrs **Ascent:** 1,900ft (580m)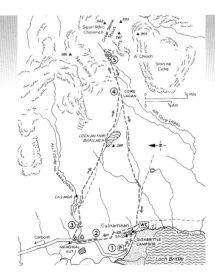
Paths: Mountain paths, one boggy and tough, 2 stiles
Suggested map: aqua3 OS Explorer 411 Skye – Cuillin Hills
Grid reference: NG 409206
Parking: Walkers' pull-off before gate into Glenbrittle campsite

Classic rock climbing country.
❶ From parking area, track leads on through **Glenbrittle** campsite to gate with kissing gate. Pass to L of toilet block to cross stile. Turn **L** along stony track just above, which runs gently downhill above campsite, to rejoin Glenbrittle road.
❷ Continue over bridge with white **Memorial Hut** just ahead. On **R** are stone buchts (sheep-handling enclosures) and here waymarked path heads uphill to reach footbridge over **Allt Coire na Banachdich**.
❸ Cross footbridge and head up to **R** of stream's deep ravine. Look out for short side-path on **L** for best view of waterfall. Above, path bears **R**, to slant up hillside. This part of path has never been built or repaired and is rough and boulder. It passes above **Loch an Fhir-bhallaich** and forks, with **L-H** higher branch being drier but with loose eroded scree. It rounds shoulder into lower part of **Coire Lagan** and meets much larger and better path.

❹ Turn uphill on this path, until belt of bare rock blocks way into upper corrie. This rock has been smoothed by a glacier into gently-rounded swells, known as 'boiler-plates'. Scree field runs up into boiler-plate rocks. Best route keeps up L edge, below slab wall with small waterslide, to highest point of scree. Head up **L** for few steps on bare rock, then back **R** on ledges to an eroded scree above boiler-plate obstruction. Look back down your upward route to note it for your return. Trodden way slants up to **R**. With main stream near by on **R**, it goes up to rim of upper corrie.
❺ Boiler-plate slabs at lochan's outflow are excellent for picnics. Walking mainly on bare rock, it's easy to make circuit of lochan. For return journey, retrace your steps to Point ❹. Ignoring R fork of route you came up by, keep straight downhill on main path. It runs straight down to toilet block at **Glenbrittle** campsite at start.

991 QUIRAING *PRISON AND PINNACLE*

5¼ miles (8.4km) 3hrs **Ascent:** 1,200ft (365m) ▲
Paths: Well-used path, 1 stile
Suggested map: aqua3 OS Explorer 408 Skye – Trotternish & the Storr
Grid reference: NG 440679
Parking: Pull-in, top of pass on Staffin–Uig road. Overflow parking at cemetery ¼ mile (400m) on Staffin side (not during funerals)

Skye's northern peninsula's lava landscape.
❶ Well-built path starts at 'bendy road' sign opposite lay-by. Jagged tower of grass and rock on skyline is **the Prison**. Path crosses steep landslip slope towards it, with awkward crossing of small stream gully on bare rock, then passes small waterfall high above and heads to **R** rather than up into rocky gap. It turns uphill into wide col to **L** of **the Prison**.
❷ Main path does not drop, but goes forward, slightly uphill, crossing old fence line at crag foot. It crosses foot of steep ground, then passes above small peat pool. Ignore path forking down **R**; main path slants up **L** into col where old wall runs across.
❸ Path descends into landslip valley that runs across hillside, then slants up **L** to col with stile.
❹ Cross and turn **R** for excursion to **Sron Vourlinn**. Follow crest over slightly rocky section with short descent beyond, then join main path along grassy

meadow with sudden edge on **R**. After highest point, continue slightly downhill to north top. Here see that land is still slipping, with crevasse beside cliff edge where another narrow section is shortly to peel away.
❺ Return to col with stile (Point ❹) and continue uphill. Drops are now on **L**, as you look down towards pinnacles surrounding **the Table**. After passing broken ground on **R**, come to fallen wall, part of which appears from below as cairn. Path continues next to cliff edge on **L**; you can fork off **R**, directly uphill, to summit trig point on **Meall na Suiramach**.
❻ Follow broad path slightly downhill to cairn at cliff edge. Look straight down on to **the Table**, 100ft (30m) below. Turn **R** on wide path. After 1 mile (1.6km), path descends alongside cliff edge. As edge turns half-**R**, you should turn fully **R**. Path is faint, but reappears ahead contouring around steep grass slope. Above car park it turns straight downhill for final steep descent.

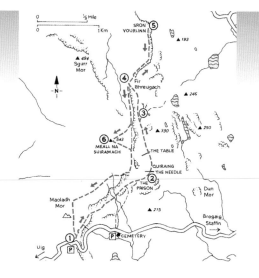

992 RAASAY *A ROYAL REFUGE*

7¾ miles (12.5km) 3hrs 45min **Ascent:** 820ft (250m) ▲
Paths: Small but clear paths, some tracks, 1 stile
Suggested map: aqua3 OS Explorer 409 Raasay, Rona & Scalpay or 410 Skye – Portree & Bracadale
Grid reference: NG 555342 (on OS Explorer 410)
Parking: Ferry terminal at Sconser, Skye (or lay-by to east); Calmac ferries run each hour to Raasay

To Raasay's old iron mining railway.
❶ On Raasay, turn **L** on road. At **Inverarish**, turn **L** over bridge and divert **L** along shore. After playing field rejoin road, pass **Isle of Raasay Hotel** to junction.
❷ Continue ahead past neglected stable block, towards **Raasay House**, now outdoor centre. Just before it, turn **L** to **old pier**. Track continues below ramparts of old gun battery. Follow path around bay, until gate leads to shoreline path to **Eilean Aird nan Gobhar**. Check tides before crossing to tidal island.
❸ Head inland over rock knoll, then pass along **L-H** edge of plantation on muddy path overhung by rhododendron. Continue along shore of **North Bay**, with pine plantation on your **R**, round to headland. Go up briefly through low basalt cliff and return along its top. Head along **L** edge of plantation, to emerge through iron gate on to road.
❹ Turn **L** for 180yds (165m) to grey gate on **R**. Green track leads up and to **R** into craggy valley. At

walled paddock it turns **L** to join tarred road. Follow this down past lily lochan and **L** across dam. Join wide path running up under larch and rhododendron but, in 100yds (91m), bear **R** ('Temptation Hill Trail'). Side path on **R** leads to remains of Iron-Age broch (tower). Main path leads down to pass white church, then bends **R** and drops to tarred road.
❺ Turn sharp **L** up road for 200yds (183m), then **R** at white-topped waymark. Track shrinks to path as it bends **L** and climbs. It becomes forest track, passing more white waymarkers, finally reaching abandoned buildings of old iron **mine**.
❻ At tarred road beyond, turn up **L** to signpost for Miners' Trail. Turn **R** on green track of former **railway**. Where **viaduct** has been removed, path scrambles down steeply and then climbs again to regain railed. Blue-waymarked Miners' Trail turns off, but your route follows **railway** onwards, across stretch of moor and down to **ferry** terminal.

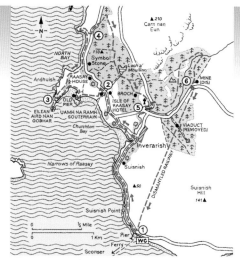

993 PORTREE *SEEING SEA EAGLES*

2¾ miles (4.4km) 1hr 15min **Ascent:** 400ft (122m) ▲
Paths: Smooth, well-made paths, farm track, 3 stiles
Suggested map: aqua3 OS Explorer 409 Raasay, Rona & Scalpay or 410 Skye – Portree & Bracadale
Grid reference: NG 485436 (on OS Explorer 410)
Parking: Daytime-only parking on main A855 above Portree Harbour. Small parking area at slipway

A lovely coastal walk to a raised beach called the Bile.
❶ Turn off **A855** on lane ('Budh Mor'), walk to shoreline then continue to small parking area. Tarred path continues along shore. After crossing footbridge, it passes under hazels. Path rounds headland to reach edge of level green field called **the Bile**.
❷ Wall runs up edge of **the Bile**. Ignore small gate, but turn **L** with wall on your **R**. Just before field corner pass large fuchsia bush. About 25yds (23m) later path forks. Turn **R**, crossing small stream and wall, to head along top edge of **the Bile**. Turn **R**, down fence, to field gate. Cross top of next field on old green path, to stile at its corner. See track just beyond.
❸ Turn sharp **L**, up track. At top it passes through 2 gates to reach stony road just to **R** of **Torvaig**. Turn **L** past house and cross foot of tarred road into gently descending track. It runs down between 2 large corrugated sheds and through gate with stile.

❹ Grassy path ahead leads down into **Portree**, but you can take short, rough, diversion to **Dun Torvaig** (ancient fortified hilltop) above. For **dun**, turn **L** along fence, and then **L** again on well-made path above. It leads to kissing gate above 2 sheds. Turn sharp **R** along fence for a few steps and then bear **L** around base of small outcrop and head up on tiny path to **dun**. Remnants of dry-stone walling can be seen around summit. Return to gravel path, passing above Point ❹ to join wall on your **R**. Path leads down under goat willows into wood where it splits; stay close to wall and continue ahead.
❺ At 1st houses (The Parks Bungalow 5), keep downhill on tarred street. On **L** is entrance to **Cuillin Hills Hotel**. A few steps later, fork **R** on stony path. At shore road, turn **R** across stream and at once turn **R** again on to path that runs up for 60yds (55m) to craggy little **waterfall**. Return to shore road and turn **R** to walk start.

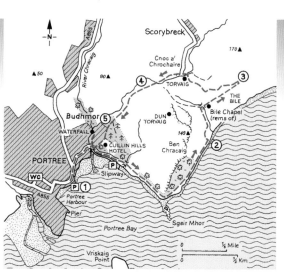

Highland

RAMASAIG WATERSTEIN HEAD

5¾ miles (9.2km) 3hrs 30min **Ascent:** 1,500ft (457m)
Paths: Grassy clifftops and moorland, 1 stile
Suggested map: aqua3 OS Explorer 407 Skye – Dunvegan
Grid reference: NG 163443
Parking: Ramasaig road end or pull-ins at pass ¾ mile (1.2km) north

Through crofting country and peat moors to a 1,000ft (305m) sea cliff.

❶ From end of tarmac, road continues as track between farm buildings, with bridge over **Ramasaig Burn**. After gate it reaches shed with tin roof. Bear **R** here and follow **L** bank of **Ramasaig Burn** to shore.

❷ Cross **burn** at ford and head up very steep meadow beside fence that protects cliff edge. There's awkward fence to cross half way up. At top, above **Ramasaig Cliff**, keep following fence on **L**. It cuts across to **R** to protect notch in cliff edge. From here (Point ❸), you could cut down to parking areas at road pass near by.

❸ Keep downhill alongside cliffside fence. At bottom, turf wall off to **R** provides another short-cut back to road. Clifftop walk now bears slightly **R** around V-notch of **Moonen Burn**. Small path crosses stream and continues uphill to rejoin clifftop fence, which soon turns slightly inland around another cliff notch.

Cliff-edge fence leads up and to **L**, to reach **Waterstein Head**. Here there is a **trig point**, 971ft (296m) above the sea – the 2nd highest sea cliff on Skye. Below you will see Neist Point lighthouse.

❹ Return for ¼ mile (400m) down to where fence bends to **R**, then continue ahead through shallow grassy col for slight rise to **Beinn Charnach**. Here bear **R** to follow gently rounded grass ridge line parallel with cliffs. Highest line along ridge is driest. Fence runs across, with grey gate at its highest point where it passes through col. Climb over gate and on up to cairn on **Beinn na Coinnich**.

❺ Continue along slightly rocky plateau for 300yds (274m) to southeast top. Now **Ramasaig** road is visible ¼ mile (400m) away on **L**. Go down to join quad bike track heading towards road. Just before reaching road, bike track crosses swampy col. This shows old and recent peat workings. Turn **R**, along road, passing above **Loch Eishort** to start.

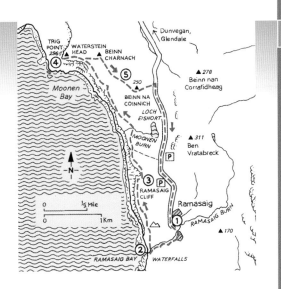

STRATH CARRON SOUTH TORRIDON MOUNTAINS

9 miles (14.5km) 5hrs **Ascent:** 1,700ft (518m)
Paths: Well-made path, then track, no stiles. Note: During stalking season on Achnashellach Estate (15 September–20 October, not Sundays), keep strictly to route, which is right of way.
Suggested map: aqua3 OS Explorer 429 Glen Carron & West Monar
Grid reference: NH 005484 **Parking:** On A890 below Achnashellach Station

Deer stalkers' paths lead into the mountains.

❶ Track runs up behind red phone box, then turns **R** to platform end. Cross line through 2 gates and head up stony track opposite, past waymarker arrow. After 100yds (91m) reach junction under power lines. Turn **L** on smooth gravel road to gate through deer fence. After ¼ mile (400m), look for cairn where new path turns back to **L**.

❷ Path goes back through deer fence at kissing gate, then runs up alongside **River Lair**. As slope steepens above tree-line, short side path on **L** gives view of waterfall. Well-maintained stalkers' path runs over slabs of bare sandstone. Cairn marks point where it arrives in upper valley, Coire Lair, with view to high pass at its head, 2 miles (3.2km) away.

❸ About 200yds (183m) after this 1st cairn, another marks junction of paths. Bear **R**, between 2 pools. Shortly there is 2nd junction with cairn. Bear **R**, on path that leaves corrie through wide, shallow col

350yds (320m) above. Conical cairn marks highest point. Path descends among drumlins and sandstone boulders, slanting down to **R** to join wooded **Allt nan Dearcag**. Path now runs down alongside this stream. Scattered forest damaged by fire and grazing deer is on opposite side as path drops to footbridge. Bridge crosses side stream, **Allt Coire Beinne Leithe**, with **Easan Geal**, White Waterfalls, just above.

❹ At locked estate **hut**, track continues downhill, with gorge of **Easan Dorcha** (Dark Waterfalls) on **R**. After 1 mile (1.6km) turn **R** over stone bridge on **R** on to track that runs up valley to **Coulin Pass** at its head.

❺ After pass, track goes through gate into plantations, then bends **R** to slant down side of Strath Carron. At Scottish Rights of Way Society signpost, follow main track ahead towards **Achnashellach**. Enter clear-felled area then cross bridge to reach mobile phone mast. Fork **L**, passing 2nd mast, and descend to reach junction above **station**.

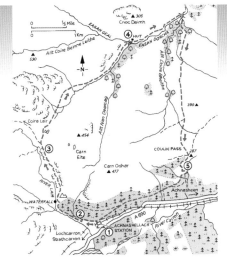

LOCH TORRIDON THE DIABAIG COAST PATH

9½ miles (15.3km) 6hrs **Ascent:** 1,805ft (550m)
Paths: Narrow, rough and wet in places, no stiles
Suggested map: aqua3 OS Explorer 433 Torridon – Beinn Eighe & Liathach
Grid reference: NG 840575
Parking: Informal camp and caravan site above Inveralligin

In the footsteps of the fairy folk.

❶ Follow road **R**, past village green, over Abhainn Alligin, along shoreline for 100yds (91m), then up **R** among sandstone outcrops. Bear **L** under power line to join corner of tarmac driveway. Keep ahead to **Alligin Shuas**.

❷ Turn up road and then **L**, on road for Diabaig. As road steepens, you can take path ahead, rejoining road as it crosses high pass and runs down past linked **Loch Diabaigas Airde** and **Loch a'Mhullaich**.

❸ Turn off **L**, cross footbridge. Clear path leads out along high wall of valley, then zig-zags down spur, to grey gate. Descend through woods to white house, No 1 Diabaig. Turn **R** to old stone **pier**.

❹ Return up path you just came down to pass stone shed. Sign indicates turn to **R**, under outcrop and between boulders. Path heads up to small rock step with arrow mark, up to gate in fence and zig-zags into open gully, large crag on **R**. At top of this, it turns **R**

along shelf, with more crag above. Path slants gently down along foot of another crag, then up to col.

❺ From here path is small but clear. It bends **R** to **Loch a' Bhealaich Mhoir** then **L** below it to small **loch**. Follow stream down towards cottage, **Port Lair**.

❻ Pass above house, then slant gradually up away from sea. Path crosses head of bracken valley with ruined croft house into knolly area. Cross 2 branches of stream and ascend to cairn which marks where path bears **L** up spur. It now contours across meadow among knolls, at end of which it climbs pink rocks over final spur, with view up Loch Torridon to Liathach.

❼ Path descends slightly to cross high, steep slope of heather. Near end of slope, path forks. Take upper branch, through wide col. Boggy path descends towards **Alligin Shuas**. From gate above village, faint path runs down in direction of distant green shed. It descends through wood, then contours just above village to road above Point ❷. Retrace steps to start.

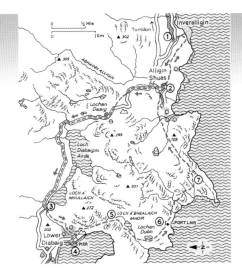

Highland

997 GAIRLOCH FLOWERDALE FALLS

5¼ miles (8.4km) 2hrs 45min **Ascent:** 800ft (244m)
Paths: Tracks and smooth paths, mostly waymarked, no stiles
Suggested map: aqua3 OS Explorer 433 Torridon – Beinn Eighe & Liathach or 434 Gairloch & Loch Ewe
Grid reference: NG 807756 on OS Explorer 433
Parking: Beach car park, southern end of Gairloch

Porpoise-watching along the Gairloch shore.
❶ Cross road and head up to R of cemetery. Turn **L** at corner, into trees to track above. Turn **R** until footbridge leads on to wide path that descends. With wall corner ahead, turn **R** ('**Flowerdale Waterfall**'). Track descends to tarred driveway.
❷ Turn **L** to pass **Flowerdale House**. Way is marked with red-topped poles. Track passes to L of old barn and turns **R** at sign for **waterfall** to pass **Flowerdale Mains**. In ¼ mile (400m) pass concrete bridge on R.
❸ Follow main path, still to L of stream to footbridge, just before you get to **Flowerdale Waterfall**.
❹ Path leads up past **waterfall** to cross footbridge above. It runs up into pine clump, then turns back down valley. After another footbridge it joins rough track, to meet forest road beside Point **❸**. Turn **L**, away from concrete bridge, through felled forest.
❺ Look for blue-topped pole marking path on **R** with

footbridge. It leads through meadowland and bracken with blue waymarker poles. Path bends **R** at old fence cornerpost and descends through bracken and birch to pass above and to L of enclosed field. Turn **R** under 2 large oak trees and cross stream to earth track.
❻ Turn **L** for few steps, until small bracken path runs up to R past waymarked power pole. Path bends **L** under oaks, then drops to rejoin earth track. This soon meets larger track, old road from Loch Maree to Gairloch. Turn **R** along this, through couple of gates, to **Old Inn** at **Charlestown**.
❼ Cross old bridge, and main road, to **pier**. Turn **R** at sign for Gairloch Chandlery, to tarmac path ('beach'). This passes to L of pinewood, then turns **R** into trees. It bends **L** and emerges to run along spine of small headland. Just before being carried out to sea it turns sharp **R**, and crosses above rocky bay to fort (An Dun). Duckboard path runs along back of beach, then turns **R** to car park.

998 POOLEWE GREAT WILDERNESS

6½ miles (10.4km) 2hrs 45min **Ascent:** 250ft (76m)
Paths: Mostly good, but one short rough, wet section, 3 stiles
Suggested map: aqua3 OS Explorer 434 Gairloch & Loch Ewe
Grid reference: NG 857808
Parking: In Poolewe, just up B8057 side street

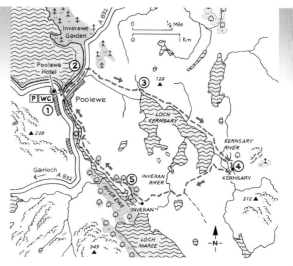

A pleasant walk around Loch Kernsary.
❶ Kissing gate beside public toilets leads to path that crosses Marie Curie Field of Hope to main road. Turn **L** to cross bridge over **River Ewe** then continue through village. At 40mph derestriction sign, there's white cottage on R. Beside it, tarred trackway has Scottish Rights of Way Society signpost for **Kernsary**.
❷ Follow track over cattle grid to new track that forks **L**. After 50yds (46m), keep ahead on path with wall on L. It passes through kissing gate into Cnoc na Lise, Garden Hill. This has been replanted as community wood with oak and birch trees. Another kissing gate leads path out of young wood. Reconstructed path runs over bare sandstone slabs and under low-voltage power line. It crosses low spur to fine view of **Loch Kernsary** and remote, steep-sided hills of Great Wilderness, then goes over stream to **loch** side.
❸ Path follows L-H shore of **loch**, passing through patches of birch scrub. About half-way along **loch**, it

suddenly deteriorates, becoming braided trod of boulder and bog. From stile at **loch** head, slant to **L** down meadow to footbridge under oak tree. Head up, with fence on R, to join track beside **Kernsary** farm.
❹ Turn **R**, through gate. Follow track past farm, to culvert crossing of **Kernsary River**. This becomes ford only after heavy rain. If needed, you will find footbridge 70yds (64m) upstream. After crossing, turn **R** on smooth track. New track bears **L**, away from **Loch Kernsary** towards hollow containing **Loch Maree**. After bridge over Inveran River is gate with ladder stile. Signs welcoming responsible walkers (and cyclists) reflect principles of Letterewe Accord. Soon come views of **Loch Maree**. The driveway of **Inveran** house joins from L and track starts being tarred.
❺ At sign, 'Blind Corners', green track on **L** leads down to point where narrow **loch** becomes wide river. Return to main track and follow it above then beside **River Ewe**. It reaches **Poolewe** just beside bridge.

999 LOCH NESS MONSTERS AND BEASTIES

4¼ miles (6.8km) 2hrs 15min **Ascent:** 700ft (213m)
Paths: Waymarked paths and tracks, no stiles
Suggested map: aqua3 OS Explorer 416 Inverness, Loch Ness & Culloden
Grid reference: NH 522237 **Parking:** Forest Enterprise car park

Overlooking Loch Ness and past the home of the Beast of Boleskine.
❶ From car park follow yellow waymarkers uphill near stream. After 100yds (91m), take path on **R** ('Loch View'). After bench, path contours briefly then turns up **L**, to higher viewpoint, then turns back sharply **R** and descends on earth steps through little crag to forest road. Turn **R** for 200yds (183m).
❷ Turn up **L** on footpath with more yellow waymarkers. Path has low, mossed wall alongside as it bends up to higher forest road. Turn **R** and walk for 150yds (137m) to sharp L-H bend. Keep ahead on small footpath through area of cleared forestry, then go steeply up to **L** under trees. At top, bear **L** along little ridge, dropping gently downhill to viewpoint.
❸ Return for 100yds (91m); bear **L** down other side of ridge. Path descends steeply to forest road. Sign indicates **Lochan Torr** an Tuill (picnic table near by).
❹ Return down forest road, past where you joined it. It climbs gently, then descends to sharp **R** bend where

you turned off earlier ('to Car Park') on side now facing you. After 150yds (137m), at another 'to Car Park' waymarker, turn **L** down path with low mossed wall to forest road below (Point **❷**). Turn **L**, past red/green waymarker. Track kinks **L** past **quarry**.
❺ Where main track bends R, downhill, keep ahead on green track with red/green waymarker to emerge from trees at signpost. Follow this down to **R** towards **Easter Boleskine** house. Green waymarkers indicate diversion to **L** of house, to join its driveway track below. Follow this down to B852.
❻ Turn **R** for 50yds (46m). Below L edge of road is tarred track. Turn down past blue/green waymarker to cross this track, with two blue waymarkers leading into path beyond. Pass down to **R** of electricity transformers. At foot of slope, main path bears **R** with blue waymarker. It runs above **loch** shore and joins gravel track just below **Lower Birchwood House**. Tarred lane ahead leads up to B852, with car park just above on R.

STRATHPEFFER *The Falls of Rogie*

10 miles (16.1km) 5hrs **Ascent:** 1,200ft (365m)
Paths: Waymarked paths and track, no stiles
Suggested map: aqua3 OS Explorer 437 Ben Wyvis & Strathpeffer
Grid reference: NH 483582 **Parking:** Main square, Strathpeffer

From a spa to a salmon-leaping waterfall.

1 Head along main road towards **Contin**. At edge of town, turn **R** at signpost for Garve then, at bend in lane, turn **L**, following another signpost.

2 Pass round to **L** of **Loch Kinellan**, then keep ahead up faint path through gorse to corner of plantation. Join larger track leading into forest. After ¼ mile (400m) reach signpost.

3 Turn **L** for **View Rock** on good path with green waymarkers. At **View Rock**, side-path diverts to **R** for viewpoint. After steep descent, ignore green path turning off to **L** and follow green waymarkers downhill. At forest road turn **L**, then back **R** for 60yds (55m) to path on **L**. Cross another forest road to car park.

4 At end of car park pick up wide path ('River Walk'). After stream culvert, main path bends up to **R**, past waymark to forest road. Turn **L** ('Garve'), and in 80yds (73m) bear **L**, heading slightly downhill.

5 Go on for 600yds (549m), to small track on **L** ('**Falls of Rogie**'). At its foot, cross footbridge below falls; turn **R**, upstream. Path has green waymarkers and after ¼ mile (400m) bends **L** away from river. Cross rocky ground to junction. Turn up **R**, to car park.

6 Leave car park through wooden arch and follow green waymarkers back to bridge. Retrace outward route to Point **5** and turn sharp **L** up forest road, leading uphill to 4-way junction.

7 Turn **R** on smaller track to pass between boulders, then **L** on rutted path to rejoin same track higher up. After 600yds (549m) reach signpost at Point **3**. Keep ahead and retrace outward route to Point **2**. Turn **L** on tarred lane, which becomes track. Keep ahead towards house, but before it, turn **L** through kissing gate, with 2nd one beyond leading into plantation ('**Strathpeffer**').

8 Follow main track straight ahead until you see **Strathpeffer** down on right. At next junction bear **R** down wood edge and turn **R** into town. Street on **L** leads past church with square steeple, where you turn down **R** to main square.

MAINLAND ORKNEY *The Gloup Loop*

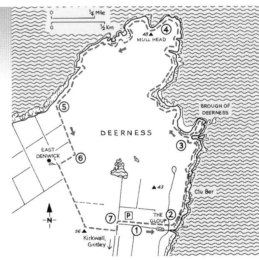

4 miles (6.4km) 2hrs 30min **Ascent:** 93ft (28m)
Paths: Continuous, 4 kissing gates, 2 stiles
Suggested map: aqua3 OS Explorer 461 Orkney – East Mainland
Grid reference: HY 590079
Parking: Mull Head car park (free)
Note: Dogs are not allowed on this walk due to wildlife

An easy walk with an abundance of wildlife.

1 Leave car park at R-H corner and follow direction sign along gravel path to **The Gloup**, where you will find 2 viewing platforms and information plaque. The word 'Gloup' comes from the old Norse word 'gluppa' meaning chasm and at 100ft (30m) deep it is a remarkable feat, formed by the force of the North Sea.

2 Past **The Gloup** you will see red-painted kissing gate and directional sign pointing **L**. This will lead you along grassy footpath to **Brough of Deerness** (pronounced 'broch'), but a more interesting route, perhaps, is straight ahead and then **L** along cliff edge, also following grassy path.

3 At **Brough** is another information plaque and, in cliff edge, precipitous stone staircase which takes you down cliff (take care here) and, by turning **R** at beach, into sheltered stony bay, Little Burra Geo. You will see, in edge of **Brough** wall, steep dirt path, which you can climb with help of chain set into rock. This will take you to top of **Brough** so that you can explore ancient site here.

4 Having climbed back to main route, another red-painted kissing gate on your **R** shows footpath leading along to cairn at **Mull Head**. From cairn path turns **L** and becomes much narrower, although still clear, taking you along northern cliff edge.

5 Path turns sharp **L** just before wire fence and climbs uphill through moorland to another red-painted kissing gate.

6 Turn **R** here and go down to yet another gate you can see in fencing above derelict farmhouse, **East Denwick**. Here turn **L** along wide track and climb hill until track becomes very overgrown and **L** turn travels downhill to small red-painted gate on your **L**.

7 Narrow grass path through gate and between wire fences turns **R** and leads back into car park.

walking in safety

Walking is the number one activity in Britain, with many more participants than angling, golf or even watching football. According to official figures, as many as 15 million people regularly take a walk of 2 miles (3.2km) or more every month, either individually, in families, or in organised groups or clubs.

PRACTICALITIES

There are 140,000 miles (225,300 km) of public rights of way in England and Wales, and in most mountain areas and Scotland there is a de facto right of access above the enclosed foothills. In some hill areas, particularly in the Peak District, access agreements are in force which allow the walker virtually unlimited right to roam, and the Government has announced that it intends to introduce this right to all mountains, moorlands and uncultivated land in due course.

Elsewhere, it is the law of the land that you should stick to those rights of way, which, it should be noted, have the same status in law as a public highway (like the M1). Therefore, if you find one that is blocked, you have the right to clear it to allow your passage, although we do not recommend that you argue or try to force a way. It is better to report the blockage to the responsible authority (usually the county council or unitary authority highways department). If you stray from a right of way, technically you will be trespassing, but unless you do any damage you cannot be prosecuted, despite what some signs still say. All the routes in this book have been checked and are either on rights of way or on well-established legal paths.

When out in the country, you should respect the life of the people who live and work there, especially the farmers, who have to a large extent created the landscapes which offer such scenic walking.

Keep your dog under control at all times, especially around livestock, and obey local bylaws and other dog control notices. Remember it is against the law to let your dog foul in many public areas, especially in villages and towns.

WALKING IN SAFETY

All these walks are suitable for any reasonably fit person. Route finding is usually straightforward, but we strongly recommend that you carry the relevant Ordnance Survey map with you in addition to the route and walk description.

Although each walk has been researched with a view to minimising the risks to the walkers who follow its route, no walk in the countryside can be considered to be completely free from risk. Walking in the outdoors will always require a degree of common sense and judgement to ensure that it is as safe as possible.

Be aware of the consequences of changes of weather and tides. Check the forecast and tides, if applicable, before you set off. Carry spare clothing and a torch if you are walking in the winter months.

Remember that the weather can change very quickly at any time of the year, and in moorland and heathland areas, mist and fog can make route finding much harder. Don't set out in these conditions unless you are confident of your navigation skills in poor visibility. In summer remember to take account of the heat and sun; wear a hat and carry drinking water.

On walks in more isolated areas you should carry a whistle and survival bag. If you have an accident and require the help of the emergency services, make a note of your position as accurately as possible and contact the emergency services. (Don't rely on your mobile phone as it may not work in some areas.)

EQUIPMENT AND SAFETY

The most important single item of equipment for country walking is good pair of sturdy boots or walking shoes. Boots give better support to your ankles, especially in rough or hill country, and your feet need to be kept warm and dry in all conditions.

Britain's climate is unpredictable, so warm and waterproof clothing is the next essential, but you don't need to spend a fortune on an Everest-specification jacket for strolling in the Cotswolds. There are many efficient and breathable alternatives which need not cost the earth. Waterproof trousers or gaiters are also a good idea and, as up to 40 per cent of body heat is lost through the head, a warm hat is essential. Some of the mountain walks in this book should not be attempted in winter conditions or in poor visibility unless you are confident of your navigation skills.

None of the walks in this book will take more than a day, but you will need a rucksack to hold extra clothing, food and drink for the longer walks. Look for one with about a 20–35-litre capacity, with stormproof pockets for your map, compass (a good idea on any hill walk), camera and other bits and pieces.

REMEMBER

- Be particularly careful on cliff paths and in upland terrain, where the consequences of a slip can be very serious.
- Remember to check tidal conditions before walking along the seashore.
- Some sections of route are by, or cross roads. Take care and remember traffic is a danger even on minor country lanes.
- Be careful around farmyard machinery and livestock, especially if you have children or a dog with you.

Index of Walks